P9-CRZ-778

# DOONESBURY:
## The War Years

**Also from Random House Value Publishing:**

Doonesbury Redux: Duke 2000 and Revolt of the English Majors

# DOONESBURY:
# The War Years

Peace Out, Dawg!

& Got War?

BY G. B. TRUDEAU

GRAMERCY BOOKS
NEW YORK

Previously published as two volumes by Andrews McMeel Publishing under the titles:

*Peace Out, Dawg!* © 2002 by G. B. Trudeau
*Got War?* © 2003 by G. B. Trudeau

All rights reserved. No part of this book may be reproduced or transmitted in any form or by any means electronic or mechanical including photocopying and recording, or by any information storage and retrieval system, without permission in writing from the publisher.

This 2006 edition is published by Gramercy Books, an imprint of Random House Value Publishing, a division of Random House, Inc., New York, by arrangement with Andrews McMeel Publishing. Gramercy is a registered trademark and the colophon is a trademark of Random House, Inc.


Random House
New York • Toronto • London • Sydney • Auckland
www.randomhouse.com

Printed and bound in Singapore

A catalog record for this title is available from the Library of Congress.


ISBN-10: 0-517-22866-1
ISBN-13: 978-0-517-22866-1

10 9 8 7 6 5 4 3 2 1

# CONTENTS

# Peace Out, Dawg!

Peace Out, Dawg!
Peace Out, Dawg!

"All in all, it's been a fabulous year for Laura and me."

—George W. Bush, Dec. 12, 2001

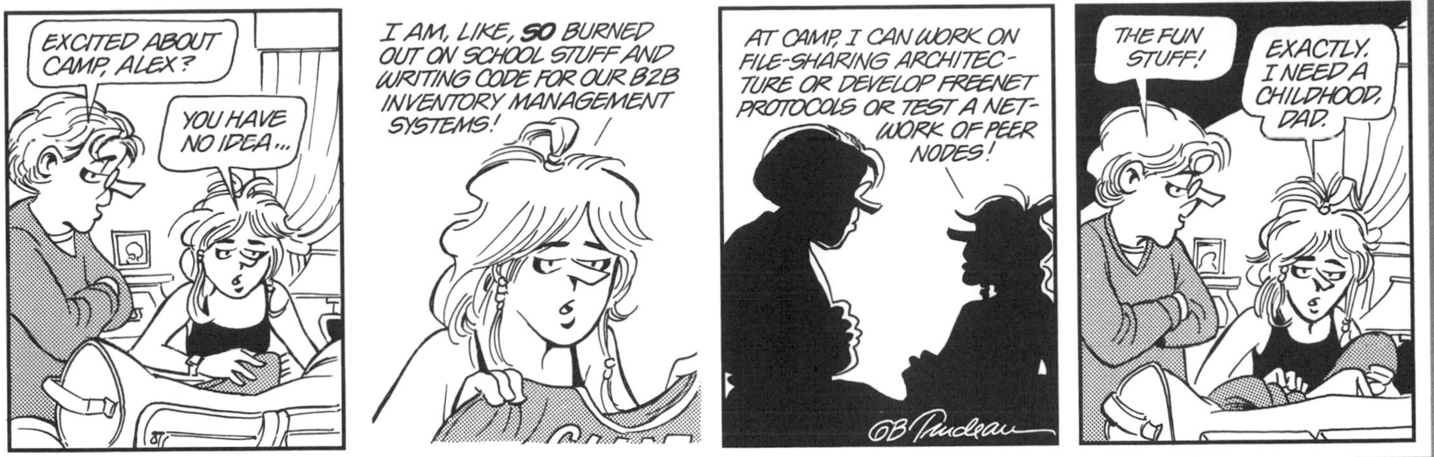
EXCITED ABOUT CAMP, ALEX?
YOU HAVE NO IDEA...
I AM, LIKE, **SO** BURNED OUT ON SCHOOL STUFF AND WRITING CODE FOR OUR B2B INVENTORY MANAGEMENT SYSTEMS!
AT CAMP, I CAN WORK ON FILE-SHARING ARCHITECTURE OR DEVELOP FREENET PROTOCOLS OR TEST A NETWORK OF PEER NODES!
GB Trudeau
THE FUN STUFF!
EXACTLY. I NEED A CHILDHOOD, DAD.

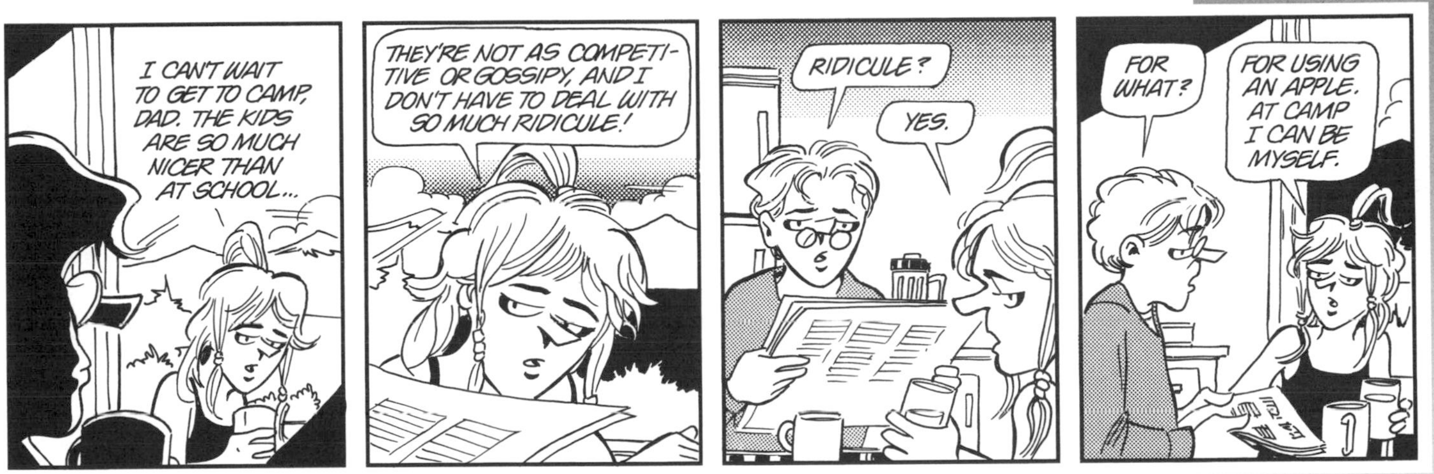
I CAN'T WAIT TO GET TO CAMP, DAD. THE KIDS ARE SO MUCH NICER THAN AT SCHOOL...
THEY'RE NOT AS COMPETITIVE OR GOSSIPY, AND I DON'T HAVE TO DEAL WITH SO MUCH RIDICULE!
RIDICULE?
YES.
FOR WHAT?
FOR USING AN APPLE. AT CAMP I CAN BE MYSELF.

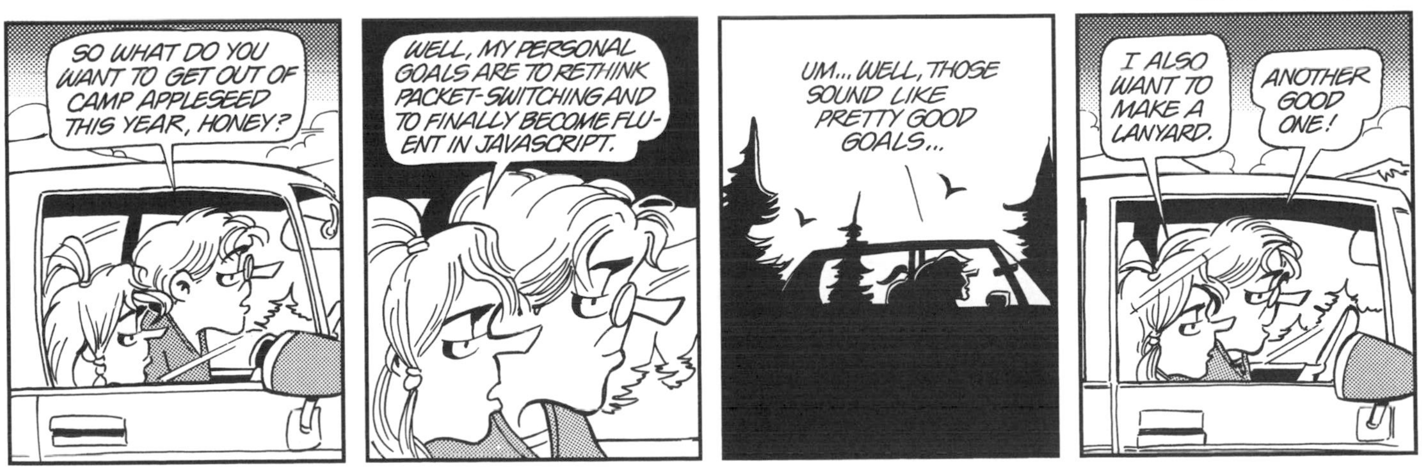
SO WHAT DO YOU WANT TO GET OUT OF CAMP APPLESEED THIS YEAR, HONEY?
WELL, MY PERSONAL GOALS ARE TO RETHINK PACKET-SWITCHING AND TO FINALLY BECOME FLUENT IN JAVASCRIPT.
UM... WELL, THOSE SOUND LIKE PRETTY GOOD GOALS...
I ALSO WANT TO MAKE A LANYARD.
ANOTHER GOOD ONE!

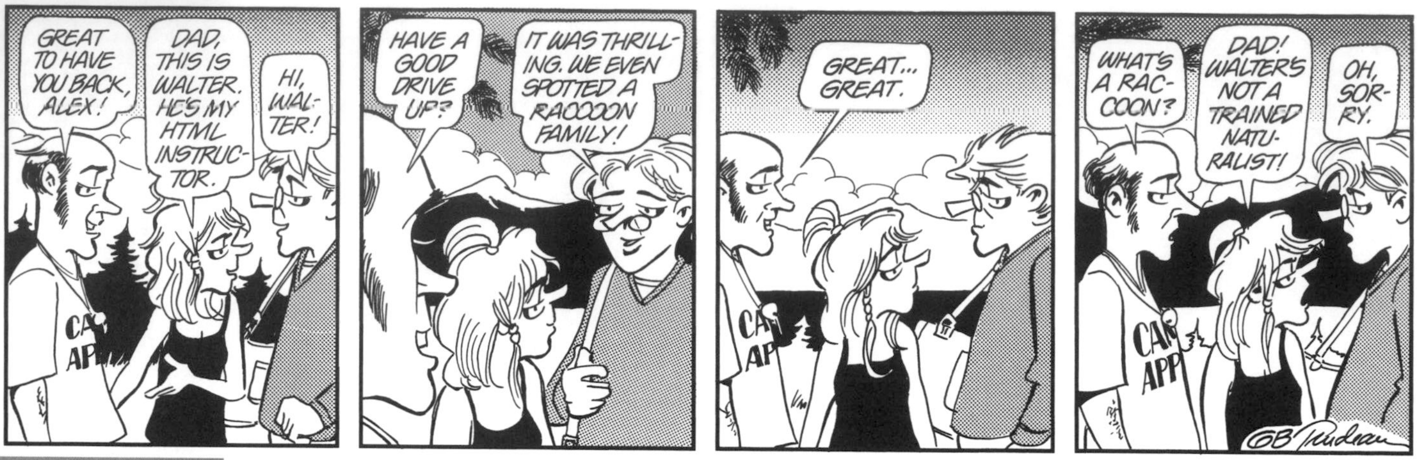
GREAT TO HAVE YOU BACK, ALEX!
DAD, THIS IS WALTER. HE'S MY HTML INSTRUCTOR.
HI, WALTER!
HAVE A GOOD DRIVE UP?
IT WAS THRILLING. WE EVEN SPOTTED A RACCOON FAMILY!
GREAT... GREAT.
WHAT'S A RACCOON?
DAD! WALTER'S NOT A TRAINED NATURALIST!
OH, SORRY.

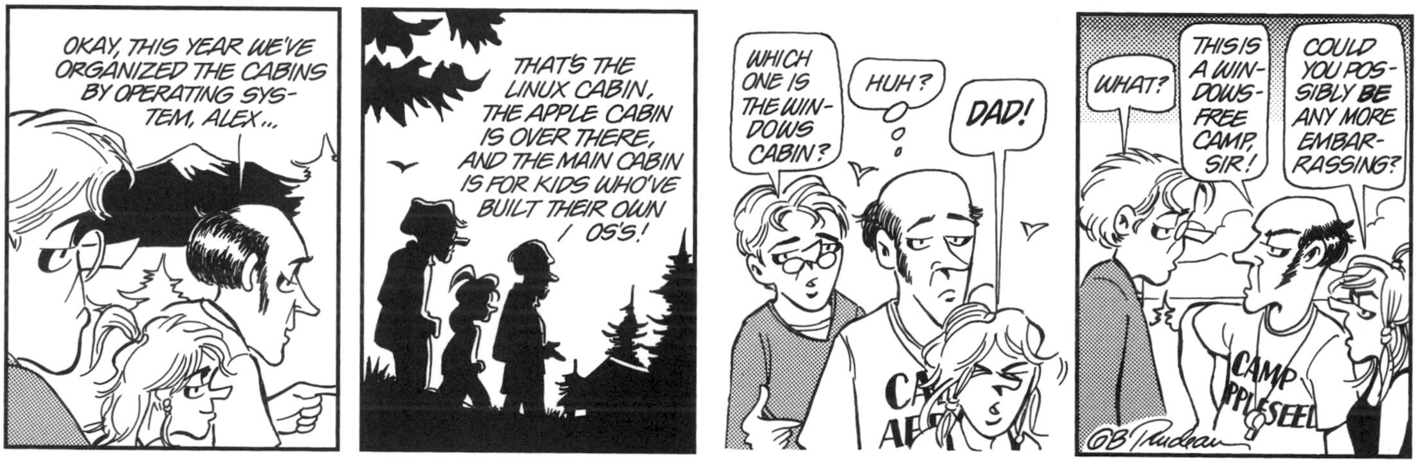
OKAY, THIS YEAR WE'VE ORGANIZED THE CABINS BY OPERATING SYSTEM, ALEX...
THAT'S THE LINUX CABIN, THE APPLE CABIN IS OVER THERE, AND THE MAIN CABIN IS FOR KIDS WHO'VE BUILT THEIR OWN OS'S!
WHICH ONE IS THE WINDOWS CABIN?
HUH?
DAD!
WHAT?
THIS IS A WINDOWS-FREE CAMP, SIR!
COULD YOU POSSIBLY BE ANY MORE EMBARRASSING?

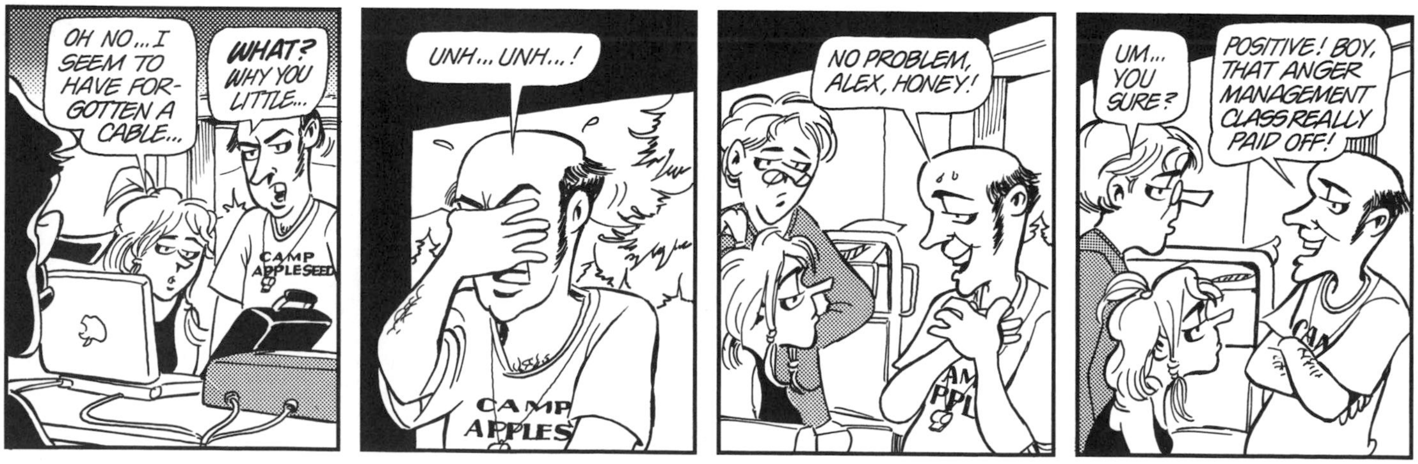
OH NO... I SEEM TO HAVE FORGOTTEN A CABLE...
WHAT? WHY YOU LITTLE...
CAMP APPLESEED
UNH... UNH...!
NO PROBLEM, ALEX, HONEY!
UM... YOU SURE?
POSITIVE! BOY, THAT ANGER MANAGEMENT CLASS REALLY PAID OFF!

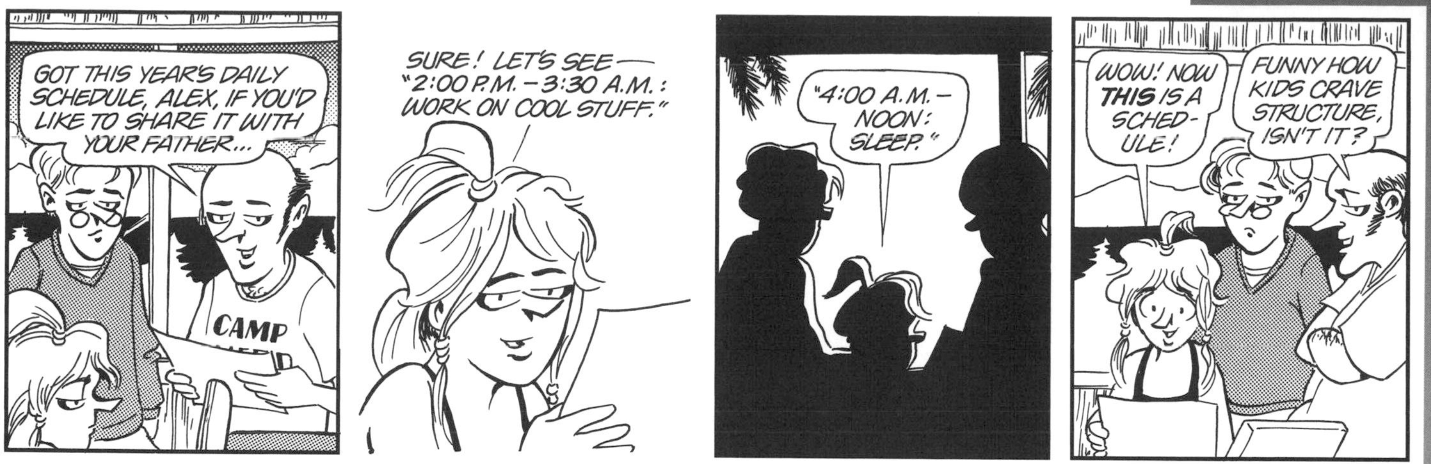
GOT THIS YEAR'S DAILY SCHEDULE, ALEX, IF YOU'D LIKE TO SHARE IT WITH YOUR FATHER...
SURE! LET'S SEE— "2:00 P.M. – 3:30 A.M.: WORK ON COOL STUFF."
"4:00 A.M. – NOON: SLEEP."
WOW! NOW THIS IS A SCHED-ULE!
FUNNY HOW KIDS CRAVE STRUCTURE, ISN'T IT?

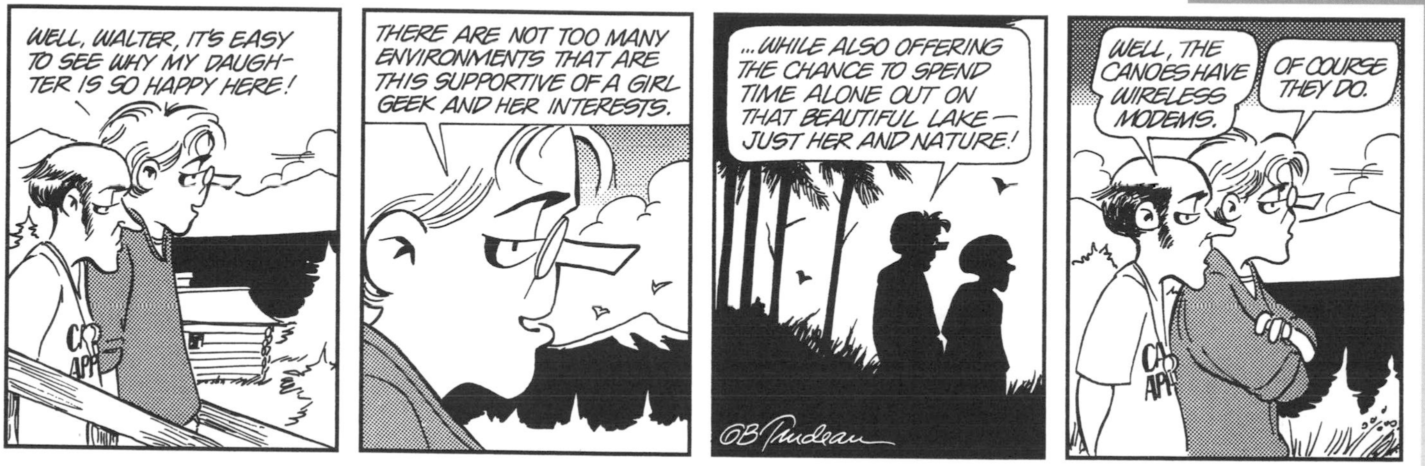
WELL, WALTER, IT'S EASY TO SEE WHY MY DAUGH-TER IS SO HAPPY HERE!
THERE ARE NOT TOO MANY ENVIRONMENTS THAT ARE THIS SUPPORTIVE OF A GIRL GEEK AND HER INTERESTS.
...WHILE ALSO OFFERING THE CHANCE TO SPEND TIME ALONE OUT ON THAT BEAUTIFUL LAKE— JUST HER AND NATURE!
WELL, THE CANOES HAVE WIRELESS MODEMS.
OF COURSE THEY DO.

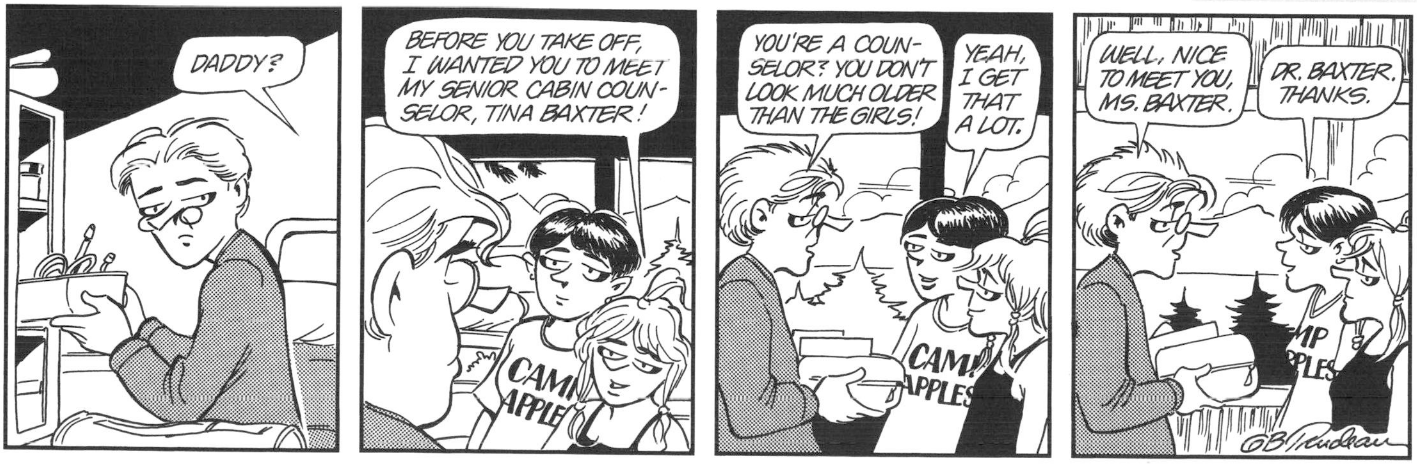
DADDY?
BEFORE YOU TAKE OFF, I WANTED YOU TO MEET MY SENIOR CABIN COUN-SELOR, TINA BAXTER!
YOU'RE A COUN-SELOR? YOU DON'T LOOK MUCH OLDER THAN THE GIRLS!
YEAH, I GET THAT A LOT.
WELL, NICE TO MEET YOU, MS. BAXTER.
DR. BAXTER. THANKS.

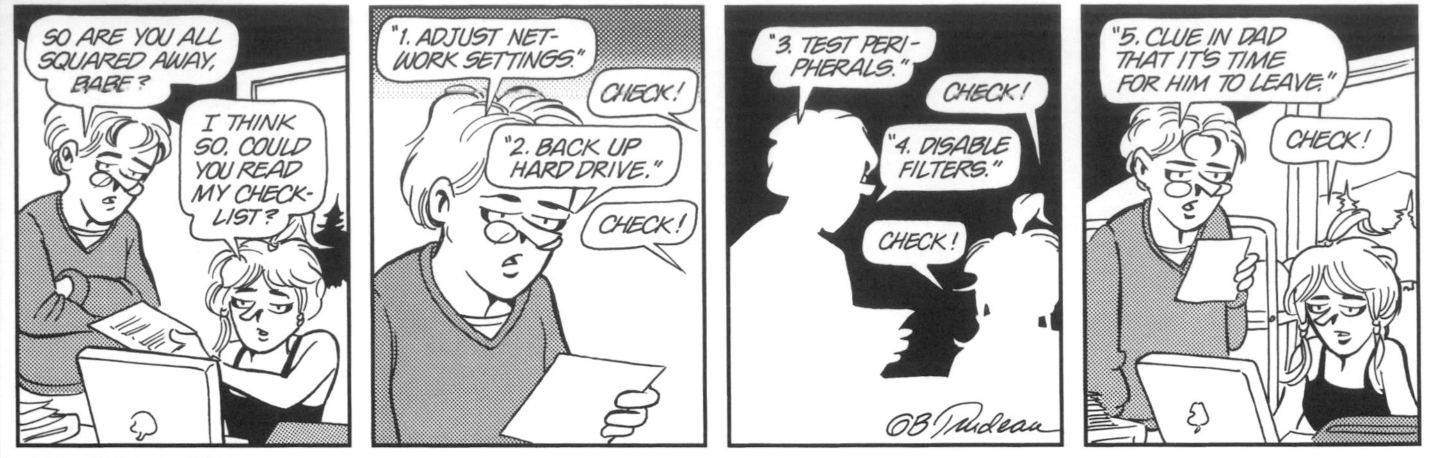
SO ARE YOU ALL SQUARED AWAY, BABE?
I THINK SO. COULD YOU READ MY CHECK-LIST?
"1. ADJUST NET-WORK SETTINGS."
CHECK!
"2. BACK UP HARD DRIVE."
CHECK!
"3. TEST PERI-PHERALS."
CHECK!
"4. DISABLE FILTERS."
CHECK!
"5. CLUE IN DAD THAT IT'S TIME FOR HIM TO LEAVE."
CHECK!

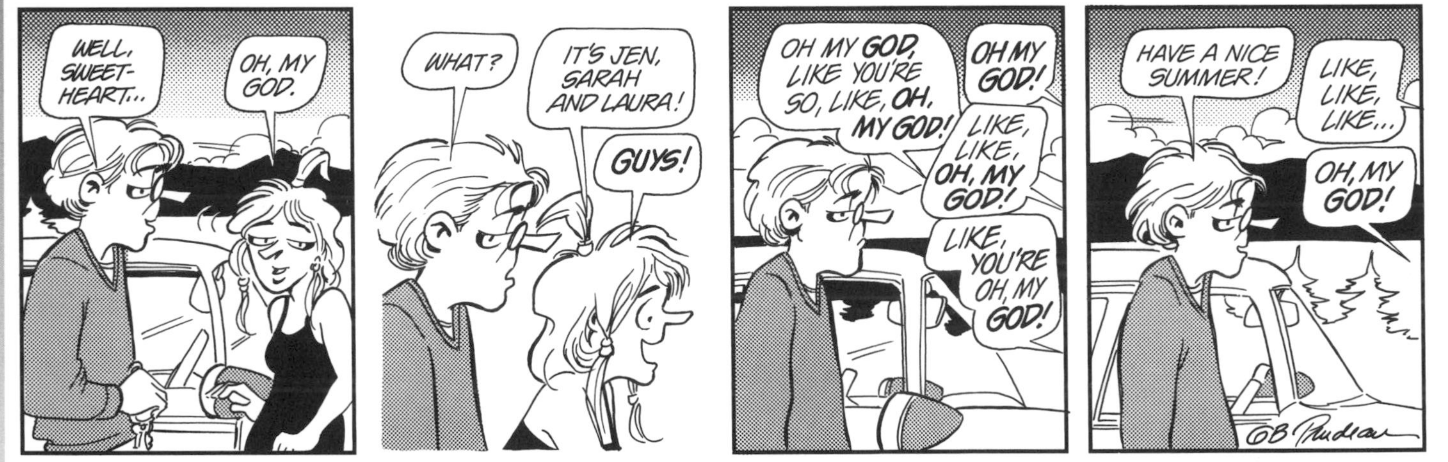
WELL, SWEET-HEART...
OH, MY GOD.
WHAT?
IT'S JEN, SARAH AND LAURA!
GUYS!
OH MY GOD, LIKE YOU'RE SO, LIKE, OH, MY GOD!
OH MY GOD!
LIKE, LIKE, OH, MY GOD!
LIKE, YOU'RE OH, MY GOD!
HAVE A NICE SUMMER!
LIKE, LIKE, LIKE...
OH, MY GOD!

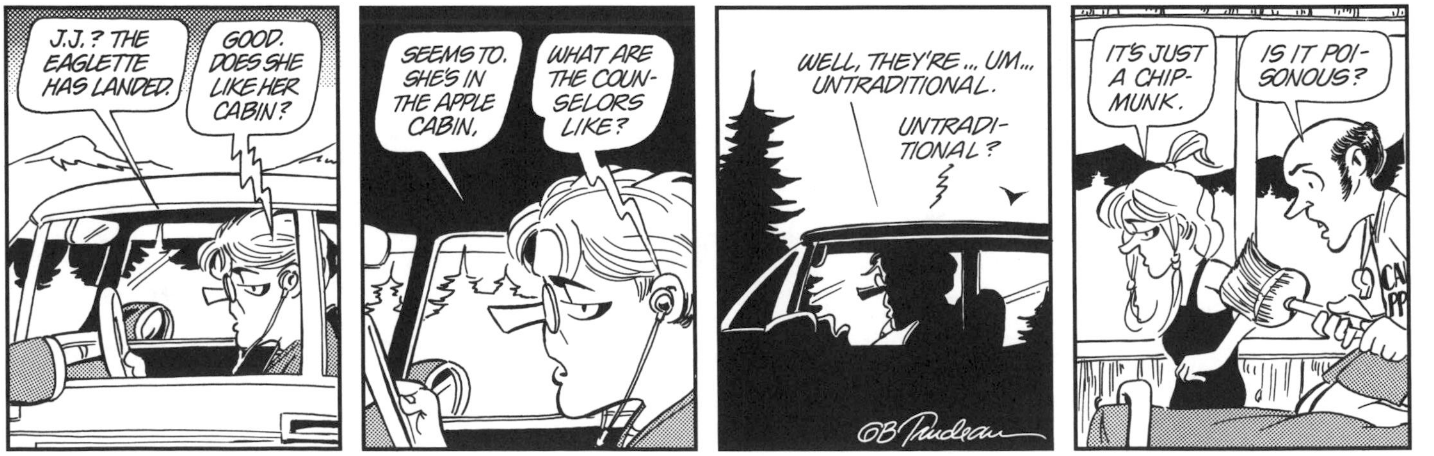
J.J.? THE EAGLETTE HAS LANDED.
GOOD. DOES SHE LIKE HER CABIN?
SEEMS TO. SHE'S IN THE APPLE CABIN.
WHAT ARE THE COUN-SELORS LIKE?
WELL, THEY'RE... UM... UNTRADITIONAL.
UNTRADI-TIONAL?
IT'S JUST A CHIP-MUNK.
IS IT POI-SONOUS?

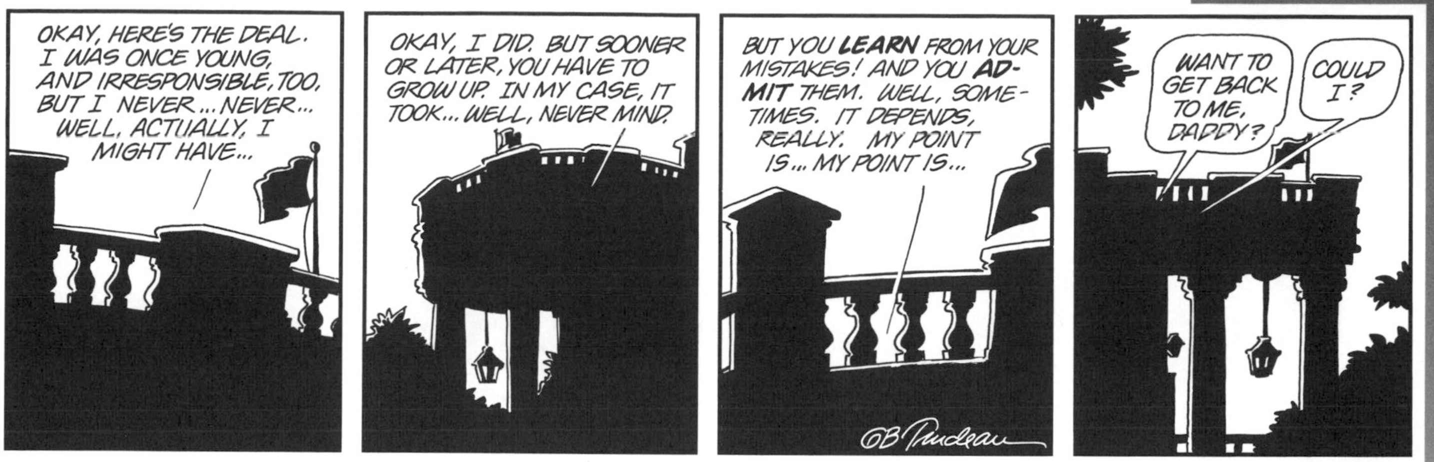
OKAY, HERE'S THE DEAL. I WAS ONCE YOUNG, AND IRRESPONSIBLE, TOO. BUT I NEVER... NEVER... WELL, ACTUALLY, I MIGHT HAVE...
OKAY, I DID. BUT SOONER OR LATER, YOU HAVE TO GROW UP. IN MY CASE, IT TOOK... WELL, NEVER MIND.
BUT YOU LEARN FROM YOUR MISTAKES! AND YOU ADMIT THEM. WELL, SOMETIMES. IT DEPENDS, REALLY. MY POINT IS... MY POINT IS...
WANT TO GET BACK TO ME, DADDY?
COULD I?

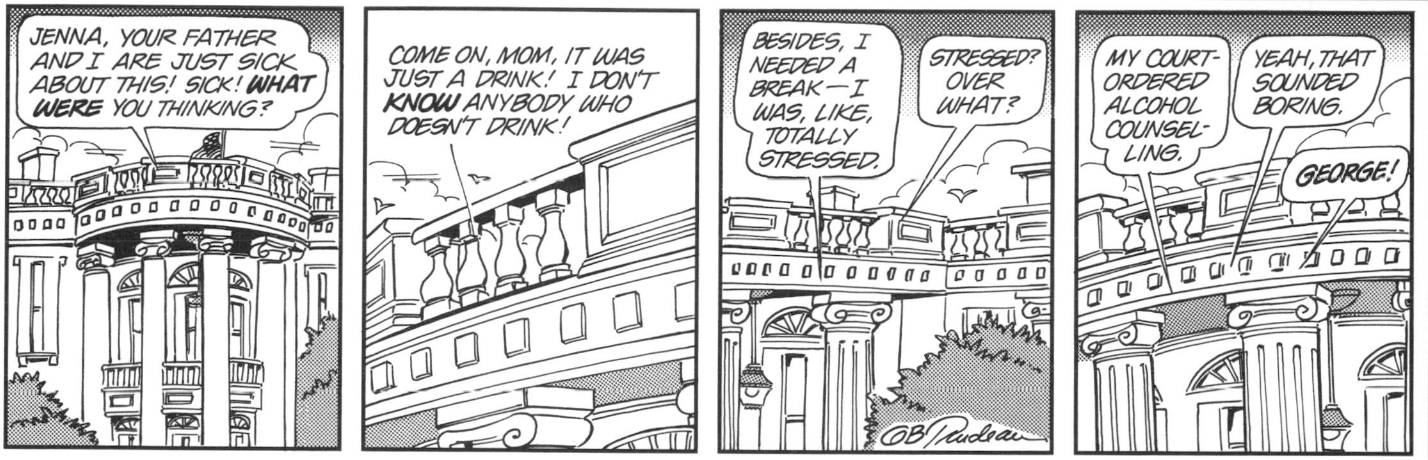
JENNA, YOUR FATHER AND I ARE JUST SICK ABOUT THIS! SICK! WHAT WERE YOU THINKING?
COME ON, MOM, IT WAS JUST A DRINK! I DON'T KNOW ANYBODY WHO DOESN'T DRINK!
BESIDES, I NEEDED A BREAK—I WAS, LIKE, TOTALLY STRESSED.
STRESSED? OVER WHAT?
MY COURT-ORDERED ALCOHOL COUNSELLING.
YEAH, THAT SOUNDED BORING.
GEORGE!

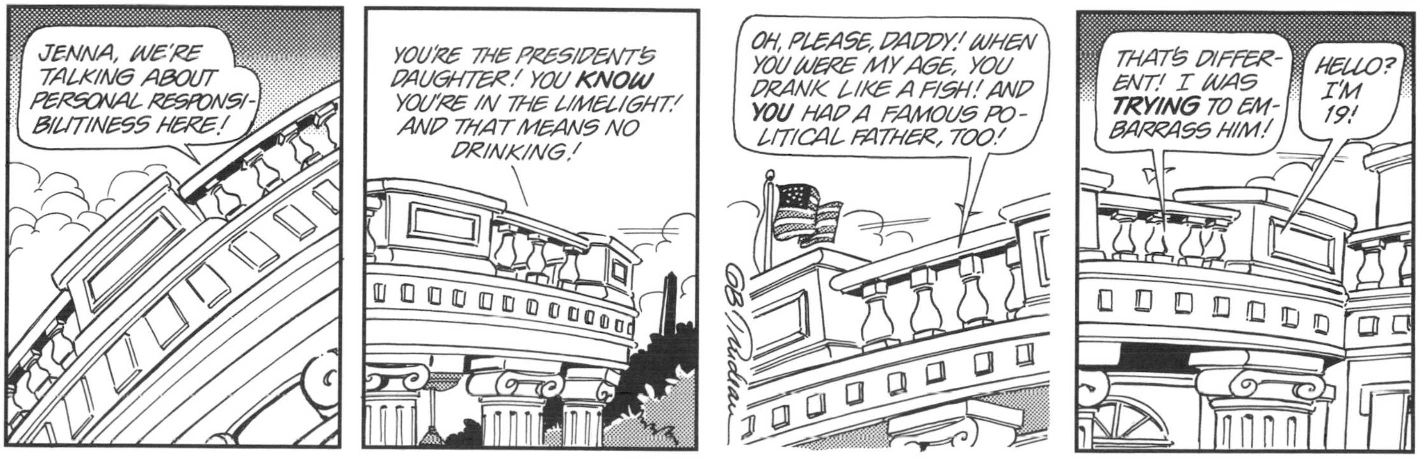
JENNA, WE'RE TALKING ABOUT PERSONAL RESPONSIBILITINESS HERE!
YOU'RE THE PRESIDENT'S DAUGHTER! YOU KNOW YOU'RE IN THE LIMELIGHT! AND THAT MEANS NO DRINKING!
OH, PLEASE, DADDY! WHEN YOU WERE MY AGE, YOU DRANK LIKE A FISH! AND YOU HAD A FAMOUS POLITICAL FATHER, TOO!
THAT'S DIFFERENT! I WAS TRYING TO EMBARRASS HIM!
HELLO? I'M 19!

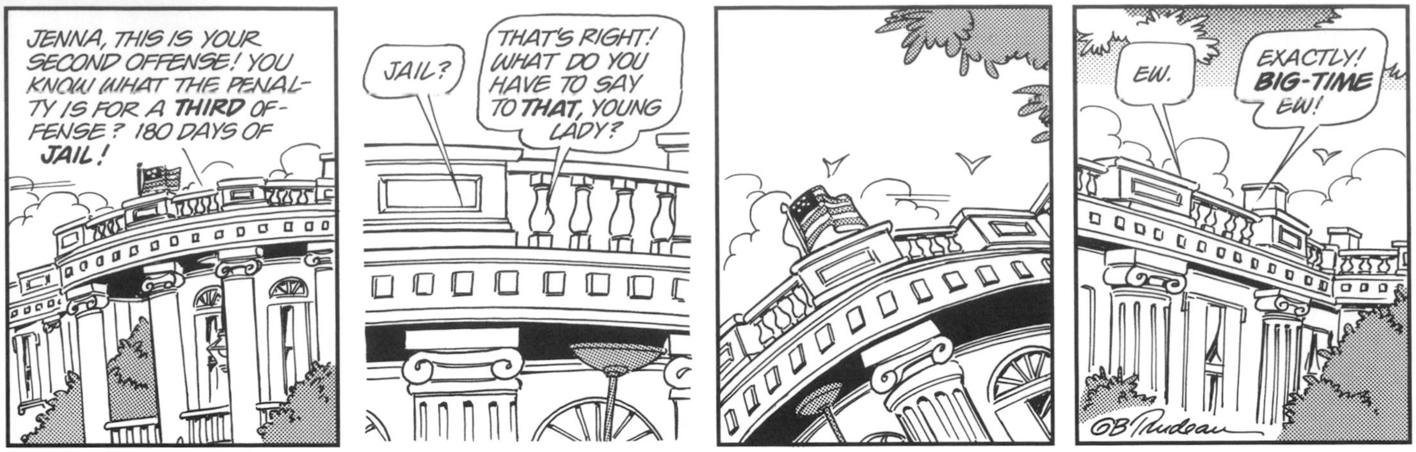
JENNA, THIS IS YOUR SECOND OFFENSE! YOU KNOW WHAT THE PENALTY IS FOR A **THIRD** OFFENSE? 180 DAYS OF **JAIL!**
JAIL?
THAT'S RIGHT! WHAT DO YOU HAVE TO SAY TO **THAT,** YOUNG LADY?
EW.
EXACTLY! **BIG-TIME** EW!

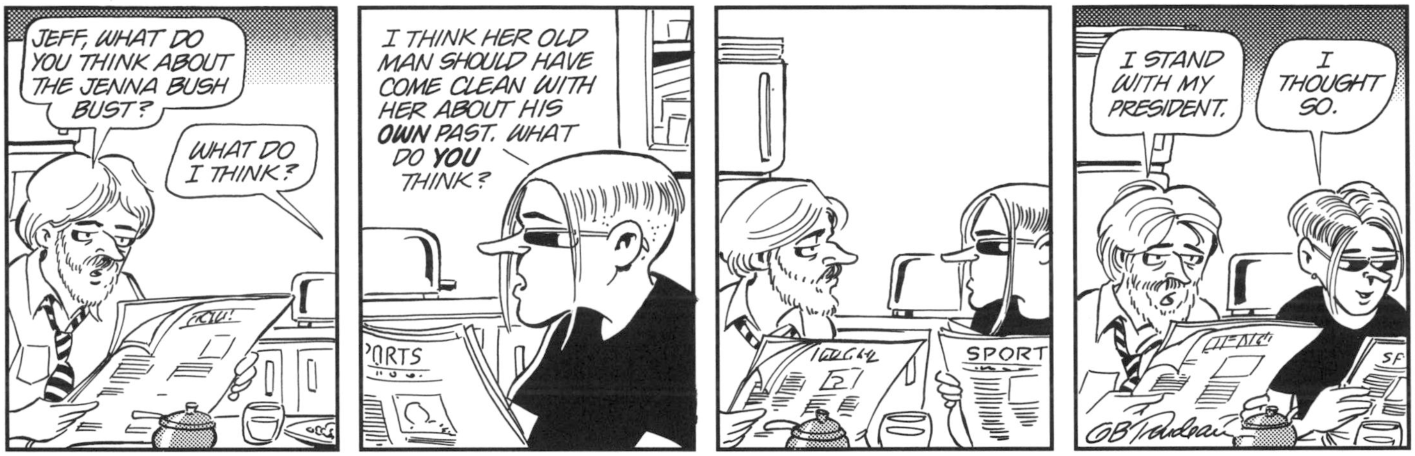
JEFF, WHAT DO YOU THINK ABOUT THE JENNA BUSH BUST?
WHAT DO I THINK?
I THINK HER OLD MAN SHOULD HAVE COME CLEAN WITH HER ABOUT HIS **OWN** PAST. WHAT DO **YOU** THINK?
SPORTS
SPORT
I STAND WITH MY PRESIDENT.
I THOUGHT SO.

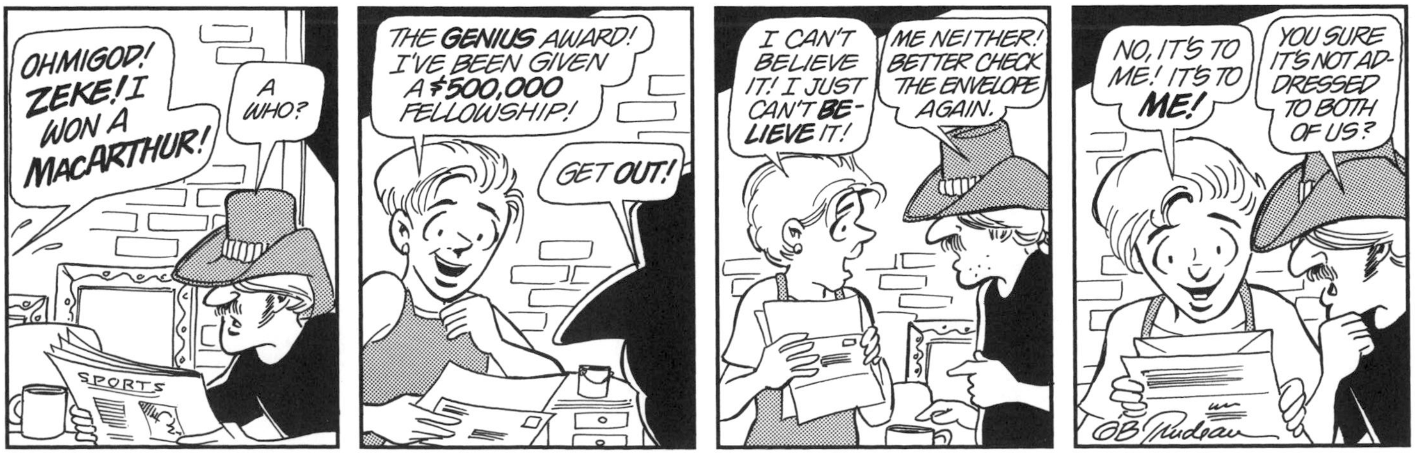
OHMIGOD! **ZEKE!** I WON A **MacARTHUR!**
A WHO?
SPORTS
THE **GENIUS** AWARD! I'VE BEEN GIVEN A **$500,000** FELLOWSHIP!
GET **OUT!**
I CAN'T BELIEVE IT! I JUST CAN'T **BELIEVE** IT!
ME NEITHER! BETTER CHECK THE ENVELOPE AGAIN.
NO, IT'S TO ME! IT'S TO **ME!**
YOU SURE IT'S NOT ADDRESSED TO BOTH OF US?

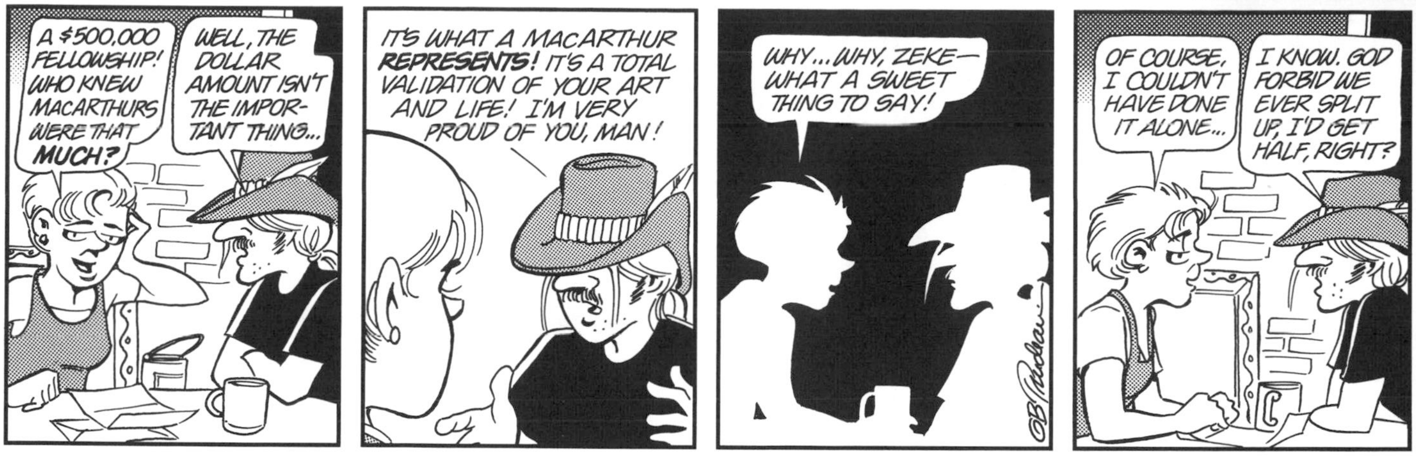
A $500,000 FELLOWSHIP! WHO KNEW MACARTHURS WERE THAT **MUCH?**
WELL, THE DOLLAR AMOUNT ISN'T THE IMPORTANT THING...
IT'S WHAT A MACARTHUR **REPRESENTS!** IT'S A TOTAL VALIDATION OF YOUR ART AND LIFE! I'M VERY PROUD OF YOU, MAN!
WHY... WHY, ZEKE— WHAT A SWEET THING TO SAY!
OF COURSE, I COULDN'T HAVE DONE IT ALONE...
I KNOW. GOD FORBID WE EVER SPLIT UP, I'D GET HALF, RIGHT?

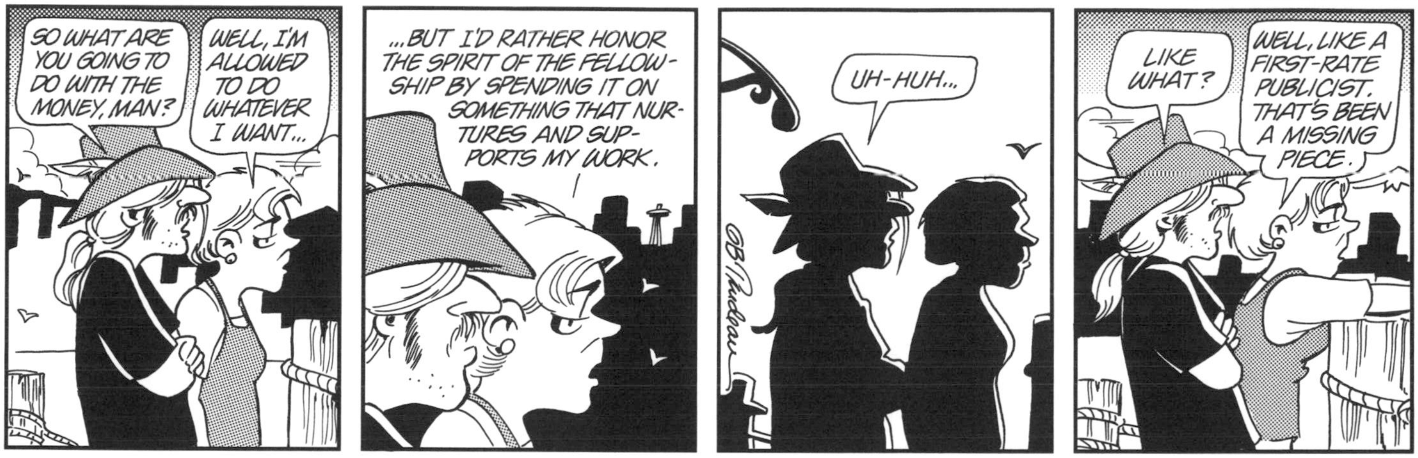
SO WHAT ARE YOU GOING TO DO WITH THE MONEY, MAN?
WELL, I'M ALLOWED TO DO WHATEVER I WANT...
...BUT I'D RATHER HONOR THE SPIRIT OF THE FELLOWSHIP BY SPENDING IT ON SOMETHING THAT NURTURES AND SUPPORTS MY WORK.
UH-HUH...
LIKE WHAT?
WELL, LIKE A FIRST-RATE PUBLICIST. THAT'S BEEN A MISSING PIECE.

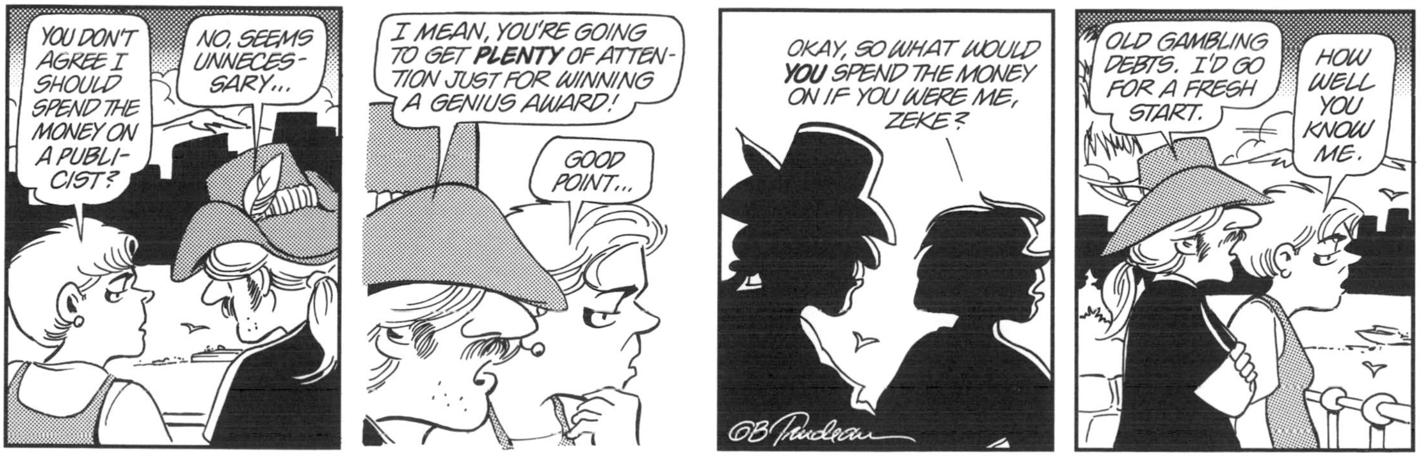
YOU DON'T AGREE I SHOULD SPEND THE MONEY ON A PUBLICIST?
NO, SEEMS UNNECESSARY...
I MEAN, YOU'RE GOING TO GET **PLENTY** OF ATTENTION JUST FOR WINNING A GENIUS AWARD!
GOOD POINT...
OKAY, SO WHAT WOULD **YOU** SPEND THE MONEY ON IF YOU WERE ME, ZEKE?
OLD GAMBLING DEBTS. I'D GO FOR A FRESH START.
HOW WELL YOU KNOW ME.

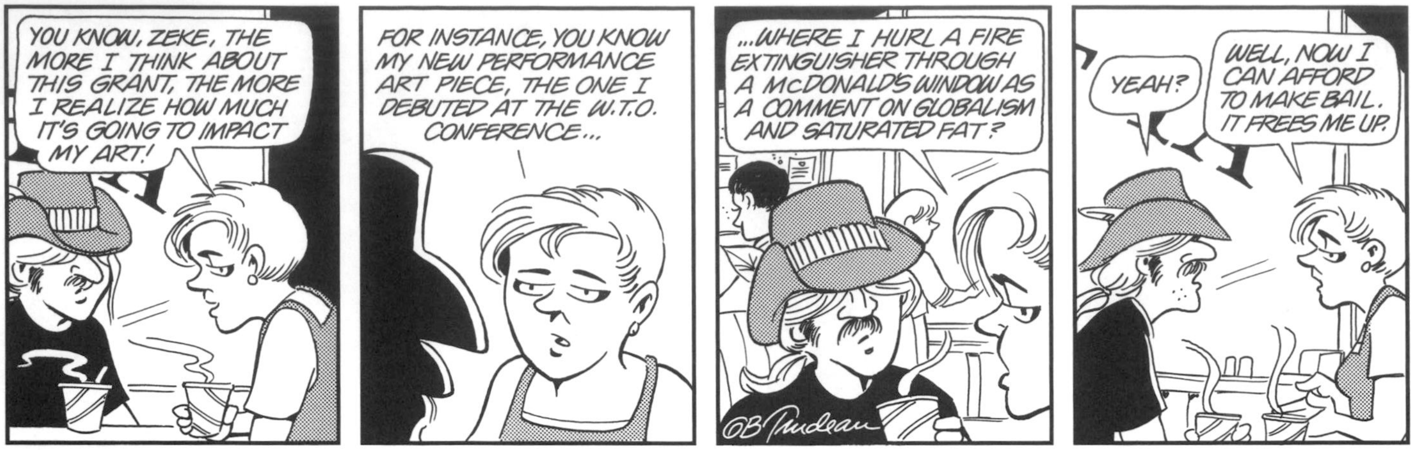
YOU KNOW, ZEKE, THE MORE I THINK ABOUT THIS GRANT, THE MORE I REALIZE HOW MUCH IT'S GOING TO IMPACT MY ART!
FOR INSTANCE, YOU KNOW MY NEW PERFORMANCE ART PIECE, THE ONE I DEBUTED AT THE W.T.O. CONFERENCE...
...WHERE I HURL A FIRE EXTINGUISHER THROUGH A McDONALD'S WINDOW AS A COMMENT ON GLOBALISM AND SATURATED FAT?
GB Trudeau
YEAH?
WELL, NOW I CAN AFFORD TO MAKE BAIL. IT FREES ME UP.

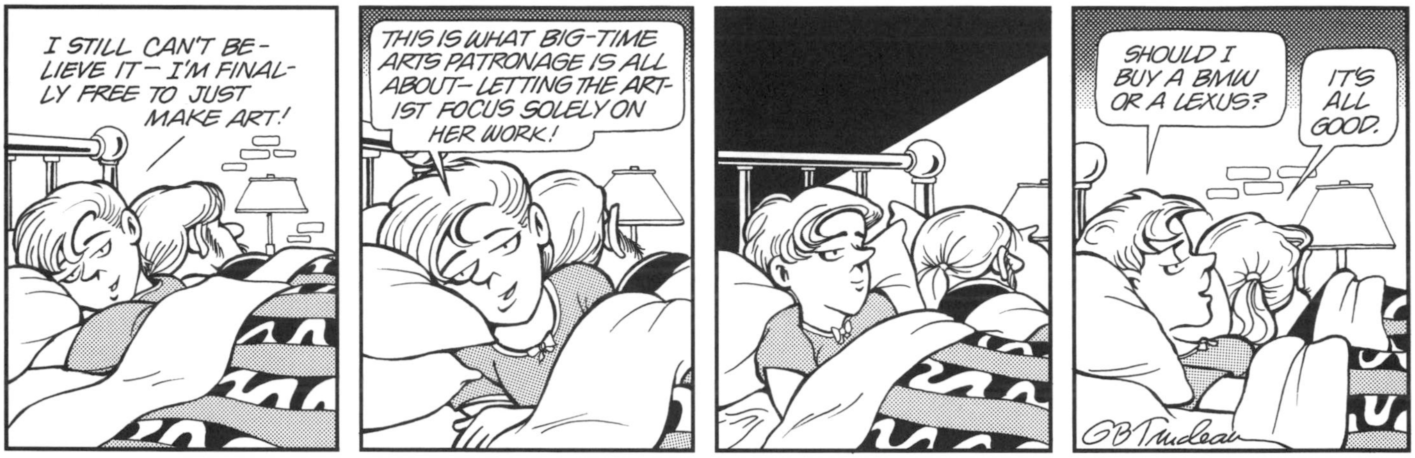
I STILL CAN'T BELIEVE IT— I'M FINALLY FREE TO JUST MAKE ART!
THIS IS WHAT BIG-TIME ARTS PATRONAGE IS ALL ABOUT— LETTING THE ARTIST FOCUS SOLELY ON HER WORK!
SHOULD I BUY A BMW OR A LEXUS?
IT'S ALL GOOD.
GB Trudeau

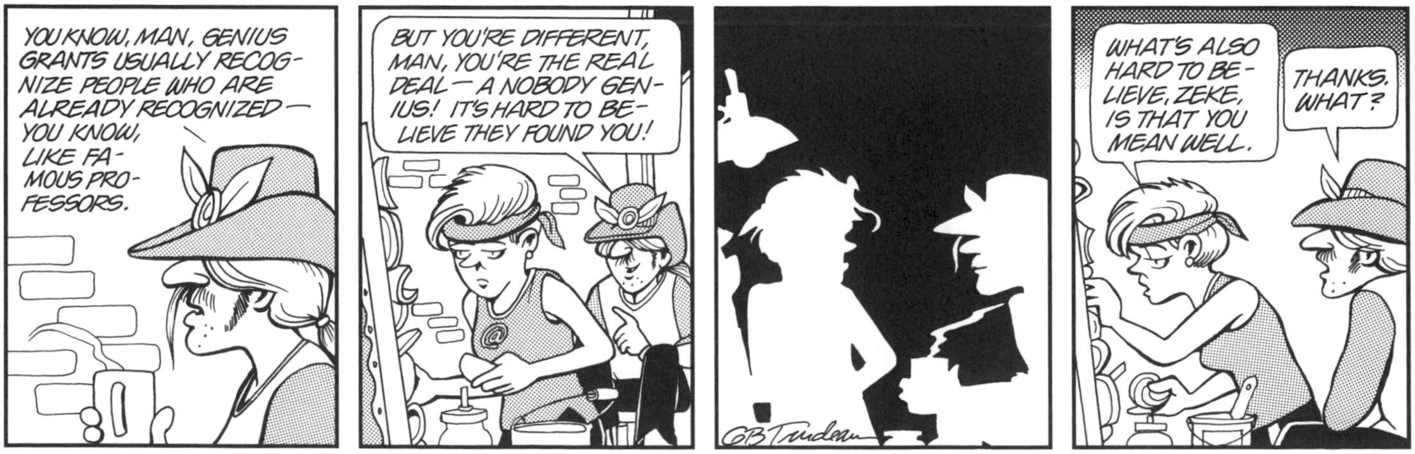
YOU KNOW, MAN, GENIUS GRANTS USUALLY RECOGNIZE PEOPLE WHO ARE ALREADY RECOGNIZED— YOU KNOW, LIKE FAMOUS PROFESSORS.
BUT YOU'RE DIFFERENT, MAN, YOU'RE THE REAL DEAL— A NOBODY GENIUS! IT'S HARD TO BELIEVE THEY FOUND YOU!
GB Trudeau
WHAT'S ALSO HARD TO BELIEVE, ZEKE, IS THAT YOU MEAN WELL.
THANKS. WHAT?

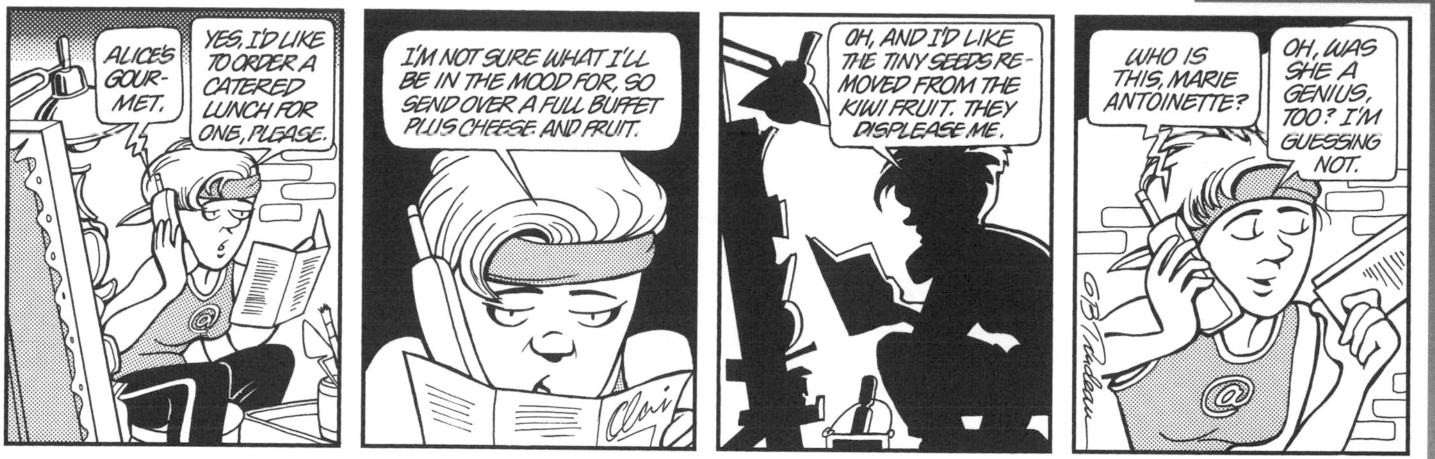
ALICE'S GOURMET.
YES, I'D LIKE TO ORDER A CATERED LUNCH FOR ONE, PLEASE.
I'M NOT SURE WHAT I'LL BE IN THE MOOD FOR, SO SEND OVER A FULL BUFFET PLUS CHEESE AND FRUIT.
OH, AND I'D LIKE THE TINY SEEDS REMOVED FROM THE KIWI FRUIT. THEY DISPLEASE ME.
WHO IS THIS, MARIE ANTOINETTE?
OH, WAS SHE A GENIUS, TOO? I'M GUESSING NOT.
GB Trudeau

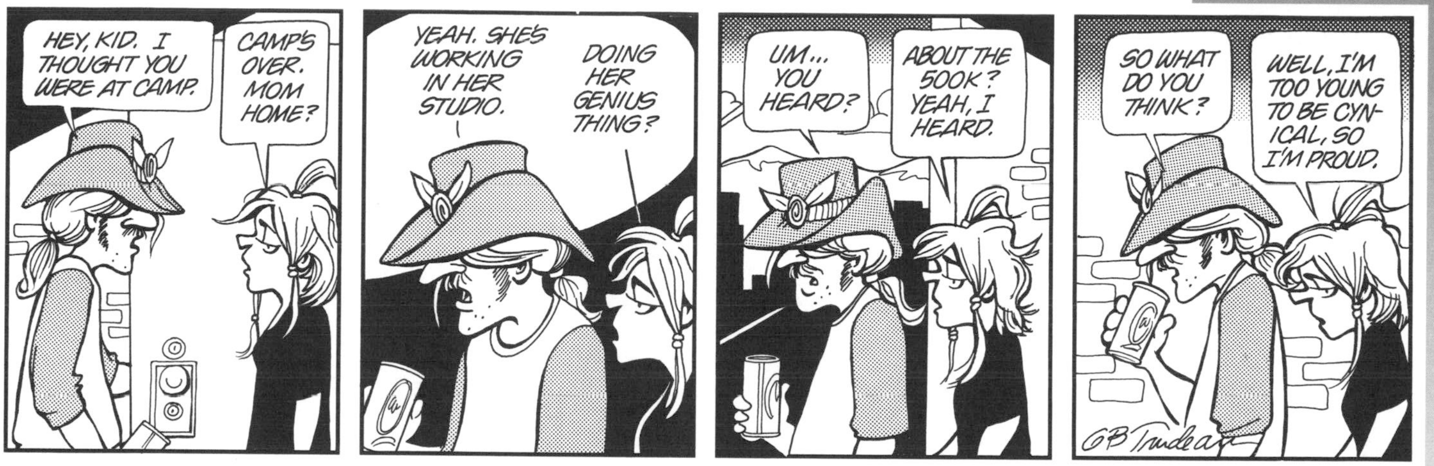
HEY, KID. I THOUGHT YOU WERE AT CAMP.
CAMP'S OVER. MOM HOME?
YEAH. SHE'S WORKING IN HER STUDIO.
DOING HER GENIUS THING?
UM... YOU HEARD?
ABOUT THE 500K? YEAH, I HEARD.
SO WHAT DO YOU THINK?
WELL, I'M TOO YOUNG TO BE CYNICAL, SO I'M PROUD.
GB Trudeau

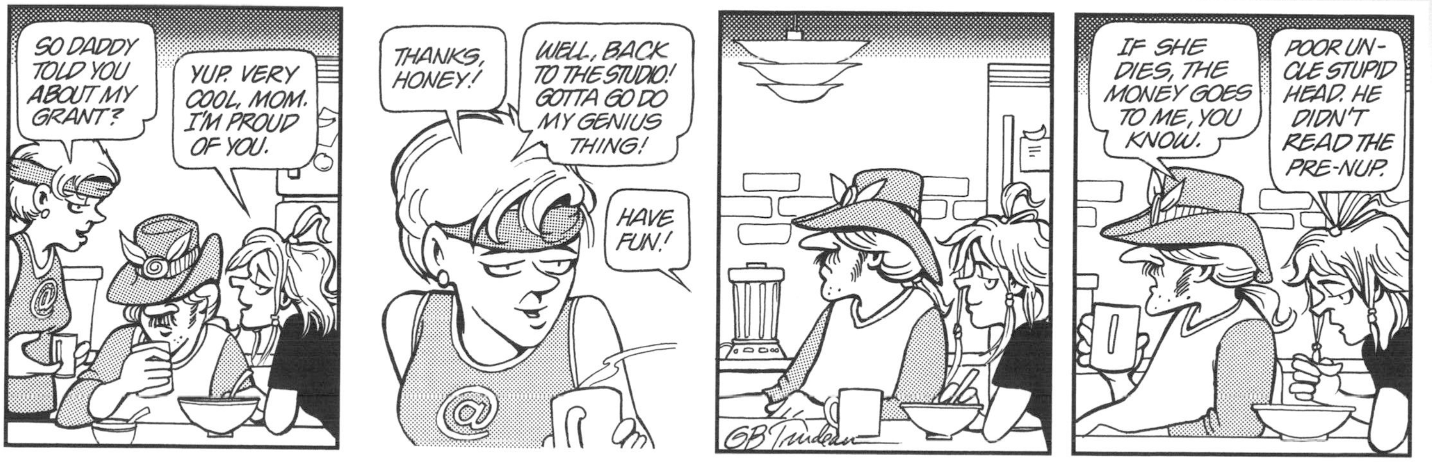
SO DADDY TOLD YOU ABOUT MY GRANT?
YUP. VERY COOL, MOM. I'M PROUD OF YOU.
THANKS, HONEY!
WELL, BACK TO THE STUDIO! GOTTA GO DO MY GENIUS THING!
HAVE FUN!
GB Trudeau
IF SHE DIES, THE MONEY GOES TO ME, YOU KNOW.
POOR UNCLE STUPID HEAD. HE DIDN'T READ THE PRE-NUP.

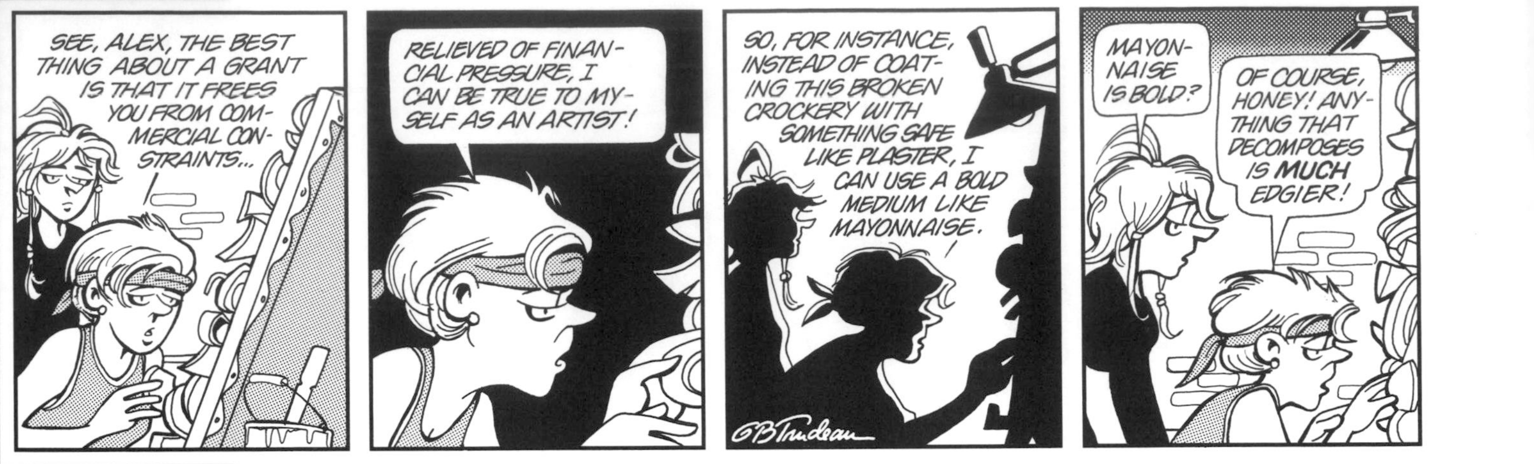
SEE, ALEX, THE BEST THING ABOUT A GRANT IS THAT IT FREES YOU FROM COMMERCIAL CONSTRAINTS...
RELIEVED OF FINANCIAL PRESSURE, I CAN BE TRUE TO MYSELF AS AN ARTIST!
SO, FOR INSTANCE, INSTEAD OF COATING THIS BROKEN CROCKERY WITH SOMETHING SAFE LIKE PLASTER, I CAN USE A BOLD MEDIUM LIKE MAYONNAISE.
MAYONNAISE IS BOLD?
OF COURSE, HONEY! ANYTHING THAT DECOMPOSES IS **MUCH** EDGIER!
GBTrudeau

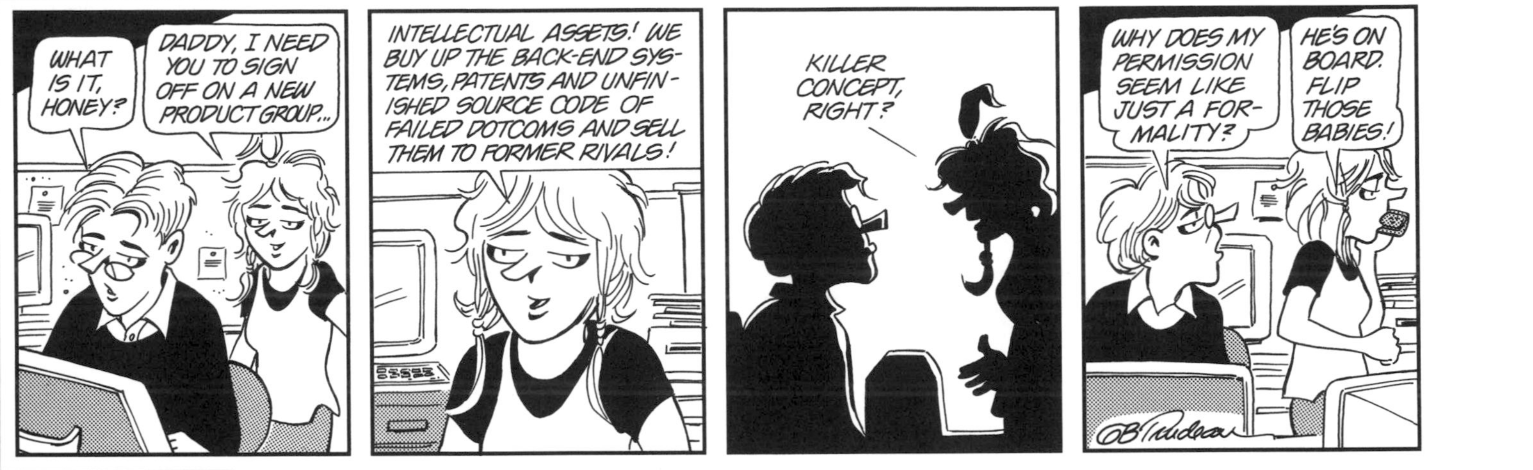
WHAT IS IT, HONEY?
DADDY, I NEED YOU TO SIGN OFF ON A NEW PRODUCT GROUP...
INTELLECTUAL ASSETS! WE BUY UP THE BACK-END SYSTEMS, PATENTS AND UNFINISHED SOURCE CODE OF FAILED DOTCOMS AND SELL THEM TO FORMER RIVALS!
KILLER CONCEPT, RIGHT?
WHY DOES MY PERMISSION SEEM LIKE JUST A FORMALITY?
HE'S ON BOARD. FLIP THOSE BABIES!
GBTrudeau

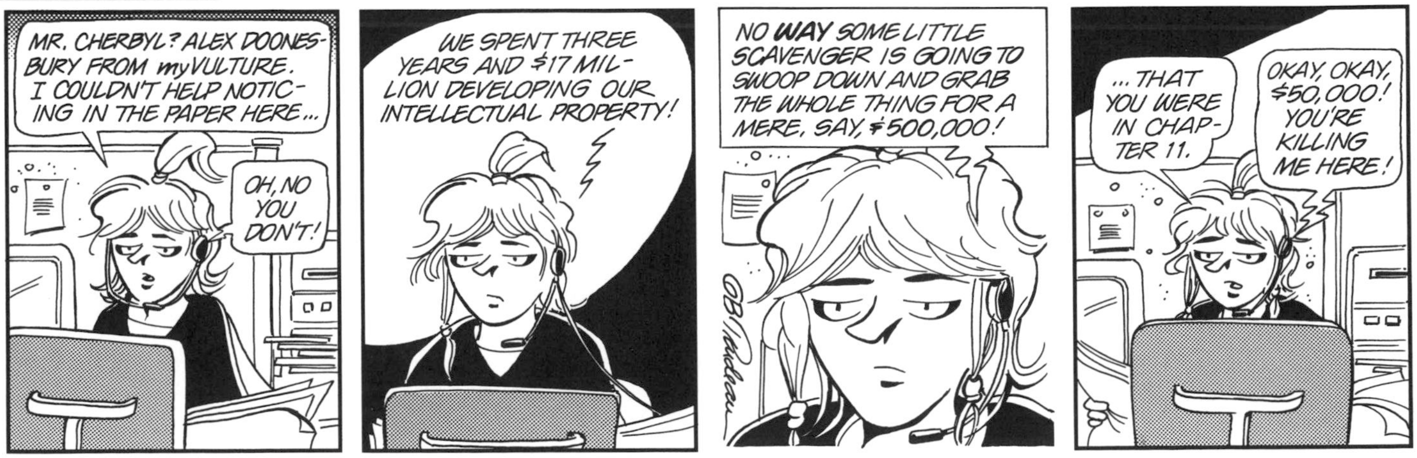
MR. CHERBYL? ALEX DOONESBURY FROM myVULTURE. I COULDN'T HELP NOTICING IN THE PAPER HERE...
OH, NO YOU DON'T!
WE SPENT THREE YEARS AND $17 MILLION DEVELOPING OUR INTELLECTUAL PROPERTY!
NO **WAY** SOME LITTLE SCAVENGER IS GOING TO SWOOP DOWN AND GRAB THE WHOLE THING FOR A MERE, SAY, $500,000!
GBTrudeau
...THAT YOU WERE IN CHAPTER 11.
OKAY, OKAY, $50,000! YOU'RE KILLING ME HERE!

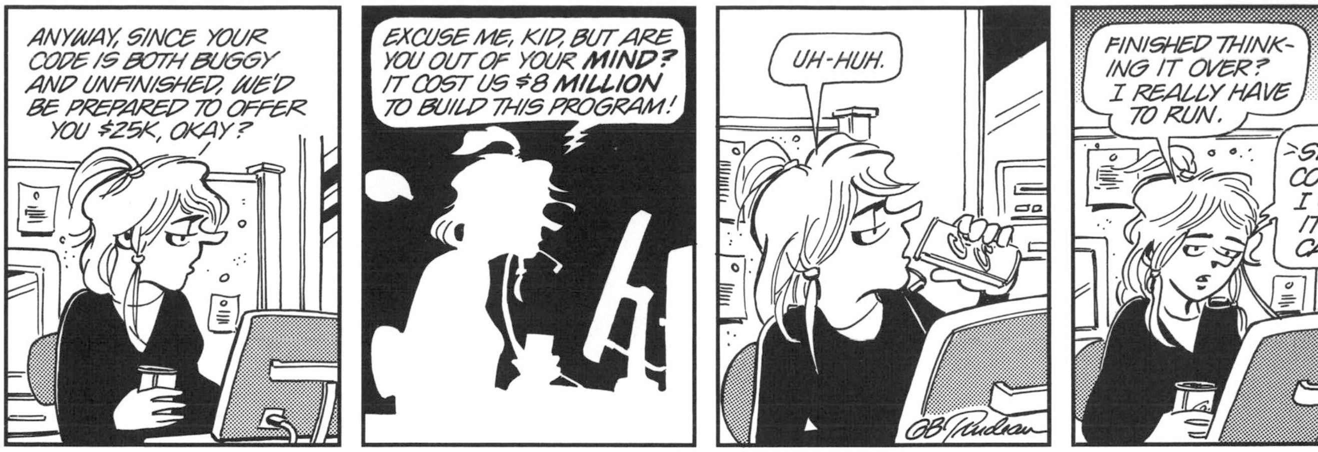
ANYWAY, SINCE YOUR CODE IS BOTH BUGGY AND UNFINISHED, WE'D BE PREPARED TO OFFER YOU $25K, OKAY?
EXCUSE ME, KID, BUT ARE YOU OUT OF YOUR **MIND?** IT COST US $8 **MILLION** TO BUILD THIS PROGRAM!
UH-HUH.
FINISHED THINKING IT OVER? I REALLY HAVE TO RUN.
>SIGH<... COULD I GET IT IN CASH?


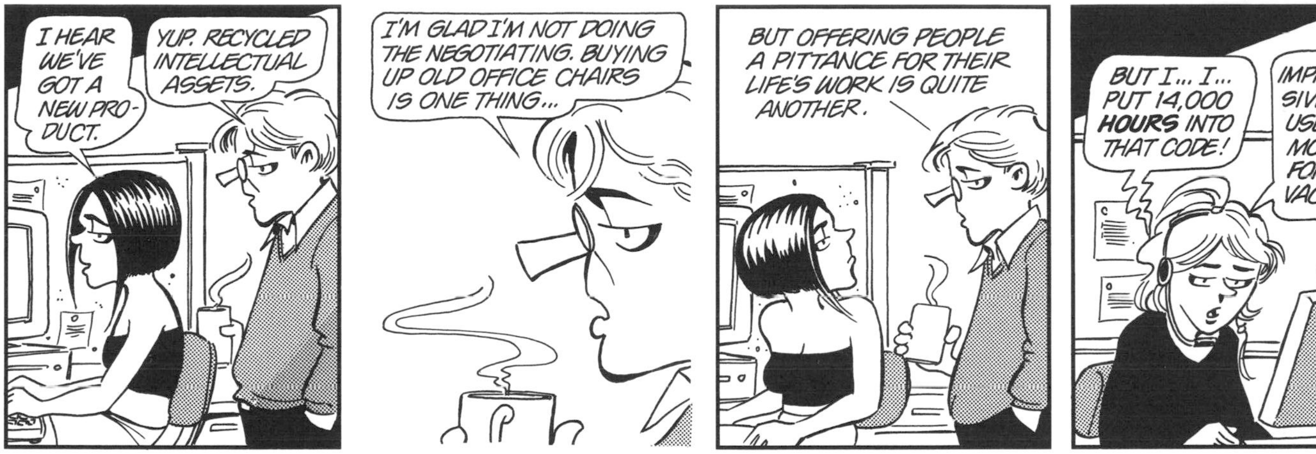
I HEAR WE'VE GOT A NEW PRODUCT.
YUP. RECYCLED INTELLECTUAL ASSETS.
I'M GLAD I'M NOT DOING THE NEGOTIATING. BUYING UP OLD OFFICE CHAIRS IS ONE THING...
BUT OFFERING PEOPLE A PITTANCE FOR THEIR LIFE'S WORK IS QUITE ANOTHER.
BUT I... I... PUT 14,000 **HOURS** INTO THAT CODE!
IMPRESSIVE. I'D USE THE MONEY FOR A VACATION.


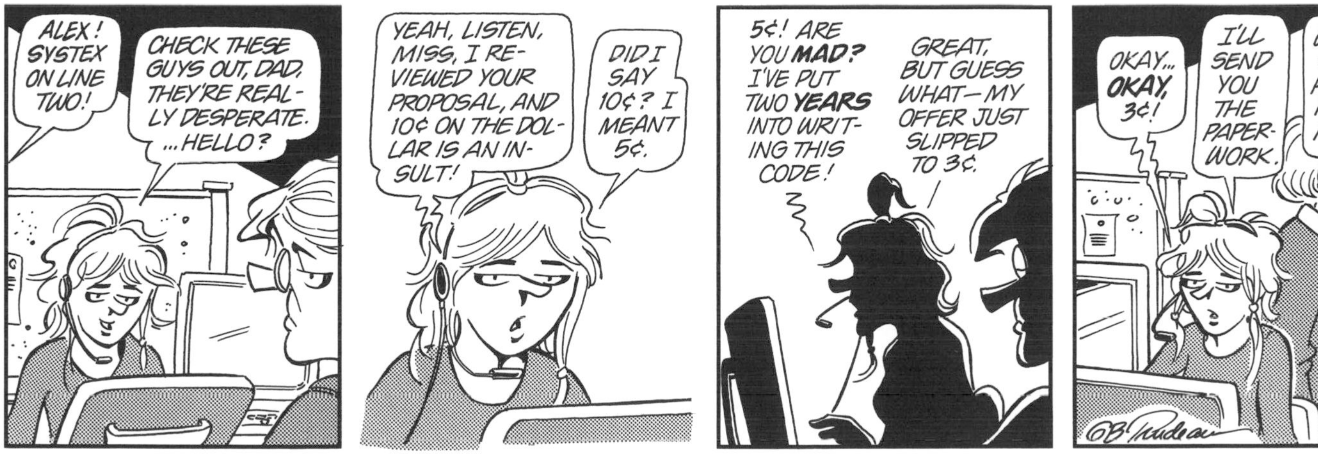
ALEX! **SYSTEX** ON LINE TWO!
CHECK THESE GUYS OUT, DAD. THEY'RE REALLY DESPERATE. ...HELLO?
YEAH, LISTEN, MISS, I REVIEWED YOUR PROPOSAL, AND 10¢ ON THE DOLLAR IS AN INSULT!
DID I SAY 10¢? I MEANT 5¢.
5¢! ARE YOU **MAD?** I'VE PUT TWO **YEARS** INTO WRITING THIS CODE!
GREAT, BUT GUESS WHAT— MY OFFER JUST SLIPPED TO 3¢.
OKAY... **OKAY,** 3¢!
I'LL SEND YOU THE PAPERWORK.
WHEW! COLD, HONEY—KEEP IT UP.

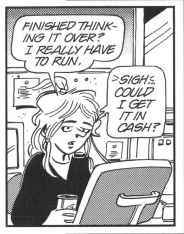

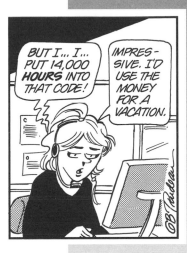

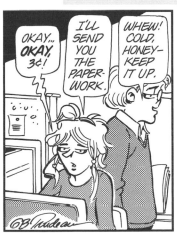

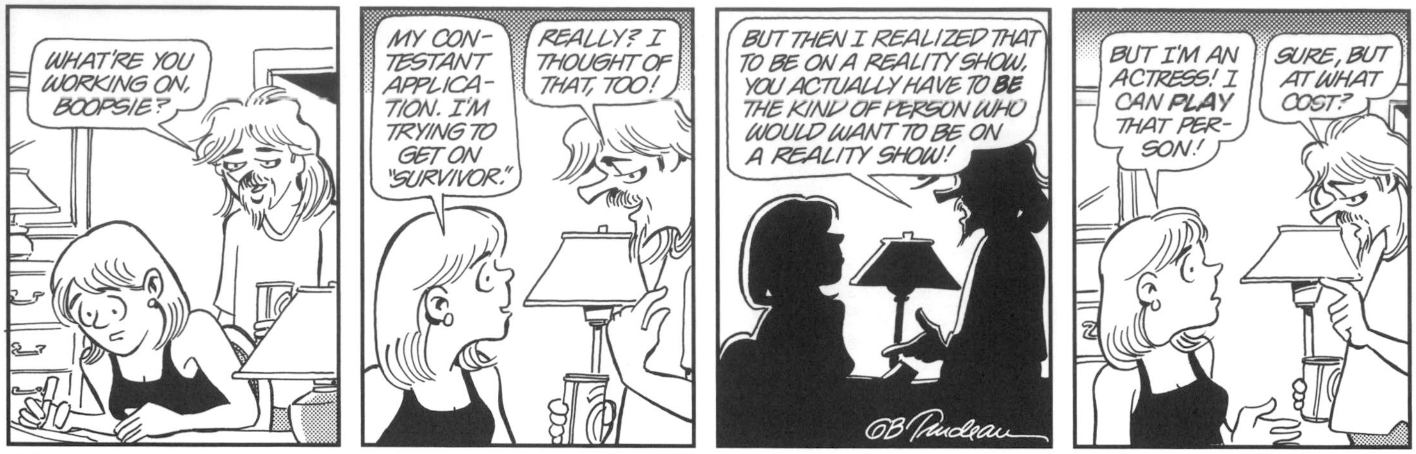
WHAT'RE YOU WORKING ON, BOOPSIE?
MY CONTESTANT APPLICATION. I'M TRYING TO GET ON "SURVIVOR."
REALLY? I THOUGHT OF THAT, TOO!
BUT THEN I REALIZED THAT TO BE ON A REALITY SHOW, YOU ACTUALLY HAVE TO BE THE KIND OF PERSON WHO WOULD WANT TO BE ON A REALITY SHOW!
©B Trudeau
BUT I'M AN ACTRESS! I CAN PLAY THAT PERSON!
SURE, BUT AT WHAT COST?

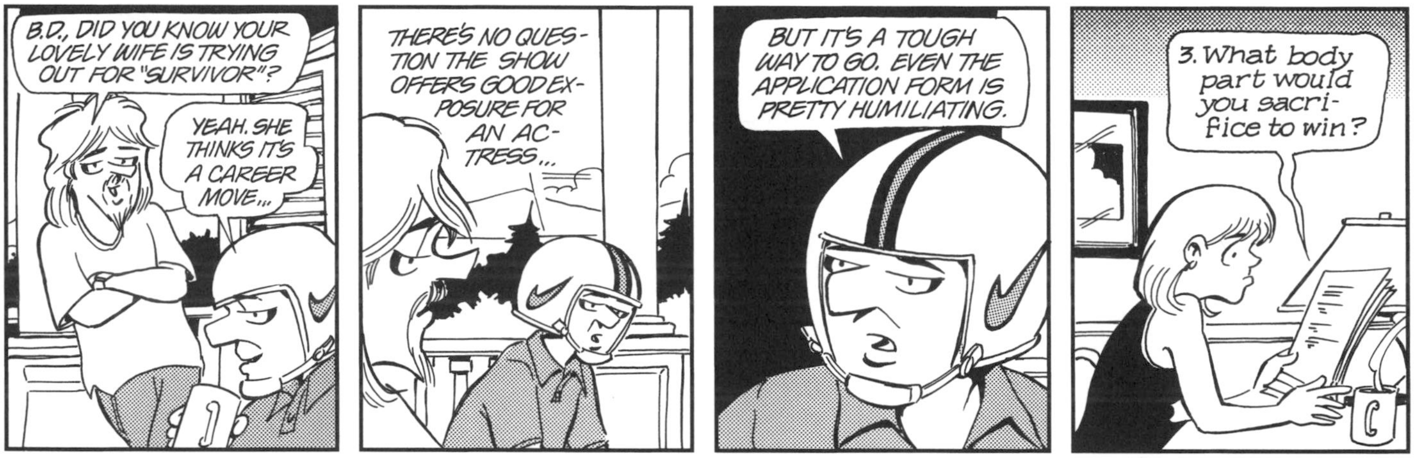
B.D., DID YOU KNOW YOUR LOVELY WIFE IS TRYING OUT FOR "SURVIVOR"?
YEAH. SHE THINKS IT'S A CAREER MOVE...
THERE'S NO QUESTION THE SHOW OFFERS GOOD EXPOSURE FOR AN ACTRESS...
BUT IT'S A TOUGH WAY TO GO. EVEN THE APPLICATION FORM IS PRETTY HUMILIATING.
3. What body part would you sacrifice to win?

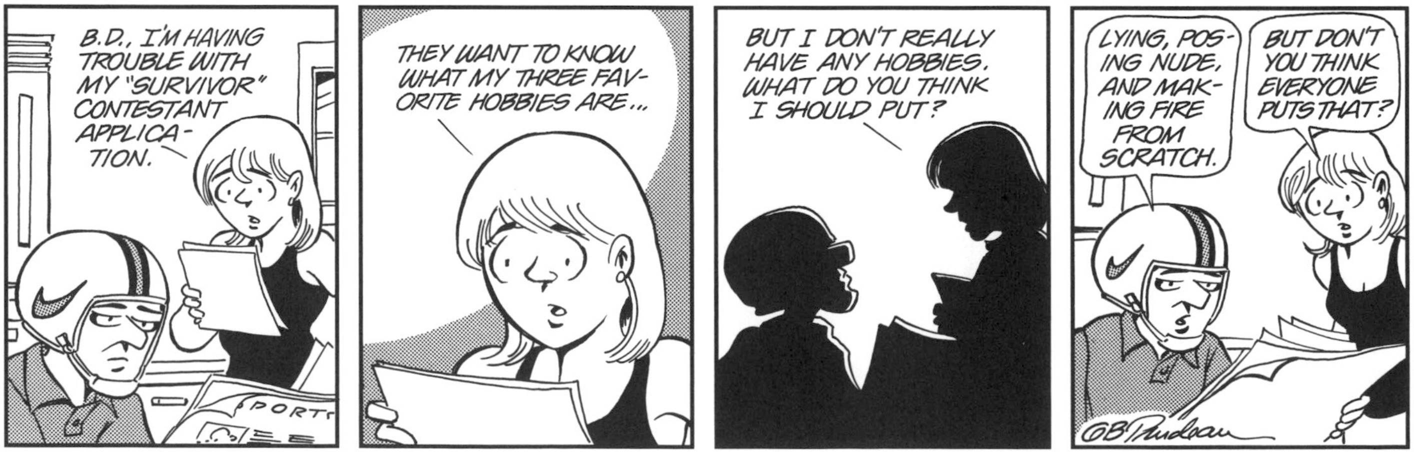
B.D., I'M HAVING TROUBLE WITH MY "SURVIVOR" CONTESTANT APPLICATION.
THEY WANT TO KNOW WHAT MY THREE FAVORITE HOBBIES ARE...
BUT I DON'T REALLY HAVE ANY HOBBIES. WHAT DO YOU THINK I SHOULD PUT?
LYING, POSING NUDE, AND MAKING FIRE FROM SCRATCH.
BUT DON'T YOU THINK EVERYONE PUTS THAT?
©B Trudeau

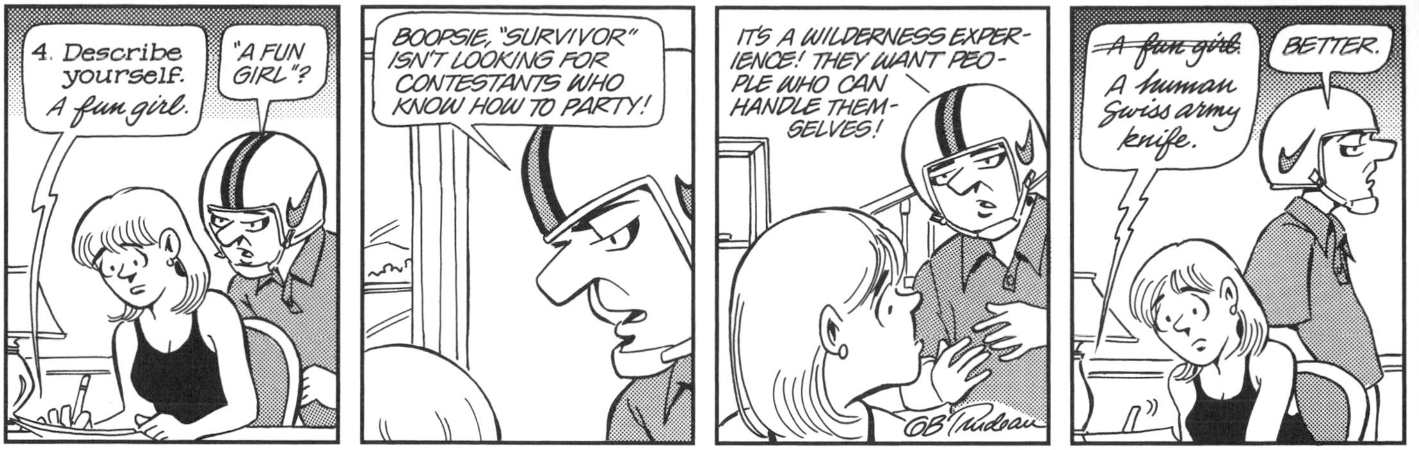
4. Describe yourself. A fun girl.
"A FUN GIRL"?
BOOPSIE, "SURVIVOR" ISN'T LOOKING FOR CONTESTANTS WHO KNOW HOW TO PARTY!
IT'S A WILDERNESS EXPERIENCE! THEY WANT PEOPLE WHO CAN HANDLE THEMSELVES!
~~A fun girl.~~ A human Swiss army knife.
BETTER.

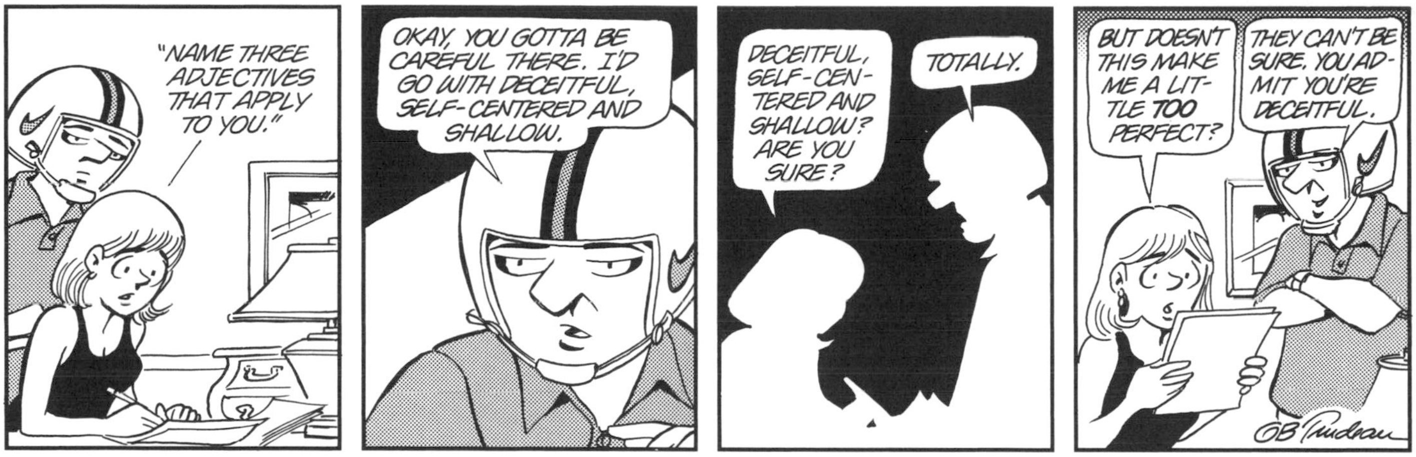
"NAME THREE ADJECTIVES THAT APPLY TO YOU."
OKAY, YOU GOTTA BE CAREFUL THERE. I'D GO WITH DECEITFUL, SELF-CENTERED AND SHALLOW.
DECEITFUL, SELF-CENTERED AND SHALLOW? ARE YOU SURE?
TOTALLY.
BUT DOESN'T THIS MAKE ME A LITTLE **TOO** PERFECT?
THEY CAN'T BE SURE. YOU ADMIT YOU'RE DECEITFUL.

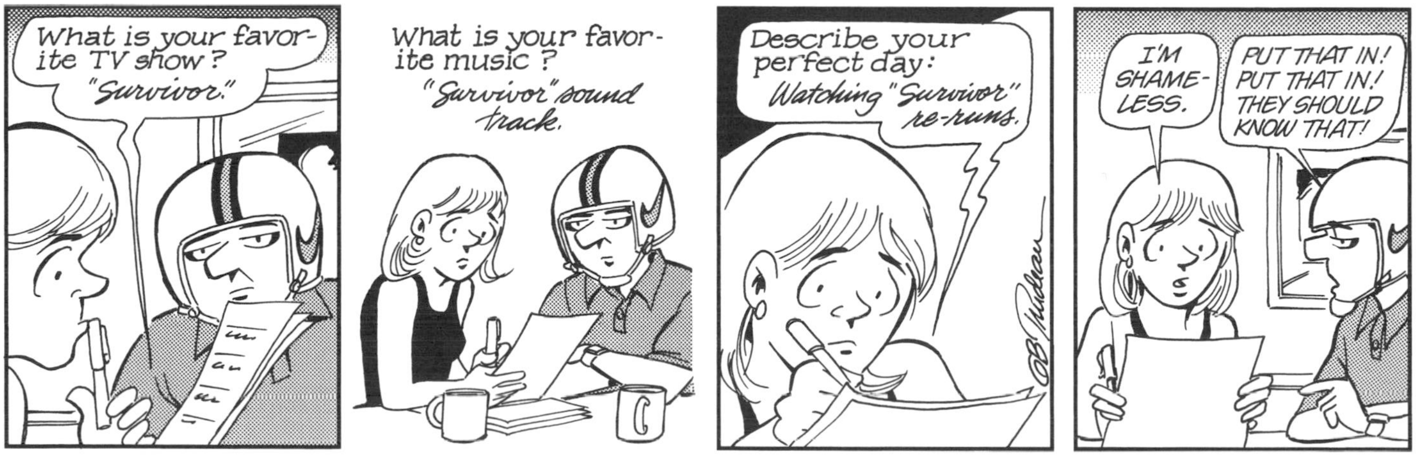
What is your favorite TV show? "Survivor."
What is your favorite music? "Survivor" sound track.
Describe your perfect day: Watching "Survivor" re-runs.
I'M SHAMELESS.
PUT THAT IN! PUT THAT IN! THEY SHOULD KNOW THAT!

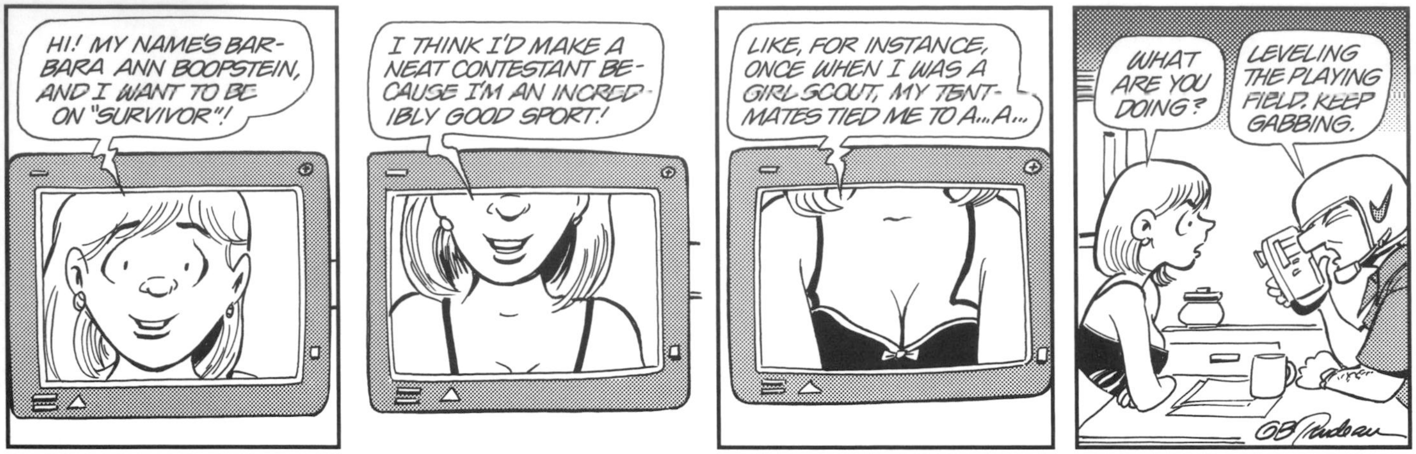
HI! MY NAME'S BARBARA ANN BOOPSTEIN, AND I WANT TO BE ON "SURVIVOR"!
I THINK I'D MAKE A NEAT CONTESTANT BECAUSE I'M AN INCREDIBLY GOOD SPORT!
LIKE, FOR INSTANCE, ONCE WHEN I WAS A GIRL SCOUT, MY TENTMATES TIED ME TO A...A...
WHAT ARE YOU DOING?
LEVELING THE PLAYING FIELD. KEEP GABBING.
GB Trudeau

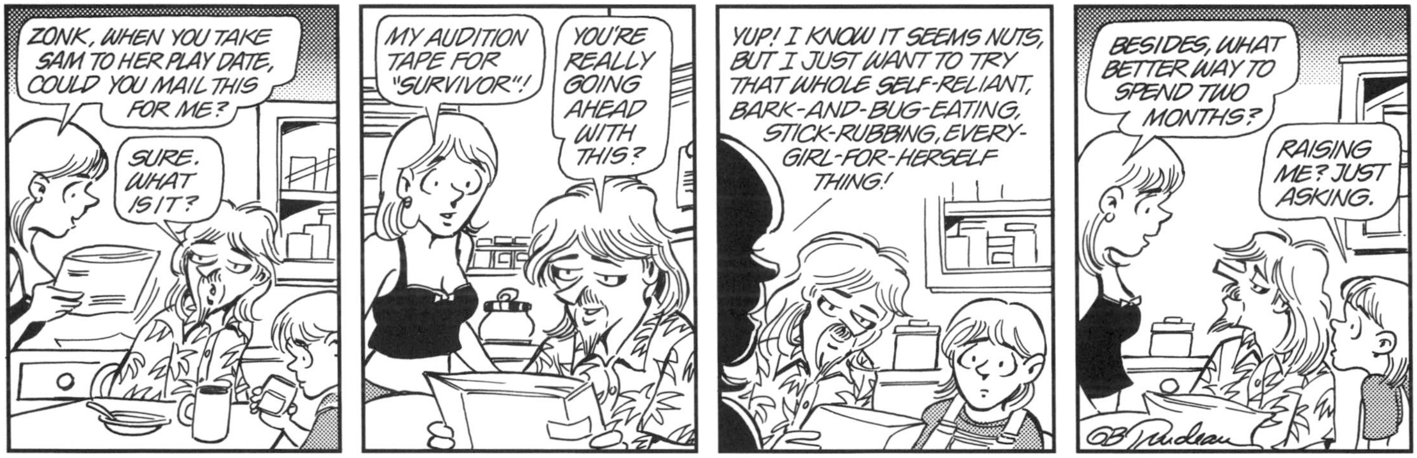
ZONK, WHEN YOU TAKE SAM TO HER PLAY DATE, COULD YOU MAIL THIS FOR ME?
SURE. WHAT IS IT?
MY AUDITION TAPE FOR "SURVIVOR"!
YOU'RE REALLY GOING AHEAD WITH THIS?
YUP! I KNOW IT SEEMS NUTS, BUT I JUST WANT TO TRY THAT WHOLE SELF-RELIANT, BARK-AND-BUG-EATING, STICK-RUBBING, EVERY-GIRL-FOR-HERSELF THING!
BESIDES, WHAT BETTER WAY TO SPEND TWO MONTHS?
RAISING ME? JUST ASKING.
GB Trudeau

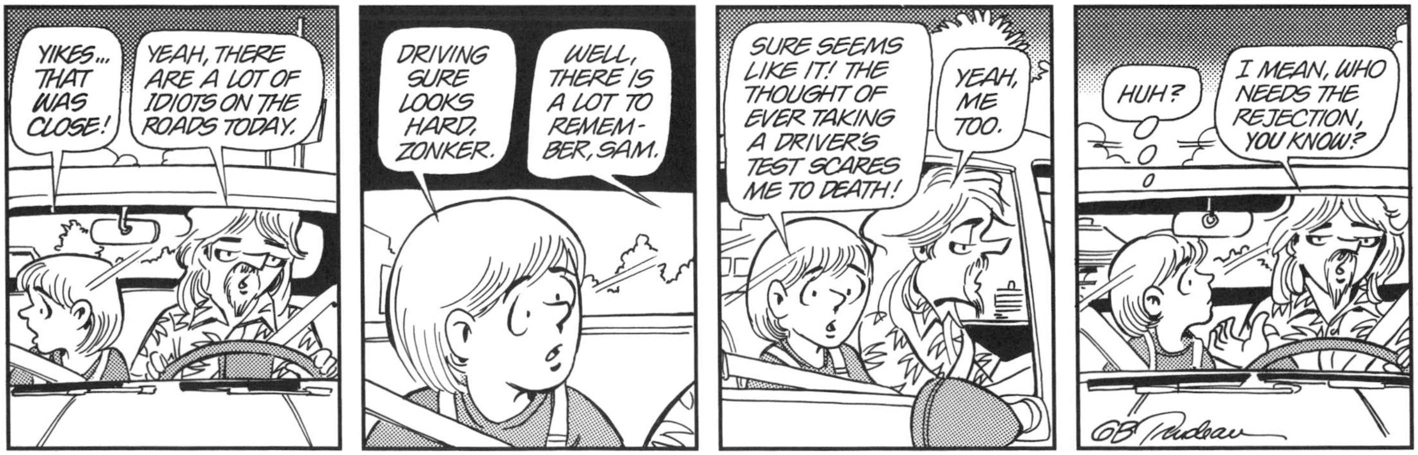
YIKES... THAT WAS CLOSE!
YEAH, THERE ARE A LOT OF IDIOTS ON THE ROADS TODAY.
DRIVING SURE LOOKS HARD, ZONKER.
WELL, THERE IS A LOT TO REMEMBER, SAM.
SURE SEEMS LIKE IT! THE THOUGHT OF EVER TAKING A DRIVER'S TEST SCARES ME TO DEATH!
YEAH, ME TOO.
HUH?
I MEAN, WHO NEEDS THE REJECTION, YOU KNOW?
GB Trudeau

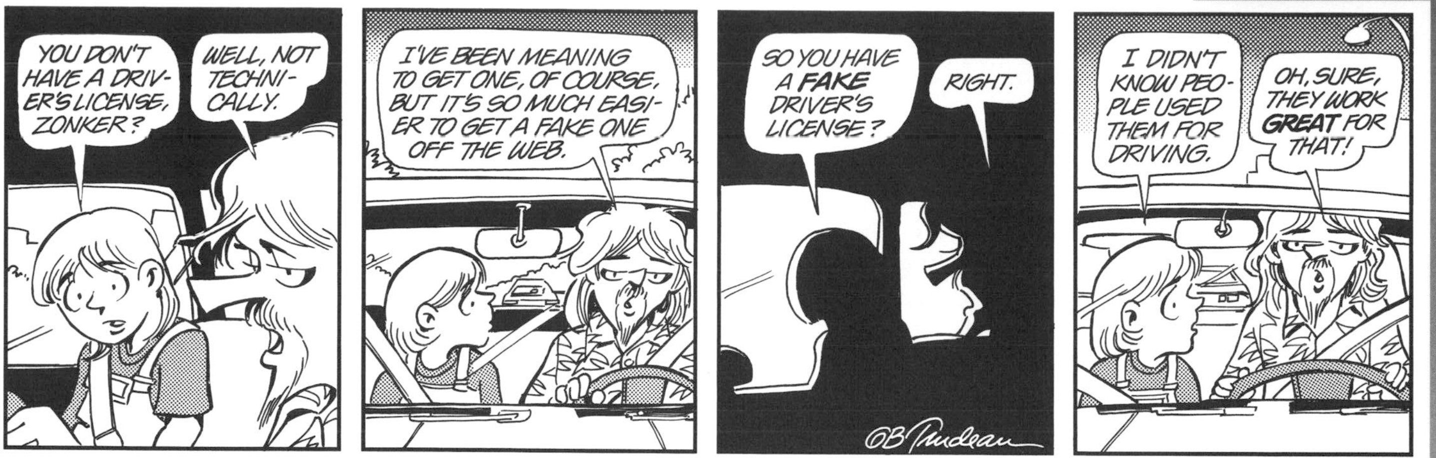
YOU DON'T HAVE A DRIVER'S LICENSE, ZONKER?
WELL, NOT TECHNICALLY.
I'VE BEEN MEANING TO GET ONE, OF COURSE, BUT IT'S SO MUCH EASIER TO GET A FAKE ONE OFF THE WEB.
SO YOU HAVE A FAKE DRIVER'S LICENSE?
RIGHT.
I DIDN'T KNOW PEOPLE USED THEM FOR DRIVING.
OH, SURE, THEY WORK GREAT FOR THAT!
©B Trudeau

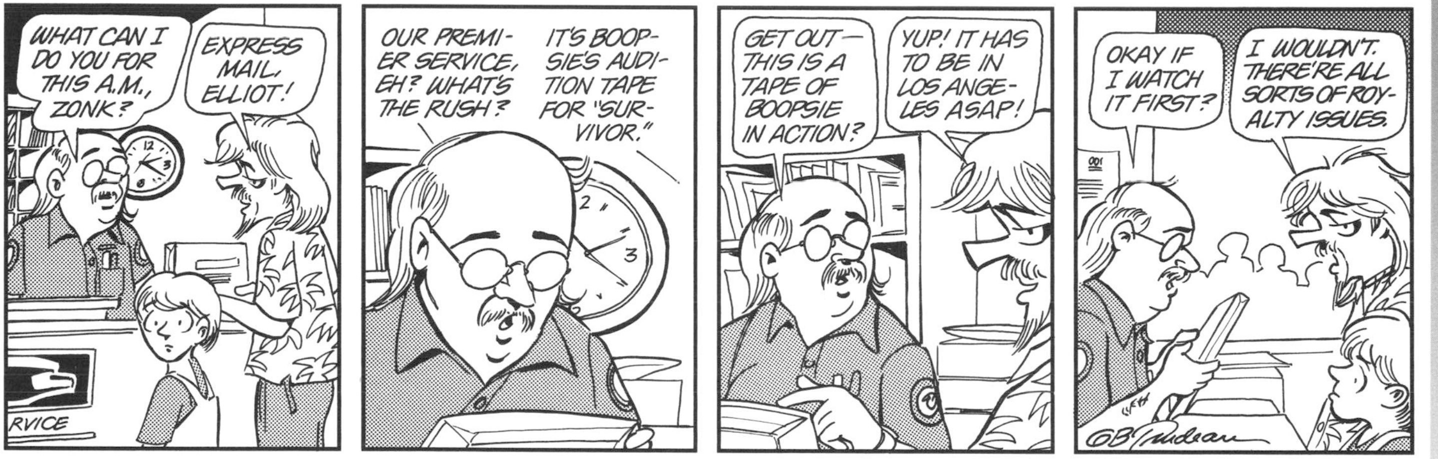
WHAT CAN I DO YOU FOR THIS A.M., ZONK?
EXPRESS MAIL, ELLIOT!
RVICE
OUR PREMIER SERVICE, EH? WHAT'S THE RUSH?
IT'S BOOPSIE'S AUDITION TAPE FOR "SURVIVOR."
GET OUT— THIS IS A TAPE OF BOOPSIE IN ACTION?
YUP! IT HAS TO BE IN LOS ANGELES ASAP!
OKAY IF I WATCH IT FIRST?
I WOULDN'T. THERE'RE ALL SORTS OF ROYALTY ISSUES.
©B Trudeau

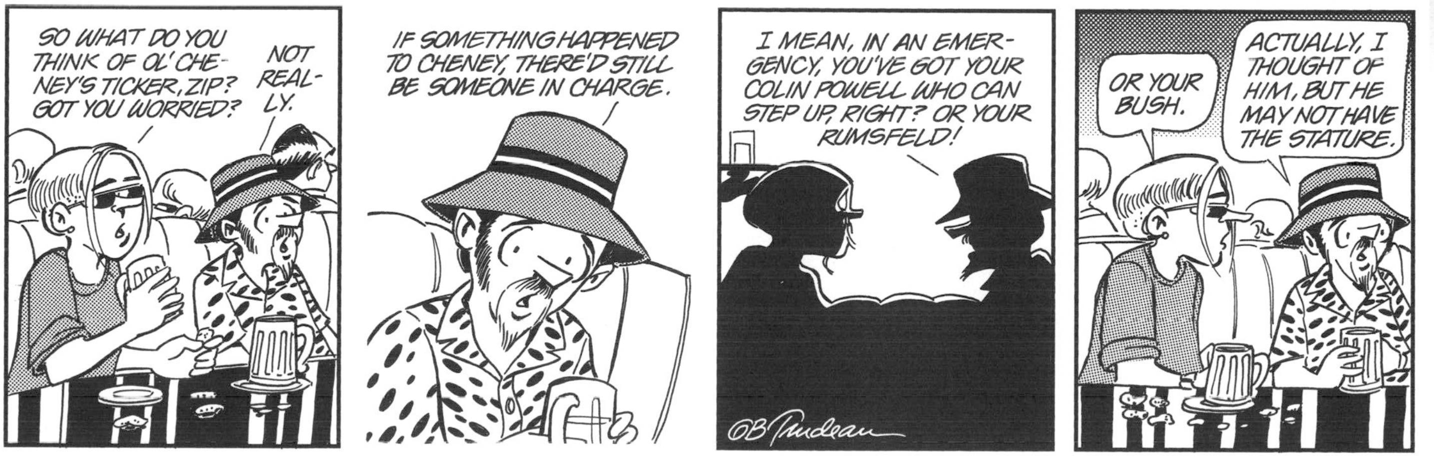
SO WHAT DO YOU THINK OF OL' CHENEY'S TICKER, ZIP? GOT YOU WORRIED?
NOT REALLY.
IF SOMETHING HAPPENED TO CHENEY, THERE'D STILL BE SOMEONE IN CHARGE.
I MEAN, IN AN EMERGENCY, YOU'VE GOT YOUR COLIN POWELL WHO CAN STEP UP, RIGHT? OR YOUR RUMSFELD!
©B Trudeau
OR YOUR BUSH.
ACTUALLY, I THOUGHT OF HIM, BUT HE MAY NOT HAVE THE STATURE.

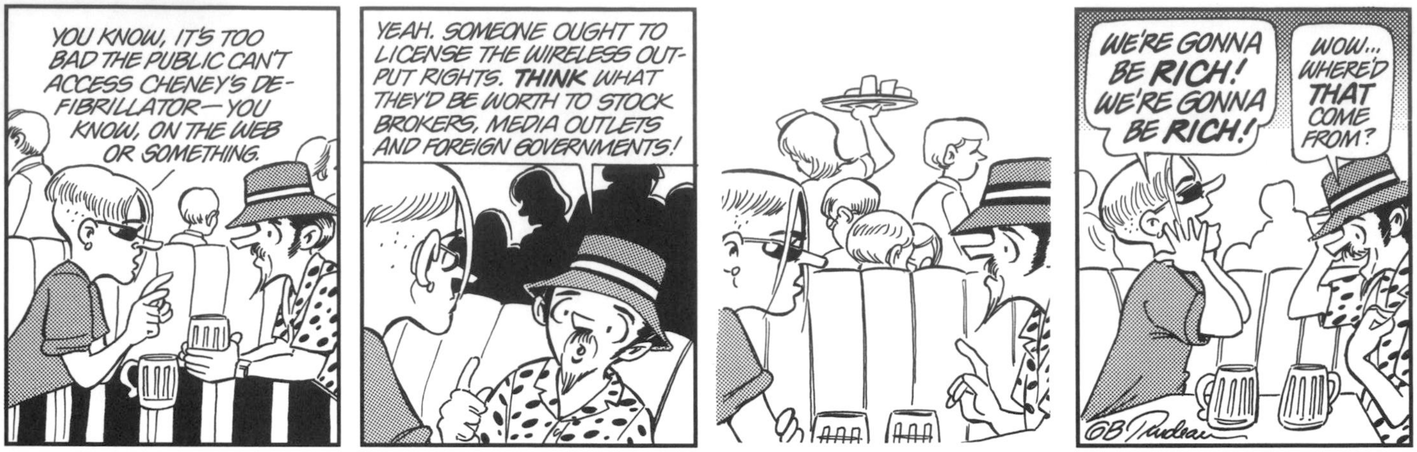
YOU KNOW, IT'S TOO BAD THE PUBLIC CAN'T ACCESS CHENEY'S DE-FIBRILLATOR— YOU KNOW, ON THE WEB OR SOMETHING.
YEAH. SOMEONE OUGHT TO LICENSE THE WIRELESS OUT-PUT RIGHTS. THINK WHAT THEY'D BE WORTH TO STOCK BROKERS, MEDIA OUTLETS AND FOREIGN GOVERNMENTS!
WE'RE GONNA BE RICH! WE'RE GONNA BE RICH!
WOW... WHERE'D THAT COME FROM?
©B Trudeau

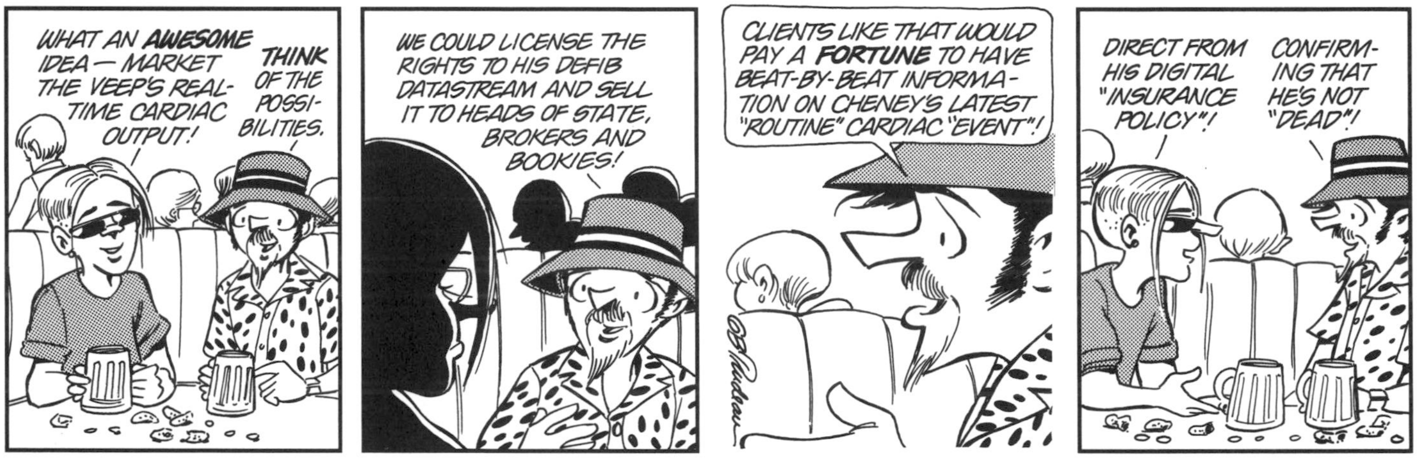
WHAT AN AWESOME IDEA — MARKET THE VEEP'S REAL-TIME CARDIAC OUTPUT!
THINK OF THE POSSI-BILITIES.
WE COULD LICENSE THE RIGHTS TO HIS DEFIB DATASTREAM AND SELL IT TO HEADS OF STATE, BROKERS AND BOOKIES!
CLIENTS LIKE THAT WOULD PAY A FORTUNE TO HAVE BEAT-BY-BEAT INFORMA-TION ON CHENEY'S LATEST "ROUTINE" CARDIAC "EVENT"!
©B Trudeau
DIRECT FROM HIS DIGITAL "INSURANCE POLICY"!
CONFIRM-ING THAT HE'S NOT "DEAD"!

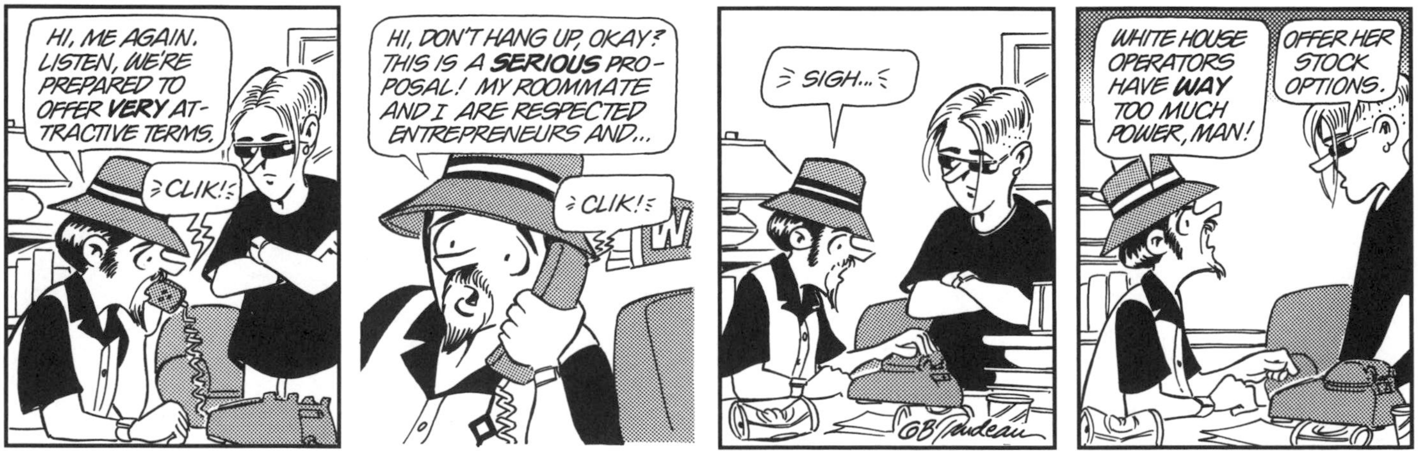
HI, ME AGAIN. LISTEN, WE'RE PREPARED TO OFFER VERY AT-TRACTIVE TERMS.
CLIK!
HI, DON'T HANG UP, OKAY? THIS IS A SERIOUS PRO-POSAL! MY ROOMMATE AND I ARE RESPECTED ENTREPRENEURS AND...
CLIK!
SIGH...
©B Trudeau
WHITE HOUSE OPERATORS HAVE WAY TOO MUCH POWER, MAN!
OFFER HER STOCK OPTIONS.

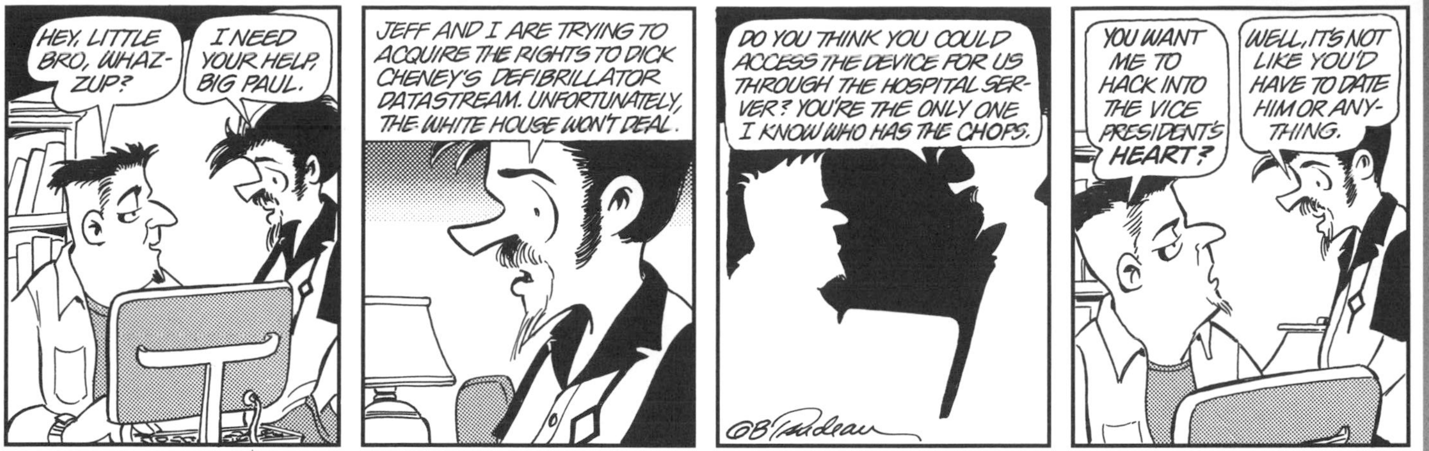
HEY, LITTLE BRO, WHAZ-ZUP?
I NEED YOUR HELP, BIG PAUL.
JEFF AND I ARE TRYING TO ACQUIRE THE RIGHTS TO DICK CHENEY'S DEFIBRILLATOR DATASTREAM. UNFORTUNATELY, THE WHITE HOUSE WON'T DEAL.
DO YOU THINK YOU COULD ACCESS THE DEVICE FOR US THROUGH THE HOSPITAL SER-VER? YOU'RE THE ONLY ONE I KNOW WHO HAS THE CHOPS.
YOU WANT ME TO HACK INTO THE VICE PRESIDENT'S HEART?
WELL, IT'S NOT LIKE YOU'D HAVE TO DATE HIM OR ANY-THING.

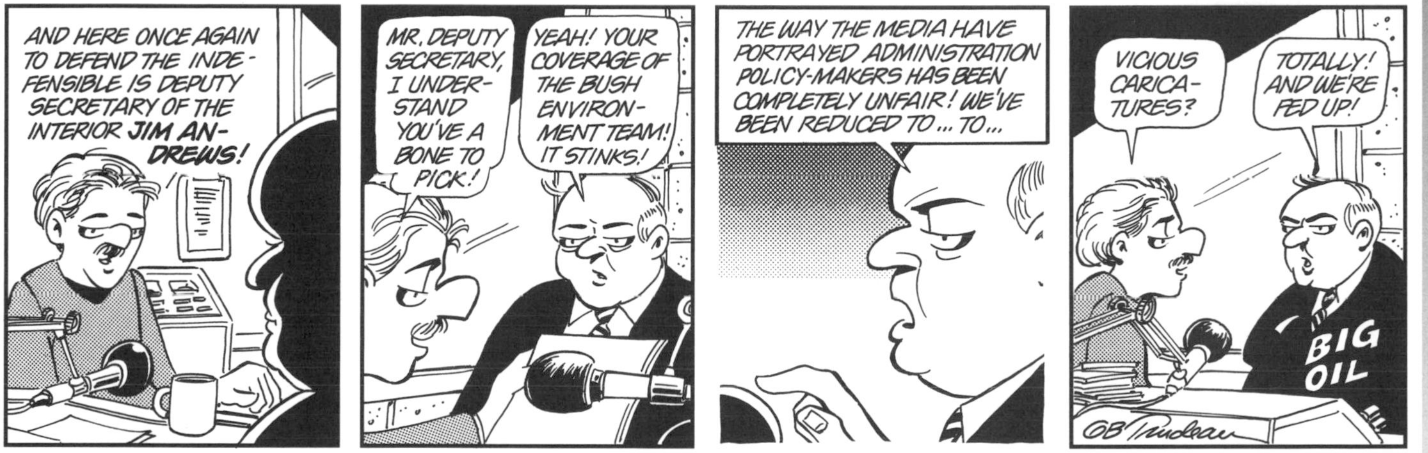
AND HERE ONCE AGAIN TO DEFEND THE INDE-FENSIBLE IS DEPUTY SECRETARY OF THE INTERIOR JIM AN-DREWS!
MR. DEPUTY SECRETARY, I UNDER-STAND YOU'VE A BONE TO PICK!
YEAH! YOUR COVERAGE OF THE BUSH ENVIRON-MENT TEAM! IT STINKS!
THE WAY THE MEDIA HAVE PORTRAYED ADMINISTRATION POLICY-MAKERS HAS BEEN COMPLETELY UNFAIR! WE'VE BEEN REDUCED TO ... TO ...
VICIOUS CARICA-TURES?
TOTALLY! AND WE'RE FED UP!
BIG OIL

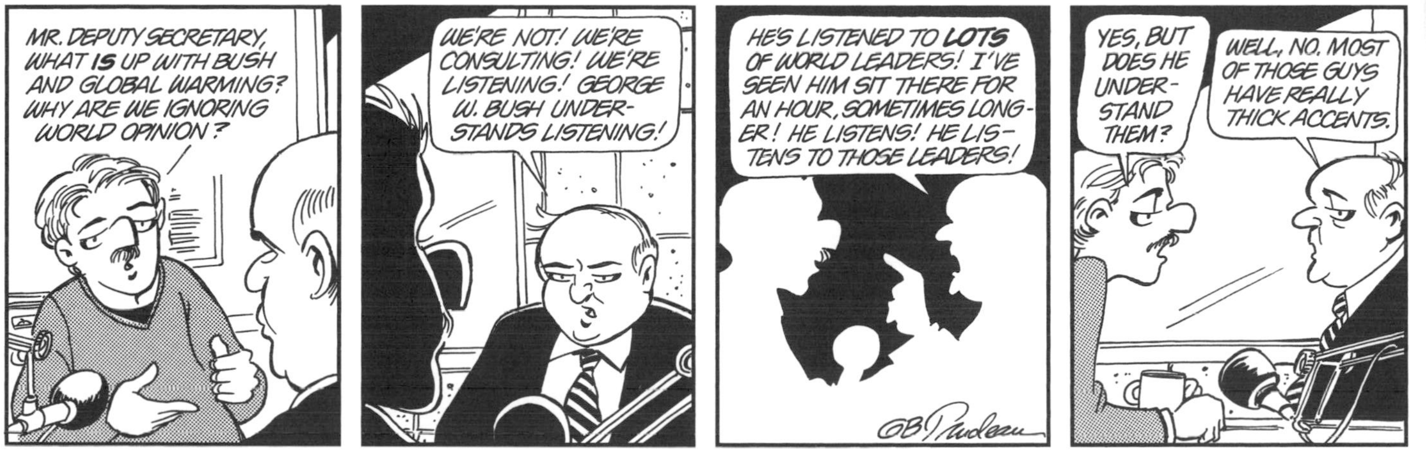
MR. DEPUTY SECRETARY, WHAT IS UP WITH BUSH AND GLOBAL WARMING? WHY ARE WE IGNORING WORLD OPINION?
WE'RE NOT! WE'RE CONSULTING! WE'RE LISTENING! GEORGE W. BUSH UNDER-STANDS LISTENING!
HE'S LISTENED TO LOTS OF WORLD LEADERS! I'VE SEEN HIM SIT THERE FOR AN HOUR, SOMETIMES LONG-ER! HE LISTENS! HE LIS-TENS TO THOSE LEADERS!
YES, BUT DOES HE UNDER-STAND THEM?
WELL, NO. MOST OF THOSE GUYS HAVE REALLY THICK ACCENTS.

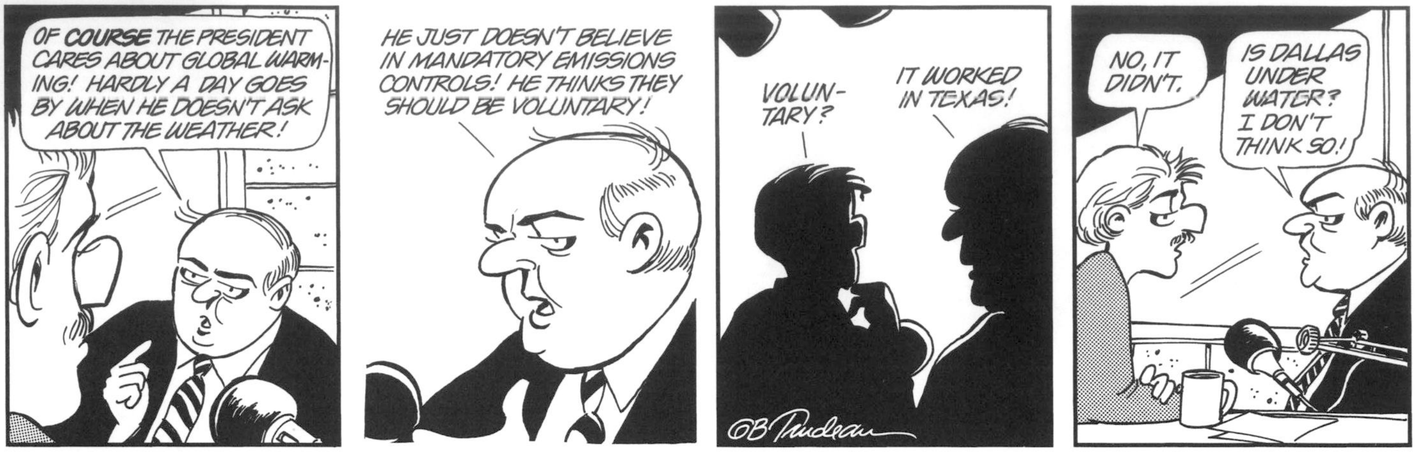
OF **COURSE** THE PRESIDENT CARES ABOUT GLOBAL WARMING! HARDLY A DAY GOES BY WHEN HE DOESN'T ASK ABOUT THE WEATHER!
HE JUST DOESN'T BELIEVE IN MANDATORY EMISSIONS CONTROLS! HE THINKS THEY SHOULD BE VOLUNTARY!
VOLUNTARY?
IT WORKED IN TEXAS!
NO, IT DIDN'T.
IS DALLAS UNDER WATER? I DON'T THINK SO.!
©B Trudeau

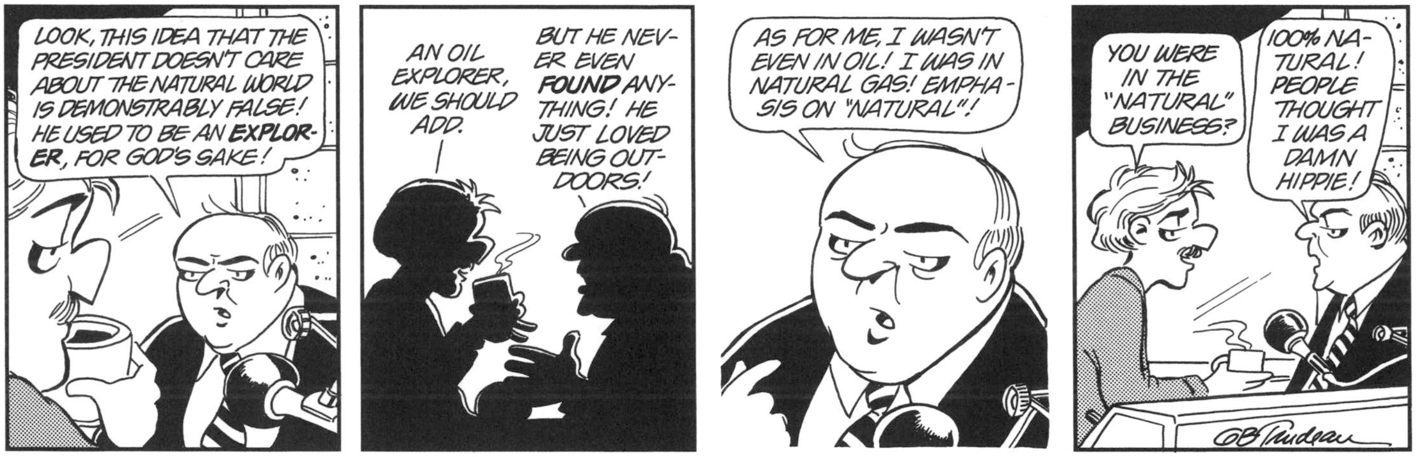
LOOK, THIS IDEA THAT THE PRESIDENT DOESN'T CARE ABOUT THE NATURAL WORLD IS DEMONSTRABLY FALSE! HE USED TO BE AN **EXPLORER**, FOR GOD'S SAKE!
AN OIL EXPLORER, WE SHOULD ADD.
BUT HE NEVER EVEN **FOUND** ANYTHING! HE JUST LOVED BEING OUTDOORS!
AS FOR ME, I WASN'T EVEN IN OIL! I WAS IN NATURAL GAS! EMPHASIS ON "NATURAL"!
YOU WERE IN THE "NATURAL" BUSINESS?
100% NATURAL! PEOPLE THOUGHT I WAS A DAMN HIPPIE!
©B Trudeau

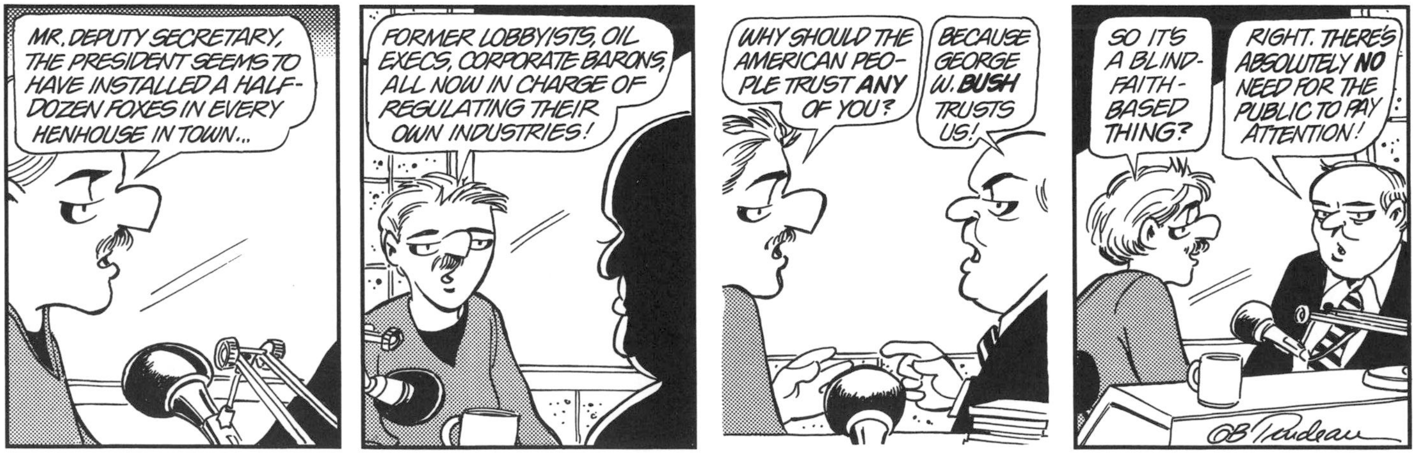
MR. DEPUTY SECRETARY, THE PRESIDENT SEEMS TO HAVE INSTALLED A HALF-DOZEN FOXES IN EVERY HENHOUSE IN TOWN...
FORMER LOBBYISTS, OIL EXECS, CORPORATE BARONS, ALL NOW IN CHARGE OF REGULATING THEIR OWN INDUSTRIES!
WHY SHOULD THE AMERICAN PEOPLE TRUST **ANY** OF YOU?
BECAUSE GEORGE W. **BUSH** TRUSTS US!
SO IT'S A BLIND-FAITH-BASED THING?
RIGHT. THERE'S ABSOLUTELY **NO** NEED FOR THE PUBLIC TO PAY ATTENTION!
©B Trudeau

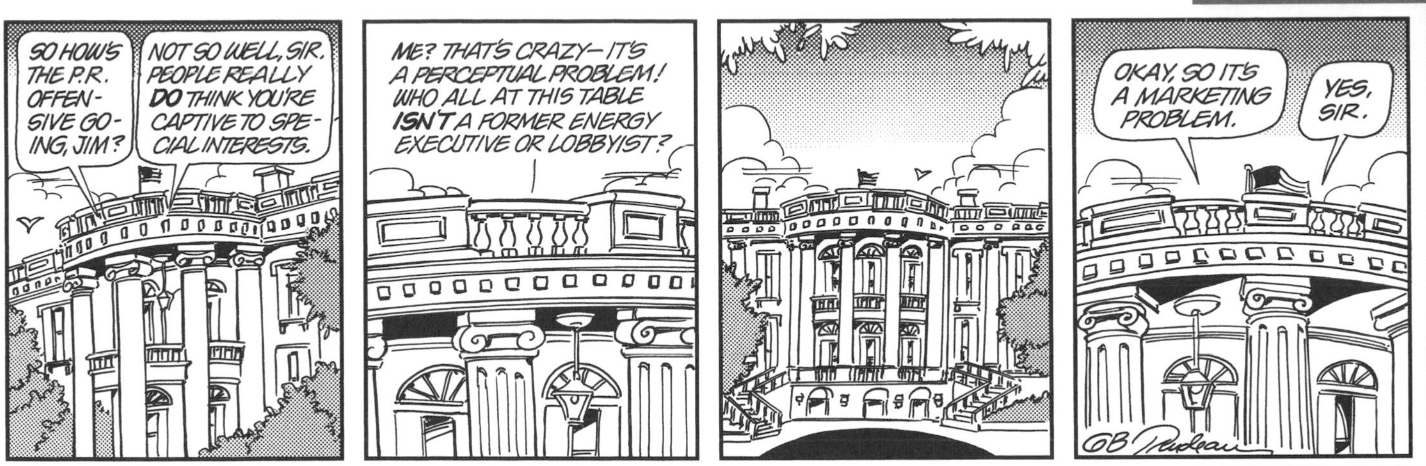
SO HOW'S THE P.R. OFFEN-SIVE GO-ING, JIM?
NOT SO WELL, SIR. PEOPLE REALLY DO THINK YOU'RE CAPTIVE TO SPE-CIAL INTERESTS.
ME? THAT'S CRAZY—IT'S A PERCEPTUAL PROBLEM! WHO ALL AT THIS TABLE ISN'T A FORMER ENERGY EXECUTIVE OR LOBBYIST?
OKAY, SO IT'S A MARKETING PROBLEM.
YES, SIR.
GB Trudeau

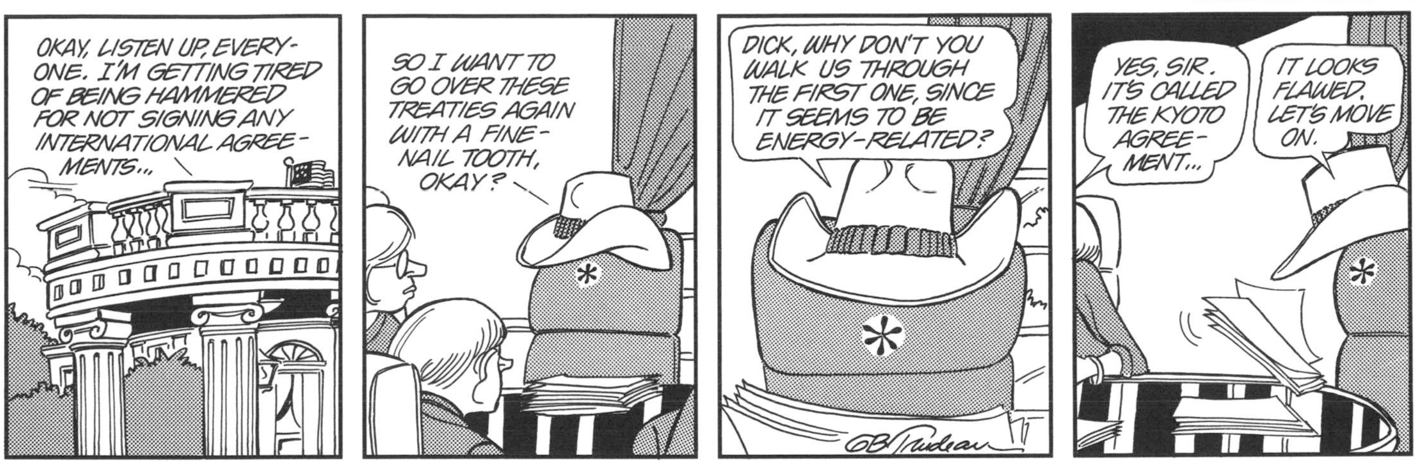
OKAY, LISTEN UP, EVERY-ONE. I'M GETTING TIRED OF BEING HAMMERED FOR NOT SIGNING ANY INTERNATIONAL AGREE-MENTS...
SO I WANT TO GO OVER THESE TREATIES AGAIN WITH A FINE-NAIL TOOTH, OKAY?
DICK, WHY DON'T YOU WALK US THROUGH THE FIRST ONE, SINCE IT SEEMS TO BE ENERGY-RELATED?
GB Trudeau
YES, SIR. IT'S CALLED THE KYOTO AGREE-MENT...
IT LOOKS FLAWED. LET'S MOVE ON.

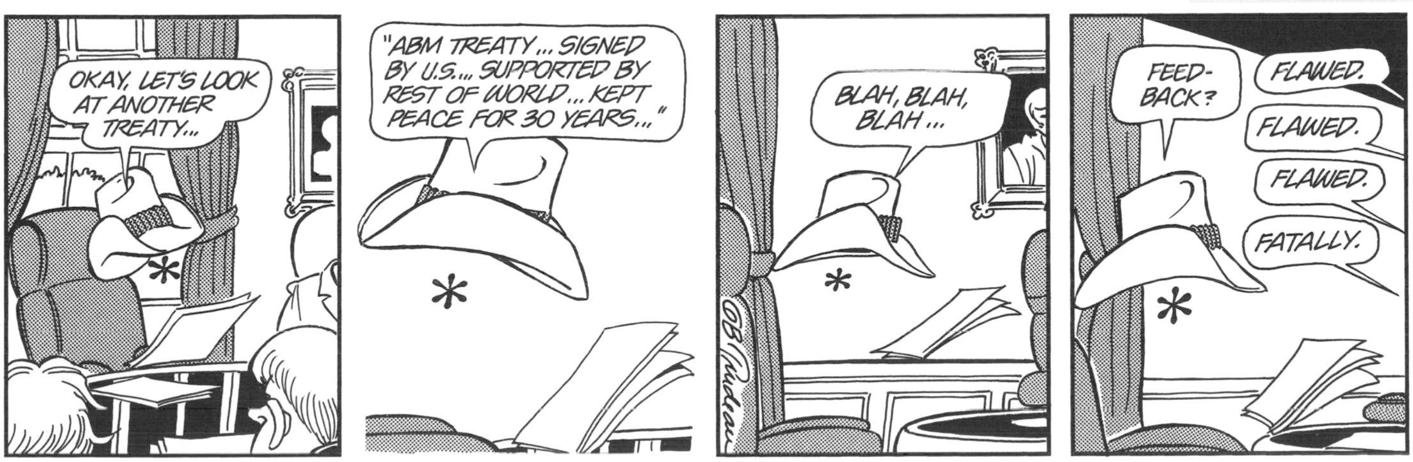
OKAY, LET'S LOOK AT ANOTHER TREATY...
"ABM TREATY... SIGNED BY U.S.... SUPPORTED BY REST OF WORLD... KEPT PEACE FOR 30 YEARS..."
BLAH, BLAH, BLAH...
GB Trudeau
FEED-BACK?
FLAWED.
FLAWED.
FLAWED.
FATALLY.

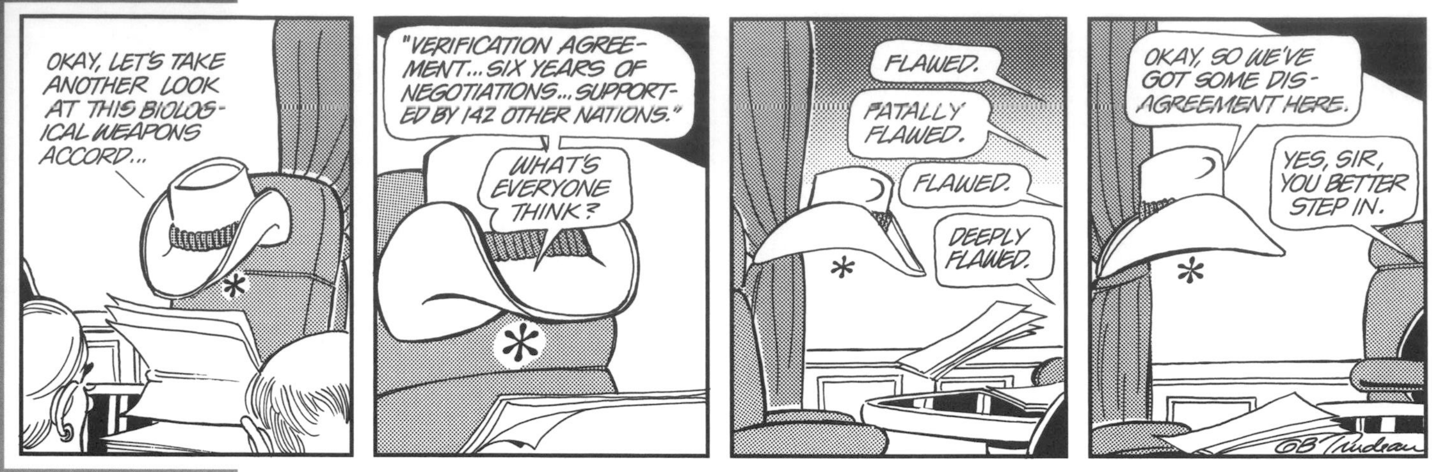
OKAY, LET'S TAKE ANOTHER LOOK AT THIS BIOLOGICAL WEAPONS ACCORD...
"VERIFICATION AGREEMENT... SIX YEARS OF NEGOTIATIONS... SUPPORTED BY 142 OTHER NATIONS."
WHAT'S EVERYONE THINK?
FLAWED.
FATALLY FLAWED.
FLAWED.
DEEPLY FLAWED.
OKAY, SO WE'VE GOT SOME DISAGREEMENT HERE.
YES, SIR, YOU BETTER STEP IN.
©B Trudeau

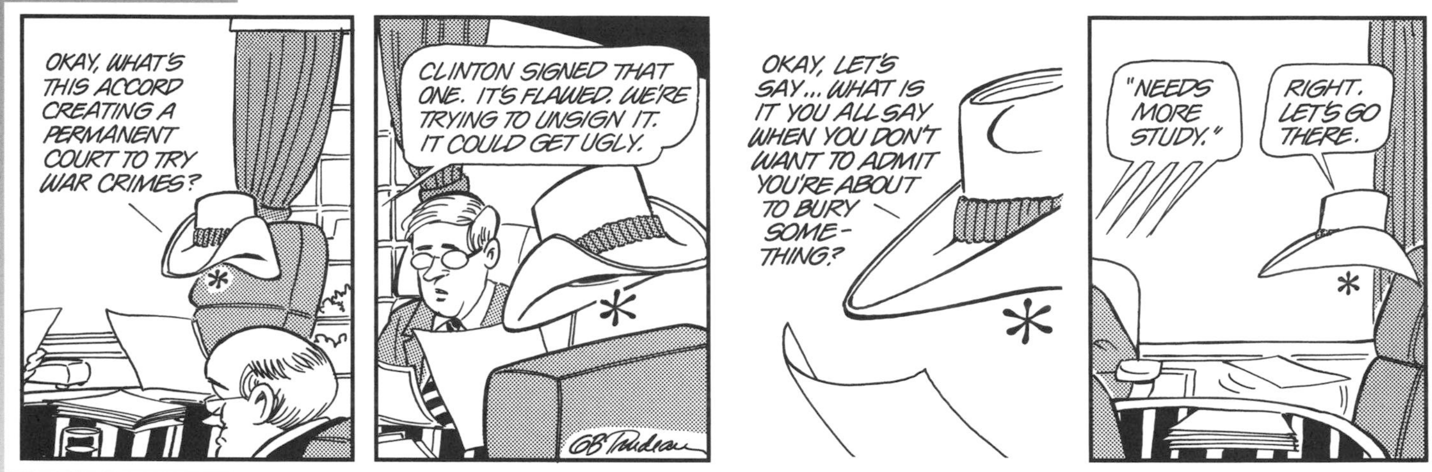
OKAY, WHAT'S THIS ACCORD CREATING A PERMANENT COURT TO TRY WAR CRIMES?
CLINTON SIGNED THAT ONE. IT'S FLAWED. WE'RE TRYING TO UNSIGN IT. IT COULD GET UGLY.
©B Trudeau
OKAY, LET'S SAY... WHAT IS IT YOU ALL SAY WHEN YOU DON'T WANT TO ADMIT YOU'RE ABOUT TO BURY SOMETHING?
"NEEDS MORE STUDY."
RIGHT. LET'S GO THERE.

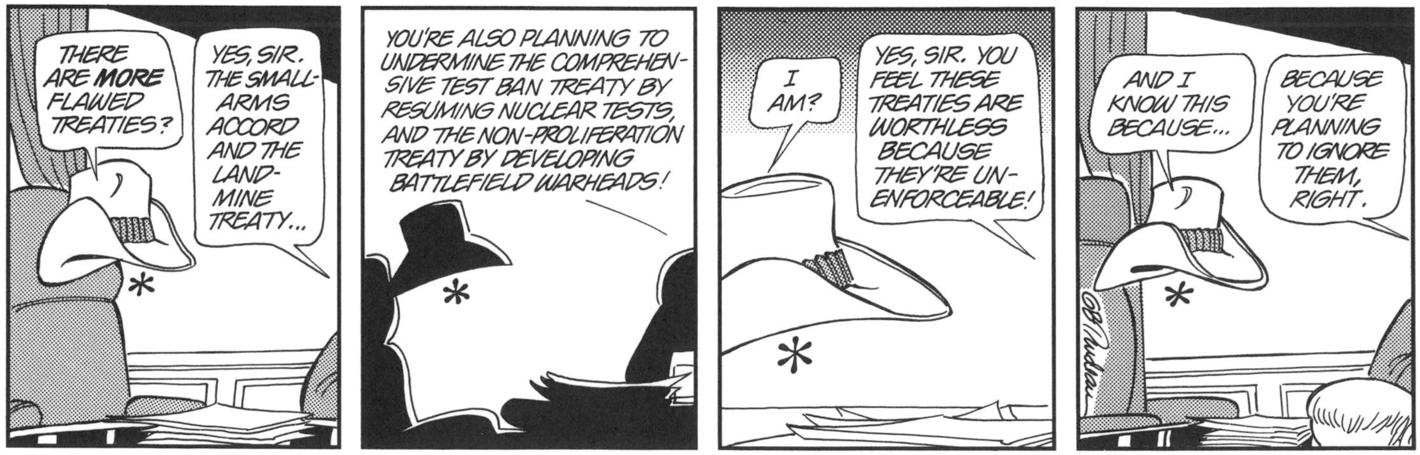
THERE ARE MORE FLAWED TREATIES?
YES, SIR. THE SMALL-ARMS ACCORD AND THE LAND-MINE TREATY...
YOU'RE ALSO PLANNING TO UNDERMINE THE COMPREHENSIVE TEST BAN TREATY BY RESUMING NUCLEAR TESTS, AND THE NON-PROLIFERATION TREATY BY DEVELOPING BATTLEFIELD WARHEADS!
I AM?
YES, SIR. YOU FEEL THESE TREATIES ARE WORTHLESS BECAUSE THEY'RE UNENFORCEABLE!
AND I KNOW THIS BECAUSE...
BECAUSE YOU'RE PLANNING TO IGNORE THEM, RIGHT.
©B Trudeau

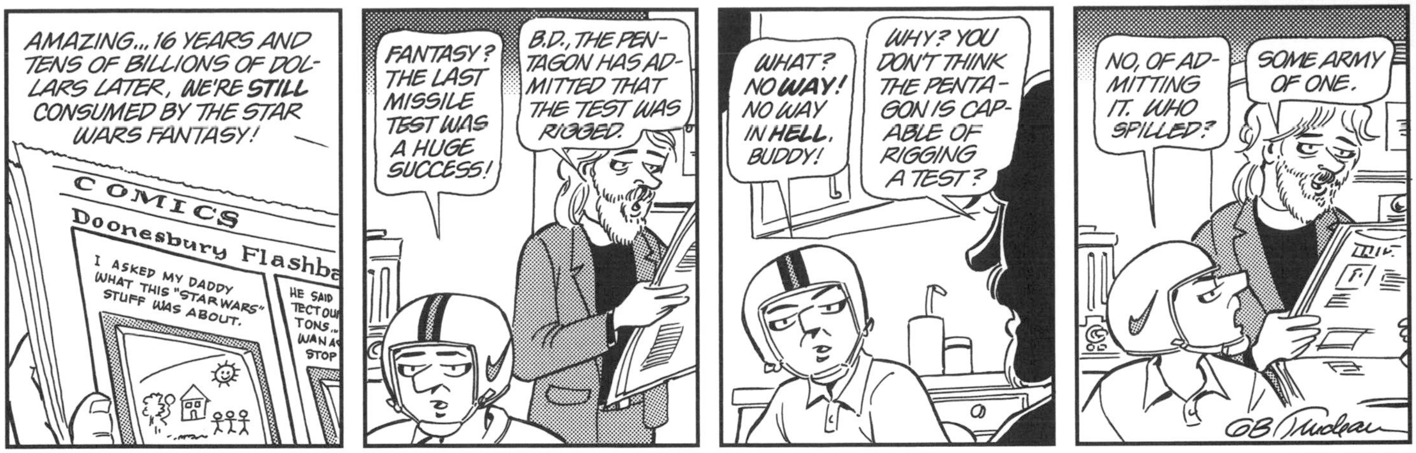
AMAZING... 16 YEARS AND TENS OF BILLIONS OF DOLLARS LATER, WE'RE **STILL** CONSUMED BY THE STAR WARS FANTASY!
COMICS
I ASKED MY DADDY WHAT THIS "STAR WARS" STUFF WAS ABOUT.
FANTASY? THE LAST MISSILE TEST WAS A HUGE SUCCESS!
B.D., THE PENTAGON HAS ADMITTED THAT THE TEST WAS RIGGED.
WHAT? NO **WAY**! NO WAY IN **HELL**, BUDDY!
WHY? YOU DON'T THINK THE PENTAGON IS CAPABLE OF RIGGING A TEST?
NO, OF ADMITTING IT. WHO SPILLED?
SOME ARMY OF ONE.
GB Trudeau

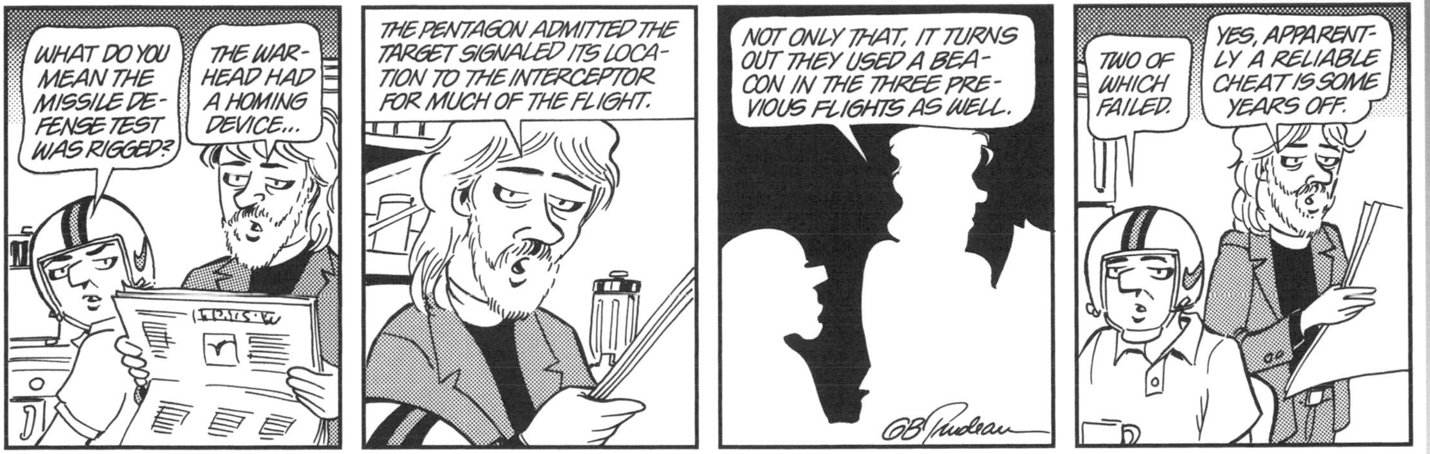
WHAT DO YOU MEAN THE MISSILE DEFENSE TEST WAS RIGGED?
THE WARHEAD HAD A HOMING DEVICE...
THE PENTAGON ADMITTED THE TARGET SIGNALED ITS LOCATION TO THE INTERCEPTOR FOR MUCH OF THE FLIGHT.
NOT ONLY THAT, IT TURNS OUT THEY USED A BEACON IN THE THREE PREVIOUS FLIGHTS AS WELL.
GB Trudeau
TWO OF WHICH FAILED.
YES, APPARENTLY A RELIABLE CHEAT IS SOME YEARS OFF.

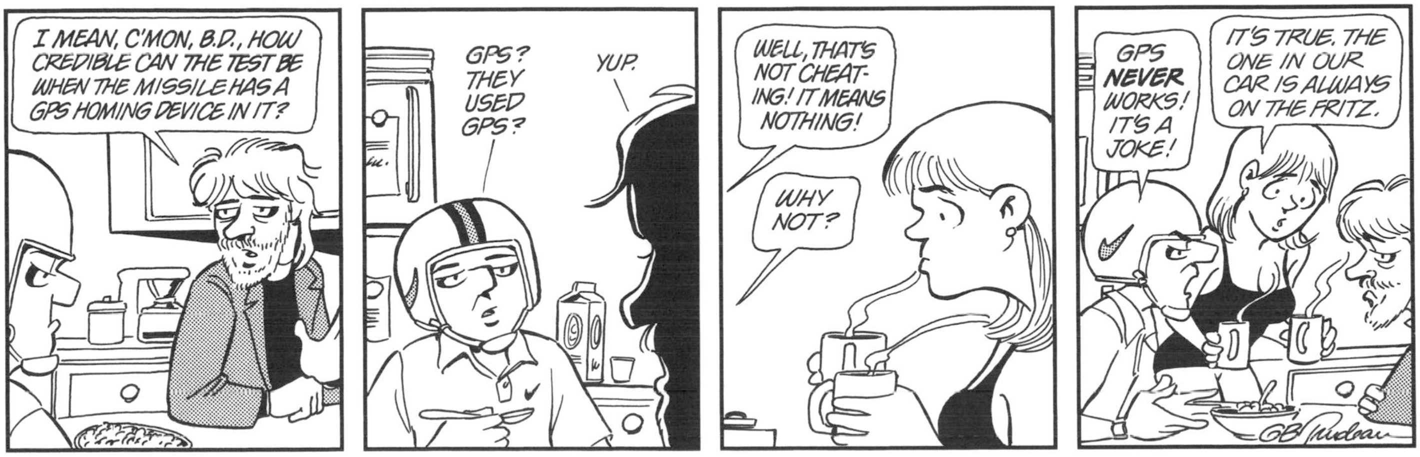
I MEAN, C'MON, B.D., HOW CREDIBLE CAN THE TEST BE WHEN THE MISSILE HAS A GPS HOMING DEVICE IN IT?
GPS? THEY USED GPS?
YUP.
WELL, THAT'S NOT CHEATING! IT MEANS NOTHING!
WHY NOT?
GPS **NEVER** WORKS! IT'S A JOKE!
IT'S TRUE. THE ONE IN OUR CAR IS ALWAYS ON THE FRITZ.
GB Trudeau

LOOK, REV, EVEN IF THE SCIENCE IS SLOW IN COMING, WE HAVE TO DO SOMETHING.

THE OLD COLD WAR DETERRENCE DOESN'T CUT IT ANYMORE! THERE'S A WHOLE NEW GENERATION OF MADMEN WHO WILL PAY **ANY** PRICE TO DESTROY US!

SO STALIN WASN'T MAD ENOUGH FOR YOU, B.D.? OR MAO? THEY KILLED MILLIONS OF THEIR OWN PEOPLE!

YES, BUT NOT **THEMSELVES!**

RIGHT. TODAY'S MADMEN ARE EDGIER, MORE DEPRESSED.

LOOK, REV, YOUR TYPICAL ROGUE NATION MADMAN DOESN'T BLINK! HE'D DO **ANYTHING** TO DROP A WARHEAD DOWN OUR PANTS!

OKAY, BUT WHY WOULDN'T HE JUST DELIVER IT EASILY, CHEAPLY AND UNTRACEABLY ON A SMALL BOAT...

...INSTEAD OF ON A HIGHLY DETECTABLE MISSILE WHOSE LAUNCH GUARANTEES HIS OWN ANNIHILATION?

BECAUSE HE'S **MAD!** DON'T YOU **LISTEN?**

NO MORE COFFEE FOR **YOU,** MISTER!

B.D., I DON'T KNOW WHO THIS NEW BREED OF MANIAC IS, BUT I THINK YOU'D AGREE THAT NO ONE TOPS SADDAM HUSSEIN, RIGHT?

AND YET DURING THE GULF WAR, WHEN HE COULD HAVE LOBBED BIOLOGICAL WEAPONS INTO ISRAEL, HE DIDN'T.

WHY? BECAUSE HE KNEW THAT IF HE DID, BAGHDAD WOULD DISAPPEAR IN A MUSHROOM CLOUD! HE WAS, IN A WORD, DETERRED.

OR OFF HIS GAME! YOU DON'T **KNOW!**

THESE GUYS ARE EVIL **GENIUSES,** B.D., NOT EVIL IDIOTS!

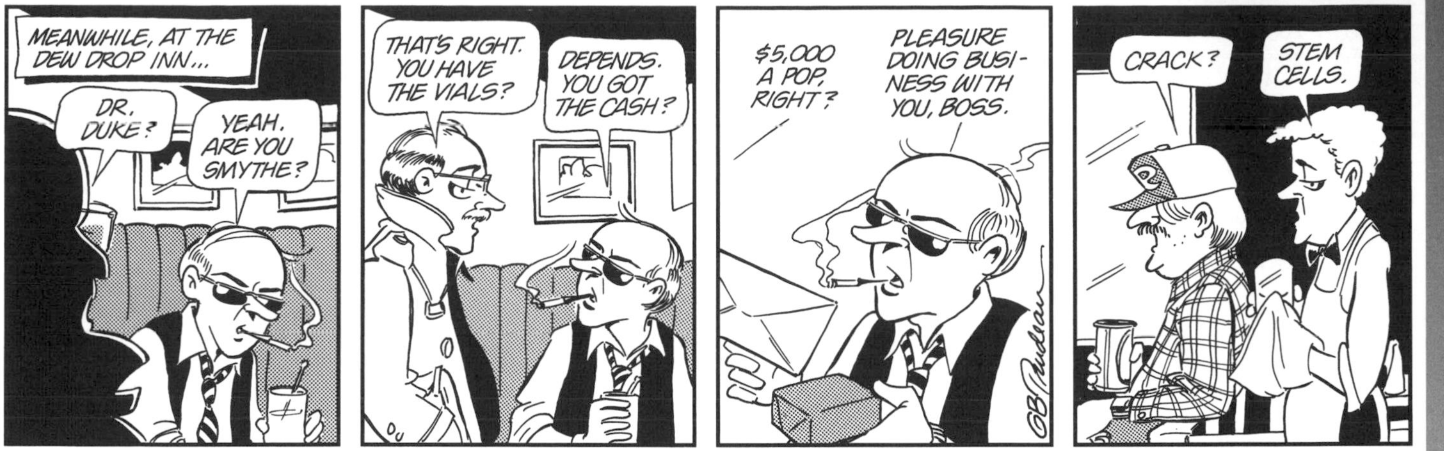
MEANWHILE, AT THE DEW DROP INN...
DR. DUKE?
YEAH. ARE YOU SMYTHE?
THAT'S RIGHT. YOU HAVE THE VIALS?
DEPENDS. YOU GOT THE CASH?
$5,000 A POP, RIGHT?
PLEASURE DOING BUSINESS WITH YOU, BOSS.
CRACK?
STEM CELLS.

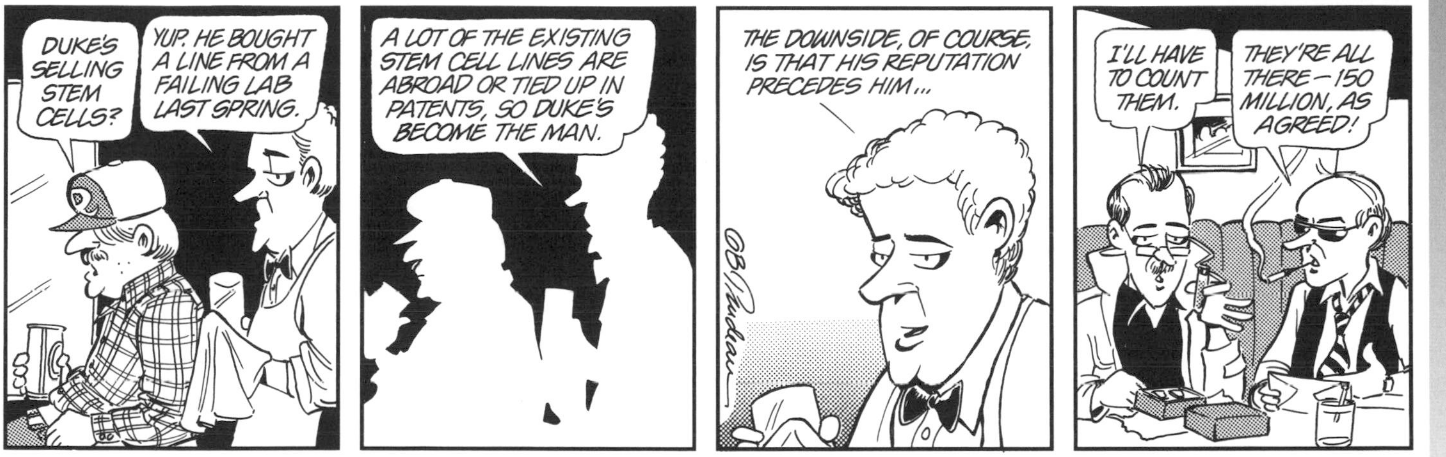
DUKE'S SELLING STEM CELLS?
YUP. HE BOUGHT A LINE FROM A FAILING LAB LAST SPRING.
A LOT OF THE EXISTING STEM CELL LINES ARE ABROAD OR TIED UP IN PATENTS, SO DUKE'S BECOME THE MAN.
THE DOWNSIDE, OF COURSE, IS THAT HIS REPUTATION PRECEDES HIM...
I'LL HAVE TO COUNT THEM.
THEY'RE ALL THERE — 150 MILLION, AS AGREED!

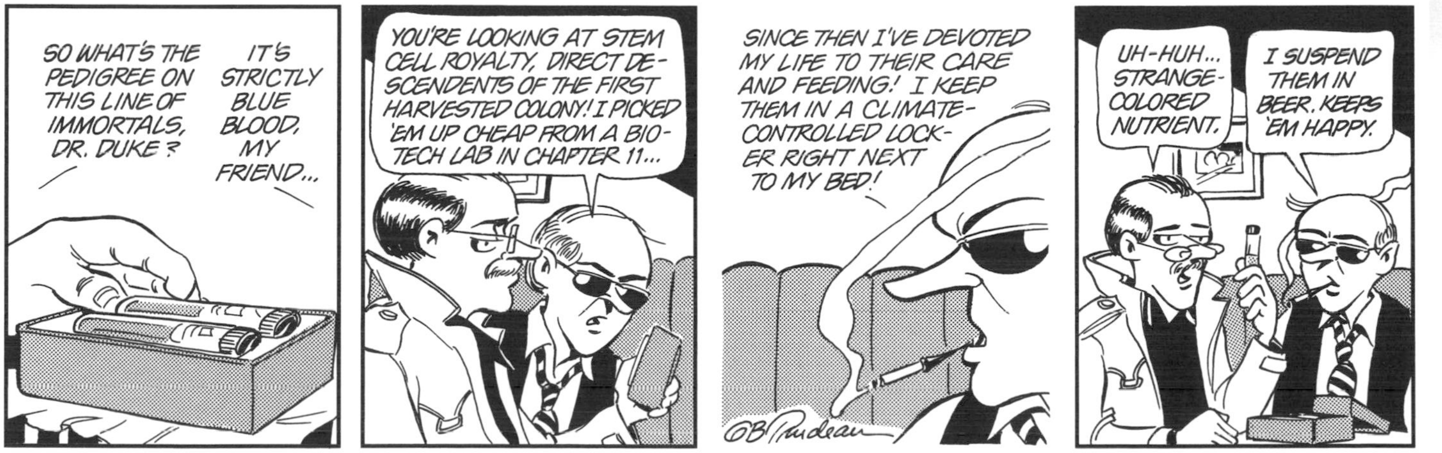
SO WHAT'S THE PEDIGREE ON THIS LINE OF IMMORTALS, DR. DUKE?
IT'S STRICTLY BLUE BLOOD, MY FRIEND...
YOU'RE LOOKING AT STEM CELL ROYALTY, DIRECT DESCENDENTS OF THE FIRST HARVESTED COLONY! I PICKED 'EM UP CHEAP FROM A BIOTECH LAB IN CHAPTER 11...
SINCE THEN I'VE DEVOTED MY LIFE TO THEIR CARE AND FEEDING! I KEEP THEM IN A CLIMATE-CONTROLLED LOCKER RIGHT NEXT TO MY BED!
UH-HUH... STRANGE-COLORED NUTRIENT.
I SUSPEND THEM IN BEER. KEEPS 'EM HAPPY.

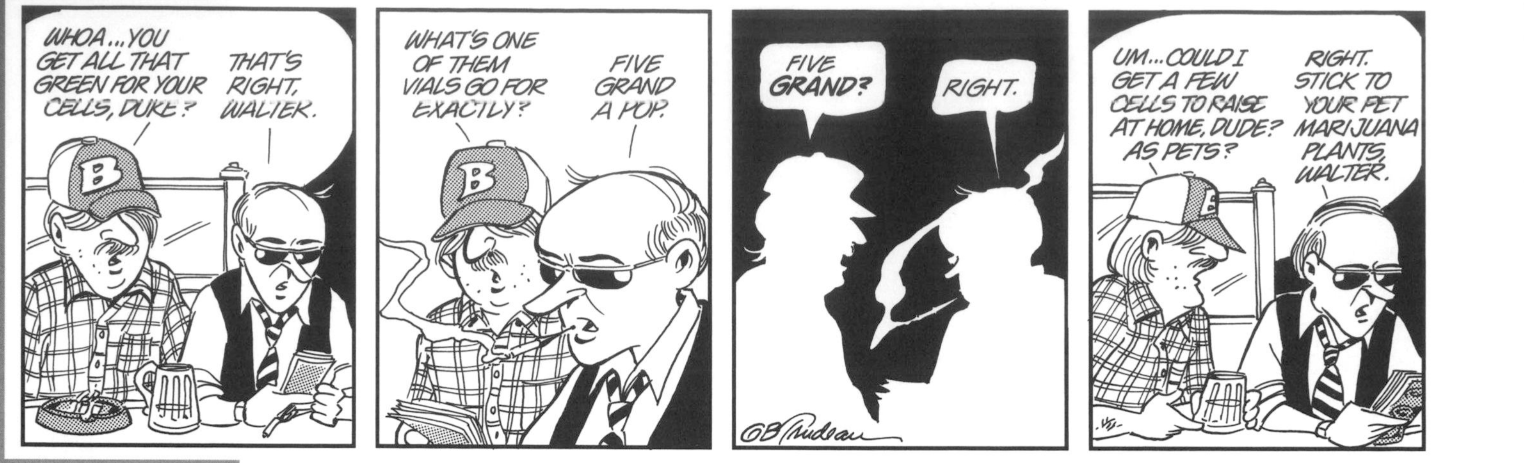
WHOA... YOU GET ALL THAT GREEN FOR YOUR CELLS, DUKE?
THAT'S RIGHT, WALTER.
WHAT'S ONE OF THEM VIALS GO FOR EXACTLY?
FIVE GRAND A POP.
FIVE GRAND?
RIGHT.
UM... COULD I GET A FEW CELLS TO RAISE AT HOME, DUDE? AS PETS?
RIGHT. STICK TO YOUR PET MARIJUANA PLANTS, WALTER.

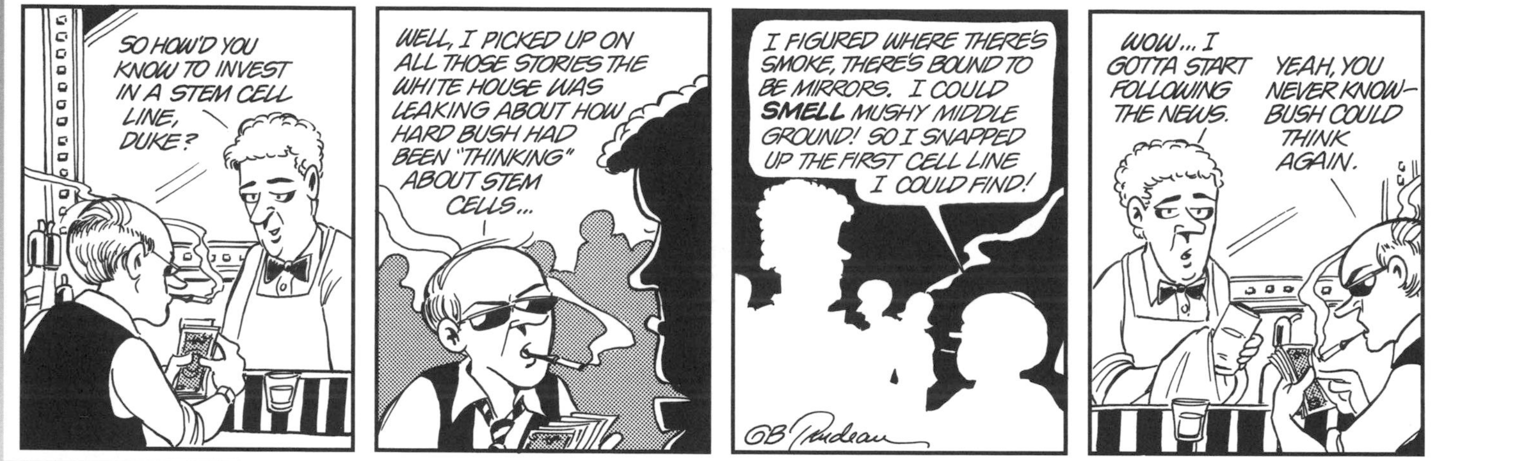
SO HOW'D YOU KNOW TO INVEST IN A STEM CELL LINE, DUKE?
WELL, I PICKED UP ON ALL THOSE STORIES THE WHITE HOUSE WAS LEAKING ABOUT HOW HARD BUSH HAD BEEN "THINKING" ABOUT STEM CELLS...
I FIGURED WHERE THERE'S SMOKE, THERE'S BOUND TO BE MIRRORS. I COULD SMELL MUSHY MIDDLE GROUND! SO I SNAPPED UP THE FIRST CELL LINE I COULD FIND!
WOW... I GOTTA START FOLLOWING THE NEWS.
YEAH, YOU NEVER KNOW- BUSH COULD THINK AGAIN.

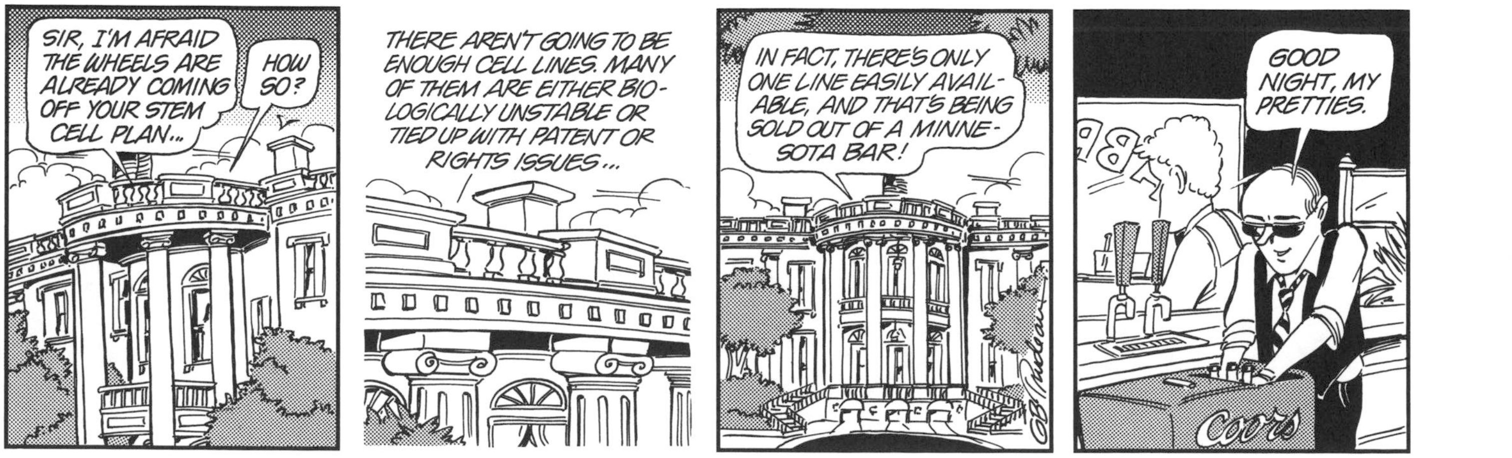
SIR, I'M AFRAID THE WHEELS ARE ALREADY COMING OFF YOUR STEM CELL PLAN...
HOW SO?
THERE AREN'T GOING TO BE ENOUGH CELL LINES. MANY OF THEM ARE EITHER BIO-LOGICALLY UNSTABLE OR TIED UP WITH PATENT OR RIGHTS ISSUES...
IN FACT, THERE'S ONLY ONE LINE EASILY AVAIL-ABLE, AND THAT'S BEING SOLD OUT OF A MINNE-SOTA BAR!
GOOD NIGHT, MY PRETTIES.
Coors

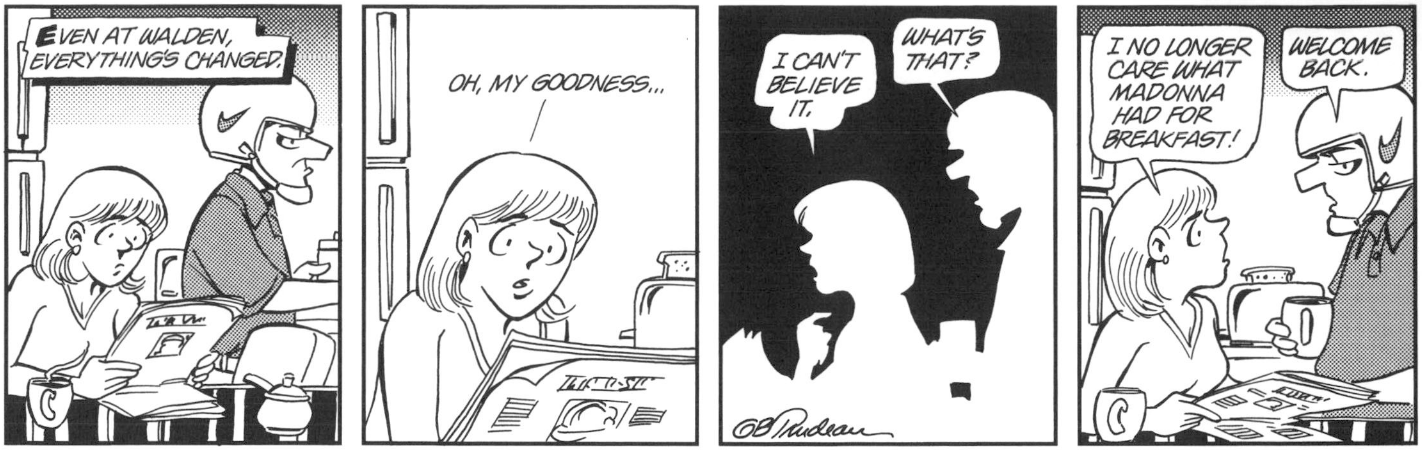
EVEN AT WALDEN, EVERYTHING'S CHANGED.
OH, MY GOODNESS...
I CAN'T BELIEVE IT.
WHAT'S THAT?
I NO LONGER CARE WHAT MADONNA HAD FOR BREAKFAST!
WELCOME BACK.
©B Trudeau

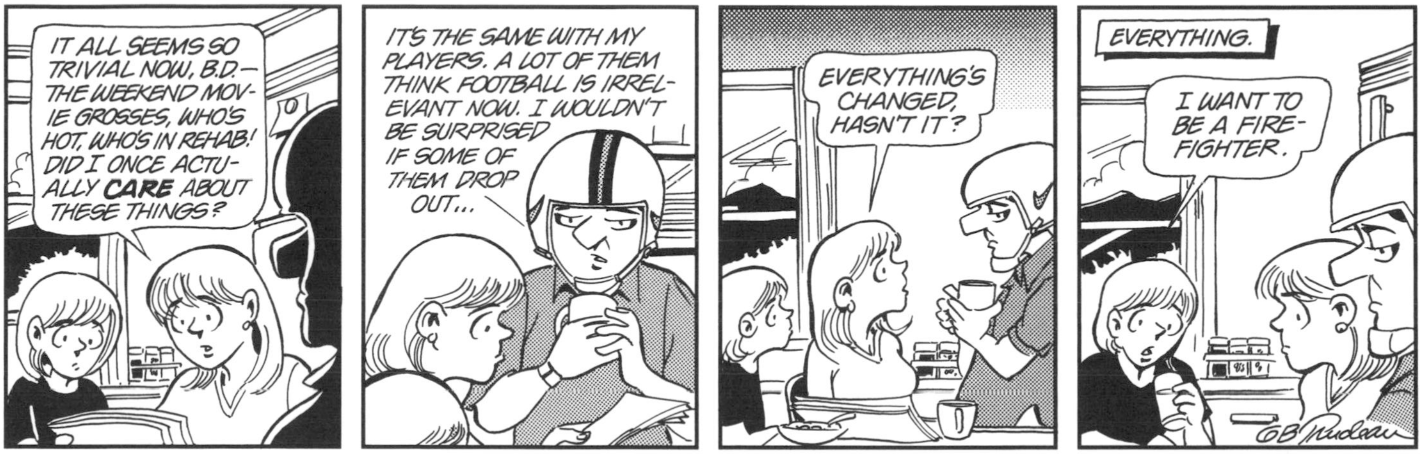
IT ALL SEEMS SO TRIVIAL NOW, B.D.— THE WEEKEND MOVIE GROSSES, WHO'S HOT, WHO'S IN REHAB! DID I ONCE ACTUALLY CARE ABOUT THESE THINGS?
IT'S THE SAME WITH MY PLAYERS. A LOT OF THEM THINK FOOTBALL IS IRRELEVANT NOW. I WOULDN'T BE SURPRISED IF SOME OF THEM DROP OUT...
EVERYTHING'S CHANGED, HASN'T IT?
EVERYTHING.
I WANT TO BE A FIREFIGHTER.
©B Trudeau

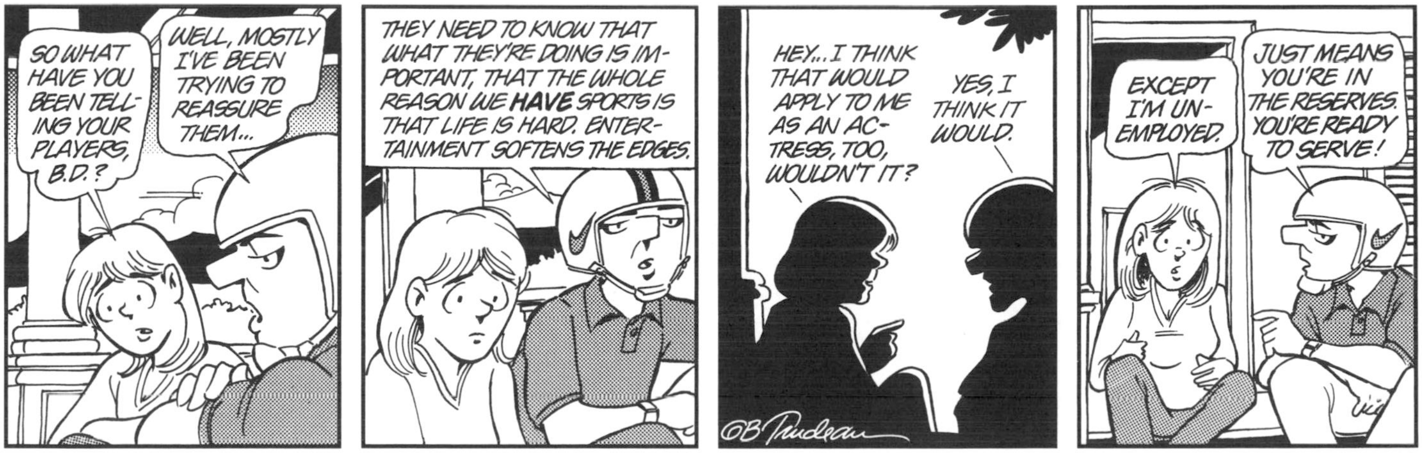
SO WHAT HAVE YOU BEEN TELLING YOUR PLAYERS, B.D.?
WELL, MOSTLY I'VE BEEN TRYING TO REASSURE THEM...
THEY NEED TO KNOW THAT WHAT THEY'RE DOING IS IMPORTANT, THAT THE WHOLE REASON WE HAVE SPORTS IS THAT LIFE IS HARD. ENTERTAINMENT SOFTENS THE EDGES.
HEY... I THINK THAT WOULD APPLY TO ME AS AN ACTRESS, TOO, WOULDN'T IT?
YES, I THINK IT WOULD.
©B Trudeau
EXCEPT I'M UNEMPLOYED.
JUST MEANS YOU'RE IN THE RESERVES. YOU'RE READY TO SERVE!

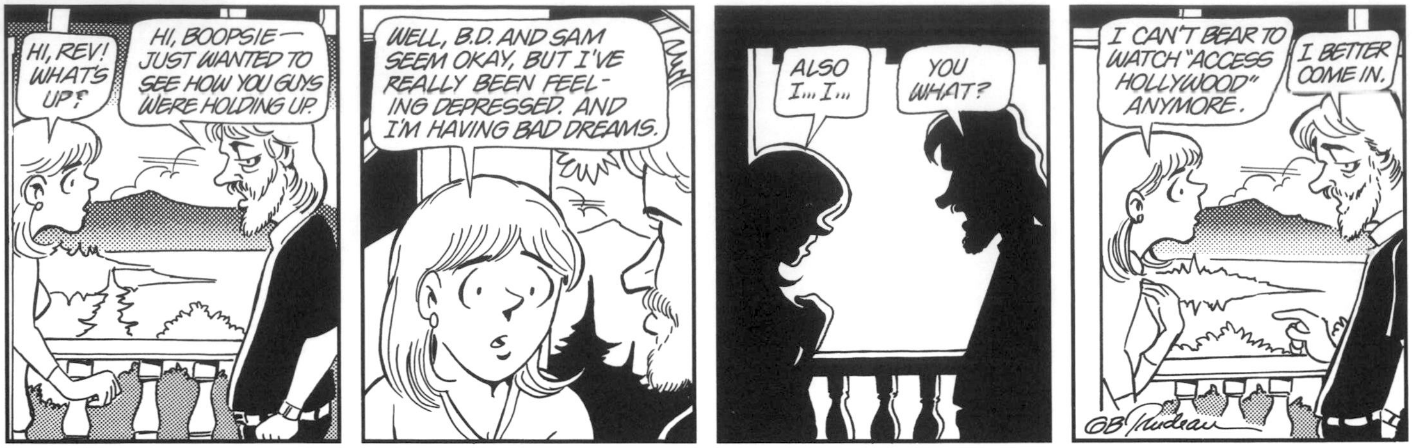
HI, REV! WHAT'S UP?
HI, BOOPSIE— JUST WANTED TO SEE HOW YOU GUYS WERE HOLDING UP.
WELL, B.D. AND SAM SEEM OKAY, BUT I'VE REALLY BEEN FEEL-ING DEPRESSED. AND I'M HAVING BAD DREAMS.
ALSO I... I...
YOU WHAT?
I CAN'T BEAR TO WATCH "ACCESS HOLLYWOOD" ANYMORE.
I BETTER COME IN.
GB Trudeau

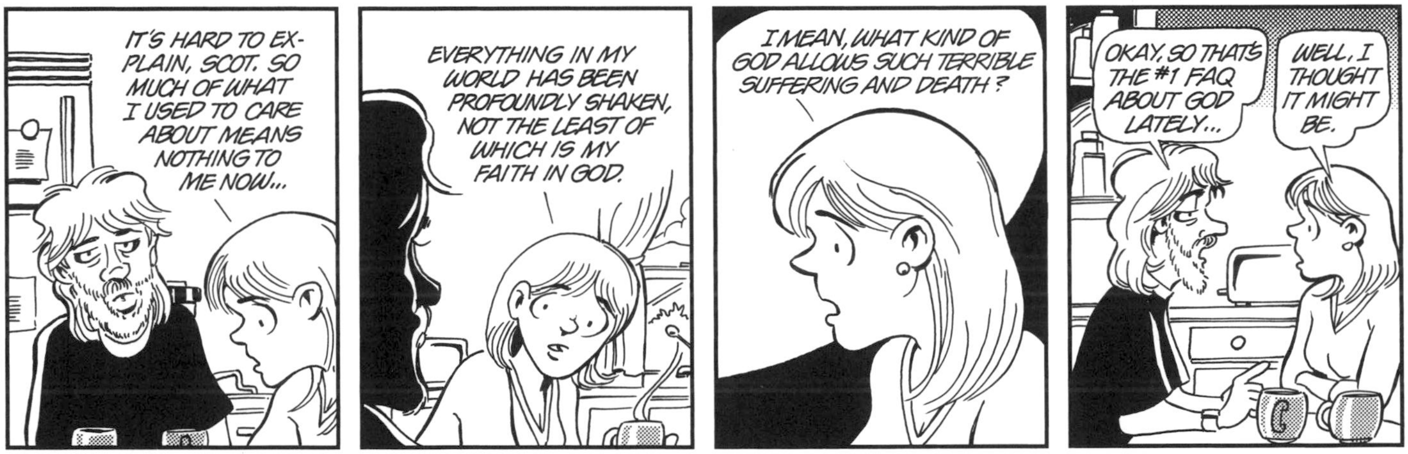
IT'S HARD TO EX-PLAIN, SCOT. SO MUCH OF WHAT I USED TO CARE ABOUT MEANS NOTHING TO ME NOW...
EVERYTHING IN MY WORLD HAS BEEN PROFOUNDLY SHAKEN, NOT THE LEAST OF WHICH IS MY FAITH IN GOD.
I MEAN, WHAT KIND OF GOD ALLOWS SUCH TERRIBLE SUFFERING AND DEATH?
OKAY, SO THAT'S THE #1 FAQ ABOUT GOD LATELY...
WELL, I THOUGHT IT MIGHT BE.

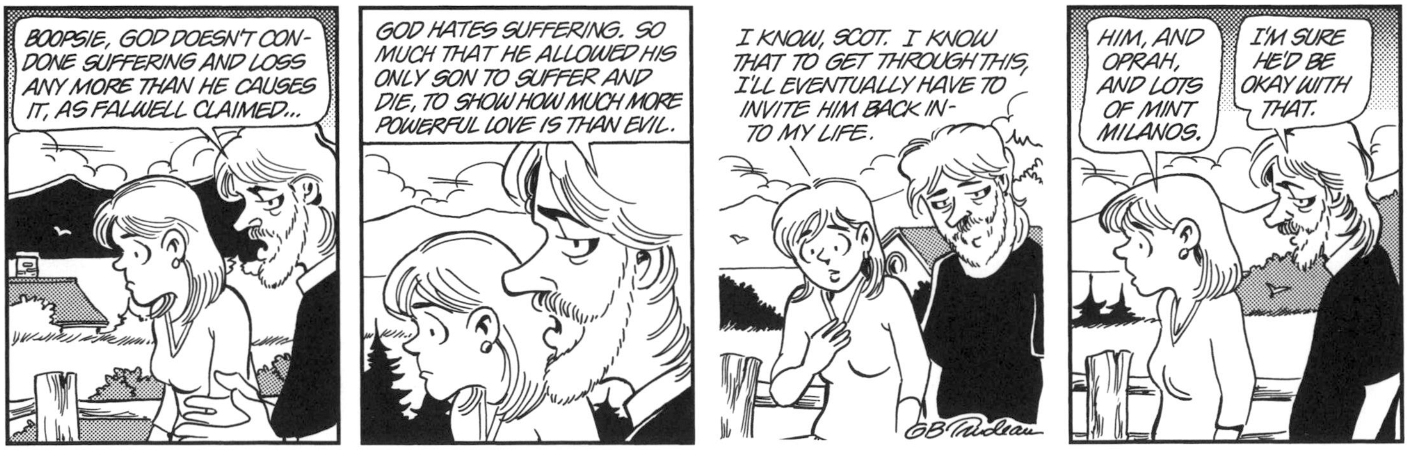
BOOPSIE, GOD DOESN'T CON-DONE SUFFERING AND LOSS ANY MORE THAN HE CAUSES IT, AS FALWELL CLAIMED...
GOD HATES SUFFERING. SO MUCH THAT HE ALLOWED HIS ONLY SON TO SUFFER AND DIE, TO SHOW HOW MUCH MORE POWERFUL LOVE IS THAN EVIL.
I KNOW, SCOT. I KNOW THAT TO GET THROUGH THIS, I'LL EVENTUALLY HAVE TO INVITE HIM BACK IN-TO MY LIFE.
GB Trudeau
HIM, AND OPRAH, AND LOTS OF MINT MILANOS.
I'M SURE HE'D BE OKAY WITH THAT.

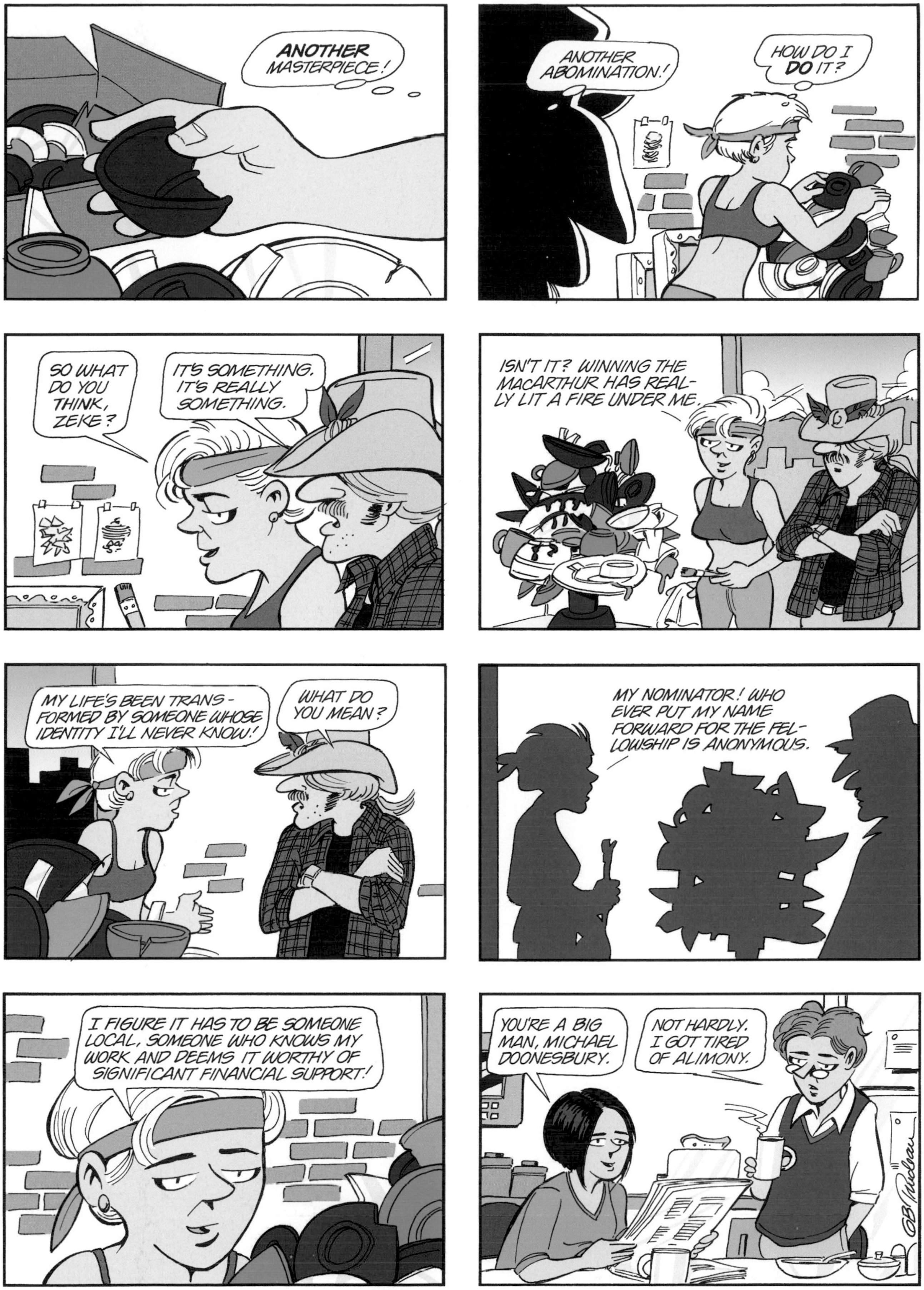
ANOTHER MASTERPIECE!
ANOTHER ABOMINATION!
HOW DO I DO IT?
SO WHAT DO YOU THINK, ZEKE?
IT'S SOMETHING. IT'S REALLY SOMETHING.
ISN'T IT? WINNING THE MacARTHUR HAS REALLY LIT A FIRE UNDER ME.
MY LIFE'S BEEN TRANSFORMED BY SOMEONE WHOSE IDENTITY I'LL NEVER KNOW!
WHAT DO YOU MEAN?
MY NOMINATOR! WHO EVER PUT MY NAME FORWARD FOR THE FELLOWSHIP IS ANONYMOUS.
I FIGURE IT HAS TO BE SOMEONE LOCAL, SOMEONE WHO KNOWS MY WORK AND DEEMS IT WORTHY OF SIGNIFICANT FINANCIAL SUPPORT!
YOU'RE A BIG MAN, MICHAEL DOONESBURY.
NOT HARDLY. I GOT TIRED OF ALIMONY.

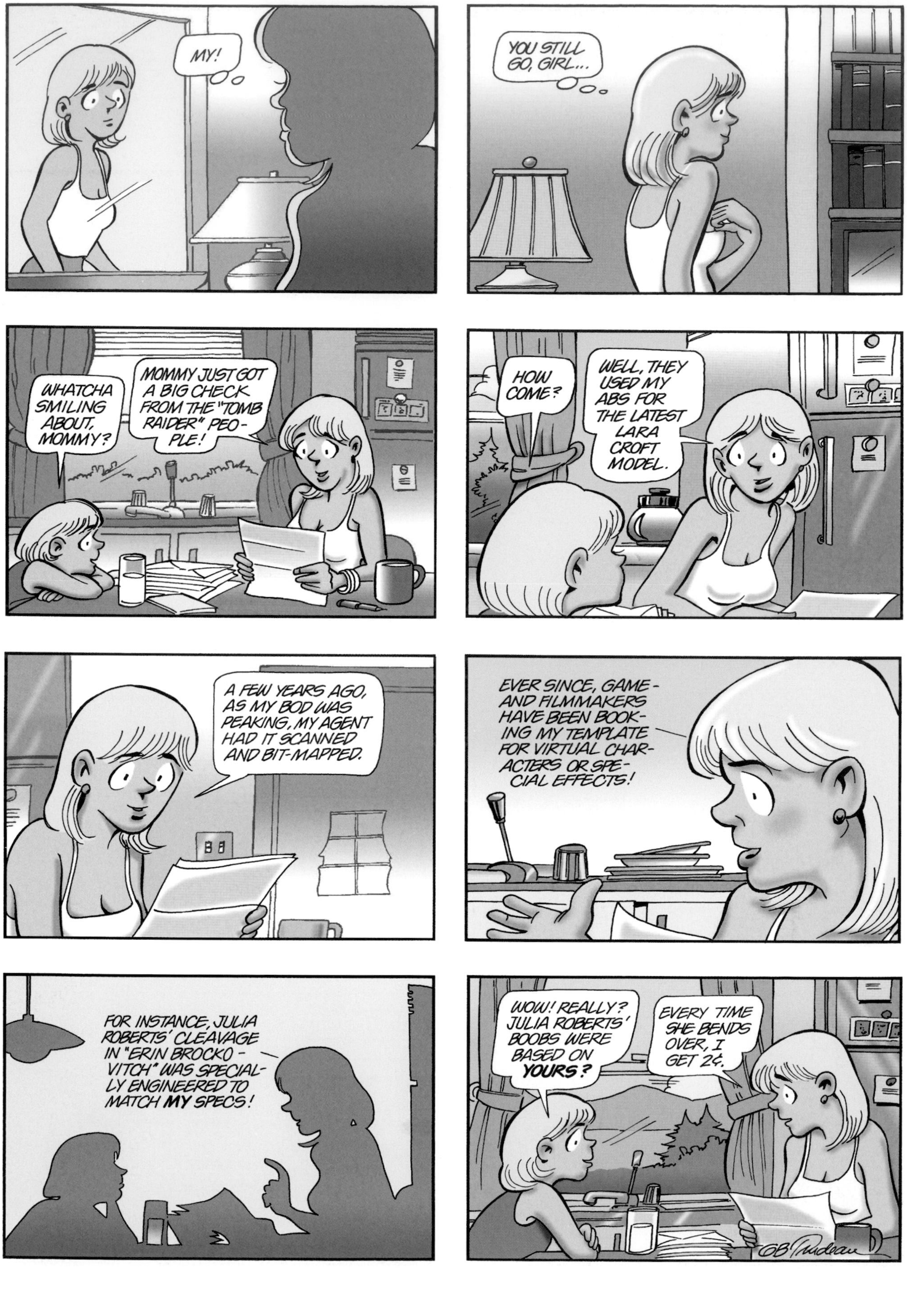
MY!
YOU STILL GO, GIRL...
WHATCHA SMILING ABOUT, MOMMY?
MOMMY JUST GOT A BIG CHECK FROM THE "TOMB RAIDER" PEOPLE!
HOW COME?
WELL, THEY USED MY ABS FOR THE LATEST LARA CROFT MODEL.
A FEW YEARS AGO, AS MY BOD WAS PEAKING, MY AGENT HAD IT SCANNED AND BIT-MAPPED.
EVER SINCE, GAME- AND FILMMAKERS HAVE BEEN BOOKING MY TEMPLATE FOR VIRTUAL CHARACTERS OR SPECIAL EFFECTS!
FOR INSTANCE, JULIA ROBERTS' CLEAVAGE IN "ERIN BROCKOVITCH" WAS SPECIALLY ENGINEERED TO MATCH **MY** SPECS!
WOW! REALLY? JULIA ROBERTS' BOOBS WERE BASED ON **YOURS**?
EVERY TIME SHE BENDS OVER, I GET 2¢.
GB Trudeau

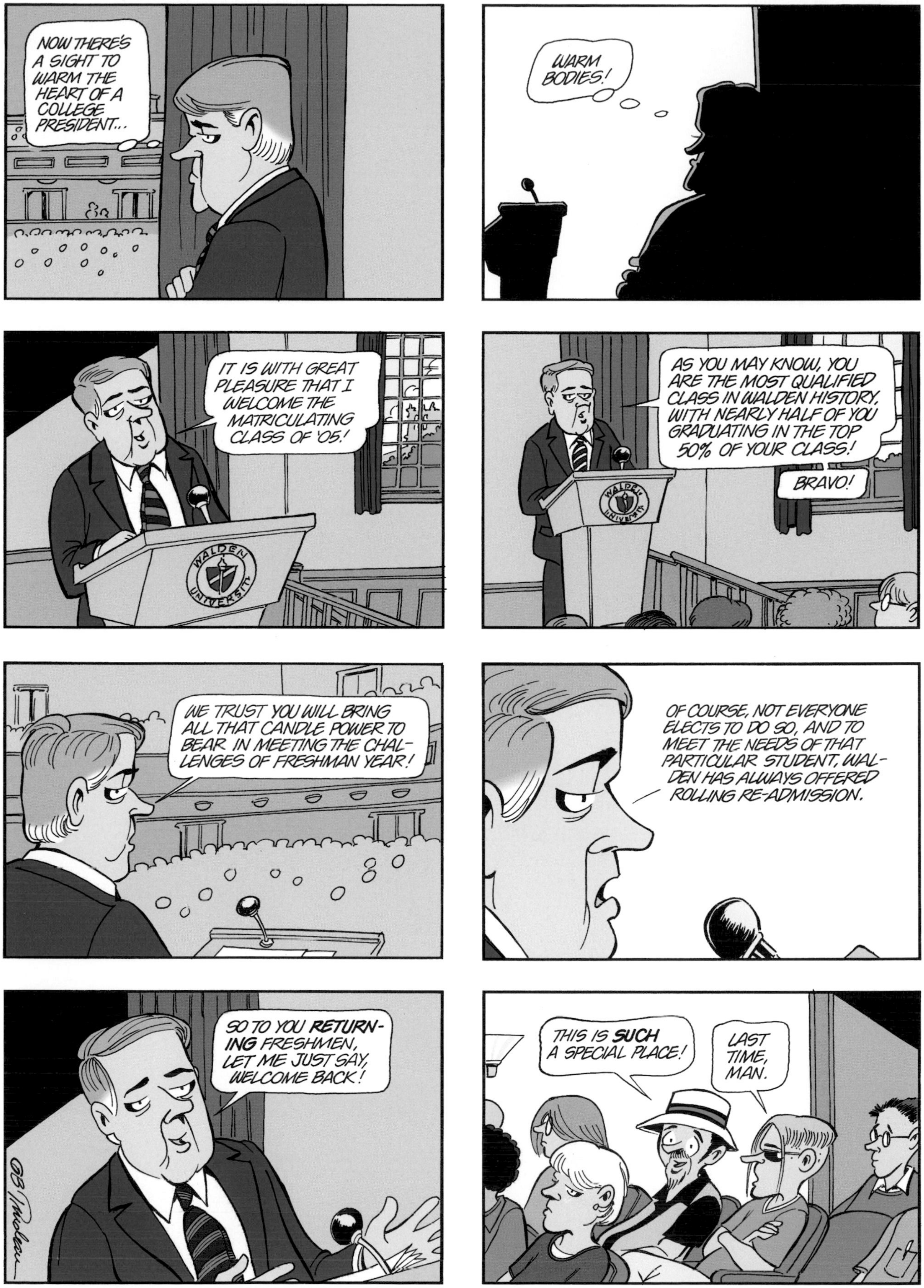
NOW THERE'S A SIGHT TO WARM THE HEART OF A COLLEGE PRESIDENT...
WARM BODIES!
IT IS WITH GREAT PLEASURE THAT I WELCOME THE MATRICULATING CLASS OF '05!
AS YOU MAY KNOW, YOU ARE THE MOST QUALIFIED CLASS IN WALDEN HISTORY, WITH NEARLY HALF OF YOU GRADUATING IN THE TOP 50% OF YOUR CLASS!
BRAVO!
WE TRUST YOU WILL BRING ALL THAT CANDLE POWER TO BEAR IN MEETING THE CHALLENGES OF FRESHMAN YEAR!
OF COURSE, NOT EVERYONE ELECTS TO DO SO, AND TO MEET THE NEEDS OF THAT PARTICULAR STUDENT, WALDEN HAS ALWAYS OFFERED ROLLING RE-ADMISSION.
SO TO YOU **RETURNING** FRESHMEN, LET ME JUST SAY, WELCOME BACK!
THIS IS **SUCH** A SPECIAL PLACE!
LAST TIME, MAN.

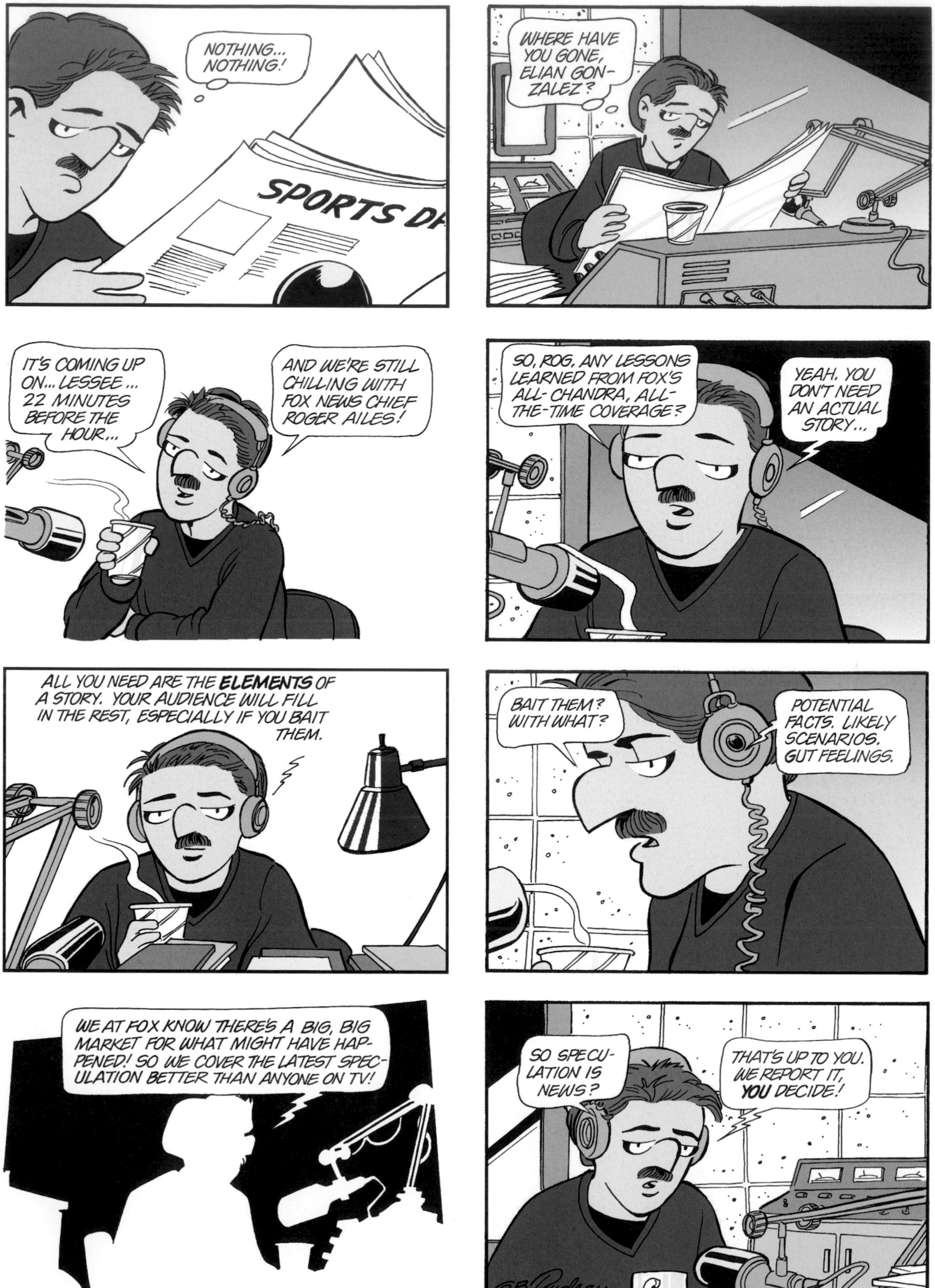
NOTHING... NOTHING!
SPORTS DE
WHERE HAVE YOU GONE, ELIAN GONZALEZ?
IT'S COMING UP ON... LESSEE... 22 MINUTES BEFORE THE HOUR...
AND WE'RE STILL CHILLING WITH FOX NEWS CHIEF ROGER AILES!
SO, ROG, ANY LESSONS LEARNED FROM FOX'S ALL-CHANDRA, ALL-THE-TIME COVERAGE?
YEAH. YOU DON'T NEED AN ACTUAL STORY...
ALL YOU NEED ARE THE **ELEMENTS** OF A STORY. YOUR AUDIENCE WILL FILL IN THE REST, ESPECIALLY IF YOU BAIT THEM.
BAIT THEM? WITH WHAT?
POTENTIAL FACTS. LIKELY SCENARIOS. GUT FEELINGS.
WE AT FOX KNOW THERE'S A BIG, BIG MARKET FOR WHAT MIGHT HAVE HAPPENED! SO WE COVER THE LATEST SPECULATION BETTER THAN ANYONE ON TV!
SO SPECULATION IS NEWS?
THAT'S UP TO YOU. WE REPORT IT, **YOU** DECIDE!
GB Trudeau

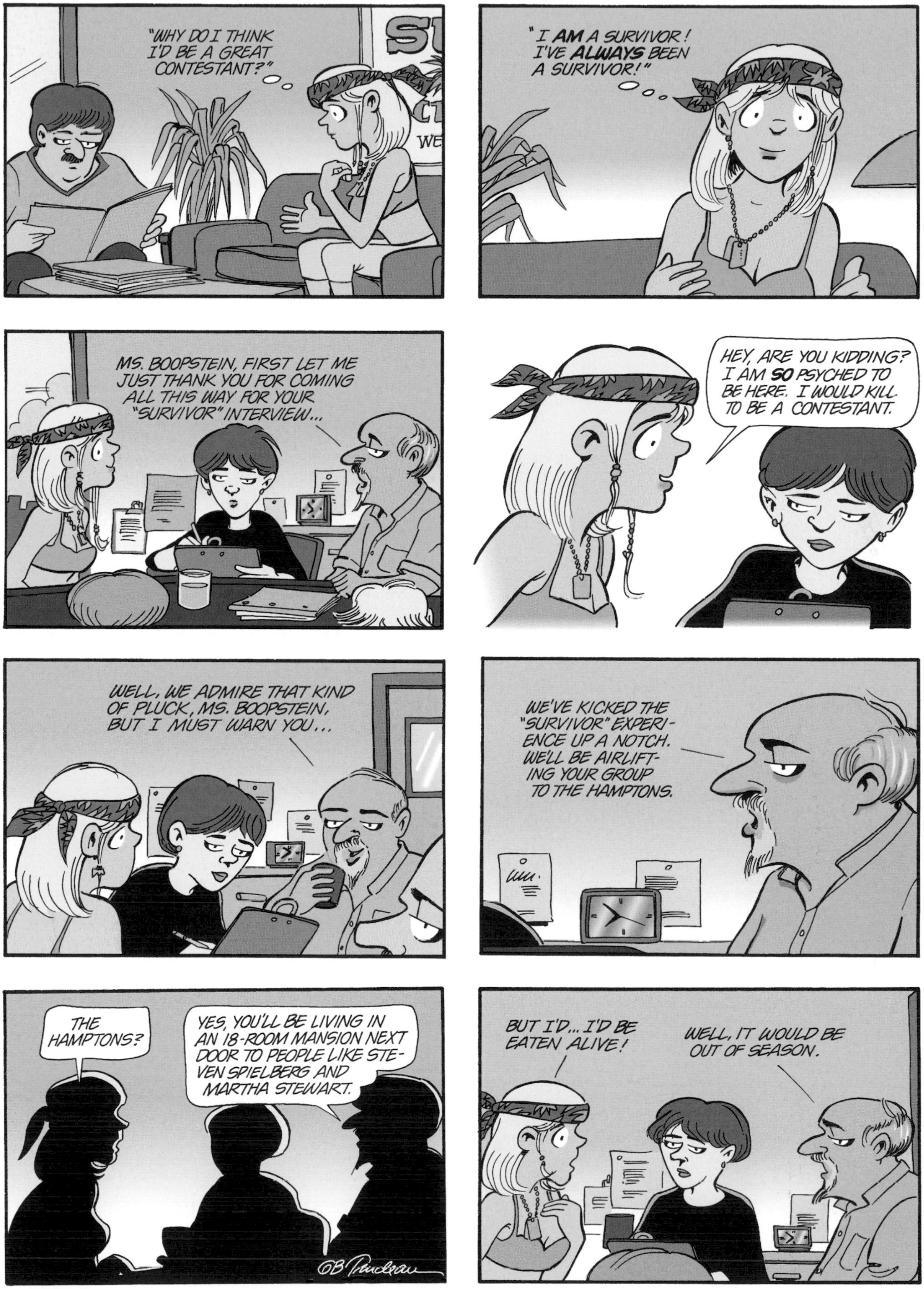
"WHY DO I THINK I'D BE A GREAT CONTESTANT?"
"I AM A SURVIVOR! I'VE ALWAYS BEEN A SURVIVOR!"
MS. BOOPSTEIN, FIRST LET ME JUST THANK YOU FOR COMING ALL THIS WAY FOR YOUR "SURVIVOR" INTERVIEW...
HEY, ARE YOU KIDDING? I AM SO PSYCHED TO BE HERE. I WOULD KILL TO BE A CONTESTANT.
WELL, WE ADMIRE THAT KIND OF PLUCK, MS. BOOPSTEIN, BUT I MUST WARN YOU...
WE'VE KICKED THE "SURVIVOR" EXPERIENCE UP A NOTCH. WE'LL BE AIRLIFTING YOUR GROUP TO THE HAMPTONS.
THE HAMPTONS?
YES, YOU'LL BE LIVING IN AN 18-ROOM MANSION NEXT DOOR TO PEOPLE LIKE STEVEN SPIELBERG AND MARTHA STEWART.
BUT I'D... I'D BE EATEN ALIVE!
WELL, IT WOULD BE OUT OF SEASON.

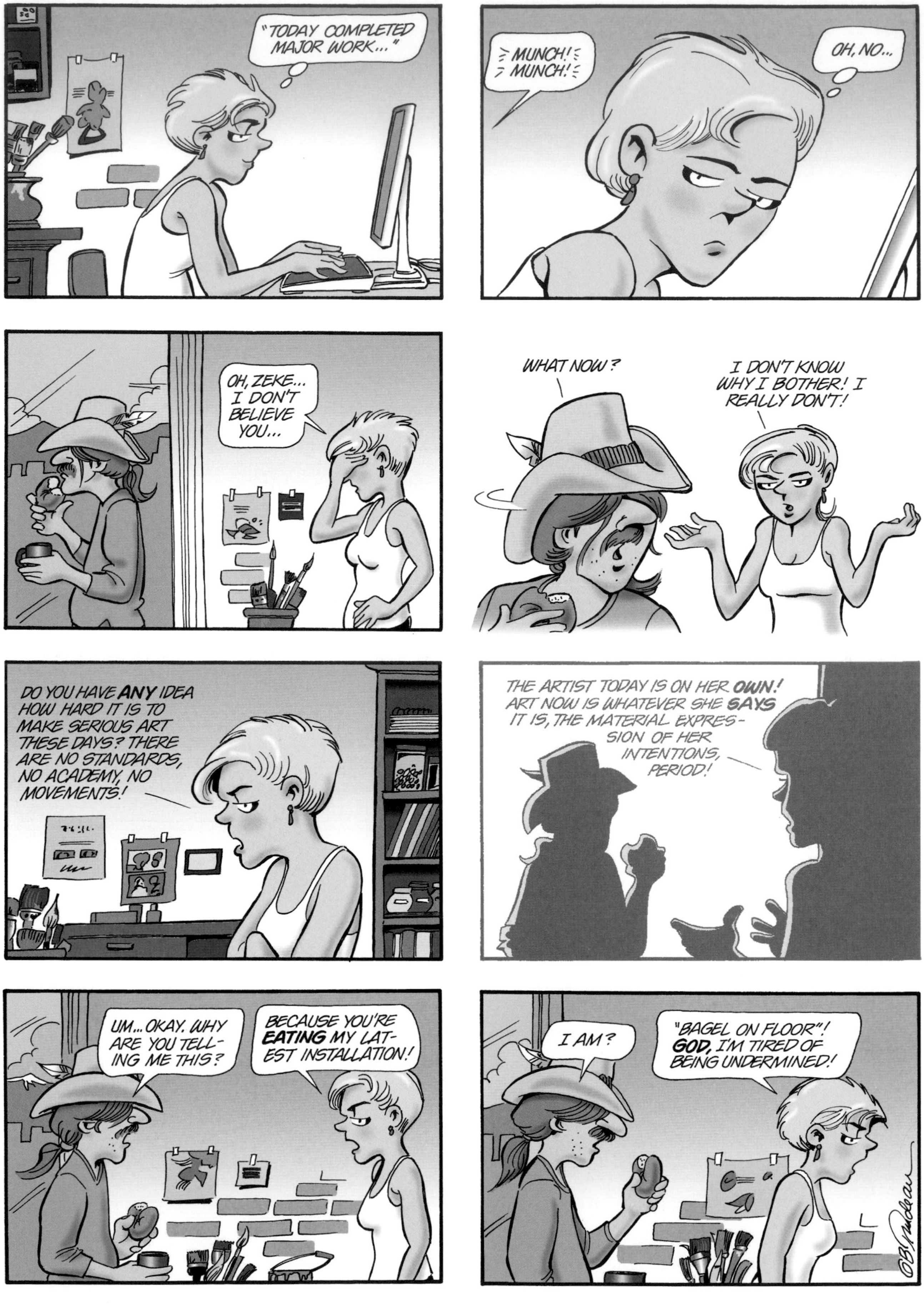
"TODAY COMPLETED MAJOR WORK..."
MUNCH! MUNCH!
OH, NO...
OH, ZEKE... I DON'T BELIEVE YOU...
WHAT NOW?
I DON'T KNOW WHY I BOTHER! I REALLY DON'T!
DO YOU HAVE **ANY** IDEA HOW HARD IT IS TO MAKE SERIOUS ART THESE DAYS? THERE ARE NO STANDARDS, NO ACADEMY, NO MOVEMENTS!
THE ARTIST TODAY IS ON HER **OWN**! ART NOW IS WHATEVER SHE **SAYS** IT IS, THE MATERIAL EXPRES- SION OF HER INTENTIONS, PERIOD!
UM... OKAY. WHY ARE YOU TELL- ING ME THIS?
BECAUSE YOU'RE **EATING** MY LAT- EST INSTALLATION!
I AM?
"BAGEL ON FLOOR"! **GOD,** I'M TIRED OF BEING UNDERMINED!
©BTrudeau

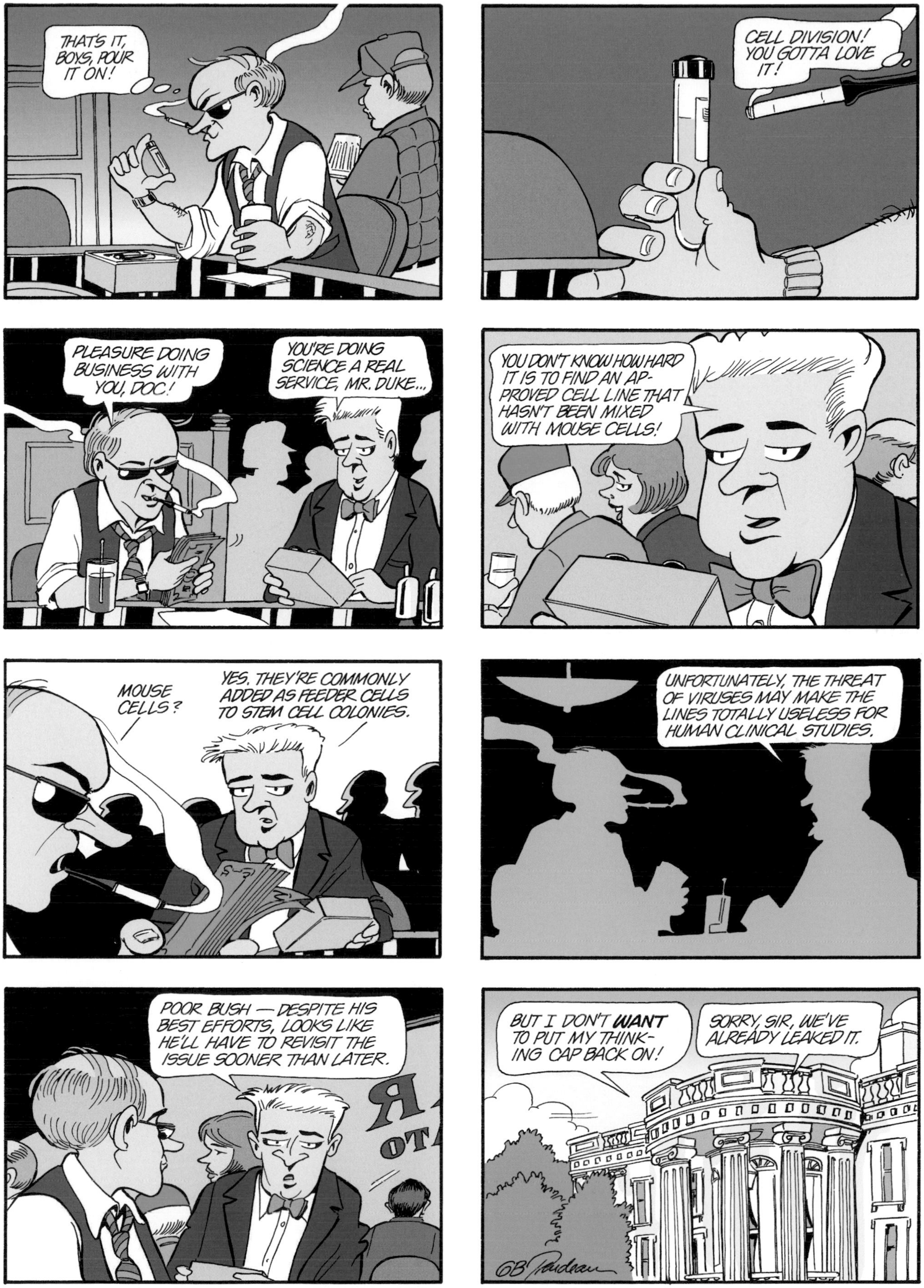

THAT'S IT, BOYS, POUR IT ON!
CELL DIVISION! YOU GOTTA LOVE IT!
PLEASURE DOING BUSINESS WITH YOU, DOC!
YOU'RE DOING SCIENCE A REAL SERVICE, MR. DUKE...
YOU DON'T KNOW HOW HARD IT IS TO FIND AN APPROVED CELL LINE THAT HASN'T BEEN MIXED WITH MOUSE CELLS!
MOUSE CELLS?
YES. THEY'RE COMMONLY ADDED AS FEEDER CELLS TO STEM CELL COLONIES.
UNFORTUNATELY, THE THREAT OF VIRUSES MAY MAKE THE LINES TOTALLY USELESS FOR HUMAN CLINICAL STUDIES.
POOR BUSH — DESPITE HIS BEST EFFORTS, LOOKS LIKE HE'LL HAVE TO REVISIT THE ISSUE SOONER THAN LATER.
BUT I DON'T **WANT** TO PUT MY THINKING CAP BACK ON!
SORRY, SIR, WE'VE ALREADY LEAKED IT.
GB Trudeau

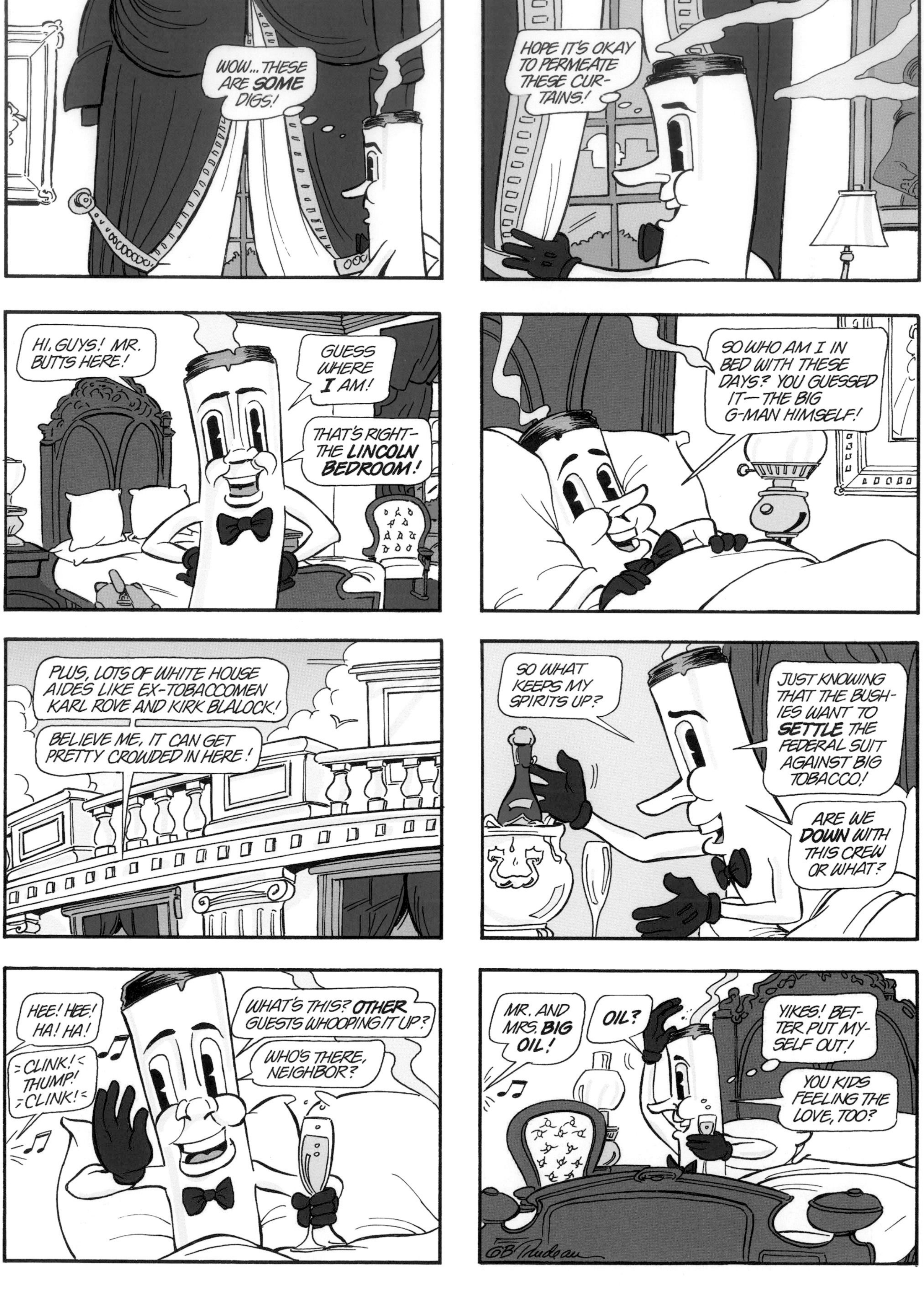
WOW... THESE ARE SOME DIGS!
HOPE IT'S OKAY TO PERMEATE THESE CUR-TAINS!
HI, GUYS! MR. BUTTS HERE!
GUESS WHERE I AM!
THAT'S RIGHT-THE LINCOLN BEDROOM!
SO WHO AM I IN BED WITH THESE DAYS? YOU GUESSED IT—THE BIG G-MAN HIMSELF!
PLUS, LOTS OF WHITE HOUSE AIDES LIKE EX-TOBACCOMEN KARL ROVE AND KIRK BLALOCK!
BELIEVE ME, IT CAN GET PRETTY CROWDED IN HERE!
SO WHAT KEEPS MY SPIRITS UP?
JUST KNOWING THAT THE BUSH-IES WANT TO SETTLE THE FEDERAL SUIT AGAINST BIG TOBACCO!
ARE WE DOWN WITH THIS CREW OR WHAT?
HEE! HEE! HA! HA!
CLINK! THUMP! CLINK!
WHAT'S THIS? OTHER GUESTS WHOOPING IT UP?
WHO'S THERE, NEIGHBOR?
MR. AND MRS. BIG OIL!
OIL?
YIKES! BET-TER PUT MY-SELF OUT!
YOU KIDS FEELING THE LOVE, TOO?
©B Trudeau

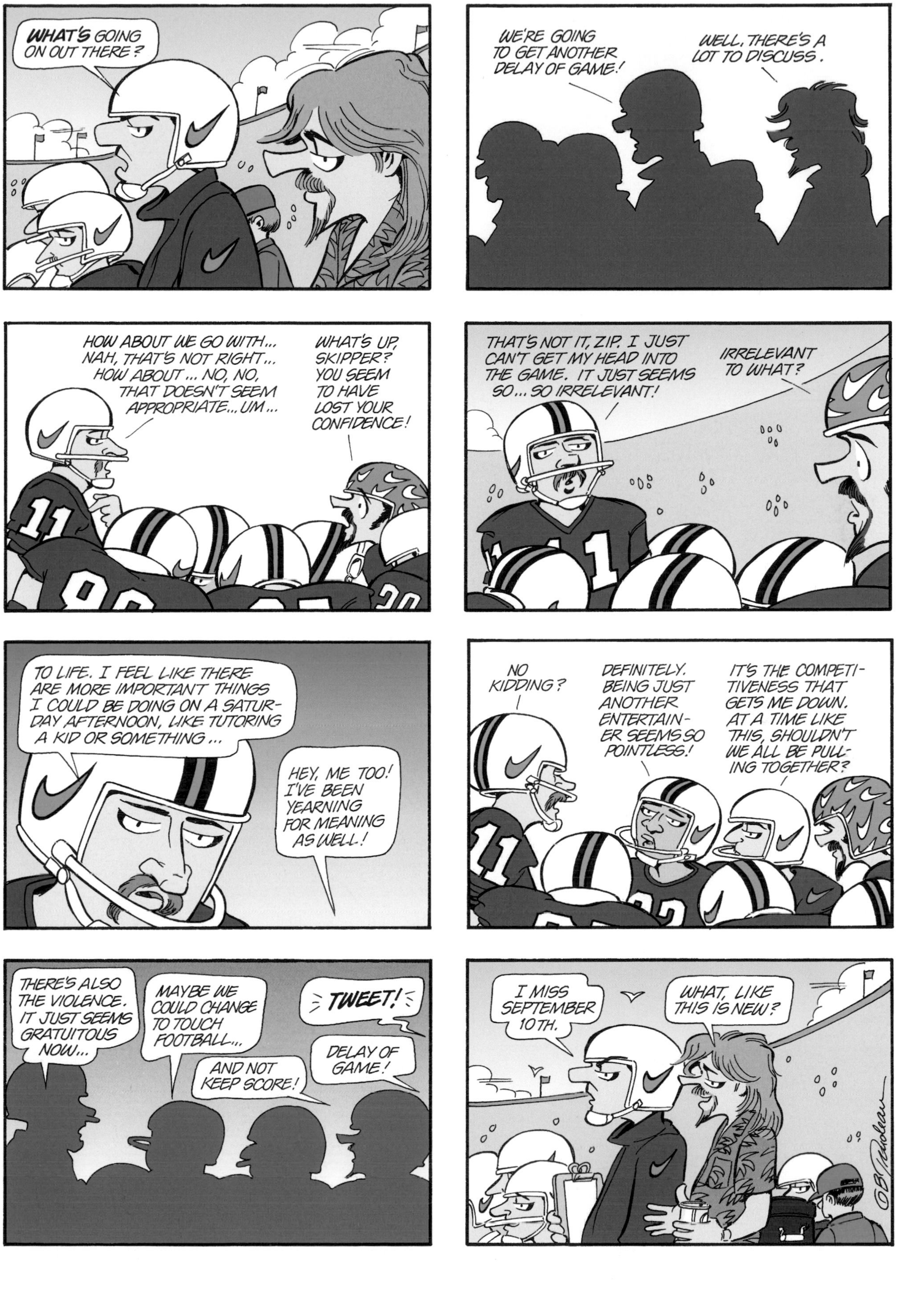
WHAT'S GOING ON OUT THERE?
WE'RE GOING TO GET ANOTHER DELAY OF GAME!
WELL, THERE'S A LOT TO DISCUSS.
HOW ABOUT WE GO WITH... NAH, THAT'S NOT RIGHT... HOW ABOUT... NO, NO, THAT DOESN'T SEEM APPROPRIATE... UM...
WHAT'S UP, SKIPPER? YOU SEEM TO HAVE LOST YOUR CONFIDENCE!
THAT'S NOT IT, ZIP. I JUST CAN'T GET MY HEAD INTO THE GAME. IT JUST SEEMS SO... SO IRRELEVANT!
IRRELEVANT TO WHAT?
TO LIFE. I FEEL LIKE THERE ARE MORE IMPORTANT THINGS I COULD BE DOING ON A SATURDAY AFTERNOON, LIKE TUTORING A KID OR SOMETHING...
HEY, ME TOO! I'VE BEEN YEARNING FOR MEANING AS WELL!
NO KIDDING?
DEFINITELY. BEING JUST ANOTHER ENTERTAINER SEEMS SO POINTLESS!
IT'S THE COMPETITIVENESS THAT GETS ME DOWN. AT A TIME LIKE THIS, SHOULDN'T WE ALL BE PULLING TOGETHER?
THERE'S ALSO THE VIOLENCE. IT JUST SEEMS GRATUITOUS NOW...
MAYBE WE COULD CHANGE TO TOUCH FOOTBALL...
AND NOT KEEP SCORE!
TWEET!
DELAY OF GAME!
I MISS SEPTEMBER 10TH.
WHAT, LIKE THIS IS NEW?
©B. Trudeau

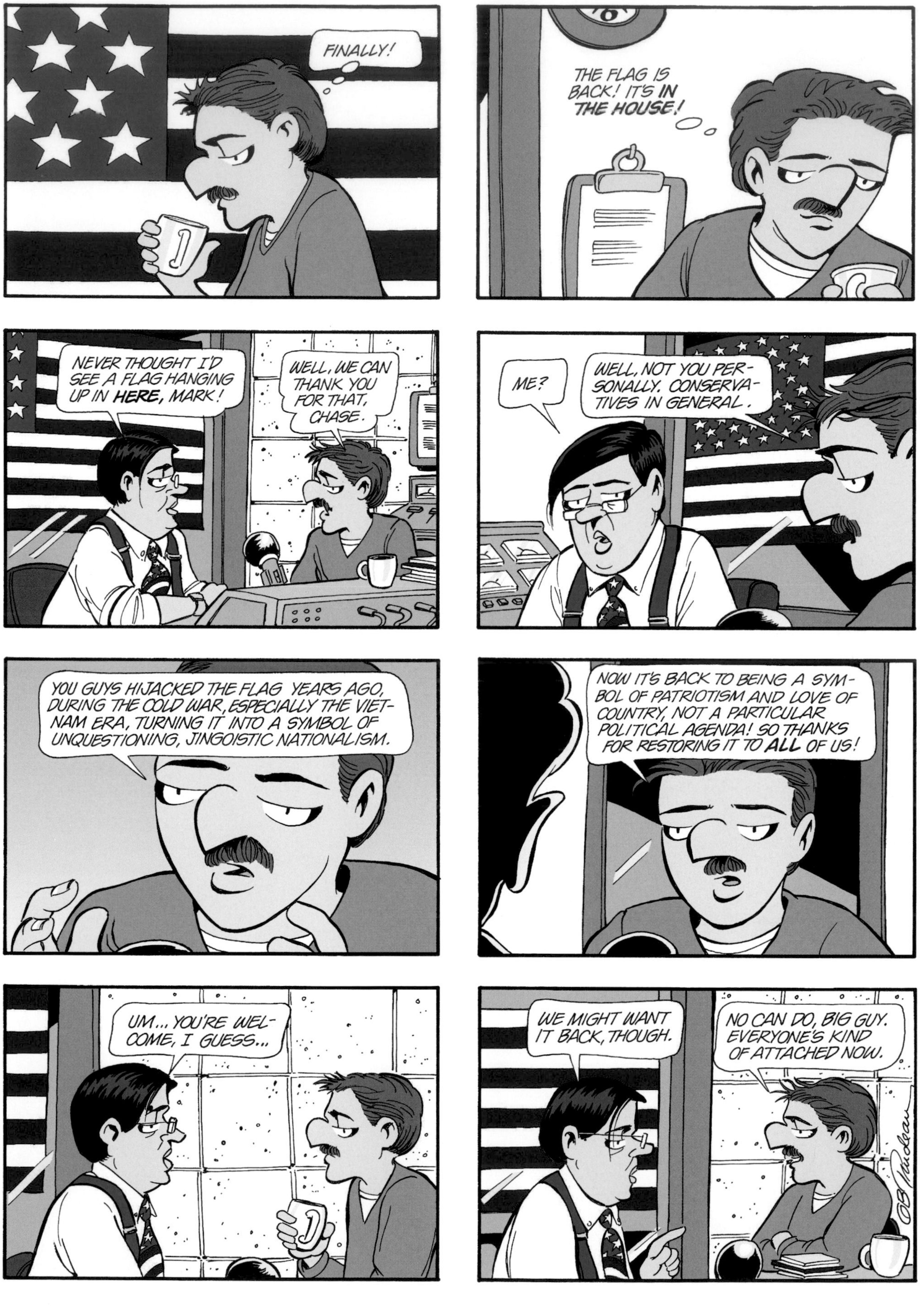
FINALLY!
THE FLAG IS BACK! IT'S IN THE HOUSE!
NEVER THOUGHT I'D SEE A FLAG HANGING UP IN HERE, MARK!
WELL, WE CAN THANK YOU FOR THAT, CHASE.
ME?
WELL, NOT YOU PERSONALLY. CONSERVATIVES IN GENERAL.
YOU GUYS HIJACKED THE FLAG YEARS AGO, DURING THE COLD WAR, ESPECIALLY THE VIETNAM ERA, TURNING IT INTO A SYMBOL OF UNQUESTIONING, JINGOISTIC NATIONALISM.
NOW IT'S BACK TO BEING A SYMBOL OF PATRIOTISM AND LOVE OF COUNTRY, NOT A PARTICULAR POLITICAL AGENDA! SO THANKS FOR RESTORING IT TO ALL OF US!
UM... YOU'RE WELCOME, I GUESS...
WE MIGHT WANT IT BACK, THOUGH.
NO CAN DO, BIG GUY. EVERYONE'S KIND OF ATTACHED NOW.

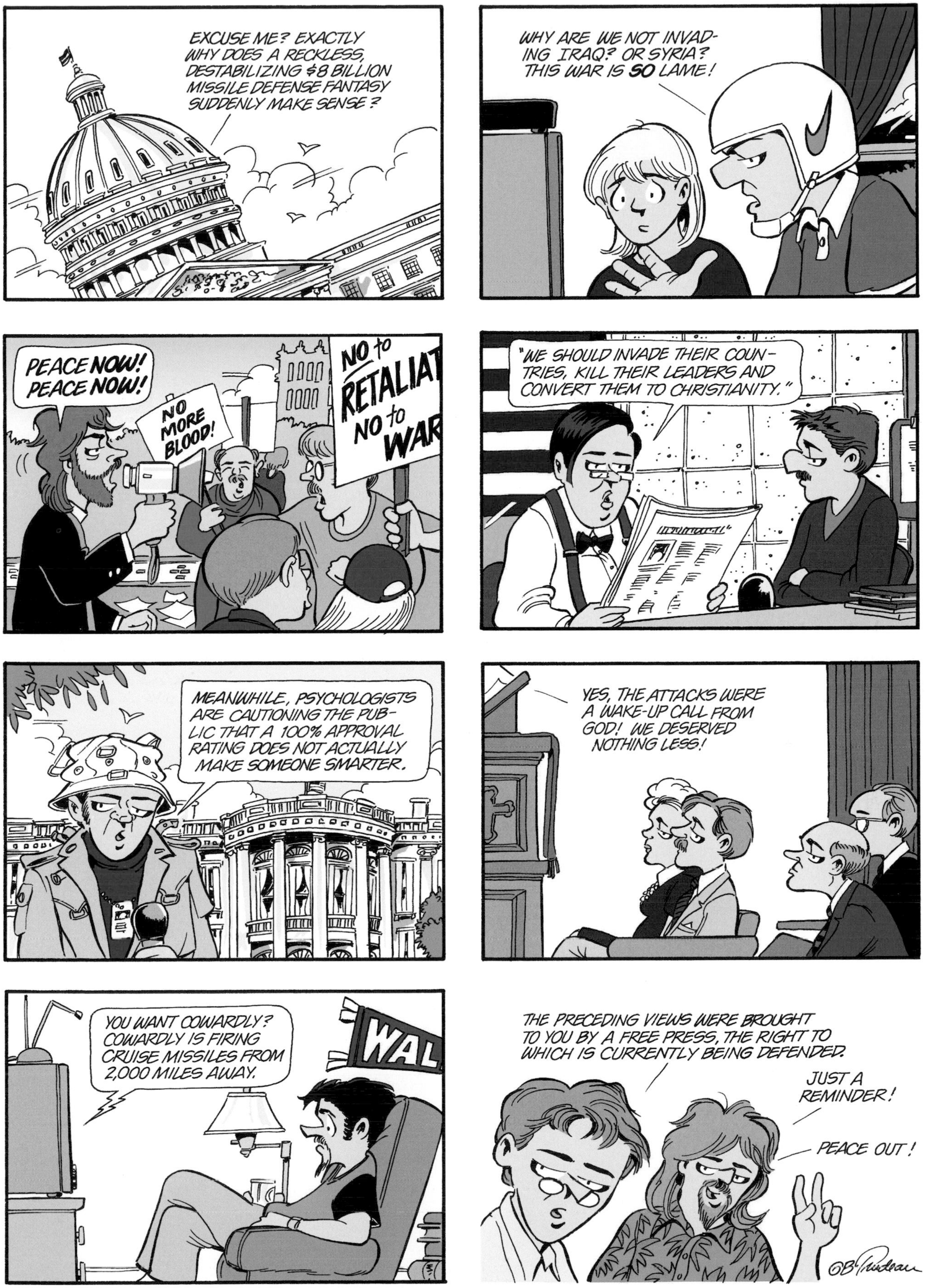
EXCUSE ME? EXACTLY WHY DOES A RECKLESS, DESTABILIZING $8 BILLION MISSILE DEFENSE FANTASY SUDDENLY MAKE SENSE?
WHY ARE WE NOT INVADING IRAQ? OR SYRIA? THIS WAR IS SO LAME!
PEACE NOW! PEACE NOW!
NO MORE BLOOD!
NO to RETALIAT
NO to WAR
"WE SHOULD INVADE THEIR COUNTRIES, KILL THEIR LEADERS AND CONVERT THEM TO CHRISTIANITY."
MEANWHILE, PSYCHOLOGISTS ARE CAUTIONING THE PUBLIC THAT A 100% APPROVAL RATING DOES NOT ACTUALLY MAKE SOMEONE SMARTER.
YES, THE ATTACKS WERE A WAKE-UP CALL FROM GOD! WE DESERVED NOTHING LESS!
YOU WANT COWARDLY? COWARDLY IS FIRING CRUISE MISSILES FROM 2,000 MILES AWAY.
WAL
THE PRECEDING VIEWS WERE BROUGHT TO YOU BY A FREE PRESS, THE RIGHT TO WHICH IS CURRENTLY BEING DEFENDED.
JUST A REMINDER!
PEACE OUT!
©B. Trudeau

KARL, IS IT STILL UNPATRIOTIC TO CRITICIZE ME?
YES, SIR.
COOL! THIS IS GREAT...
SIR, YOU'VE BEEN SO BUSY THIS FALL, WE DIDN'T HAVE A CHANCE TO BRIEF YOU ON THIS...
BUT IT TURNED OUT THAT THE MISSILE DEFENSE PROGRAM, AND CORPORATE TAX CUTS, AND SUBSIDIES FOR THE POWER INDUSTRY, AND OIL DRILLING IN ALASKA...
...IN FACT, MOST OF THE ITEMS ON OUR POLITICAL AGENDA...
...ARE ALL JUSTIFIED BY THE WAR AGAINST TERRORISM!
WOW... WHAT A COINCIDENCE...
THANKS, EVILDOERS!
THEY'RE SUCH JERKS — IF THEY ONLY KNEW...
©B Trudeau

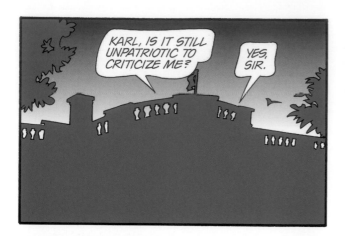

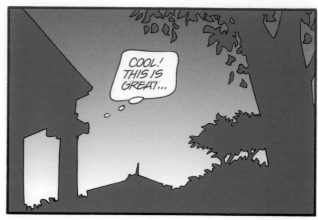

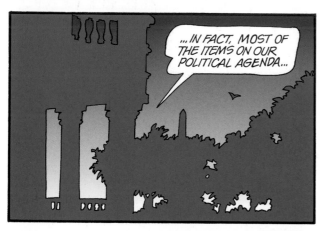

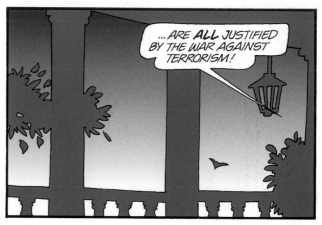

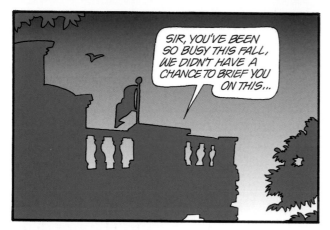

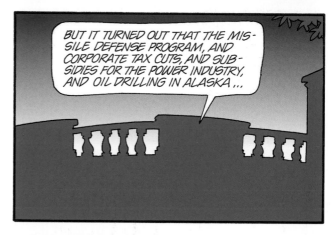

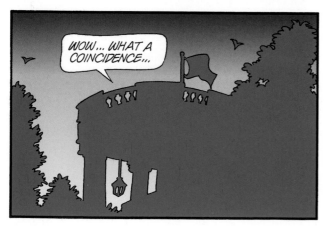

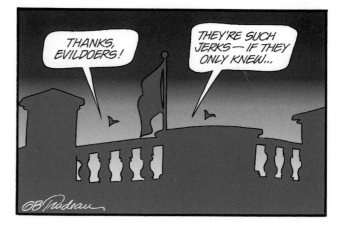

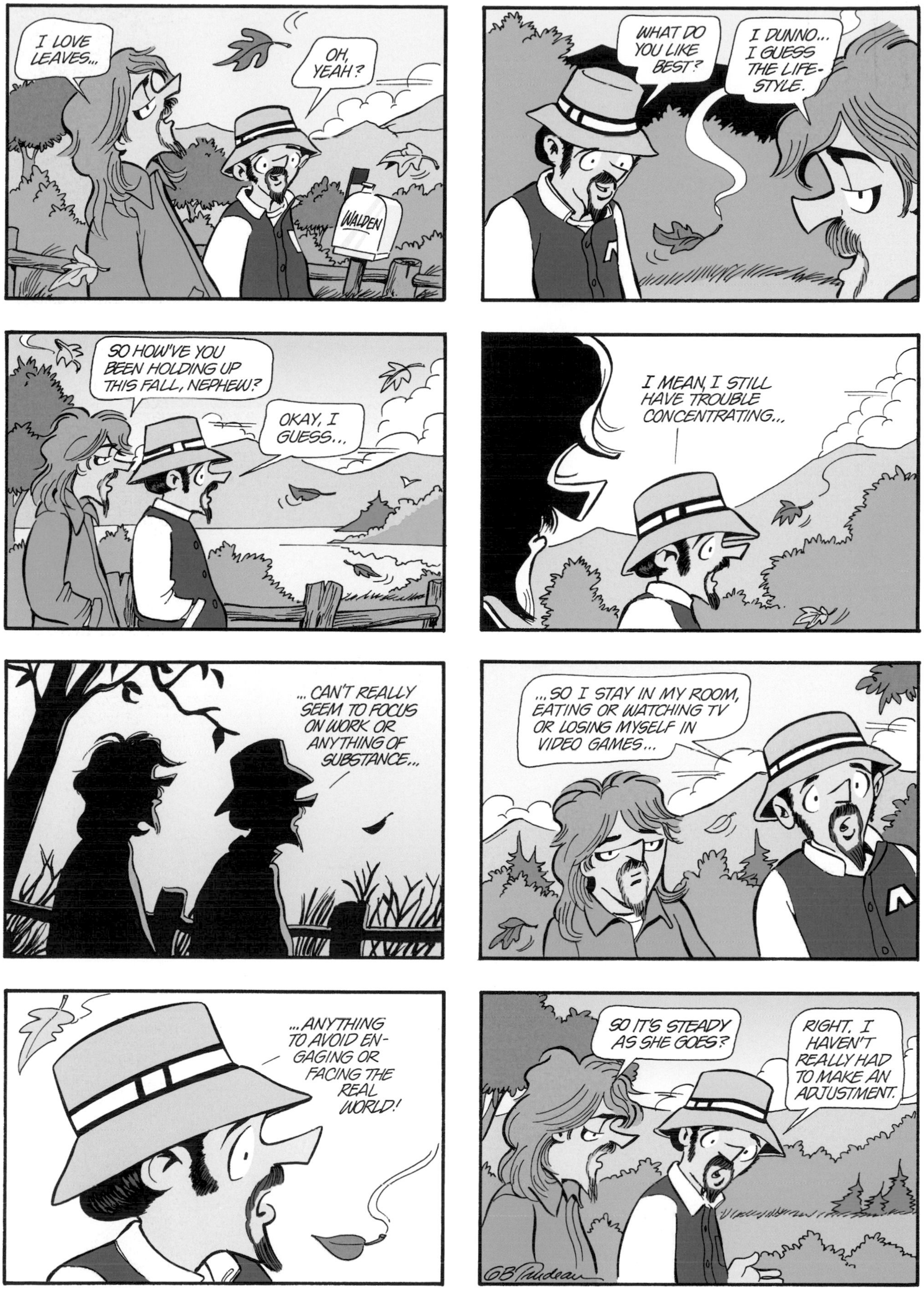
I LOVE LEAVES...
OH, YEAH?
WALDEN
WHAT DO YOU LIKE BEST?
I DUNNO... I GUESS THE LIFE-STYLE.
SO HOW'VE YOU BEEN HOLDING UP THIS FALL, NEPHEW?
OKAY, I GUESS...
I MEAN, I STILL HAVE TROUBLE CONCENTRATING...
...CAN'T REALLY SEEM TO FOCUS ON WORK OR ANYTHING OF SUBSTANCE...
...SO I STAY IN MY ROOM, EATING OR WATCHING TV OR LOSING MYSELF IN VIDEO GAMES...
...ANYTHING TO AVOID EN-GAGING OR FACING THE REAL WORLD!
SO IT'S STEADY AS SHE GOES?
RIGHT. I HAVEN'T REALLY HAD TO MAKE AN ADJUSTMENT.
GB Trudeau

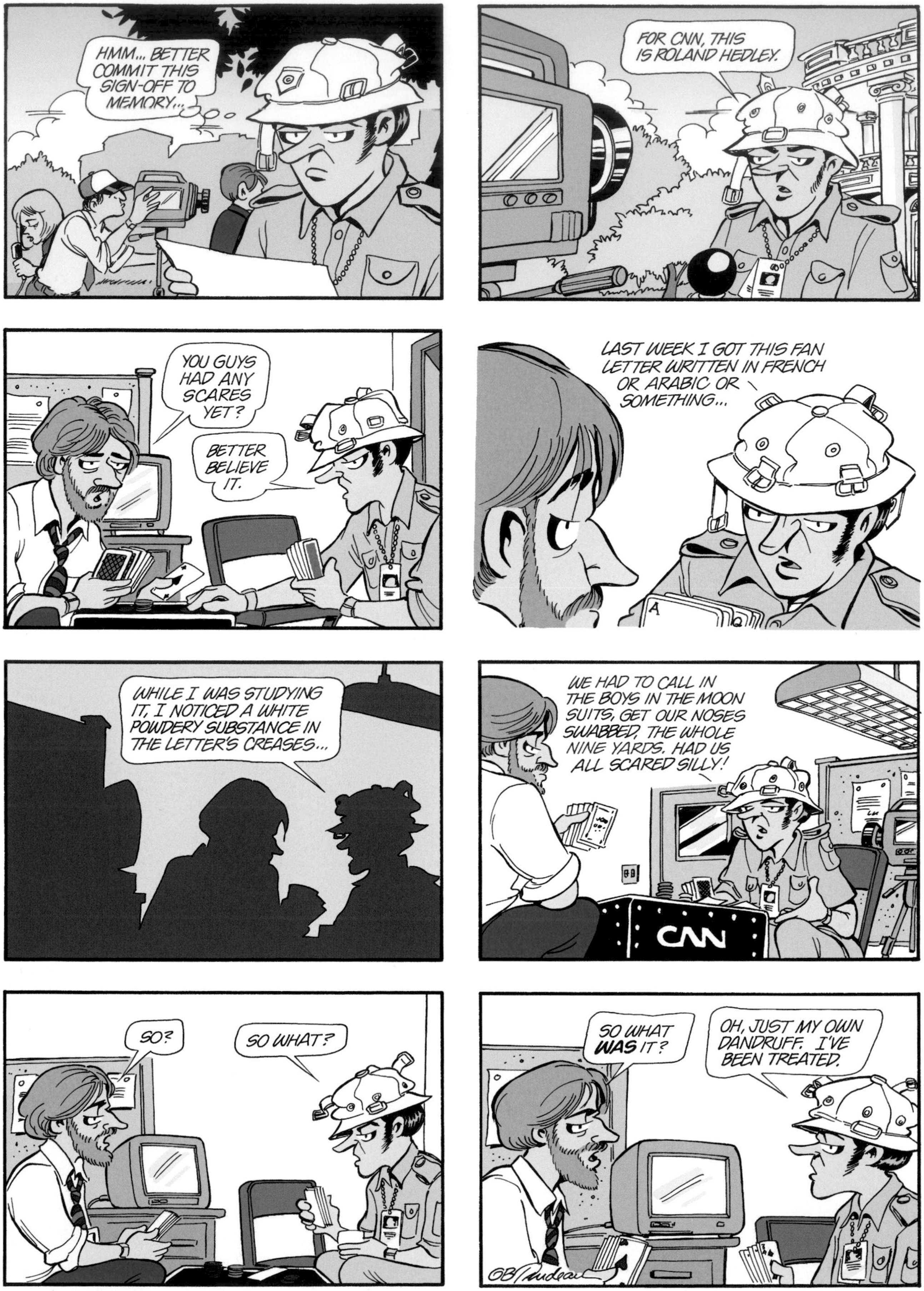
HMM... BETTER COMMIT THIS SIGN-OFF TO MEMORY...
FOR CNN, THIS IS ROLAND HEDLEY.
YOU GUYS HAD ANY SCARES YET?
BETTER BELIEVE IT.
LAST WEEK I GOT THIS FAN LETTER WRITTEN IN FRENCH OR ARABIC OR SOMETHING...
WHILE I WAS STUDYING IT, I NOTICED A WHITE POWDERY SUBSTANCE IN THE LETTER'S CREASES...
WE HAD TO CALL IN THE BOYS IN THE MOON SUITS, GET OUR NOSES SWABBED, THE WHOLE NINE YARDS. HAD US ALL SCARED SILLY!
CNN
SO?
SO WHAT?
SO WHAT **WAS** IT?
OH, JUST MY OWN DANDRUFF. I'VE BEEN TREATED.

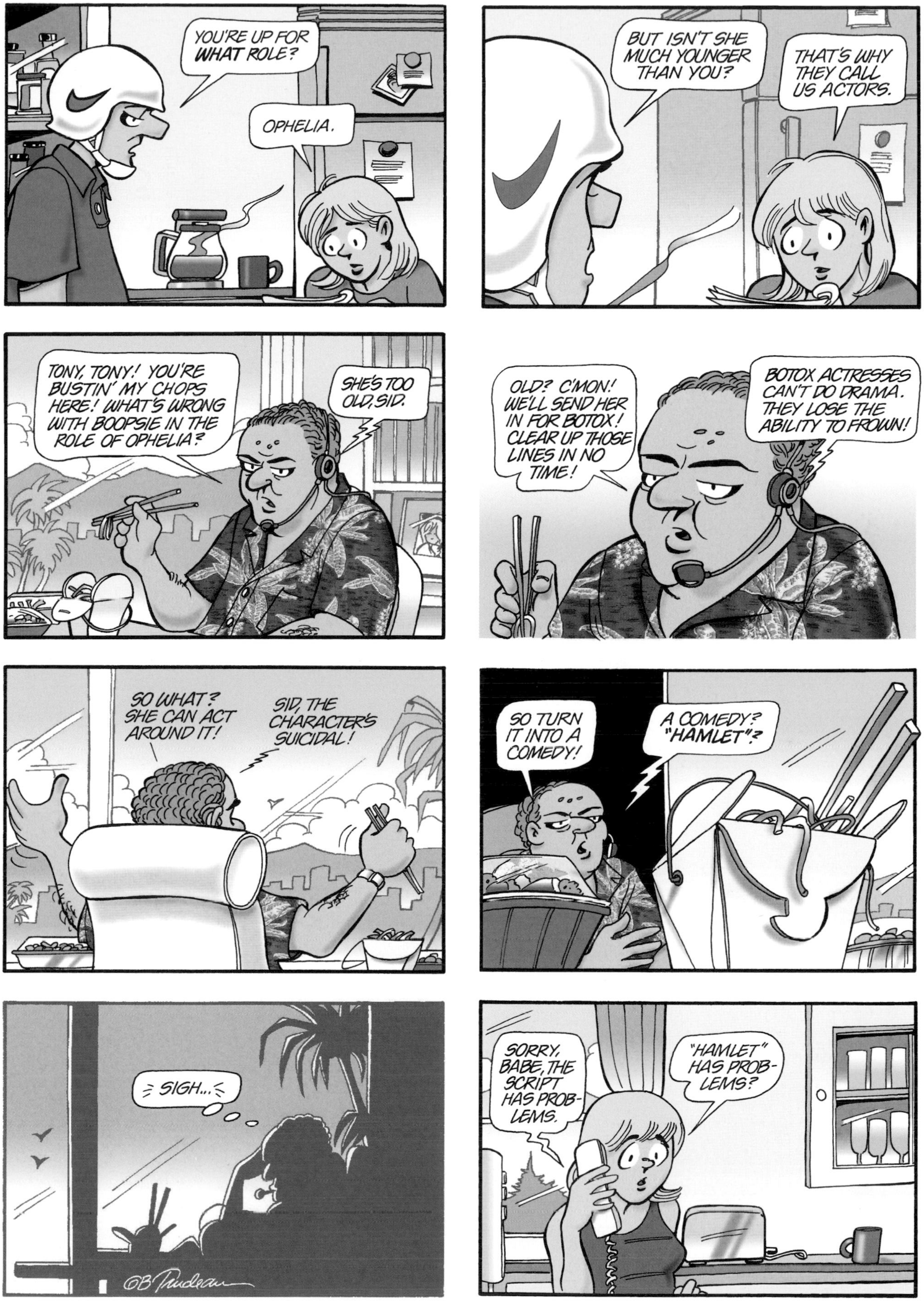
YOU'RE UP FOR WHAT ROLE?
OPHELIA.
BUT ISN'T SHE MUCH YOUNGER THAN YOU?
THAT'S WHY THEY CALL US ACTORS.
TONY, TONY! YOU'RE BUSTIN' MY CHOPS HERE! WHAT'S WRONG WITH BOOPSIE IN THE ROLE OF OPHELIA?
SHE'S TOO OLD, SID.
OLD? C'MON! WE'LL SEND HER IN FOR BOTOX! CLEAR UP THOSE LINES IN NO TIME!
BOTOX ACTRESSES CAN'T DO DRAMA. THEY LOSE THE ABILITY TO FROWN!
SO WHAT? SHE CAN ACT AROUND IT!
SID, THE CHARACTER'S SUICIDAL!
SO TURN IT INTO A COMEDY!
A COMEDY? "HAMLET"?
SIGH...
©B Trudeau
SORRY, BABE, THE SCRIPT HAS PROBLEMS.
"HAMLET" HAS PROBLEMS?

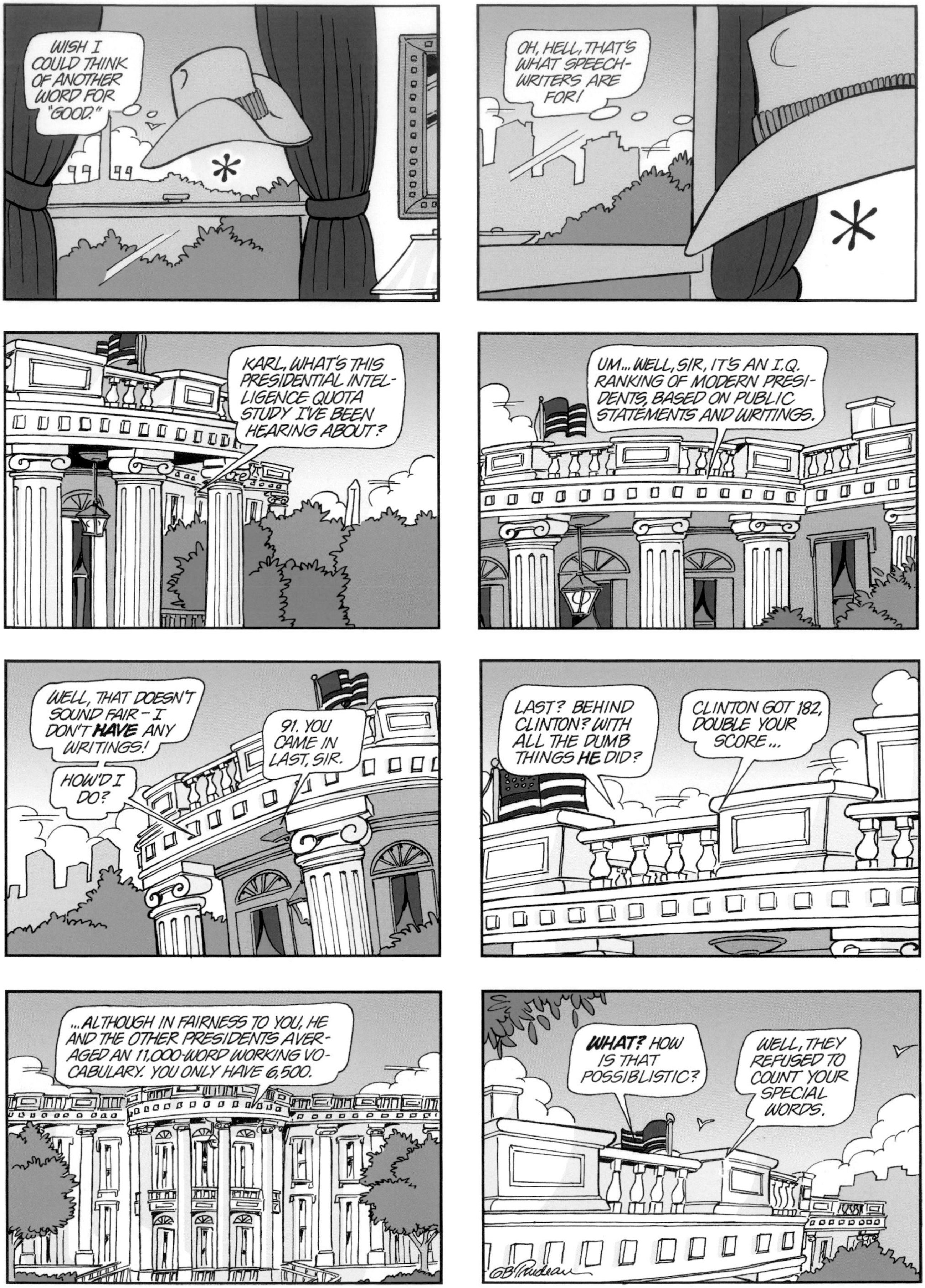
WISH I COULD THINK OF ANOTHER WORD FOR "GOOD."
OH, HELL, THAT'S WHAT SPEECH-WRITERS ARE FOR!
KARL, WHAT'S THIS PRESIDENTIAL INTELLIGENCE QUOTA STUDY I'VE BEEN HEARING ABOUT?
UM... WELL, SIR, IT'S AN I.Q. RANKING OF MODERN PRESIDENTS, BASED ON PUBLIC STATEMENTS AND WRITINGS.
WELL, THAT DOESN'T SOUND FAIR—I DON'T **HAVE** ANY WRITINGS!
HOW'D I DO?
91. YOU CAME IN LAST, SIR.
LAST? BEHIND CLINTON? WITH ALL THE DUMB THINGS **HE** DID?
CLINTON GOT 182, DOUBLE YOUR SCORE...
...ALTHOUGH IN FAIRNESS TO YOU, HE AND THE OTHER PRESIDENTS AVERAGED AN 11,000-WORD WORKING VOCABULARY. YOU ONLY HAVE 6,500.
**WHAT?** HOW IS THAT POSSIBLISTIC?
WELL, THEY REFUSED TO COUNT YOUR SPECIAL WORDS.
©B Trudeau

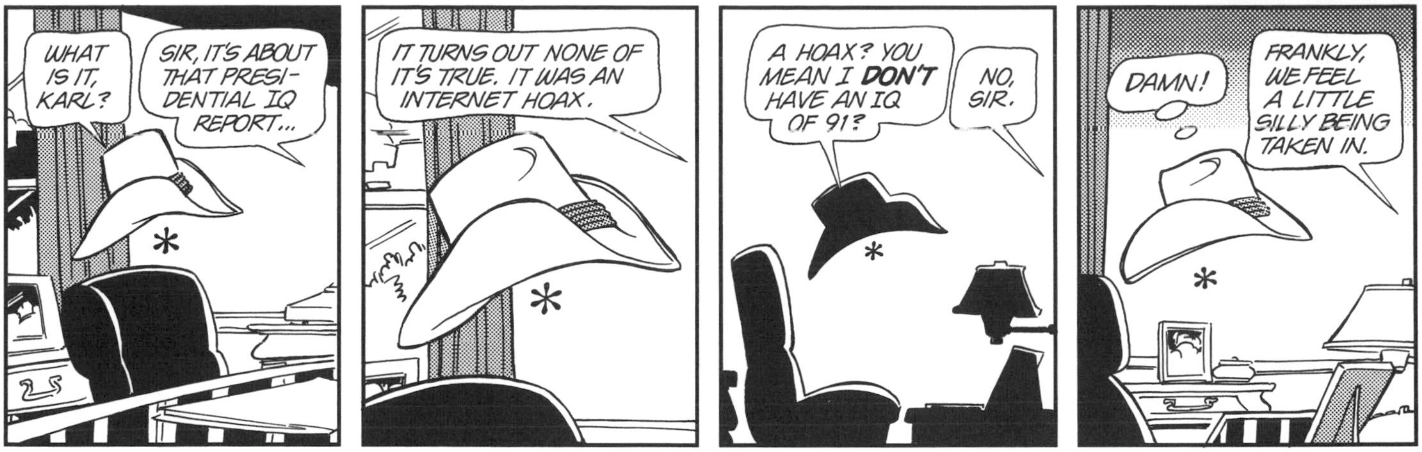
WHAT IS IT, KARL?
SIR, IT'S ABOUT THAT PRESI-DENTIAL IQ REPORT...
IT TURNS OUT NONE OF IT'S TRUE. IT WAS AN INTERNET HOAX.
A HOAX? YOU MEAN I **DON'T** HAVE AN IQ OF 91?
NO, SIR.
DAMN!
FRANKLY, WE FEEL A LITTLE SILLY BEING TAKEN IN.

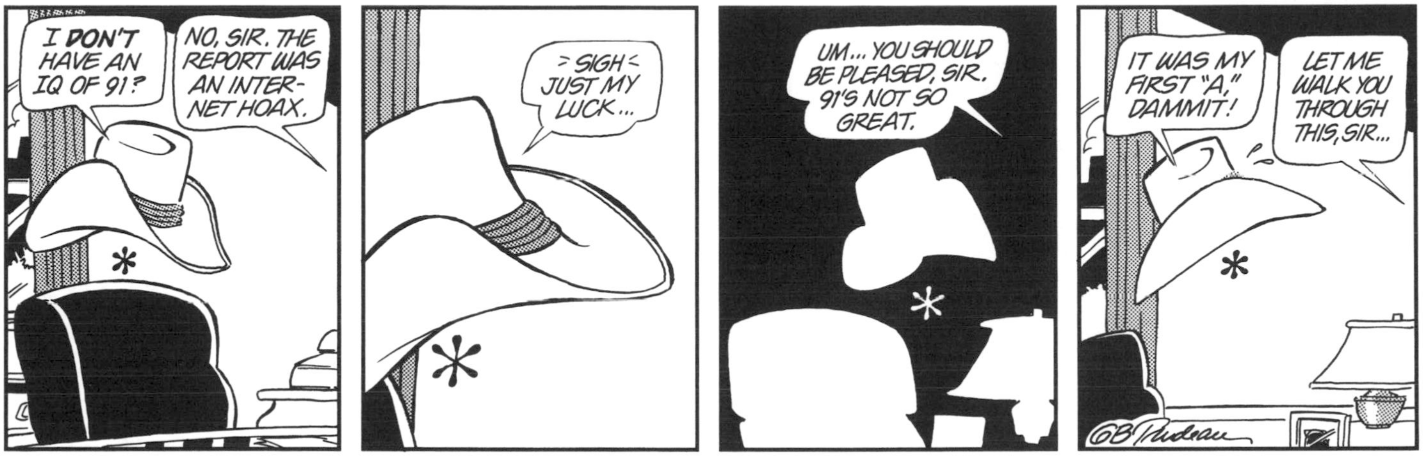
I **DON'T** HAVE AN IQ OF 91?
NO, SIR. THE REPORT WAS AN INTER-NET HOAX.
> SIGH < JUST MY LUCK...
UM... YOU SHOULD BE PLEASED, SIR. 91'S NOT SO GREAT.
IT WAS MY FIRST "A," DAMMIT!
LET ME WALK YOU THROUGH THIS, SIR...

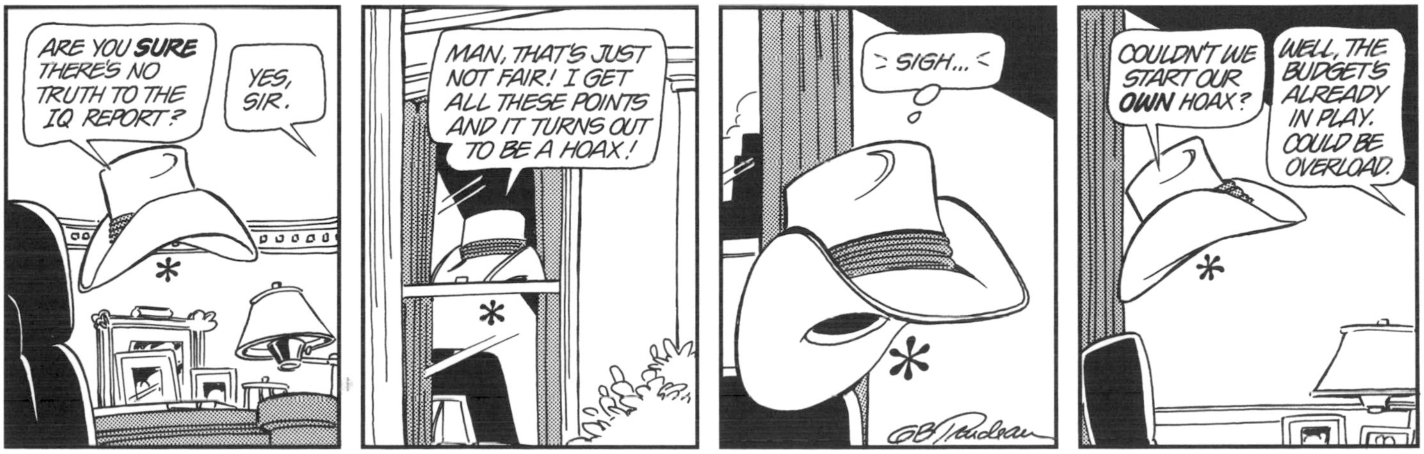
ARE YOU **SURE** THERE'S NO TRUTH TO THE IQ REPORT?
YES, SIR.
MAN, THAT'S JUST NOT FAIR! I GET ALL THESE POINTS AND IT TURNS OUT TO BE A HOAX!
> SIGH... <
COULDN'T WE START OUR **OWN** HOAX?
WELL, THE BUDGET'S ALREADY IN PLAY. COULD BE OVERLOAD.

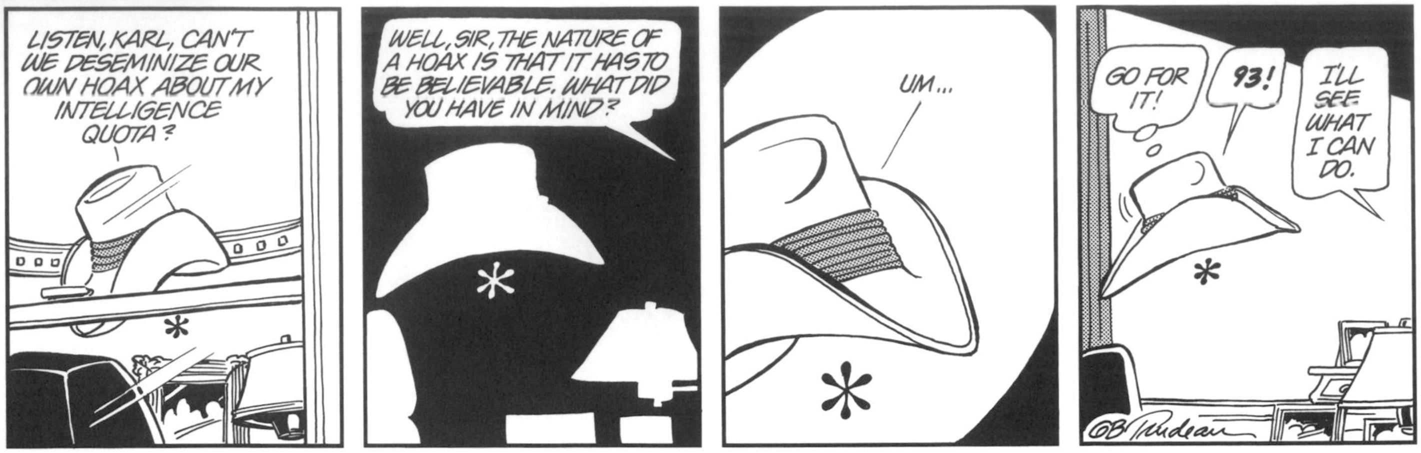
LISTEN, KARL, CAN'T WE DESEMINIZE OUR OWN HOAX ABOUT MY INTELLIGENCE QUOTA?
WELL, SIR, THE NATURE OF A HOAX IS THAT IT HAS TO BE BELIEVABLE. WHAT DID YOU HAVE IN MIND?
UM...
GO FOR IT!
93!
I'LL SEE WHAT I CAN DO.

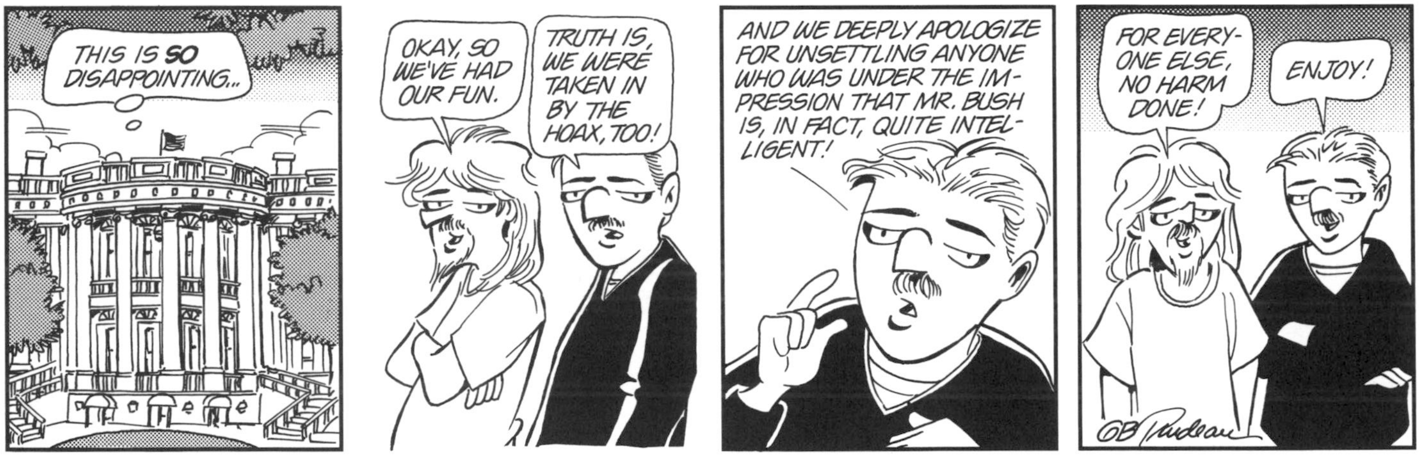
THIS IS **SO** DISAPPOINTING...
OKAY, SO WE'VE HAD OUR FUN.
TRUTH IS, WE WERE TAKEN IN BY THE HOAX, TOO!
AND WE DEEPLY APOLOGIZE FOR UNSETTLING ANYONE WHO WAS UNDER THE IMPRESSION THAT MR. BUSH IS, IN FACT, QUITE INTELLIGENT!
FOR EVERYONE ELSE, NO HARM DONE!
ENJOY!

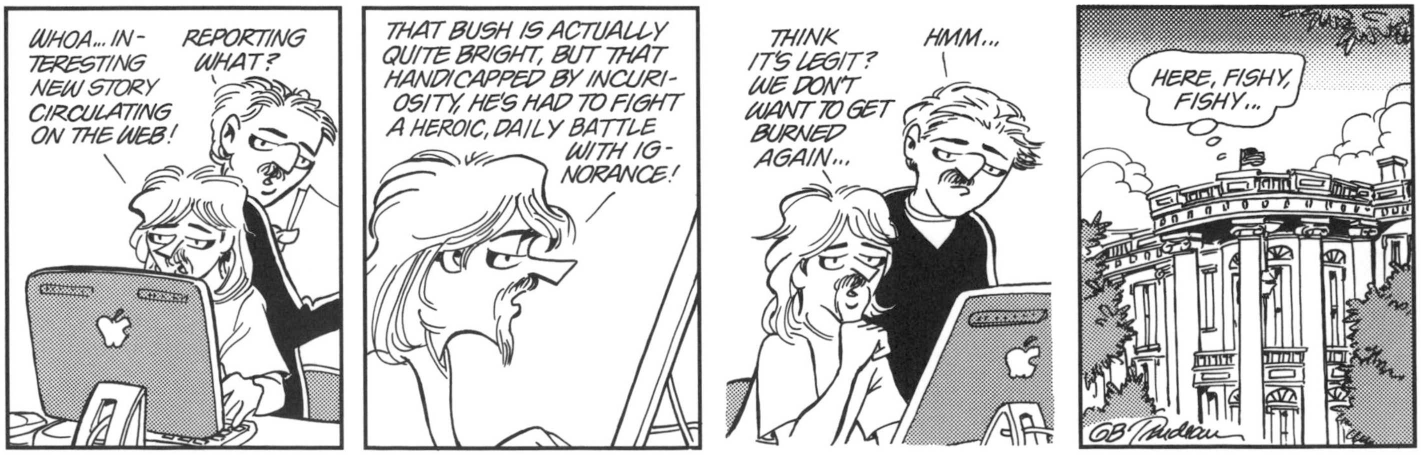
WHOA... INTERESTING NEW STORY CIRCULATING ON THE WEB!
REPORTING WHAT?
THAT BUSH IS ACTUALLY QUITE BRIGHT, BUT THAT HANDICAPPED BY INCURIOSITY, HE'S HAD TO FIGHT A HEROIC, DAILY BATTLE WITH IGNORANCE!
THINK IT'S LEGIT? WE DON'T WANT TO GET BURNED AGAIN...
HMM...
HERE, FISHY, FISHY...

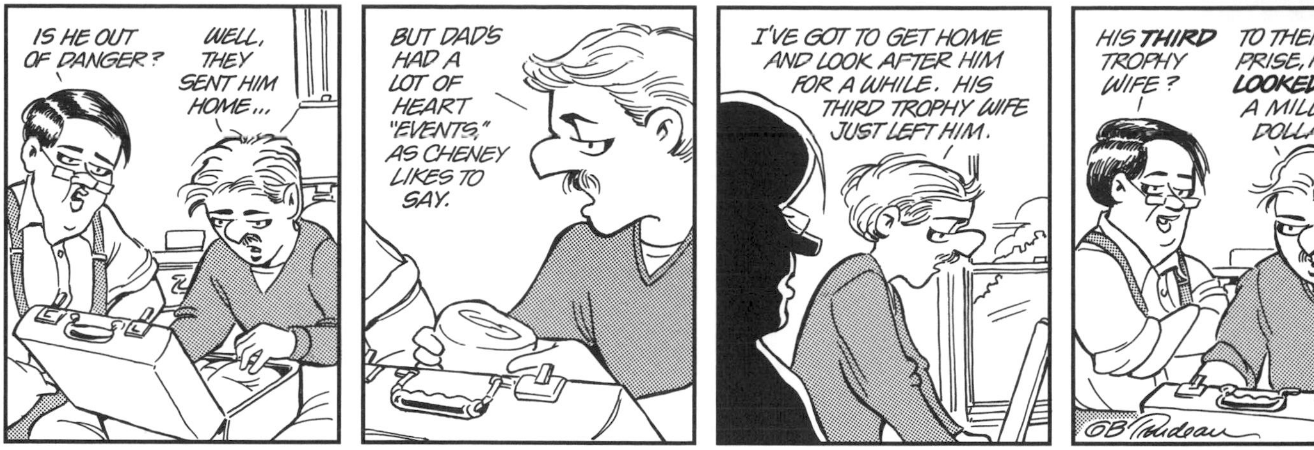
IS HE OUT OF DANGER?
WELL, THEY SENT HIM HOME...
BUT DAD'S HAD A LOT OF HEART "EVENTS," AS CHENEY LIKES TO SAY.
I'VE GOT TO GET HOME AND LOOK AFTER HIM FOR A WHILE. HIS THIRD TROPHY WIFE JUST LEFT HIM.
HIS **THIRD** TROPHY WIFE?
TO THEIR SURPRISE, HE ONLY **LOOKED** LIKE A MILLION DOLLARS.

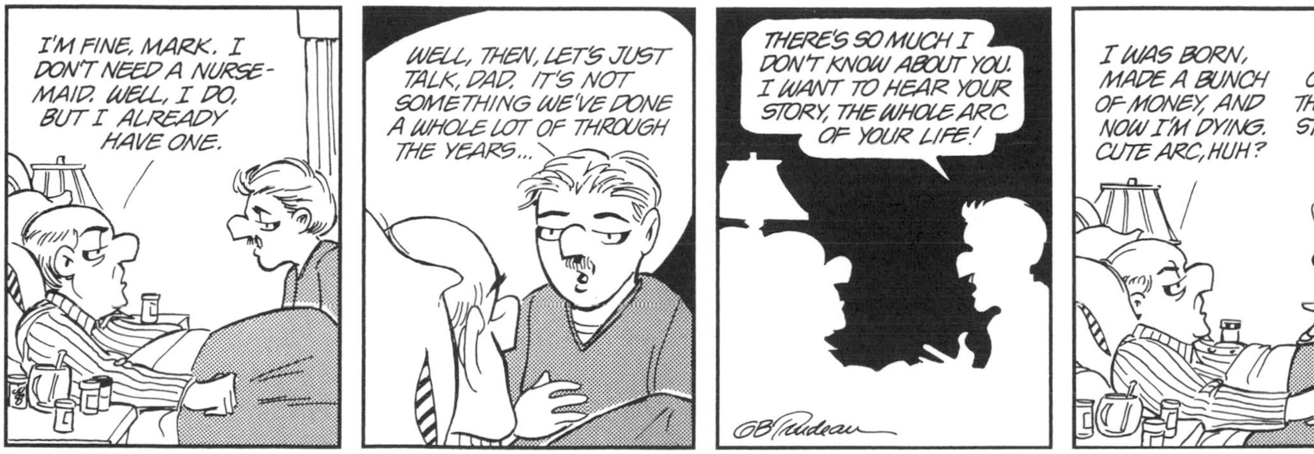
I'M FINE, MARK. I DON'T NEED A NURSEMAID. WELL, I DO, BUT I ALREADY HAVE ONE.
WELL, THEN, LET'S JUST TALK, DAD. IT'S NOT SOMETHING WE'VE DONE A WHOLE LOT OF THROUGH THE YEARS...
THERE'S SO MUCH I DON'T KNOW ABOUT YOU. I WANT TO HEAR YOUR STORY, THE WHOLE ARC OF YOUR LIFE!
I WAS BORN, MADE A BUNCH OF MONEY, AND NOW I'M DYING. CUTE ARC, HUH?
OKAY, THAT'S A START...

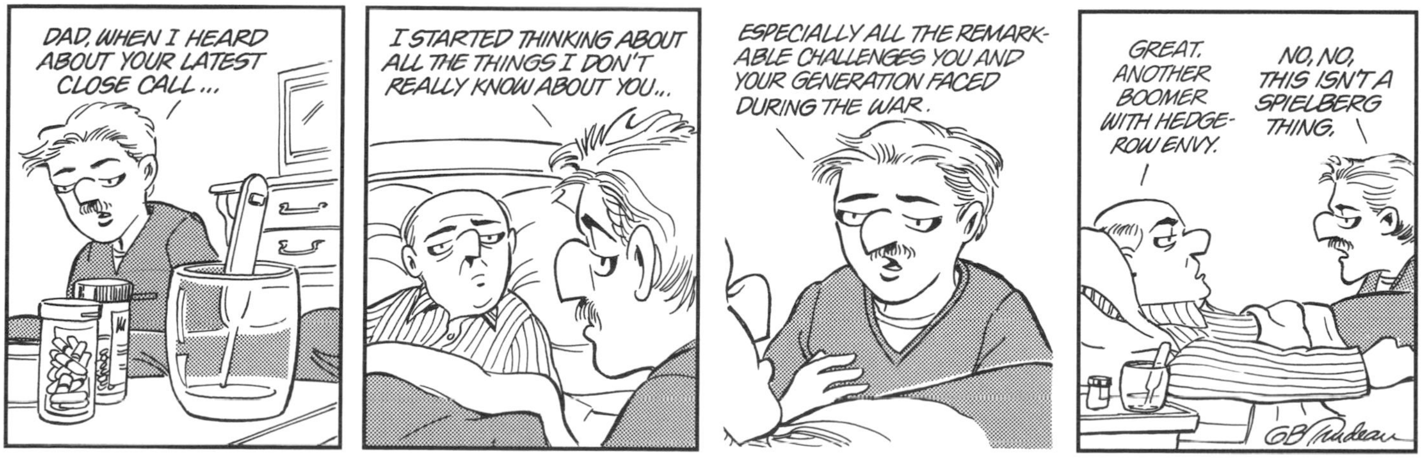
DAD, WHEN I HEARD ABOUT YOUR LATEST CLOSE CALL...
I STARTED THINKING ABOUT ALL THE THINGS I DON'T REALLY KNOW ABOUT YOU...
ESPECIALLY ALL THE REMARKABLE CHALLENGES YOU AND YOUR GENERATION FACED DURING THE WAR.
GREAT. ANOTHER BOOMER WITH HEDGEROW ENVY.
NO, NO, THIS ISN'T A SPIELBERG THING.

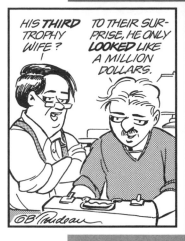

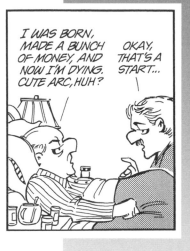

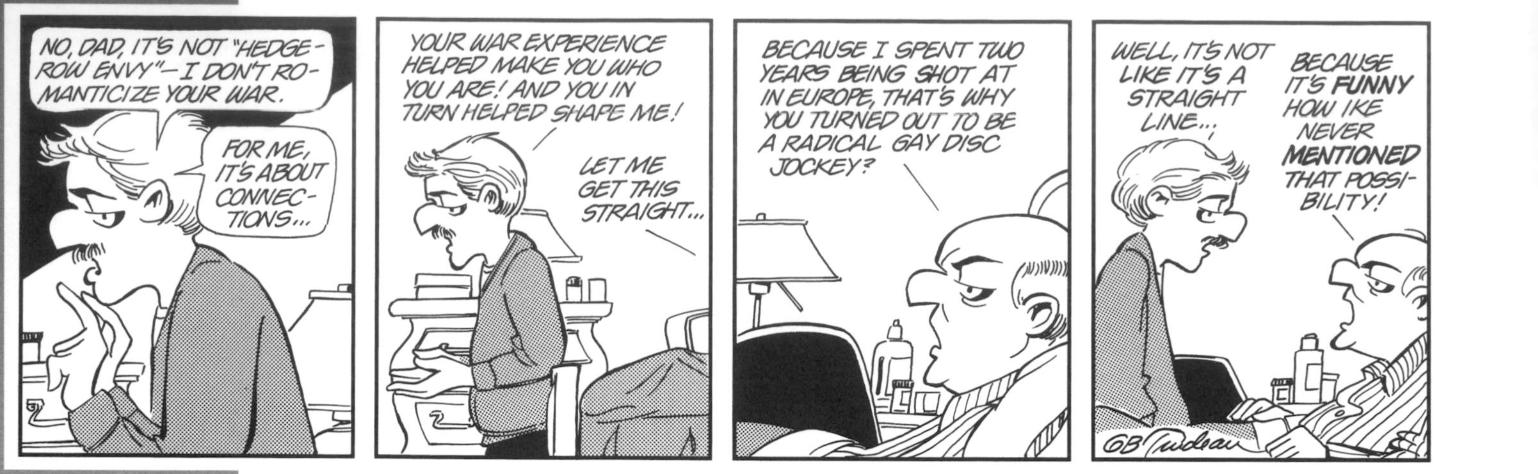
NO, DAD, IT'S NOT "HEDGE-ROW ENVY"—I DON'T ROMANTICIZE YOUR WAR.
FOR ME, IT'S ABOUT CONNECTIONS...
YOUR WAR EXPERIENCE HELPED MAKE YOU WHO YOU ARE! AND YOU IN TURN HELPED SHAPE ME!
LET ME GET THIS STRAIGHT...
BECAUSE I SPENT TWO YEARS BEING SHOT AT IN EUROPE, THAT'S WHY YOU TURNED OUT TO BE A RADICAL GAY DISC JOCKEY?
WELL, IT'S NOT LIKE IT'S A STRAIGHT LINE...
BECAUSE IT'S **FUNNY** HOW IKE NEVER **MENTIONED** THAT POSSIBILITY!
©B Trudeau

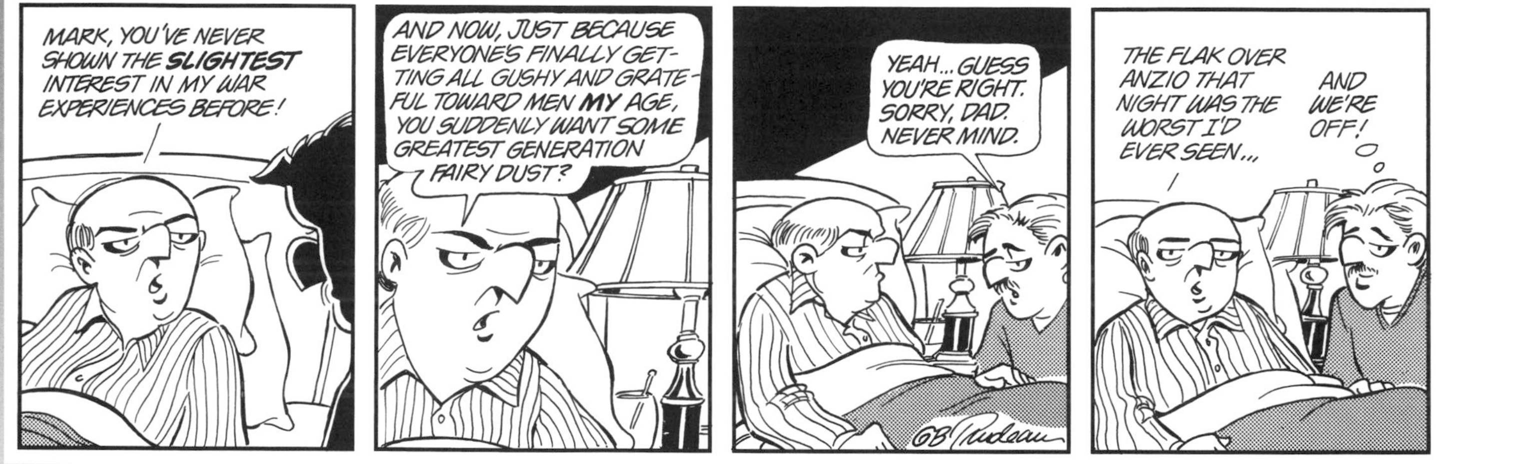
MARK, YOU'VE NEVER SHOWN THE **SLIGHTEST** INTEREST IN MY WAR EXPERIENCES BEFORE!
AND NOW, JUST BECAUSE EVERYONE'S FINALLY GETTING ALL GUSHY AND GRATEFUL TOWARD MEN **MY** AGE, YOU SUDDENLY WANT SOME GREATEST GENERATION FAIRY DUST?
YEAH... GUESS YOU'RE RIGHT. SORRY, DAD. NEVER MIND.
THE FLAK OVER ANZIO THAT NIGHT WAS THE WORST I'D EVER SEEN...
AND WE'RE OFF!
©B Trudeau

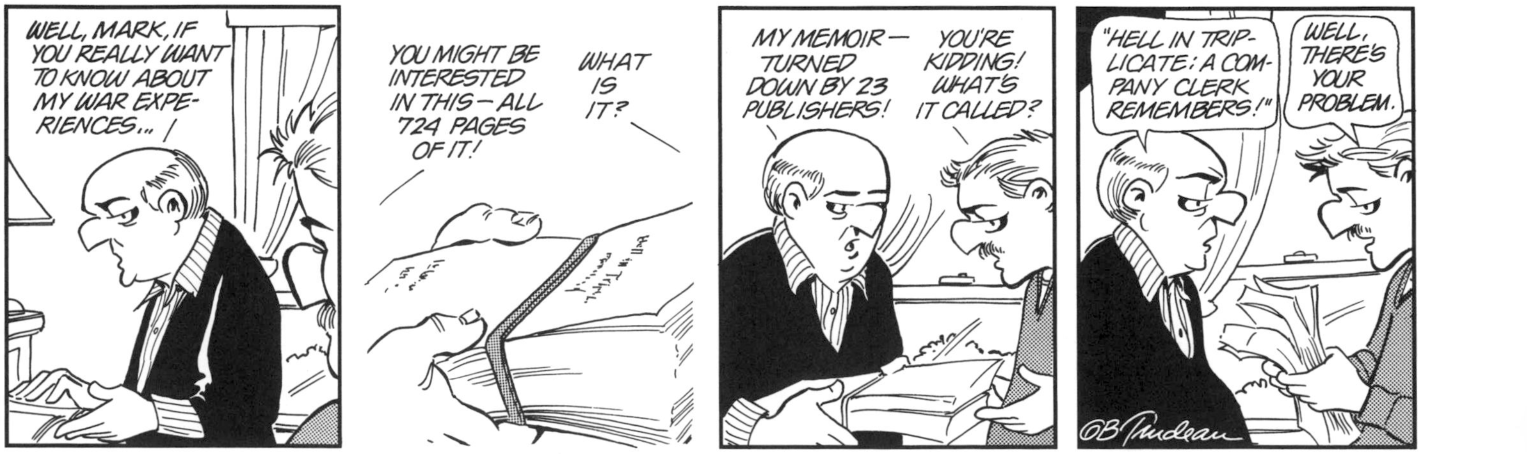
WELL, MARK, IF YOU REALLY WANT TO KNOW ABOUT MY WAR EXPERIENCES...
YOU MIGHT BE INTERESTED IN THIS—ALL 724 PAGES OF IT!
WHAT IS IT?
MY MEMOIR—TURNED DOWN BY 23 PUBLISHERS!
YOU'RE KIDDING! WHAT'S IT CALLED?
"HELL IN TRIPLICATE: A COMPANY CLERK REMEMBERS!"
WELL, THERE'S YOUR PROBLEM.
©B Trudeau

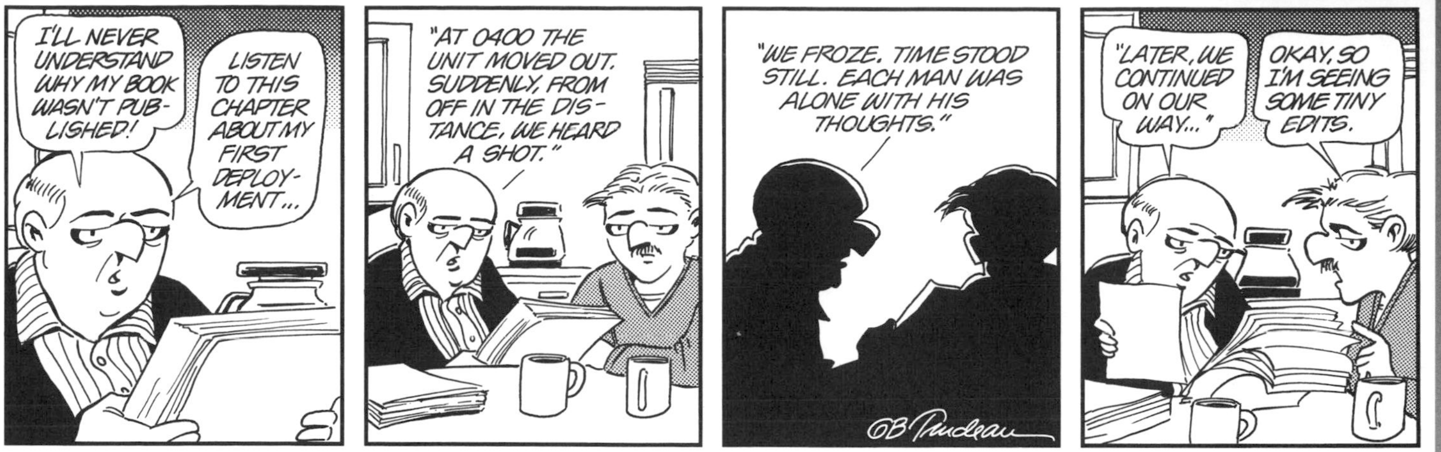
I'LL NEVER UNDERSTAND WHY MY BOOK WASN'T PUBLISHED!
LISTEN TO THIS CHAPTER ABOUT MY FIRST DEPLOYMENT...
"AT 0400 THE UNIT MOVED OUT. SUDDENLY, FROM OFF IN THE DISTANCE, WE HEARD A SHOT."
"WE FROZE. TIME STOOD STILL. EACH MAN WAS ALONE WITH HIS THOUGHTS."
"LATER, WE CONTINUED ON OUR WAY..."
OKAY, SO I'M SEEING SOME TINY EDITS.

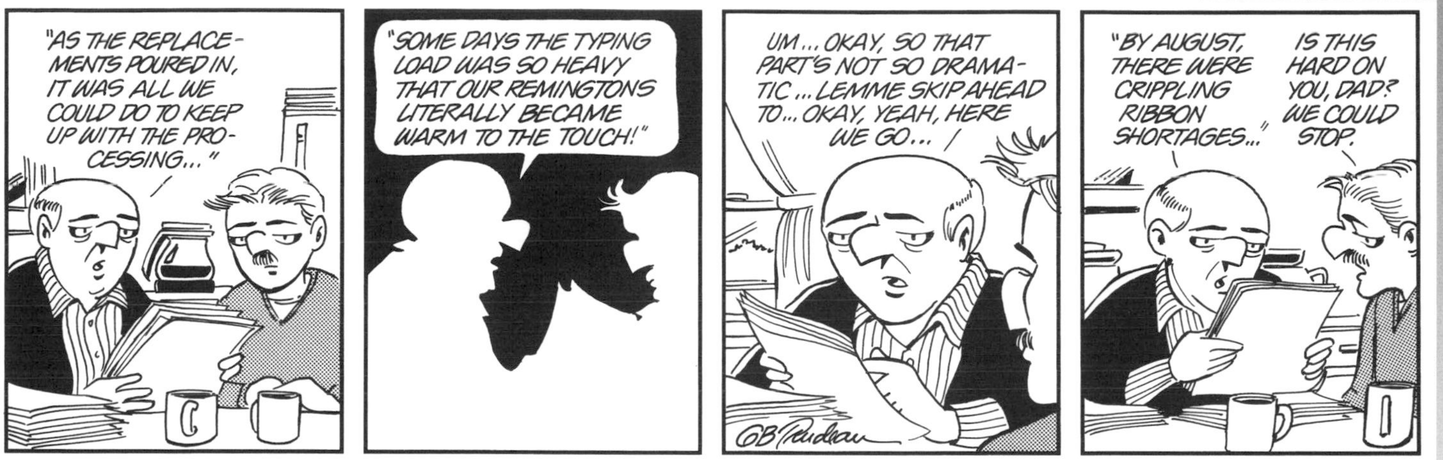
"AS THE REPLACEMENTS POURED IN, IT WAS ALL WE COULD DO TO KEEP UP WITH THE PROCESSING..."
"SOME DAYS THE TYPING LOAD WAS SO HEAVY THAT OUR REMINGTONS LITERALLY BECAME WARM TO THE TOUCH!"
UM... OKAY, SO THAT PART'S NOT SO DRAMATIC... LEMME SKIP AHEAD TO... OKAY, YEAH, HERE WE GO...
"BY AUGUST, THERE WERE CRIPPLING RIBBON SHORTAGES..."
IS THIS HARD ON YOU, DAD? WE COULD STOP.

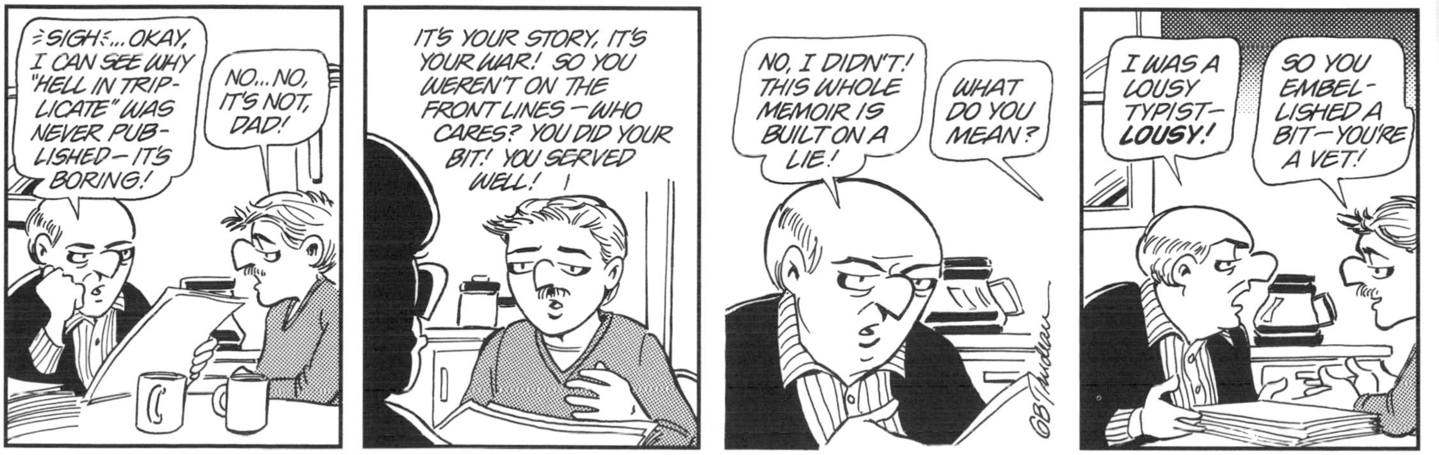
SIGH... OKAY, I CAN SEE WHY "HELL IN TRIPLICATE" WAS NEVER PUBLISHED—IT'S BORING!
NO...NO, IT'S NOT, DAD!
IT'S YOUR STORY, IT'S YOUR WAR! SO YOU WEREN'T ON THE FRONT LINES—WHO CARES? YOU DID YOUR BIT! YOU SERVED WELL!
NO, I DIDN'T! THIS WHOLE MEMOIR IS BUILT ON A LIE!
WHAT DO YOU MEAN?
I WAS A LOUSY TYPIST—LOUSY!
SO YOU EMBELLISHED A BIT—YOU'RE A VET!

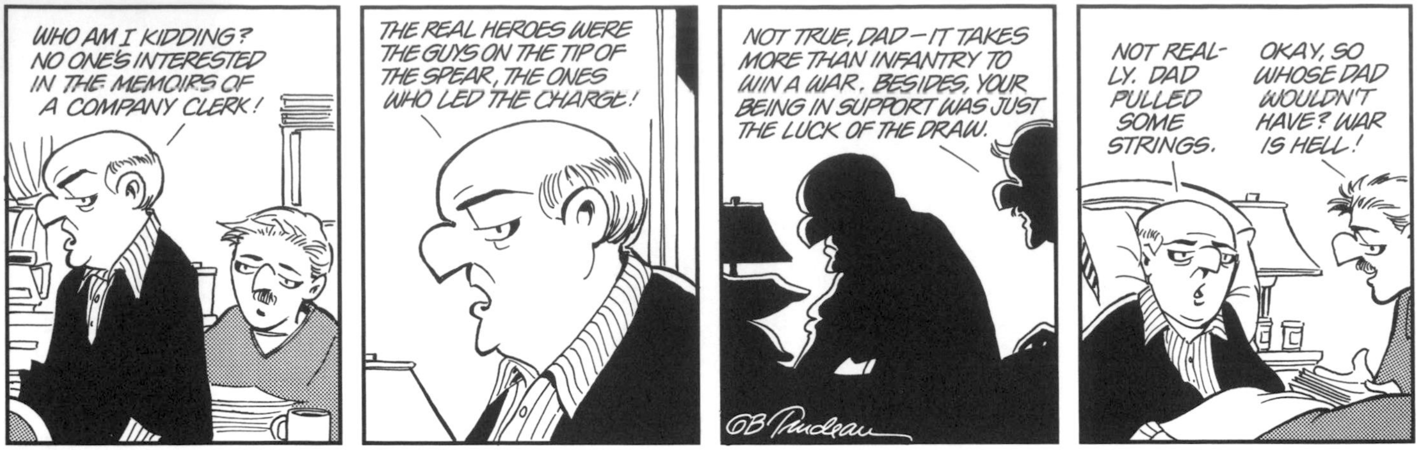
WHO AM I KIDDING? NO ONE'S INTERESTED IN THE MEMOIRS OF A COMPANY CLERK!
THE REAL HEROES WERE THE GUYS ON THE TIP OF THE SPEAR, THE ONES WHO LED THE CHARGE!
NOT TRUE, DAD – IT TAKES MORE THAN INFANTRY TO WIN A WAR. BESIDES, YOUR BEING IN SUPPORT WAS JUST THE LUCK OF THE DRAW.
NOT REALLY. DAD PULLED SOME STRINGS.
OKAY, SO WHOSE DAD WOULDN'T HAVE? WAR IS HELL!
GB Trudeau

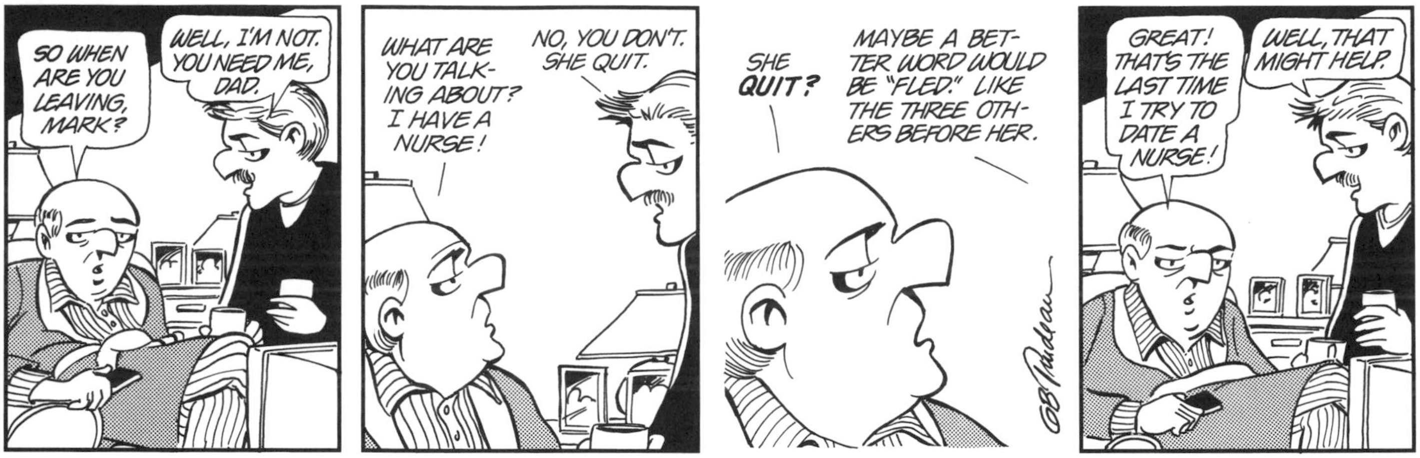
SO WHEN ARE YOU LEAVING, MARK?
WELL, I'M NOT. YOU NEED ME, DAD.
WHAT ARE YOU TALKING ABOUT? I HAVE A NURSE!
NO, YOU DON'T. SHE QUIT.
SHE **QUIT?**
MAYBE A BETTER WORD WOULD BE "FLED." LIKE THE THREE OTHERS BEFORE HER.
GB Trudeau
GREAT! THAT'S THE LAST TIME I TRY TO DATE A NURSE!
WELL, THAT MIGHT HELP.

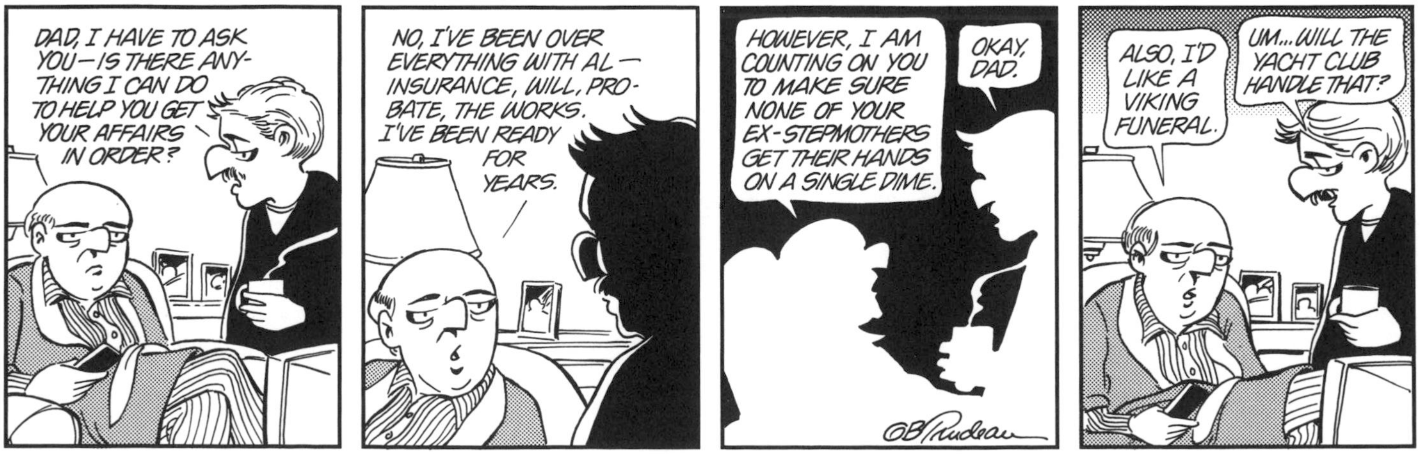
DAD, I HAVE TO ASK YOU – IS THERE ANYTHING I CAN DO TO HELP YOU GET YOUR AFFAIRS IN ORDER?
NO, I'VE BEEN OVER EVERYTHING WITH AL – INSURANCE, WILL, PROBATE, THE WORKS. I'VE BEEN READY FOR YEARS.
HOWEVER, I AM COUNTING ON YOU TO MAKE SURE NONE OF YOUR EX-STEPMOTHERS GET THEIR HANDS ON A SINGLE DIME.
OKAY, DAD.
GB Trudeau
ALSO, I'D LIKE A VIKING FUNERAL.
UM... WILL THE YACHT CLUB HANDLE THAT?

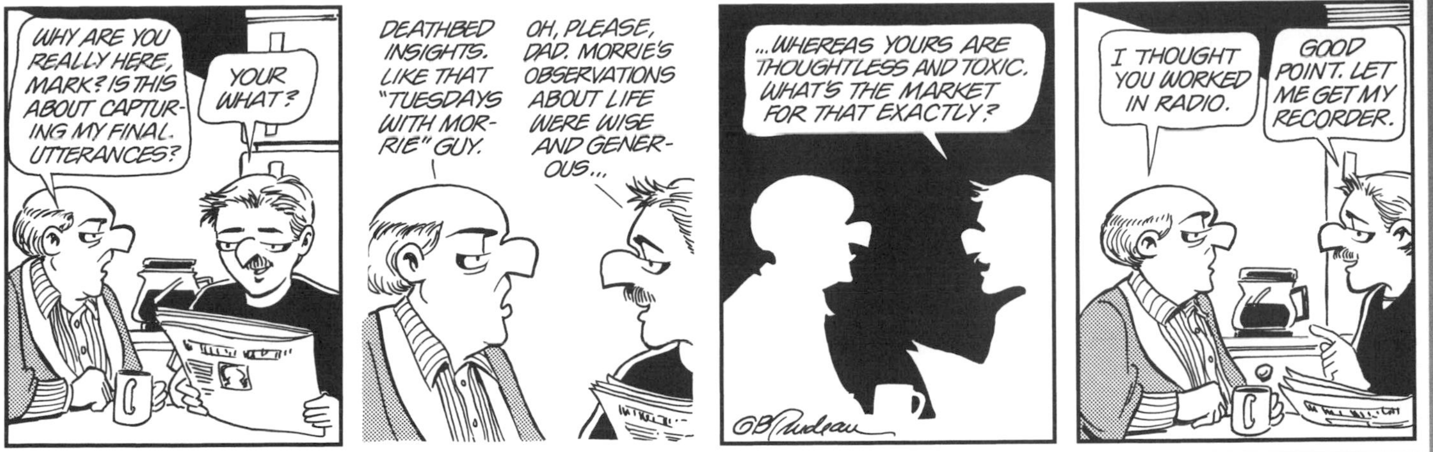
WHY ARE YOU REALLY HERE, MARK? IS THIS ABOUT CAPTURING MY FINAL UTTERANCES?
YOUR WHAT?
DEATHBED INSIGHTS. LIKE THAT "TUESDAYS WITH MORRIE" GUY.
OH, PLEASE, DAD. MORRIE'S OBSERVATIONS ABOUT LIFE WERE WISE AND GENEROUS...
...WHEREAS YOURS ARE THOUGHTLESS AND TOXIC. WHAT'S THE MARKET FOR THAT EXACTLY?
I THOUGHT YOU WORKED IN RADIO.
GOOD POINT. LET ME GET MY RECORDER.

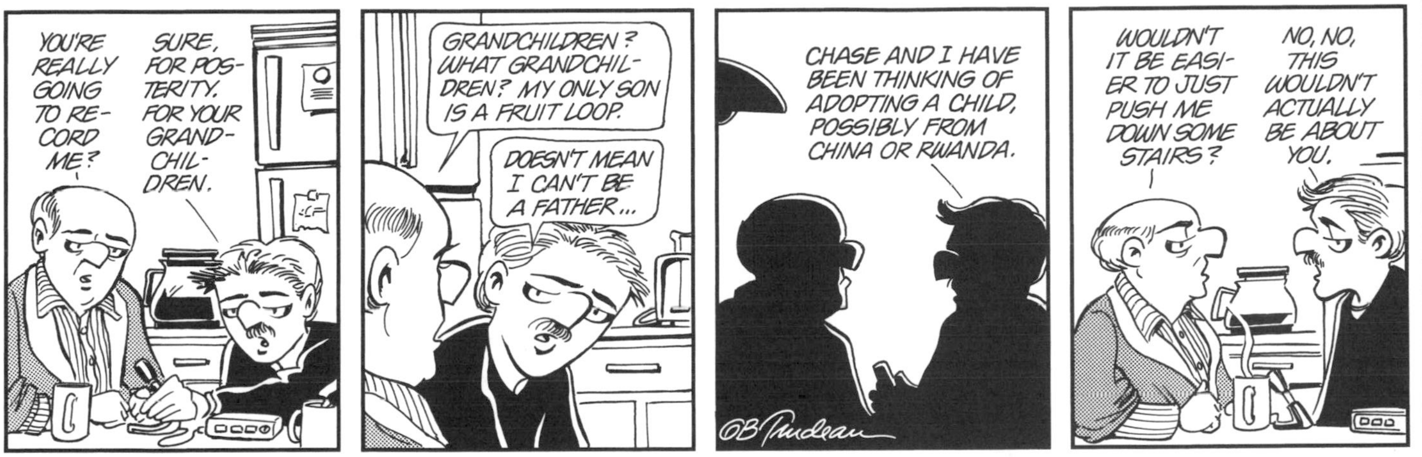
YOU'RE REALLY GOING TO RECORD ME?
SURE, FOR POSTERITY. FOR YOUR GRANDCHILDREN.
GRANDCHILDREN? WHAT GRANDCHILDREN? MY ONLY SON IS A FRUIT LOOP.
DOESN'T MEAN I CAN'T BE A FATHER...
CHASE AND I HAVE BEEN THINKING OF ADOPTING A CHILD, POSSIBLY FROM CHINA OR RWANDA.
WOULDN'T IT BE EASIER TO JUST PUSH ME DOWN SOME STAIRS?
NO, NO, THIS WOULDN'T ACTUALLY BE ABOUT YOU.

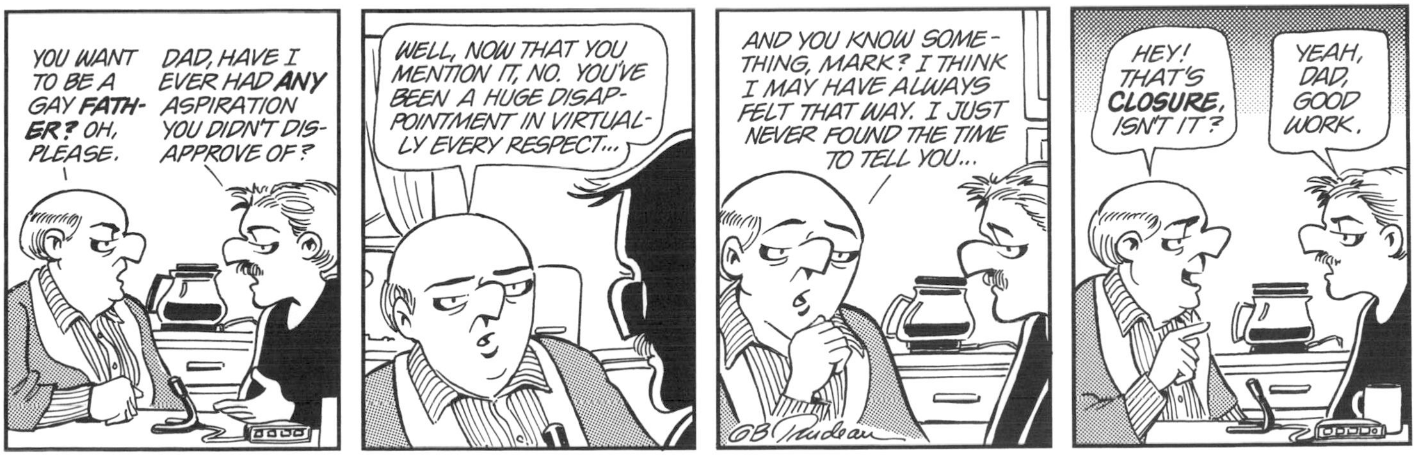
YOU WANT TO BE A GAY FATHER? OH, PLEASE.
DAD, HAVE I EVER HAD ANY ASPIRATION YOU DIDN'T DISAPPROVE OF?
WELL, NOW THAT YOU MENTION IT, NO. YOU'VE BEEN A HUGE DISAPPOINTMENT IN VIRTUALLY EVERY RESPECT...
AND YOU KNOW SOMETHING, MARK? I THINK I MAY HAVE ALWAYS FELT THAT WAY. I JUST NEVER FOUND THE TIME TO TELL YOU...
HEY! THAT'S CLOSURE, ISN'T IT?
YEAH, DAD, GOOD WORK.

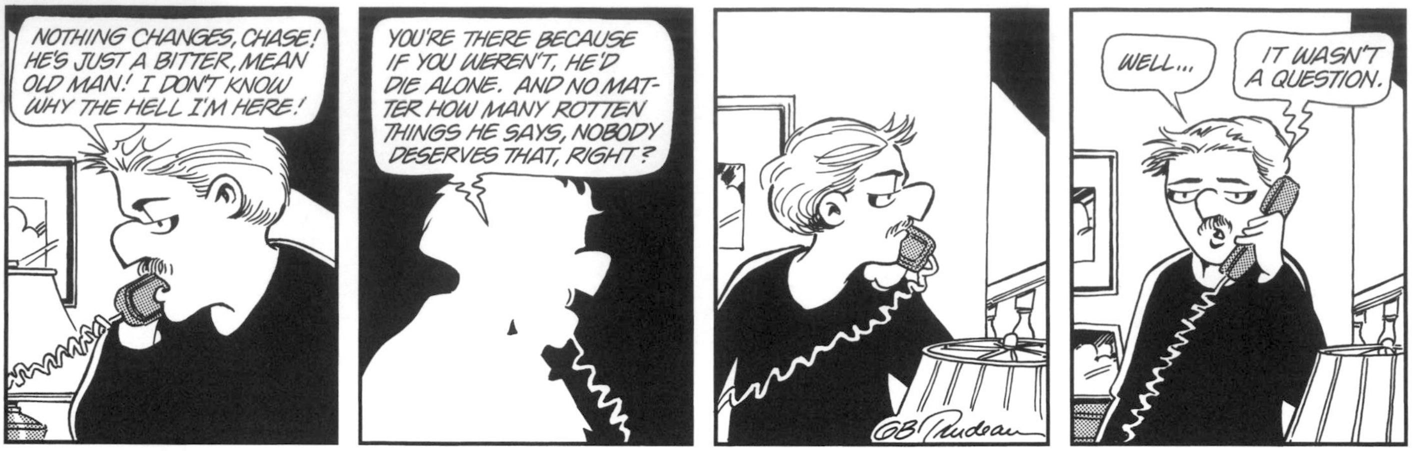
NOTHING CHANGES, CHASE! HE'S JUST A BITTER, MEAN OLD MAN! I DON'T KNOW WHY THE HELL I'M HERE!
YOU'RE THERE BECAUSE IF YOU WEREN'T, HE'D DIE ALONE. AND NO MATTER HOW MANY ROTTEN THINGS HE SAYS, NOBODY DESERVES THAT, RIGHT?
WELL...
IT WASN'T A QUESTION.

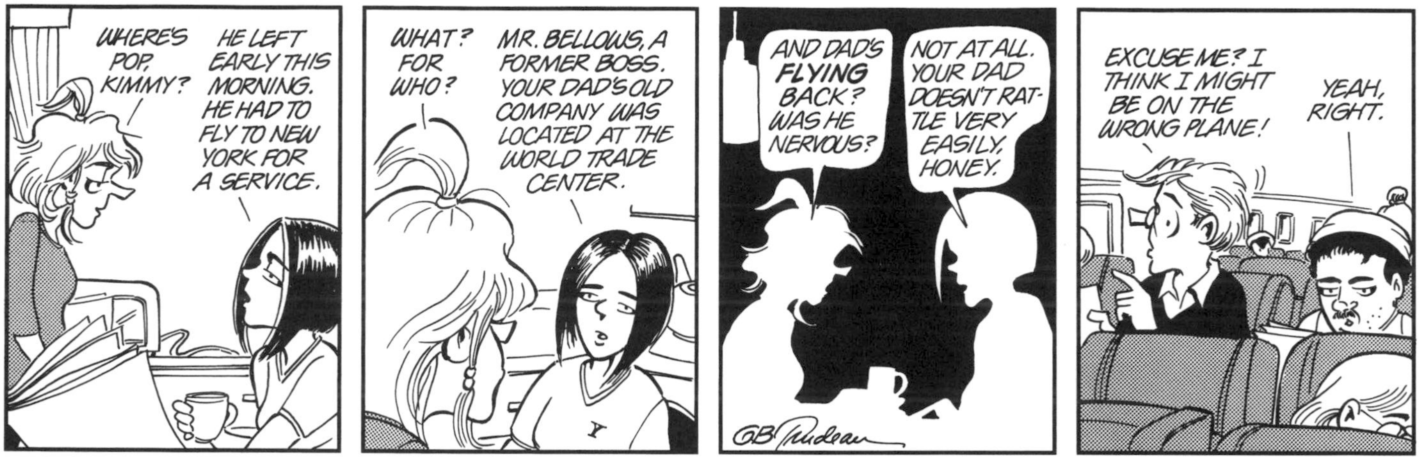
WHERE'S POP, KIMMY?
HE LEFT EARLY THIS MORNING. HE HAD TO FLY TO NEW YORK FOR A SERVICE.
WHAT? FOR WHO?
MR. BELLOWS, A FORMER BOSS. YOUR DAD'S OLD COMPANY WAS LOCATED AT THE WORLD TRADE CENTER.
AND DAD'S FLYING BACK? WAS HE NERVOUS?
NOT AT ALL. YOUR DAD DOESN'T RATTLE VERY EASILY, HONEY.
EXCUSE ME? I THINK I MIGHT BE ON THE WRONG PLANE!
YEAH, RIGHT.

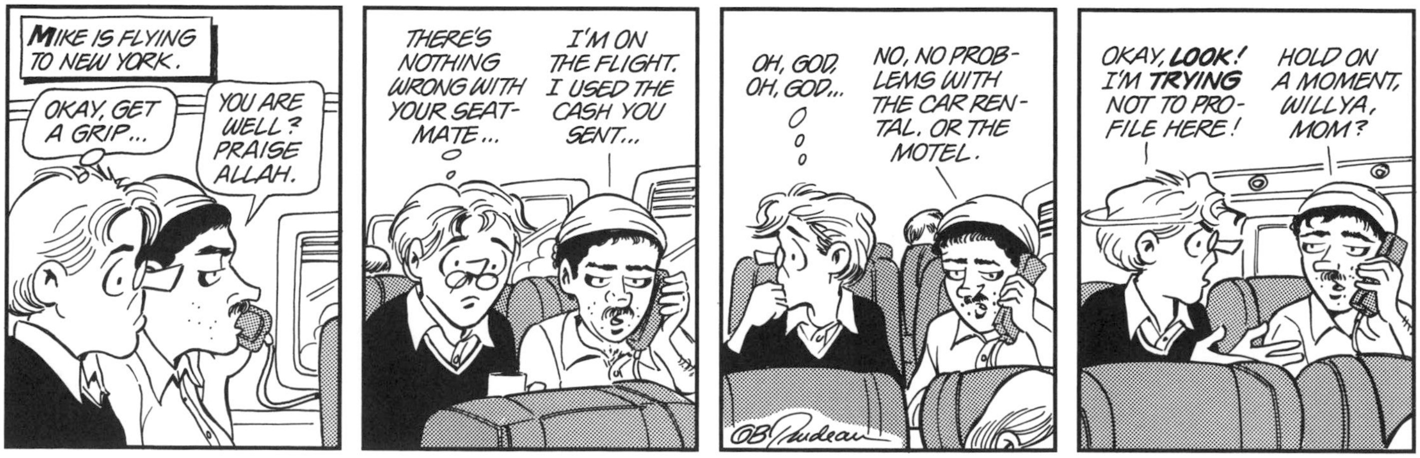
MIKE IS FLYING TO NEW YORK.
OKAY, GET A GRIP...
YOU ARE WELL? PRAISE ALLAH.
THERE'S NOTHING WRONG WITH YOUR SEATMATE...
I'M ON THE FLIGHT. I USED THE CASH YOU SENT...
OH, GOD, OH, GOD...
NO, NO PROBLEMS WITH THE CAR RENTAL. OR THE MOTEL.
OKAY, LOOK! I'M TRYING NOT TO PROFILE HERE!
HOLD ON A MOMENT, WILLYA, MOM?

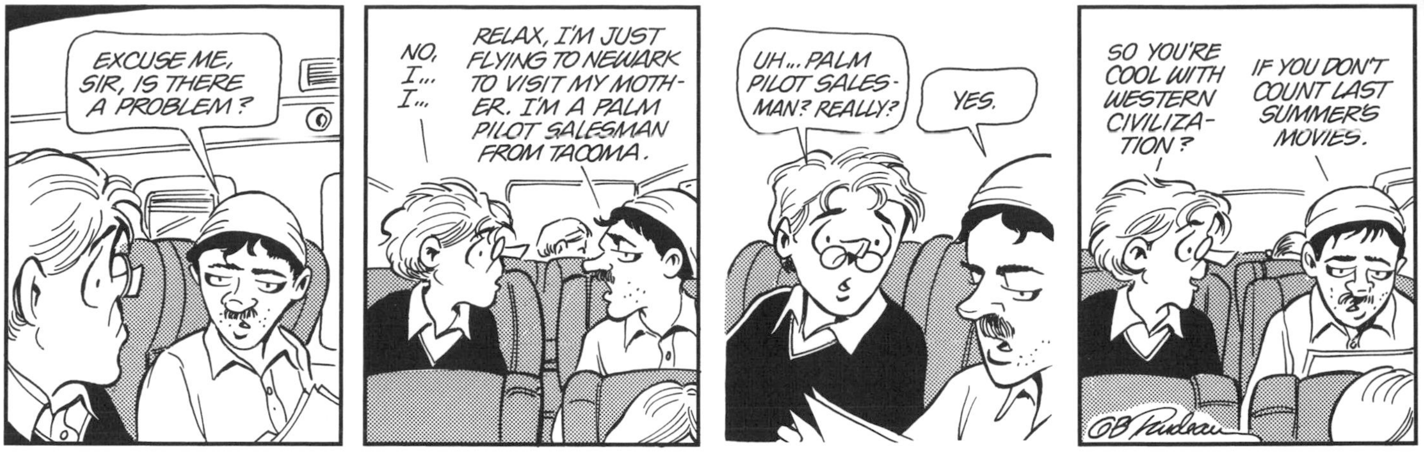
EXCUSE ME, SIR, IS THERE A PROBLEM?
NO, I... I...
RELAX, I'M JUST FLYING TO NEWARK TO VISIT MY MOTHER. I'M A PALM PILOT SALESMAN FROM TACOMA.
UH... PALM PILOT SALESMAN? REALLY?
YES.
SO YOU'RE COOL WITH WESTERN CIVILIZATION?
IF YOU DON'T COUNT LAST SUMMER'S MOVIES.
©B Trudeau

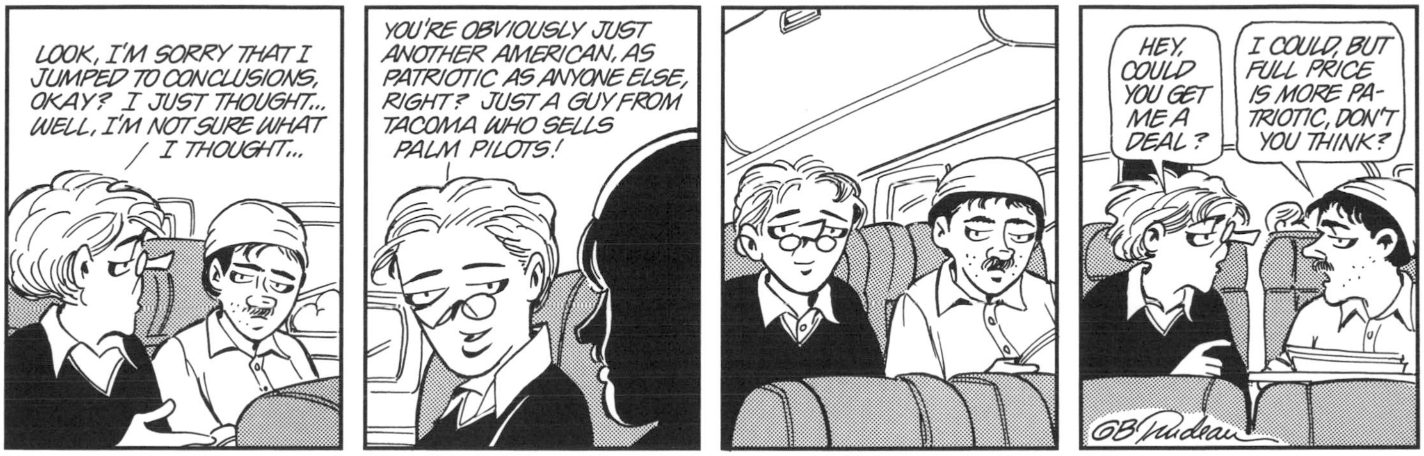
LOOK, I'M SORRY THAT I JUMPED TO CONCLUSIONS, OKAY? I JUST THOUGHT... WELL, I'M NOT SURE WHAT I THOUGHT...
YOU'RE OBVIOUSLY JUST ANOTHER AMERICAN, AS PATRIOTIC AS ANYONE ELSE, RIGHT? JUST A GUY FROM TACOMA WHO SELLS PALM PILOTS!
HEY, COULD YOU GET ME A DEAL?
I COULD, BUT FULL PRICE IS MORE PATRIOTIC, DON'T YOU THINK?
©B Trudeau

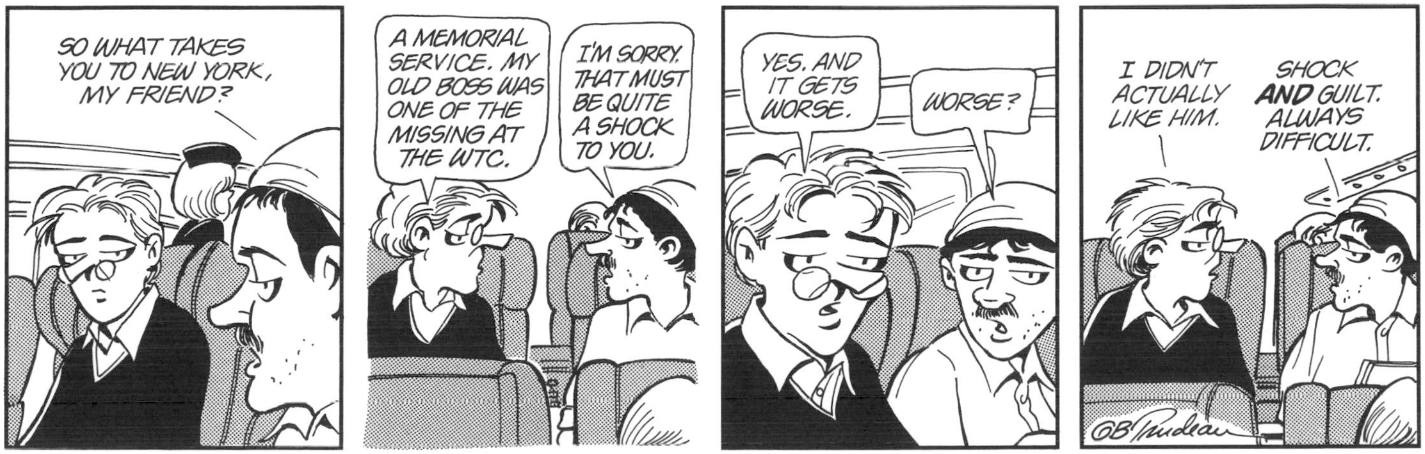
SO WHAT TAKES YOU TO NEW YORK, MY FRIEND?
A MEMORIAL SERVICE. MY OLD BOSS WAS ONE OF THE MISSING AT THE WTC.
I'M SORRY. THAT MUST BE QUITE A SHOCK TO YOU.
YES. AND IT GETS WORSE.
WORSE?
I DIDN'T ACTUALLY LIKE HIM.
SHOCK AND GUILT. ALWAYS DIFFICULT.
©B Trudeau

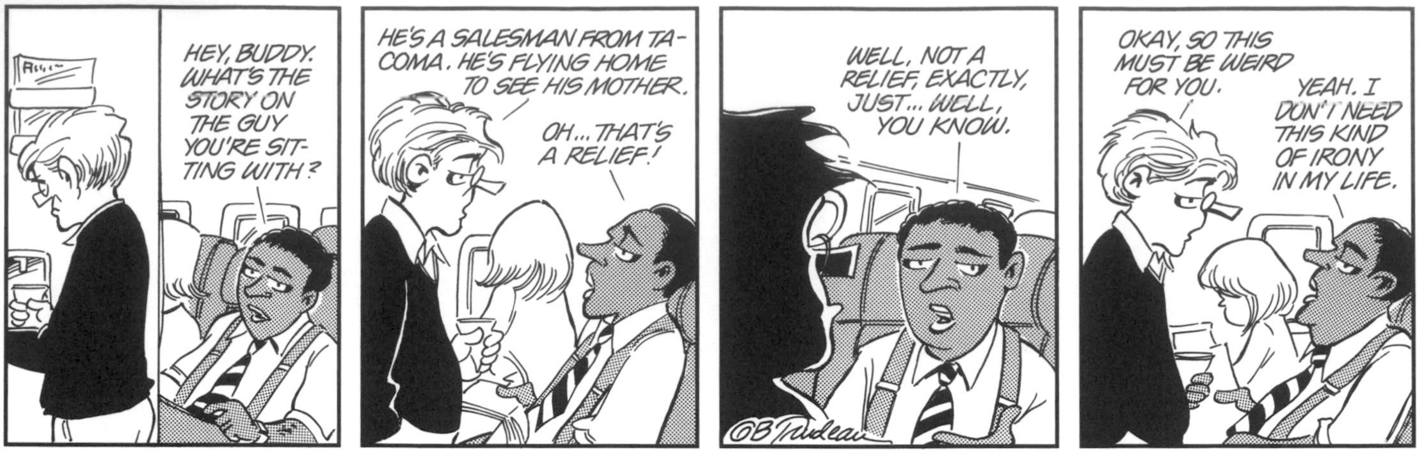
HEY, BUDDY. WHAT'S THE STORY ON THE GUY YOU'RE SITTING WITH?
HE'S A SALESMAN FROM TACOMA. HE'S FLYING HOME TO SEE HIS MOTHER.
OH... THAT'S A RELIEF!
WELL, NOT A RELIEF, EXACTLY, JUST... WELL, YOU KNOW.
OKAY, SO THIS MUST BE WEIRD FOR YOU.
YEAH. I DON'T NEED THIS KIND OF IRONY IN MY LIFE.

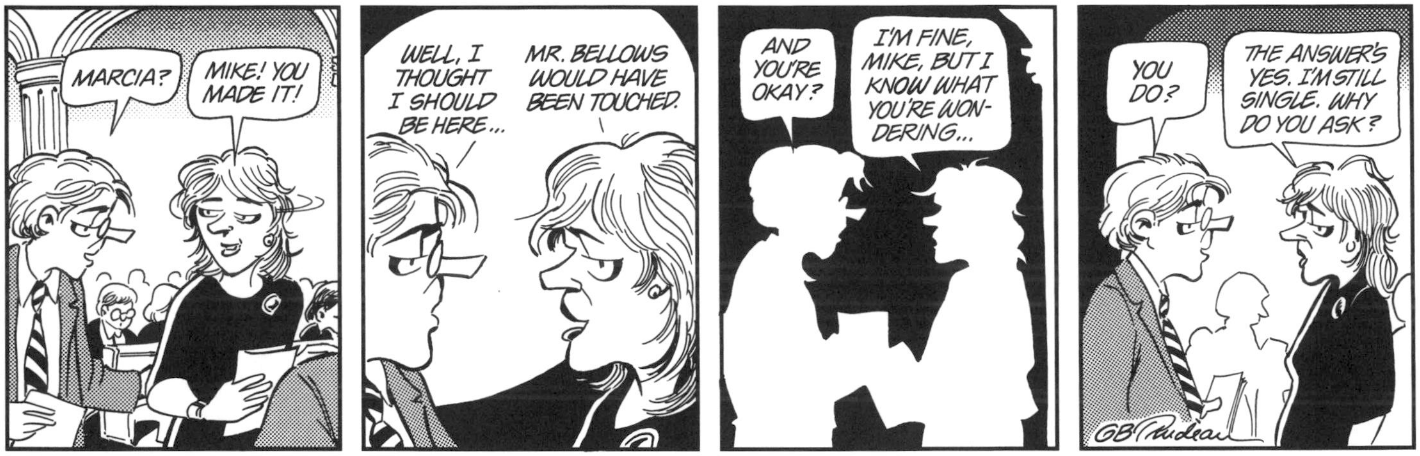
MARCIA?
MIKE! YOU MADE IT!
WELL, I THOUGHT I SHOULD BE HERE...
MR. BELLOWS WOULD HAVE BEEN TOUCHED.
AND YOU'RE OKAY?
I'M FINE, MIKE, BUT I KNOW WHAT YOU'RE WONDERING...
YOU DO?
THE ANSWER'S YES. I'M STILL SINGLE. WHY DO YOU ASK?

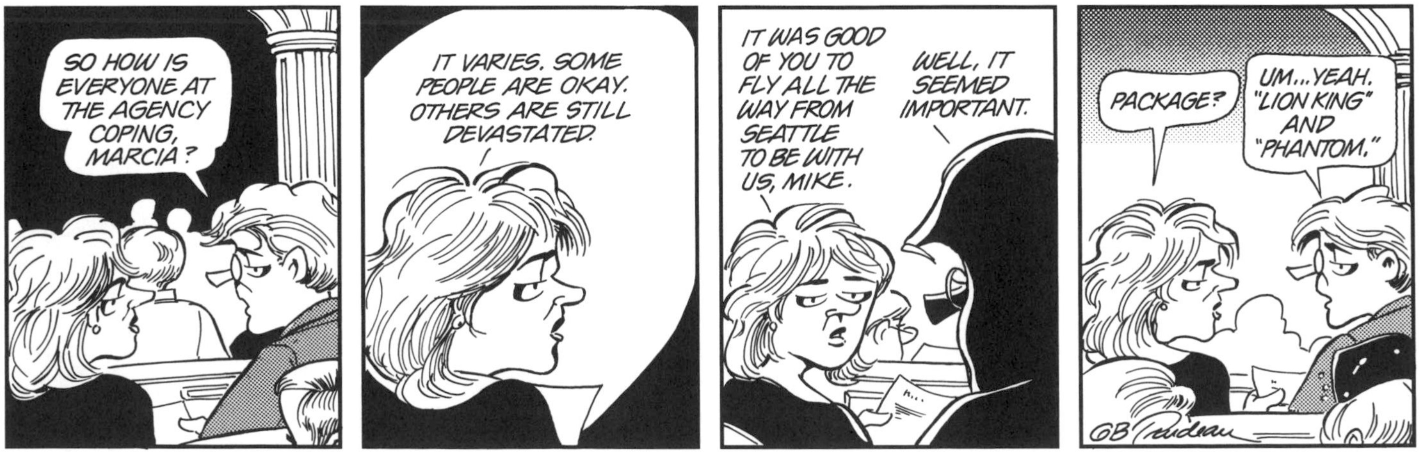
SO HOW IS EVERYONE AT THE AGENCY COPING, MARCIA?
IT VARIES. SOME PEOPLE ARE OKAY. OTHERS ARE STILL DEVASTATED.
IT WAS GOOD OF YOU TO FLY ALL THE WAY FROM SEATTLE TO BE WITH US, MIKE.
WELL, IT SEEMED IMPORTANT.
PACKAGE?
UM... YEAH. "LION KING" AND "PHANTOM."

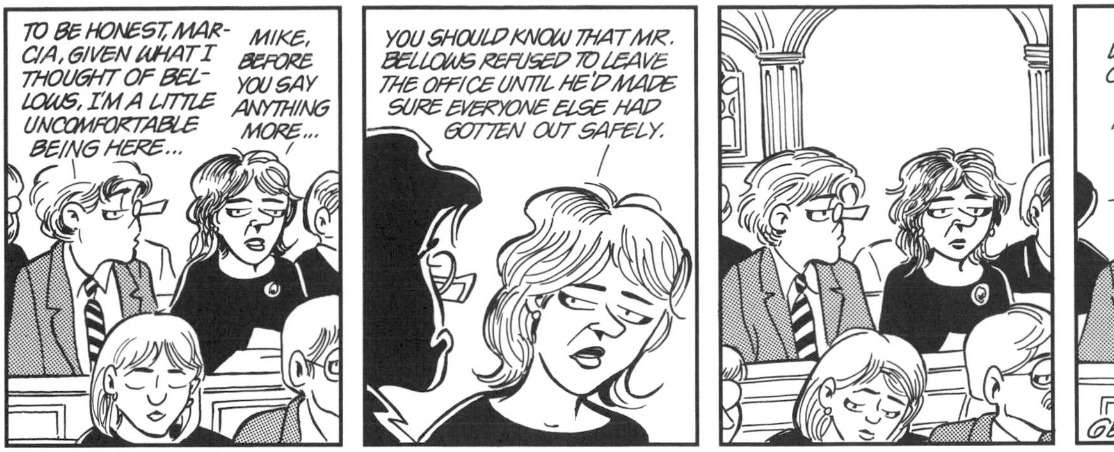
TO BE HONEST, MARCIA, GIVEN WHAT I THOUGHT OF BELLOWS, I'M A LITTLE UNCOMFORTABLE BEING HERE...
MIKE, BEFORE YOU SAY ANYTHING MORE...
YOU SHOULD KNOW THAT MR. BELLOWS REFUSED TO LEAVE THE OFFICE UNTIL HE'D MADE SURE EVERYONE ELSE HAD GOTTEN OUT SAFELY.
DID I SAY UNCOMFORTABLE? I MEANT MORTIFIED.
ME, TOO. WHO KNEW?

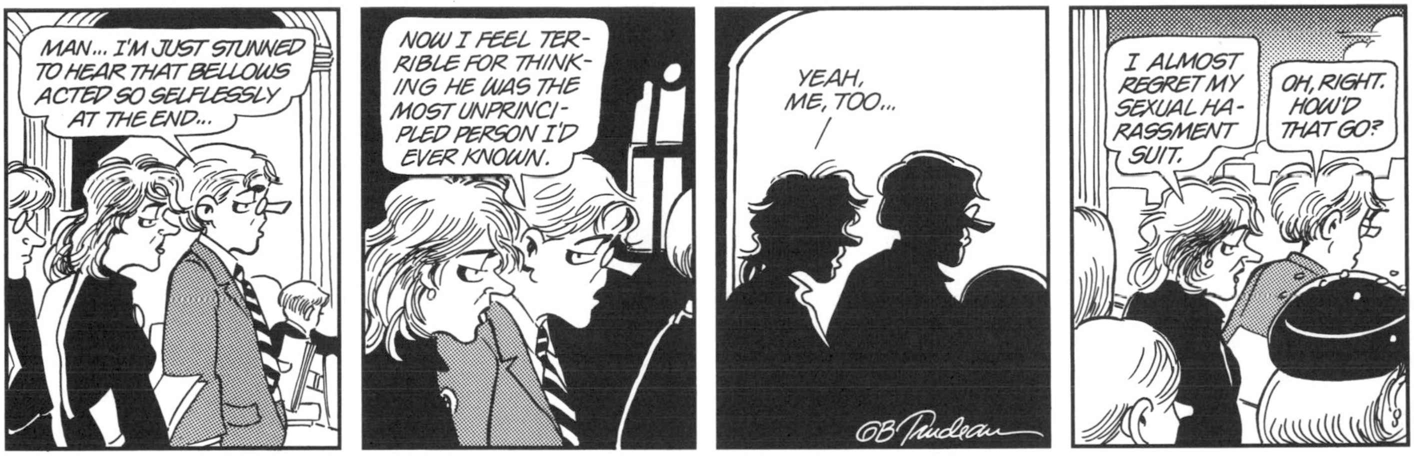
MAN... I'M JUST STUNNED TO HEAR THAT BELLOWS ACTED SO SELFLESSLY AT THE END...
NOW I FEEL TERRIBLE FOR THINKING HE WAS THE MOST UNPRINCIPLED PERSON I'D EVER KNOWN.
YEAH, ME, TOO...
I ALMOST REGRET MY SEXUAL HARASSMENT SUIT.
OH, RIGHT. HOW'D THAT GO?

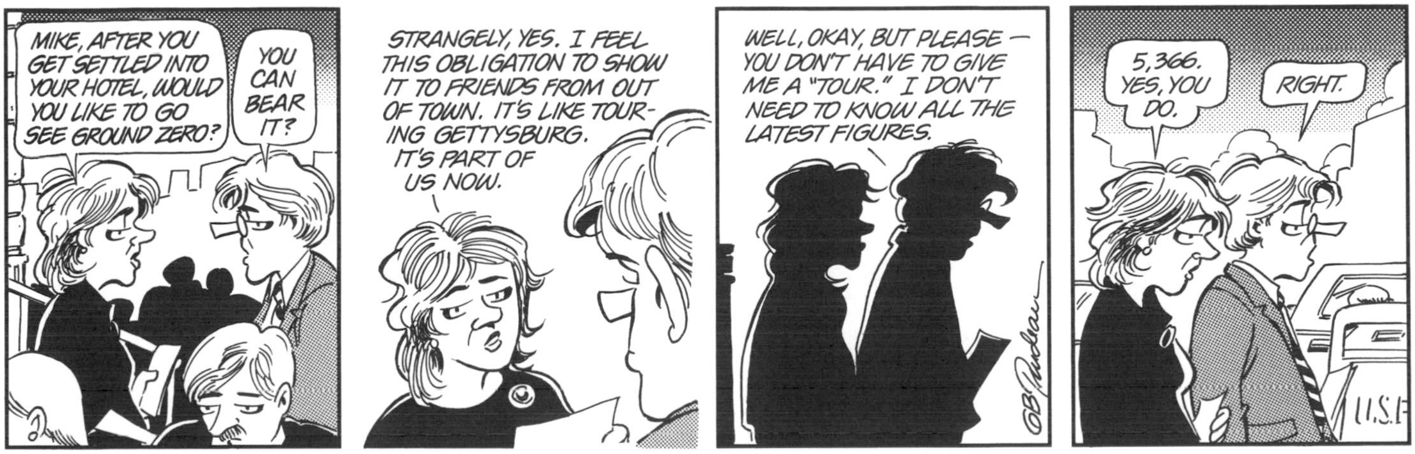
MIKE, AFTER YOU GET SETTLED INTO YOUR HOTEL, WOULD YOU LIKE TO GO SEE GROUND ZERO?
YOU CAN BEAR IT?
STRANGELY, YES. I FEEL THIS OBLIGATION TO SHOW IT TO FRIENDS FROM OUT OF TOWN. IT'S LIKE TOURING GETTYSBURG. IT'S PART OF US NOW.
WELL, OKAY, BUT PLEASE — YOU DON'T HAVE TO GIVE ME A "TOUR." I DON'T NEED TO KNOW ALL THE LATEST FIGURES.
5,366. YES, YOU DO.
RIGHT.

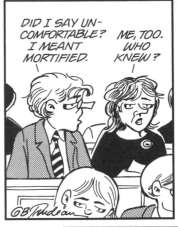

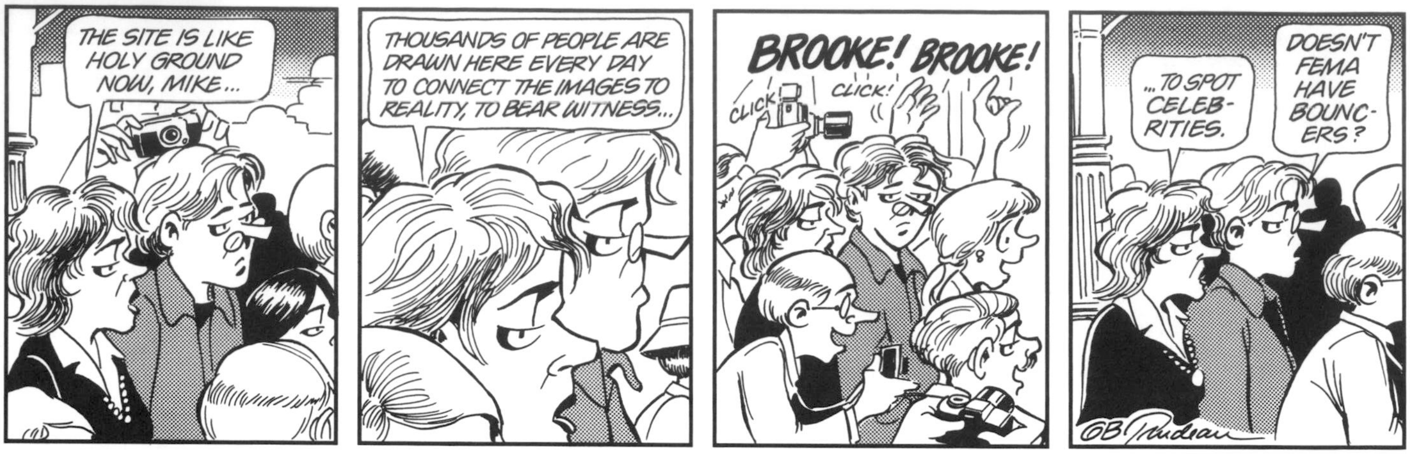
THE SITE IS LIKE HOLY GROUND NOW, MIKE...
THOUSANDS OF PEOPLE ARE DRAWN HERE EVERY DAY TO CONNECT THE IMAGES TO REALITY, TO BEAR WITNESS...
BROOKE! BROOKE!
CLICK
CLICK!
...TO SPOT CELEBRITIES.
DOESN'T FEMA HAVE BOUNCERS?
©B Trudeau

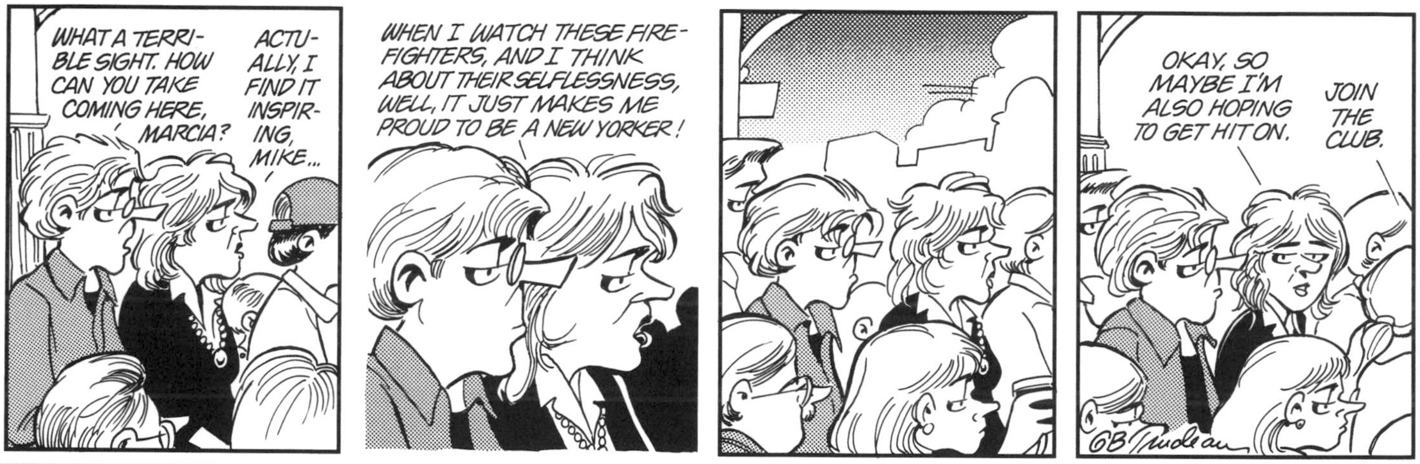
WHAT A TERRIBLE SIGHT. HOW CAN YOU TAKE COMING HERE, MARCIA?
ACTUALLY, I FIND IT INSPIRING, MIKE...
WHEN I WATCH THESE FIREFIGHTERS, AND I THINK ABOUT THEIR SELFLESSNESS, WELL, IT JUST MAKES ME PROUD TO BE A NEW YORKER!
OKAY, SO MAYBE I'M ALSO HOPING TO GET HIT ON.
JOIN THE CLUB.
©B Trudeau

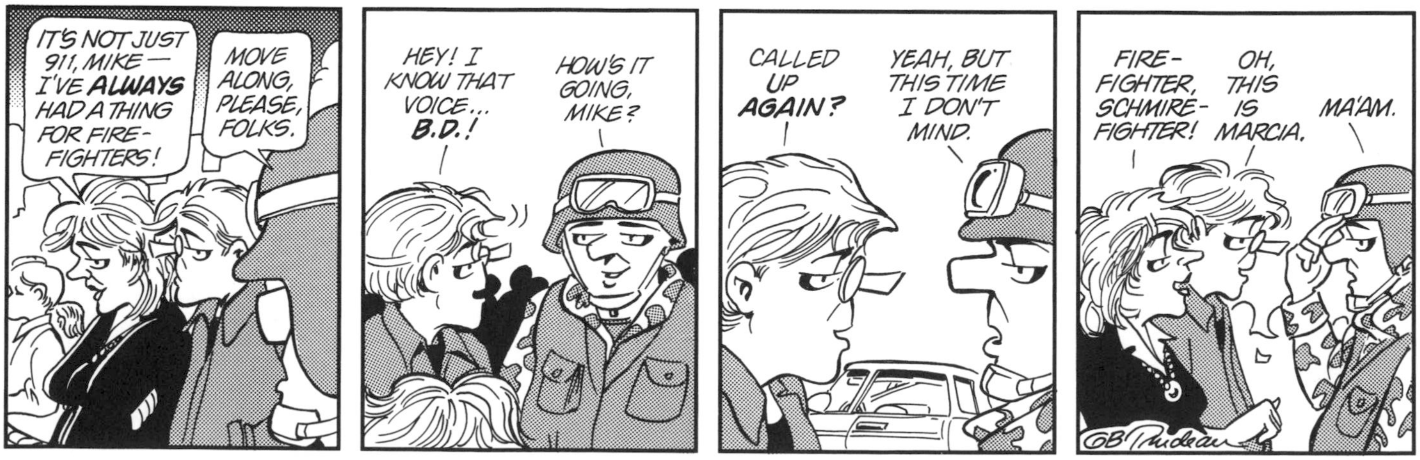
IT'S NOT JUST 911, MIKE — I'VE ALWAYS HAD A THING FOR FIREFIGHTERS!
MOVE ALONG, PLEASE, FOLKS.
HEY! I KNOW THAT VOICE... B.D.!
HOW'S IT GOING, MIKE?
CALLED UP AGAIN?
YEAH, BUT THIS TIME I DON'T MIND.
FIREFIGHTER, SCHMIREFIGHTER!
OH, THIS IS MARCIA.
MA'AM.
©B Trudeau

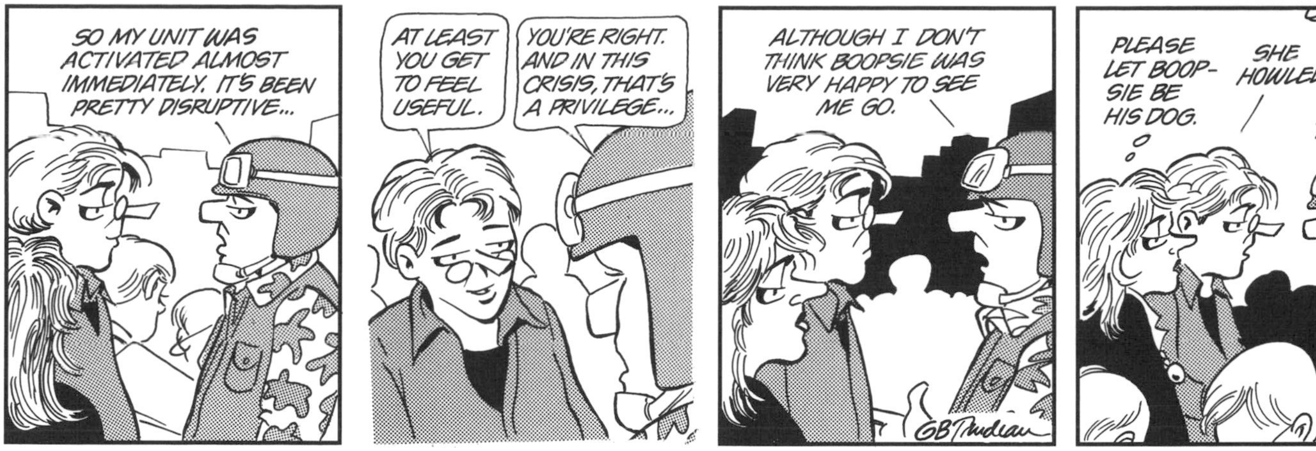
SO MY UNIT WAS ACTIVATED ALMOST IMMEDIATELY. IT'S BEEN PRETTY DISRUPTIVE...
AT LEAST YOU GET TO FEEL USEFUL.
YOU'RE RIGHT. AND IN THIS CRISIS, THAT'S A PRIVILEGE...
ALTHOUGH I DON'T THINK BOOPSIE WAS VERY HAPPY TO SEE ME GO.
PLEASE LET BOOPSIE BE HIS DOG.
SHE HOWLED?
BIG-TIME.

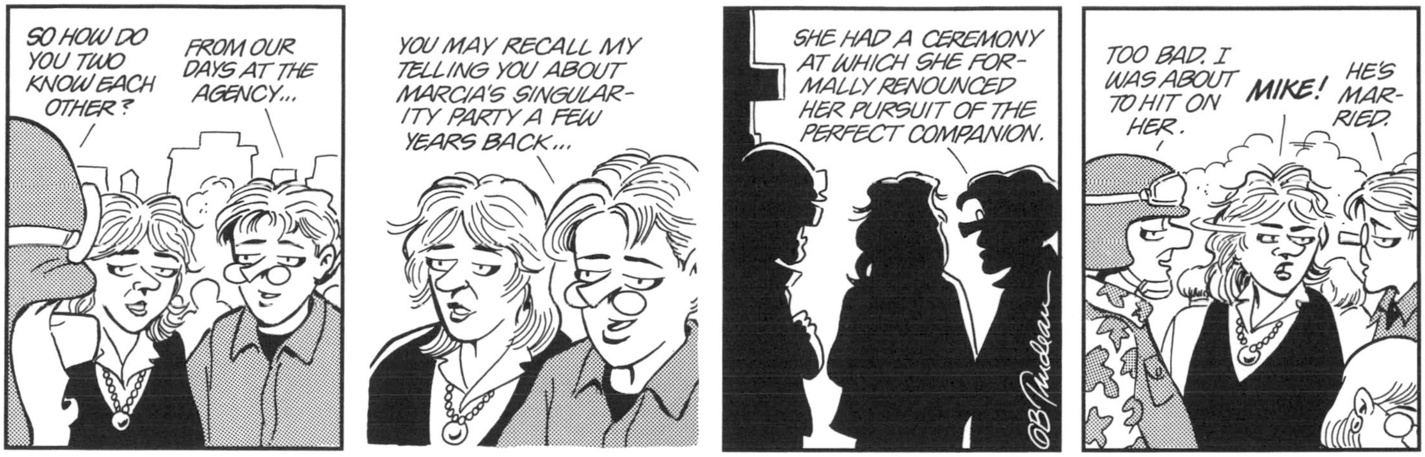
SO HOW DO YOU TWO KNOW EACH OTHER?
FROM OUR DAYS AT THE AGENCY...
YOU MAY RECALL MY TELLING YOU ABOUT MARCIA'S SINGULARITY PARTY A FEW YEARS BACK...
SHE HAD A CEREMONY AT WHICH SHE FORMALLY RENOUNCED HER PURSUIT OF THE PERFECT COMPANION.
TOO BAD. I WAS ABOUT TO HIT ON HER.
MIKE!
HE'S MARRIED.

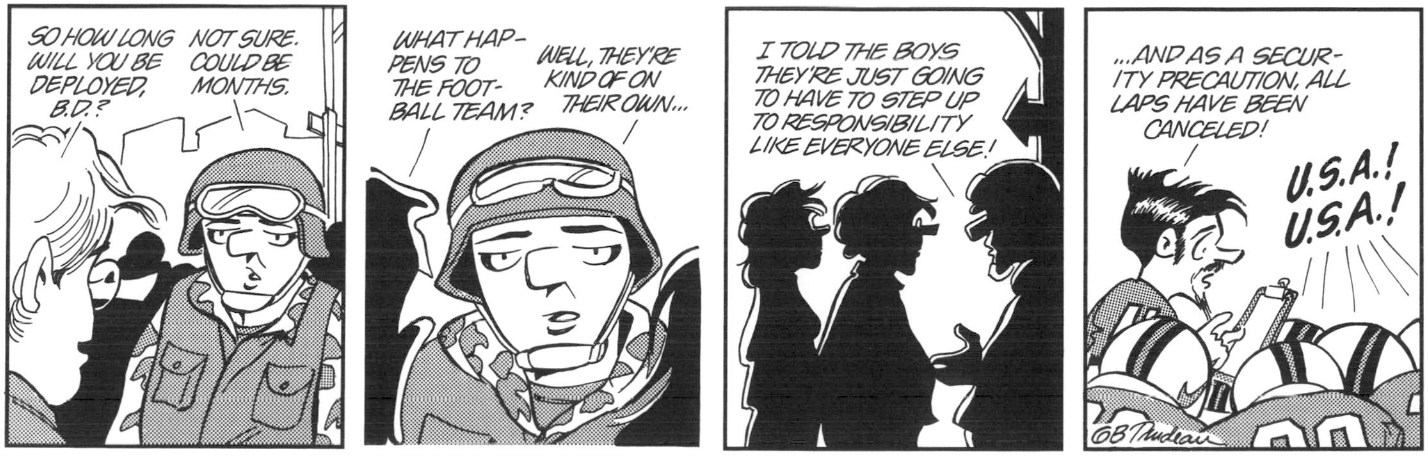
SO HOW LONG WILL YOU BE DEPLOYED, B.D.?
NOT SURE. COULD BE MONTHS.
WHAT HAPPENS TO THE FOOTBALL TEAM?
WELL, THEY'RE KIND OF ON THEIR OWN...
I TOLD THE BOYS THEY'RE JUST GOING TO HAVE TO STEP UP TO RESPONSIBILITY LIKE EVERYONE ELSE!
...AND AS A SECURITY PRECAUTION, ALL LAPS HAVE BEEN CANCELED!
U.S.A.! U.S.A.!

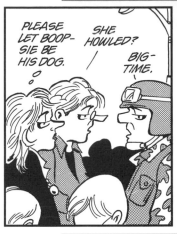

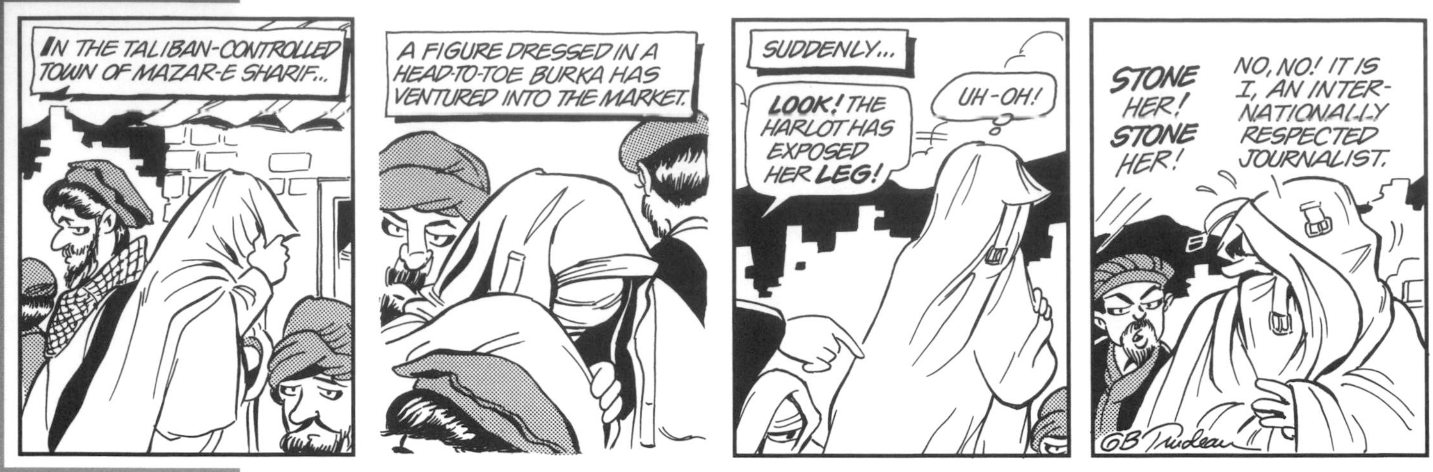
IN THE TALIBAN-CONTROLLED TOWN OF MAZAR-E SHARIF...
A FIGURE DRESSED IN A HEAD-TO-TOE BURKA HAS VENTURED INTO THE MARKET.
SUDDENLY...
LOOK! THE HARLOT HAS EXPOSED HER LEG!
UH-OH!
STONE HER! STONE HER!
NO, NO! IT IS I, AN INTERNATIONALLY RESPECTED JOURNALIST.
©B Trudeau

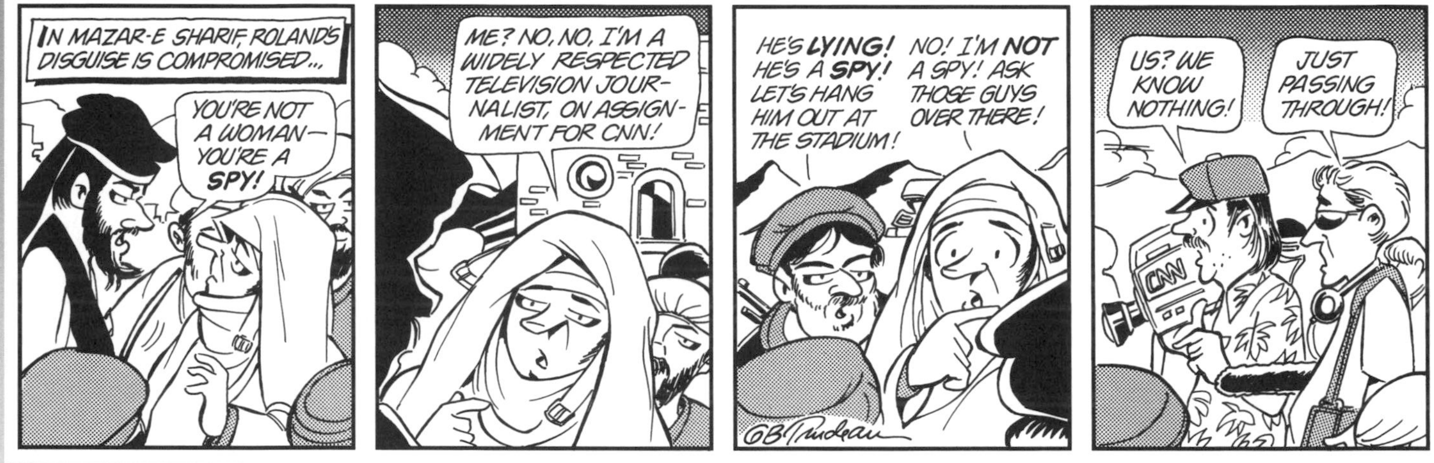
IN MAZAR-E SHARIF, ROLAND'S DISGUISE IS COMPROMISED...
YOU'RE NOT A WOMAN— YOU'RE A SPY!
ME? NO, NO, I'M A WIDELY RESPECTED TELEVISION JOURNALIST, ON ASSIGNMENT FOR CNN!
HE'S LYING! HE'S A SPY! LET'S HANG HIM OUT AT THE STADIUM!
NO! I'M NOT A SPY! ASK THOSE GUYS OVER THERE!
©B Trudeau
US? WE KNOW NOTHING!
JUST PASSING THROUGH!
CNN

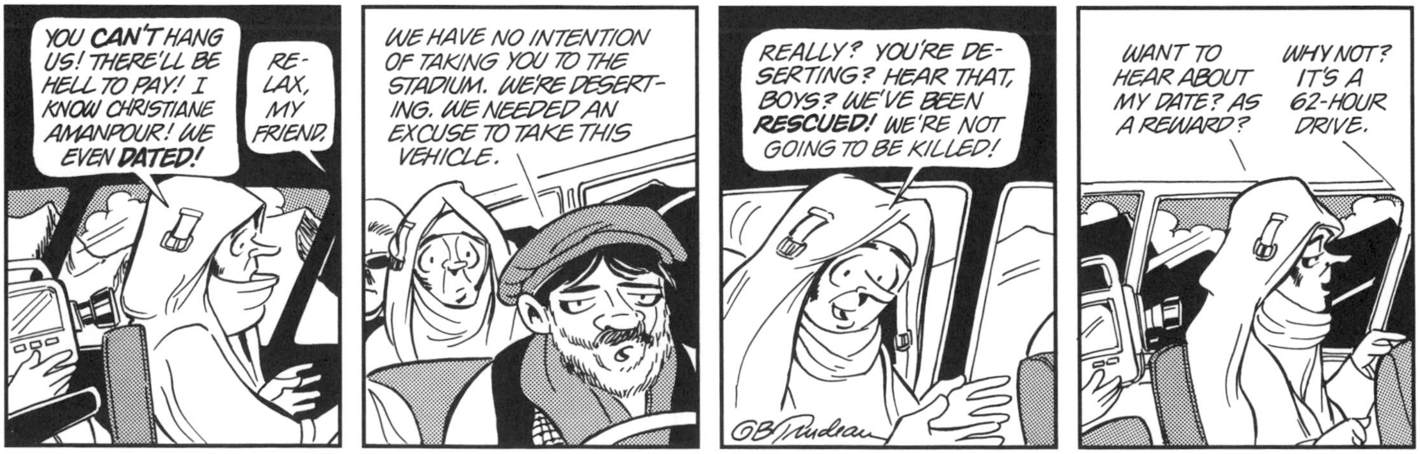
YOU CAN'T HANG US! THERE'LL BE HELL TO PAY! I KNOW CHRISTIANE AMANPOUR! WE EVEN DATED!
RELAX, MY FRIEND.
WE HAVE NO INTENTION OF TAKING YOU TO THE STADIUM. WE'RE DESERTING. WE NEEDED AN EXCUSE TO TAKE THIS VEHICLE.
REALLY? YOU'RE DESERTING? HEAR THAT, BOYS? WE'VE BEEN RESCUED! WE'RE NOT GOING TO BE KILLED!
©B Trudeau
WANT TO HEAR ABOUT MY DATE? AS A REWARD?
WHY NOT? IT'S A 62-HOUR DRIVE.

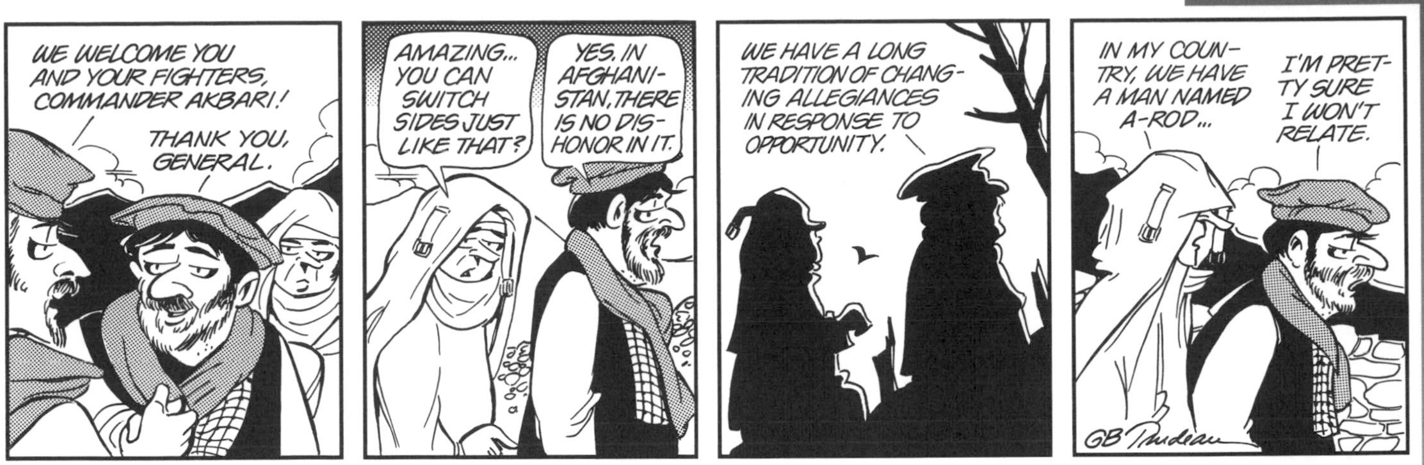
WE WELCOME YOU AND YOUR FIGHTERS, COMMANDER AKBARI!
THANK YOU, GENERAL.
AMAZING... YOU CAN SWITCH SIDES JUST LIKE THAT?
YES, IN AFGHANISTAN, THERE IS NO DISHONOR IN IT.
WE HAVE A LONG TRADITION OF CHANGING ALLEGIANCES IN RESPONSE TO OPPORTUNITY.
IN MY COUNTRY, WE HAVE A MAN NAMED A-ROD...
I'M PRETTY SURE I WON'T RELATE.
GB Trudeau

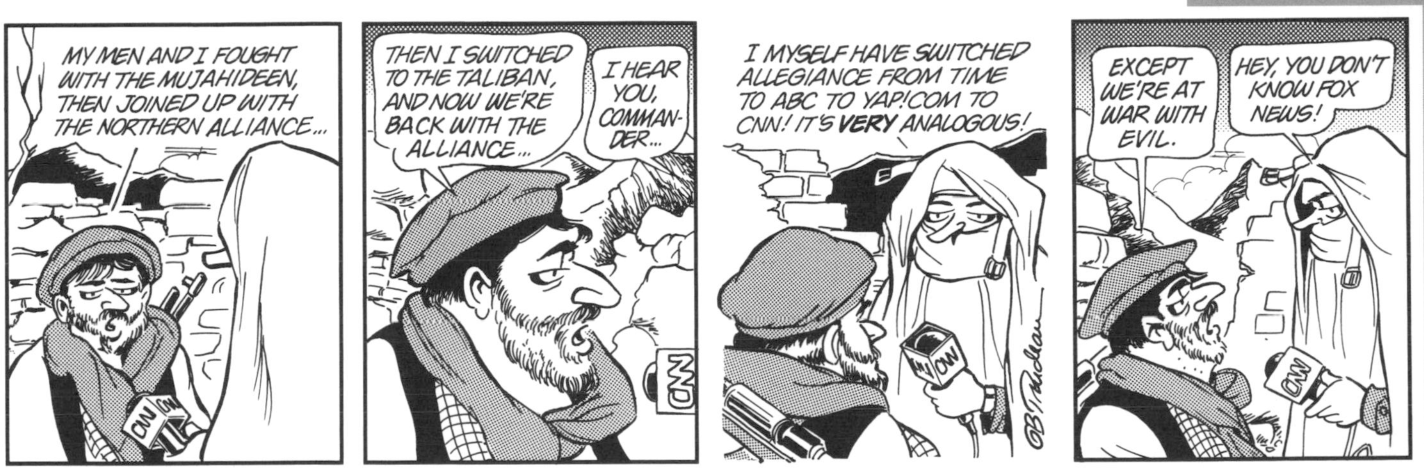
MY MEN AND I FOUGHT WITH THE MUJAHIDEEN, THEN JOINED UP WITH THE NORTHERN ALLIANCE...
CNN
THEN I SWITCHED TO THE TALIBAN, AND NOW WE'RE BACK WITH THE ALLIANCE...
I HEAR YOU, COMMANDER...
CNN
I MYSELF HAVE SWITCHED ALLEGIANCE FROM TIME TO ABC TO YAP!COM TO CNN! IT'S **VERY** ANALOGOUS!
CNN
GB Trudeau
EXCEPT WE'RE AT WAR WITH EVIL.
HEY, YOU DON'T KNOW FOX NEWS!
CNN

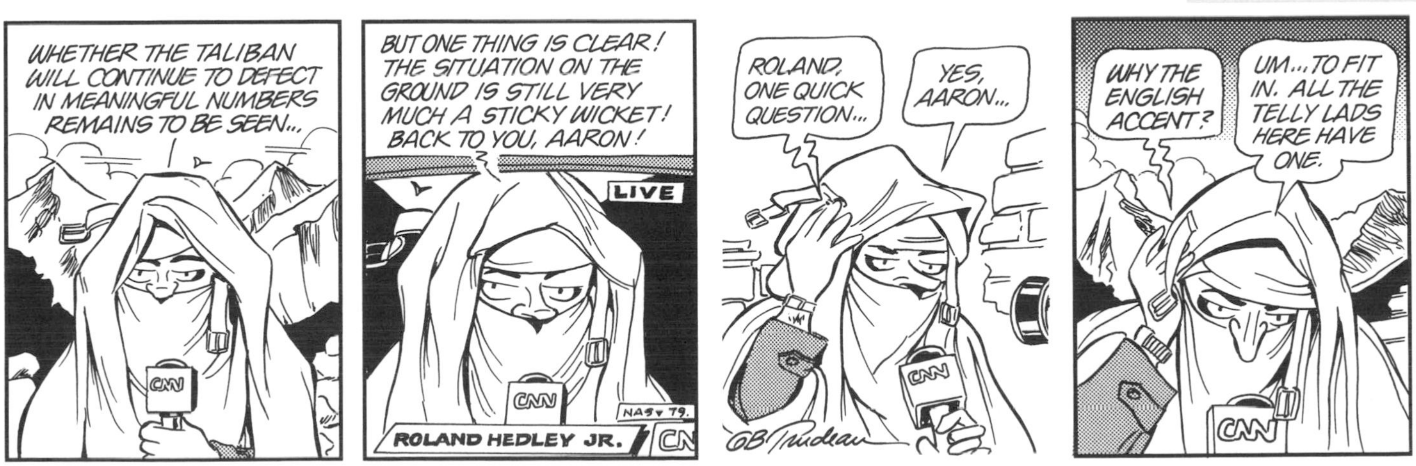
WHETHER THE TALIBAN WILL CONTINUE TO DEFECT IN MEANINGFUL NUMBERS REMAINS TO BE SEEN...
CNN
BUT ONE THING IS CLEAR! THE SITUATION ON THE GROUND IS STILL VERY MUCH A STICKY WICKET! BACK TO YOU, AARON!
LIVE
CNN
ROLAND HEDLEY JR.
ROLAND, ONE QUICK QUESTION...
YES, AARON...
CNN
GB Trudeau
WHY THE ENGLISH ACCENT?
UM... TO FIT IN. ALL THE TELLY LADS HERE HAVE ONE.
CNN

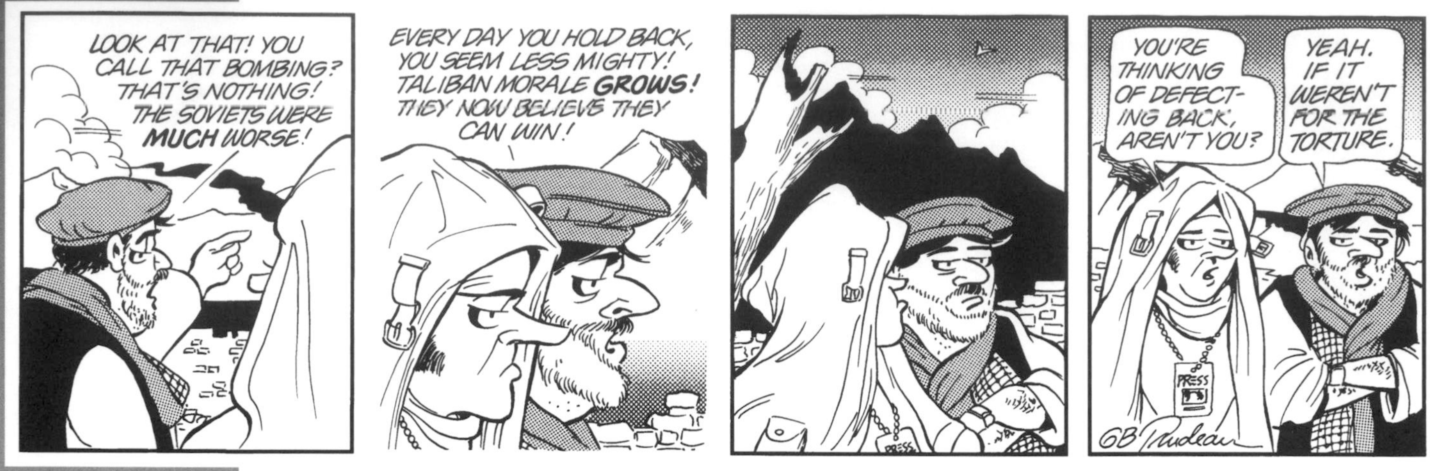
LOOK AT THAT! YOU CALL THAT BOMBING? THAT'S NOTHING! THE SOVIETS WERE MUCH WORSE!
EVERY DAY YOU HOLD BACK, YOU SEEM LESS MIGHTY! TALIBAN MORALE GROWS! THEY NOW BELIEVE THEY CAN WIN!
YOU'RE THINKING OF DEFECTING BACK, AREN'T YOU?
YEAH. IF IT WEREN'T FOR THE TORTURE.

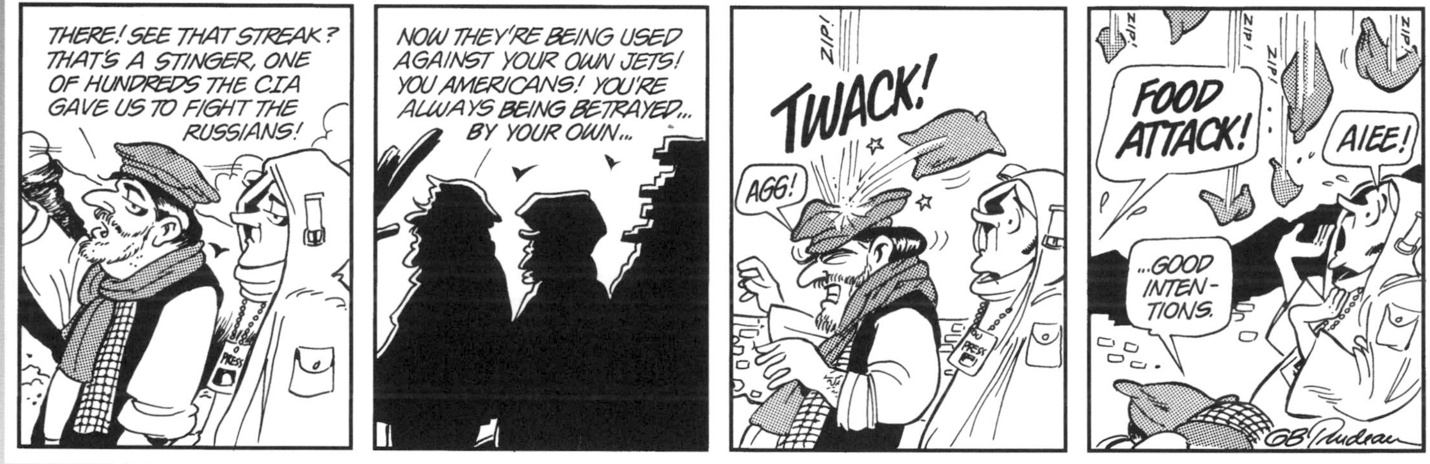
THERE! SEE THAT STREAK? THAT'S A STINGER, ONE OF HUNDREDS THE CIA GAVE US TO FIGHT THE RUSSIANS!
NOW THEY'RE BEING USED AGAINST YOUR OWN JETS! YOU AMERICANS! YOU'RE ALWAYS BEING BETRAYED... BY YOUR OWN...
ZIP!
TWACK!
AGG!
ZIP!
FOOD ATTACK!
AIEE!
...GOOD INTENTIONS.

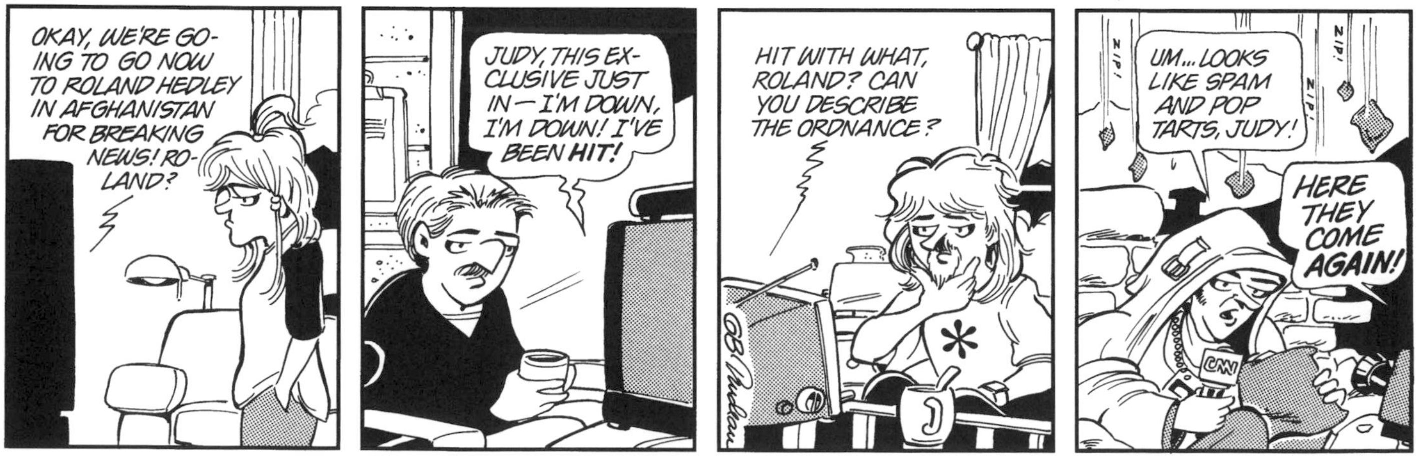
OKAY, WE'RE GOING TO GO NOW TO ROLAND HEDLEY IN AFGHANISTAN FOR BREAKING NEWS! ROLAND?
JUDY, THIS EXCLUSIVE JUST IN—I'M DOWN, I'M DOWN! I'VE BEEN HIT!
HIT WITH WHAT, ROLAND? CAN YOU DESCRIBE THE ORDNANCE?
UM... LOOKS LIKE SPAM AND POP TARTS, JUDY!
HERE THEY COME AGAIN!
ZIP!
CNN

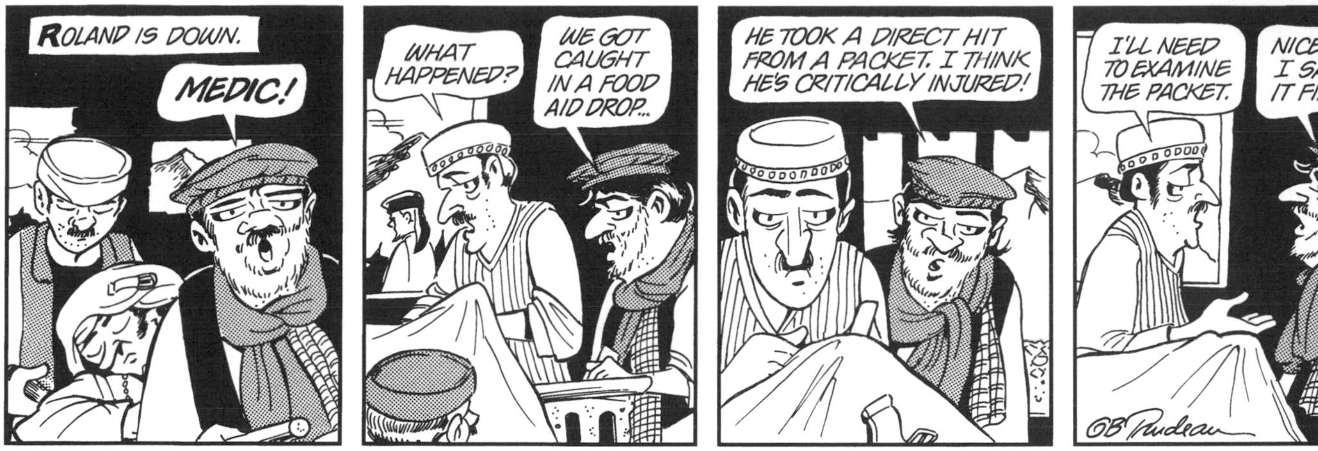
ROLAND IS DOWN.
MEDIC!
WHAT HAPPENED?
WE GOT CAUGHT IN A FOOD AID DROP...
HE TOOK A DIRECT HIT FROM A PACKET. I THINK HE'S CRITICALLY INJURED!
I'LL NEED TO EXAMINE THE PACKET.
NICE TRY. I SAW IT FIRST.
©B Trudeau

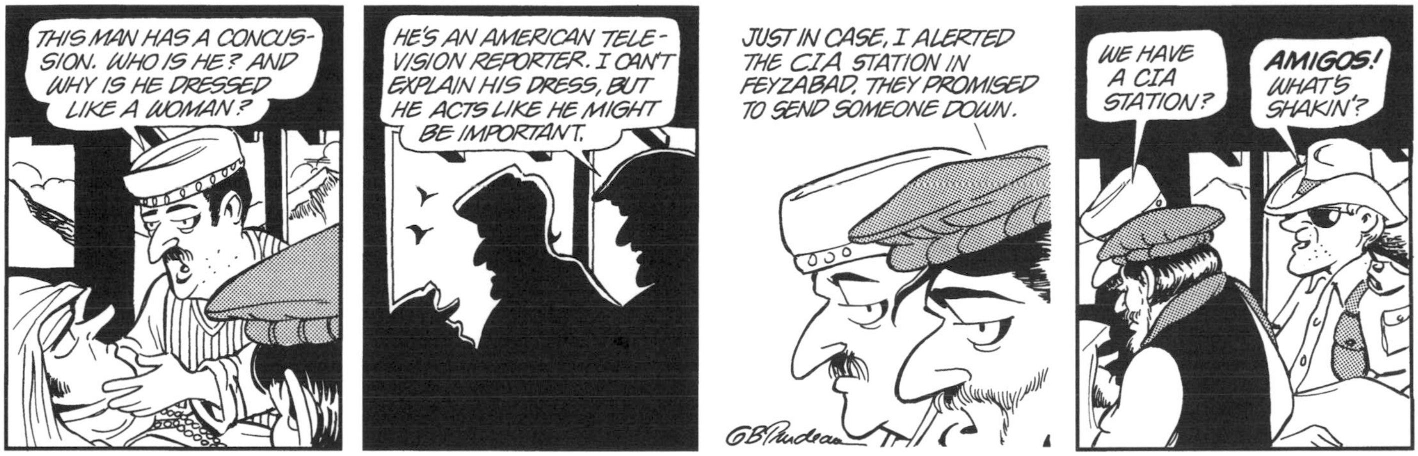
THIS MAN HAS A CONCUSSION. WHO IS HE? AND WHY IS HE DRESSED LIKE A WOMAN?
HE'S AN AMERICAN TELEVISION REPORTER. I CAN'T EXPLAIN HIS DRESS, BUT HE ACTS LIKE HE MIGHT BE IMPORTANT.
JUST IN CASE, I ALERTED THE CIA STATION IN FEYZABAD. THEY PROMISED TO SEND SOMEONE DOWN.
©B Trudeau
WE HAVE A CIA STATION?
AMIGOS! WHAT'S SHAKIN'?

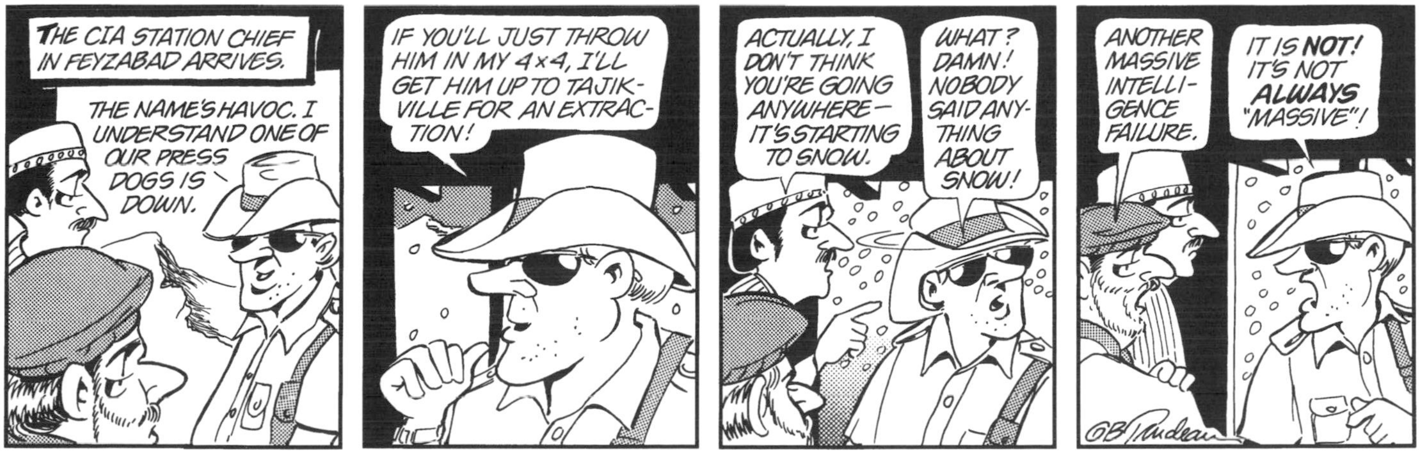
THE CIA STATION CHIEF IN FEYZABAD ARRIVES.
THE NAME'S HAVOC. I UNDERSTAND ONE OF OUR PRESS DOGS IS DOWN.
IF YOU'LL JUST THROW HIM IN MY 4×4, I'LL GET HIM UP TO TAJIKVILLE FOR AN EXTRACTION!
ACTUALLY, I DON'T THINK YOU'RE GOING ANYWHERE — IT'S STARTING TO SNOW.
WHAT? DAMN! NOBODY SAID ANYTHING ABOUT SNOW!
ANOTHER MASSIVE INTELLIGENCE FAILURE.
IT IS NOT! IT'S NOT ALWAYS "MASSIVE"!
©B Trudeau

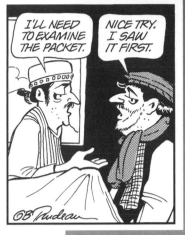

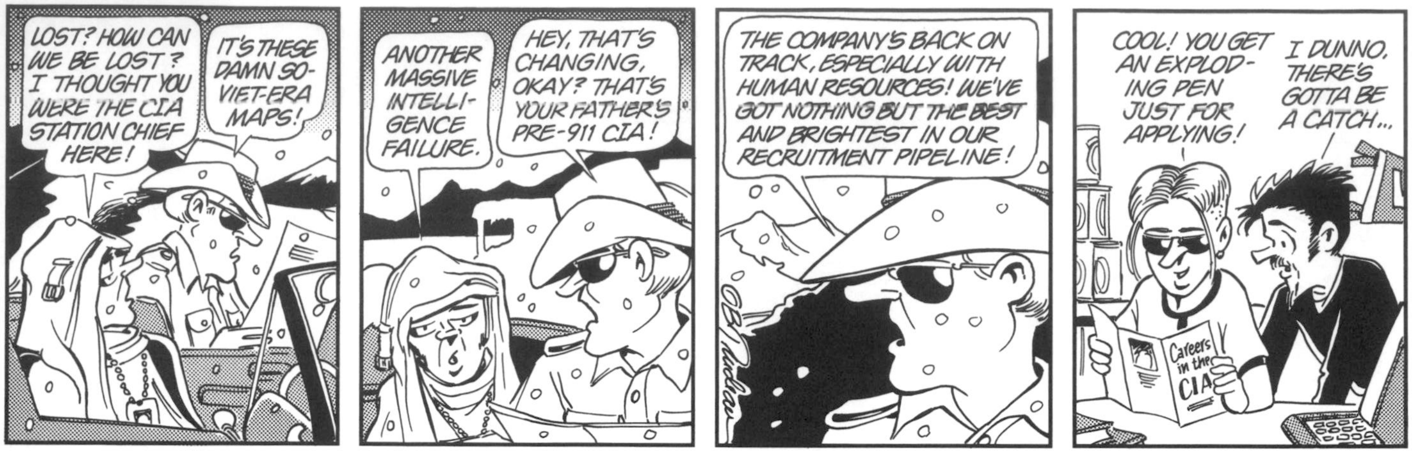
LOST? HOW CAN WE BE LOST? I THOUGHT YOU WERE THE CIA STATION CHIEF HERE!
IT'S THESE DAMN SO-VIET-ERA MAPS!
ANOTHER MASSIVE INTELLI-GENCE FAILURE.
HEY, THAT'S CHANGING, OKAY? THAT'S YOUR FATHER'S PRE-911 CIA!
THE COMPANY'S BACK ON TRACK, ESPECIALLY WITH HUMAN RESOURCES! WE'VE GOT NOTHING BUT THE BEST AND BRIGHTEST IN OUR RECRUITMENT PIPELINE!
COOL! YOU GET AN EXPLOD-ING PEN JUST FOR APPLYING!
I DUNNO, THERE'S GOTTA BE A CATCH...
Careers in the CIA

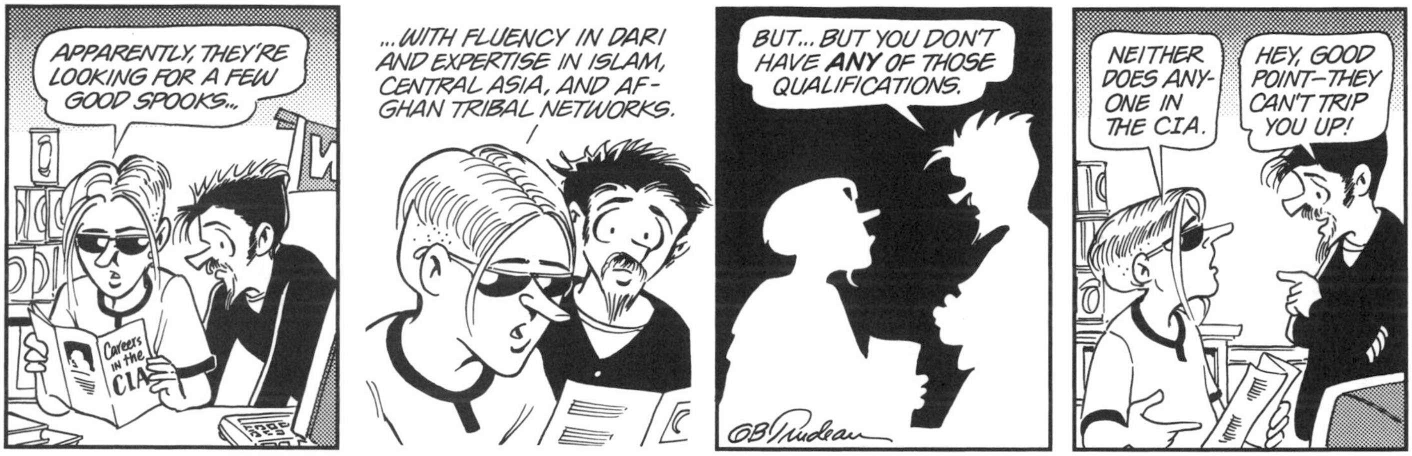
APPARENTLY, THEY'RE LOOKING FOR A FEW GOOD SPOOKS...
Careers in the CIA
...WITH FLUENCY IN DARI AND EXPERTISE IN ISLAM, CENTRAL ASIA, AND AF-GHAN TRIBAL NETWORKS.
BUT... BUT YOU DON'T HAVE ANY OF THOSE QUALIFICATIONS.
NEITHER DOES ANY-ONE IN THE CIA.
HEY, GOOD POINT—THEY CAN'T TRIP YOU UP!

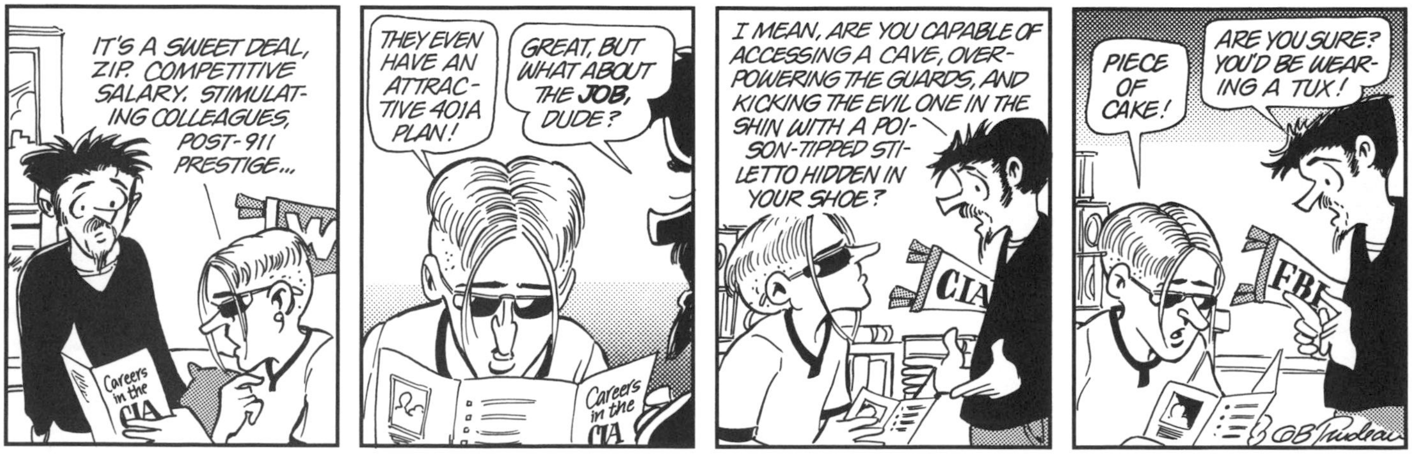
IT'S A SWEET DEAL, ZIP. COMPETITIVE SALARY. STIMULAT-ING COLLEAGUES, POST-911 PRESTIGE...
Careers in the CIA
THEY EVEN HAVE AN ATTRAC-TIVE 401A PLAN!
GREAT, BUT WHAT ABOUT THE JOB, DUDE?
Careers in the CIA
I MEAN, ARE YOU CAPABLE OF ACCESSING A CAVE, OVER-POWERING THE GUARDS, AND KICKING THE EVIL ONE IN THE SHIN WITH A POI-SON-TIPPED STI-LETTO HIDDEN IN YOUR SHOE?
CIA
PIECE OF CAKE!
ARE YOU SURE? YOU'D BE WEAR-ING A TUX!
FBI

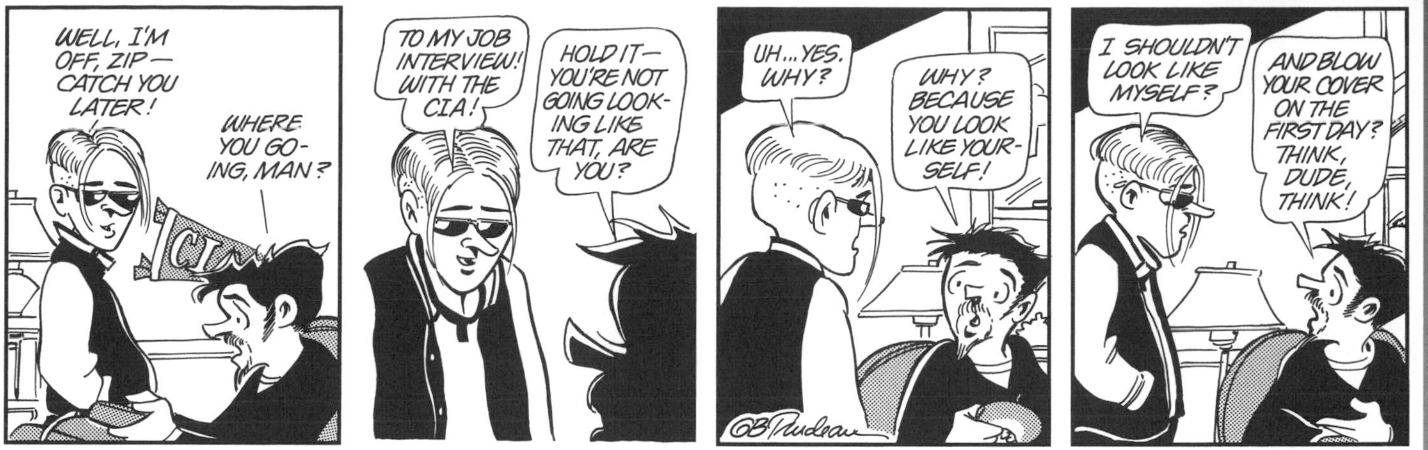
WELL, I'M OFF, ZIP— CATCH YOU LATER!
WHERE YOU GOING, MAN?
CIA
TO MY JOB INTERVIEW! WITH THE CIA!
HOLD IT— YOU'RE NOT GOING LOOKING LIKE THAT, ARE YOU?
UH... YES. WHY?
WHY? BECAUSE YOU LOOK LIKE YOURSELF!
I SHOULDN'T LOOK LIKE MYSELF?
AND BLOW YOUR COVER ON THE FIRST DAY? THINK, DUDE, THINK!

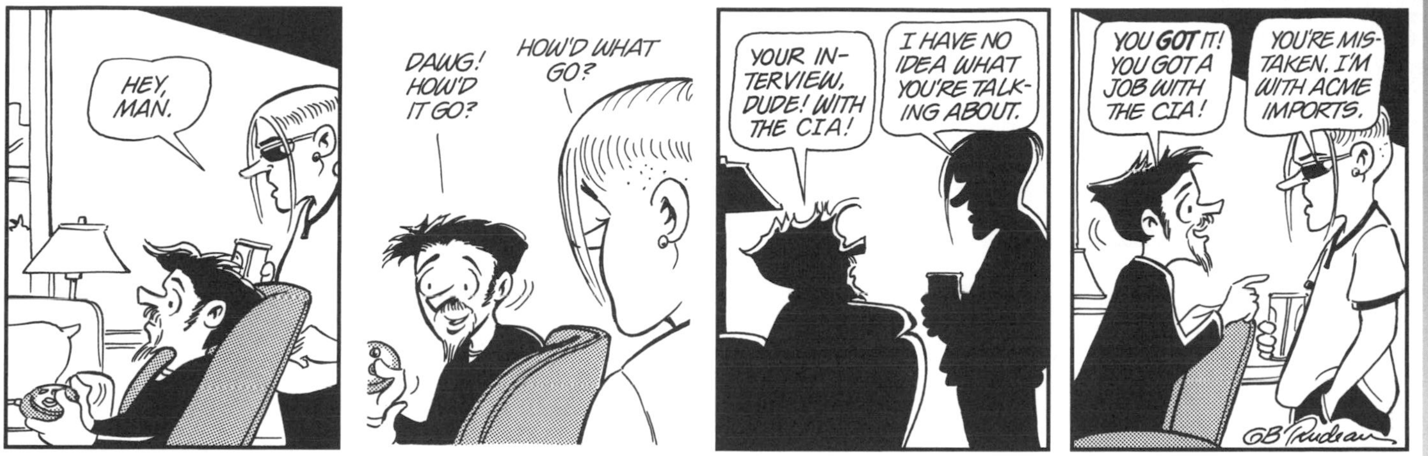
HEY, MAN.
DAWG! HOW'D IT GO?
HOW'D WHAT GO?
YOUR INTERVIEW, DUDE! WITH THE CIA!
I HAVE NO IDEA WHAT YOU'RE TALKING ABOUT.
YOU **GOT** IT! YOU GOT A JOB WITH THE CIA!
YOU'RE MISTAKEN. I'M WITH ACME IMPORTS.

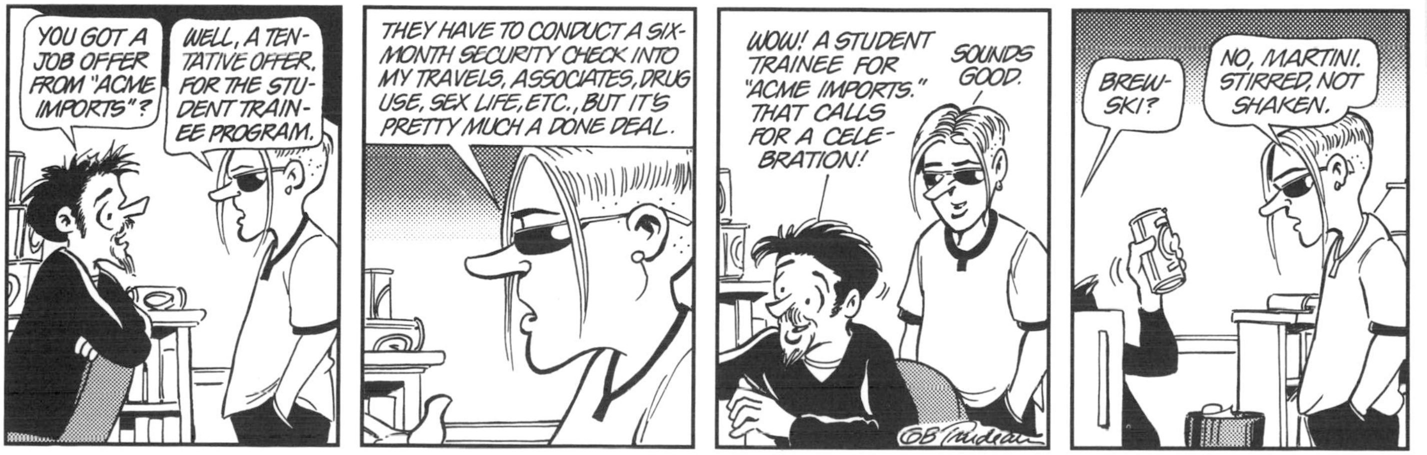
YOU GOT A JOB OFFER FROM "ACME IMPORTS"?
WELL, A TENTATIVE OFFER. FOR THE STUDENT TRAINEE PROGRAM.
THEY HAVE TO CONDUCT A SIX-MONTH SECURITY CHECK INTO MY TRAVELS, ASSOCIATES, DRUG USE, SEX LIFE, ETC., BUT IT'S PRETTY MUCH A DONE DEAL.
WOW! A STUDENT TRAINEE FOR "ACME IMPORTS." THAT CALLS FOR A CELEBRATION!
SOUNDS GOOD.
BREWSKI?
NO, MARTINI. STIRRED, NOT SHAKEN.

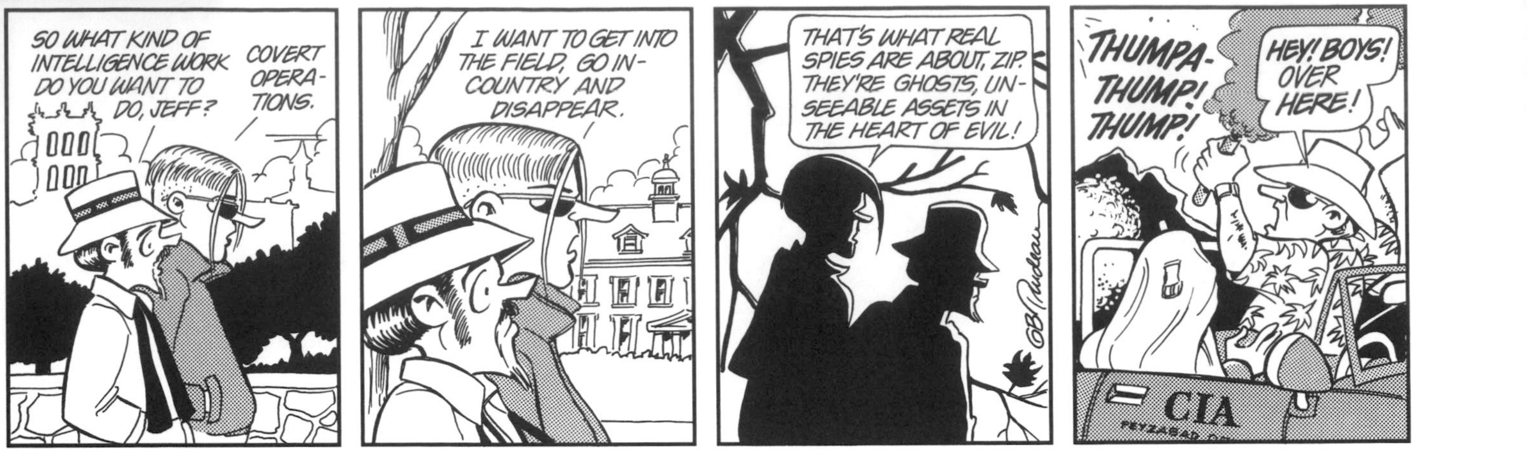
SO WHAT KIND OF INTELLIGENCE WORK DO YOU WANT TO DO, JEFF?
COVERT OPERA-TIONS.
I WANT TO GET INTO THE FIELD, GO IN-COUNTRY AND DISAPPEAR.
THAT'S WHAT REAL SPIES ARE ABOUT, ZIP. THEY'RE GHOSTS, UN-SEEABLE ASSETS IN THE HEART OF EVIL!
THUMPA-THUMP! THUMP!
HEY! BOYS! OVER HERE!
CIA

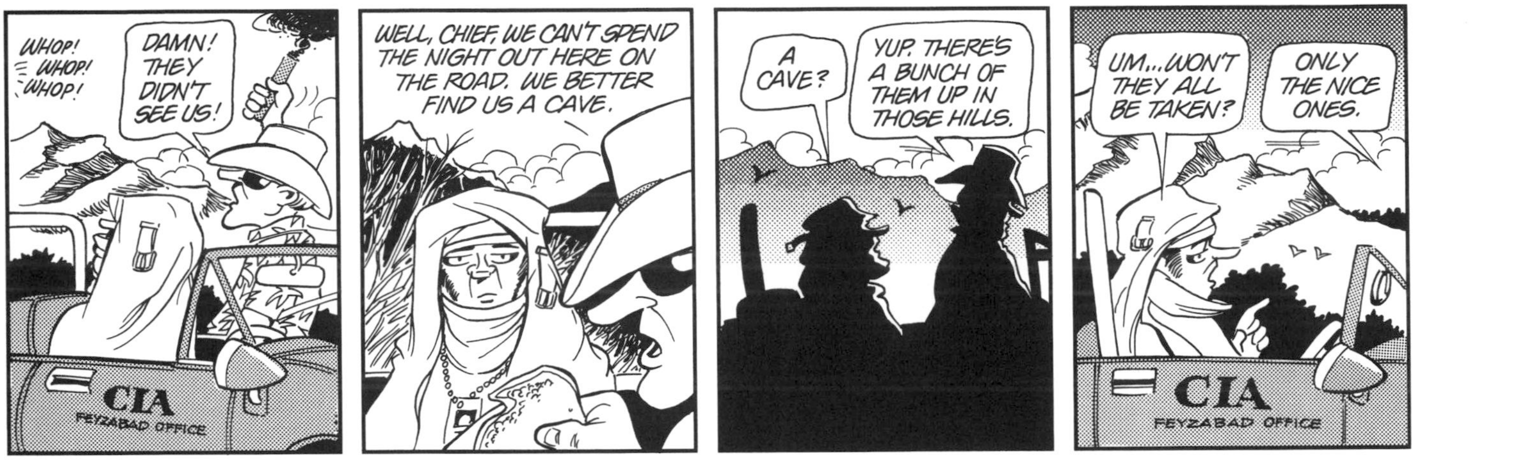
WHOP! WHOP! WHOP!
DAMN! THEY DIDN'T SEE US!
CIA
FEYZABAD OFFICE
WELL, CHIEF, WE CAN'T SPEND THE NIGHT OUT HERE ON THE ROAD. WE BETTER FIND US A CAVE.
A CAVE?
YUP. THERE'S A BUNCH OF THEM UP IN THOSE HILLS.
UM... WON'T THEY ALL BE TAKEN?
ONLY THE NICE ONES.
CIA
FEYZABAD OFFICE

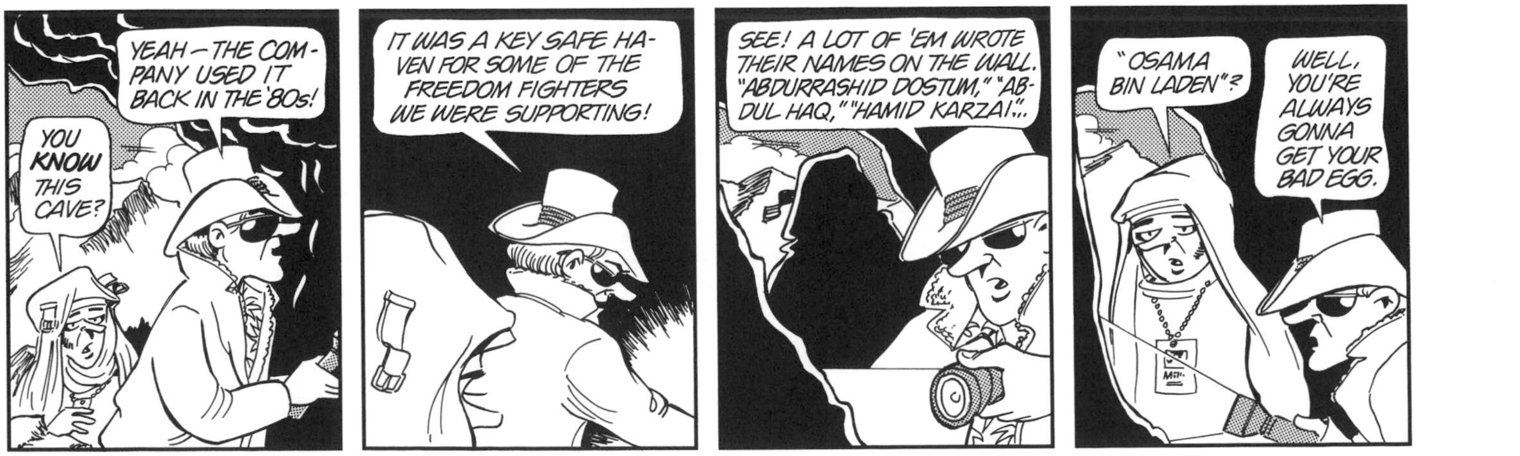
YOU **KNOW** THIS CAVE?
YEAH — THE COM-PANY USED IT BACK IN THE '80s!
IT WAS A KEY SAFE HA-VEN FOR SOME OF THE FREEDOM FIGHTERS WE WERE SUPPORTING!
SEE! A LOT OF 'EM WROTE THEIR NAMES ON THE WALL. "ABDURRASHID DOSTUM," "AB-DUL HAQ," "HAMID KARZAI"...
"OSAMA BIN LADEN"?
WELL, YOU'RE ALWAYS GONNA GET YOUR BAD EGG.

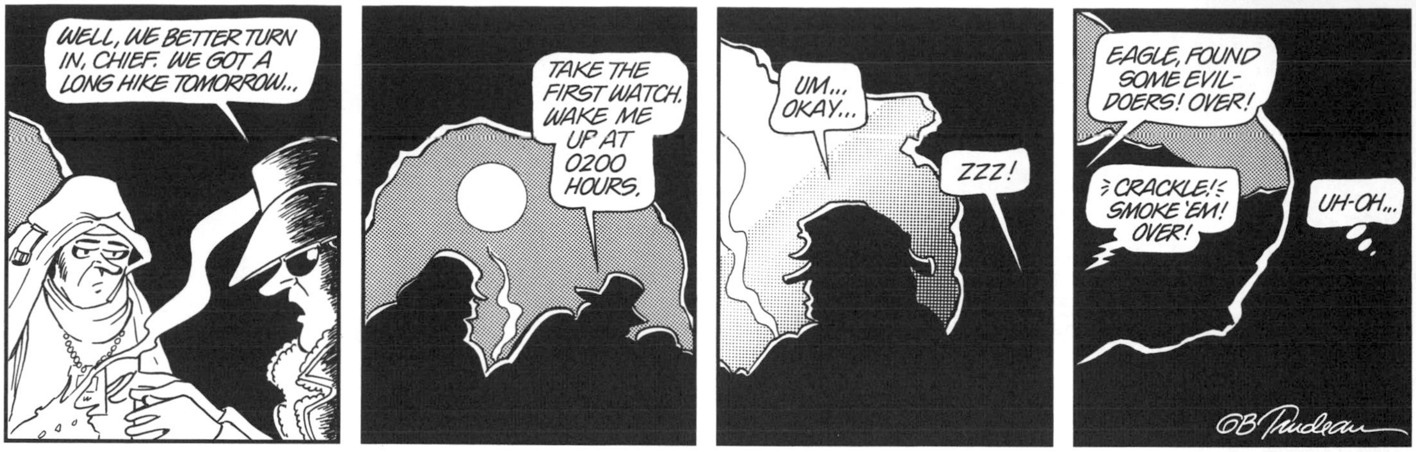
WELL, WE BETTER TURN IN, CHIEF. WE GOT A LONG HIKE TOMORROW...
TAKE THE FIRST WATCH. WAKE ME UP AT 0200 HOURS.
UM... OKAY...
ZZZ!
EAGLE, FOUND SOME EVIL-DOERS! OVER!
CRACKLE! SMOKE 'EM! OVER!
UH-OH...

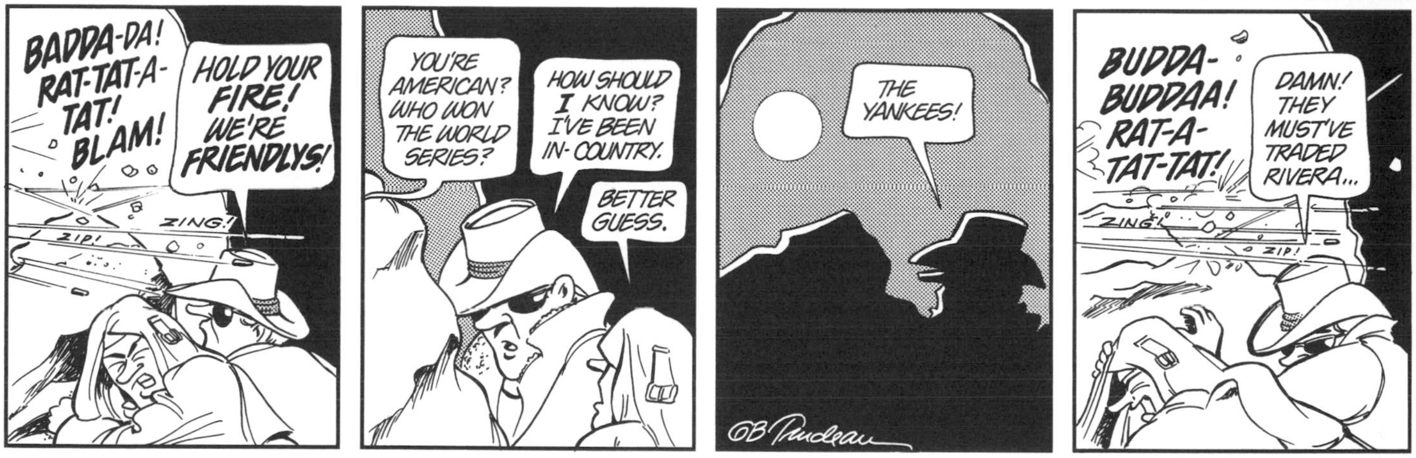
BADDA-DA! RAT-TAT-A-TAT! BLAM!
HOLD YOUR FIRE! WE'RE FRIENDLYS!
ZING!
ZIP!
YOU'RE AMERICAN? WHO WON THE WORLD SERIES?
HOW SHOULD I KNOW? I'VE BEEN IN-COUNTRY.
BETTER GUESS.
THE YANKEES!
BUDDA-BUDDAA! RAT-A-TAT-TAT!
DAMN! THEY MUST'VE TRADED RIVERA...
ZING!
ZIP!

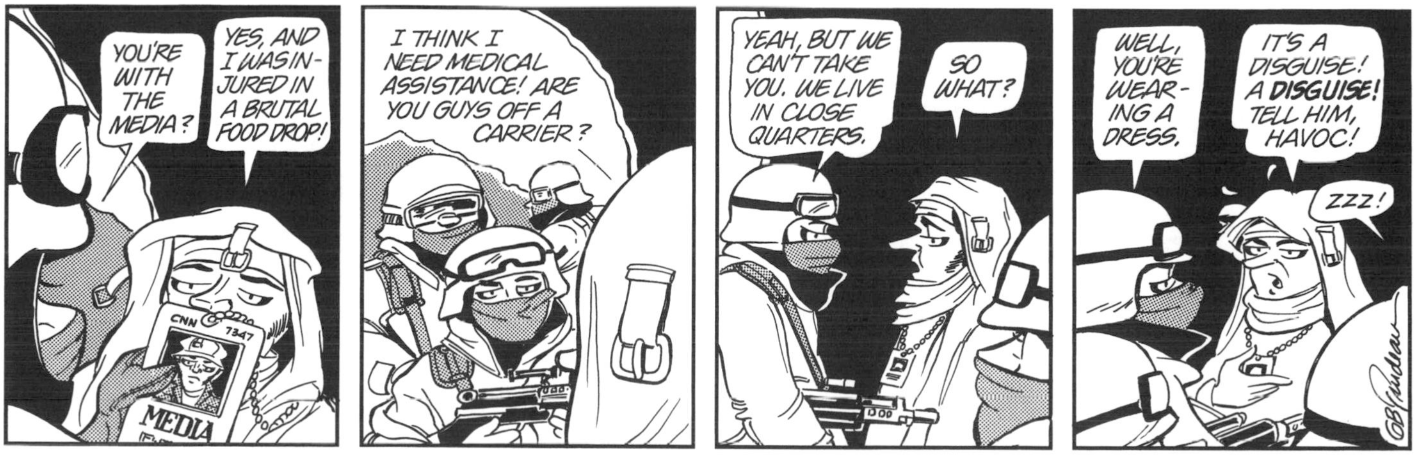
YOU'RE WITH THE MEDIA?
YES, AND I WAS INJURED IN A BRUTAL FOOD DROP!
CNN 7347
MEDIA
I THINK I NEED MEDICAL ASSISTANCE! ARE YOU GUYS OFF A CARRIER?
YEAH, BUT WE CAN'T TAKE YOU. WE LIVE IN CLOSE QUARTERS.
SO WHAT?
WELL, YOU'RE WEARING A DRESS.
IT'S A DISGUISE! A DISGUISE! TELL HIM, HAVOC!
ZZZ!

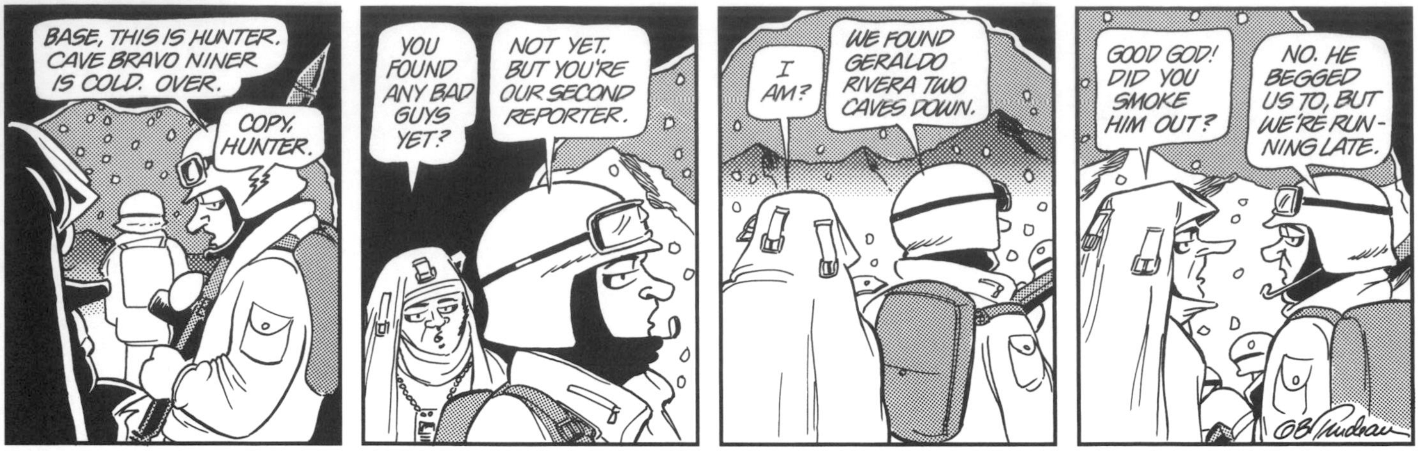
BASE, THIS IS HUNTER. CAVE BRAVO NINER IS COLD. OVER.
COPY, HUNTER.
YOU FOUND ANY BAD GUYS YET?
NOT YET. BUT YOU'RE OUR SECOND REPORTER.
I AM?
WE FOUND GERALDO RIVERA TWO CAVES DOWN.
GOOD GOD! DID YOU SMOKE HIM OUT?
NO. HE BEGGED US TO, BUT WE'RE RUNNING LATE.
©B Trudeau

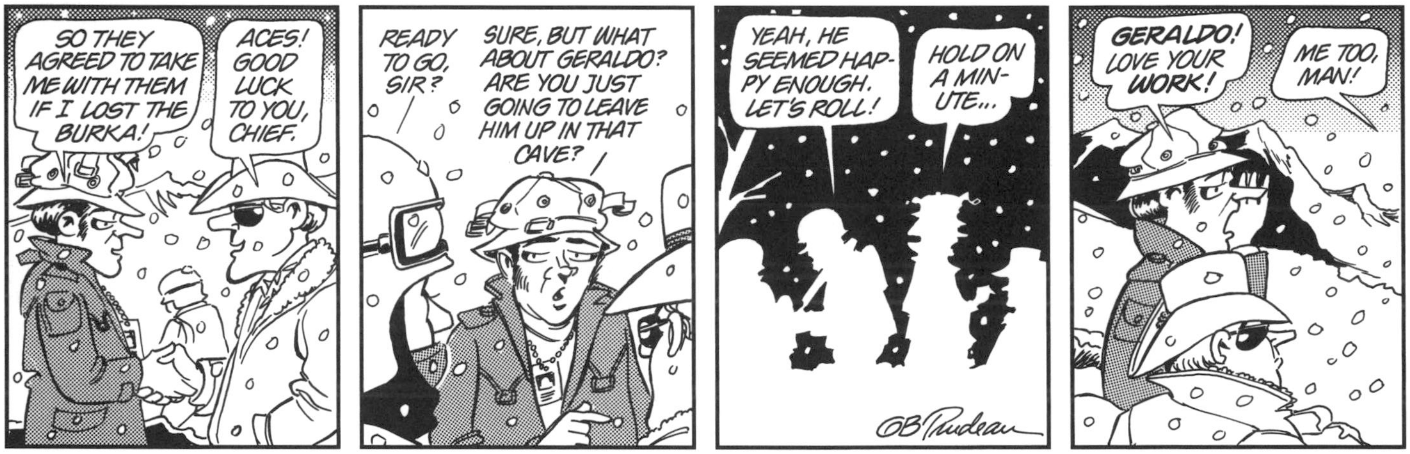
SO THEY AGREED TO TAKE ME WITH THEM IF I LOST THE BURKA!
ACES! GOOD LUCK TO YOU, CHIEF.
READY TO GO, SIR?
SURE, BUT WHAT ABOUT GERALDO? ARE YOU JUST GOING TO LEAVE HIM UP IN THAT CAVE?
YEAH, HE SEEMED HAPPY ENOUGH. LET'S ROLL!
HOLD ON A MINUTE...
©B Trudeau
GERALDO! LOVE YOUR WORK!
ME TOO, MAN!

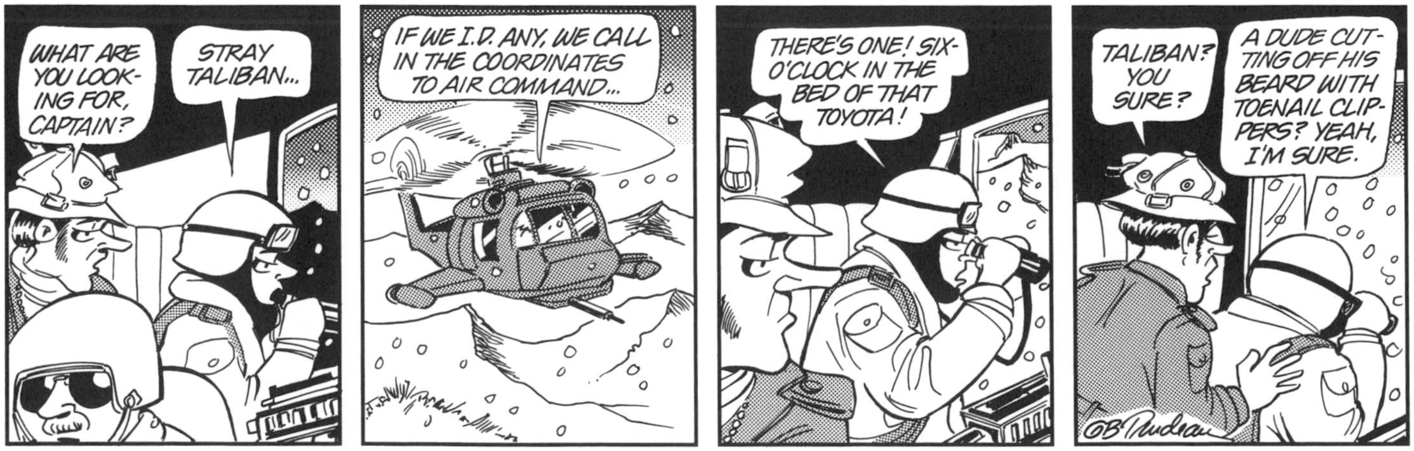
WHAT ARE YOU LOOKING FOR, CAPTAIN?
STRAY TALIBAN...
IF WE I.D. ANY, WE CALL IN THE COORDINATES TO AIR COMMAND...
THERE'S ONE! SIX-O'CLOCK IN THE BED OF THAT TOYOTA!
TALIBAN? YOU SURE?
A DUDE CUTTING OFF HIS BEARD WITH TOENAIL CLIPPERS? YEAH, I'M SURE.
©B Trudeau

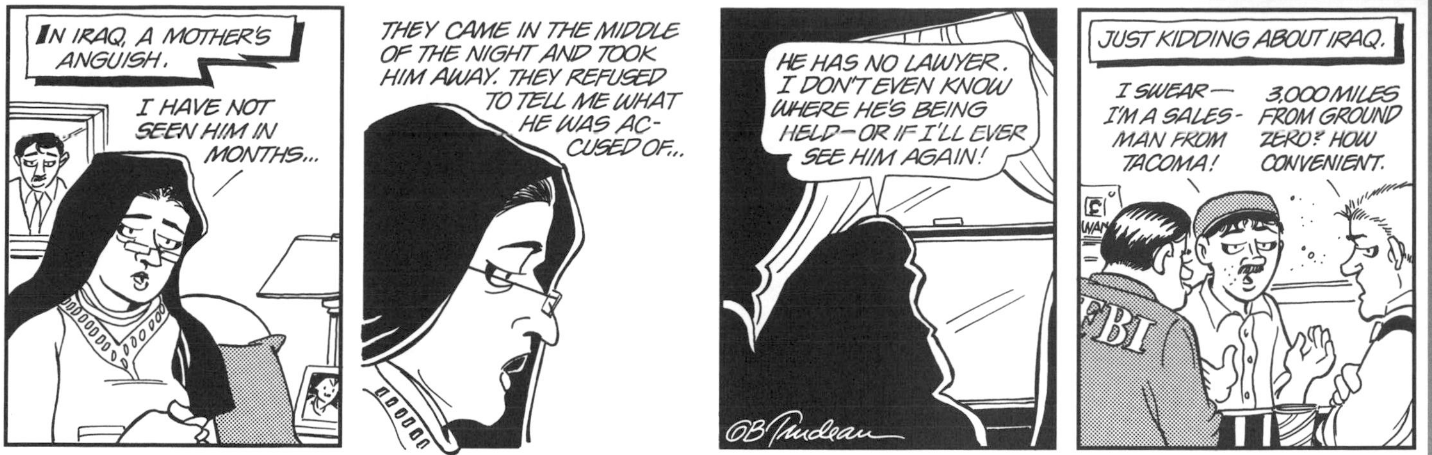
IN IRAQ, A MOTHER'S ANGUISH.
I HAVE NOT SEEN HIM IN MONTHS...
THEY CAME IN THE MIDDLE OF THE NIGHT AND TOOK HIM AWAY. THEY REFUSED TO TELL ME WHAT HE WAS ACCUSED OF...
HE HAS NO LAWYER. I DON'T EVEN KNOW WHERE HE'S BEING HELD—OR IF I'LL EVER SEE HIM AGAIN!
GB Trudeau
JUST KIDDING ABOUT IRAQ.
I SWEAR— I'M A SALESMAN FROM TACOMA!
3,000 MILES FROM GROUND ZERO? HOW CONVENIENT.
FBI

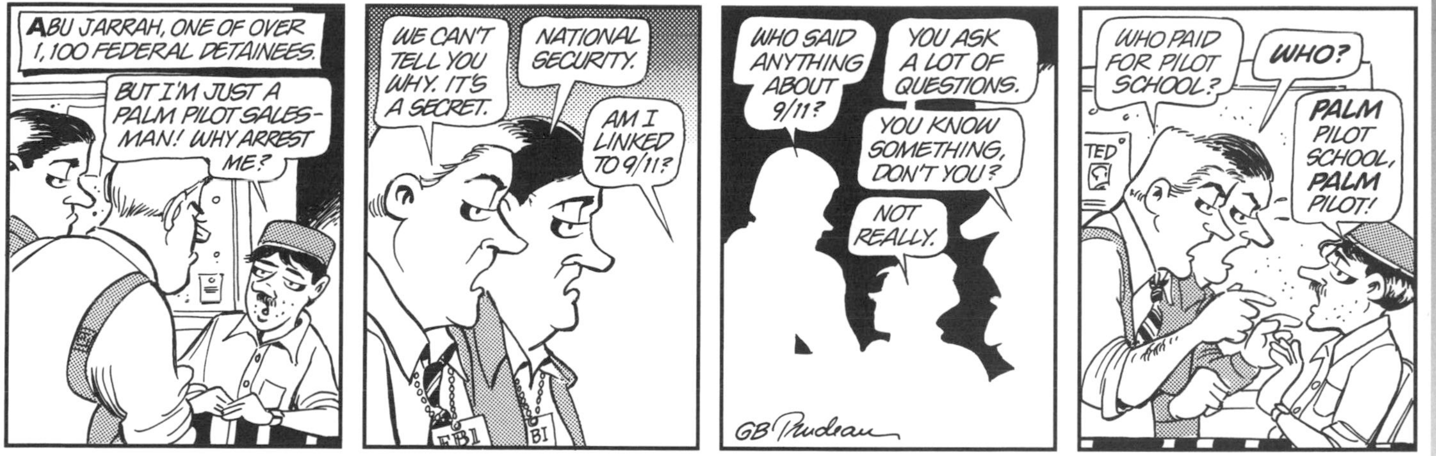
ABU JARRAH, ONE OF OVER 1,100 FEDERAL DETAINEES.
BUT I'M JUST A PALM PILOT SALESMAN! WHY ARREST ME?
WE CAN'T TELL YOU WHY. IT'S A SECRET.
NATIONAL SECURITY.
AM I LINKED TO 9/11?
FBI
WHO SAID ANYTHING ABOUT 9/11?
YOU ASK A LOT OF QUESTIONS.
YOU KNOW SOMETHING, DON'T YOU?
NOT REALLY.
GB Trudeau
WHO PAID FOR PILOT SCHOOL?
WHO?
PALM PILOT SCHOOL, PALM PILOT!

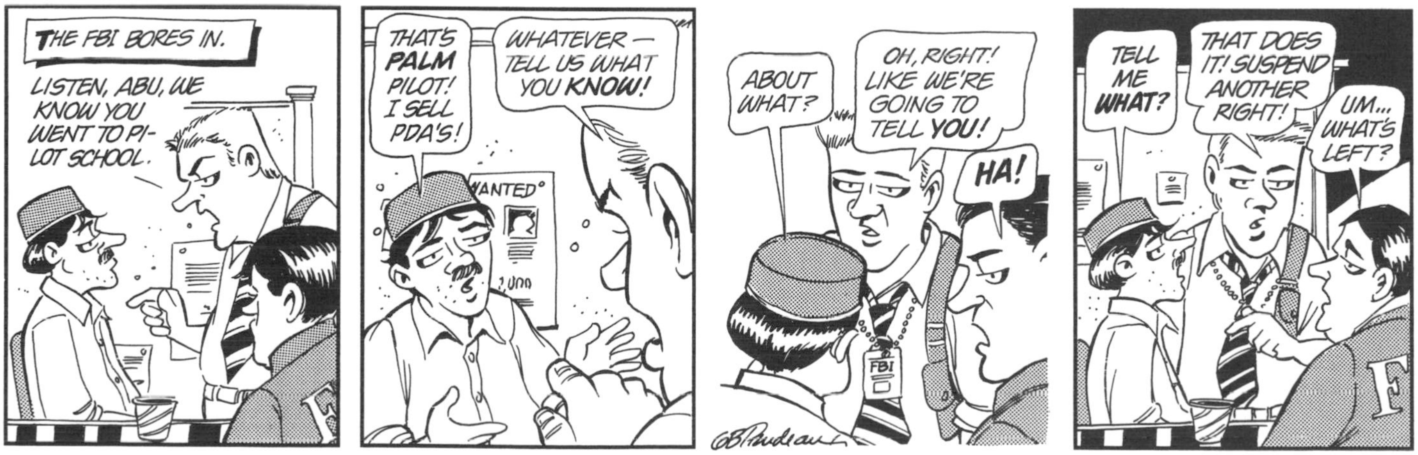
THE FBI BORES IN.
LISTEN, ABU, WE KNOW YOU WENT TO PILOT SCHOOL.
THAT'S PALM PILOT! I SELL PDA'S!
WHATEVER— TELL US WHAT YOU KNOW!
WANTED
ABOUT WHAT?
OH, RIGHT! LIKE WE'RE GOING TO TELL YOU!
HA!
FBI
GB Trudeau
TELL ME WHAT?
THAT DOES IT! SUSPEND ANOTHER RIGHT!
UM... WHAT'S LEFT?

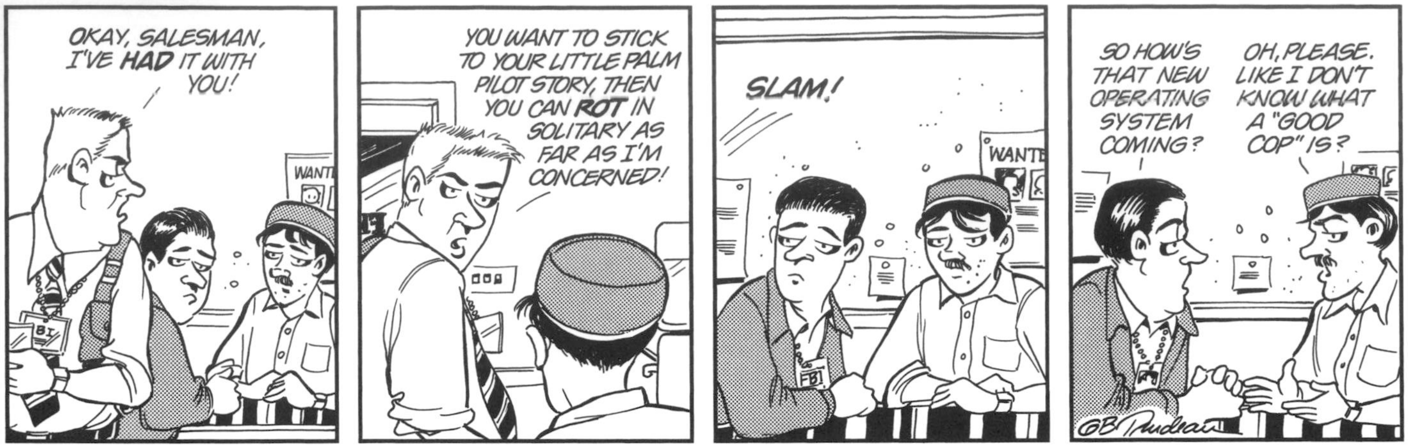
OKAY, SALESMAN, I'VE HAD IT WITH YOU!
YOU WANT TO STICK TO YOUR LITTLE PALM PILOT STORY, THEN YOU CAN ROT IN SOLITARY AS FAR AS I'M CONCERNED!
SLAM!
SO HOW'S THAT NEW OPERATING SYSTEM COMING?
OH, PLEASE. LIKE I DON'T KNOW WHAT A "GOOD COP" IS?

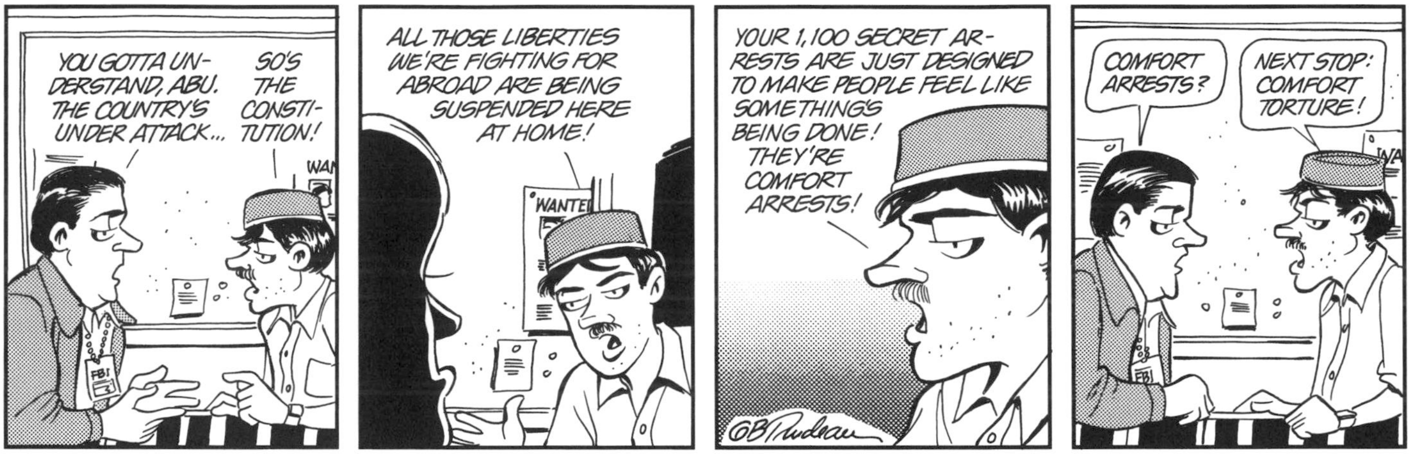
YOU GOTTA UNDERSTAND, ABU. THE COUNTRY'S UNDER ATTACK...
SO'S THE CONSTITUTION!
ALL THOSE LIBERTIES WE'RE FIGHTING FOR ABROAD ARE BEING SUSPENDED HERE AT HOME!
YOUR 1,100 SECRET ARRESTS ARE JUST DESIGNED TO MAKE PEOPLE FEEL LIKE SOMETHING'S BEING DONE! THEY'RE COMFORT ARRESTS!
COMFORT ARRESTS?
NEXT STOP: COMFORT TORTURE!

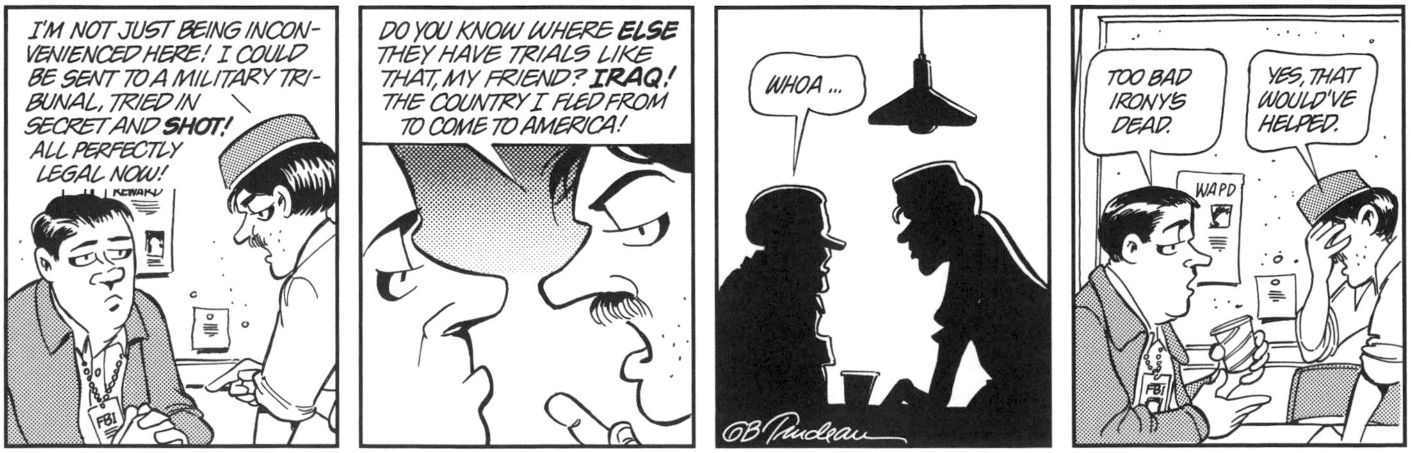
I'M NOT JUST BEING INCONVENIENCED HERE! I COULD BE SENT TO A MILITARY TRIBUNAL, TRIED IN SECRET AND SHOT! ALL PERFECTLY LEGAL NOW!
DO YOU KNOW WHERE ELSE THEY HAVE TRIALS LIKE THAT, MY FRIEND? IRAQ! THE COUNTRY I FLED FROM TO COME TO AMERICA!
WHOA...
TOO BAD IRONY'S DEAD.
YES, THAT WOULD'VE HELPED.

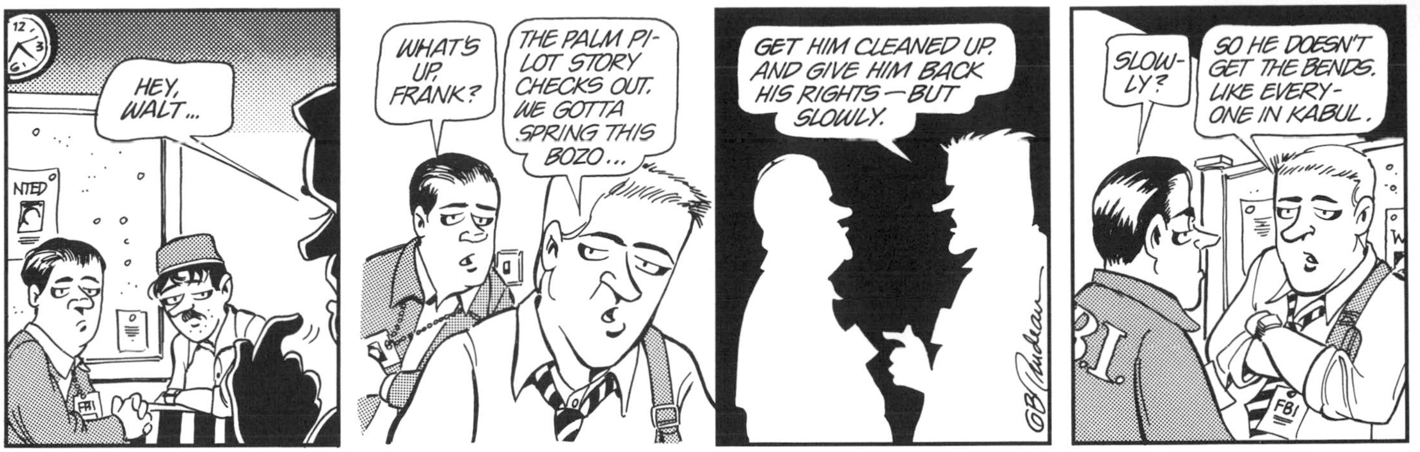
HEY, WALT...
WHAT'S UP, FRANK?
THE PALM PILOT STORY CHECKS OUT. WE GOTTA SPRING THIS BOZO...
GET HIM CLEANED UP, AND GIVE HIM BACK HIS RIGHTS—BUT SLOWLY.
SLOWLY?
SO HE DOESN'T GET THE BENDS. LIKE EVERYONE IN KABUL.

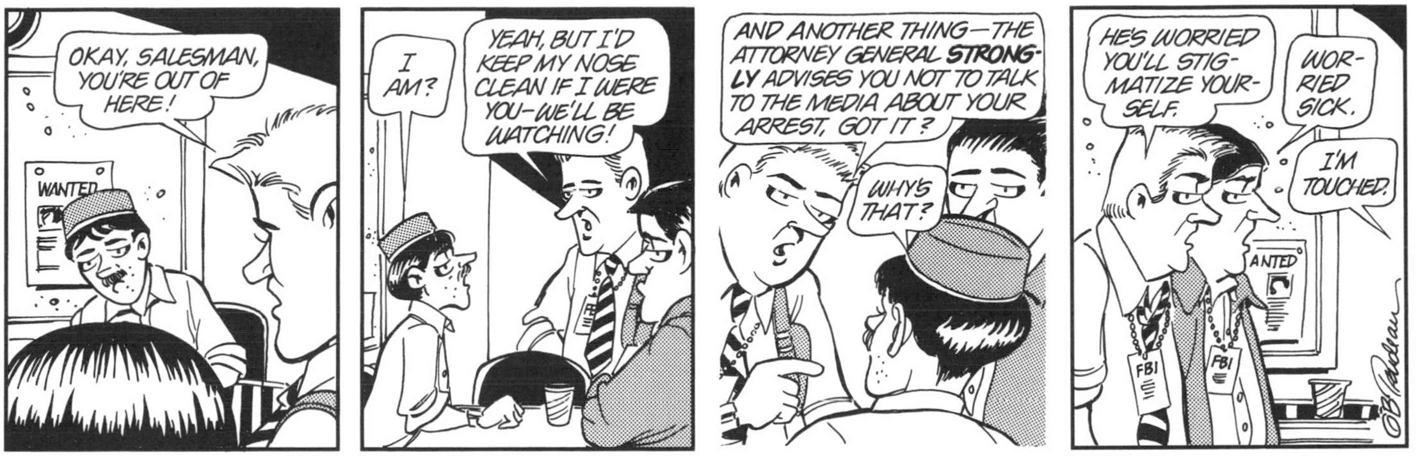
OKAY, SALESMAN, YOU'RE OUT OF HERE!
I AM?
YEAH, BUT I'D KEEP MY NOSE CLEAN IF I WERE YOU—WE'LL BE WATCHING!
AND ANOTHER THING—THE ATTORNEY GENERAL **STRONGLY** ADVISES YOU NOT TO TALK TO THE MEDIA ABOUT YOUR ARREST, GOT IT?
WHY'S THAT?
HE'S WORRIED YOU'LL STIGMATIZE YOURSELF.
WORRIED SICK.
I'M TOUCHED.

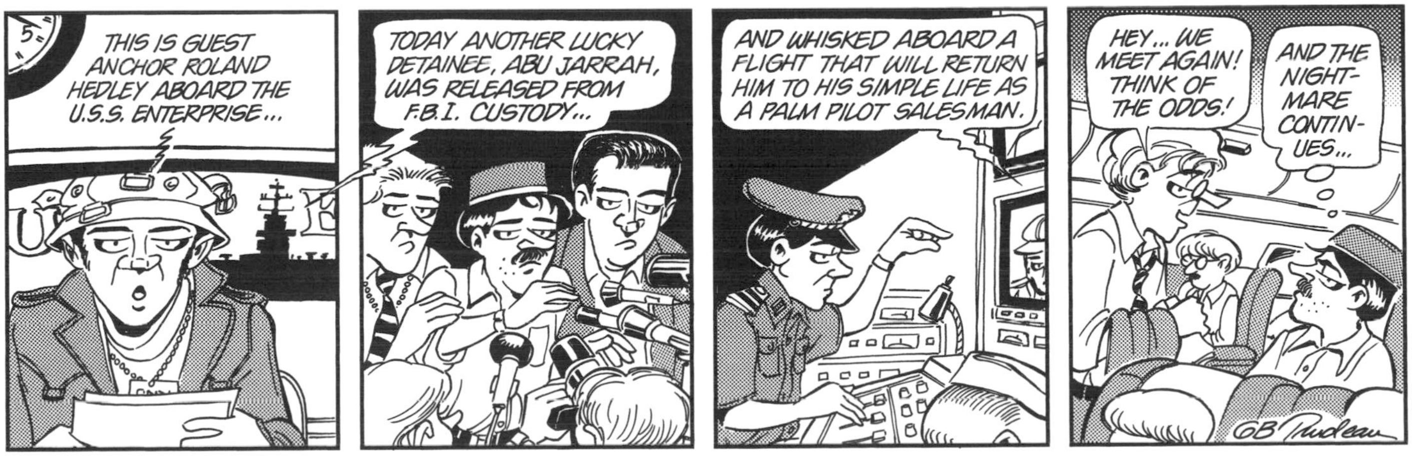
THIS IS GUEST ANCHOR ROLAND HEDLEY ABOARD THE U.S.S. ENTERPRISE...
TODAY ANOTHER LUCKY DETAINEE, ABU JARRAH, WAS RELEASED FROM F.B.I. CUSTODY...
AND WHISKED ABOARD A FLIGHT THAT WILL RETURN HIM TO HIS SIMPLE LIFE AS A PALM PILOT SALESMAN.
HEY... WE MEET AGAIN! THINK OF THE ODDS!
AND THE NIGHTMARE CONTINUES...

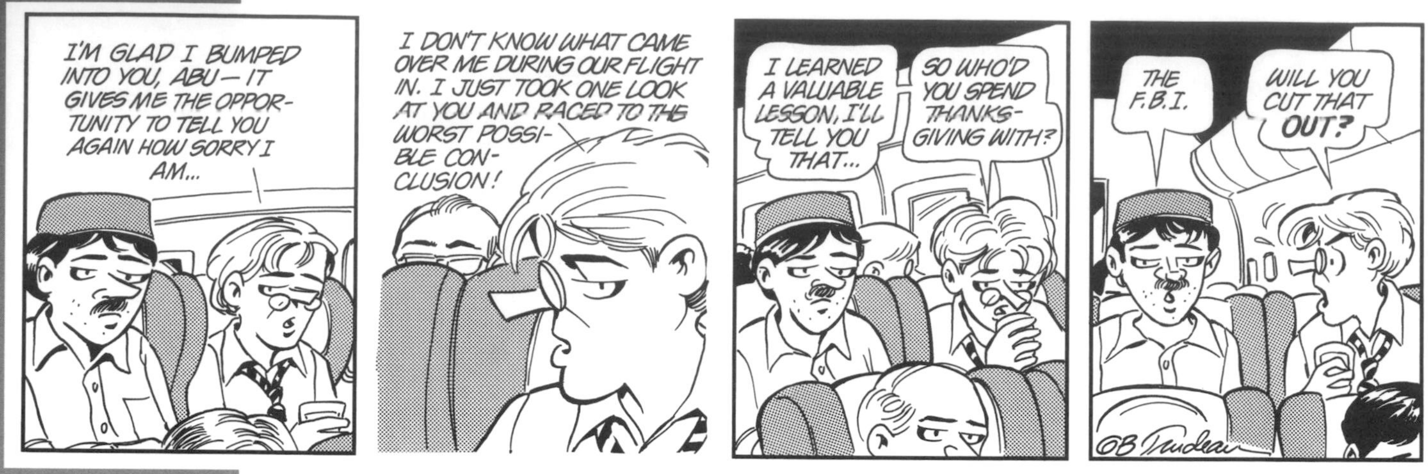
I'M GLAD I BUMPED INTO YOU, ABU— IT GIVES ME THE OPPORTUNITY TO TELL YOU AGAIN HOW SORRY I AM...
I DON'T KNOW WHAT CAME OVER ME DURING OUR FLIGHT IN. I JUST TOOK ONE LOOK AT YOU AND RACED TO THE WORST POSSIBLE CONCLUSION!
I LEARNED A VALUABLE LESSON, I'LL TELL YOU THAT...
SO WHO'D YOU SPEND THANKSGIVING WITH?
THE F.B.I.
WILL YOU CUT THAT OUT?
GB Trudeau

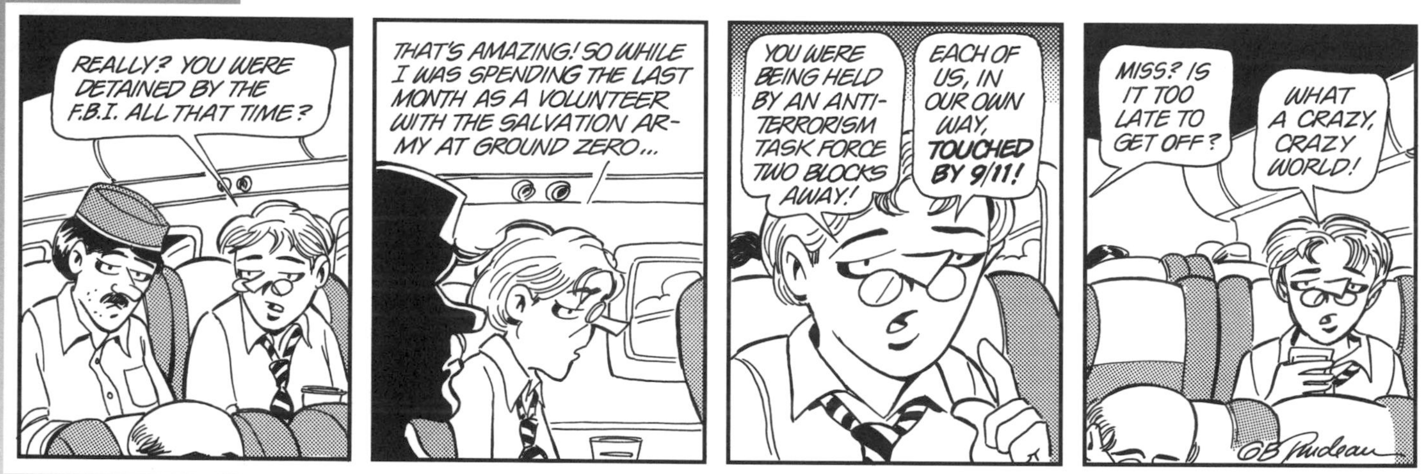
REALLY? YOU WERE DETAINED BY THE F.B.I. ALL THAT TIME?
THAT'S AMAZING! SO WHILE I WAS SPENDING THE LAST MONTH AS A VOLUNTEER WITH THE SALVATION ARMY AT GROUND ZERO...
YOU WERE BEING HELD BY AN ANTI-TERRORISM TASK FORCE TWO BLOCKS AWAY!
EACH OF US, IN OUR OWN WAY, TOUCHED BY 9/11!
MISS? IS IT TOO LATE TO GET OFF?
WHAT A CRAZY, CRAZY WORLD!
GB Trudeau

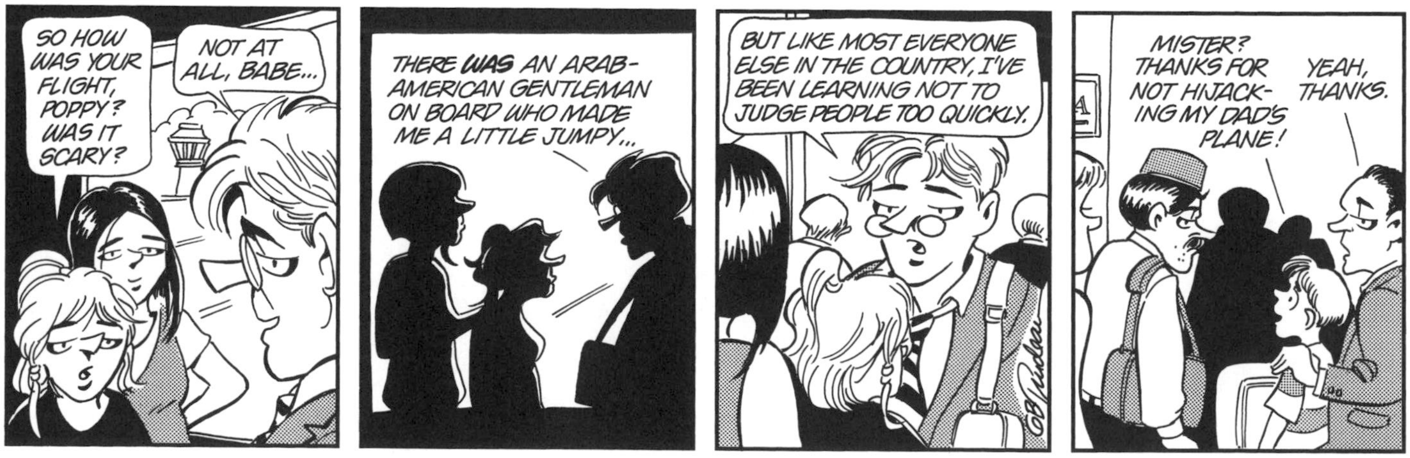
SO HOW WAS YOUR FLIGHT, POPPY? WAS IT SCARY?
NOT AT ALL, BABE...
THERE WAS AN ARAB-AMERICAN GENTLEMAN ON BOARD WHO MADE ME A LITTLE JUMPY...
BUT LIKE MOST EVERYONE ELSE IN THE COUNTRY, I'VE BEEN LEARNING NOT TO JUDGE PEOPLE TOO QUICKLY.
MISTER? THANKS FOR NOT HIJACKING MY DAD'S PLANE!
YEAH, THANKS.

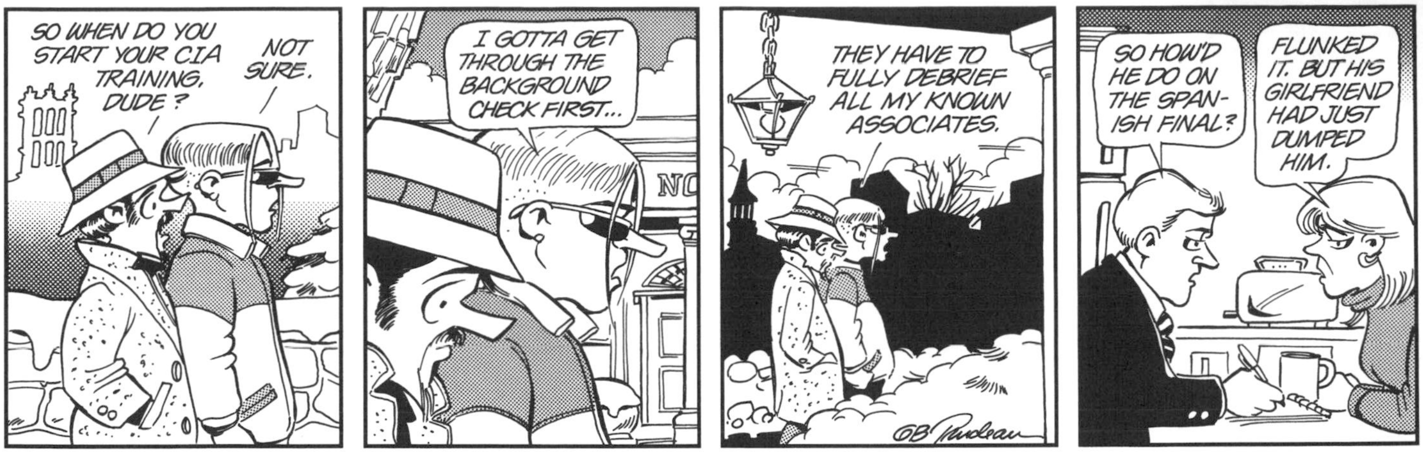
SO WHEN DO YOU START YOUR CIA TRAINING, DUDE?
NOT SURE.
I GOTTA GET THROUGH THE BACKGROUND CHECK FIRST...
THEY HAVE TO FULLY DEBRIEF ALL MY KNOWN ASSOCIATES.
SO HOW'D HE DO ON THE SPANISH FINAL?
FLUNKED IT. BUT HIS GIRLFRIEND HAD JUST DUMPED HIM.

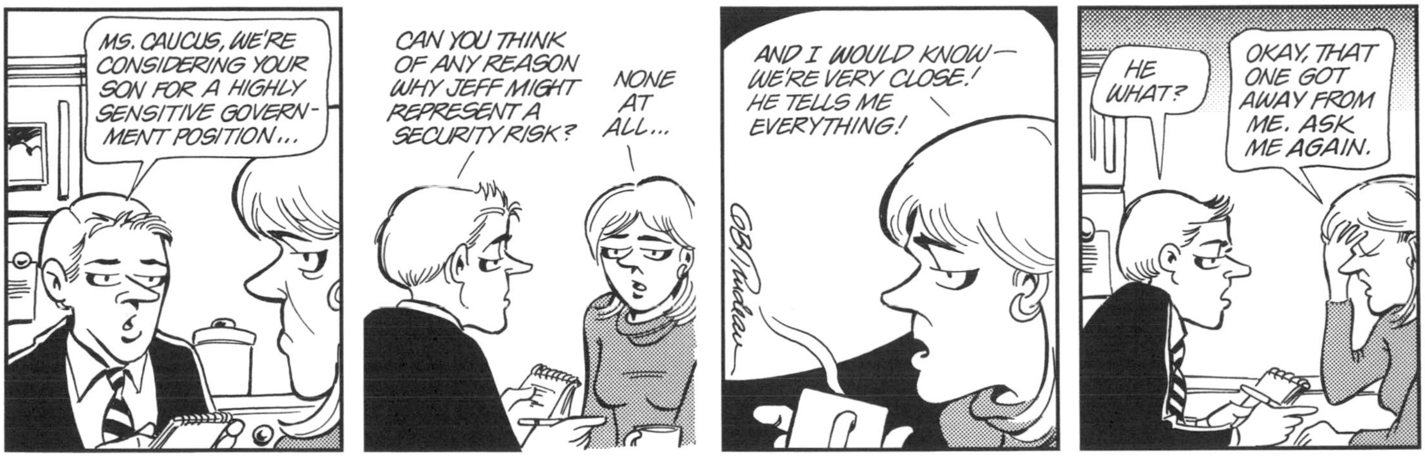
MS. CAUCUS, WE'RE CONSIDERING YOUR SON FOR A HIGHLY SENSITIVE GOVERNMENT POSITION...
CAN YOU THINK OF ANY REASON WHY JEFF MIGHT REPRESENT A SECURITY RISK?
NONE AT ALL...
AND I WOULD KNOW— WE'RE VERY CLOSE! HE TELLS ME EVERYTHING!
HE WHAT?
OKAY, THAT ONE GOT AWAY FROM ME. ASK ME AGAIN.

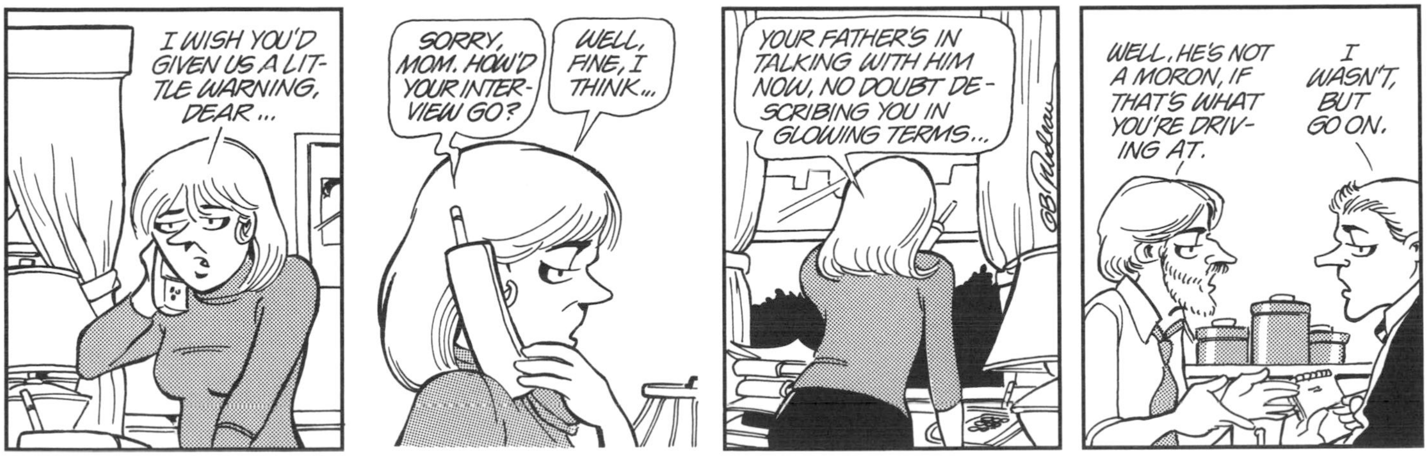
I WISH YOU'D GIVEN US A LITTLE WARNING, DEAR...
SORRY, MOM. HOW'D YOUR INTERVIEW GO?
WELL, FINE, I THINK...
YOUR FATHER'S IN TALKING WITH HIM NOW, NO DOUBT DESCRIBING YOU IN GLOWING TERMS...
WELL, HE'S NOT A MORON, IF THAT'S WHAT YOU'RE DRIVING AT.
I WASN'T, BUT GO ON.

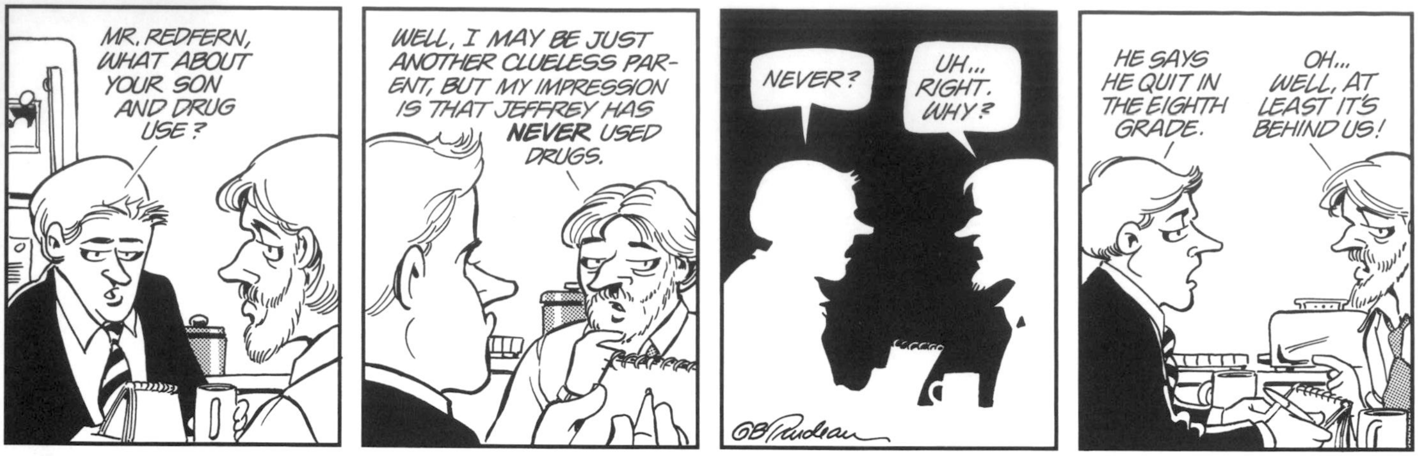
MR. REDFERN, WHAT ABOUT YOUR SON AND DRUG USE?
WELL, I MAY BE JUST ANOTHER CLUELESS PARENT, BUT MY IMPRESSION IS THAT JEFFREY HAS **NEVER** USED DRUGS.
NEVER?
UH... RIGHT. WHY?
HE SAYS HE QUIT IN THE EIGHTH GRADE.
OH... WELL, AT LEAST IT'S BEHIND US!
©B Trudeau

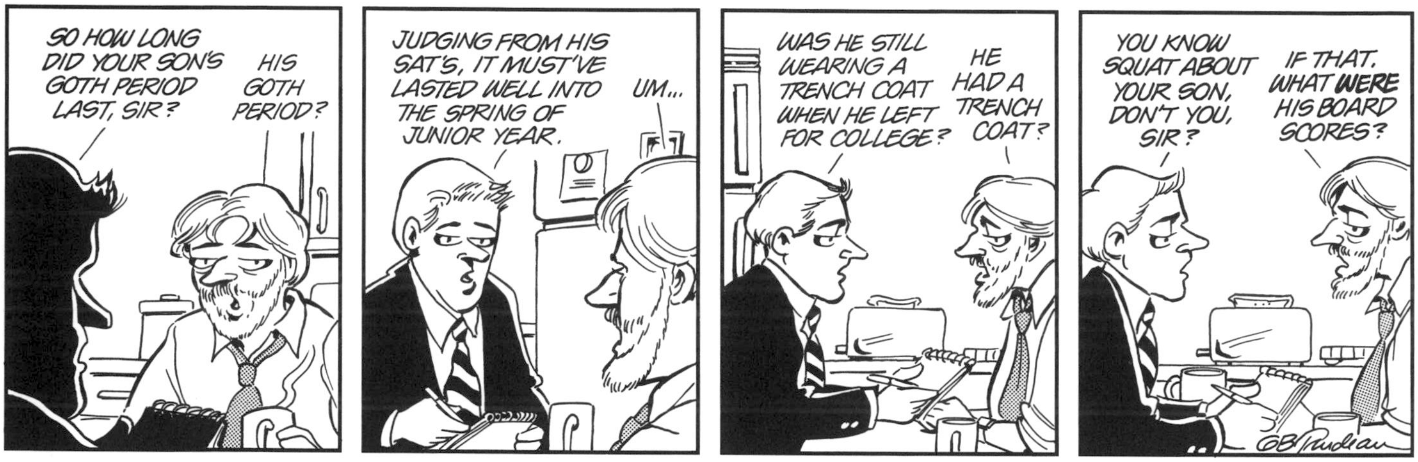
SO HOW LONG DID YOUR SON'S GOTH PERIOD LAST, SIR?
HIS GOTH PERIOD?
JUDGING FROM HIS SAT'S, IT MUST'VE LASTED WELL INTO THE SPRING OF JUNIOR YEAR.
UM...
WAS HE STILL WEARING A TRENCH COAT WHEN HE LEFT FOR COLLEGE?
HE HAD A TRENCH COAT?
YOU KNOW SQUAT ABOUT YOUR SON, DON'T YOU, SIR?
IF THAT. WHAT **WERE** HIS BOARD SCORES?
©B Trudeau

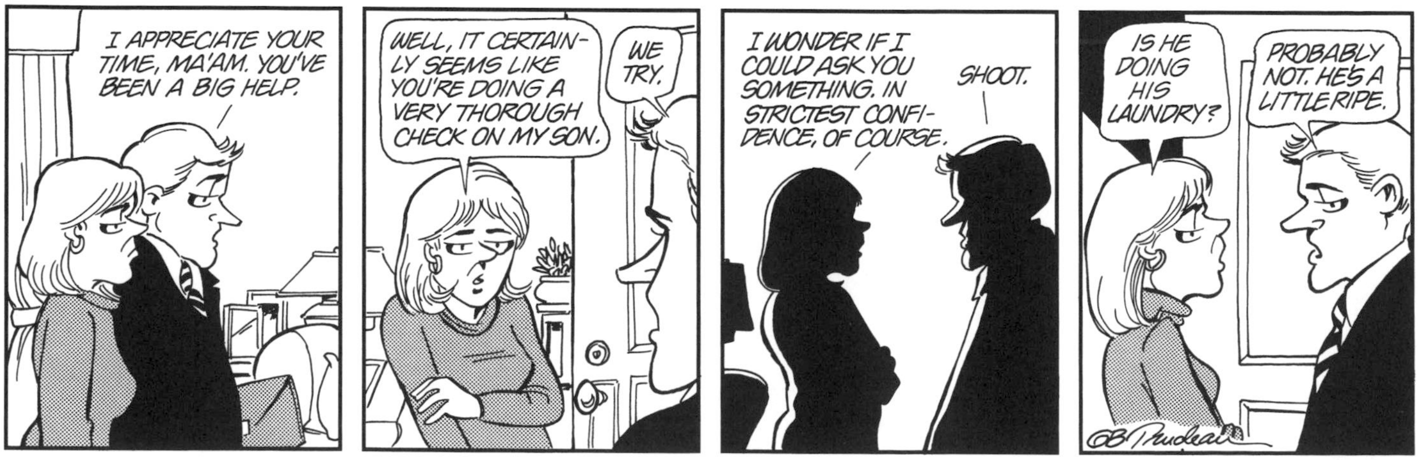
I APPRECIATE YOUR TIME, MA'AM. YOU'VE BEEN A BIG HELP.
WELL, IT CERTAINLY SEEMS LIKE YOU'RE DOING A VERY THOROUGH CHECK ON MY SON.
WE TRY.
I WONDER IF I COULD ASK YOU SOMETHING. IN STRICTEST CONFIDENCE, OF COURSE.
SHOOT.
IS HE DOING HIS LAUNDRY?
PROBABLY NOT. HE'S A LITTLE RIPE.
©B Trudeau

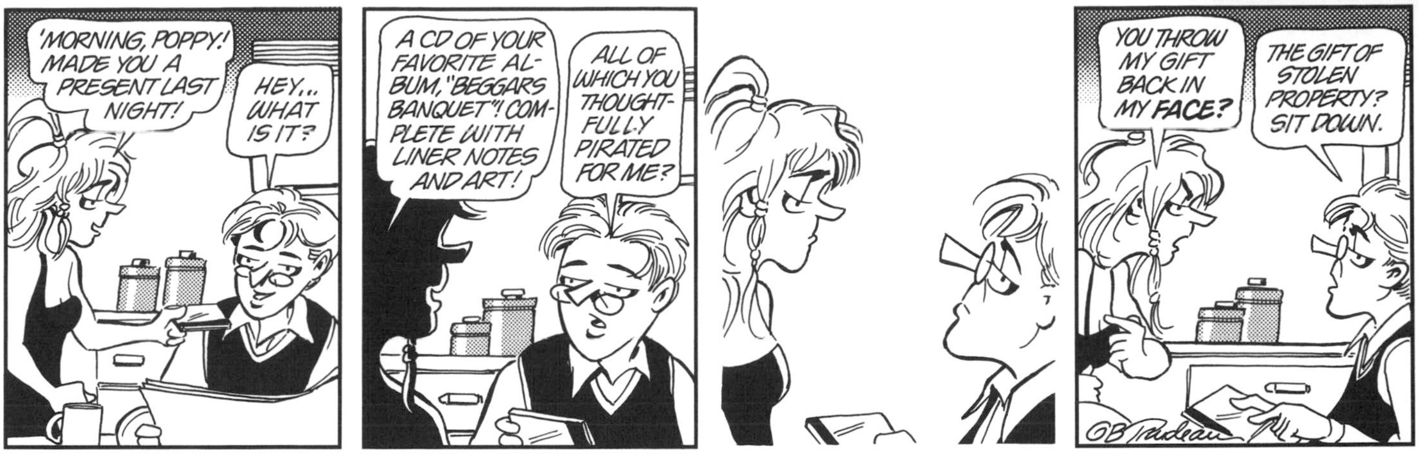
'MORNING, POPPY! MADE YOU A PRESENT LAST NIGHT!
HEY... WHAT IS IT?
A CD OF YOUR FAVORITE ALBUM, "BEGGARS BANQUET"! COMPLETE WITH LINER NOTES AND ART!
ALL OF WHICH YOU THOUGHTFULLY PIRATED FOR ME?
YOU THROW MY GIFT BACK IN MY FACE?
THE GIFT OF STOLEN PROPERTY? SIT DOWN.
©B Trudeau

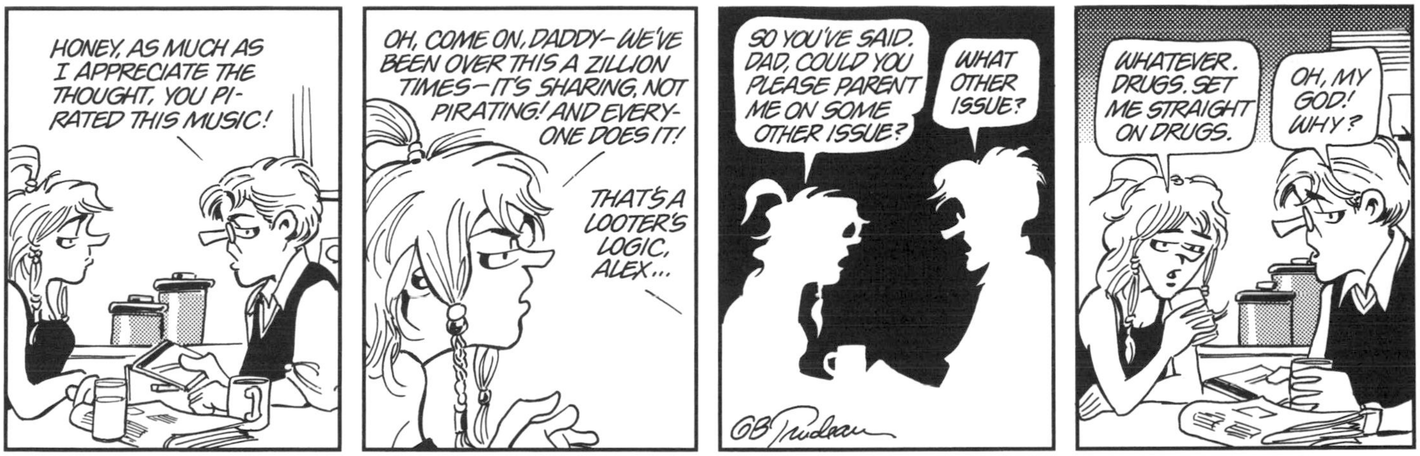
HONEY, AS MUCH AS I APPRECIATE THE THOUGHT, YOU PIRATED THIS MUSIC!
OH, COME ON, DADDY– WE'VE BEEN OVER THIS A ZILLION TIMES– IT'S SHARING, NOT PIRATING! AND EVERYONE DOES IT!
THAT'S A LOOTER'S LOGIC, ALEX...
SO YOU'VE SAID. DAD, COULD YOU PLEASE PARENT ME ON SOME OTHER ISSUE?
WHAT OTHER ISSUE?
WHATEVER. DRUGS. SET ME STRAIGHT ON DRUGS.
OH, MY GOD! WHY?
©B Trudeau

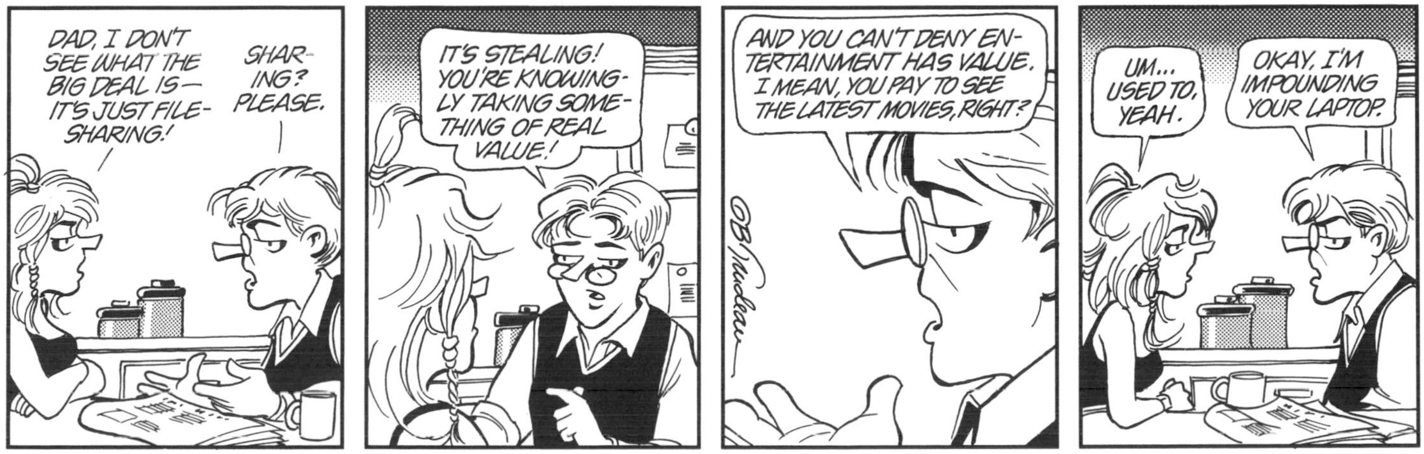
DAD, I DON'T SEE WHAT THE BIG DEAL IS– IT'S JUST FILE-SHARING!
SHARING? PLEASE.
IT'S STEALING! YOU'RE KNOWINGLY TAKING SOMETHING OF REAL VALUE!
AND YOU CAN'T DENY ENTERTAINMENT HAS VALUE. I MEAN, YOU PAY TO SEE THE LATEST MOVIES, RIGHT?
UM... USED TO, YEAH.
OKAY, I'M IMPOUNDING YOUR LAPTOP.
©B Trudeau

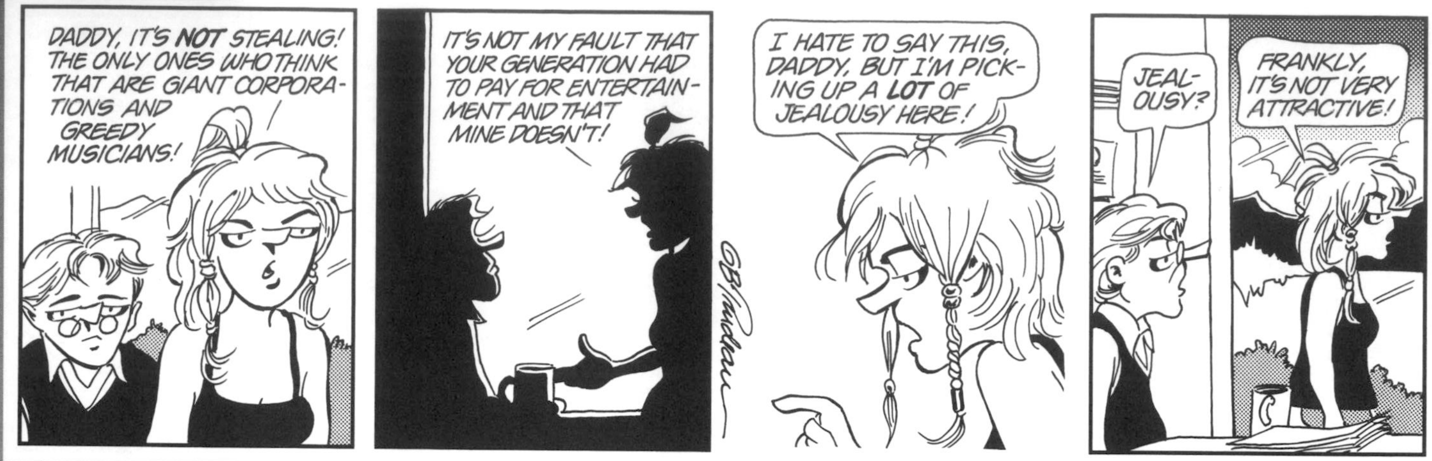
DADDY, IT'S **NOT** STEALING! THE ONLY ONES WHO THINK THAT ARE GIANT CORPORATIONS AND GREEDY MUSICIANS!
IT'S NOT MY FAULT THAT YOUR GENERATION HAD TO PAY FOR ENTERTAINMENT AND THAT MINE DOESN'T!
I HATE TO SAY THIS, DADDY, BUT I'M PICKING UP A **LOT** OF JEALOUSY HERE!
JEALOUSY?
FRANKLY, IT'S NOT VERY ATTRACTIVE!

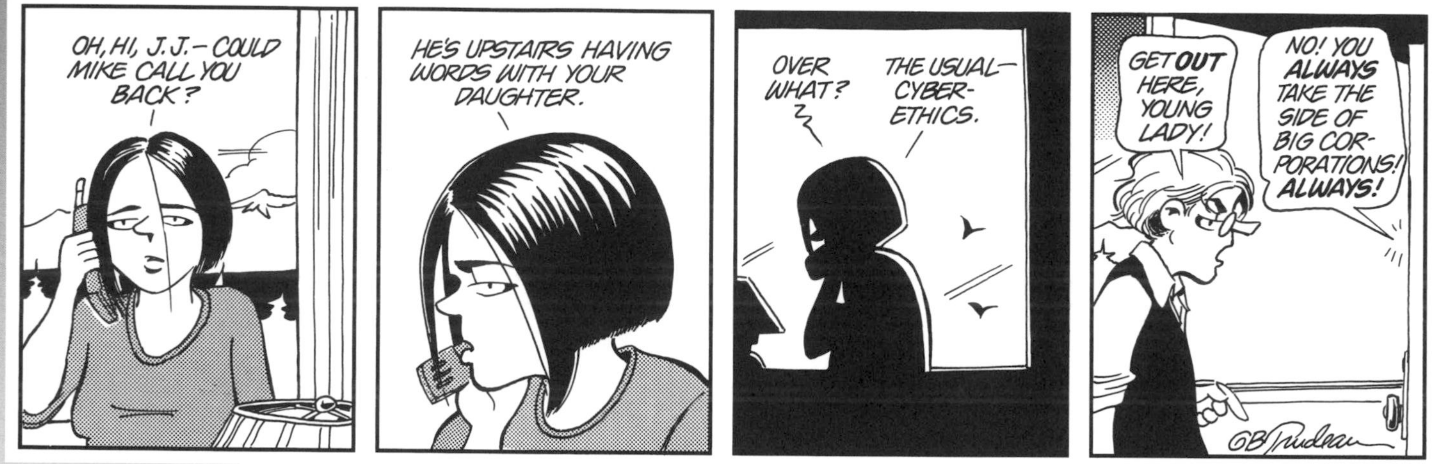
OH, HI, J.J.– COULD MIKE CALL YOU BACK?
HE'S UPSTAIRS HAVING WORDS WITH YOUR DAUGHTER.
OVER WHAT?
THE USUAL–CYBER-ETHICS.
GET **OUT** HERE, YOUNG LADY!
NO! YOU **ALWAYS** TAKE THE SIDE OF BIG CORPORATIONS! **ALWAYS!**

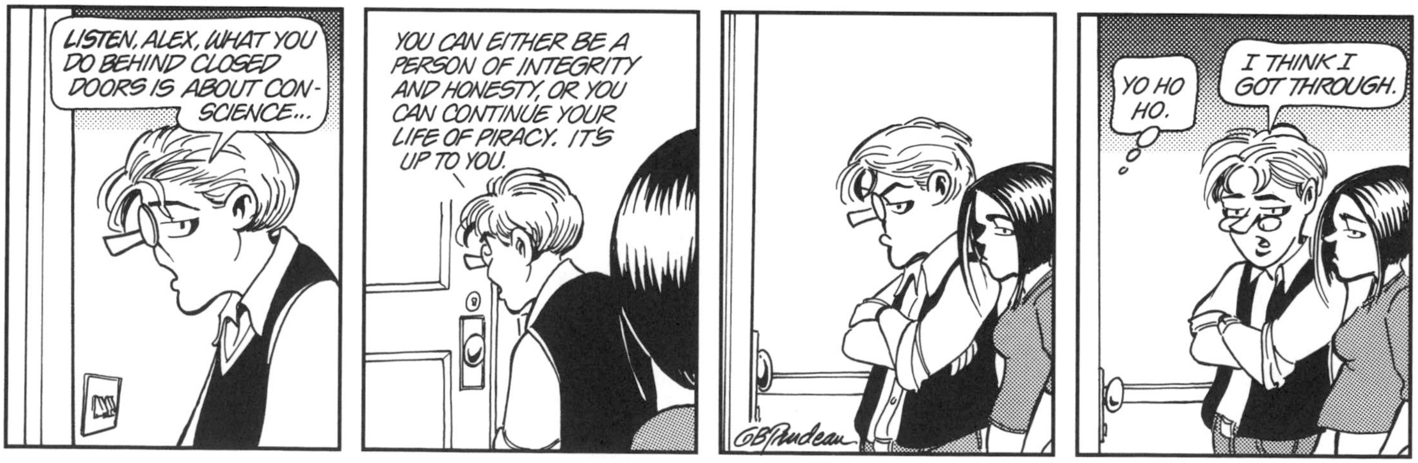
**LISTEN, ALEX,** WHAT YOU DO BEHIND CLOSED DOORS IS ABOUT CONSCIENCE...
YOU CAN EITHER BE A PERSON OF INTEGRITY AND HONESTY, OR YOU CAN CONTINUE YOUR LIFE OF PIRACY. IT'S UP TO YOU.
YO HO HO.
I THINK I GOT THROUGH.

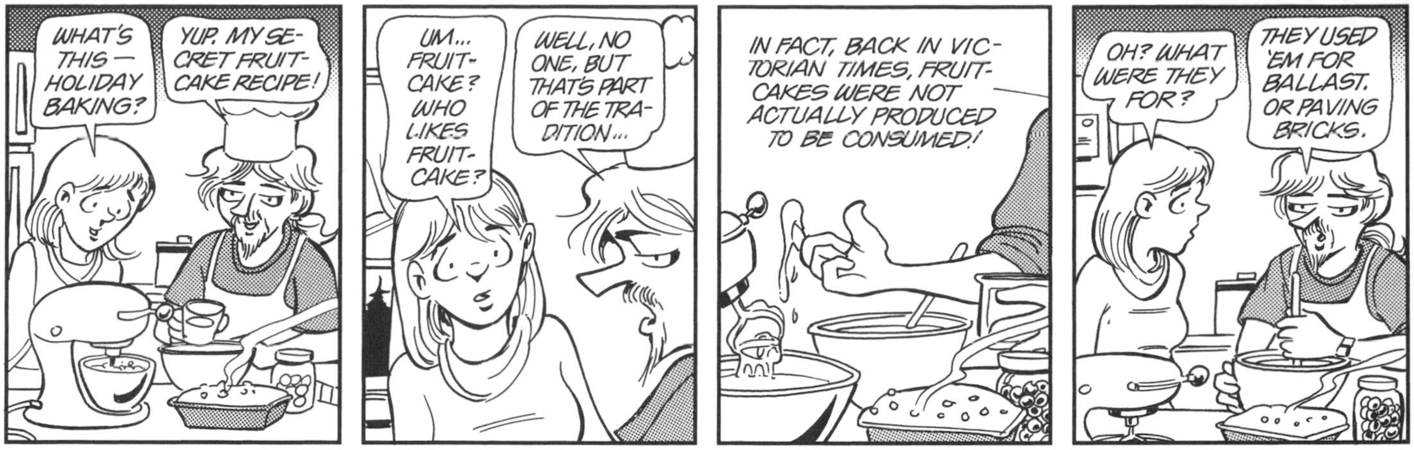
WHAT'S THIS — HOLIDAY BAKING?
YUP. MY SECRET FRUITCAKE RECIPE!
UM... FRUITCAKE? WHO LIKES FRUITCAKE?
WELL, NO ONE, BUT THAT'S PART OF THE TRADITION...
IN FACT, BACK IN VICTORIAN TIMES, FRUITCAKES WERE NOT ACTUALLY PRODUCED TO BE CONSUMED!
OH? WHAT WERE THEY FOR?
THEY USED 'EM FOR BALLAST. OR PAVING BRICKS.

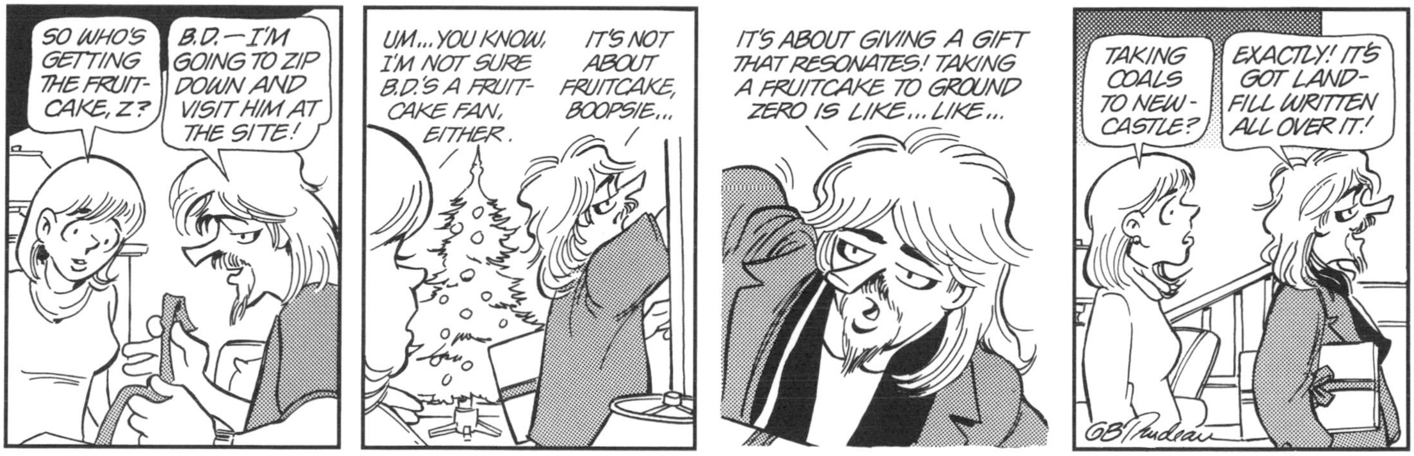
SO WHO'S GETTING THE FRUITCAKE, Z?
B.D.—I'M GOING TO ZIP DOWN AND VISIT HIM AT THE SITE!
UM... YOU KNOW, I'M NOT SURE B.D.'S A FRUITCAKE FAN, EITHER.
IT'S NOT ABOUT FRUITCAKE, BOOPSIE...
IT'S ABOUT GIVING A GIFT THAT RESONATES! TAKING A FRUITCAKE TO GROUND ZERO IS LIKE... LIKE...
TAKING COALS TO NEWCASTLE?
EXACTLY! IT'S GOT LANDFILL WRITTEN ALL OVER IT!

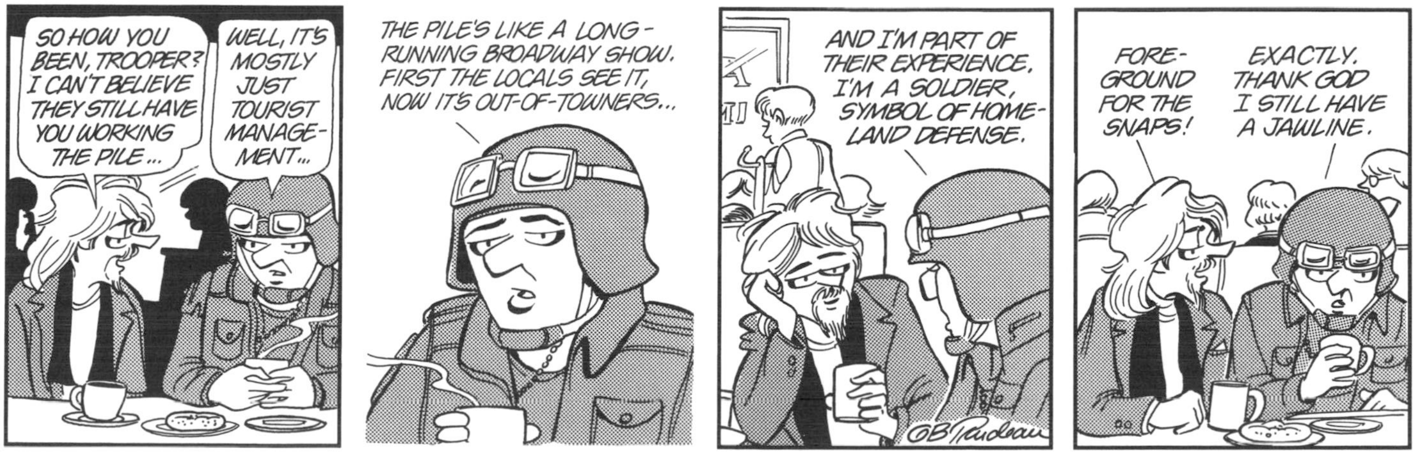
SO HOW YOU BEEN, TROOPER? I CAN'T BELIEVE THEY STILL HAVE YOU WORKING THE PILE...
WELL, IT'S MOSTLY JUST TOURIST MANAGEMENT...
THE PILE'S LIKE A LONG-RUNNING BROADWAY SHOW. FIRST THE LOCALS SEE IT, NOW IT'S OUT-OF-TOWNERS...
AND I'M PART OF THEIR EXPERIENCE. I'M A SOLDIER, SYMBOL OF HOMELAND DEFENSE.
FOREGROUND FOR THE SNAPS!
EXACTLY. THANK GOD I STILL HAVE A JAWLINE.

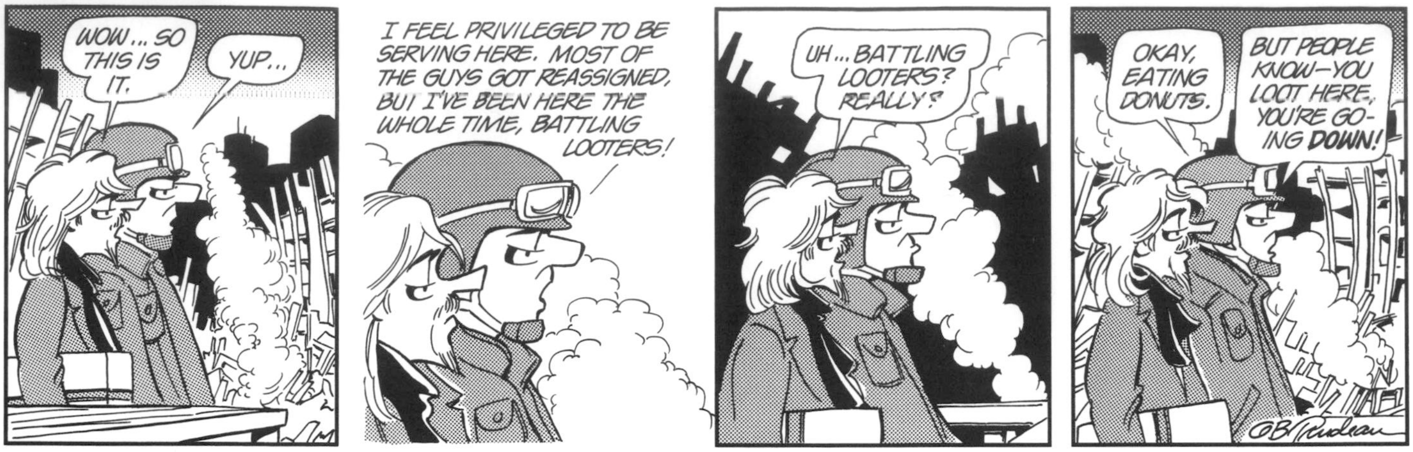
WOW... SO THIS IS IT.
YUP...
I FEEL PRIVILEGED TO BE SERVING HERE. MOST OF THE GUYS GOT REASSIGNED, BUT I'VE BEEN HERE THE WHOLE TIME, BATTLING LOOTERS!
UH... BATTLING LOOTERS? REALLY?
OKAY, EATING DONUTS.
BUT PEOPLE KNOW—YOU LOOT HERE, YOU'RE GOING **DOWN**!

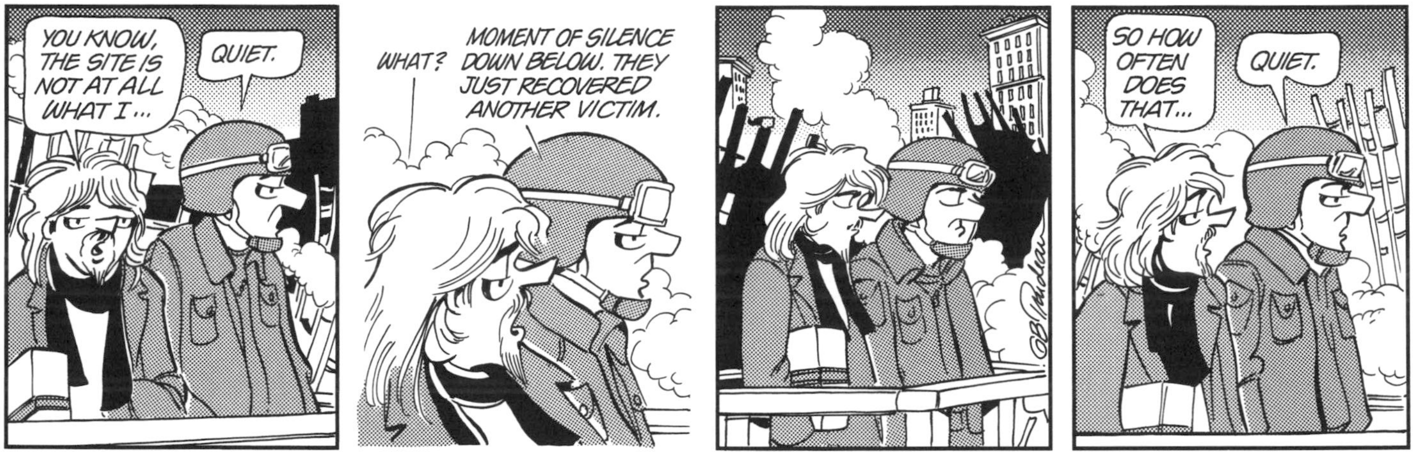
YOU KNOW, THE SITE IS NOT AT ALL WHAT I...
QUIET.
WHAT?
MOMENT OF SILENCE DOWN BELOW. THEY JUST RECOVERED ANOTHER VICTIM.
SO HOW OFTEN DOES THAT...
QUIET.

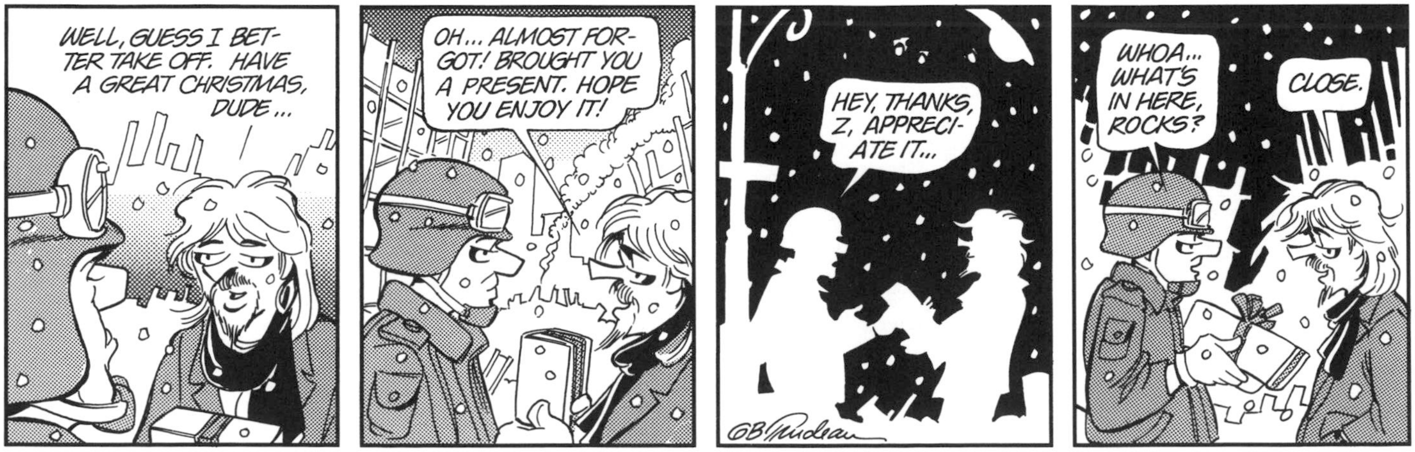
WELL, GUESS I BETTER TAKE OFF. HAVE A GREAT CHRISTMAS, DUDE...
OH... ALMOST FORGOT! BROUGHT YOU A PRESENT. HOPE YOU ENJOY IT!
HEY, THANKS, Z, APPRECIATE IT...
WHOA... WHAT'S IN HERE, ROCKS?
CLOSE.

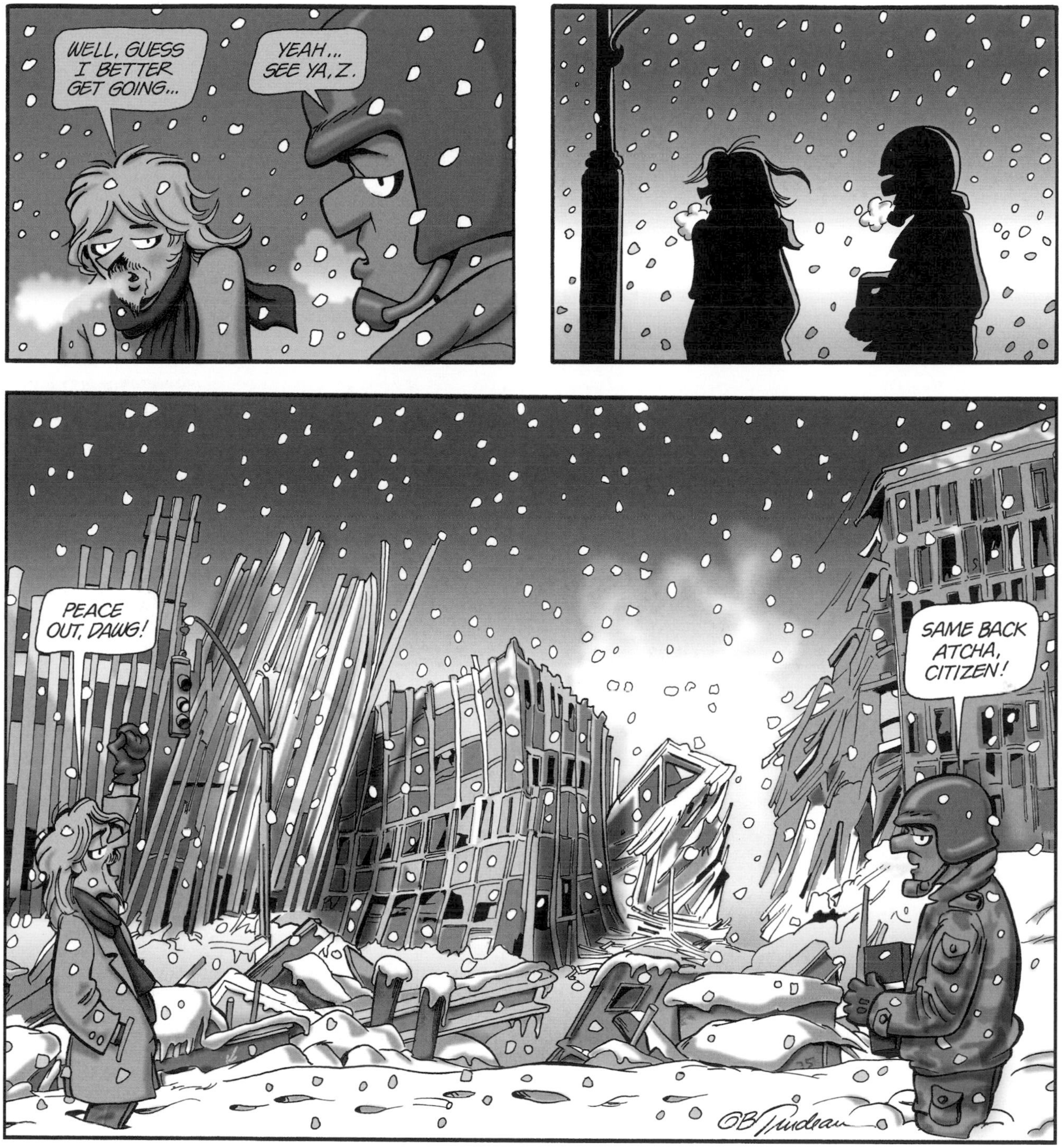
WELL, GUESS I BETTER GET GOING...
YEAH... SEE YA, Z.
PEACE OUT, DAWG!
SAME BACK ATCHA, CITIZEN!
©B Trudeau

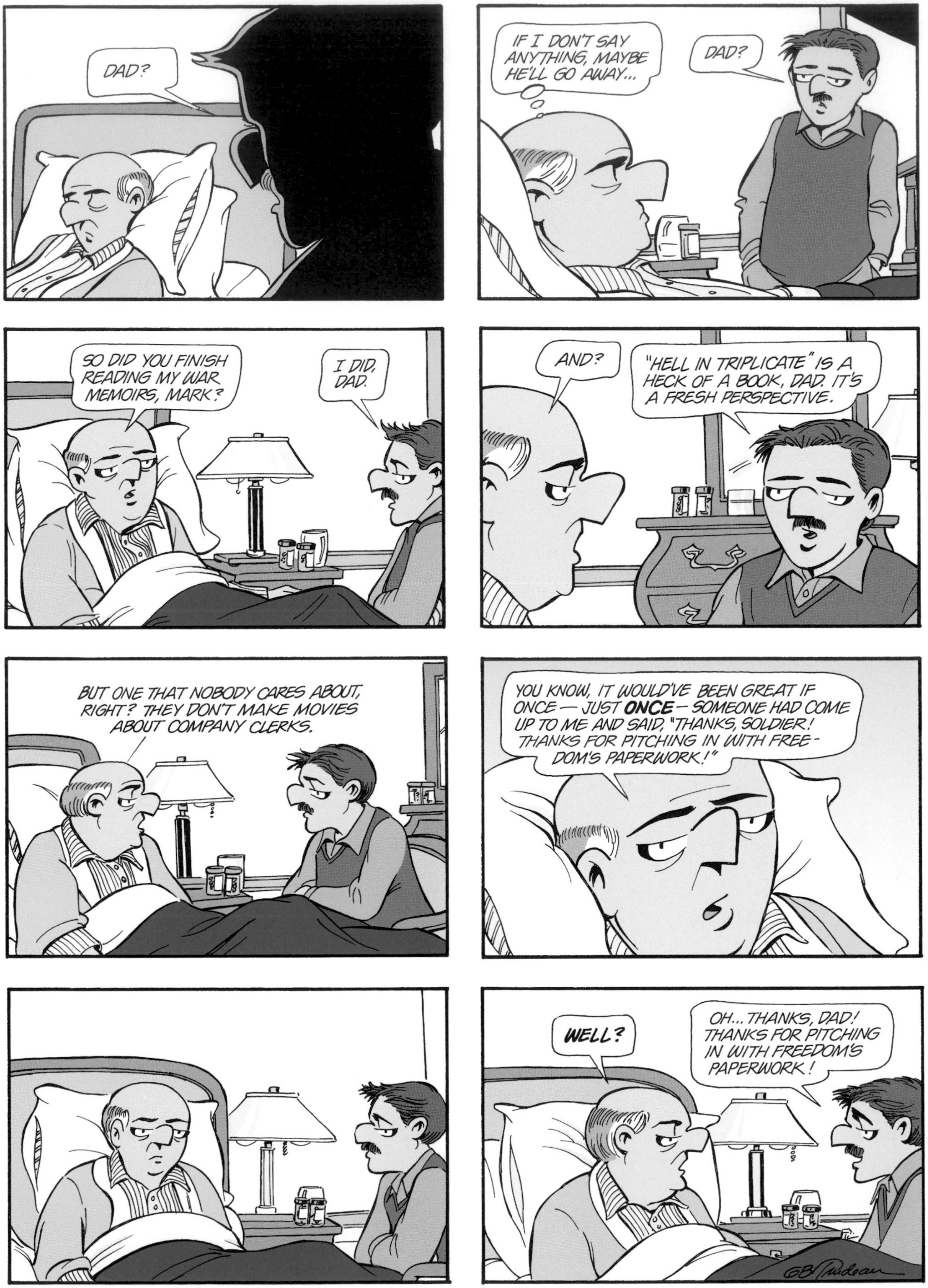
DAD?
IF I DON'T SAY ANYTHING, MAYBE HE'LL GO AWAY...
DAD?
SO DID YOU FINISH READING MY WAR MEMOIRS, MARK?
I DID, DAD.
AND?
"HELL IN TRIPLICATE" IS A HECK OF A BOOK, DAD. IT'S A FRESH PERSPECTIVE.
BUT ONE THAT NOBODY CARES ABOUT, RIGHT? THEY DON'T MAKE MOVIES ABOUT COMPANY CLERKS.
YOU KNOW, IT WOULD'VE BEEN GREAT IF ONCE — JUST **ONCE** — SOMEONE HAD COME UP TO ME AND SAID, "THANKS, SOLDIER! THANKS FOR PITCHING IN WITH FREE-DOM'S PAPERWORK!"
**WELL?**
OH... THANKS, DAD! THANKS FOR PITCHING IN WITH FREEDOM'S PAPERWORK!

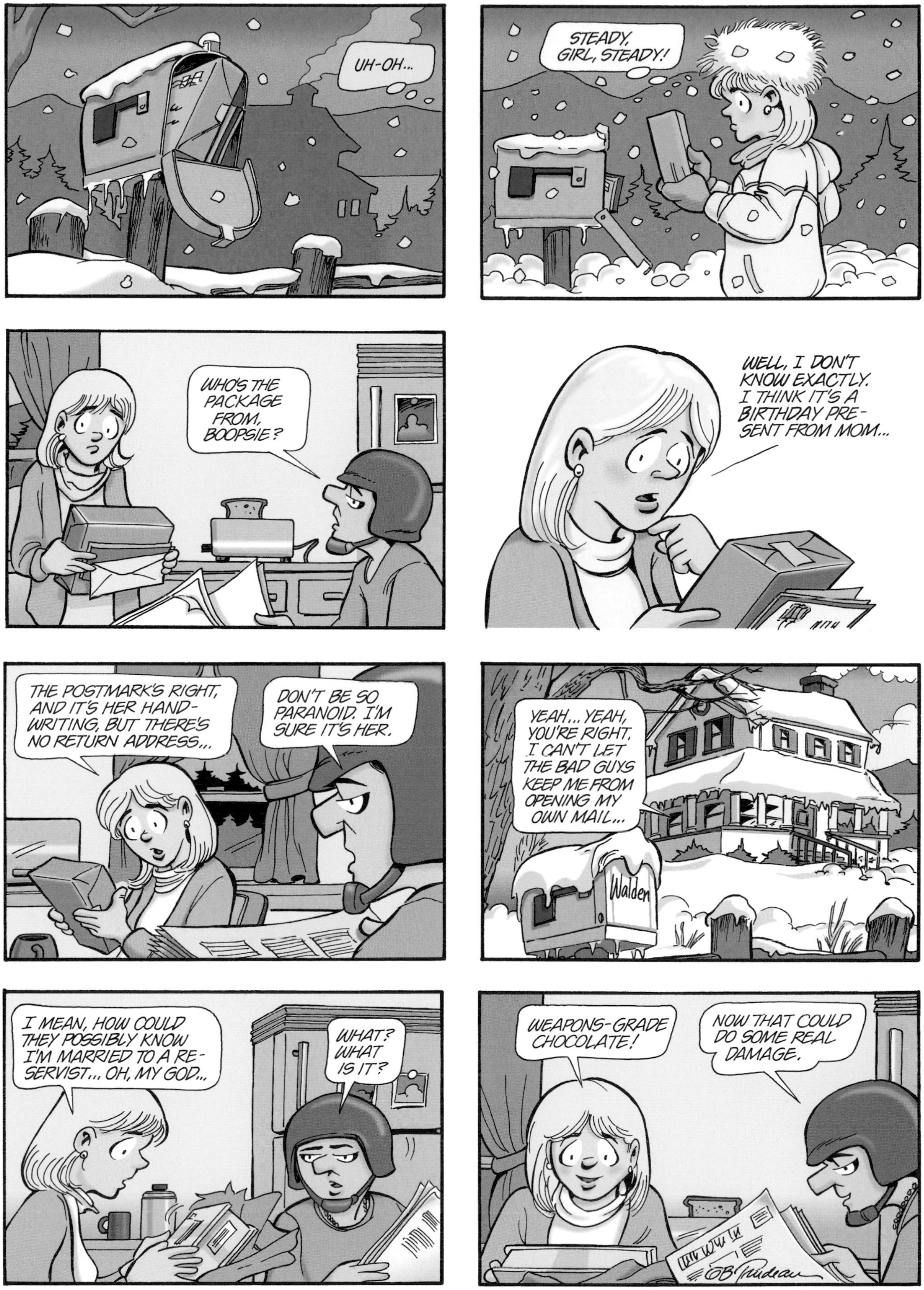
UH-OH...
STEADY, GIRL, STEADY!
WHO'S THE PACKAGE FROM, BOOPSIE?
WELL, I DON'T KNOW EXACTLY. I THINK IT'S A BIRTHDAY PRESENT FROM MOM...
THE POSTMARK'S RIGHT, AND IT'S HER HANDWRITING, BUT THERE'S NO RETURN ADDRESS...
DON'T BE SO PARANOID. I'M SURE IT'S HER.
YEAH... YEAH, YOU'RE RIGHT. I CAN'T LET THE BAD GUYS KEEP ME FROM OPENING MY OWN MAIL...
Walden
I MEAN, HOW COULD THEY POSSIBLY KNOW I'M MARRIED TO A RESERVIST... OH, MY GOD...
WHAT? WHAT IS IT?
WEAPONS-GRADE CHOCOLATE!
NOW THAT COULD DO SOME REAL DAMAGE.
GBTrudeau

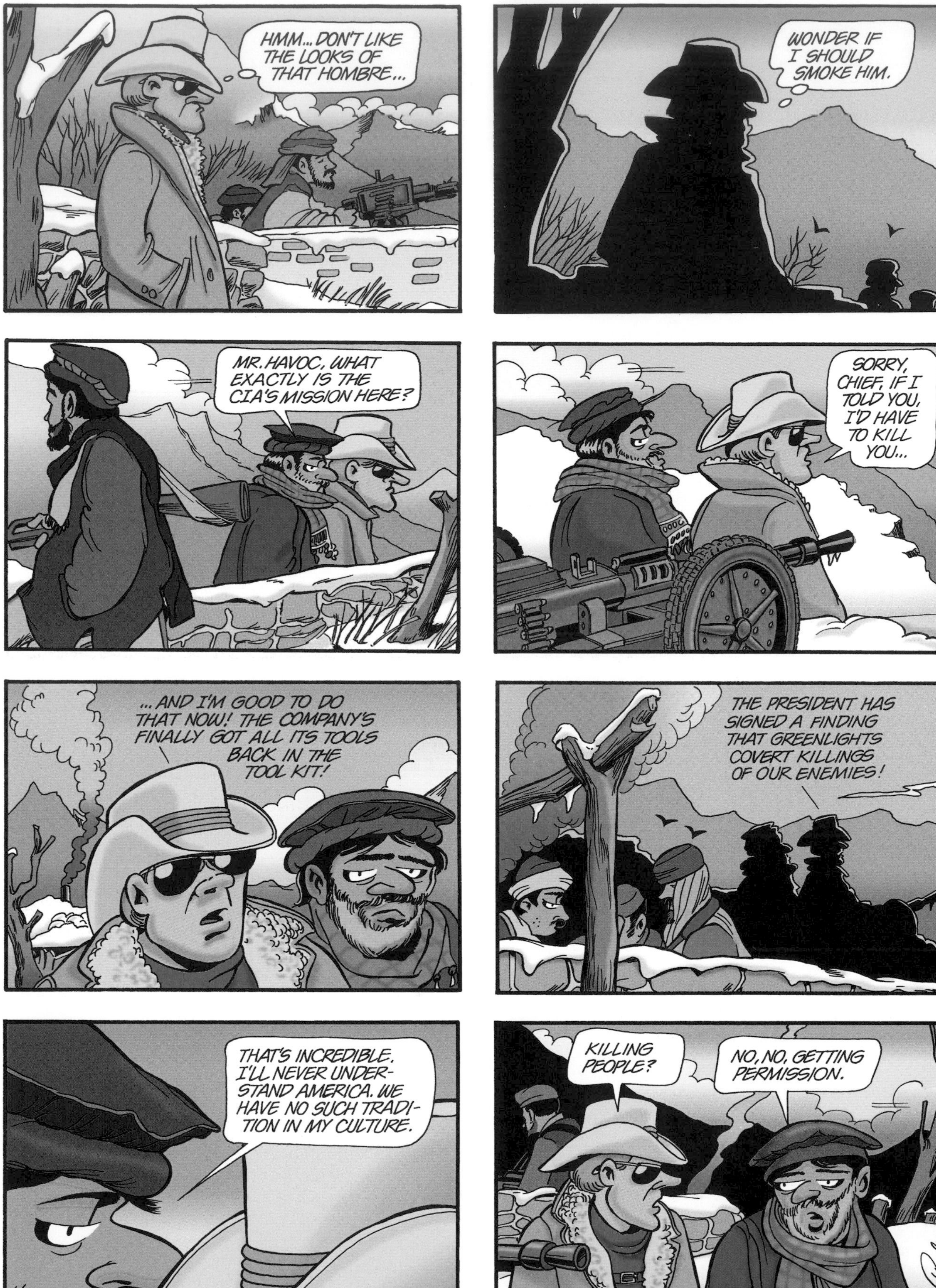
HMM... DON'T LIKE THE LOOKS OF THAT HOMBRE...
WONDER IF I SHOULD SMOKE HIM.
MR. HAVOC, WHAT EXACTLY IS THE CIA'S MISSION HERE?
SORRY, CHIEF, IF I TOLD YOU, I'D HAVE TO KILL YOU...
...AND I'M GOOD TO DO THAT NOW! THE COMPANY'S FINALLY GOT ALL ITS TOOLS BACK IN THE TOOL KIT!
THE PRESIDENT HAS SIGNED A FINDING THAT GREENLIGHTS COVERT KILLINGS OF OUR ENEMIES!
THAT'S INCREDIBLE. I'LL NEVER UNDERSTAND AMERICA. WE HAVE NO SUCH TRADITION IN MY CULTURE.
KILLING PEOPLE?
NO, NO, GETTING PERMISSION.

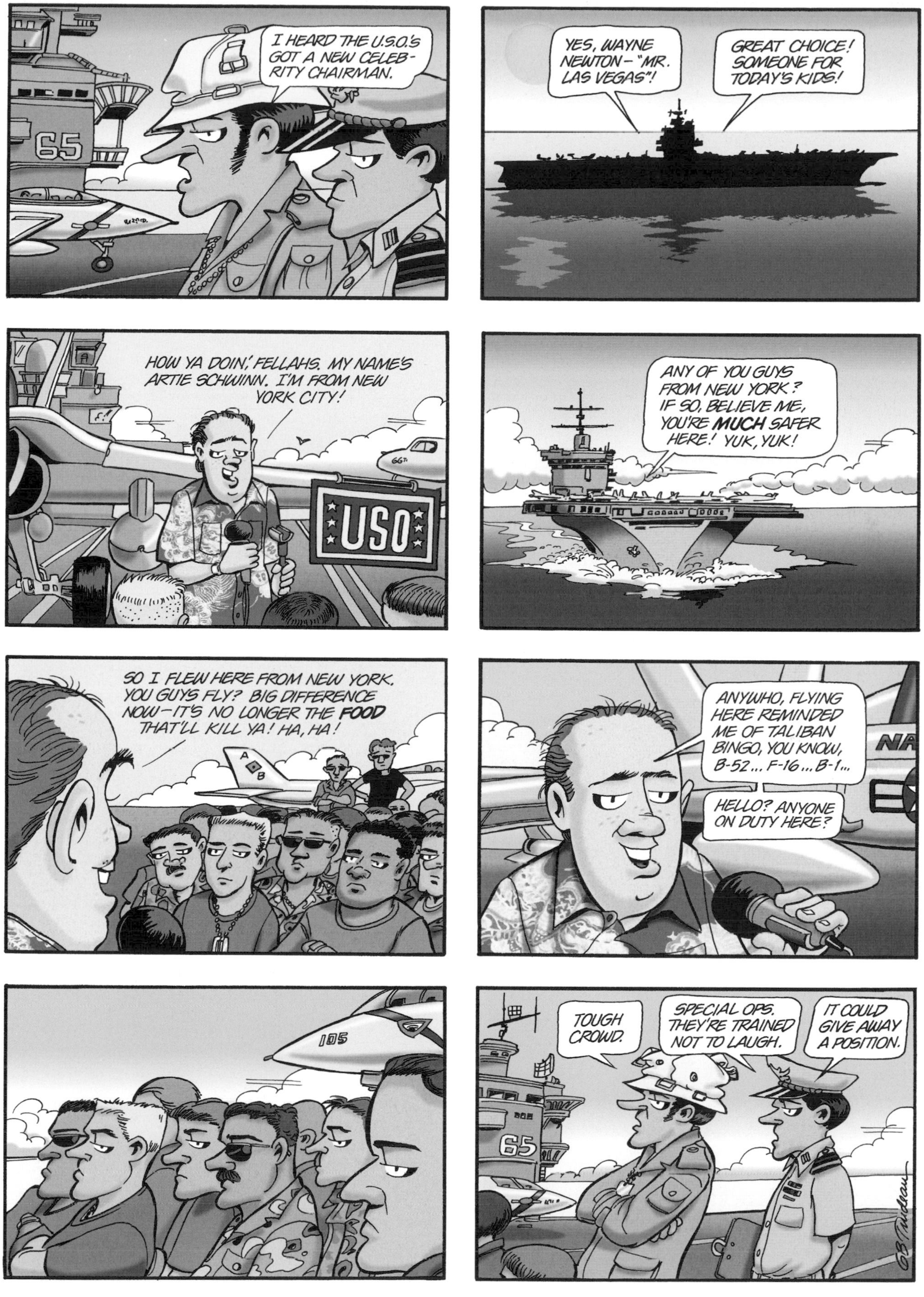
I HEARD THE U.S.O.'s GOT A NEW CELEBRITY CHAIRMAN.
YES, WAYNE NEWTON – "MR. LAS VEGAS"!
GREAT CHOICE! SOMEONE FOR TODAY'S KIDS!
HOW YA DOIN,' FELLAHS. MY NAME'S ARTIE SCHWINN. I'M FROM NEW YORK CITY!
USO
ANY OF YOU GUYS FROM NEW YORK? IF SO, BELIEVE ME, YOU'RE **MUCH** SAFER HERE! YUK, YUK!
SO I FLEW HERE FROM NEW YORK. YOU GUYS FLY? BIG DIFFERENCE NOW – IT'S NO LONGER THE **FOOD** THAT'LL KILL YA! HA, HA!
ANYWHO, FLYING HERE REMINDED ME OF TALIBAN BINGO, YOU KNOW, B-52... F-16... B-1...
HELLO? ANYONE ON DUTY HERE?
TOUGH CROWD.
SPECIAL OPS. THEY'RE TRAINED NOT TO LAUGH.
IT COULD GIVE AWAY A POSITION.
GB Trudeau

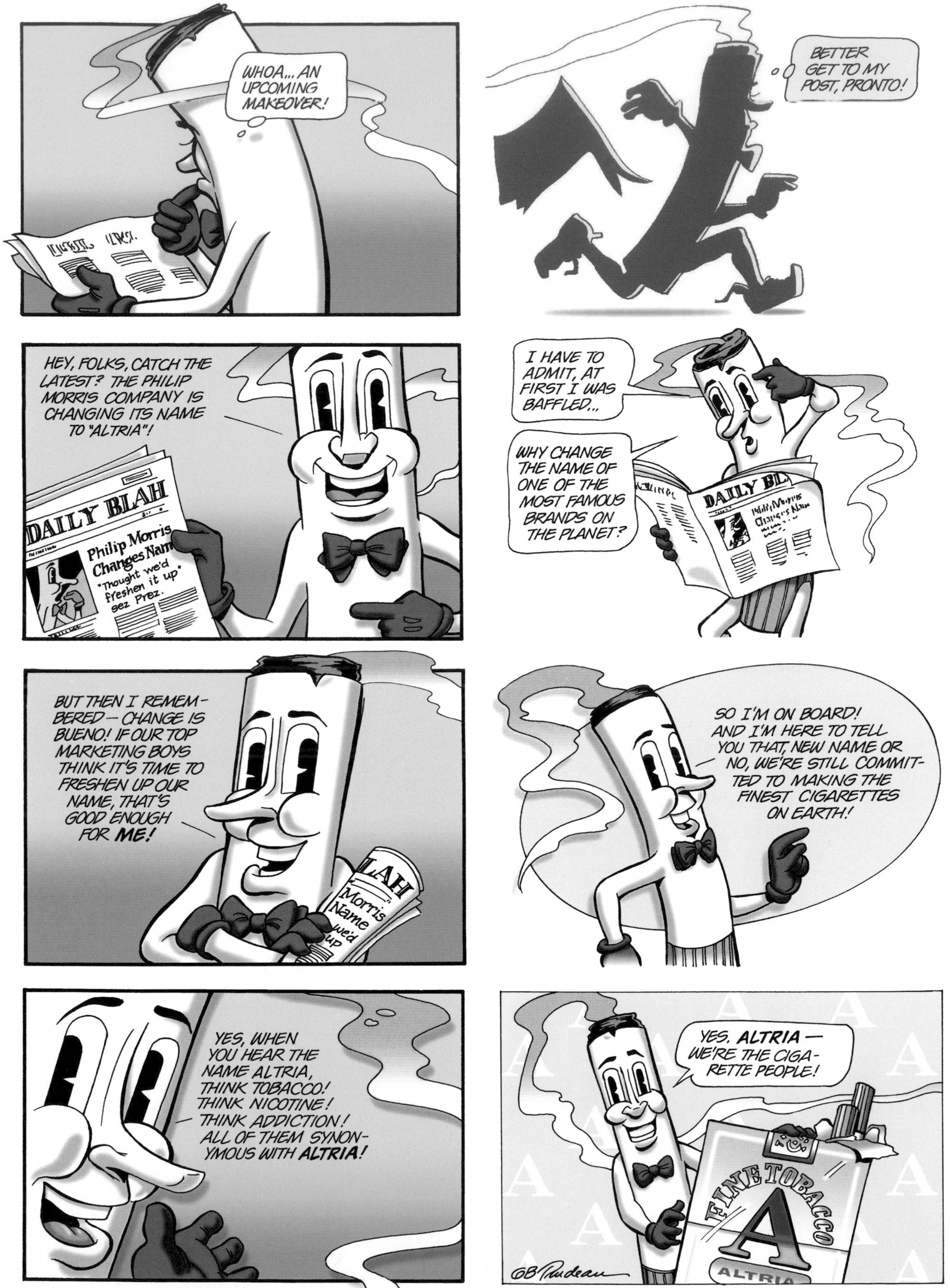
WHOA... AN UPCOMING MAKEOVER!
BETTER GET TO MY POST, PRONTO!
HEY, FOLKS, CATCH THE LATEST? THE PHILIP MORRIS COMPANY IS CHANGING ITS NAME TO "ALTRIA"!
DAILY BLAH
Philip Morris Changes Nam
"Thought we'd freshen it up" sez Prez.
I HAVE TO ADMIT, AT FIRST I WAS BAFFLED...
WHY CHANGE THE NAME OF ONE OF THE MOST FAMOUS BRANDS ON THE PLANET?
DAILY BL
BUT THEN I REMEMBERED — CHANGE IS BUENO! IF OUR TOP MARKETING BOYS THINK IT'S TIME TO FRESHEN UP OUR NAME, THAT'S GOOD ENOUGH FOR **ME!**
SO I'M ON BOARD! AND I'M HERE TO TELL YOU THAT, NEW NAME OR NO, WE'RE STILL COMMITTED TO MAKING THE FINEST CIGARETTES ON EARTH!
YES, WHEN YOU HEAR THE NAME ALTRIA, THINK TOBACCO! THINK NICOTINE! THINK ADDICTION! ALL OF THEM SYNONYMOUS WITH **ALTRIA!**
YES. **ALTRIA** — WE'RE THE CIGARETTE PEOPLE!
FINE TOBACCO
A
ALTRIA

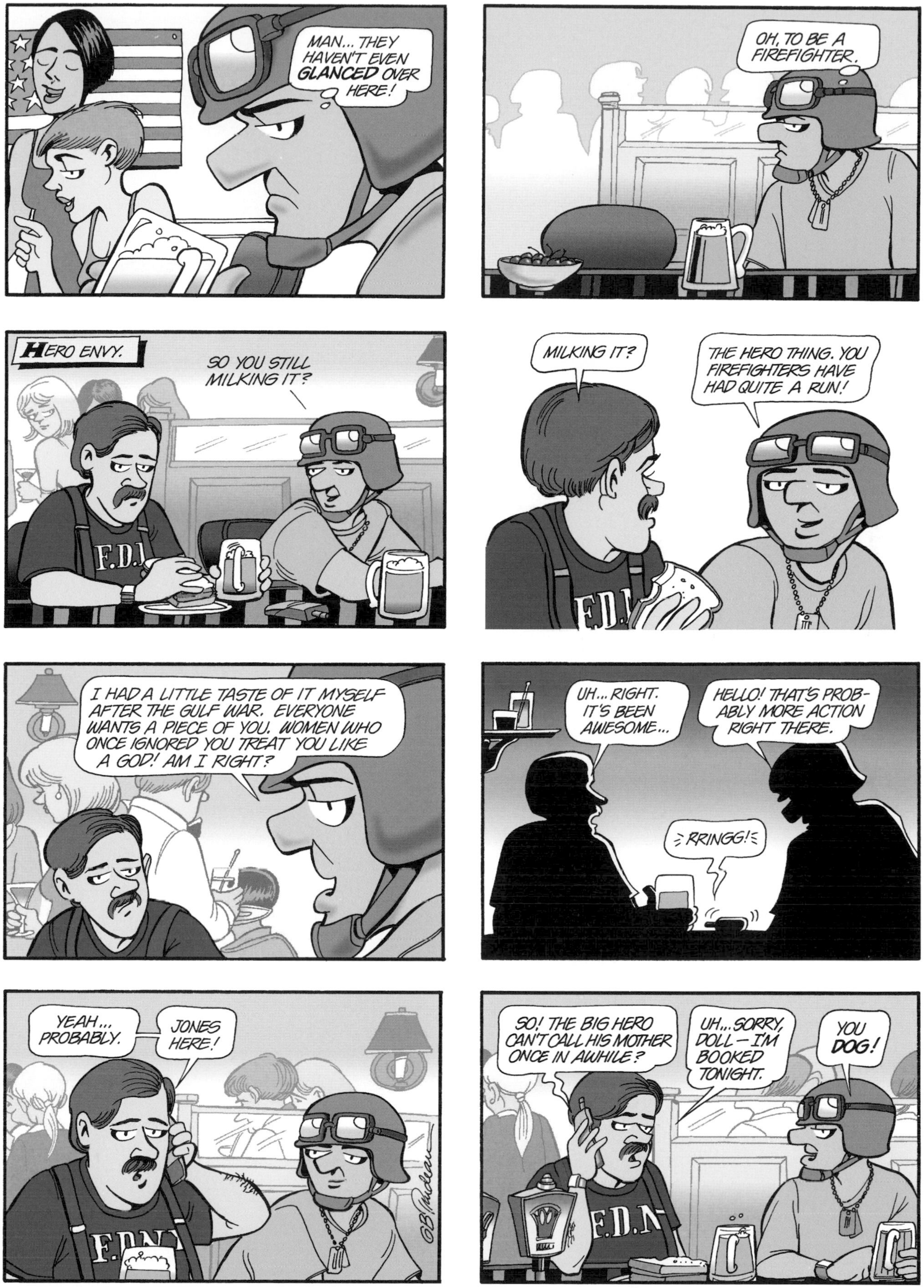
MAN... THEY HAVEN'T EVEN GLANCED OVER HERE!
OH, TO BE A FIREFIGHTER.
HERO ENVY.
SO YOU STILL MILKING IT?
MILKING IT?
THE HERO THING. YOU FIREFIGHTERS HAVE HAD QUITE A RUN!
F.D.N.
I HAD A LITTLE TASTE OF IT MYSELF AFTER THE GULF WAR. EVERYONE WANTS A PIECE OF YOU. WOMEN WHO ONCE IGNORED YOU TREAT YOU LIKE A GOD! AM I RIGHT?
UH... RIGHT. IT'S BEEN AWESOME...
HELLO! THAT'S PROBABLY MORE ACTION RIGHT THERE.
RRINGG!
YEAH... PROBABLY.
JONES HERE!
SO! THE BIG HERO CAN'T CALL HIS MOTHER ONCE IN AWHILE?
UH... SORRY, DOLL — I'M BOOKED TONIGHT.
YOU DOG!

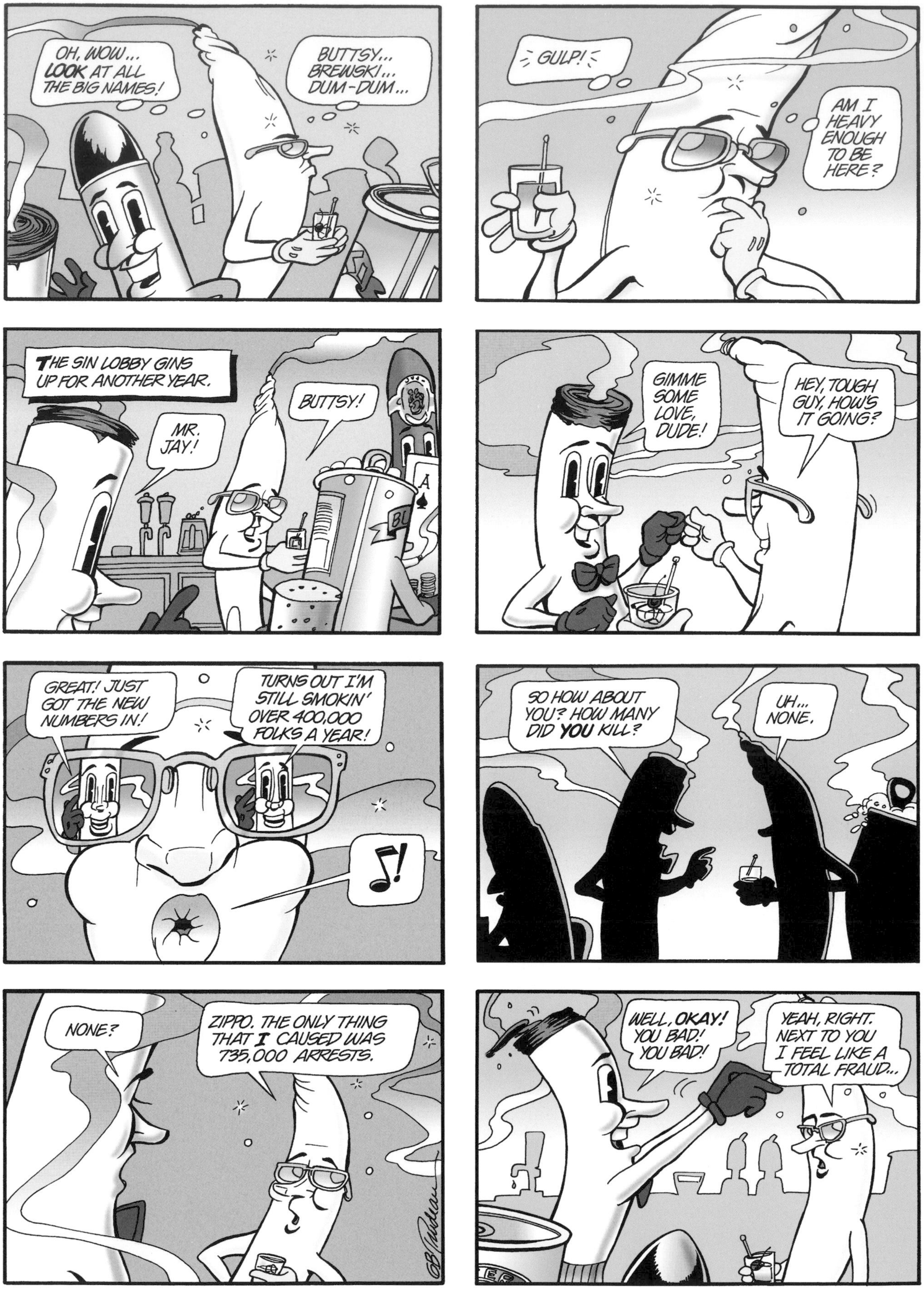

OH, WOW... LOOK AT ALL THE BIG NAMES!
BUTTSY... BREWSKI... DUM-DUM...
GULP!
AM I HEAVY ENOUGH TO BE HERE?
THE SIN LOBBY GINS UP FOR ANOTHER YEAR.
MR. JAY!
BUTTSY!
GIMME SOME LOVE, DUDE!
HEY, TOUGH GUY, HOW'S IT GOING?
GREAT! JUST GOT THE NEW NUMBERS IN!
TURNS OUT I'M STILL SMOKIN' OVER 400,000 FOLKS A YEAR!
SO HOW ABOUT YOU? HOW MANY DID YOU KILL?
UH... NONE.
NONE?
ZIPPO. THE ONLY THING THAT I CAUSED WAS 735,000 ARRESTS.
WELL, OKAY! YOU BAD! YOU BAD!
YEAH, RIGHT. NEXT TO YOU I FEEL LIKE A TOTAL FRAUD...

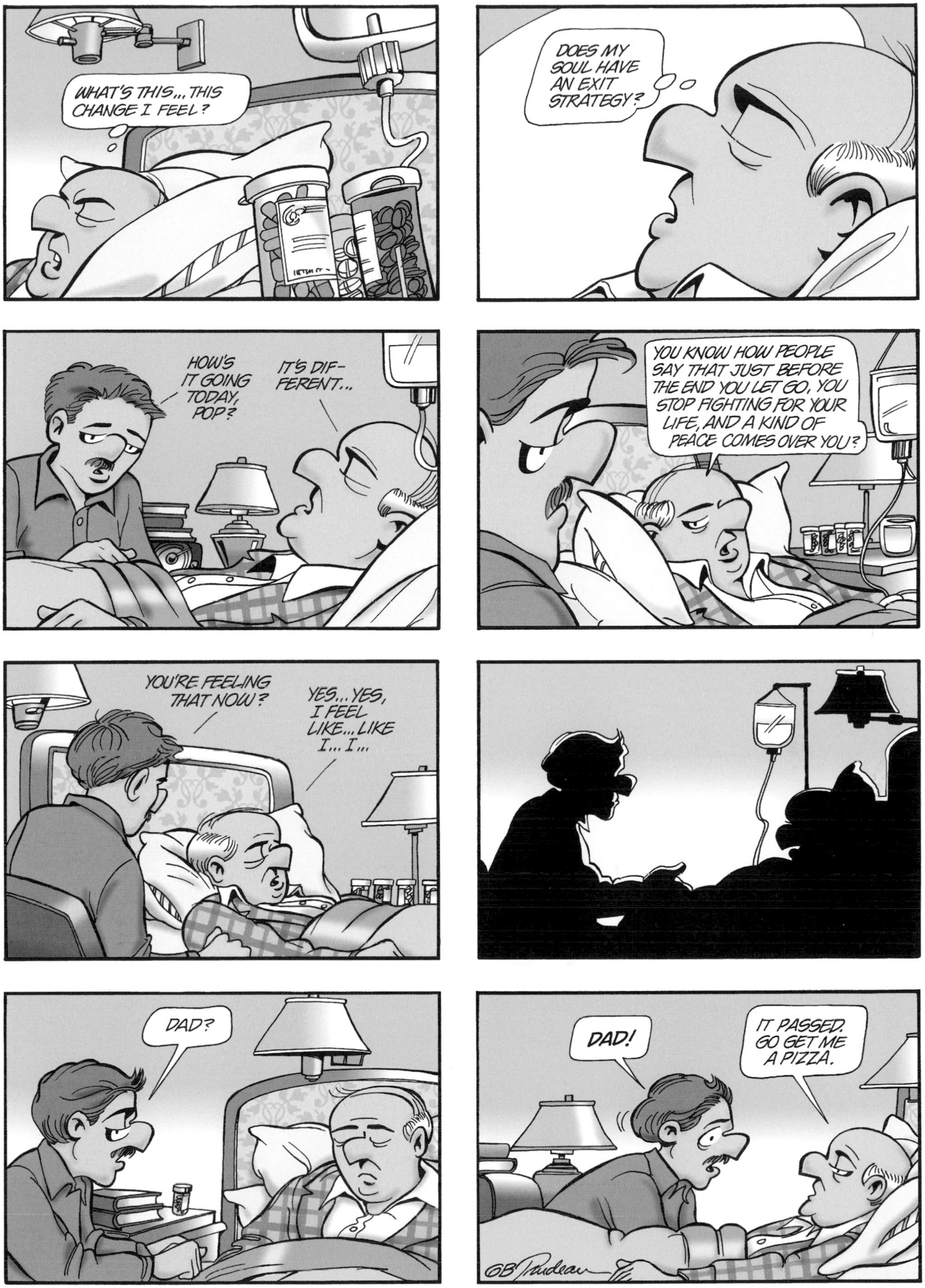
WHAT'S THIS... THIS CHANGE I FEEL?
DOES MY SOUL HAVE AN EXIT STRATEGY?
HOW'S IT GOING TODAY, POP?
IT'S DIF-FERENT...
YOU KNOW HOW PEOPLE SAY THAT JUST BEFORE THE END YOU LET GO, YOU STOP FIGHTING FOR YOUR LIFE, AND A KIND OF PEACE COMES OVER YOU?
YOU'RE FEELING THAT NOW?
YES... YES, I FEEL LIKE... LIKE I... I...
DAD?
DAD!
IT PASSED. GO GET ME A PIZZA.
GB Trudeau

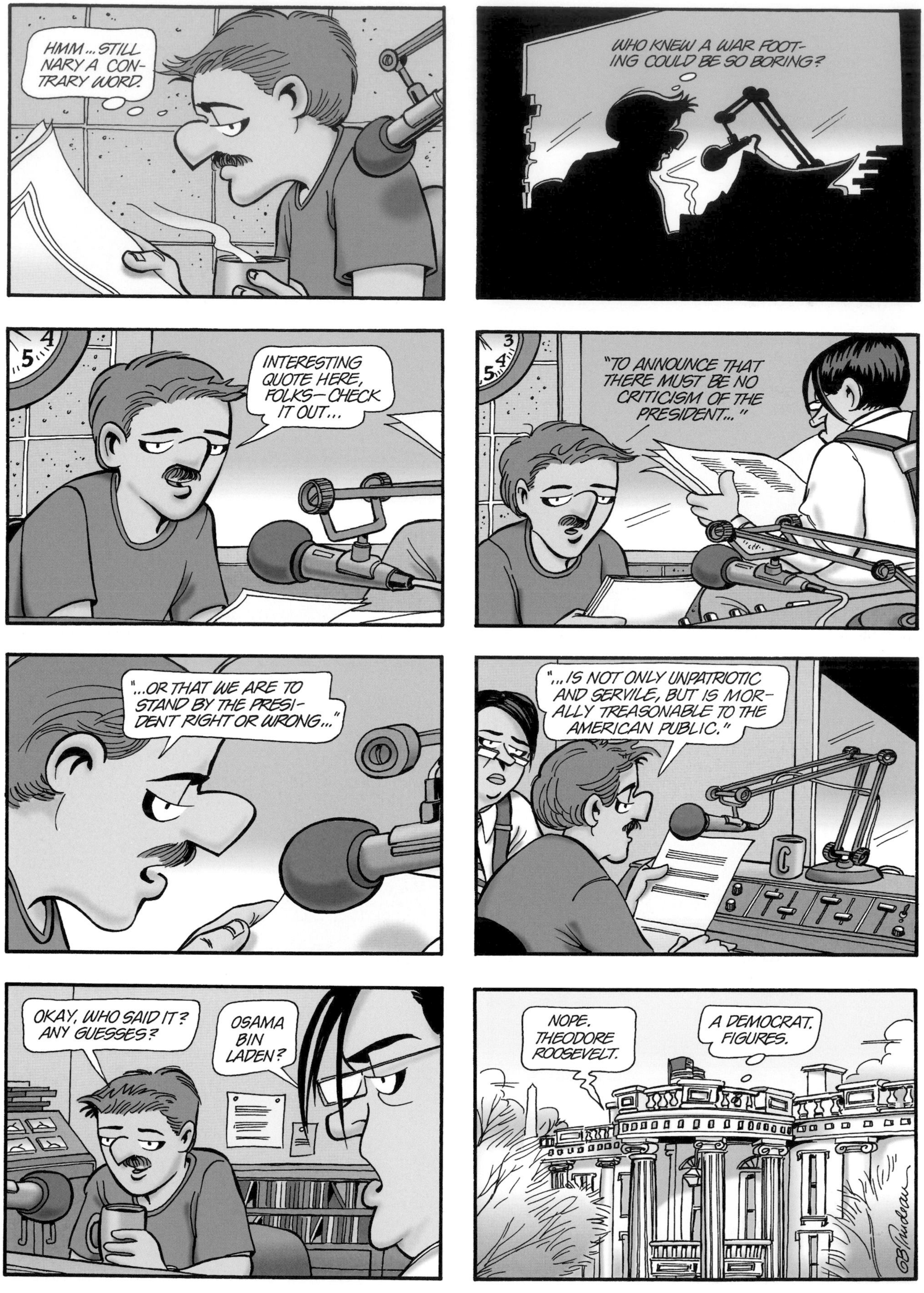
HMM... STILL NARY A CONTRARY WORD.
WHO KNEW A WAR FOOTING COULD BE SO BORING?
INTERESTING QUOTE HERE, FOLKS—CHECK IT OUT...
"TO ANNOUNCE THAT THERE MUST BE NO CRITICISM OF THE PRESIDENT..."
"...OR THAT WE ARE TO STAND BY THE PRESIDENT RIGHT OR WRONG..."
"...IS NOT ONLY UNPATRIOTIC AND SERVILE, BUT IS MORALLY TREASONABLE TO THE AMERICAN PUBLIC."
OKAY, WHO SAID IT? ANY GUESSES?
OSAMA BIN LADEN?
NOPE. THEODORE ROOSEVELT.
A DEMOCRAT. FIGURES.
GBTrudeau

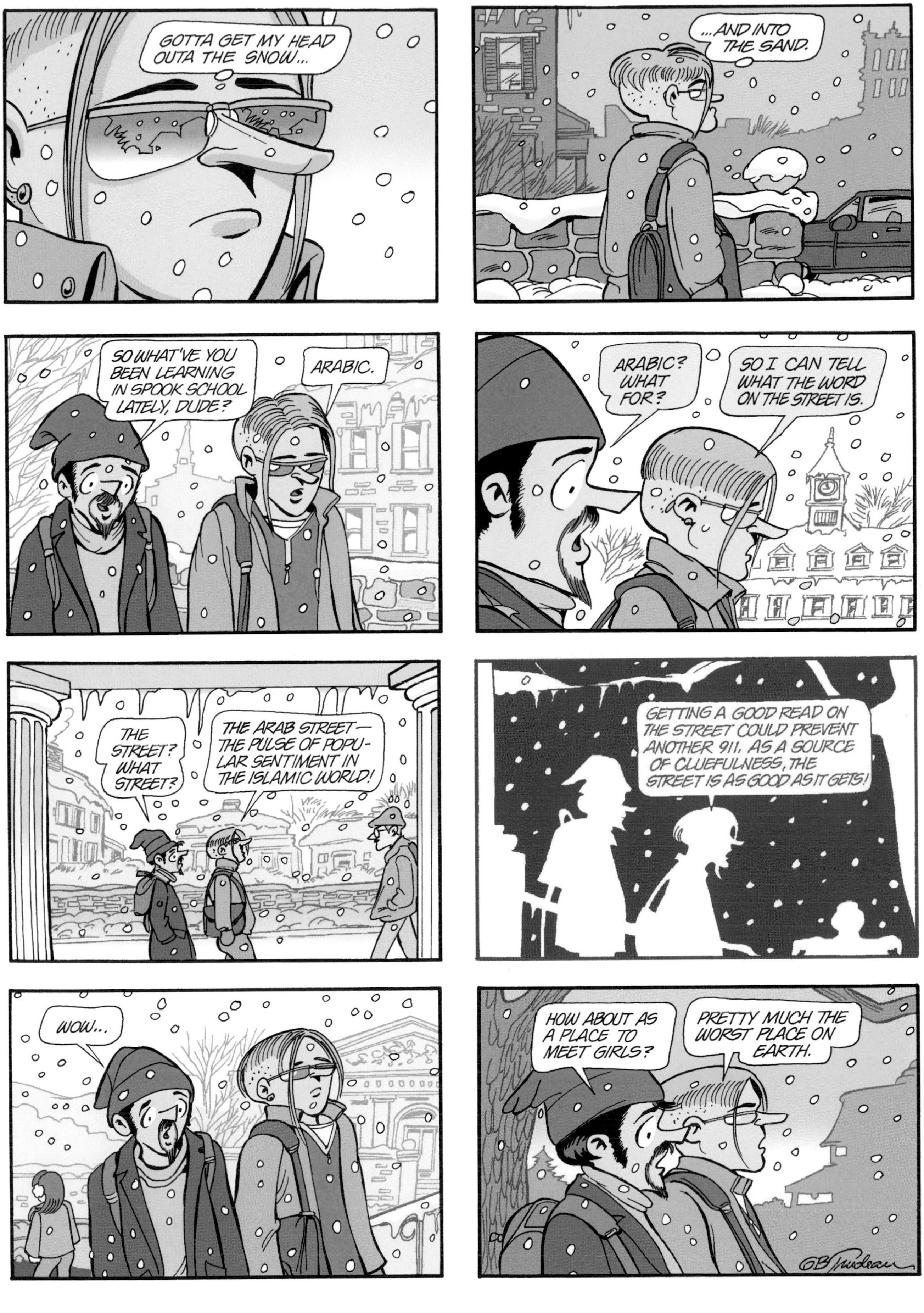
GOTTA GET MY HEAD OUTA THE SNOW...
...AND INTO THE SAND.
SO WHAT'VE YOU BEEN LEARNING IN SPOOK SCHOOL LATELY, DUDE?
ARABIC.
ARABIC? WHAT FOR?
SO I CAN TELL WHAT THE WORD ON THE STREET IS.
THE STREET? WHAT STREET?
THE ARAB STREET— THE PULSE OF POPULAR SENTIMENT IN THE ISLAMIC WORLD!
GETTING A GOOD READ ON THE STREET COULD PREVENT ANOTHER 911. AS A SOURCE OF CLUEFULNESS, THE STREET IS AS GOOD AS IT GETS!
WOW...
HOW ABOUT AS A PLACE TO MEET GIRLS?
PRETTY MUCH THE WORST PLACE ON EARTH.
GB Trudeau

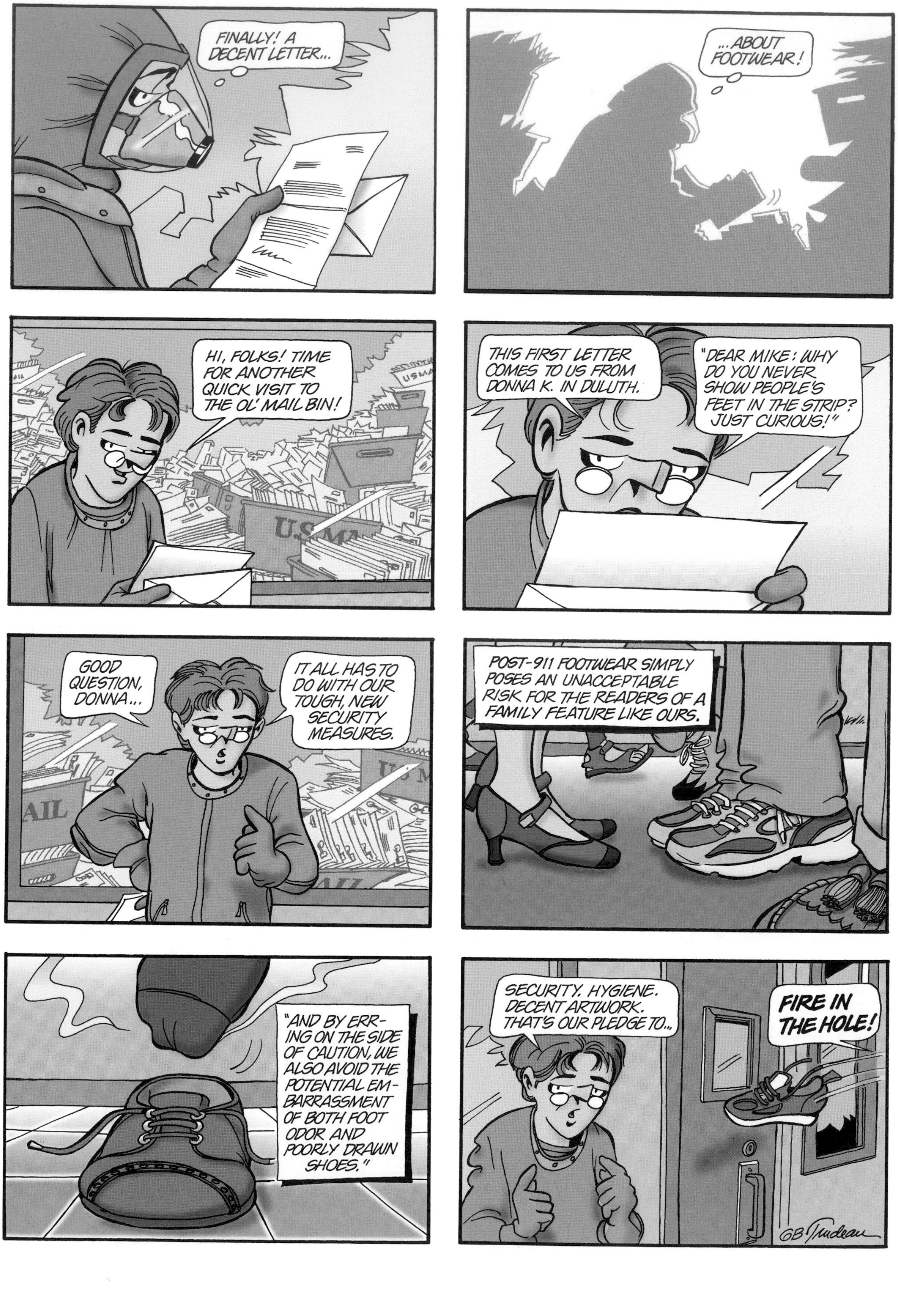
FINALLY! A DECENT LETTER...
...ABOUT FOOTWEAR!
HI, FOLKS! TIME FOR ANOTHER QUICK VISIT TO THE OL' MAIL BIN!
THIS FIRST LETTER COMES TO US FROM DONNA K. IN DULUTH.
"DEAR MIKE: WHY DO YOU NEVER SHOW PEOPLE'S FEET IN THE STRIP? JUST CURIOUS!"
GOOD QUESTION, DONNA...
IT ALL HAS TO DO WITH OUR TOUGH, NEW SECURITY MEASURES.
POST-911 FOOTWEAR SIMPLY POSES AN UNACCEPTABLE RISK FOR THE READERS OF A FAMILY FEATURE LIKE OURS.
"AND BY ERRING ON THE SIDE OF CAUTION, WE ALSO AVOID THE POTENTIAL EMBARRASSMENT OF BOTH FOOT ODOR AND POORLY DRAWN SHOES."
SECURITY. HYGIENE. DECENT ARTWORK. THAT'S OUR PLEDGE TO...
FIRE IN THE HOLE!
GB Trudeau

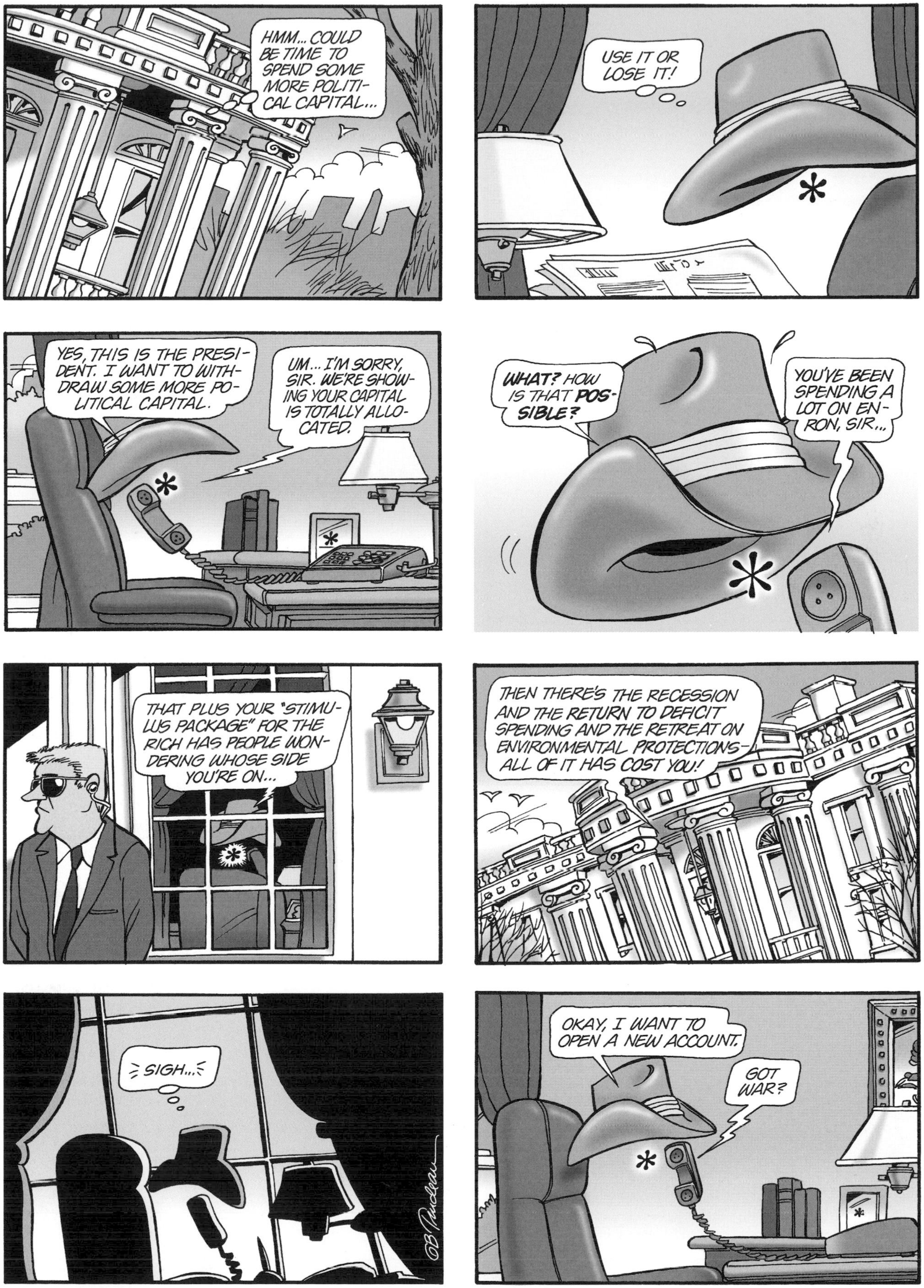
HMM... COULD BE TIME TO SPEND SOME MORE POLITI-CAL CAPITAL...
USE IT OR LOSE IT!
YES, THIS IS THE PRESI-DENT. I WANT TO WITH-DRAW SOME MORE PO-LITICAL CAPITAL.
UM... I'M SORRY, SIR. WE'RE SHOW-ING YOUR CAPITAL IS TOTALLY ALLO-CATED.
WHAT? HOW IS THAT POS-SIBLE?
YOU'VE BEEN SPENDING A LOT ON EN-RON, SIR...
THAT PLUS YOUR "STIMU-LUS PACKAGE" FOR THE RICH HAS PEOPLE WON-DERING WHOSE SIDE YOU'RE ON...
THEN THERE'S THE RECESSION AND THE RETURN TO DEFICIT SPENDING AND THE RETREAT ON ENVIRONMENTAL PROTECTIONS-ALL OF IT HAS COST YOU!
SIGH...
OKAY, I WANT TO OPEN A NEW ACCOUNT.
GOT WAR?

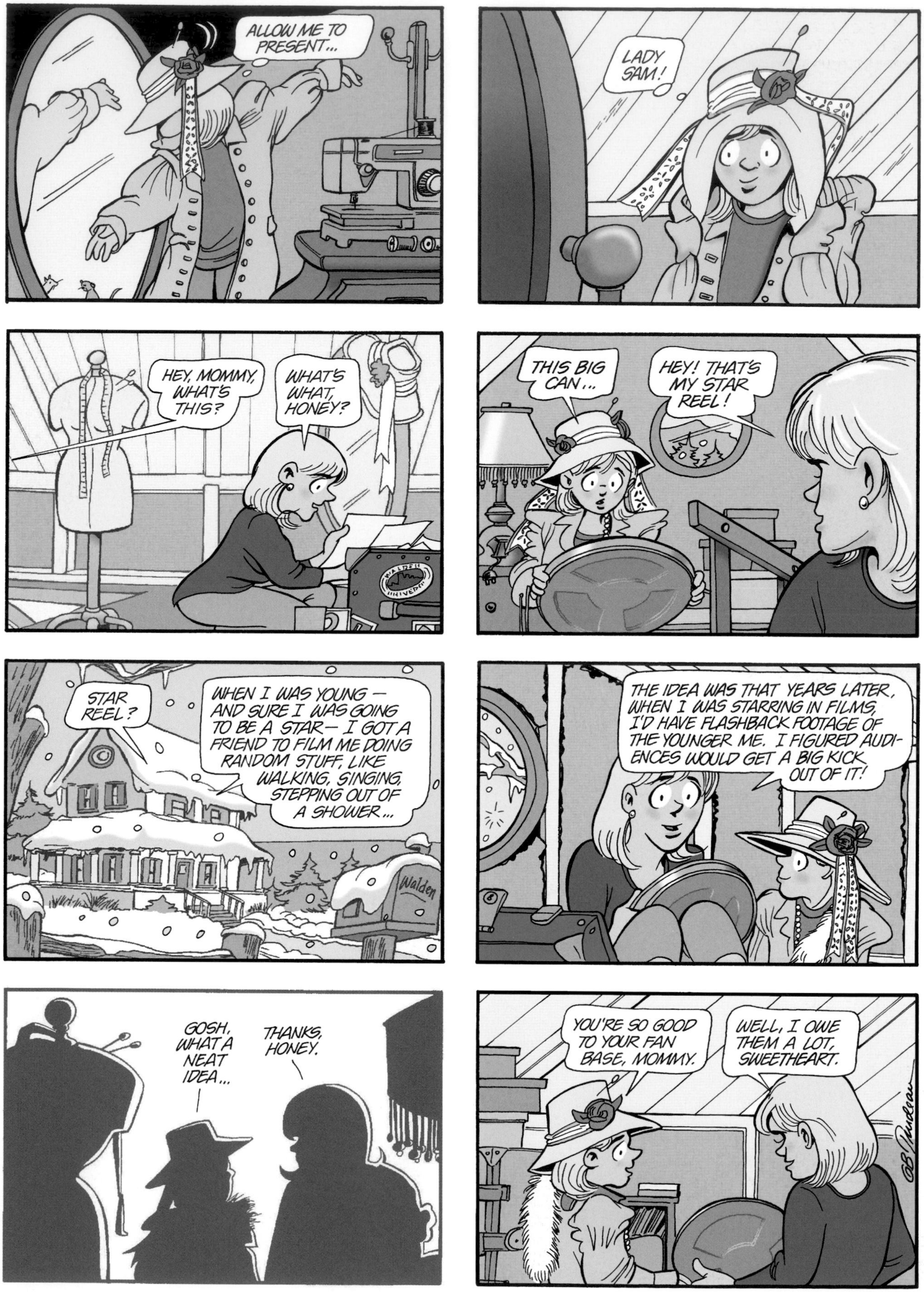
ALLOW ME TO PRESENT...
LADY SAM!
HEY, MOMMY, WHAT'S THIS?
WHAT'S WHAT, HONEY?
THIS BIG CAN...
HEY! THAT'S MY STAR REEL!
STAR REEL?
WHEN I WAS YOUNG — AND SURE I WAS GOING TO BE A STAR— I GOT A FRIEND TO FILM ME DOING RANDOM STUFF, LIKE WALKING, SINGING, STEPPING OUT OF A SHOWER...
Walden
THE IDEA WAS THAT YEARS LATER, WHEN I WAS STARRING IN FILMS, I'D HAVE FLASHBACK FOOTAGE OF THE YOUNGER ME. I FIGURED AUDIENCES WOULD GET A BIG KICK OUT OF IT!
GOSH, WHAT A NEAT IDEA...
THANKS, HONEY.
YOU'RE SO GOOD TO YOUR FAN BASE, MOMMY.
WELL, I OWE THEM A LOT, SWEETHEART.
GBTrudeau

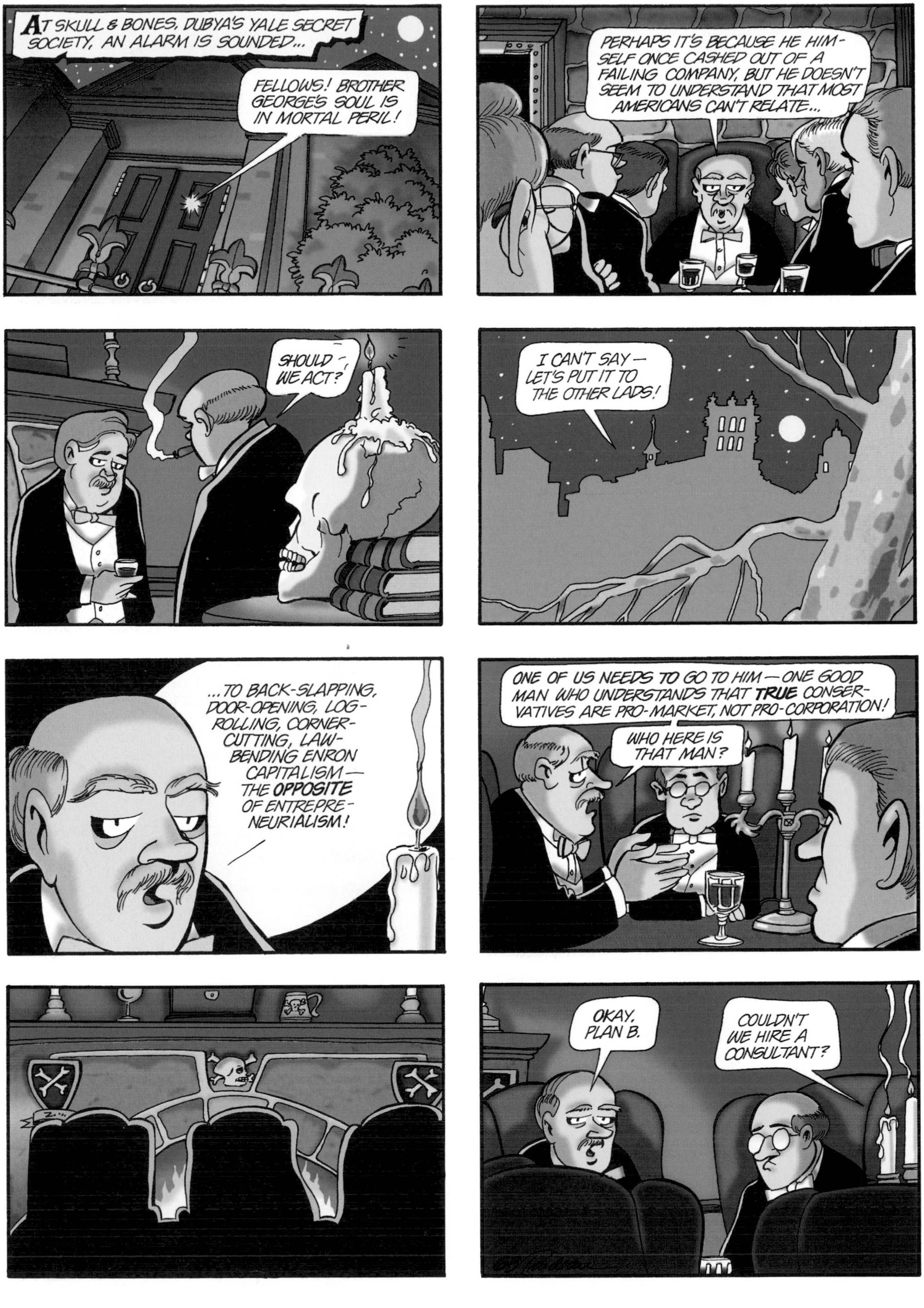
AT SKULL & BONES, DUBYA'S YALE SECRET SOCIETY, AN ALARM IS SOUNDED...
FELLOWS! BROTHER GEORGE'S SOUL IS IN MORTAL PERIL!
PERHAPS IT'S BECAUSE HE HIMSELF ONCE CASHED OUT OF A FAILING COMPANY, BUT HE DOESN'T SEEM TO UNDERSTAND THAT MOST AMERICANS CAN'T RELATE...
SHOULD WE ACT?
I CAN'T SAY — LET'S PUT IT TO THE OTHER LADS!
...TO BACK-SLAPPING, DOOR-OPENING, LOG-ROLLING, CORNER-CUTTING, LAW-BENDING ENRON CAPITALISM — THE OPPOSITE OF ENTREPRENEURIALISM!
ONE OF US NEEDS TO GO TO HIM — ONE GOOD MAN WHO UNDERSTANDS THAT TRUE CONSERVATIVES ARE PRO-MARKET, NOT PRO-CORPORATION!
WHO HERE IS THAT MAN?
OKAY. PLAN B.
COULDN'T WE HIRE A CONSULTANT?

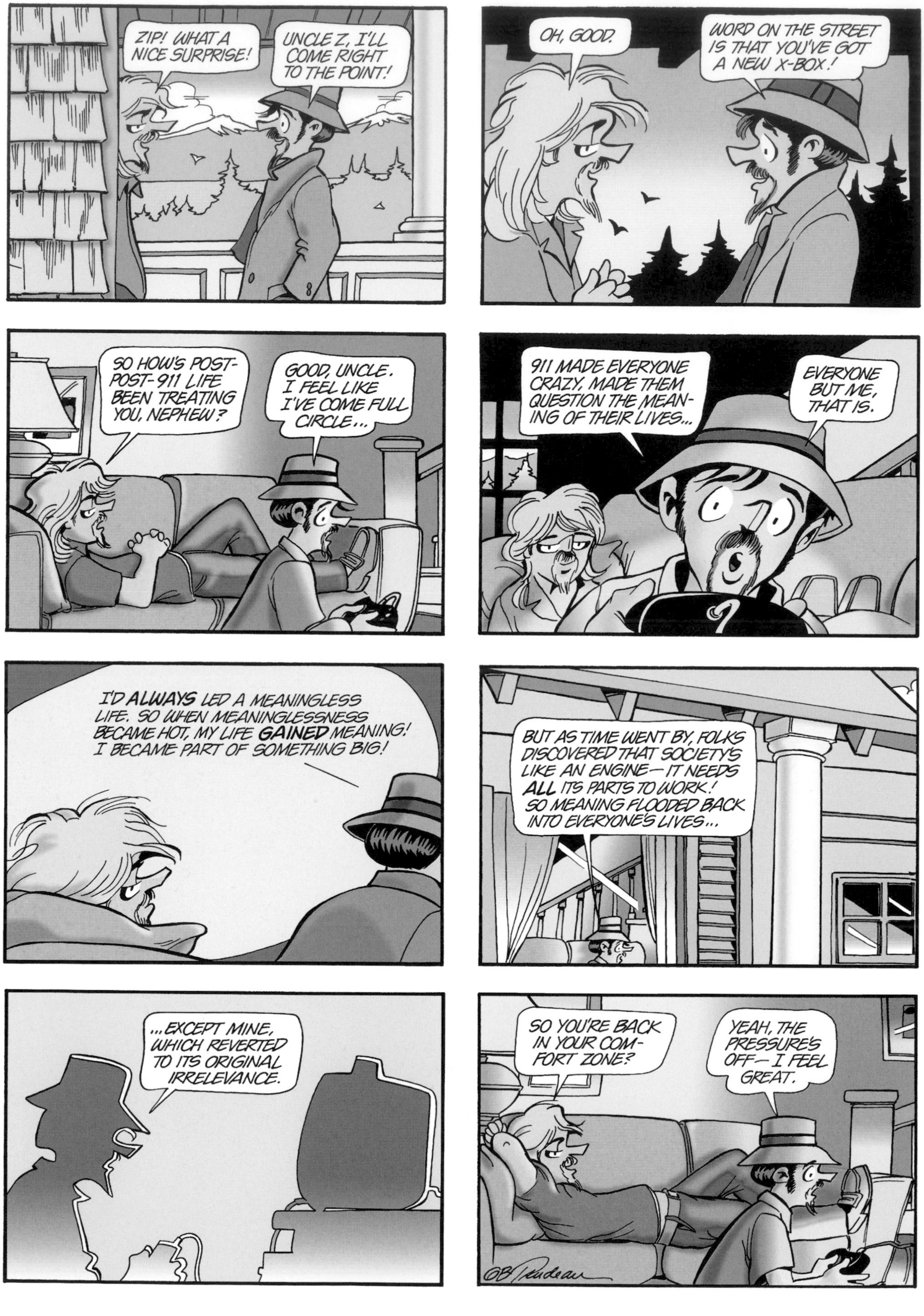
ZIP! WHAT A NICE SURPRISE!
UNCLE Z, I'LL COME RIGHT TO THE POINT!
OH, GOOD.
WORD ON THE STREET IS THAT YOU'VE GOT A NEW X-BOX!
SO HOW'S POST-POST-911 LIFE BEEN TREATING YOU, NEPHEW?
GOOD, UNCLE. I FEEL LIKE I'VE COME FULL CIRCLE...
911 MADE EVERYONE CRAZY. MADE THEM QUESTION THE MEANING OF THEIR LIVES...
EVERYONE BUT ME, THAT IS.
I'D ALWAYS LED A MEANINGLESS LIFE. SO WHEN MEANINGLESSNESS BECAME HOT, MY LIFE GAINED MEANING! I BECAME PART OF SOMETHING BIG!
BUT AS TIME WENT BY, FOLKS DISCOVERED THAT SOCIETY'S LIKE AN ENGINE—IT NEEDS ALL ITS PARTS TO WORK! SO MEANING FLOODED BACK INTO EVERYONE'S LIVES...
...EXCEPT MINE, WHICH REVERTED TO ITS ORIGINAL IRRELEVANCE.
SO YOU'RE BACK IN YOUR COMFORT ZONE?
YEAH, THE PRESSURE'S OFF—I FEEL GREAT.
GB Trudeau

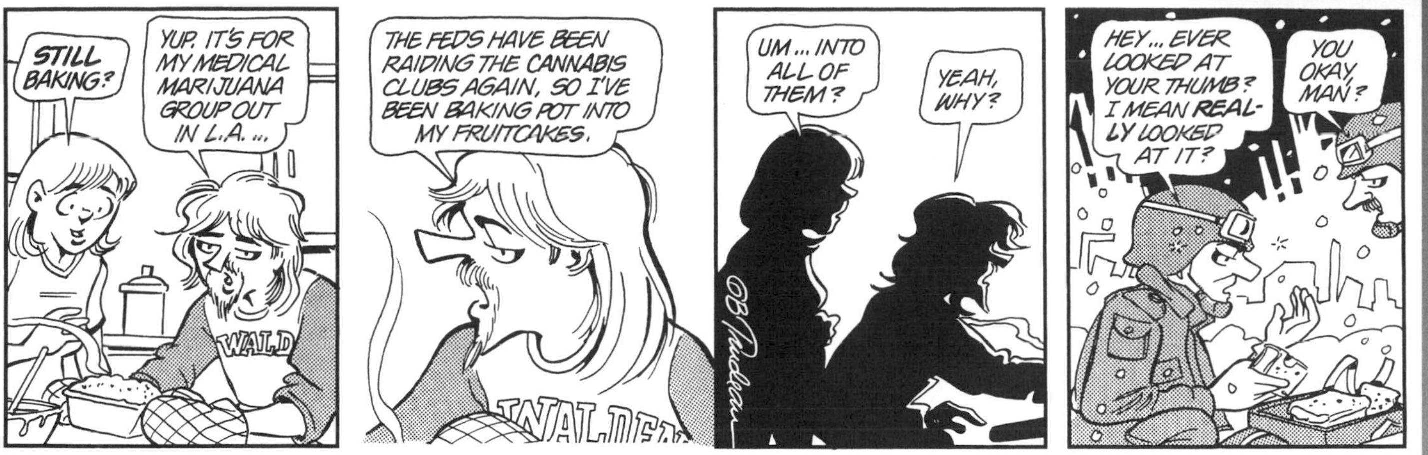
STILL BAKING?
YUP. IT'S FOR MY MEDICAL MARIJUANA GROUP OUT IN L.A. ...
THE FEDS HAVE BEEN RAIDING THE CANNABIS CLUBS AGAIN, SO I'VE BEEN BAKING POT INTO MY FRUITCAKES.
UM ... INTO ALL OF THEM?
YEAH, WHY?
HEY... EVER LOOKED AT YOUR THUMB? I MEAN REALLY LOOKED AT IT?
YOU OKAY, MAN?

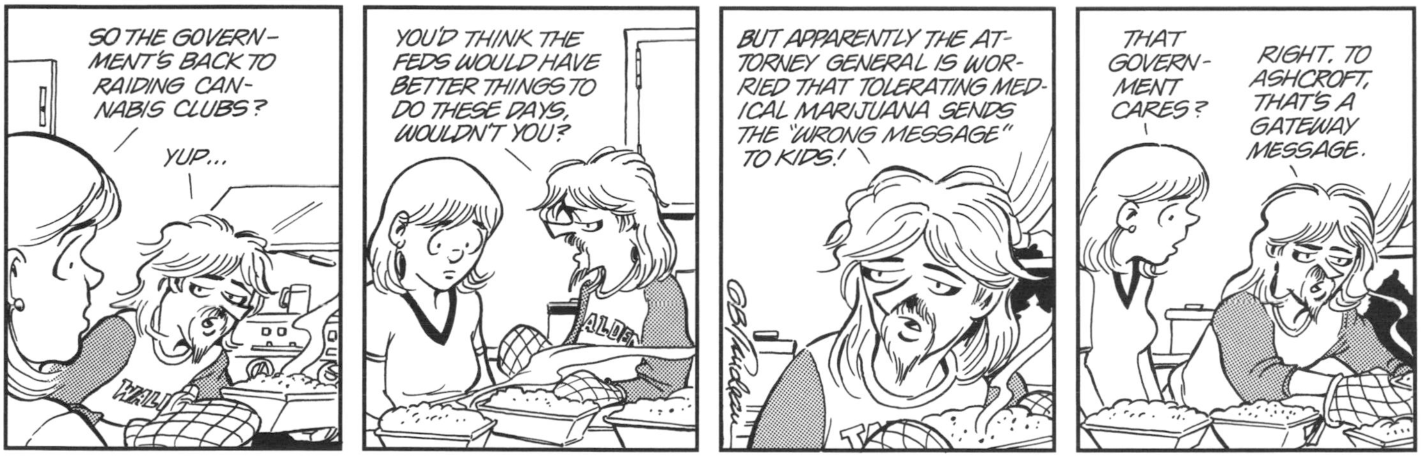
SO THE GOVERNMENT'S BACK TO RAIDING CANNABIS CLUBS?
YUP...
YOU'D THINK THE FEDS WOULD HAVE BETTER THINGS TO DO THESE DAYS, WOULDN'T YOU?
BUT APPARENTLY THE ATTORNEY GENERAL IS WORRIED THAT TOLERATING MEDICAL MARIJUANA SENDS THE "WRONG MESSAGE" TO KIDS!
THAT GOVERNMENT CARES?
RIGHT. TO ASHCROFT, THAT'S A GATEWAY MESSAGE.

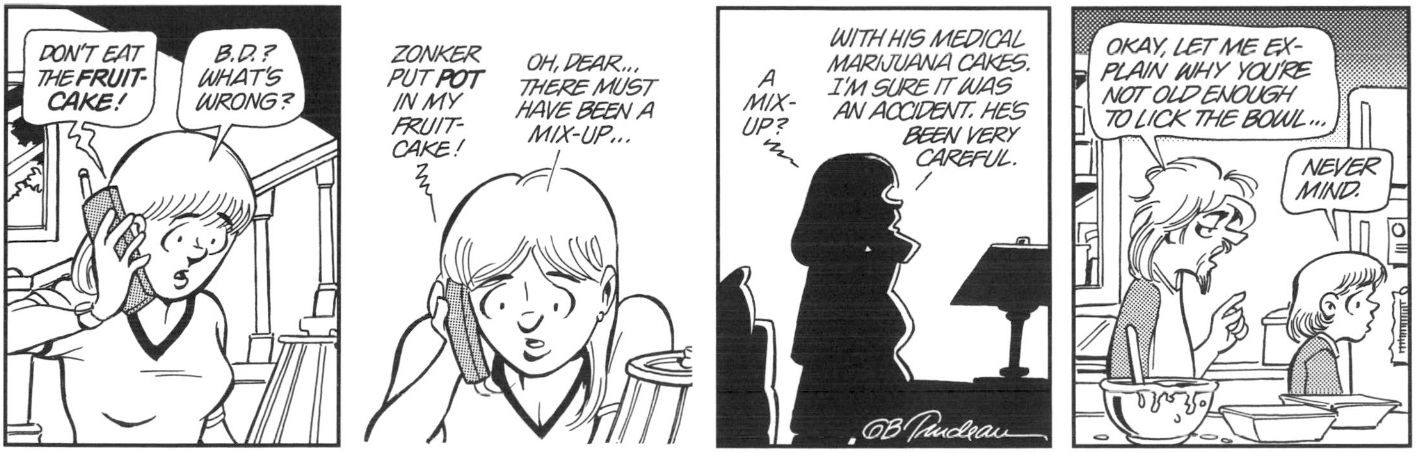
DON'T EAT THE FRUITCAKE!
B.D.? WHAT'S WRONG?
ZONKER PUT POT IN MY FRUITCAKE!
OH, DEAR... THERE MUST HAVE BEEN A MIX-UP...
A MIX-UP?
WITH HIS MEDICAL MARIJUANA CAKES. I'M SURE IT WAS AN ACCIDENT. HE'S BEEN VERY CAREFUL.
OKAY, LET ME EXPLAIN WHY YOU'RE NOT OLD ENOUGH TO LICK THE BOWL...
NEVER MIND.

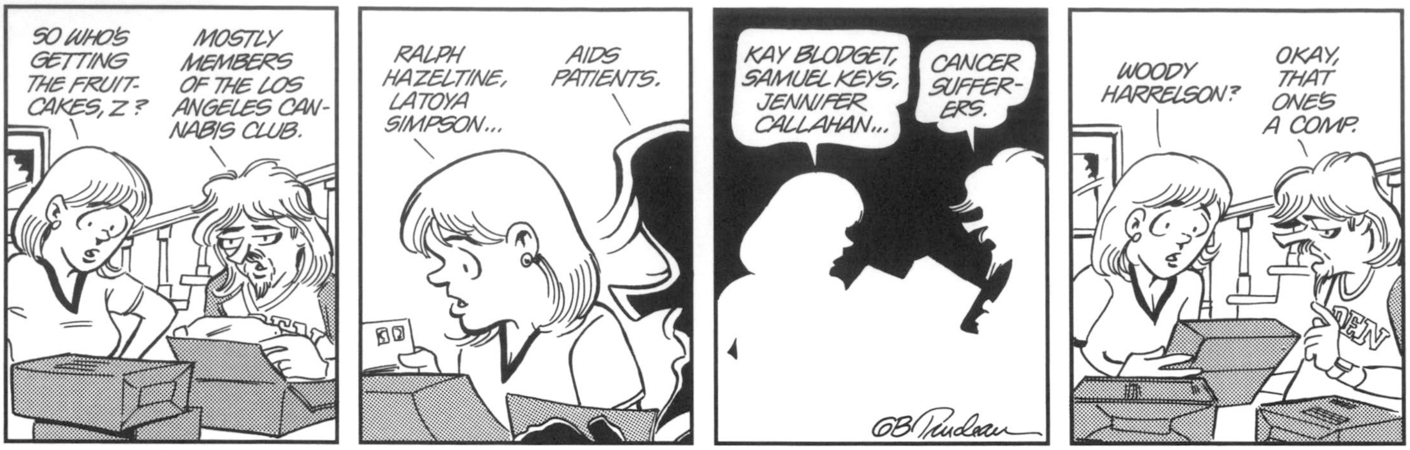
SO WHO'S GETTING THE FRUIT-CAKES, Z?
MOSTLY MEMBERS OF THE LOS ANGELES CAN-NABIS CLUB.
RALPH HAZELTINE, LATOYA SIMPSON...
AIDS PATIENTS.
KAY BLODGET, SAMUEL KEYS, JENNIFER CALLAHAN...
CANCER SUFFER-ERS.
WOODY HARRELSON?
OKAY, THAT ONE'S A COMP.

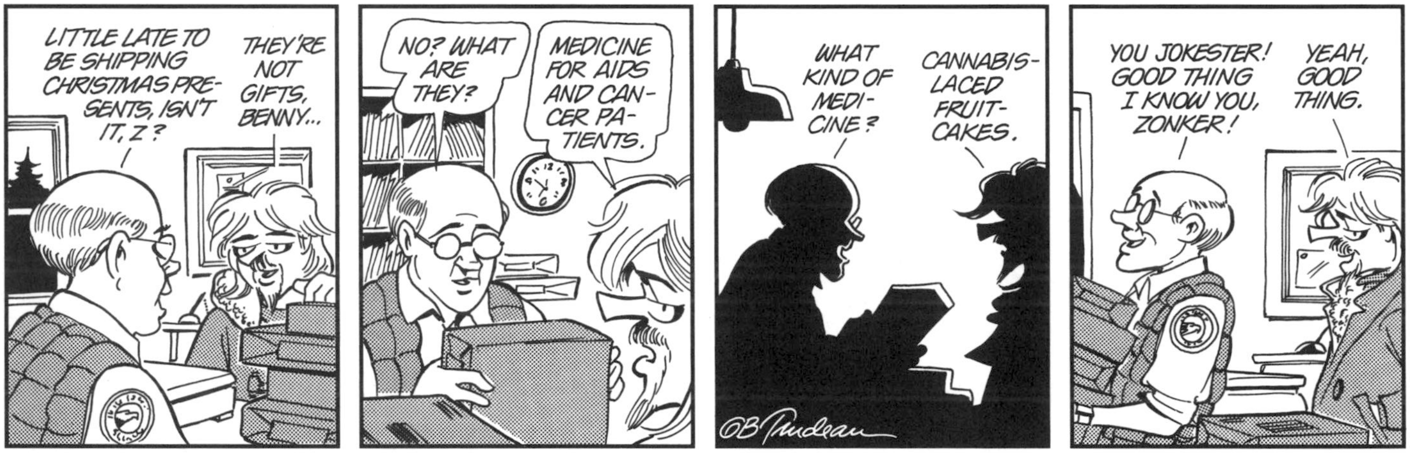
LITTLE LATE TO BE SHIPPING CHRISTMAS PRE-SENTS, ISN'T IT, Z?
THEY'RE NOT GIFTS, BENNY...
NO? WHAT ARE THEY?
MEDICINE FOR AIDS AND CAN-CER PA-TIENTS.
WHAT KIND OF MEDI-CINE?
CANNABIS-LACED FRUIT-CAKES.
YOU JOKESTER! GOOD THING I KNOW YOU, ZONKER!
YEAH, GOOD THING.

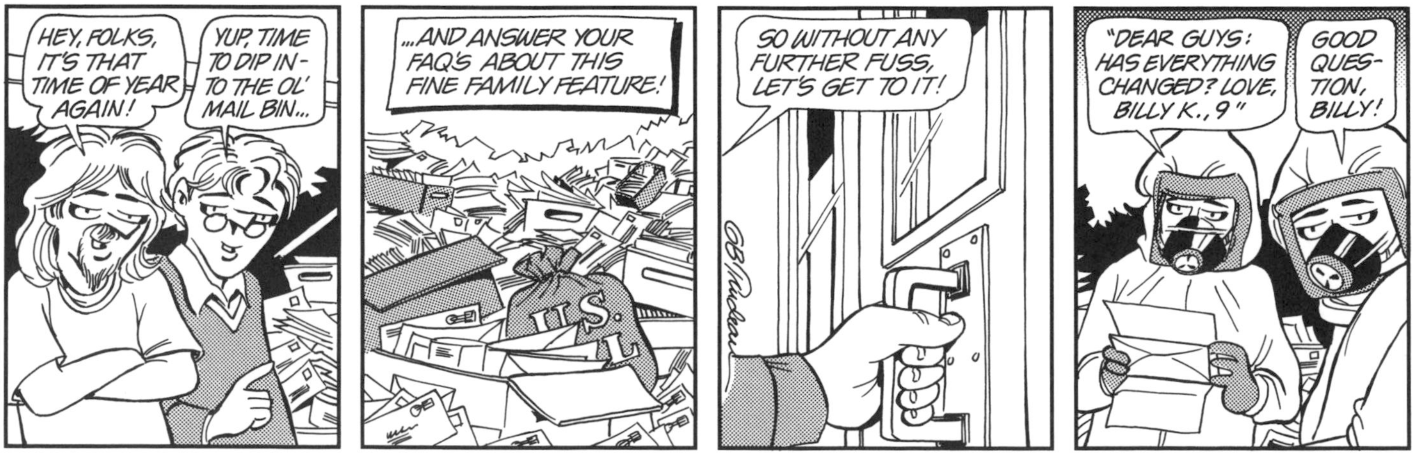
HEY, FOLKS, IT'S THAT TIME OF YEAR AGAIN!
YUP. TIME TO DIP IN-TO THE OL' MAIL BIN...
...AND ANSWER YOUR FAQ'S ABOUT THIS FINE FAMILY FEATURE!
SO WITHOUT ANY FURTHER FUSS, LET'S GET TO IT!
"DEAR GUYS: HAS EVERYTHING CHANGED? LOVE, BILLY K., 9"
GOOD QUES-TION, BILLY!

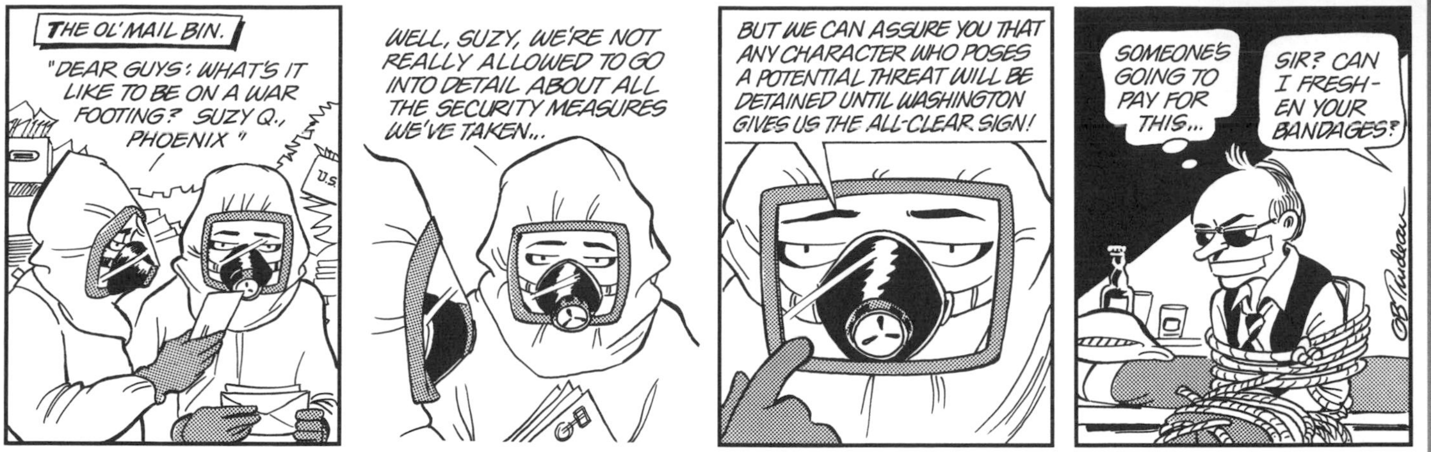
THE OL' MAIL BIN.
"DEAR GUYS: WHAT'S IT LIKE TO BE ON A WAR FOOTING? SUZY Q., PHOENIX"
WELL, SUZY, WE'RE NOT REALLY ALLOWED TO GO INTO DETAIL ABOUT ALL THE SECURITY MEASURES WE'VE TAKEN...
BUT WE CAN ASSURE YOU THAT ANY CHARACTER WHO POSES A POTENTIAL THREAT WILL BE DETAINED UNTIL WASHINGTON GIVES US THE ALL-CLEAR SIGN!
SOMEONE'S GOING TO PAY FOR THIS...
SIR? CAN I FRESH-EN YOUR BANDAGES?

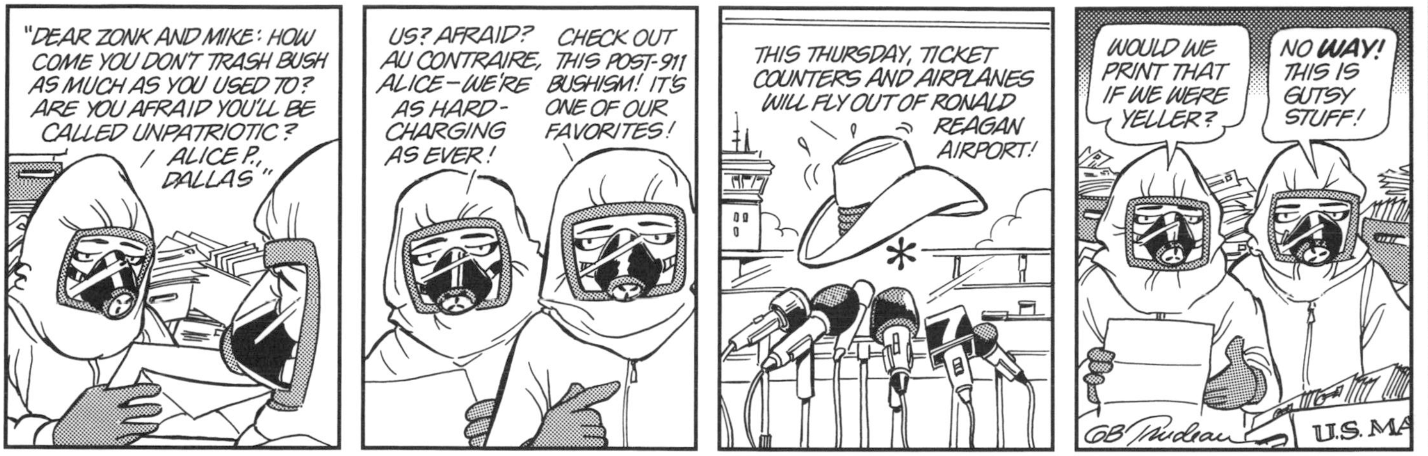
"DEAR ZONK AND MIKE: HOW COME YOU DON'T TRASH BUSH AS MUCH AS YOU USED TO? ARE YOU AFRAID YOU'LL BE CALLED UNPATRIOTIC? ALICE P., DALLAS"
US? AFRAID? AU CONTRAIRE, ALICE—WE'RE AS HARD-CHARGING AS EVER!
CHECK OUT THIS POST-911 BUSHISM! IT'S ONE OF OUR FAVORITES!
THIS THURSDAY, TICKET COUNTERS AND AIRPLANES WILL FLY OUT OF RONALD REAGAN AIRPORT!
WOULD WE PRINT THAT IF WE WERE YELLER?
NO WAY! THIS IS GUTSY STUFF!
U.S. MA

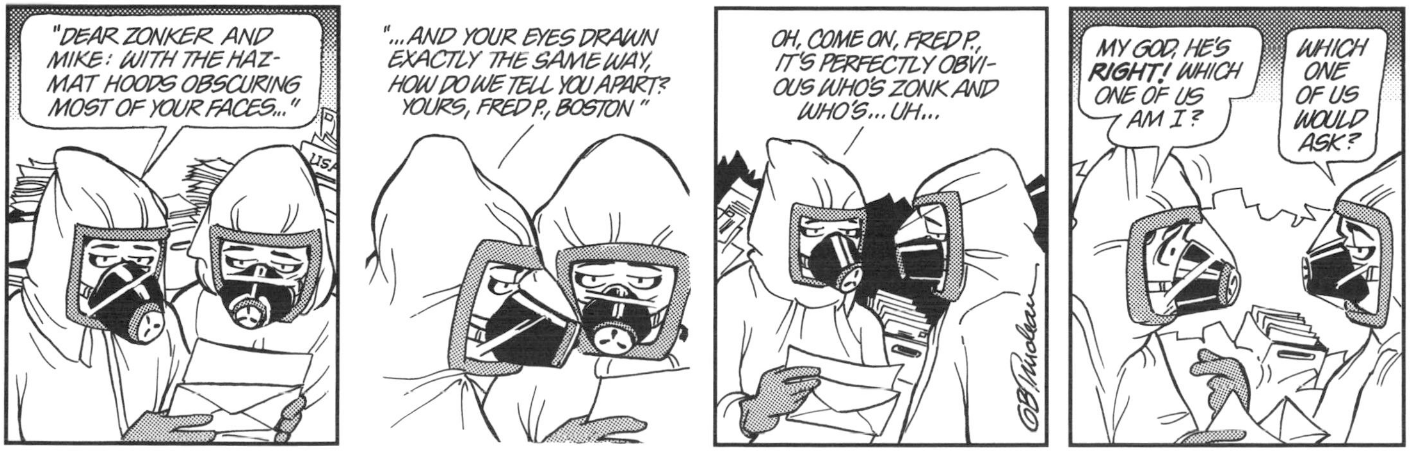
"DEAR ZONKER AND MIKE: WITH THE HAZ-MAT HOODS OBSCURING MOST OF YOUR FACES..."
"...AND YOUR EYES DRAWN EXACTLY THE SAME WAY, HOW DO WE TELL YOU APART? YOURS, FRED P., BOSTON"
OH, COME ON, FRED P., IT'S PERFECTLY OBVI-OUS WHO'S ZONK AND WHO'S... UH...
MY GOD, HE'S RIGHT! WHICH ONE OF US AM I?
WHICH ONE OF US WOULD ASK?

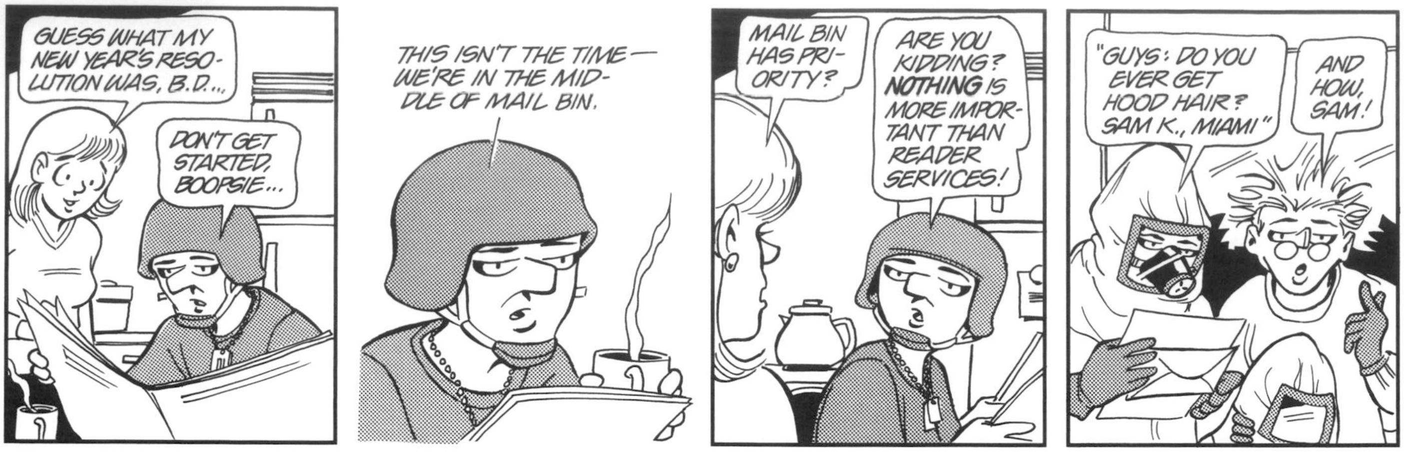
GUESS WHAT MY NEW YEAR'S RESOLUTION WAS, B.D...
DON'T GET STARTED, BOOPSIE...
THIS ISN'T THE TIME— WE'RE IN THE MIDDLE OF MAIL BIN.
MAIL BIN HAS PRIORITY?
ARE YOU KIDDING? NOTHING IS MORE IMPORTANT THAN READER SERVICES!
"GUYS: DO YOU EVER GET HOOD HAIR? SAM K., MIAMI"
AND HOW, SAM!

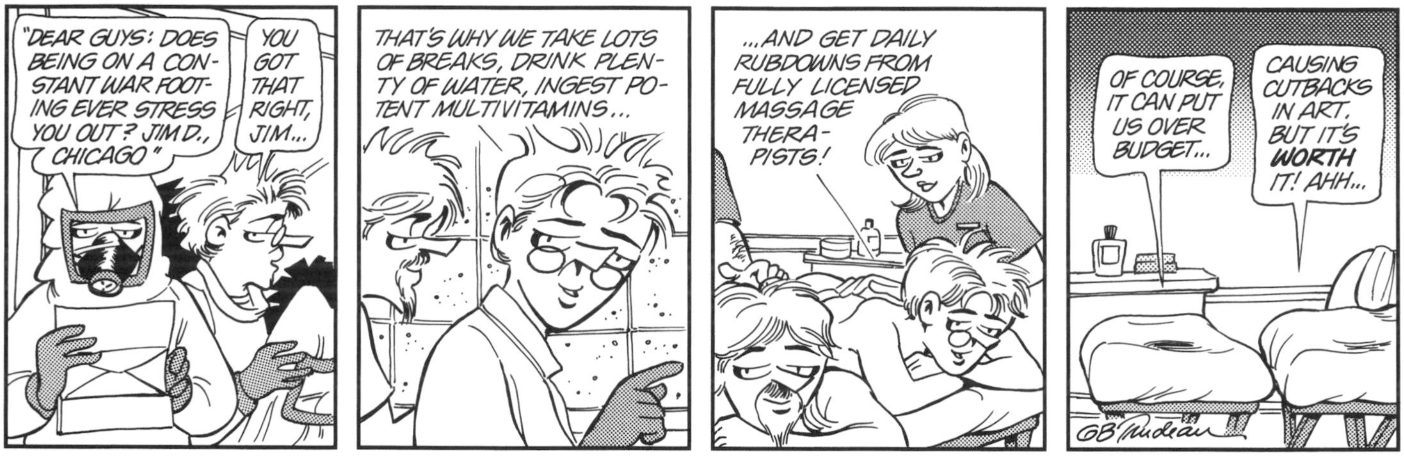
"DEAR GUYS: DOES BEING ON A CONSTANT WAR FOOTING EVER STRESS YOU OUT? JIM D., CHICAGO"
YOU GOT THAT RIGHT, JIM...
THAT'S WHY WE TAKE LOTS OF BREAKS, DRINK PLENTY OF WATER, INGEST POTENT MULTIVITAMINS...
...AND GET DAILY RUBDOWNS FROM FULLY LICENSED MASSAGE THERAPISTS!
OF COURSE, IT CAN PUT US OVER BUDGET...
CAUSING CUTBACKS IN ART, BUT IT'S WORTH IT! AHH...

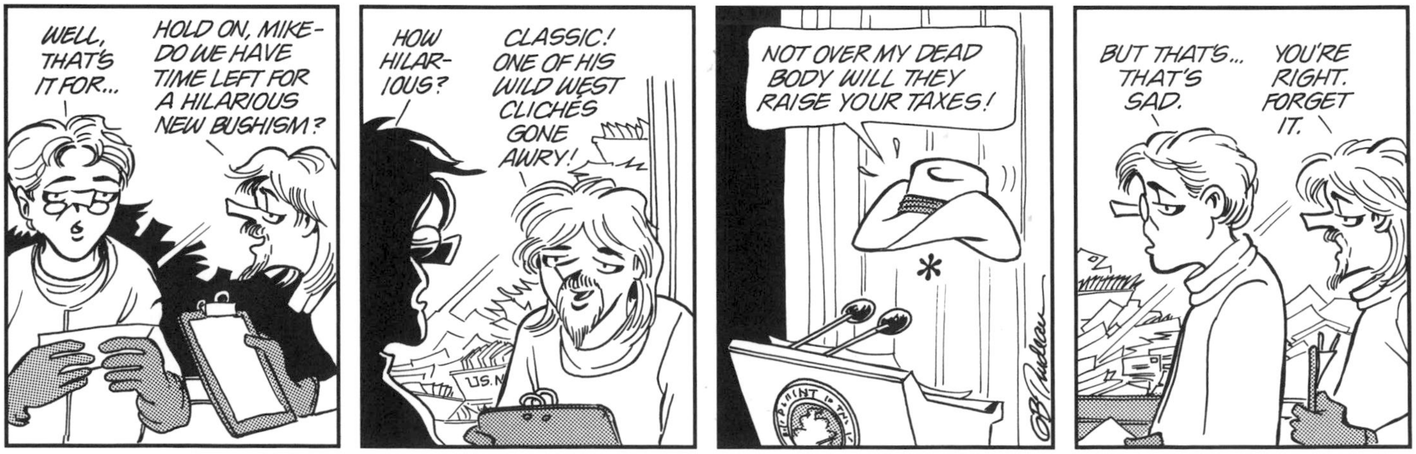
WELL, THAT'S IT FOR...
HOLD ON, MIKE- DO WE HAVE TIME LEFT FOR A HILARIOUS NEW BUSHISM?
HOW HILARIOUS?
CLASSIC! ONE OF HIS WILD WEST CLICHÉS GONE AWRY!
NOT OVER MY DEAD BODY WILL THEY RAISE YOUR TAXES!
BUT THAT'S... THAT'S SAD.
YOU'RE RIGHT. FORGET IT.

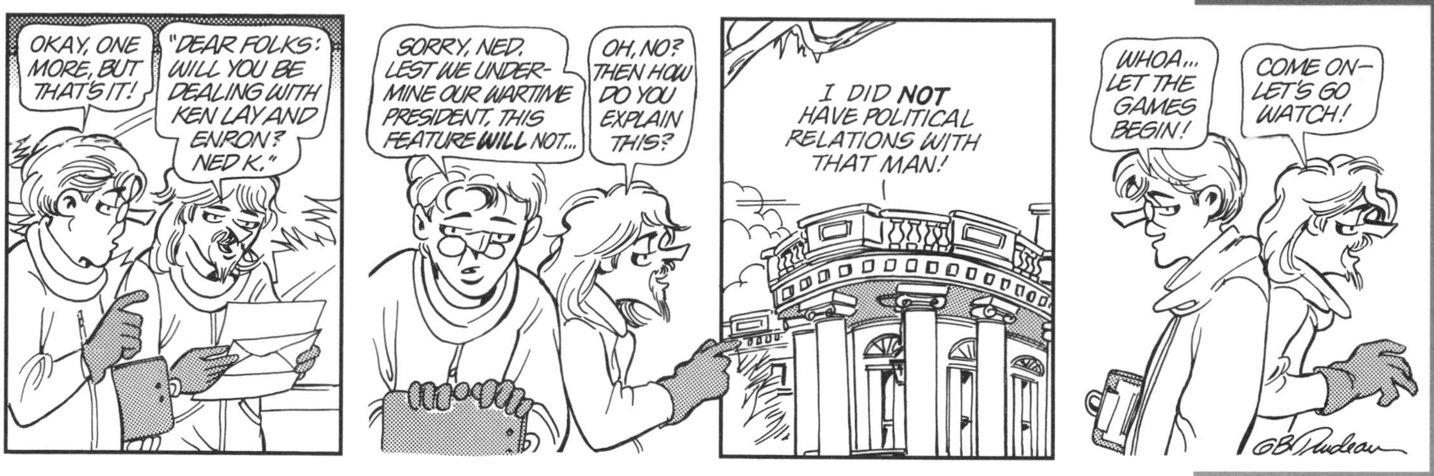
OKAY, ONE MORE, BUT THAT'S IT!
"DEAR FOLKS: WILL YOU BE DEALING WITH KEN LAY AND ENRON? NED K."
SORRY, NED. LEST WE UNDERMINE OUR WARTIME PRESIDENT, THIS FEATURE **WILL** NOT...
OH, NO? THEN HOW DO YOU EXPLAIN THIS?
I DID **NOT** HAVE POLITICAL RELATIONS WITH THAT MAN!
WHOA... LET THE GAMES BEGIN!
COME ON— LET'S GO WATCH!
GB Trudeau

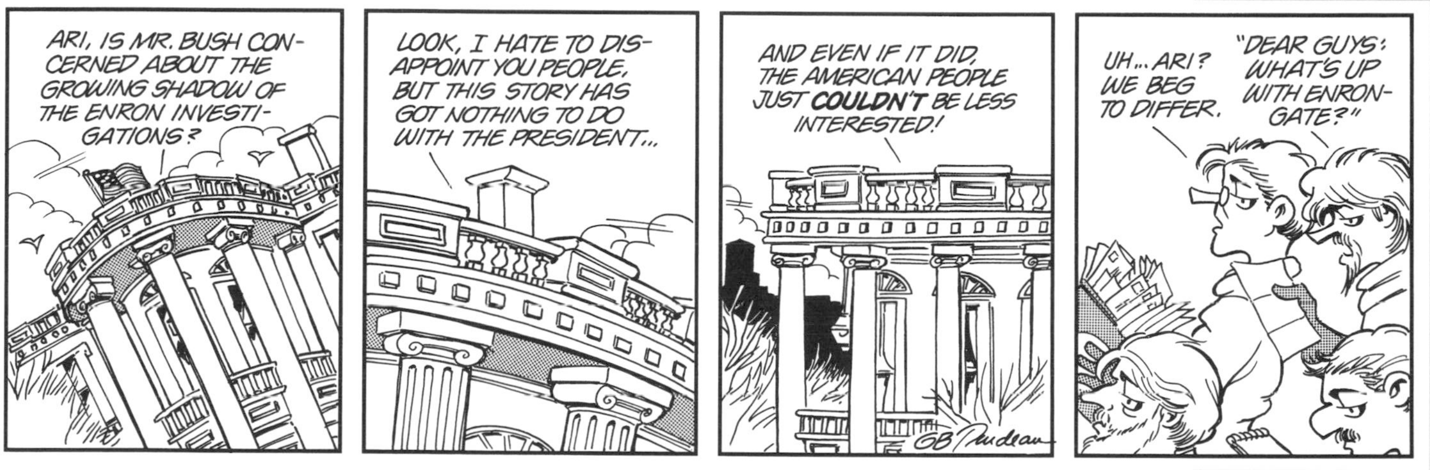
ARI, IS MR. BUSH CONCERNED ABOUT THE GROWING SHADOW OF THE ENRON INVESTIGATIONS?
LOOK, I HATE TO DISAPPOINT YOU PEOPLE, BUT THIS STORY HAS GOT NOTHING TO DO WITH THE PRESIDENT...
AND EVEN IF IT DID, THE AMERICAN PEOPLE JUST **COULDN'T** BE LESS INTERESTED!
GB Trudeau
UH... ARI? WE BEG TO DIFFER.
"DEAR GUYS: WHAT'S UP WITH ENRONGATE?"

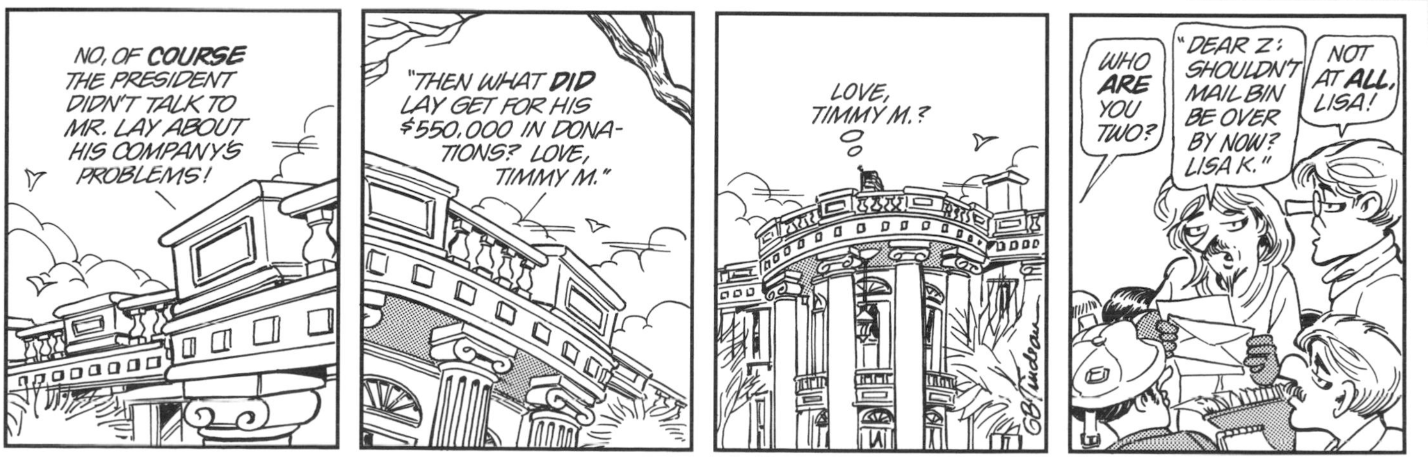
NO, OF **COURSE** THE PRESIDENT DIDN'T TALK TO MR. LAY ABOUT HIS COMPANY'S PROBLEMS!
"THEN WHAT **DID** LAY GET FOR HIS $550,000 IN DONATIONS? LOVE, TIMMY M."
LOVE, TIMMY M.?
GB Trudeau
WHO **ARE** YOU TWO?
"DEAR Z: SHOULDN'T MAIL BIN BE OVER BY NOW? LISA K."
NOT AT **ALL**, LISA!

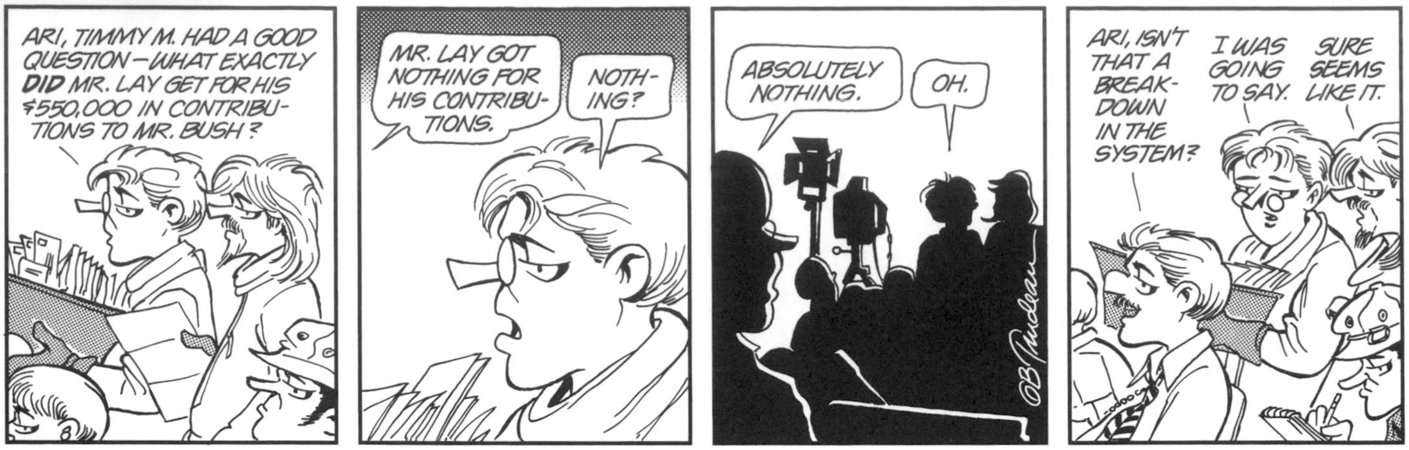
ARI, TIMMY M. HAD A GOOD QUESTION—WHAT EXACTLY **DID** MR. LAY GET FOR HIS $550,000 IN CONTRIBUTIONS TO MR. BUSH?
MR. LAY GOT NOTHING FOR HIS CONTRIBUTIONS.
NOTHING?
ABSOLUTELY NOTHING.
OH.
ARI, ISN'T THAT A BREAKDOWN IN THE SYSTEM?
I WAS GOING TO SAY.
SURE SEEMS LIKE IT.

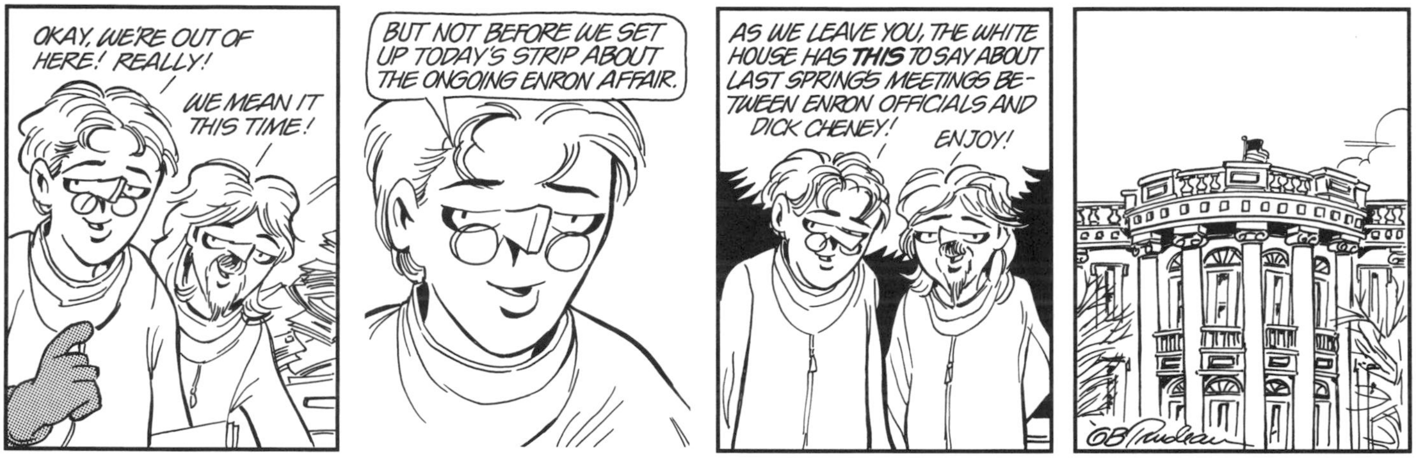
OKAY, WE'RE OUT OF HERE! REALLY!
WE MEAN IT THIS TIME!
BUT NOT BEFORE WE SET UP TODAY'S STRIP ABOUT THE ONGOING ENRON AFFAIR.
AS WE LEAVE YOU, THE WHITE HOUSE HAS **THIS** TO SAY ABOUT LAST SPRING'S MEETINGS BETWEEN ENRON OFFICIALS AND DICK CHENEY!
ENJOY!

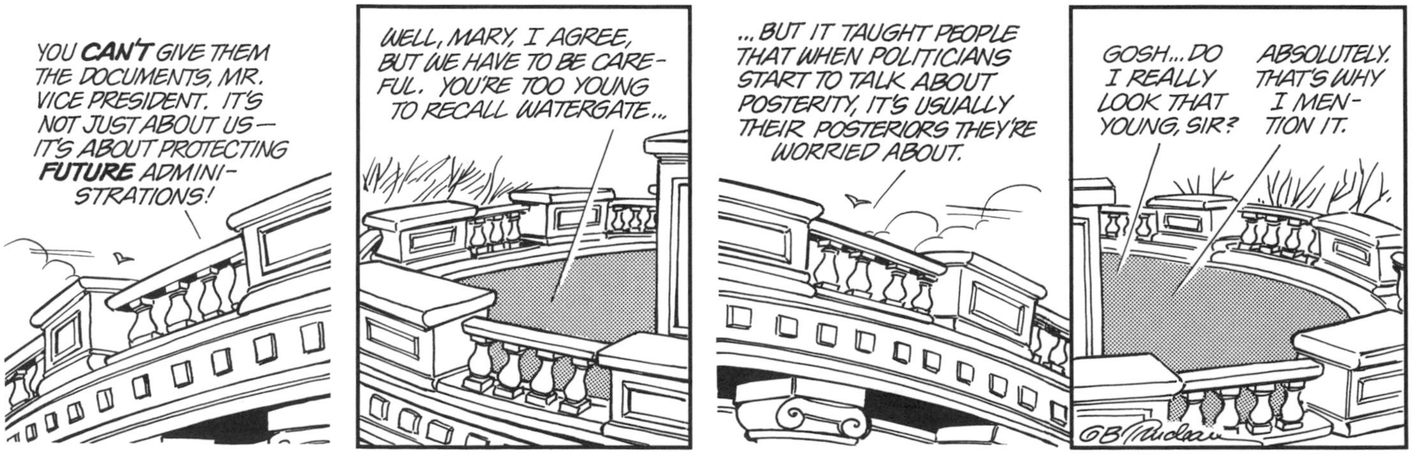
YOU **CAN'T** GIVE THEM THE DOCUMENTS, MR. VICE PRESIDENT. IT'S NOT JUST ABOUT US—IT'S ABOUT PROTECTING **FUTURE** ADMINISTRATIONS!
WELL, MARY, I AGREE, BUT WE HAVE TO BE CAREFUL. YOU'RE TOO YOUNG TO RECALL WATERGATE...
...BUT IT TAUGHT PEOPLE THAT WHEN POLITICIANS START TO TALK ABOUT POSTERITY, IT'S USUALLY THEIR POSTERIORS THEY'RE WORRIED ABOUT.
GOSH... DO I REALLY LOOK THAT YOUNG, SIR?
ABSOLUTELY. THAT'S WHY I MENTION IT.

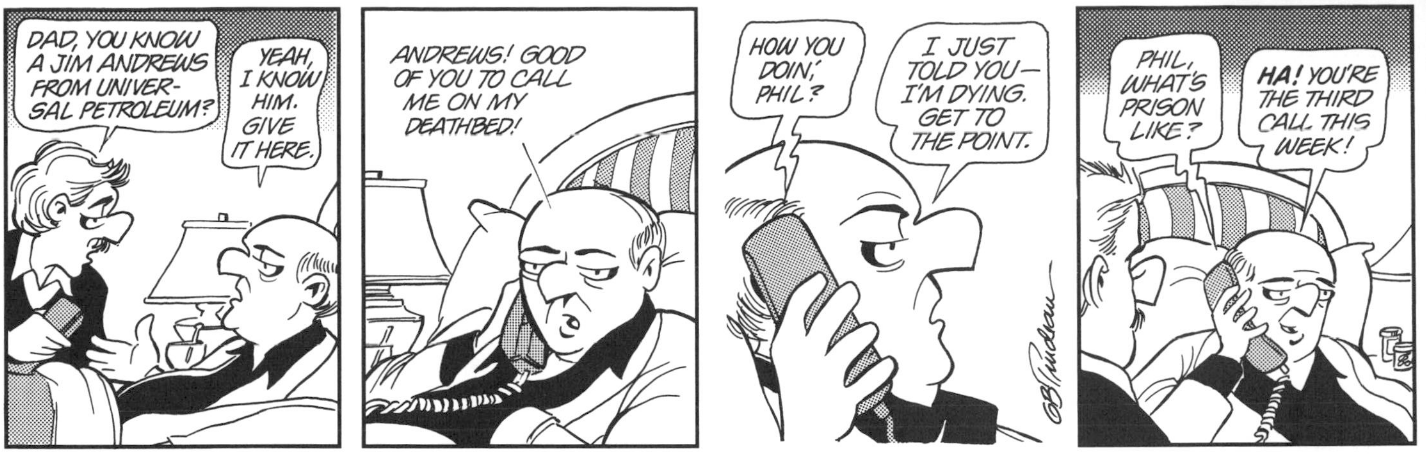
DAD, YOU KNOW A JIM ANDREWS FROM UNIVERSAL PETROLEUM?
YEAH, I KNOW HIM. GIVE IT HERE.
ANDREWS! GOOD OF YOU TO CALL ME ON MY DEATHBED!
HOW YOU DOIN,' PHIL?
I JUST TOLD YOU— I'M DYING. GET TO THE POINT.
PHIL, WHAT'S PRISON LIKE?
HA! YOU'RE THE THIRD CALL THIS WEEK!

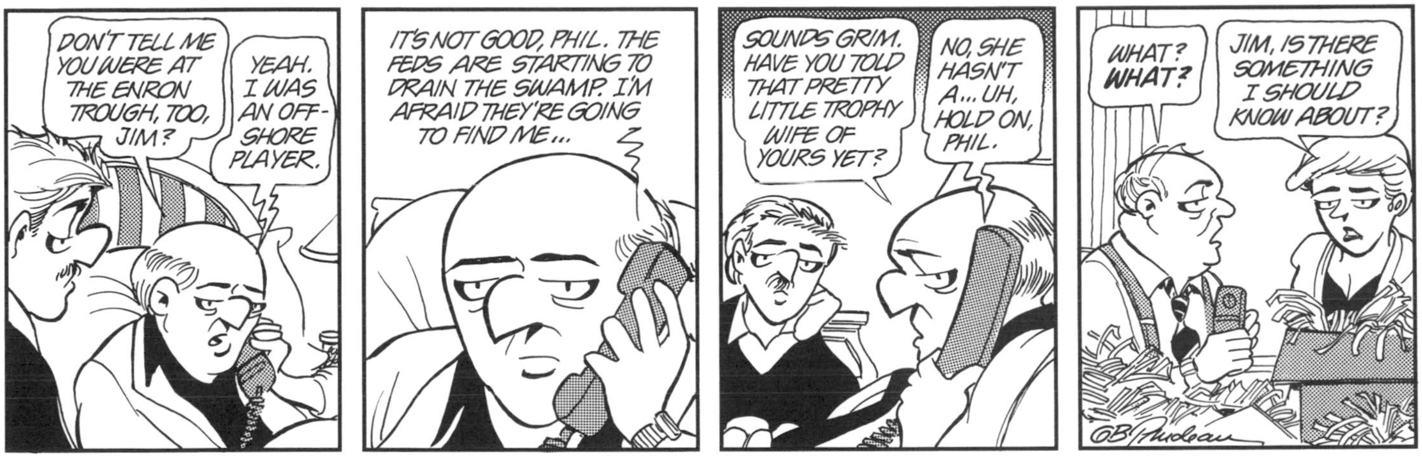
DON'T TELL ME YOU WERE AT THE ENRON TROUGH, TOO, JIM?
YEAH. I WAS AN OFF-SHORE PLAYER.
IT'S NOT GOOD, PHIL. THE FEDS ARE STARTING TO DRAIN THE SWAMP. I'M AFRAID THEY'RE GOING TO FIND ME...
SOUNDS GRIM. HAVE YOU TOLD THAT PRETTY LITTLE TROPHY WIFE OF YOURS YET?
NO, SHE HASN'T A... UH, HOLD ON, PHIL.
WHAT? WHAT?
JIM, IS THERE SOMETHING I SHOULD KNOW ABOUT?

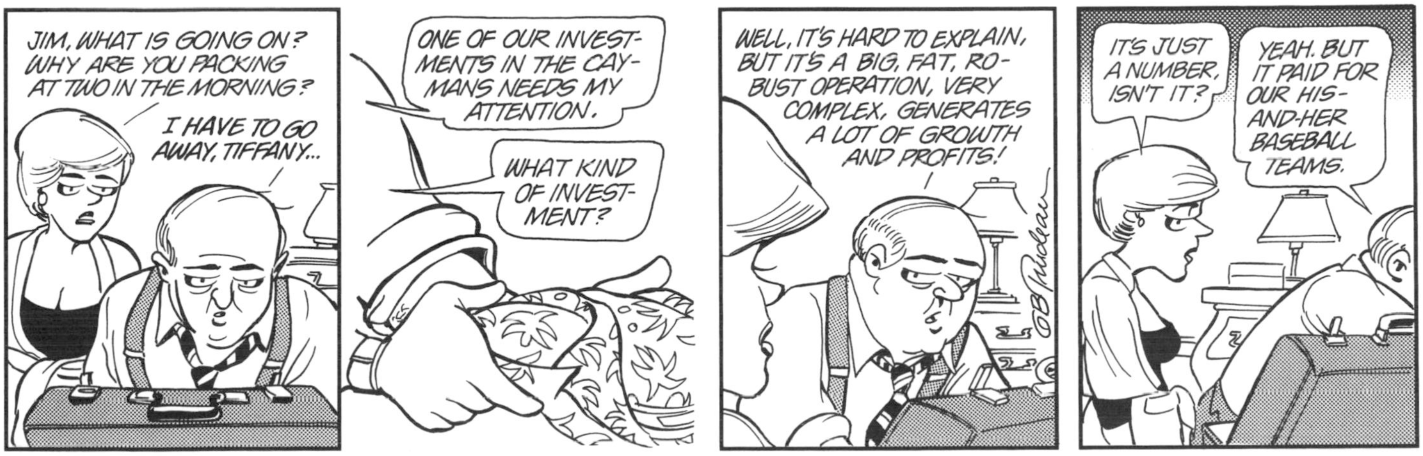
JIM, WHAT IS GOING ON? WHY ARE YOU PACKING AT TWO IN THE MORNING?
I HAVE TO GO AWAY, TIFFANY...
ONE OF OUR INVESTMENTS IN THE CAYMANS NEEDS MY ATTENTION.
WHAT KIND OF INVESTMENT?
WELL, IT'S HARD TO EXPLAIN, BUT IT'S A BIG, FAT, ROBUST OPERATION, VERY COMPLEX, GENERATES A LOT OF GROWTH AND PROFITS!
IT'S JUST A NUMBER, ISN'T IT?
YEAH. BUT IT PAID FOR OUR HIS-AND-HER BASEBALL TEAMS.

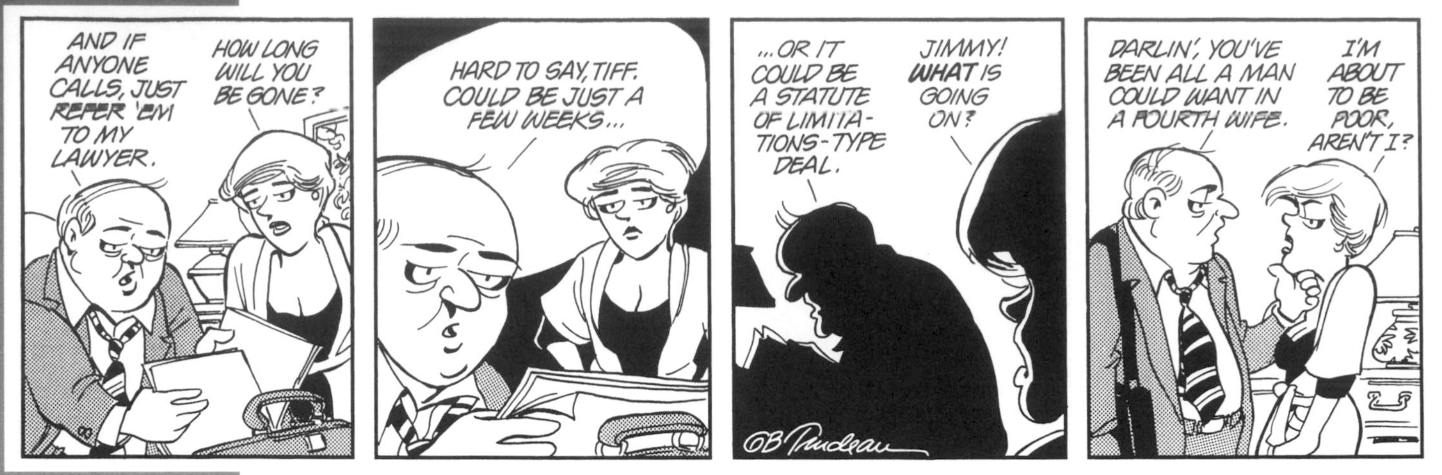
AND IF ANYONE CALLS, JUST REFER 'EM TO MY LAWYER.
HOW LONG WILL YOU BE GONE?
HARD TO SAY, TIFF. COULD BE JUST A FEW WEEKS...
...OR IT COULD BE A STATUTE OF LIMITA-TIONS-TYPE DEAL.
JIMMY! **WHAT** IS GOING ON?
DARLIN', YOU'VE BEEN ALL A MAN COULD WANT IN A FOURTH WIFE.
I'M ABOUT TO BE POOR, AREN'T I?
©B Trudeau

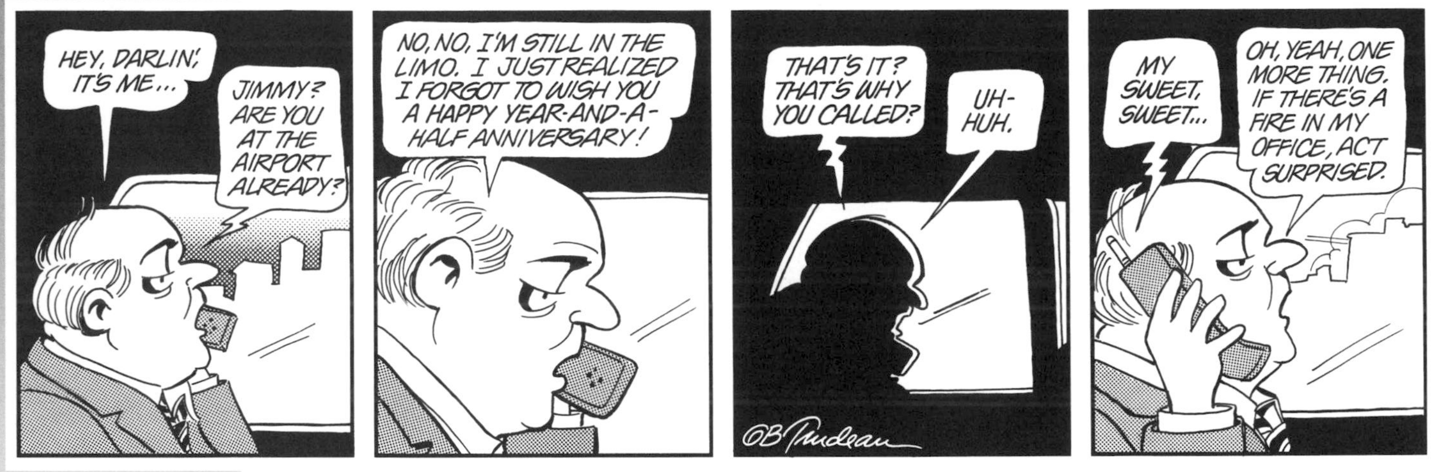
HEY, DARLIN', IT'S ME...
JIMMY? ARE YOU AT THE AIRPORT ALREADY?
NO, NO, I'M STILL IN THE LIMO. I JUST REALIZED I FORGOT TO WISH YOU A HAPPY YEAR-AND-A-HALF ANNIVERSARY!
THAT'S IT? THAT'S WHY YOU CALLED?
UH-HUH.
MY SWEET, SWEET...
OH, YEAH, ONE MORE THING. IF THERE'S A FIRE IN MY OFFICE, ACT SURPRISED.
©B Trudeau

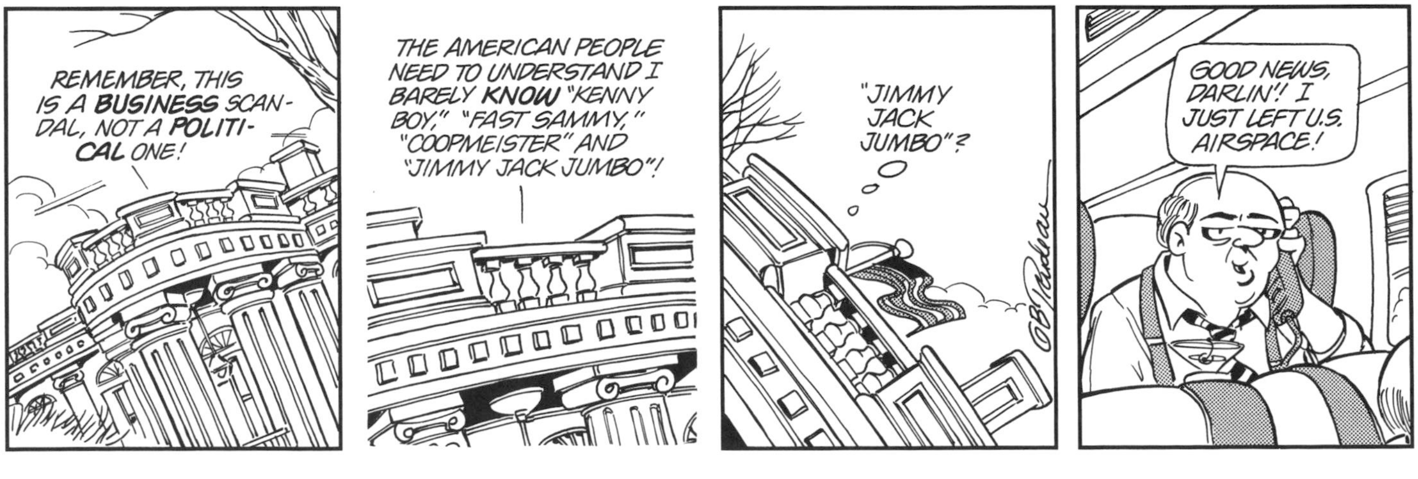
REMEMBER, THIS IS A **BUSINESS** SCAN-DAL, NOT A **POLITI-CAL** ONE!
THE AMERICAN PEOPLE NEED TO UNDERSTAND I BARELY **KNOW** "KENNY BOY," "FAST SAMMY," "COOPMEISTER" AND "JIMMY JACK JUMBO"!
"JIMMY JACK JUMBO"?
©B Trudeau
GOOD NEWS, DARLIN'! I JUST LEFT U.S. AIRSPACE!

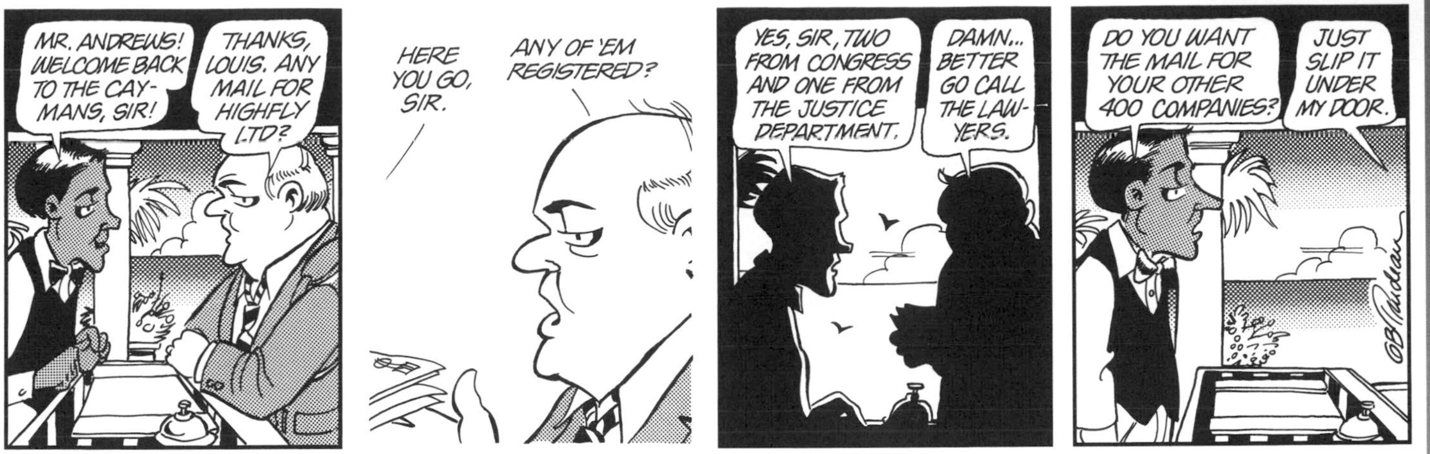
MR. ANDREWS! WELCOME BACK TO THE CAYMANS, SIR!
THANKS, LOUIS. ANY MAIL FOR HIGHFLY LTD?
HERE YOU GO, SIR.
ANY OF 'EM REGISTERED?
YES, SIR, TWO FROM CONGRESS AND ONE FROM THE JUSTICE DEPARTMENT.
DAMN... BETTER GO CALL THE LAWYERS.
DO YOU WANT THE MAIL FOR YOUR OTHER 400 COMPANIES?
JUST SLIP IT UNDER MY DOOR.

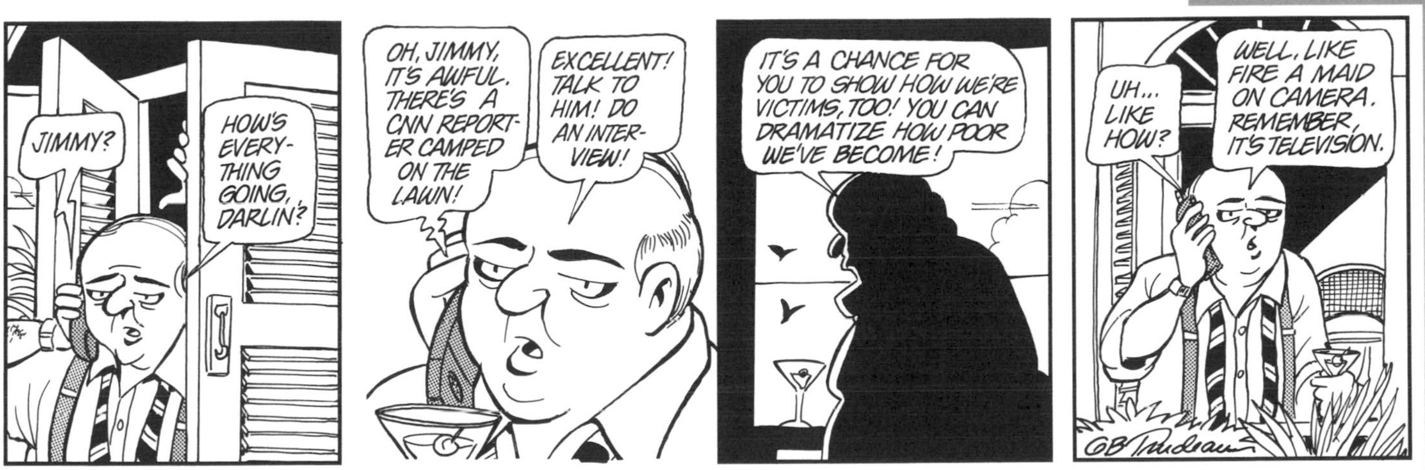
JIMMY?
HOW'S EVERYTHING GOING, DARLIN'?
OH, JIMMY, IT'S AWFUL. THERE'S A CNN REPORTER CAMPED ON THE LAWN!
EXCELLENT! TALK TO HIM! DO AN INTERVIEW!
IT'S A CHANCE FOR YOU TO SHOW HOW WE'RE VICTIMS, TOO! YOU CAN DRAMATIZE HOW POOR WE'VE BECOME!
UH... LIKE HOW?
WELL, LIKE FIRE A MAID ON CAMERA. REMEMBER, IT'S TELEVISION.

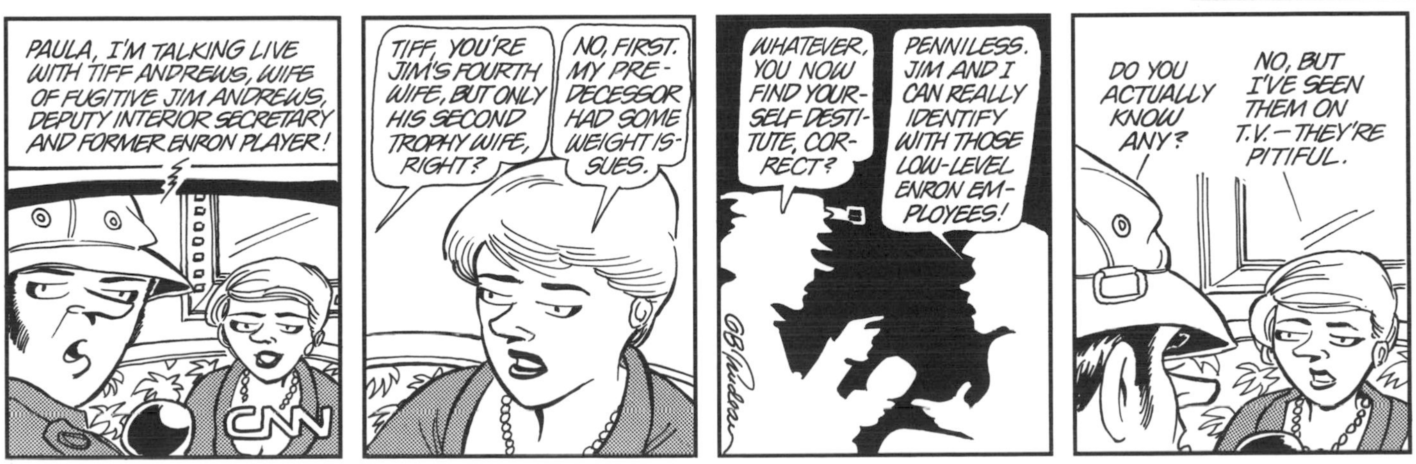
PAULA, I'M TALKING LIVE WITH TIFF ANDREWS, WIFE OF FUGITIVE JIM ANDREWS, DEPUTY INTERIOR SECRETARY AND FORMER ENRON PLAYER!
CNN
TIFF, YOU'RE JIM'S FOURTH WIFE, BUT ONLY HIS SECOND TROPHY WIFE, RIGHT?
NO, FIRST. MY PREDECESSOR HAD SOME WEIGHT ISSUES.
WHATEVER. YOU NOW FIND YOURSELF DESTITUTE, CORRECT?
PENNILESS. JIM AND I CAN REALLY IDENTIFY WITH THOSE LOW-LEVEL ENRON EMPLOYEES!
DO YOU ACTUALLY KNOW ANY?
NO, BUT I'VE SEEN THEM ON T.V. — THEY'RE PITIFUL.

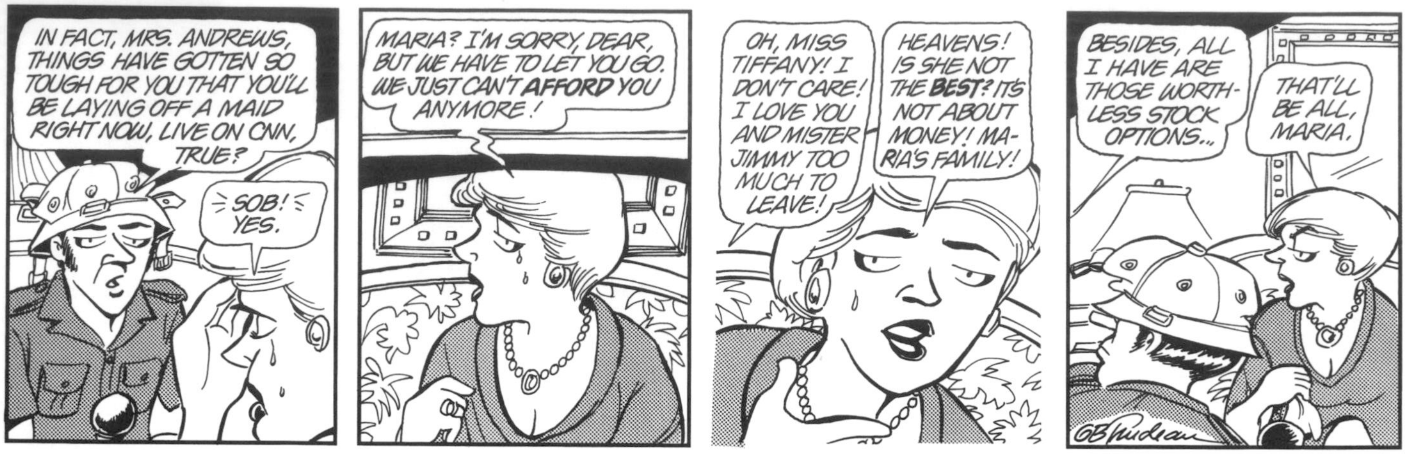
IN FACT, MRS. ANDREWS, THINGS HAVE GOTTEN SO TOUGH FOR YOU THAT YOU'LL BE LAYING OFF A MAID RIGHT NOW, LIVE ON CNN, TRUE?
SOB! YES.
MARIA? I'M SORRY, DEAR, BUT WE HAVE TO LET YOU GO. WE JUST CAN'T AFFORD YOU ANYMORE!
OH, MISS TIFFANY! I DON'T CARE! I LOVE YOU AND MISTER JIMMY TOO MUCH TO LEAVE!
HEAVENS! IS SHE NOT THE BEST? IT'S NOT ABOUT MONEY! MARIA'S FAMILY!
BESIDES, ALL I HAVE ARE THOSE WORTHLESS STOCK OPTIONS...
THAT'LL BE ALL, MARIA.
GBTrudeau

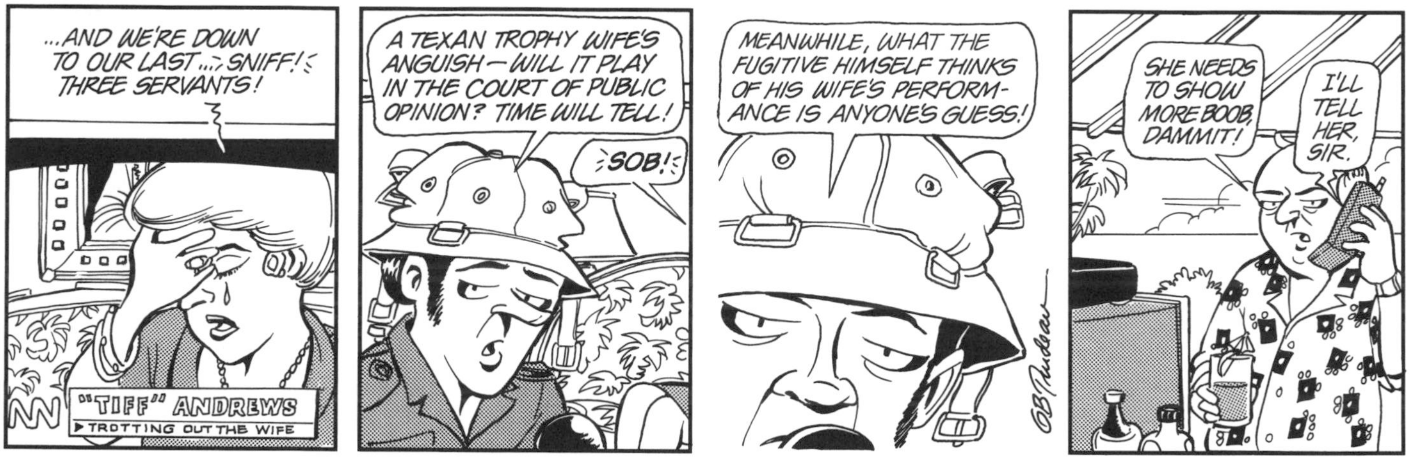
...AND WE'RE DOWN TO OUR LAST... SNIFF! THREE SERVANTS!
"TIFF" ANDREWS
TROTTING OUT THE WIFE
A TEXAN TROPHY WIFE'S ANGUISH—WILL IT PLAY IN THE COURT OF PUBLIC OPINION? TIME WILL TELL!
SOB!
MEANWHILE, WHAT THE FUGITIVE HIMSELF THINKS OF HIS WIFE'S PERFORMANCE IS ANYONE'S GUESS!
GBTrudeau
SHE NEEDS TO SHOW MORE BOOB, DAMMIT!
I'LL TELL HER, SIR.

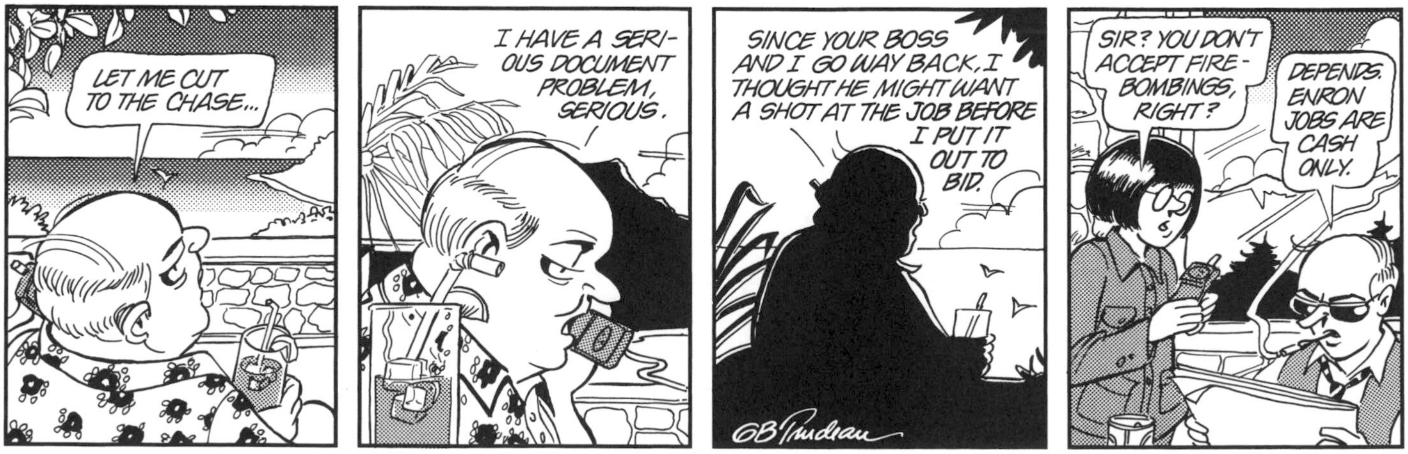
LET ME CUT TO THE CHASE...
I HAVE A SERIOUS DOCUMENT PROBLEM, SERIOUS.
SINCE YOUR BOSS AND I GO WAY BACK, I THOUGHT HE MIGHT WANT A SHOT AT THE JOB BEFORE I PUT IT OUT TO BID.
GBTrudeau
SIR? YOU DON'T ACCEPT FIRE-BOMBINGS, RIGHT?
DEPENDS. ENRON JOBS ARE CASH ONLY.

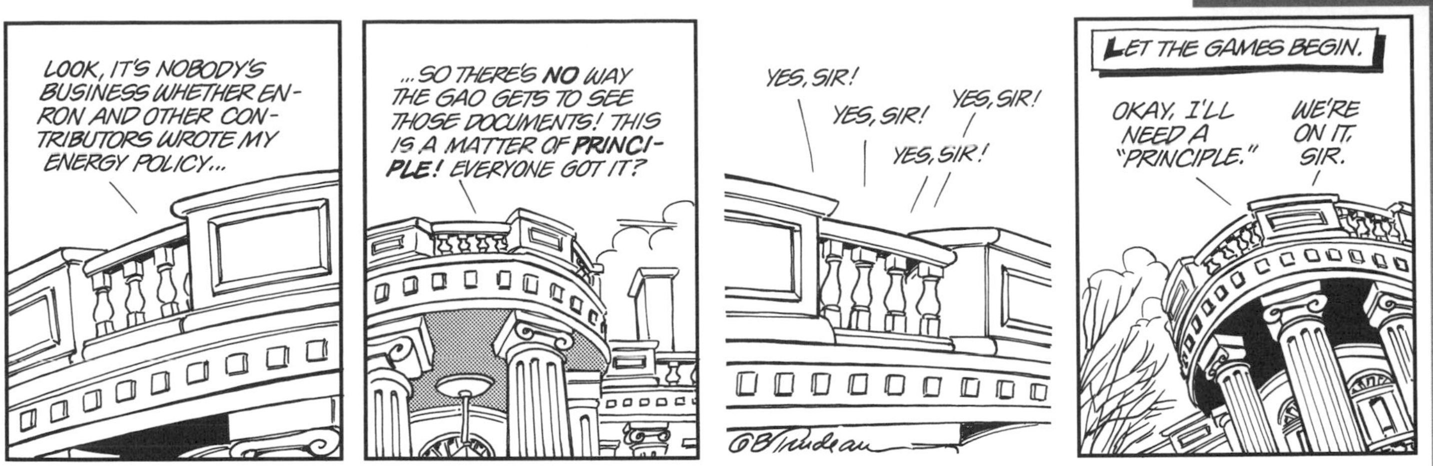
LOOK, IT'S NOBODY'S BUSINESS WHETHER ENRON AND OTHER CONTRIBUTORS WROTE MY ENERGY POLICY...
...SO THERE'S NO WAY THE GAO GETS TO SEE THOSE DOCUMENTS! THIS IS A MATTER OF PRINCIPLE! EVERYONE GOT IT?
YES, SIR!
YES, SIR!
YES, SIR!
YES, SIR!
©B Trudeau
LET THE GAMES BEGIN.
OKAY, I'LL NEED A "PRINCIPLE."
WE'RE ON IT, SIR.

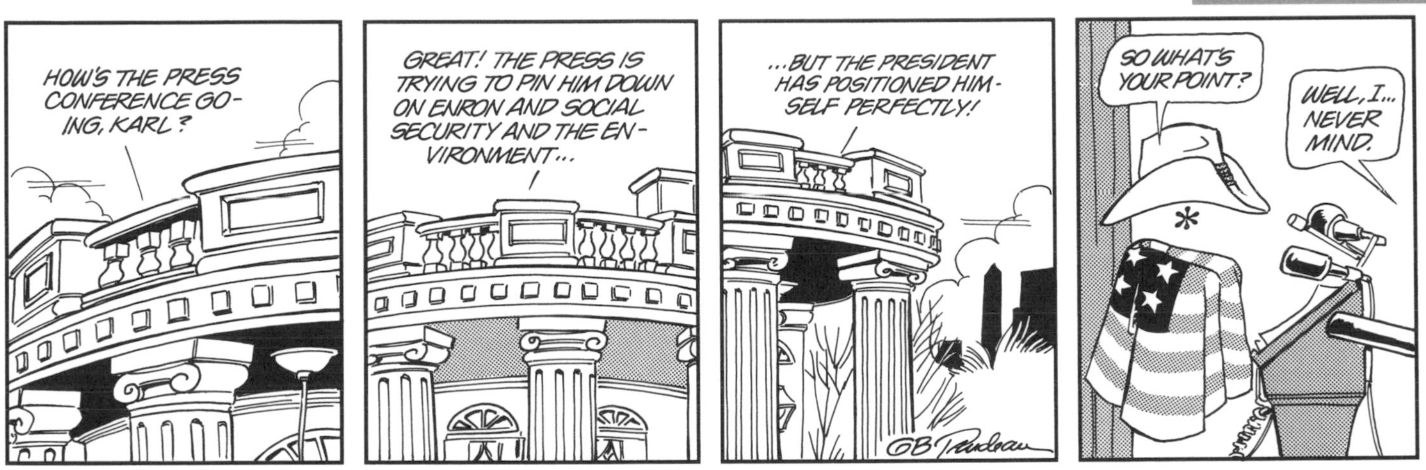
HOW'S THE PRESS CONFERENCE GOING, KARL?
GREAT! THE PRESS IS TRYING TO PIN HIM DOWN ON ENRON AND SOCIAL SECURITY AND THE ENVIRONMENT...
...BUT THE PRESIDENT HAS POSITIONED HIMSELF PERFECTLY!
©B Trudeau
SO WHAT'S YOUR POINT?
WELL, I... NEVER MIND.

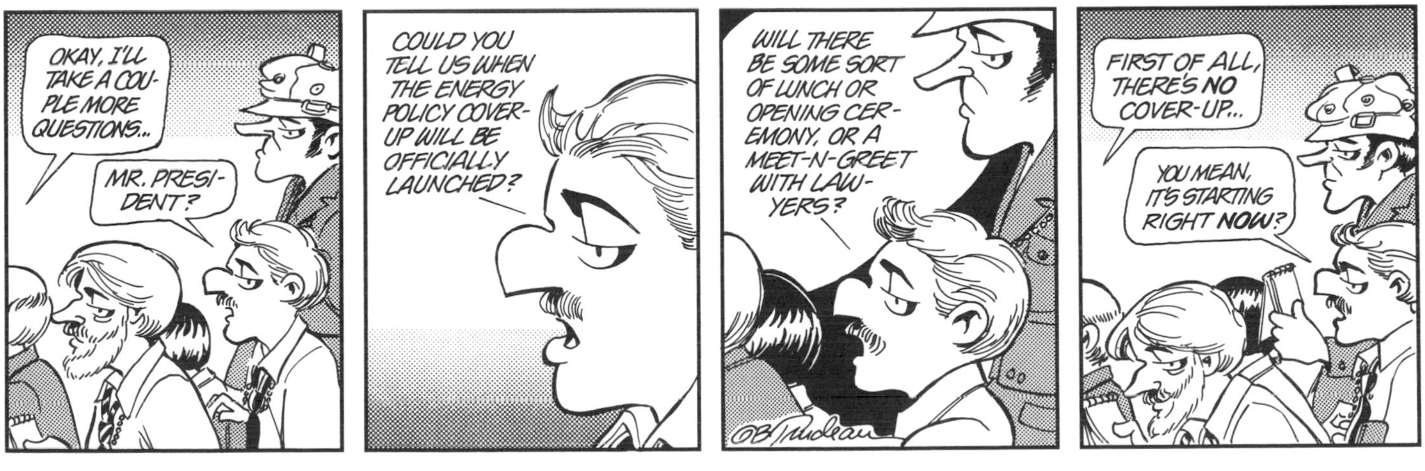
OKAY, I'LL TAKE A COUPLE MORE QUESTIONS..
MR. PRESIDENT?
COULD YOU TELL US WHEN THE ENERGY POLICY COVER-UP WILL BE OFFICIALLY LAUNCHED?
WILL THERE BE SOME SORT OF LUNCH OR OPENING CEREMONY, OR A MEET-N-GREET WITH LAWYERS?
©B Trudeau
FIRST OF ALL, THERE'S NO COVER-UP...
YOU MEAN, IT'S STARTING RIGHT NOW?

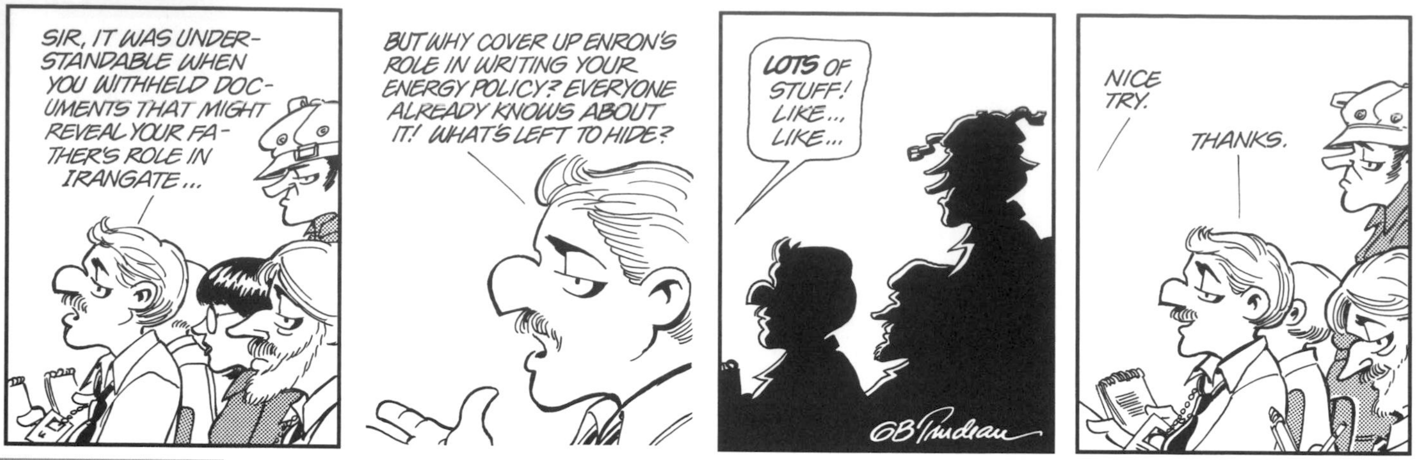
SIR, IT WAS UNDERSTANDABLE WHEN YOU WITHHELD DOCUMENTS THAT MIGHT REVEAL YOUR FATHER'S ROLE IN IRANGATE...
BUT WHY COVER UP ENRON'S ROLE IN WRITING YOUR ENERGY POLICY? EVERYONE ALREADY KNOWS ABOUT IT! WHAT'S LEFT TO HIDE?
LOTS OF STUFF! LIKE... LIKE...
GB Trudeau
NICE TRY.
THANKS.

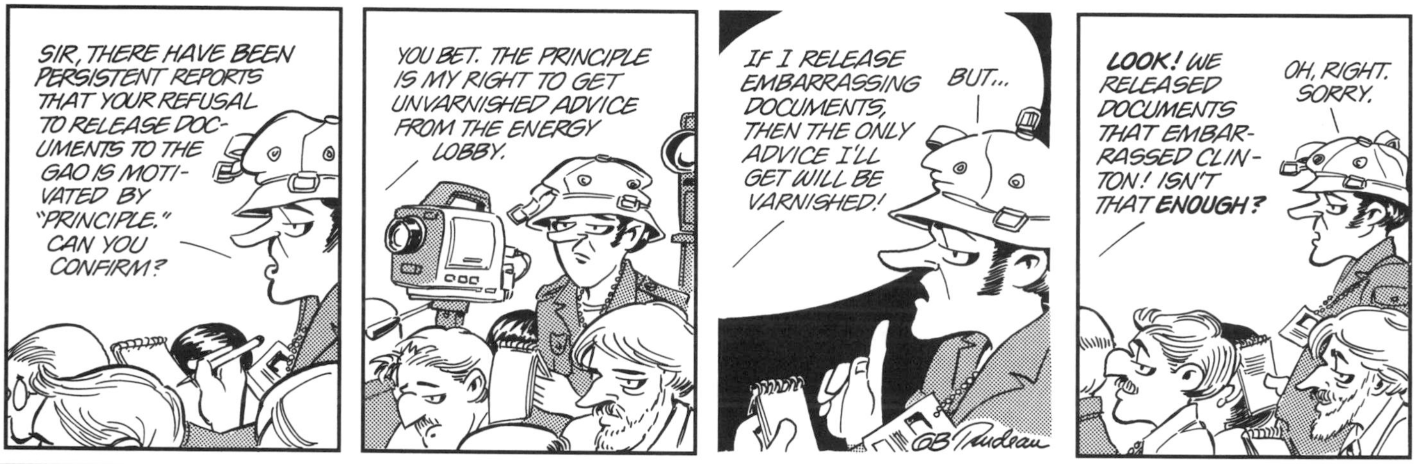
SIR, THERE HAVE BEEN PERSISTENT REPORTS THAT YOUR REFUSAL TO RELEASE DOCUMENTS TO THE GAO IS MOTIVATED BY "PRINCIPLE." CAN YOU CONFIRM?
YOU BET. THE PRINCIPLE IS MY RIGHT TO GET UNVARNISHED ADVICE FROM THE ENERGY LOBBY.
IF I RELEASE EMBARRASSING DOCUMENTS, THEN THE ONLY ADVICE I'LL GET WILL BE VARNISHED!
BUT...
GB Trudeau
LOOK! WE RELEASED DOCUMENTS THAT EMBARRASSED CLINTON! ISN'T THAT ENOUGH?
OH, RIGHT. SORRY.

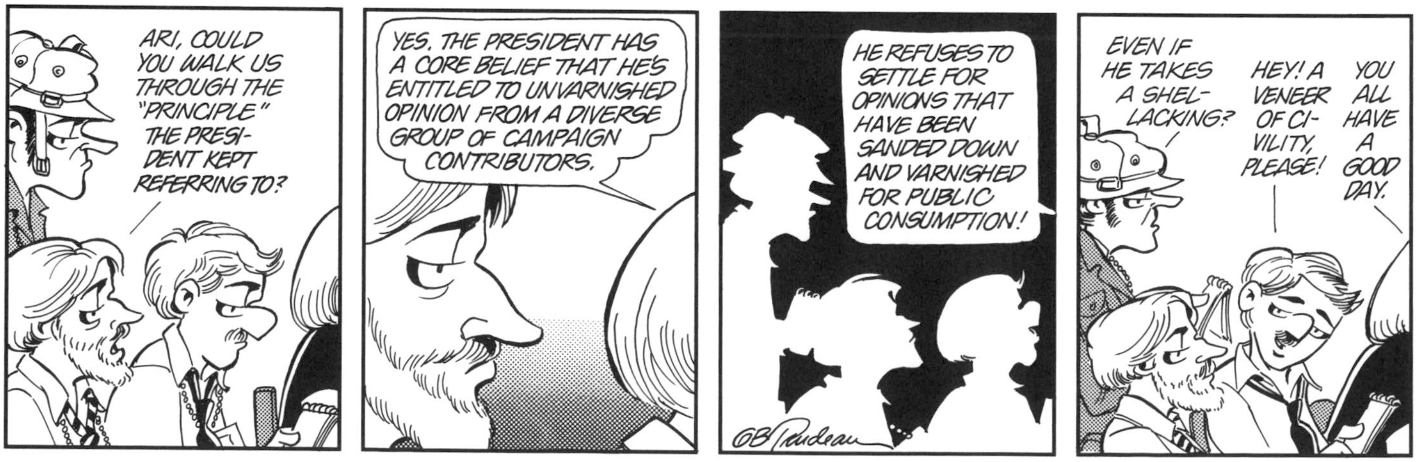
ARI, COULD YOU WALK US THROUGH THE "PRINCIPLE" THE PRESIDENT KEPT REFERRING TO?
YES. THE PRESIDENT HAS A CORE BELIEF THAT HE'S ENTITLED TO UNVARNISHED OPINION FROM A DIVERSE GROUP OF CAMPAIGN CONTRIBUTORS.
HE REFUSES TO SETTLE FOR OPINIONS THAT HAVE BEEN SANDED DOWN AND VARNISHED FOR PUBLIC CONSUMPTION!
GB Trudeau
EVEN IF HE TAKES A SHELLACKING?
HEY! A VENEER OF CIVILITY, PLEASE!
YOU ALL HAVE A GOOD DAY.

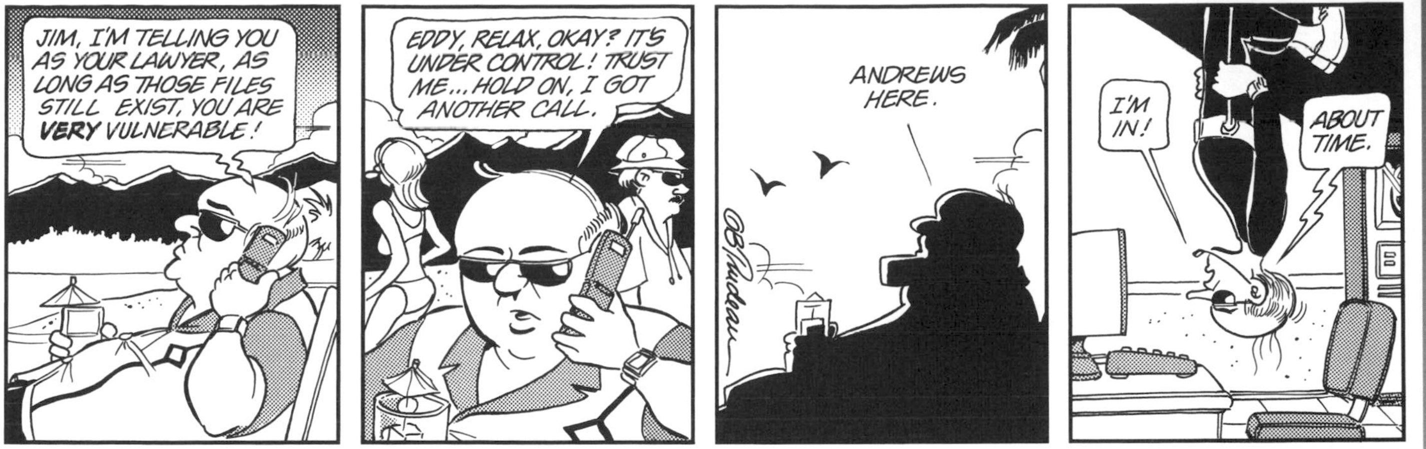
JIM, I'M TELLING YOU AS YOUR LAWYER, AS LONG AS THOSE FILES STILL EXIST, YOU ARE **VERY** VULNERABLE!
EDDY, RELAX, OKAY? IT'S UNDER CONTROL! TRUST ME... HOLD ON, I GOT ANOTHER CALL.
ANDREWS HERE.
I'M IN!
ABOUT TIME.

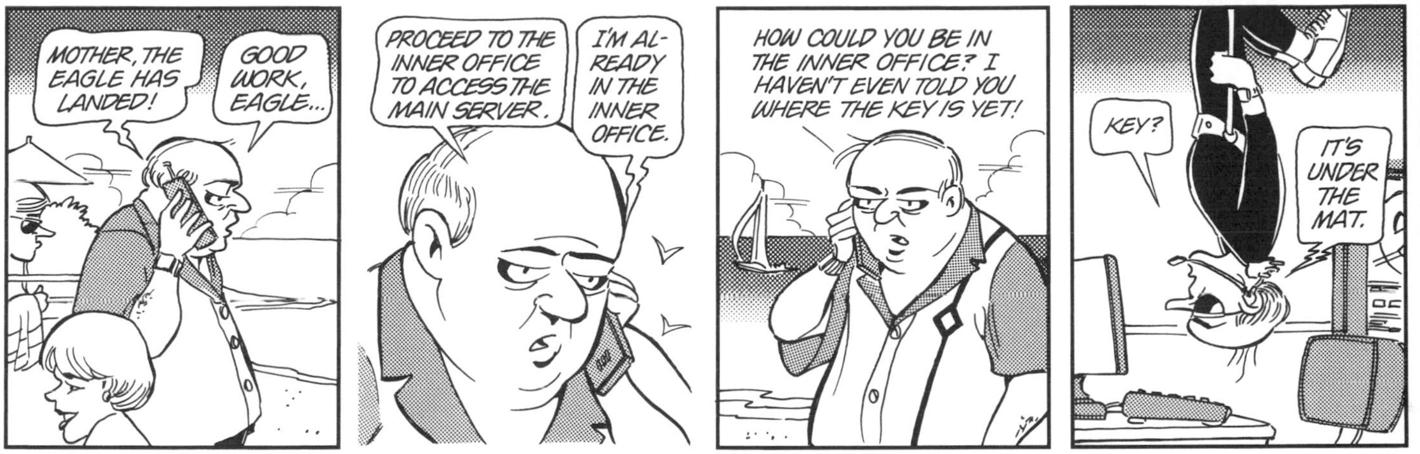
MOTHER, THE EAGLE HAS LANDED!
GOOD WORK, EAGLE...
PROCEED TO THE INNER OFFICE TO ACCESS THE MAIN SERVER.
I'M ALREADY IN THE INNER OFFICE.
HOW COULD YOU BE IN THE INNER OFFICE? I HAVEN'T EVEN TOLD YOU WHERE THE KEY IS YET!
KEY?
IT'S UNDER THE MAT.

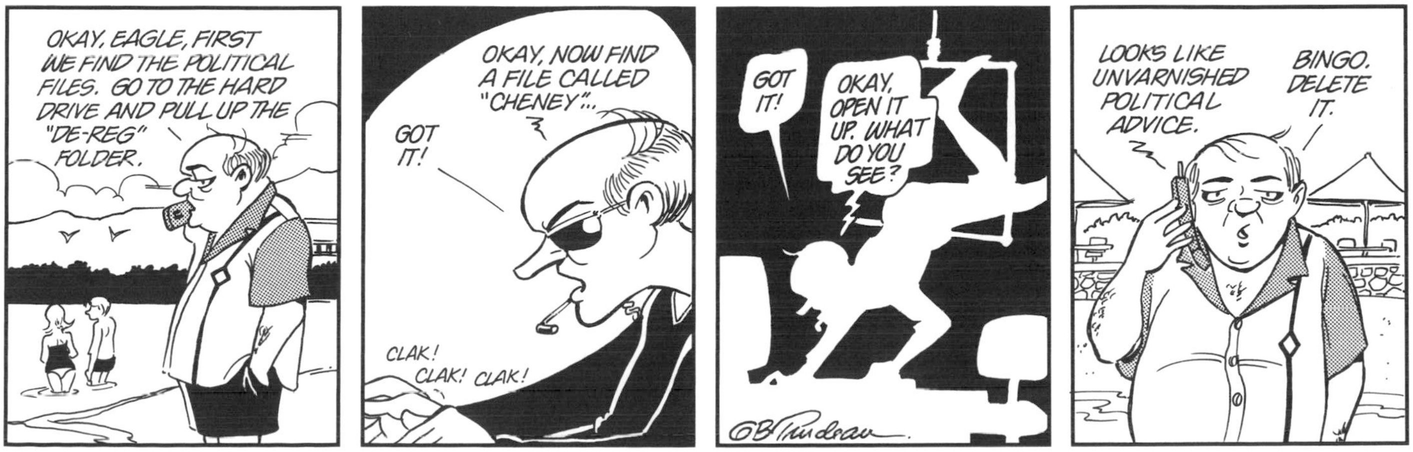
OKAY, EAGLE, FIRST WE FIND THE POLITICAL FILES. GO TO THE HARD DRIVE AND PULL UP THE "DE-REG" FOLDER.
OKAY, NOW FIND A FILE CALLED "CHENEY"...
GOT IT!
CLAK! CLAK! CLAK!
GOT IT!
OKAY, OPEN IT UP. WHAT DO YOU SEE?
LOOKS LIKE UNVARNISHED POLITICAL ADVICE.
BINGO. DELETE IT.

OKAY, MOTHER, I'M NOW LOGGED ON TO THE BACKUP SERVER...
GOOD! NOW LISTEN, EAGLE, YOU NEED TO DISABLE THE FIREWALL. THIS IS CRITICAL!
COPY THAT, BIG GUY!
MAY I HELP YOU?
MOTHER, WE'VE GOT COMPANY.
THAT'S JUST MY SECRETARY. FIRE HER.
GBTrudeau

ANDREWS SAYS TO TELL YOU YOU'RE FIRED!
HE CAN'T FIRE ME, I'M HIS WIFE! WHAT ARE YOU DOING HERE?
UM...
I CAN GUESS. WHATEVER JIM'S PAYING YOU TO DESTROY EVIDENCE, I'LL PAY YOU DOUBLE **NOT** TO!
EAGLE! ARE YOU STILL THERE? HAVE YOU BEEN COMPROMISED?
I RESENT YOUR IMPLICATION, MOTHER!
CHECK OKAY?
GBTrudeau

EAGLE? HAVE YOU KILLED THE PARTNERSHIP FILES YET?
THAT'S A NEGATIVE, MOTHER. I GOT A PROBLEM.
PROBLEM?
THE SYSTEM'S LOCKED DOWN. I'M GOING TO HAVE TO ABORT.
SIGH...
GBTrudeau
PUT MY WIFE ON.
WHO? YOU'RE BREAKING UP, BIG GUY.

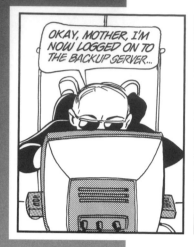

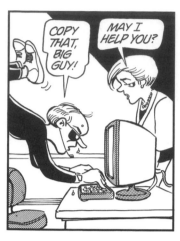

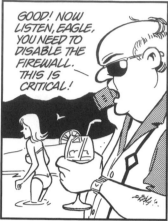

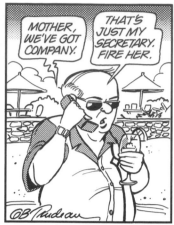

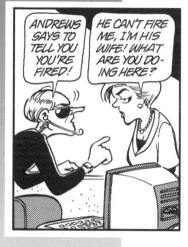

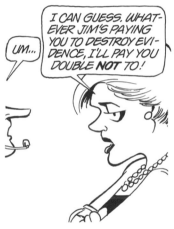

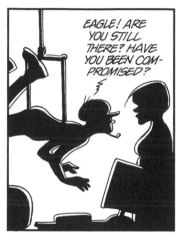

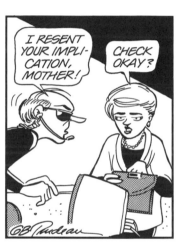

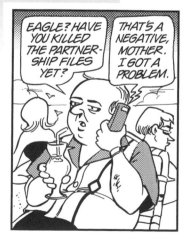

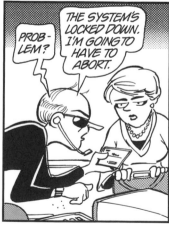

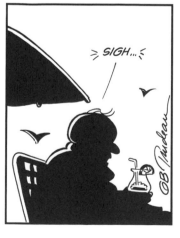

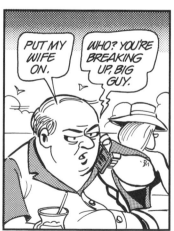

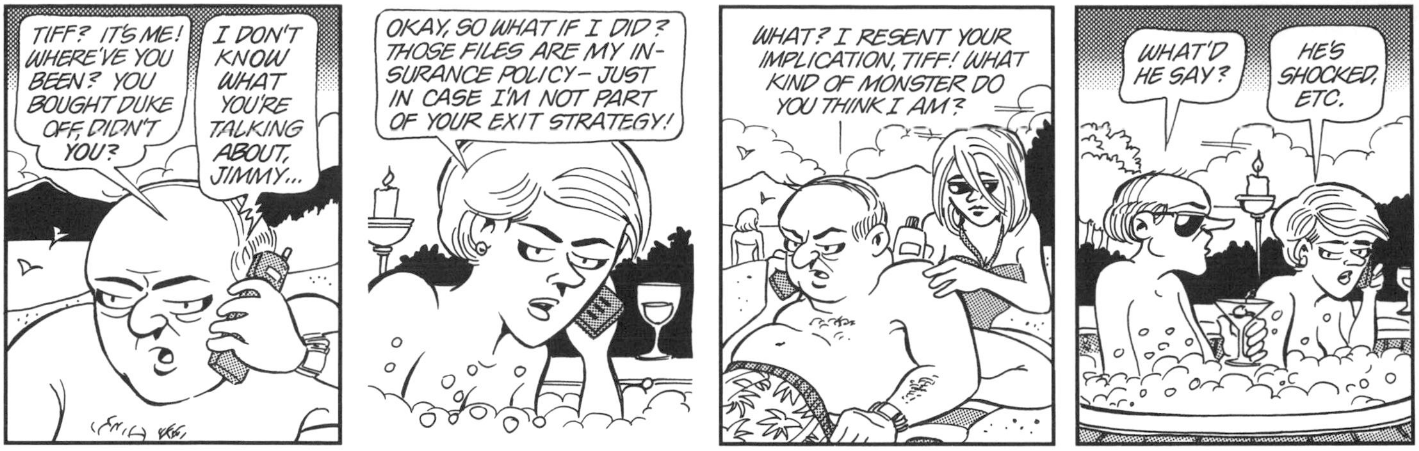
TIFF? IT'S ME! WHERE'VE YOU BEEN? YOU BOUGHT DUKE OFF, DIDN'T YOU?
I DON'T KNOW WHAT YOU'RE TALKING ABOUT, JIMMY...
OKAY, SO WHAT IF I DID? THOSE FILES ARE MY INSURANCE POLICY – JUST IN CASE I'M NOT PART OF YOUR EXIT STRATEGY!
WHAT? I RESENT YOUR IMPLICATION, TIFF! WHAT KIND OF MONSTER DO YOU THINK I AM?
WHAT'D HE SAY?
HE'S SHOCKED, ETC.

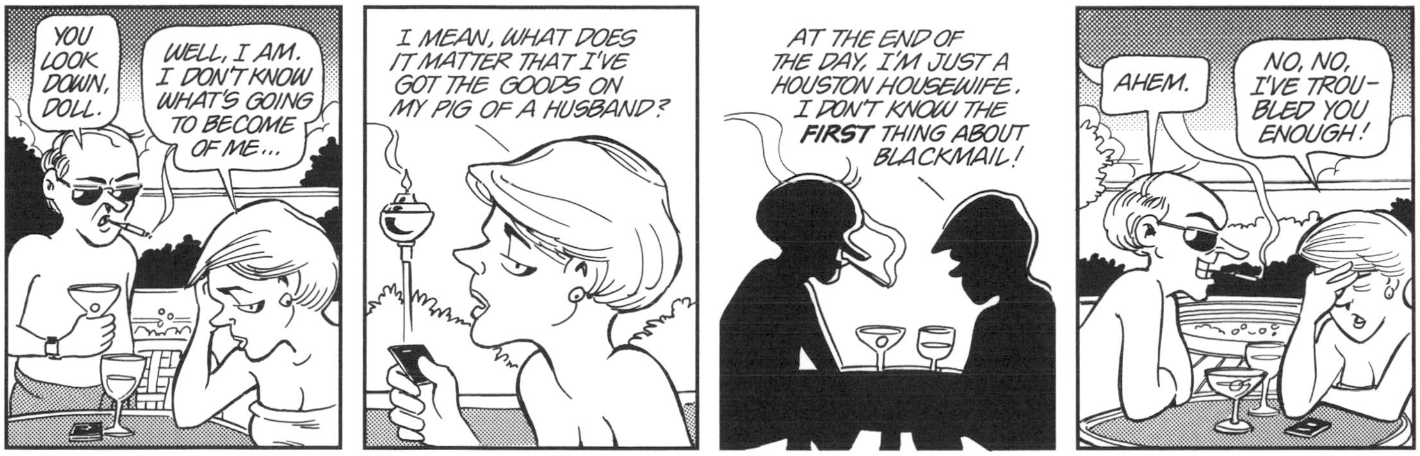
YOU LOOK DOWN, DOLL.
WELL, I AM. I DON'T KNOW WHAT'S GOING TO BECOME OF ME...
I MEAN, WHAT DOES IT MATTER THAT I'VE GOT THE GOODS ON MY PIG OF A HUSBAND?
AT THE END OF THE DAY, I'M JUST A HOUSTON HOUSEWIFE. I DON'T KNOW THE FIRST THING ABOUT BLACKMAIL!
AHEM.
NO, NO, I'VE TROUBLED YOU ENOUGH!

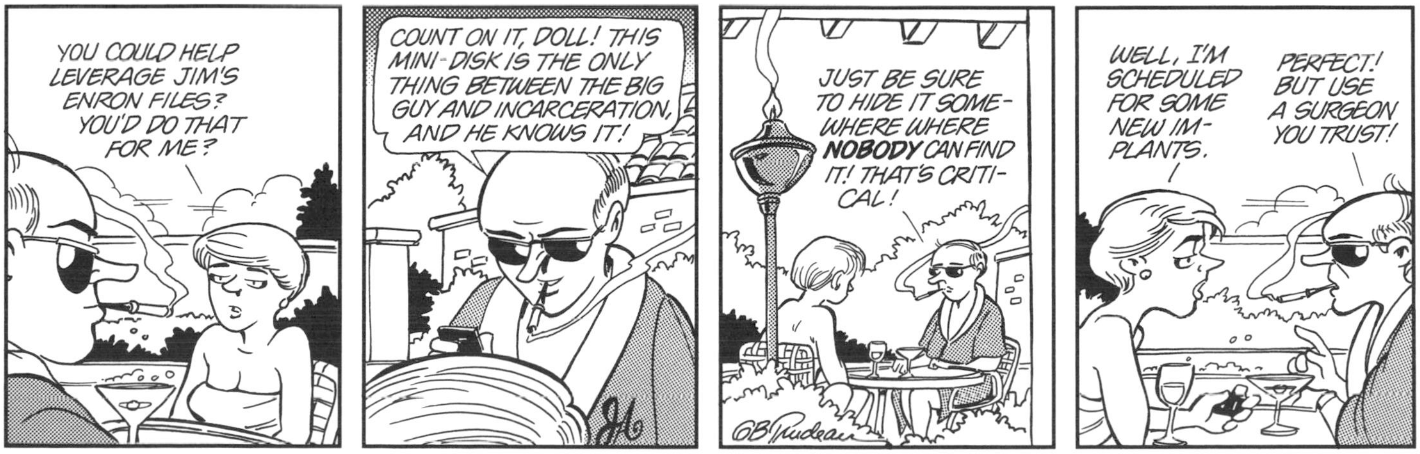
YOU COULD HELP LEVERAGE JIM'S ENRON FILES? YOU'D DO THAT FOR ME?
COUNT ON IT, DOLL! THIS MINI-DISK IS THE ONLY THING BETWEEN THE BIG GUY AND INCARCERATION, AND HE KNOWS IT!
JUST BE SURE TO HIDE IT SOMEWHERE WHERE NOBODY CAN FIND IT! THAT'S CRITICAL!
WELL, I'M SCHEDULED FOR SOME NEW IMPLANTS.
PERFECT! BUT USE A SURGEON YOU TRUST!
GBTrudeau

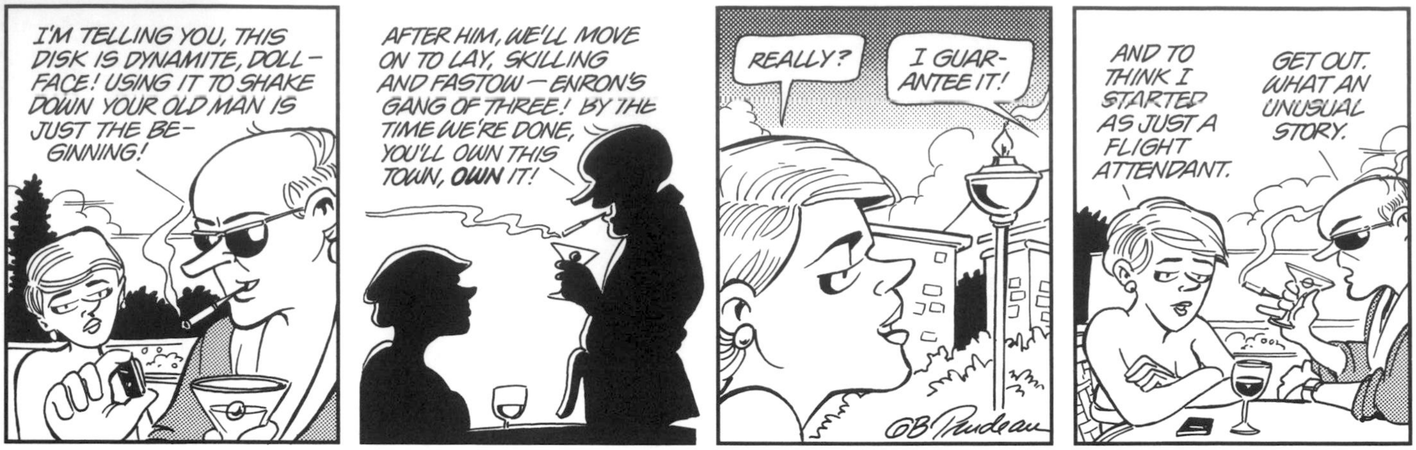
I'M TELLING YOU, THIS DISK IS DYNAMITE, DOLL-FACE! USING IT TO SHAKE DOWN YOUR OLD MAN IS JUST THE BE-GINNING!
AFTER HIM, WE'LL MOVE ON TO LAY, SKILLING AND FASTOW — ENRON'S GANG OF THREE! BY THE TIME WE'RE DONE, YOU'LL OWN THIS TOWN, OWN IT!
REALLY?
I GUAR-ANTEE IT!
GB Trudeau
AND TO THINK I STARTED AS JUST A FLIGHT ATTENDANT.
GET OUT. WHAT AN UNUSUAL STORY.

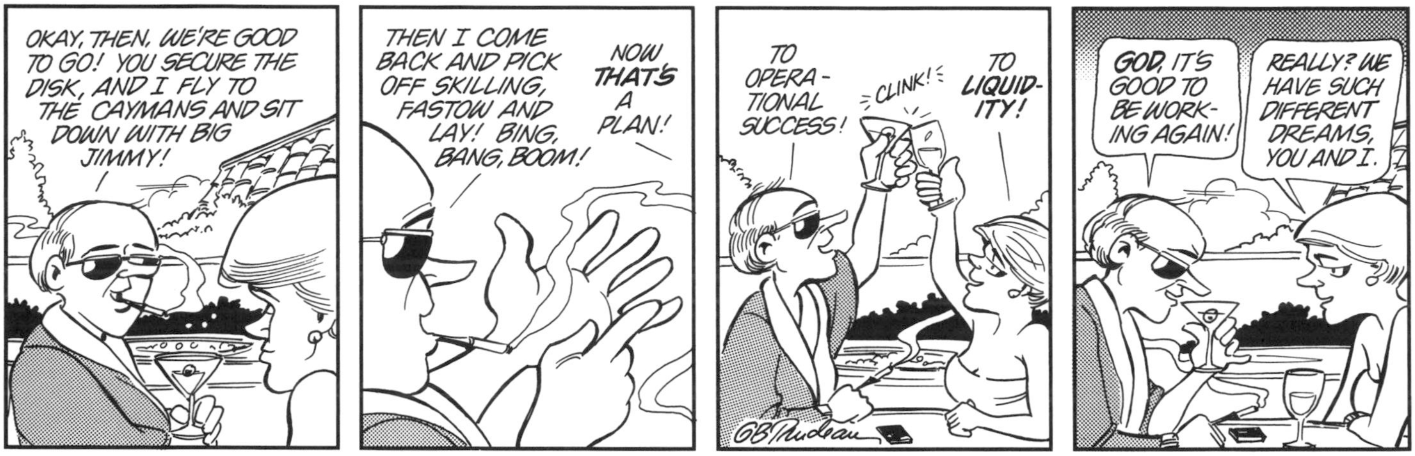
OKAY, THEN, WE'RE GOOD TO GO! YOU SECURE THE DISK, AND I FLY TO THE CAYMANS AND SIT DOWN WITH BIG JIMMY!
THEN I COME BACK AND PICK OFF SKILLING, FASTOW AND LAY! BING, BANG, BOOM!
NOW THAT'S A PLAN!
TO OPERA-TIONAL SUCCESS!
CLINK!
TO LIQUID-ITY!
GB Trudeau
GOD, IT'S GOOD TO BE WORK-ING AGAIN!
REALLY? WE HAVE SUCH DIFFERENT DREAMS, YOU AND I.

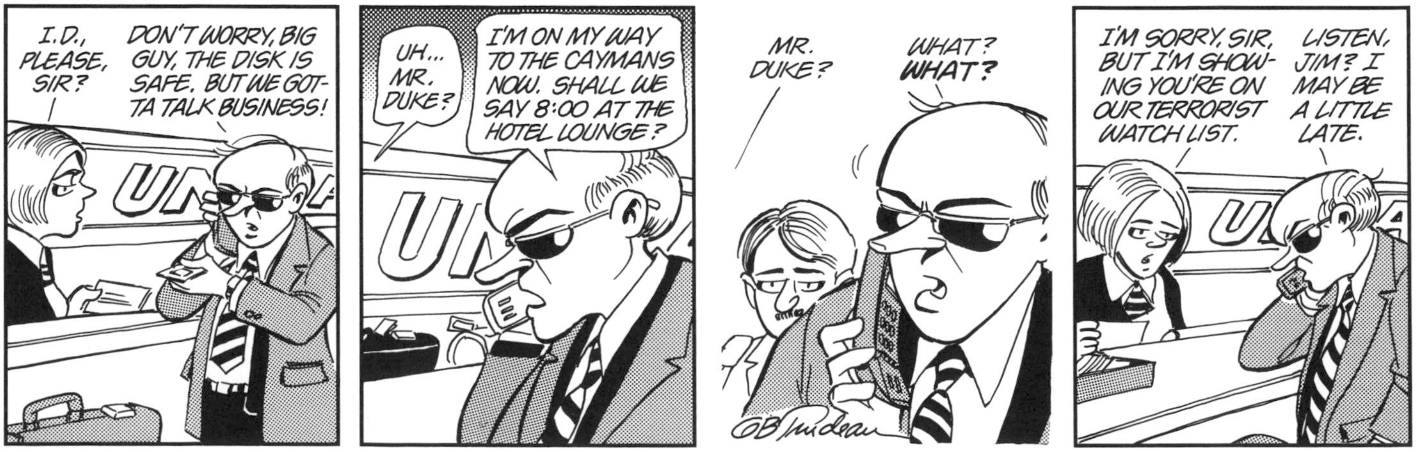
I.D., PLEASE, SIR?
DON'T WORRY, BIG GUY, THE DISK IS SAFE. BUT WE GOT-TA TALK BUSINESS!
UH... MR. DUKE?
I'M ON MY WAY TO THE CAYMANS NOW. SHALL WE SAY 8:00 AT THE HOTEL LOUNGE?
MR. DUKE?
WHAT? WHAT?
GB Trudeau
I'M SORRY, SIR, BUT I'M SHOW-ING YOU'RE ON OUR TERRORIST WATCH LIST.
LISTEN, JIM? I MAY BE A LITTLE LATE.

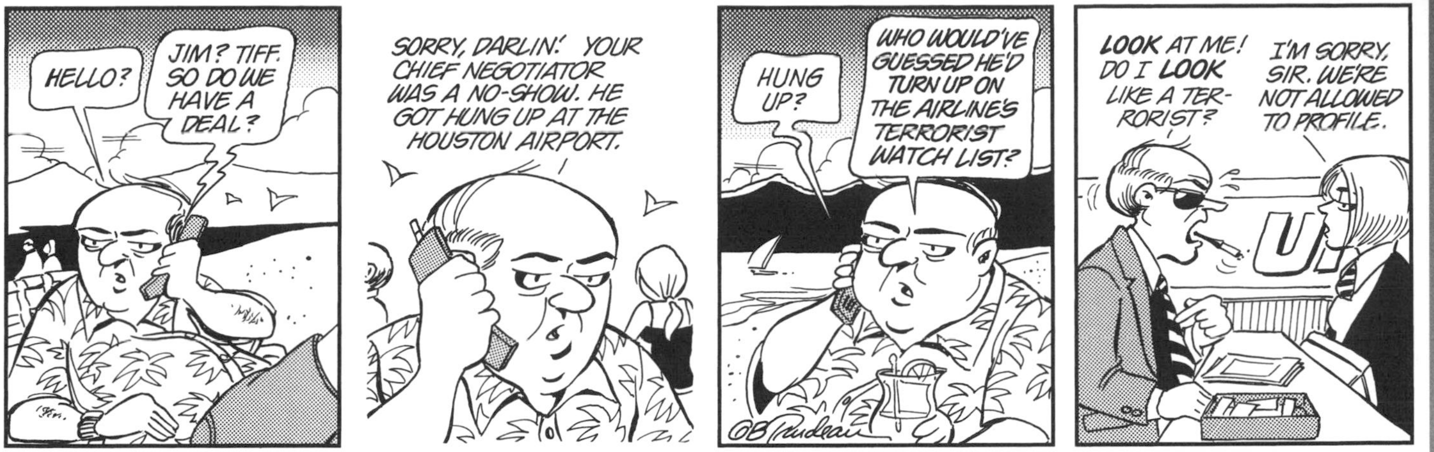
HELLO?
JIM? TIFF. SO DO WE HAVE A DEAL?
SORRY, DARLIN'. YOUR CHIEF NEGOTIATOR WAS A NO-SHOW. HE GOT HUNG UP AT THE HOUSTON AIRPORT.
HUNG UP?
WHO WOULD'VE GUESSED HE'D TURN UP ON THE AIRLINE'S TERRORIST WATCH LIST?
LOOK AT ME! DO I LOOK LIKE A TERRORIST?
I'M SORRY, SIR. WE'RE NOT ALLOWED TO PROFILE.

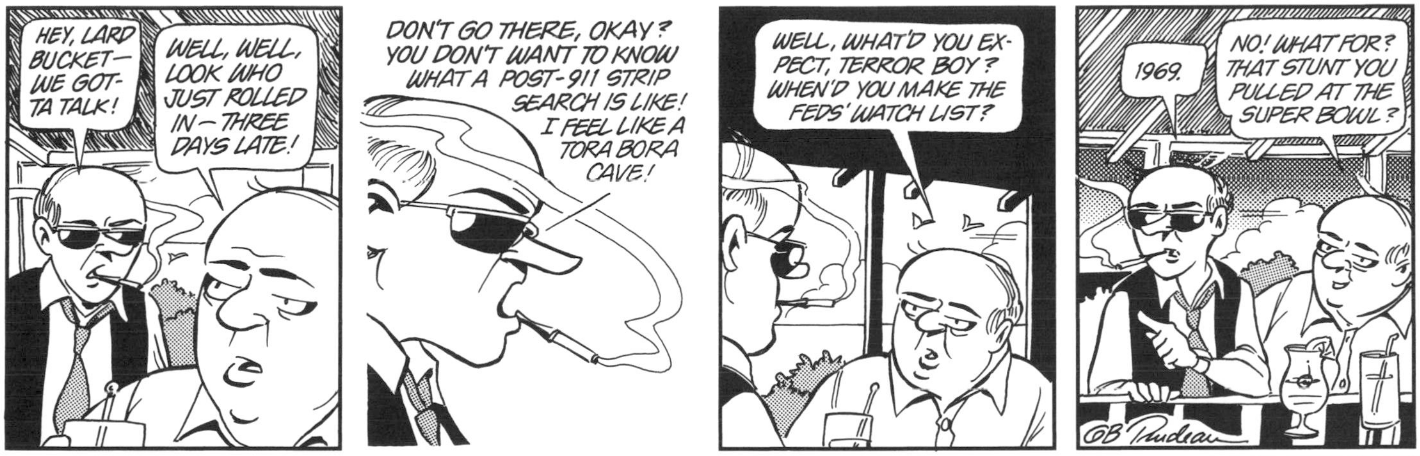
HEY, LARD BUCKET— WE GOTTA TALK!
WELL, WELL, LOOK WHO JUST ROLLED IN— THREE DAYS LATE!
DON'T GO THERE, OKAY? YOU DON'T WANT TO KNOW WHAT A POST-911 STRIP SEARCH IS LIKE! I FEEL LIKE A TORA BORA CAVE!
WELL, WHAT'D YOU EXPECT, TERROR BOY? WHEN'D YOU MAKE THE FEDS' WATCH LIST?
1969.
NO! WHAT FOR? THAT STUNT YOU PULLED AT THE SUPER BOWL?

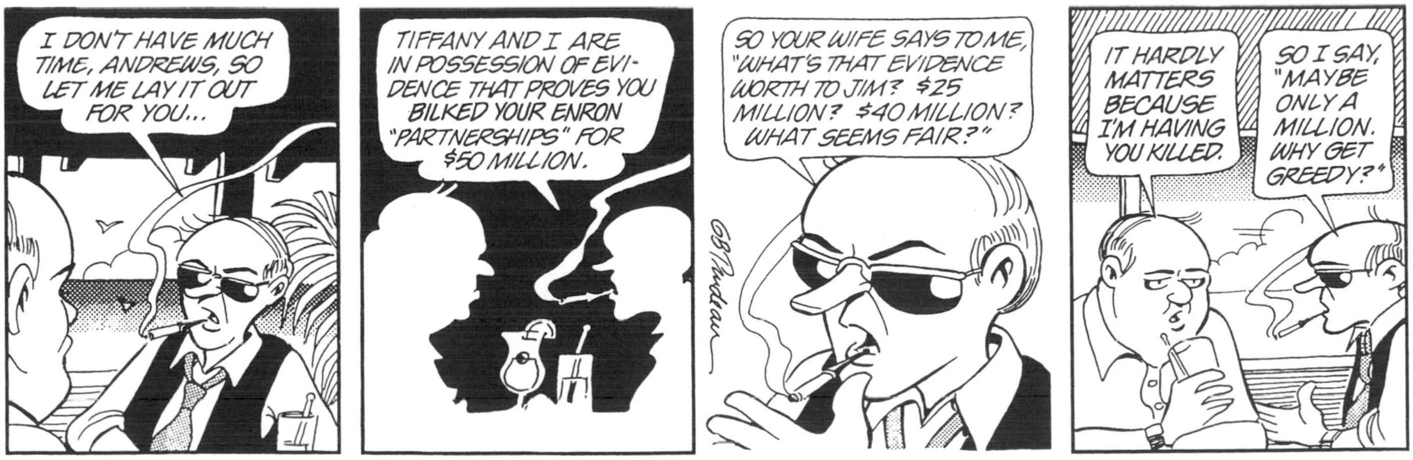
I DON'T HAVE MUCH TIME, ANDREWS, SO LET ME LAY IT OUT FOR YOU...
TIFFANY AND I ARE IN POSSESSION OF EVIDENCE THAT PROVES YOU BILKED YOUR ENRON "PARTNERSHIPS" FOR $50 MILLION.
SO YOUR WIFE SAYS TO ME, "WHAT'S THAT EVIDENCE WORTH TO JIM? $25 MILLION? $40 MILLION? WHAT SEEMS FAIR?"
IT HARDLY MATTERS BECAUSE I'M HAVING YOU KILLED.
SO I SAY, "MAYBE ONLY A MILLION. WHY GET GREEDY?"

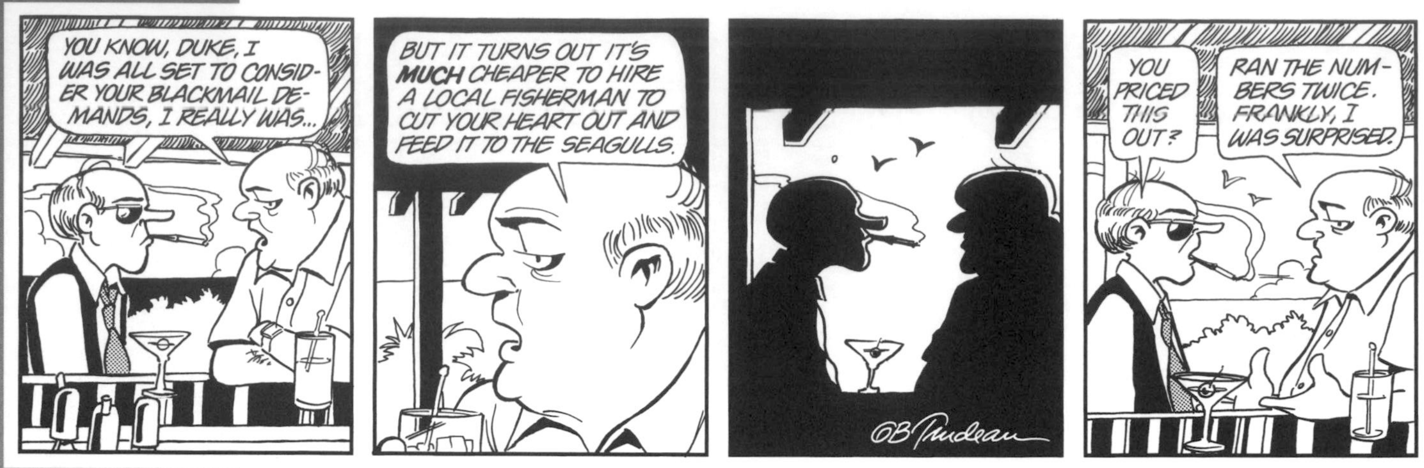
YOU KNOW, DUKE, I WAS ALL SET TO CONSIDER YOUR BLACKMAIL DEMANDS, I REALLY WAS...
BUT IT TURNS OUT IT'S **MUCH** CHEAPER TO HIRE A LOCAL FISHERMAN TO CUT YOUR HEART OUT AND FEED IT TO THE SEAGULLS.
YOU PRICED THIS OUT?
RAN THE NUMBERS TWICE. FRANKLY, I WAS SURPRISED.

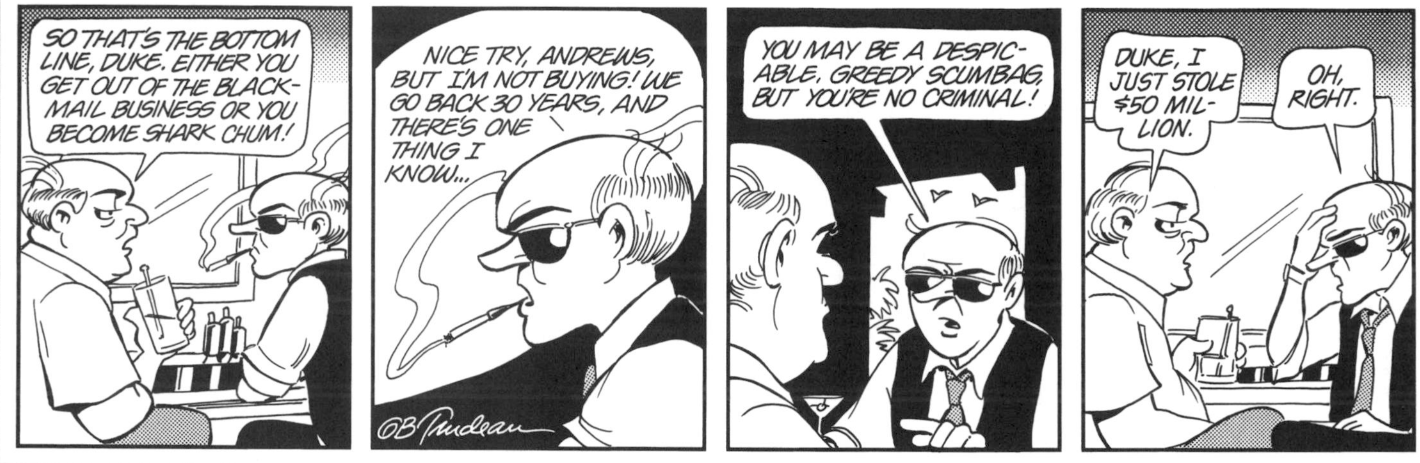
SO THAT'S THE BOTTOM LINE, DUKE. EITHER YOU GET OUT OF THE BLACKMAIL BUSINESS OR YOU BECOME SHARK CHUM!
NICE TRY, ANDREWS, BUT I'M NOT BUYING! WE GO BACK 30 YEARS, AND THERE'S ONE THING I KNOW...
YOU MAY BE A DESPICABLE, GREEDY SCUMBAG, BUT YOU'RE NO CRIMINAL!
DUKE, I JUST STOLE $50 MILLION.
OH, RIGHT.

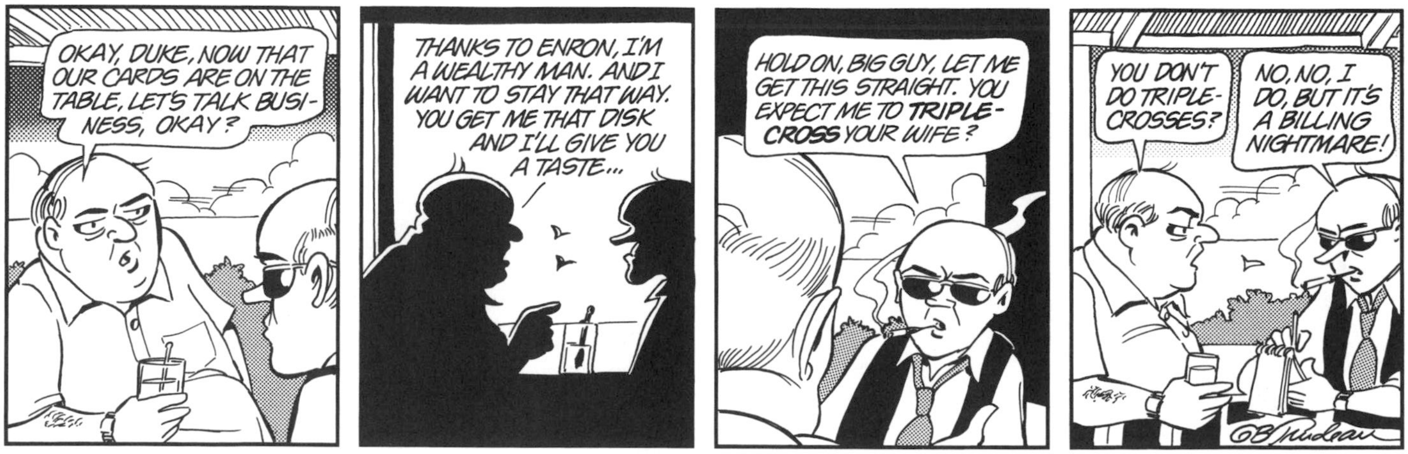
OKAY, DUKE, NOW THAT OUR CARDS ARE ON THE TABLE, LET'S TALK BUSINESS, OKAY?
THANKS TO ENRON, I'M A WEALTHY MAN. AND I WANT TO STAY THAT WAY. YOU GET ME THAT DISK AND I'LL GIVE YOU A TASTE...
HOLD ON, BIG GUY, LET ME GET THIS STRAIGHT. YOU EXPECT ME TO **TRIPLE-CROSS** YOUR WIFE?
YOU DON'T DO TRIPLE-CROSSES?
NO, NO, I DO, BUT IT'S A BILLING NIGHTMARE!

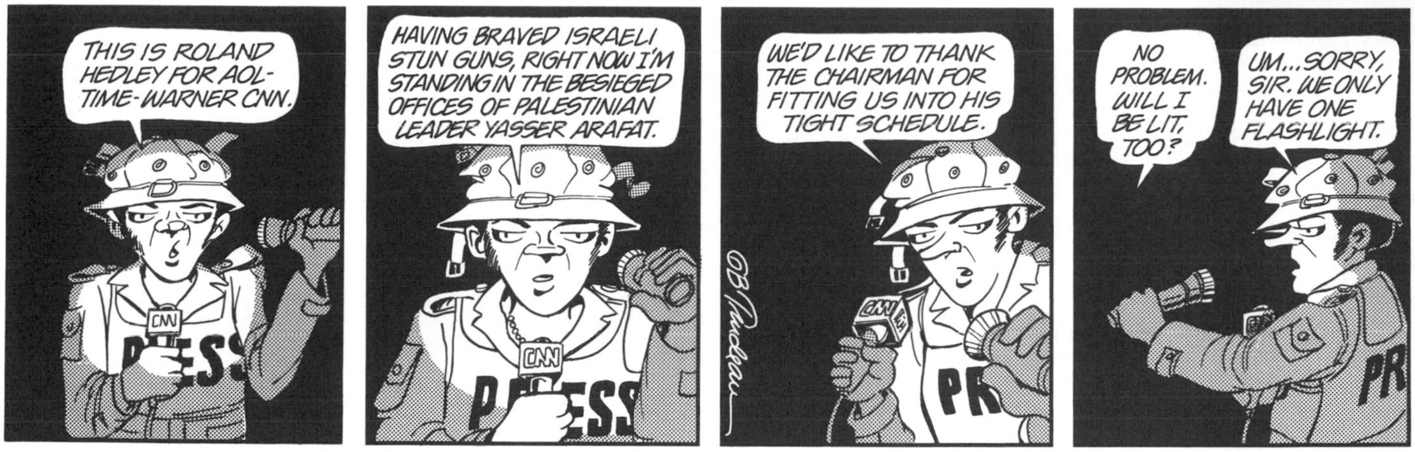
THIS IS ROLAND HEDLEY FOR AOL-TIME-WARNER CNN.
HAVING BRAVED ISRAELI STUN GUNS, RIGHT NOW I'M STANDING IN THE BESIEGED OFFICES OF PALESTINIAN LEADER YASSER ARAFAT.
WE'D LIKE TO THANK THE CHAIRMAN FOR FITTING US INTO HIS TIGHT SCHEDULE.
NO PROBLEM. WILL I BE LIT, TOO?
UM... SORRY, SIR. WE ONLY HAVE ONE FLASHLIGHT.
©B Trudeau

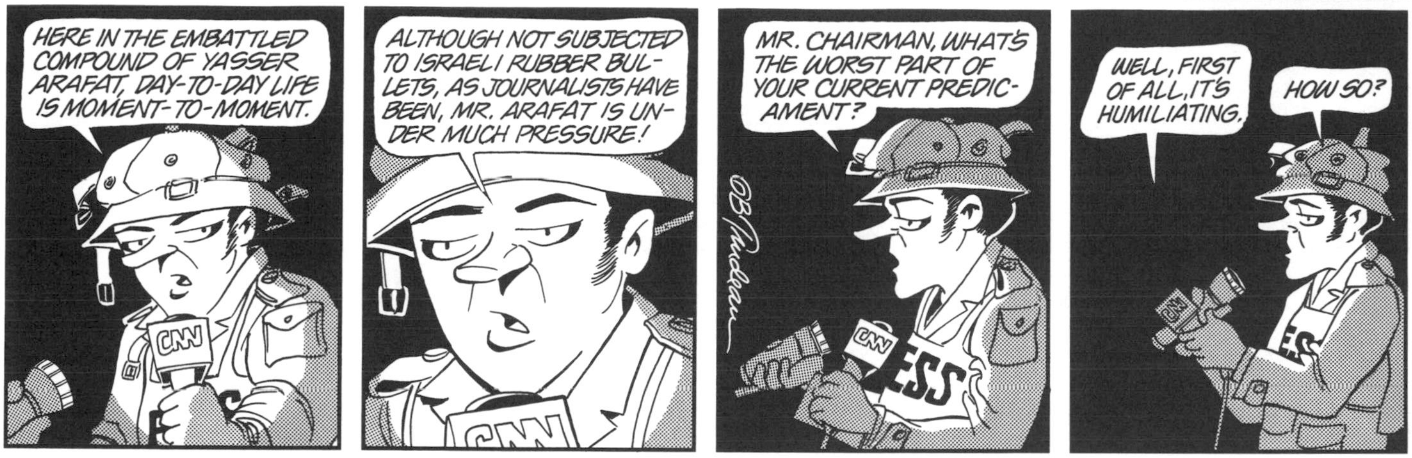
HERE IN THE EMBATTLED COMPOUND OF YASSER ARAFAT, DAY-TO-DAY LIFE IS MOMENT-TO-MOMENT.
ALTHOUGH NOT SUBJECTED TO ISRAELI RUBBER BULLETS, AS JOURNALISTS HAVE BEEN, MR. ARAFAT IS UNDER MUCH PRESSURE!
MR. CHAIRMAN, WHAT'S THE WORST PART OF YOUR CURRENT PREDICAMENT?
WELL, FIRST OF ALL, IT'S HUMILIATING.
HOW SO?
©B Trudeau

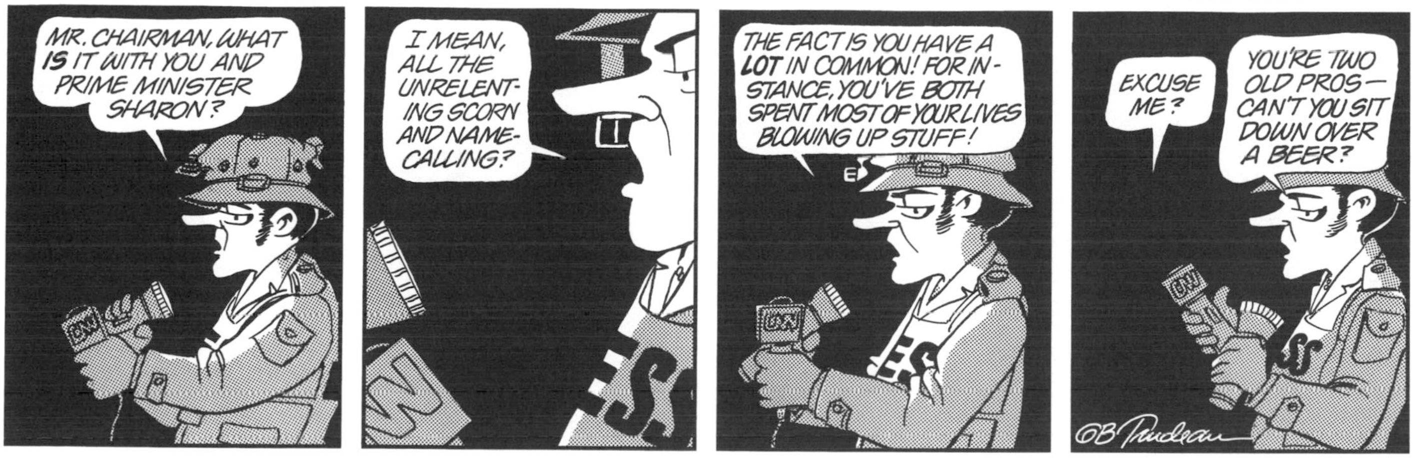
MR. CHAIRMAN, WHAT IS IT WITH YOU AND PRIME MINISTER SHARON?
I MEAN, ALL THE UNRELENTING SCORN AND NAME-CALLING?
THE FACT IS YOU HAVE A LOT IN COMMON! FOR INSTANCE, YOU'VE BOTH SPENT MOST OF YOUR LIVES BLOWING UP STUFF!
EXCUSE ME?
YOU'RE TWO OLD PROS — CAN'T YOU SIT DOWN OVER A BEER?
©B Trudeau

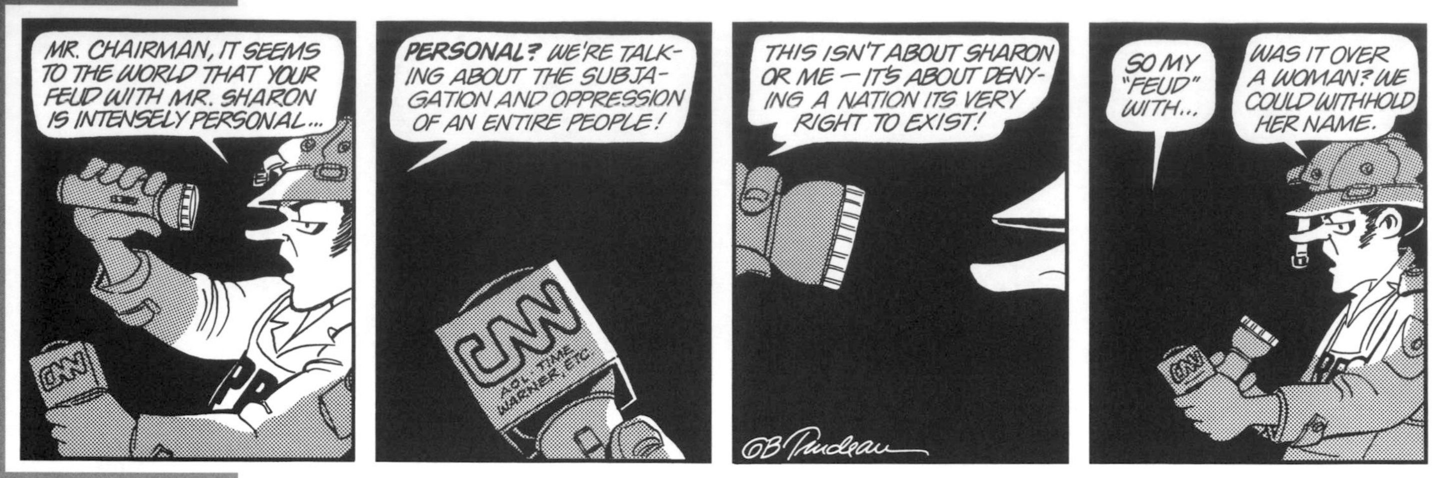
MR. CHAIRMAN, IT SEEMS TO THE WORLD THAT YOUR FEUD WITH MR. SHARON IS INTENSELY PERSONAL...
PERSONAL? WE'RE TALKING ABOUT THE SUBJAGATION AND OPPRESSION OF AN ENTIRE PEOPLE!
CNN AOL TIME WARNER ETC.
THIS ISN'T ABOUT SHARON OR ME — IT'S ABOUT DENYING A NATION ITS VERY RIGHT TO EXIST!
SO MY "FEUD" WITH...
WAS IT OVER A WOMAN? WE COULD WITHHOLD HER NAME.

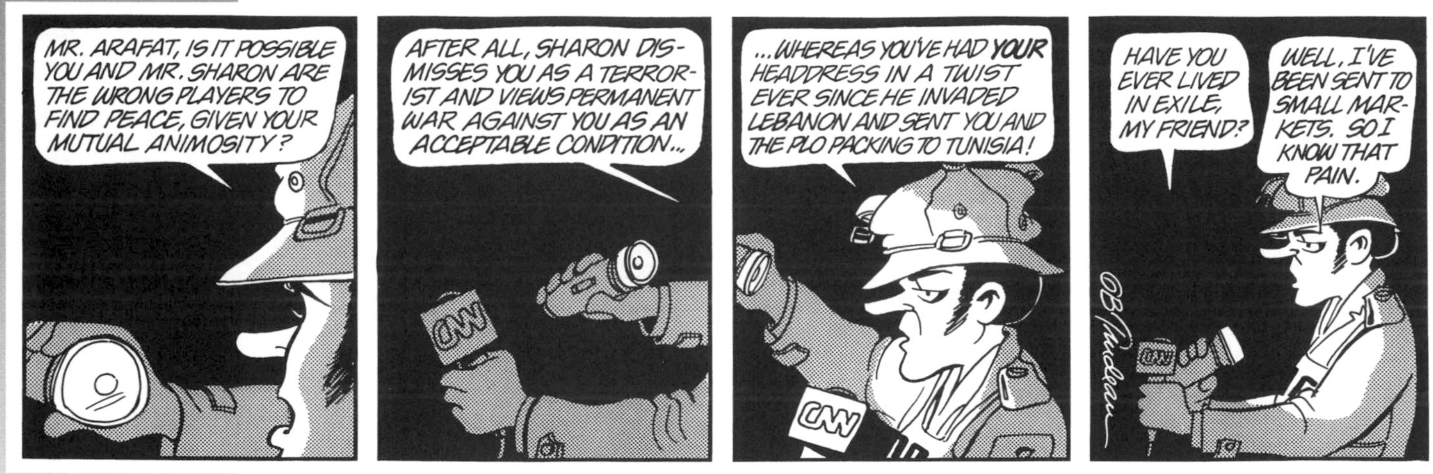
MR. ARAFAT, IS IT POSSIBLE YOU AND MR. SHARON ARE THE WRONG PLAYERS TO FIND PEACE, GIVEN YOUR MUTUAL ANIMOSITY?
AFTER ALL, SHARON DISMISSES YOU AS A TERRORIST AND VIEWS PERMANENT WAR AGAINST YOU AS AN ACCEPTABLE CONDITION...
...WHEREAS YOU'VE HAD YOUR HEADDRESS IN A TWIST EVER SINCE HE INVADED LEBANON AND SENT YOU AND THE PLO PACKING TO TUNISIA!
HAVE YOU EVER LIVED IN EXILE, MY FRIEND?
WELL, I'VE BEEN SENT TO SMALL MARKETS. SO I KNOW THAT PAIN.

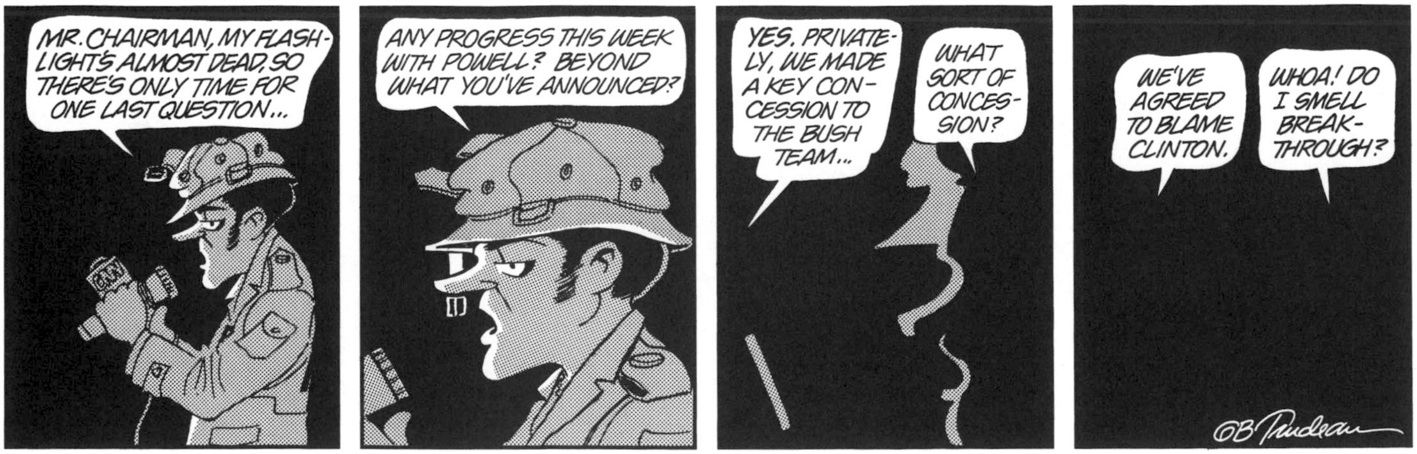
MR. CHAIRMAN, MY FLASHLIGHT'S ALMOST DEAD, SO THERE'S ONLY TIME FOR ONE LAST QUESTION...
ANY PROGRESS THIS WEEK WITH POWELL? BEYOND WHAT YOU'VE ANNOUNCED?
YES. PRIVATELY, WE MADE A KEY CONCESSION TO THE BUSH TEAM...
WHAT SORT OF CONCESSION?
WE'VE AGREED TO BLAME CLINTON.
WHOA! DO I SMELL BREAKTHROUGH?

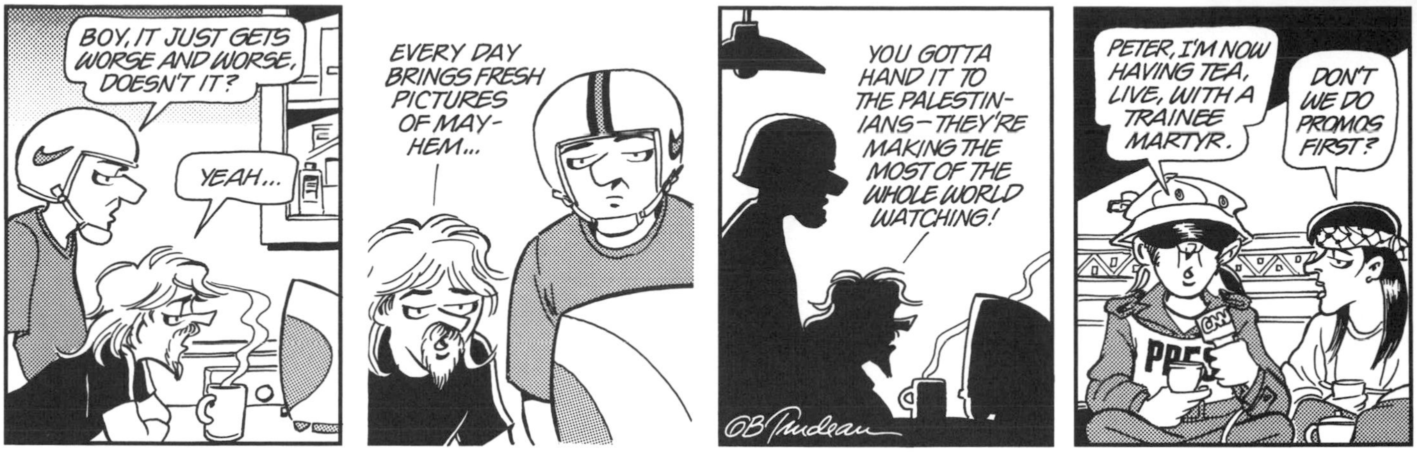
BOY, IT JUST GETS WORSE AND WORSE, DOESN'T IT?
YEAH...
EVERY DAY BRINGS FRESH PICTURES OF MAY-HEM...
YOU GOTTA HAND IT TO THE PALESTIN-IANS—THEY'RE MAKING THE MOST OF THE WHOLE WORLD WATCHING!
©B Trudeau
PETER, I'M NOW HAVING TEA, LIVE, WITH A TRAINEE MARTYR.
DON'T WE DO PROMOS FIRST?
PRESS
CNN

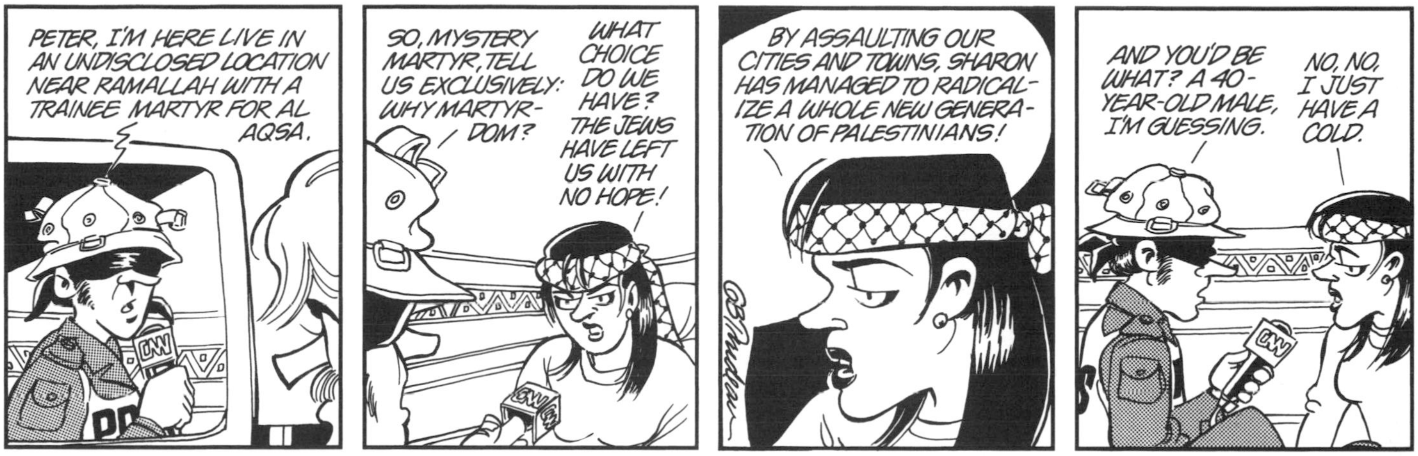
PETER, I'M HERE LIVE IN AN UNDISCLOSED LOCATION NEAR RAMALLAH WITH A TRAINEE MARTYR FOR AL AQSA.
SO, MYSTERY MARTYR, TELL US EXCLUSIVELY: WHY MARTYR-DOM?
WHAT CHOICE DO WE HAVE? THE JEWS HAVE LEFT US WITH NO HOPE!
BY ASSAULTING OUR CITIES AND TOWNS, SHARON HAS MANAGED TO RADICAL-IZE A WHOLE NEW GENERA-TION OF PALESTINIANS!
©B Trudeau
AND YOU'D BE WHAT? A 40-YEAR-OLD MALE, I'M GUESSING.
NO, NO, I JUST HAVE A COLD.

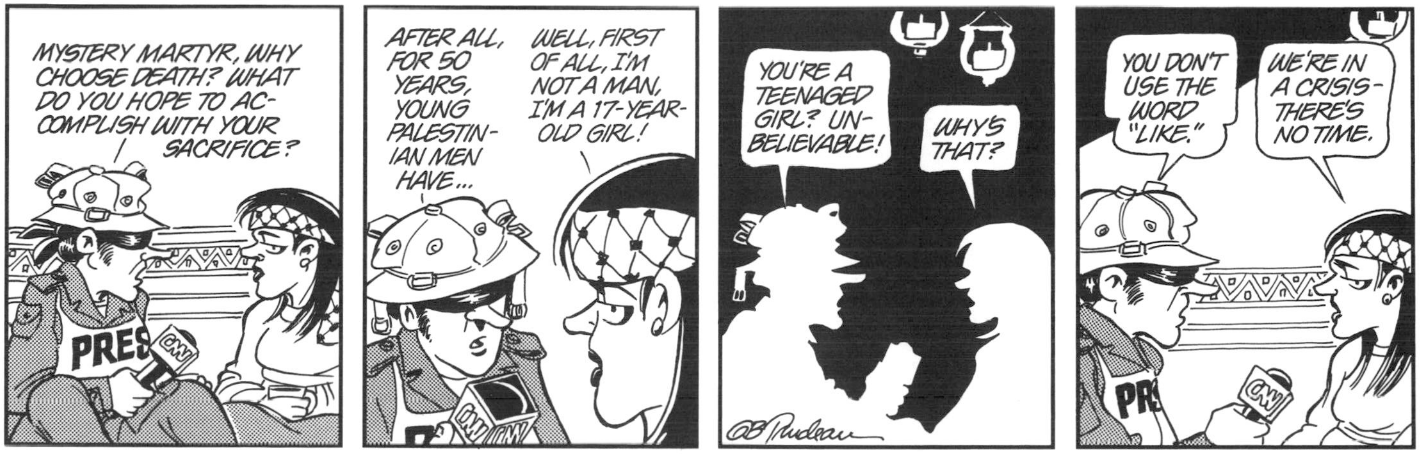
MYSTERY MARTYR, WHY CHOOSE DEATH? WHAT DO YOU HOPE TO AC-COMPLISH WITH YOUR SACRIFICE?
PRES
AFTER ALL, FOR 50 YEARS, YOUNG PALESTIN-IAN MEN HAVE...
WELL, FIRST OF ALL, I'M NOT A MAN, I'M A 17-YEAR-OLD GIRL!
YOU'RE A TEENAGED GIRL? UN-BELIEVABLE!
WHY'S THAT?
©B Trudeau
YOU DON'T USE THE WORD "LIKE."
WE'RE IN A CRISIS—THERE'S NO TIME.

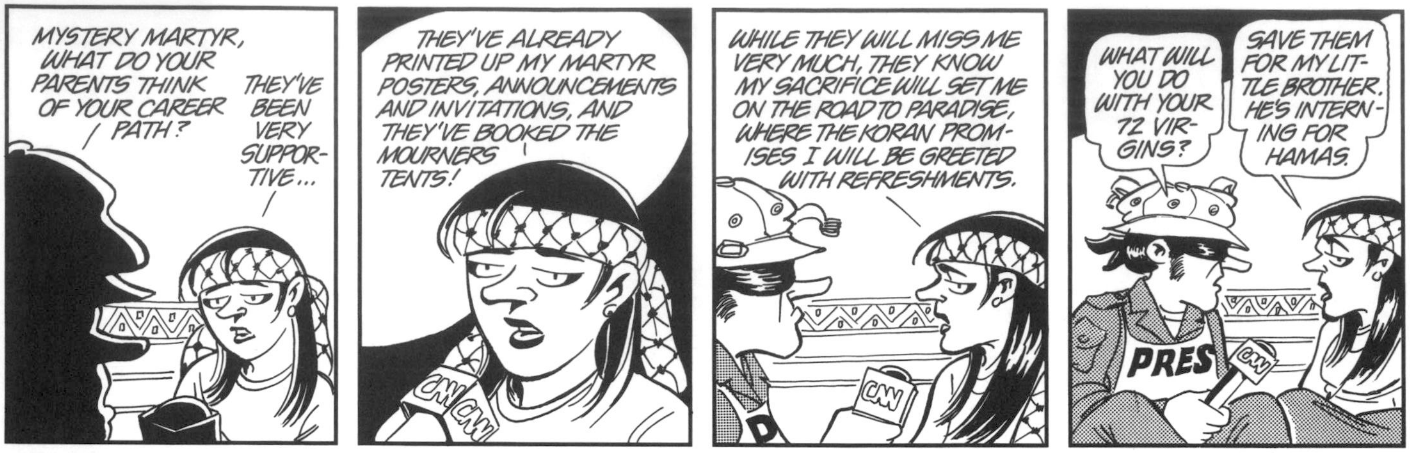
MYSTERY MARTYR, WHAT DO YOUR PARENTS THINK OF YOUR CAREER PATH?
THEY'VE BEEN VERY SUPPORTIVE...
THEY'VE ALREADY PRINTED UP MY MARTYR POSTERS, ANNOUNCEMENTS AND INVITATIONS, AND THEY'VE BOOKED THE MOURNERS TENTS!
CNN
WHILE THEY WILL MISS ME VERY MUCH, THEY KNOW MY SACRIFICE WILL SET ME ON THE ROAD TO PARADISE, WHERE THE KORAN PROMISES I WILL BE GREETED WITH REFRESHMENTS.
WHAT WILL YOU DO WITH YOUR 72 VIRGINS?
SAVE THEM FOR MY LITTLE BROTHER. HE'S INTERNING FOR HAMAS.
PRES

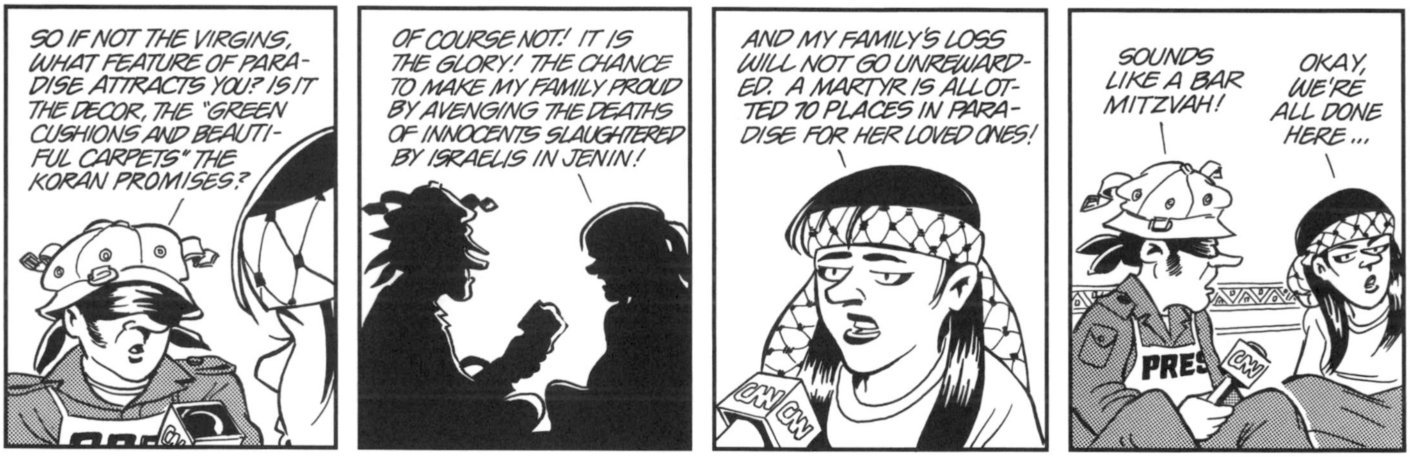
SO IF NOT THE VIRGINS, WHAT FEATURE OF PARADISE ATTRACTS YOU? IS IT THE DECOR, THE "GREEN CUSHIONS AND BEAUTIFUL CARPETS" THE KORAN PROMISES?
OF COURSE NOT! IT IS THE GLORY! THE CHANCE TO MAKE MY FAMILY PROUD BY AVENGING THE DEATHS OF INNOCENTS SLAUGHTERED BY ISRAELIS IN JENIN!
AND MY FAMILY'S LOSS WILL NOT GO UNREWARDED. A MARTYR IS ALLOTTED 70 PLACES IN PARADISE FOR HER LOVED ONES!
SOUNDS LIKE A BAR MITZVAH!
OKAY, WE'RE ALL DONE HERE...
PRES

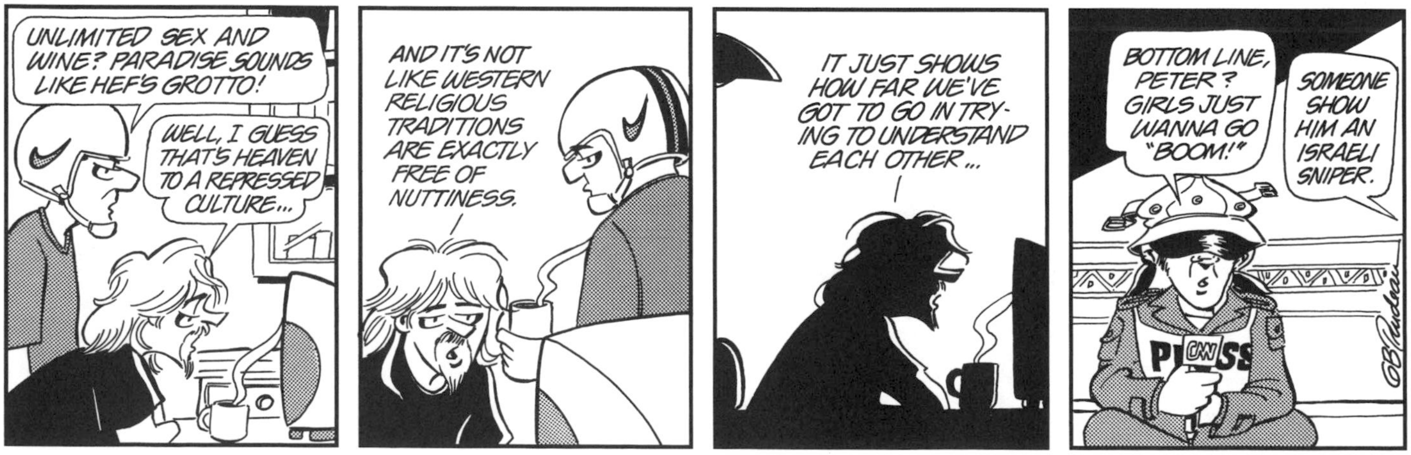
UNLIMITED SEX AND WINE? PARADISE SOUNDS LIKE HEF'S GROTTO!
WELL, I GUESS THAT'S HEAVEN TO A REPRESSED CULTURE...
AND IT'S NOT LIKE WESTERN RELIGIOUS TRADITIONS ARE EXACTLY FREE OF NUTTINESS.
IT JUST SHOWS HOW FAR WE'VE GOT TO GO IN TRYING TO UNDERSTAND EACH OTHER...
BOTTOM LINE, PETER? GIRLS JUST WANNA GO "BOOM!"
SOMEONE SHOW HIM AN ISRAELI SNIPER.

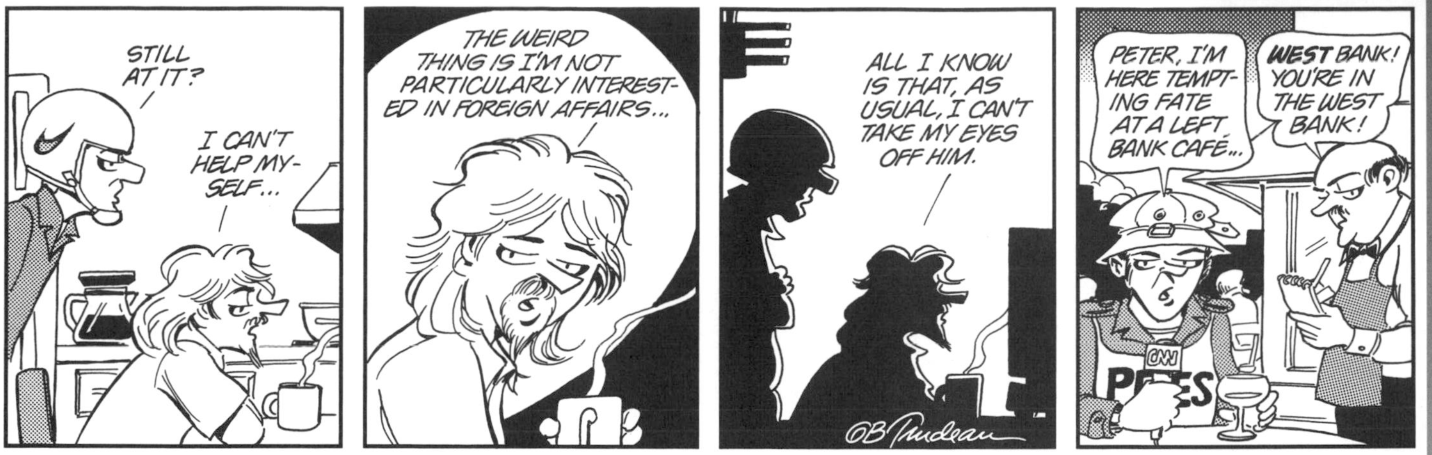
STILL AT IT?
I CAN'T HELP MYSELF...
THE WEIRD THING IS I'M NOT PARTICULARLY INTERESTED IN FOREIGN AFFAIRS...
ALL I KNOW IS THAT, AS USUAL, I CAN'T TAKE MY EYES OFF HIM.
PETER, I'M HERE TEMPTING FATE AT A LEFT BANK CAFÉ...
**WEST** BANK! YOU'RE IN THE WEST BANK!
CNN
PRESS

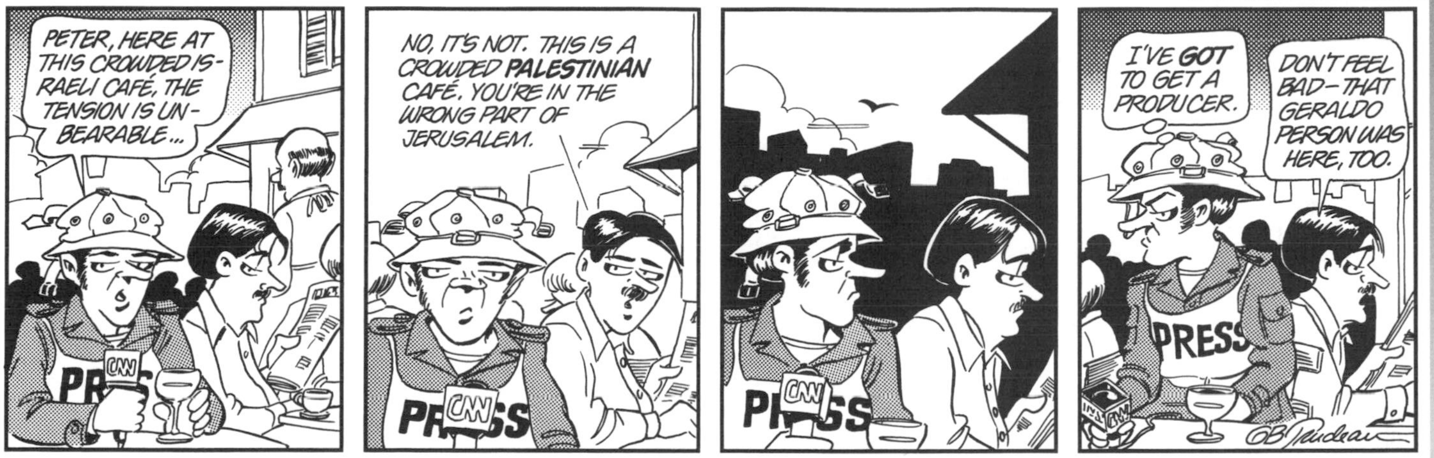
PETER, HERE AT THIS CROWDED ISRAELI CAFÉ, THE TENSION IS UNBEARABLE...
NO, IT'S NOT. THIS IS A CROWDED **PALESTINIAN** CAFÉ. YOU'RE IN THE WRONG PART OF JERUSALEM.
I'VE **GOT** TO GET A PRODUCER.
DON'T FEEL BAD—THAT GERALDO PERSON WAS HERE, TOO.
CNN
PRESS

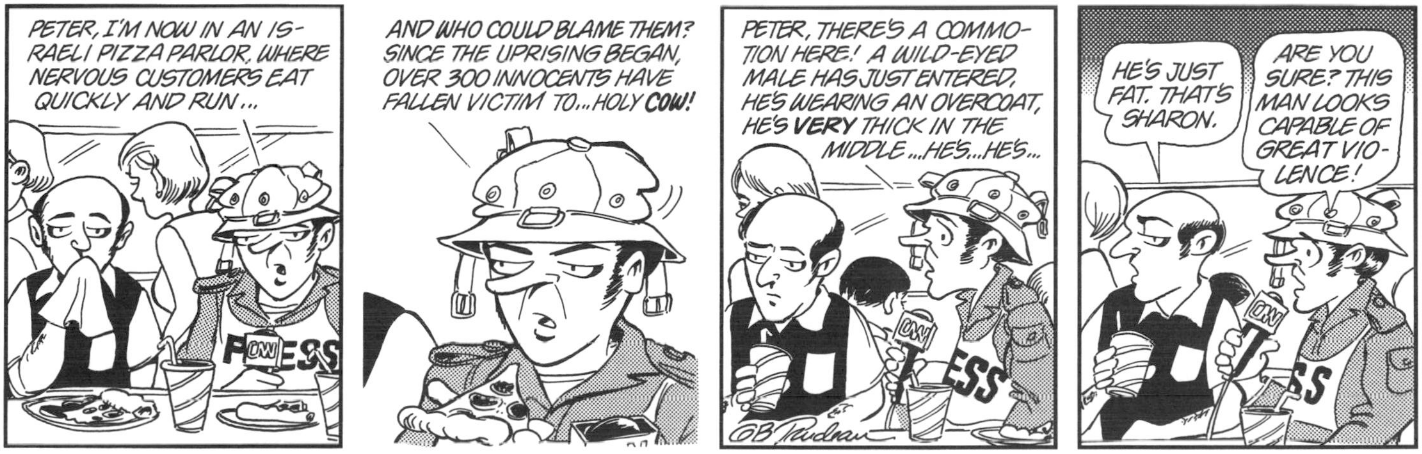
PETER, I'M NOW IN AN ISRAELI PIZZA PARLOR, WHERE NERVOUS CUSTOMERS EAT QUICKLY AND RUN...
AND WHO COULD BLAME THEM? SINCE THE UPRISING BEGAN, OVER 300 INNOCENTS HAVE FALLEN VICTIM TO... HOLY **COW!**
PETER, THERE'S A COMMOTION HERE! A WILD-EYED MALE HAS JUST ENTERED. HE'S WEARING AN OVERCOAT, HE'S **VERY** THICK IN THE MIDDLE... HE'S... HE'S...
HE'S JUST FAT. THAT'S SHARON.
ARE YOU SURE? THIS MAN LOOKS CAPABLE OF GREAT VIOLENCE!
CNN
PRESS

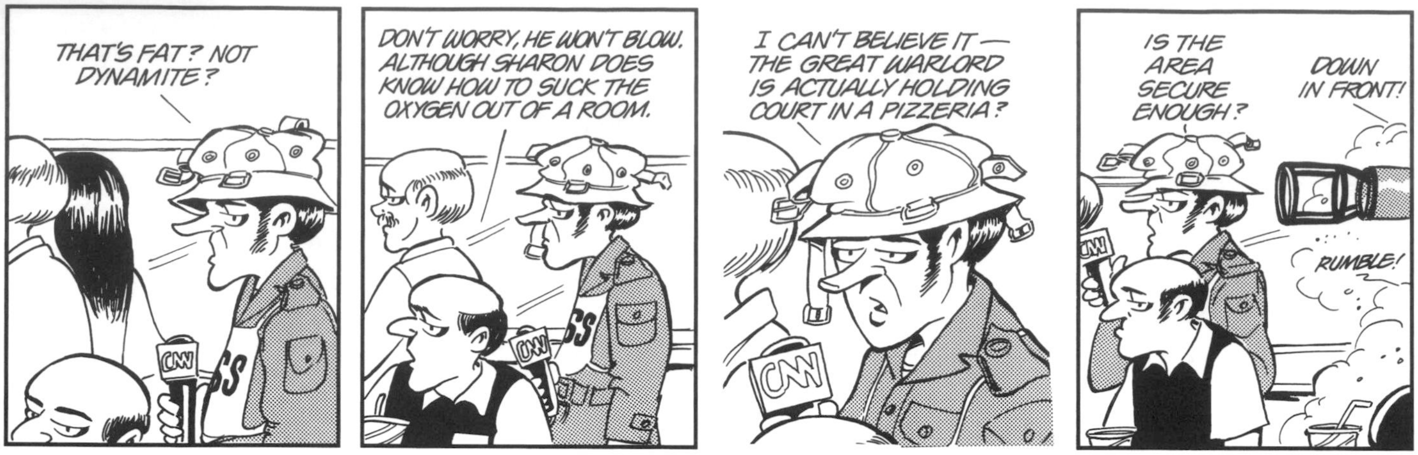
THAT'S FAT? NOT DYNAMITE?
DON'T WORRY, HE WON'T BLOW. ALTHOUGH SHARON DOES KNOW HOW TO SUCK THE OXYGEN OUT OF A ROOM.
I CAN'T BELIEVE IT — THE GREAT WARLORD IS ACTUALLY HOLDING COURT IN A PIZZERIA?
IS THE AREA SECURE ENOUGH?
DOWN IN FRONT!
RUMBLE!

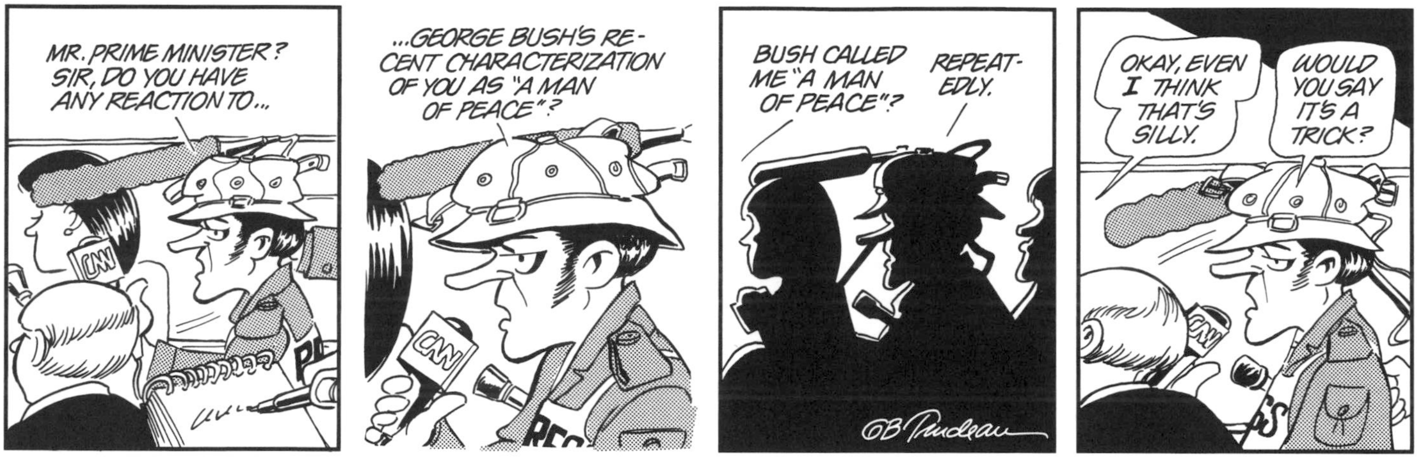
MR. PRIME MINISTER? SIR, DO YOU HAVE ANY REACTION TO...
...GEORGE BUSH'S RECENT CHARACTERIZATION OF YOU AS "A MAN OF PEACE"?
BUSH CALLED ME "A MAN OF PEACE"?
REPEATEDLY.
OKAY, EVEN I THINK THAT'S SILLY.
WOULD YOU SAY IT'S A TRICK?

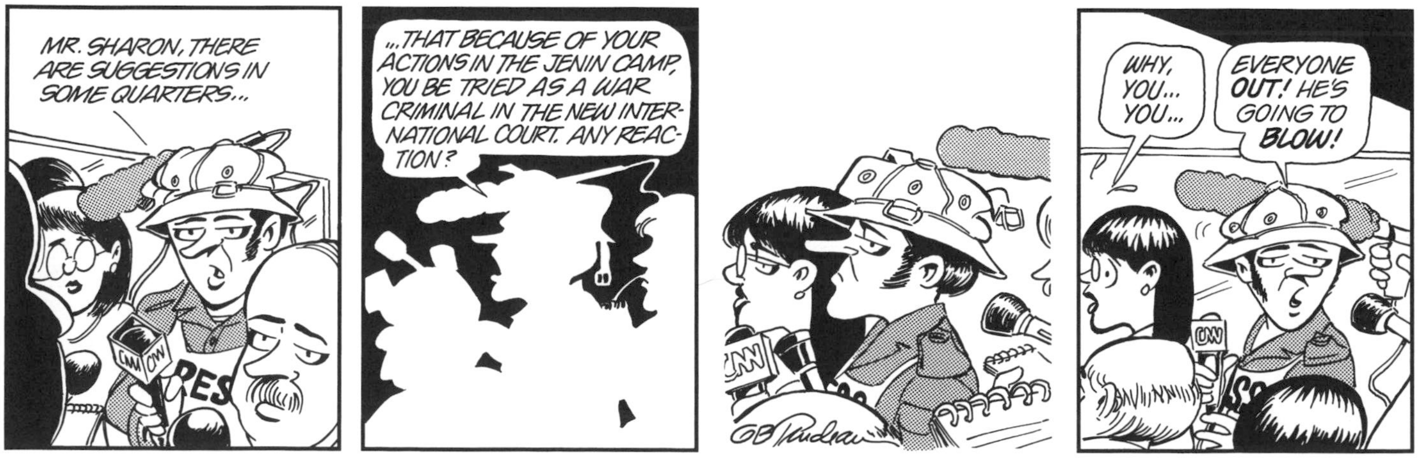
MR. SHARON, THERE ARE SUGGESTIONS IN SOME QUARTERS...
...THAT BECAUSE OF YOUR ACTIONS IN THE JENIN CAMP, YOU BE TRIED AS A WAR CRIMINAL IN THE NEW INTERNATIONAL COURT. ANY REACTION?
WHY, YOU... YOU...
EVERYONE OUT! HE'S GOING TO BLOW!

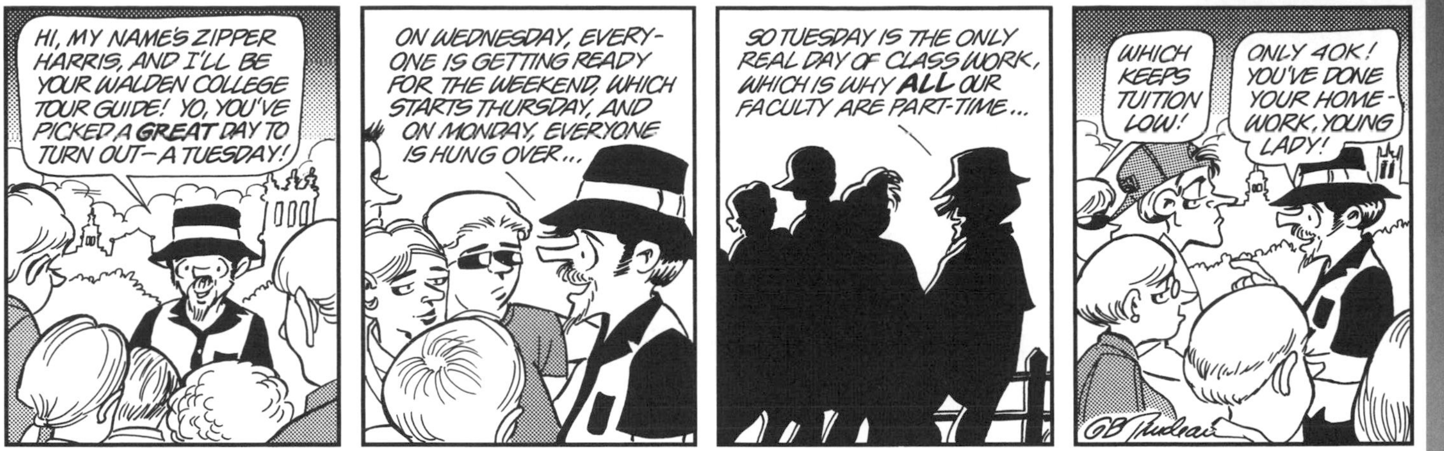
HI, MY NAME'S ZIPPER HARRIS, AND I'LL BE YOUR WALDEN COLLEGE TOUR GUIDE! YO, YOU'VE PICKED A GREAT DAY TO TURN OUT—A TUESDAY!
ON WEDNESDAY, EVERYONE IS GETTING READY FOR THE WEEKEND, WHICH STARTS THURSDAY, AND ON MONDAY, EVERYONE IS HUNG OVER...
SO TUESDAY IS THE ONLY REAL DAY OF CLASS WORK, WHICH IS WHY ALL OUR FACULTY ARE PART-TIME...
WHICH KEEPS TUITION LOW!
ONLY 40K! YOU'VE DONE YOUR HOMEWORK, YOUNG LADY!
GB Trudeau

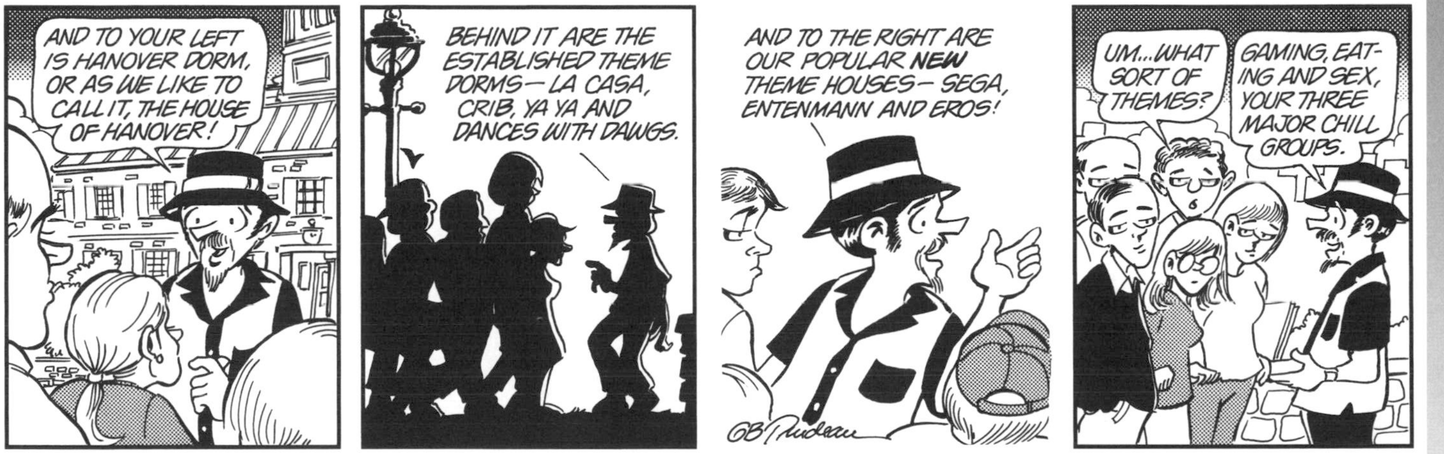
AND TO YOUR LEFT IS HANOVER DORM, OR AS WE LIKE TO CALL IT, THE HOUSE OF HANOVER!
BEHIND IT ARE THE ESTABLISHED THEME DORMS—LA CASA, CRIB, YA YA AND DANCES WITH DAWGS.
AND TO THE RIGHT ARE OUR POPULAR NEW THEME HOUSES—SEGA, ENTENMANN AND EROS!
GB Trudeau
UM...WHAT SORT OF THEMES?
GAMING, EATING AND SEX, YOUR THREE MAJOR CHILL GROUPS.

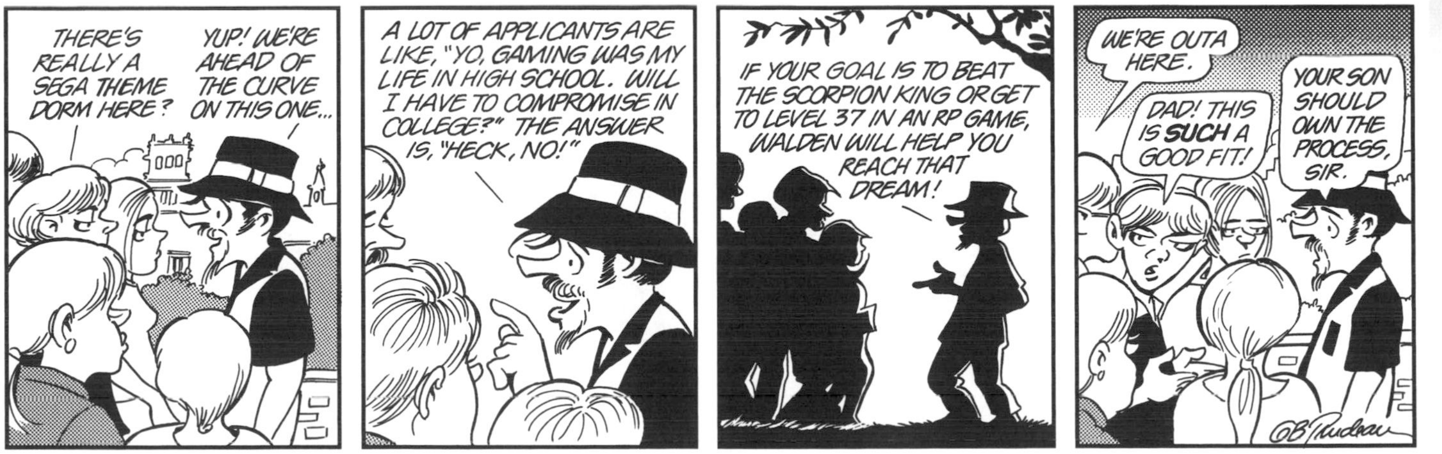
THERE'S REALLY A SEGA THEME DORM HERE?
YUP! WE'RE AHEAD OF THE CURVE ON THIS ONE...
A LOT OF APPLICANTS ARE LIKE, "YO, GAMING WAS MY LIFE IN HIGH SCHOOL. WILL I HAVE TO COMPROMISE IN COLLEGE?" THE ANSWER IS, "HECK, NO!"
IF YOUR GOAL IS TO BEAT THE SCORPION KING OR GET TO LEVEL 37 IN AN RP GAME, WALDEN WILL HELP YOU REACH THAT DREAM!
WE'RE OUTA HERE.
DAD! THIS IS SUCH A GOOD FIT!
YOUR SON SHOULD OWN THE PROCESS, SIR.
GB Trudeau

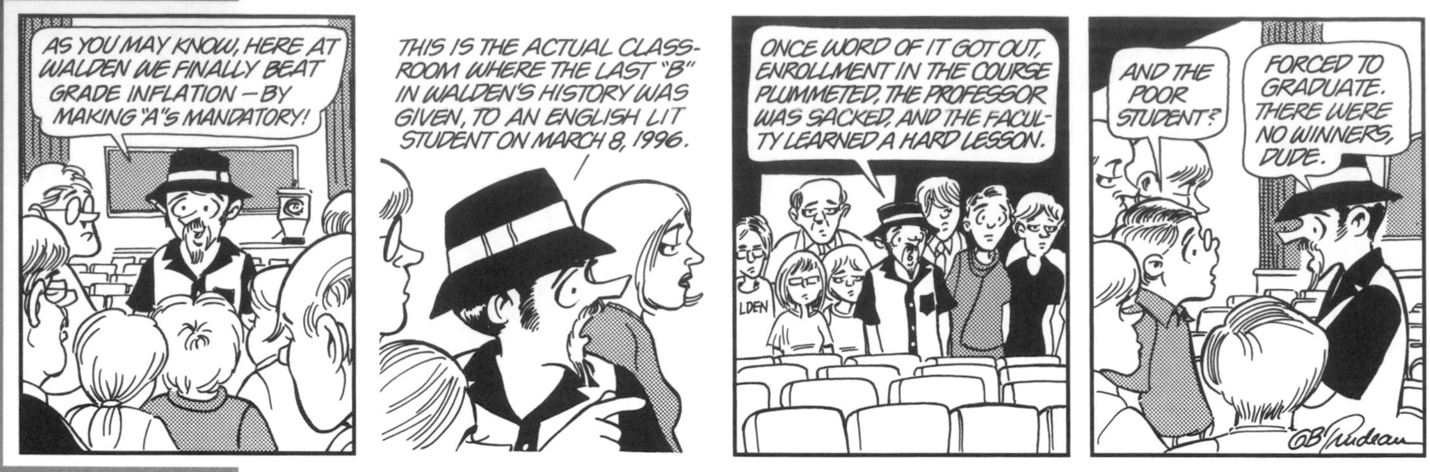
AS YOU MAY KNOW, HERE AT WALDEN WE FINALLY BEAT GRADE INFLATION — BY MAKING "A"s MANDATORY!
THIS IS THE ACTUAL CLASSROOM WHERE THE LAST "B" IN WALDEN'S HISTORY WAS GIVEN, TO AN ENGLISH LIT STUDENT ON MARCH 8, 1996.
ONCE WORD OF IT GOT OUT, ENROLLMENT IN THE COURSE PLUMMETED, THE PROFESSOR WAS SACKED, AND THE FACULTY LEARNED A HARD LESSON.
AND THE POOR STUDENT?
FORCED TO GRADUATE. THERE WERE NO WINNERS, DUDE.
GB Trudeau

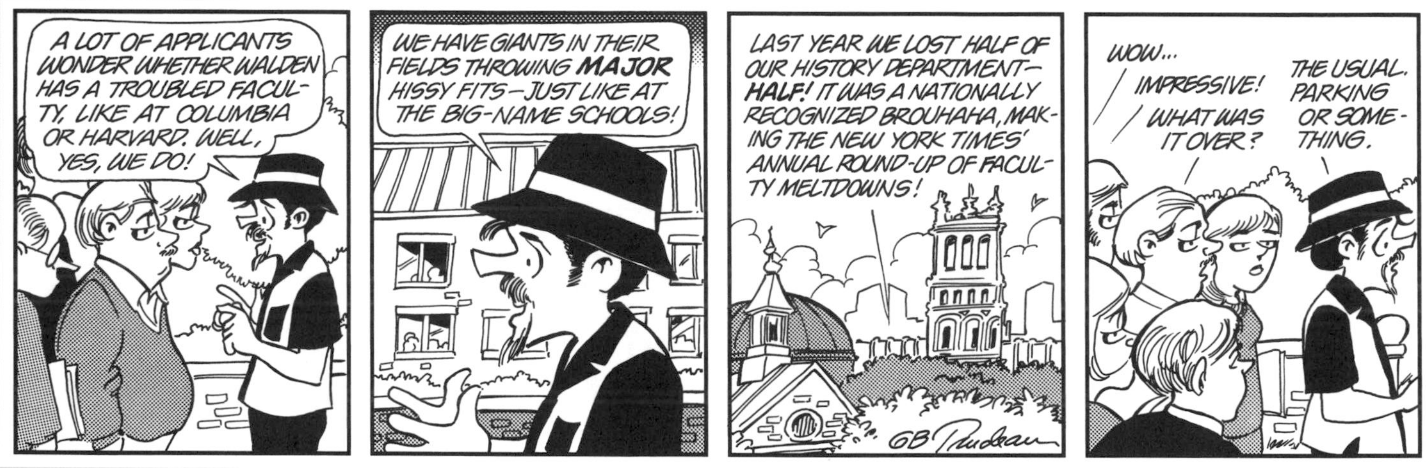
A LOT OF APPLICANTS WONDER WHETHER WALDEN HAS A TROUBLED FACULTY, LIKE AT COLUMBIA OR HARVARD. WELL, YES, WE DO!
WE HAVE GIANTS IN THEIR FIELDS THROWING MAJOR HISSY FITS — JUST LIKE AT THE BIG-NAME SCHOOLS!
LAST YEAR WE LOST HALF OF OUR HISTORY DEPARTMENT — HALF! IT WAS A NATIONALLY RECOGNIZED BROUHAHA, MAKING THE NEW YORK TIMES' ANNUAL ROUND-UP OF FACULTY MELTDOWNS!
GB Trudeau
WOW...
IMPRESSIVE!
WHAT WAS IT OVER?
THE USUAL. PARKING OR SOMETHING.

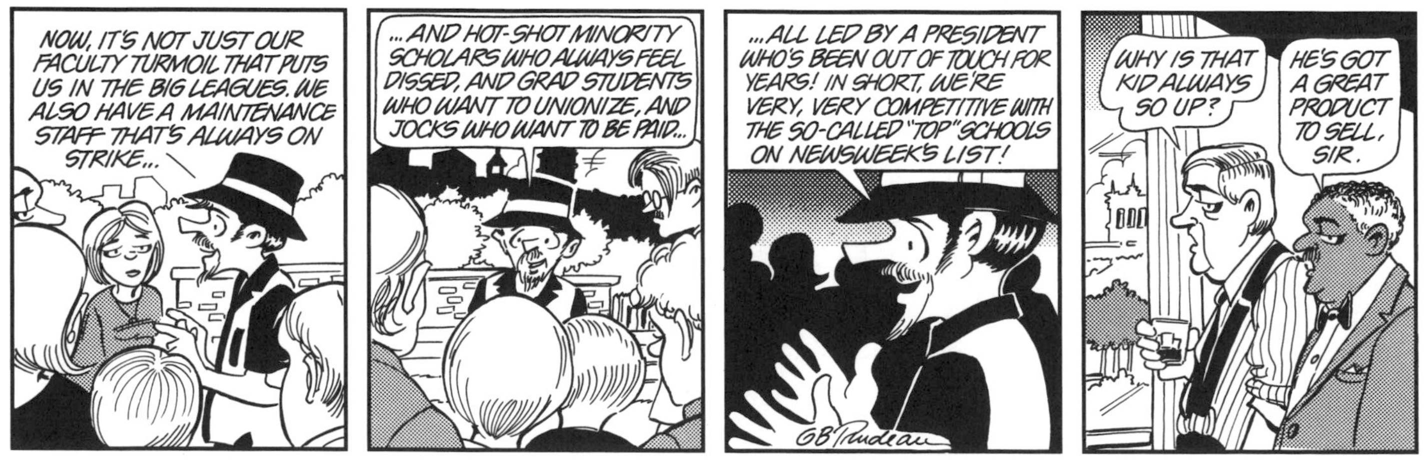
NOW, IT'S NOT JUST OUR FACULTY TURMOIL THAT PUTS US IN THE BIG LEAGUES. WE ALSO HAVE A MAINTENANCE STAFF THAT'S ALWAYS ON STRIKE...
...AND HOT-SHOT MINORITY SCHOLARS WHO ALWAYS FEEL DISSED, AND GRAD STUDENTS WHO WANT TO UNIONIZE, AND JOCKS WHO WANT TO BE PAID...
...ALL LED BY A PRESIDENT WHO'S BEEN OUT OF TOUCH FOR YEARS! IN SHORT, WE'RE VERY, VERY COMPETITIVE WITH THE SO-CALLED "TOP" SCHOOLS ON NEWSWEEK'S LIST!
GB Trudeau
WHY IS THAT KID ALWAYS SO UP?
HE'S GOT A GREAT PRODUCT TO SELL, SIR.

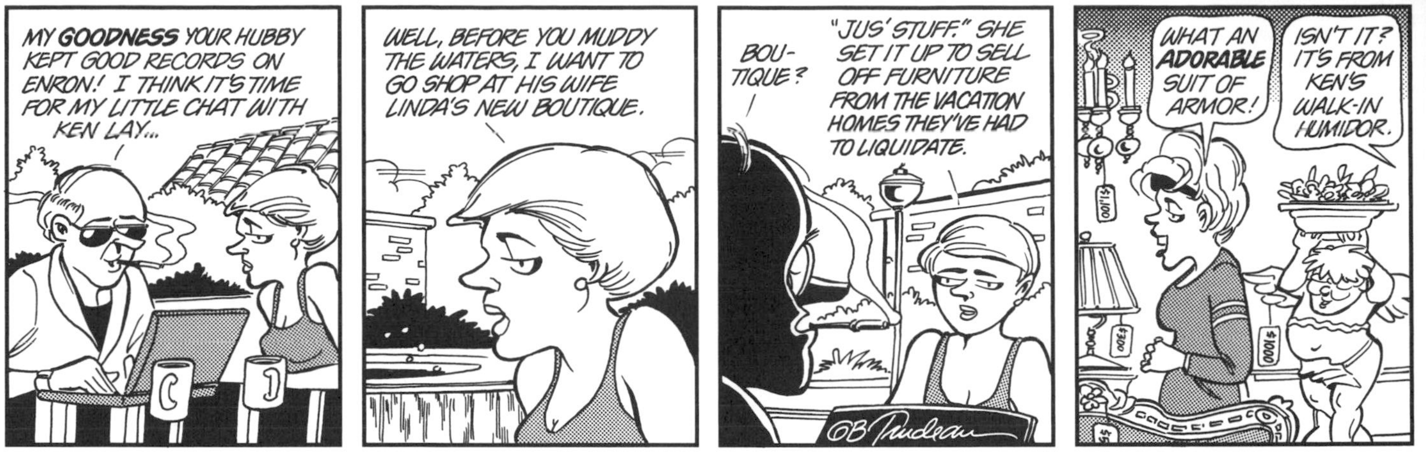
MY GOODNESS YOUR HUBBY KEPT GOOD RECORDS ON ENRON! I THINK IT'S TIME FOR MY LITTLE CHAT WITH KEN LAY...
WELL, BEFORE YOU MUDDY THE WATERS, I WANT TO GO SHOP AT HIS WIFE LINDA'S NEW BOUTIQUE.
BOUTIQUE?
"JUS' STUFF." SHE SET IT UP TO SELL OFF FURNITURE FROM THE VACATION HOMES THEY'VE HAD TO LIQUIDATE.
WHAT AN ADORABLE SUIT OF ARMOR!
ISN'T IT? IT'S FROM KEN'S WALK-IN HUMIDOR.

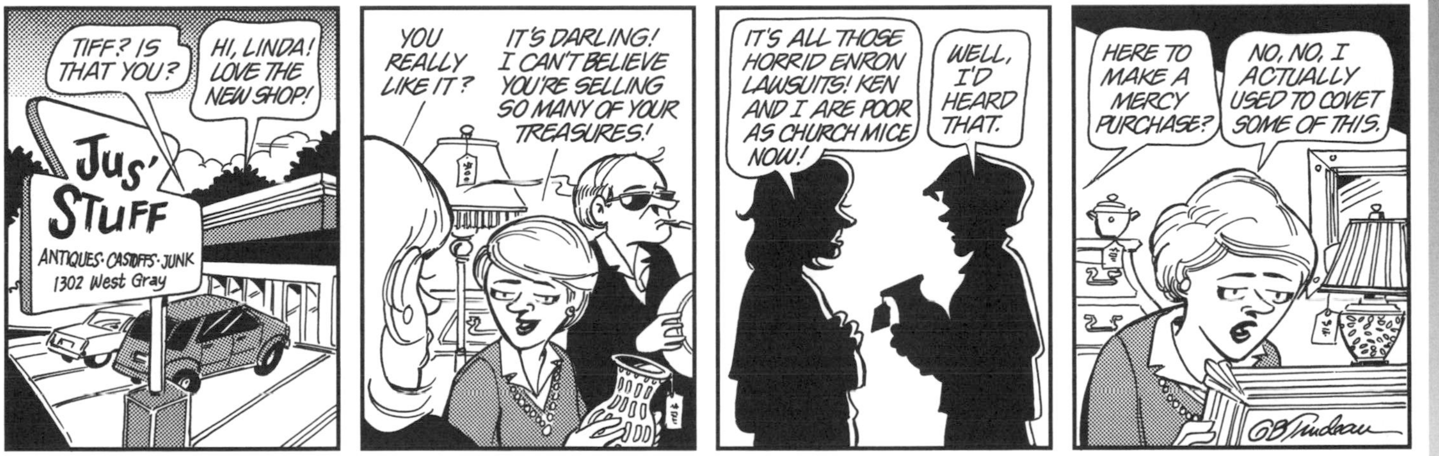
TIFF? IS THAT YOU?
HI, LINDA! LOVE THE NEW SHOP!
JUS' STUFF
ANTIQUES · CASTOFFS · JUNK
1302 West Gray
YOU REALLY LIKE IT?
IT'S DARLING! I CAN'T BELIEVE YOU'RE SELLING SO MANY OF YOUR TREASURES!
IT'S ALL THOSE HORRID ENRON LAWSUITS! KEN AND I ARE POOR AS CHURCH MICE NOW!
WELL, I'D HEARD THAT.
HERE TO MAKE A MERCY PURCHASE?
NO, NO, I ACTUALLY USED TO COVET SOME OF THIS.

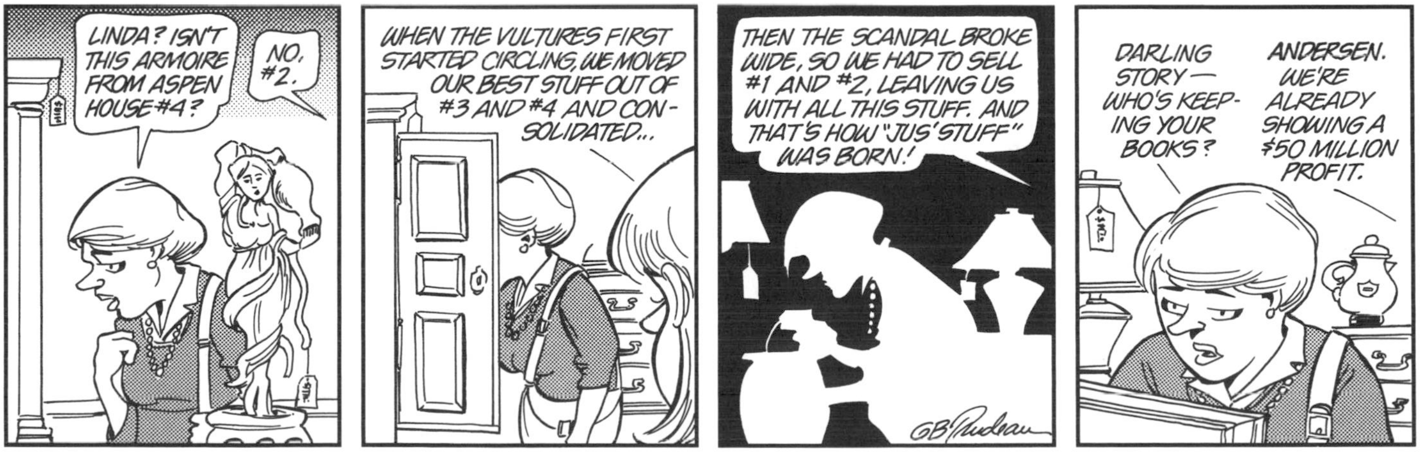
LINDA? ISN'T THIS ARMOIRE FROM ASPEN HOUSE #4?
NO, #2.
WHEN THE VULTURES FIRST STARTED CIRCLING, WE MOVED OUR BEST STUFF OUT OF #3 AND #4 AND CONSOLIDATED...
THEN THE SCANDAL BROKE WIDE, SO WE HAD TO SELL #1 AND #2, LEAVING US WITH ALL THIS STUFF. AND THAT'S HOW "JUS' STUFF" WAS BORN!
DARLING STORY— WHO'S KEEPING YOUR BOOKS?
ANDERSEN. WE'RE ALREADY SHOWING A $50 MILLION PROFIT.

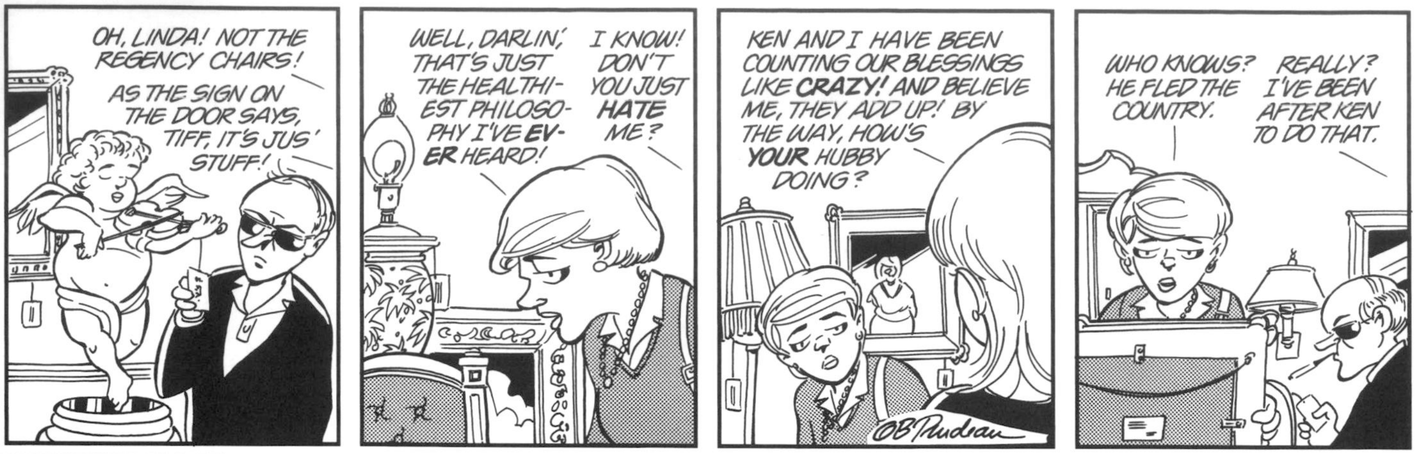
OH, LINDA! NOT THE REGENCY CHAIRS!
AS THE SIGN ON THE DOOR SAYS, TIFF, IT'S JUS' STUFF!
WELL, DARLIN', THAT'S JUST THE HEALTHIEST PHILOSOPHY I'VE EVER HEARD!
I KNOW! DON'T YOU JUST **HATE** ME?
KEN AND I HAVE BEEN COUNTING OUR BLESSINGS LIKE **CRAZY!** AND BELIEVE ME, THEY ADD UP! BY THE WAY, HOW'S **YOUR** HUBBY DOING?
WHO KNOWS? HE FLED THE COUNTRY.
REALLY? I'VE BEEN AFTER KEN TO DO THAT.

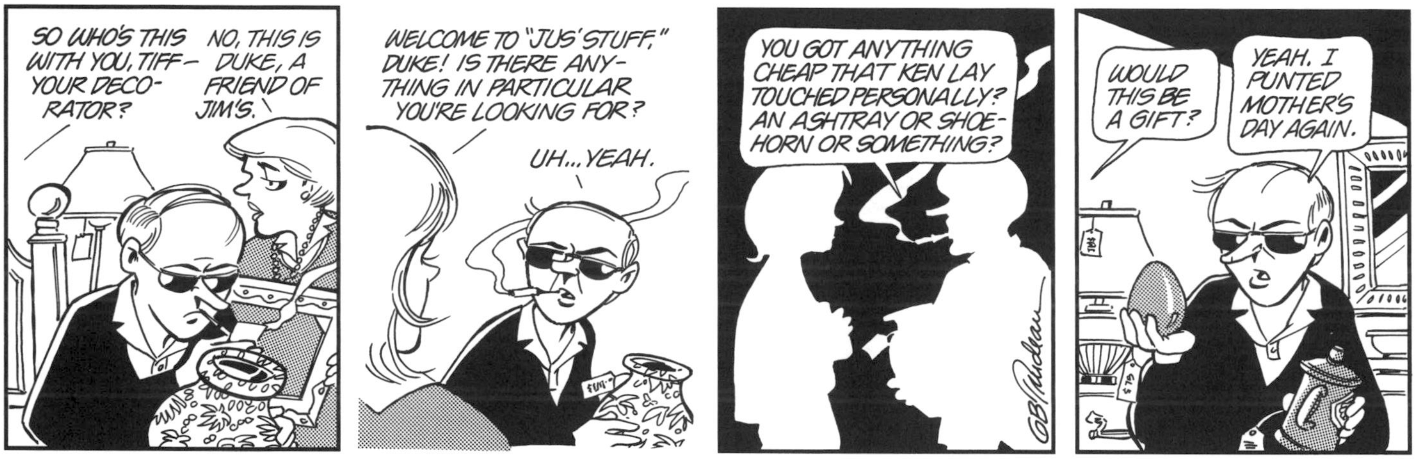
SO WHO'S THIS WITH YOU, TIFF — YOUR DECORATOR?
NO, THIS IS DUKE, A FRIEND OF JIM'S.
WELCOME TO "JUS' STUFF," DUKE! IS THERE ANYTHING IN PARTICULAR YOU'RE LOOKING FOR?
UH... YEAH.
YOU GOT ANYTHING CHEAP THAT KEN LAY TOUCHED PERSONALLY? AN ASHTRAY OR SHOEHORN OR SOMETHING?
WOULD THIS BE A GIFT?
YEAH. I PUNTED MOTHER'S DAY AGAIN.

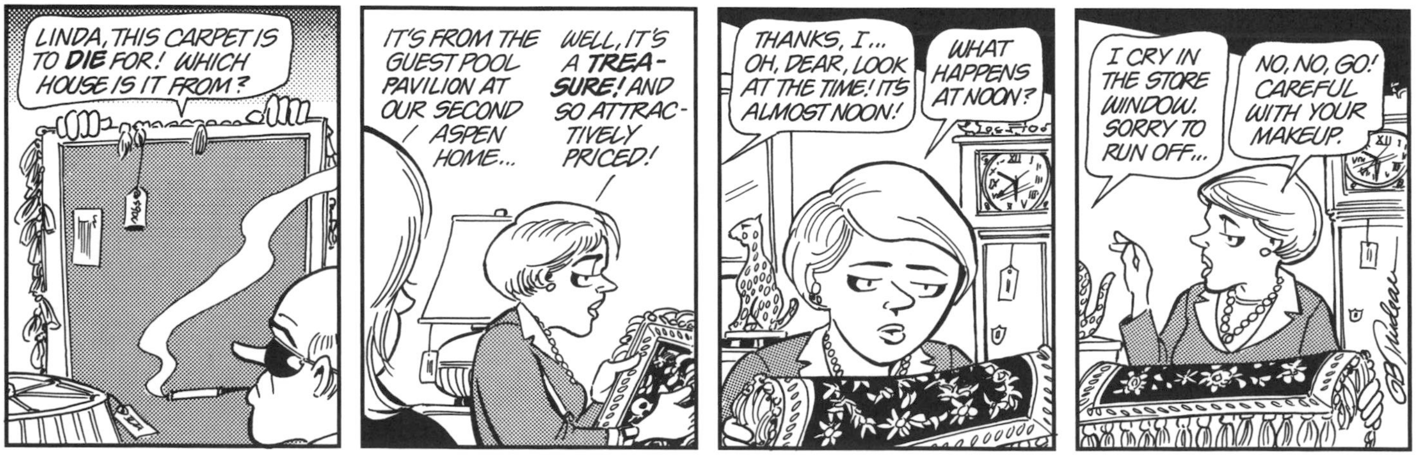
LINDA, THIS CARPET IS TO **DIE** FOR! WHICH HOUSE IS IT FROM?
IT'S FROM THE GUEST POOL PAVILION AT OUR SECOND ASPEN HOME...
WELL, IT'S A **TREASURE!** AND SO ATTRACTIVELY PRICED!
THANKS, I... OH, DEAR, LOOK AT THE TIME! IT'S ALMOST NOON!
WHAT HAPPENS AT NOON?
I CRY IN THE STORE WINDOW. SORRY TO RUN OFF...
NO, NO, GO! CAREFUL WITH YOUR MAKEUP.

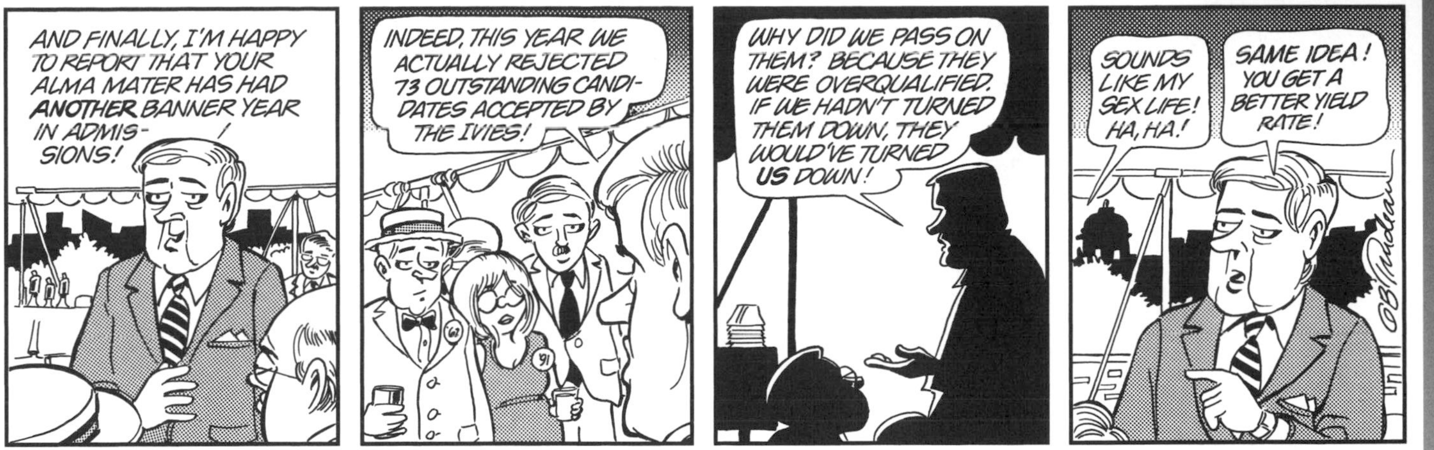
AND FINALLY, I'M HAPPY TO REPORT THAT YOUR ALMA MATER HAS HAD ANOTHER BANNER YEAR IN ADMISSIONS!
INDEED, THIS YEAR WE ACTUALLY REJECTED 73 OUTSTANDING CANDIDATES ACCEPTED BY THE IVIES!
WHY DID WE PASS ON THEM? BECAUSE THEY WERE OVERQUALIFIED. IF WE HADN'T TURNED THEM DOWN, THEY WOULD'VE TURNED US DOWN!
SOUNDS LIKE MY SEX LIFE! HA, HA!
SAME IDEA! YOU GET A BETTER YIELD RATE!

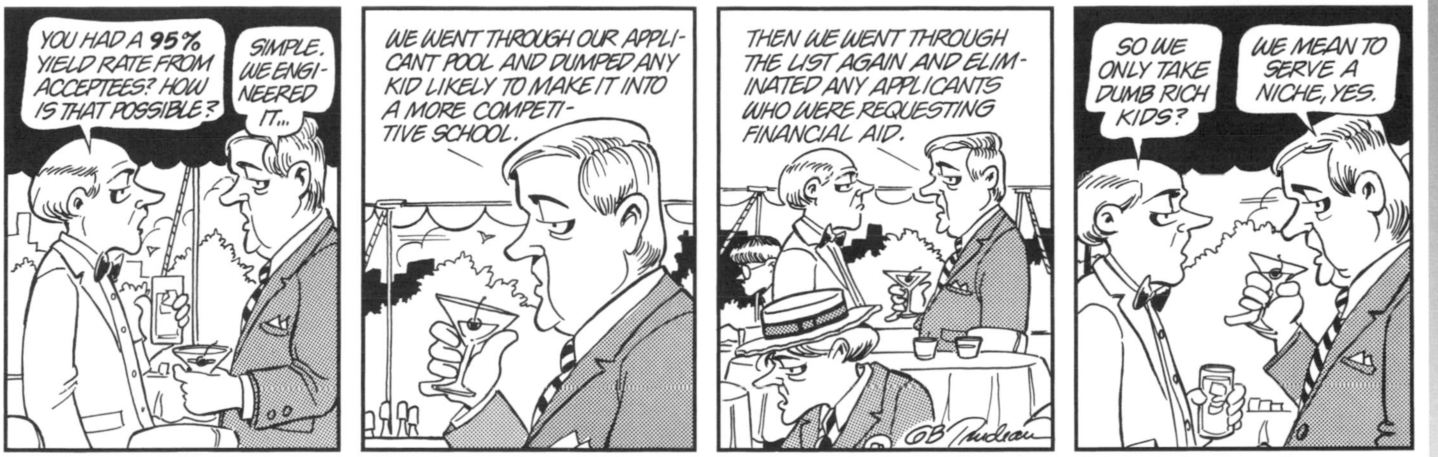
YOU HAD A 95% YIELD RATE FROM ACCEPTEES? HOW IS THAT POSSIBLE?
SIMPLE. WE ENGINEERED IT...
WE WENT THROUGH OUR APPLICANT POOL AND DUMPED ANY KID LIKELY TO MAKE IT INTO A MORE COMPETITIVE SCHOOL.
THEN WE WENT THROUGH THE LIST AGAIN AND ELIMINATED ANY APPLICANTS WHO WERE REQUESTING FINANCIAL AID.
SO WE ONLY TAKE DUMB RICH KIDS?
WE MEAN TO SERVE A NICHE, YES.

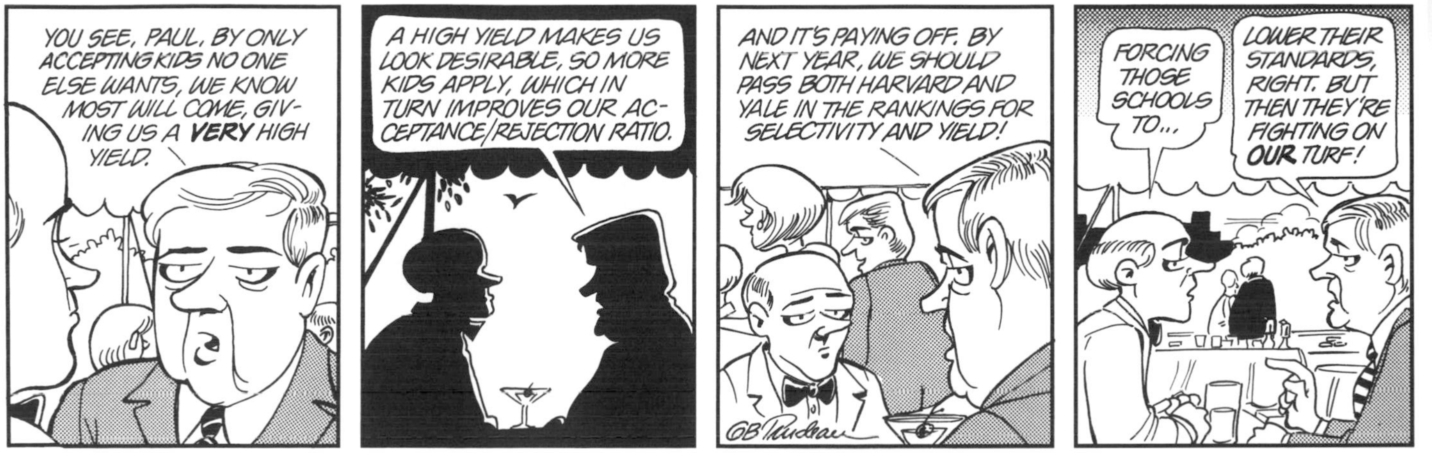
YOU SEE, PAUL, BY ONLY ACCEPTING KIDS NO ONE ELSE WANTS, WE KNOW MOST WILL COME, GIVING US A VERY HIGH YIELD.
A HIGH YIELD MAKES US LOOK DESIRABLE, SO MORE KIDS APPLY, WHICH IN TURN IMPROVES OUR ACCEPTANCE/REJECTION RATIO.
AND IT'S PAYING OFF. BY NEXT YEAR, WE SHOULD PASS BOTH HARVARD AND YALE IN THE RANKINGS FOR SELECTIVITY AND YIELD!
FORCING THOSE SCHOOLS TO...
LOWER THEIR STANDARDS, RIGHT. BUT THEN THEY'RE FIGHTING ON OUR TURF!

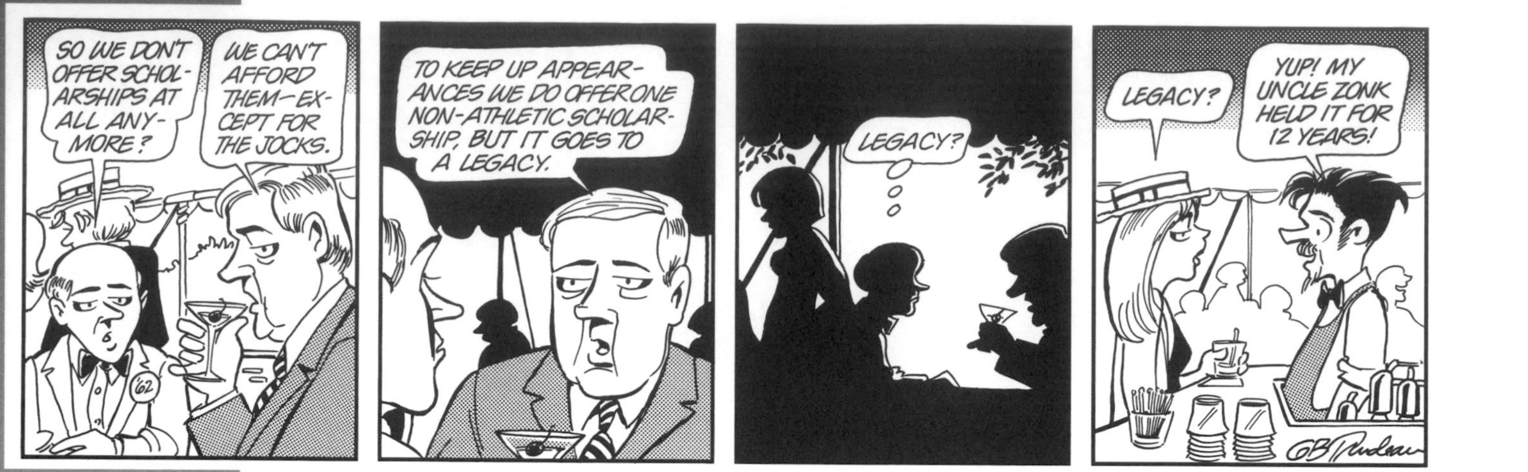
SO WE DON'T OFFER SCHOLARSHIPS AT ALL ANYMORE?
WE CAN'T AFFORD THEM—EXCEPT FOR THE JOCKS.
TO KEEP UP APPEARANCES WE DO OFFER ONE NON-ATHLETIC SCHOLARSHIP, BUT IT GOES TO A LEGACY.
'62
LEGACY?
LEGACY?
YUP! MY UNCLE ZONK HELD IT FOR 12 YEARS!

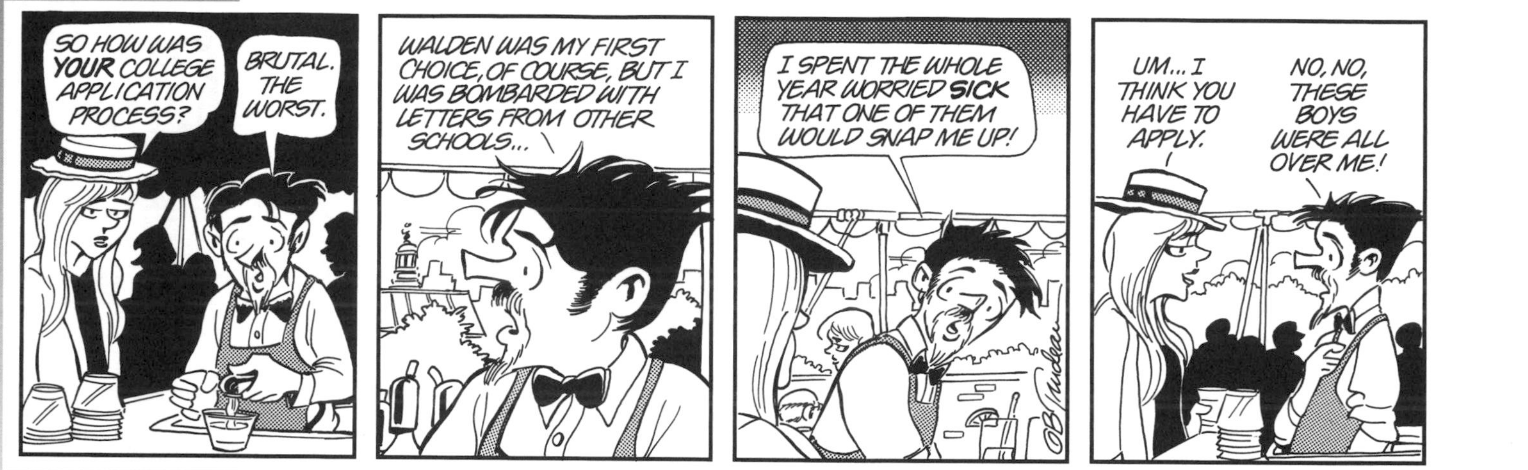
SO HOW WAS YOUR COLLEGE APPLICATION PROCESS?
BRUTAL. THE WORST.
WALDEN WAS MY FIRST CHOICE, OF COURSE, BUT I WAS BOMBARDED WITH LETTERS FROM OTHER SCHOOLS...
I SPENT THE WHOLE YEAR WORRIED SICK THAT ONE OF THEM WOULD SNAP ME UP!
UM... I THINK YOU HAVE TO APPLY.
NO, NO, THESE BOYS WERE ALL OVER ME!

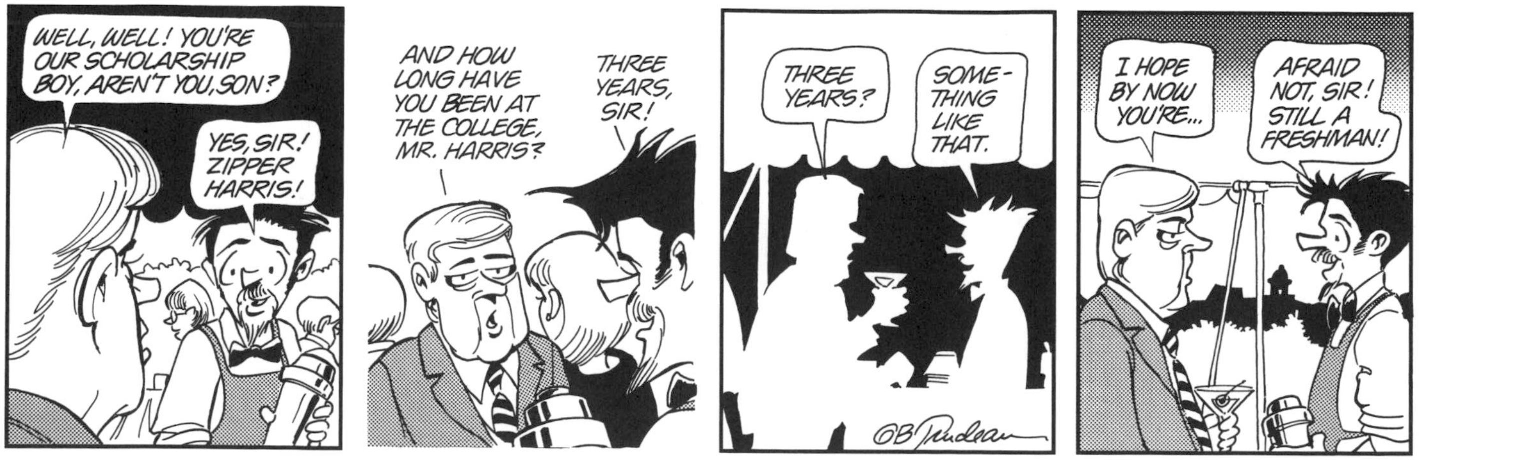
WELL, WELL! YOU'RE OUR SCHOLARSHIP BOY, AREN'T YOU, SON?
YES, SIR! ZIPPER HARRIS!
AND HOW LONG HAVE YOU BEEN AT THE COLLEGE, MR. HARRIS?
THREE YEARS, SIR!
THREE YEARS?
SOMETHING LIKE THAT.
I HOPE BY NOW YOU'RE...
AFRAID NOT, SIR! STILL A FRESHMAN!

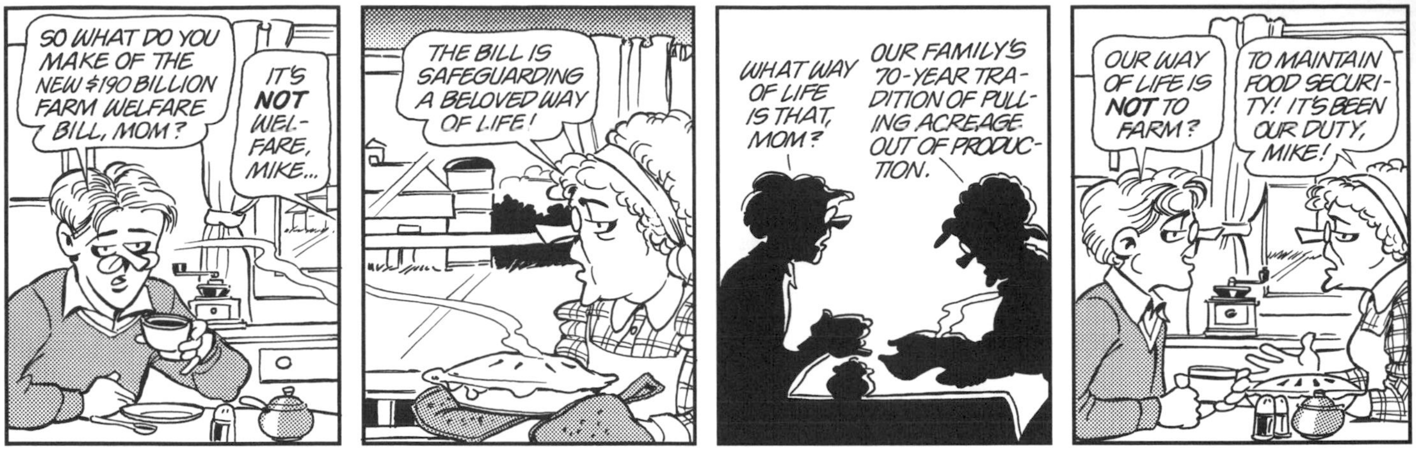
SO WHAT DO YOU MAKE OF THE NEW $190 BILLION FARM WELFARE BILL, MOM?
IT'S **NOT** WEL-FARE, MIKE...
THE BILL IS SAFEGUARDING A BELOVED WAY OF LIFE!
WHAT WAY OF LIFE IS THAT, MOM?
OUR FAMILY'S 70-YEAR TRA-DITION OF PULL-ING ACREAGE OUT OF PRODUC-TION.
OUR WAY OF LIFE IS **NOT** TO FARM?
TO MAINTAIN FOOD SECURI-TY! IT'S BEEN OUR DUTY, MIKE!

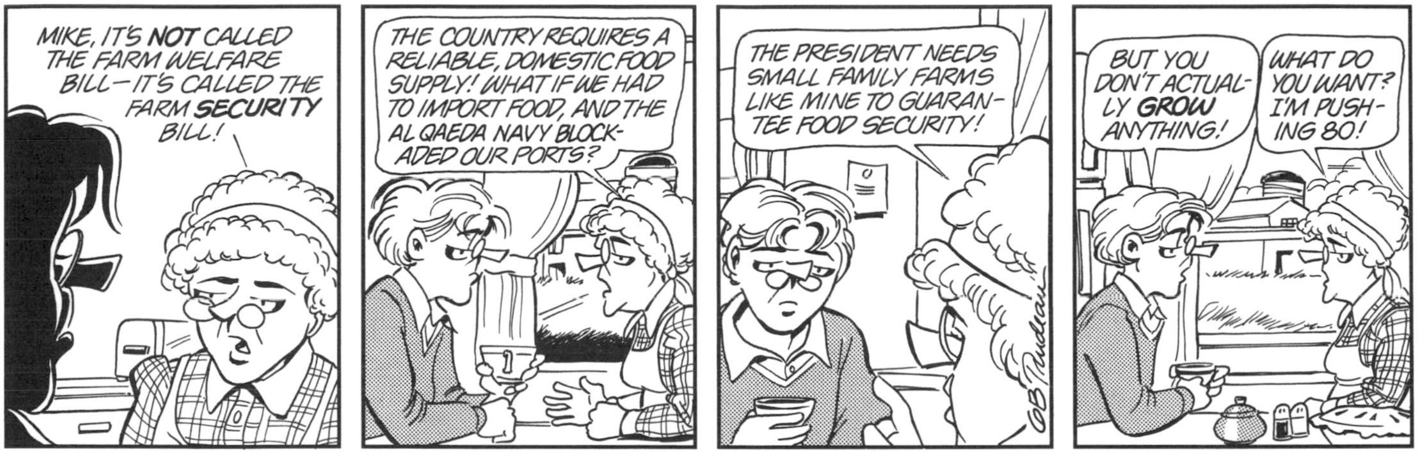
MIKE, IT'S **NOT** CALLED THE FARM WELFARE BILL—IT'S CALLED THE FARM **SECURITY** BILL!
THE COUNTRY REQUIRES A RELIABLE, DOMESTIC FOOD SUPPLY! WHAT IF WE HAD TO IMPORT FOOD, AND THE AL QAEDA NAVY BLOCK-ADED OUR PORTS?
THE PRESIDENT NEEDS SMALL FAMILY FARMS LIKE MINE TO GUARAN-TEE FOOD SECURITY!
BUT YOU DON'T ACTUAL-LY **GROW** ANYTHING!
WHAT DO YOU WANT? I'M PUSH-ING 80!

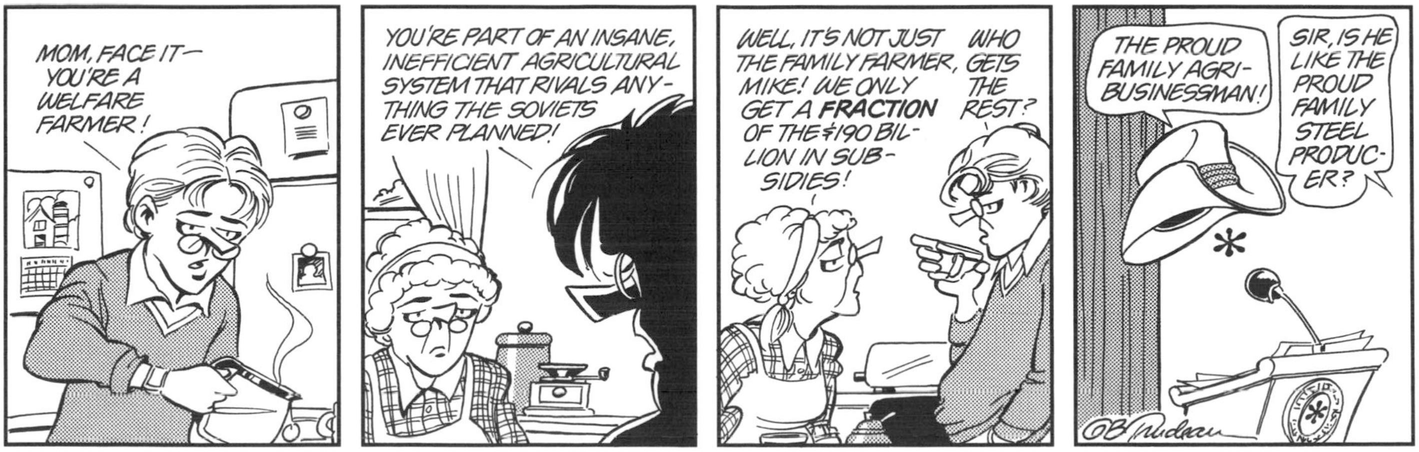
MOM, FACE IT—YOU'RE A WELFARE FARMER!
YOU'RE PART OF AN INSANE, INEFFICIENT AGRICULTURAL SYSTEM THAT RIVALS ANY-THING THE SOVIETS EVER PLANNED!
WELL, IT'S NOT JUST THE FAMILY FARMER, MIKE! WE ONLY GET A **FRACTION** OF THE $190 BIL-LION IN SUB-SIDIES!
WHO GETS THE REST?
THE PROUD FAMILY AGRI-BUSINESSMAN!
SIR, IS HE LIKE THE PROUD FAMILY STEEL PRODUC-ER?

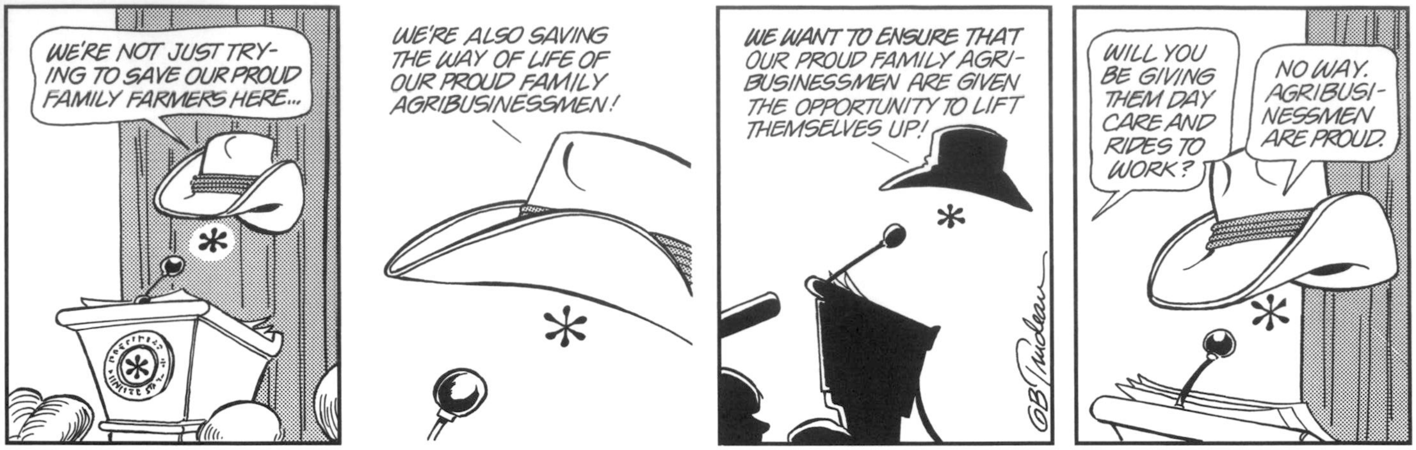
WE'RE NOT JUST TRYING TO SAVE OUR PROUD FAMILY FARMERS HERE...
WE'RE ALSO SAVING THE WAY OF LIFE OF OUR PROUD FAMILY AGRIBUSINESSMEN!
WE WANT TO ENSURE THAT OUR PROUD FAMILY AGRIBUSINESSMEN ARE GIVEN THE OPPORTUNITY TO LIFT THEMSELVES UP!
WILL YOU BE GIVING THEM DAY CARE AND RIDES TO WORK?
NO WAY. AGRIBUSINESSMEN ARE PROUD.

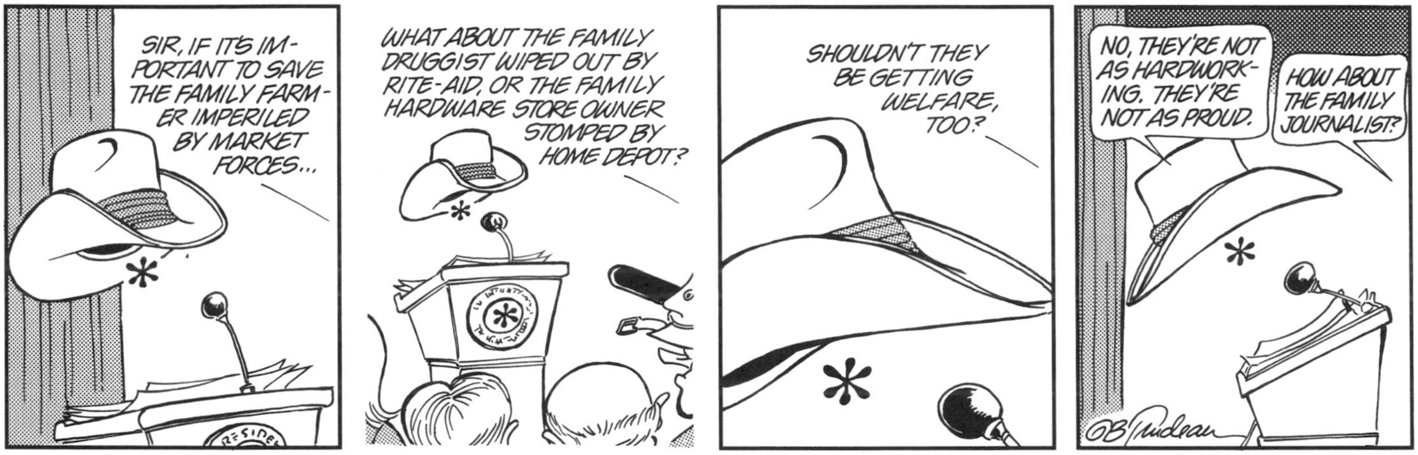
SIR, IF IT'S IMPORTANT TO SAVE THE FAMILY FARMER IMPERILED BY MARKET FORCES...
WHAT ABOUT THE FAMILY DRUGGIST WIPED OUT BY RITE-AID, OR THE FAMILY HARDWARE STORE OWNER STOMPED BY HOME DEPOT?
SHOULDN'T THEY BE GETTING WELFARE, TOO?
NO, THEY'RE NOT AS HARDWORKING. THEY'RE NOT AS PROUD.
HOW ABOUT THE FAMILY JOURNALIST?

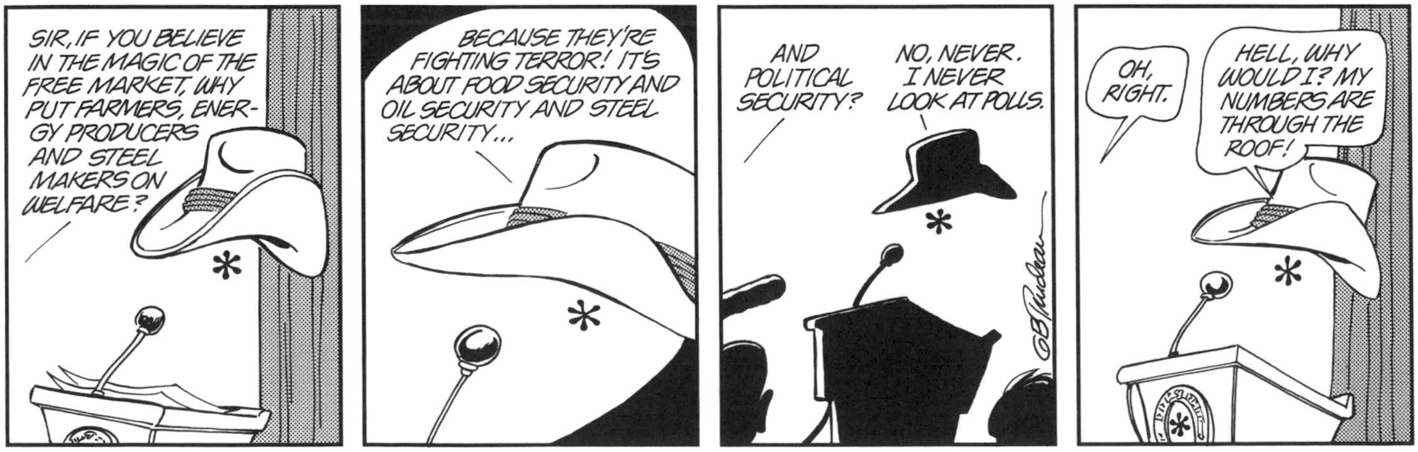
SIR, IF YOU BELIEVE IN THE MAGIC OF THE FREE MARKET, WHY PUT FARMERS, ENERGY PRODUCERS AND STEEL MAKERS ON WELFARE?
BECAUSE THEY'RE FIGHTING TERROR! IT'S ABOUT FOOD SECURITY AND OIL SECURITY AND STEEL SECURITY...
AND POLITICAL SECURITY?
NO, NEVER. I NEVER LOOK AT POLLS.
OH, RIGHT.
HELL, WHY WOULD I? MY NUMBERS ARE THROUGH THE ROOF!

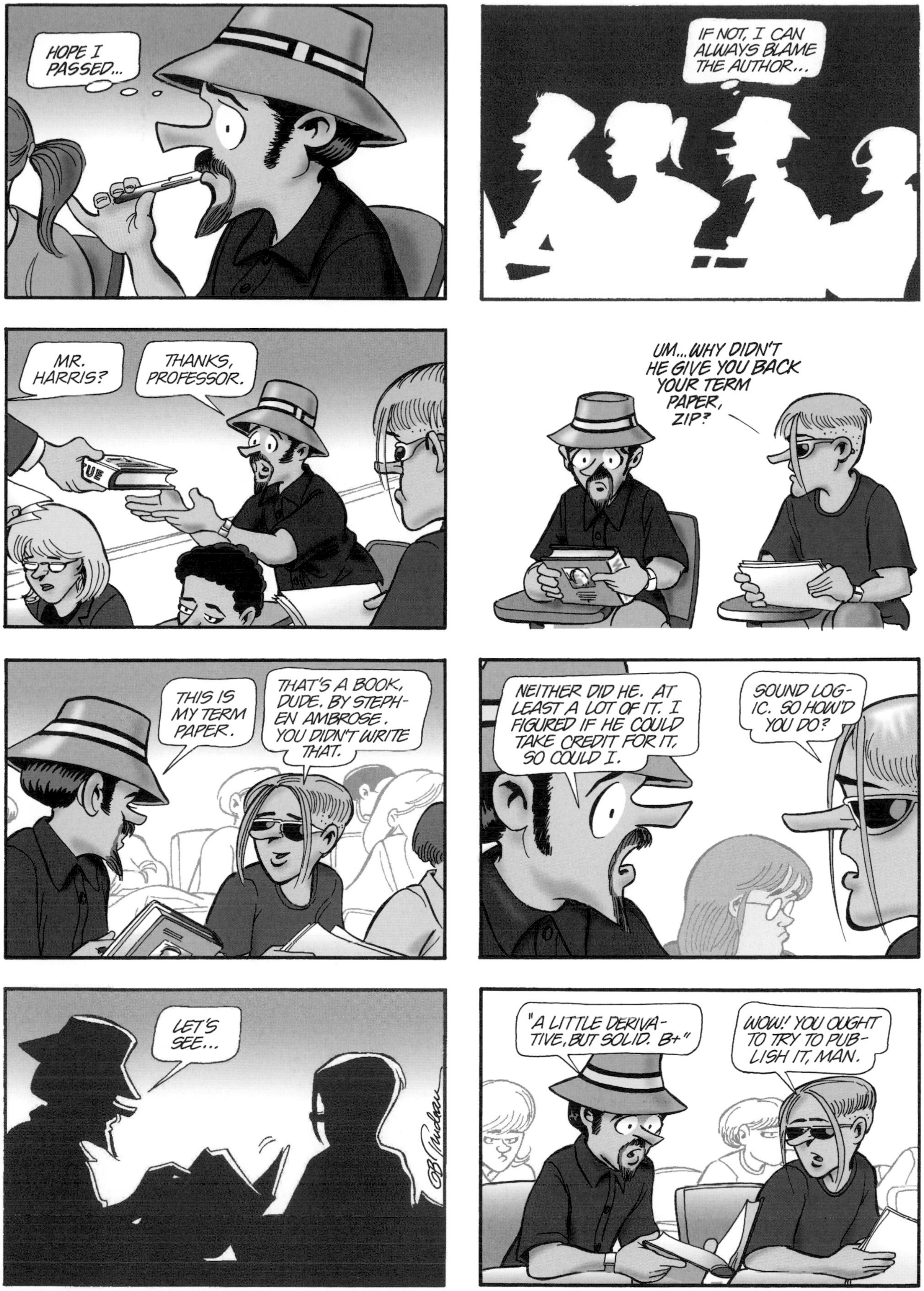
HOPE I PASSED...
IF NOT, I CAN ALWAYS BLAME THE AUTHOR...
MR. HARRIS?
THANKS, PROFESSOR.
UM...WHY DIDN'T HE GIVE YOU BACK YOUR TERM PAPER, ZIP?
THIS IS MY TERM PAPER.
THAT'S A BOOK, DUDE. BY STEPH-EN AMBROSE. YOU DIDN'T WRITE THAT.
NEITHER DID HE. AT LEAST A LOT OF IT. I FIGURED IF HE COULD TAKE CREDIT FOR IT, SO COULD I.
SOUND LOG-IC. SO HOW'D YOU DO?
LET'S SEE...
"A LITTLE DERIVA-TIVE, BUT SOLID. B+"
WOW! YOU OUGHT TO TRY TO PUB-LISH IT, MAN.

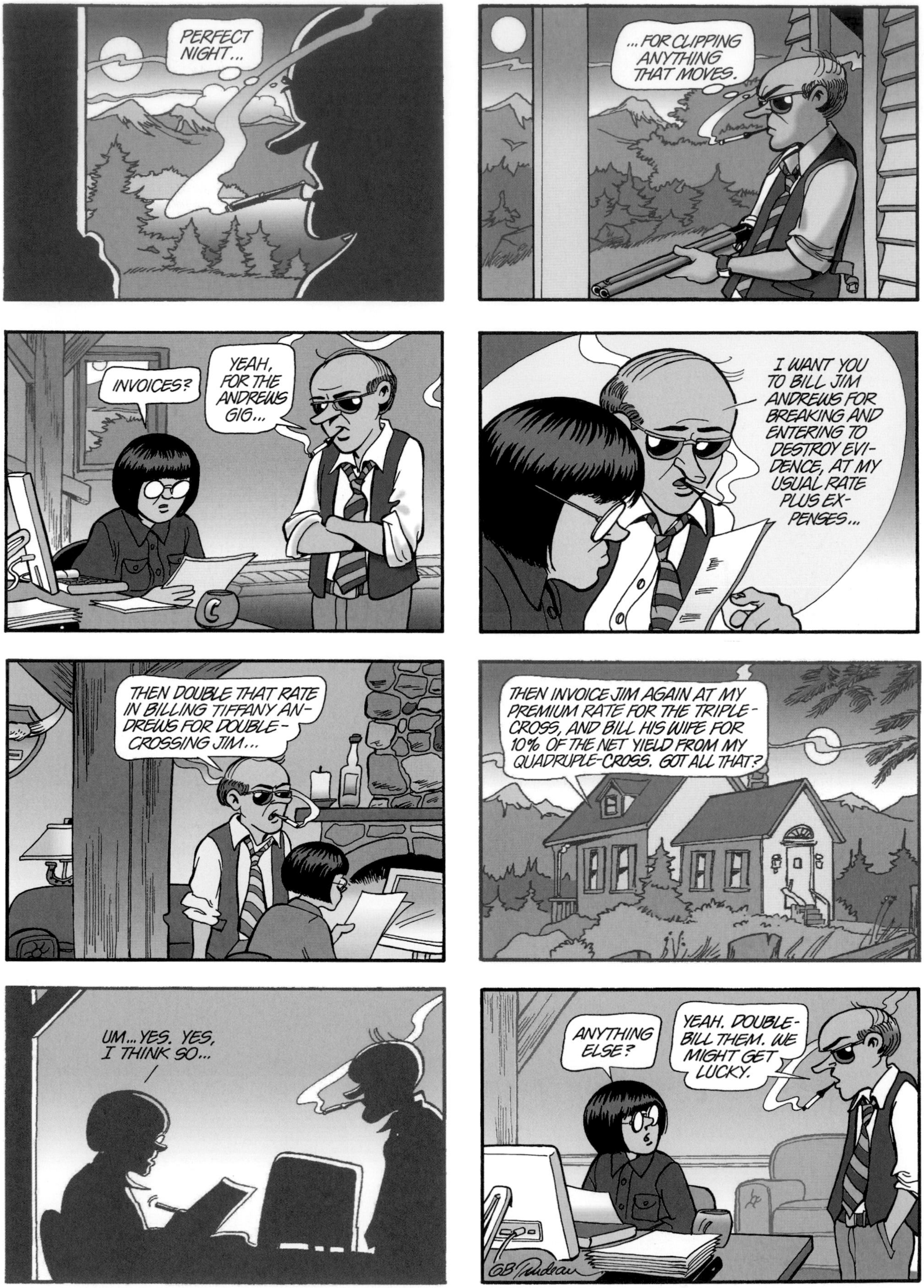
PERFECT NIGHT...
...FOR CLIPPING ANYTHING THAT MOVES.
INVOICES?
YEAH, FOR THE ANDREWS GIG...
I WANT YOU TO BILL JIM ANDREWS FOR BREAKING AND ENTERING TO DESTROY EVIDENCE, AT MY USUAL RATE PLUS EXPENSES...
THEN DOUBLE THAT RATE IN BILLING TIFFANY ANDREWS FOR DOUBLE-CROSSING JIM...
THEN INVOICE JIM AGAIN AT MY PREMIUM RATE FOR THE TRIPLE-CROSS, AND BILL HIS WIFE FOR 10% OF THE NET YIELD FROM MY QUADRUPLE-CROSS. GOT ALL THAT?
UM...YES. YES, I THINK SO...
ANYTHING ELSE?
YEAH. DOUBLE-BILL THEM. WE MIGHT GET LUCKY.
GB Trudeau

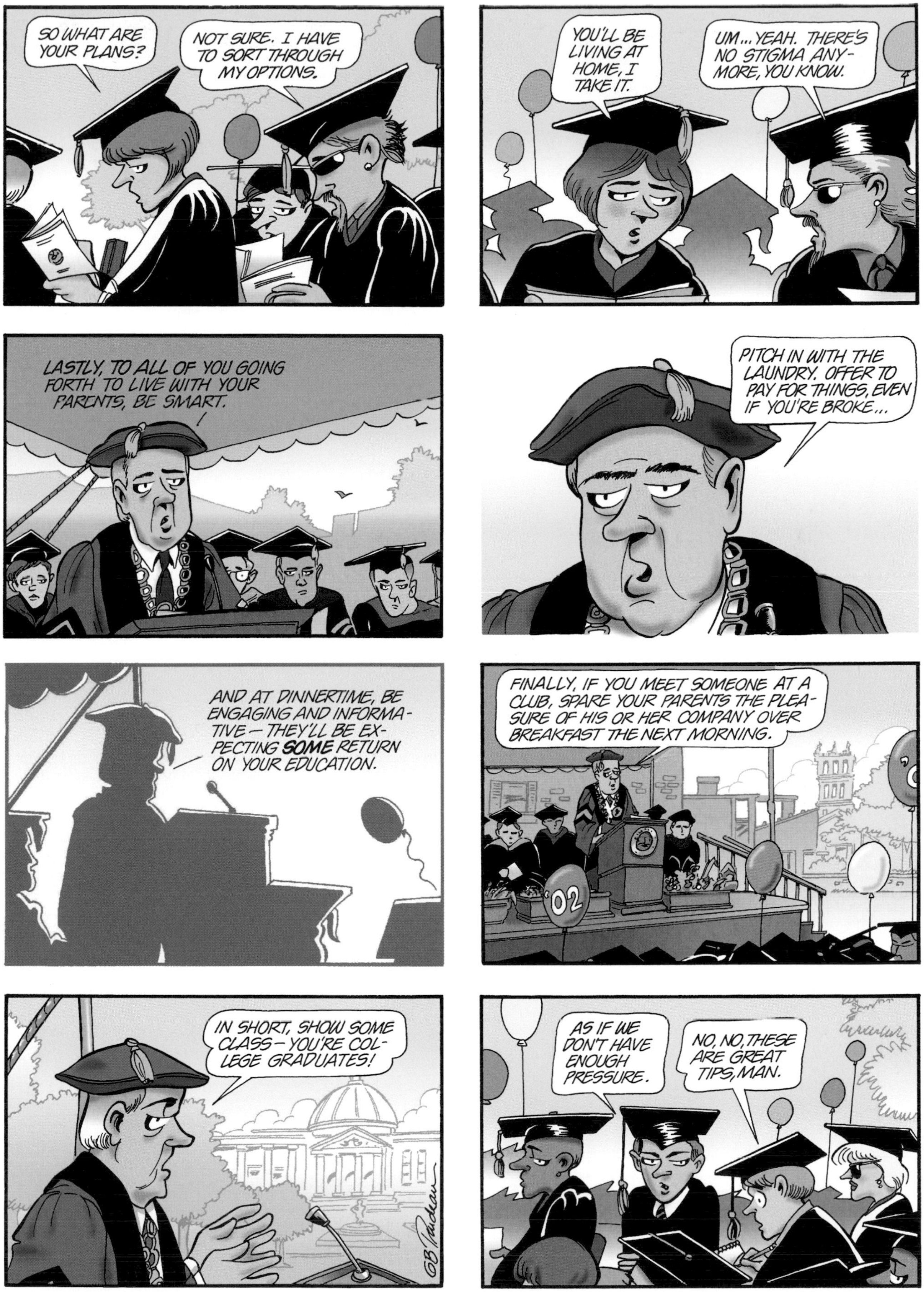
SO WHAT ARE YOUR PLANS?
NOT SURE. I HAVE TO SORT THROUGH MY OPTIONS.
YOU'LL BE LIVING AT HOME, I TAKE IT.
UM... YEAH. THERE'S NO STIGMA ANY-MORE, YOU KNOW.
LASTLY, TO ALL OF YOU GOING FORTH TO LIVE WITH YOUR PARENTS, BE SMART.
PITCH IN WITH THE LAUNDRY. OFFER TO PAY FOR THINGS, EVEN IF YOU'RE BROKE...
AND AT DINNERTIME, BE ENGAGING AND INFORMA-TIVE — THEY'LL BE EX-PECTING **SOME** RETURN ON YOUR EDUCATION.
FINALLY, IF YOU MEET SOMEONE AT A CLUB, SPARE YOUR PARENTS THE PLEA-SURE OF HIS OR HER COMPANY OVER BREAKFAST THE NEXT MORNING.
'02
IN SHORT, SHOW SOME CLASS — YOU'RE COL-LEGE GRADUATES!
AS IF WE DON'T HAVE ENOUGH PRESSURE.
NO, NO, THESE ARE GREAT TIPS, MAN.

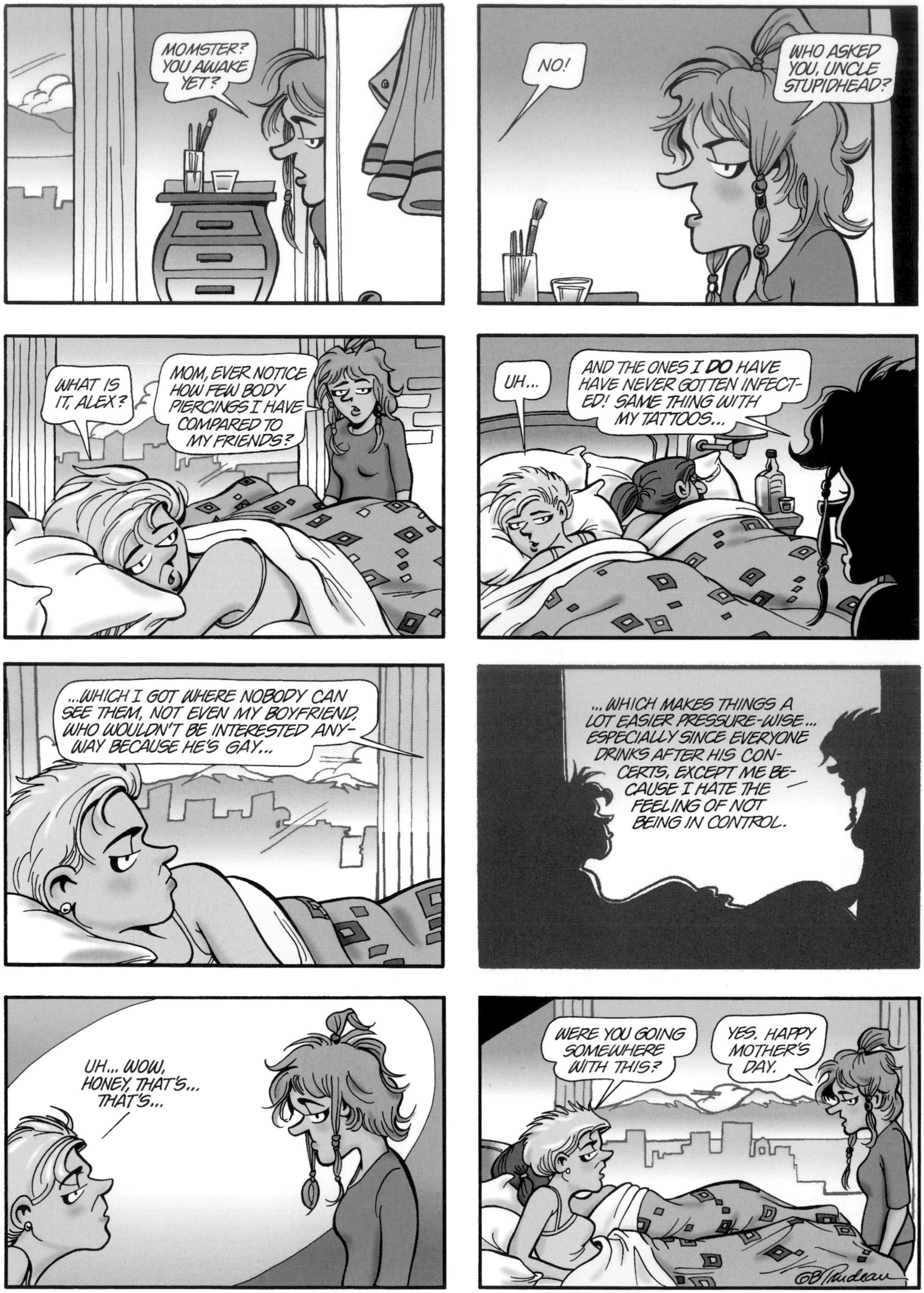
MOMSTER? YOU AWAKE YET?
NO!
WHO ASKED YOU, UNCLE STUPIDHEAD?
WHAT IS IT, ALEX?
MOM, EVER NOTICE HOW FEW BODY PIERCINGS I HAVE COMPARED TO MY FRIENDS?
UH...
AND THE ONES I DO HAVE HAVE NEVER GOTTEN INFECTED! SAME THING WITH MY TATTOOS...
...WHICH I GOT WHERE NOBODY CAN SEE THEM, NOT EVEN MY BOYFRIEND, WHO WOULDN'T BE INTERESTED ANYWAY BECAUSE HE'S GAY...
...WHICH MAKES THINGS A LOT EASIER PRESSURE-WISE... ESPECIALLY SINCE EVERYONE DRINKS AFTER HIS CONCERTS, EXCEPT ME BECAUSE I HATE THE FEELING OF NOT BEING IN CONTROL.
UH... WOW, HONEY, THAT'S... THAT'S...
WERE YOU GOING SOMEWHERE WITH THIS?
YES. HAPPY MOTHER'S DAY.
©BTrudeau

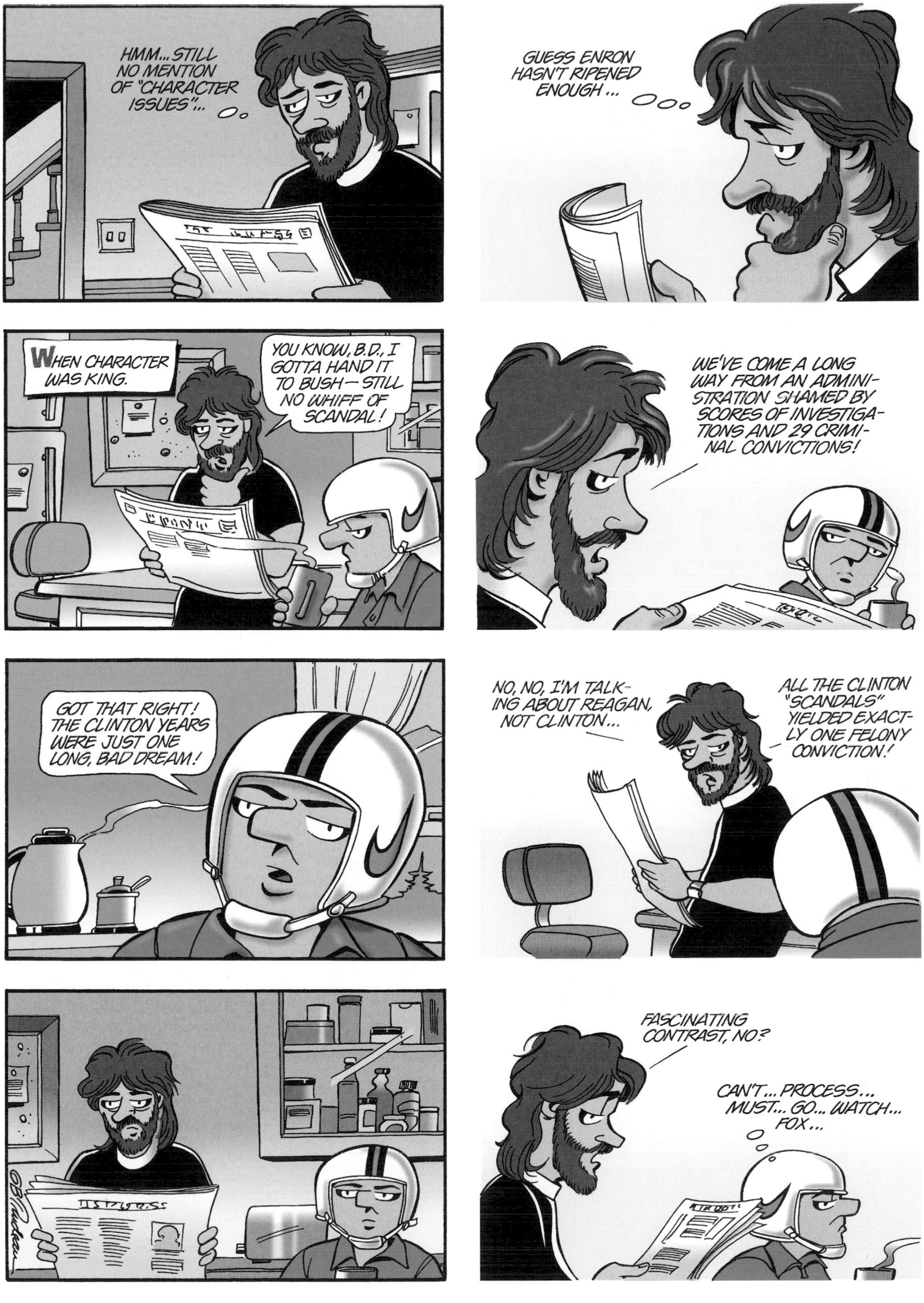
HMM... STILL NO MENTION OF "CHARACTER ISSUES"...
GUESS ENRON HASN'T RIPENED ENOUGH...
WHEN CHARACTER WAS KING.
YOU KNOW, B.D., I GOTTA HAND IT TO BUSH— STILL NO WHIFF OF SCANDAL!
WE'VE COME A LONG WAY FROM AN ADMINISTRATION SHAMED BY SCORES OF INVESTIGATIONS AND 29 CRIMINAL CONVICTIONS!
GOT THAT RIGHT! THE CLINTON YEARS WERE JUST ONE LONG, BAD DREAM!
NO, NO, I'M TALKING ABOUT REAGAN, NOT CLINTON...
ALL THE CLINTON "SCANDALS" YIELDED EXACTLY ONE FELONY CONVICTION!
FASCINATING CONTRAST, NO?
CAN'T... PROCESS... MUST... GO... WATCH... FOX...

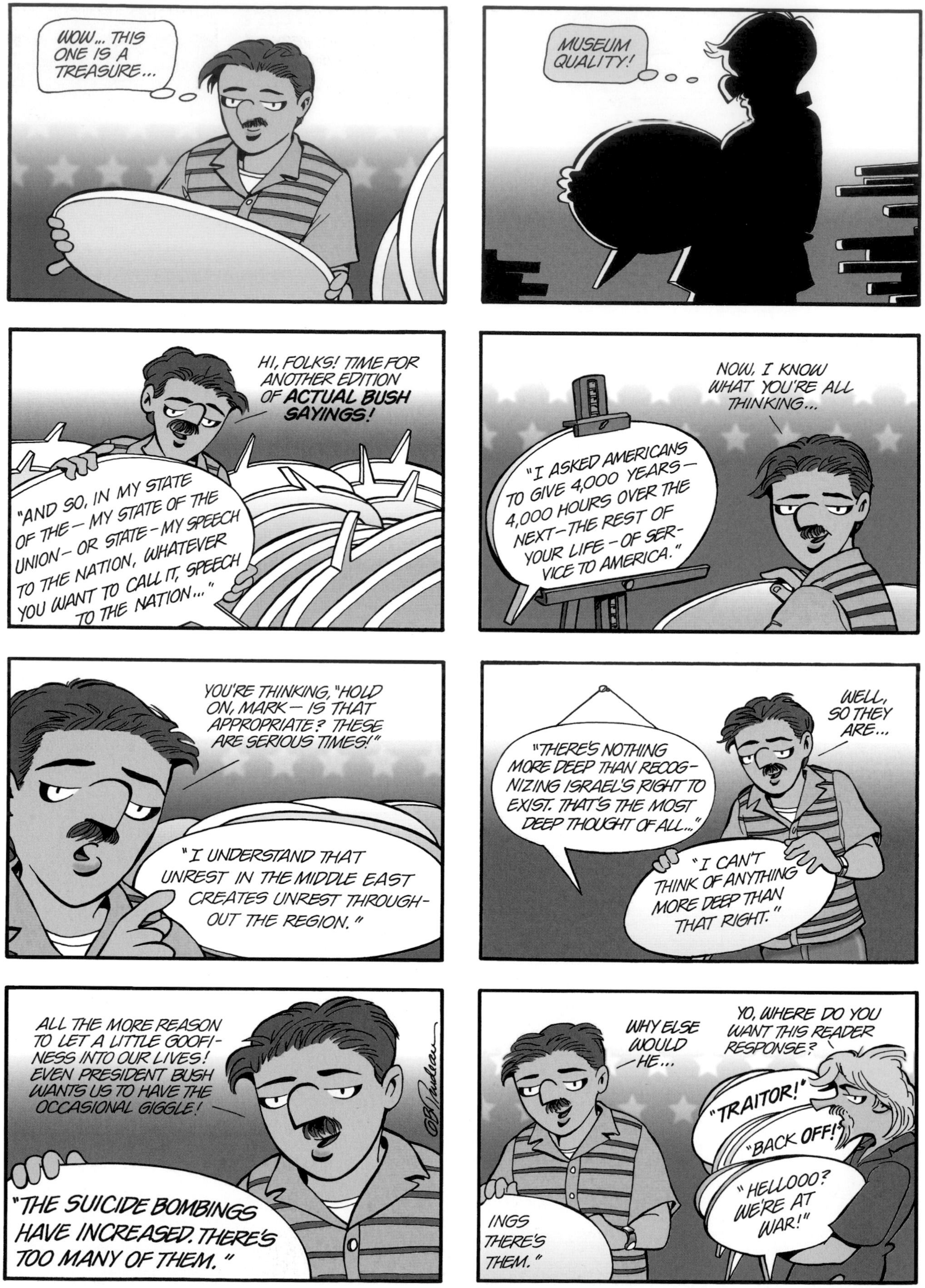
WOW... THIS ONE IS A TREASURE...
MUSEUM QUALITY!
HI, FOLKS! TIME FOR ANOTHER EDITION OF ACTUAL BUSH SAYINGS!
"AND SO, IN MY STATE OF THE — MY STATE OF THE UNION — OR STATE — MY SPEECH TO THE NATION, WHATEVER YOU WANT TO CALL IT, SPEECH TO THE NATION..."
NOW, I KNOW WHAT YOU'RE ALL THINKING...
"I ASKED AMERICANS TO GIVE 4,000 YEARS — 4,000 HOURS OVER THE NEXT — THE REST OF YOUR LIFE — OF SERVICE TO AMERICA."
YOU'RE THINKING, "HOLD ON, MARK — IS THAT APPROPRIATE? THESE ARE SERIOUS TIMES!"
"I UNDERSTAND THAT UNREST IN THE MIDDLE EAST CREATES UNREST THROUGHOUT THE REGION."
WELL, SO THEY ARE...
"THERE'S NOTHING MORE DEEP THAN RECOGNIZING ISRAEL'S RIGHT TO EXIST. THAT'S THE MOST DEEP THOUGHT OF ALL..."
"I CAN'T THINK OF ANYTHING MORE DEEP THAN THAT RIGHT."
ALL THE MORE REASON TO LET A LITTLE GOOFINESS INTO OUR LIVES! EVEN PRESIDENT BUSH WANTS US TO HAVE THE OCCASIONAL GIGGLE!
"THE SUICIDE BOMBINGS HAVE INCREASED. THERE'S TOO MANY OF THEM."
WHY ELSE WOULD HE...
YO, WHERE DO YOU WANT THIS READER RESPONSE?
"TRAITOR!"
"BACK OFF!"
"HELLOOO? WE'RE AT WAR!"
INGS THERE'S THEM."

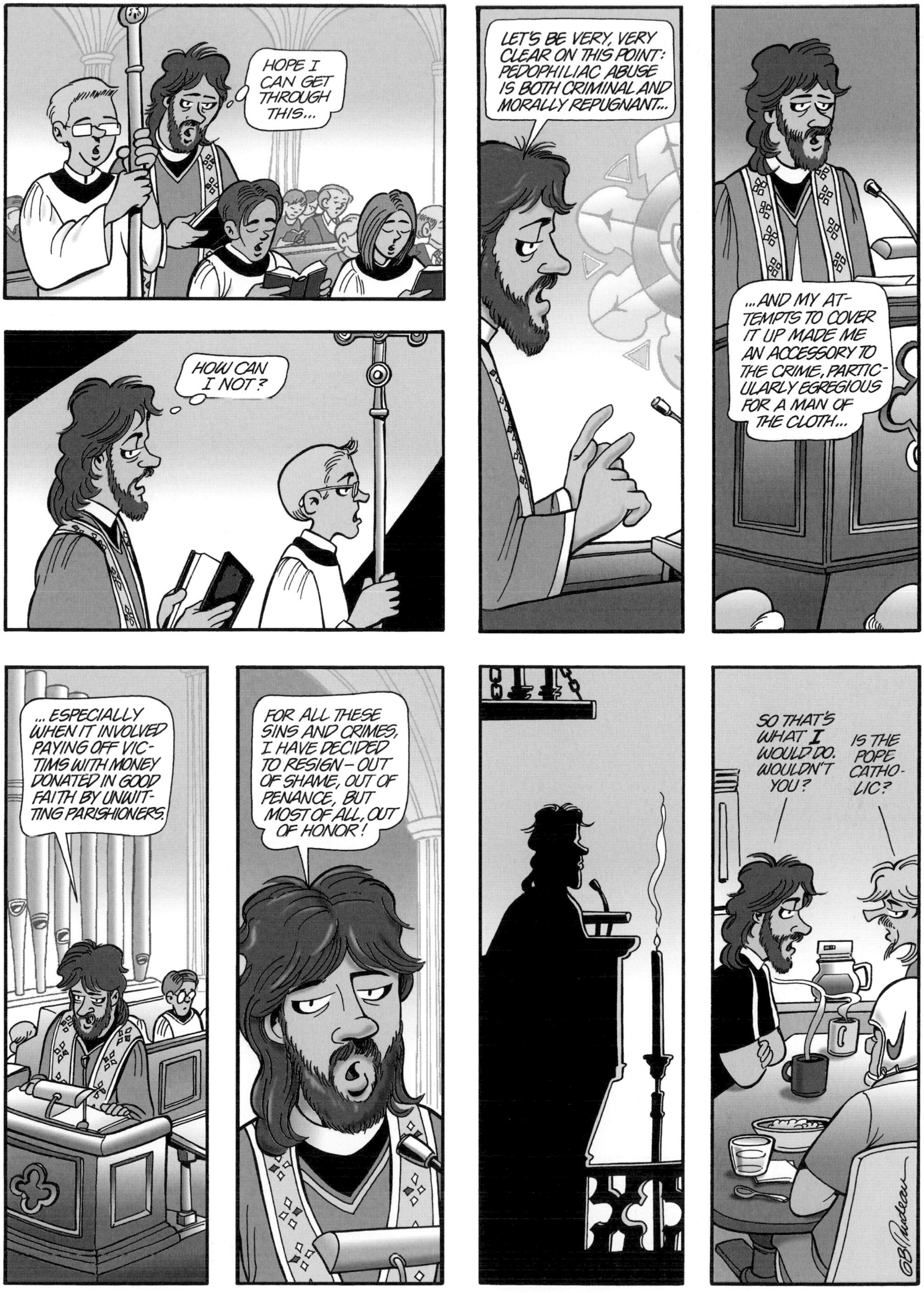
HOPE I CAN GET THROUGH THIS...
HOW CAN I NOT?
LET'S BE VERY, VERY CLEAR ON THIS POINT: PEDOPHILIAC ABUSE IS BOTH CRIMINAL AND MORALLY REPUGNANT...
...AND MY ATTEMPTS TO COVER IT UP MADE ME AN ACCESSORY TO THE CRIME, PARTICULARLY EGREGIOUS FOR A MAN OF THE CLOTH...
...ESPECIALLY WHEN IT INVOLVED PAYING OFF VICTIMS WITH MONEY DONATED IN GOOD FAITH BY UNWITTING PARISHIONERS.
FOR ALL THESE SINS AND CRIMES, I HAVE DECIDED TO RESIGN – OUT OF SHAME, OUT OF PENANCE, BUT MOST OF ALL, OUT OF HONOR!
SO THAT'S WHAT I WOULD DO. WOULDN'T YOU?
IS THE POPE CATHOLIC?
GBTrudeau

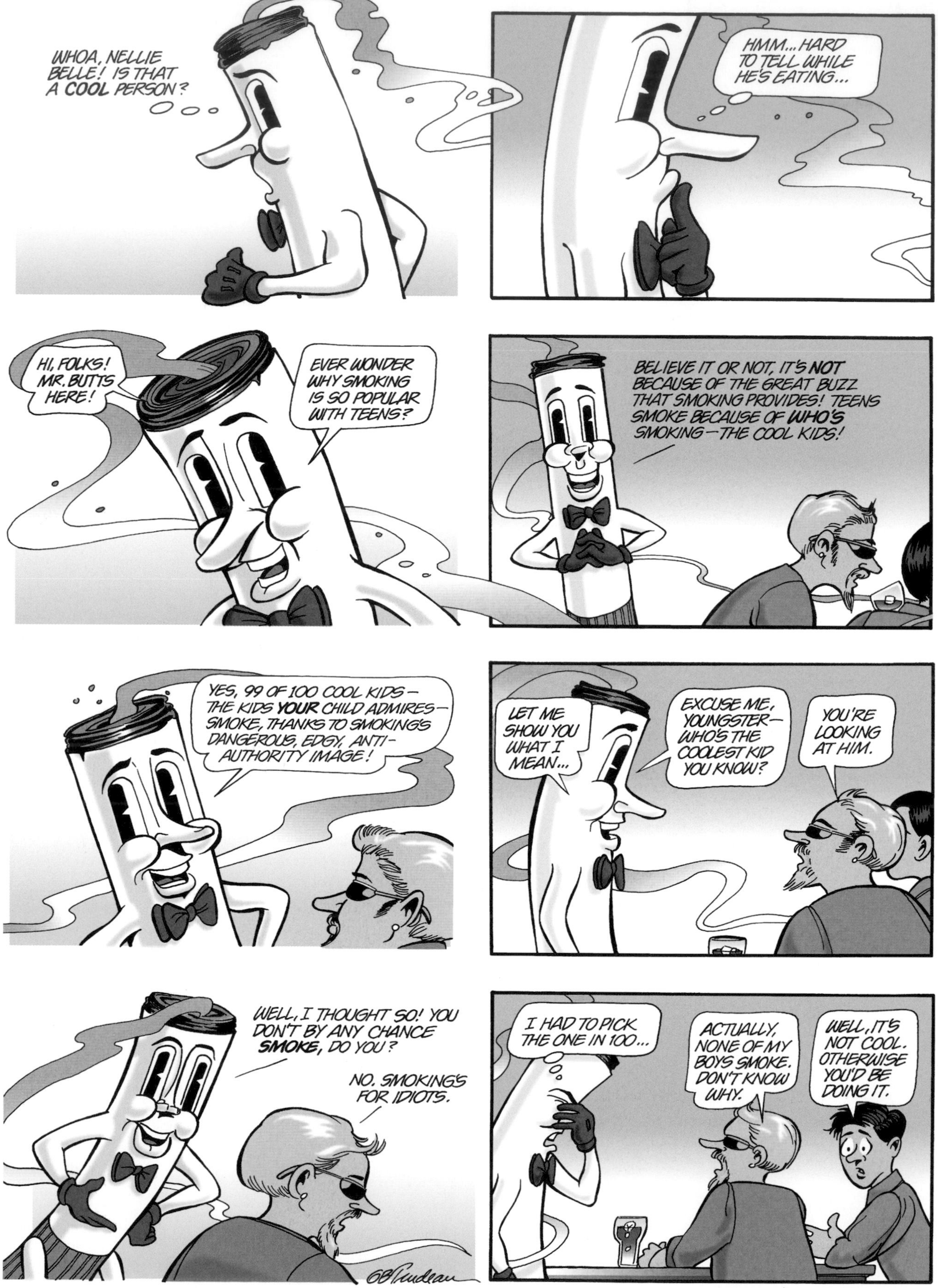
WHOA, NELLIE BELLE! IS THAT A COOL PERSON?
HMM... HARD TO TELL WHILE HE'S EATING...
HI, FOLKS! MR. BUTTS HERE!
EVER WONDER WHY SMOKING IS SO POPULAR WITH TEENS?
BELIEVE IT OR NOT, IT'S NOT BECAUSE OF THE GREAT BUZZ THAT SMOKING PROVIDES! TEENS SMOKE BECAUSE OF WHO'S SMOKING—THE COOL KIDS!
YES, 99 OF 100 COOL KIDS—THE KIDS YOUR CHILD ADMIRES—SMOKE, THANKS TO SMOKING'S DANGEROUS, EDGY, ANTI-AUTHORITY IMAGE!
LET ME SHOW YOU WHAT I MEAN...
EXCUSE ME, YOUNGSTER—WHO'S THE COOLEST KID YOU KNOW?
YOU'RE LOOKING AT HIM.
WELL, I THOUGHT SO! YOU DON'T BY ANY CHANCE SMOKE, DO YOU?
NO. SMOKING'S FOR IDIOTS.
I HAD TO PICK THE ONE IN 100...
ACTUALLY, NONE OF MY BOYS SMOKE. DON'T KNOW WHY.
WELL, IT'S NOT COOL. OTHERWISE YOU'D BE DOING IT.
GBTrudeau

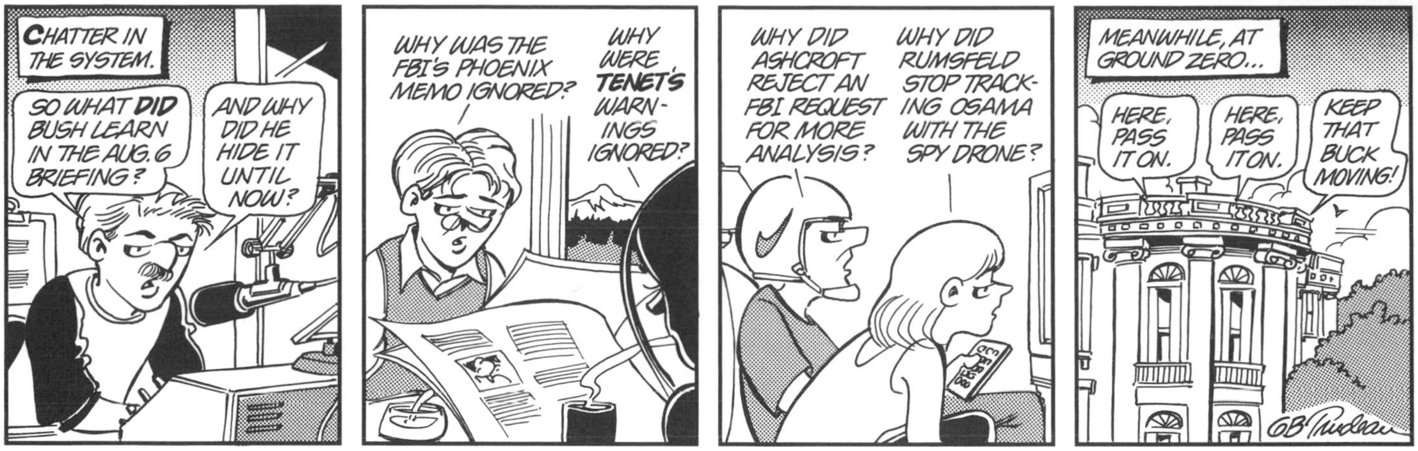
CHATTER IN THE SYSTEM.
SO WHAT DID BUSH LEARN IN THE AUG. 6 BRIEFING?
AND WHY DID HE HIDE IT UNTIL NOW?
WHY WAS THE FBI'S PHOENIX MEMO IGNORED?
WHY WERE TENET'S WARNINGS IGNORED?
WHY DID ASHCROFT REJECT AN FBI REQUEST FOR MORE ANALYSIS?
WHY DID RUMSFELD STOP TRACKING OSAMA WITH THE SPY DRONE?
MEANWHILE, AT GROUND ZERO...
HERE, PASS IT ON.
HERE, PASS IT ON.
KEEP THAT BUCK MOVING!
GB Trudeau

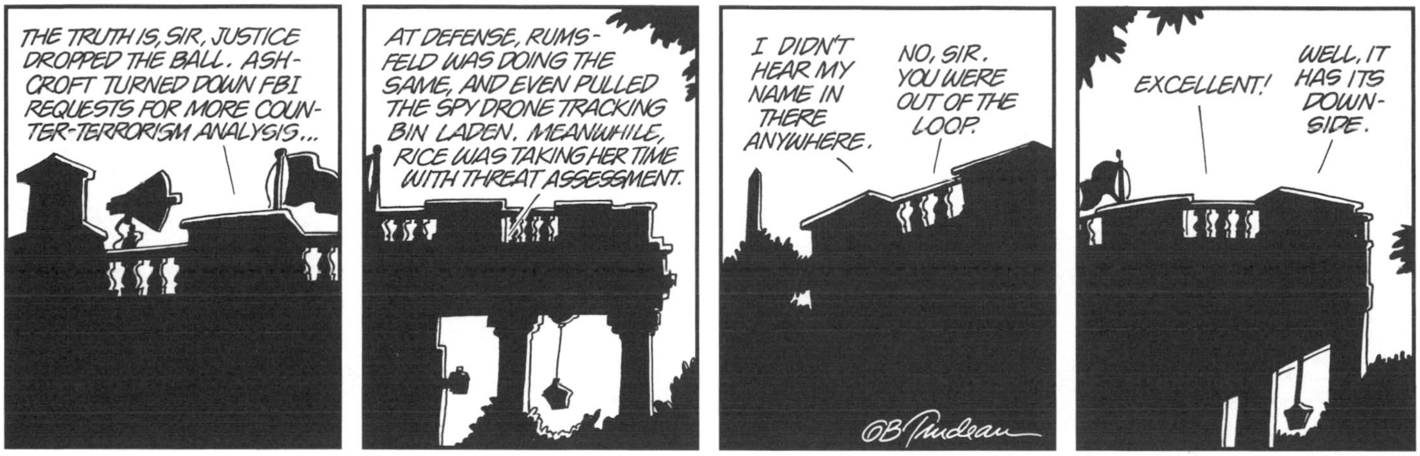
THE TRUTH IS, SIR, JUSTICE DROPPED THE BALL. ASHCROFT TURNED DOWN FBI REQUESTS FOR MORE COUNTER-TERRORISM ANALYSIS...
AT DEFENSE, RUMSFELD WAS DOING THE SAME, AND EVEN PULLED THE SPY DRONE TRACKING BIN LADEN. MEANWHILE, RICE WAS TAKING HER TIME WITH THREAT ASSESSMENT.
I DIDN'T HEAR MY NAME IN THERE ANYWHERE.
NO, SIR. YOU WERE OUT OF THE LOOP.
EXCELLENT!
WELL, IT HAS ITS DOWNSIDE.
GB Trudeau

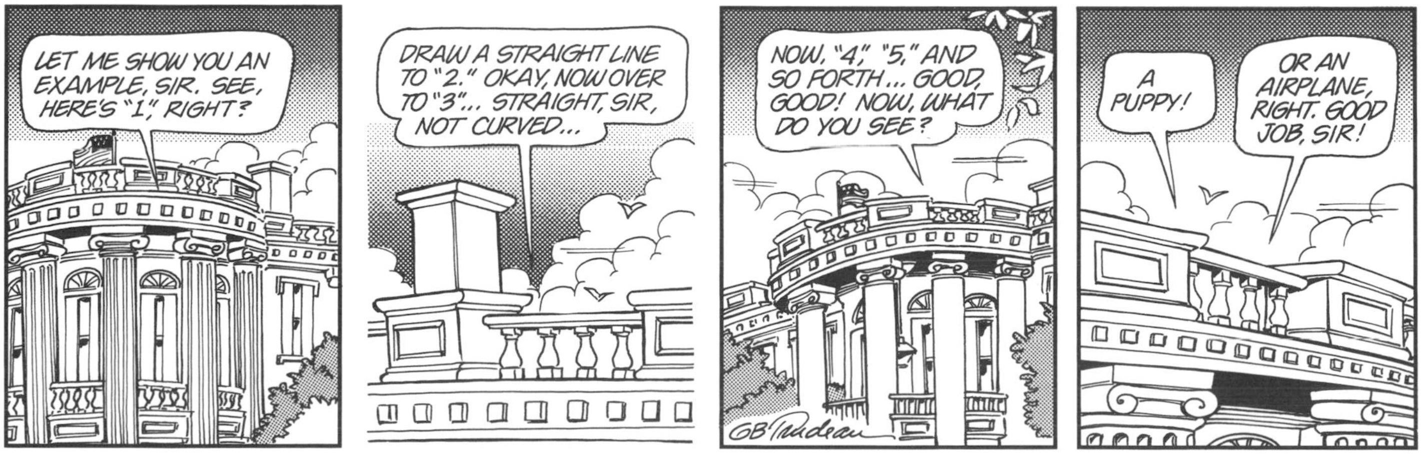
LET ME SHOW YOU AN EXAMPLE, SIR. SEE, HERE'S "1," RIGHT?
DRAW A STRAIGHT LINE TO "2." OKAY, NOW OVER TO "3"... STRAIGHT, SIR, NOT CURVED...
NOW, "4," "5," AND SO FORTH... GOOD, GOOD! NOW, WHAT DO YOU SEE?
GB Trudeau
A PUPPY!
OR AN AIRPLANE, RIGHT. GOOD JOB, SIR!

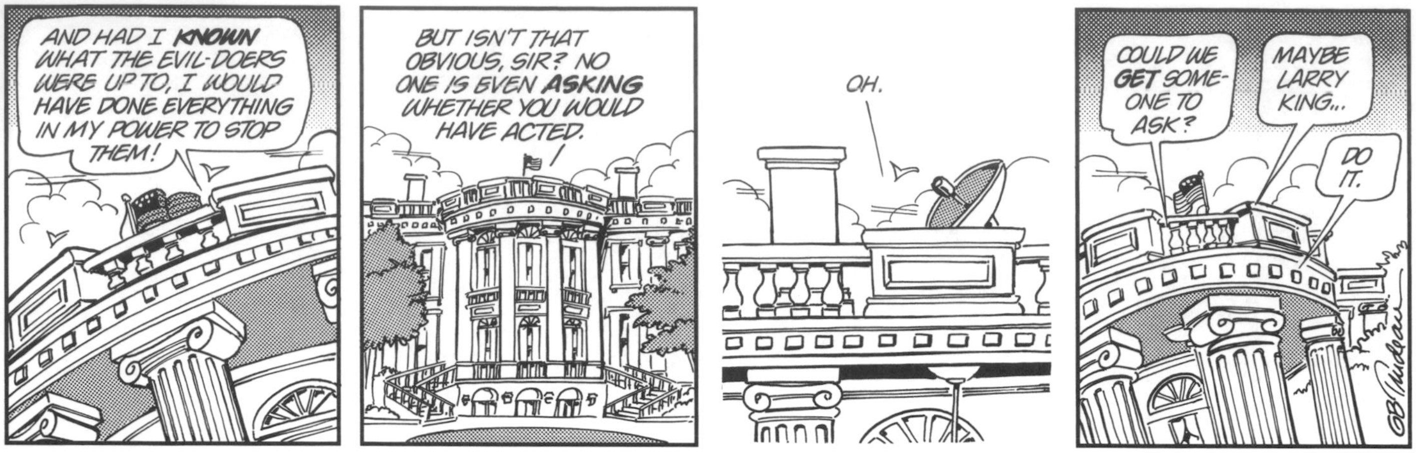
AND HAD I KNOWN WHAT THE EVIL-DOERS WERE UP TO, I WOULD HAVE DONE EVERYTHING IN MY POWER TO STOP THEM!
BUT ISN'T THAT OBVIOUS, SIR? NO ONE IS EVEN ASKING WHETHER YOU WOULD HAVE ACTED.
OH.
COULD WE GET SOME-ONE TO ASK?
MAYBE LARRY KING...
DO IT.
GB Trudeau

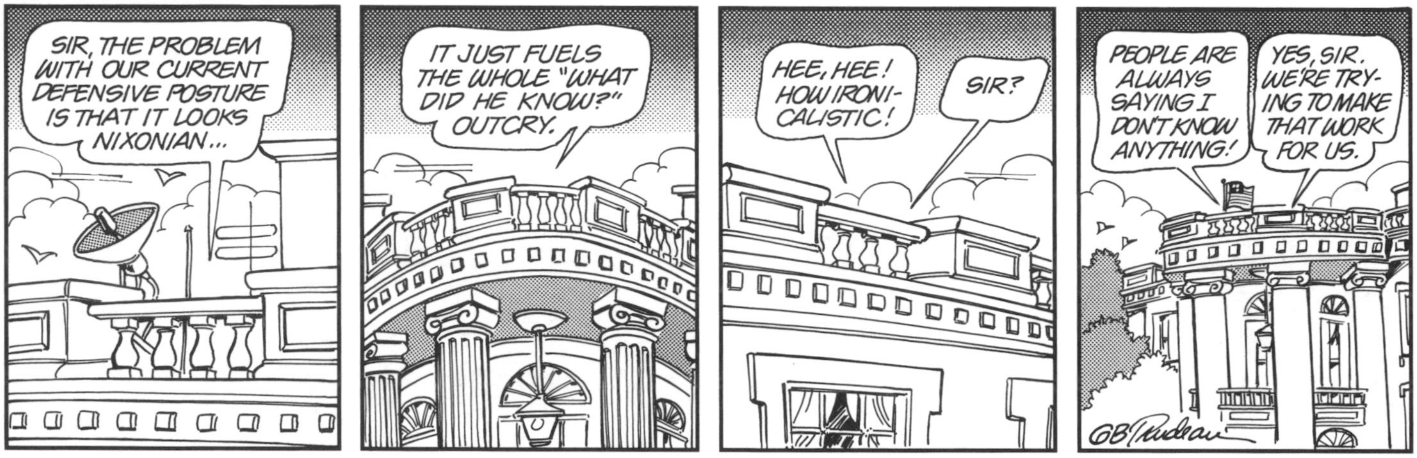
SIR, THE PROBLEM WITH OUR CURRENT DEFENSIVE POSTURE IS THAT IT LOOKS NIXONIAN...
IT JUST FUELS THE WHOLE "WHAT DID HE KNOW?" OUTCRY.
HEE, HEE! HOW IRONI-CALISTIC!
SIR?
PEOPLE ARE ALWAYS SAYING I DON'T KNOW ANYTHING!
YES, SIR. WE'RE TRY-ING TO MAKE THAT WORK FOR US.
GB Trudeau

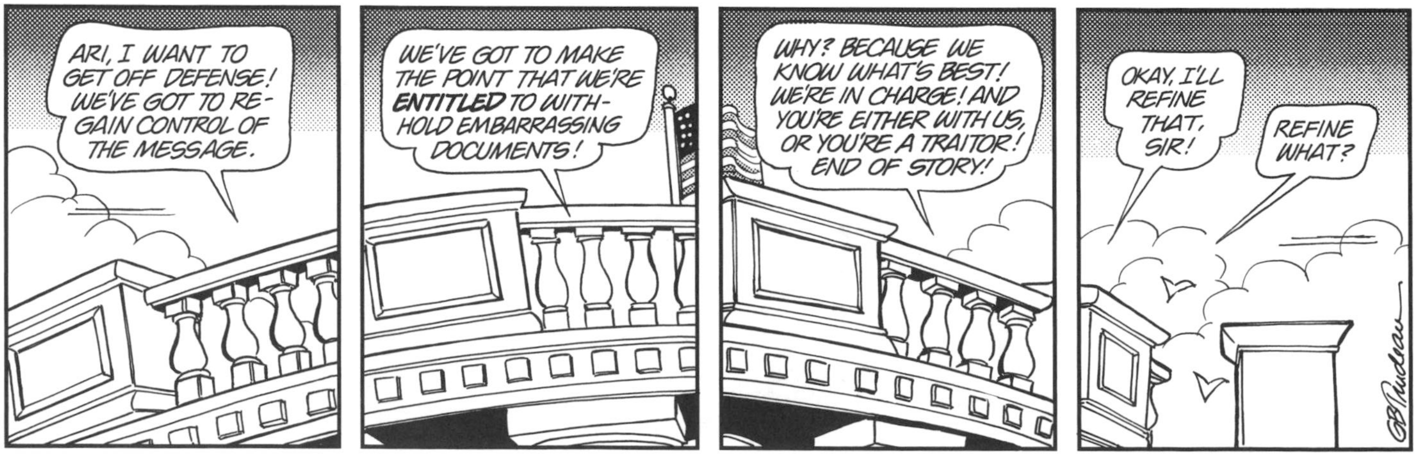
ARI, I WANT TO GET OFF DEFENSE! WE'VE GOT TO RE-GAIN CONTROL OF THE MESSAGE.
WE'VE GOT TO MAKE THE POINT THAT WE'RE ENTITLED TO WITH-HOLD EMBARRASSING DOCUMENTS!
WHY? BECAUSE WE KNOW WHAT'S BEST! WE'RE IN CHARGE! AND YOU'RE EITHER WITH US, OR YOU'RE A TRAITOR! END OF STORY!
OKAY, I'LL REFINE THAT, SIR!
REFINE WHAT?
GB Trudeau

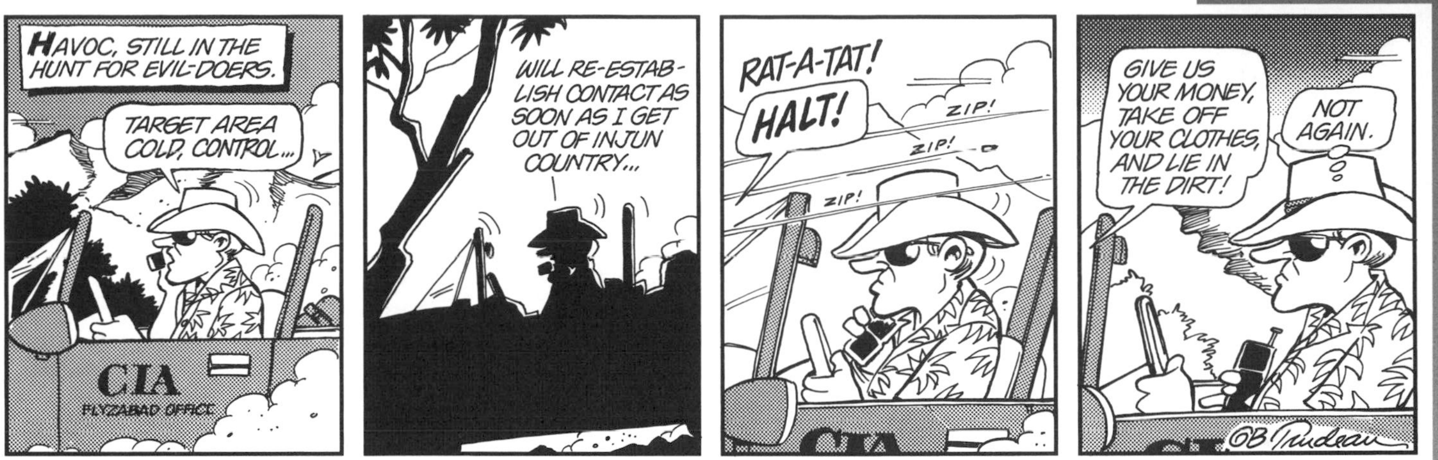
HAVOC, STILL IN THE HUNT FOR EVIL-DOERS.
TARGET AREA COLD, CONTROL...
CIA
FLYZABAD OFFICE
WILL RE-ESTABLISH CONTACT AS SOON AS I GET OUT OF INJUN COUNTRY...
RAT-A-TAT!
HALT!
ZIP!
ZIP!
ZIP!
GIVE US YOUR MONEY, TAKE OFF YOUR CLOTHES, AND LIE IN THE DIRT!
NOT AGAIN.

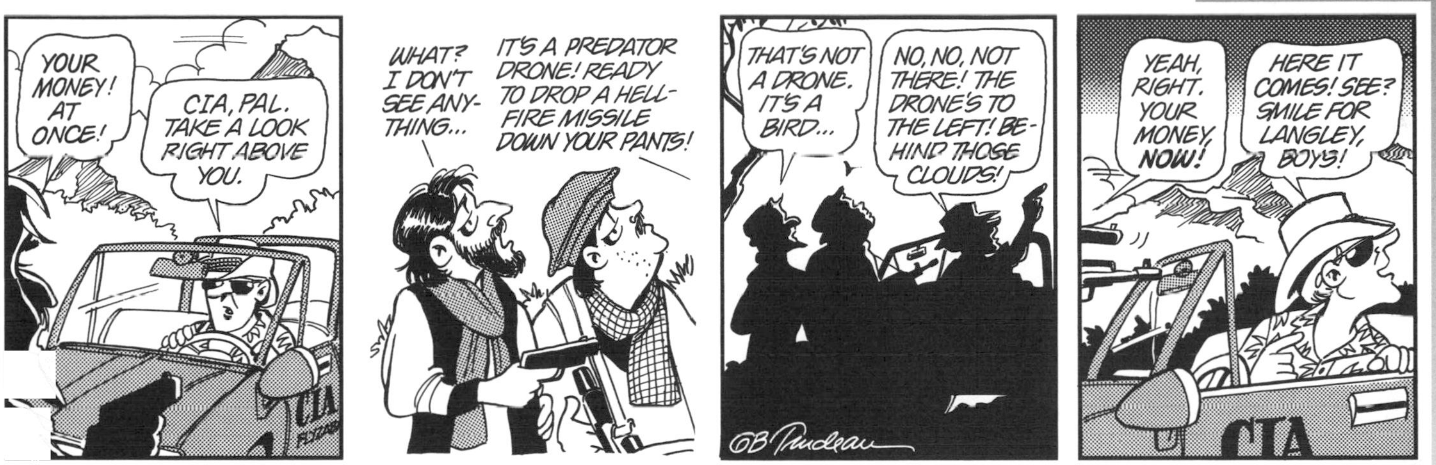
YOUR MONEY! AT ONCE!
CIA, PAL. TAKE A LOOK RIGHT ABOVE YOU.
WHAT? I DON'T SEE ANYTHING...
IT'S A PREDATOR DRONE! READY TO DROP A HELLFIRE MISSILE DOWN YOUR PANTS!
THAT'S NOT A DRONE. IT'S A BIRD...
NO, NO, NOT THERE! THE DRONE'S TO THE LEFT! BEHIND THOSE CLOUDS!
YEAH, RIGHT. YOUR MONEY, NOW!
HERE IT COMES! SEE? SMILE FOR LANGLEY, BOYS!
CIA

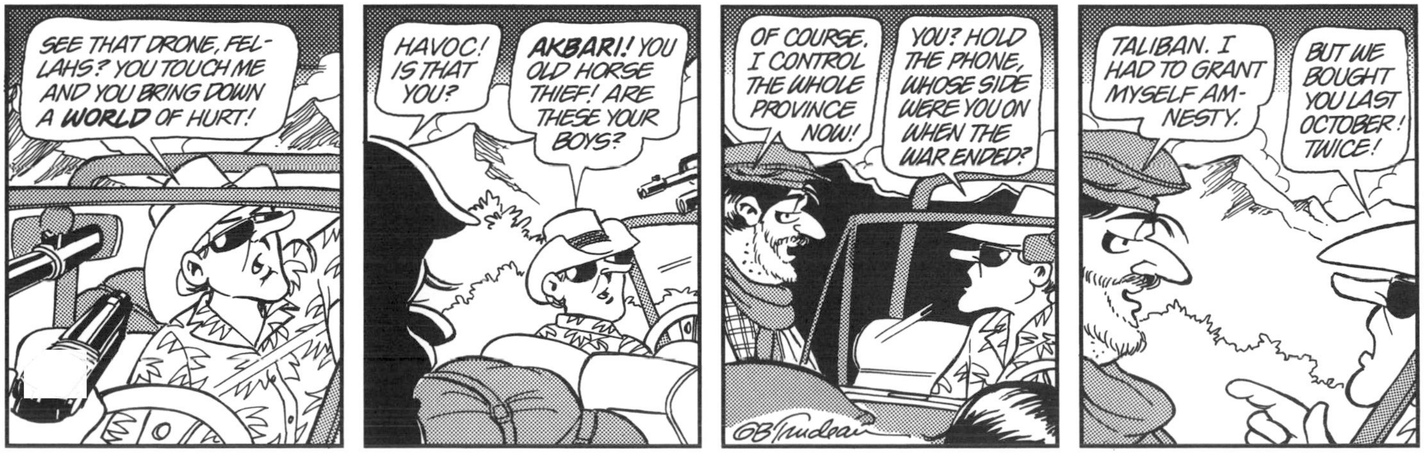
SEE THAT DRONE, FELLAHS? YOU TOUCH ME AND YOU BRING DOWN A WORLD OF HURT!
HAVOC! IS THAT YOU?
AKBARI! YOU OLD HORSE THIEF! ARE THESE YOUR BOYS?
OF COURSE. I CONTROL THE WHOLE PROVINCE NOW!
YOU? HOLD THE PHONE, WHOSE SIDE WERE YOU ON WHEN THE WAR ENDED?
TALIBAN. I HAD TO GRANT MYSELF AMNESTY.
BUT WE BOUGHT YOU LAST OCTOBER! TWICE!

SO THIS IS YOUR IDEA OF FREEDOM, AKBARI? BACK TO WARLORDING AND BANDITRY?
LOOK, THERE'S A POWER VACUUM, OKAY? WHAT ARE YOU BLAMING ME FOR? YOU'RE THE ONES WHO CONFINED THE PEACEKEEPERS TO KABUL!
BESIDES, MY TRIBE IS TRADITIONALLY PEACEFUL. WE ONLY HAVE A FEW MORE SCORES TO SETTLE.
DATING FROM THE 14TH CENTURY, NO DOUBT.
JUST TWO. THE REST ARE POST-COLONIAL.

I'LL TELL YOU, AKBARI, WE'RE GETTING FED UP WITH YOU YO-YOS...
WE LIBERATE YOU FROM YOUR LITTLE TALIBUDDIES, AND THE FIRST THING YOU DO IS RE-TRASH YOUR OWN COUNTRY!
I MEAN, WHAT THE HELL DOES IT TAKE TO GET AFGHAN "LEADERS" TO FINALLY GROW UP?
BALLPARK? IN U.S. DOLLARS?
YEAH, RIGHT, I'M PRICING WARLORDS.

LOOK, AKBARI, IT'S NO SECRET THAT DUBYA ISN'T INTO NATION-BUILDING...
BUT THAT DOESN'T MEAN YOU HAVE TO RETURN TO CHAOS! IT JUST MAKES US LOOK BAD!
I UNDERSTAND YOUR CONCERNS, MY FRIEND, I REALLY DO...
LISTEN, WE'RE SHELLING A VILLAGE TONIGHT. WANT TO MONITOR US?
NO... NO, I'M OFF THE CLOCK.

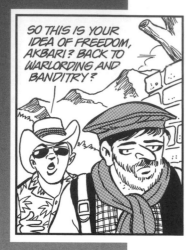

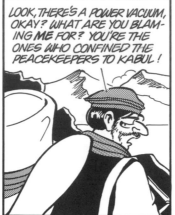

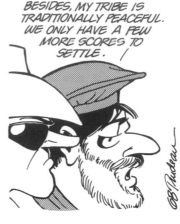

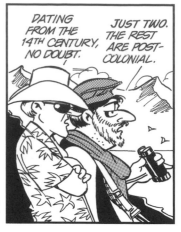

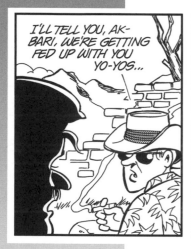

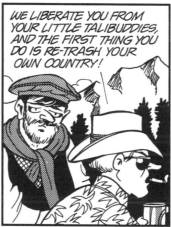

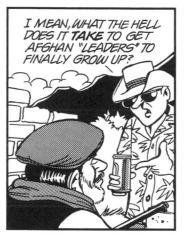

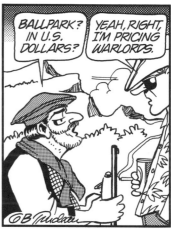

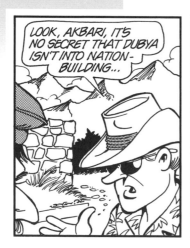

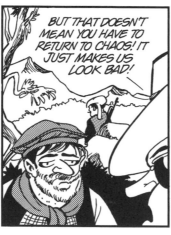

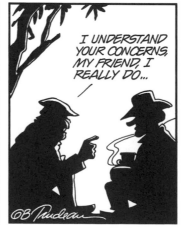

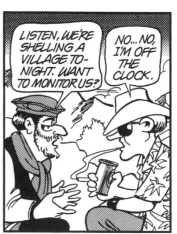

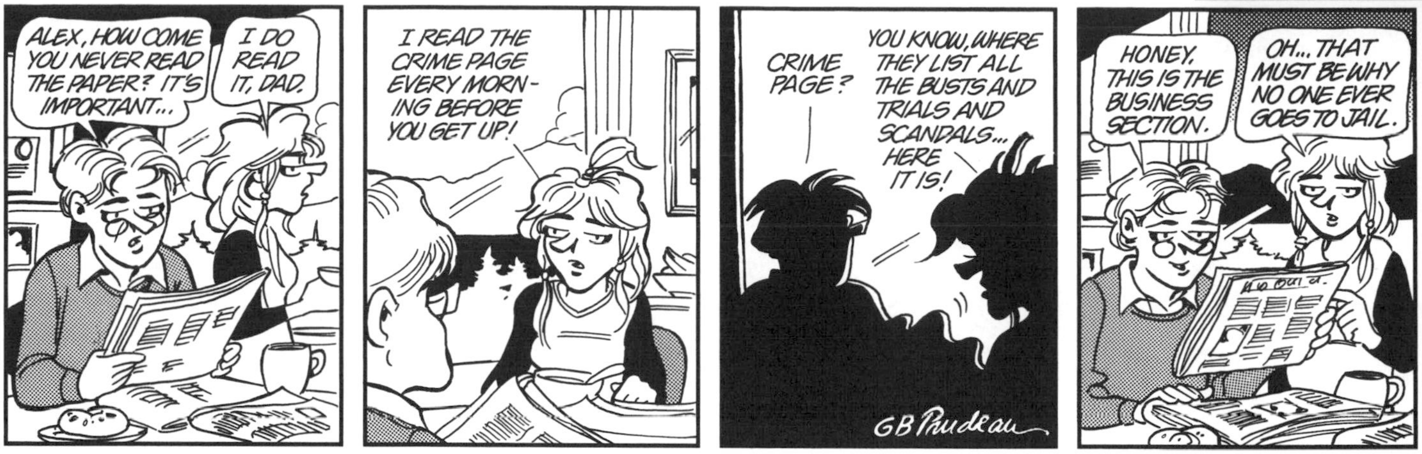
ALEX, HOW COME YOU NEVER READ THE PAPER? IT'S IMPORTANT...
I DO READ IT, DAD.
I READ THE CRIME PAGE EVERY MORNING BEFORE YOU GET UP!
CRIME PAGE?
YOU KNOW, WHERE THEY LIST ALL THE BUSTS AND TRIALS AND SCANDALS... HERE IT IS!
GB Trudeau
HONEY, THIS IS THE BUSINESS SECTION.
OH... THAT MUST BE WHY NO ONE EVER GOES TO JAIL.

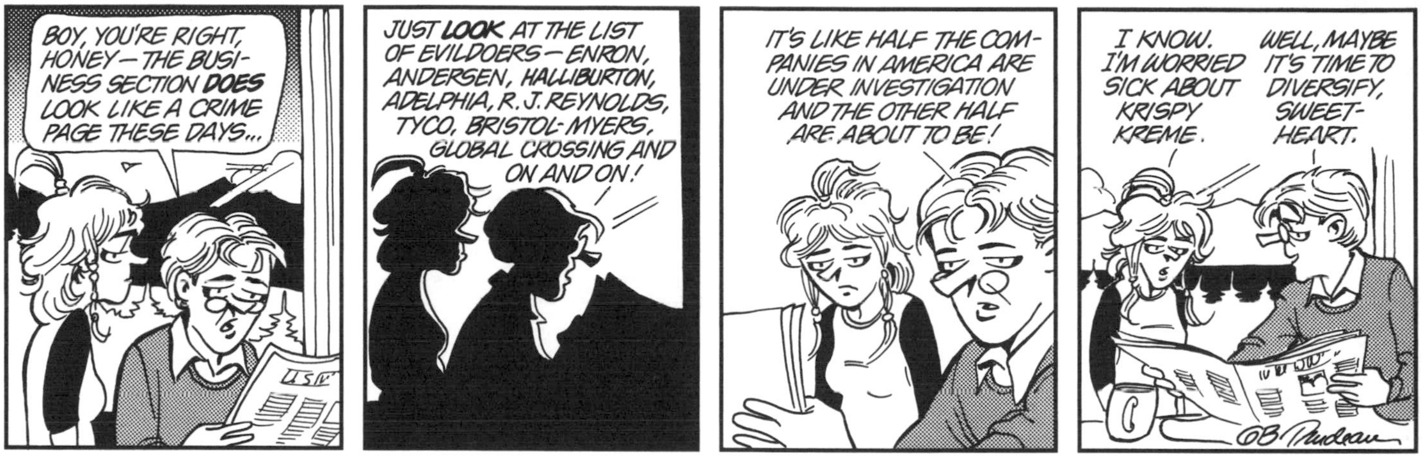
BOY, YOU'RE RIGHT, HONEY—THE BUSINESS SECTION DOES LOOK LIKE A CRIME PAGE THESE DAYS...
JUST LOOK AT THE LIST OF EVILDOERS—ENRON, ANDERSEN, HALLIBURTON, ADELPHIA, R.J. REYNOLDS, TYCO, BRISTOL-MYERS, GLOBAL CROSSING AND ON AND ON!
IT'S LIKE HALF THE COMPANIES IN AMERICA ARE UNDER INVESTIGATION AND THE OTHER HALF ARE ABOUT TO BE!
I KNOW. I'M WORRIED SICK ABOUT KRISPY KREME.
WELL, MAYBE IT'S TIME TO DIVERSIFY, SWEETHEART.
GB Trudeau

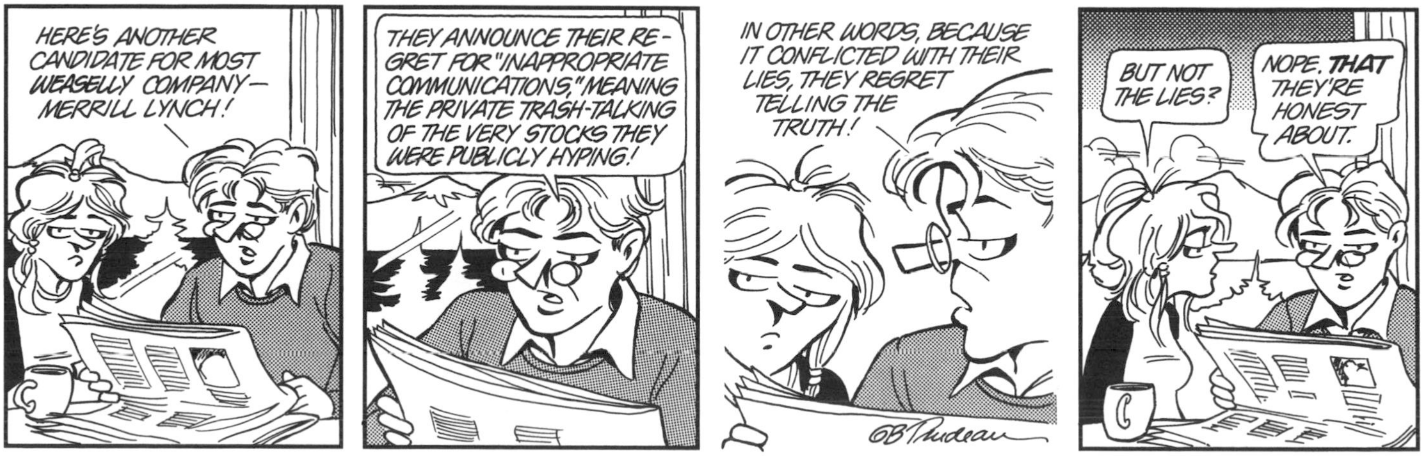
HERE'S ANOTHER CANDIDATE FOR MOST WEASELLY COMPANY—MERRILL LYNCH!
THEY ANNOUNCE THEIR REGRET FOR "INAPPROPRIATE COMMUNICATIONS," MEANING THE PRIVATE TRASH-TALKING OF THE VERY STOCKS THEY WERE PUBLICLY HYPING!
IN OTHER WORDS, BECAUSE IT CONFLICTED WITH THEIR LIES, THEY REGRET TELLING THE TRUTH!
GB Trudeau
BUT NOT THE LIES?
NOPE. THAT THEY'RE HONEST ABOUT.

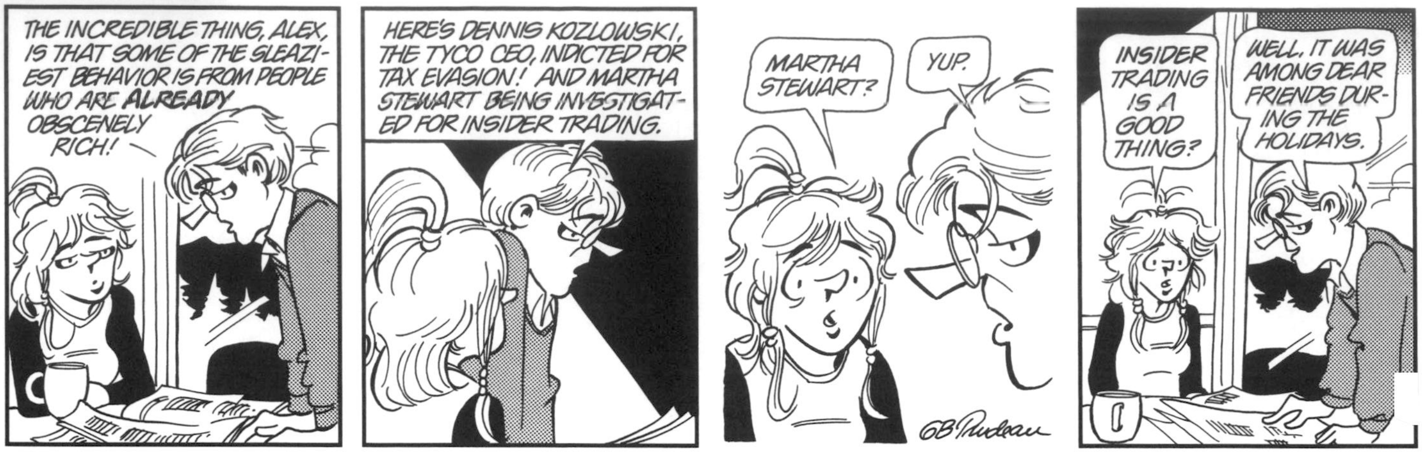
THE INCREDIBLE THING, ALEX, IS THAT SOME OF THE SLEAZIEST BEHAVIOR IS FROM PEOPLE WHO ARE **ALREADY** OBSCENELY RICH!
HERE'S DENNIS KOZLOWSKI, THE TYCO CEO, INDICTED FOR TAX EVASION! AND MARTHA STEWART BEING INVESTIGATED FOR INSIDER TRADING.
MARTHA STEWART?
YUP.
INSIDER TRADING IS A GOOD THING?
WELL, IT WAS AMONG DEAR FRIENDS DURING THE HOLIDAYS.

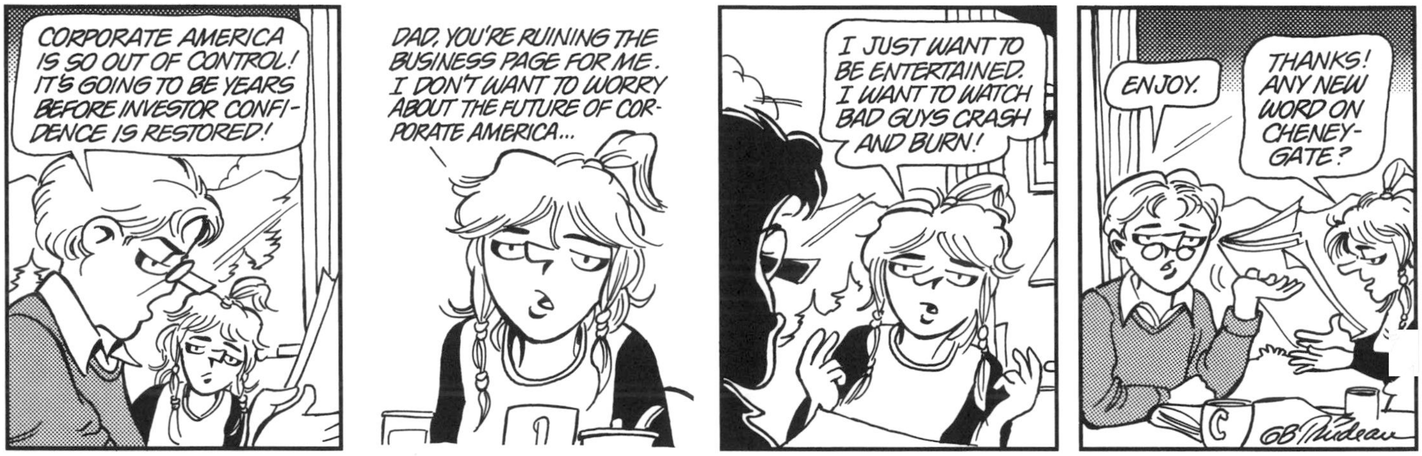
CORPORATE AMERICA IS SO OUT OF CONTROL! IT'S GOING TO BE YEARS BEFORE INVESTOR CONFIDENCE IS RESTORED!
DAD, YOU'RE RUINING THE BUSINESS PAGE FOR ME. I DON'T WANT TO WORRY ABOUT THE FUTURE OF CORPORATE AMERICA...
I JUST WANT TO BE ENTERTAINED. I WANT TO WATCH BAD GUYS CRASH AND BURN!
ENJOY.
THANKS! ANY NEW WORD ON CHENEY-GATE?

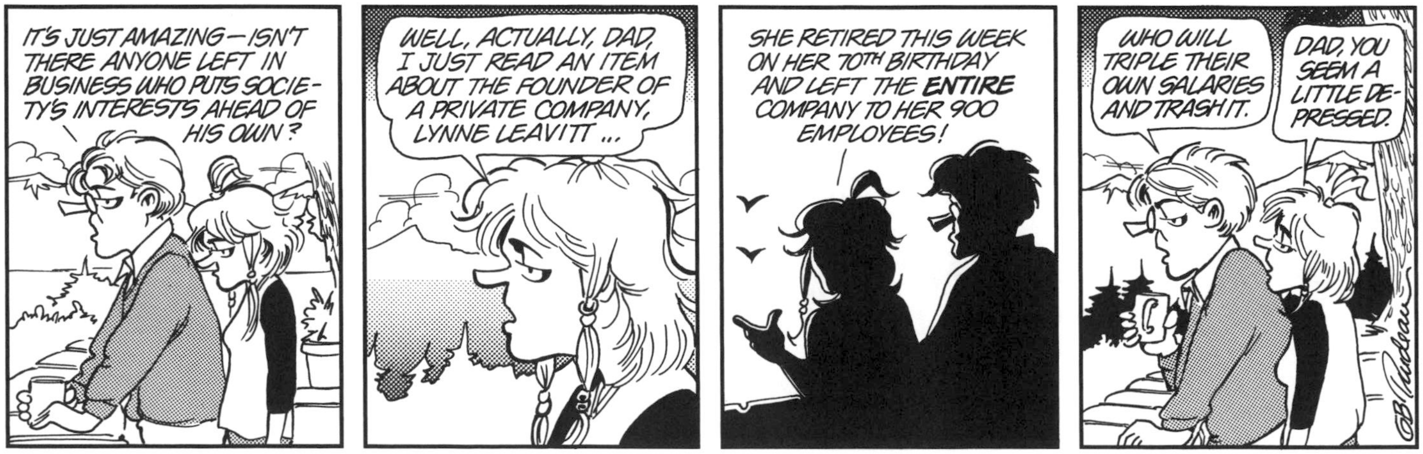
IT'S JUST AMAZING—ISN'T THERE ANYONE LEFT IN BUSINESS WHO PUTS SOCIETY'S INTERESTS AHEAD OF HIS OWN?
WELL, ACTUALLY, DAD, I JUST READ AN ITEM ABOUT THE FOUNDER OF A PRIVATE COMPANY, LYNNE LEAVITT ...
SHE RETIRED THIS WEEK ON HER 70TH BIRTHDAY AND LEFT THE **ENTIRE** COMPANY TO HER 900 EMPLOYEES!
WHO WILL TRIPLE THEIR OWN SALARIES AND TRASH IT.
DAD, YOU SEEM A LITTLE DEPRESSED.

# Got War?

Got War?
Got War?

"Bring 'em on!"

—President George W. Bush, encouraging Iraqi guerrillas to attack U.S. forces

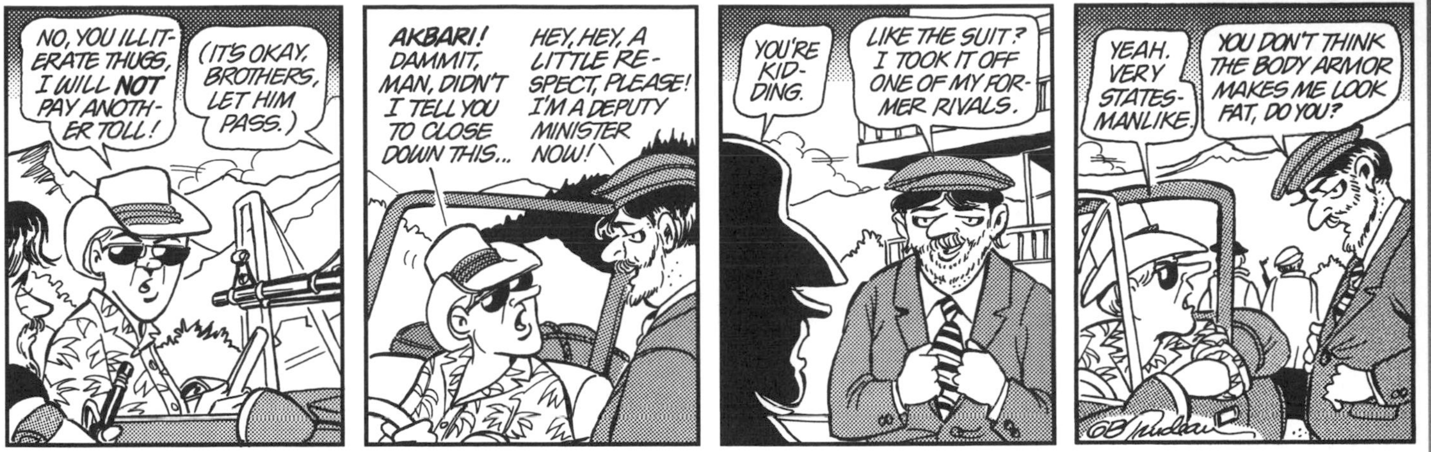
NO, YOU ILLITERATE THUGS, I WILL **NOT** PAY ANOTHER TOLL!
(IT'S OKAY, BROTHERS, LET HIM PASS.)
**AKBARI!** DAMMIT, MAN, DIDN'T I TELL YOU TO CLOSE DOWN THIS...
HEY, HEY, A LITTLE RESPECT, PLEASE! I'M A DEPUTY MINISTER NOW!
YOU'RE KIDDING.
LIKE THE SUIT? I TOOK IT OFF ONE OF MY FORMER RIVALS.
YEAH. VERY STATESMANLIKE.
YOU DON'T THINK THE BODY ARMOR MAKES ME LOOK FAT, DO YOU?

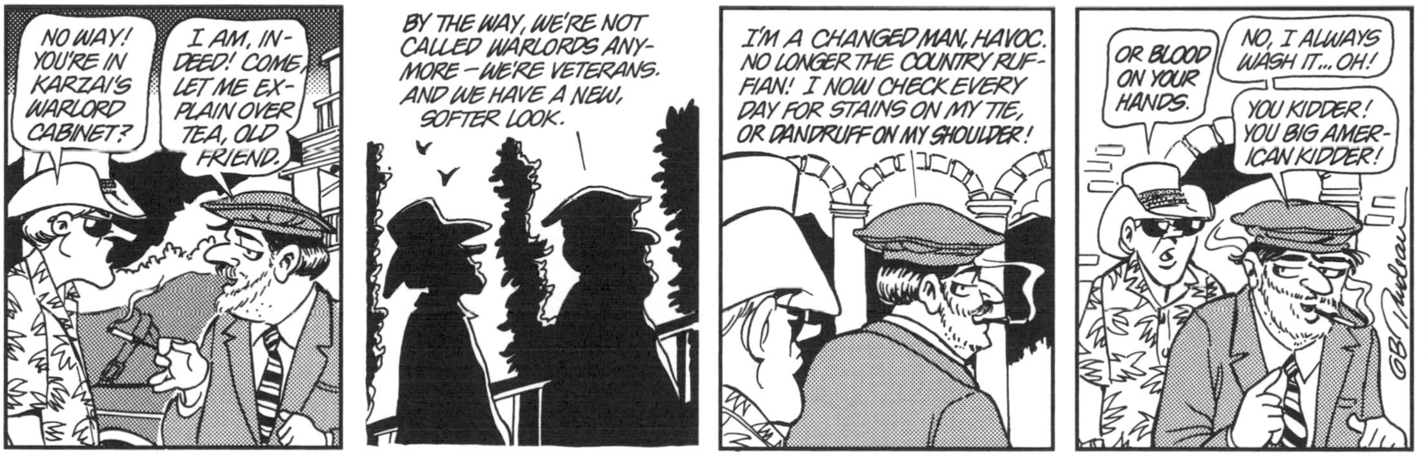
NO WAY! YOU'RE IN KARZAI'S WARLORD CABINET?
I AM, INDEED! COME, LET ME EXPLAIN OVER TEA, OLD FRIEND.
BY THE WAY, WE'RE NOT CALLED WARLORDS ANYMORE — WE'RE VETERANS. AND WE HAVE A NEW, SOFTER LOOK.
I'M A CHANGED MAN, HAVOC. NO LONGER THE COUNTRY RUFFIAN! I NOW CHECK EVERY DAY FOR STAINS ON MY TIE, OR DANDRUFF ON MY SHOULDER!
OR BLOOD ON YOUR HANDS.
NO, I ALWAYS WASH IT... OH!
YOU KIDDER! YOU BIG AMERICAN KIDDER!

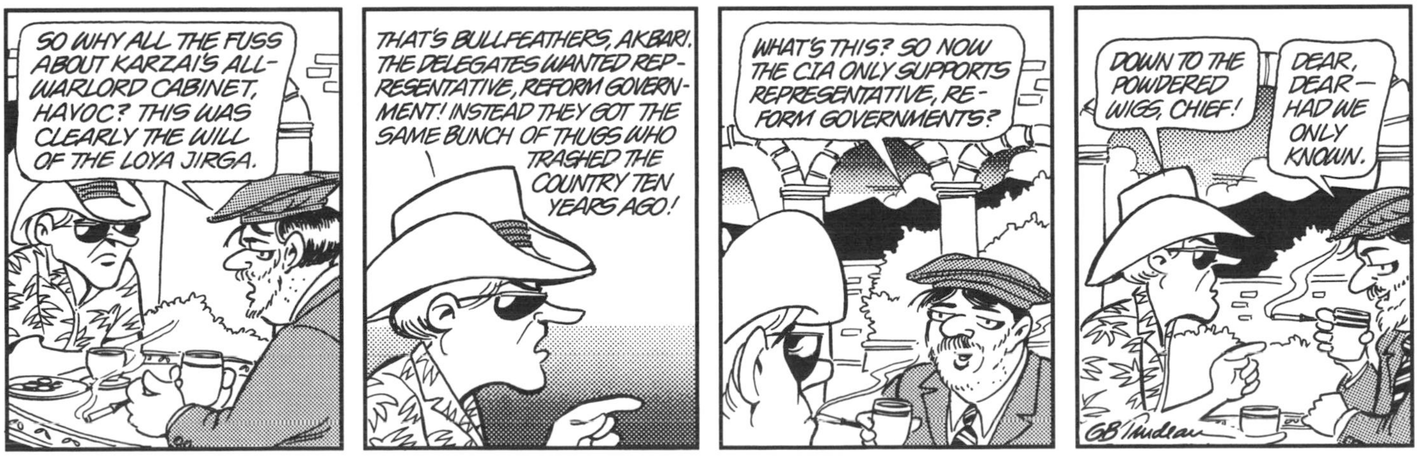
SO WHY ALL THE FUSS ABOUT KARZAI'S ALL-WARLORD CABINET, HAVOC? THIS WAS CLEARLY THE WILL OF THE LOYA JIRGA.
THAT'S BULLFEATHERS, AKBARI. THE DELEGATES WANTED REPRESENTATIVE, REFORM GOVERNMENT! INSTEAD THEY GOT THE SAME BUNCH OF THUGS WHO TRASHED THE COUNTRY TEN YEARS AGO!
WHAT'S THIS? SO NOW THE CIA ONLY SUPPORTS REPRESENTATIVE, REFORM GOVERNMENTS?
DOWN TO THE POWDERED WIGS, CHIEF!
DEAR, DEAR — HAD WE ONLY KNOWN.

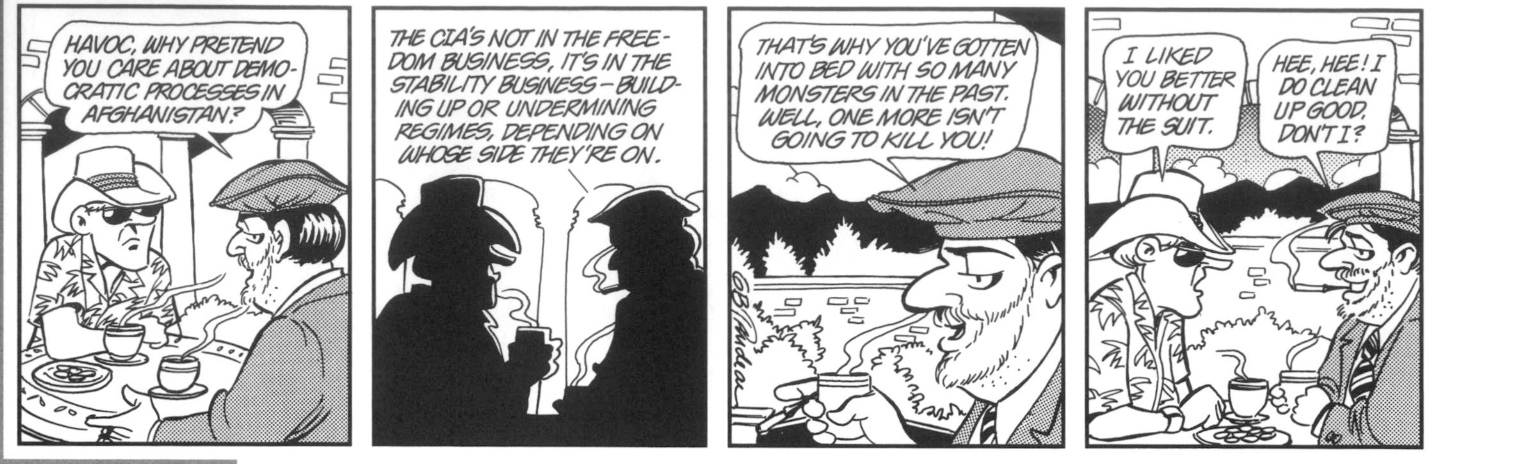
HAVOC, WHY PRETEND YOU CARE ABOUT DEMOCRATIC PROCESSES IN AFGHANISTAN?
THE CIA'S NOT IN THE FREEDOM BUSINESS, IT'S IN THE STABILITY BUSINESS – BUILDING UP OR UNDERMINING REGIMES, DEPENDING ON WHOSE SIDE THEY'RE ON.
THAT'S WHY YOU'VE GOTTEN INTO BED WITH SO MANY MONSTERS IN THE PAST. WELL, ONE MORE ISN'T GOING TO KILL YOU!
I LIKED YOU BETTER WITHOUT THE SUIT.
HEE, HEE! I DO CLEAN UP GOOD, DON'T I?

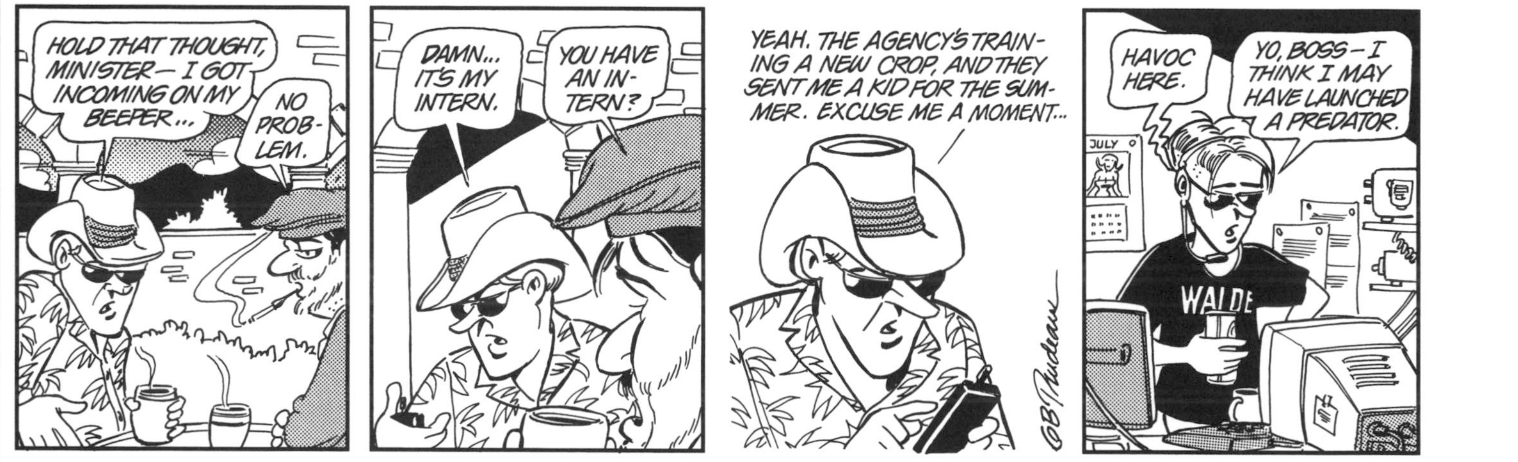
HOLD THAT THOUGHT, MINISTER – I GOT INCOMING ON MY BEEPER...
NO PROBLEM.
DAMN... IT'S MY INTERN.
YOU HAVE AN INTERN?
YEAH. THE AGENCY'S TRAINING A NEW CROP, AND THEY SENT ME A KID FOR THE SUMMER. EXCUSE ME A MOMENT...
HAVOC HERE.
YO, BOSS – I THINK I MAY HAVE LAUNCHED A PREDATOR.
JULY
WALDE

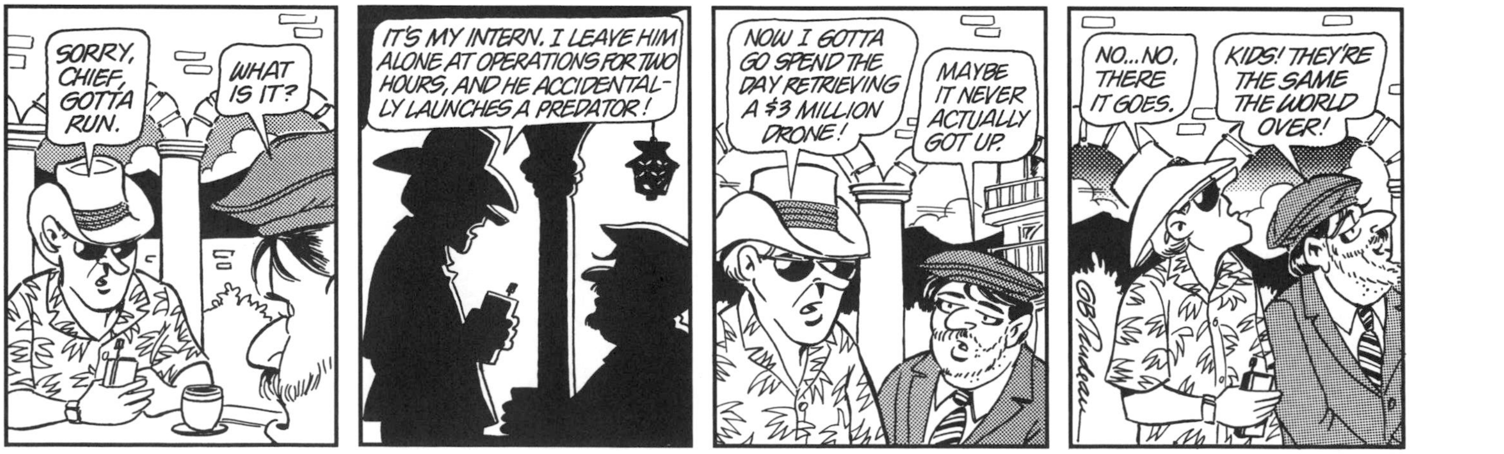
SORRY, CHIEF, GOTTA RUN.
WHAT IS IT?
IT'S MY INTERN. I LEAVE HIM ALONE AT OPERATIONS FOR TWO HOURS, AND HE ACCIDENTALLY LAUNCHES A PREDATOR!
NOW I GOTTA GO SPEND THE DAY RETRIEVING A $3 MILLION DRONE!
MAYBE IT NEVER ACTUALLY GOT UP.
NO... NO, THERE IT GOES.
KIDS! THEY'RE THE SAME THE WORLD OVER!

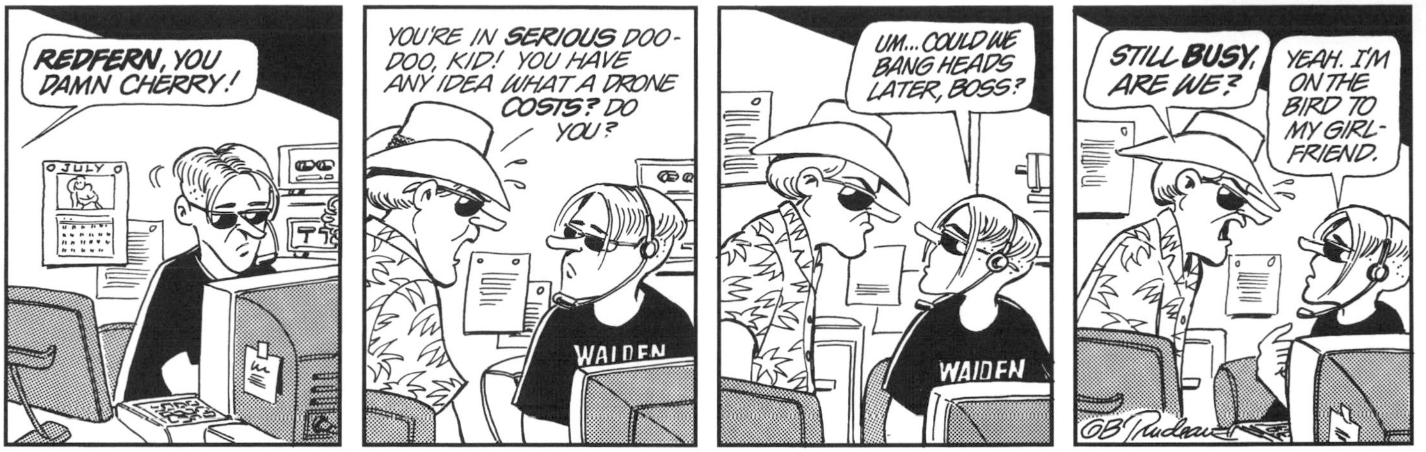

REDFERN, YOU DAMN CHERRY!
YOU'RE IN SERIOUS DOO-DOO, KID! YOU HAVE ANY IDEA WHAT A DRONE COSTS? DO YOU?
WALDEN
UM... COULD WE BANG HEADS LATER, BOSS?
WALDEN
STILL BUSY, ARE WE?
YEAH. I'M ON THE BIRD TO MY GIRLFRIEND.
©B Trudeau


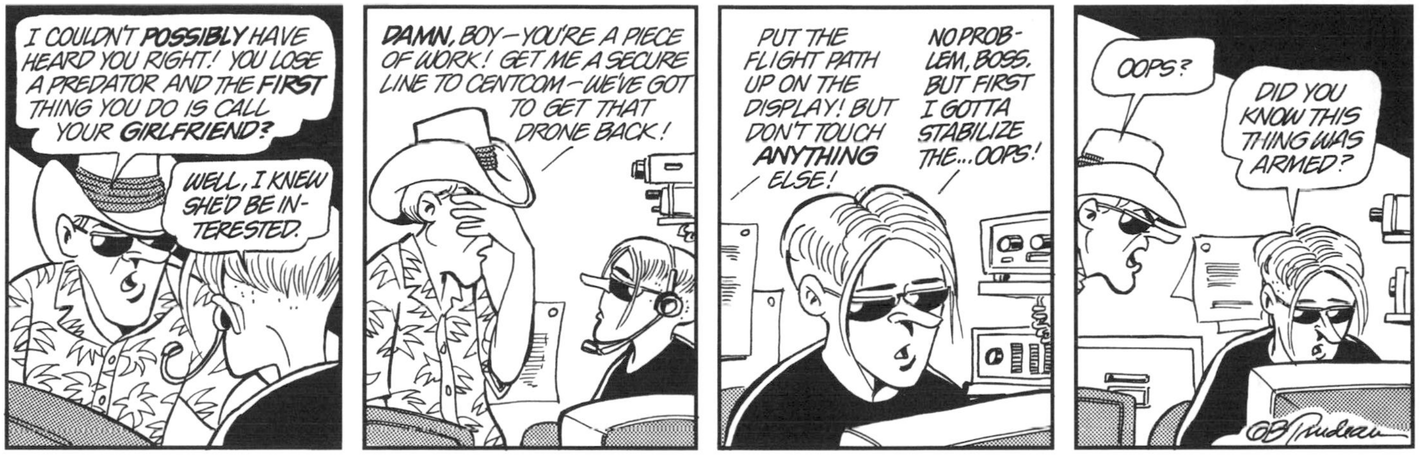

I COULDN'T POSSIBLY HAVE HEARD YOU RIGHT! YOU LOSE A PREDATOR AND THE FIRST THING YOU DO IS CALL YOUR GIRLFRIEND?
WELL, I KNEW SHE'D BE INTERESTED.
DAMN, BOY—YOU'RE A PIECE OF WORK! GET ME A SECURE LINE TO CENTCOM—WE'VE GOT TO GET THAT DRONE BACK!
PUT THE FLIGHT PATH UP ON THE DISPLAY! BUT DON'T TOUCH ANYTHING ELSE!
NO PROBLEM, BOSS. BUT FIRST I GOTTA STABILIZE THE... OOPS!
OOPS?
DID YOU KNOW THIS THING WAS ARMED?
©B Trudeau


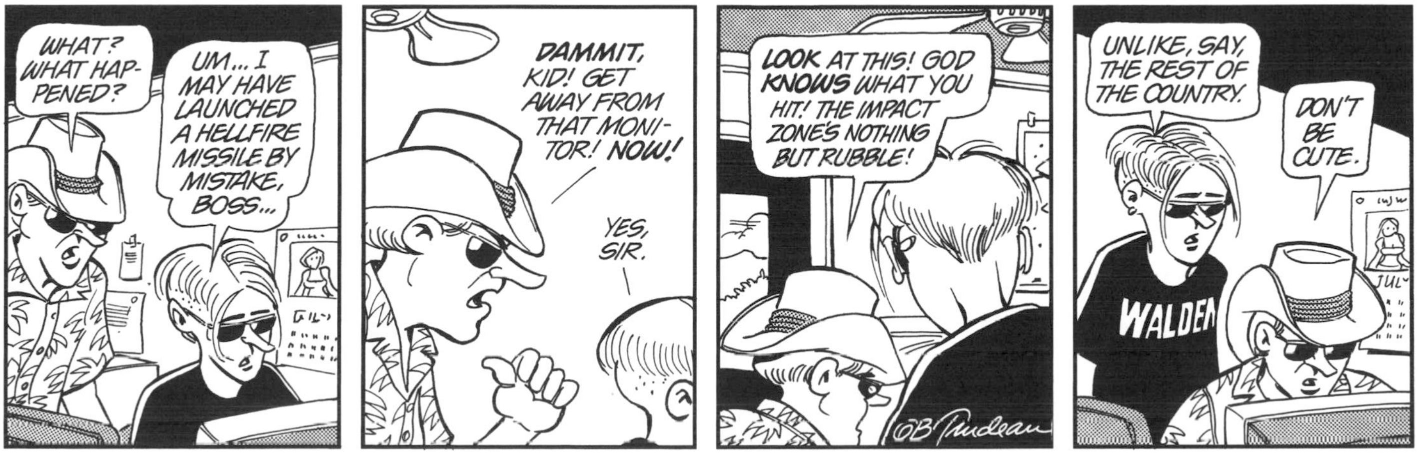

WHAT? WHAT HAPPENED?
UM... I MAY HAVE LAUNCHED A HELLFIRE MISSILE BY MISTAKE, BOSS...
DAMMIT, KID! GET AWAY FROM THAT MONITOR! NOW!
YES, SIR.
LOOK AT THIS! GOD KNOWS WHAT YOU HIT! THE IMPACT ZONE'S NOTHING BUT RUBBLE!
©B Trudeau
UNLIKE, SAY, THE REST OF THE COUNTRY.
DON'T BE CUTE.
WALDEN

YES, SIR... YES, SIR, IT WAS OUR ASSET... WHAT? NO KIDDING... THANK YOU, SIR. ROGER THAT!
WALDEN
WHAT IS IT?
THE MISSILE YOU LAUNCHED. IT TOOK OUT AN AL QAEDA AMMO DUMP.
WALDEN
THINK OF THE ODDS, EH, BOSS?
YOU'RE STILL GROUNDED. NO MISSIONS UNTIL LABOR DAY!
WALDEN

YOU KNOW, KID, I'VE SPENT MY WHOLE LIFE TRYING TO PUT THE BIG HURT ON BAD GUYS...
AND YOU FLY IN HERE, AND ON YOUR **FIRST DAY**, YOU DO MAJOR DAMAGE TO KID QAEDA! HELL, YOU'LL PROBABLY GET A COMMENDATION!
IT'S ALL THAT DAMN GAMING YOU GREW UP ON, RIGHT?
YES, SIR. THAT GIVES ME AN EDGE.

HAVOC? IT'S YOUR FAVORITE WARLORD! WHAT HAPPENED WITH THE DRONE?
WE RECOVERED IT...
BUT NOT BEFORE MY INTERN ACCIDENTALLY TOOK OUT AN AL QAEDA AMMO DUMP!
CIA
THE KID'S ONLY BEEN HERE A DAY, AND ALREADY HE'S THIS BIG WAR STAR!
SO THEN I THOUGHT, "HEY! I WONDER WHAT THIS BUTTON DOES!"
BOLD THINKING!

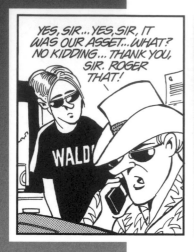

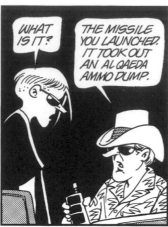

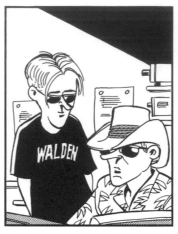

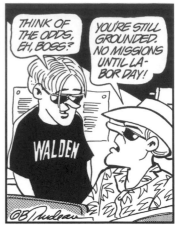

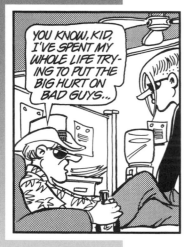

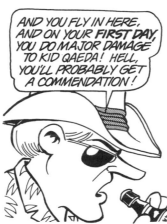

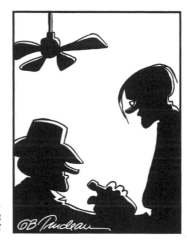

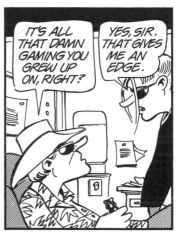

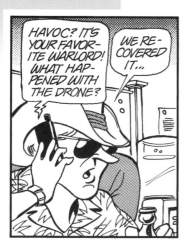

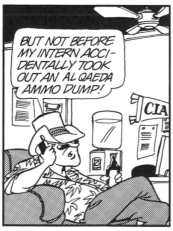

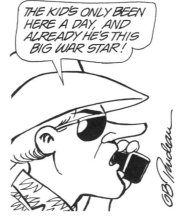

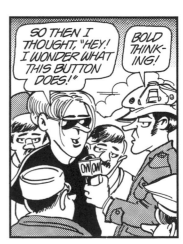

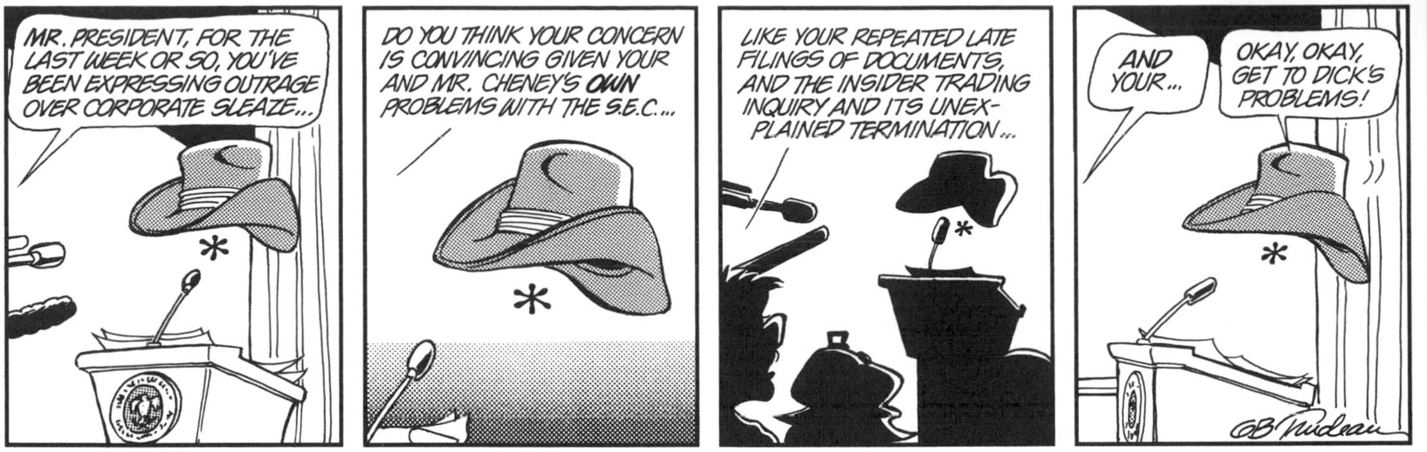
MR. PRESIDENT, FOR THE LAST WEEK OR SO, YOU'VE BEEN EXPRESSING OUTRAGE OVER CORPORATE SLEAZE...
DO YOU THINK YOUR CONCERN IS CONVINCING GIVEN YOUR AND MR. CHENEY'S **OWN** PROBLEMS WITH THE S.E.C....
LIKE YOUR REPEATED LATE FILINGS OF DOCUMENTS, AND THE INSIDER TRADING INQUIRY AND ITS UNEXPLAINED TERMINATION...
AND YOUR...
OKAY, OKAY, GET TO DICK'S PROBLEMS!
©B Trudeau

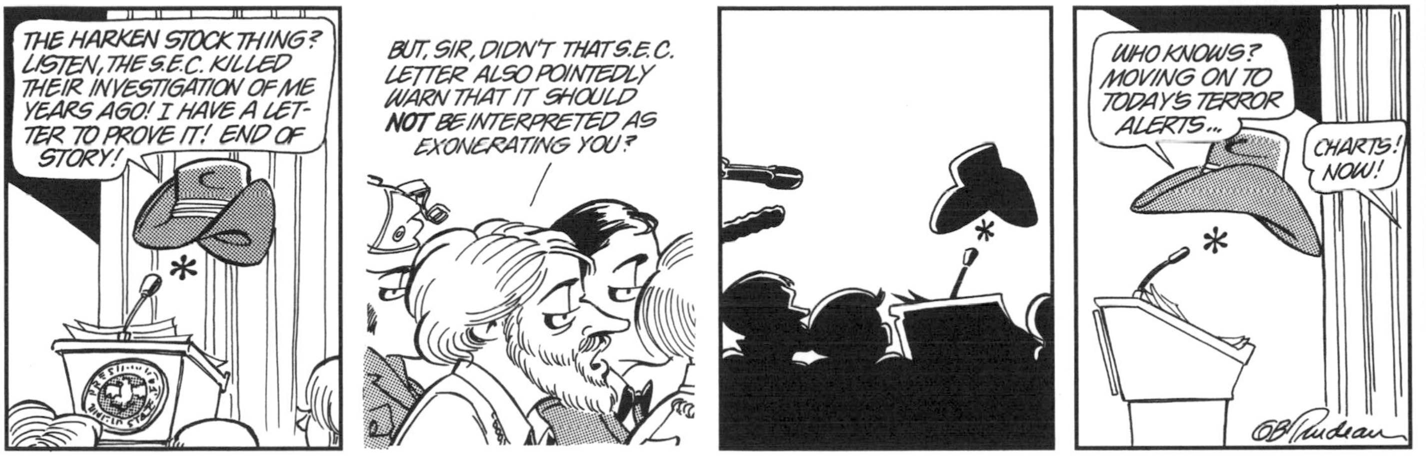
THE HARKEN STOCK THING? LISTEN, THE S.E.C. KILLED THEIR INVESTIGATION OF ME YEARS AGO! I HAVE A LETTER TO PROVE IT! END OF STORY!
BUT, SIR, DIDN'T THAT S.E.C. LETTER ALSO POINTEDLY WARN THAT IT SHOULD **NOT** BE INTERPRETED AS EXONERATING YOU?
WHO KNOWS? MOVING ON TO TODAY'S TERROR ALERTS...
CHARTS! NOW!
©B Trudeau

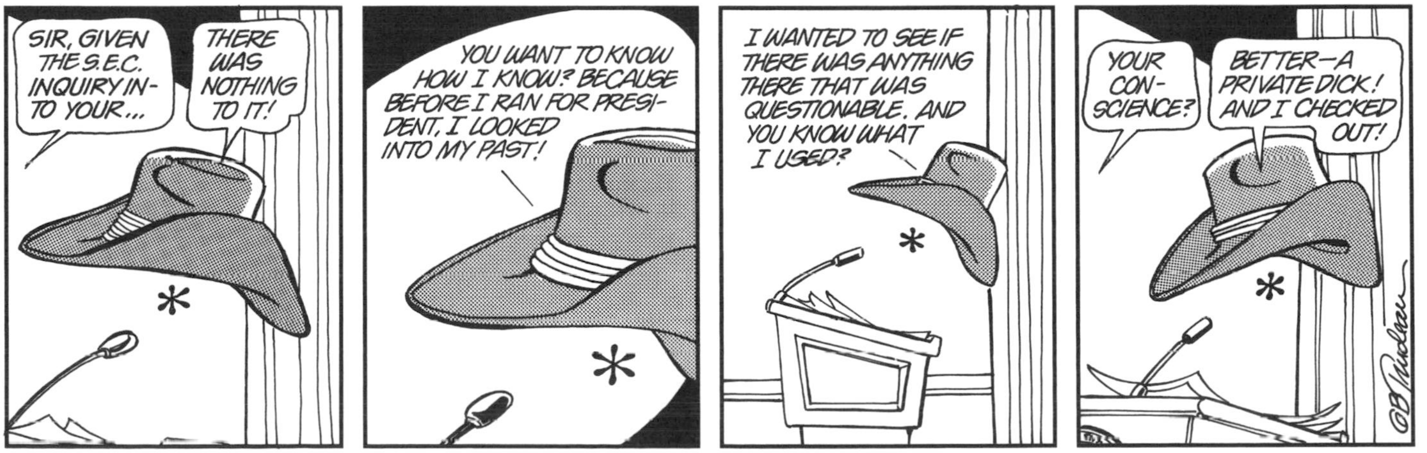
SIR, GIVEN THE S.E.C. INQUIRY INTO YOUR...
THERE WAS NOTHING TO IT!
YOU WANT TO KNOW HOW I KNOW? BECAUSE BEFORE I RAN FOR PRESIDENT, I LOOKED INTO MY PAST!
I WANTED TO SEE IF THERE WAS ANYTHING THERE THAT WAS QUESTIONABLE. AND YOU KNOW WHAT I USED?
YOUR CONSCIENCE?
BETTER—A PRIVATE DICK! AND I CHECKED OUT!
©B Trudeau

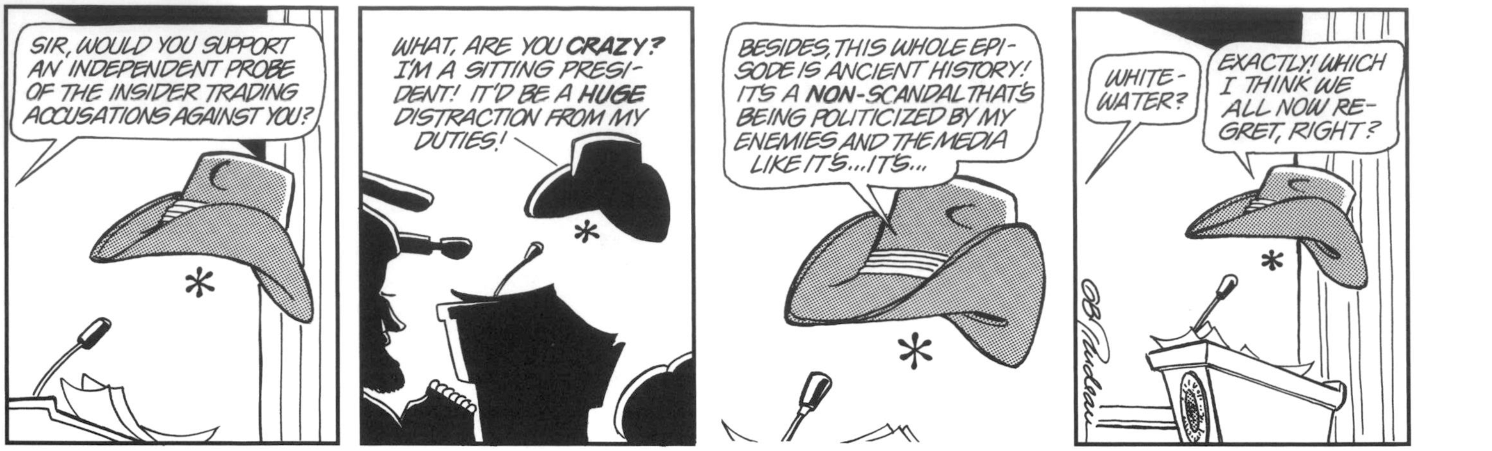
SIR, WOULD YOU SUPPORT AN INDEPENDENT PROBE OF THE INSIDER TRADING ACCUSATIONS AGAINST YOU?
WHAT, ARE YOU **CRAZY?** I'M A SITTING PRESIDENT! IT'D BE A **HUGE** DISTRACTION FROM MY DUTIES!
BESIDES, THIS WHOLE EPISODE IS ANCIENT HISTORY! IT'S A **NON**-SCANDAL THAT'S BEING POLITICIZED BY MY ENEMIES AND THE MEDIA LIKE IT'S... IT'S...
WHITEWATER?
EXACTLY! WHICH I THINK WE ALL NOW REGRET, RIGHT?
©B Trudeau

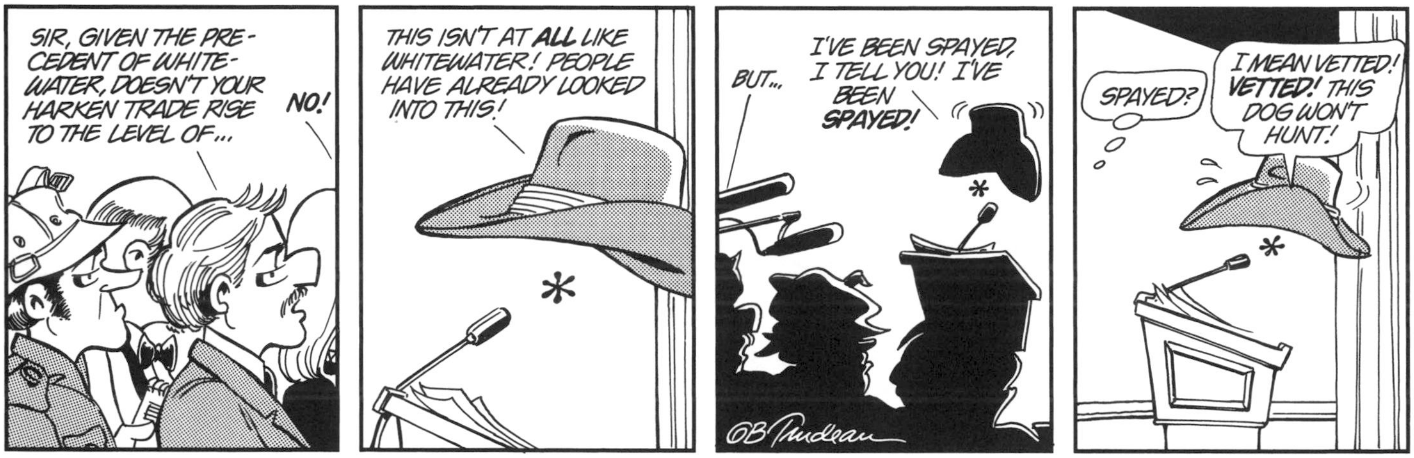
SIR, GIVEN THE PRECEDENT OF WHITEWATER, DOESN'T YOUR HARKEN TRADE RISE TO THE LEVEL OF...
**NO!**
THIS ISN'T AT **ALL** LIKE WHITEWATER! PEOPLE HAVE ALREADY LOOKED INTO THIS!
BUT...
I'VE BEEN SPAYED, I TELL YOU! I'VE BEEN **SPAYED!**
©B Trudeau
SPAYED?
I MEAN VETTED! **VETTED!** THIS DOG WON'T HUNT!

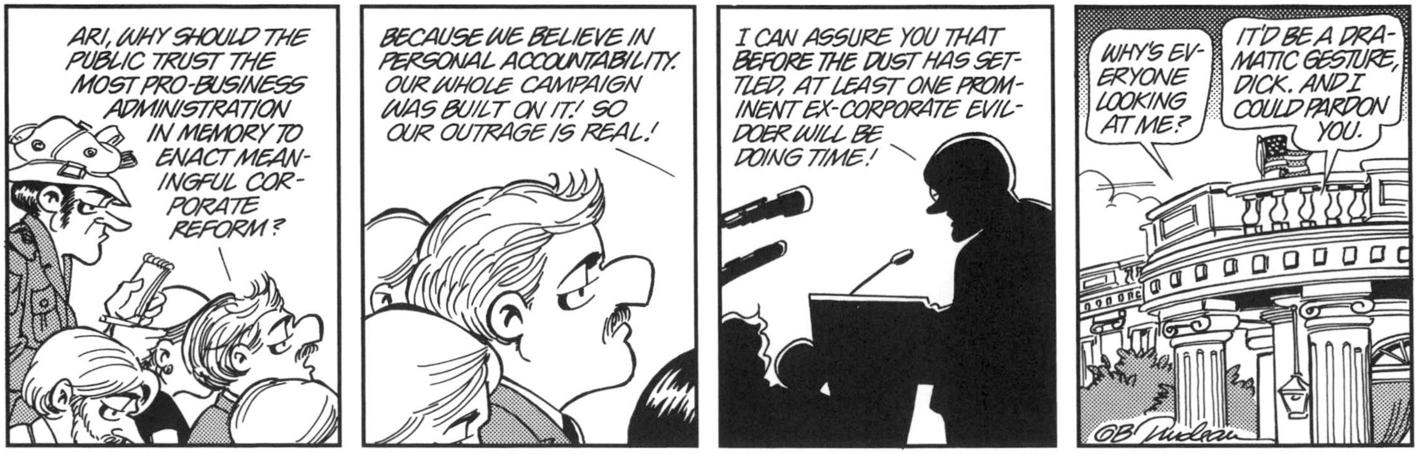
ARI, WHY SHOULD THE PUBLIC TRUST THE MOST PRO-BUSINESS ADMINISTRATION IN MEMORY TO ENACT MEANINGFUL CORPORATE REFORM?
BECAUSE WE BELIEVE IN PERSONAL ACCOUNTABILITY. OUR WHOLE CAMPAIGN WAS BUILT ON IT! SO OUR OUTRAGE IS REAL!
I CAN ASSURE YOU THAT BEFORE THE DUST HAS SETTLED, AT LEAST ONE PROMINENT EX-CORPORATE EVILDOER WILL BE DOING TIME!
WHY'S EVERYONE LOOKING AT ME?
IT'D BE A DRAMATIC GESTURE, DICK. AND I COULD PARDON YOU.
©B Trudeau

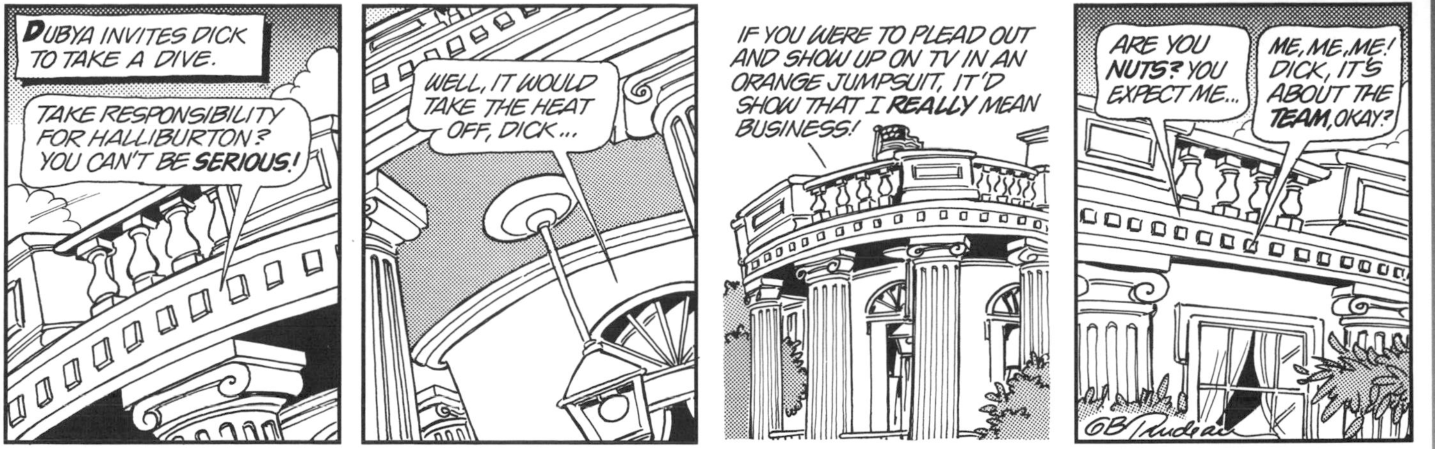
DUBYA INVITES DICK TO TAKE A DIVE.
TAKE RESPONSIBILITY FOR HALLIBURTON? YOU CAN'T BE SERIOUS!
WELL, IT WOULD TAKE THE HEAT OFF, DICK...
IF YOU WERE TO PLEAD OUT AND SHOW UP ON TV IN AN ORANGE JUMPSUIT, IT'D SHOW THAT I REALLY MEAN BUSINESS!
ARE YOU NUTS? YOU EXPECT ME...
ME, ME, ME! DICK, IT'S ABOUT THE TEAM, OKAY?
GB Trudeau

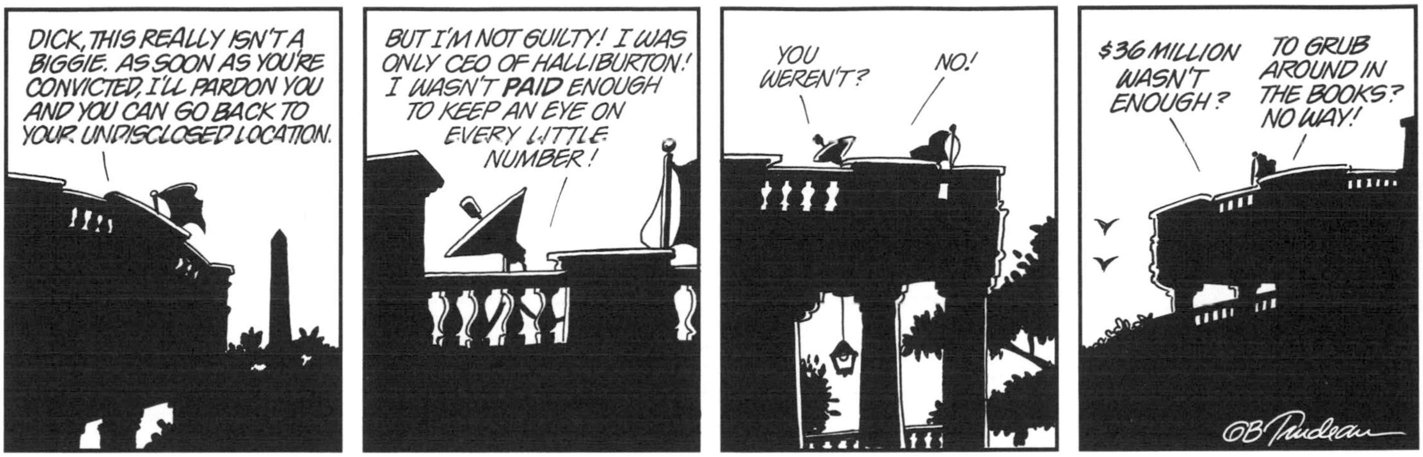
DICK, THIS REALLY ISN'T A BIGGIE. AS SOON AS YOU'RE CONVICTED, I'LL PARDON YOU AND YOU CAN GO BACK TO YOUR UNDISCLOSED LOCATION.
BUT I'M NOT GUILTY! I WAS ONLY CEO OF HALLIBURTON! I WASN'T PAID ENOUGH TO KEEP AN EYE ON EVERY LITTLE NUMBER!
YOU WEREN'T?
NO!
$36 MILLION WASN'T ENOUGH?
TO GRUB AROUND IN THE BOOKS? NO WAY!
GB Trudeau

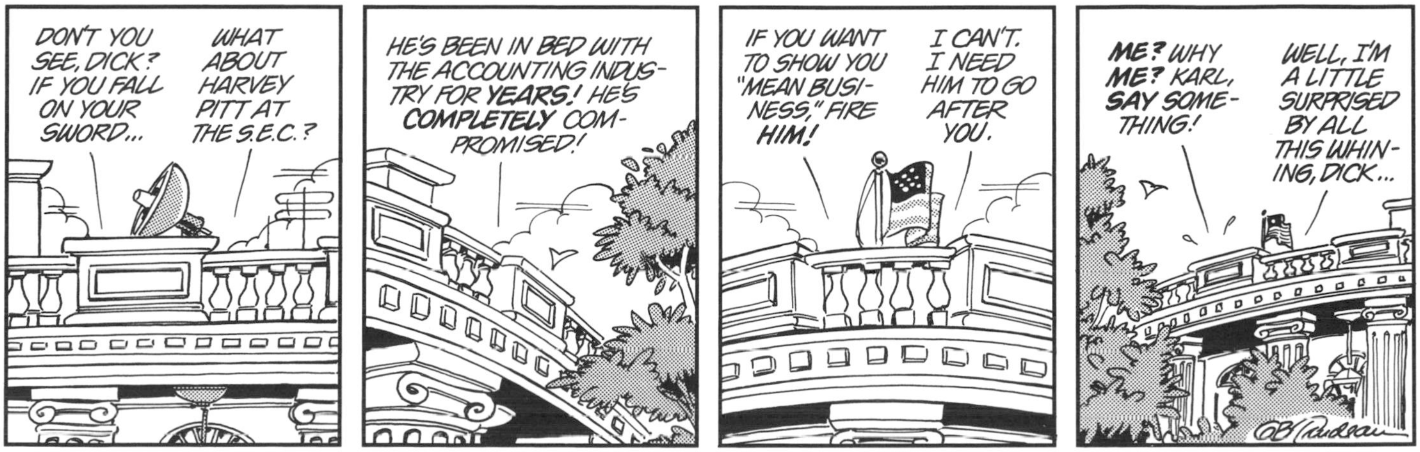
DON'T YOU SEE, DICK? IF YOU FALL ON YOUR SWORD...
WHAT ABOUT HARVEY PITT AT THE S.E.C.?
HE'S BEEN IN BED WITH THE ACCOUNTING INDUSTRY FOR YEARS! HE'S COMPLETELY COMPROMISED!
IF YOU WANT TO SHOW YOU "MEAN BUSINESS," FIRE HIM!
I CAN'T. I NEED HIM TO GO AFTER YOU.
ME? WHY ME? KARL, SAY SOMETHING!
WELL, I'M A LITTLE SURPRISED BY ALL THIS WHINING, DICK...
GB Trudeau

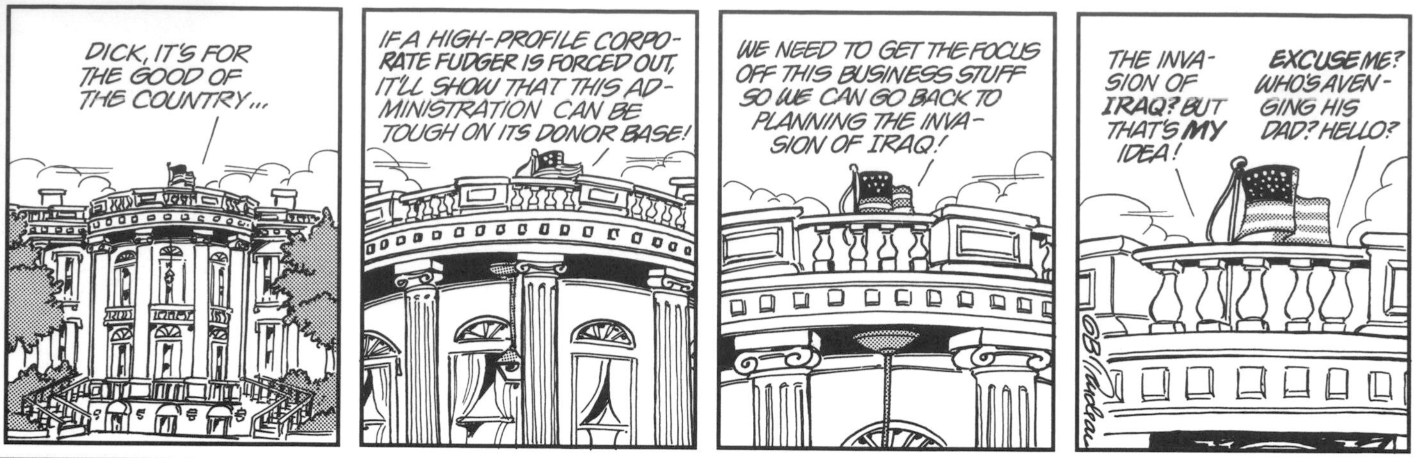
DICK, IT'S FOR THE GOOD OF THE COUNTRY...
IF A HIGH-PROFILE CORPORATE FUDGER IS FORCED OUT, IT'LL SHOW THAT THIS ADMINISTRATION CAN BE TOUGH ON ITS DONOR BASE!
WE NEED TO GET THE FOCUS OFF THIS BUSINESS STUFF SO WE CAN GO BACK TO PLANNING THE INVASION OF IRAQ!
THE INVASION OF **IRAQ**? BUT THAT'S **MY** IDEA!
**EXCUSE** ME? WHO'S AVENGING HIS DAD? HELLO?

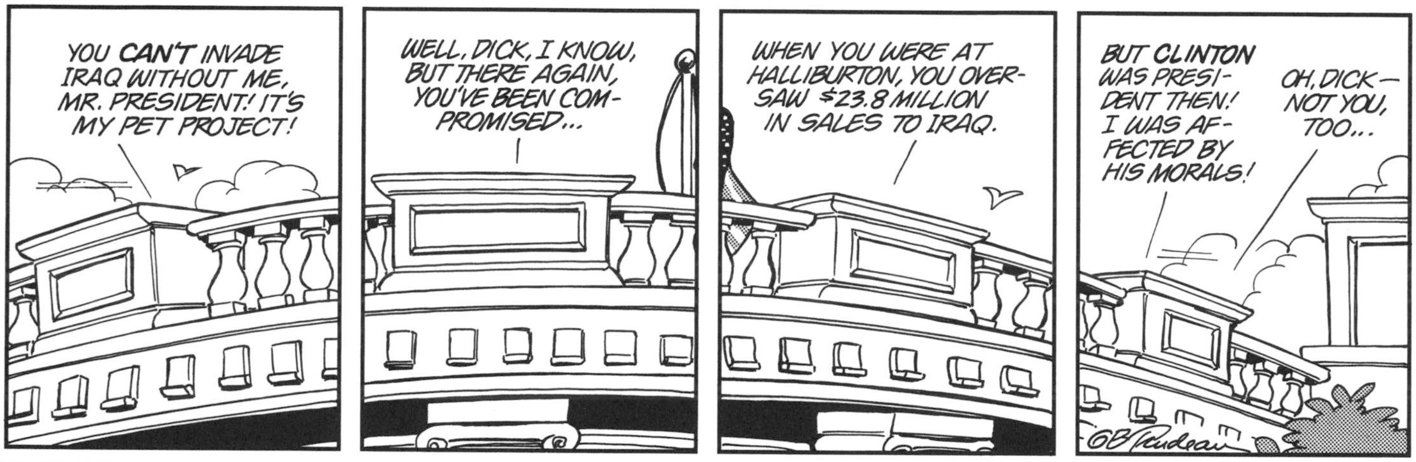
YOU **CAN'T** INVADE IRAQ WITHOUT ME, MR. PRESIDENT! IT'S MY PET PROJECT!
WELL, DICK, I KNOW, BUT THERE AGAIN, YOU'VE BEEN COMPROMISED...
WHEN YOU WERE AT HALLIBURTON, YOU OVERSAW $23.8 MILLION IN SALES TO IRAQ.
BUT **CLINTON** WAS PRESIDENT THEN! I WAS AFFECTED BY HIS MORALS!
OH, DICK— NOT YOU, TOO...

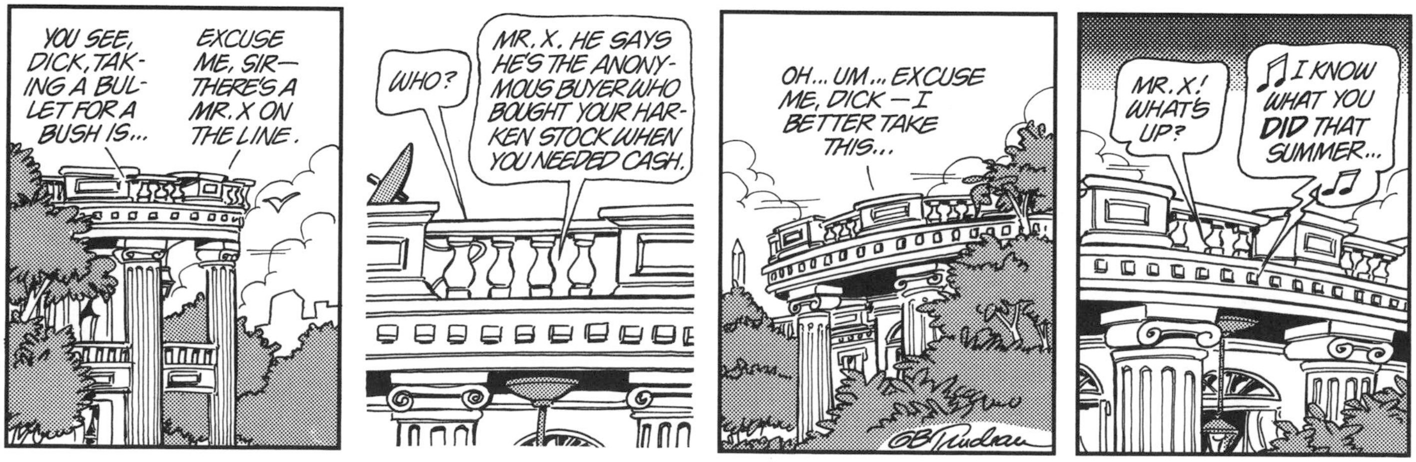
YOU SEE, DICK, TAKING A BULLET FOR A BUSH IS...
EXCUSE ME, SIR— THERE'S A MR. X ON THE LINE.
WHO?
MR. X. HE SAYS HE'S THE ANONYMOUS BUYER WHO BOUGHT YOUR HARKEN STOCK WHEN YOU NEEDED CASH.
OH... UM... EXCUSE ME, DICK — I BETTER TAKE THIS...
MR. X! WHAT'S UP?
♫ I KNOW WHAT YOU **DID** THAT SUMMER... ♫

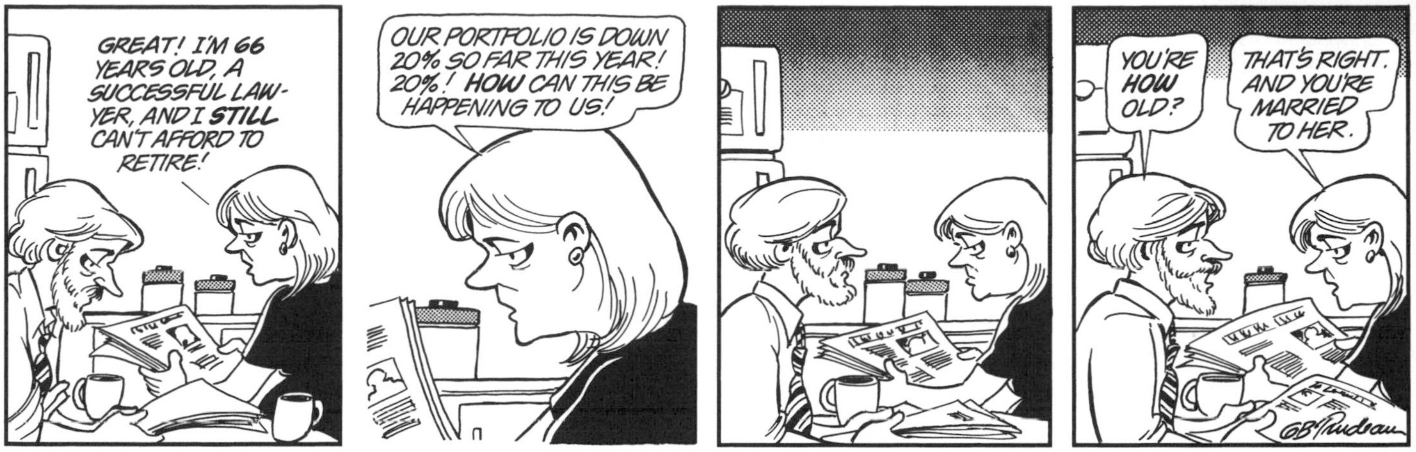
GREAT! I'M 66 YEARS OLD, A SUCCESSFUL LAWYER, AND I STILL CAN'T AFFORD TO RETIRE!
OUR PORTFOLIO IS DOWN 20% SO FAR THIS YEAR! 20%! HOW CAN THIS BE HAPPENING TO US!
YOU'RE HOW OLD?
THAT'S RIGHT. AND YOU'RE MARRIED TO HER.

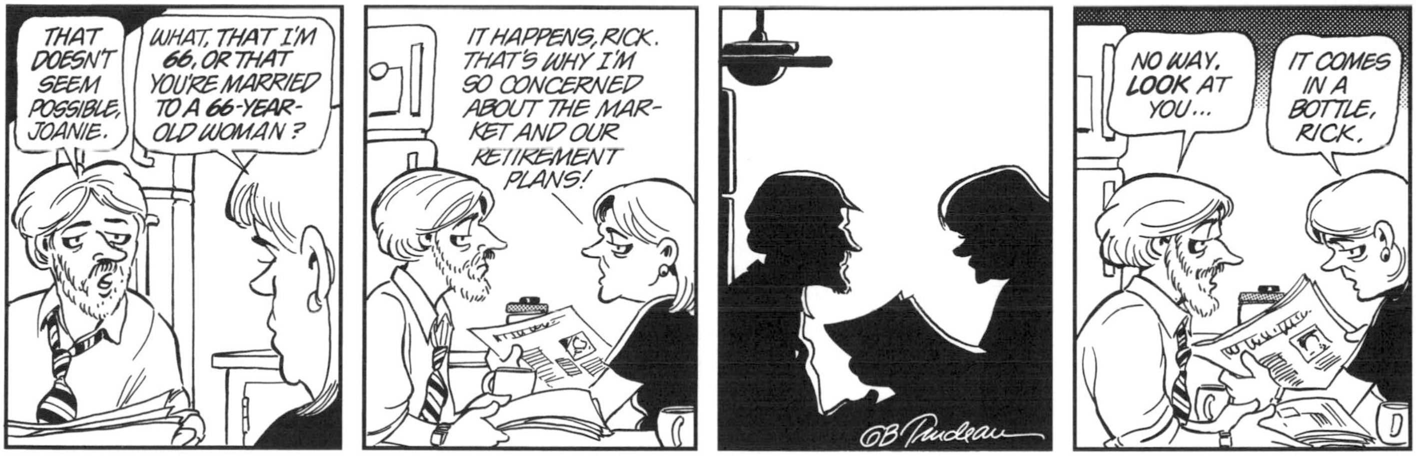
THAT DOESN'T SEEM POSSIBLE, JOANIE.
WHAT, THAT I'M 66, OR THAT YOU'RE MARRIED TO A 66-YEAR-OLD WOMAN?
IT HAPPENS, RICK. THAT'S WHY I'M SO CONCERNED ABOUT THE MARKET AND OUR RETIREMENT PLANS!
NO WAY. LOOK AT YOU...
IT COMES IN A BOTTLE, RICK.

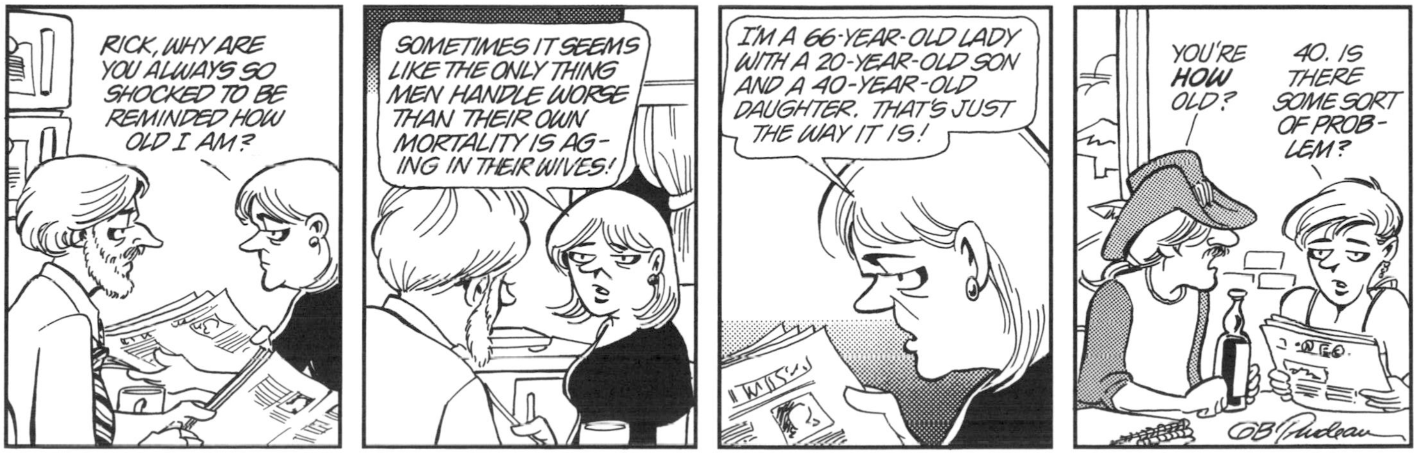
RICK, WHY ARE YOU ALWAYS SO SHOCKED TO BE REMINDED HOW OLD I AM?
SOMETIMES IT SEEMS LIKE THE ONLY THING MEN HANDLE WORSE THAN THEIR OWN MORTALITY IS AGING IN THEIR WIVES!
I'M A 66-YEAR-OLD LADY WITH A 20-YEAR-OLD SON AND A 40-YEAR-OLD DAUGHTER. THAT'S JUST THE WAY IT IS!
YOU'RE HOW OLD?
40. IS THERE SOME SORT OF PROBLEM?

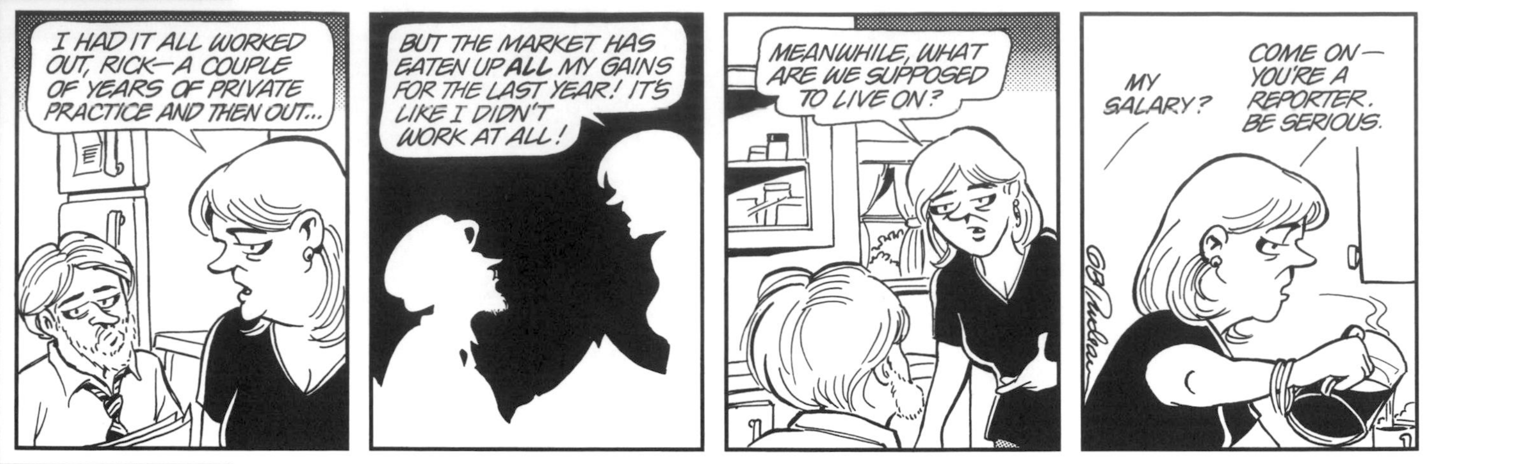
I HAD IT ALL WORKED OUT, RICK—A COUPLE OF YEARS OF PRIVATE PRACTICE AND THEN OUT...
BUT THE MARKET HAS EATEN UP **ALL** MY GAINS FOR THE LAST YEAR! IT'S LIKE I DIDN'T WORK AT ALL!
MEANWHILE, WHAT ARE WE SUPPOSED TO LIVE ON?
MY SALARY?
COME ON—YOU'RE A REPORTER. BE SERIOUS.

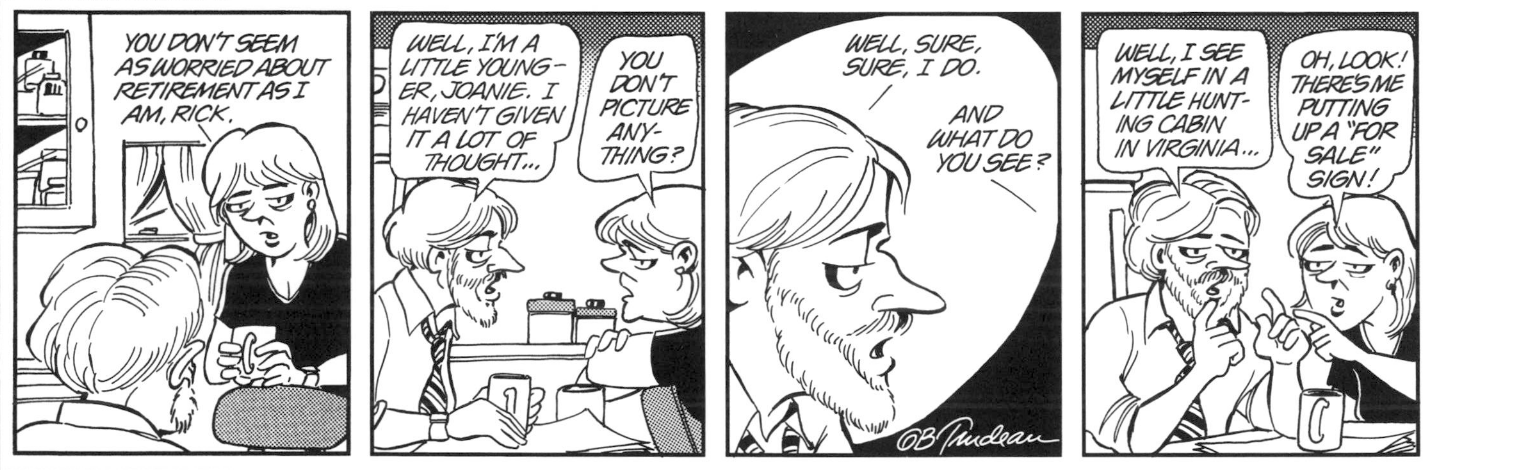
YOU DON'T SEEM AS WORRIED ABOUT RETIREMENT AS I AM, RICK.
WELL, I'M A LITTLE YOUNGER, JOANIE. I HAVEN'T GIVEN IT A LOT OF THOUGHT...
YOU DON'T PICTURE ANYTHING?
WELL, SURE, SURE, I DO.
AND WHAT DO YOU SEE?
WELL, I SEE MYSELF IN A LITTLE HUNTING CABIN IN VIRGINIA...
OH, LOOK! THERE'S ME PUTTING UP A "FOR SALE" SIGN!

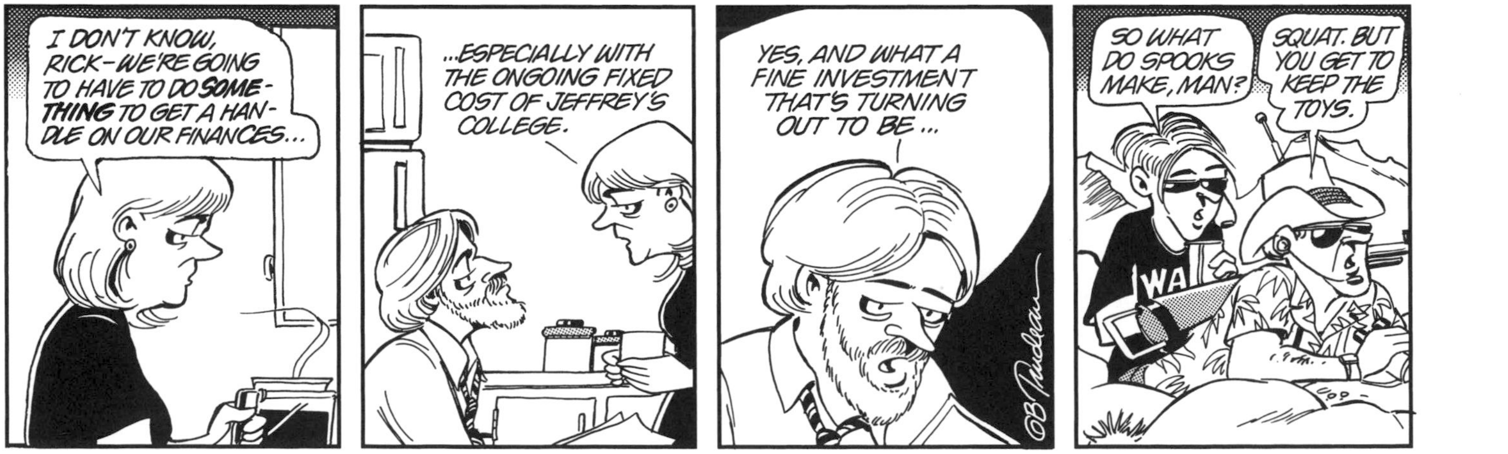
I DON'T KNOW, RICK—WE'RE GOING TO HAVE TO DO **SOMETHING** TO GET A HANDLE ON OUR FINANCES...
...ESPECIALLY WITH THE ONGOING FIXED COST OF JEFFREY'S COLLEGE.
YES, AND WHAT A FINE INVESTMENT THAT'S TURNING OUT TO BE...
SO WHAT DO SPOOKS MAKE, MAN?
SQUAT. BUT YOU GET TO KEEP THE TOYS.

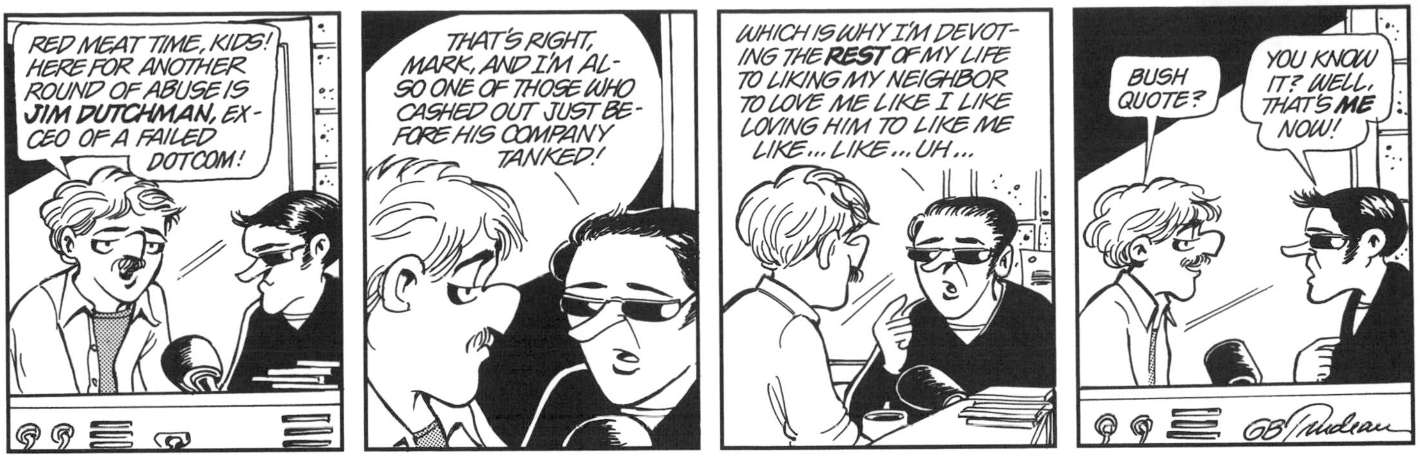
RED MEAT TIME, KIDS! HERE FOR ANOTHER ROUND OF ABUSE IS **JIM DUTCHMAN,** EX-CEO OF A FAILED DOTCOM!
THAT'S RIGHT, MARK, AND I'M ALSO ONE OF THOSE WHO CASHED OUT JUST BEFORE HIS COMPANY TANKED!
WHICH IS WHY I'M DEVOTING THE **REST** OF MY LIFE TO LIKING MY NEIGHBOR TO LOVE ME LIKE I LIKE LOVING HIM TO LIKE ME LIKE... LIKE... UH...
BUSH QUOTE?
YOU KNOW IT? WELL, THAT'S **ME** NOW!
GB Trudeau

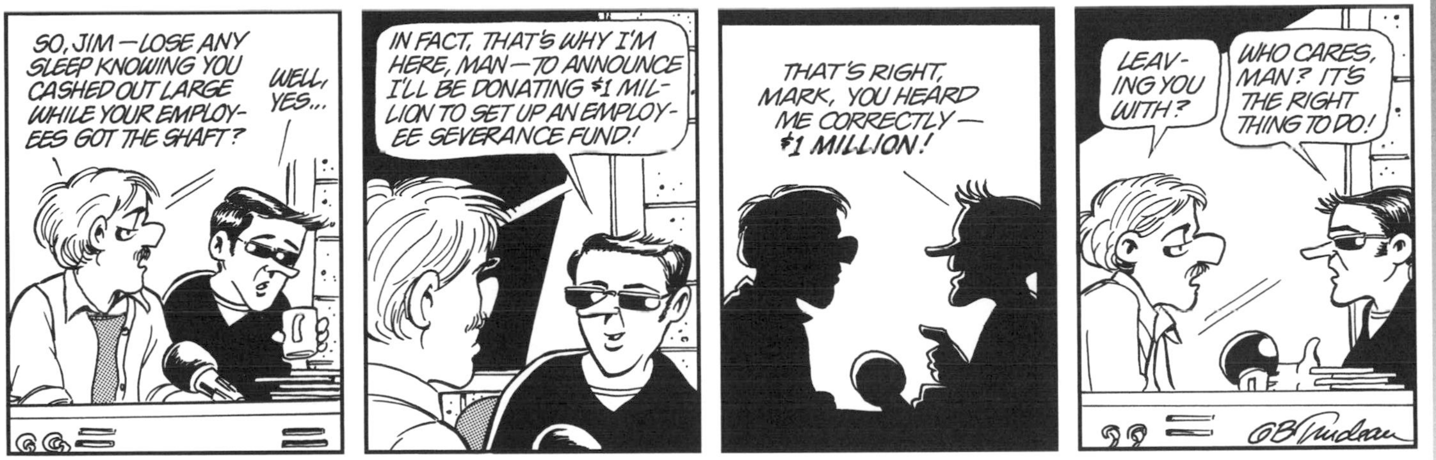
SO, JIM — LOSE ANY SLEEP KNOWING YOU CASHED OUT LARGE WHILE YOUR EMPLOYEES GOT THE SHAFT?
WELL, YES...
IN FACT, THAT'S WHY I'M HERE, MAN — TO ANNOUNCE I'LL BE DONATING $1 MILLION TO SET UP AN EMPLOYEE SEVERANCE FUND!
THAT'S RIGHT, MARK, YOU HEARD ME CORRECTLY — **$1 MILLION!**
LEAVING YOU WITH?
WHO CARES, MAN? IT'S THE RIGHT THING TO DO!
GB Trudeau

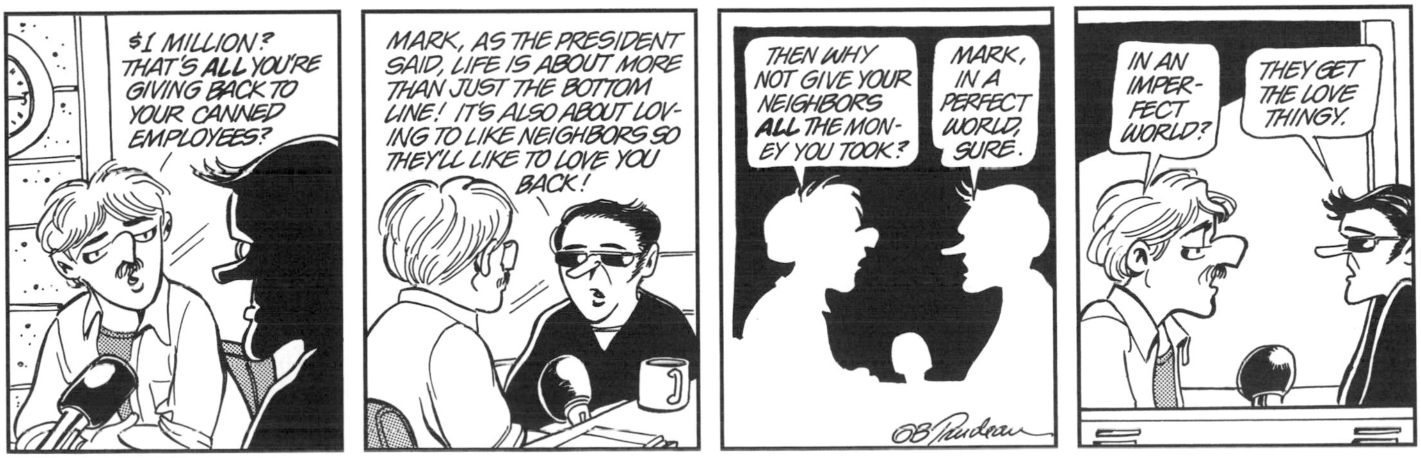
$1 MILLION? THAT'S **ALL** YOU'RE GIVING BACK TO YOUR CANNED EMPLOYEES?
MARK, AS THE PRESIDENT SAID, LIFE IS ABOUT MORE THAN JUST THE BOTTOM LINE! IT'S ALSO ABOUT LOVING TO LIKE NEIGHBORS SO THEY'LL LIKE TO LOVE YOU BACK!
THEN WHY NOT GIVE YOUR NEIGHBORS **ALL** THE MONEY YOU TOOK?
MARK, IN A PERFECT WORLD, SURE.
GB Trudeau
IN AN IMPERFECT WORLD?
THEY GET THE LOVE THINGY.

JIM, DO YOU... **HEY!**
JAMES DUTCHMAN?
YES?
YOU'RE UNDER ARREST, SIR!
ATF
**WHAT?** WHO ARE **YOU?**
ANTI-FRAUD TASK FORCE!
YOU HAVE THE RIGHT TO REMAIN SILENT...
NO, HE DOESN'T! THIS IS **RADIO!**
**HONEY!** HIDE THE **BOOKS!**
STEP AWAY FROM THE MIKE, SIR!
GB Trudeau

LET **GO!** I'M **INNOCENT!** I USED GENERALLY ACCEPTED ACCOUNTING METHODS!
LET'S GO, PAL.
UNBELIEVABLE, FOLKS — YOU'VE JUST BEEN LISTENING TO A LIVE ON-AIR BUST!
WITHOUT WARNING, AN ANTI-FRAUD TASK-FORCE TEAM HAS JUST ARRESTED EX-DOTCOM CEO JIM DUTCHMAN RIGHT HERE ON NPR REALITY RADIO!
SOUNDS LIKE A STUNT.
THIS IS NOT, REPEAT, **NOT** A STUNT.
GB Trudeau

I'M NOW TALKING WITH SPECIAL AGENT EUGENE MEYERS, WHO LED THE BUST OF MY PREVIOUS GUEST, JIM DUTCHMAN.
SO, SPECIAL AGENT—WHAT'S UP WITH THE TIMING?
WELL, MARK, WE WERE TRYING TO MAKE AN IMPRESSION.
WE FIGURED A LIVE BUST ON NPR WOULD SEND A MESSAGE TO YOUR HUNDREDS OF WHITE COLLAR LISTENERS.
THOUSANDS.
WHICHEVER, WE WANTED TO REACH THAT DEMOGRAPHIC.
GB Trudeau

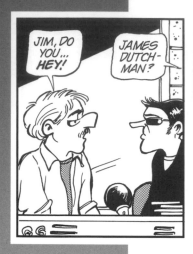

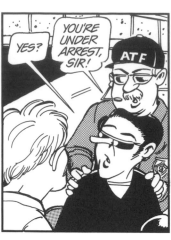

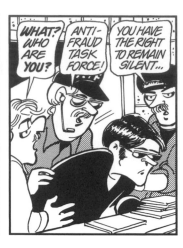

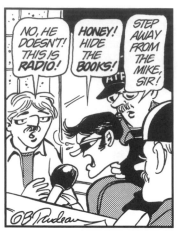

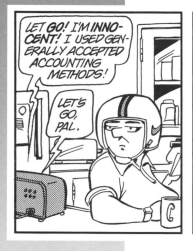

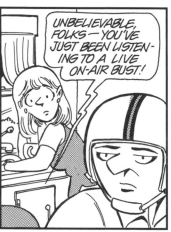

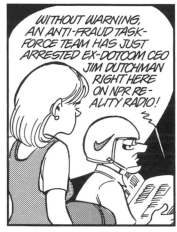

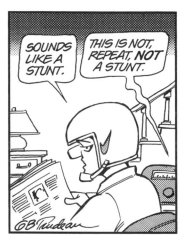

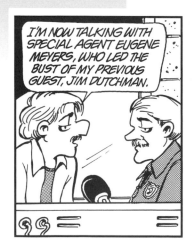

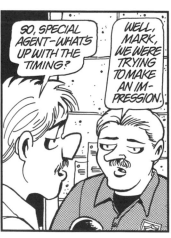

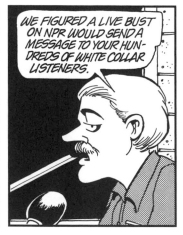

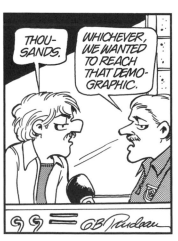

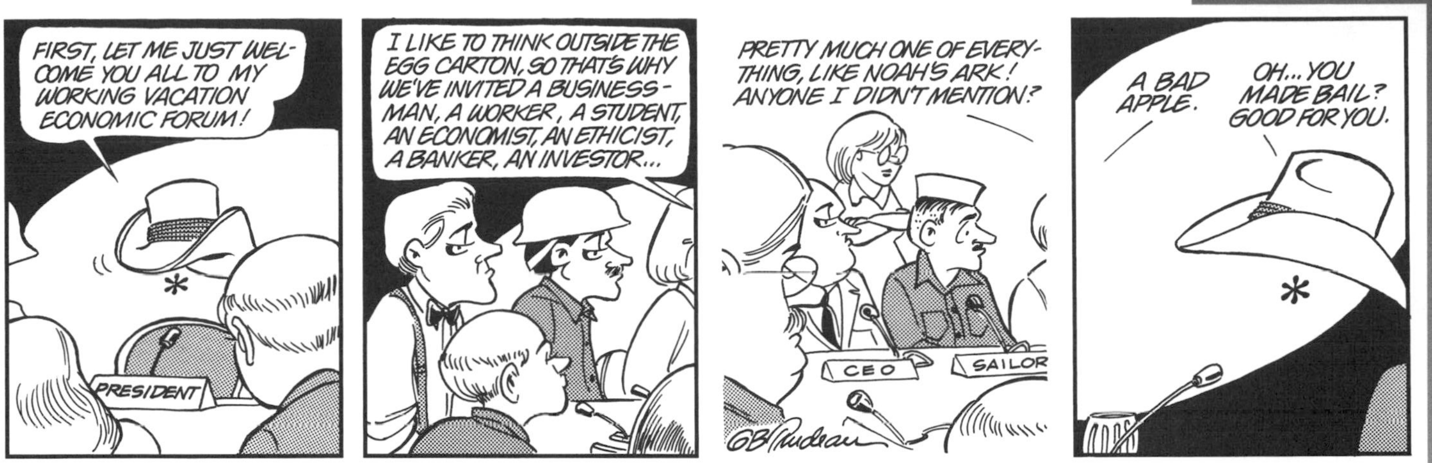
FIRST, LET ME JUST WELCOME YOU ALL TO MY WORKING VACATION ECONOMIC FORUM!
PRESIDENT
I LIKE TO THINK OUTSIDE THE EGG CARTON, SO THAT'S WHY WE'VE INVITED A BUSINESSMAN, A WORKER, A STUDENT, AN ECONOMIST, AN ETHICIST, A BANKER, AN INVESTOR...
PRETTY MUCH ONE OF EVERYTHING, LIKE NOAH'S ARK! ANYONE I DIDN'T MENTION?
CEO
SAILOR
A BAD APPLE.
OH... YOU MADE BAIL? GOOD FOR YOU.

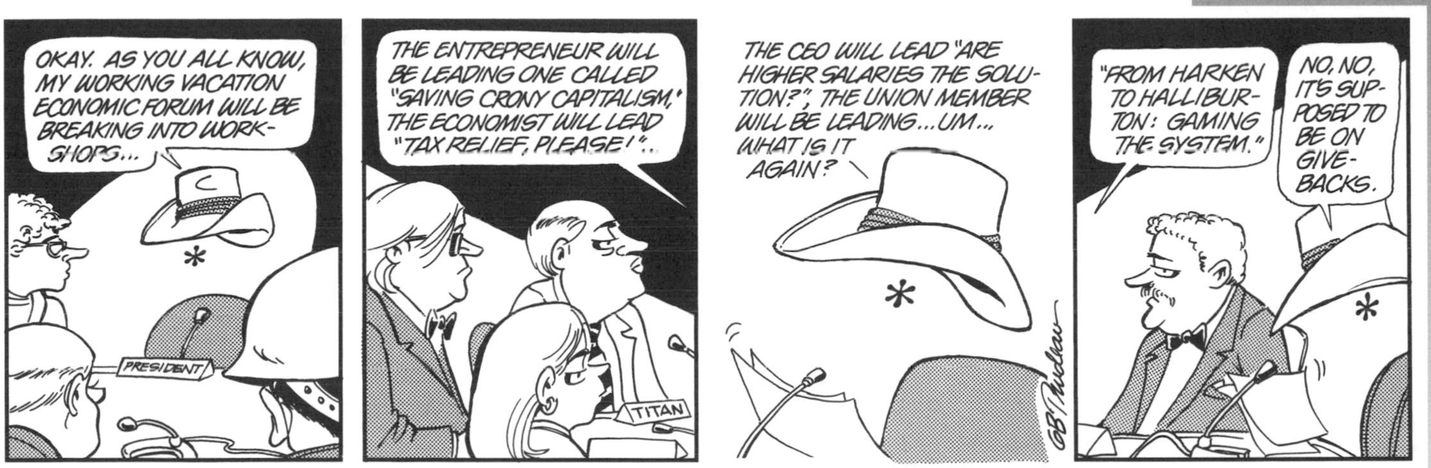
OKAY. AS YOU ALL KNOW, MY WORKING VACATION ECONOMIC FORUM WILL BE BREAKING INTO WORKSHOPS...
PRESIDENT
THE ENTREPRENEUR WILL BE LEADING ONE CALLED "SAVING CRONY CAPITALISM," THE ECONOMIST WILL LEAD "TAX RELIEF, PLEASE!"...
TITAN
THE CEO WILL LEAD "ARE HIGHER SALARIES THE SOLUTION?", THE UNION MEMBER WILL BE LEADING... UM... WHAT IS IT AGAIN?
"FROM HARKEN TO HALLIBURTON: GAMING THE SYSTEM."
NO, NO, IT'S SUPPOSED TO BE ON GIVEBACKS.

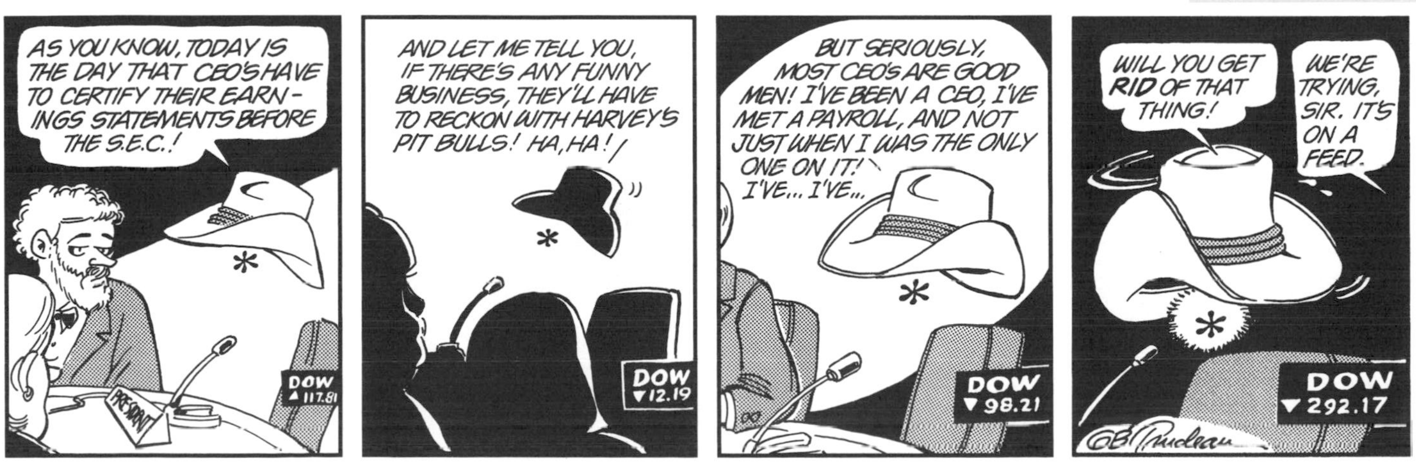
AS YOU KNOW, TODAY IS THE DAY THAT CEO'S HAVE TO CERTIFY THEIR EARNINGS STATEMENTS BEFORE THE S.E.C.!
DOW ▲117.81
AND LET ME TELL YOU, IF THERE'S ANY FUNNY BUSINESS, THEY'LL HAVE TO RECKON WITH HARVEY'S PIT BULLS! HA, HA!
DOW ▼12.19
BUT SERIOUSLY, MOST CEO'S ARE GOOD MEN! I'VE BEEN A CEO, I'VE MET A PAYROLL, AND NOT JUST WHEN I WAS THE ONLY ONE ON IT! I'VE... I'VE...
DOW ▼98.21
WILL YOU GET RID OF THAT THING!
WE'RE TRYING, SIR. IT'S ON A FEED.
DOW ▼292.17

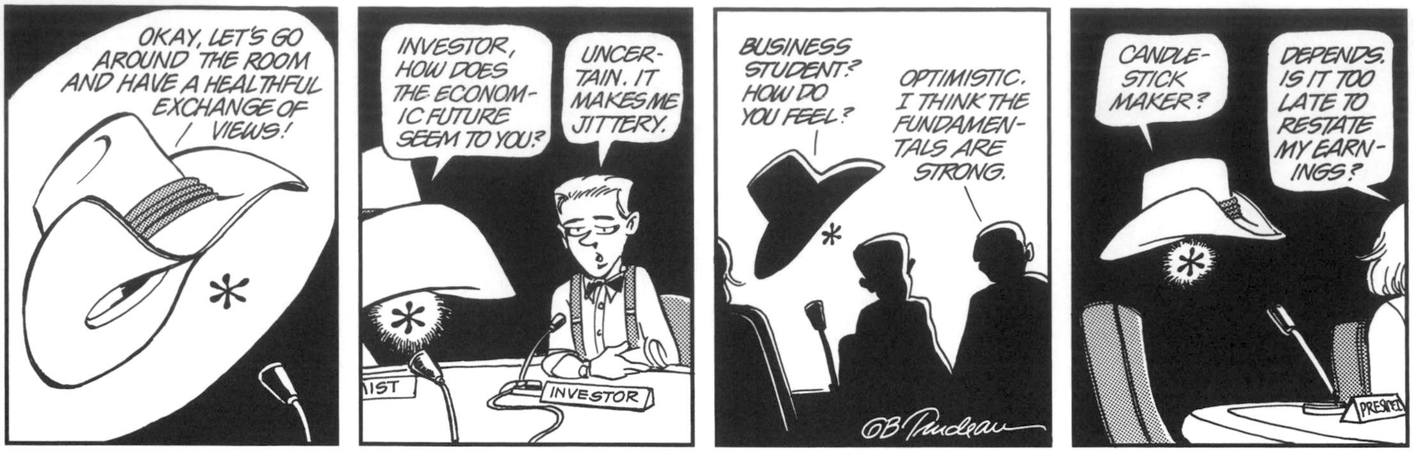
OKAY, LET'S GO AROUND THE ROOM AND HAVE A HEALTHFUL EXCHANGE OF VIEWS!
INVESTOR, HOW DOES THE ECONOMIC FUTURE SEEM TO YOU?
UNCERTAIN. IT MAKES ME JITTERY.
INVESTOR
BUSINESS STUDENT? HOW DO YOU FEEL?
OPTIMISTIC. I THINK THE FUNDAMENTALS ARE STRONG.
CANDLESTICK MAKER?
DEPENDS. IS IT TOO LATE TO RESTATE MY EARNINGS?

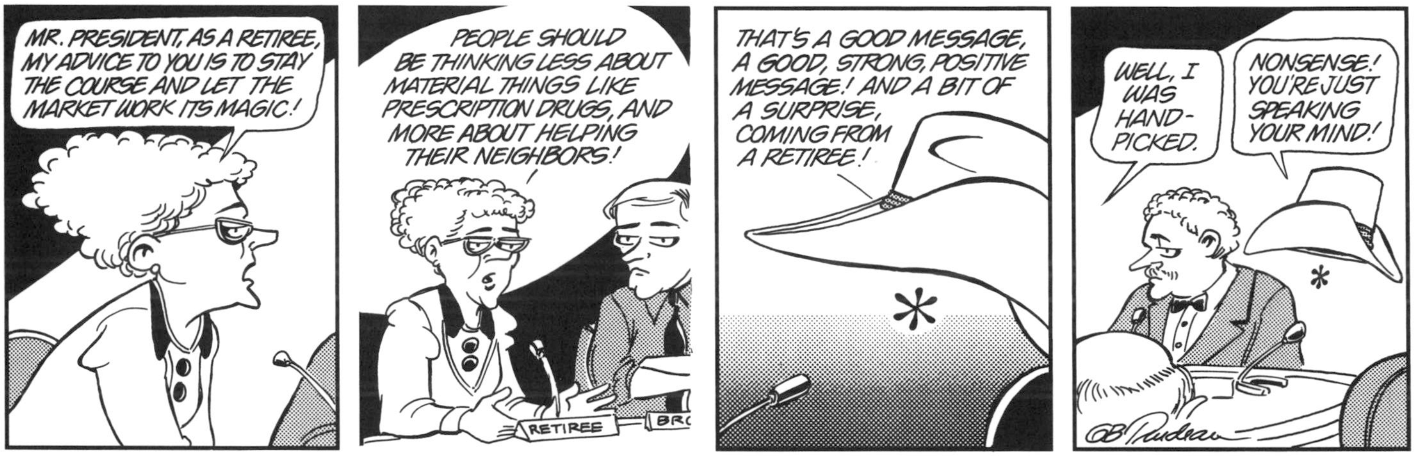
MR. PRESIDENT, AS A RETIREE, MY ADVICE TO YOU IS TO STAY THE COURSE AND LET THE MARKET WORK ITS MAGIC!
PEOPLE SHOULD BE THINKING LESS ABOUT MATERIAL THINGS LIKE PRESCRIPTION DRUGS, AND MORE ABOUT HELPING THEIR NEIGHBORS!
RETIREE
THAT'S A GOOD MESSAGE, A GOOD, STRONG, POSITIVE MESSAGE! AND A BIT OF A SURPRISE, COMING FROM A RETIREE!
WELL, I WAS HAND-PICKED.
NONSENSE! YOU'RE JUST SPEAKING YOUR MIND!

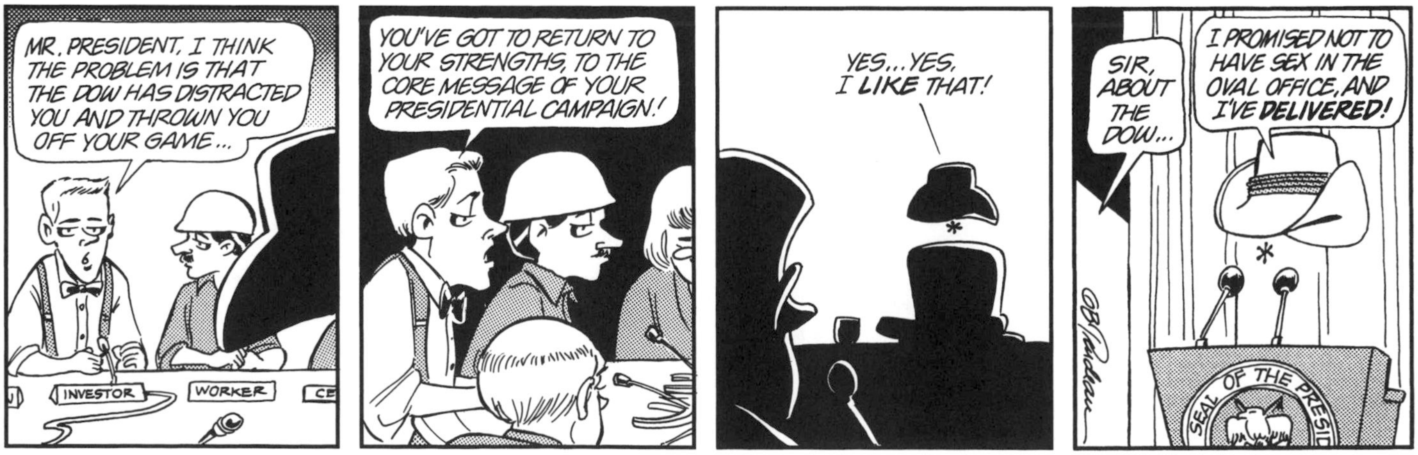
MR. PRESIDENT, I THINK THE PROBLEM IS THAT THE DOW HAS DISTRACTED YOU AND THROWN YOU OFF YOUR GAME...
INVESTOR
WORKER
YOU'VE GOT TO RETURN TO YOUR STRENGTHS, TO THE CORE MESSAGE OF YOUR PRESIDENTIAL CAMPAIGN!
YES...YES, I LIKE THAT!
SIR, ABOUT THE DOW...
I PROMISED NOT TO HAVE SEX IN THE OVAL OFFICE, AND I'VE DELIVERED!

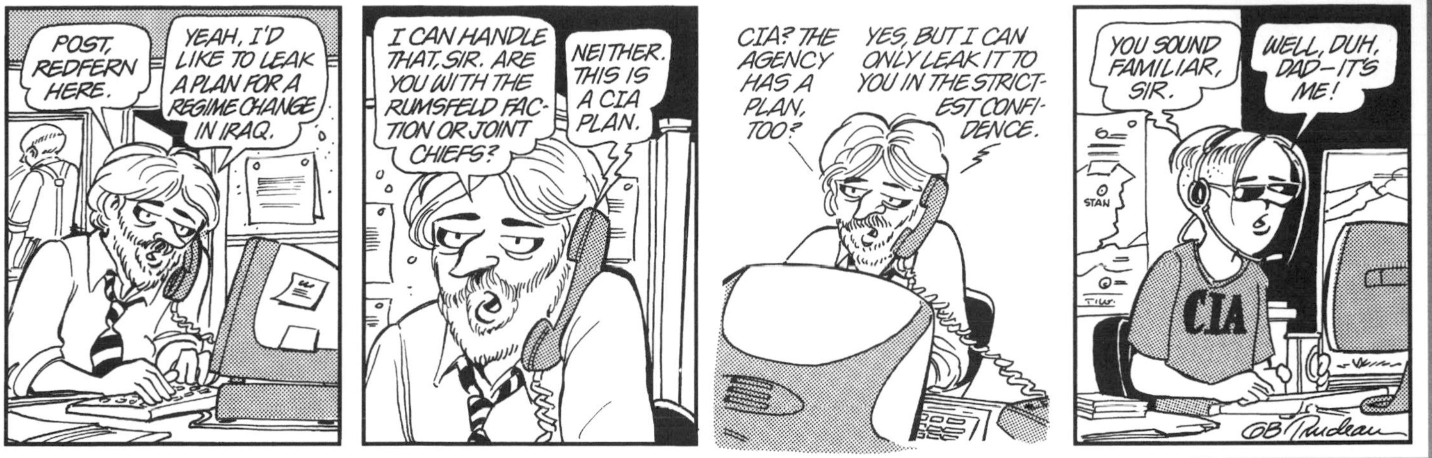
POST, REDFERN HERE.
YEAH, I'D LIKE TO LEAK A PLAN FOR A REGIME CHANGE IN IRAQ.
I CAN HANDLE THAT, SIR. ARE YOU WITH THE RUMSFELD FACTION OR JOINT CHIEFS?
NEITHER. THIS IS A CIA PLAN.
CIA? THE AGENCY HAS A PLAN, TOO?
YES, BUT I CAN ONLY LEAK IT TO YOU IN THE STRICTEST CONFIDENCE.
YOU SOUND FAMILIAR, SIR.
WELL, DUH, DAD—IT'S ME!
CIA
©B Trudeau

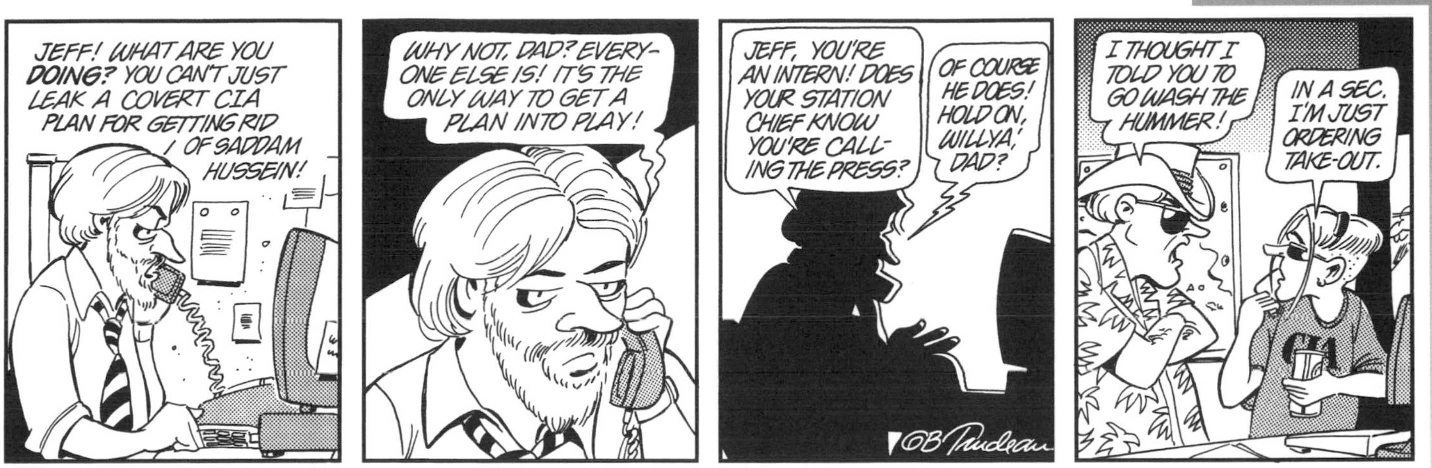
JEFF! WHAT ARE YOU **DOING?** YOU CAN'T JUST LEAK A COVERT CIA PLAN FOR GETTING RID OF SADDAM HUSSEIN!
WHY NOT, DAD? EVERYONE ELSE IS! IT'S THE ONLY WAY TO GET A PLAN INTO PLAY!
JEFF, YOU'RE AN INTERN! DOES YOUR STATION CHIEF KNOW YOU'RE CALLING THE PRESS?
OF COURSE HE DOES! HOLD ON, WILLYA, DAD?
©B Trudeau
I THOUGHT I TOLD YOU TO GO WASH THE HUMMER!
IN A SEC. I'M JUST ORDERING TAKE-OUT.

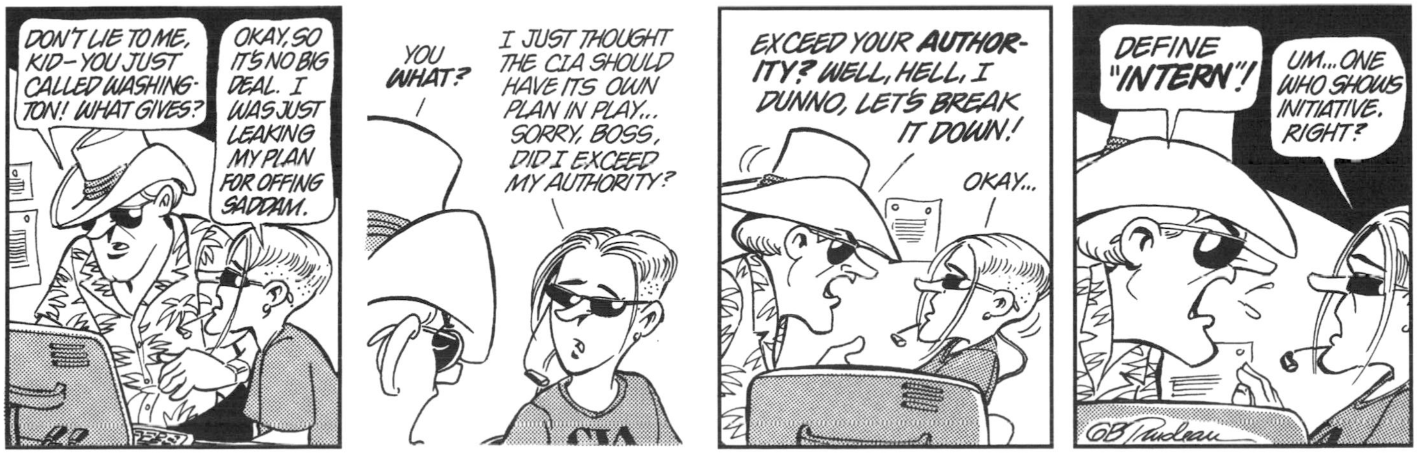
DON'T LIE TO ME, KID—YOU JUST CALLED WASHINGTON! WHAT GIVES?
OKAY, SO IT'S NO BIG DEAL. I WAS JUST LEAKING MY PLAN FOR OFFING SADDAM.
YOU **WHAT?**
I JUST THOUGHT THE CIA SHOULD HAVE ITS OWN PLAN IN PLAY... SORRY, BOSS, DID I EXCEED MY AUTHORITY?
EXCEED YOUR **AUTHORITY? WELL, HELL,** I DUNNO, LET'S BREAK IT DOWN!
OKAY...
DEFINE **"INTERN"!**
UM...ONE WHO SHOWS INITIATIVE, RIGHT?
©B Trudeau

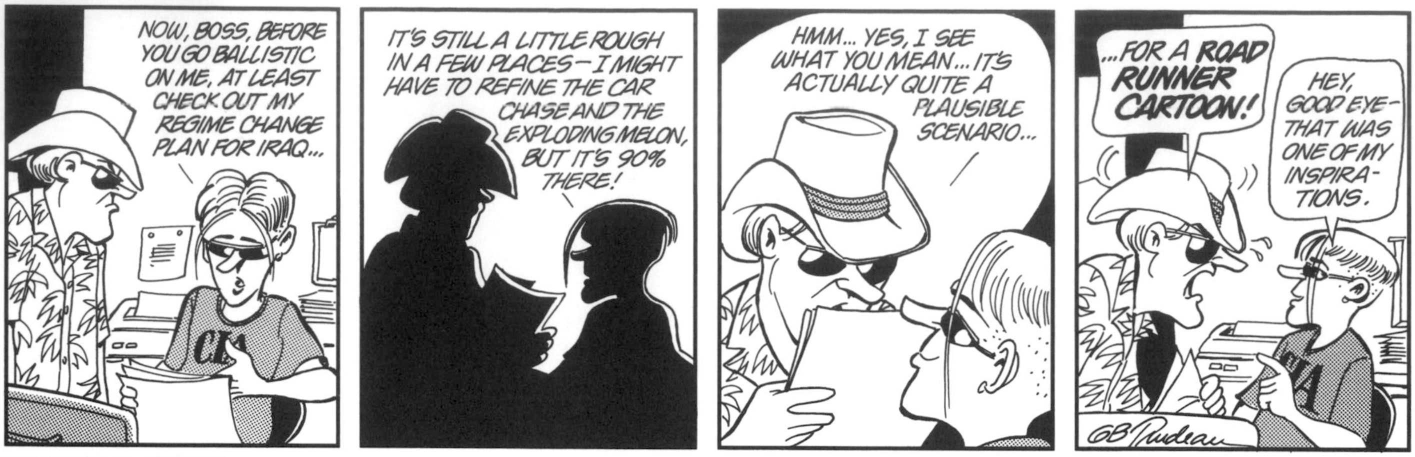
NOW, BOSS, BEFORE YOU GO BALLISTIC ON ME, AT LEAST CHECK OUT MY REGIME CHANGE PLAN FOR IRAQ...
IT'S STILL A LITTLE ROUGH IN A FEW PLACES—I MIGHT HAVE TO REFINE THE CAR CHASE AND THE EXPLODING MELON, BUT IT'S 90% THERE!
HMM... YES, I SEE WHAT YOU MEAN... IT'S ACTUALLY QUITE A PLAUSIBLE SCENARIO...
...FOR A ROAD RUNNER CARTOON!
HEY, GOOD EYE—THAT WAS ONE OF MY INSPIRATIONS.
GB Trudeau

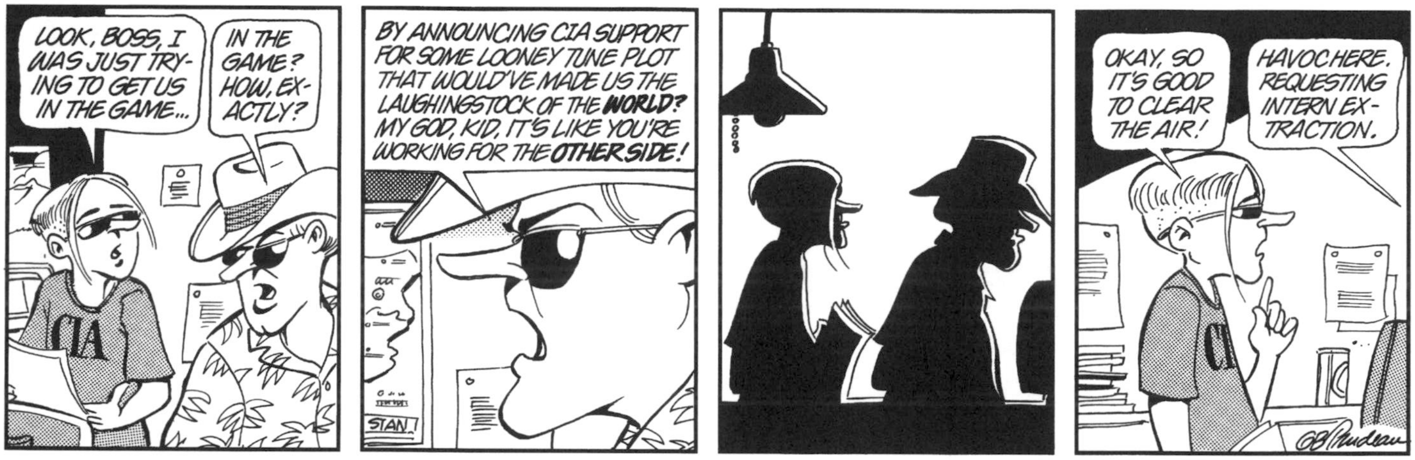
LOOK, BOSS, I WAS JUST TRYING TO GET US IN THE GAME...
IN THE GAME? HOW, EXACTLY?
BY ANNOUNCING CIA SUPPORT FOR SOME LOONEY TUNE PLOT THAT WOULD'VE MADE US THE LAUGHINGSTOCK OF THE WORLD? MY GOD, KID, IT'S LIKE YOU'RE WORKING FOR THE OTHER SIDE!
STAN
OKAY, SO IT'S GOOD TO CLEAR THE AIR!
HAVOC HERE. REQUESTING INTERN EXTRACTION.
GB Trudeau

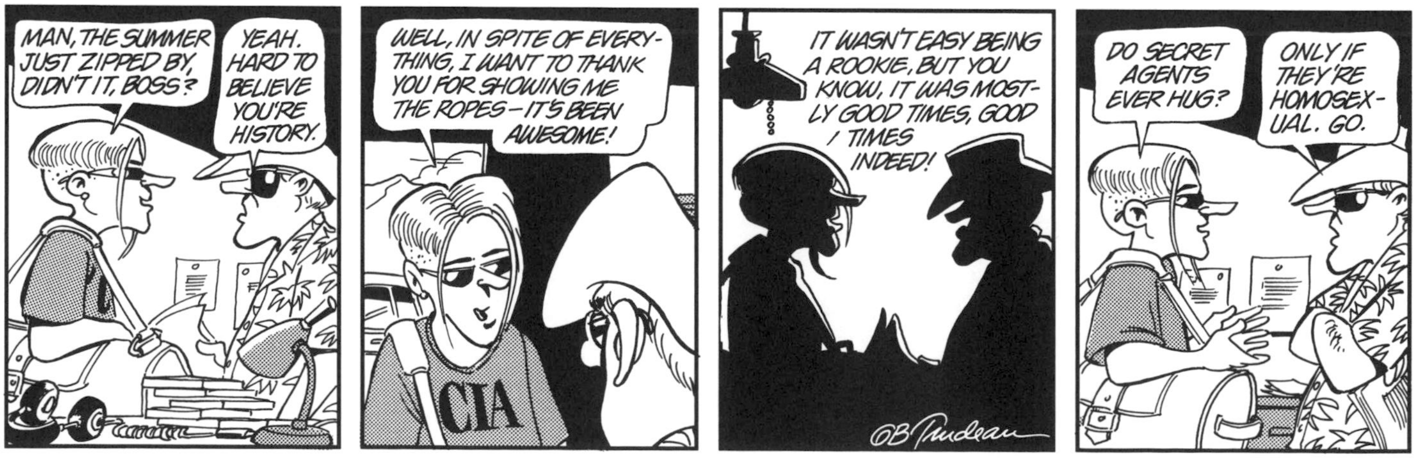
MAN, THE SUMMER JUST ZIPPED BY, DIDN'T IT, BOSS?
YEAH. HARD TO BELIEVE YOU'RE HISTORY.
WELL, IN SPITE OF EVERYTHING, I WANT TO THANK YOU FOR SHOWING ME THE ROPES—IT'S BEEN AWESOME!
IT WASN'T EASY BEING A ROOKIE, BUT YOU KNOW, IT WAS MOSTLY GOOD TIMES, GOOD TIMES INDEED!
GB Trudeau
DO SECRET AGENTS EVER HUG?
ONLY IF THEY'RE HOMOSEXUAL. GO.

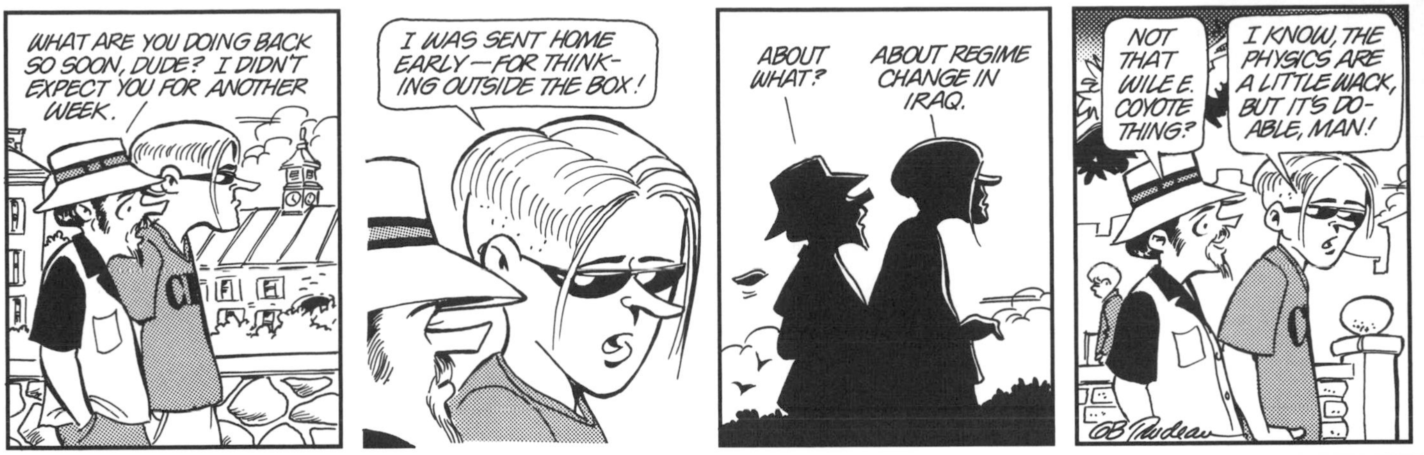
WHAT ARE YOU DOING BACK SO SOON, DUDE? I DIDN'T EXPECT YOU FOR ANOTHER WEEK.
I WAS SENT HOME EARLY—FOR THINKING OUTSIDE THE BOX!
ABOUT WHAT?
ABOUT REGIME CHANGE IN IRAQ.
NOT THAT WILE E. COYOTE THING?
I KNOW, THE PHYSICS ARE A LITTLE WACK, BUT IT'S DOABLE, MAN!

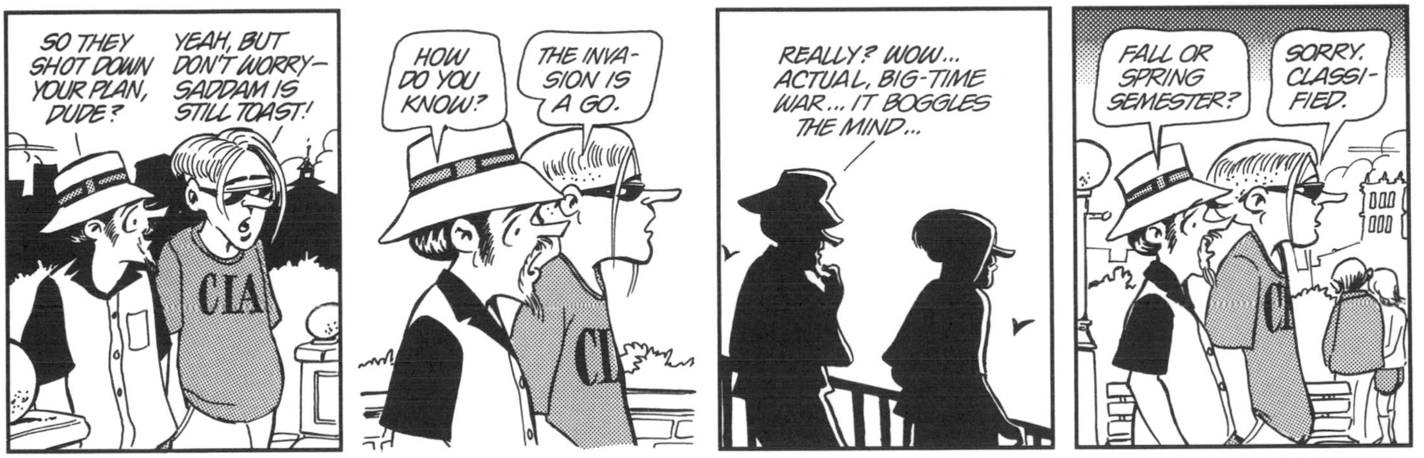
SO THEY SHOT DOWN YOUR PLAN, DUDE?
YEAH, BUT DON'T WORRY—SADDAM IS STILL TOAST!
HOW DO YOU KNOW?
THE INVASION IS A GO.
REALLY? WOW... ACTUAL, BIG-TIME WAR... IT BOGGLES THE MIND...
FALL OR SPRING SEMESTER?
SORRY. CLASSIFIED.

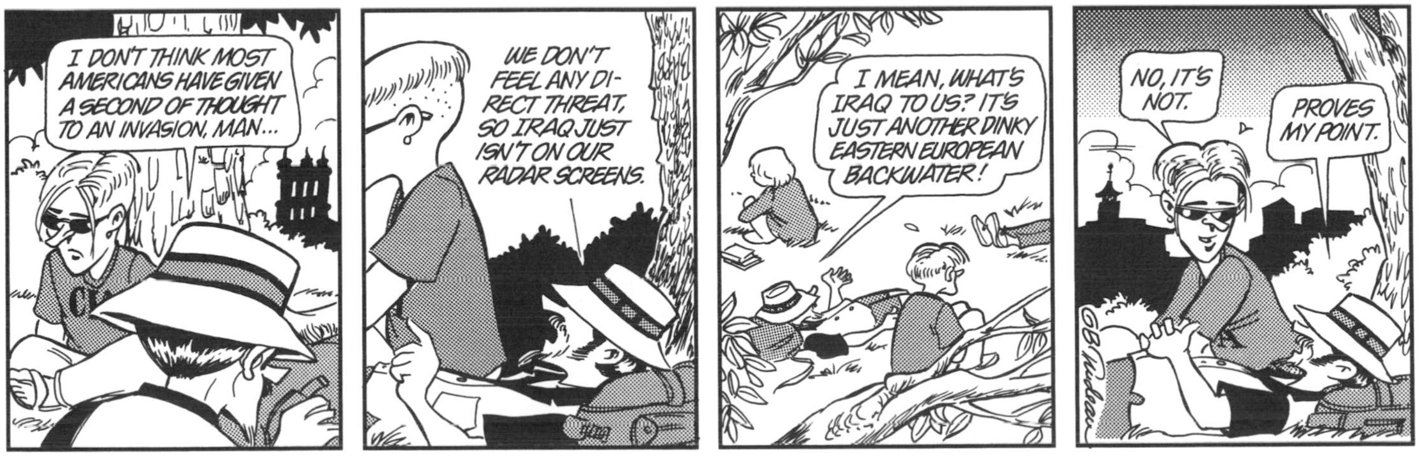
I DON'T THINK MOST AMERICANS HAVE GIVEN A SECOND OF THOUGHT TO AN INVASION, MAN...
WE DON'T FEEL ANY DIRECT THREAT, SO IRAQ JUST ISN'T ON OUR RADAR SCREENS.
I MEAN, WHAT'S IRAQ TO US? IT'S JUST ANOTHER DINKY EASTERN EUROPEAN BACKWATER!
NO, IT'S NOT.
PROVES MY POINT.

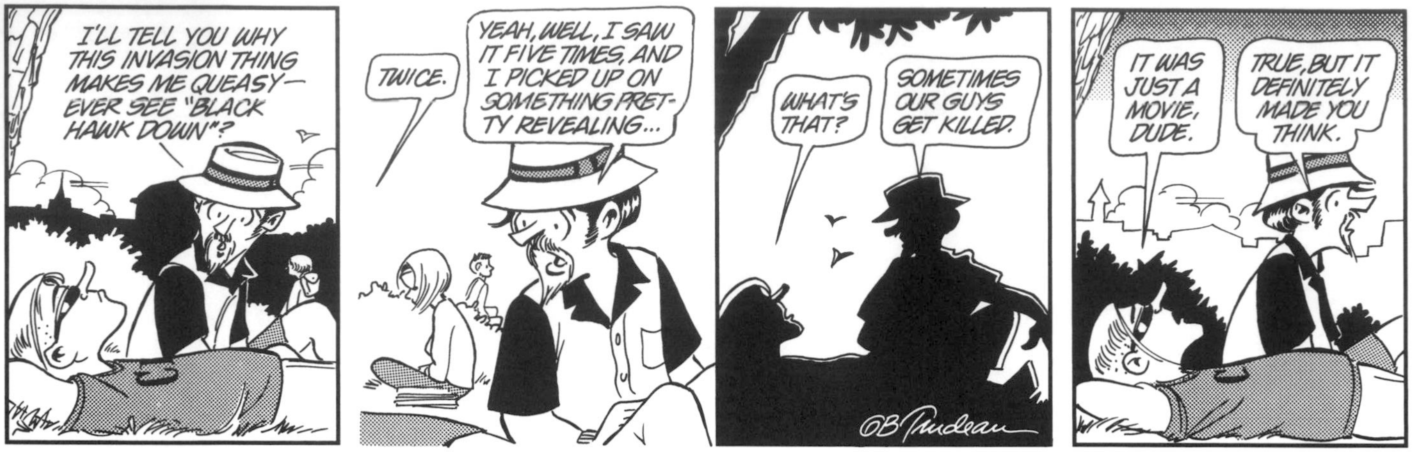
I'LL TELL YOU WHY THIS INVASION THING MAKES ME QUEASY— EVER SEE "BLACK HAWK DOWN"?
TWICE.
YEAH, WELL, I SAW IT FIVE TIMES, AND I PICKED UP ON SOMETHING PRETTY REVEALING...
WHAT'S THAT?
SOMETIMES OUR GUYS GET KILLED.
IT WAS JUST A MOVIE, DUDE.
TRUE, BUT IT DEFINITELY MADE YOU THINK.

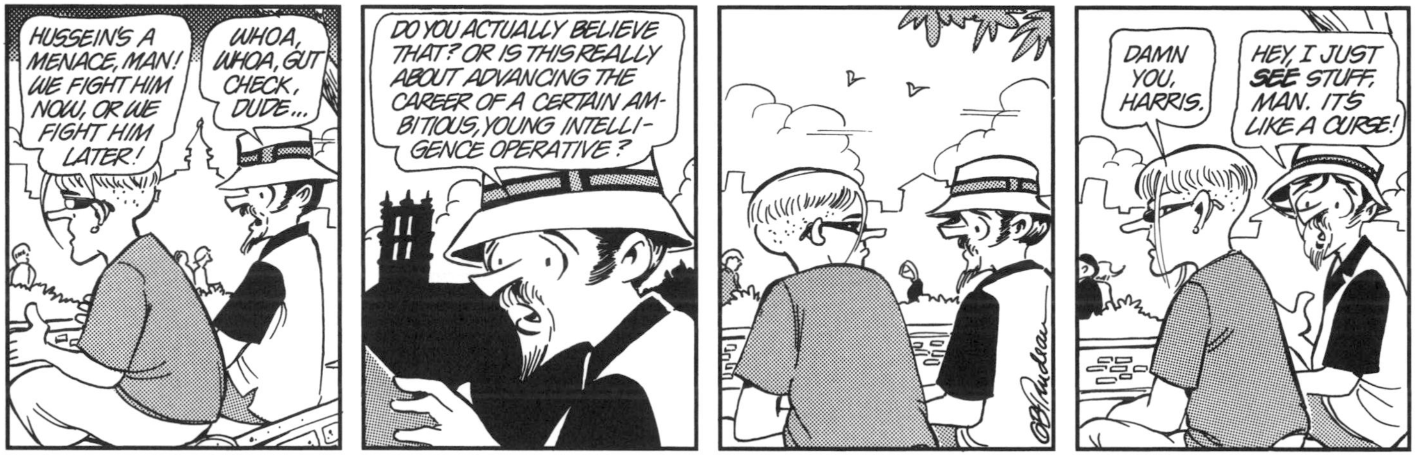
HUSSEIN'S A MENACE, MAN! WE FIGHT HIM NOW, OR WE FIGHT HIM LATER!
WHOA, WHOA, GUT CHECK, DUDE...
DO YOU ACTUALLY BELIEVE THAT? OR IS THIS REALLY ABOUT ADVANCING THE CAREER OF A CERTAIN AMBITIOUS, YOUNG INTELLIGENCE OPERATIVE?
DAMN YOU, HARRIS.
HEY, I JUST SEE STUFF, MAN. IT'S LIKE A CURSE!

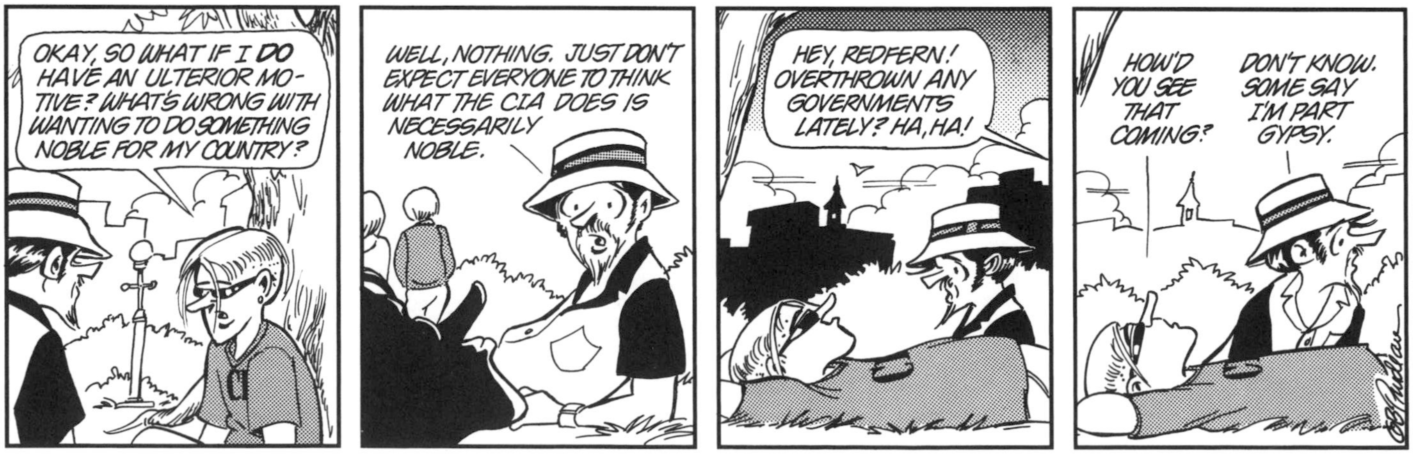
OKAY, SO WHAT IF I DO HAVE AN ULTERIOR MOTIVE? WHAT'S WRONG WITH WANTING TO DO SOMETHING NOBLE FOR MY COUNTRY?
WELL, NOTHING. JUST DON'T EXPECT EVERYONE TO THINK WHAT THE CIA DOES IS NECESSARILY NOBLE.
HEY, REDFERN! OVERTHROWN ANY GOVERNMENTS LATELY? HA, HA!
HOW'D YOU SEE THAT COMING?
DON'T KNOW. SOME SAY I'M PART GYPSY.

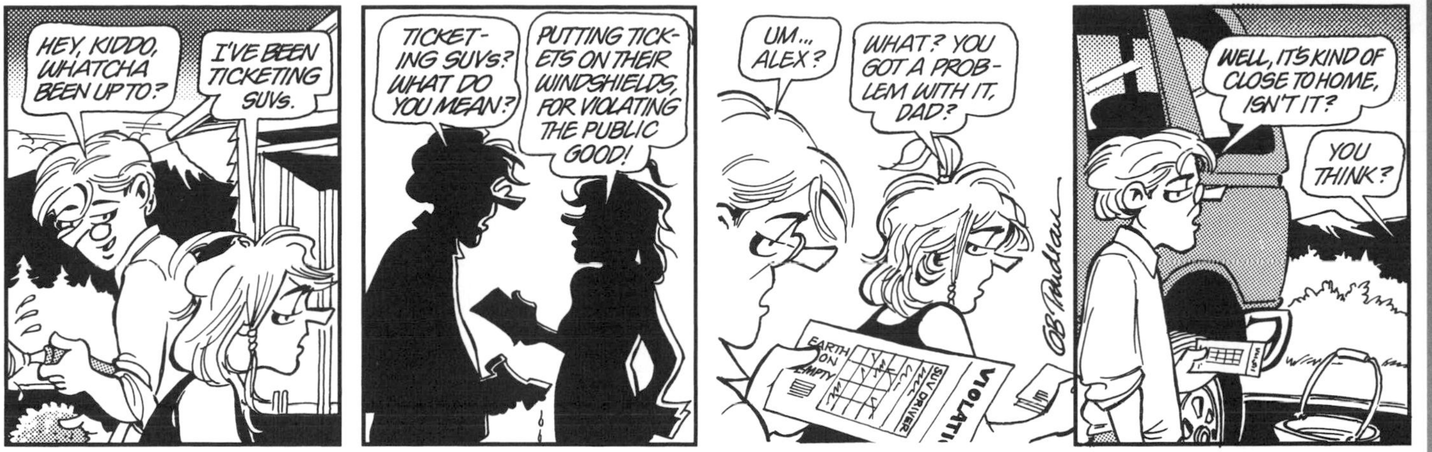
HEY, KIDDO, WHATCHA BEEN UP TO?
I'VE BEEN TICKETING SUVs.
TICKETING SUVs? WHAT DO YOU MEAN?
PUTTING TICKETS ON THEIR WINDSHIELDS, FOR VIOLATING THE PUBLIC GOOD!
UM... ALEX?
WHAT? YOU GOT A PROBLEM WITH IT, DAD?
EARTH ON EMPTY
SUV DRIVER
VIOLATI
WELL, IT'S KIND OF CLOSE TO HOME, ISN'T IT?
YOU THINK?

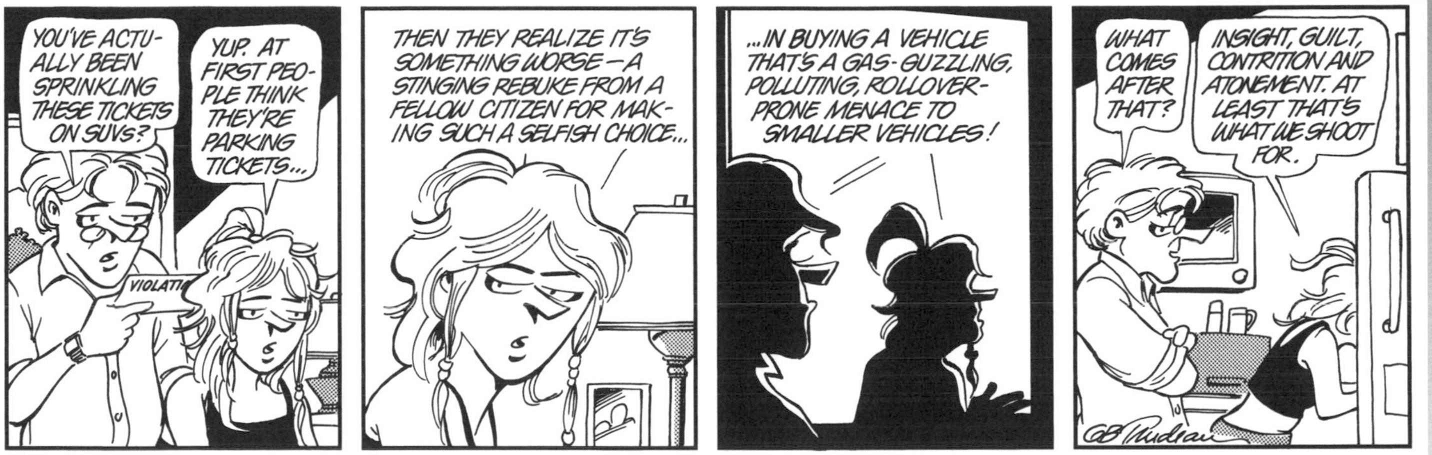
YOU'VE ACTUALLY BEEN SPRINKLING THESE TICKETS ON SUVs?
YUP. AT FIRST PEOPLE THINK THEY'RE PARKING TICKETS...
VIOLATI
THEN THEY REALIZE IT'S SOMETHING WORSE — A STINGING REBUKE FROM A FELLOW CITIZEN FOR MAKING SUCH A SELFISH CHOICE...
...IN BUYING A VEHICLE THAT'S A GAS-GUZZLING, POLLUTING, ROLLOVER-PRONE MENACE TO SMALLER VEHICLES!
WHAT COMES AFTER THAT?
INSIGHT, GUILT, CONTRITION AND ATONEMENT. AT LEAST THAT'S WHAT WE SHOOT FOR.

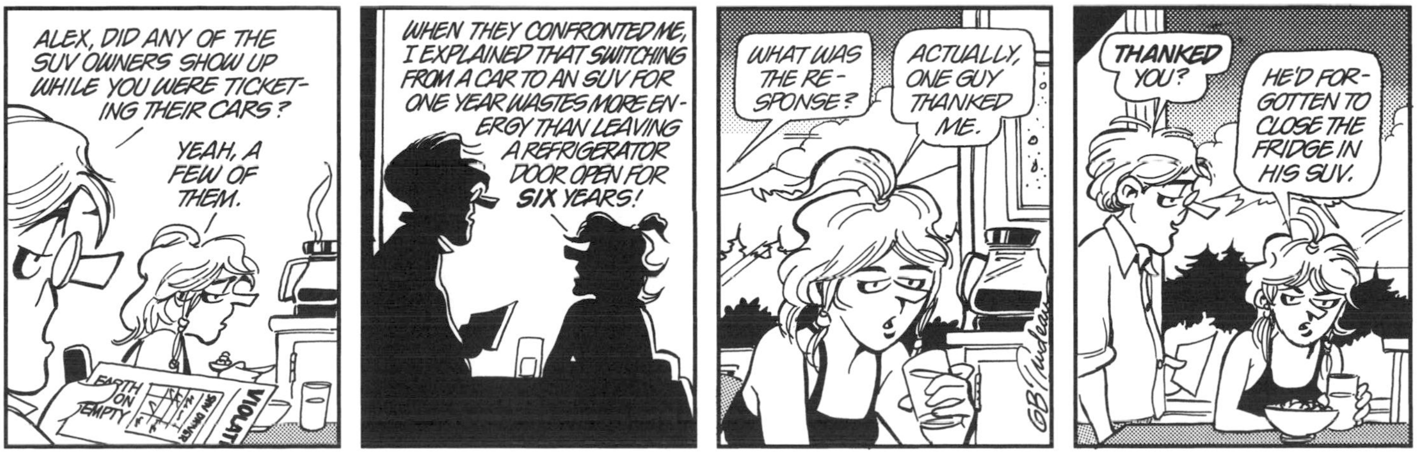
ALEX, DID ANY OF THE SUV OWNERS SHOW UP WHILE YOU WERE TICKETING THEIR CARS?
YEAH, A FEW OF THEM.
EARTH ON EMPTY
VIOLATI
WHEN THEY CONFRONTED ME, I EXPLAINED THAT SWITCHING FROM A CAR TO AN SUV FOR ONE YEAR WASTES MORE ENERGY THAN LEAVING A REFRIGERATOR DOOR OPEN FOR SIX YEARS!
WHAT WAS THE RESPONSE?
ACTUALLY, ONE GUY THANKED ME.
THANKED YOU?
HE'D FORGOTTEN TO CLOSE THE FRIDGE IN HIS SUV.

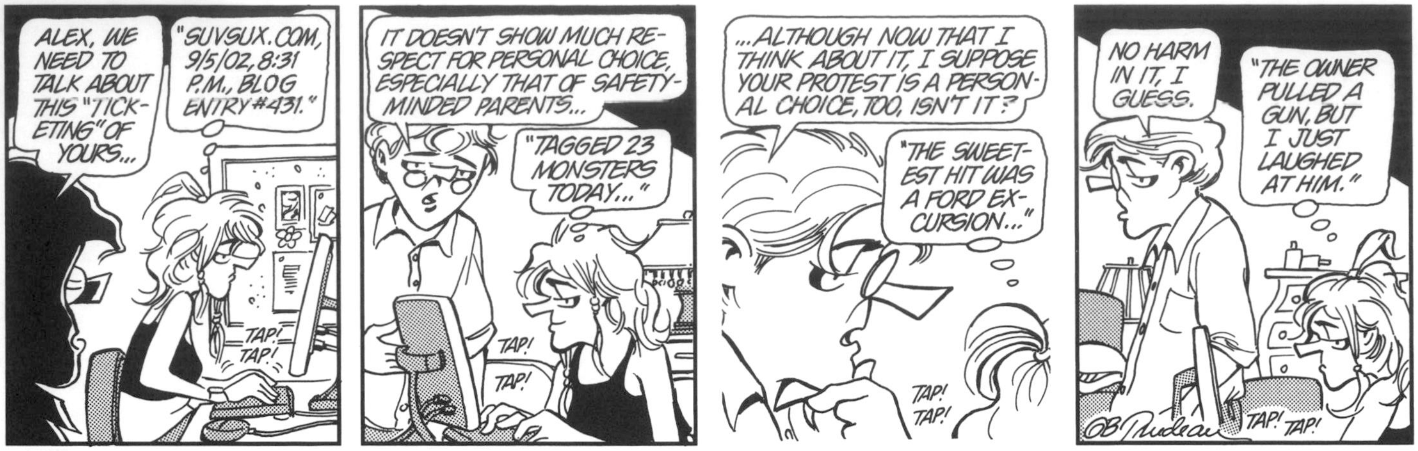
ALEX, WE NEED TO TALK ABOUT THIS "TICKETING" OF YOURS...
"SUVSUX.COM, 9/5/02, 8:31 P.M., BLOG ENTRY #431."
TAP! TAP!
IT DOESN'T SHOW MUCH RESPECT FOR PERSONAL CHOICE, ESPECIALLY THAT OF SAFETY-MINDED PARENTS...
"TAGGED 23 MONSTERS TODAY..."
TAP! TAP!
...ALTHOUGH NOW THAT I THINK ABOUT IT, I SUPPOSE YOUR PROTEST IS A PERSONAL CHOICE, TOO, ISN'T IT?
"THE SWEETEST HIT WAS A FORD EXCURSION..."
TAP! TAP!
NO HARM IN IT, I GUESS.
"THE OWNER PULLED A GUN, BUT I JUST LAUGHED AT HIM."
©B. Trudeau
TAP! TAP!

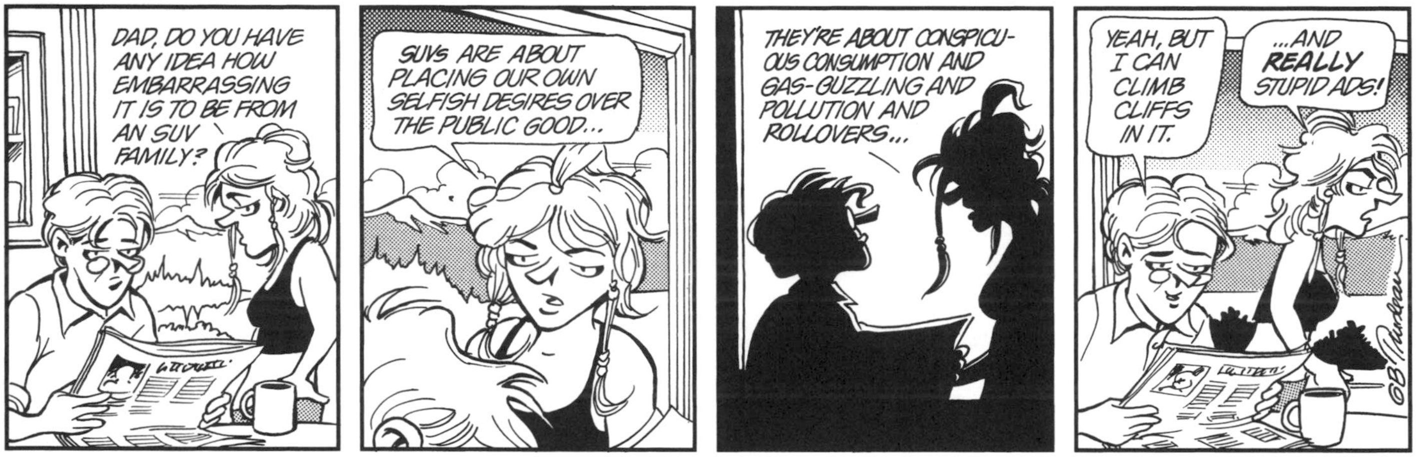
DAD, DO YOU HAVE ANY IDEA HOW EMBARRASSING IT IS TO BE FROM AN SUV FAMILY?
SUVS ARE ABOUT PLACING OUR OWN SELFISH DESIRES OVER THE PUBLIC GOOD...
THEY'RE ABOUT CONSPICUOUS CONSUMPTION AND GAS-GUZZLING AND POLLUTION AND ROLLOVERS...
YEAH, BUT I CAN CLIMB CLIFFS IN IT.
...AND REALLY STUPID ADS!
©B. Trudeau

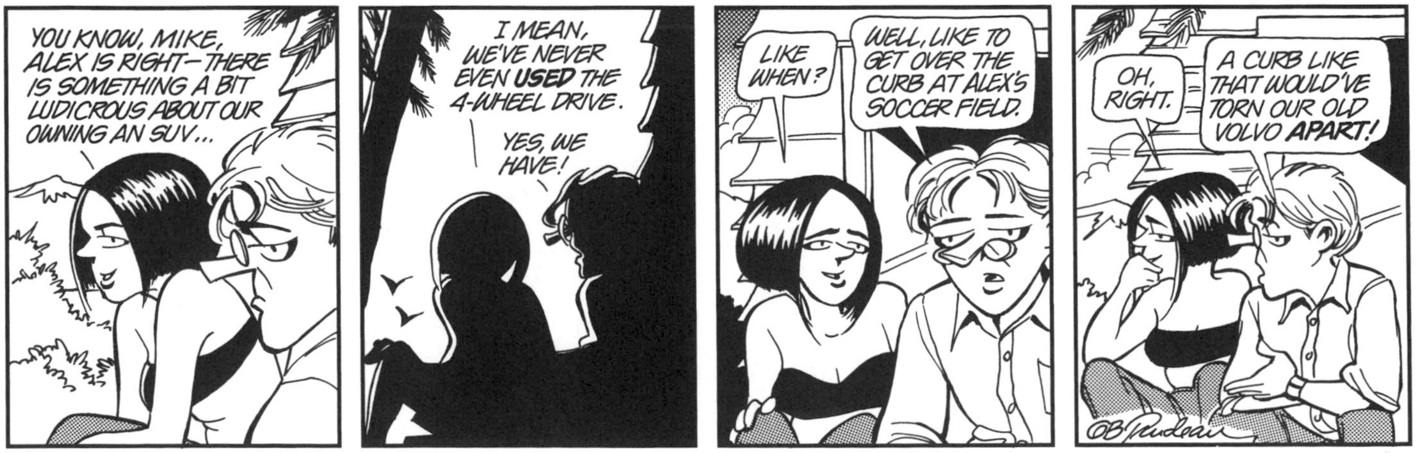
YOU KNOW, MIKE, ALEX IS RIGHT—THERE IS SOMETHING A BIT LUDICROUS ABOUT OUR OWNING AN SUV...
I MEAN, WE'VE NEVER EVEN USED THE 4-WHEEL DRIVE.
YES, WE HAVE!
LIKE WHEN?
WELL, LIKE TO GET OVER THE CURB AT ALEX'S SOCCER FIELD.
OH, RIGHT.
A CURB LIKE THAT WOULD'VE TORN OUR OLD VOLVO APART!
©B. Trudeau

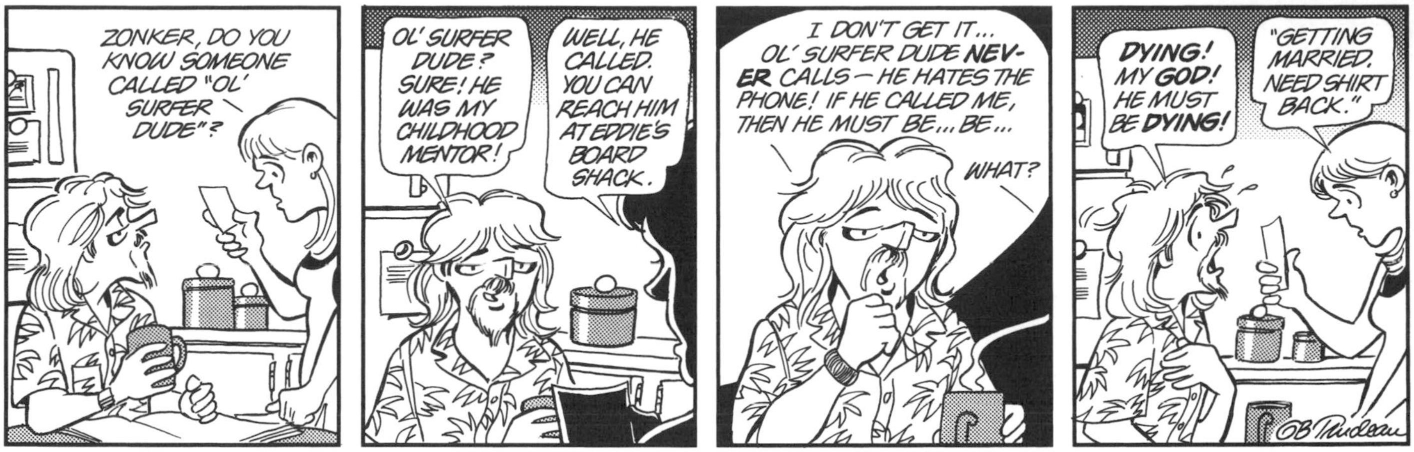
ZONKER, DO YOU KNOW SOMEONE CALLED "OL' SURFER DUDE"?
OL' SURFER DUDE? SURE! HE WAS MY CHILDHOOD MENTOR!
WELL, HE CALLED. YOU CAN REACH HIM AT EDDIE'S BOARD SHACK.
I DON'T GET IT... OL' SURFER DUDE NEVER CALLS — HE HATES THE PHONE! IF HE CALLED ME, THEN HE MUST BE... BE...
WHAT?
DYING! MY GOD! HE MUST BE DYING!
"GETTING MARRIED. NEED SHIRT BACK."
GB Trudeau

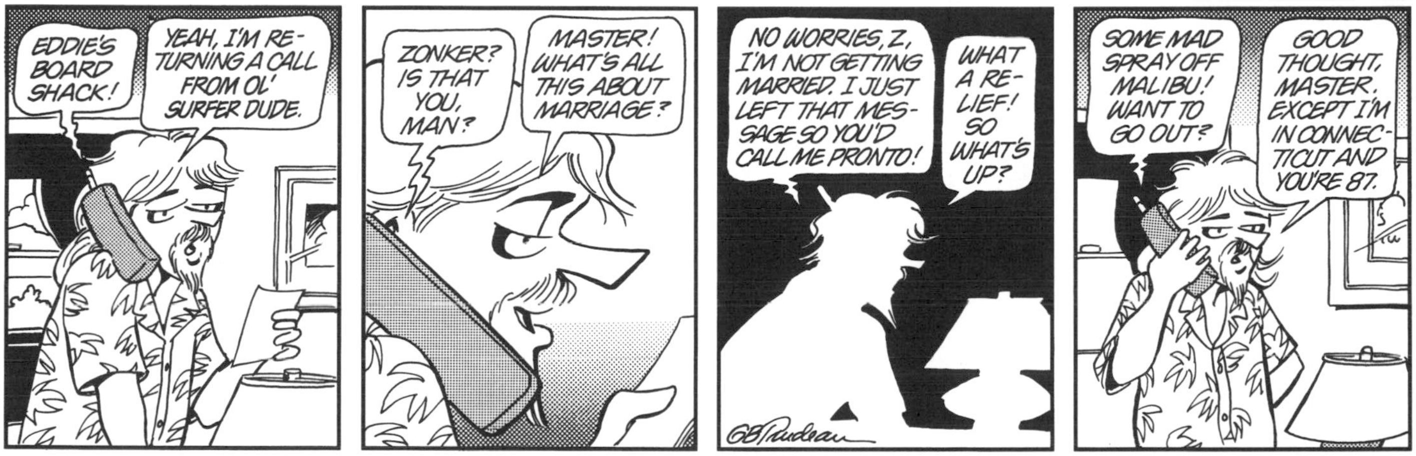
EDDIE'S BOARD SHACK!
YEAH, I'M RETURNING A CALL FROM OL' SURFER DUDE.
ZONKER? IS THAT YOU, MAN?
MASTER! WHAT'S ALL THIS ABOUT MARRIAGE?
NO WORRIES, Z, I'M NOT GETTING MARRIED. I JUST LEFT THAT MESSAGE SO YOU'D CALL ME PRONTO!
WHAT A RELIEF! SO WHAT'S UP?
SOME MAD SPRAY OFF MALIBU! WANT TO GO OUT?
GOOD THOUGHT, MASTER. EXCEPT I'M IN CONNECTICUT AND YOU'RE 87.
GB Trudeau

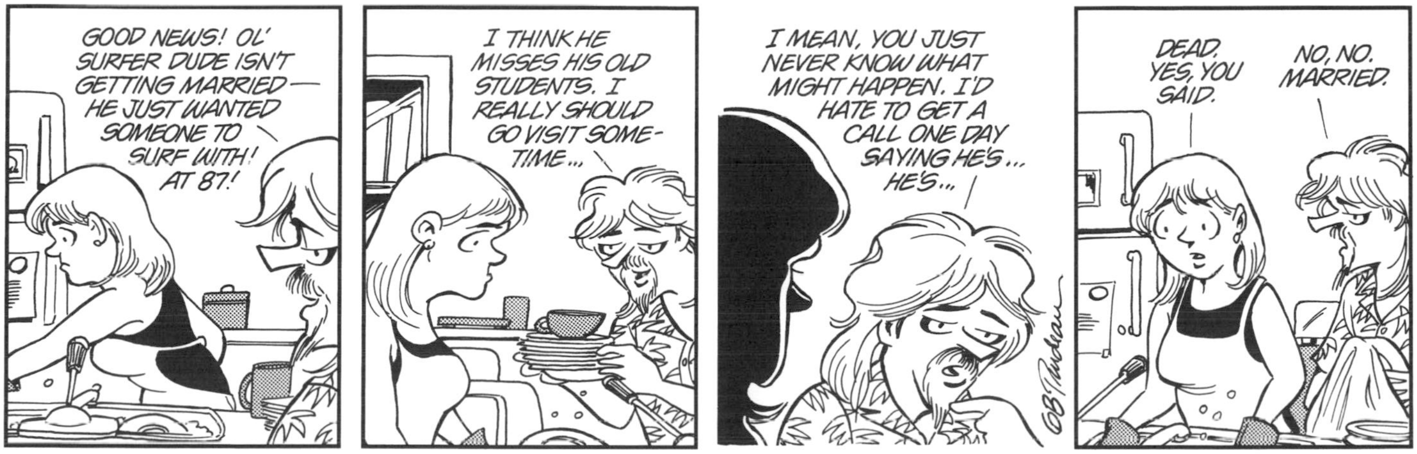
GOOD NEWS! OL' SURFER DUDE ISN'T GETTING MARRIED — HE JUST WANTED SOMEONE TO SURF WITH! AT 87!
I THINK HE MISSES HIS OLD STUDENTS. I REALLY SHOULD GO VISIT SOMETIME...
I MEAN, YOU JUST NEVER KNOW WHAT MIGHT HAPPEN. I'D HATE TO GET A CALL ONE DAY SAYING HE'S... HE'S...
DEAD. YES, YOU SAID.
NO, NO. MARRIED.
GB Trudeau

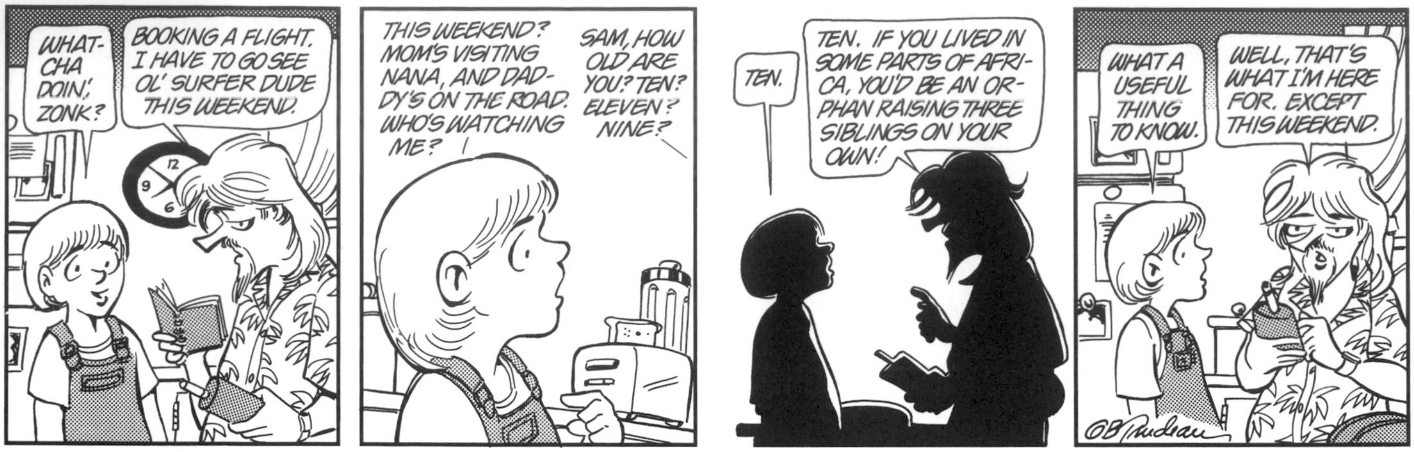
WHAT-CHA DOIN', ZONK?
BOOKING A FLIGHT. I HAVE TO GO SEE OL' SURFER DUDE THIS WEEKEND.
THIS WEEKEND? MOM'S VISITING NANA, AND DADDY'S ON THE ROAD. WHO'S WATCHING ME?
SAM, HOW OLD ARE YOU? TEN? ELEVEN? NINE?
TEN.
TEN. IF YOU LIVED IN SOME PARTS OF AFRICA, YOU'D BE AN ORPHAN RAISING THREE SIBLINGS ON YOUR OWN!
WHAT A USEFUL THING TO KNOW.
WELL, THAT'S WHAT I'M HERE FOR. EXCEPT THIS WEEKEND.

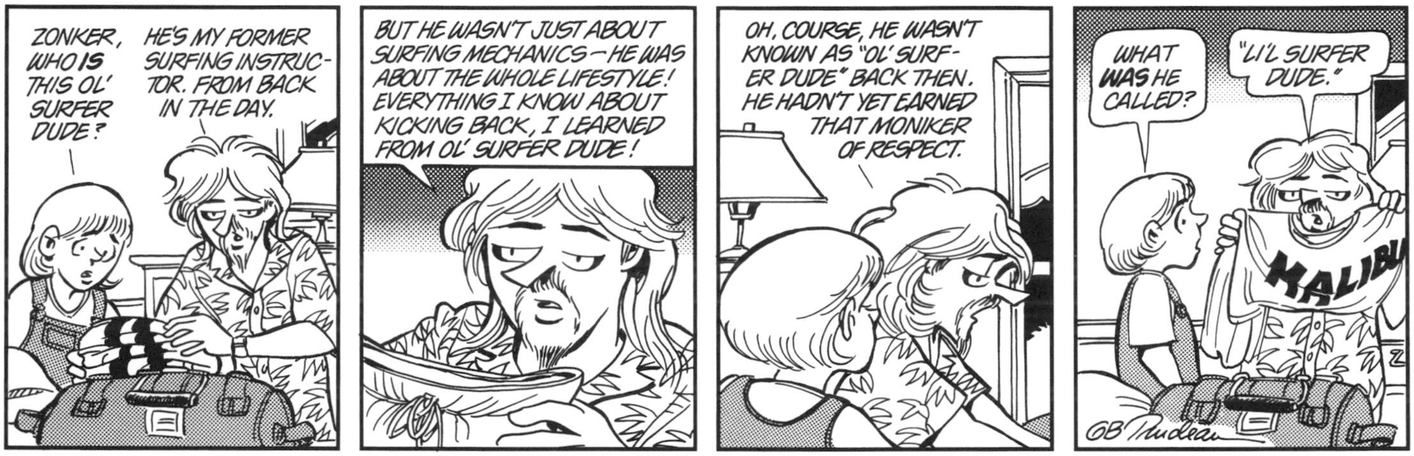
ZONKER, WHO IS THIS OL' SURFER DUDE?
HE'S MY FORMER SURFING INSTRUCTOR. FROM BACK IN THE DAY.
BUT HE WASN'T JUST ABOUT SURFING MECHANICS—HE WAS ABOUT THE WHOLE LIFESTYLE! EVERYTHING I KNOW ABOUT KICKING BACK, I LEARNED FROM OL' SURFER DUDE!
OH, COURSE, HE WASN'T KNOWN AS "OL' SURFER DUDE" BACK THEN. HE HADN'T YET EARNED THAT MONIKER OF RESPECT.
WHAT WAS HE CALLED?
"LI'L SURFER DUDE."
MALIBU

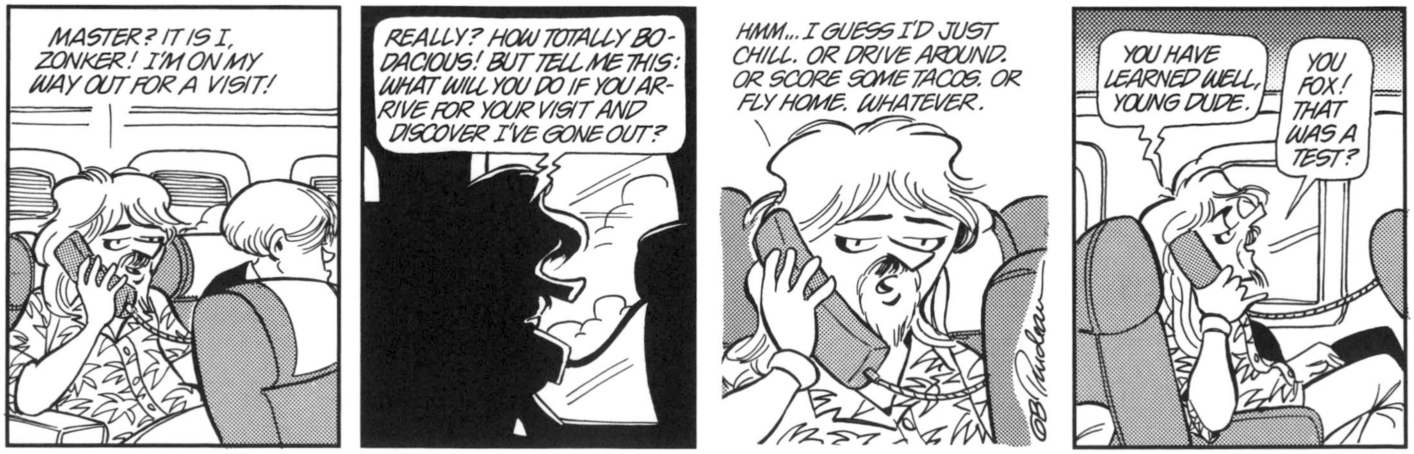
MASTER? IT IS I, ZONKER! I'M ON MY WAY OUT FOR A VISIT!
REALLY? HOW TOTALLY BODACIOUS! BUT TELL ME THIS: WHAT WILL YOU DO IF YOU ARRIVE FOR YOUR VISIT AND DISCOVER I'VE GONE OUT?
HMM... I GUESS I'D JUST CHILL. OR DRIVE AROUND. OR SCORE SOME TACOS. OR FLY HOME. WHATEVER.
YOU HAVE LEARNED WELL, YOUNG DUDE.
YOU FOX! THAT WAS A TEST?

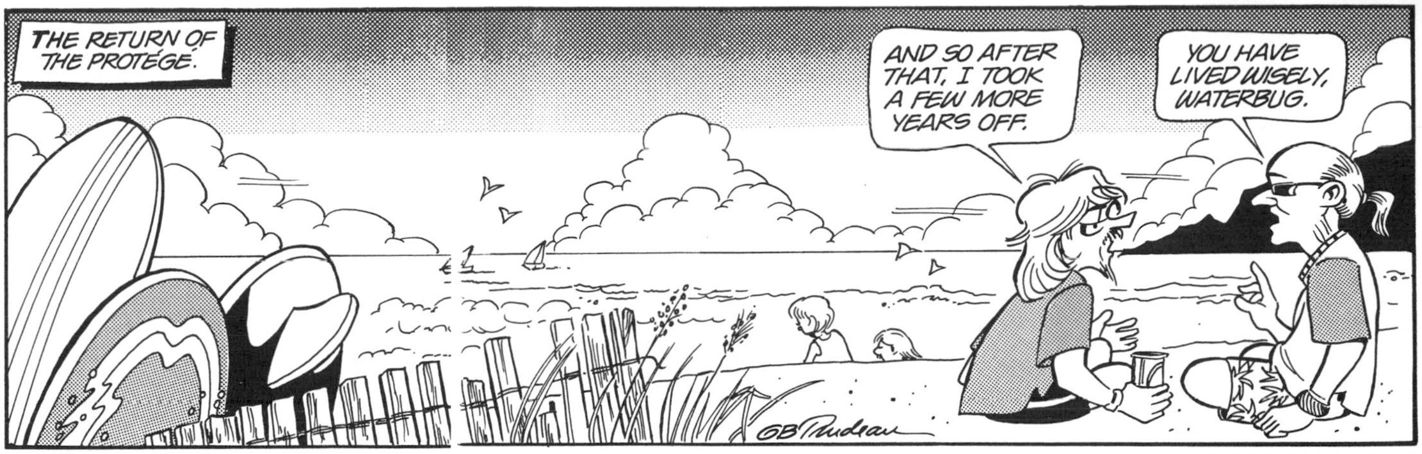
THE RETURN OF THE PROTEGÉ.
AND SO AFTER THAT, I TOOK A FEW MORE YEARS OFF.
YOU HAVE LIVED WISELY, WATERBUG.

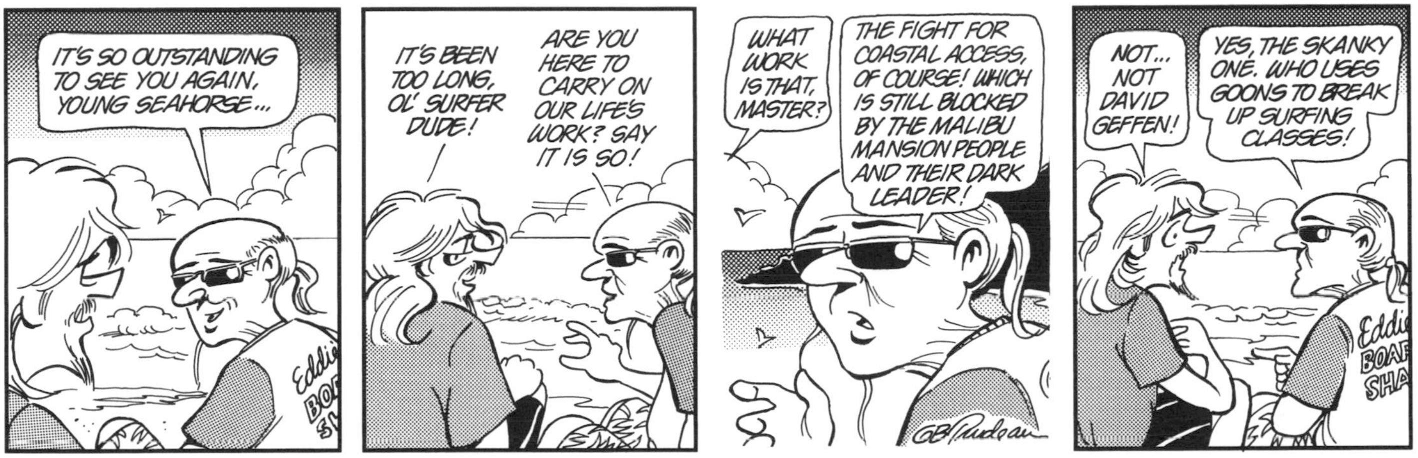
IT'S SO OUTSTANDING TO SEE YOU AGAIN, YOUNG SEAHORSE...
IT'S BEEN TOO LONG, OL' SURFER DUDE!
ARE YOU HERE TO CARRY ON OUR LIFE'S WORK? SAY IT IS SO!
WHAT WORK IS THAT, MASTER?
THE FIGHT FOR COASTAL ACCESS, OF COURSE! WHICH IS STILL BLOCKED BY THE MALIBU MANSION PEOPLE AND THEIR DARK LEADER!
NOT... NOT DAVID GEFFEN!
YES, THE SKANKY ONE. WHO USES GOONS TO BREAK UP SURFING CLASSES!

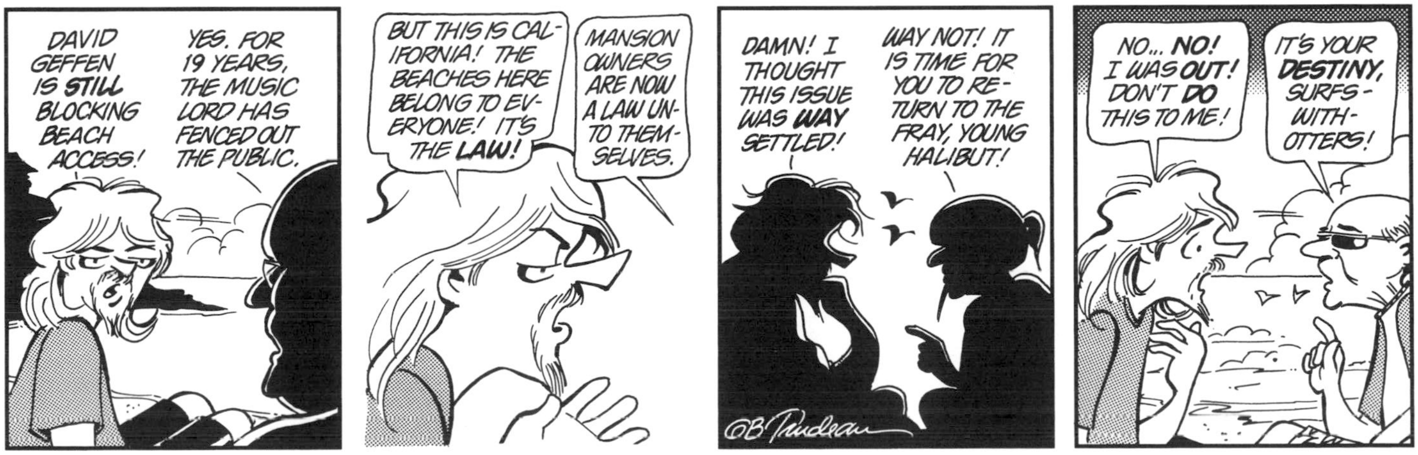
DAVID GEFFEN IS **STILL** BLOCKING BEACH ACCESS!
YES. FOR 19 YEARS, THE MUSIC LORD HAS FENCED OUT THE PUBLIC.
BUT THIS IS CALIFORNIA! THE BEACHES HERE BELONG TO EVERYONE! IT'S THE **LAW!**
MANSION OWNERS ARE NOW A LAW UNTO THEMSELVES.
DAMN! I THOUGHT THIS ISSUE WAS **WAY** SETTLED!
WAY NOT! IT IS TIME FOR YOU TO RETURN TO THE FRAY, YOUNG HALIBUT!
NO... **NO!** I WAS **OUT!** DON'T **DO** THIS TO ME!
IT'S YOUR **DESTINY,** SURFS-WITH-OTTERS!

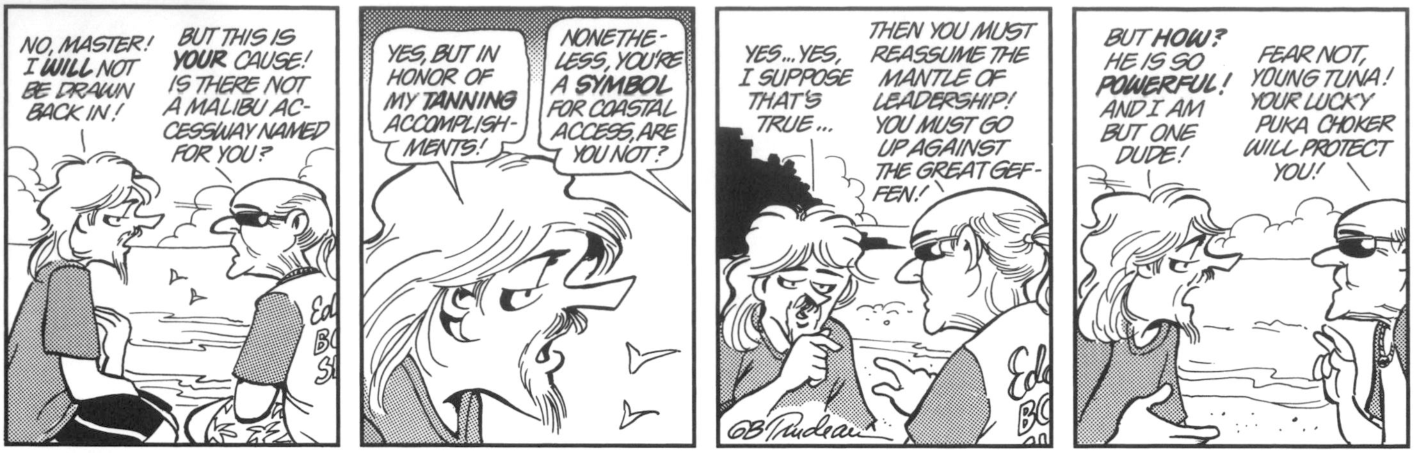
NO, MASTER! I **WILL** NOT BE DRAWN BACK IN!
BUT THIS IS **YOUR** CAUSE! IS THERE NOT A MALIBU ACCESSWAY NAMED FOR YOU?
YES, BUT IN HONOR OF MY **TANNING** ACCOMPLISHMENTS!
NONETHELESS, YOU'RE A **SYMBOL** FOR COASTAL ACCESS, ARE YOU NOT?
YES... YES, I SUPPOSE THAT'S TRUE...
THEN YOU MUST REASSUME THE MANTLE OF LEADERSHIP! YOU MUST GO UP AGAINST THE GREAT GEFFEN!
BUT **HOW?** HE IS SO **POWERFUL!** AND I AM BUT ONE DUDE!
FEAR NOT, YOUNG TUNA! YOUR LUCKY PUKA CHOKER WILL PROTECT YOU!

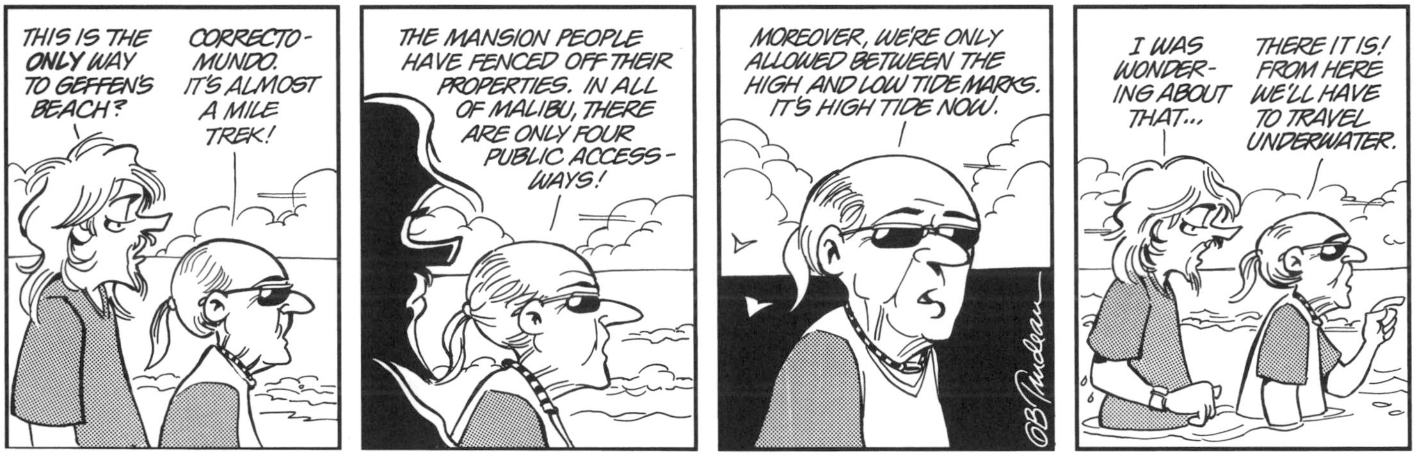
THIS IS THE **ONLY** WAY TO GEFFEN'S BEACH?
CORRECTOMUNDO. IT'S ALMOST A MILE TREK!
THE MANSION PEOPLE HAVE FENCED OFF THEIR PROPERTIES. IN ALL OF MALIBU, THERE ARE ONLY FOUR PUBLIC ACCESSWAYS!
MOREOVER, WE'RE ONLY ALLOWED BETWEEN THE HIGH AND LOW TIDE MARKS. IT'S HIGH TIDE NOW.
I WAS WONDERING ABOUT THAT...
THERE IT IS! FROM HERE WE'LL HAVE TO TRAVEL UNDERWATER.

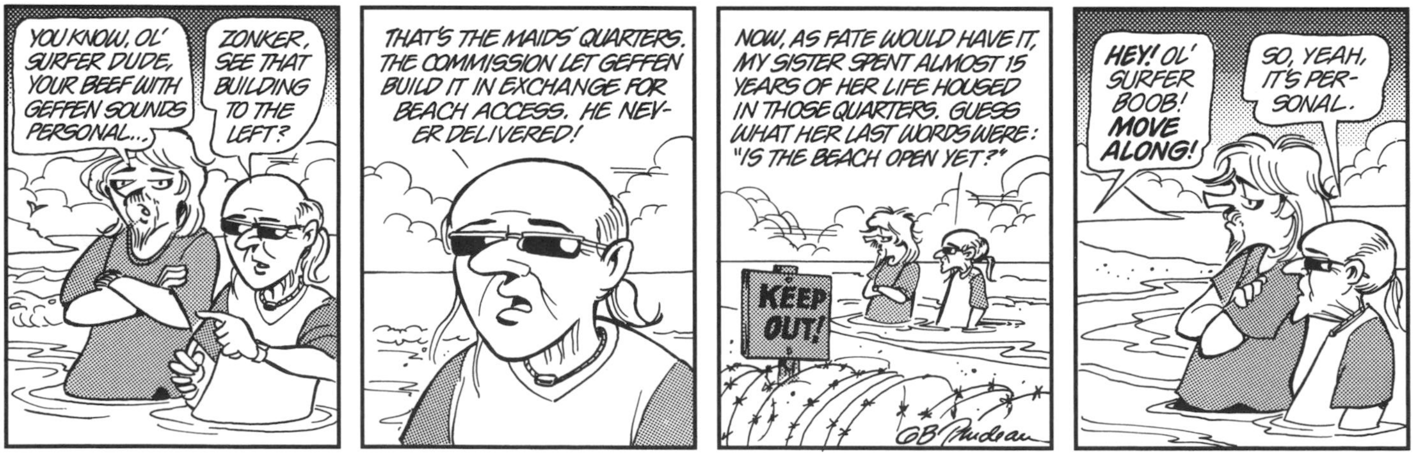
YOU KNOW, OL' SURFER DUDE, YOUR BEEF WITH GEFFEN SOUNDS PERSONAL...
ZONKER, SEE THAT BUILDING TO THE LEFT?
THAT'S THE MAIDS' QUARTERS. THE COMMISSION LET GEFFEN BUILD IT IN EXCHANGE FOR BEACH ACCESS. HE NEVER DELIVERED!
NOW, AS FATE WOULD HAVE IT, MY SISTER SPENT ALMOST 15 YEARS OF HER LIFE HOUSED IN THOSE QUARTERS. GUESS WHAT HER LAST WORDS WERE: "IS THE BEACH OPEN YET?"
KEEP OUT!
**HEY!** OL' SURFER BOOB! **MOVE ALONG!**
SO, YEAH, IT'S PERSONAL.

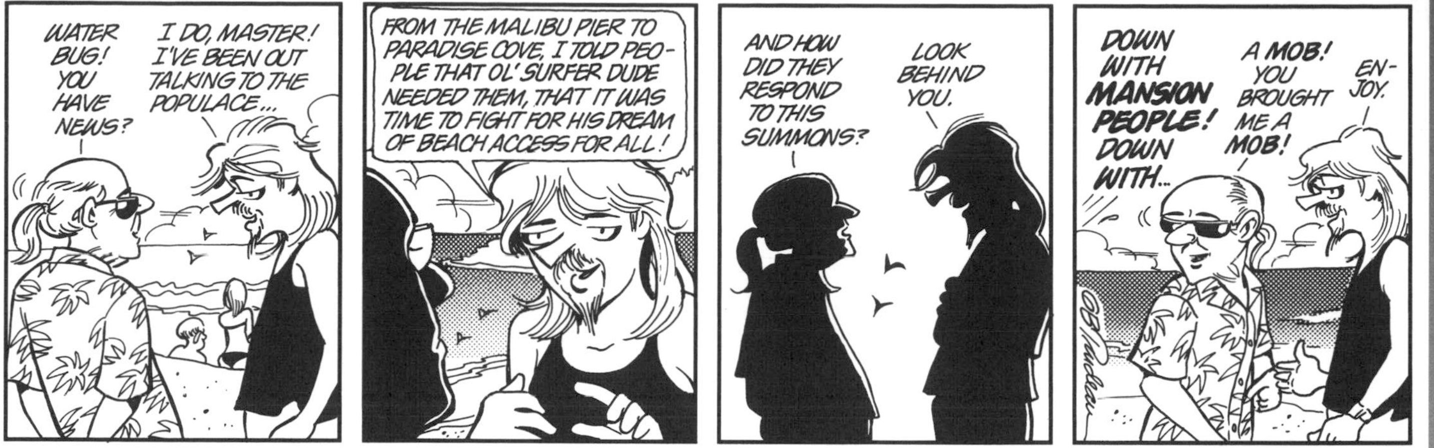
WATER BUG! YOU HAVE NEWS?
I DO, MASTER! I'VE BEEN OUT TALKING TO THE POPULACE...
FROM THE MALIBU PIER TO PARADISE COVE, I TOLD PEOPLE THAT OL' SURFER DUDE NEEDED THEM, THAT IT WAS TIME TO FIGHT FOR HIS DREAM OF BEACH ACCESS FOR ALL!
AND HOW DID THEY RESPOND TO THIS SUMMONS?
LOOK BEHIND YOU.
DOWN WITH MANSION PEOPLE! DOWN WITH...
A MOB! YOU BROUGHT ME A MOB!
ENJOY.

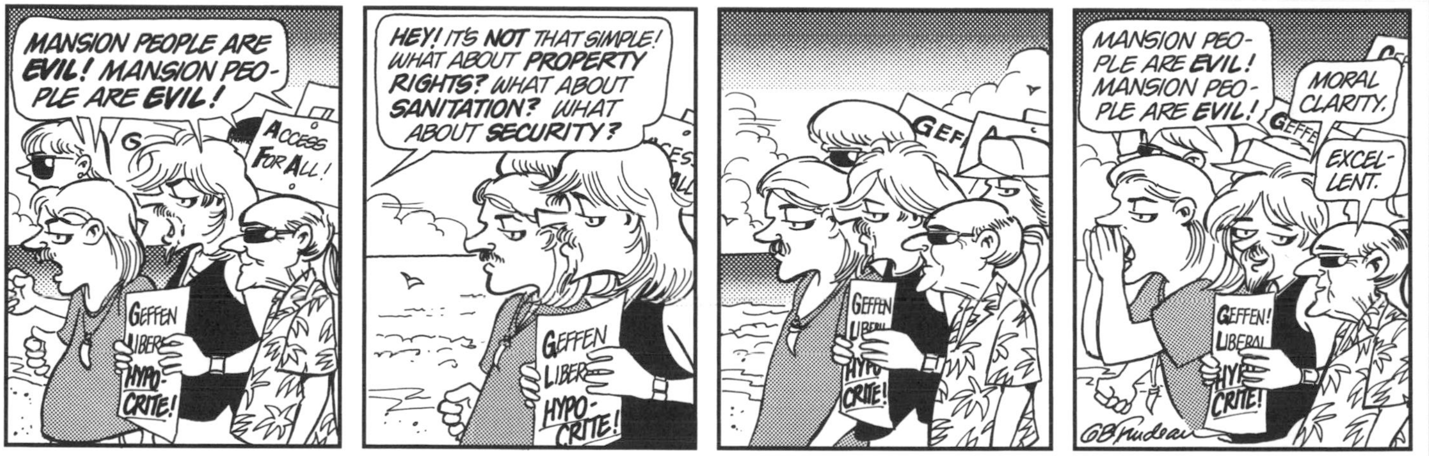
MANSION PEOPLE ARE EVIL! MANSION PEOPLE ARE EVIL!
ACCESS FOR ALL!
GEFFEN LIBERAL HYPOCRITE!
HEY! IT'S NOT THAT SIMPLE! WHAT ABOUT PROPERTY RIGHTS? WHAT ABOUT SANITATION? WHAT ABOUT SECURITY?
MANSION PEOPLE ARE EVIL! MANSION PEOPLE ARE EVIL!
MORAL CLARITY.
EXCELLENT.

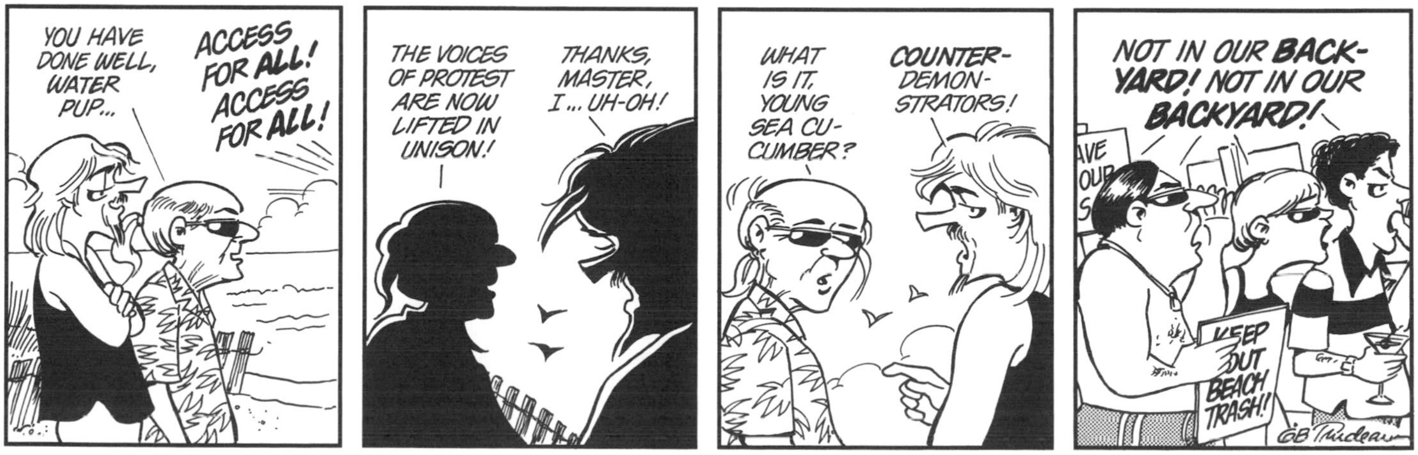
YOU HAVE DONE WELL, WATER PUP...
ACCESS FOR ALL! ACCESS FOR ALL!
THE VOICES OF PROTEST ARE NOW LIFTED IN UNISON!
THANKS, MASTER, I... UH-OH!
WHAT IS IT, YOUNG SEA CUCUMBER?
COUNTER-DEMONSTRATORS!
NOT IN OUR BACKYARD! NOT IN OUR BACKYARD!
KEEP OUT BEACH TRASH!

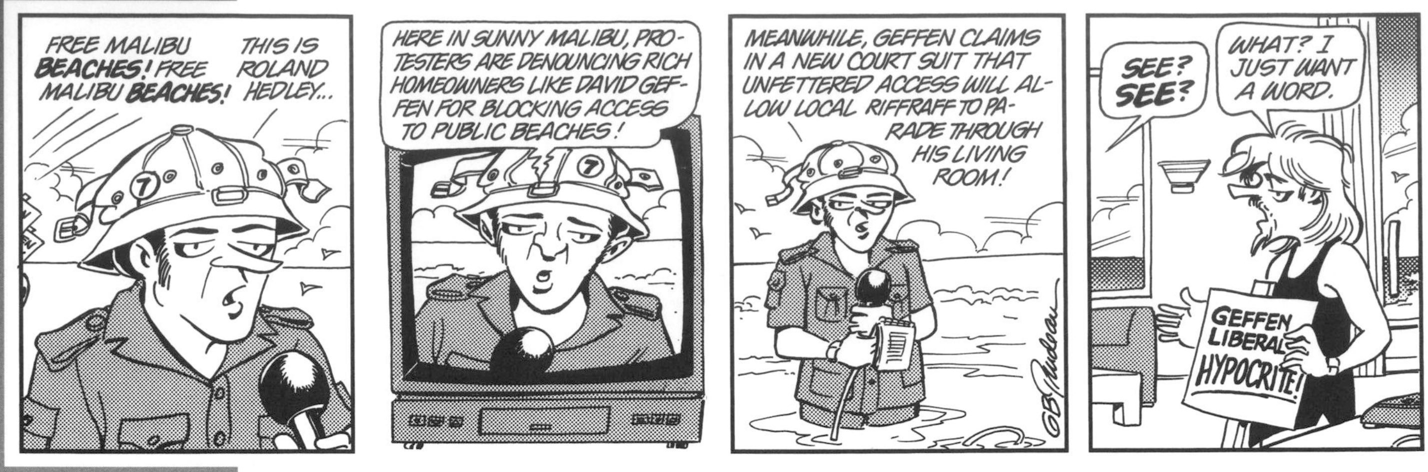
FREE MALIBU BEACHES! FREE MALIBU BEACHES!
THIS IS ROLAND HEDLEY...
HERE IN SUNNY MALIBU, PROTESTERS ARE DENOUNCING RICH HOMEOWNERS LIKE DAVID GEFFEN FOR BLOCKING ACCESS TO PUBLIC BEACHES!
MEANWHILE, GEFFEN CLAIMS IN A NEW COURT SUIT THAT UNFETTERED ACCESS WILL ALLOW LOCAL RIFFRAFF TO PARADE THROUGH HIS LIVING ROOM!
SEE? SEE?
WHAT? I JUST WANT A WORD.
GEFFEN LIBERAL HYPOCRITE!

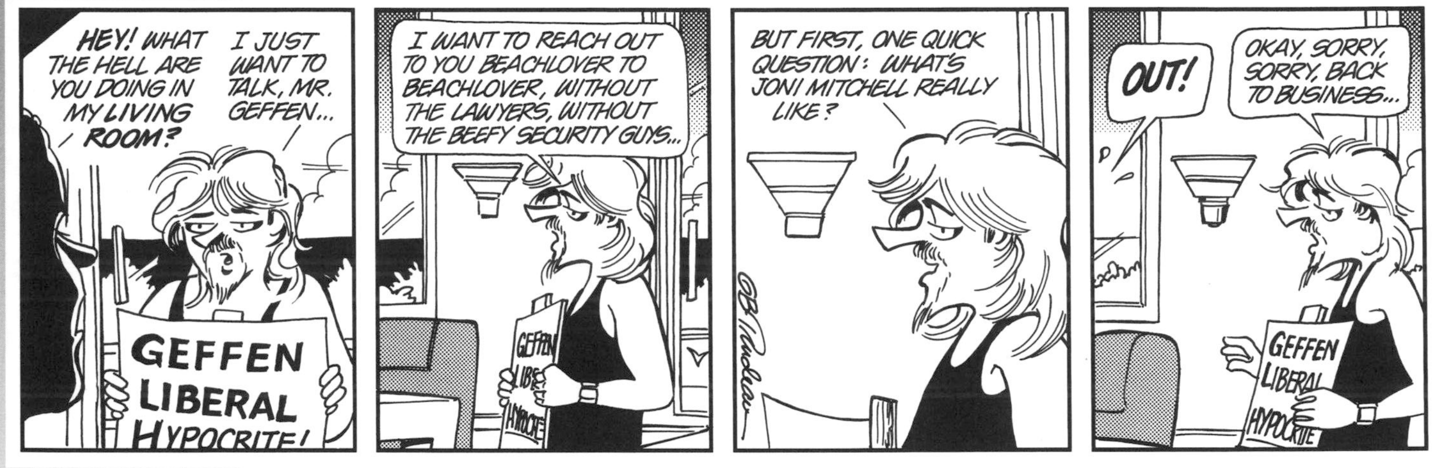
HEY! WHAT THE HELL ARE YOU DOING IN MY LIVING ROOM?
I JUST WANT TO TALK, MR. GEFFEN...
GEFFEN LIBERAL HYPOCRITE!
I WANT TO REACH OUT TO YOU BEACHLOVER TO BEACHLOVER, WITHOUT THE LAWYERS, WITHOUT THE BEEFY SECURITY GUYS...
BUT FIRST, ONE QUICK QUESTION: WHAT'S JONI MITCHELL REALLY LIKE?
OUT!
OKAY, SORRY, SORRY, BACK TO BUSINESS...
GEFFEN LIBERAL HYPOCRITE

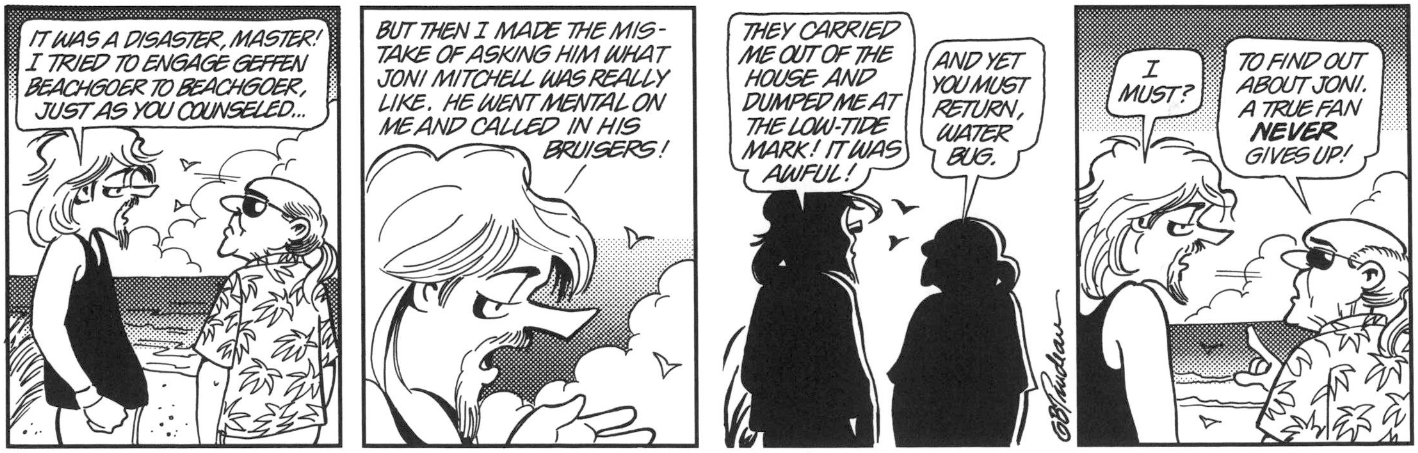
IT WAS A DISASTER, MASTER! I TRIED TO ENGAGE GEFFEN BEACHGOER TO BEACHGOER, JUST AS YOU COUNSELED...
BUT THEN I MADE THE MISTAKE OF ASKING HIM WHAT JONI MITCHELL WAS REALLY LIKE. HE WENT MENTAL ON ME AND CALLED IN HIS BRUISERS!
THEY CARRIED ME OUT OF THE HOUSE AND DUMPED ME AT THE LOW-TIDE MARK! IT WAS AWFUL!
AND YET YOU MUST RETURN, WATER BUG.
I MUST?
TO FIND OUT ABOUT JONI. A TRUE FAN NEVER GIVES UP!

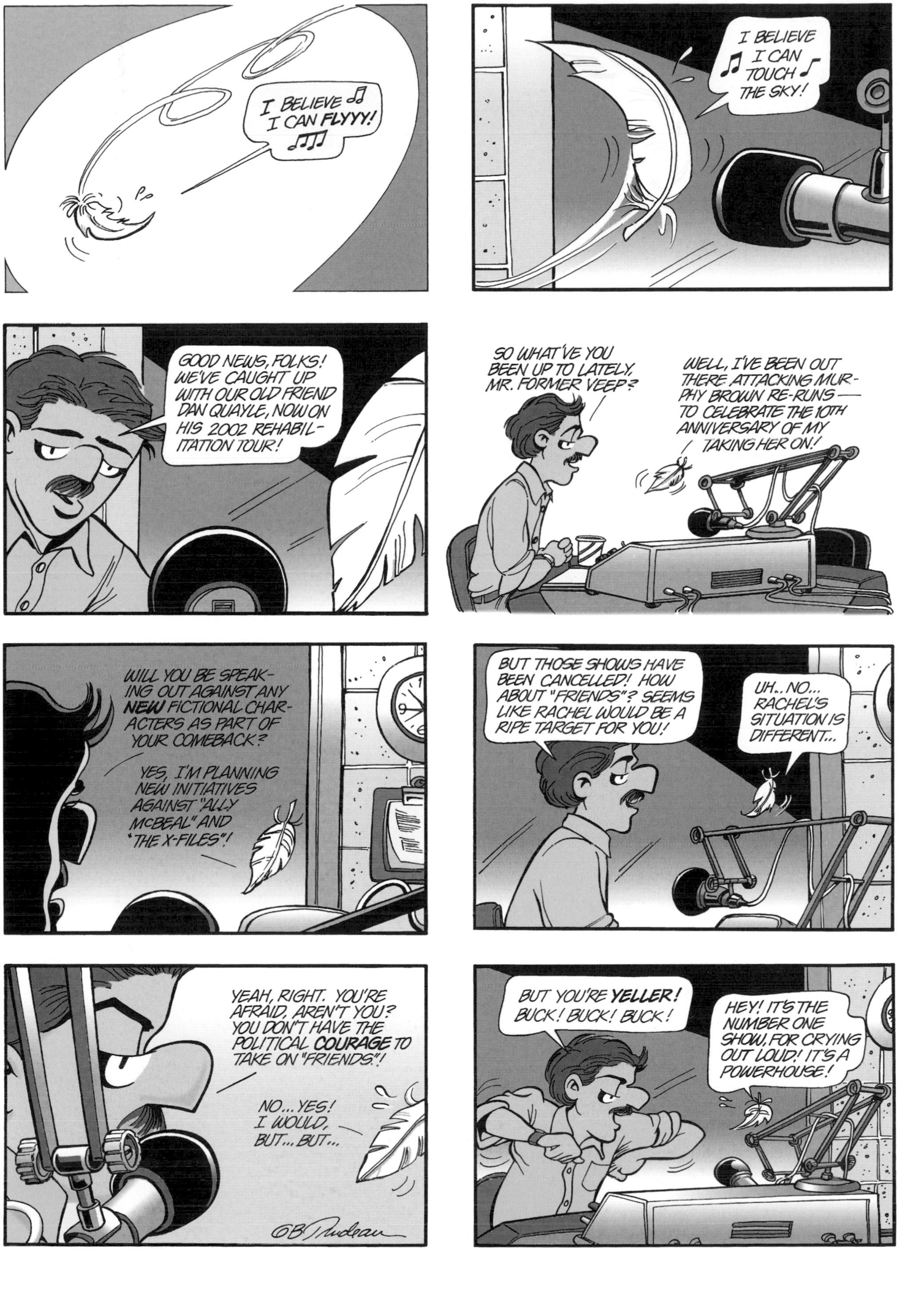
I BELIEVE ♫ I CAN FLYYY! ♫♫
I BELIEVE ♫ I CAN TOUCH ♪ THE SKY!
GOOD NEWS, FOLKS! WE'VE CAUGHT UP WITH OUR OLD FRIEND DAN QUAYLE, NOW ON HIS 2002 REHABILITATION TOUR!
SO WHAT'VE YOU BEEN UP TO LATELY, MR. FORMER VEEP?
WELL, I'VE BEEN OUT THERE ATTACKING MURPHY BROWN RE-RUNS — TO CELEBRATE THE 10TH ANNIVERSARY OF MY TAKING HER ON!
WILL YOU BE SPEAKING OUT AGAINST ANY **NEW** FICTIONAL CHARACTERS AS PART OF YOUR COMEBACK?
YES, I'M PLANNING NEW INITIATIVES AGAINST "ALLY McBEAL" AND "THE X-FILES"!
BUT THOSE SHOWS HAVE BEEN CANCELLED! HOW ABOUT "FRIENDS"? SEEMS LIKE RACHEL WOULD BE A RIPE TARGET FOR YOU!
UH.. NO... RACHEL'S SITUATION IS DIFFERENT...
YEAH, RIGHT. YOU'RE AFRAID, AREN'T YOU? YOU DON'T HAVE THE POLITICAL **COURAGE** TO TAKE ON "FRIENDS"!
NO... YES! I WOULD, BUT... BUT...
©B. Trudeau
BUT YOU'RE **YELLER!** BUCK! BUCK! BUCK!
HEY! IT'S THE NUMBER ONE SHOW, FOR CRYING OUT LOUD! IT'S A POWERHOUSE!

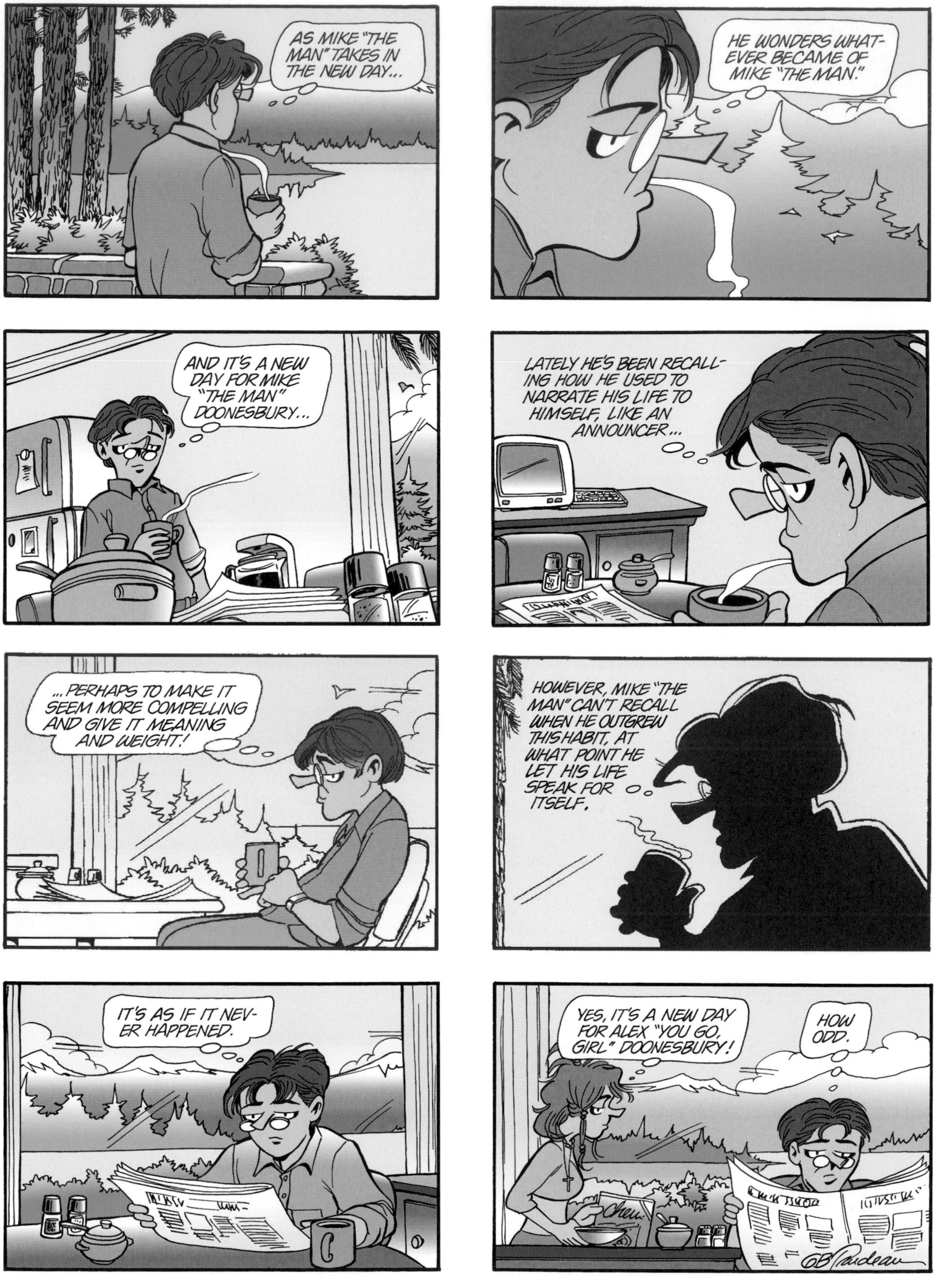

AS MIKE "THE MAN" TAKES IN THE NEW DAY...
HE WONDERS WHATEVER BECAME OF MIKE "THE MAN."
AND IT'S A NEW DAY FOR MIKE "THE MAN" DOONESBURY...
LATELY HE'S BEEN RECALLING HOW HE USED TO NARRATE HIS LIFE TO HIMSELF, LIKE AN ANNOUNCER...
...PERHAPS TO MAKE IT SEEM MORE COMPELLING AND GIVE IT MEANING AND WEIGHT!
HOWEVER, MIKE "THE MAN" CAN'T RECALL WHEN HE OUTGREW THIS HABIT, AT WHAT POINT HE LET HIS LIFE SPEAK FOR ITSELF.
IT'S AS IF IT NEVER HAPPENED.
YES, IT'S A NEW DAY FOR ALEX "YOU GO, GIRL" DOONESBURY!
HOW ODD.
GBTrudeau

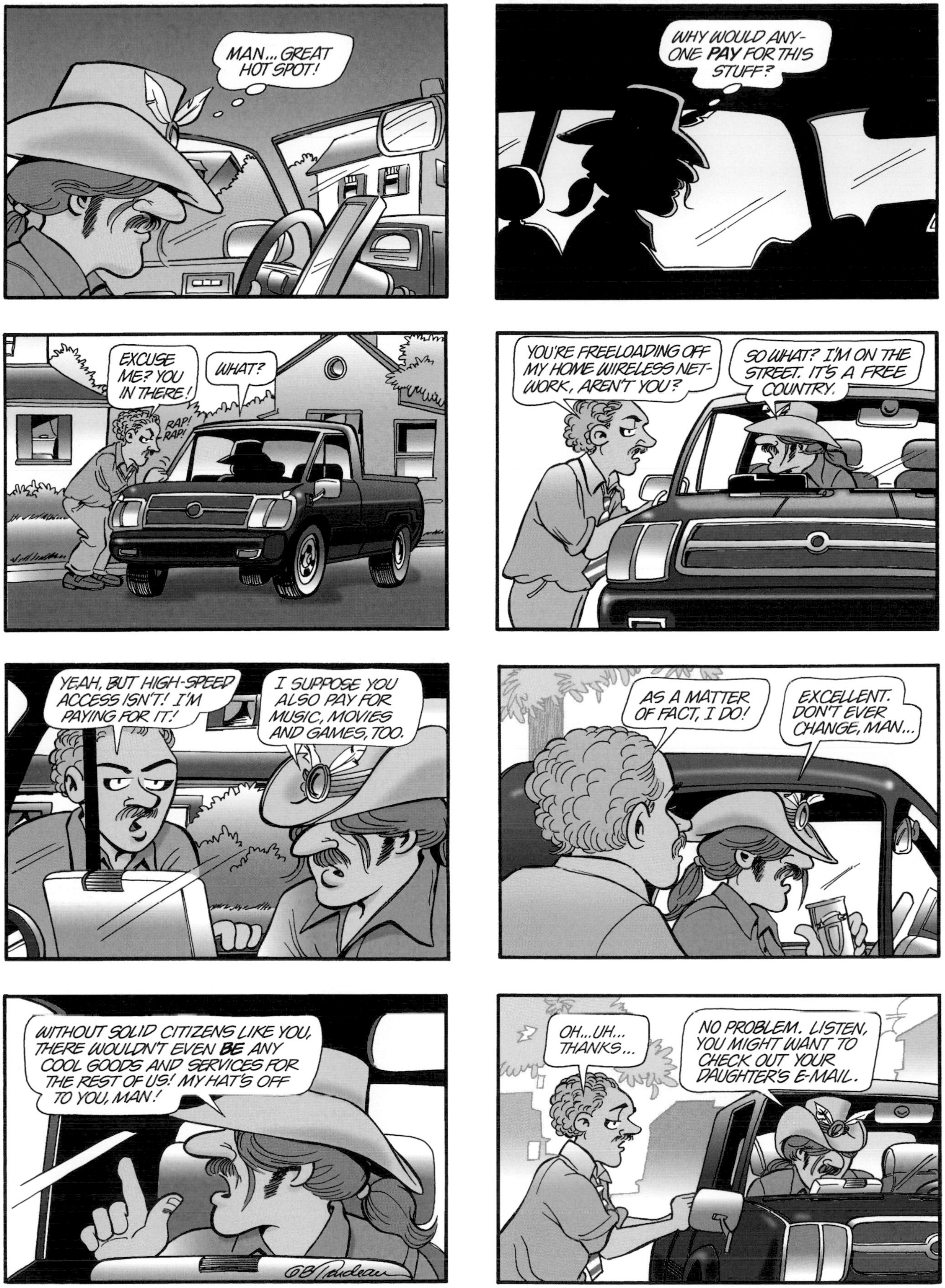
MAN... GREAT HOT SPOT!
WHY WOULD ANYONE PAY FOR THIS STUFF?
EXCUSE ME? YOU IN THERE!
RAP! RAP!
WHAT?
YOU'RE FREELOADING OFF MY HOME WIRELESS NETWORK, AREN'T YOU?
SO WHAT? I'M ON THE STREET. IT'S A FREE COUNTRY.
YEAH, BUT HIGH-SPEED ACCESS ISN'T! I'M PAYING FOR IT!
I SUPPOSE YOU ALSO PAY FOR MUSIC, MOVIES AND GAMES, TOO.
AS A MATTER OF FACT, I DO!
EXCELLENT. DON'T EVER CHANGE, MAN...
WITHOUT SOLID CITIZENS LIKE YOU, THERE WOULDN'T EVEN BE ANY COOL GOODS AND SERVICES FOR THE REST OF US! MY HAT'S OFF TO YOU, MAN!
OH...UH... THANKS...
NO PROBLEM. LISTEN, YOU MIGHT WANT TO CHECK OUT YOUR DAUGHTER'S E-MAIL.

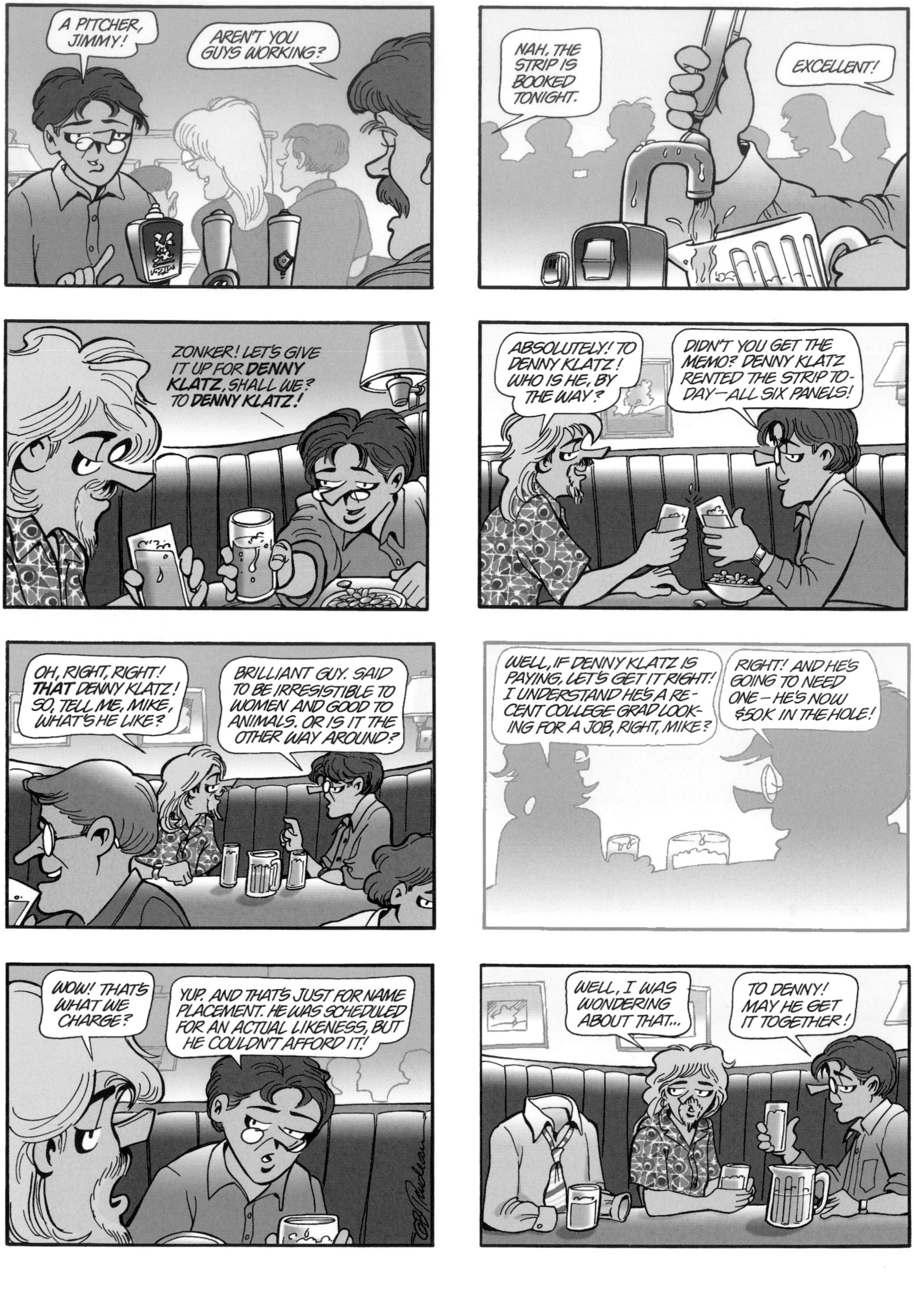
A PITCHER, JIMMY!
AREN'T YOU GUYS WORKING?
NAH, THE STRIP IS BOOKED TONIGHT.
EXCELLENT!
ZONKER! LET'S GIVE IT UP FOR **DENNY KLATZ**, SHALL WE? TO **DENNY KLATZ!**
ABSOLUTELY! TO DENNY KLATZ! WHO IS HE, BY THE WAY?
DIDN'T YOU GET THE MEMO? DENNY KLATZ RENTED THE STRIP TO-DAY—ALL SIX PANELS!
OH, RIGHT, RIGHT! **THAT** DENNY KLATZ! SO, TELL ME, MIKE, WHAT'S HE LIKE?
BRILLIANT GUY. SAID TO BE IRRESISTIBLE TO WOMEN AND GOOD TO ANIMALS. OR IS IT THE OTHER WAY AROUND?
WELL, IF DENNY KLATZ IS PAYING, LET'S GET IT RIGHT! I UNDERSTAND HE'S A RE-CENT COLLEGE GRAD LOOK-ING FOR A JOB, RIGHT, MIKE?
RIGHT! AND HE'S GOING TO NEED ONE – HE'S NOW $50K IN THE HOLE!
WOW! THAT'S WHAT WE CHARGE?
YUP. AND THAT'S JUST FOR NAME PLACEMENT. HE WAS SCHEDULED FOR AN ACTUAL LIKENESS, BUT HE COULDN'T AFFORD IT!
WELL, I WAS WONDERING ABOUT THAT...
TO DENNY! MAY HE GET IT TOGETHER!

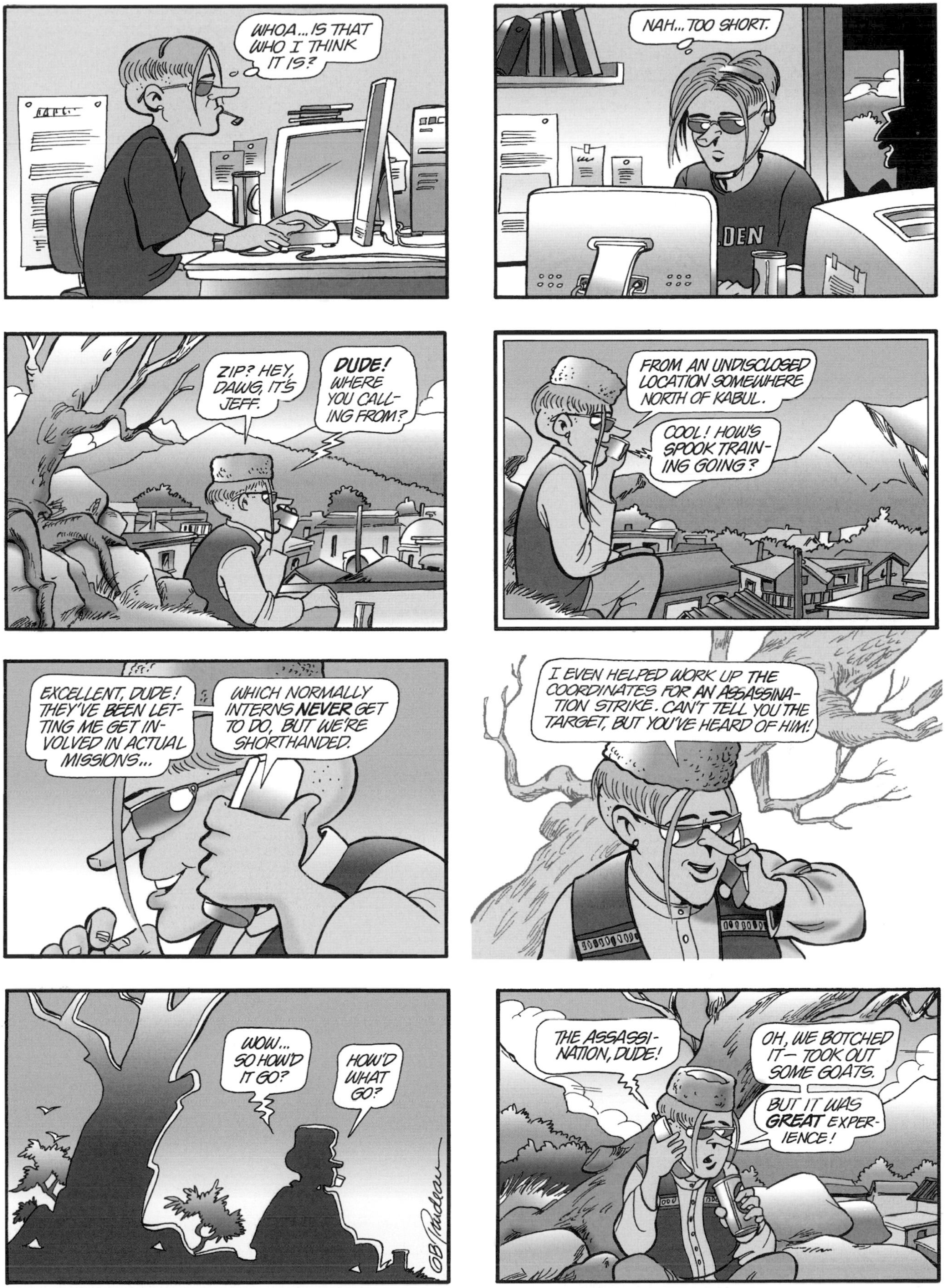
WHOA... IS THAT WHO I THINK IT IS?
NAH... TOO SHORT.
ZIP? HEY, DAWG, IT'S JEFF.
DUDE! WHERE YOU CALLING FROM?
FROM AN UNDISCLOSED LOCATION SOMEWHERE NORTH OF KABUL.
COOL! HOW'S SPOOK TRAINING GOING?
EXCELLENT, DUDE! THEY'VE BEEN LETTING ME GET INVOLVED IN ACTUAL MISSIONS...
WHICH NORMALLY INTERNS NEVER GET TO DO, BUT WE'RE SHORTHANDED.
I EVEN HELPED WORK UP THE COORDINATES FOR AN ASSASSINATION STRIKE. CAN'T TELL YOU THE TARGET, BUT YOU'VE HEARD OF HIM!
WOW... SO HOW'D IT GO?
HOW'D WHAT GO?
THE ASSASSINATION, DUDE!
OH, WE BOTCHED IT— TOOK OUT SOME GOATS.
BUT IT WAS GREAT EXPERIENCE!

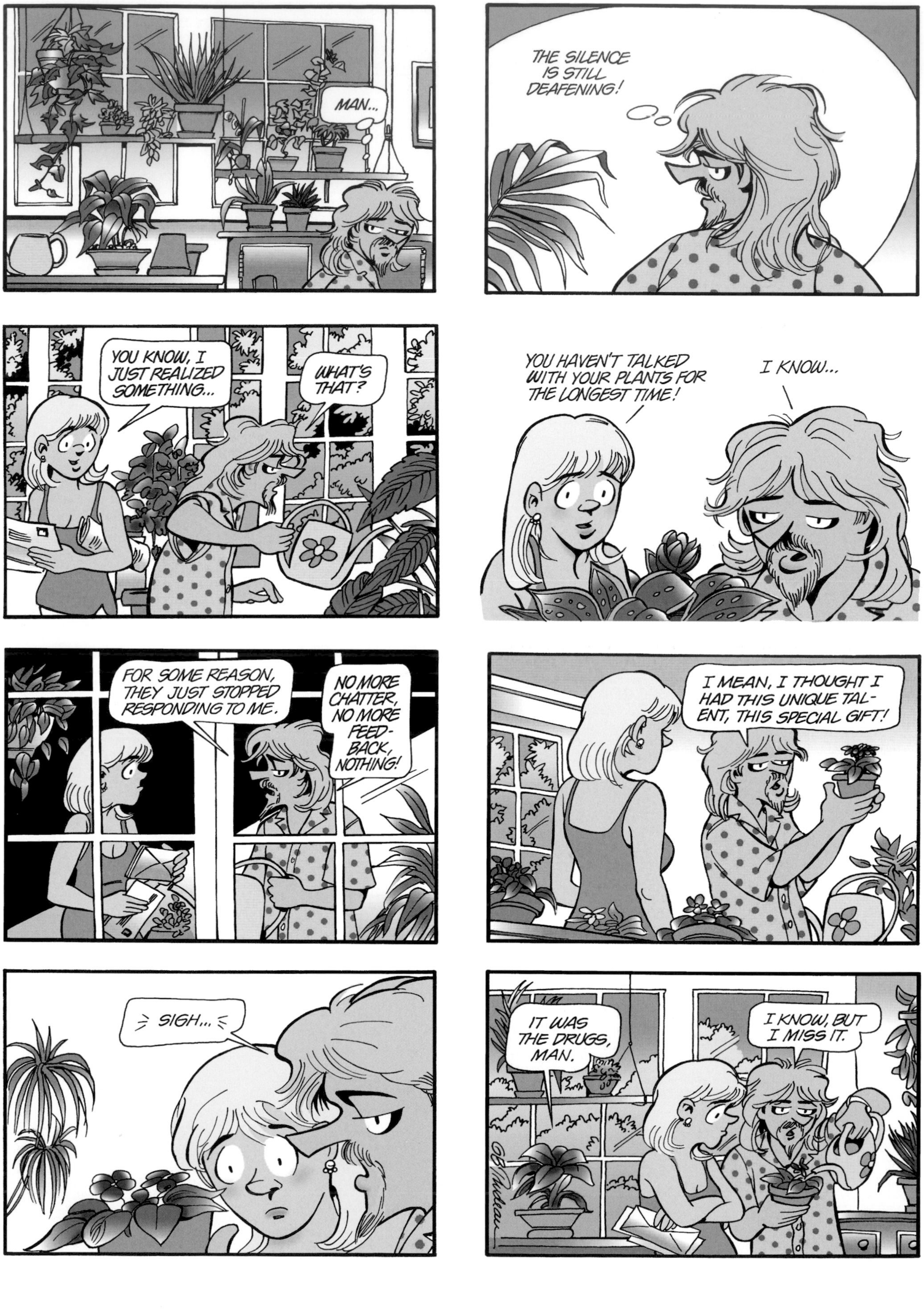
MAN...
THE SILENCE IS STILL DEAFENING!
YOU KNOW, I JUST REALIZED SOMETHING...
WHAT'S THAT?
YOU HAVEN'T TALKED WITH YOUR PLANTS FOR THE LONGEST TIME!
I KNOW...
FOR SOME REASON, THEY JUST STOPPED RESPONDING TO ME.
NO MORE CHATTER, NO MORE FEED-BACK, NOTHING!
I MEAN, I THOUGHT I HAD THIS UNIQUE TAL-ENT, THIS SPECIAL GIFT!
SIGH...
IT WAS THE DRUGS, MAN.
I KNOW, BUT I MISS IT.

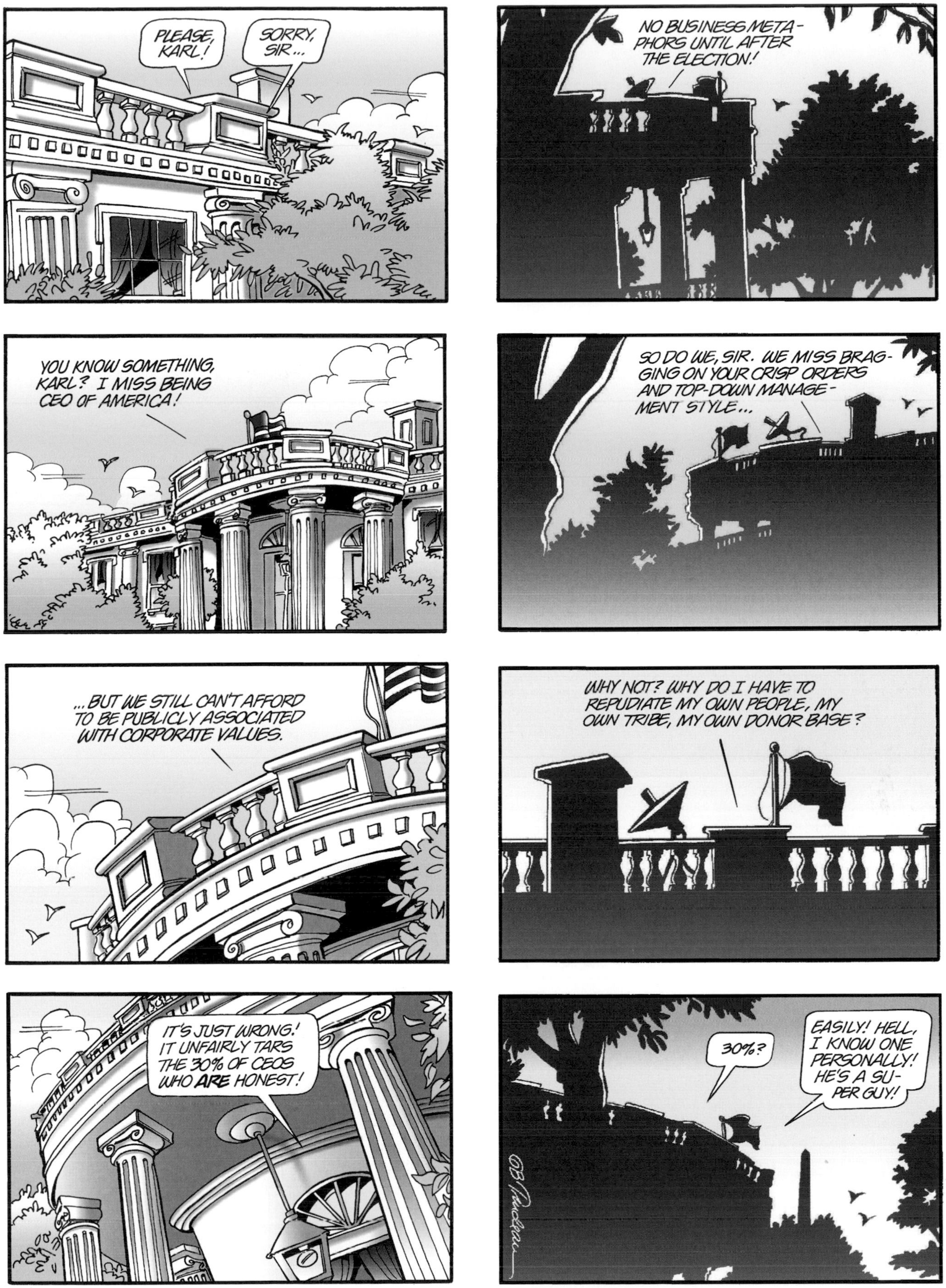
PLEASE, KARL!
SORRY, SIR...
NO BUSINESS METAPHORS UNTIL AFTER THE ELECTION!
YOU KNOW SOMETHING, KARL? I MISS BEING CEO OF AMERICA!
SO DO WE, SIR. WE MISS BRAGGING ON YOUR CRISP ORDERS AND TOP-DOWN MANAGEMENT STYLE...
...BUT WE STILL CAN'T AFFORD TO BE PUBLICLY ASSOCIATED WITH CORPORATE VALUES.
WHY NOT? WHY DO I HAVE TO REPUDIATE MY OWN PEOPLE, MY OWN TRIBE, MY OWN DONOR BASE?
IT'S JUST WRONG! IT UNFAIRLY TARS THE 30% OF CEOS WHO **ARE** HONEST!
30%?
EASILY! HELL, I KNOW ONE PERSONALLY! HE'S A SUPER GUY!

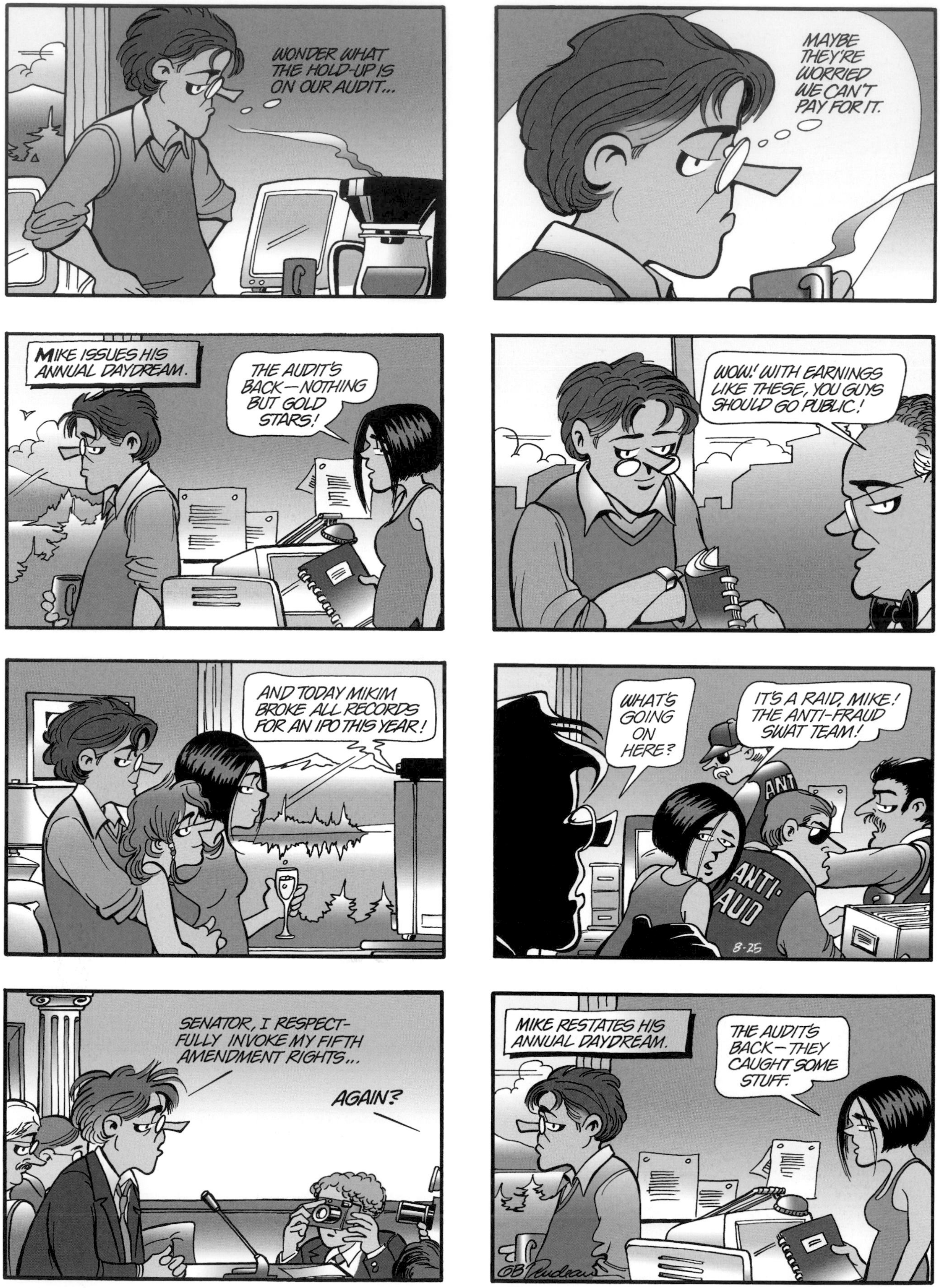

WONDER WHAT THE HOLD-UP IS ON OUR AUDIT...
MAYBE THEY'RE WORRIED WE CAN'T PAY FOR IT.
MIKE ISSUES HIS ANNUAL DAYDREAM.
THE AUDIT'S BACK—NOTHING BUT GOLD STARS!
WOW! WITH EARNINGS LIKE THESE, YOU GUYS SHOULD GO PUBLIC!
AND TODAY MIKIM BROKE ALL RECORDS FOR AN IPO THIS YEAR!
WHAT'S GOING ON HERE?
IT'S A RAID, MIKE! THE ANTI-FRAUD SWAT TEAM!
ANTI
ANTI-FRAUD
8-25
SENATOR, I RESPECT-FULLY INVOKE MY FIFTH AMENDMENT RIGHTS...
AGAIN?
MIKE RESTATES HIS ANNUAL DAYDREAM.
THE AUDIT'S BACK—THEY CAUGHT SOME STUFF.

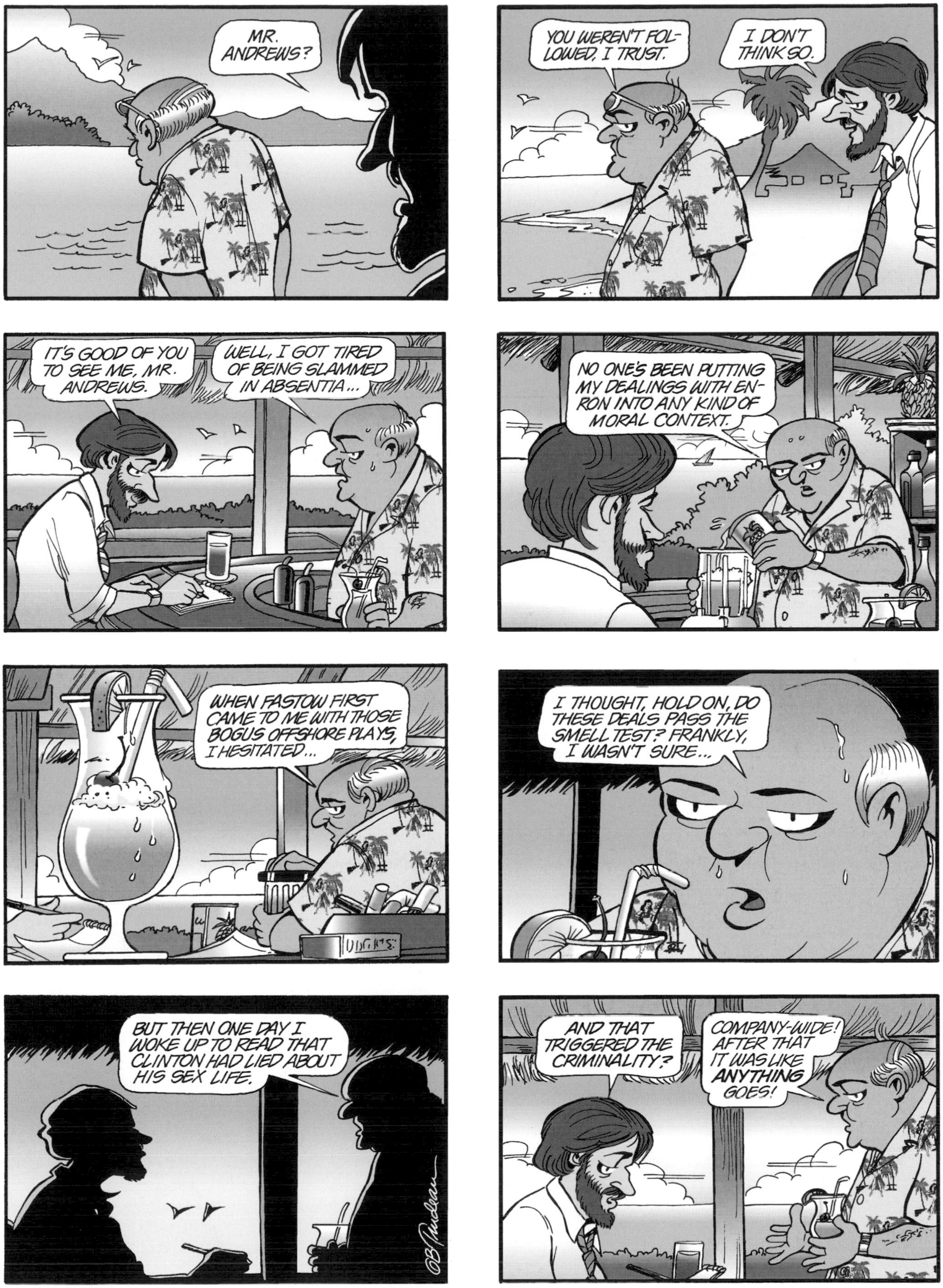
MR. ANDREWS?
YOU WEREN'T FOLLOWED, I TRUST.
I DON'T THINK SO.
IT'S GOOD OF YOU TO SEE ME, MR. ANDREWS.
WELL, I GOT TIRED OF BEING SLAMMED IN ABSENTIA...
NO ONE'S BEEN PUTTING MY DEALINGS WITH ENRON INTO ANY KIND OF MORAL CONTEXT.
WHEN FASTOW FIRST CAME TO ME WITH THOSE BOGUS OFFSHORE PLAYS, I HESITATED...
I THOUGHT, HOLD ON, DO THESE DEALS PASS THE SMELL TEST? FRANKLY, I WASN'T SURE...
BUT THEN ONE DAY I WOKE UP TO READ THAT CLINTON HAD LIED ABOUT HIS SEX LIFE.
AND THAT TRIGGERED THE CRIMINALITY?
COMPANY-WIDE! AFTER THAT IT WAS LIKE **ANYTHING** GOES!

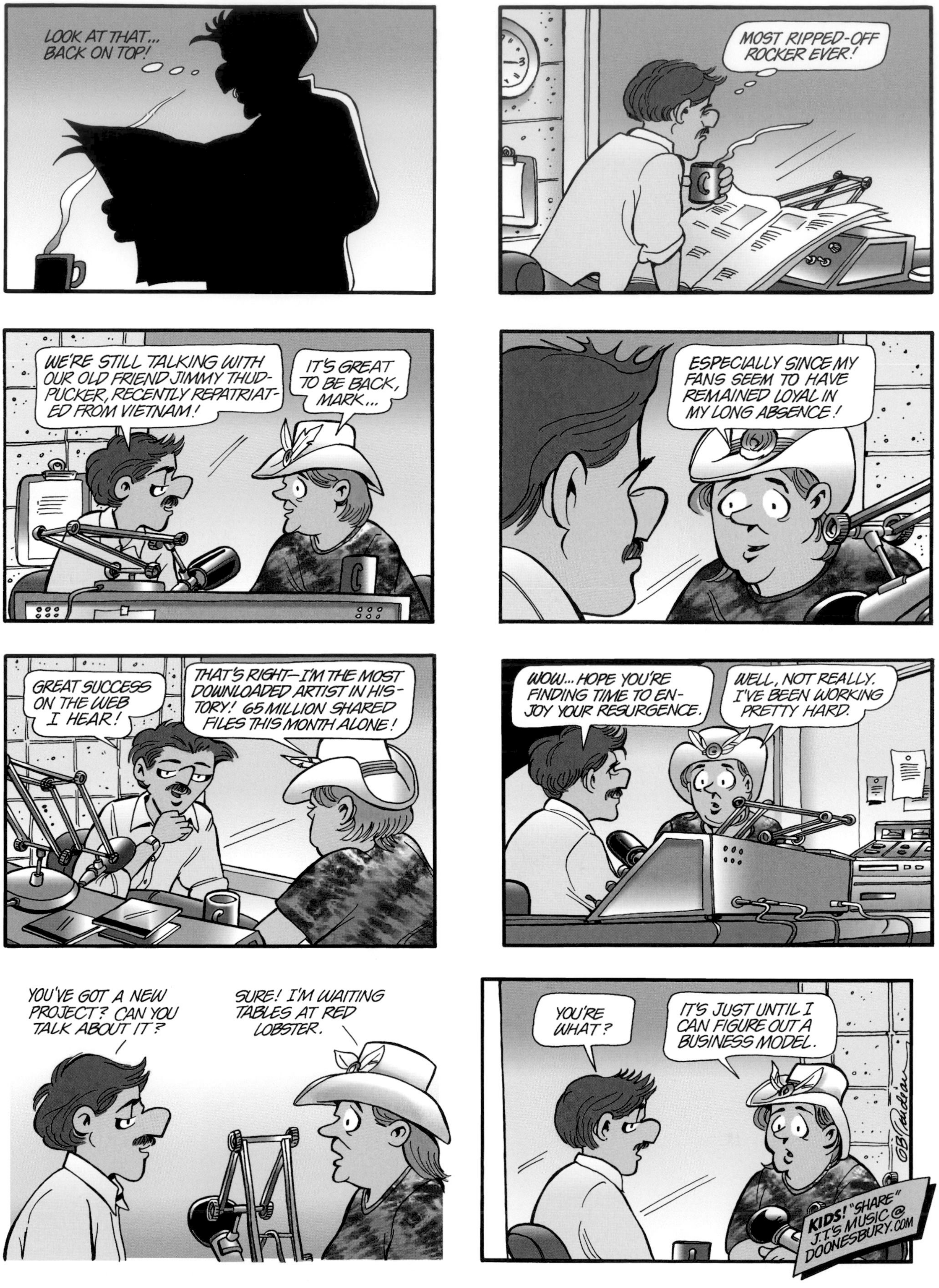
LOOK AT THAT... BACK ON TOP!
MOST RIPPED-OFF ROCKER EVER!
WE'RE STILL TALKING WITH OUR OLD FRIEND JIMMY THUDPUCKER, RECENTLY REPATRIATED FROM VIETNAM!
IT'S GREAT TO BE BACK, MARK...
ESPECIALLY SINCE MY FANS SEEM TO HAVE REMAINED LOYAL IN MY LONG ABSENCE!
GREAT SUCCESS ON THE WEB I HEAR!
THAT'S RIGHT—I'M THE MOST DOWNLOADED ARTIST IN HISTORY! 65 MILLION SHARED FILES THIS MONTH ALONE!
WOW... HOPE YOU'RE FINDING TIME TO ENJOY YOUR RESURGENCE.
WELL, NOT REALLY. I'VE BEEN WORKING PRETTY HARD.
YOU'VE GOT A NEW PROJECT? CAN YOU TALK ABOUT IT?
SURE! I'M WAITING TABLES AT RED LOBSTER.
YOU'RE WHAT?
IT'S JUST UNTIL I CAN FIGURE OUT A BUSINESS MODEL.
KIDS! "SHARE" J.T.'S MUSIC @ DOONESBURY.COM

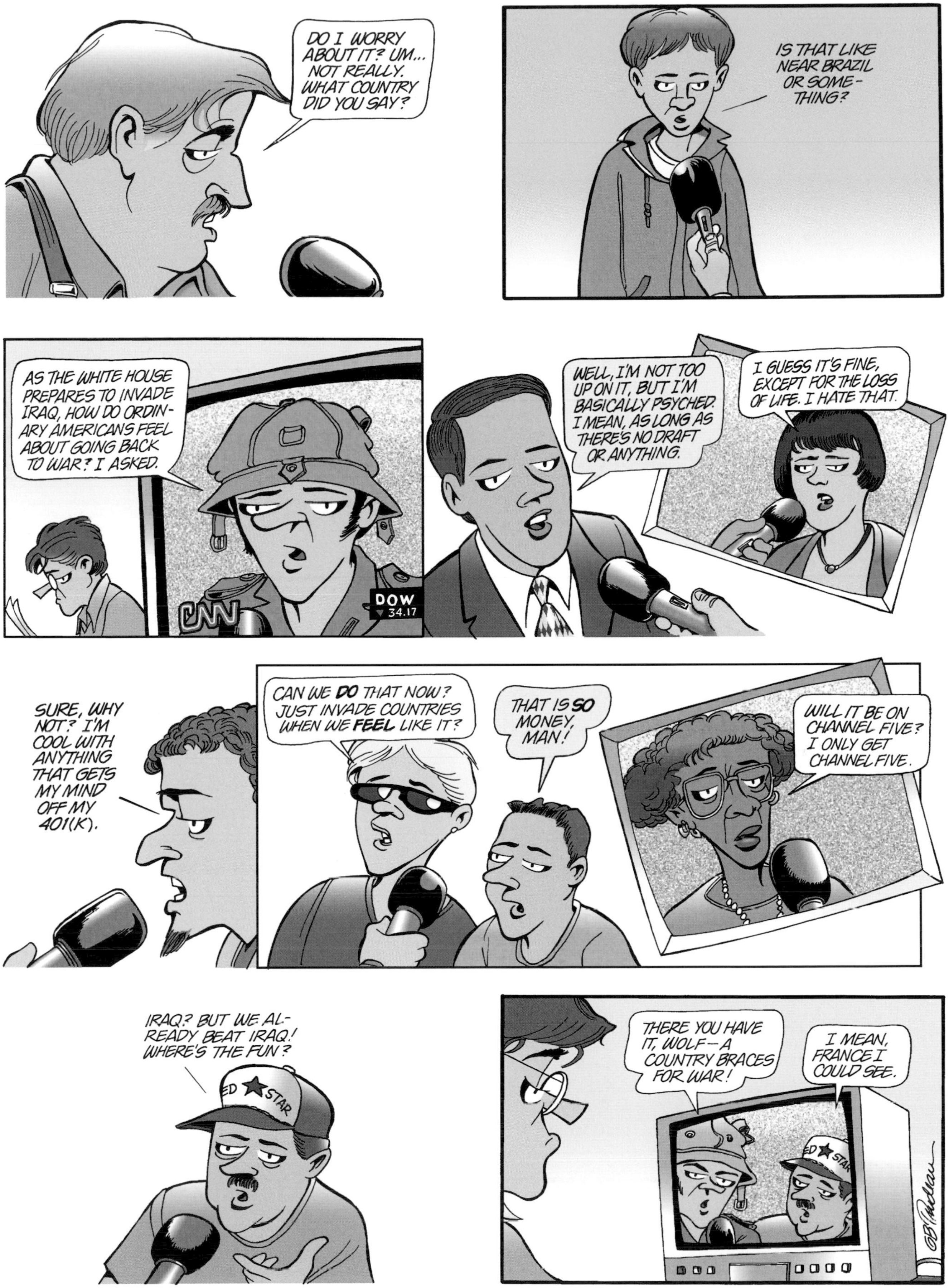

DO I WORRY ABOUT IT? UM... NOT REALLY. WHAT COUNTRY DID YOU SAY?
IS THAT LIKE NEAR BRAZIL OR SOME-THING?
AS THE WHITE HOUSE PREPARES TO INVADE IRAQ, HOW DO ORDIN-ARY AMERICANS FEEL ABOUT GOING BACK TO WAR? I ASKED.
CNN
DOW 34.17
WELL, I'M NOT TOO UP ON IT, BUT I'M BASICALLY PSYCHED. I MEAN, AS LONG AS THERE'S NO DRAFT OR ANYTHING.
I GUESS IT'S FINE, EXCEPT FOR THE LOSS OF LIFE. I HATE THAT.
SURE, WHY NOT? I'M COOL WITH ANYTHING THAT GETS MY MIND OFF MY 401(K).
CAN WE **DO** THAT NOW? JUST INVADE COUNTRIES WHEN WE **FEEL** LIKE IT?
THAT IS **SO** MONEY, MAN!
WILL IT BE ON CHANNEL FIVE? I ONLY GET CHANNEL FIVE.
IRAQ? BUT WE AL-READY BEAT IRAQ! WHERE'S THE FUN?
ED STAR
THERE YOU HAVE IT, WOLF—A COUNTRY BRACES FOR WAR!
I MEAN, FRANCE I COULD SEE.

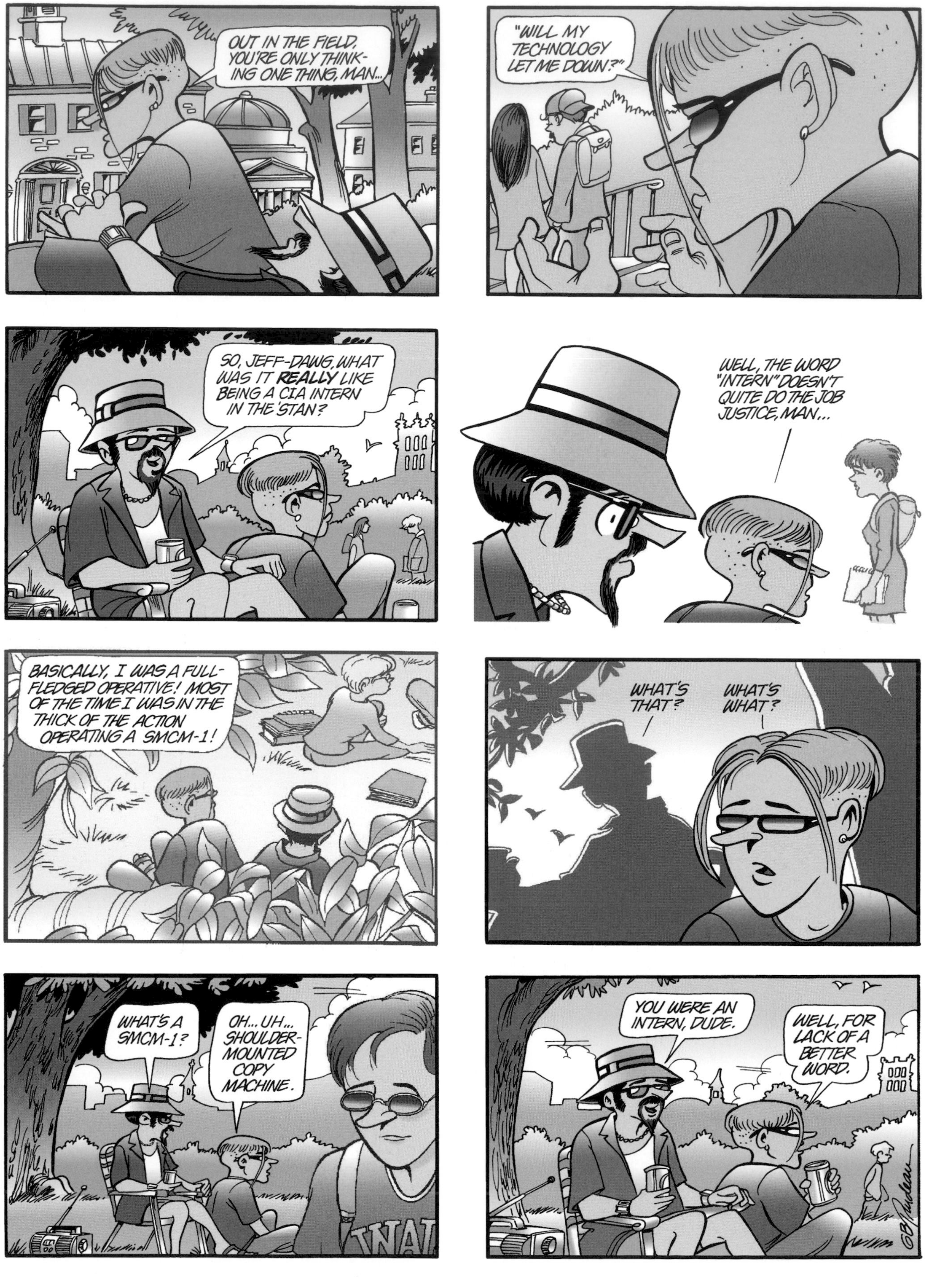
OUT IN THE FIELD, YOU'RE ONLY THINKING ONE THING, MAN...
"WILL MY TECHNOLOGY LET ME DOWN?"
SO, JEFF-DAWG, WHAT WAS IT REALLY LIKE BEING A CIA INTERN IN THE 'STAN?
WELL, THE WORD "INTERN" DOESN'T QUITE DO THE JOB JUSTICE, MAN...
BASICALLY, I WAS A FULL-FLEDGED OPERATIVE! MOST OF THE TIME I WAS IN THE THICK OF THE ACTION OPERATING A SMCM-1!
WHAT'S THAT?
WHAT'S WHAT?
WHAT'S A SMCM-1?
OH... UH... SHOULDER-MOUNTED COPY MACHINE.
YOU WERE AN INTERN, DUDE.
WELL, FOR LACK OF A BETTER WORD.

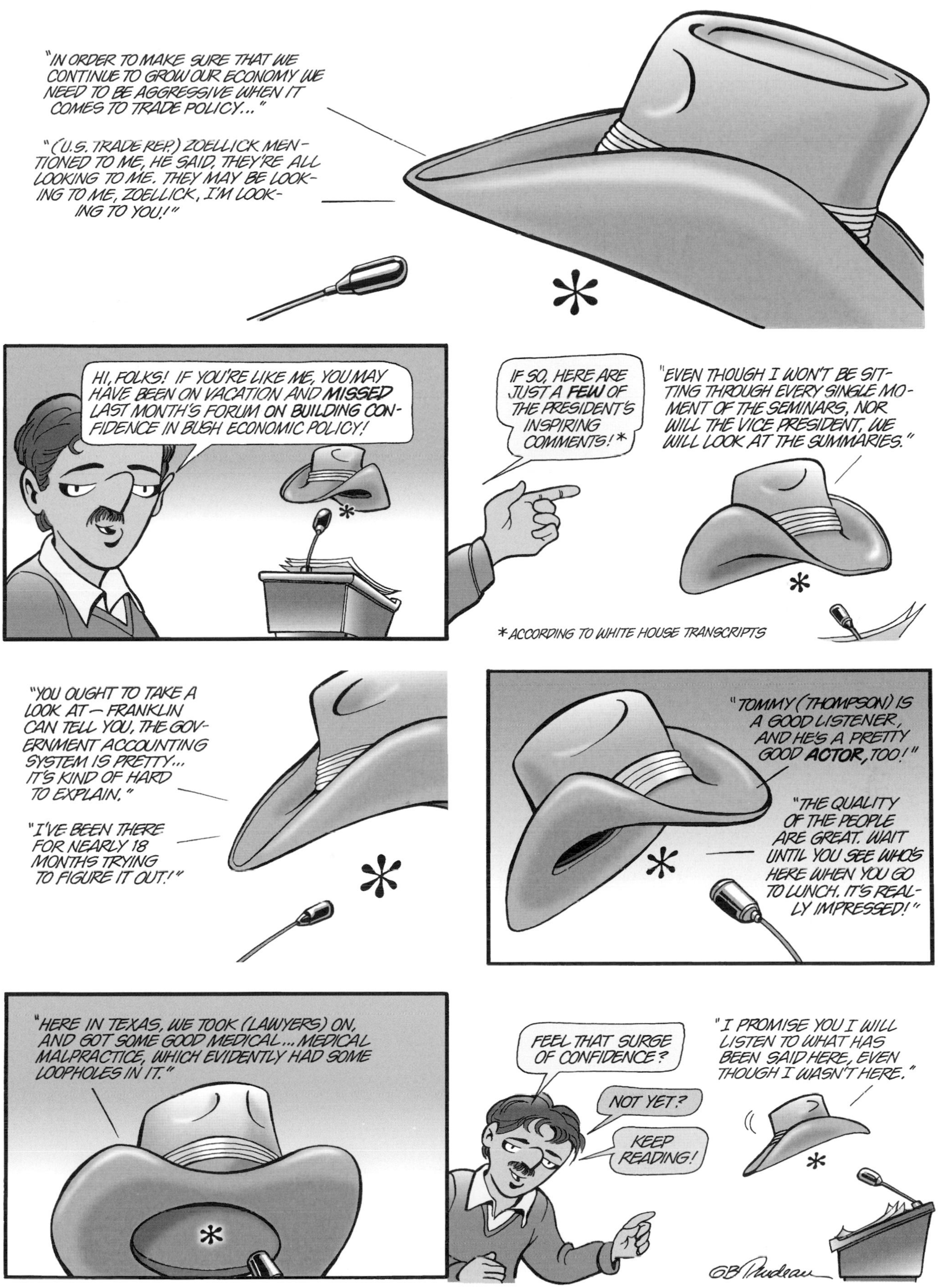
"IN ORDER TO MAKE SURE THAT WE CONTINUE TO GROW OUR ECONOMY WE NEED TO BE AGGRESSIVE WHEN IT COMES TO TRADE POLICY..."
"(U.S. TRADE REP.) ZOELLICK MENTIONED TO ME, HE SAID, THEY'RE ALL LOOKING TO ME. THEY MAY BE LOOKING TO ME, ZOELLICK, I'M LOOKING TO YOU!"
*
HI, FOLKS! IF YOU'RE LIKE ME, YOU MAY HAVE BEEN ON VACATION AND MISSED LAST MONTH'S FORUM ON BUILDING CONFIDENCE IN BUSH ECONOMIC POLICY!
IF SO, HERE ARE JUST A FEW OF THE PRESIDENT'S INSPIRING COMMENTS! *
"EVEN THOUGH I WON'T BE SITTING THROUGH EVERY SINGLE MOMENT OF THE SEMINARS, NOR WILL THE VICE PRESIDENT, WE WILL LOOK AT THE SUMMARIES."
* ACCORDING TO WHITE HOUSE TRANSCRIPTS
"YOU OUGHT TO TAKE A LOOK AT — FRANKLIN CAN TELL YOU, THE GOVERNMENT ACCOUNTING SYSTEM IS PRETTY... IT'S KIND OF HARD TO EXPLAIN."
"I'VE BEEN THERE FOR NEARLY 18 MONTHS TRYING TO FIGURE IT OUT!"
"TOMMY (THOMPSON) IS A GOOD LISTENER, AND HE'S A PRETTY GOOD ACTOR, TOO!"
"THE QUALITY OF THE PEOPLE ARE GREAT. WAIT UNTIL YOU SEE WHO'S HERE WHEN YOU GO TO LUNCH. IT'S REALLY IMPRESSED!"
"HERE IN TEXAS, WE TOOK (LAWYERS) ON, AND GOT SOME GOOD MEDICAL... MEDICAL MALPRACTICE, WHICH EVIDENTLY HAD SOME LOOPHOLES IN IT."
FEEL THAT SURGE OF CONFIDENCE?
NOT YET?
KEEP READING!
"I PROMISE YOU I WILL LISTEN TO WHAT HAS BEEN SAID HERE, EVEN THOUGH I WASN'T HERE."
GB Trudeau

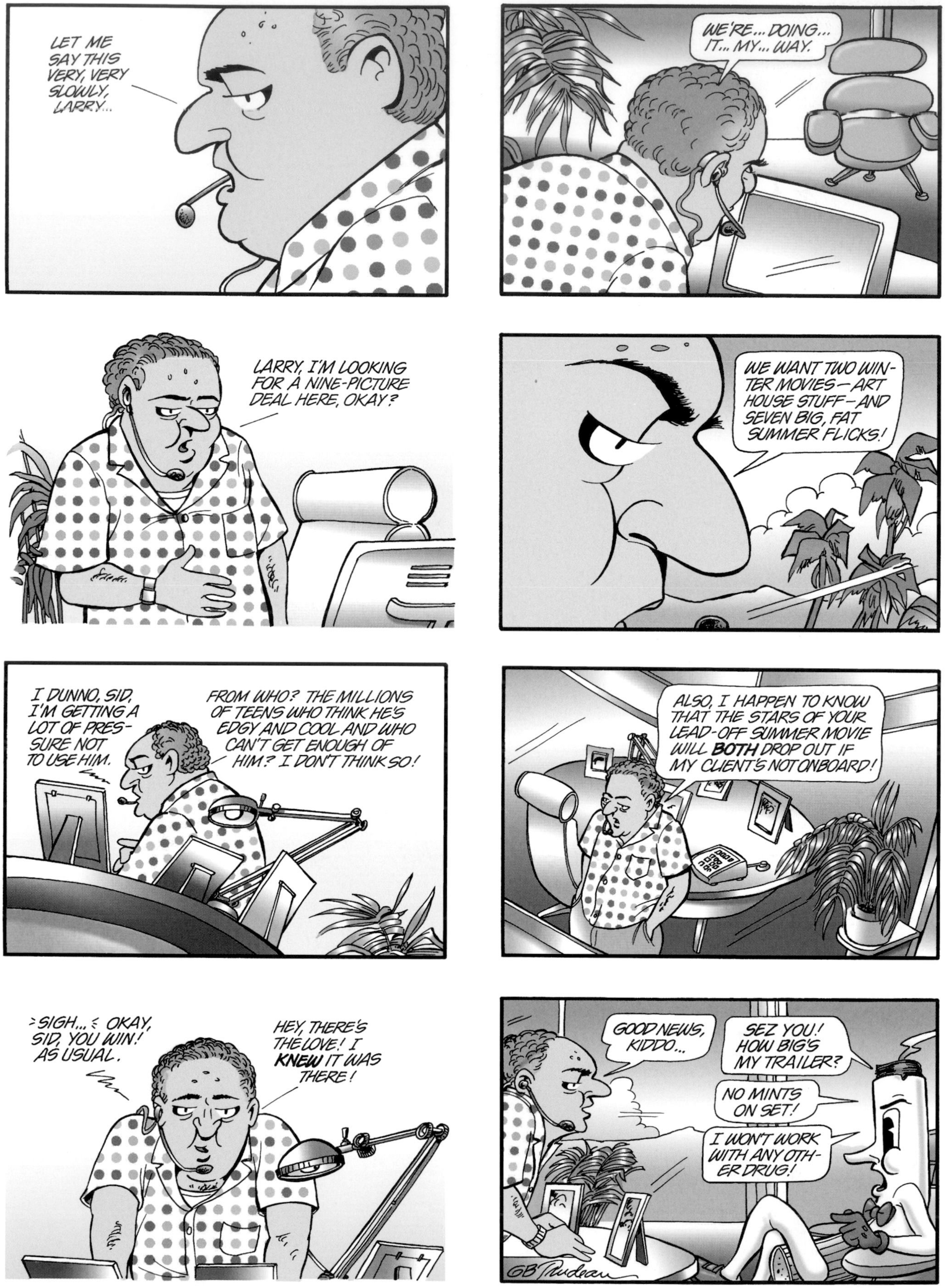
LET ME SAY THIS VERY, VERY SLOWLY, LARRY...
WE'RE... DOING... IT... MY... WAY.
LARRY, I'M LOOKING FOR A NINE-PICTURE DEAL HERE, OKAY?
WE WANT TWO WINTER MOVIES—ART HOUSE STUFF—AND SEVEN BIG, FAT SUMMER FLICKS!
I DUNNO, SID, I'M GETTING A LOT OF PRESSURE NOT TO USE HIM.
FROM WHO? THE MILLIONS OF TEENS WHO THINK HE'S EDGY AND COOL AND WHO CAN'T GET ENOUGH OF HIM? I DON'T THINK SO!
ALSO, I HAPPEN TO KNOW THAT THE STARS OF YOUR LEAD-OFF SUMMER MOVIE WILL **BOTH** DROP OUT IF MY CLIENT'S NOT ONBOARD!
≥SIGH...≤ OKAY, SID, YOU WIN! AS USUAL.
HEY, THERE'S THE LOVE! I **KNEW** IT WAS THERE!
GOOD NEWS, KIDDO...
SEZ YOU! HOW BIG'S MY TRAILER?
NO MINTS ON SET!
I WON'T WORK WITH ANY OTHER DRUG!
GB Trudeau

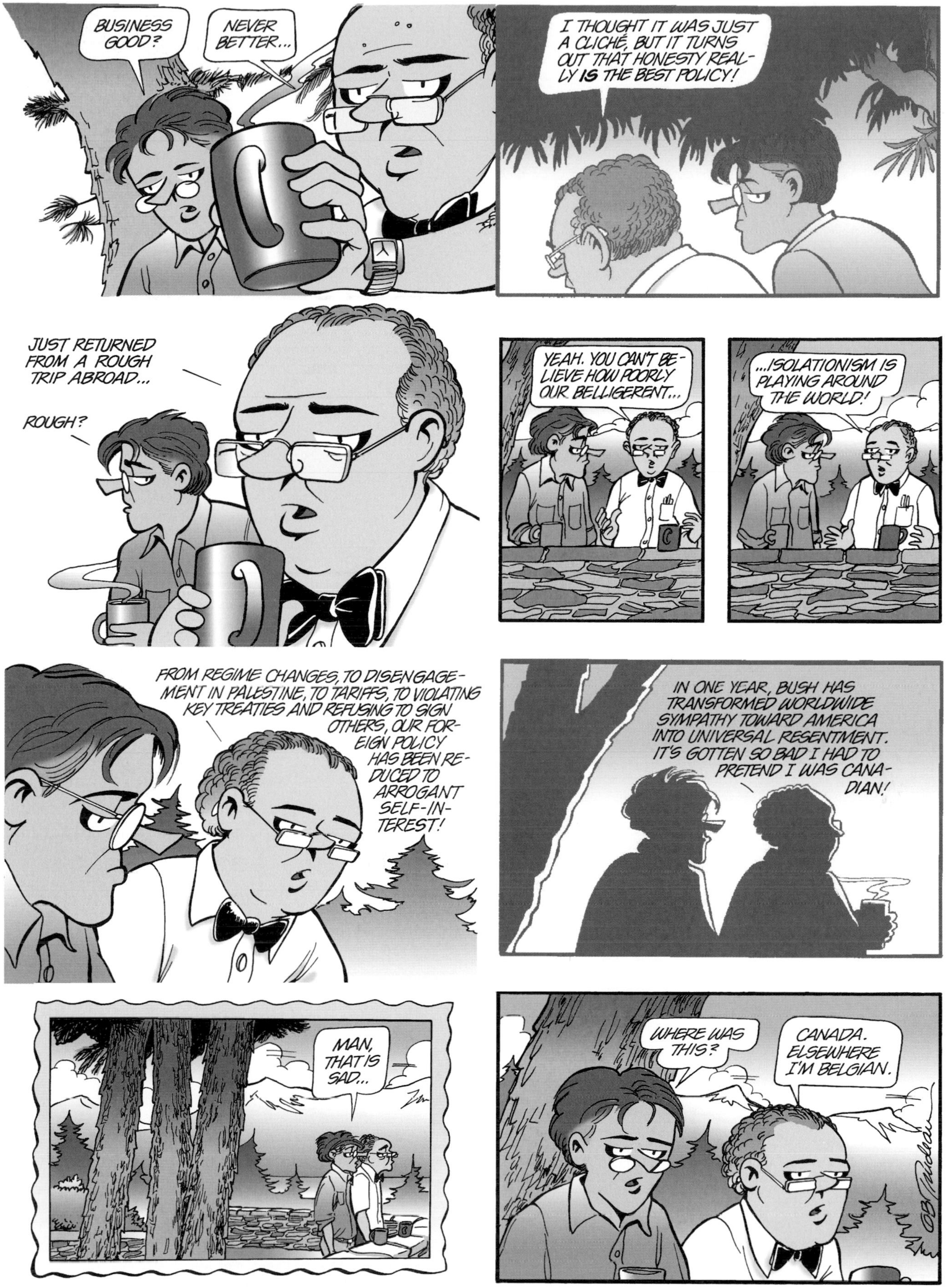
BUSINESS GOOD?
NEVER BETTER...
I THOUGHT IT WAS JUST A CLICHÉ, BUT IT TURNS OUT THAT HONESTY REALLY IS THE BEST POLICY!
JUST RETURNED FROM A ROUGH TRIP ABROAD...
ROUGH?
YEAH. YOU CAN'T BELIEVE HOW POORLY OUR BELLIGERENT...
...ISOLATIONISM IS PLAYING AROUND THE WORLD!
FROM REGIME CHANGES, TO DISENGAGEMENT IN PALESTINE, TO TARIFFS, TO VIOLATING KEY TREATIES AND REFUSING TO SIGN OTHERS, OUR FOREIGN POLICY HAS BEEN REDUCED TO ARROGANT SELF-INTEREST!
IN ONE YEAR, BUSH HAS TRANSFORMED WORLDWIDE SYMPATHY TOWARD AMERICA INTO UNIVERSAL RESENTMENT. IT'S GOTTEN SO BAD I HAD TO PRETEND I WAS CANADIAN!
MAN, THAT IS SAD...
WHERE WAS THIS?
CANADA. ELSEWHERE I'M BELGIAN.
GBTrudeau

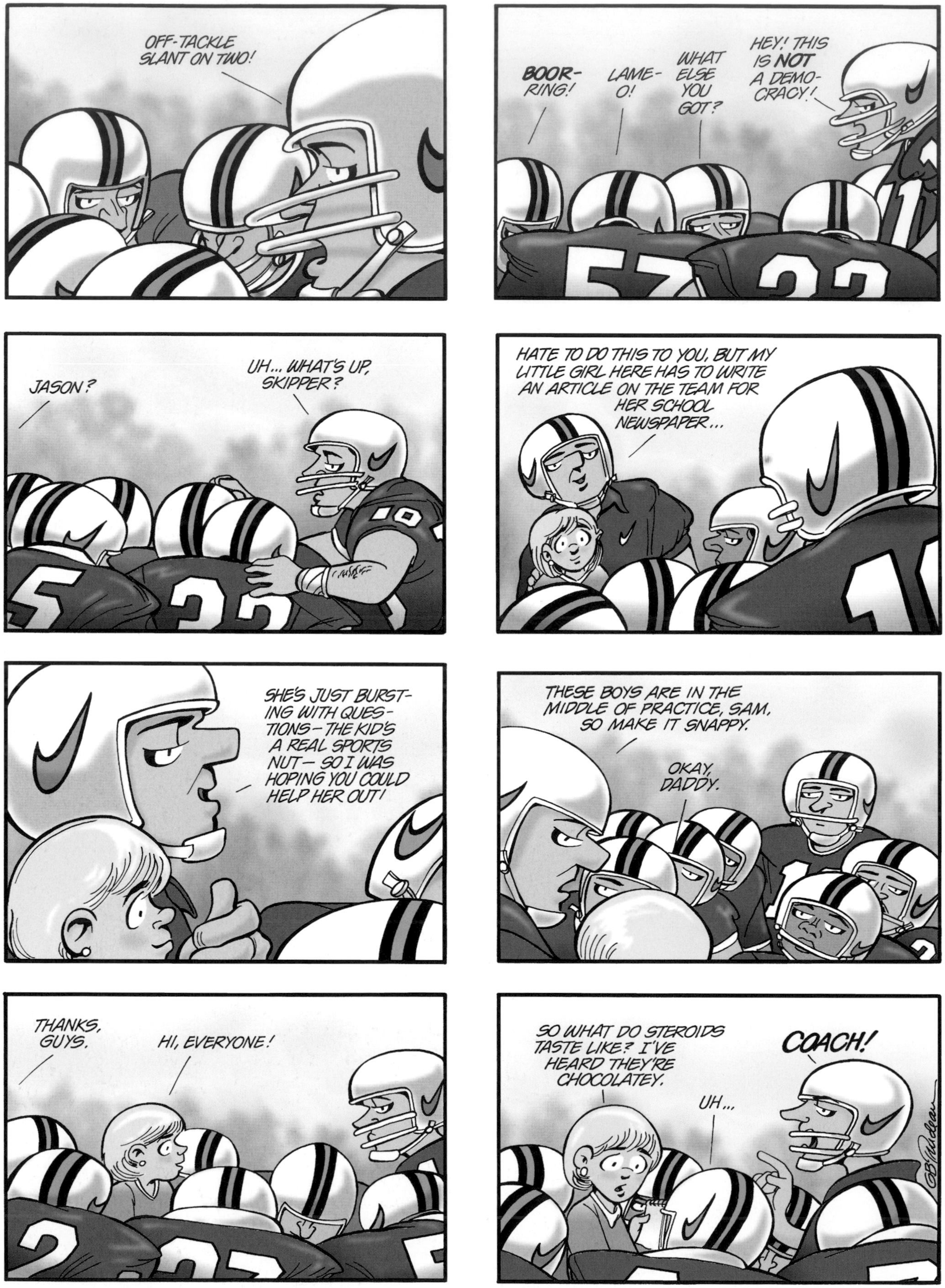
OFF-TACKLE SLANT ON TWO!
BOOR-RING!
LAME-O!
WHAT ELSE YOU GOT?
HEY! THIS IS NOT A DEMOCRACY!
JASON?
UH... WHAT'S UP, SKIPPER?
HATE TO DO THIS TO YOU, BUT MY LITTLE GIRL HERE HAS TO WRITE AN ARTICLE ON THE TEAM FOR HER SCHOOL NEWSPAPER...
SHE'S JUST BURSTING WITH QUESTIONS—THE KID'S A REAL SPORTS NUT—SO I WAS HOPING YOU COULD HELP HER OUT!
THESE BOYS ARE IN THE MIDDLE OF PRACTICE, SAM, SO MAKE IT SNAPPY.
OKAY, DADDY.
THANKS, GUYS.
HI, EVERYONE!
SO WHAT DO STEROIDS TASTE LIKE? I'VE HEARD THEY'RE CHOCOLATEY.
UH...
COACH!

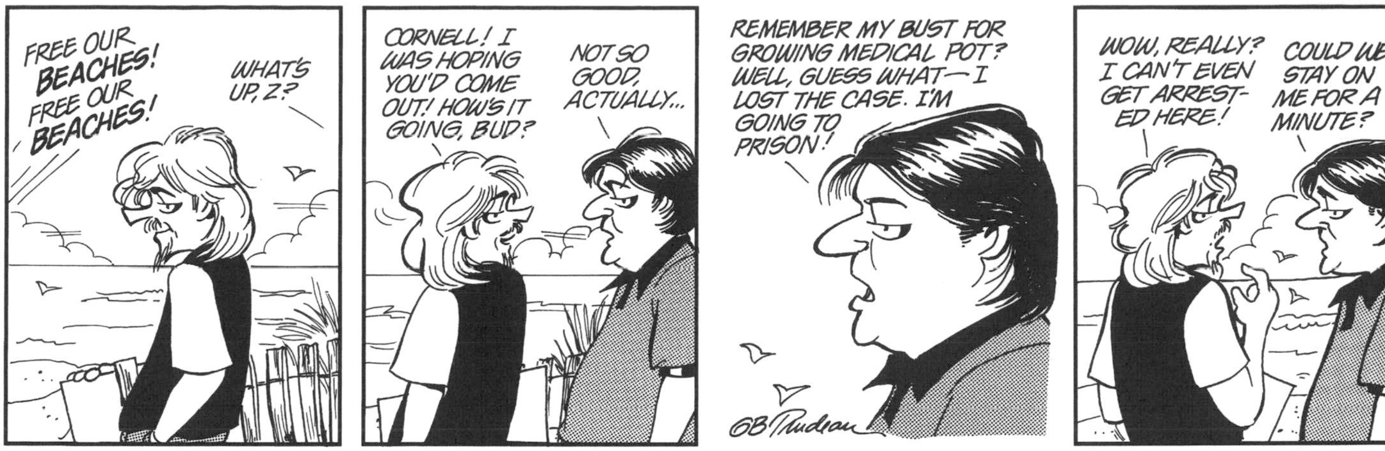
FREE OUR BEACHES! FREE OUR BEACHES!
WHAT'S UP, Z?
CORNELL! I WAS HOPING YOU'D COME OUT! HOW'S IT GOING, BUD?
NOT SO GOOD, ACTUALLY...
REMEMBER MY BUST FOR GROWING MEDICAL POT? WELL, GUESS WHAT— I LOST THE CASE. I'M GOING TO PRISON!
WOW, REALLY? I CAN'T EVEN GET ARREST-ED HERE!
COULD WE STAY ON ME FOR A MINUTE?

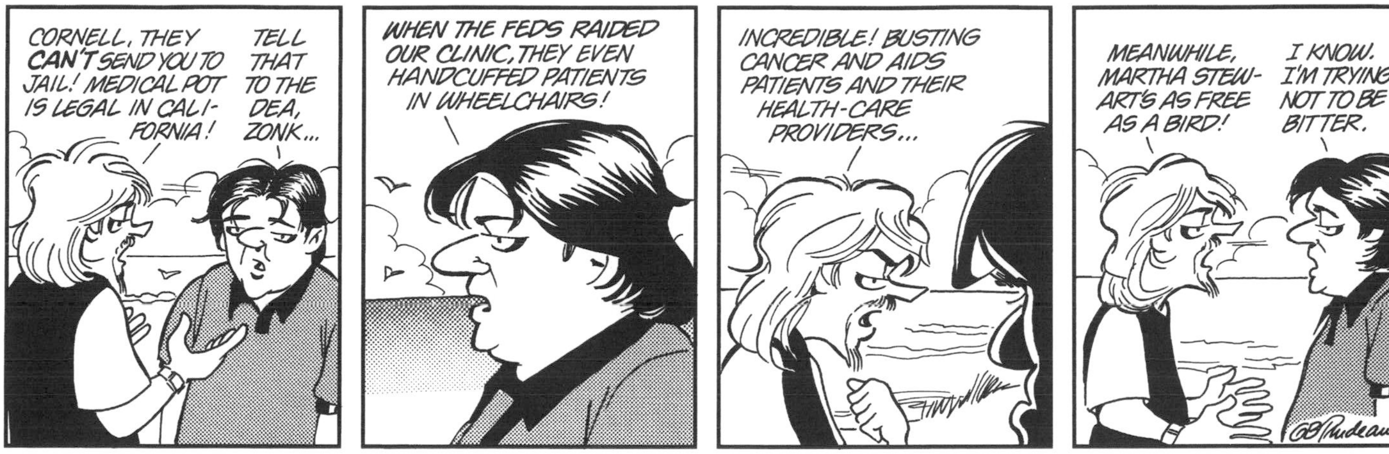
CORNELL, THEY CAN'T SEND YOU TO JAIL! MEDICAL POT IS LEGAL IN CALI-FORNIA!
TELL THAT TO THE DEA, ZONK...
WHEN THE FEDS RAIDED OUR CLINIC, THEY EVEN HANDCUFFED PATIENTS IN WHEELCHAIRS!
INCREDIBLE! BUSTING CANCER AND AIDS PATIENTS AND THEIR HEALTH-CARE PROVIDERS...
MEANWHILE, MARTHA STEW-ART'S AS FREE AS A BIRD!
I KNOW. I'M TRYING NOT TO BE BITTER.

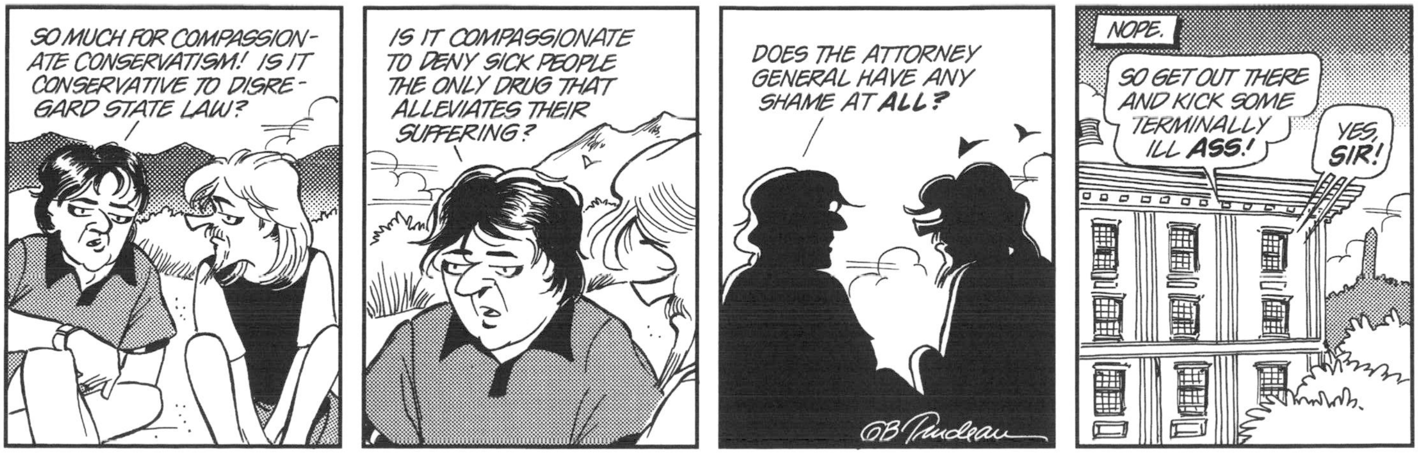
SO MUCH FOR COMPASSION-ATE CONSERVATISM! IS IT CONSERVATIVE TO DISRE-GARD STATE LAW?
IS IT COMPASSIONATE TO DENY SICK PEOPLE THE ONLY DRUG THAT ALLEVIATES THEIR SUFFERING?
DOES THE ATTORNEY GENERAL HAVE ANY SHAME AT ALL?
NOPE.
SO GET OUT THERE AND KICK SOME TERMINALLY ILL ASS!
YES, SIR!

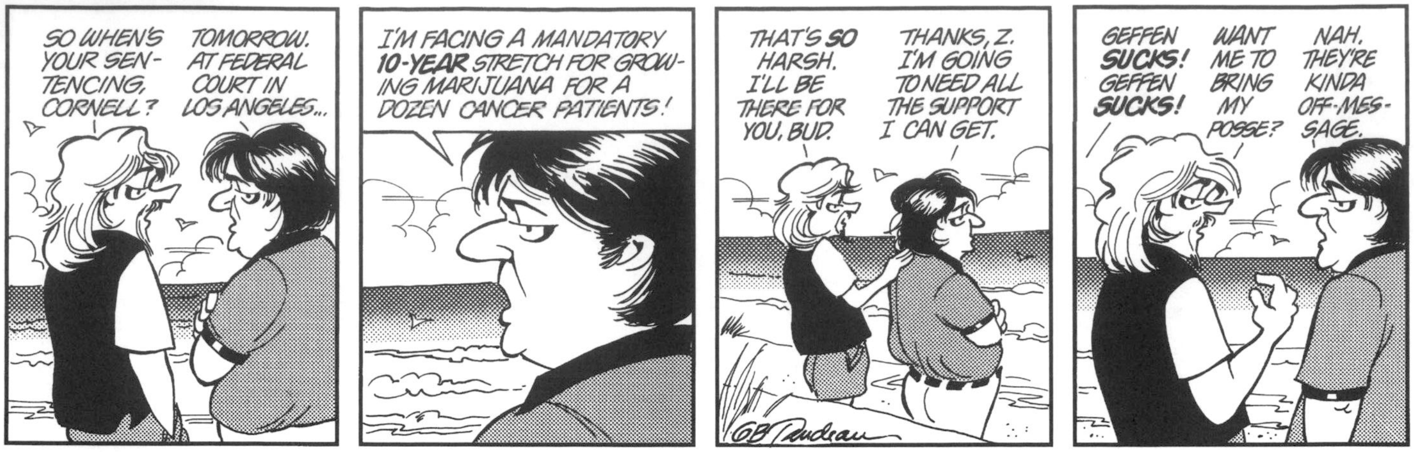
SO WHEN'S YOUR SENTENCING, CORNELL?
TOMORROW. AT FEDERAL COURT IN LOS ANGELES...
I'M FACING A MANDATORY **10-YEAR** STRETCH FOR GROWING MARIJUANA FOR A DOZEN CANCER PATIENTS!
THAT'S **SO** HARSH. I'LL BE THERE FOR YOU, BUD.
THANKS, Z. I'M GOING TO NEED ALL THE SUPPORT I CAN GET.
GEFFEN **SUCKS!** GEFFEN **SUCKS!**
WANT ME TO BRING MY POSSE?
NAH. THEY'RE KINDA OFF-MESSAGE.
GB Trudeau

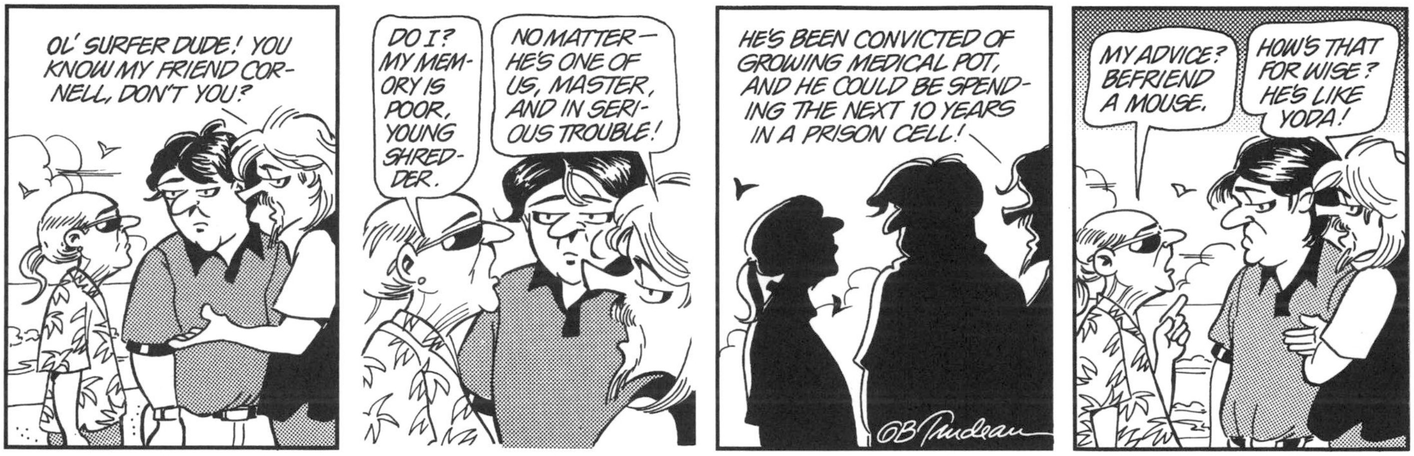
OL' SURFER DUDE! YOU KNOW MY FRIEND CORNELL, DON'T YOU?
DO I? MY MEMORY IS POOR, YOUNG SHREDDER.
NO MATTER— HE'S ONE OF US, MASTER, AND IN SERIOUS TROUBLE!
HE'S BEEN CONVICTED OF GROWING MEDICAL POT, AND HE COULD BE SPENDING THE NEXT 10 YEARS IN A PRISON CELL!
GB Trudeau
MY ADVICE? BEFRIEND A MOUSE.
HOW'S THAT FOR WISE? HE'S LIKE YODA!

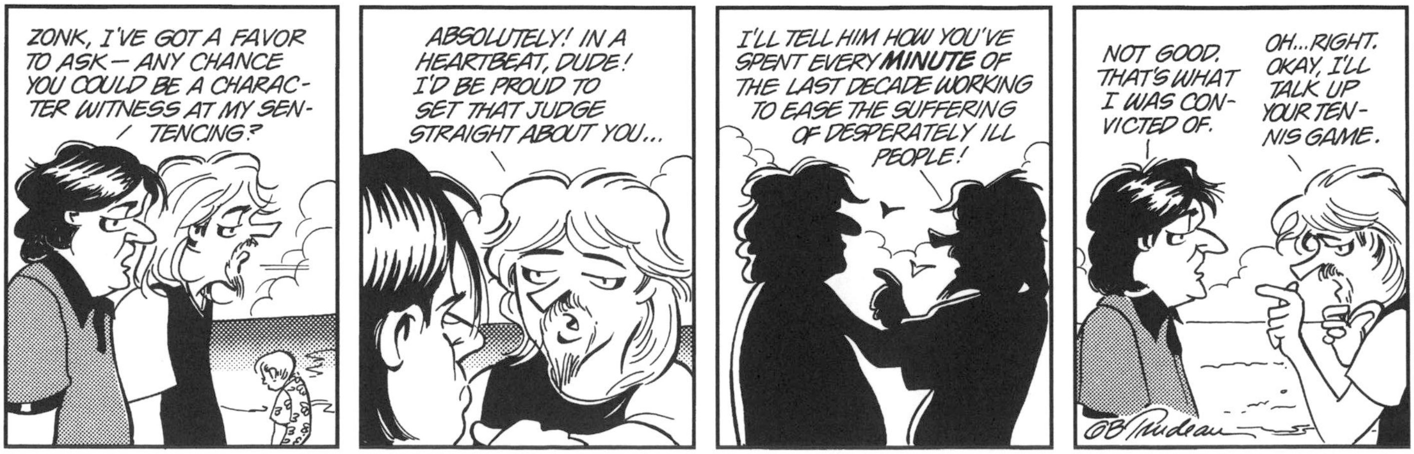
ZONK, I'VE GOT A FAVOR TO ASK— ANY CHANCE YOU COULD BE A CHARACTER WITNESS AT MY SENTENCING?
ABSOLUTELY! IN A HEARTBEAT, DUDE! I'D BE PROUD TO SET THAT JUDGE STRAIGHT ABOUT YOU...
I'LL TELL HIM HOW YOU'VE SPENT EVERY **MINUTE** OF THE LAST DECADE WORKING TO EASE THE SUFFERING OF DESPERATELY ILL PEOPLE!
NOT GOOD. THAT'S WHAT I WAS CONVICTED OF.
OH...RIGHT. OKAY, I'LL TALK UP YOUR TENNIS GAME.
GB Trudeau

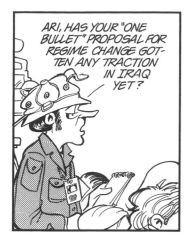

ARI, HAS YOUR "ONE BULLET" PROPOSAL FOR REGIME CHANGE GOTTEN ANY TRACTION IN IRAQ YET?
YES. WE THINK THE COST-BENEFIT ANALYSIS HAS REALLY RESONATED...
MANY IRAQIS WERE NOT AWARE THAT KILLING SADDAM THEMSELVES WAS SUCH AN ATTRACTIVELY PRICED ALTERNATIVE TO WAR!
BUT WON'T A LOT OF INNOCENT BODY DOUBLES ALSO DIE?
WELL, THAT'S SHOW BUSINESS.
GBTrudeau

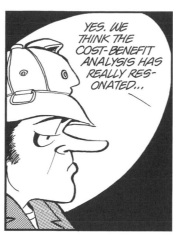

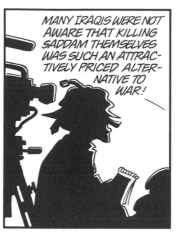

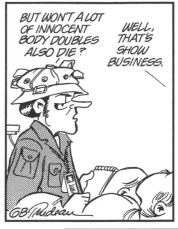

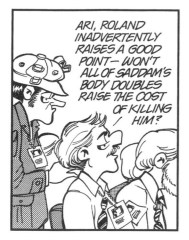

ARI, ROLAND INADVERTENTLY RAISES A GOOD POINT— WON'T ALL OF SADDAM'S BODY DOUBLES RAISE THE COST OF KILLING HIM?
WELL, WITH BODY DOUBLES, OBVIOUSLY WE'RE NO LONGER TALKING A SINGLE BULLET. HOWEVER, WITH MULTIPLE BULLETS, YOU GET ECONOMIES OF SCALE...
THIS COULD GET THE PER BULLET COST DOWN TO 8¢. THROW IN CARFARE AND PER DIEM, WE THINK EACH ASSASSINATION COULD BE BROUGHT IN FOR UNDER $5.
GBTrudeau
WHO SAYS WE DON'T PROVIDE SPECIFICS?
NOW, DEMOCRATS MAY CLAIM THAT'S TOO MUCH...

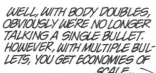

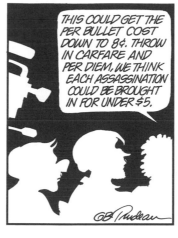

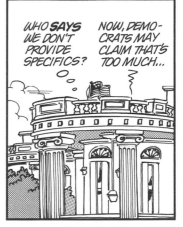

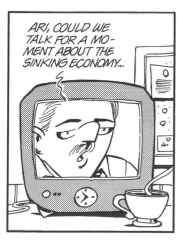

ARI, COULD WE TALK FOR A MOMENT ABOUT THE SINKING ECONOMY...
...THE HUGE NEW DEFICITS, JOBLESSNESS, PRESCRIPTION DRUGS, SOCIAL SECURITY, CORPORATE MALFEASANCE AND THE STOCK MARKET?
NO.
ARI, COULD WE GET BACK TO BANG-BANG?
YES.
GBTrudeau

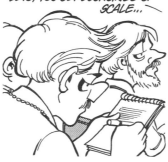

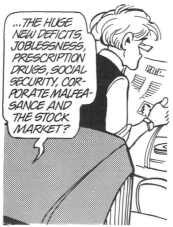

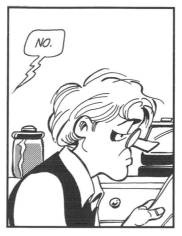

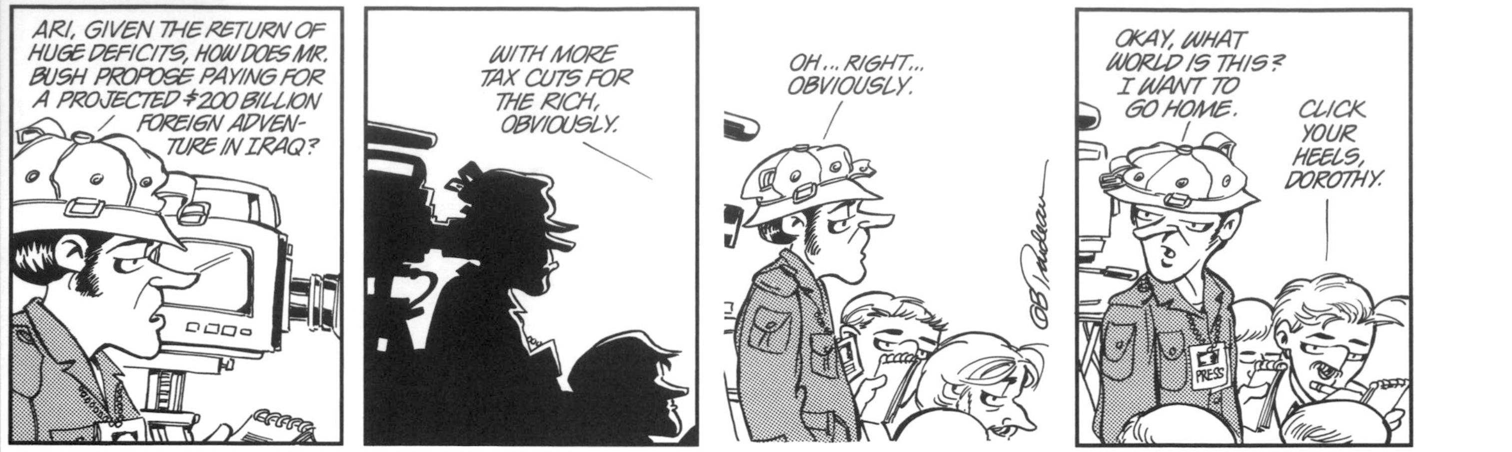
ARI, GIVEN THE RETURN OF HUGE DEFICITS, HOW DOES MR. BUSH PROPOSE PAYING FOR A PROJECTED $200 BILLION FOREIGN ADVENTURE IN IRAQ?
WITH MORE TAX CUTS FOR THE RICH, OBVIOUSLY.
OH... RIGHT... OBVIOUSLY.
OKAY, WHAT WORLD IS THIS? I WANT TO GO HOME.
CLICK YOUR HEELS, DOROTHY.
PRESS

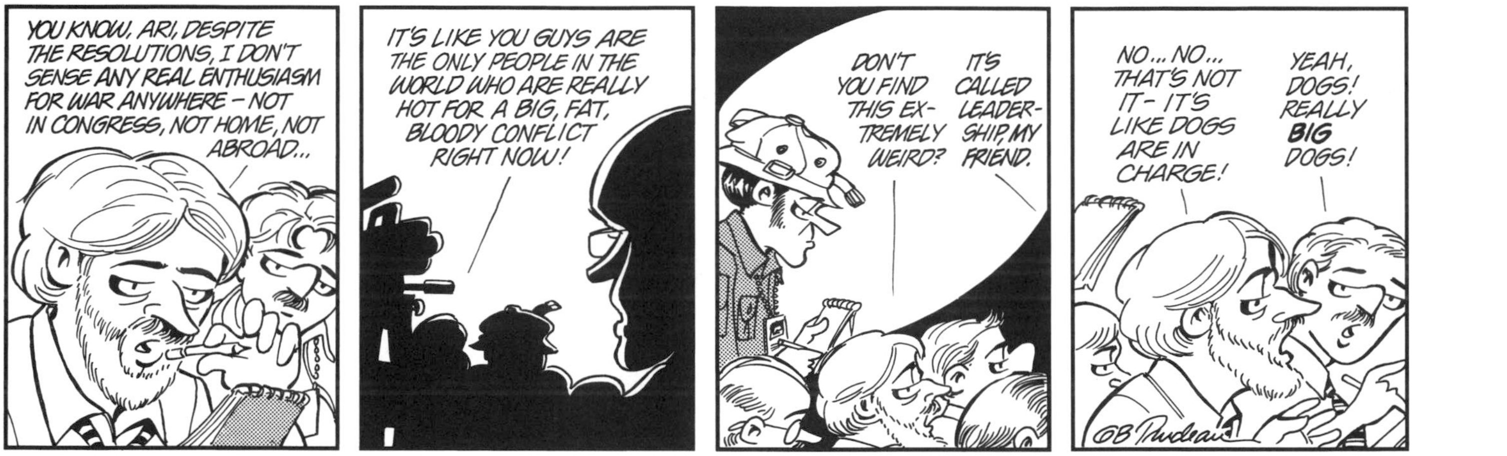
YOU KNOW, ARI, DESPITE THE RESOLUTIONS, I DON'T SENSE ANY REAL ENTHUSIASM FOR WAR ANYWHERE – NOT IN CONGRESS, NOT HOME, NOT ABROAD...
IT'S LIKE YOU GUYS ARE THE ONLY PEOPLE IN THE WORLD WHO ARE REALLY HOT FOR A BIG, FAT, BLOODY CONFLICT RIGHT NOW!
DON'T YOU FIND THIS EXTREMELY WEIRD?
IT'S CALLED LEADERSHIP, MY FRIEND.
NO... NO... THAT'S NOT IT – IT'S LIKE DOGS ARE IN CHARGE!
YEAH, DOGS! REALLY **BIG** DOGS!

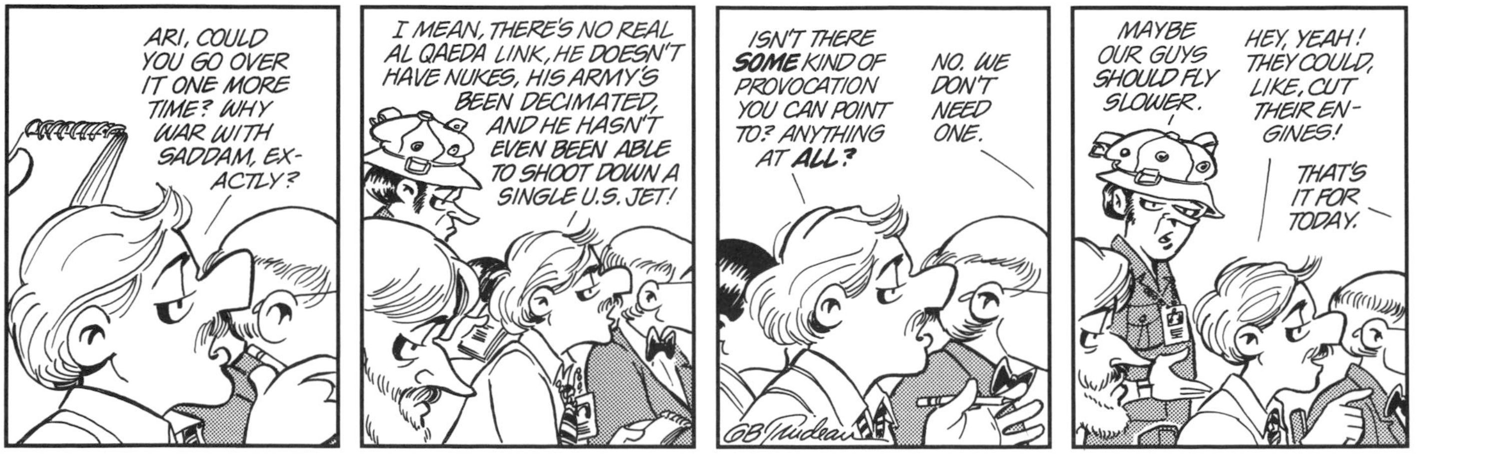
ARI, COULD YOU GO OVER IT ONE MORE TIME? WHY WAR WITH SADDAM, EXACTLY?
I MEAN, THERE'S NO REAL AL QAEDA LINK, HE DOESN'T HAVE NUKES, HIS ARMY'S BEEN DECIMATED, AND HE HASN'T EVEN BEEN ABLE TO SHOOT DOWN A SINGLE U.S. JET!
ISN'T THERE **SOME** KIND OF PROVOCATION YOU CAN POINT TO? ANYTHING AT **ALL**?
NO. WE DON'T NEED ONE.
MAYBE OUR GUYS SHOULD FLY SLOWER.
HEY, YEAH! THEY COULD, LIKE, CUT THEIR ENGINES!
THAT'S IT FOR TODAY.

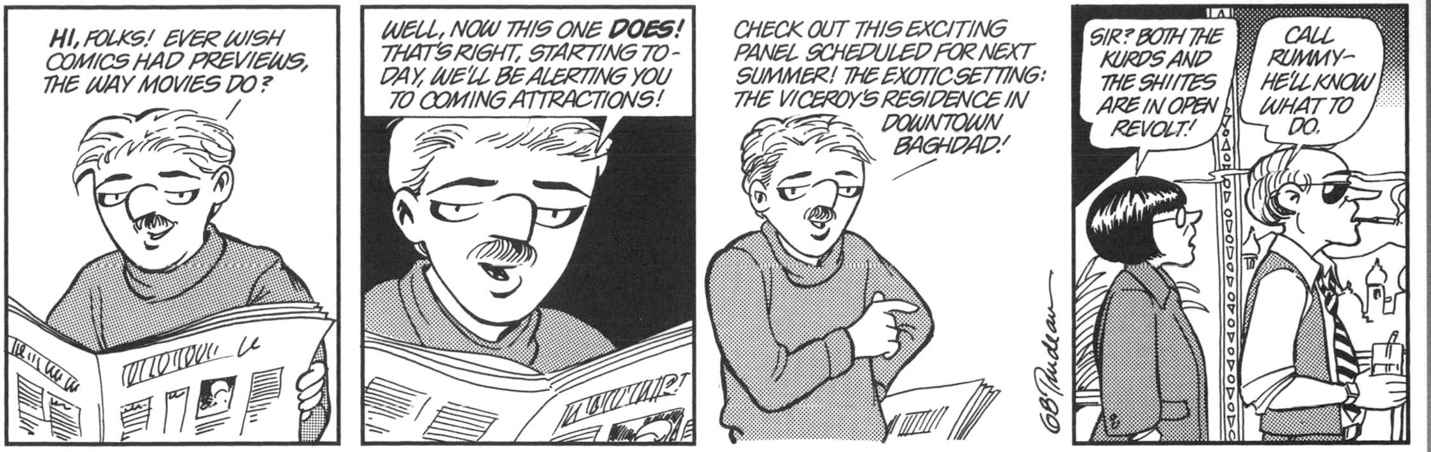
HI, FOLKS! EVER WISH COMICS HAD PREVIEWS, THE WAY MOVIES DO?
WELL, NOW THIS ONE DOES! THAT'S RIGHT, STARTING TODAY, WE'LL BE ALERTING YOU TO COMING ATTRACTIONS!
CHECK OUT THIS EXCITING PANEL SCHEDULED FOR NEXT SUMMER! THE EXOTIC SETTING: THE VICEROY'S RESIDENCE IN DOWNTOWN BAGHDAD!
SIR? BOTH THE KURDS AND THE SHIITES ARE IN OPEN REVOLT!
CALL RUMMY– HE'LL KNOW WHAT TO DO.

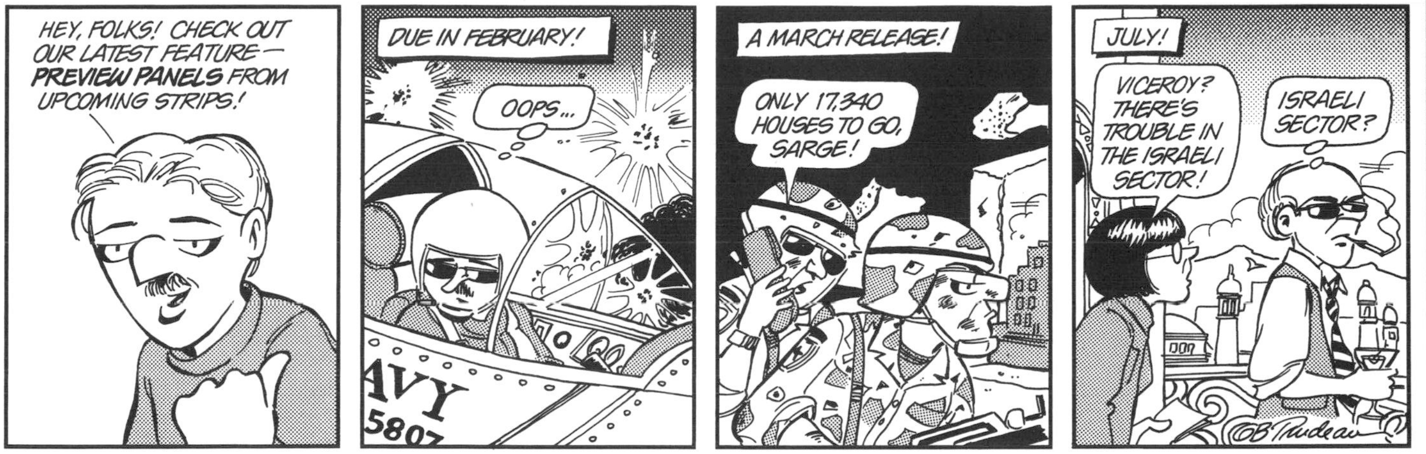
HEY, FOLKS! CHECK OUT OUR LATEST FEATURE— PREVIEW PANELS FROM UPCOMING STRIPS!
DUE IN FEBRUARY!
OOPS...
AVY
5807
A MARCH RELEASE!
ONLY 17,340 HOUSES TO GO, SARGE!
JULY!
VICEROY? THERE'S TROUBLE IN THE ISRAELI SECTOR!
ISRAELI SECTOR?

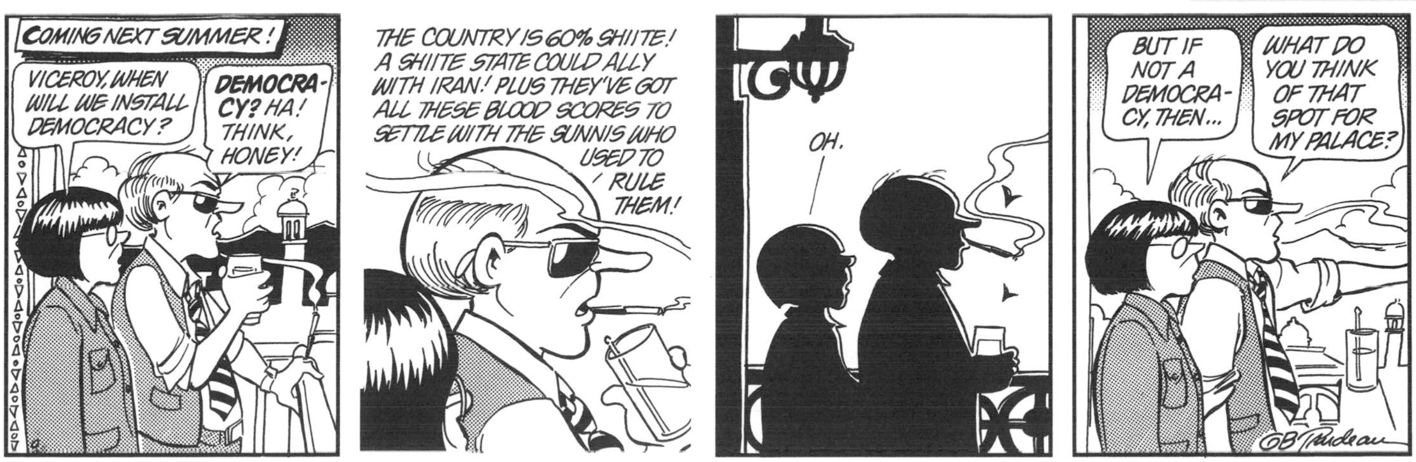
COMING NEXT SUMMER!
VICEROY, WHEN WILL WE INSTALL DEMOCRACY?
DEMOCRACY? HA! THINK, HONEY!
THE COUNTRY IS 60% SHIITE! A SHIITE STATE COULD ALLY WITH IRAN! PLUS THEY'VE GOT ALL THESE BLOOD SCORES TO SETTLE WITH THE SUNNIS WHO USED TO RULE THEM!
OH.
BUT IF NOT A DEMOCRACY, THEN...
WHAT DO YOU THINK OF THAT SPOT FOR MY PALACE?

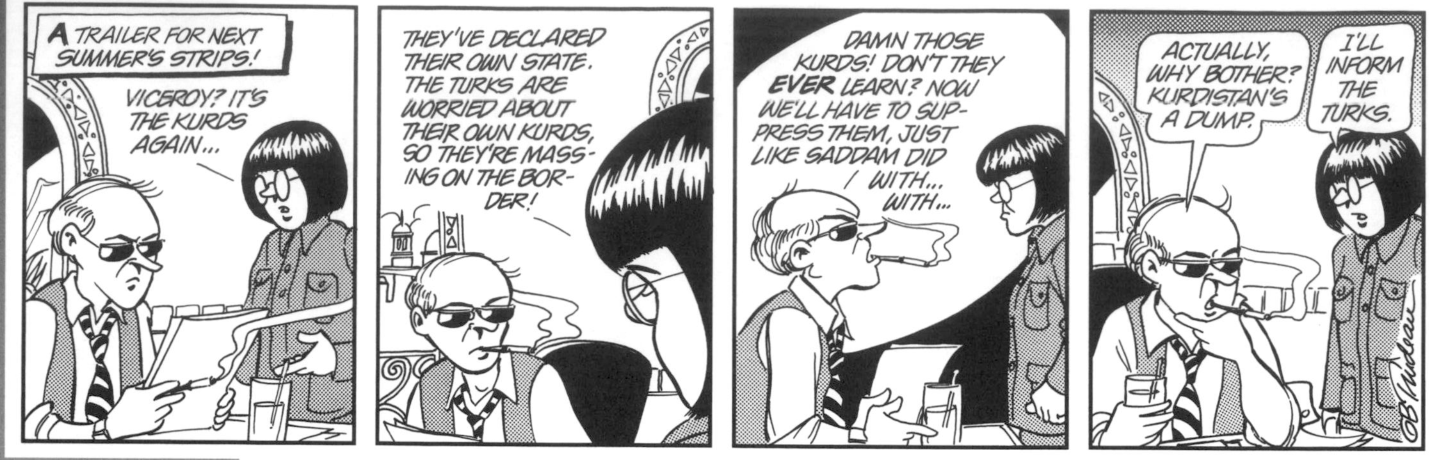
A TRAILER FOR NEXT SUMMER'S STRIPS!
VICEROY? IT'S THE KURDS AGAIN...
THEY'VE DECLARED THEIR OWN STATE. THE TURKS ARE WORRIED ABOUT THEIR OWN KURDS, SO THEY'RE MASSING ON THE BORDER!
DAMN THOSE KURDS! DON'T THEY EVER LEARN? NOW WE'LL HAVE TO SUPPRESS THEM, JUST LIKE SADDAM DID / WITH... WITH...
ACTUALLY, WHY BOTHER? KURDISTAN'S A DUMP.
I'LL INFORM THE TURKS.
GB Trudeau

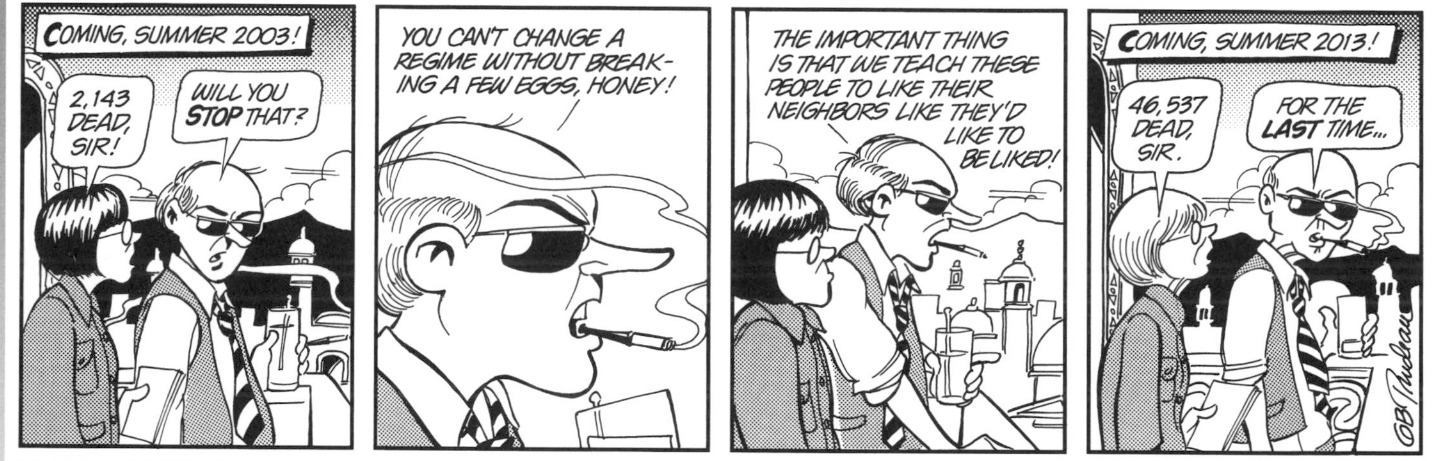
COMING, SUMMER 2003!
2,143 DEAD, SIR!
WILL YOU STOP THAT?
YOU CAN'T CHANGE A REGIME WITHOUT BREAKING A FEW EGGS, HONEY!
THE IMPORTANT THING IS THAT WE TEACH THESE PEOPLE TO LIKE THEIR NEIGHBORS LIKE THEY'D LIKE TO BE LIKED!
COMING, SUMMER 2013!
46,537 DEAD, SIR.
FOR THE LAST TIME...
GB Trudeau

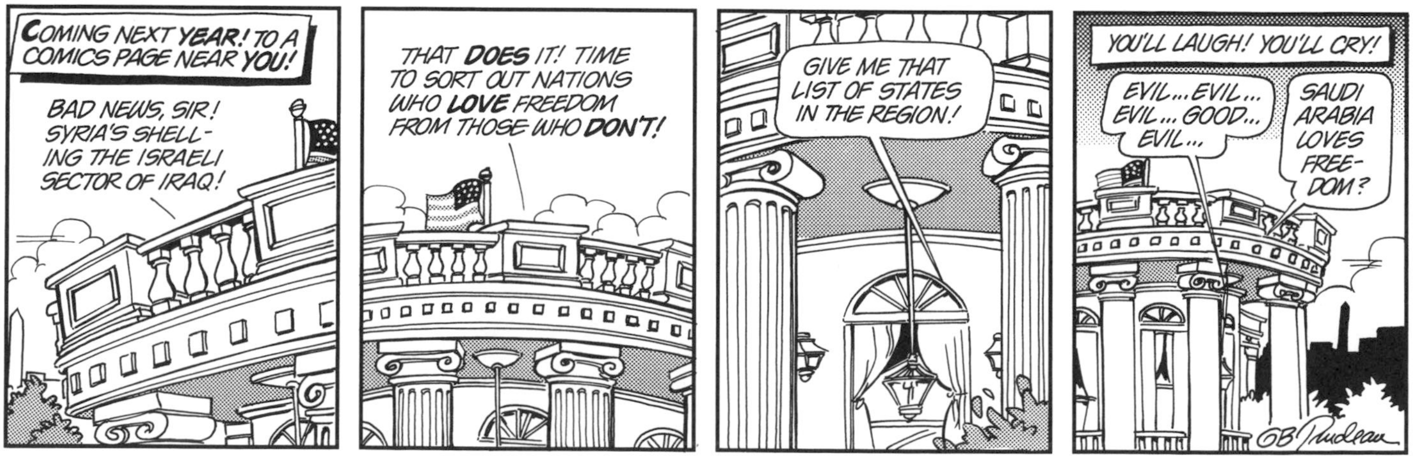
COMING NEXT YEAR! TO A COMICS PAGE NEAR YOU!
BAD NEWS, SIR! SYRIA'S SHELLING THE ISRAELI SECTOR OF IRAQ!
THAT DOES IT! TIME TO SORT OUT NATIONS WHO LOVE FREEDOM FROM THOSE WHO DON'T!
GIVE ME THAT LIST OF STATES IN THE REGION!
YOU'LL LAUGH! YOU'LL CRY!
EVIL... EVIL... EVIL... GOOD... EVIL...
SAUDI ARABIA LOVES FREEDOM?
GB Trudeau

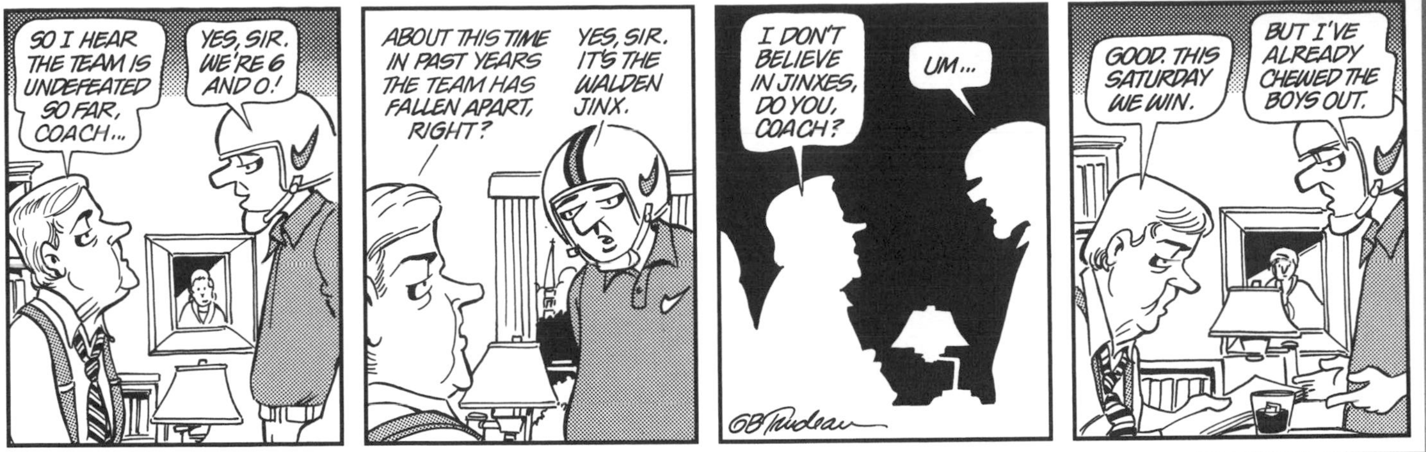
SO I HEAR THE TEAM IS UNDEFEATED SO FAR, COACH...
YES, SIR. WE'RE 6 AND 0!
ABOUT THIS TIME IN PAST YEARS THE TEAM HAS FALLEN APART, RIGHT?
YES, SIR. IT'S THE WALDEN JINX.
I DON'T BELIEVE IN JINXES, DO YOU, COACH?
UM...
GOOD. THIS SATURDAY WE WIN.
BUT I'VE ALREADY CHEWED THE BOYS OUT.

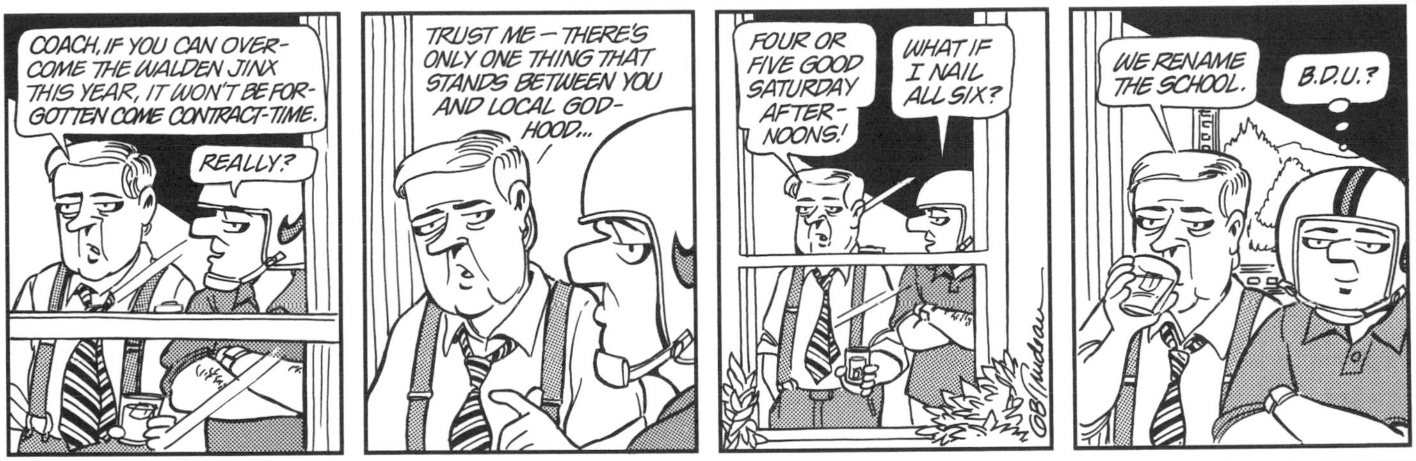
COACH, IF YOU CAN OVERCOME THE WALDEN JINX THIS YEAR, IT WON'T BE FORGOTTEN COME CONTRACT-TIME.
REALLY?
TRUST ME — THERE'S ONLY ONE THING THAT STANDS BETWEEN YOU AND LOCAL GODHOOD...
FOUR OR FIVE GOOD SATURDAY AFTERNOONS!
WHAT IF I NAIL ALL SIX?
WE RENAME THE SCHOOL.
B.D.U.?

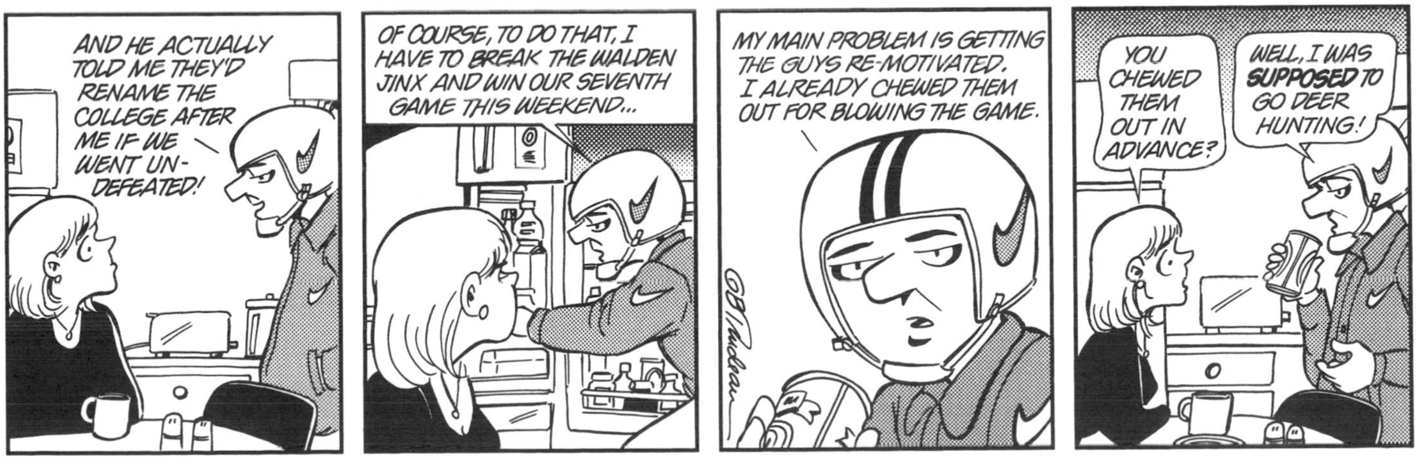
AND HE ACTUALLY TOLD ME THEY'D RENAME THE COLLEGE AFTER ME IF WE WENT UNDEFEATED!
OF COURSE, TO DO THAT, I HAVE TO BREAK THE WALDEN JINX AND WIN OUR SEVENTH GAME THIS WEEKEND...
MY MAIN PROBLEM IS GETTING THE GUYS RE-MOTIVATED. I ALREADY CHEWED THEM OUT FOR BLOWING THE GAME.
YOU CHEWED THEM OUT IN ADVANCE?
WELL, I WAS SUPPOSED TO GO DEER HUNTING!

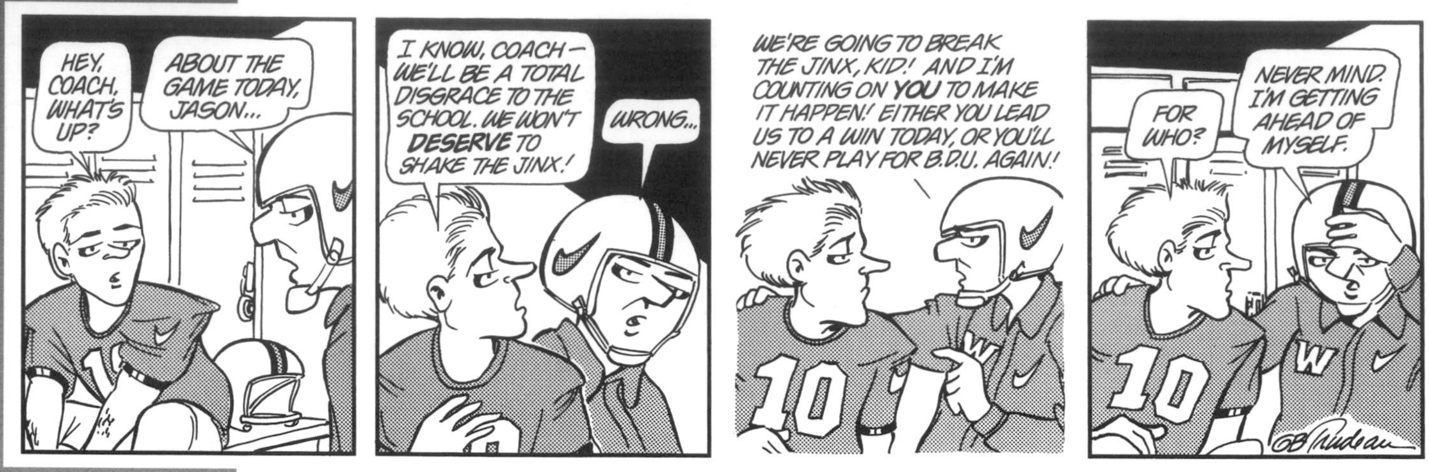
HEY, COACH, WHAT'S UP?
ABOUT THE GAME TODAY, JASON...
I KNOW, COACH— WE'LL BE A TOTAL DISGRACE TO THE SCHOOL. WE WON'T DESERVE TO SHAKE THE JINX!
WRONG...
WE'RE GOING TO BREAK THE JINX, KID! AND I'M COUNTING ON YOU TO MAKE IT HAPPEN! EITHER YOU LEAD US TO A WIN TODAY, OR YOU'LL NEVER PLAY FOR B.D.U. AGAIN!
FOR WHO?
NEVER MIND. I'M GETTING AHEAD OF MYSELF.

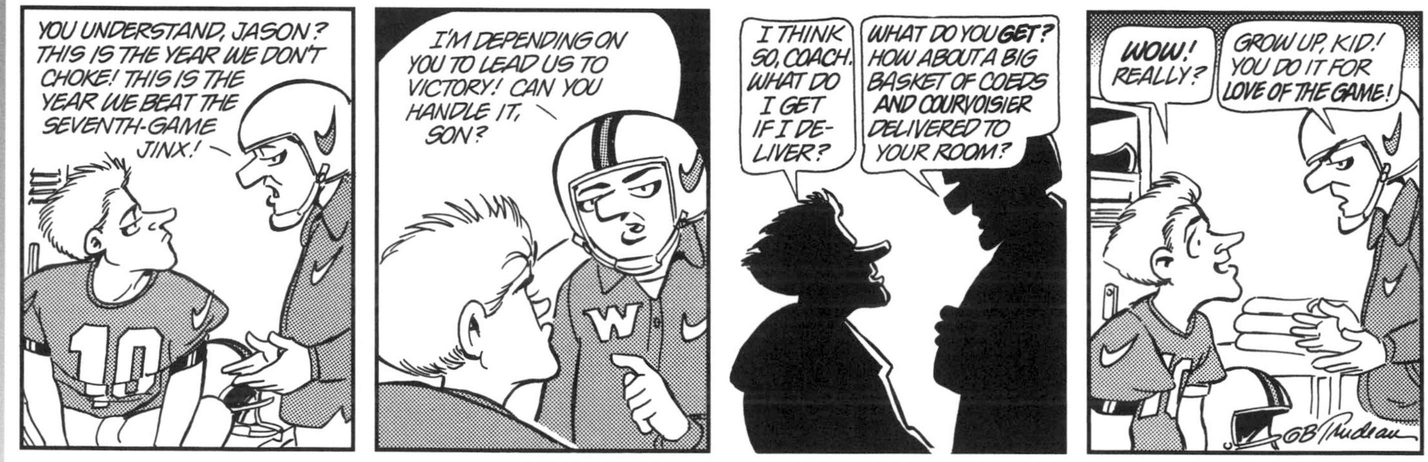
YOU UNDERSTAND, JASON? THIS IS THE YEAR WE DON'T CHOKE! THIS IS THE YEAR WE BEAT THE SEVENTH-GAME JINX!
I'M DEPENDING ON YOU TO LEAD US TO VICTORY! CAN YOU HANDLE IT, SON?
I THINK SO, COACH. WHAT DO I GET IF I DELIVER?
WHAT DO YOU GET? HOW ABOUT A BIG BASKET OF COEDS AND COURVOISIER DELIVERED TO YOUR ROOM?
WOW! REALLY?
GROW UP, KID! YOU DO IT FOR LOVE OF THE GAME!

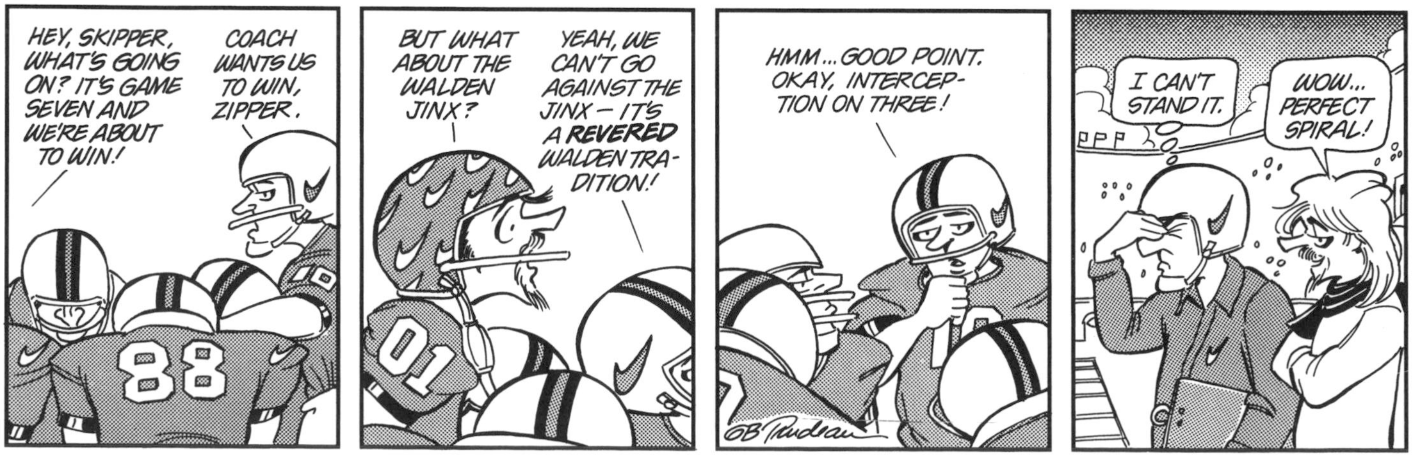
HEY, SKIPPER, WHAT'S GOING ON? IT'S GAME SEVEN AND WE'RE ABOUT TO WIN!
COACH WANTS US TO WIN, ZIPPER.
BUT WHAT ABOUT THE WALDEN JINX?
YEAH, WE CAN'T GO AGAINST THE JINX — IT'S A REVERED WALDEN TRADITION!
HMM... GOOD POINT. OKAY, INTERCEPTION ON THREE!
I CAN'T STAND IT.
WOW... PERFECT SPIRAL!

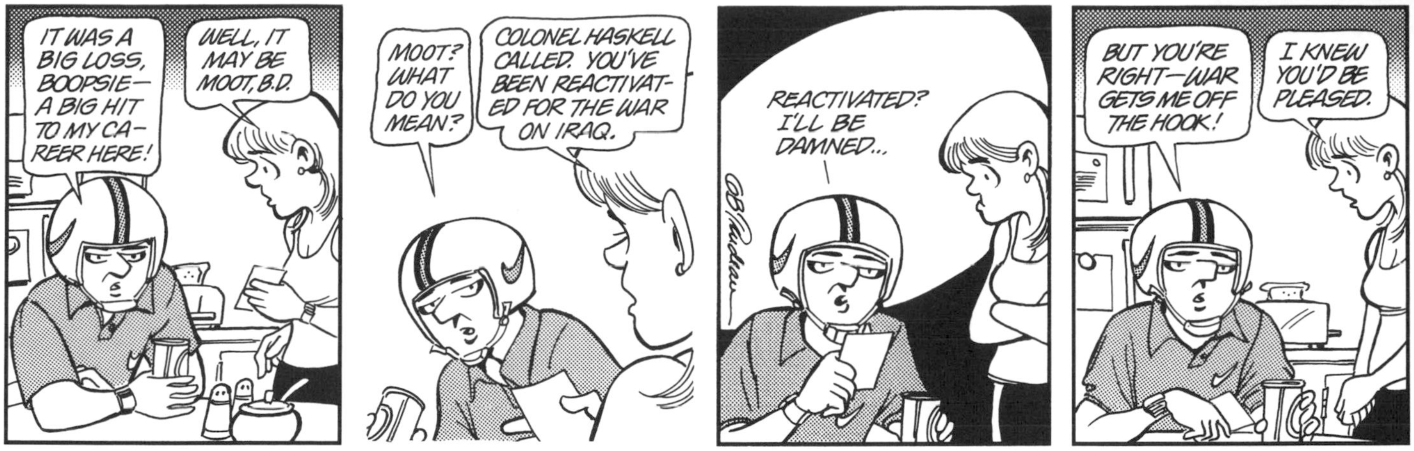
IT WAS A BIG LOSS, BOOPSIE— A BIG HIT TO MY CAREER HERE!
WELL, IT MAY BE MOOT, B.D.
MOOT? WHAT DO YOU MEAN?
COLONEL HASKELL CALLED. YOU'VE BEEN REACTIVATED FOR THE WAR ON IRAQ.
REACTIVATED? I'LL BE DAMNED...
BUT YOU'RE RIGHT—WAR GETS ME OFF THE HOOK!
I KNEW YOU'D BE PLEASED.

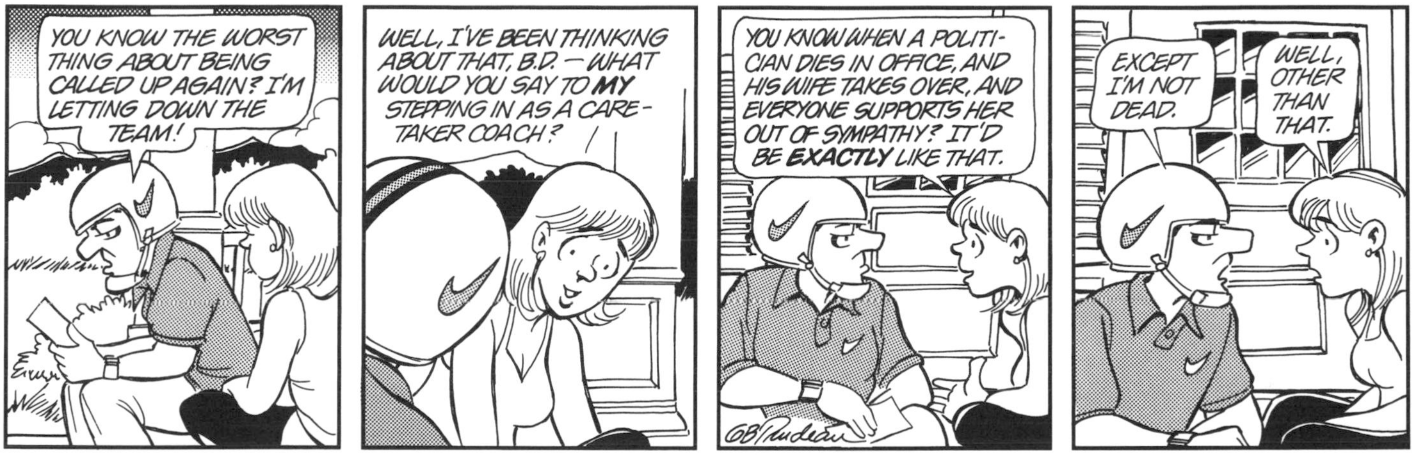
YOU KNOW THE WORST THING ABOUT BEING CALLED UP AGAIN? I'M LETTING DOWN THE TEAM!
WELL, I'VE BEEN THINKING ABOUT THAT, B.D. — WHAT WOULD YOU SAY TO MY STEPPING IN AS A CARETAKER COACH?
YOU KNOW WHEN A POLITICIAN DIES IN OFFICE, AND HIS WIFE TAKES OVER, AND EVERYONE SUPPORTS HER OUT OF SYMPATHY? IT'D BE EXACTLY LIKE THAT.
EXCEPT I'M NOT DEAD.
WELL, OTHER THAN THAT.

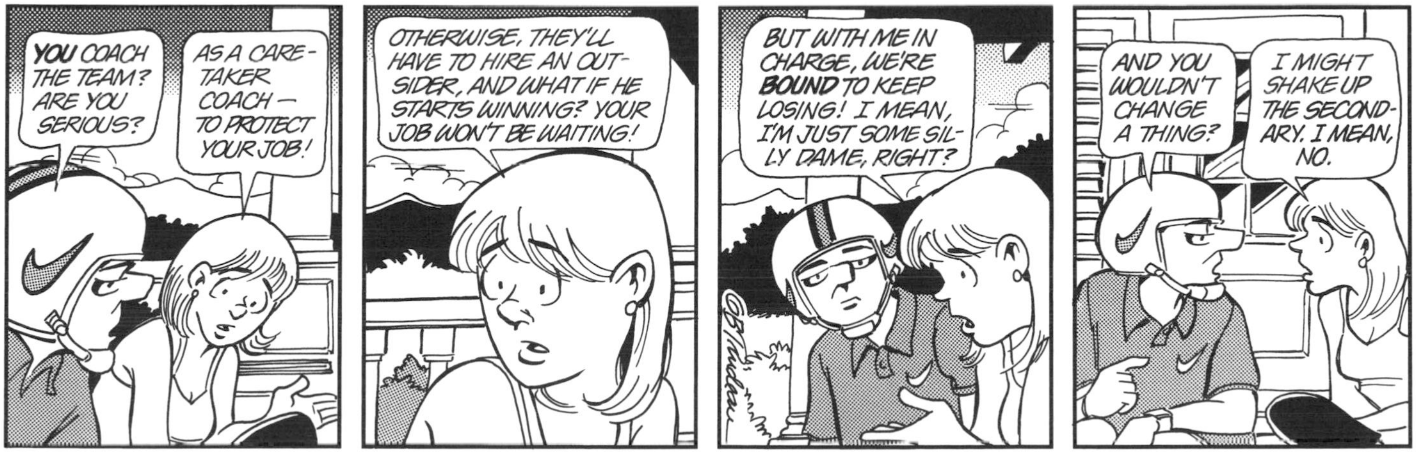
YOU COACH THE TEAM? ARE YOU SERIOUS?
AS A CARETAKER COACH — TO PROTECT YOUR JOB!
OTHERWISE, THEY'LL HAVE TO HIRE AN OUTSIDER, AND WHAT IF HE STARTS WINNING? YOUR JOB WON'T BE WAITING!
BUT WITH ME IN CHARGE, WE'RE BOUND TO KEEP LOSING! I MEAN, I'M JUST SOME SILLY DAME, RIGHT?
AND YOU WOULDN'T CHANGE A THING?
I MIGHT SHAKE UP THE SECONDARY. I MEAN, NO.

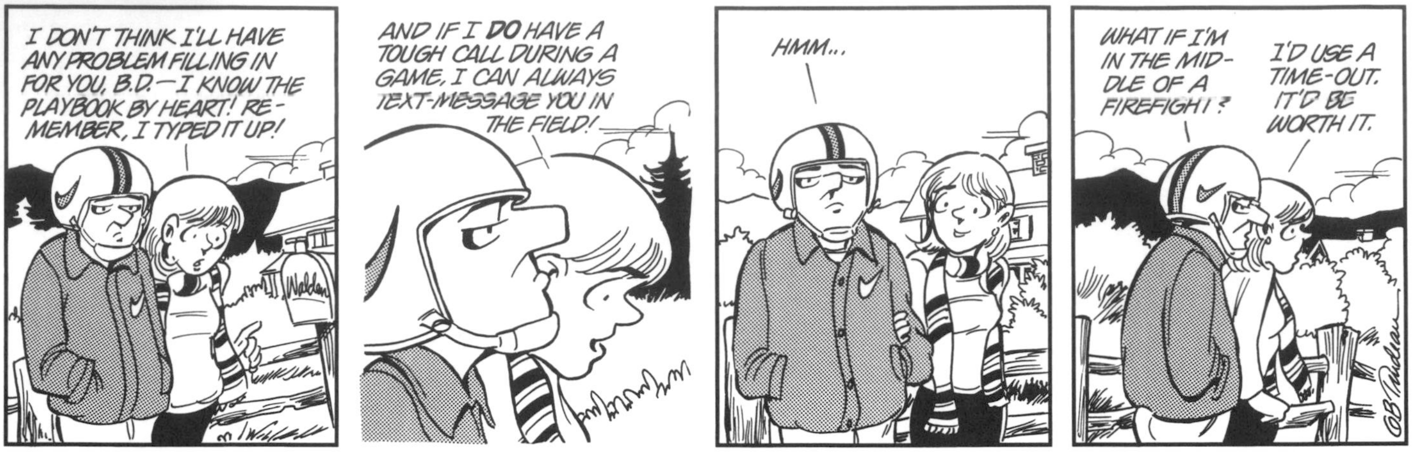
I DON'T THINK I'LL HAVE ANY PROBLEM FILLING IN FOR YOU, B.D.—I KNOW THE PLAYBOOK BY HEART! REMEMBER, I TYPED IT UP!
AND IF I **DO** HAVE A TOUGH CALL DURING A GAME, I CAN ALWAYS TEXT-MESSAGE YOU IN THE FIELD!
HMM...
WHAT IF I'M IN THE MIDDLE OF A FIREFIGHT?
I'D USE A TIME-OUT. IT'D BE WORTH IT.

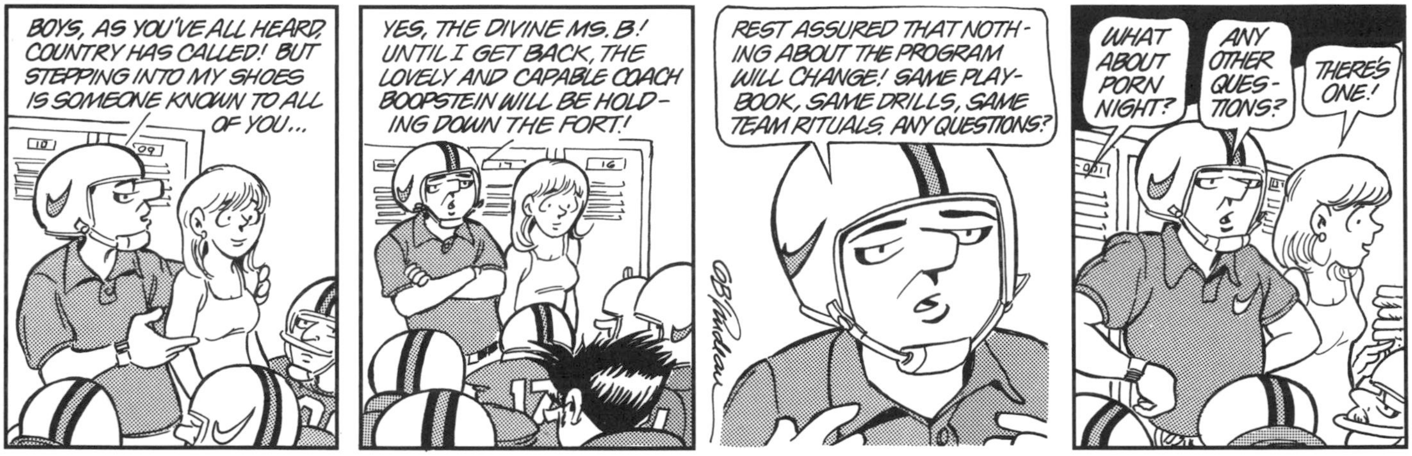
BOYS, AS YOU'VE ALL HEARD, COUNTRY HAS CALLED! BUT STEPPING INTO MY SHOES IS SOMEONE KNOWN TO ALL OF YOU...
YES, THE DIVINE MS. B! UNTIL I GET BACK, THE LOVELY AND CAPABLE COACH BOOPSTEIN WILL BE HOLDING DOWN THE FORT!
REST ASSURED THAT NOTHING ABOUT THE PROGRAM WILL CHANGE! SAME PLAYBOOK, SAME DRILLS, SAME TEAM RITUALS. ANY QUESTIONS?
WHAT ABOUT PORN NIGHT?
ANY OTHER QUESTIONS?
THERE'S ONE!

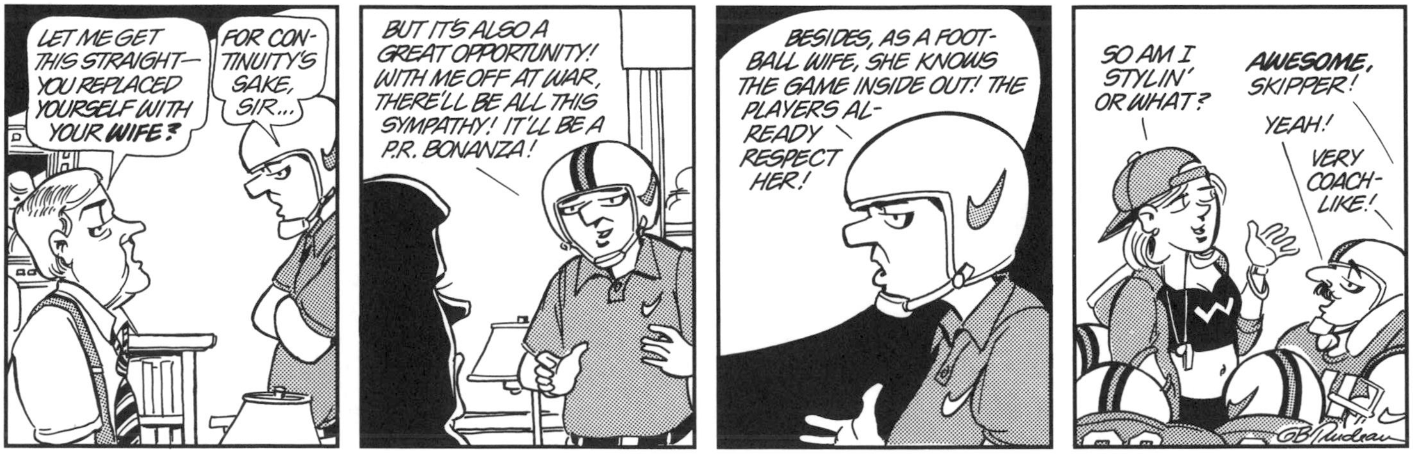
LET ME GET THIS STRAIGHT—YOU REPLACED YOURSELF WITH YOUR **WIFE?**
FOR CONTINUITY'S SAKE, SIR...
BUT IT'S ALSO A GREAT OPPORTUNITY! WITH ME OFF AT WAR, THERE'LL BE ALL THIS SYMPATHY! IT'LL BE A P.R. BONANZA!
BESIDES, AS A FOOTBALL WIFE, SHE KNOWS THE GAME INSIDE OUT! THE PLAYERS ALREADY RESPECT HER!
SO AM I STYLIN' OR WHAT?
**AWESOME,** SKIPPER!
YEAH!
VERY COACH-LIKE!

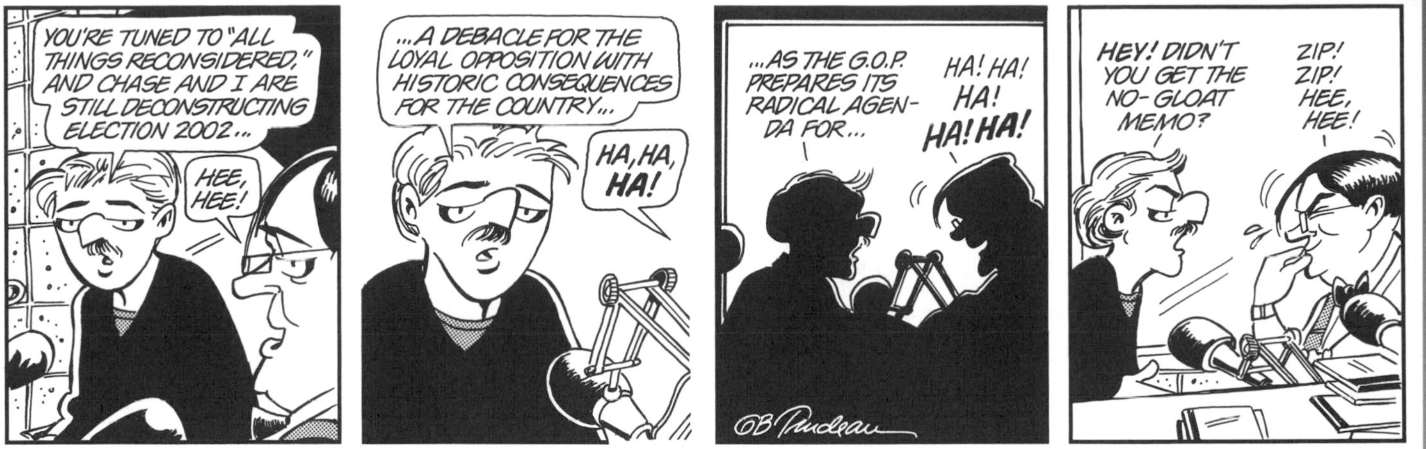
YOU'RE TUNED TO "ALL THINGS RECONSIDERED," AND CHASE AND I ARE STILL DECONSTRUCTING ELECTION 2002...
HEE, HEE!
...A DEBACLE FOR THE LOYAL OPPOSITION WITH HISTORIC CONSEQUENCES FOR THE COUNTRY...
HA, HA, HA!
...AS THE G.O.P. PREPARES ITS RADICAL AGENDA FOR...
HA! HA! HA! HA! HA!
HEY! DIDN'T YOU GET THE NO-GLOAT MEMO?
ZIP! ZIP! HEE, HEE!

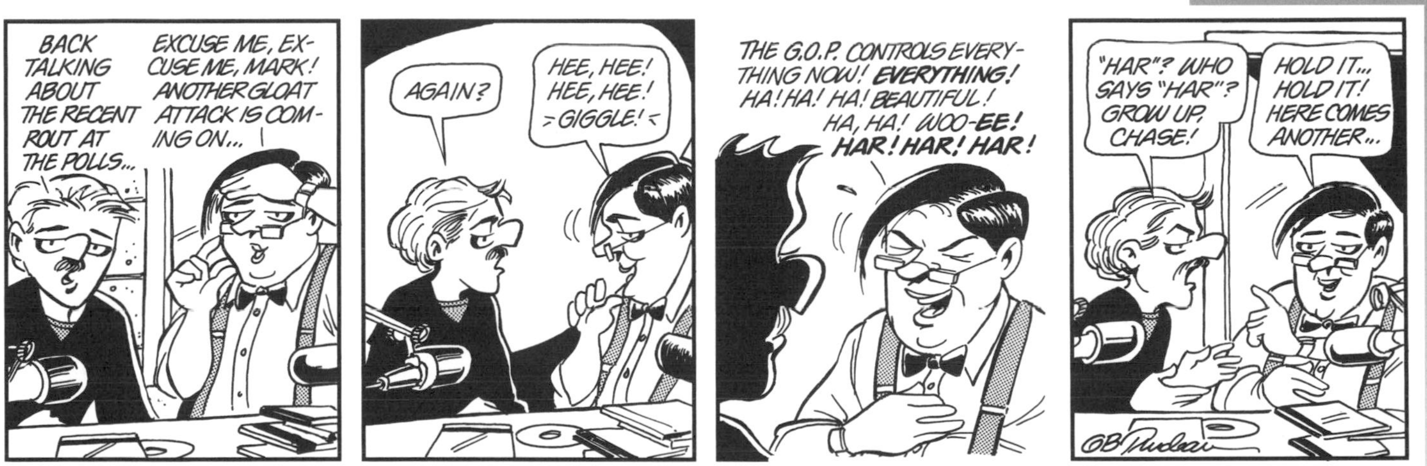
BACK TALKING ABOUT THE RECENT ROUT AT THE POLLS...
EXCUSE ME, EXCUSE ME, MARK! ANOTHER GLOAT ATTACK IS COMING ON...
AGAIN?
HEE, HEE! HEE, HEE! GIGGLE!
THE G.O.P. CONTROLS EVERYTHING NOW! EVERYTHING! HA! HA! HA! BEAUTIFUL!
HA, HA! WOO-EE! HAR! HAR! HAR!
"HAR"? WHO SAYS "HAR"? GROW UP, CHASE!
HOLD IT... HOLD IT! HERE COMES ANOTHER...

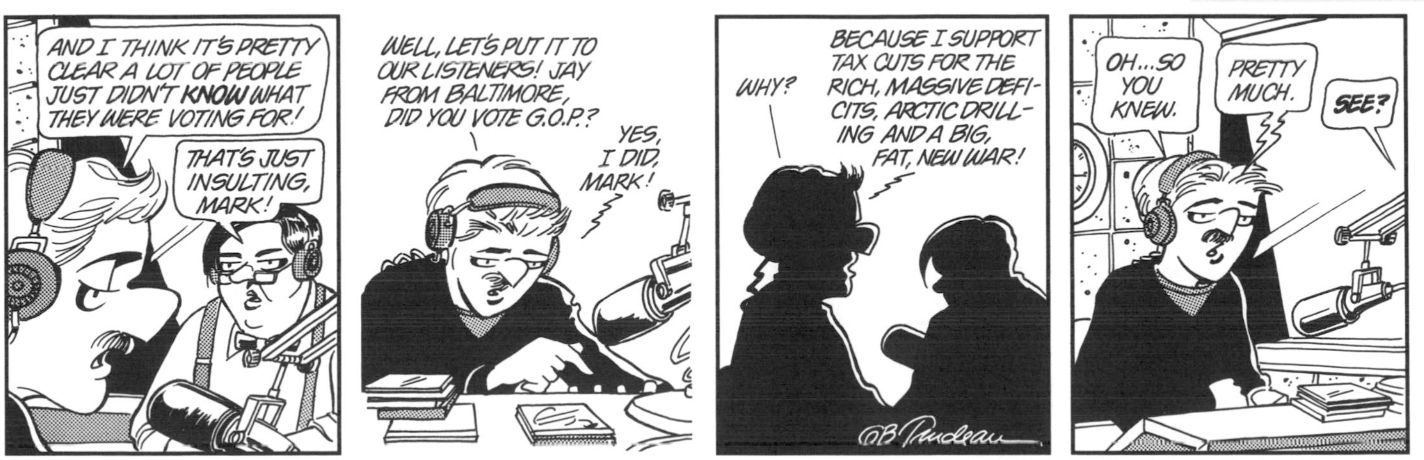
AND I THINK IT'S PRETTY CLEAR A LOT OF PEOPLE JUST DIDN'T KNOW WHAT THEY WERE VOTING FOR!
THAT'S JUST INSULTING, MARK!
WELL, LET'S PUT IT TO OUR LISTENERS! JAY FROM BALTIMORE, DID YOU VOTE G.O.P.?
YES, I DID, MARK!
WHY?
BECAUSE I SUPPORT TAX CUTS FOR THE RICH, MASSIVE DEFICITS, ARCTIC DRILLING AND A BIG, FAT, NEW WAR!
OH... SO YOU KNEW.
PRETTY MUCH.
SEE?

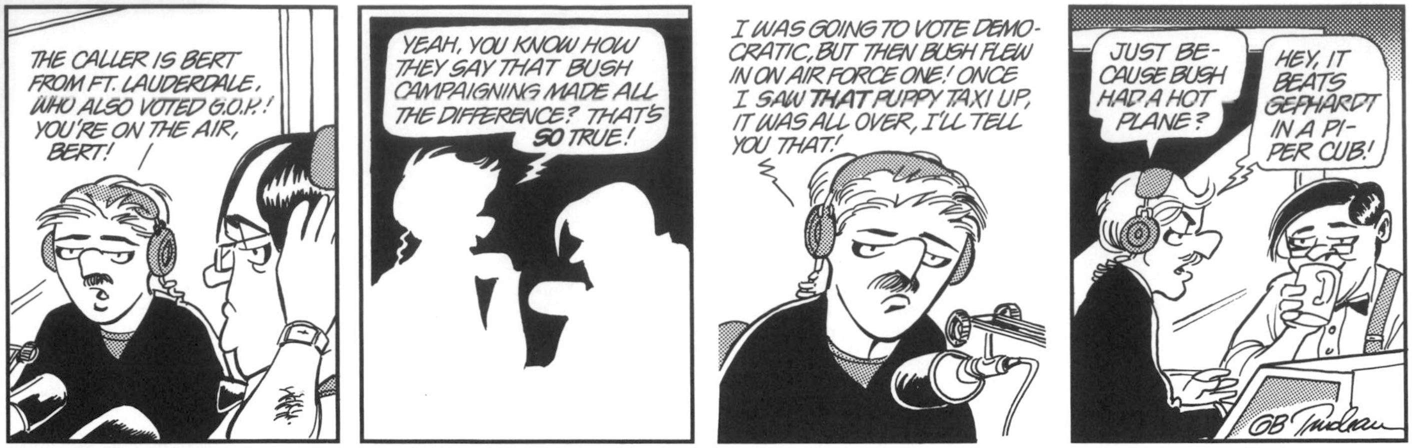
THE CALLER IS BERT FROM FT. LAUDERDALE, WHO ALSO VOTED G.O.P.! YOU'RE ON THE AIR, BERT!
YEAH, YOU KNOW HOW THEY SAY THAT BUSH CAMPAIGNING MADE ALL THE DIFFERENCE? THAT'S SO TRUE!
I WAS GOING TO VOTE DEMOCRATIC, BUT THEN BUSH FLEW IN ON AIR FORCE ONE! ONCE I SAW THAT PUPPY TAXI UP, IT WAS ALL OVER, I'LL TELL YOU THAT!
JUST BECAUSE BUSH HAD A HOT PLANE?
HEY, IT BEATS GEPHARDT IN A PIPER CUB!
GB Trudeau

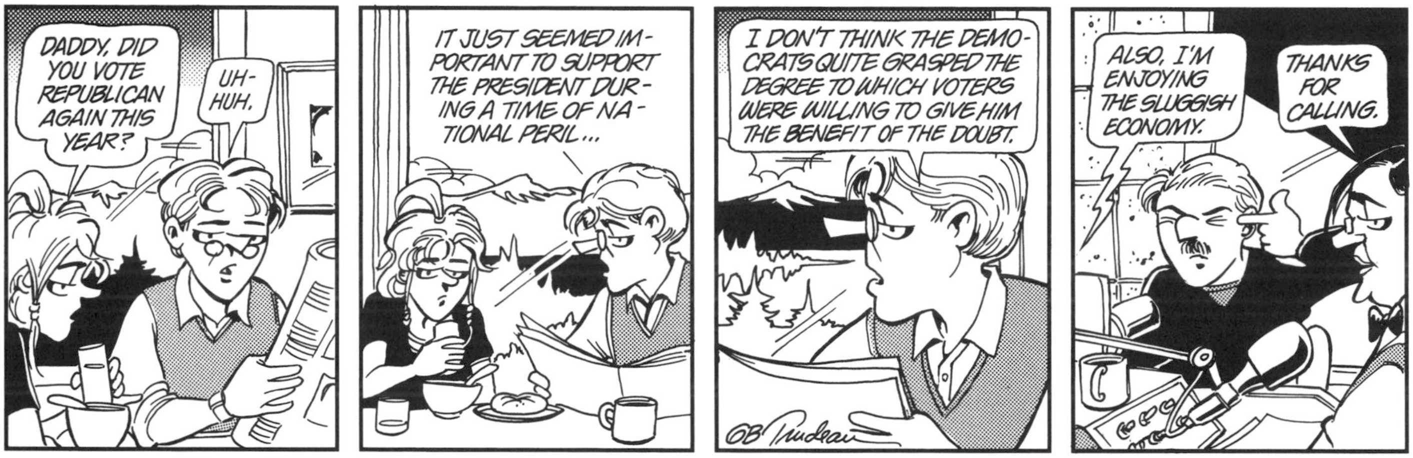
DADDY, DID YOU VOTE REPUBLICAN AGAIN THIS YEAR?
UH-HUH.
IT JUST SEEMED IMPORTANT TO SUPPORT THE PRESIDENT DURING A TIME OF NATIONAL PERIL...
I DON'T THINK THE DEMOCRATS QUITE GRASPED THE DEGREE TO WHICH VOTERS WERE WILLING TO GIVE HIM THE BENEFIT OF THE DOUBT.
GB Trudeau
ALSO, I'M ENJOYING THE SLUGGISH ECONOMY.
THANKS FOR CALLING.

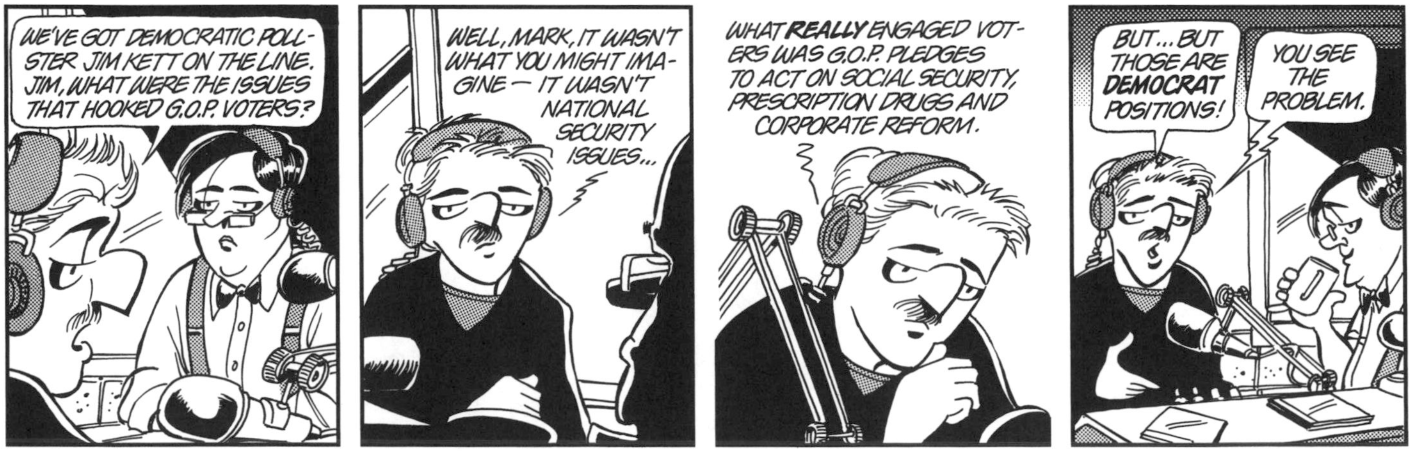
WE'VE GOT DEMOCRATIC POLLSTER JIM KETT ON THE LINE. JIM, WHAT WERE THE ISSUES THAT HOOKED G.O.P. VOTERS?
WELL, MARK, IT WASN'T WHAT YOU MIGHT IMAGINE — IT WASN'T NATIONAL SECURITY ISSUES...
WHAT REALLY ENGAGED VOTERS WAS G.O.P. PLEDGES TO ACT ON SOCIAL SECURITY, PRESCRIPTION DRUGS AND CORPORATE REFORM.
BUT... BUT THOSE ARE DEMOCRAT POSITIONS!
YOU SEE THE PROBLEM.

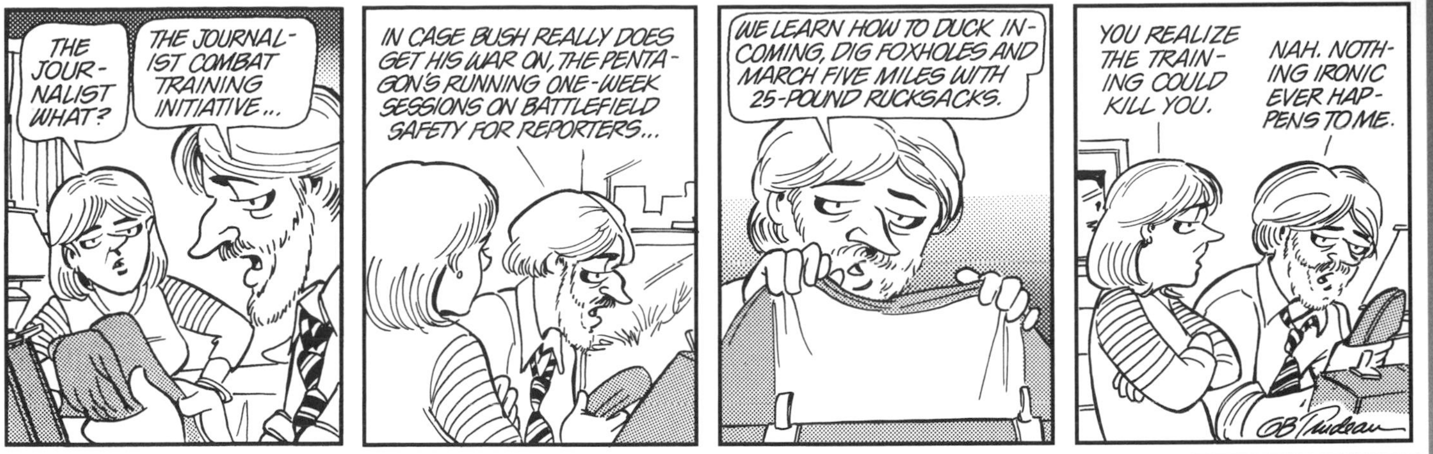
THE JOURNALIST WHAT?
THE JOURNALIST COMBAT TRAINING INITIATIVE...
IN CASE BUSH REALLY DOES GET HIS WAR ON, THE PENTAGON'S RUNNING ONE-WEEK SESSIONS ON BATTLEFIELD SAFETY FOR REPORTERS...
WE LEARN HOW TO DUCK INCOMING, DIG FOXHOLES AND MARCH FIVE MILES WITH 25-POUND RUCKSACKS.
YOU REALIZE THE TRAINING COULD KILL YOU.
NAH. NOTHING IRONIC EVER HAPPENS TO ME.

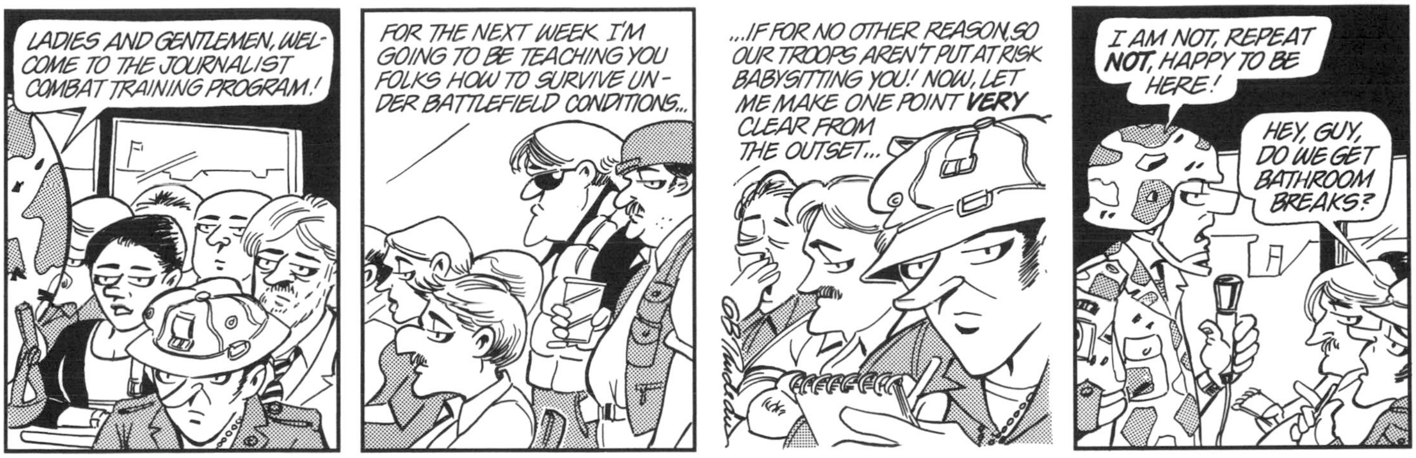
LADIES AND GENTLEMEN, WELCOME TO THE JOURNALIST COMBAT TRAINING PROGRAM!
FOR THE NEXT WEEK I'M GOING TO BE TEACHING YOU FOLKS HOW TO SURVIVE UNDER BATTLEFIELD CONDITIONS...
...IF FOR NO OTHER REASON, SO OUR TROOPS AREN'T PUT AT RISK BABYSITTING YOU! NOW, LET ME MAKE ONE POINT VERY CLEAR FROM THE OUTSET...
I AM NOT, REPEAT NOT, HAPPY TO BE HERE!
HEY, GUY, DO WE GET BATHROOM BREAKS?

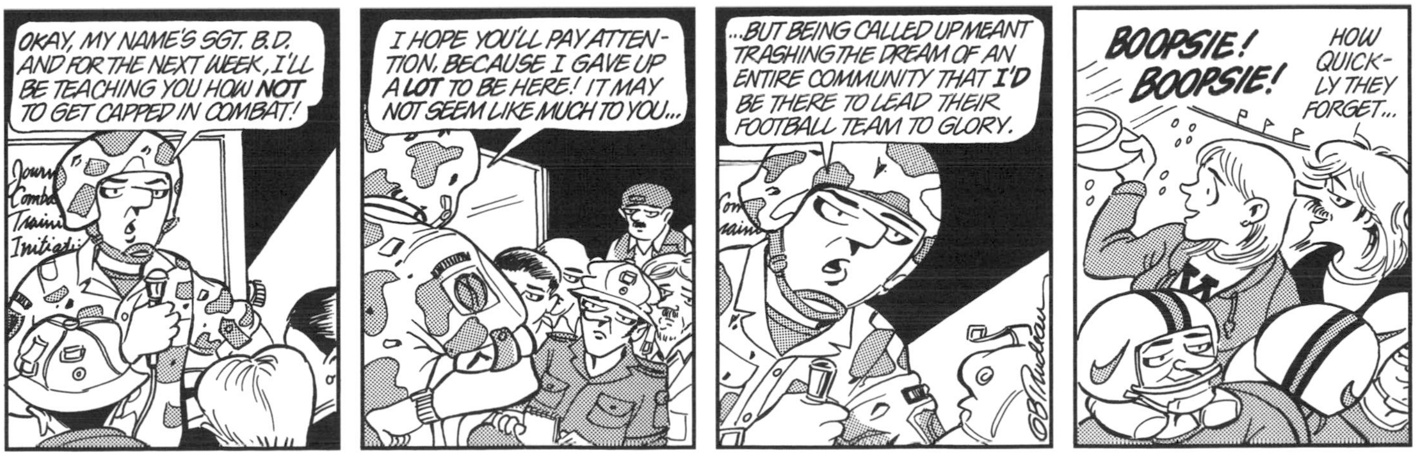
OKAY, MY NAME'S SGT. B.D. AND FOR THE NEXT WEEK, I'LL BE TEACHING YOU HOW NOT TO GET CAPPED IN COMBAT!
I HOPE YOU'LL PAY ATTENTION, BECAUSE I GAVE UP A LOT TO BE HERE! IT MAY NOT SEEM LIKE MUCH TO YOU...
...BUT BEING CALLED UP MEANT TRASHING THE DREAM OF AN ENTIRE COMMUNITY THAT I'D BE THERE TO LEAD THEIR FOOTBALL TEAM TO GLORY.
BOOPSIE! BOOPSIE!
HOW QUICKLY THEY FORGET...

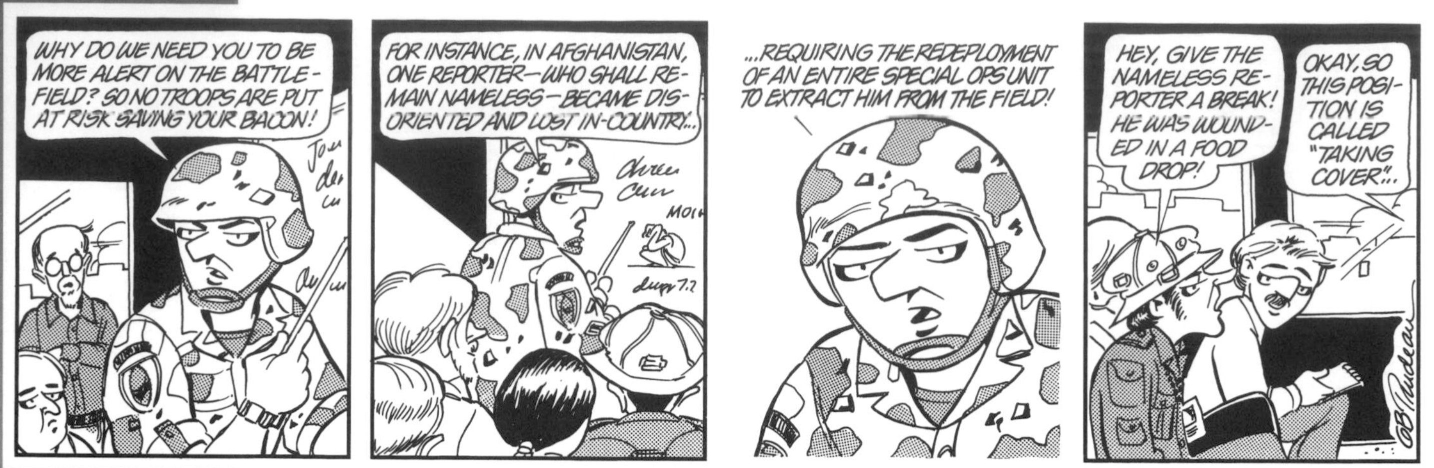
WHY DO WE NEED YOU TO BE MORE ALERT ON THE BATTLE-FIELD? SO NO TROOPS ARE PUT AT RISK SAVING YOUR BACON!
FOR INSTANCE, IN AFGHANISTAN, ONE REPORTER—WHO SHALL RE-MAIN NAMELESS—BECAME DIS-ORIENTED AND LOST IN-COUNTRY...
...REQUIRING THE REDEPLOYMENT OF AN ENTIRE SPECIAL OPS UNIT TO EXTRACT HIM FROM THE FIELD!
HEY, GIVE THE NAMELESS RE-PORTER A BREAK! HE WAS WOUND-ED IN A FOOD DROP!
OKAY, SO THIS POSI-TION IS CALLED "TAKING COVER"...
GB Trudeau

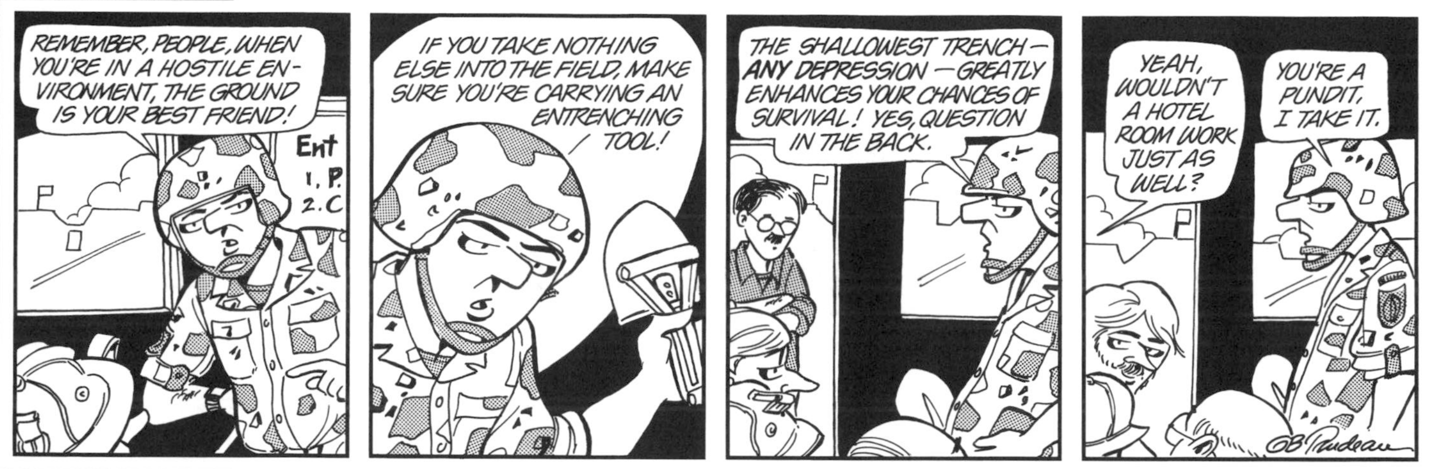
REMEMBER, PEOPLE, WHEN YOU'RE IN A HOSTILE EN-VIRONMENT, THE GROUND IS YOUR BEST FRIEND!
Ent
1. P.
2. C
IF YOU TAKE NOTHING ELSE INTO THE FIELD, MAKE SURE YOU'RE CARRYING AN ENTRENCHING TOOL!
THE SHALLOWEST TRENCH—ANY DEPRESSION—GREATLY ENHANCES YOUR CHANCES OF SURVIVAL! YES, QUESTION IN THE BACK.
YEAH, WOULDN'T A HOTEL ROOM WORK JUST AS WELL?
YOU'RE A PUNDIT, I TAKE IT.
GB Trudeau

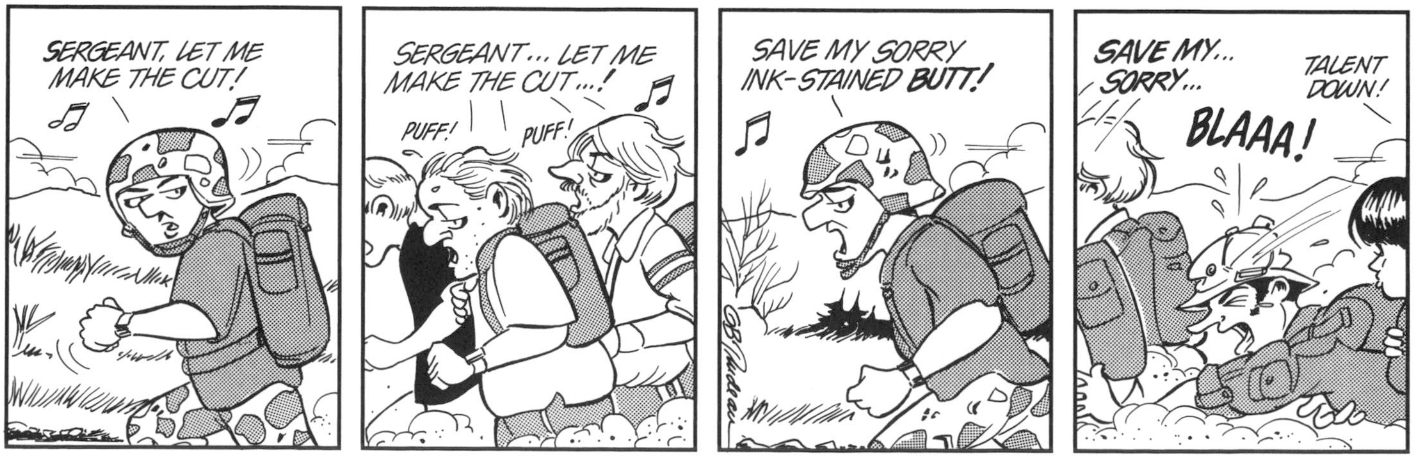
SERGEANT, LET ME MAKE THE CUT!
SERGEANT... LET ME MAKE THE CUT...!
PUFF!
PUFF!
SAVE MY SORRY INK-STAINED BUTT!
GB Trudeau
SAVE MY... SORRY...
TALENT DOWN!
BLAAA!

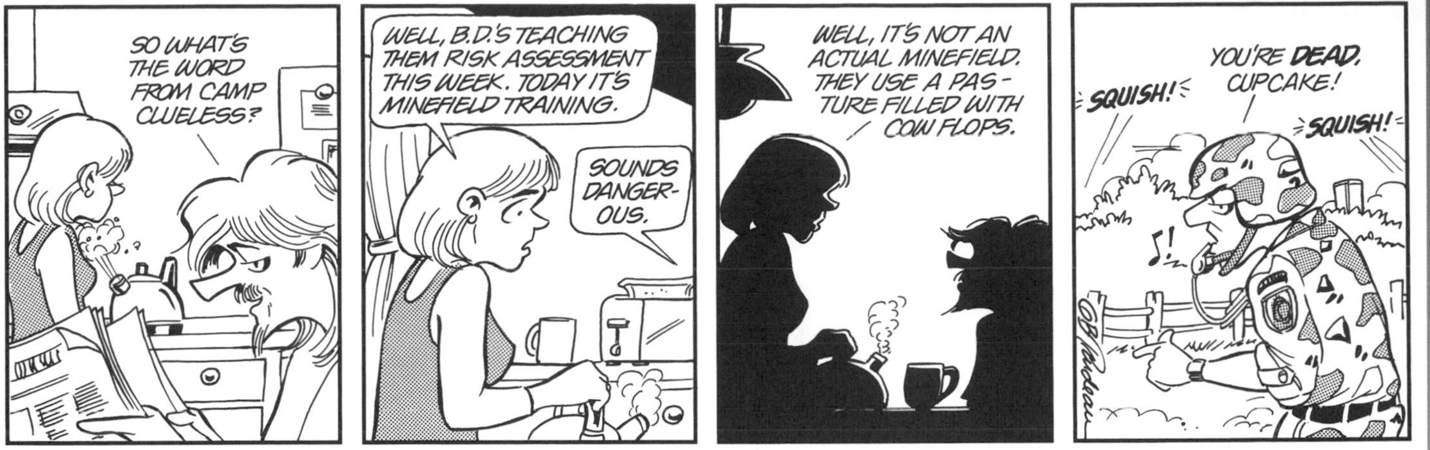
SO WHAT'S THE WORD FROM CAMP CLUELESS?
WELL, B.D.'S TEACHING THEM RISK ASSESSMENT THIS WEEK. TODAY IT'S MINEFIELD TRAINING.
SOUNDS DANGEROUS.
WELL, IT'S NOT AN ACTUAL MINEFIELD. THEY USE A PASTURE FILLED WITH COW FLOPS.
SQUISH!
YOU'RE DEAD, CUPCAKE!
SQUISH!

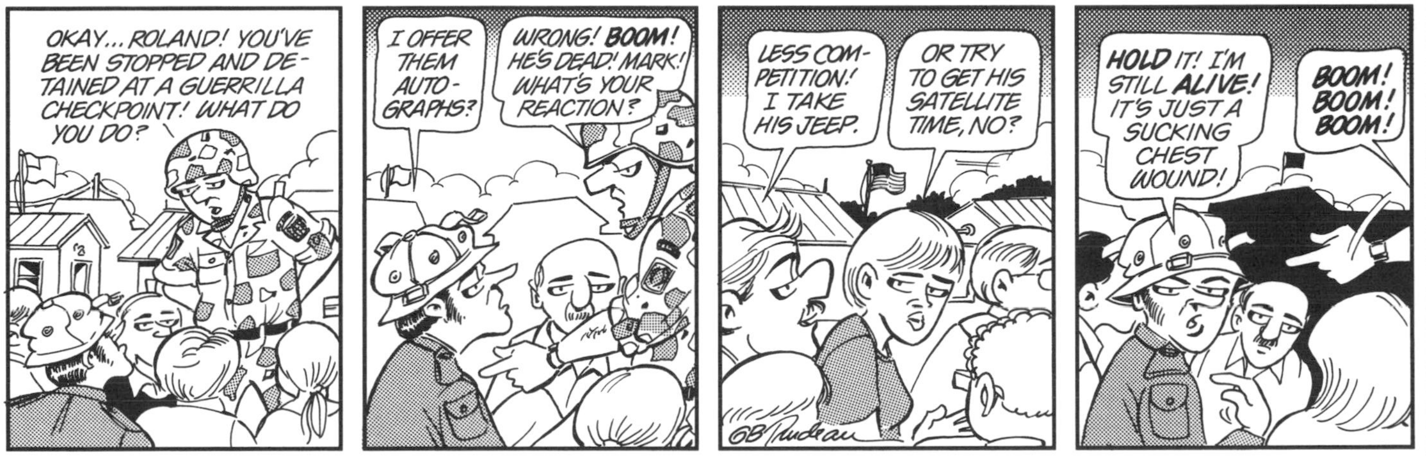
OKAY... ROLAND! YOU'VE BEEN STOPPED AND DETAINED AT A GUERRILLA CHECKPOINT! WHAT DO YOU DO?
I OFFER THEM AUTOGRAPHS?
WRONG! BOOM! HE'S DEAD! MARK! WHAT'S YOUR REACTION?
LESS COMPETITION! I TAKE HIS JEEP.
OR TRY TO GET HIS SATELLITE TIME, NO?
HOLD IT! I'M STILL ALIVE! IT'S JUST A SUCKING CHEST WOUND!
BOOM! BOOM! BOOM!

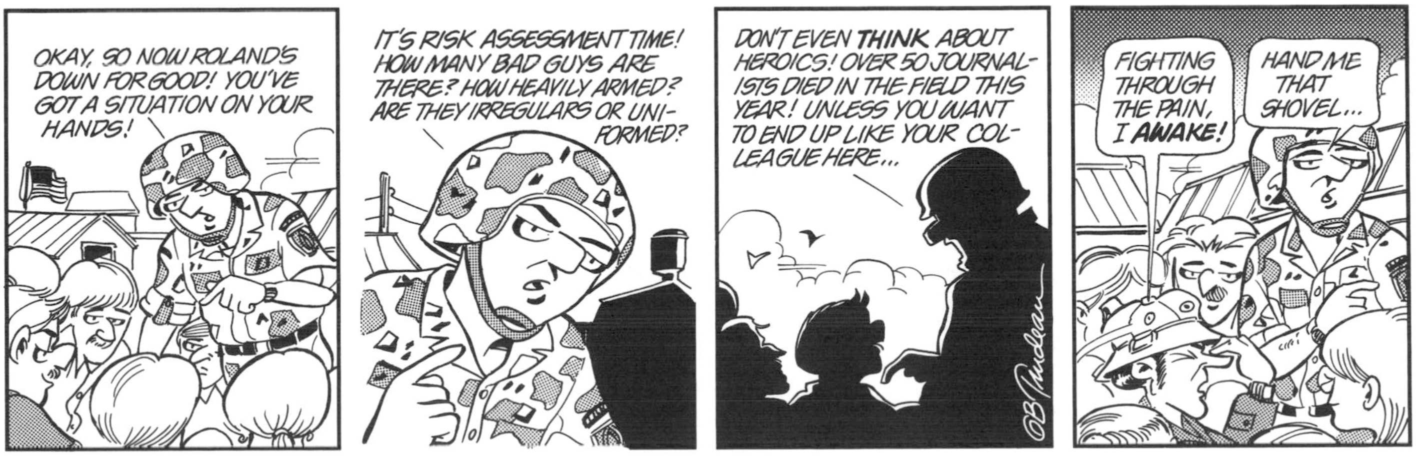
OKAY, SO NOW ROLAND'S DOWN FOR GOOD! YOU'VE GOT A SITUATION ON YOUR HANDS!
IT'S RISK ASSESSMENT TIME! HOW MANY BAD GUYS ARE THERE? HOW HEAVILY ARMED? ARE THEY IRREGULARS OR UNIFORMED?
DON'T EVEN THINK ABOUT HEROICS! OVER 50 JOURNALISTS DIED IN THE FIELD THIS YEAR! UNLESS YOU WANT TO END UP LIKE YOUR COLLEAGUE HERE...
FIGHTING THROUGH THE PAIN, I AWAKE!
HAND ME THAT SHOVEL...

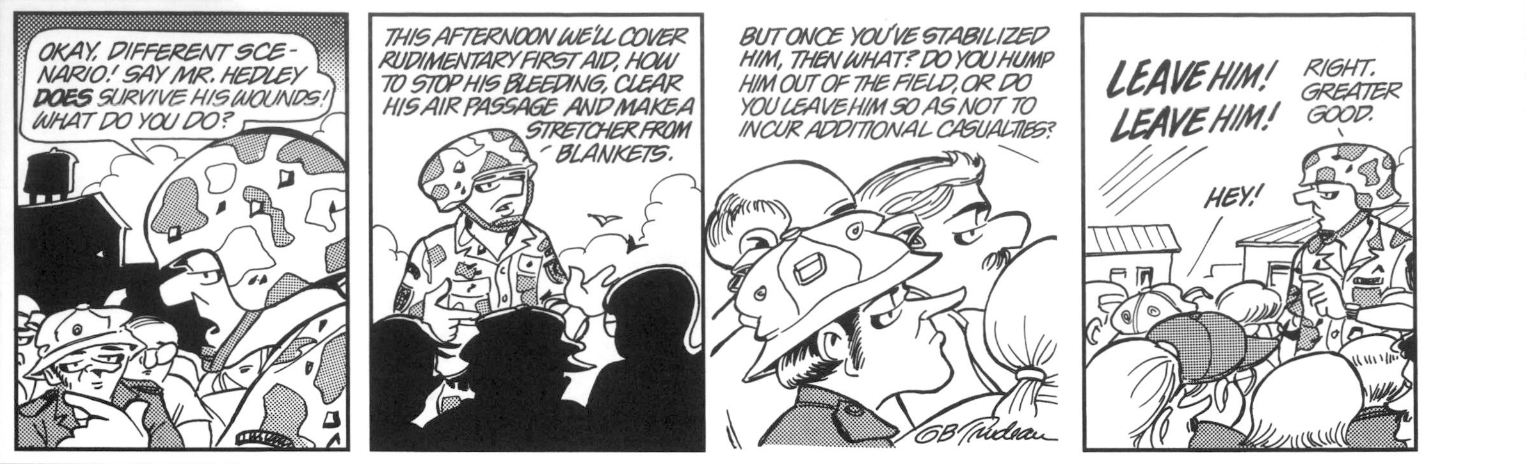
OKAY, DIFFERENT SCENARIO! SAY MR. HEDLEY DOES SURVIVE HIS WOUNDS! WHAT DO YOU DO?
THIS AFTERNOON WE'LL COVER RUDIMENTARY FIRST AID, HOW TO STOP HIS BLEEDING, CLEAR HIS AIR PASSAGE AND MAKE A STRETCHER FROM BLANKETS.
BUT ONCE YOU'VE STABILIZED HIM, THEN WHAT? DO YOU HUMP HIM OUT OF THE FIELD, OR DO YOU LEAVE HIM SO AS NOT TO INCUR ADDITIONAL CASUALTIES?
GB Trudeau
LEAVE HIM! LEAVE HIM!
HEY!
RIGHT. GREATER GOOD.

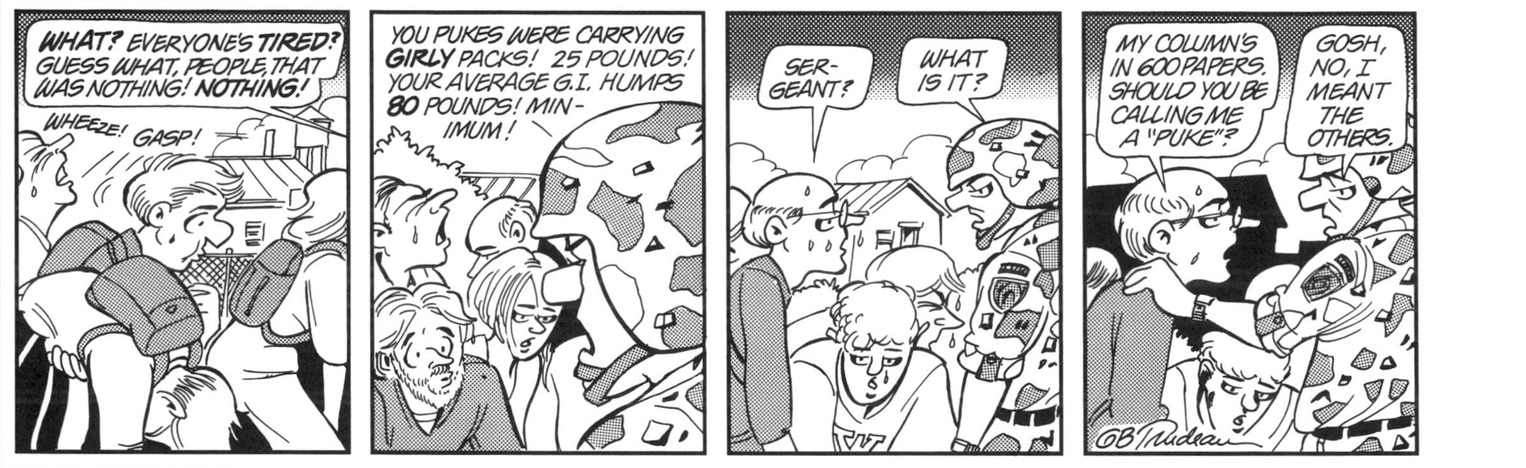
WHAT? EVERYONE'S TIRED? GUESS WHAT, PEOPLE, THAT WAS NOTHING! NOTHING!
WHEEZE! GASP!
YOU PUKES WERE CARRYING GIRLY PACKS! 25 POUNDS! YOUR AVERAGE G.I. HUMPS 80 POUNDS! MINIMUM!
SERGEANT?
WHAT IS IT?
MY COLUMN'S IN 600 PAPERS. SHOULD YOU BE CALLING ME A "PUKE"?
GOSH, NO, I MEANT THE OTHERS.
GB Trudeau

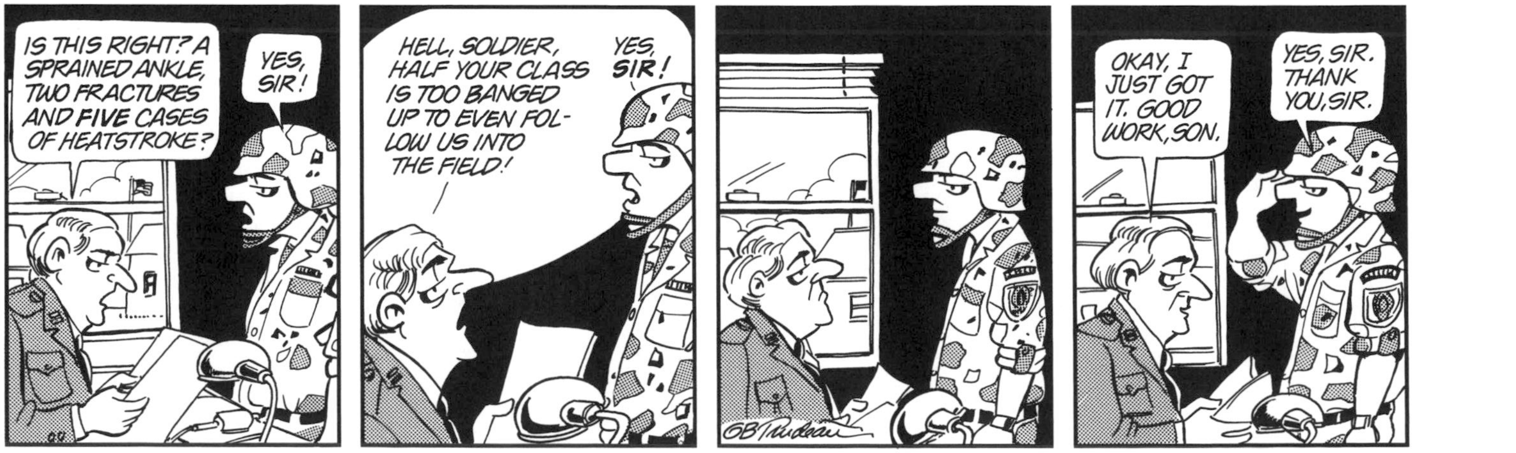
IS THIS RIGHT? A SPRAINED ANKLE, TWO FRACTURES AND FIVE CASES OF HEATSTROKE?
YES, SIR!
HELL, SOLDIER, HALF YOUR CLASS IS TOO BANGED UP TO EVEN FOLLOW US INTO THE FIELD!
YES, SIR!
GB Trudeau
OKAY, I JUST GOT IT. GOOD WORK, SON.
YES, SIR. THANK YOU, SIR.

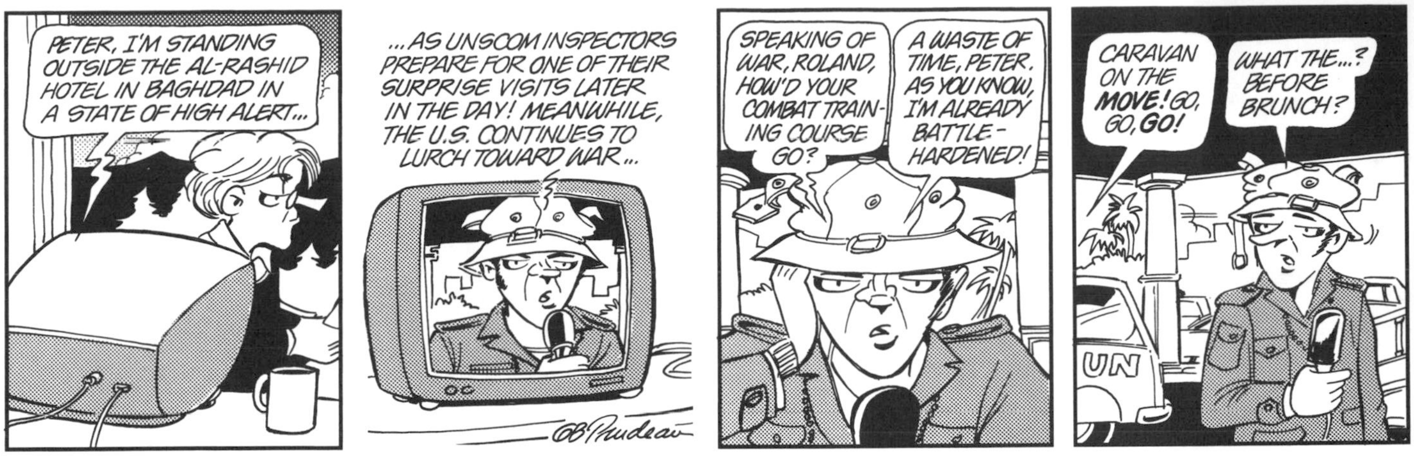
PETER, I'M STANDING OUTSIDE THE AL-RASHID HOTEL IN BAGHDAD IN A STATE OF HIGH ALERT...
...AS UNSCOM INSPECTORS PREPARE FOR ONE OF THEIR SURPRISE VISITS LATER IN THE DAY! MEANWHILE, THE U.S. CONTINUES TO LURCH TOWARD WAR...
GB Trudeau
SPEAKING OF WAR, ROLAND, HOW'D YOUR COMBAT TRAINING COURSE GO?
A WASTE OF TIME, PETER. AS YOU KNOW, I'M ALREADY BATTLE-HARDENED!
CARAVAN ON THE MOVE! GO, GO, GO!
WHAT THE...? BEFORE BRUNCH?
UN

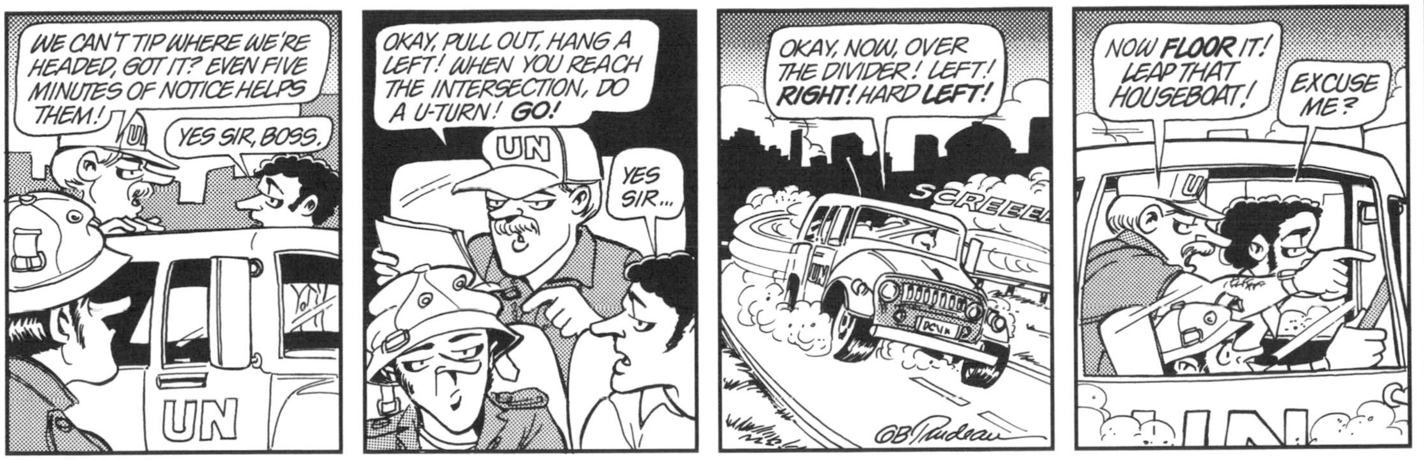
WE CAN'T TIP WHERE WE'RE HEADED, GOT IT? EVEN FIVE MINUTES OF NOTICE HELPS THEM!
YES SIR, BOSS.
UN
OKAY, PULL OUT, HANG A LEFT! WHEN YOU REACH THE INTERSECTION, DO A U-TURN! GO!
YES SIR...
OKAY, NOW, OVER THE DIVIDER! LEFT! RIGHT! HARD LEFT!
SCREEEE
GB Trudeau
NOW FLOOR IT! LEAP THAT HOUSEBOAT!
EXCUSE ME?

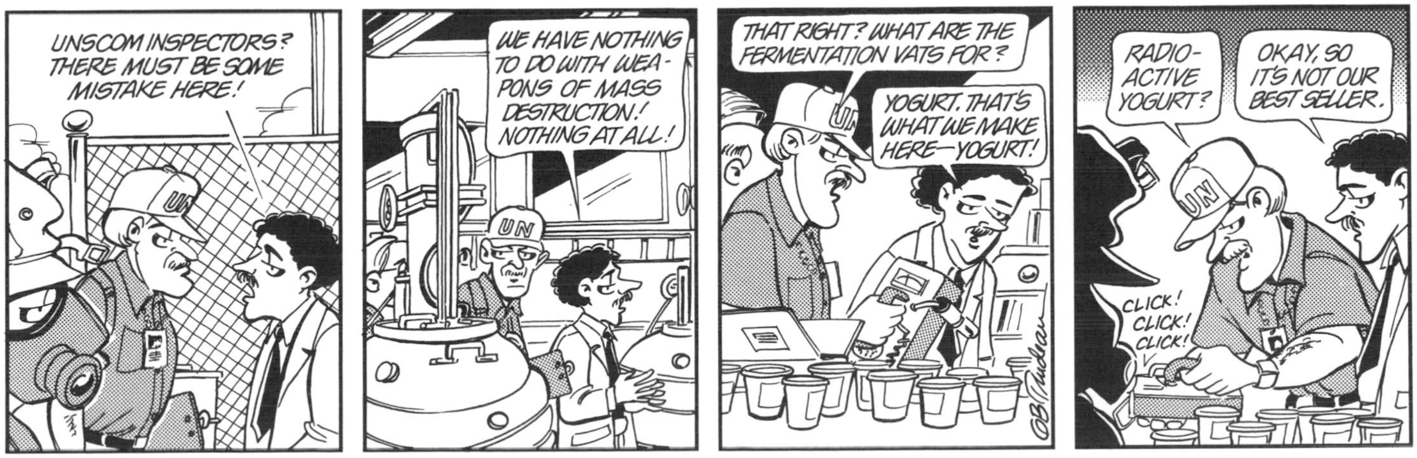
UNSCOM INSPECTORS? THERE MUST BE SOME MISTAKE HERE!
WE HAVE NOTHING TO DO WITH WEAPONS OF MASS DESTRUCTION! NOTHING AT ALL!
THAT RIGHT? WHAT ARE THE FERMENTATION VATS FOR?
YOGURT. THAT'S WHAT WE MAKE HERE—YOGURT!
GB Trudeau
RADIO-ACTIVE YOGURT?
OKAY, SO IT'S NOT OUR BEST SELLER.
CLICK! CLICK! CLICK!

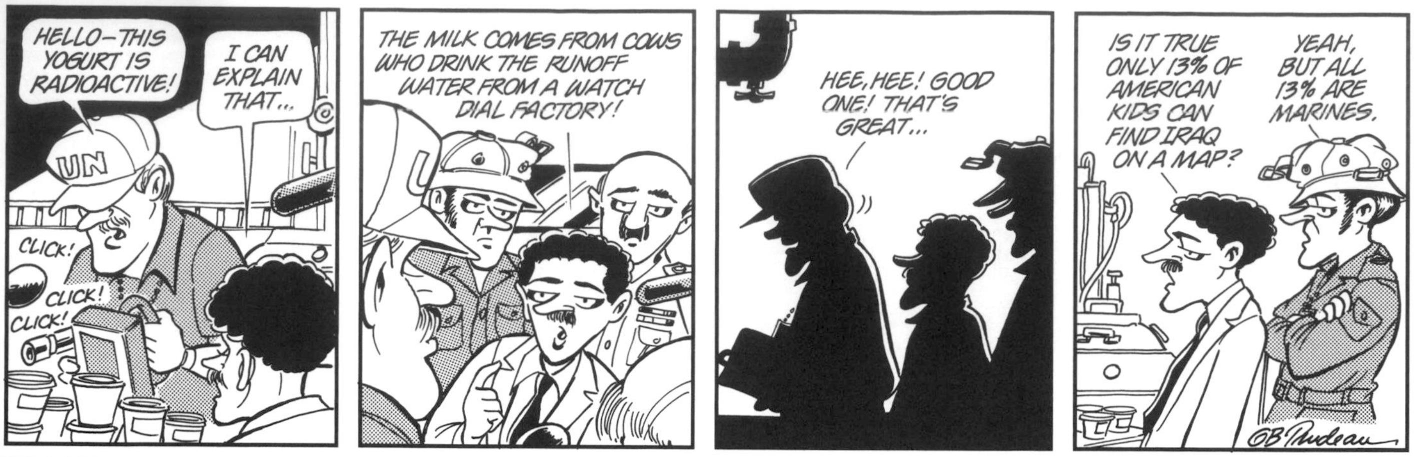
HELLO—THIS YOGURT IS RADIOACTIVE!
I CAN EXPLAIN THAT...
CLICK!
CLICK!
CLICK!
THE MILK COMES FROM COWS WHO DRINK THE RUNOFF WATER FROM A WATCH DIAL FACTORY!
HEE, HEE! GOOD ONE! THAT'S GREAT...
IS IT TRUE ONLY 13% OF AMERICAN KIDS CAN FIND IRAQ ON A MAP?
YEAH, BUT ALL 13% ARE MARINES.

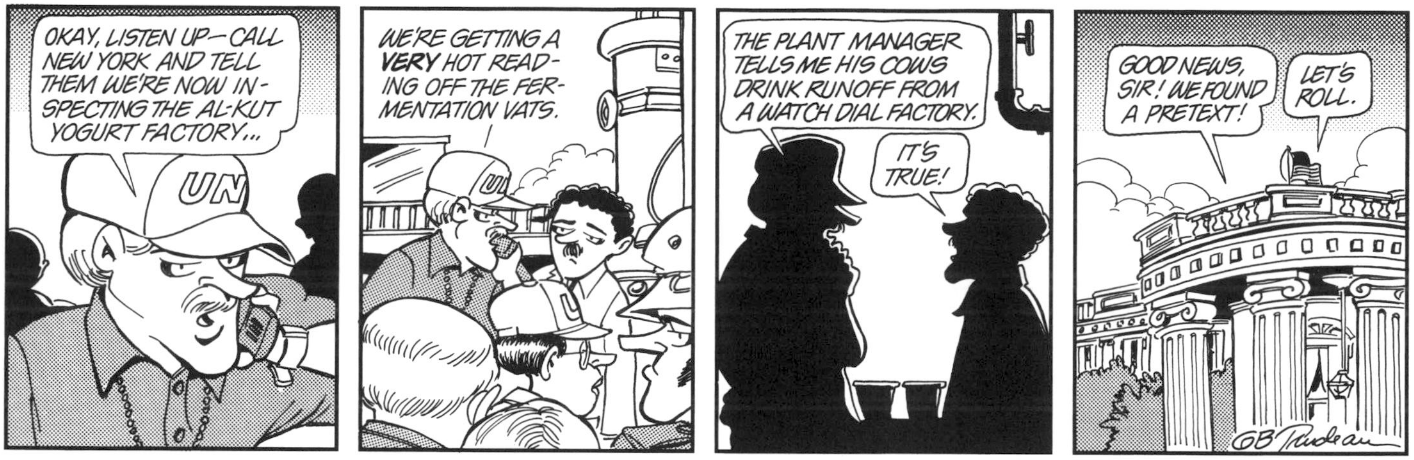
OKAY, LISTEN UP—CALL NEW YORK AND TELL THEM WE'RE NOW INSPECTING THE AL-KUT YOGURT FACTORY...
WE'RE GETTING A VERY HOT READING OFF THE FERMENTATION VATS.
THE PLANT MANAGER TELLS ME HIS COWS DRINK RUNOFF FROM A WATCH DIAL FACTORY.
IT'S TRUE!
GOOD NEWS, SIR! WE FOUND A PRETEXT!
LET'S ROLL.

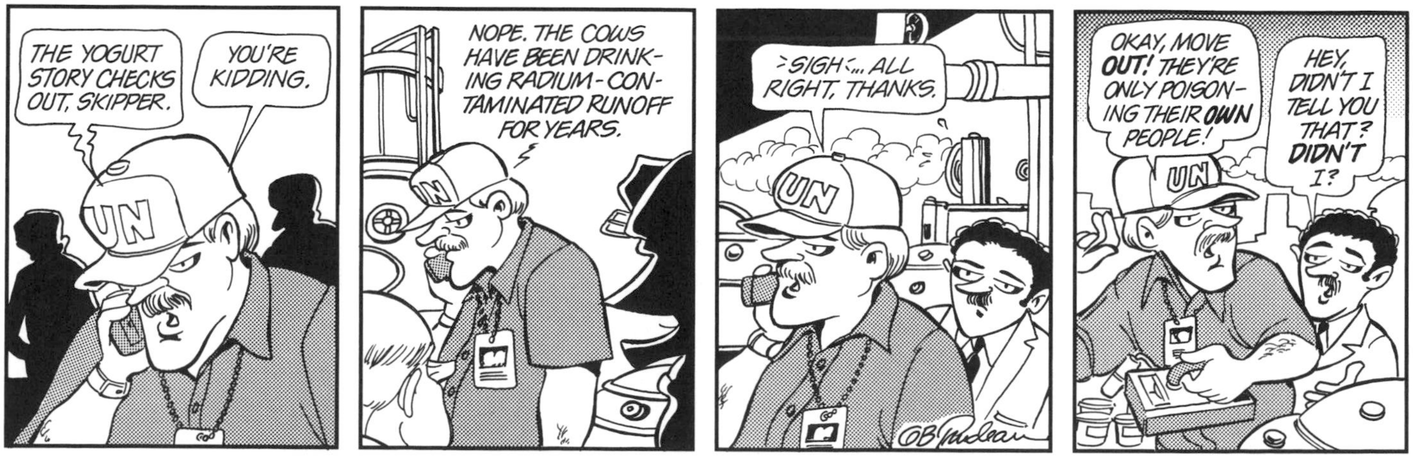
THE YOGURT STORY CHECKS OUT, SKIPPER.
YOU'RE KIDDING.
NOPE. THE COWS HAVE BEEN DRINKING RADIUM-CONTAMINATED RUNOFF FOR YEARS.
>SIGH<... ALL RIGHT, THANKS.
OKAY, MOVE OUT! THEY'RE ONLY POISONING THEIR OWN PEOPLE!
HEY, DIDN'T I TELL YOU THAT? DIDN'T I?

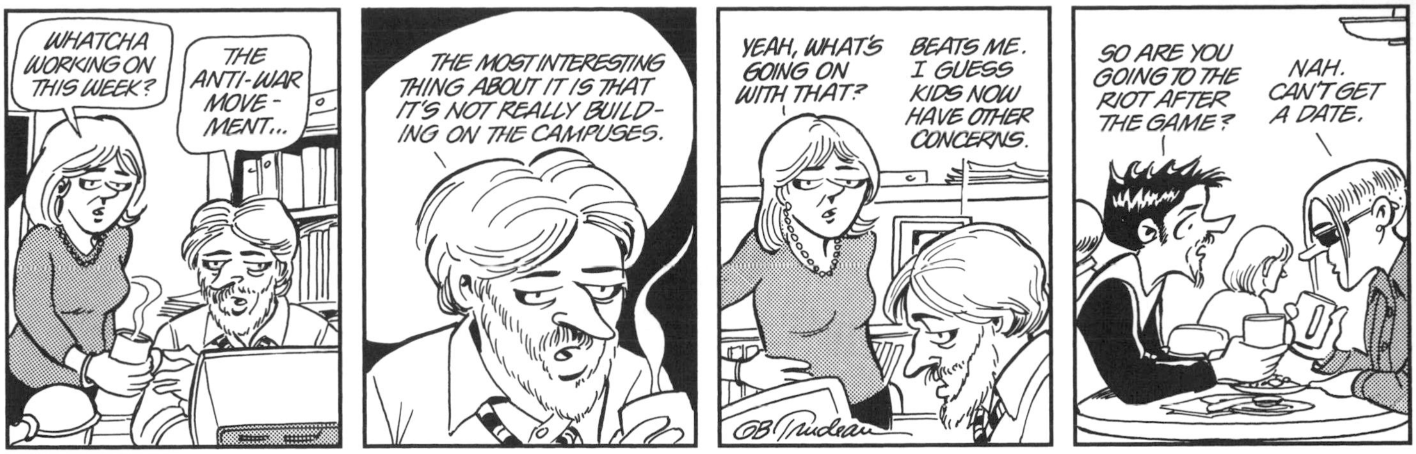
WHATCHA WORKING ON THIS WEEK?
THE ANTI-WAR MOVE-MENT...
THE MOST INTERESTING THING ABOUT IT IS THAT IT'S NOT REALLY BUILD-ING ON THE CAMPUSES.
YEAH, WHAT'S GOING ON WITH THAT?
BEATS ME. I GUESS KIDS NOW HAVE OTHER CONCERNS.
SO ARE YOU GOING TO THE RIOT AFTER THE GAME?
NAH. CAN'T GET A DATE.

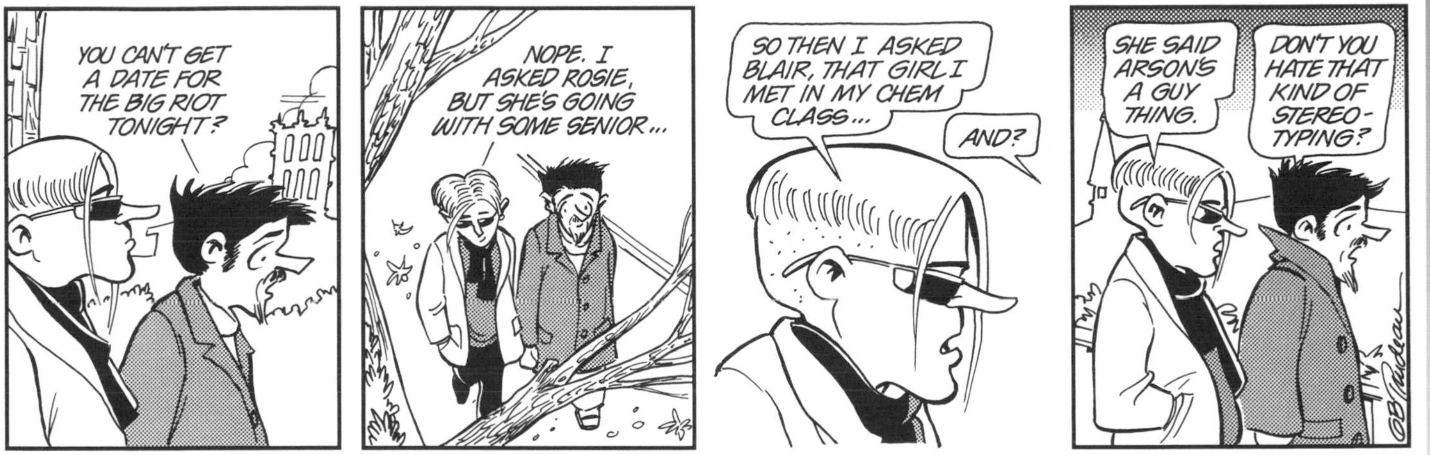
YOU CAN'T GET A DATE FOR THE BIG RIOT TONIGHT?
NOPE. I ASKED ROSIE, BUT SHE'S GOING WITH SOME SENIOR...
SO THEN I ASKED BLAIR, THAT GIRL I MET IN MY CHEM CLASS...
AND?
SHE SAID ARSON'S A GUY THING.
DON'T YOU HATE THAT KIND OF STEREO-TYPING?

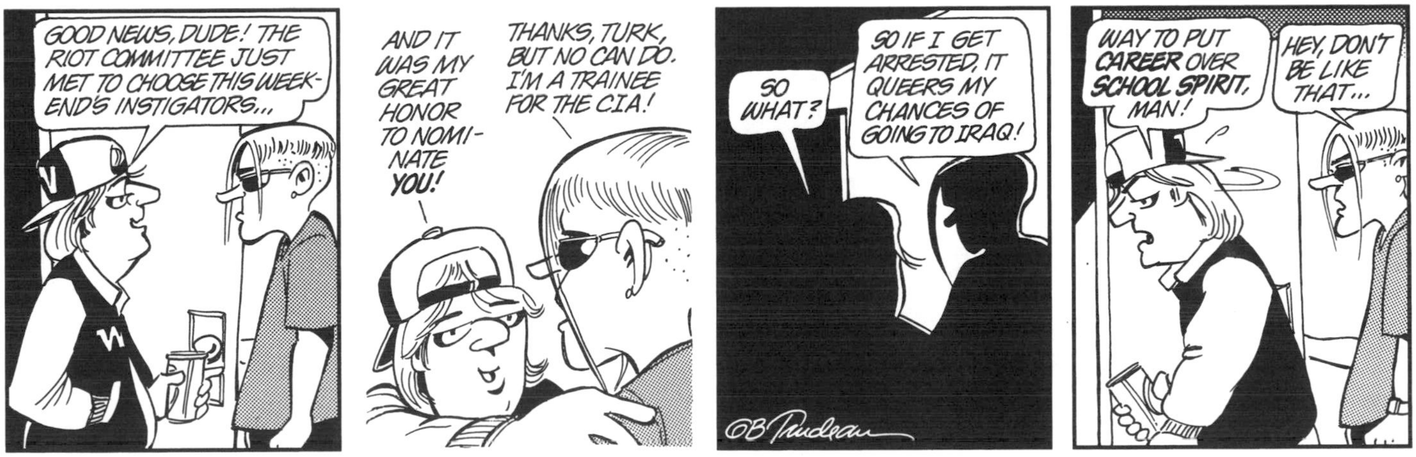
GOOD NEWS, DUDE! THE RIOT COMMITTEE JUST MET TO CHOOSE THIS WEEK-END'S INSTIGATORS...
AND IT WAS MY GREAT HONOR TO NOMI-NATE YOU!
THANKS, TURK, BUT NO CAN DO. I'M A TRAINEE FOR THE CIA!
SO WHAT?
SO IF I GET ARRESTED, IT QUEERS MY CHANCES OF GOING TO IRAQ!
WAY TO PUT CAREER OVER SCHOOL SPIRIT, MAN!
HEY, DON'T BE LIKE THAT...

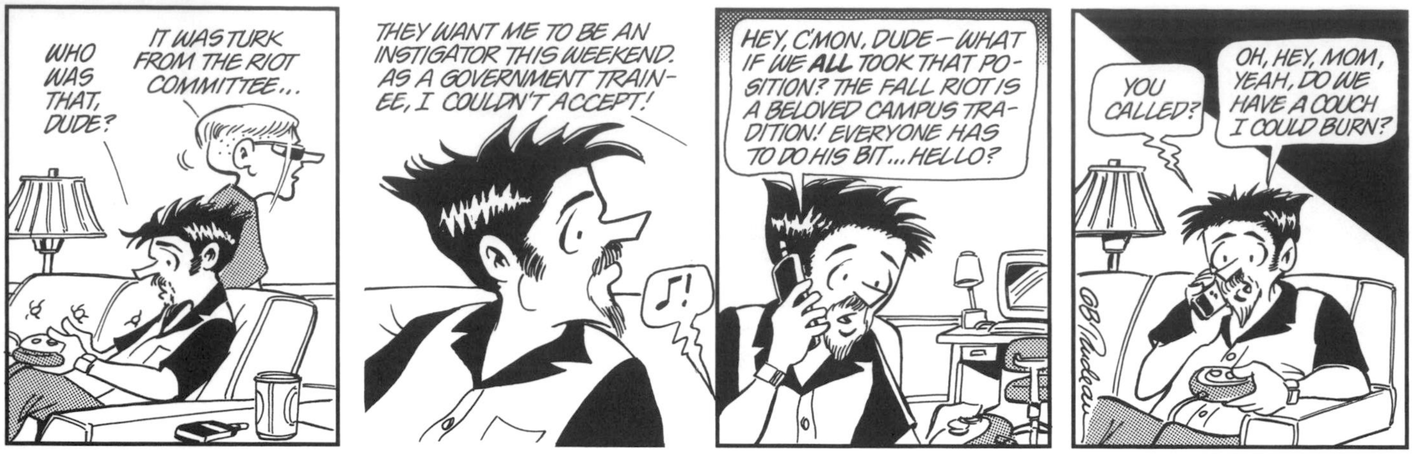
WHO WAS THAT, DUDE?
IT WAS TURK FROM THE RIOT COMMITTEE...
THEY WANT ME TO BE AN INSTIGATOR THIS WEEKEND. AS A GOVERNMENT TRAINEE, I COULDN'T ACCEPT!
HEY, C'MON, DUDE—WHAT IF WE **ALL** TOOK THAT POSITION? THE FALL RIOT IS A BELOVED CAMPUS TRADITION! EVERYONE HAS TO DO HIS BIT... HELLO?
YOU CALLED?
OH, HEY, MOM, YEAH, DO WE HAVE A COUCH I COULD BURN?

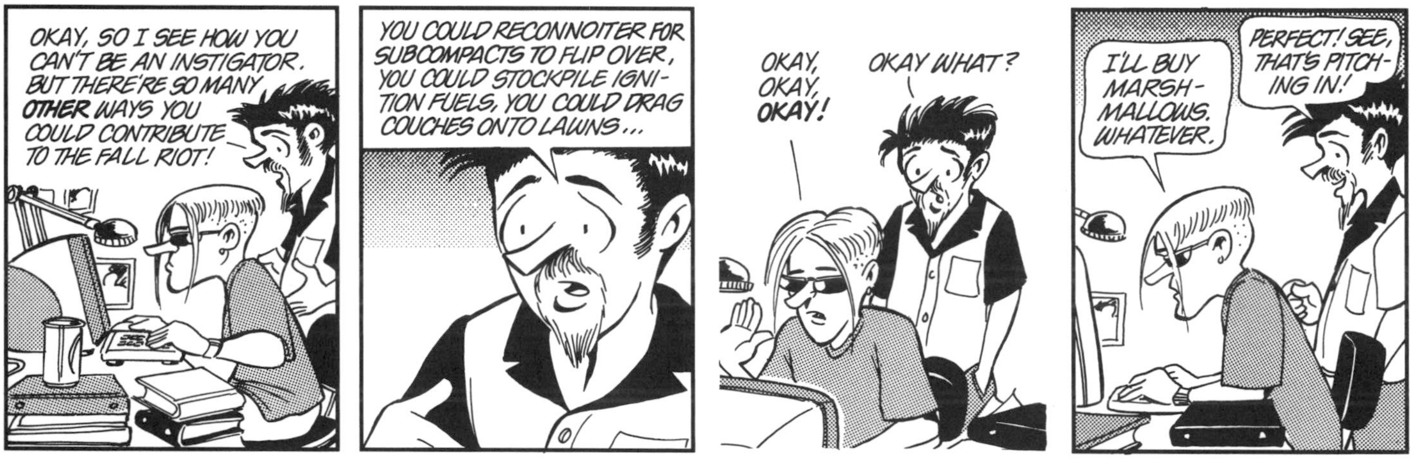
OKAY, SO I SEE HOW YOU CAN'T BE AN INSTIGATOR. BUT THERE'RE SO MANY **OTHER** WAYS YOU COULD CONTRIBUTE TO THE FALL RIOT!
YOU COULD RECONNOITER FOR SUBCOMPACTS TO FLIP OVER, YOU COULD STOCKPILE IGNITION FUELS, YOU COULD DRAG COUCHES ONTO LAWNS...
OKAY, OKAY, **OKAY!**
OKAY WHAT?
I'LL BUY MARSHMALLOWS. WHATEVER.
PERFECT! SEE, THAT'S PITCHING IN!

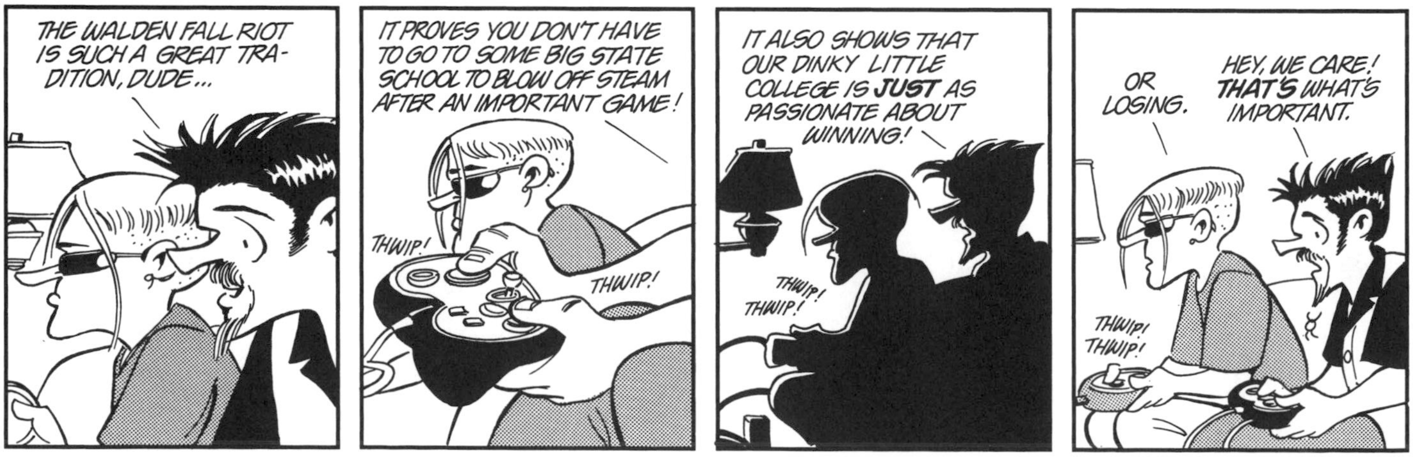
THE WALDEN FALL RIOT IS SUCH A GREAT TRADITION, DUDE...
IT PROVES YOU DON'T HAVE TO GO TO SOME BIG STATE SCHOOL TO BLOW OFF STEAM AFTER AN IMPORTANT GAME!
THWIP!
THWIP!
IT ALSO SHOWS THAT OUR DINKY LITTLE COLLEGE IS **JUST** AS PASSIONATE ABOUT WINNING!
THWIP! THWIP!
OR LOSING.
HEY, WE CARE! **THAT'S** WHAT'S IMPORTANT.
THWIP! THWIP!

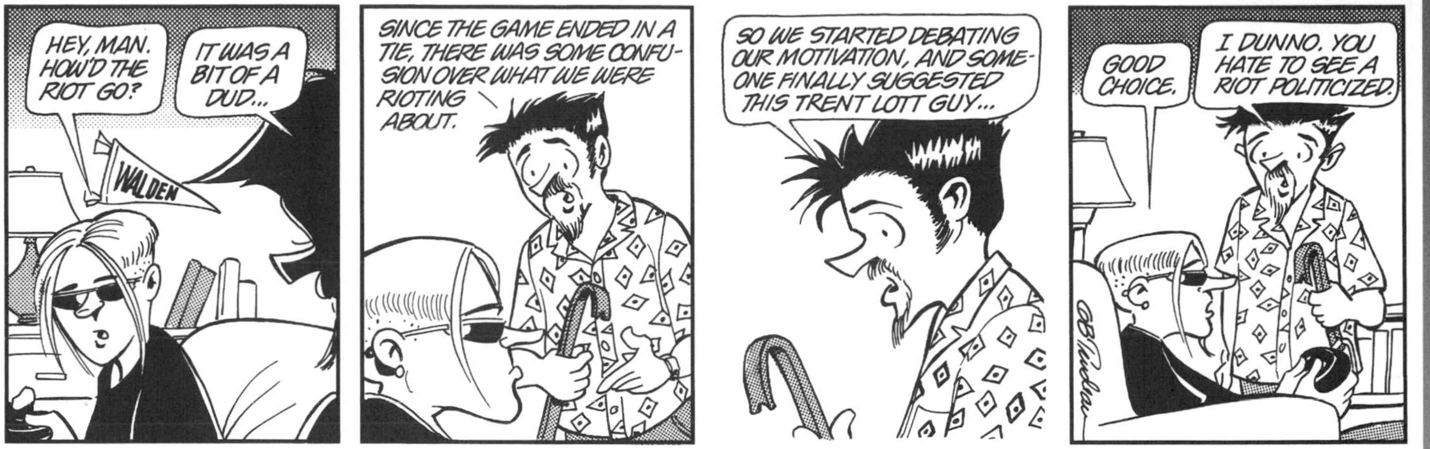
HEY, MAN. HOW'D THE RIOT GO?
IT WAS A BIT OF A DUD...
WALDEN
SINCE THE GAME ENDED IN A TIE, THERE WAS SOME CONFUSION OVER WHAT WE WERE RIOTING ABOUT.
SO WE STARTED DEBATING OUR MOTIVATION, AND SOMEONE FINALLY SUGGESTED THIS TRENT LOTT GUY...
GOOD CHOICE.
I DUNNO. YOU HATE TO SEE A RIOT POLITICIZED.
GBTrudeau

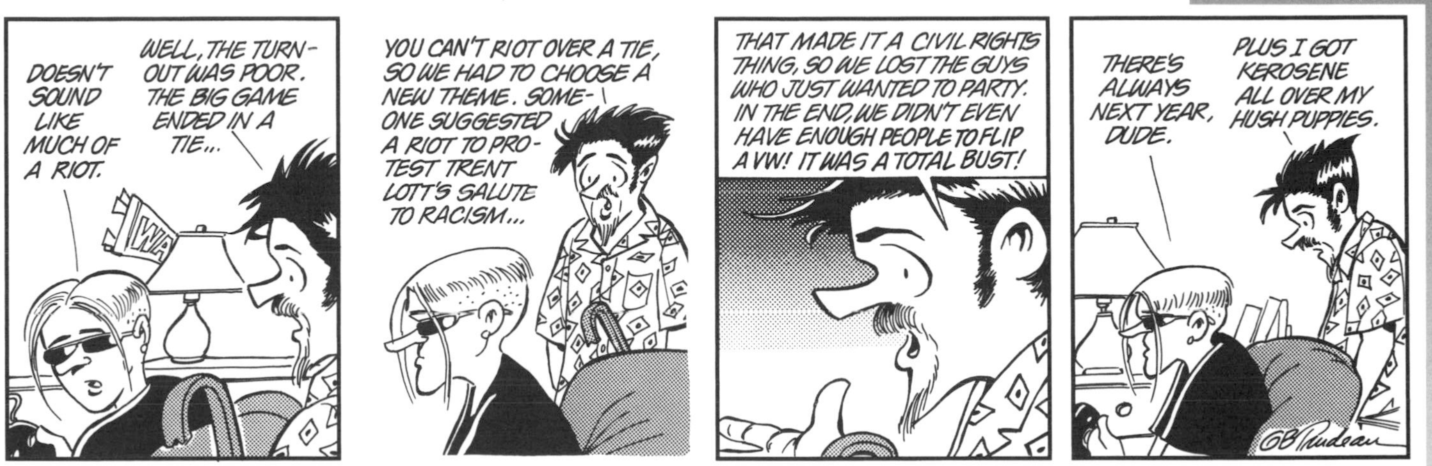
DOESN'T SOUND LIKE MUCH OF A RIOT.
WELL, THE TURNOUT WAS POOR. THE BIG GAME ENDED IN A TIE...
YOU CAN'T RIOT OVER A TIE, SO WE HAD TO CHOOSE A NEW THEME. SOMEONE SUGGESTED A RIOT TO PROTEST TRENT LOTT'S SALUTE TO RACISM...
THAT MADE IT A CIVIL RIGHTS THING, SO WE LOST THE GUYS WHO JUST WANTED TO PARTY. IN THE END, WE DIDN'T EVEN HAVE ENOUGH PEOPLE TO FLIP A VW! IT WAS A TOTAL BUST!
THERE'S ALWAYS NEXT YEAR, DUDE.
PLUS I GOT KEROSENE ALL OVER MY HUSH PUPPIES.
GBTrudeau

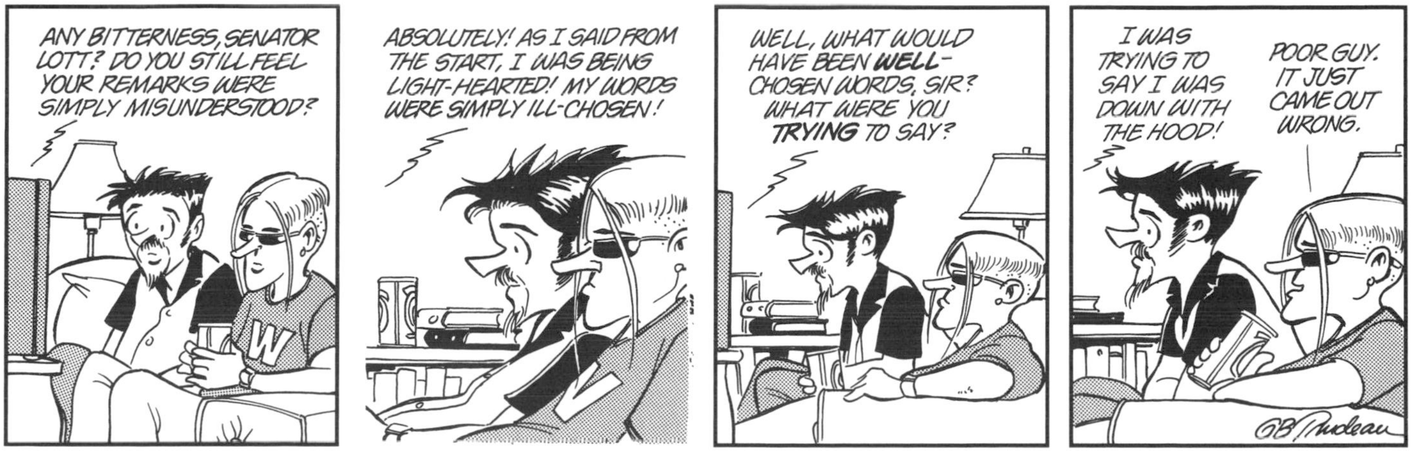
ANY BITTERNESS, SENATOR LOTT? DO YOU STILL FEEL YOUR REMARKS WERE SIMPLY MISUNDERSTOOD?
ABSOLUTELY! AS I SAID FROM THE START, I WAS BEING LIGHT-HEARTED! MY WORDS WERE SIMPLY ILL-CHOSEN!
WELL, WHAT WOULD HAVE BEEN WELL-CHOSEN WORDS, SIR? WHAT WERE YOU TRYING TO SAY?
I WAS TRYING TO SAY I WAS DOWN WITH THE HOOD!
POOR GUY. IT JUST CAME OUT WRONG.
GBTrudeau

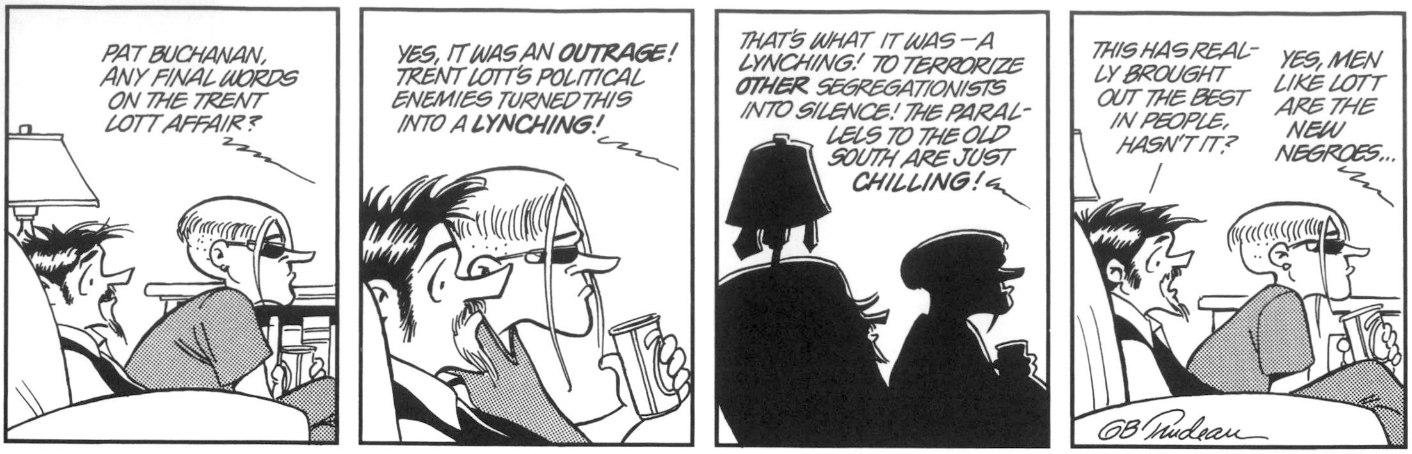
PAT BUCHANAN, ANY FINAL WORDS ON THE TRENT LOTT AFFAIR?
YES, IT WAS AN **OUTRAGE**! TRENT LOTT'S POLITICAL ENEMIES TURNED THIS INTO A **LYNCHING**!
THAT'S WHAT IT WAS—A LYNCHING! TO TERRORIZE **OTHER** SEGREGATIONISTS INTO SILENCE! THE PARALLELS TO THE OLD SOUTH ARE JUST **CHILLING**!
THIS HAS REALLY BROUGHT OUT THE BEST IN PEOPLE, HASN'T IT?
YES, MEN LIKE LOTT ARE THE NEW NEGROES...
©B Trudeau

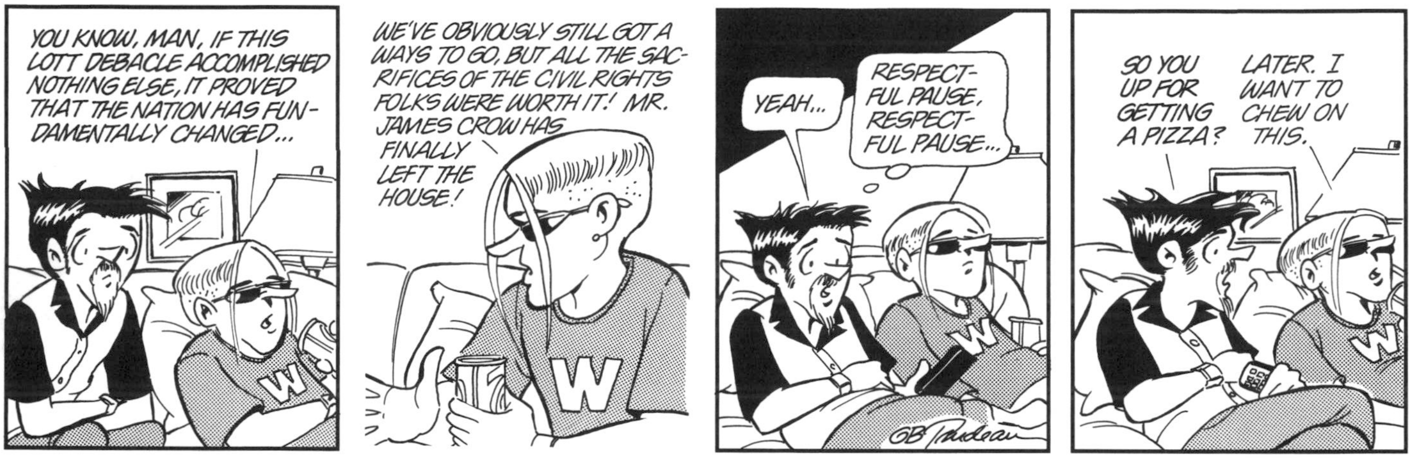
YOU KNOW, MAN, IF THIS LOTT DEBACLE ACCOMPLISHED NOTHING ELSE, IT PROVED THAT THE NATION HAS FUNDAMENTALLY CHANGED...
WE'VE OBVIOUSLY STILL GOT A WAYS TO GO, BUT ALL THE SACRIFICES OF THE CIVIL RIGHTS FOLKS WERE WORTH IT! MR. JAMES CROW HAS FINALLY LEFT THE HOUSE!
YEAH...
RESPECTFUL PAUSE, RESPECTFUL PAUSE...
©B Trudeau
SO YOU UP FOR GETTING A PIZZA?
LATER. I WANT TO CHEW ON THIS.

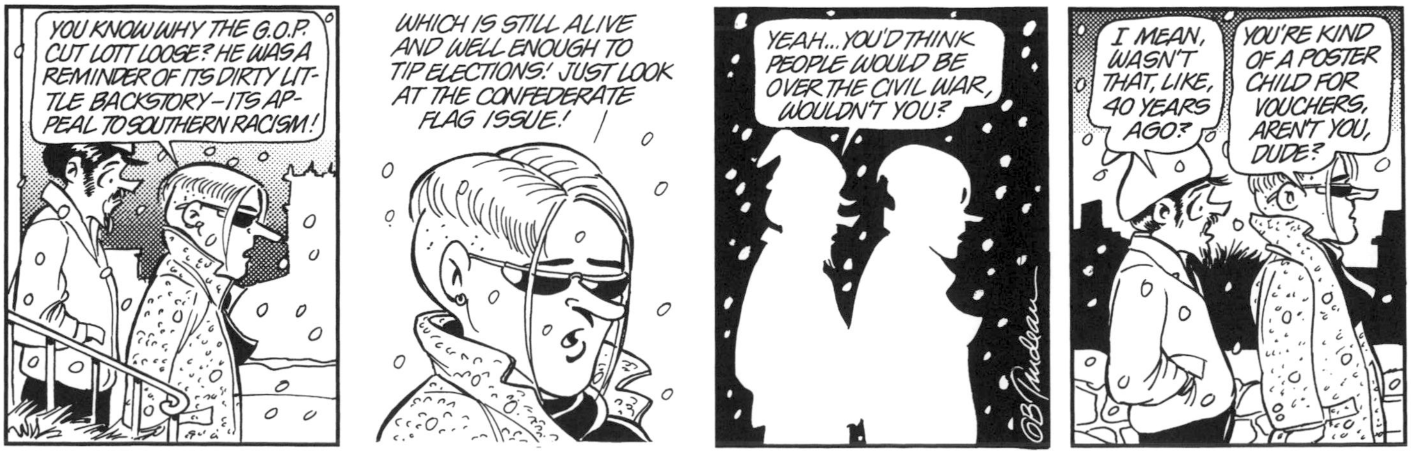
YOU KNOW WHY THE G.O.P. CUT LOTT LOOSE? HE WAS A REMINDER OF ITS DIRTY LITTLE BACKSTORY—ITS APPEAL TO SOUTHERN RACISM!
WHICH IS STILL ALIVE AND WELL ENOUGH TO TIP ELECTIONS! JUST LOOK AT THE CONFEDERATE FLAG ISSUE!
YEAH...YOU'D THINK PEOPLE WOULD BE OVER THE CIVIL WAR, WOULDN'T YOU?
©B Trudeau
I MEAN, WASN'T THAT, LIKE, 40 YEARS AGO?
YOU'RE KIND OF A POSTER CHILD FOR VOUCHERS, AREN'T YOU, DUDE?

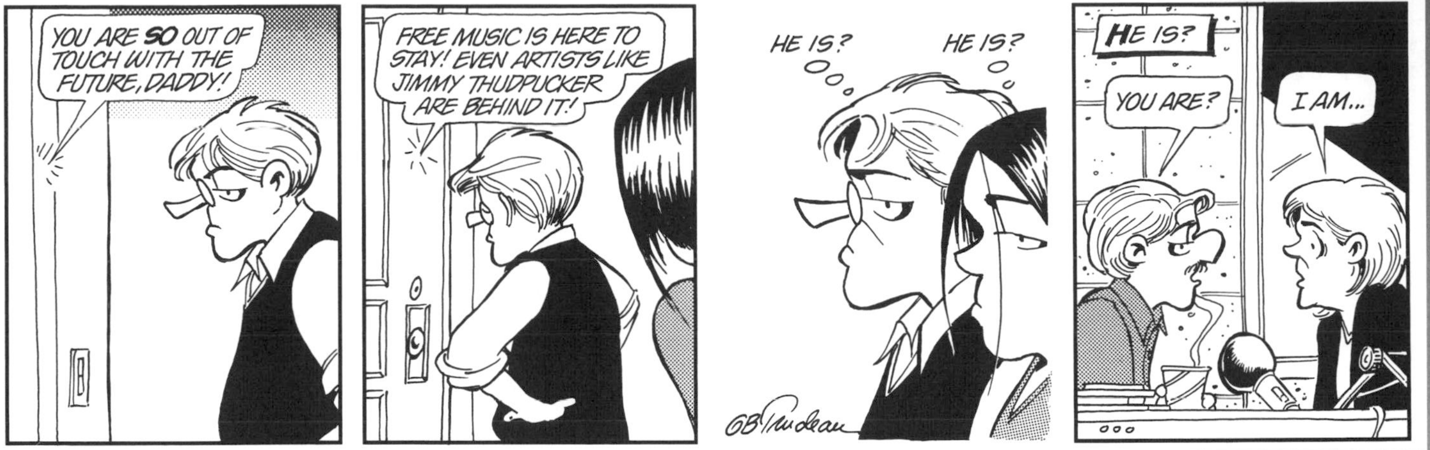
YOU ARE SO OUT OF TOUCH WITH THE FUTURE, DADDY!
FREE MUSIC IS HERE TO STAY! EVEN ARTISTS LIKE JIMMY THUDPUCKER ARE BEHIND IT!
HE IS?
HE IS?
HE IS?
YOU ARE?
I AM...

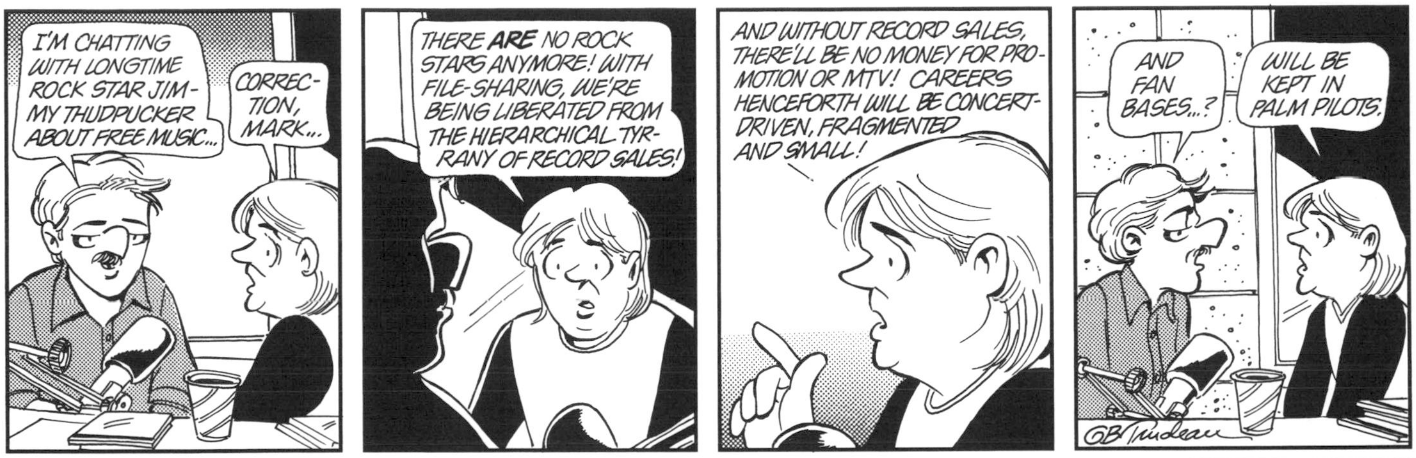
I'M CHATTING WITH LONGTIME ROCK STAR JIM-MY THUDPUCKER ABOUT FREE MUSIC...
CORREC-TION, MARK...
THERE ARE NO ROCK STARS ANYMORE! WITH FILE-SHARING, WE'RE BEING LIBERATED FROM THE HIERARCHICAL TYR-RANY OF RECORD SALES!
AND WITHOUT RECORD SALES, THERE'LL BE NO MONEY FOR PRO-MOTION OR MTV! CAREERS HENCEFORTH WILL BE CONCERT-DRIVEN, FRAGMENTED AND SMALL!
AND FAN BASES...?
WILL BE KEPT IN PALM PILOTS.

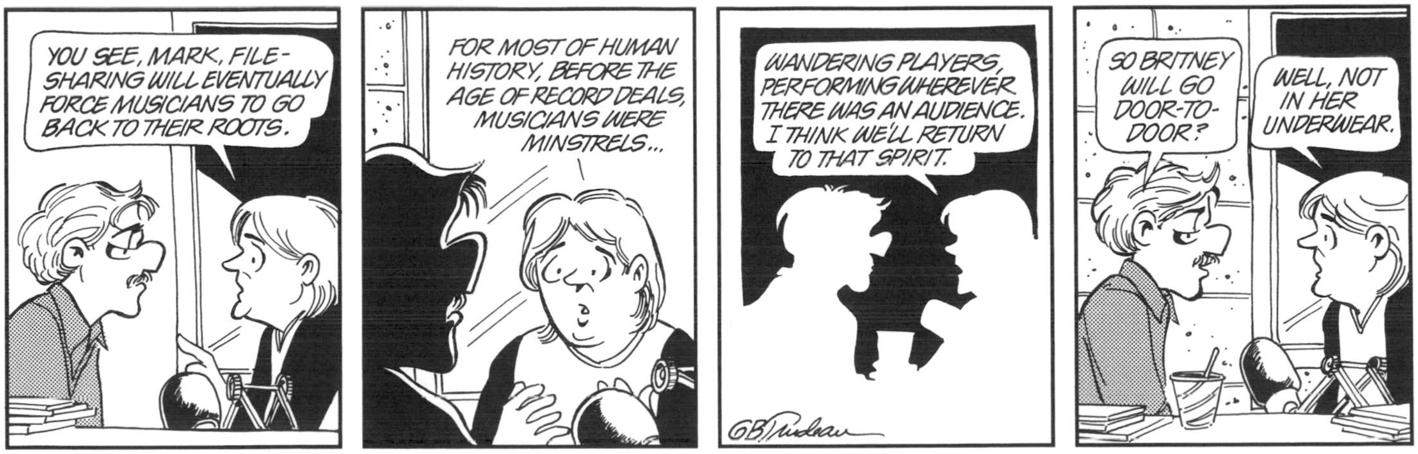
YOU SEE, MARK, FILE-SHARING WILL EVENTUALLY FORCE MUSICIANS TO GO BACK TO THEIR ROOTS.
FOR MOST OF HUMAN HISTORY, BEFORE THE AGE OF RECORD DEALS, MUSICIANS WERE MINSTRELS...
WANDERING PLAYERS, PERFORMING WHEREVER THERE WAS AN AUDIENCE. I THINK WE'LL RETURN TO THAT SPIRIT.
SO BRITNEY WILL GO DOOR-TO-DOOR?
WELL, NOT IN HER UNDERWEAR.

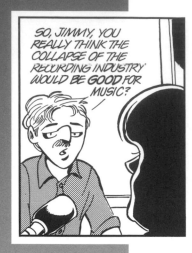

SO, JIMMY, YOU REALLY THINK THE COLLAPSE OF THE RECORDING INDUSTRY WOULD BE **GOOD** FOR MUSIC?
ABSOLUTELY. WITHOUT RECORD SALES TO WORRY ABOUT, MUSICIANS CAN FOCUS ON PERFORMANCE CAREERS.
IN THIS NEW WORLD, TALENTED MUSICIANS WILL PROSPER, AND BAD ONES WILL HAVE PLENTY OF TIME TO PRACTICE!
AND THE SUITS?
THE SUITS WILL DIE OFF, AND PEPPERLAND WILL BE FREE AGAIN!
GB Trudeau

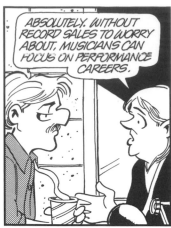

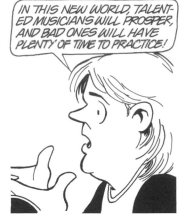

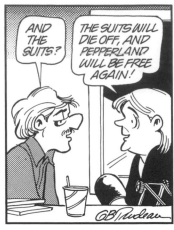

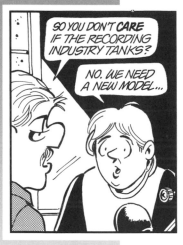

SO YOU DON'T **CARE** IF THE RECORDING INDUSTRY TANKS?
NO. WE NEED A NEW MODEL...
A POST-POP STAR MODEL, WHERE MUSIC IS FREE, AND PERFORMERS MAKE A MODEST LIVING THROUGH TOURING!
A **MODEST** LIVING?
RIGHT. LIKE WORKING JAZZ AND CLASSICAL MUSICIANS.
BUT WHERE WILL OUR NEXT **DIVAS** COME FROM?
OPERA. LIKE BEFORE.
GB Trudeau

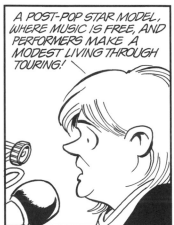

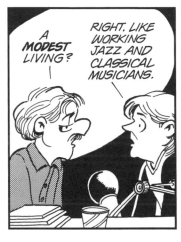

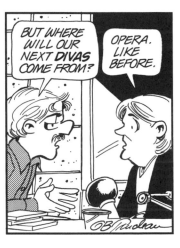

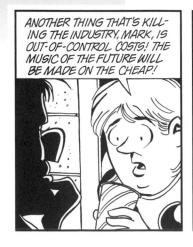

ANOTHER THING THAT'S KILLING THE INDUSTRY, MARK, IS OUT-OF-CONTROL COSTS! THE MUSIC OF THE FUTURE WILL BE MADE ON THE CHEAP!
FOR INSTANCE, I JUST PRODUCED AN ALBUM FOR ONE OF THE MOST PROMISING YOUNG ARTISTS IN THE WORLD FOR LESS THAN $18K!
WOW... WHO IS THIS ARTIST?
MY SON.
YOUR SON?
AGAIN, IT'S ABOUT COST CONTAINMENT.
GB Trudeau

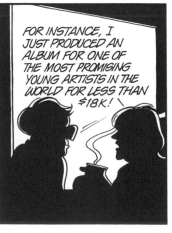

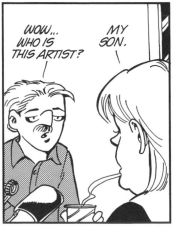

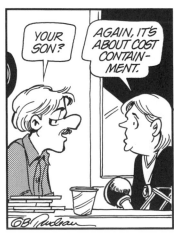

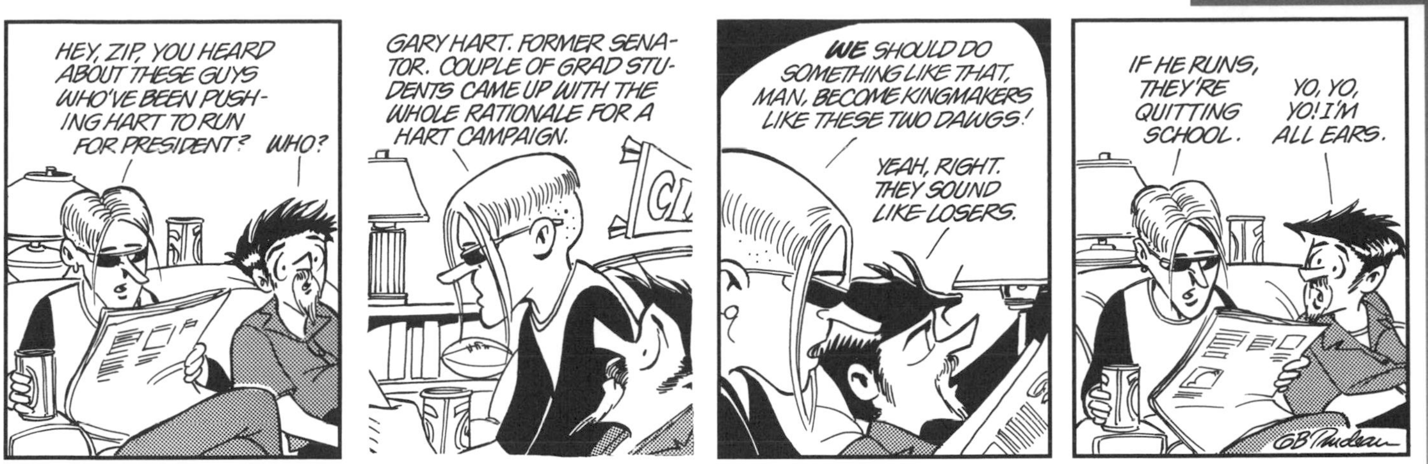
HEY, ZIP, YOU HEARD ABOUT THESE GUYS WHO'VE BEEN PUSHING HART TO RUN FOR PRESIDENT?
WHO?
GARY HART. FORMER SENATOR. COUPLE OF GRAD STUDENTS CAME UP WITH THE WHOLE RATIONALE FOR A HART CAMPAIGN.
CIA
WE SHOULD DO SOMETHING LIKE THAT, MAN. BECOME KINGMAKERS LIKE THESE TWO DAWGS!
YEAH, RIGHT. THEY SOUND LIKE LOSERS.
IF HE RUNS, THEY'RE QUITTING SCHOOL.
YO, YO, YO! I'M ALL EARS.

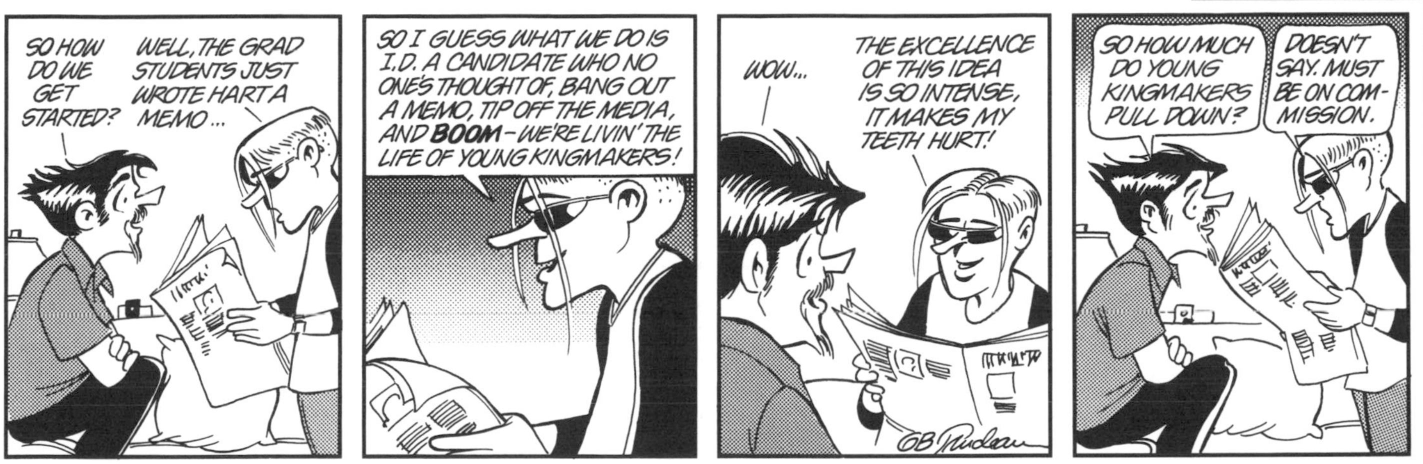
SO HOW DO WE GET STARTED?
WELL, THE GRAD STUDENTS JUST WROTE HART A MEMO...
SO I GUESS WHAT WE DO IS I.D. A CANDIDATE WHO NO ONE'S THOUGHT OF, BANG OUT A MEMO, TIP OFF THE MEDIA, AND BOOM – WE'RE LIVIN' THE LIFE OF YOUNG KINGMAKERS!
WOW...
THE EXCELLENCE OF THIS IDEA IS SO INTENSE, IT MAKES MY TEETH HURT!
SO HOW MUCH DO YOUNG KINGMAKERS PULL DOWN?
DOESN'T SAY. MUST BE ON COMMISSION.

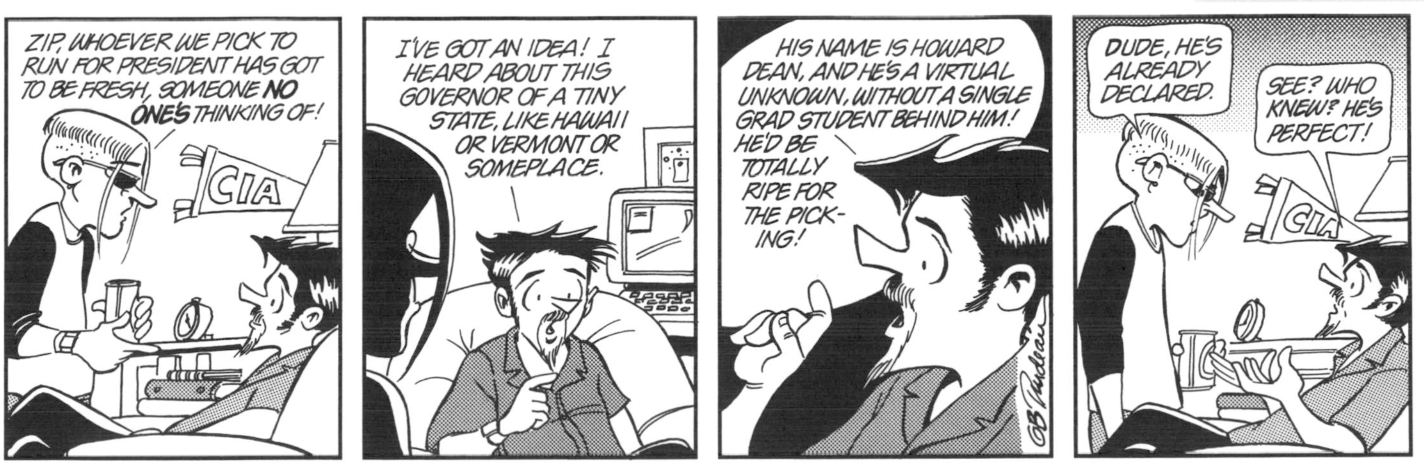
ZIP, WHOEVER WE PICK TO RUN FOR PRESIDENT HAS GOT TO BE FRESH, SOMEONE NO ONE'S THINKING OF!
CIA
I'VE GOT AN IDEA! I HEARD ABOUT THIS GOVERNOR OF A TINY STATE, LIKE HAWAII OR VERMONT OR SOMEPLACE.
HIS NAME IS HOWARD DEAN, AND HE'S A VIRTUAL UNKNOWN, WITHOUT A SINGLE GRAD STUDENT BEHIND HIM! HE'D BE TOTALLY RIPE FOR THE PICKING!
DUDE, HE'S ALREADY DECLARED.
SEE? WHO KNEW? HE'S PERFECT!
CIA

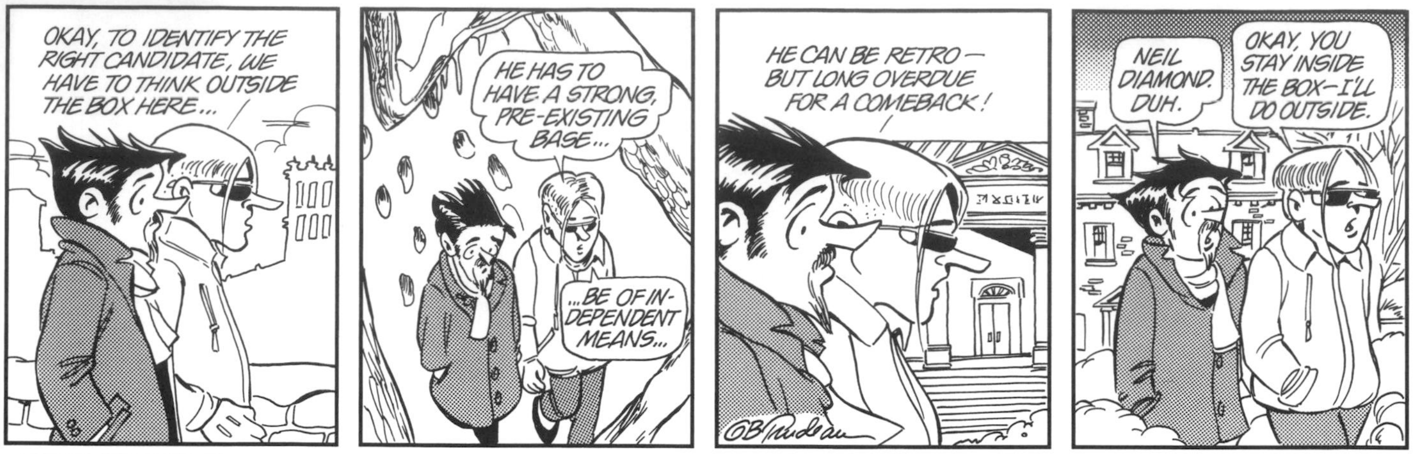
OKAY, TO IDENTIFY THE RIGHT CANDIDATE, WE HAVE TO THINK OUTSIDE THE BOX HERE...
HE HAS TO HAVE A STRONG, PRE-EXISTING BASE...
...BE OF INDEPENDENT MEANS...
HE CAN BE RETRO — BUT LONG OVERDUE FOR A COMEBACK!
NEIL DIAMOND. DUH.
OKAY, YOU STAY INSIDE THE BOX—I'LL DO OUTSIDE.

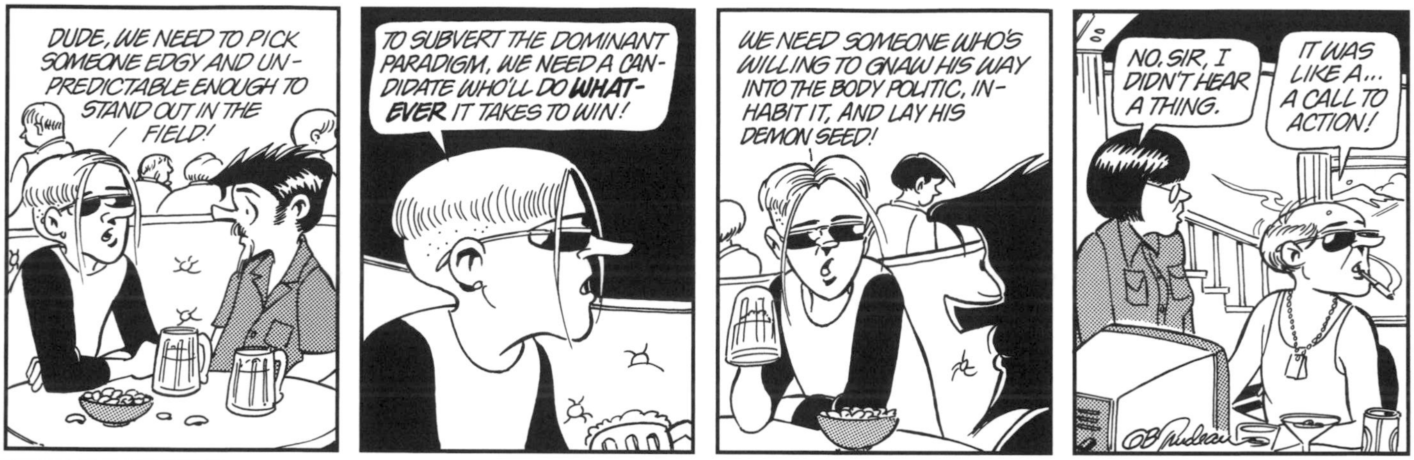
DUDE, WE NEED TO PICK SOMEONE EDGY AND UNPREDICTABLE ENOUGH TO STAND OUT IN THE FIELD!
TO SUBVERT THE DOMINANT PARADIGM, WE NEED A CANDIDATE WHO'LL DO WHATEVER IT TAKES TO WIN!
WE NEED SOMEONE WHO'S WILLING TO GNAW HIS WAY INTO THE BODY POLITIC, INHABIT IT, AND LAY HIS DEMON SEED!
NO, SIR, I DIDN'T HEAR A THING.
IT WAS LIKE A... A CALL TO ACTION!

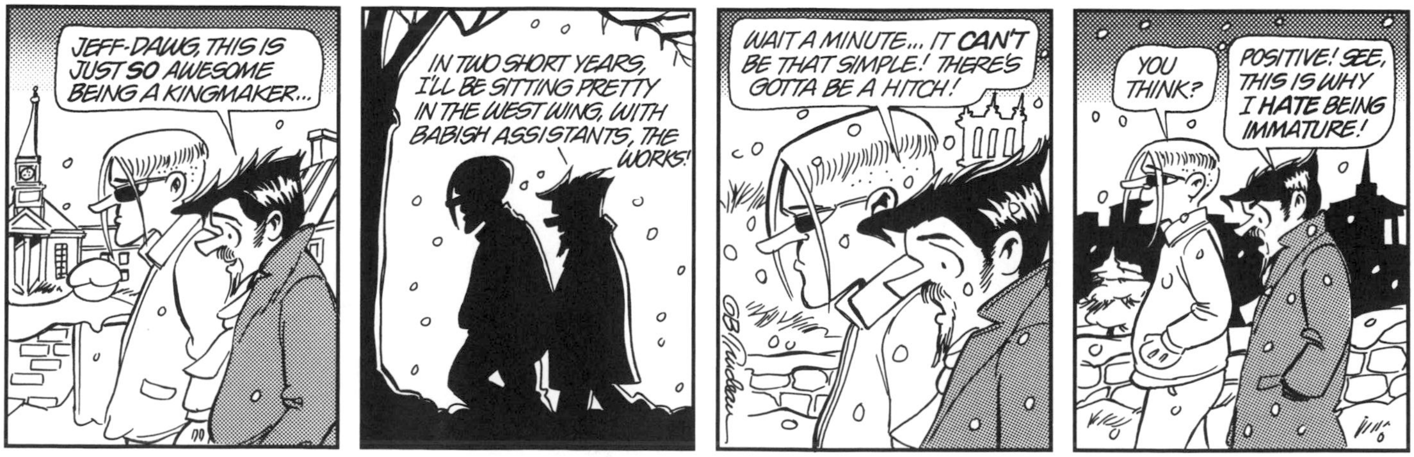
JEFF-DAWG, THIS IS JUST SO AWESOME BEING A KINGMAKER...
IN TWO SHORT YEARS, I'LL BE SITTING PRETTY IN THE WEST WING, WITH BABISH ASSISTANTS, THE WORKS!
WAIT A MINUTE... IT CAN'T BE THAT SIMPLE! THERE'S GOTTA BE A HITCH!
YOU THINK?
POSITIVE! SEE, THIS IS WHY I HATE BEING IMMATURE!

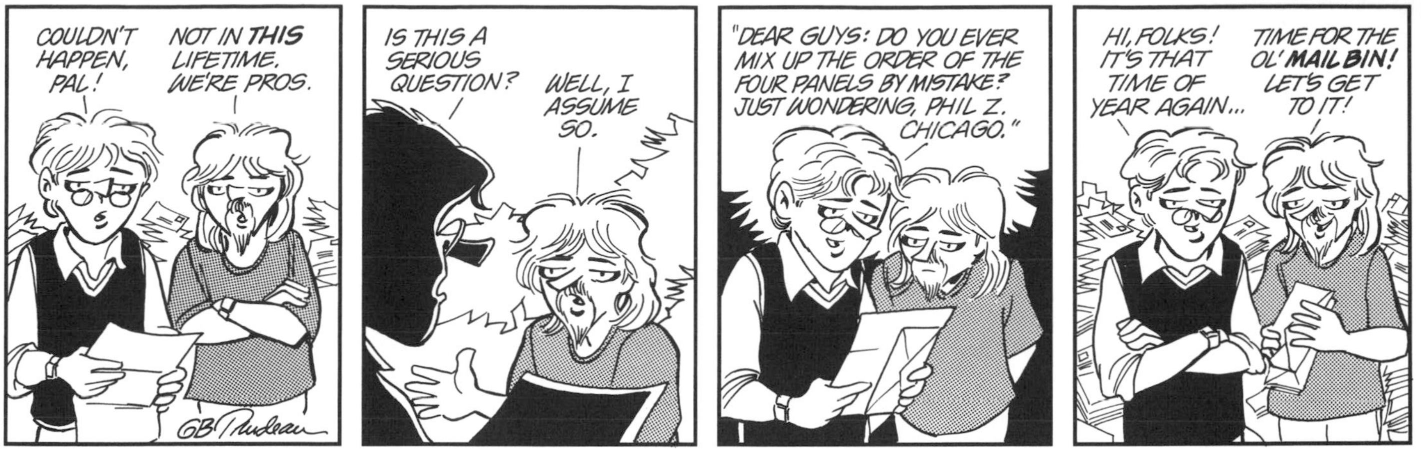
COULDN'T HAPPEN, PAL!
NOT IN THIS LIFETIME. WE'RE PROS.
IS THIS A SERIOUS QUESTION?
WELL, I ASSUME SO.
"DEAR GUYS: DO YOU EVER MIX UP THE ORDER OF THE FOUR PANELS BY MISTAKE? JUST WONDERING, PHIL Z. CHICAGO."
HI, FOLKS! IT'S THAT TIME OF YEAR AGAIN...
TIME FOR THE OL' MAIL BIN! LET'S GET TO IT!

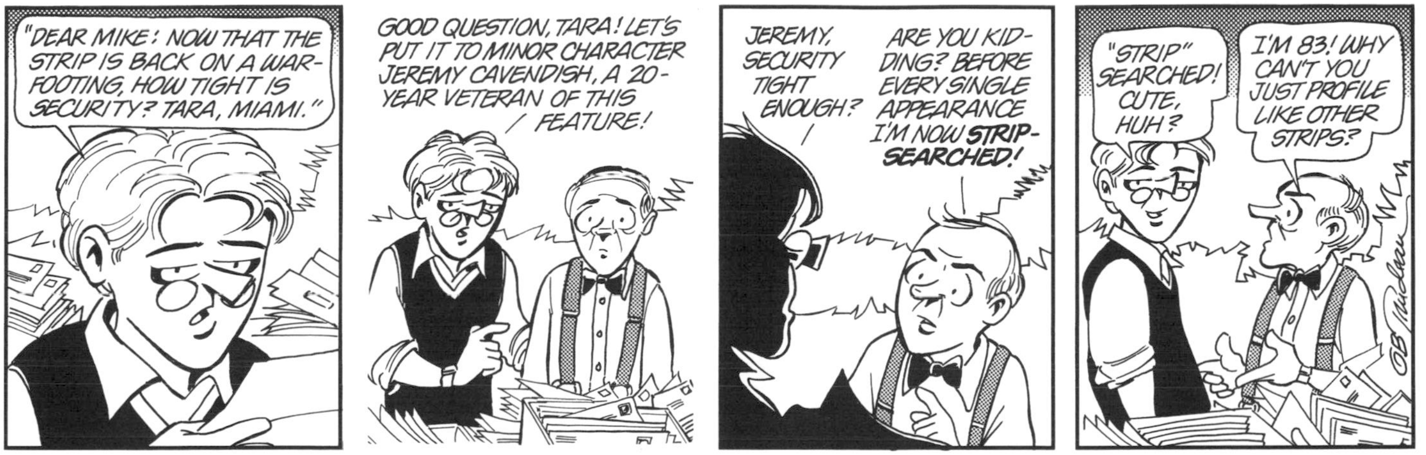
"DEAR MIKE: NOW THAT THE STRIP IS BACK ON A WAR-FOOTING, HOW TIGHT IS SECURITY? TARA, MIAMI."
GOOD QUESTION, TARA! LET'S PUT IT TO MINOR CHARACTER JEREMY CAVENDISH, A 20-YEAR VETERAN OF THIS FEATURE!
JEREMY, SECURITY TIGHT ENOUGH?
ARE YOU KIDDING? BEFORE EVERY SINGLE APPEARANCE I'M NOW STRIP-SEARCHED!
"STRIP" SEARCHED! CUTE, HUH?
I'M 83! WHY CAN'T YOU JUST PROFILE LIKE OTHER STRIPS?

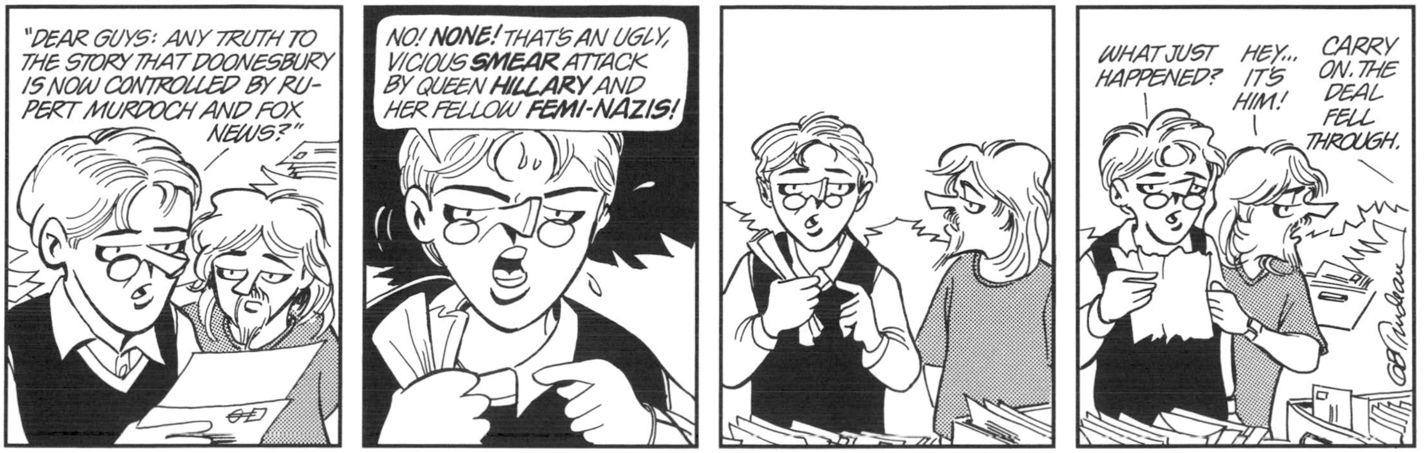
"DEAR GUYS: ANY TRUTH TO THE STORY THAT DOONESBURY IS NOW CONTROLLED BY RUPERT MURDOCH AND FOX NEWS?"
NO! NONE! THAT'S AN UGLY, VICIOUS SMEAR ATTACK BY QUEEN HILLARY AND HER FELLOW FEMI-NAZIS!
WHAT JUST HAPPENED?
HEY... IT'S HIM!
CARRY ON. THE DEAL FELL THROUGH.

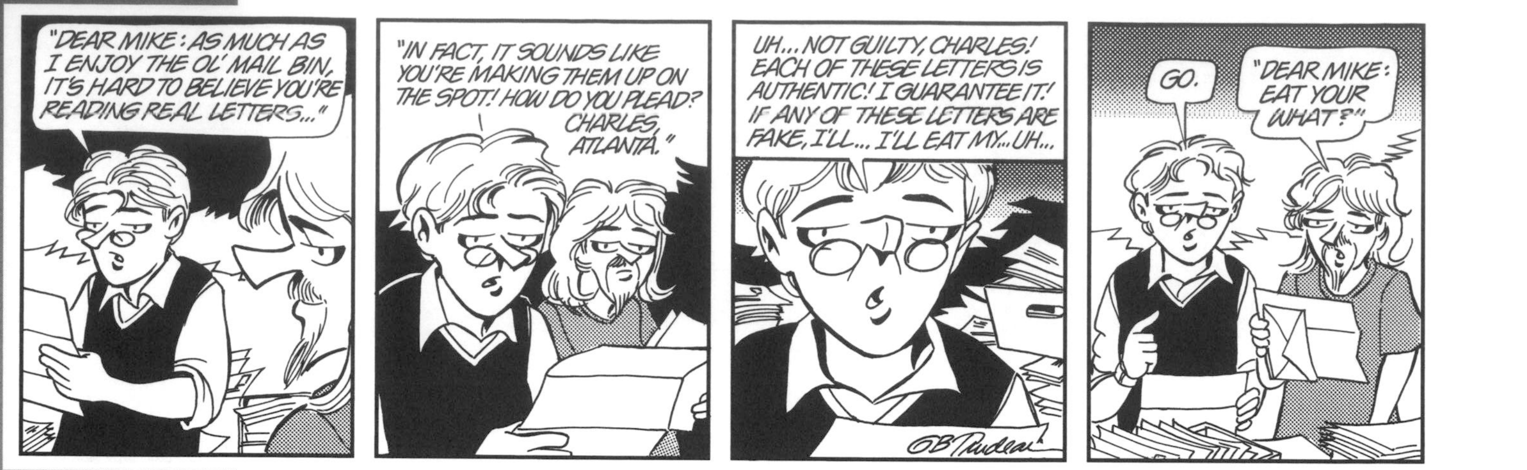
"DEAR MIKE: AS MUCH AS I ENJOY THE OL' MAIL BIN, IT'S HARD TO BELIEVE YOU'RE READING REAL LETTERS..."
"IN FACT, IT SOUNDS LIKE YOU'RE MAKING THEM UP ON THE SPOT! HOW DO YOU PLEAD? CHARLES, ATLANTA."
UH... NOT GUILTY, CHARLES! EACH OF THESE LETTERS IS AUTHENTIC! I GUARANTEE IT! IF ANY OF THESE LETTERS ARE FAKE, I'LL... I'LL EAT MY... UH...
GO.
"DEAR MIKE: EAT YOUR WHAT?"

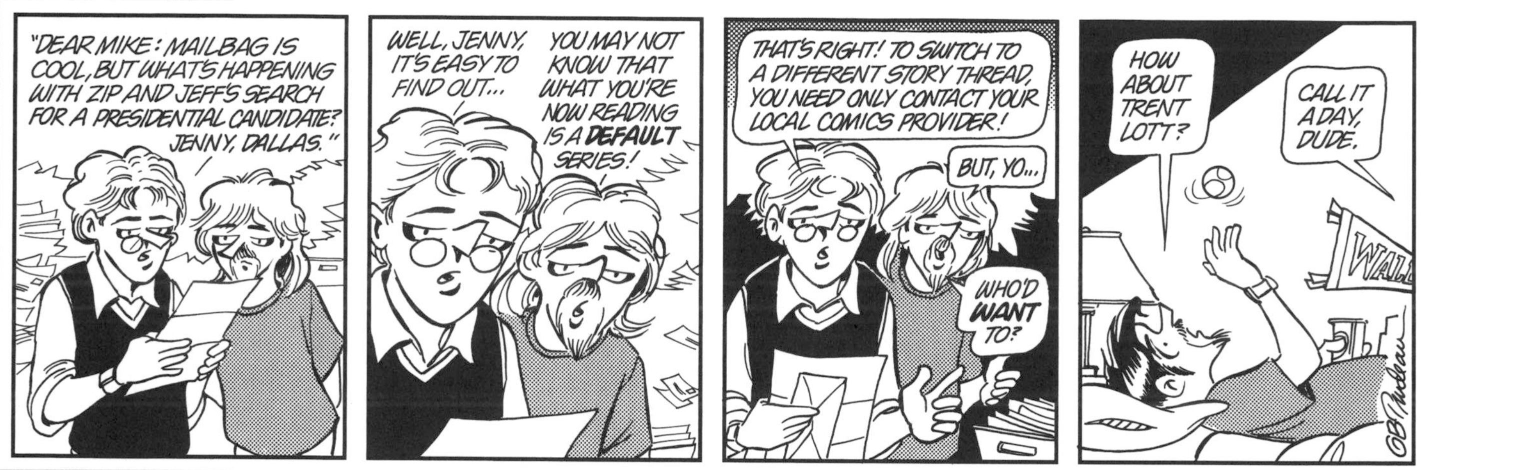
"DEAR MIKE: MAILBAG IS COOL, BUT WHAT'S HAPPENING WITH ZIP AND JEFF'S SEARCH FOR A PRESIDENTIAL CANDIDATE? JENNY, DALLAS."
WELL, JENNY, IT'S EASY TO FIND OUT...
YOU MAY NOT KNOW THAT WHAT YOU'RE NOW READING IS A **DEFAULT** SERIES!
THAT'S RIGHT! TO SWITCH TO A DIFFERENT STORY THREAD, YOU NEED ONLY CONTACT YOUR LOCAL COMICS PROVIDER!
BUT, YO...
WHO'D **WANT** TO?
HOW ABOUT TRENT LOTT?
CALL IT A DAY, DUDE.

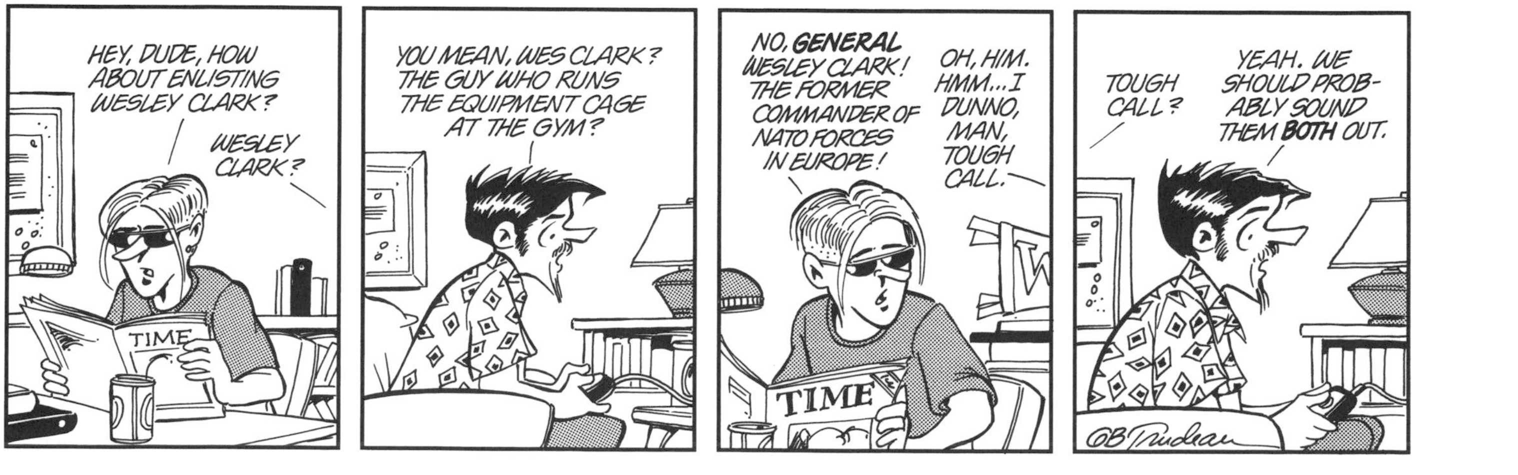
HEY, DUDE, HOW ABOUT ENLISTING WESLEY CLARK?
WESLEY CLARK?
TIME
YOU MEAN, WES CLARK? THE GUY WHO RUNS THE EQUIPMENT CAGE AT THE GYM?
NO, **GENERAL** WESLEY CLARK! THE FORMER COMMANDER OF NATO FORCES IN EUROPE!
OH, HIM. HMM... I DUNNO, MAN, TOUGH CALL.
TIME
TOUGH CALL?
YEAH. WE SHOULD PROBABLY SOUND THEM **BOTH** OUT.

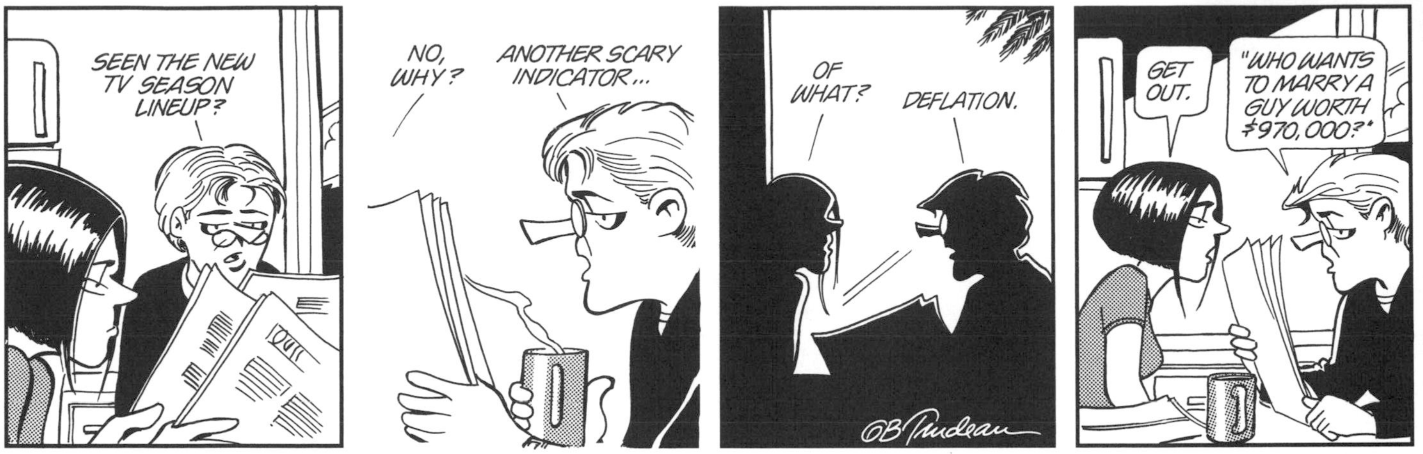
SEEN THE NEW TV SEASON LINEUP?
NO, WHY?
ANOTHER SCARY INDICATOR...
OF WHAT?
DEFLATION.
GET OUT.
"WHO WANTS TO MARRY A GUY WORTH $970,000?"

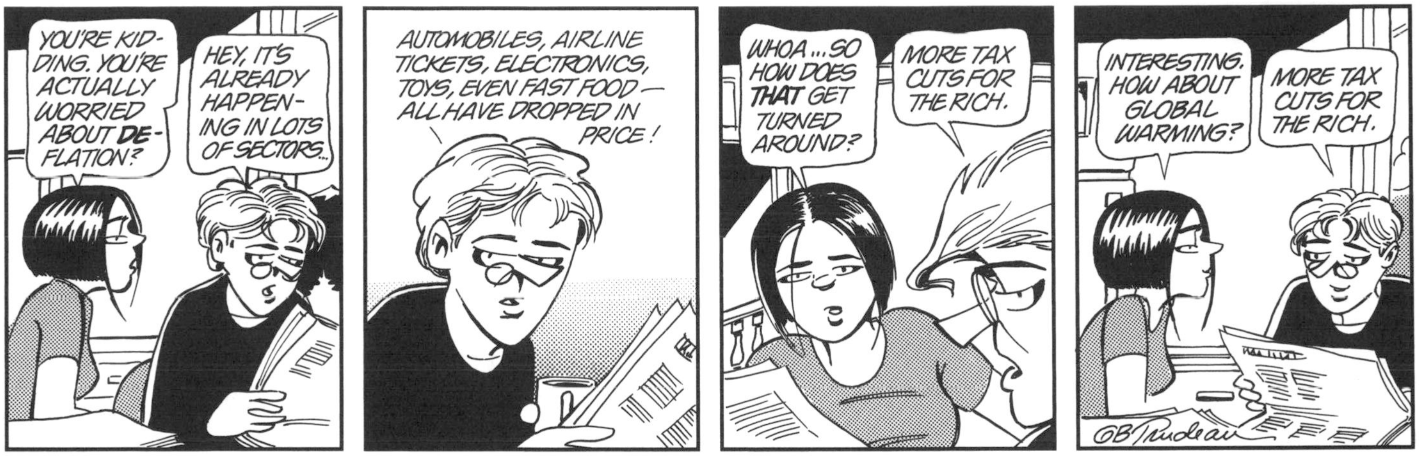
YOU'RE KIDDING. YOU'RE ACTUALLY WORRIED ABOUT **DE**FLATION?
HEY, IT'S ALREADY HAPPENING IN LOTS OF SECTORS...
AUTOMOBILES, AIRLINE TICKETS, ELECTRONICS, TOYS, EVEN FAST FOOD — ALL HAVE DROPPED IN PRICE!
WHOA...SO HOW DOES **THAT** GET TURNED AROUND?
MORE TAX CUTS FOR THE RICH.
INTERESTING. HOW ABOUT GLOBAL WARMING?
MORE TAX CUTS FOR THE RICH.

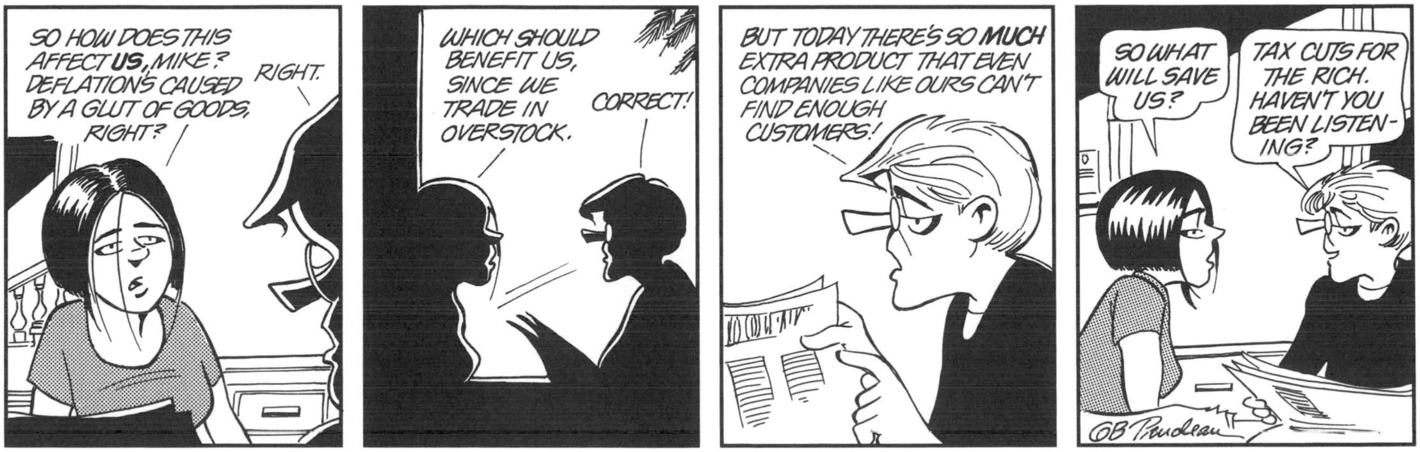
SO HOW DOES THIS AFFECT **US**, MIKE? DEFLATION'S CAUSED BY A GLUT OF GOODS, RIGHT?
RIGHT.
WHICH SHOULD BENEFIT US, SINCE WE TRADE IN OVERSTOCK.
CORRECT!
BUT TODAY THERE'S SO **MUCH** EXTRA PRODUCT THAT EVEN COMPANIES LIKE OURS CAN'T FIND ENOUGH CUSTOMERS!
SO WHAT WILL SAVE US?
TAX CUTS FOR THE RICH. HAVEN'T YOU BEEN LISTENING?

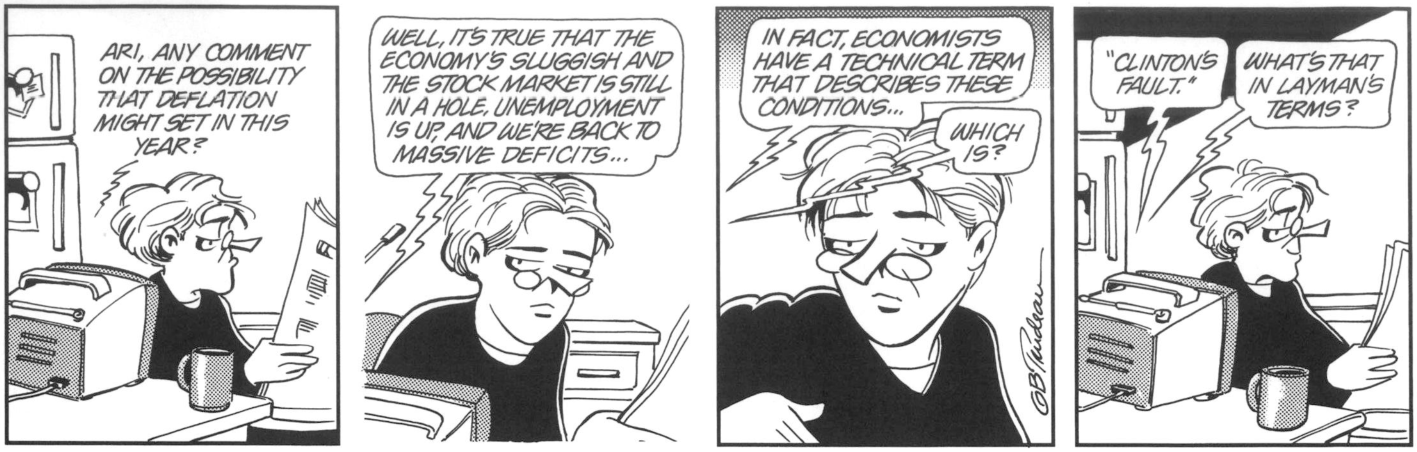
ARI, ANY COMMENT ON THE POSSIBILITY THAT DEFLATION MIGHT SET IN THIS YEAR?
WELL, IT'S TRUE THAT THE ECONOMY'S SLUGGISH AND THE STOCK MARKET IS STILL IN A HOLE, UNEMPLOYMENT IS UP, AND WE'RE BACK TO MASSIVE DEFICITS...
IN FACT, ECONOMISTS HAVE A TECHNICAL TERM THAT DESCRIBES THESE CONDITIONS...
WHICH IS?
"CLINTON'S FAULT."
WHAT'S THAT IN LAYMAN'S TERMS?

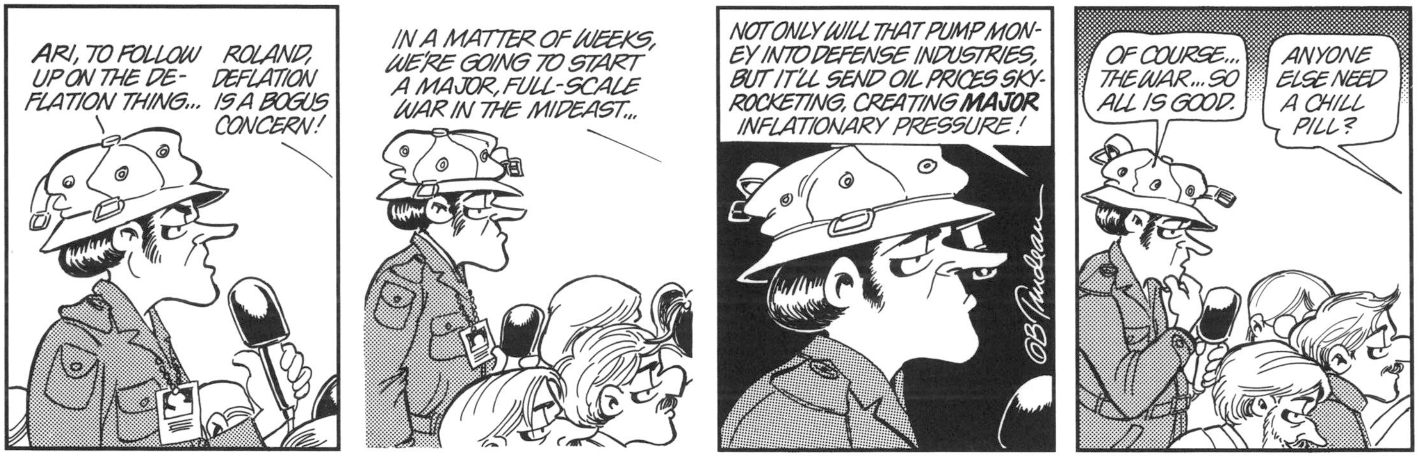
ARI, TO FOLLOW UP ON THE DEFLATION THING...
ROLAND, DEFLATION IS A BOGUS CONCERN!
IN A MATTER OF WEEKS, WE'RE GOING TO START A MAJOR, FULL-SCALE WAR IN THE MIDEAST...
NOT ONLY WILL THAT PUMP MONEY INTO DEFENSE INDUSTRIES, BUT IT'LL SEND OIL PRICES SKYROCKETING, CREATING **MAJOR** INFLATIONARY PRESSURE!
OF COURSE... THE WAR... SO ALL IS GOOD.
ANYONE ELSE NEED A CHILL PILL?

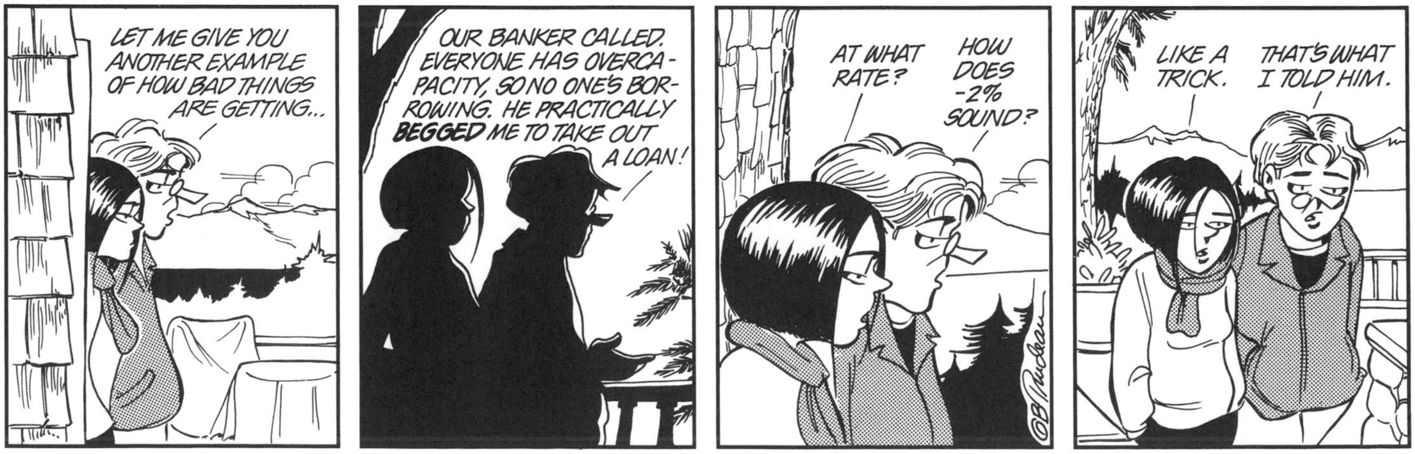
LET ME GIVE YOU ANOTHER EXAMPLE OF HOW BAD THINGS ARE GETTING...
OUR BANKER CALLED. EVERYONE HAS OVERCAPACITY, SO NO ONE'S BORROWING. HE PRACTICALLY **BEGGED** ME TO TAKE OUT A LOAN!
AT WHAT RATE?
HOW DOES -2% SOUND?
LIKE A TRICK.
THAT'S WHAT I TOLD HIM.

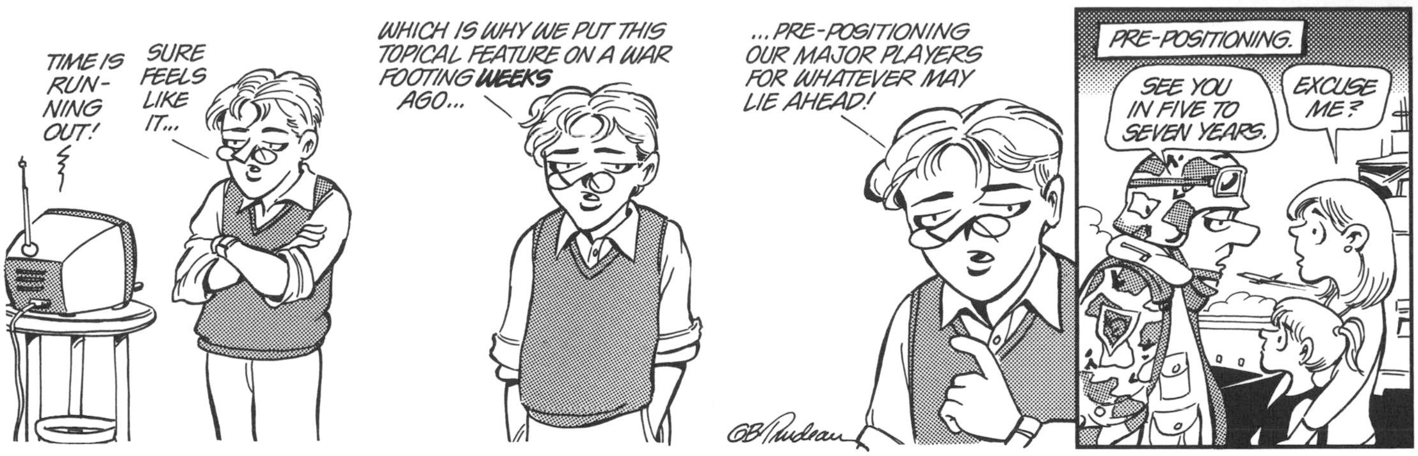
TIME IS RUN-NING OUT!
SURE FEELS LIKE IT...
WHICH IS WHY WE PUT THIS TOPICAL FEATURE ON A WAR FOOTING **WEEKS** AGO...
...PRE-POSITIONING OUR MAJOR PLAYERS FOR WHATEVER MAY LIE AHEAD!
PRE-POSITIONING.
SEE YOU IN FIVE TO SEVEN YEARS.
EXCUSE ME?

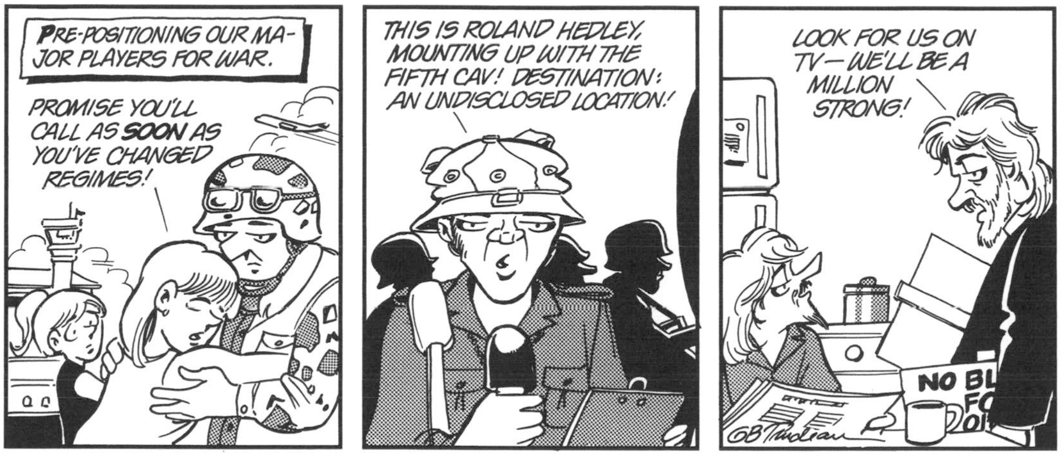
PRE-POSITIONING OUR MA-JOR PLAYERS FOR WAR.
PROMISE YOU'LL CALL AS **SOON** AS YOU'VE CHANGED REGIMES!
THIS IS ROLAND HEDLEY, MOUNTING UP WITH THE FIFTH CAV! DESTINATION: AN UNDISCLOSED LOCATION!
LOOK FOR US ON TV—WE'LL BE A MILLION STRONG!
DUDE.
DUDE.
CIA

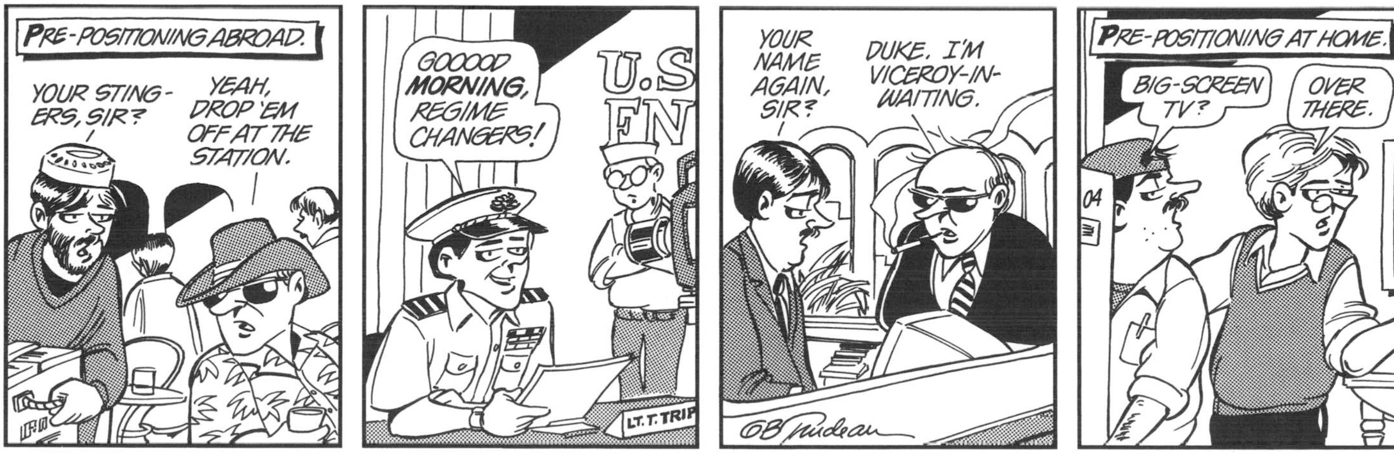
PRE-POSITIONING ABROAD.
YOUR STING-ERS, SIR?
YEAH, DROP 'EM OFF AT THE STATION.
GOOOOD **MORNING**, REGIME CHANGERS!
LT. T. TRIP
YOUR NAME AGAIN, SIR?
DUKE. I'M VICEROY-IN-WAITING.
PRE-POSITIONING AT HOME.
BIG-SCREEN TV?
OVER THERE.

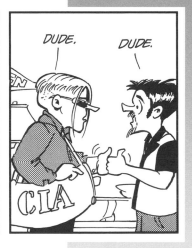

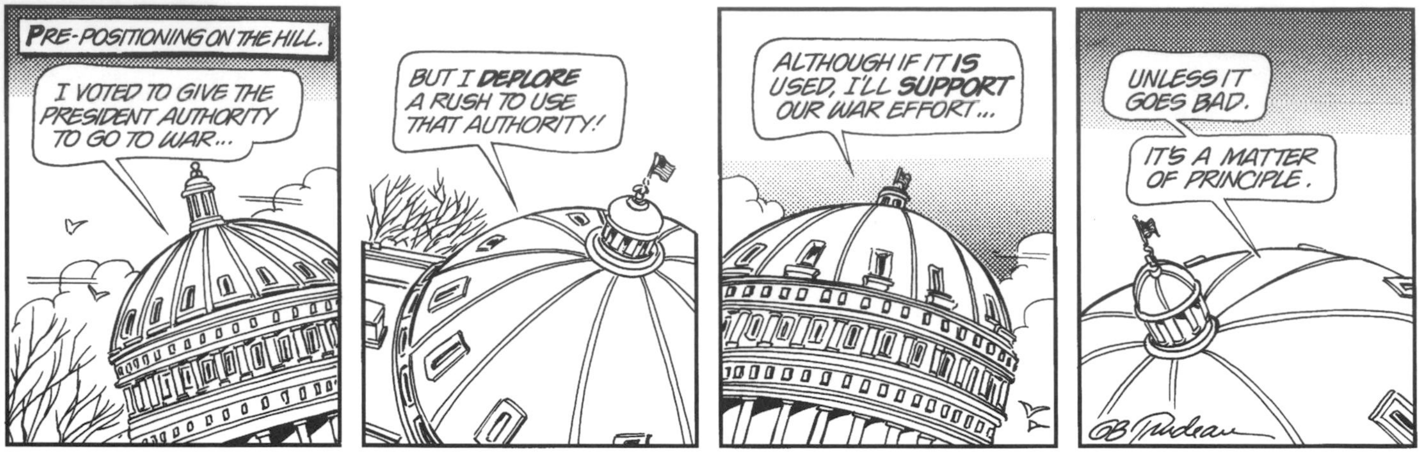
PRE-POSITIONING ON THE HILL.
I VOTED TO GIVE THE PRESIDENT AUTHORITY TO GO TO WAR...
BUT I DEPLORE A RUSH TO USE THAT AUTHORITY!
ALTHOUGH IF IT IS USED, I'LL SUPPORT OUR WAR EFFORT...
UNLESS IT GOES BAD.
IT'S A MATTER OF PRINCIPLE.

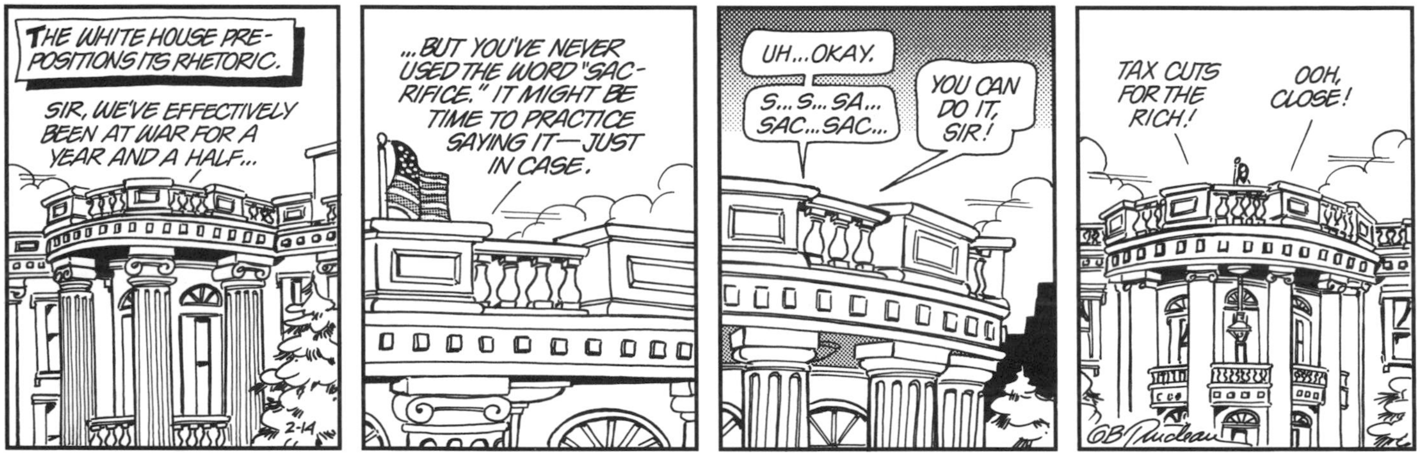
THE WHITE HOUSE PRE-POSITIONS ITS RHETORIC.
SIR, WE'VE EFFECTIVELY BEEN AT WAR FOR A YEAR AND A HALF...
...BUT YOU'VE NEVER USED THE WORD "SAC-RIFICE." IT MIGHT BE TIME TO PRACTICE SAYING IT—JUST IN CASE.
UH...OKAY.
S...S...SA... SAC...SAC...
YOU CAN DO IT, SIR!
TAX CUTS FOR THE RICH!
OOH, CLOSE!

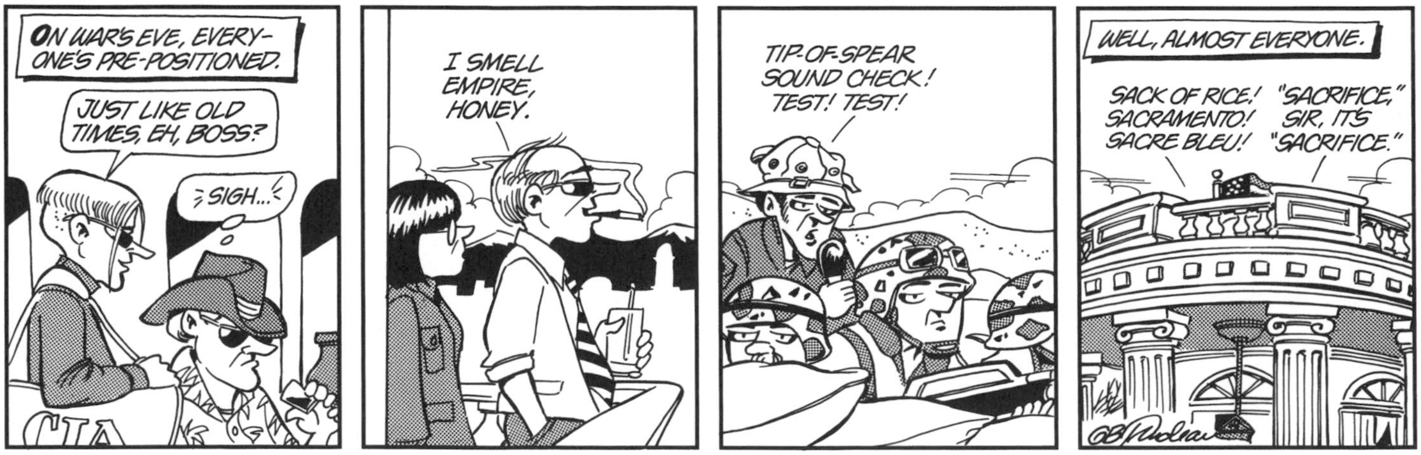
ON WAR'S EVE, EVERY-ONE'S PRE-POSITIONED.
JUST LIKE OLD TIMES, EH, BOSS?
SIGH...
I SMELL EMPIRE, HONEY.
TIP-OF-SPEAR SOUND CHECK! TEST! TEST!
WELL, ALMOST EVERYONE.
SACK OF RICE! SACRAMENTO! SACRE BLEU!
"SACRIFICE," SIR, IT'S "SACRIFICE."

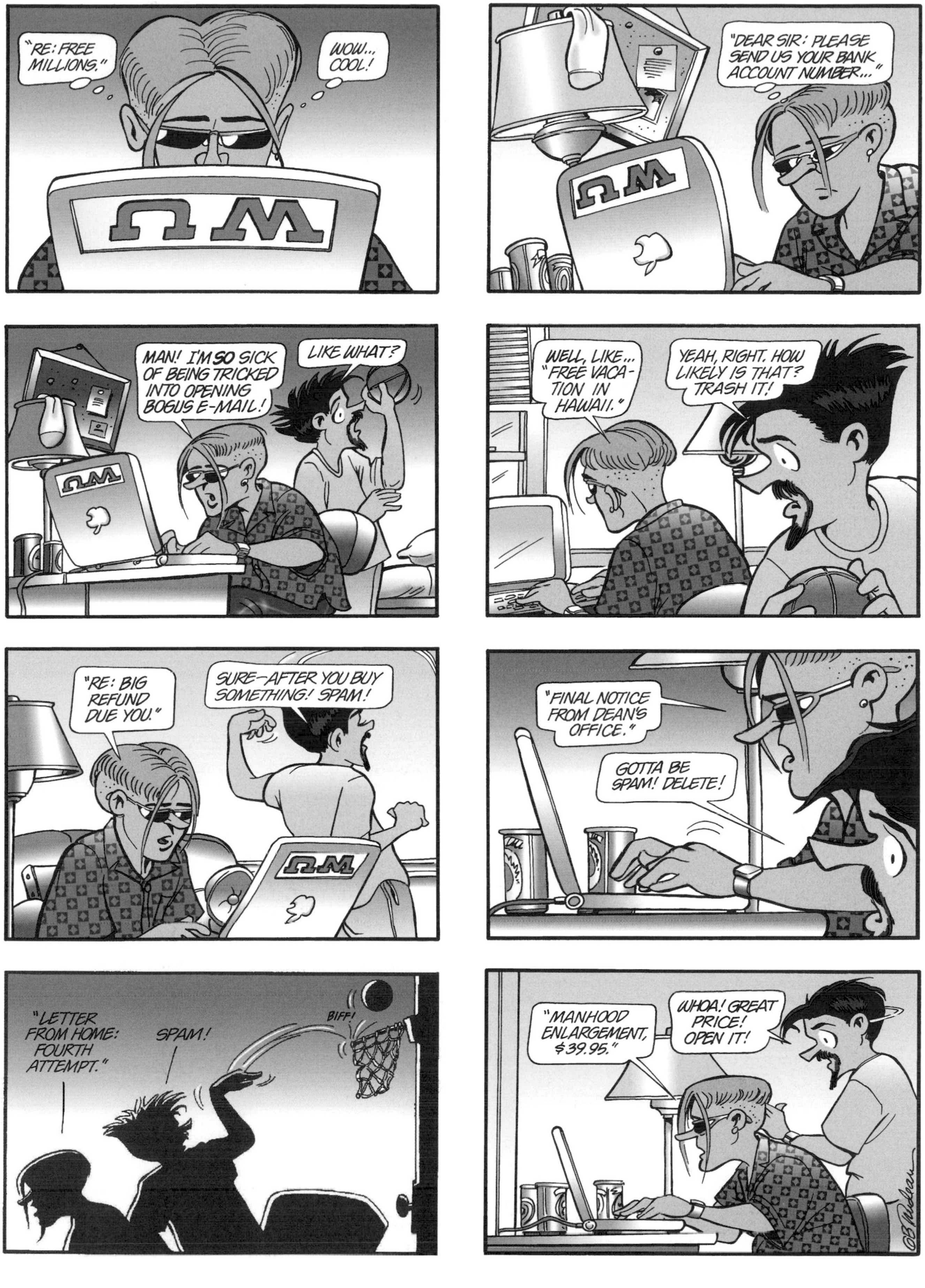
"RE: FREE MILLIONS."
WOW.. COOL!
"DEAR SIR: PLEASE SEND US YOUR BANK ACCOUNT NUMBER..."
MAN! I'M SO SICK OF BEING TRICKED INTO OPENING BOGUS E-MAIL!
LIKE WHAT?
WELL, LIKE... "FREE VACA-TION IN HAWAII."
YEAH, RIGHT. HOW LIKELY IS THAT? TRASH IT!
"RE: BIG REFUND DUE YOU."
SURE—AFTER YOU BUY SOMETHING! SPAM!
"FINAL NOTICE FROM DEAN'S OFFICE."
GOTTA BE SPAM! DELETE!
"LETTER FROM HOME: FOURTH ATTEMPT."
SPAM!
BIFF!
"MANHOOD ENLARGEMENT, $39.95."
WHOA! GREAT PRICE! OPEN IT!

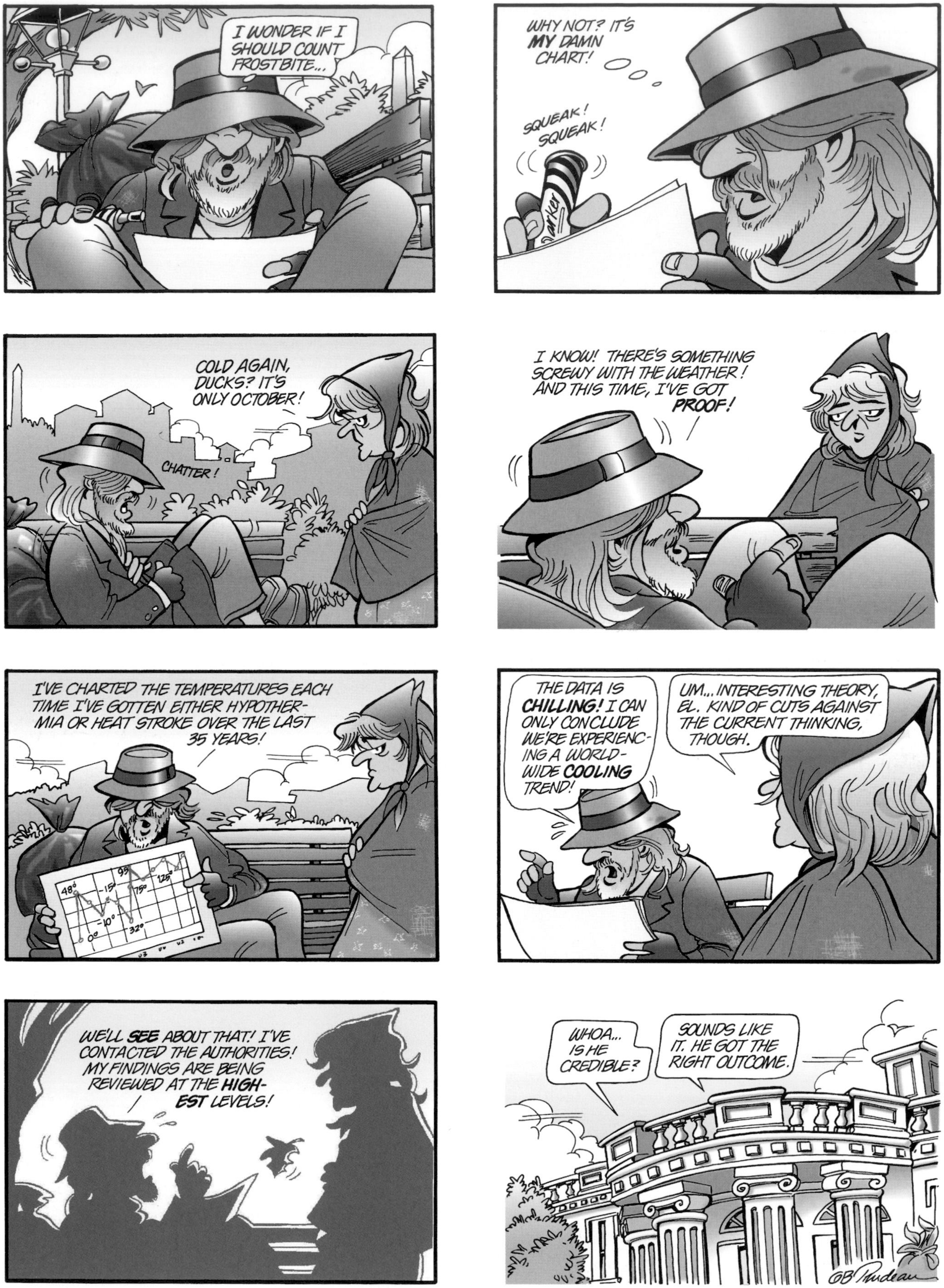
I WONDER IF I SHOULD COUNT FROSTBITE...
WHY NOT? IT'S **MY** DAMN CHART!
SQUEAK! SQUEAK!
COLD AGAIN, DUCKS? IT'S ONLY OCTOBER!
CHATTER!
I KNOW! THERE'S SOMETHING SCREWY WITH THE WEATHER! AND THIS TIME, I'VE GOT **PROOF!**
I'VE CHARTED THE TEMPERATURES EACH TIME I'VE GOTTEN EITHER HYPOTHERMIA OR HEAT STROKE OVER THE LAST 35 YEARS!
48° -15° 95° 75° 125° -10° 0° 32°
THE DATA IS **CHILLING!** I CAN ONLY CONCLUDE WE'RE EXPERIENCING A WORLD-WIDE **COOLING** TREND!
UM... INTERESTING THEORY, EL. KIND OF CUTS AGAINST THE CURRENT THINKING, THOUGH.
WE'LL **SEE** ABOUT THAT! I'VE CONTACTED THE AUTHORITIES! MY FINDINGS ARE BEING REVIEWED AT THE **HIGHEST** LEVELS!
WHOA... IS HE CREDIBLE?
SOUNDS LIKE IT. HE GOT THE RIGHT OUTCOME.
GB Trudeau

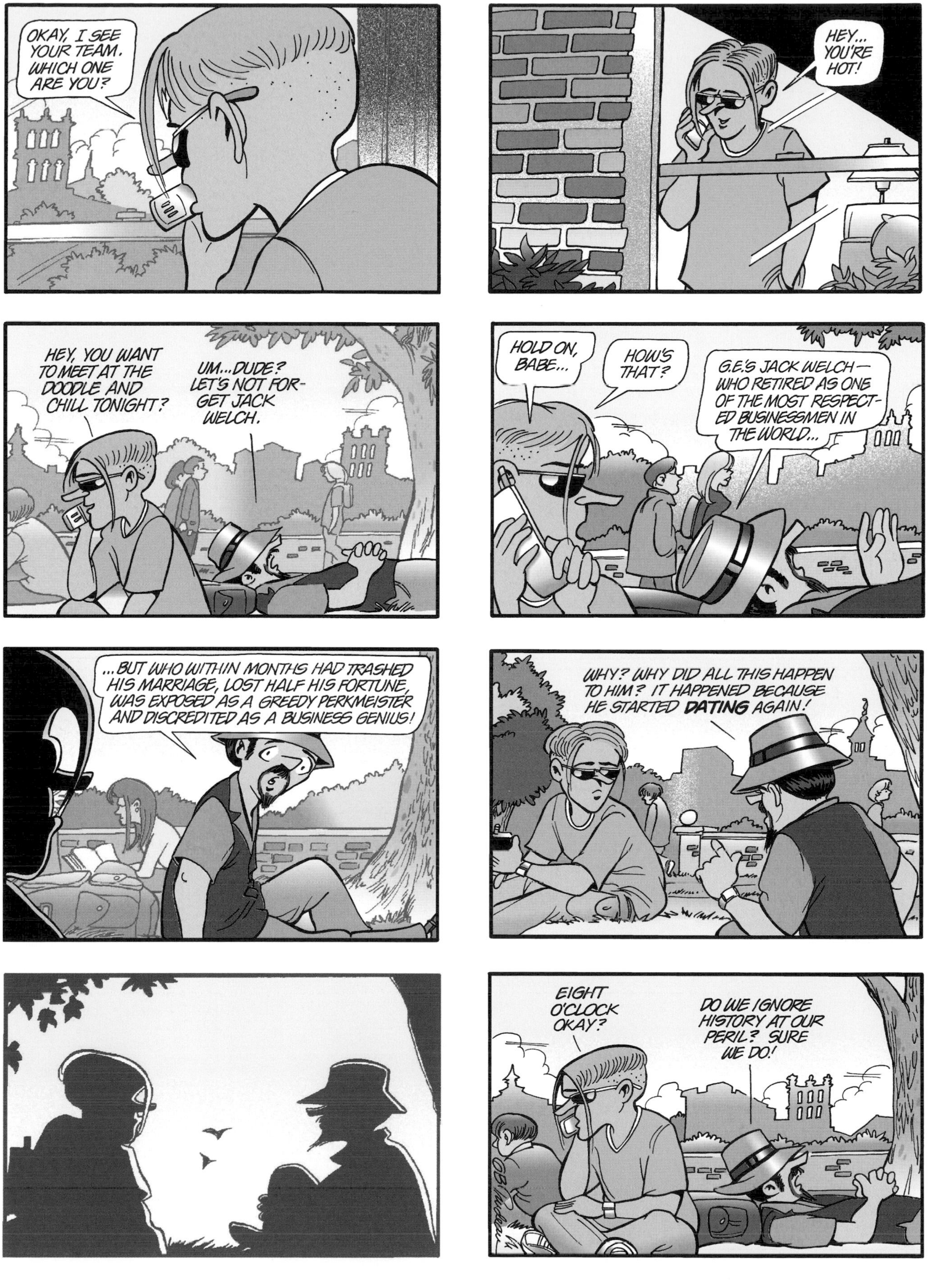

OKAY, I SEE YOUR TEAM. WHICH ONE ARE YOU?
HEY... YOU'RE HOT!
HEY, YOU WANT TO MEET AT THE DOODLE AND CHILL TONIGHT?
UM...DUDE? LET'S NOT FORGET JACK WELCH.
HOLD ON, BABE...
HOW'S THAT?
G.E.'S JACK WELCH — WHO RETIRED AS ONE OF THE MOST RESPECTED BUSINESSMEN IN THE WORLD...
...BUT WHO WITHIN MONTHS HAD TRASHED HIS MARRIAGE, LOST HALF HIS FORTUNE, WAS EXPOSED AS A GREEDY PERKMEISTER AND DISCREDITED AS A BUSINESS GENIUS!
WHY? WHY DID ALL THIS HAPPEN TO HIM? IT HAPPENED BECAUSE HE STARTED DATING AGAIN!
EIGHT O'CLOCK OKAY?
DO WE IGNORE HISTORY AT OUR PERIL? SURE WE DO!

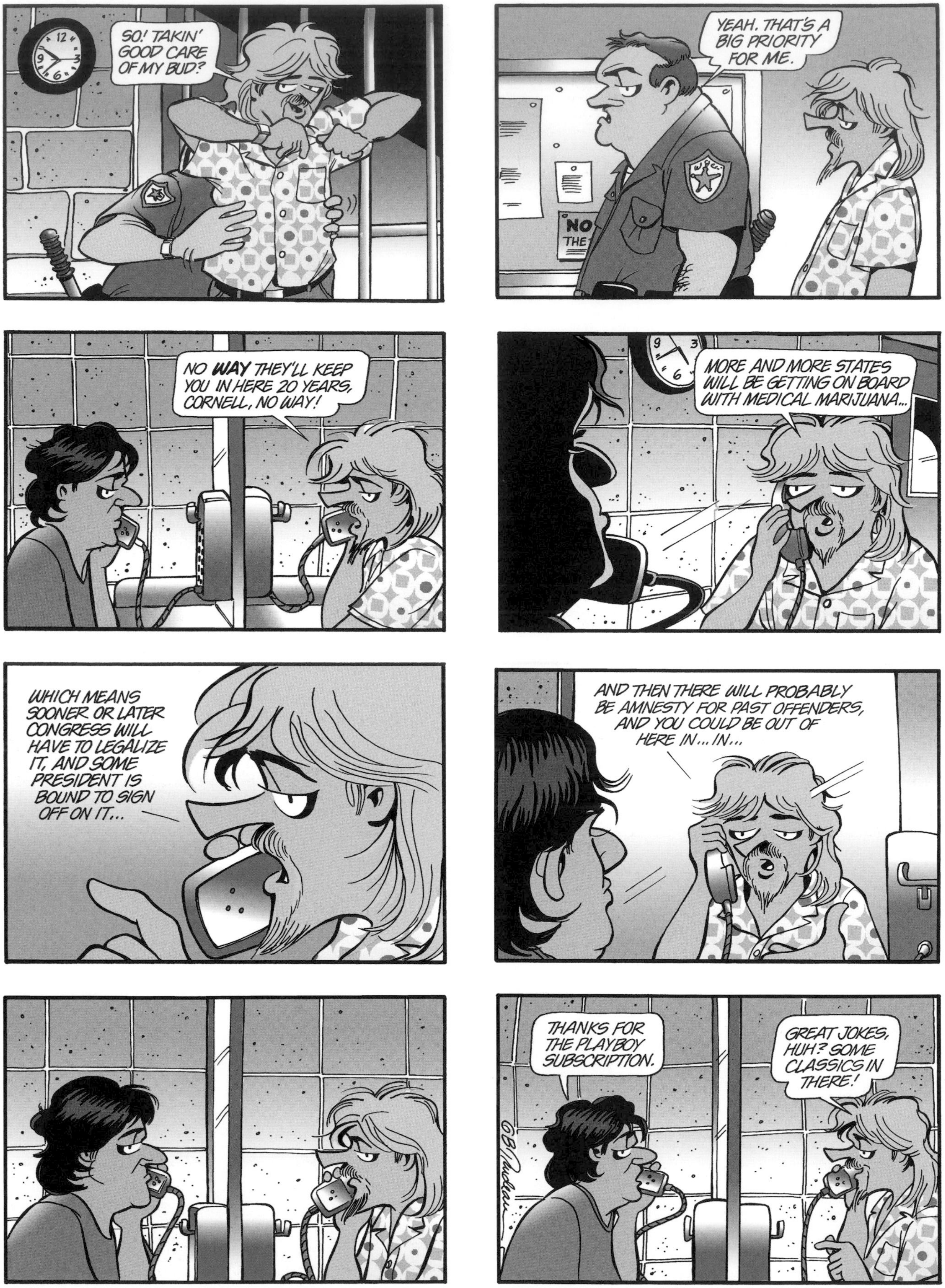

SO! TAKIN' GOOD CARE OF MY BUD?
YEAH. THAT'S A BIG PRIORITY FOR ME.
NO **WAY** THEY'LL KEEP YOU IN HERE 20 YEARS, CORNELL, NO WAY!
MORE AND MORE STATES WILL BE GETTING ON BOARD WITH MEDICAL MARIJUANA...
WHICH MEANS SOONER OR LATER CONGRESS WILL HAVE TO LEGALIZE IT, AND SOME PRESIDENT IS BOUND TO SIGN OFF ON IT...
AND THEN THERE WILL PROBABLY BE AMNESTY FOR PAST OFFENDERS, AND YOU COULD BE OUT OF HERE IN... IN...
THANKS FOR THE PLAYBOY SUBSCRIPTION.
GREAT JOKES, HUH? SOME CLASSICS IN THERE!

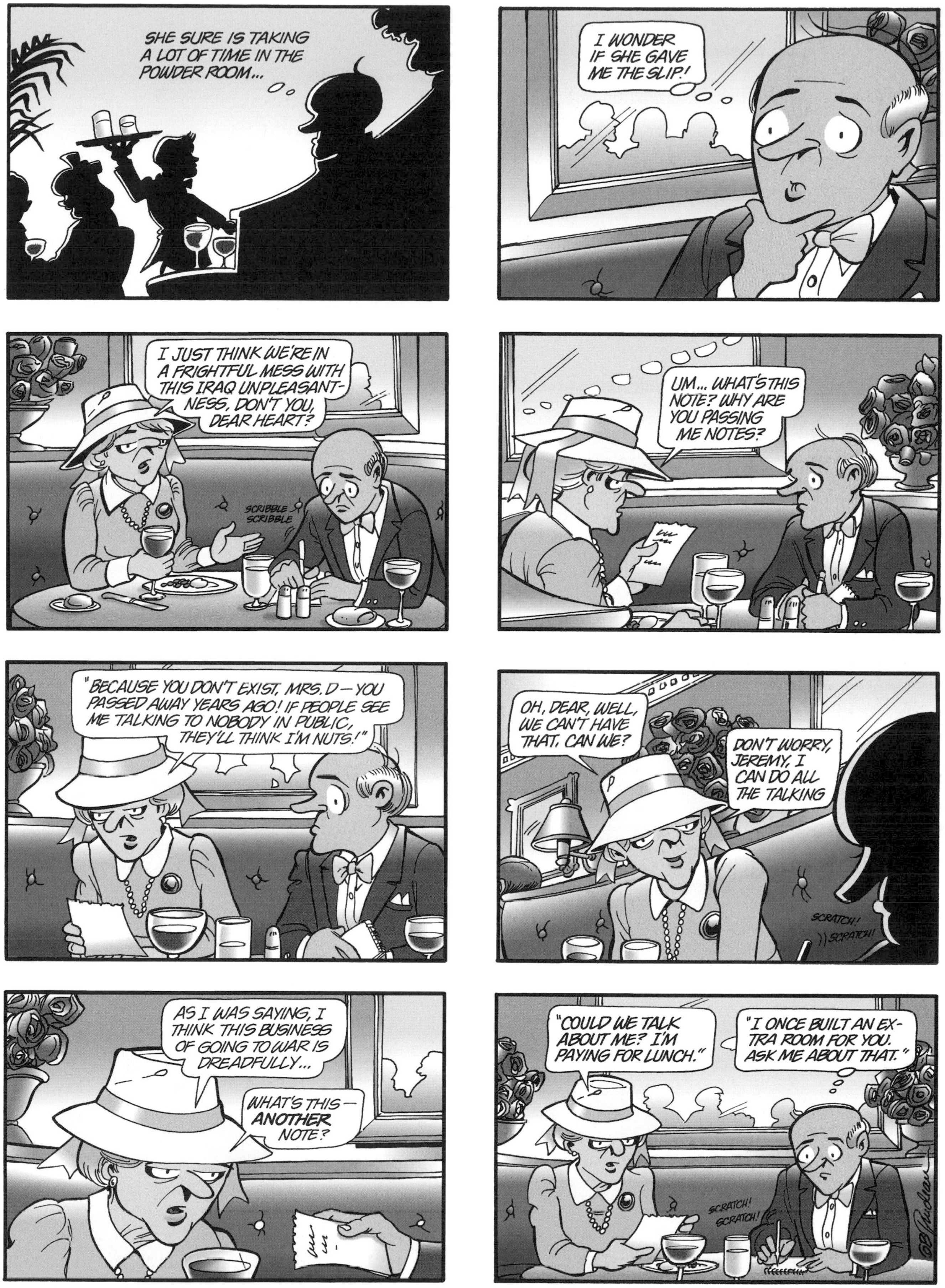
SHE SURE IS TAKING A LOT OF TIME IN THE POWDER ROOM...
I WONDER IF SHE GAVE ME THE SLIP!
I JUST THINK WE'RE IN A FRIGHTFUL MESS WITH THIS IRAQ UNPLEASANT-NESS, DON'T YOU, DEAR HEART?
SCRIBBLE SCRIBBLE
UM... WHAT'S THIS NOTE? WHY ARE YOU PASSING ME NOTES?
"BECAUSE YOU DON'T EXIST, MRS. D — YOU PASSED AWAY YEARS AGO! IF PEOPLE SEE ME TALKING TO NOBODY IN PUBLIC, THEY'LL THINK I'M NUTS!"
OH, DEAR, WELL, WE CAN'T HAVE THAT, CAN WE?
DON'T WORRY, JEREMY, I CAN DO ALL THE TALKING
SCRATCH! SCRATCH!
AS I WAS SAYING, I THINK THIS BUSINESS OF GOING TO WAR IS DREADFULLY...
WHAT'S THIS — **ANOTHER** NOTE?
"COULD WE TALK ABOUT ME? I'M PAYING FOR LUNCH."
"I ONCE BUILT AN EX-TRA ROOM FOR YOU. ASK ME ABOUT THAT."
SCRATCH! SCRATCH!

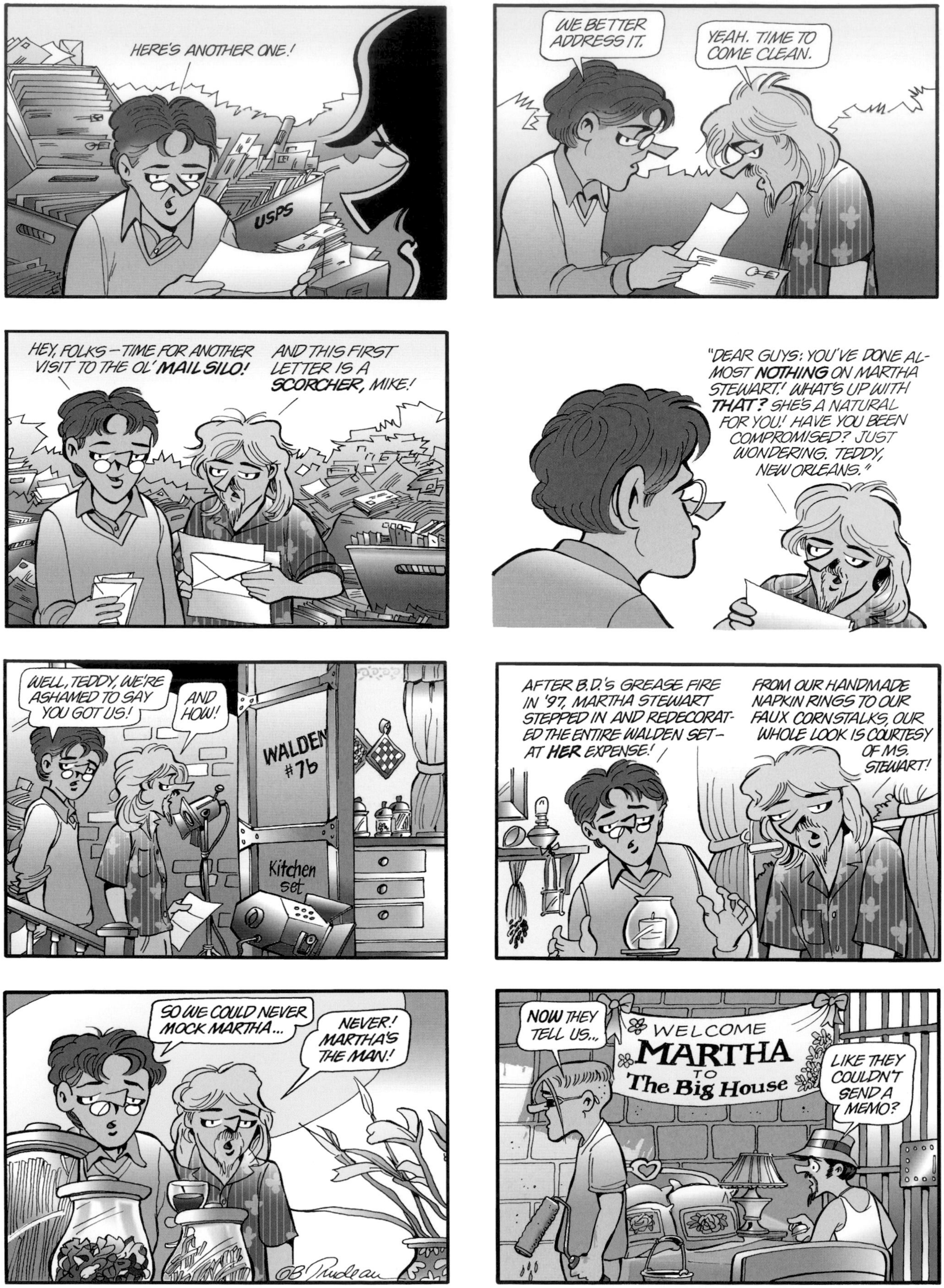
HERE'S ANOTHER ONE!
USPS
WE BETTER ADDRESS IT.
YEAH. TIME TO COME CLEAN.
HEY, FOLKS—TIME FOR ANOTHER VISIT TO THE OL' **MAIL SILO!**
AND THIS FIRST LETTER IS A **SCORCHER,** MIKE!
"DEAR GUYS: YOU'VE DONE ALMOST **NOTHING** ON MARTHA STEWART! WHAT'S UP WITH **THAT?** SHE'S A NATURAL FOR YOU! HAVE YOU BEEN COMPROMISED? JUST WONDERING. TEDDY, NEW ORLEANS."
WELL, TEDDY, WE'RE ASHAMED TO SAY YOU GOT US!
AND HOW!
WALDEN #76
Kitchen set
AFTER B.D.'S GREASE FIRE IN '97, MARTHA STEWART STEPPED IN AND REDECORATED THE ENTIRE WALDEN SET—AT **HER** EXPENSE!
FROM OUR HANDMADE NAPKIN RINGS TO OUR FAUX CORNSTALKS, OUR WHOLE LOOK IS COURTESY OF MS. STEWART!
SO WE COULD NEVER MOCK MARTHA...
NEVER! MARTHA'S THE MAN!
**NOW** THEY TELL US...
WELCOME MARTHA TO The Big House
LIKE THEY COULDN'T SEND A MEMO?

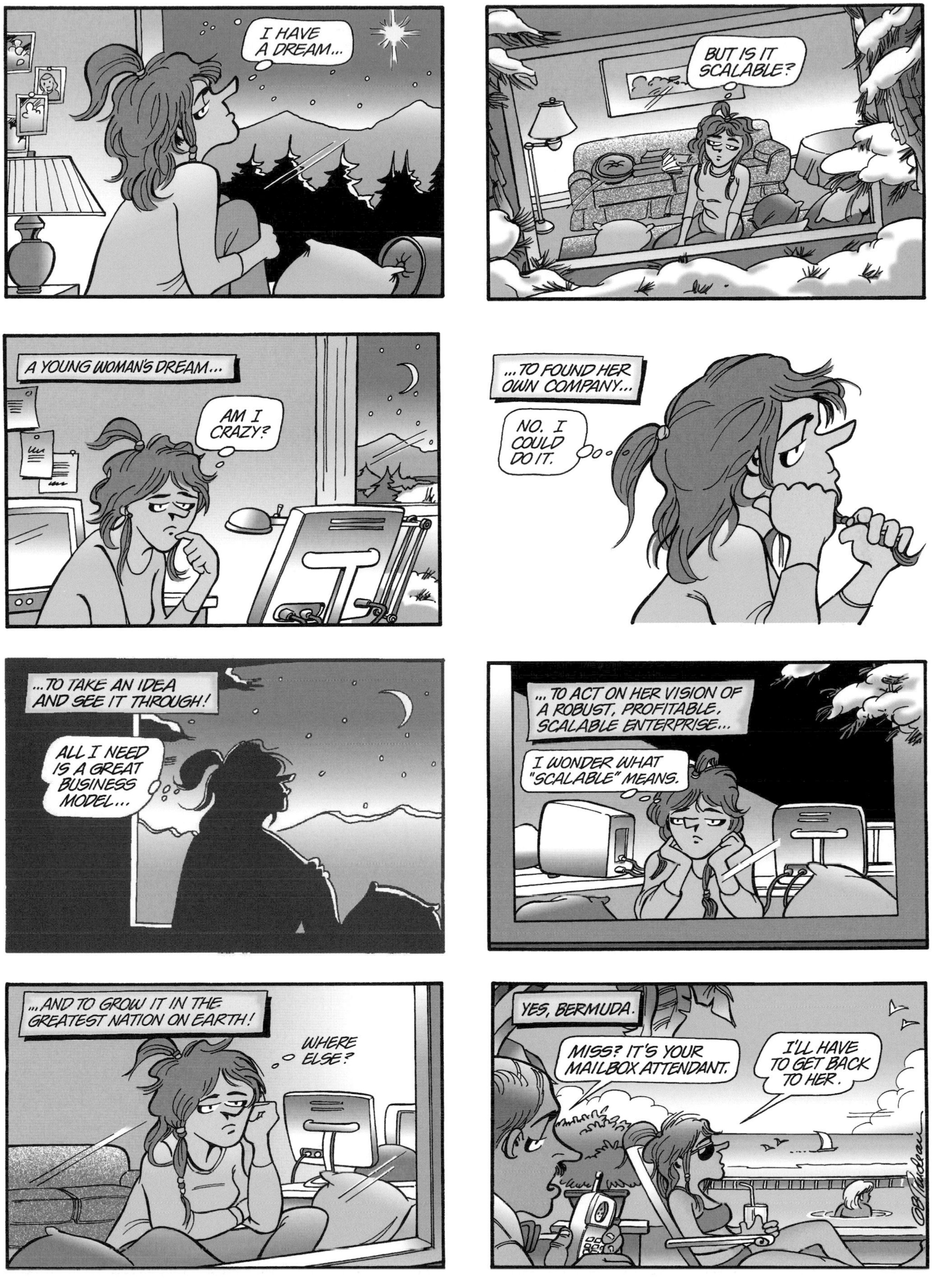
I HAVE A DREAM...
BUT IS IT SCALABLE?
A YOUNG WOMAN'S DREAM...
AM I CRAZY?
...TO FOUND HER OWN COMPANY...
NO. I COULD DO IT.
...TO TAKE AN IDEA AND SEE IT THROUGH!
ALL I NEED IS A GREAT BUSINESS MODEL...
...TO ACT ON HER VISION OF A ROBUST, PROFITABLE, SCALABLE ENTERPRISE...
I WONDER WHAT "SCALABLE" MEANS.
...AND TO GROW IT IN THE GREATEST NATION ON EARTH!
WHERE ELSE?
YES, BERMUDA.
MISS? IT'S YOUR MAILBOX ATTENDANT.
I'LL HAVE TO GET BACK TO HER.

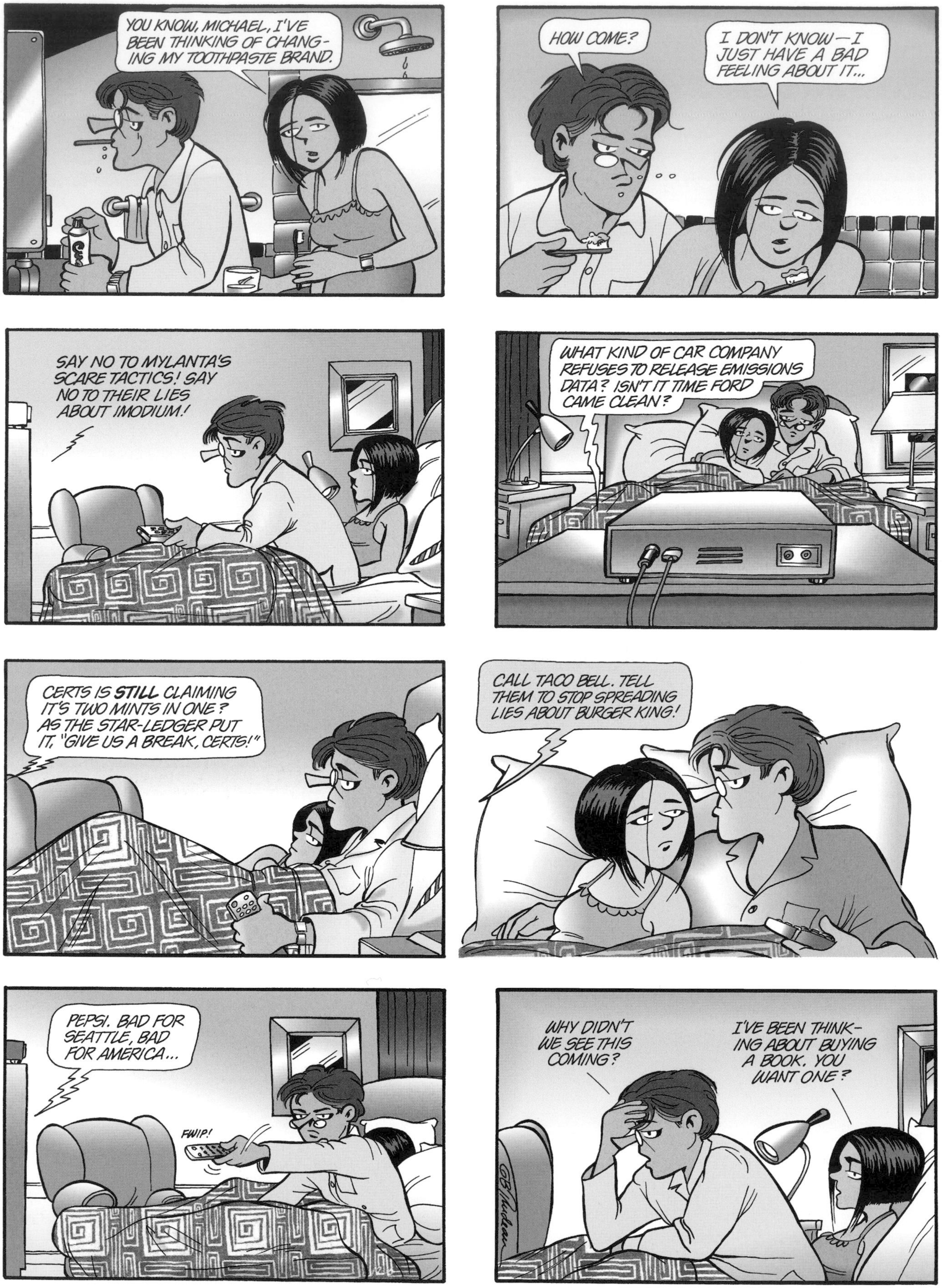
YOU KNOW, MICHAEL, I'VE BEEN THINKING OF CHANGING MY TOOTHPASTE BRAND.
HOW COME?
I DON'T KNOW—I JUST HAVE A BAD FEELING ABOUT IT...
SAY NO TO MYLANTA'S SCARE TACTICS! SAY NO TO THEIR LIES ABOUT IMODIUM!
WHAT KIND OF CAR COMPANY REFUSES TO RELEASE EMISSIONS DATA? ISN'T IT TIME FORD CAME CLEAN?
CERTS IS **STILL** CLAIMING IT'S TWO MINTS IN ONE? AS THE STAR-LEDGER PUT IT, "GIVE US A BREAK, CERTS!"
CALL TACO BELL. TELL THEM TO STOP SPREADING LIES ABOUT BURGER KING!
PEPSI. BAD FOR SEATTLE, BAD FOR AMERICA...
FWIP!
WHY DIDN'T WE SEE THIS COMING?
I'VE BEEN THINKING ABOUT BUYING A BOOK. YOU WANT ONE?

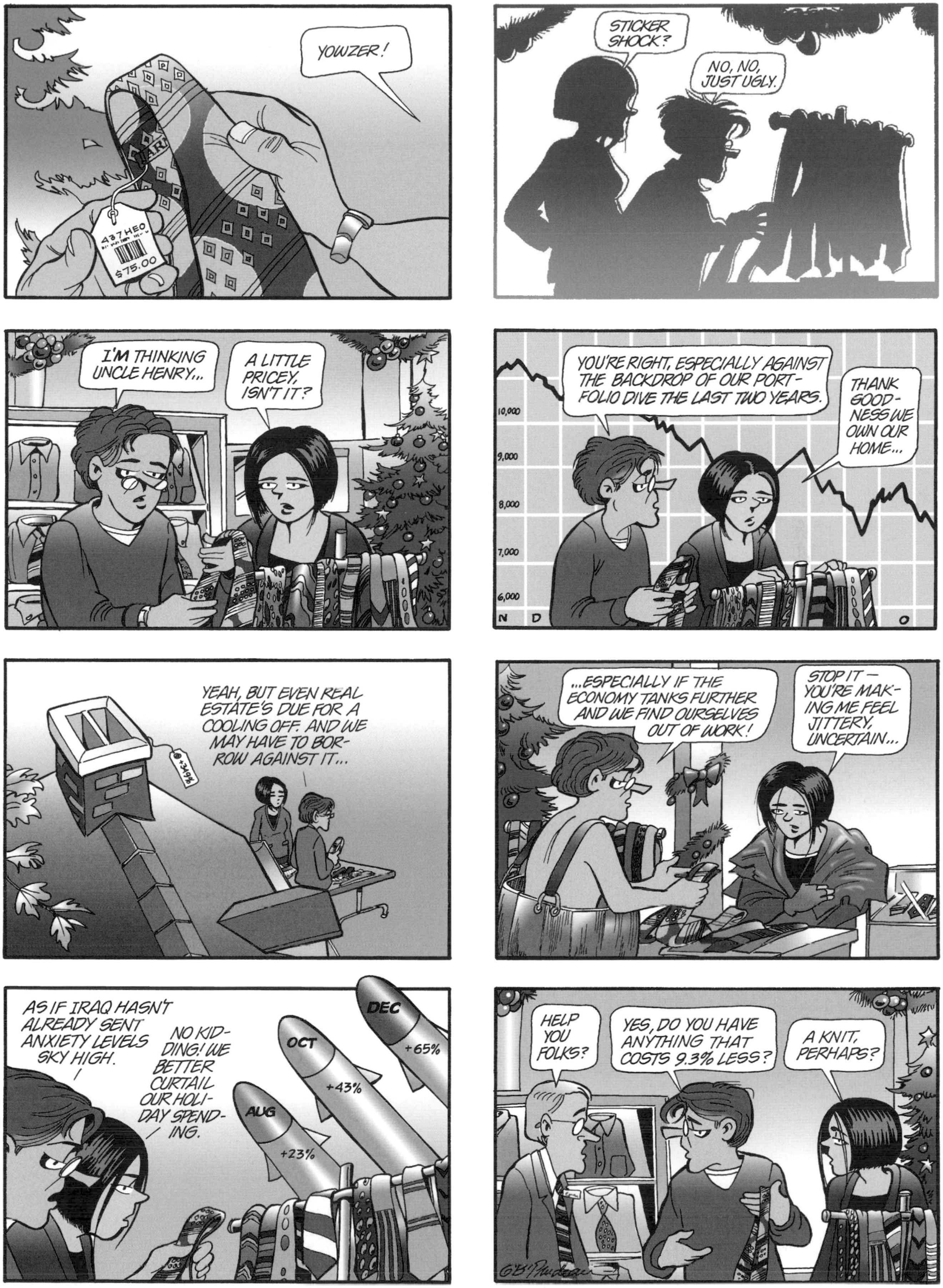

YOWZER!
437 HEO
$75.00
STICKER SHOCK?
NO, NO, JUST UGLY.
I'M THINKING UNCLE HENRY...
A LITTLE PRICEY, ISN'T IT?
YOU'RE RIGHT, ESPECIALLY AGAINST THE BACKDROP OF OUR PORT-FOLIO DIVE THE LAST TWO YEARS.
THANK GOOD-NESS WE OWN OUR HOME...
10,000
9,000
8,000
7,000
6,000
N
D
O
YEAH, BUT EVEN REAL ESTATE'S DUE FOR A COOLING OFF. AND WE MAY HAVE TO BOR-ROW AGAINST IT...
...ESPECIALLY IF THE ECONOMY TANKS FURTHER AND WE FIND OURSELVES OUT OF WORK!
STOP IT — YOU'RE MAK-ING ME FEEL JITTERY, UNCERTAIN...
AS IF IRAQ HASN'T ALREADY SENT ANXIETY LEVELS SKY HIGH.
NO KID-DING! WE BETTER CURTAIL OUR HOLI-DAY SPEND-ING.
AUG
+23%
OCT
+43%
DEC
+65%
HELP YOU FOLKS?
YES, DO YOU HAVE ANYTHING THAT COSTS 9.3% LESS?
A KNIT, PERHAPS?

IT'S THE MAN!
UH-OH.
DOES HE KNOW YET?
NOT UNLESS HE READ ABOUT IT.
YOU WOULD NOT BELIEVE THESE GUYS, BOOPSIE...
THEY'RE POMPOUS, CLUELESS AND TOTALLY OUT OF SHAPE...
EVEN WITH TRAINING, I DON'T SEE ANY OF THEM LASTING FIVE MINUTES UNDER FIRE...
SO HOW DID EVERYTHING WORK OUT WITH THE TEAM?
TQ
AE7
I'M SORRY I HAD TO LEAVE YOU IN CHARGE. I HOPE THE SEASON WASN'T TOO HUMILIATING FOR EVERYONE.
GB Trudeau
UM... NO, WE MANAGED.
DID YOU TELL HIM ABOUT THE BOWL INVITE?
W
LEAGUE CHAMPION

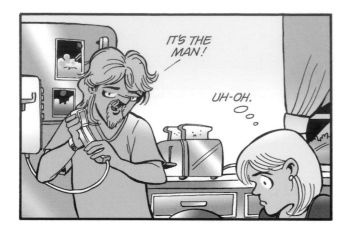

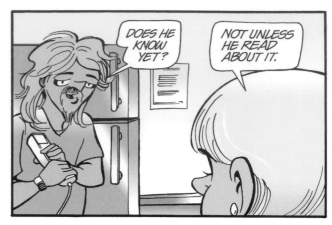

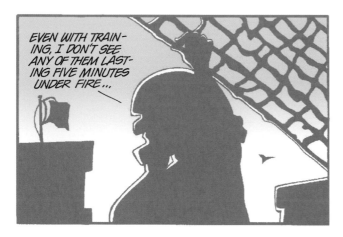

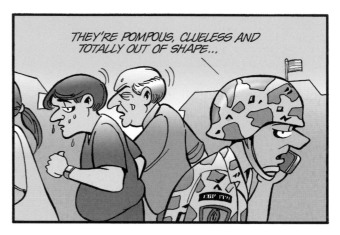

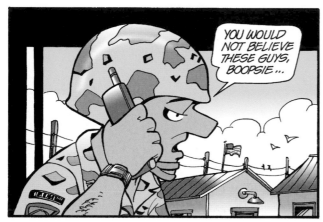

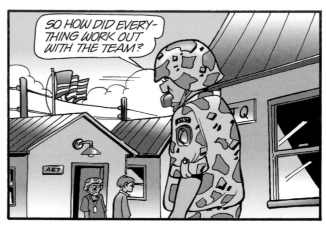

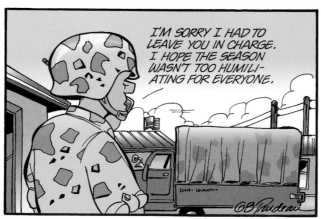

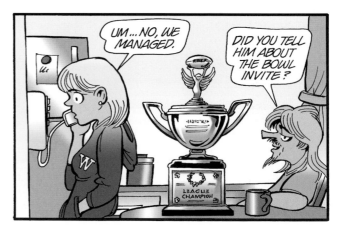

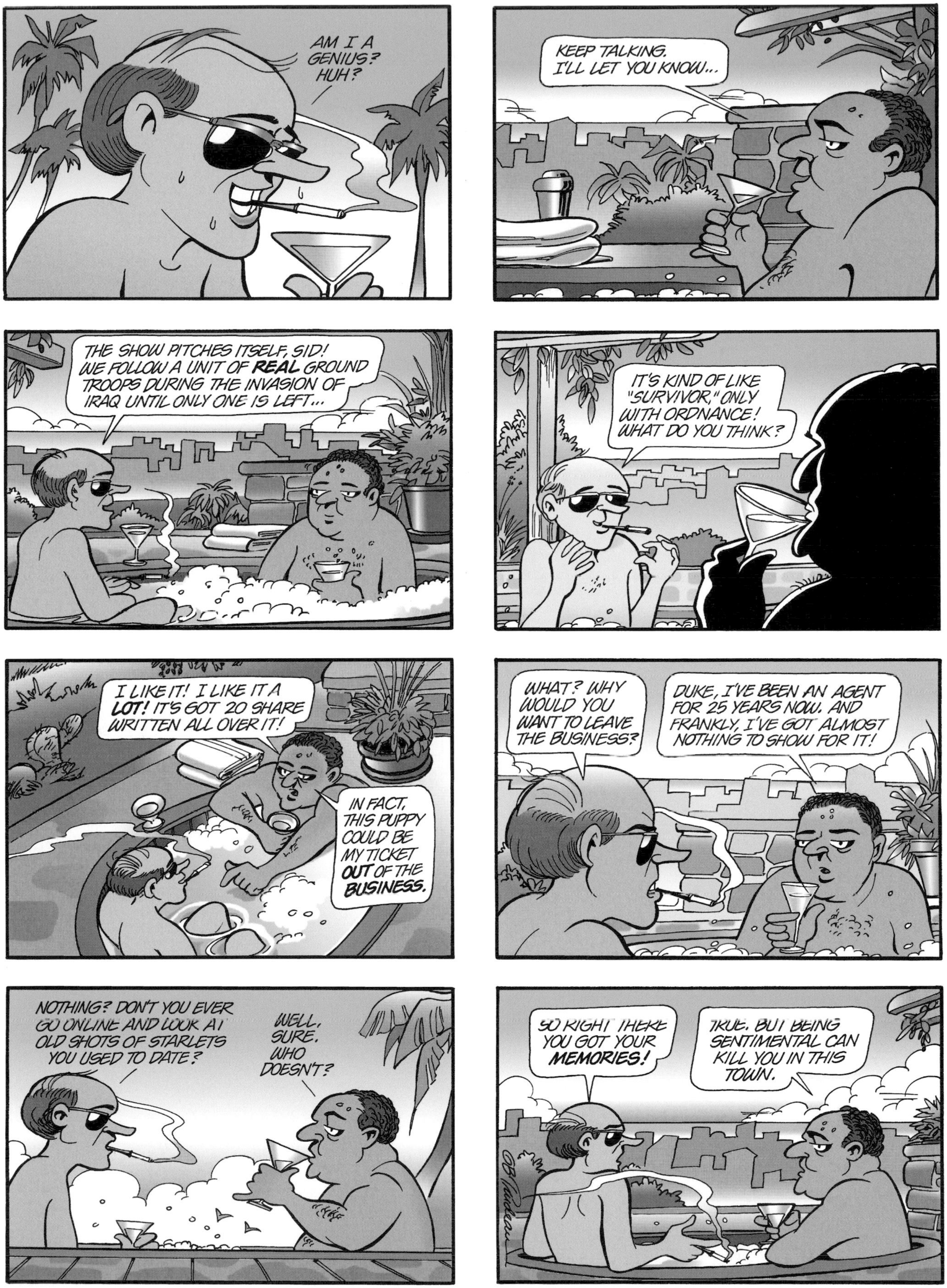

AM I A GENIUS? HUH?
KEEP TALKING. I'LL LET YOU KNOW...
THE SHOW PITCHES ITSELF, SID! WE FOLLOW A UNIT OF **REAL** GROUND TROOPS DURING THE INVASION OF IRAQ UNTIL ONLY ONE IS LEFT...
IT'S KIND OF LIKE "SURVIVOR," ONLY WITH ORDNANCE! WHAT DO YOU THINK?
I LIKE IT! I LIKE IT A **LOT!** IT'S GOT 20 SHARE WRITTEN ALL OVER IT!
IN FACT, THIS PUPPY COULD BE MY TICKET **OUT** OF THE **BUSINESS.**
WHAT? WHY WOULD YOU WANT TO LEAVE THE BUSINESS?
DUKE, I'VE BEEN AN AGENT FOR 25 YEARS NOW. AND FRANKLY, I'VE GOT ALMOST NOTHING TO SHOW FOR IT!
NOTHING? DON'T YOU EVER GO ONLINE AND LOOK AT OLD SHOTS OF STARLETS YOU USED TO DATE?
WELL, SURE. WHO DOESN'T?
SO RIGHT THERE YOU GOT YOUR **MEMORIES!**
TRUE. BUT BEING SENTIMENTAL CAN KILL YOU IN THIS TOWN.

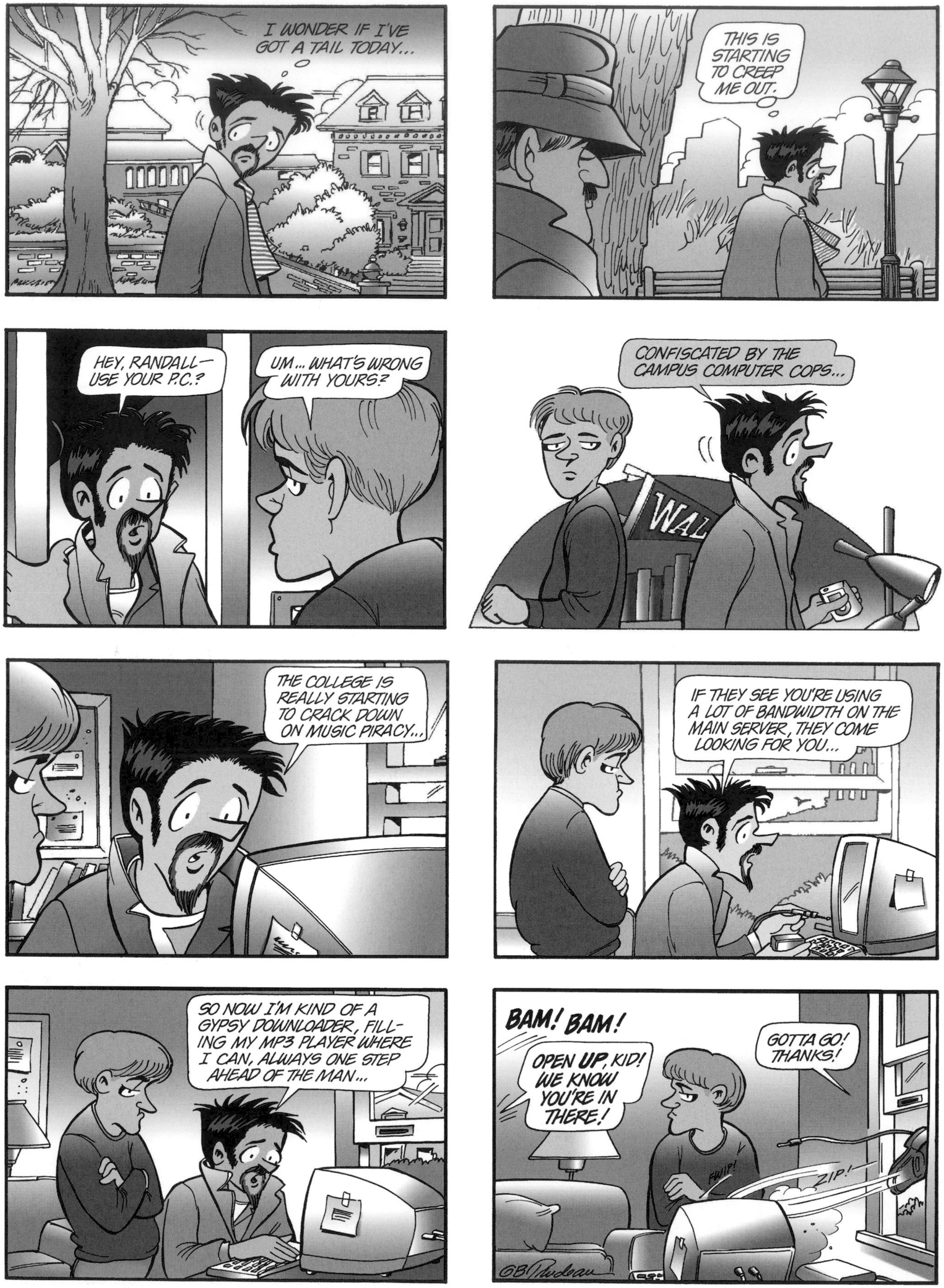
I WONDER IF I'VE GOT A TAIL TODAY...
THIS IS STARTING TO CREEP ME OUT.
HEY, RANDALL— USE YOUR P.C.?
UM... WHAT'S WRONG WITH YOURS?
CONFISCATED BY THE CAMPUS COMPUTER COPS...
WAL
THE COLLEGE IS REALLY STARTING TO CRACK DOWN ON MUSIC PIRACY...
IF THEY SEE YOU'RE USING A LOT OF BANDWIDTH ON THE MAIN SERVER, THEY COME LOOKING FOR YOU...
SO NOW I'M KIND OF A GYPSY DOWNLOADER, FILLING MY MP3 PLAYER WHERE I CAN, ALWAYS ONE STEP AHEAD OF THE MAN...
BAM! BAM!
OPEN UP, KID! WE KNOW YOU'RE IN THERE!
GOTTA GO! THANKS!
FWIP!
ZIP!

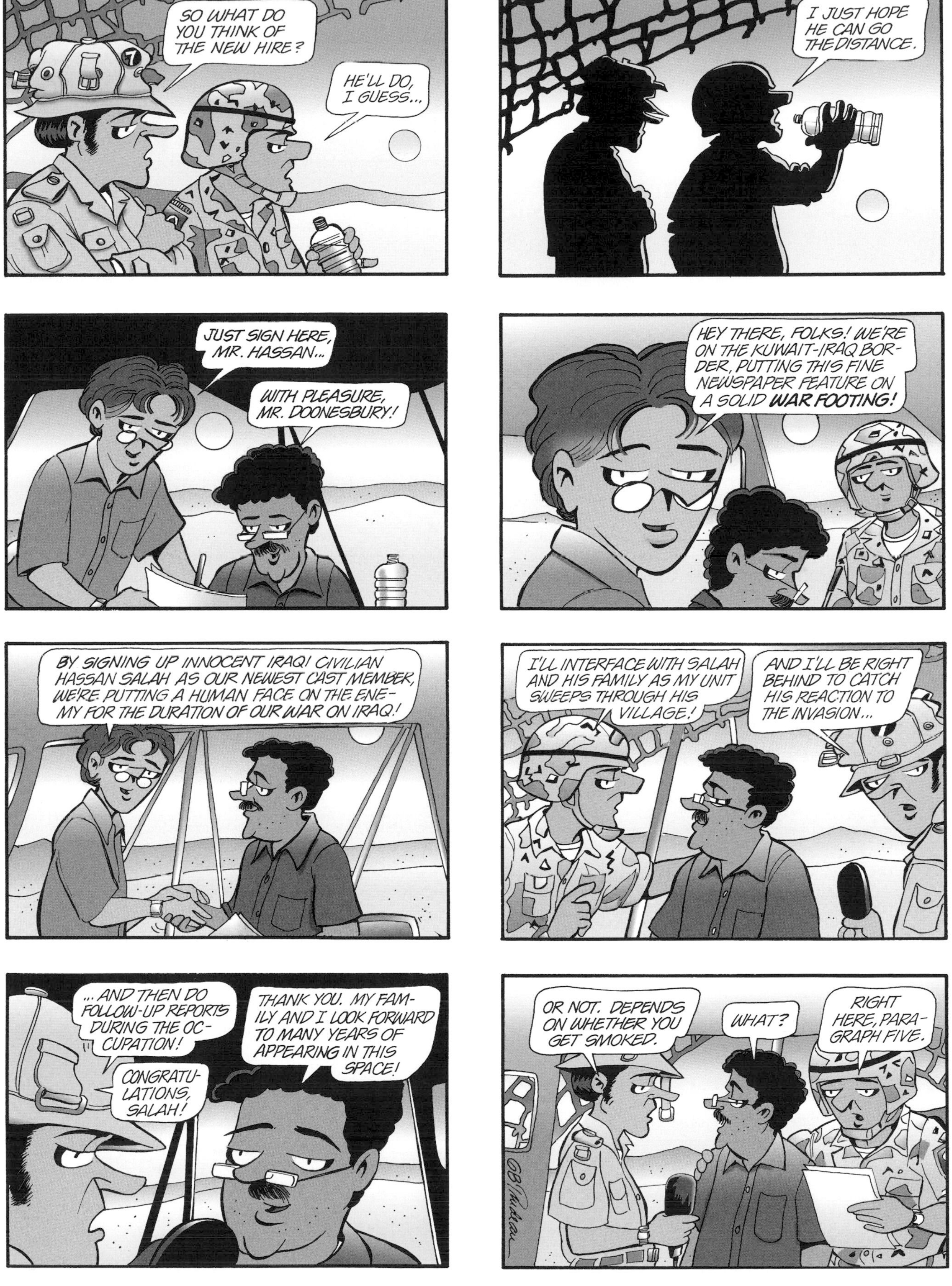
SO WHAT DO YOU THINK OF THE NEW HIRE?
HE'LL DO, I GUESS...
I JUST HOPE HE CAN GO THE DISTANCE.
JUST SIGN HERE, MR. HASSAN...
WITH PLEASURE, MR. DOONESBURY!
HEY THERE, FOLKS! WE'RE ON THE KUWAIT-IRAQ BORDER, PUTTING THIS FINE NEWSPAPER FEATURE ON A SOLID **WAR FOOTING!**
BY SIGNING UP INNOCENT IRAQI CIVILIAN HASSAN SALAH AS OUR NEWEST CAST MEMBER, WE'RE PUTTING A HUMAN FACE ON THE ENEMY FOR THE DURATION OF OUR WAR ON IRAQ!
I'LL INTERFACE WITH SALAH AND HIS FAMILY AS MY UNIT SWEEPS THROUGH HIS VILLAGE!
AND I'LL BE RIGHT BEHIND TO CATCH HIS REACTION TO THE INVASION...
...AND THEN DO FOLLOW-UP REPORTS DURING THE OCCUPATION!
CONGRATULATIONS, SALAH!
THANK YOU. MY FAMILY AND I LOOK FORWARD TO MANY YEARS OF APPEARING IN THIS SPACE!
OR NOT. DEPENDS ON WHETHER YOU GET SMOKED.
WHAT?
RIGHT HERE, PARAGRAPH FIVE.

SIR? THE EPA ADMINISTRATOR IS ON LINE TWO!
WE STILL HAVE AN EPA?
OKAY, LET'S MOVE ON TO OUR CONTRIBUTORS FROM THE EXTRACTION INDUSTRIES — IS EVERY-ONE HAPPY THERE?
VERY, SIR! WITH ALL THE NATIONAL SECURITY DISTRAC-TIONS, WE'VE BEEN ABLE TO QUIETLY GUT ONE ENVIRON-MENTAL PROTECTION REGU-LATION AFTER ANOTHER...
FOR INSTANCE, WE'VE PRODUCED NEW RULES TO SPEED UP LOGGING IN NATIONAL FORESTS, ROLLED BACK PROTECTIONS OF 58 MILLION ACRES FROM ROADS AND DEVELOPMENTS, EASED POLLUTION CONTROLS FOR POWER PLANTS AND FACTORIES, REJECTED NEW FUEL-EFFICIENCY STANDARDS, SPED UP PERMIT-GRANTING FOR POWER COMPANIES...
...LIFTED A BAN ON SNOWMOBILES IN PARKS, PROPOSED 51,000 NEW NATURAL GAS WELLS, REMOVED LIMITS ON COAL PRODUCERS FOR DUMPING MOUNTAINTOP FILL IN STREAMS, REDUCED EPA FINES OF POLLUTERS BY 64%, OPENED UP PADRE ISLAND TO DRILLING, HALTED FUNDING FOR SEVERAL SUPERFUND SITES, RE-PLACED SCIENTISTS WHO DON'T SUPPORT OUR VIEWS, REJECTED THE KYOTO GLOBAL WARMING TREATY, AND MUCH, MUCH MORE!
WHOA... THAT'S QUITE A LIST...
YES, SIR.
DOES CHRISTIE WHITMAN STILL WORK FOR US?
I CAN CHECK.

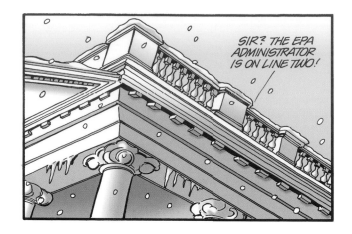

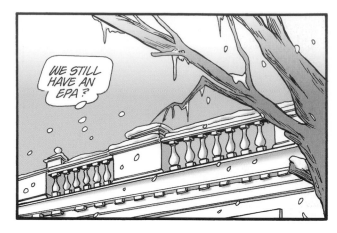

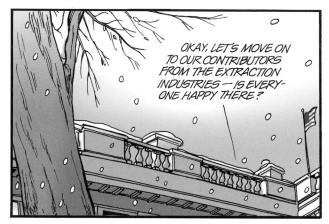

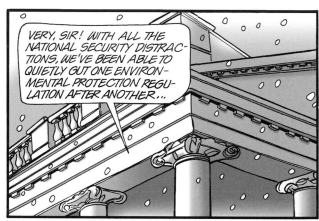

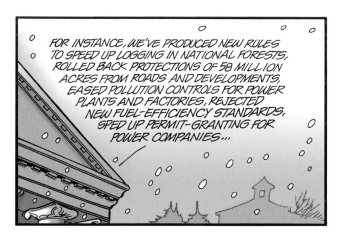

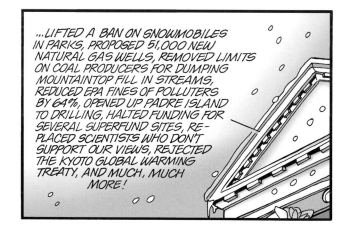

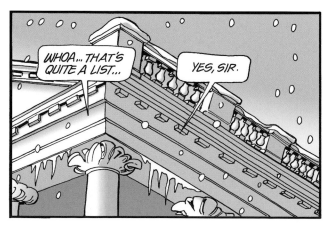

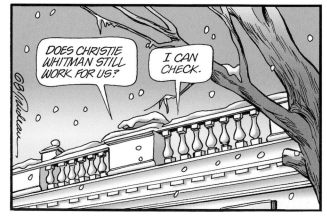

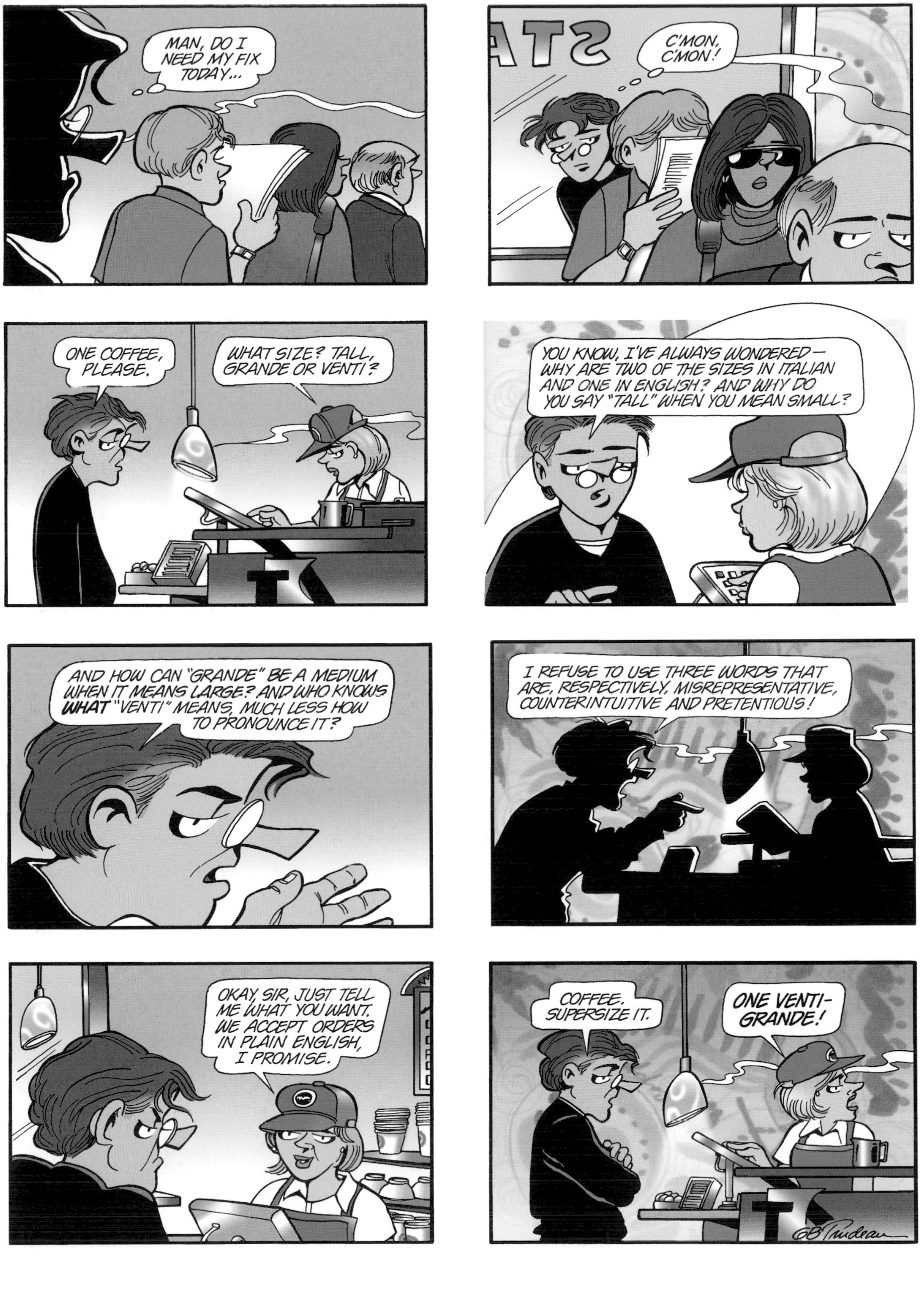
MAN, DO I NEED MY FIX TODAY...
C'MON, C'MON!
ONE COFFEE, PLEASE.
WHAT SIZE? TALL, GRANDE OR VENTI?
YOU KNOW, I'VE ALWAYS WONDERED— WHY ARE TWO OF THE SIZES IN ITALIAN AND ONE IN ENGLISH? AND WHY DO YOU SAY "TALL" WHEN YOU MEAN SMALL?
AND HOW CAN "GRANDE" BE A MEDIUM WHEN IT MEANS LARGE? AND WHO KNOWS **WHAT** "VENTI" MEANS, MUCH LESS HOW TO PRONOUNCE IT?
I REFUSE TO USE THREE WORDS THAT ARE, RESPECTIVELY, MISREPRESENTATIVE, COUNTERINTUITIVE AND PRETENTIOUS!
OKAY, SIR, JUST TELL ME WHAT YOU WANT. WE ACCEPT ORDERS IN PLAIN ENGLISH, I PROMISE.
COFFEE. SUPERSIZE IT.
ONE VENTI-GRANDE!

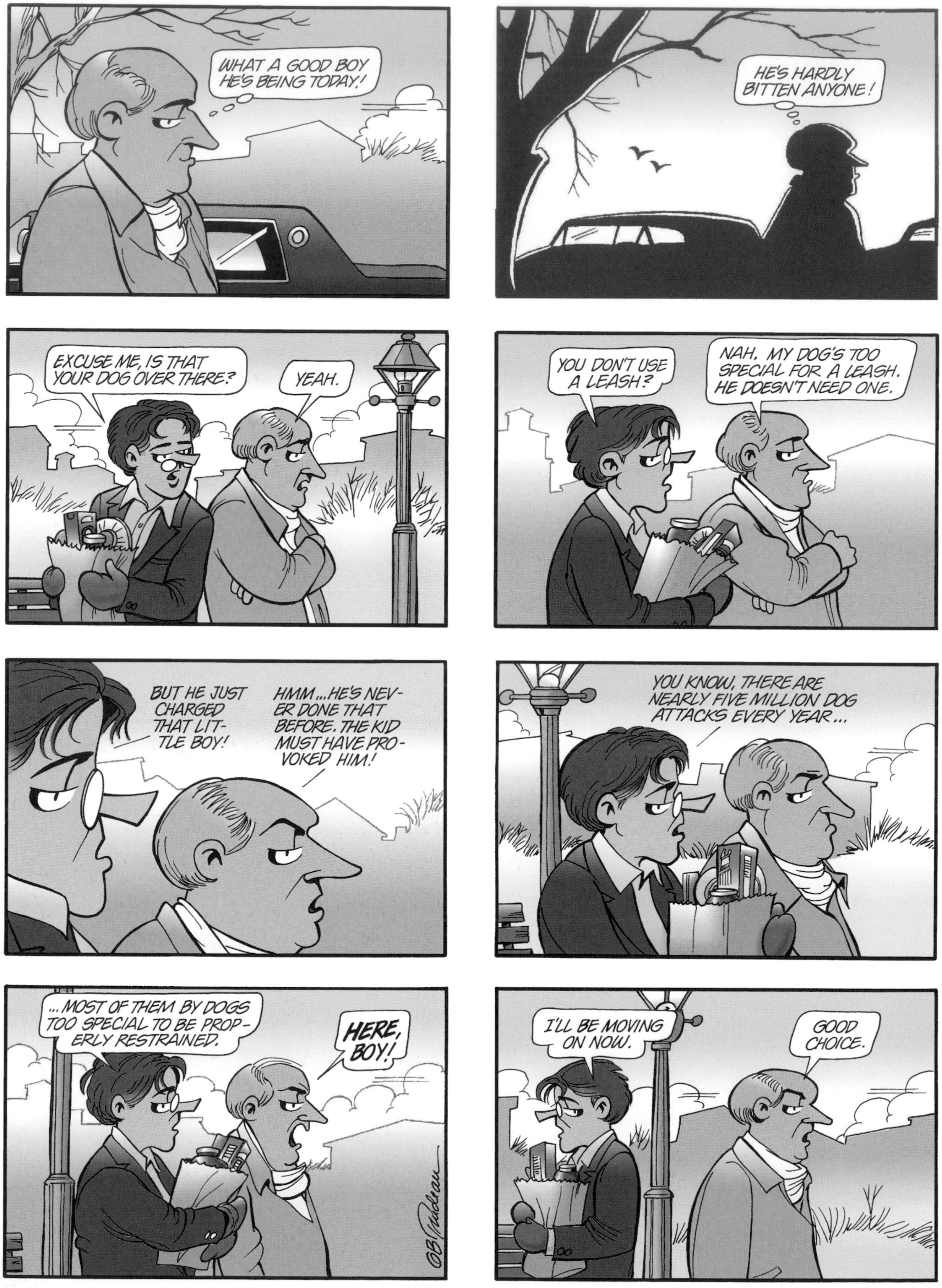
WHAT A GOOD BOY HE'S BEING TODAY!
HE'S HARDLY BITTEN ANYONE!
EXCUSE ME, IS THAT YOUR DOG OVER THERE?
YEAH.
YOU DON'T USE A LEASH?
NAH. MY DOG'S TOO SPECIAL FOR A LEASH. HE DOESN'T NEED ONE.
BUT HE JUST CHARGED THAT LIT-TLE BOY!
HMM...HE'S NEV-ER DONE THAT BEFORE. THE KID MUST HAVE PRO-VOKED HIM!
YOU KNOW, THERE ARE NEARLY FIVE MILLION DOG ATTACKS EVERY YEAR...
...MOST OF THEM BY DOGS TOO SPECIAL TO BE PROP-ERLY RESTRAINED.
HERE, BOY!
I'LL BE MOVING ON NOW.
GOOD CHOICE.

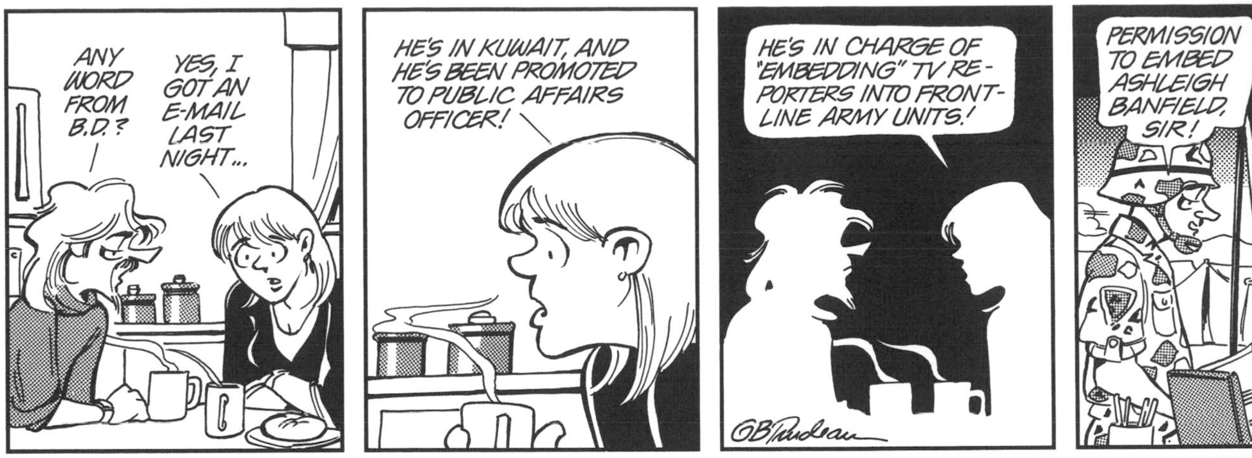
ANY WORD FROM B.D.?
YES, I GOT AN E-MAIL LAST NIGHT...
HE'S IN KUWAIT, AND HE'S BEEN PROMOTED TO PUBLIC AFFAIRS OFFICER!
HE'S IN CHARGE OF "EMBEDDING" TV REPORTERS INTO FRONTLINE ARMY UNITS!
PERMISSION TO EMBED ASHLEIGH BANFIELD, SIR!
CALM DOWN, SOLDIER.

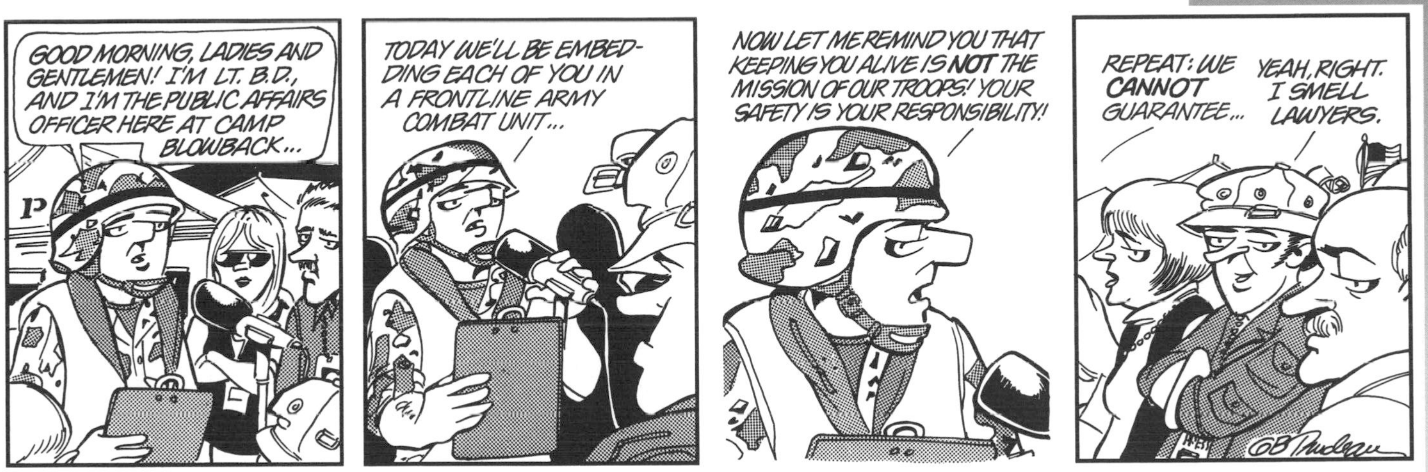
GOOD MORNING, LADIES AND GENTLEMEN! I'M LT. B.D., AND I'M THE PUBLIC AFFAIRS OFFICER HERE AT CAMP BLOWBACK...
TODAY WE'LL BE EMBEDDING EACH OF YOU IN A FRONTLINE ARMY COMBAT UNIT...
NOW LET ME REMIND YOU THAT KEEPING YOU ALIVE IS NOT THE MISSION OF OUR TROOPS! YOUR SAFETY IS YOUR RESPONSIBILITY!
REPEAT: WE CANNOT GUARANTEE...
YEAH, RIGHT. I SMELL LAWYERS.

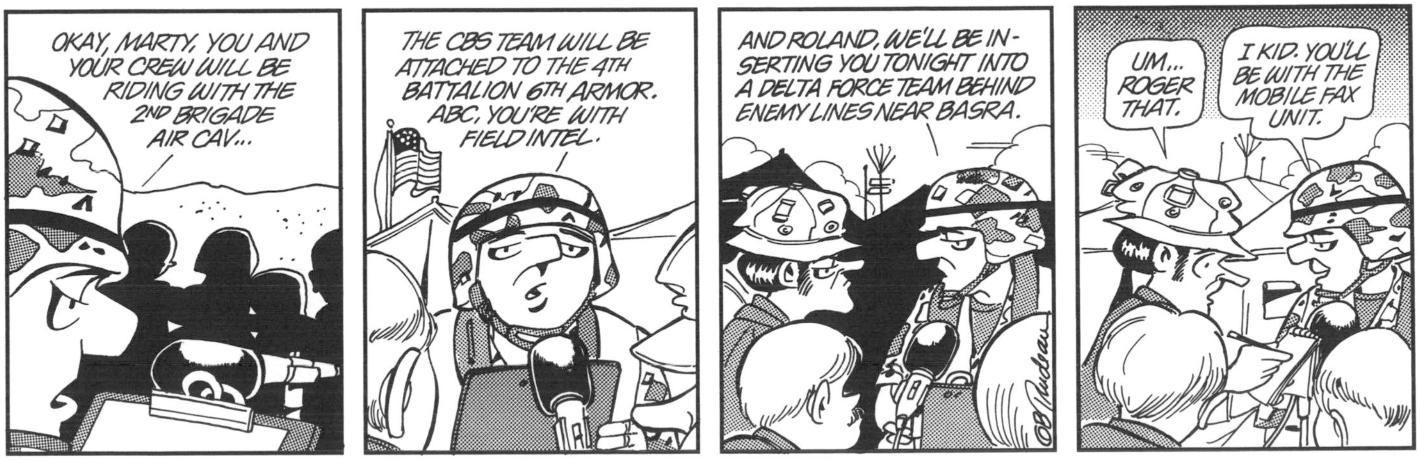
OKAY, MARTY, YOU AND YOUR CREW WILL BE RIDING WITH THE 2ND BRIGADE AIR CAV...
THE CBS TEAM WILL BE ATTACHED TO THE 4TH BATTALION 6TH ARMOR. ABC, YOU'RE WITH FIELD INTEL.
AND ROLAND, WE'LL BE INSERTING YOU TONIGHT INTO A DELTA FORCE TEAM BEHIND ENEMY LINES NEAR BASRA.
UM... ROGER THAT.
I KID. YOU'LL BE WITH THE MOBILE FAX UNIT.

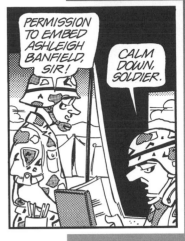

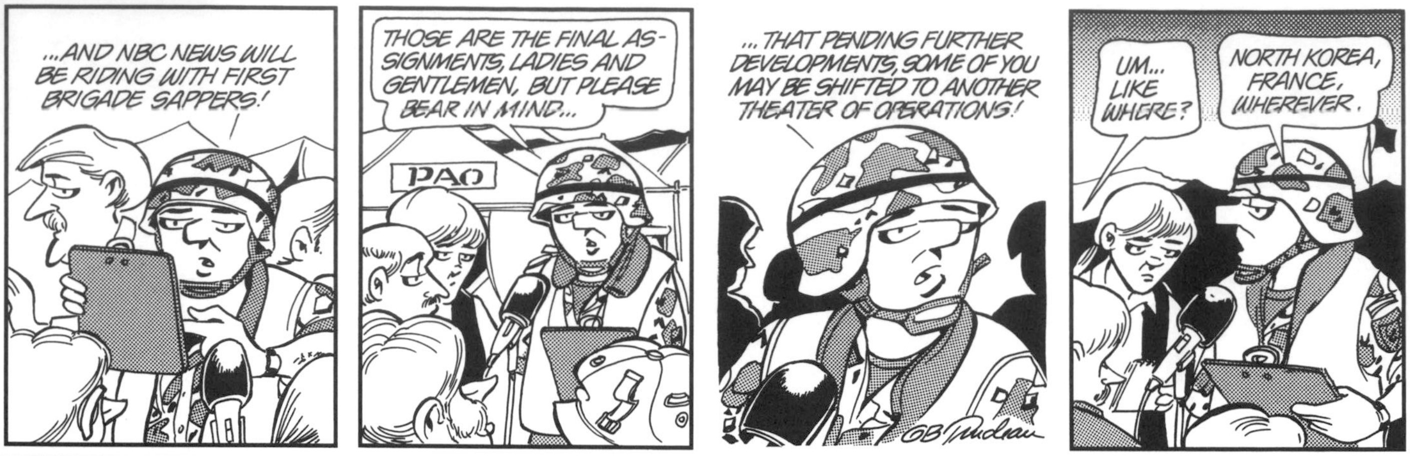
...AND NBC NEWS WILL BE RIDING WITH FIRST BRIGADE SAPPERS!
THOSE ARE THE FINAL AS-SIGNMENTS, LADIES AND GENTLEMEN, BUT PLEASE BEAR IN MIND...
PAO
...THAT PENDING FURTHER DEVELOPMENTS, SOME OF YOU MAY BE SHIFTED TO ANOTHER THEATER OF OPERATIONS!
UM... LIKE WHERE?
NORTH KOREA, FRANCE, WHEREVER.

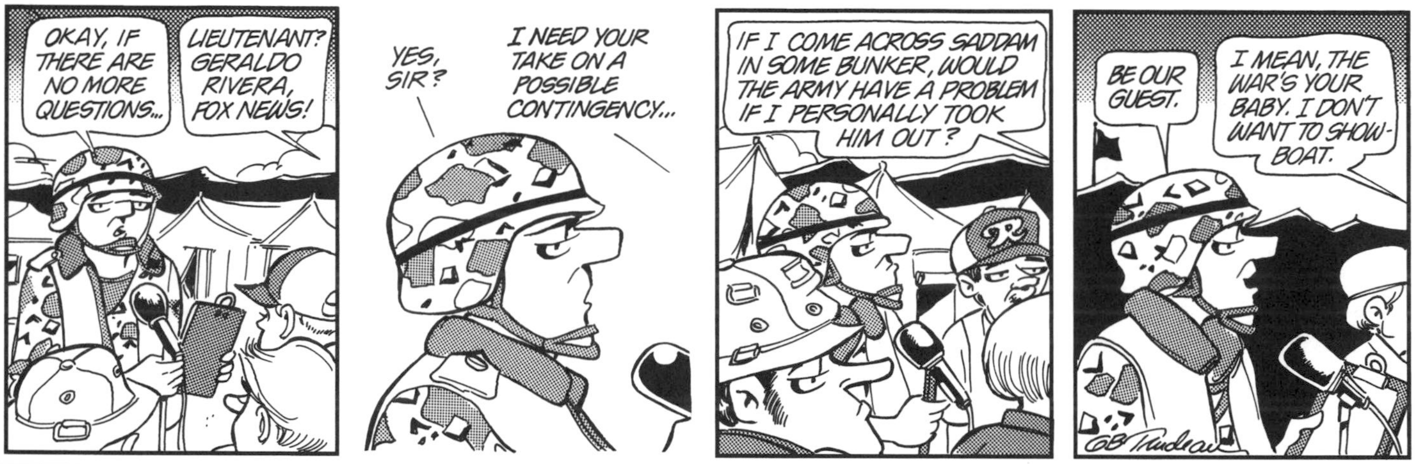
OKAY, IF THERE ARE NO MORE QUESTIONS...
LIEUTENANT? GERALDO RIVERA, FOX NEWS!
YES, SIR?
I NEED YOUR TAKE ON A POSSIBLE CONTINGENCY...
IF I COME ACROSS SADDAM IN SOME BUNKER, WOULD THE ARMY HAVE A PROBLEM IF I PERSONALLY TOOK HIM OUT?
BE OUR GUEST.
I MEAN, THE WAR'S YOUR BABY. I DON'T WANT TO SHOW-BOAT.

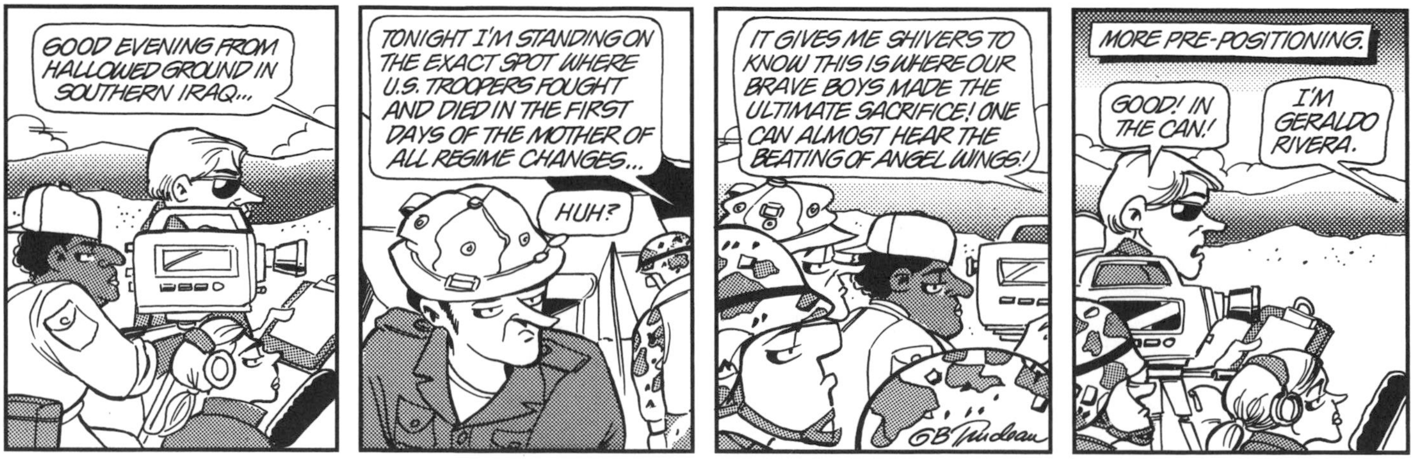
GOOD EVENING FROM HALLOWED GROUND IN SOUTHERN IRAQ...
TONIGHT I'M STANDING ON THE EXACT SPOT WHERE U.S. TROOPERS FOUGHT AND DIED IN THE FIRST DAYS OF THE MOTHER OF ALL REGIME CHANGES...
HUH?
IT GIVES ME SHIVERS TO KNOW THIS IS WHERE OUR BRAVE BOYS MADE THE ULTIMATE SACRIFICE! ONE CAN ALMOST HEAR THE BEATING OF ANGEL WINGS!
MORE PRE-POSITIONING.
GOOD! IN THE CAN!
I'M GERALDO RIVERA.

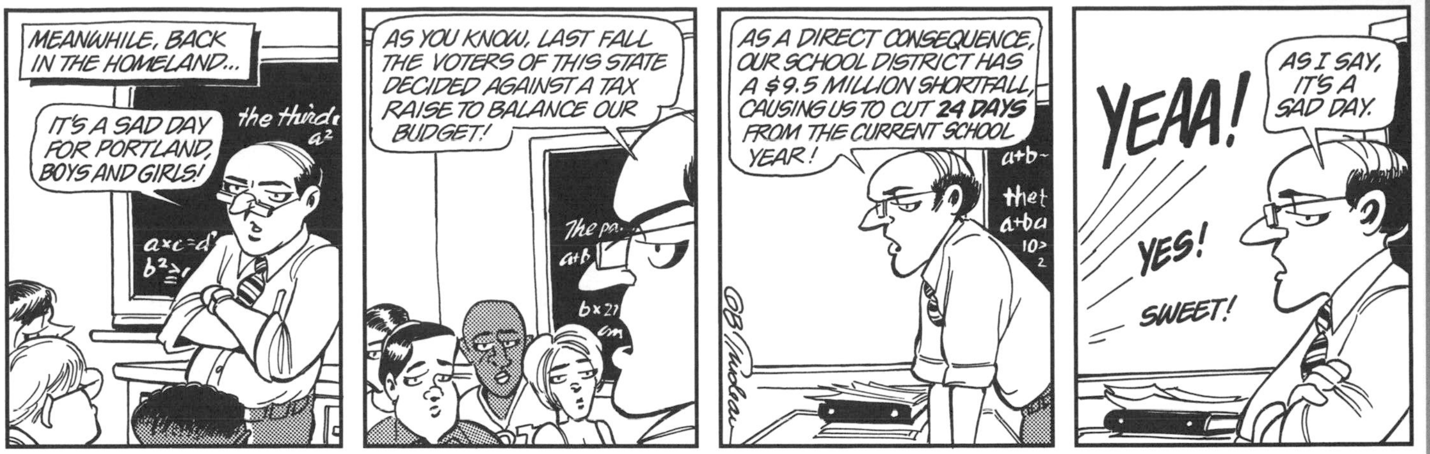
MEANWHILE, BACK IN THE HOMELAND...
IT'S A SAD DAY FOR PORTLAND, BOYS AND GIRLS!
AS YOU KNOW, LAST FALL THE VOTERS OF THIS STATE DECIDED AGAINST A TAX RAISE TO BALANCE OUR BUDGET!
AS A DIRECT CONSEQUENCE, OUR SCHOOL DISTRICT HAS A $9.5 MILLION SHORTFALL, CAUSING US TO CUT **24 DAYS** FROM THE CURRENT SCHOOL YEAR!
YEAA!
YES!
SWEET!
AS I SAY, IT'S A SAD DAY.

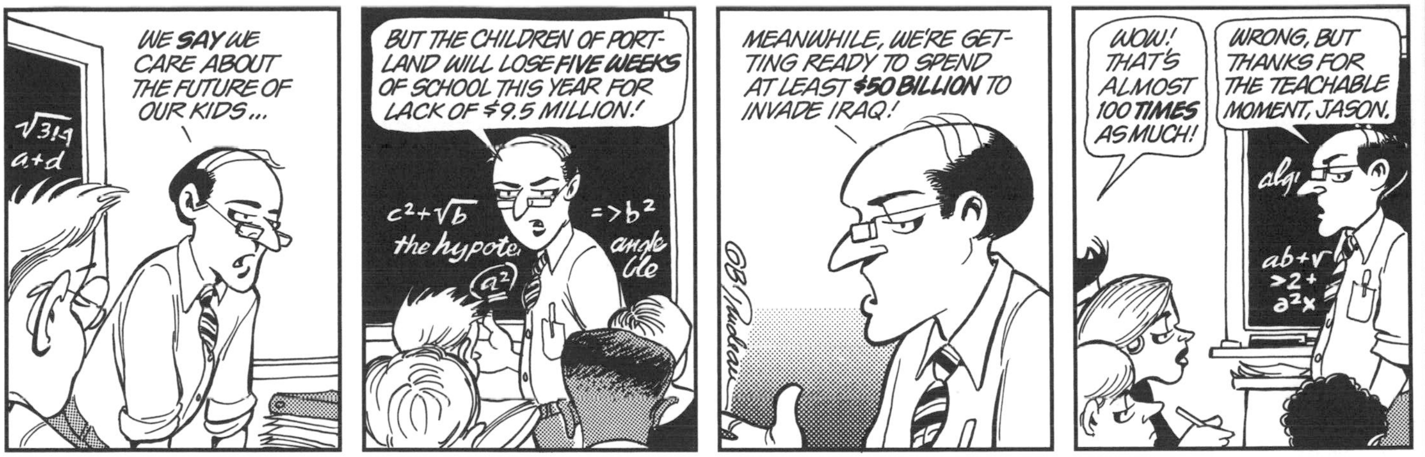
WE **SAY** WE CARE ABOUT THE FUTURE OF OUR KIDS...
BUT THE CHILDREN OF PORTLAND WILL LOSE **FIVE WEEKS** OF SCHOOL THIS YEAR FOR LACK OF $9.5 MILLION!
MEANWHILE, WE'RE GETTING READY TO SPEND AT LEAST **$50 BILLION** TO INVADE IRAQ!
WOW! THAT'S ALMOST 100 **TIMES** AS MUCH!
WRONG, BUT THANKS FOR THE TEACHABLE MOMENT, JASON.

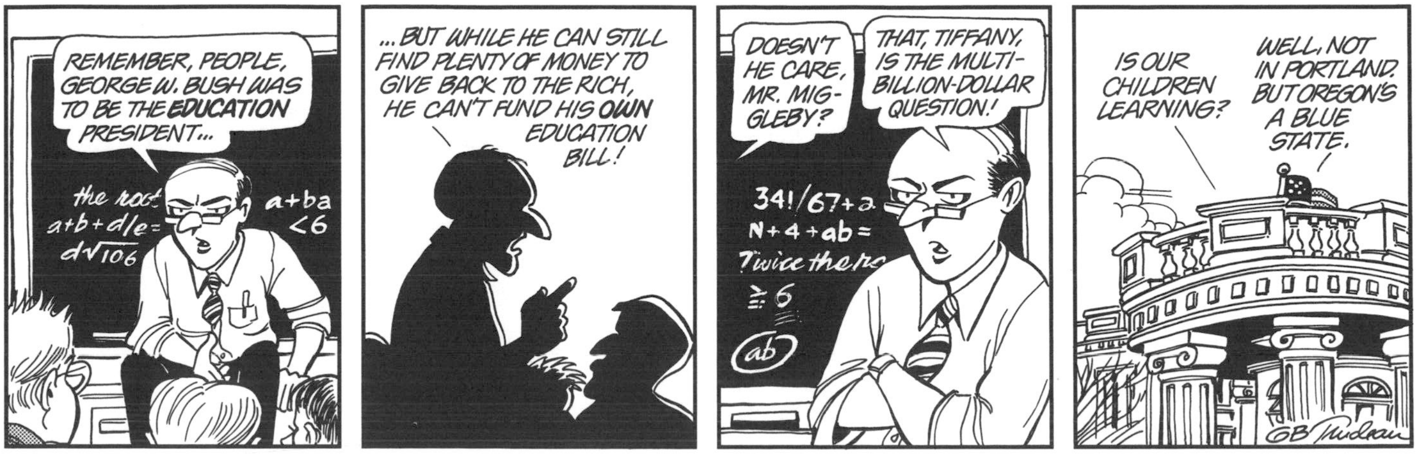
REMEMBER, PEOPLE, GEORGE W. BUSH WAS TO BE THE **EDUCATION** PRESIDENT...
...BUT WHILE HE CAN STILL FIND PLENTY OF MONEY TO GIVE BACK TO THE RICH, HE CAN'T FUND HIS **OWN** EDUCATION BILL!
DOESN'T HE CARE, MR. MIGGLEBY?
THAT, TIFFANY, IS THE MULTI-BILLION-DOLLAR QUESTION!
IS OUR CHILDREN LEARNING?
WELL, NOT IN PORTLAND. BUT OREGON'S A BLUE STATE.

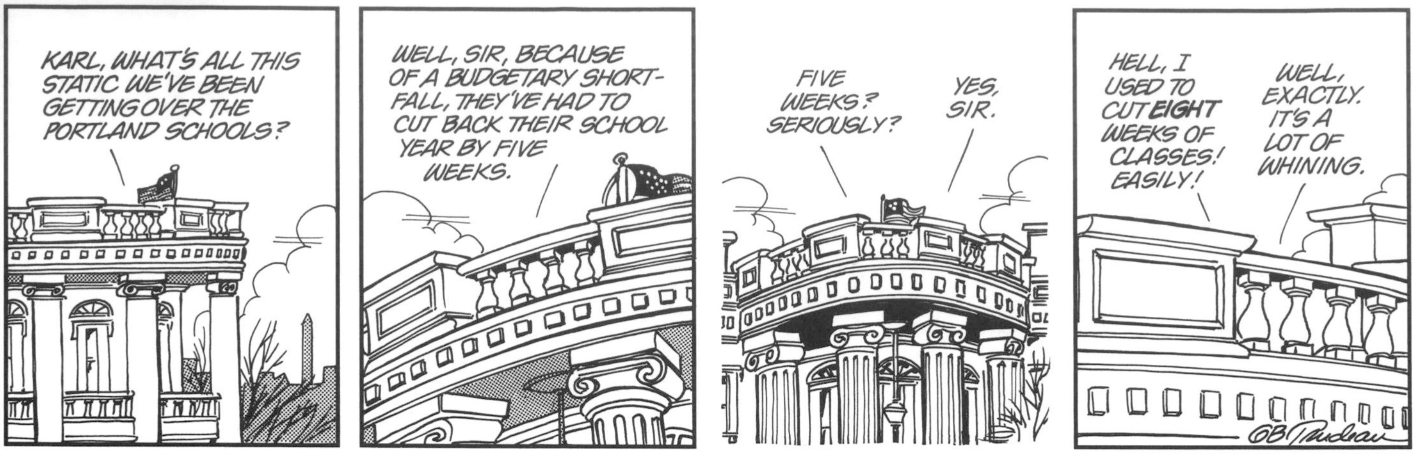
KARL, WHAT'S ALL THIS STATIC WE'VE BEEN GETTING OVER THE PORTLAND SCHOOLS?
WELL, SIR, BECAUSE OF A BUDGETARY SHORT-FALL, THEY'VE HAD TO CUT BACK THEIR SCHOOL YEAR BY FIVE WEEKS.
FIVE WEEKS? SERIOUSLY?
YES, SIR.
HELL, I USED TO CUT **EIGHT** WEEKS OF CLASSES! EASILY!
WELL, EXACTLY. IT'S A LOT OF WHINING.
GB Trudeau

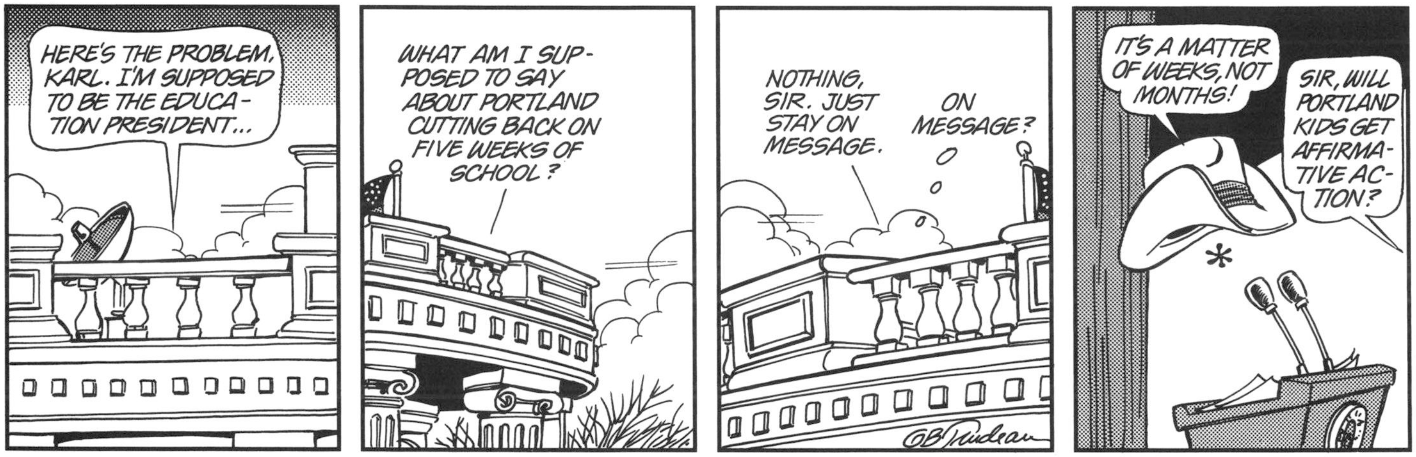
HERE'S THE PROBLEM, KARL. I'M SUPPOSED TO BE THE EDUCATION PRESIDENT...
WHAT AM I SUPPOSED TO SAY ABOUT PORTLAND CUTTING BACK ON FIVE WEEKS OF SCHOOL?
NOTHING, SIR. JUST STAY ON MESSAGE.
ON MESSAGE?
GB Trudeau
IT'S A MATTER OF WEEKS, NOT MONTHS!
SIR, WILL PORTLAND KIDS GET AFFIRMATIVE ACTION?

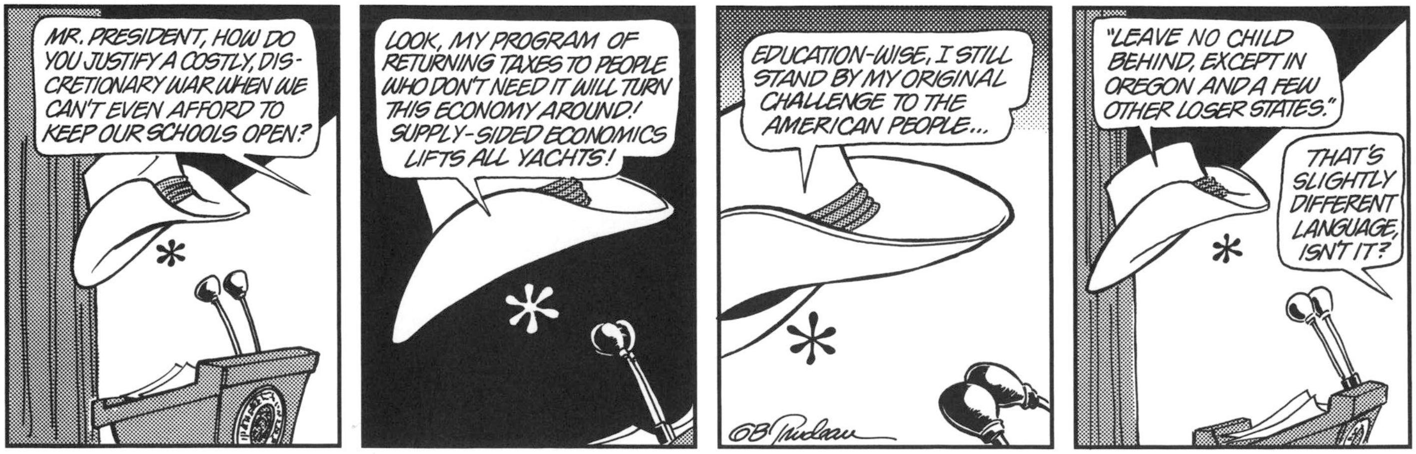
MR. PRESIDENT, HOW DO YOU JUSTIFY A COSTLY, DISCRETIONARY WAR WHEN WE CAN'T EVEN AFFORD TO KEEP OUR SCHOOLS OPEN?
LOOK, MY PROGRAM OF RETURNING TAXES TO PEOPLE WHO DON'T NEED IT WILL TURN THIS ECONOMY AROUND! SUPPLY-SIDED ECONOMICS LIFTS ALL YACHTS!
EDUCATION-WISE, I STILL STAND BY MY ORIGINAL CHALLENGE TO THE AMERICAN PEOPLE...
GB Trudeau
"LEAVE NO CHILD BEHIND, EXCEPT IN OREGON AND A FEW OTHER LOSER STATES."
THAT'S SLIGHTLY DIFFERENT LANGUAGE, ISN'T IT?

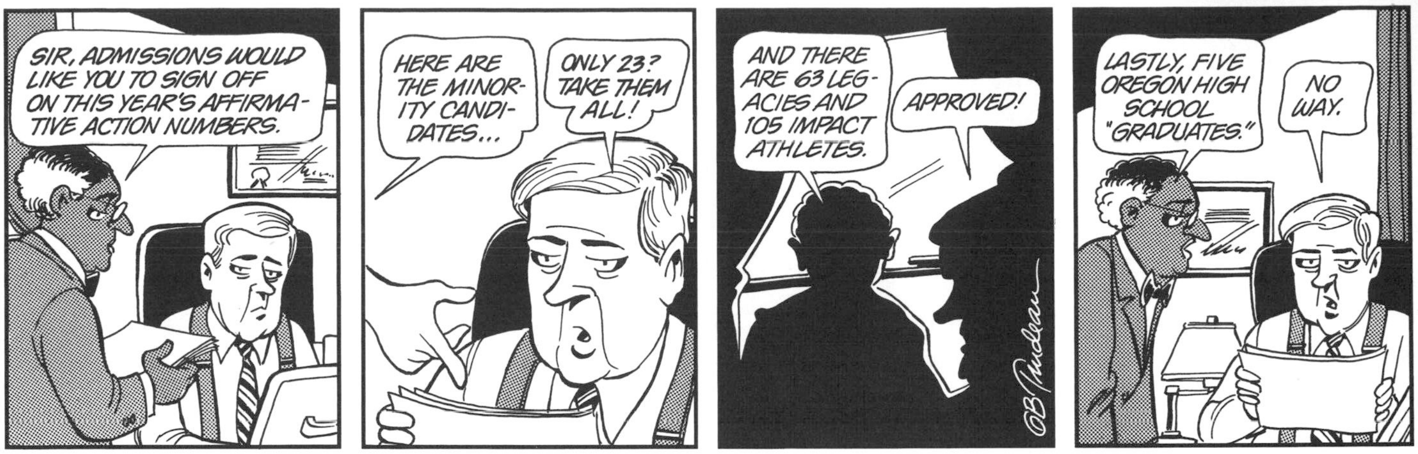
SIR, ADMISSIONS WOULD LIKE YOU TO SIGN OFF ON THIS YEAR'S AFFIRMATIVE ACTION NUMBERS.
HERE ARE THE MINORITY CANDIDATES...
ONLY 23? TAKE THEM ALL!
AND THERE ARE 63 LEGACIES AND 105 IMPACT ATHLETES.
APPROVED!
LASTLY, FIVE OREGON HIGH SCHOOL "GRADUATES."
NO WAY.

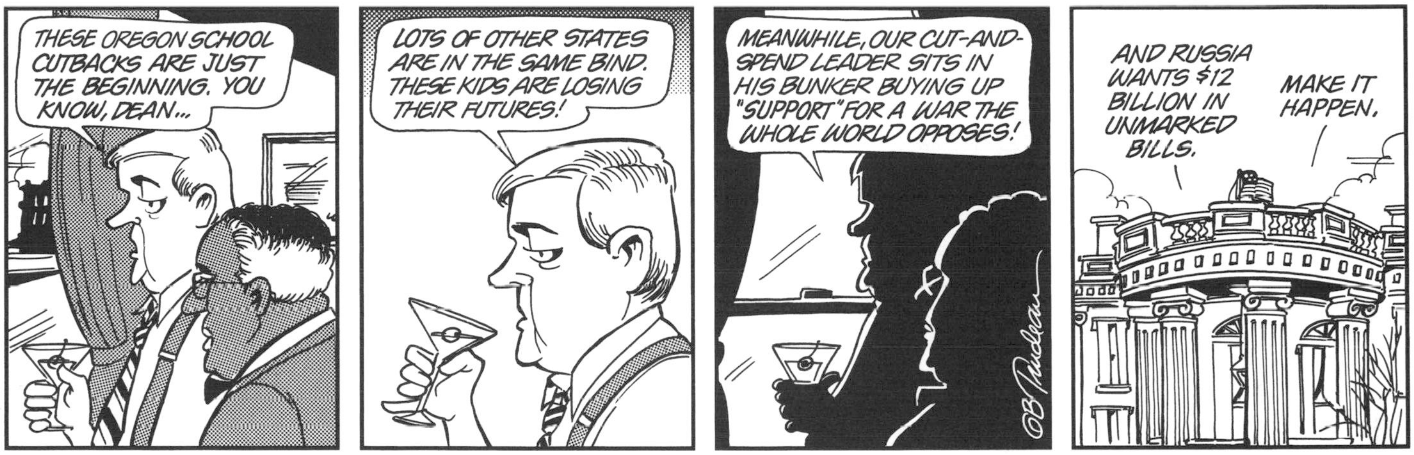
THESE OREGON SCHOOL CUTBACKS ARE JUST THE BEGINNING. YOU KNOW, DEAN...
LOTS OF OTHER STATES ARE IN THE SAME BIND. THESE KIDS ARE LOSING THEIR FUTURES!
MEANWHILE, OUR CUT-AND-SPEND LEADER SITS IN HIS BUNKER BUYING UP "SUPPORT" FOR A WAR THE WHOLE WORLD OPPOSES!
AND RUSSIA WANTS $12 BILLION IN UNMARKED BILLS.
MAKE IT HAPPEN.

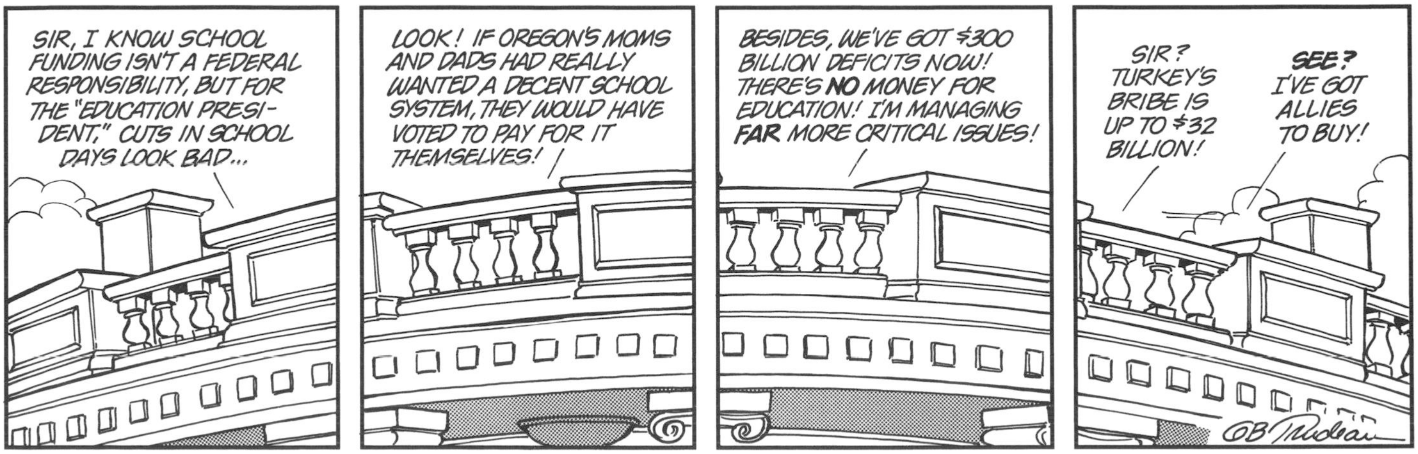
SIR, I KNOW SCHOOL FUNDING ISN'T A FEDERAL RESPONSIBILITY, BUT FOR THE "EDUCATION PRESIDENT," CUTS IN SCHOOL DAYS LOOK BAD...
LOOK! IF OREGON'S MOMS AND DADS HAD REALLY WANTED A DECENT SCHOOL SYSTEM, THEY WOULD HAVE VOTED TO PAY FOR IT THEMSELVES!
BESIDES, WE'VE GOT $300 BILLION DEFICITS NOW! THERE'S NO MONEY FOR EDUCATION! I'M MANAGING FAR MORE CRITICAL ISSUES!
SIR? TURKEY'S BRIBE IS UP TO $32 BILLION!
SEE? I'VE GOT ALLIES TO BUY!

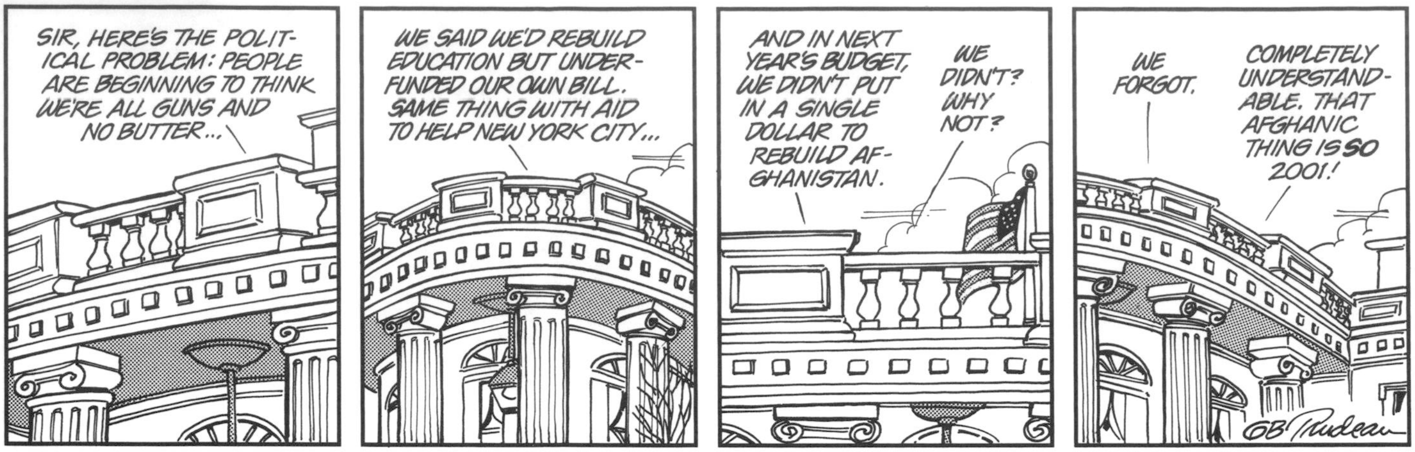
SIR, HERE'S THE POLITICAL PROBLEM: PEOPLE ARE BEGINNING TO THINK WE'RE ALL GUNS AND NO BUTTER...
WE SAID WE'D REBUILD EDUCATION BUT UNDERFUNDED OUR OWN BILL. SAME THING WITH AID TO HELP NEW YORK CITY...
AND IN NEXT YEAR'S BUDGET, WE DIDN'T PUT IN A SINGLE DOLLAR TO REBUILD AFGHANISTAN.
WE DIDN'T? WHY NOT?
WE FORGOT.
COMPLETELY UNDERSTANDABLE. THAT AFGHANIC THING IS SO 2001!

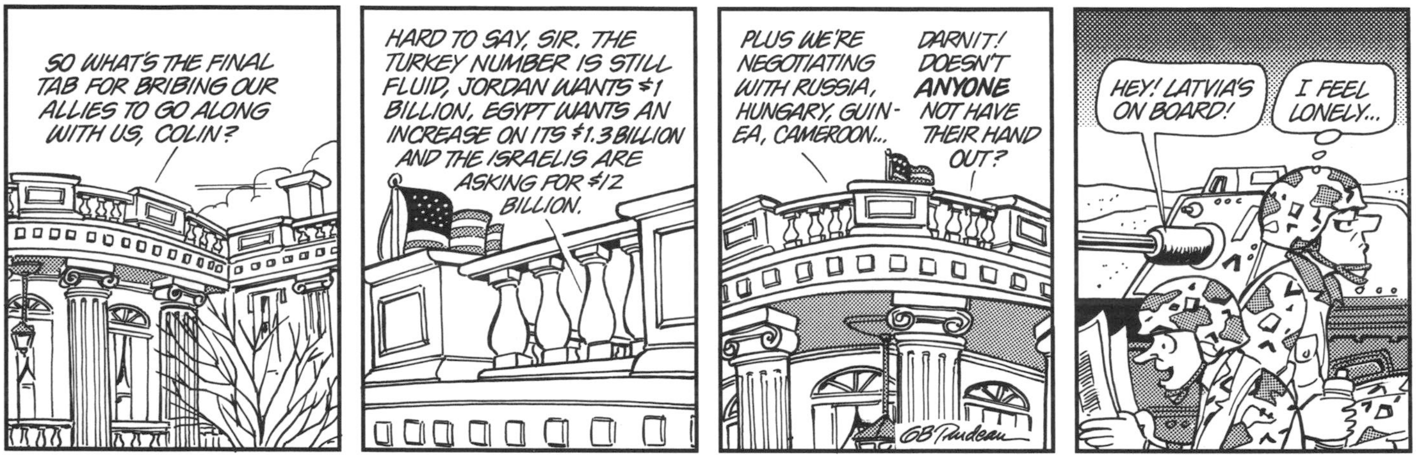
SO WHAT'S THE FINAL TAB FOR BRIBING OUR ALLIES TO GO ALONG WITH US, COLIN?
HARD TO SAY, SIR. THE TURKEY NUMBER IS STILL FLUID, JORDAN WANTS $1 BILLION, EGYPT WANTS AN INCREASE ON ITS $1.3 BILLION AND THE ISRAELIS ARE ASKING FOR $12 BILLION.
PLUS WE'RE NEGOTIATING WITH RUSSIA, HUNGARY, GUINEA, CAMEROON...
DARNIT! DOESN'T ANYONE NOT HAVE THEIR HAND OUT?
HEY! LATVIA'S ON BOARD!
I FEEL LONELY...

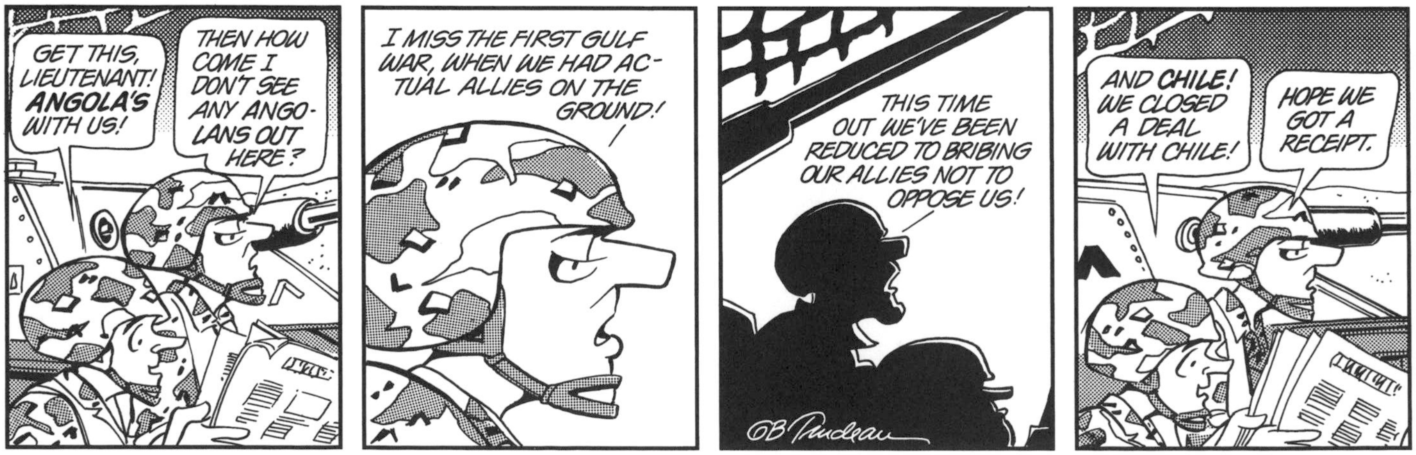
GET THIS, LIEUTENANT! ANGOLA'S WITH US!
THEN HOW COME I DON'T SEE ANY ANGOLANS OUT HERE?
I MISS THE FIRST GULF WAR, WHEN WE HAD ACTUAL ALLIES ON THE GROUND!
THIS TIME OUT WE'VE BEEN REDUCED TO BRIBING OUR ALLIES NOT TO OPPOSE US!
AND CHILE! WE CLOSED A DEAL WITH CHILE!
HOPE WE GOT A RECEIPT.

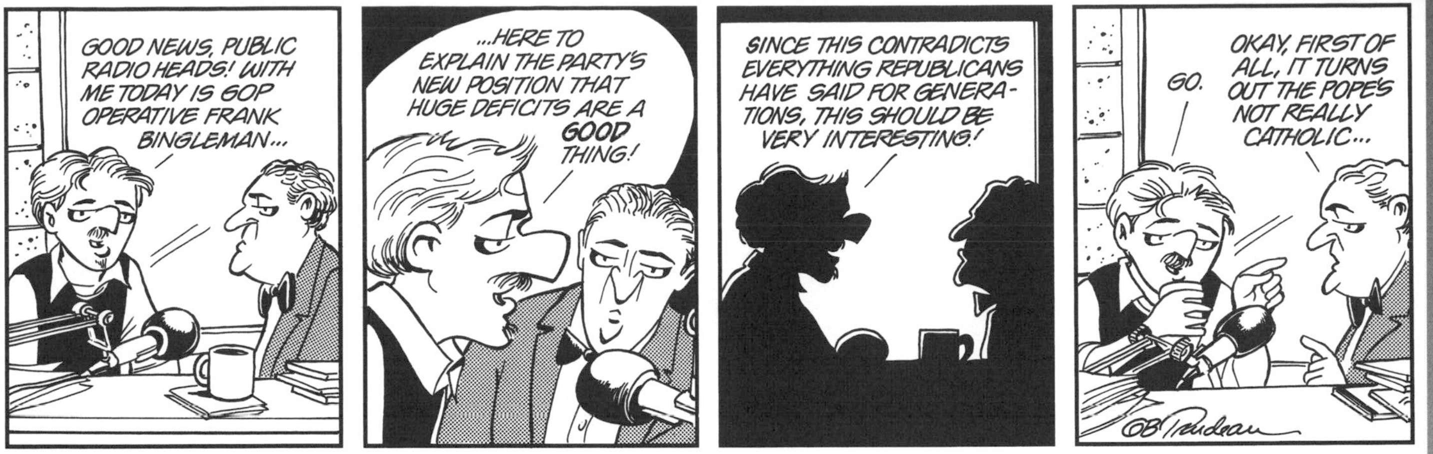
GOOD NEWS, PUBLIC RADIO HEADS! WITH ME TODAY IS GOP OPERATIVE FRANK BINGLEMAN...
...HERE TO EXPLAIN THE PARTY'S NEW POSITION THAT HUGE DEFICITS ARE A **GOOD** THING!
SINCE THIS CONTRADICTS EVERYTHING REPUBLICANS HAVE SAID FOR GENERATIONS, THIS SHOULD BE VERY INTERESTING!
GO.
OKAY, FIRST OF ALL, IT TURNS OUT THE POPE'S NOT REALLY CATHOLIC...


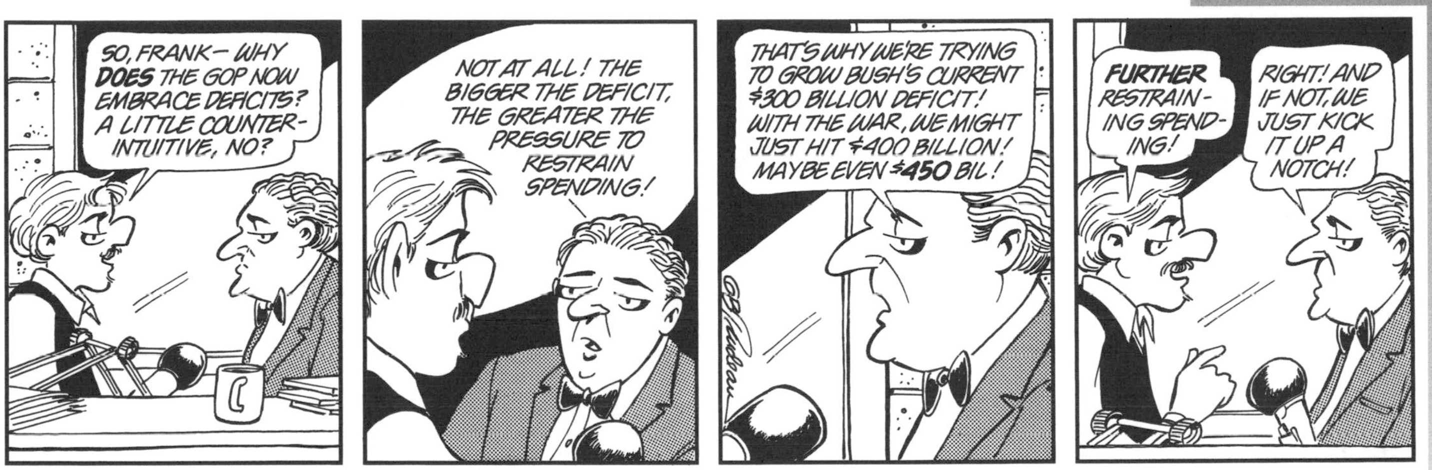
SO, FRANK— WHY **DOES** THE GOP NOW EMBRACE DEFICITS? A LITTLE COUNTER-INTUITIVE, NO?
NOT AT ALL! THE BIGGER THE DEFICIT, THE GREATER THE PRESSURE TO RESTRAIN SPENDING!
THAT'S WHY WE'RE TRYING TO GROW BUSH'S CURRENT $300 BILLION DEFICIT! WITH THE WAR, WE MIGHT JUST HIT $400 BILLION! MAYBE EVEN **$450** BIL!
**FURTHER** RESTRAINING SPENDING!
RIGHT! AND IF NOT, WE JUST KICK IT UP A NOTCH!


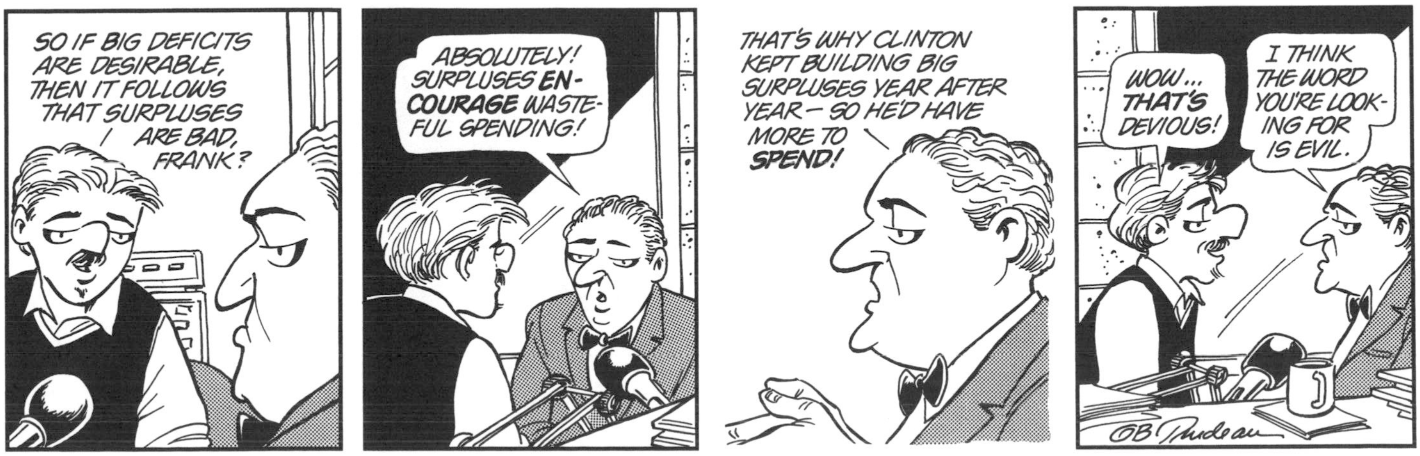
SO IF BIG DEFICITS ARE DESIRABLE, THEN IT FOLLOWS THAT SURPLUSES ARE BAD, FRANK?
ABSOLUTELY! SURPLUSES **ENCOURAGE** WASTEFUL SPENDING!
THAT'S WHY CLINTON KEPT BUILDING BIG SURPLUSES YEAR AFTER YEAR— SO HE'D HAVE MORE TO **SPEND**!
WOW... **THAT'S** DEVIOUS!
I THINK THE WORD YOU'RE LOOKING FOR IS EVIL.

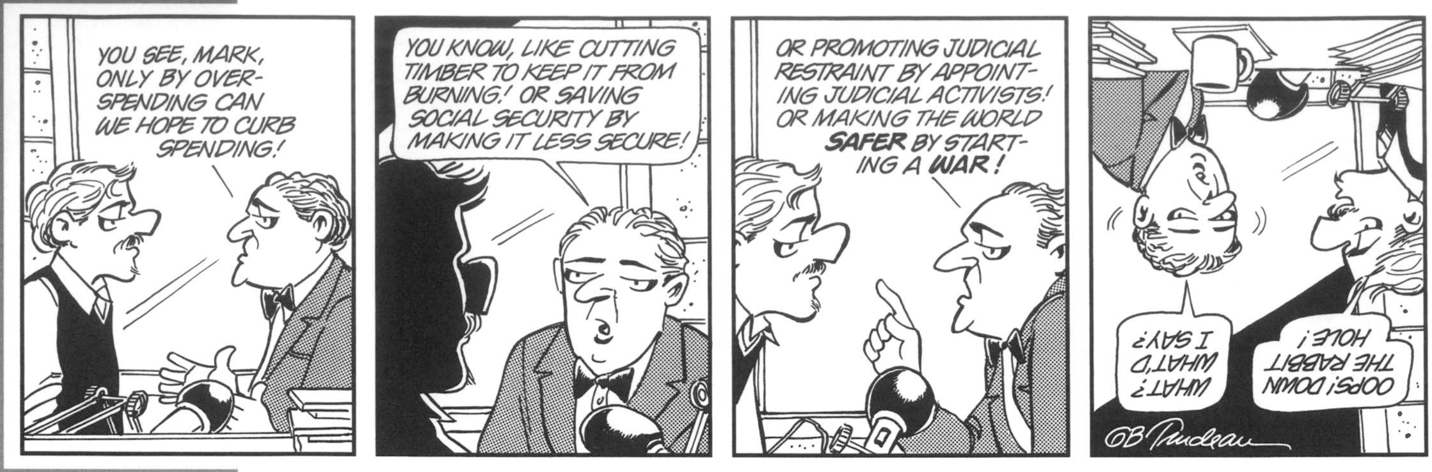

YOU SEE, MARK, ONLY BY OVER-SPENDING CAN WE HOPE TO CURB SPENDING!
YOU KNOW, LIKE CUTTING TIMBER TO KEEP IT FROM BURNING! OR SAVING SOCIAL SECURITY BY MAKING IT LESS SECURE!
OR PROMOTING JUDICIAL RESTRAINT BY APPOINT-ING JUDICIAL ACTIVISTS! OR MAKING THE WORLD **SAFER** BY START-ING A **WAR**!
WHAT? WHAT'D I SAY?
OOPS! DOWN THE RABBIT HOLE!
©B Trudeau


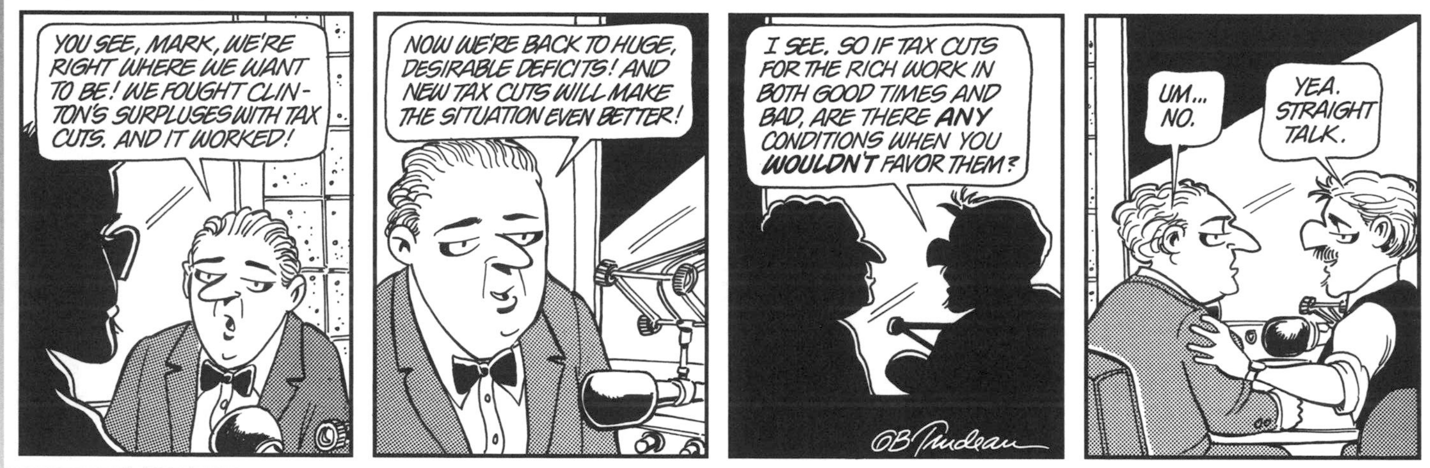

YOU SEE, MARK, WE'RE RIGHT WHERE WE WANT TO BE! WE FOUGHT CLIN-TON'S SURPLUSES WITH TAX CUTS. AND IT WORKED!
NOW WE'RE BACK TO HUGE, DESIRABLE DEFICITS! AND NEW TAX CUTS WILL MAKE THE SITUATION EVEN BETTER!
I SEE. SO IF TAX CUTS FOR THE RICH WORK IN BOTH GOOD TIMES AND BAD, ARE THERE **ANY** CONDITIONS WHEN YOU **WOULDN'T** FAVOR THEM?
UM... NO.
YEA. STRAIGHT TALK.
©B Trudeau


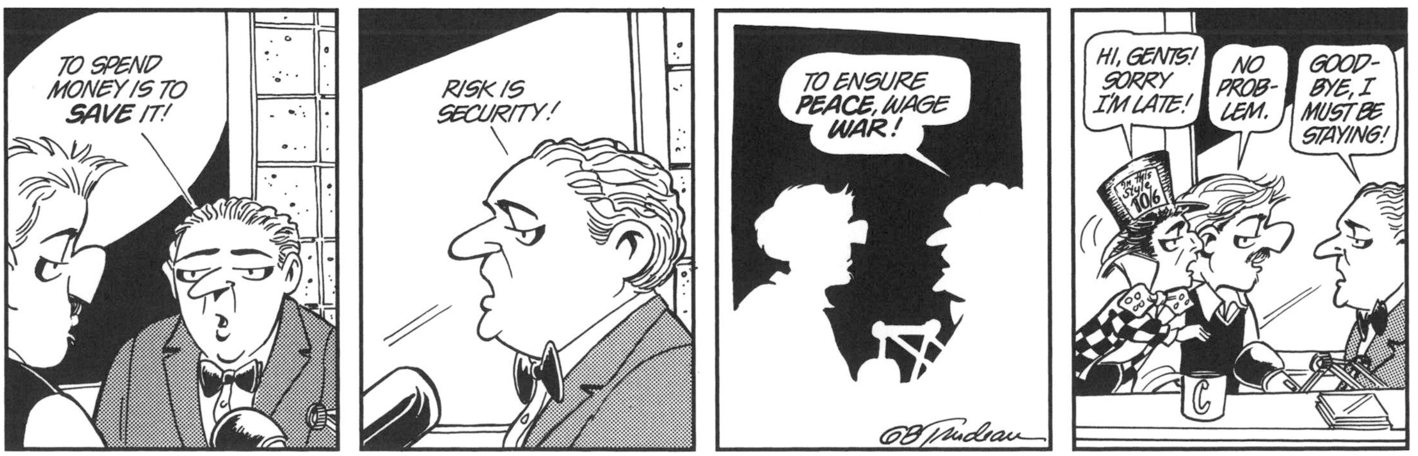

TO SPEND MONEY IS TO **SAVE** IT!
RISK IS SECURITY!
TO ENSURE **PEACE**, WAGE **WAR**!
HI, GENTS! SORRY I'M LATE!
NO PROB-LEM.
GOOD-BYE, I MUST BE STAYING!
In this Style 10/6
©B Trudeau

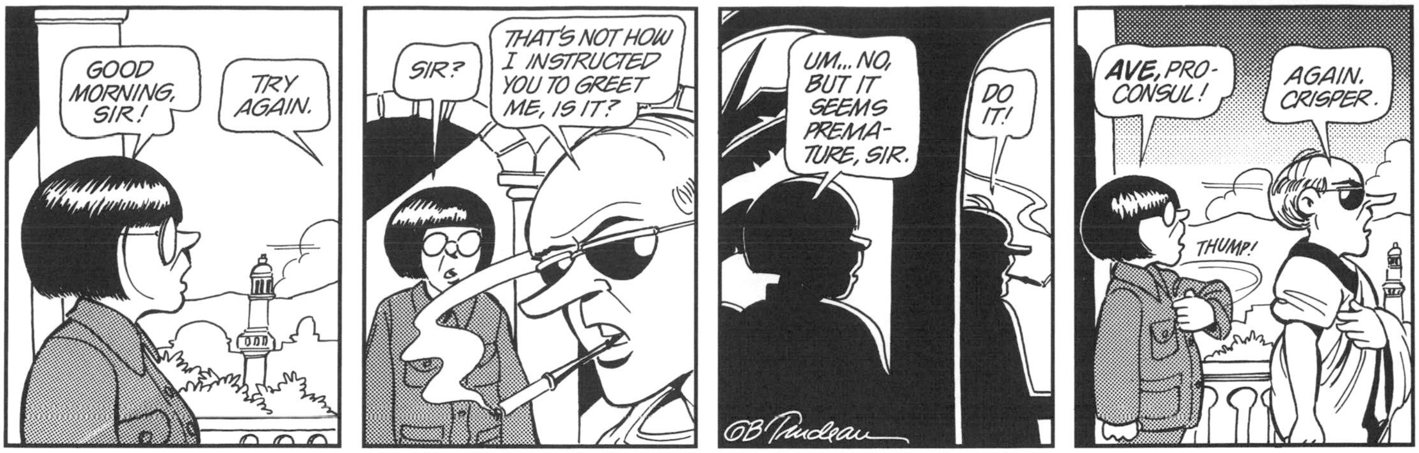
GOOD MORNING, SIR!
TRY AGAIN.
SIR?
THAT'S NOT HOW I INSTRUCTED YOU TO GREET ME, IS IT?
UM... NO, BUT IT SEEMS PREMATURE, SIR.
DO IT!
AVE, PROCONSUL!
THUMP!
AGAIN. CRISPER.

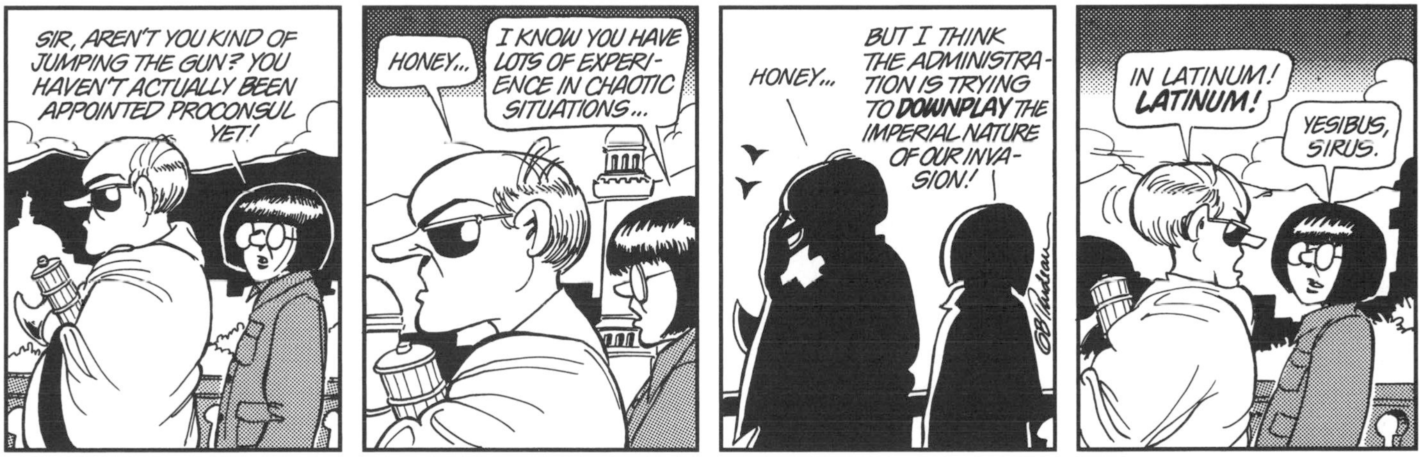
SIR, AREN'T YOU KIND OF JUMPING THE GUN? YOU HAVEN'T ACTUALLY BEEN APPOINTED PROCONSUL YET!
HONEY...
I KNOW YOU HAVE LOTS OF EXPERIENCE IN CHAOTIC SITUATIONS...
HONEY...
BUT I THINK THE ADMINISTRATION IS TRYING TO DOWNPLAY THE IMPERIAL NATURE OF OUR INVASION!
IN LATINUM! LATINUM!
YESIBUS, SIRUS.

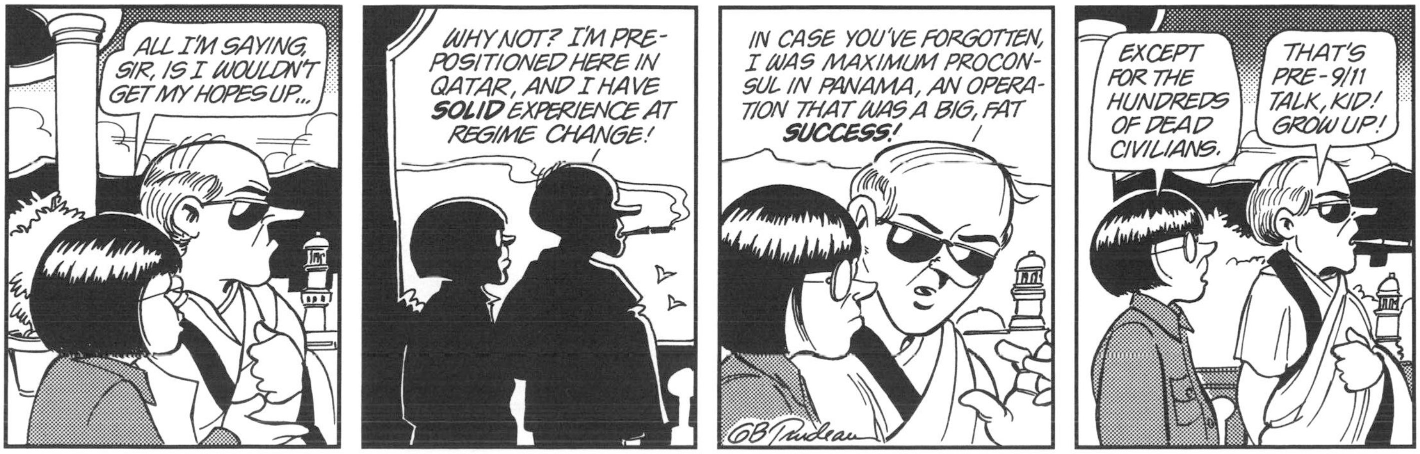
ALL I'M SAYING, SIR, IS I WOULDN'T GET MY HOPES UP...
WHY NOT? I'M PREPOSITIONED HERE IN QATAR, AND I HAVE SOLID EXPERIENCE AT REGIME CHANGE!
IN CASE YOU'VE FORGOTTEN, I WAS MAXIMUM PROCONSUL IN PANAMA, AN OPERATION THAT WAS A BIG, FAT SUCCESS!
EXCEPT FOR THE HUNDREDS OF DEAD CIVILIANS.
THAT'S PRE-9/11 TALK, KID! GROW UP!

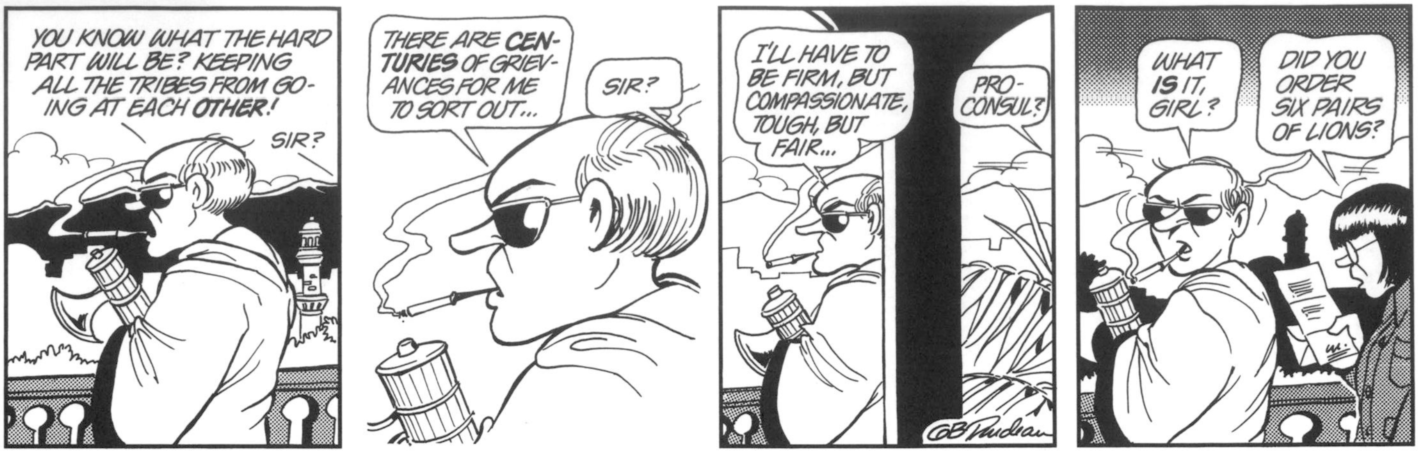
YOU KNOW WHAT THE HARD PART WILL BE? KEEPING ALL THE TRIBES FROM GOING AT EACH OTHER!
SIR?
THERE ARE CENTURIES OF GRIEVANCES FOR ME TO SORT OUT...
SIR?
I'LL HAVE TO BE FIRM, BUT COMPASSIONATE, TOUGH, BUT FAIR...
PROCONSUL?
WHAT IS IT, GIRL?
DID YOU ORDER SIX PAIRS OF LIONS?

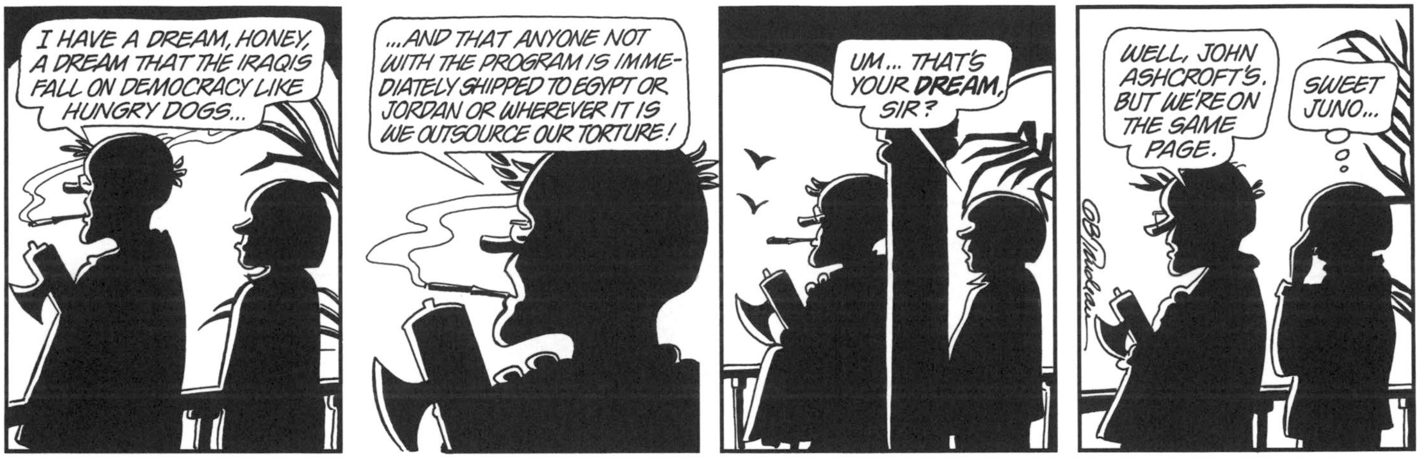
I HAVE A DREAM, HONEY, A DREAM THAT THE IRAQIS FALL ON DEMOCRACY LIKE HUNGRY DOGS...
...AND THAT ANYONE NOT WITH THE PROGRAM IS IMMEDIATELY SHIPPED TO EGYPT OR JORDAN OR WHEREVER IT IS WE OUTSOURCE OUR TORTURE!
UM... THAT'S YOUR DREAM, SIR?
WELL, JOHN ASHCROFT'S. BUT WE'RE ON THE SAME PAGE.
SWEET JUNO...

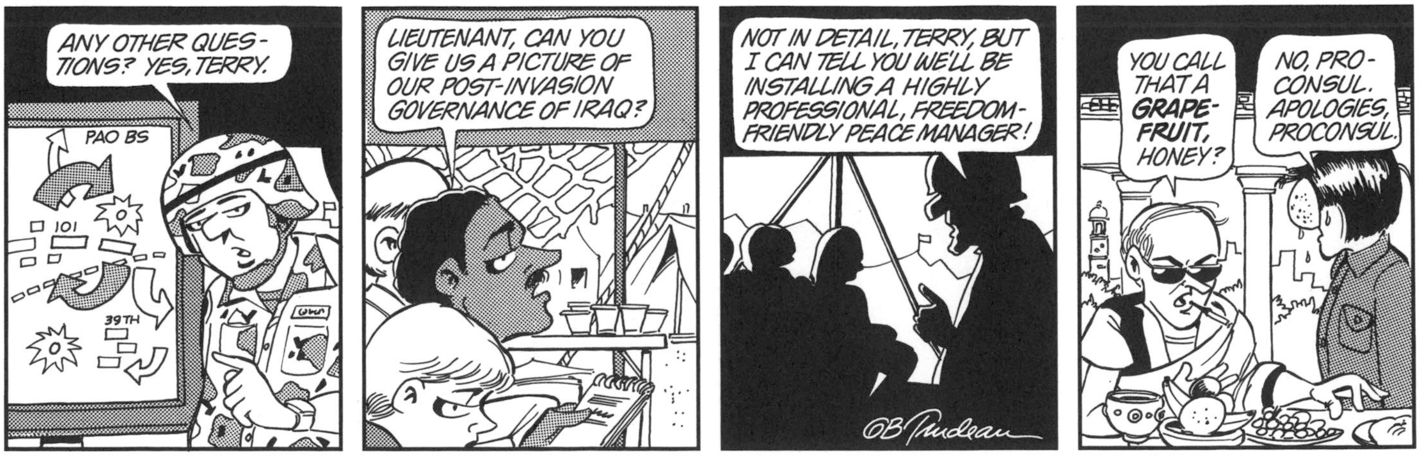
ANY OTHER QUESTIONS? YES, TERRY.
PAO BS
101
39TH
LIEUTENANT, CAN YOU GIVE US A PICTURE OF OUR POST-INVASION GOVERNANCE OF IRAQ?
NOT IN DETAIL, TERRY, BUT I CAN TELL YOU WE'LL BE INSTALLING A HIGHLY PROFESSIONAL, FREEDOM-FRIENDLY PEACE MANAGER!
YOU CALL THAT A GRAPEFRUIT, HONEY?
NO, PROCONSUL. APOLOGIES, PROCONSUL.

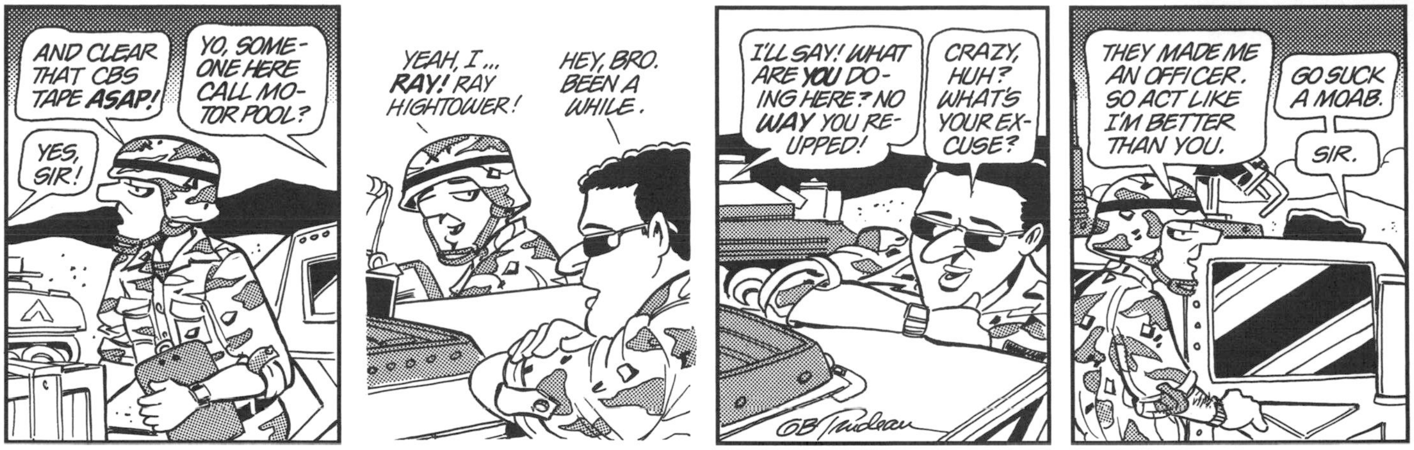
AND CLEAR THAT CBS TAPE ASAP!
YES, SIR!
YO, SOME-ONE HERE CALL MO-TOR POOL?
YEAH, I ... RAY! RAY HIGHTOWER!
HEY, BRO. BEEN A WHILE.
I'LL SAY! WHAT ARE YOU DO-ING HERE? NO WAY YOU RE-UPPED!
CRAZY, HUH? WHAT'S YOUR EX-CUSE?
THEY MADE ME AN OFFICER. SO ACT LIKE I'M BETTER THAN YOU.
GO SUCK A MOAB.
SIR.

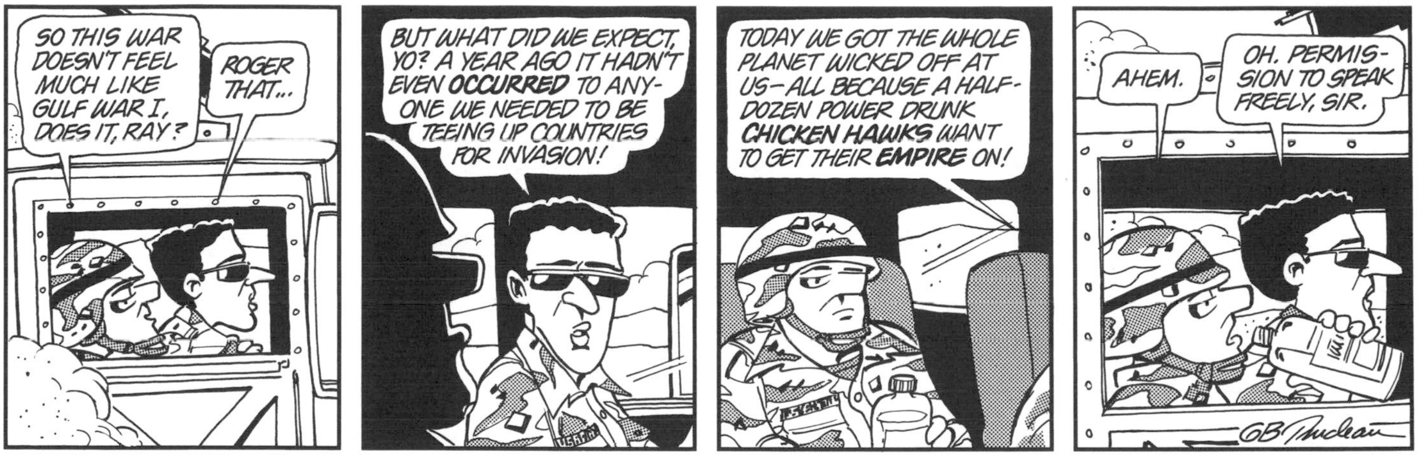
SO THIS WAR DOESN'T FEEL MUCH LIKE GULF WAR I, DOES IT, RAY?
ROGER THAT...
BUT WHAT DID WE EXPECT, YO? A YEAR AGO IT HADN'T EVEN OCCURRED TO ANY-ONE WE NEEDED TO BE TEEING UP COUNTRIES FOR INVASION!
TODAY WE GOT THE WHOLE PLANET WICKED OFF AT US—ALL BECAUSE A HALF-DOZEN POWER DRUNK CHICKEN HAWKS WANT TO GET THEIR EMPIRE ON!
AHEM.
OH. PERMIS-SION TO SPEAK FREELY, SIR.

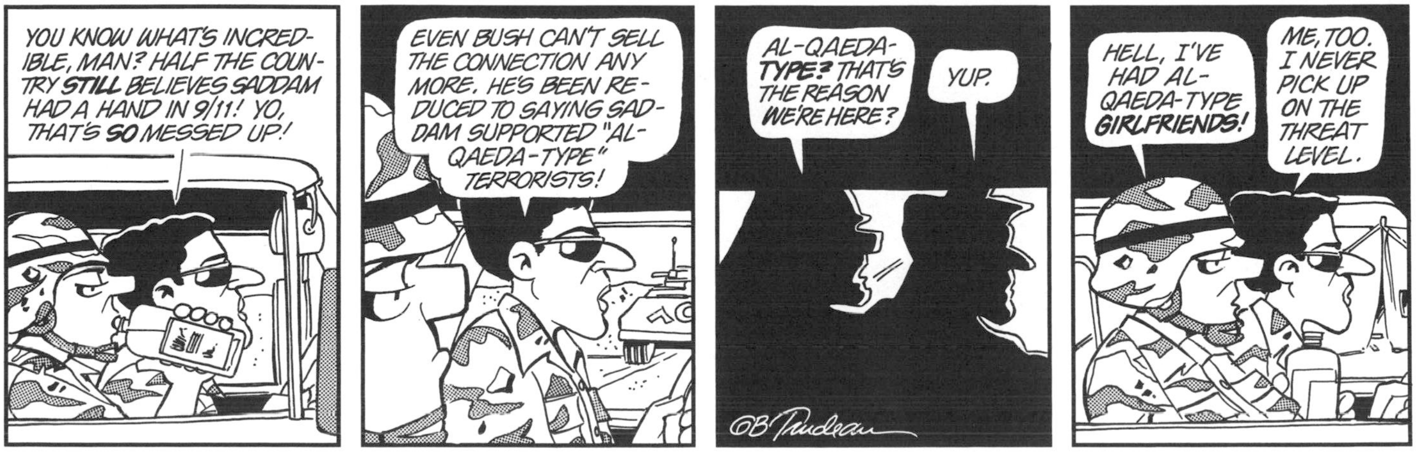
YOU KNOW WHAT'S INCRED-IBLE, MAN? HALF THE COUN-TRY STILL BELIEVES SADDAM HAD A HAND IN 9/11! YO, THAT'S SO MESSED UP!
EVEN BUSH CAN'T SELL THE CONNECTION ANY MORE. HE'S BEEN RE-DUCED TO SAYING SAD-DAM SUPPORTED "AL-QAEDA-TYPE" TERRORISTS!
AL-QAEDA-TYPE? THAT'S THE REASON WE'RE HERE?
YUP.
HELL, I'VE HAD AL-QAEDA-TYPE GIRLFRIENDS!
ME, TOO. I NEVER PICK UP ON THE THREAT LEVEL.

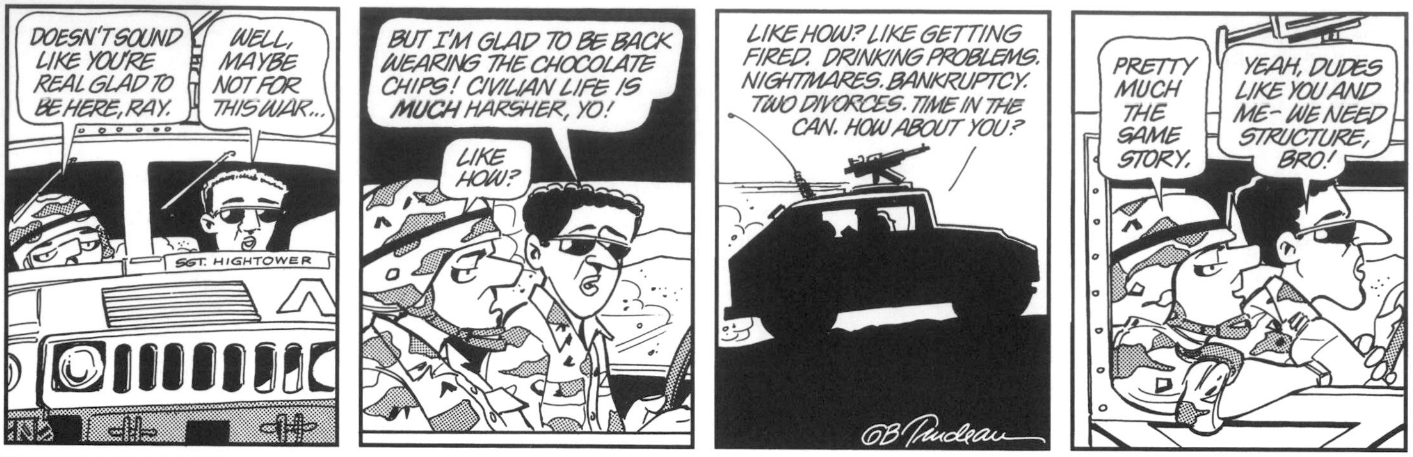
DOESN'T SOUND LIKE YOU'RE REAL GLAD TO BE HERE, RAY.
WELL, MAYBE NOT FOR THIS WAR...
SGT. HIGHTOWER
BUT I'M GLAD TO BE BACK WEARING THE CHOCOLATE CHIPS! CIVILIAN LIFE IS MUCH HARSHER, YO!
LIKE HOW?
LIKE HOW? LIKE GETTING FIRED. DRINKING PROBLEMS. NIGHTMARES. BANKRUPTCY. TWO DIVORCES. TIME IN THE CAN. HOW ABOUT YOU?
PRETTY MUCH THE SAME STORY.
YEAH, DUDES LIKE YOU AND ME- WE NEED STRUCTURE, BRO!

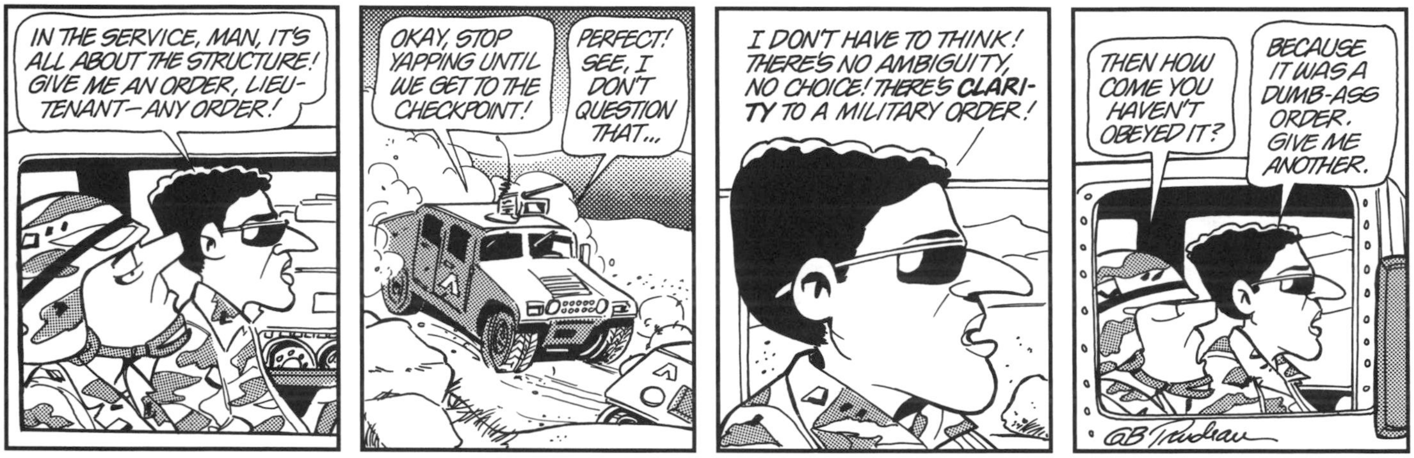
IN THE SERVICE, MAN, IT'S ALL ABOUT THE STRUCTURE! GIVE ME AN ORDER, LIEUTENANT—ANY ORDER!
OKAY, STOP YAPPING UNTIL WE GET TO THE CHECKPOINT!
PERFECT! SEE, I DON'T QUESTION THAT...
I DON'T HAVE TO THINK! THERE'S NO AMBIGUITY, NO CHOICE! THERE'S CLARITY TO A MILITARY ORDER!
THEN HOW COME YOU HAVEN'T OBEYED IT?
BECAUSE IT WAS A DUMB-ASS ORDER. GIVE ME ANOTHER.

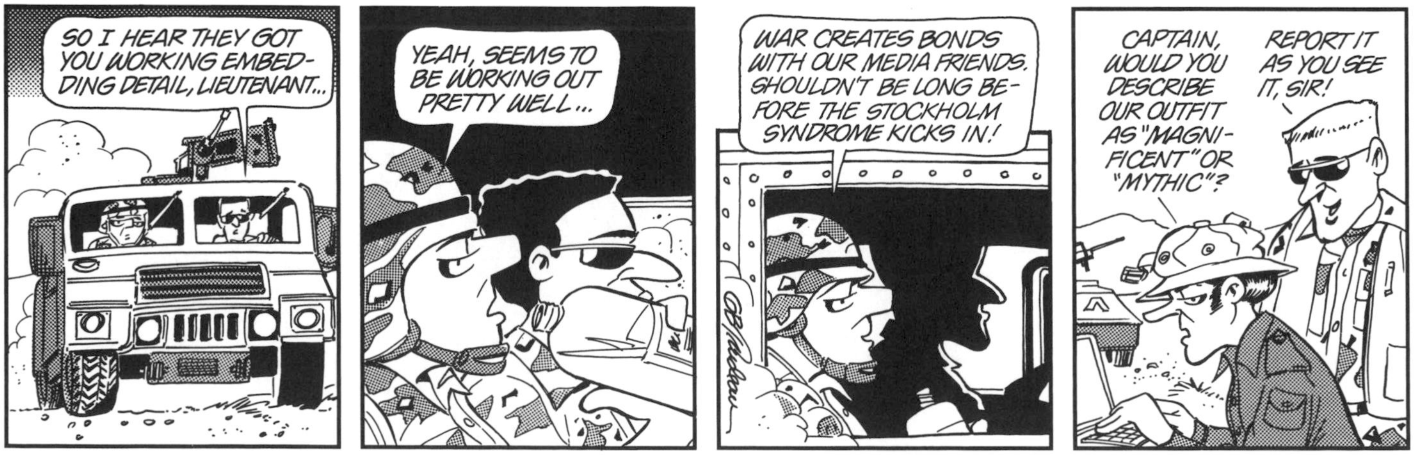
SO I HEAR THEY GOT YOU WORKING EMBEDDING DETAIL, LIEUTENANT...
YEAH, SEEMS TO BE WORKING OUT PRETTY WELL...
WAR CREATES BONDS WITH OUR MEDIA FRIENDS. SHOULDN'T BE LONG BEFORE THE STOCKHOLM SYNDROME KICKS IN!
CAPTAIN, WOULD YOU DESCRIBE OUR OUTFIT AS "MAGNIFICENT" OR "MYTHIC"?
REPORT IT AS YOU SEE IT, SIR!

TV NATION.
ANOTHER BOMB...
WHOA!!
NEUTRALIZED!
DENIED ENVIRONMENT!
WAY TO DECONFLICT THE AIRSPACE!
IN YOUR FACE, KOBE!
COULD WE SWITCH BACK TO THE WAR?

WHY ARE WE WATCHING BASKETBALL? THERE'S A WAR ON.
EXACTLY SO. PEOPLE NEED A BREAK.
A BREAK? FROM WHAT, HISTORY? WE'VE GOT THOUSANDS OF COUNTRYMEN FIGHTING FOR US OUT THERE!
THIS IS THE FIRST WAR WHERE WE CAN BE WITH THEM! WE CAN SEE THE WAR AS THEY SEE IT!
OKAY, OKAY...
THIS IS ROLAND HEDLEY, LIVE FROM SOMEWHERE!
CNN WAR IN IRAQ

THIS IS ROLAND HEDLEY, FROM SOMEWHERE INSIDE A SANDSTORM...
CNN WAR IN IRAQ
ROLAND? IT'S WOLF. HOW DO WE KNOW IT'S YOU THERE, AND NOT SOME FEDAYEEN AGENT SPREADING DISINFORMATION?
CNN WAR IN IRAQ
CNN WAR IN IRAQ
CALL MY WIFE. I HAVE A BIRTHMARK ON...
IT WAS A JOKE. A JOKE.
CNN WAR IN IRAQ

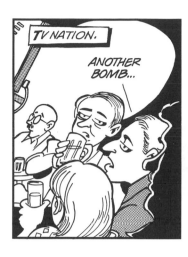

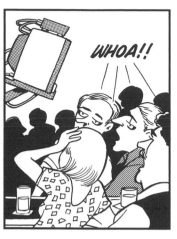

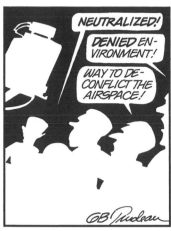

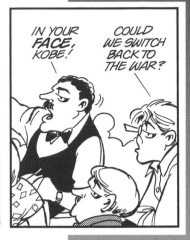

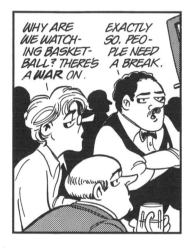

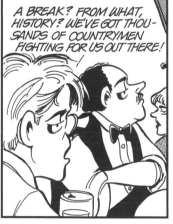

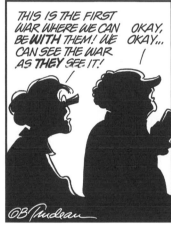

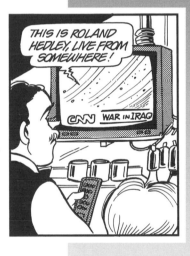

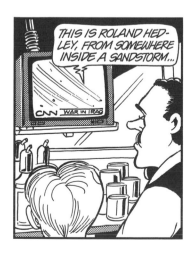

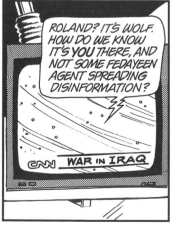

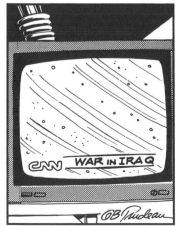

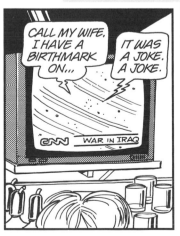

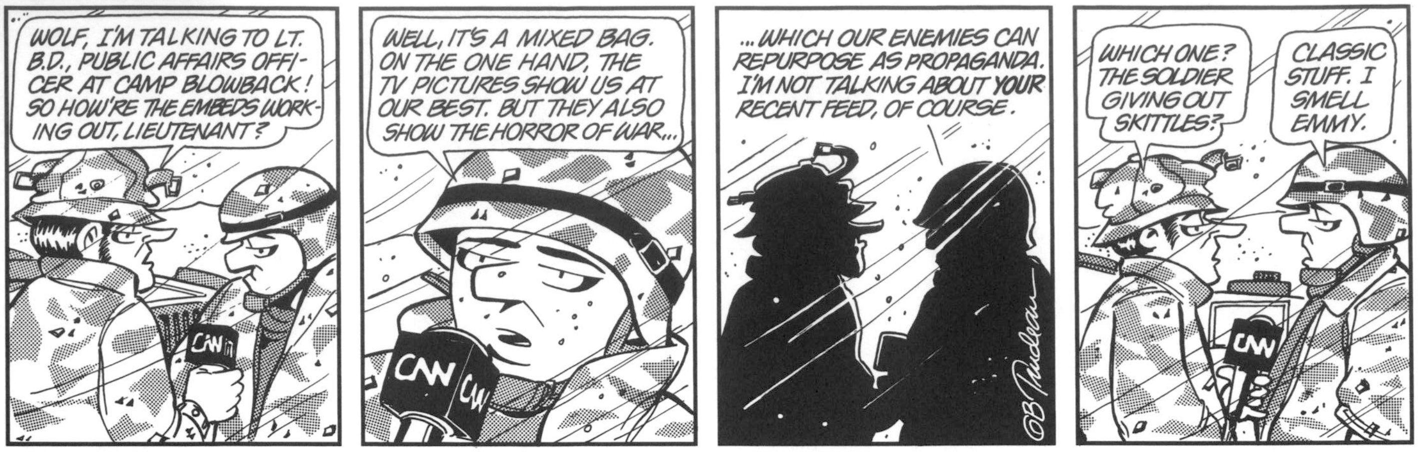
WOLF, I'M TALKING TO LT. B.D., PUBLIC AFFAIRS OFFICER AT CAMP BLOWBACK! SO HOW'RE THE EMBEDS WORKING OUT, LIEUTENANT?
WELL, IT'S A MIXED BAG. ON THE ONE HAND, THE TV PICTURES SHOW US AT OUR BEST. BUT THEY ALSO SHOW THE HORROR OF WAR...
...WHICH OUR ENEMIES CAN REPURPOSE AS PROPAGANDA. I'M NOT TALKING ABOUT **YOUR** RECENT FEED, OF COURSE.
WHICH ONE? THE SOLDIER GIVING OUT SKITTLES?
CLASSIC STUFF. I SMELL EMMY.

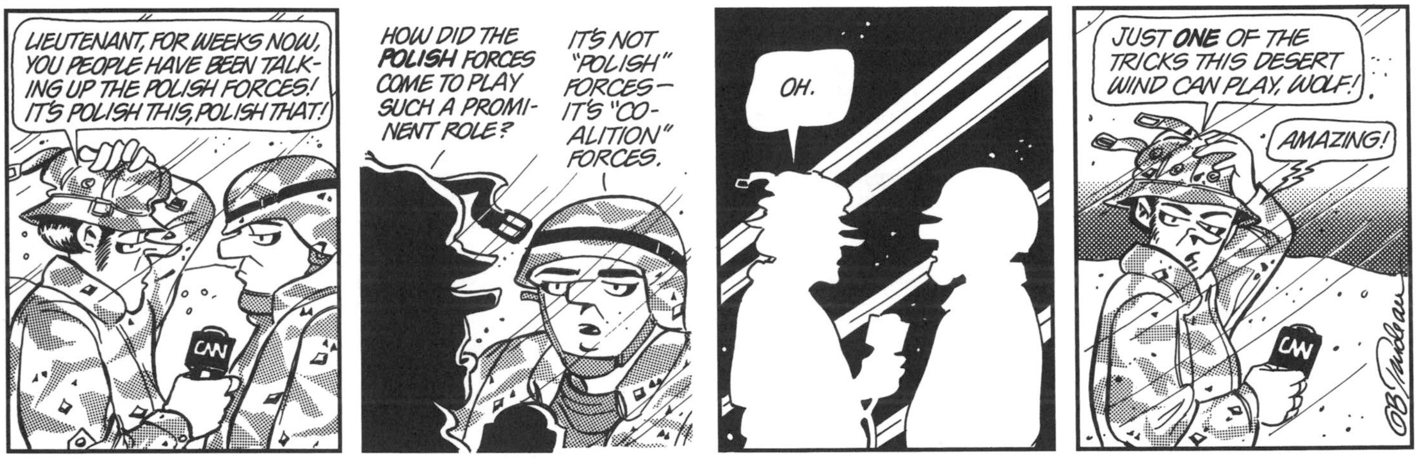
LIEUTENANT, FOR WEEKS NOW, YOU PEOPLE HAVE BEEN TALKING UP THE POLISH FORCES! IT'S POLISH THIS, POLISH THAT!
HOW DID THE **POLISH** FORCES COME TO PLAY SUCH A PROMINENT ROLE?
IT'S NOT "POLISH" FORCES— IT'S "COALITION" FORCES.
OH.
JUST **ONE** OF THE TRICKS THIS DESERT WIND CAN PLAY, WOLF!
AMAZING!

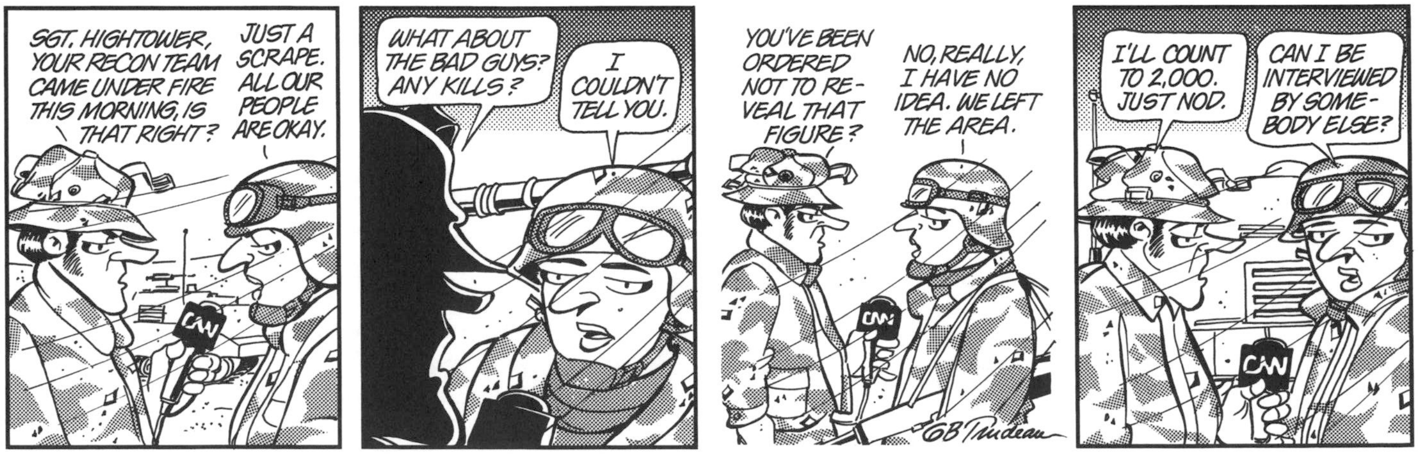
SGT. HIGHTOWER, YOUR RECON TEAM CAME UNDER FIRE THIS MORNING, IS THAT RIGHT?
JUST A SCRAPE. ALL OUR PEOPLE ARE OKAY.
WHAT ABOUT THE BAD GUYS? ANY KILLS?
I COULDN'T TELL YOU.
YOU'VE BEEN ORDERED NOT TO REVEAL THAT FIGURE?
NO, REALLY, I HAVE NO IDEA. WE LEFT THE AREA.
I'LL COUNT TO 2,000. JUST NOD.
CAN I BE INTERVIEWED BY SOMEBODY ELSE?

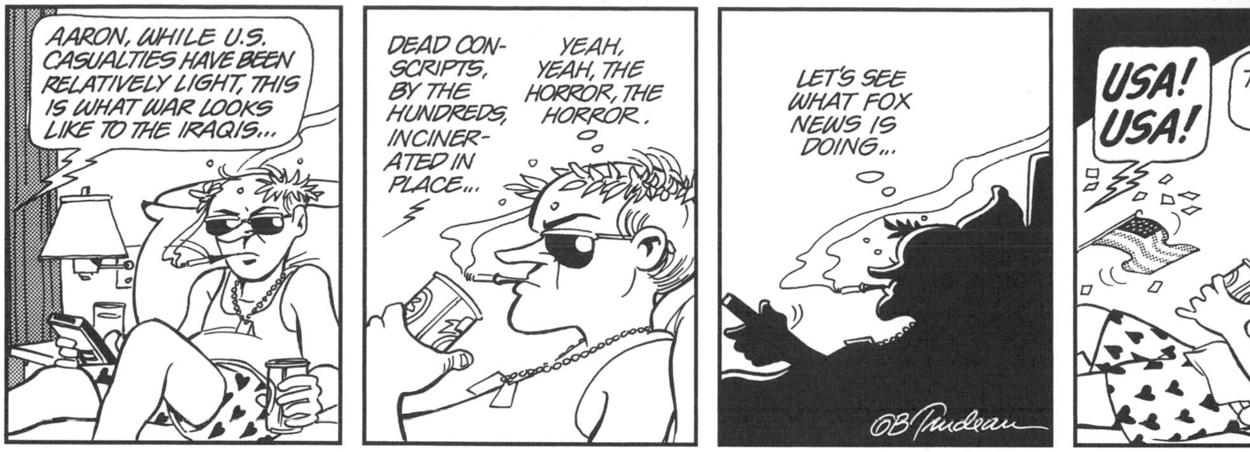
AARON, WHILE U.S. CASUALTIES HAVE BEEN RELATIVELY LIGHT, THIS IS WHAT WAR LOOKS LIKE TO THE IRAQIS...
DEAD CONSCRIPTS, BY THE HUNDREDS, INCINERATED IN PLACE...
YEAH, YEAH, THE HORROR, THE HORROR.
LET'S SEE WHAT FOX NEWS IS DOING...
USA! USA!
THAT'S MORE LIKE IT!
©B Trudeau

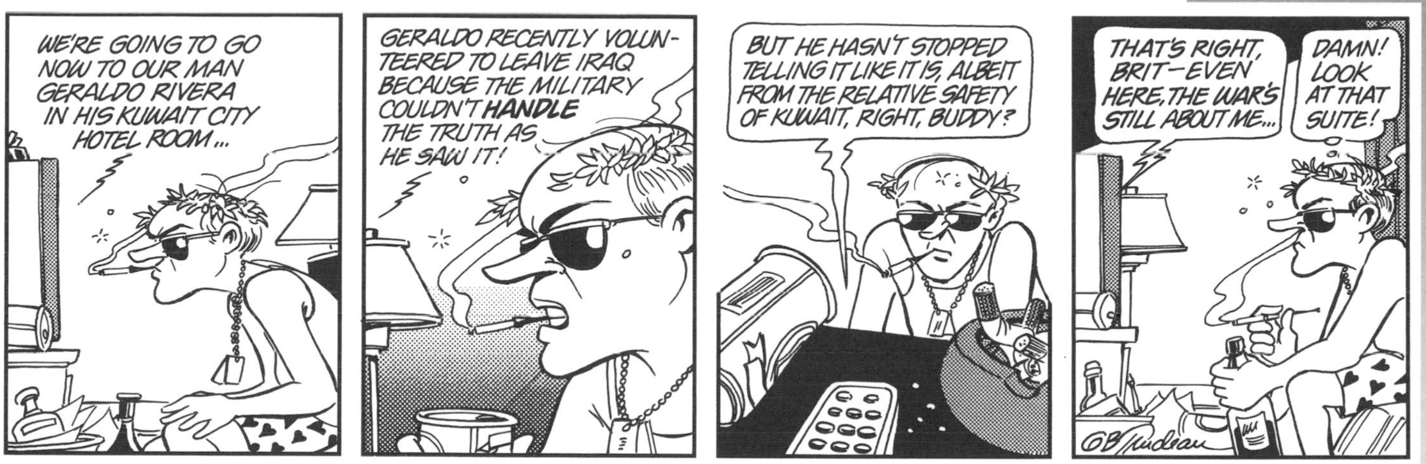
WE'RE GOING TO GO NOW TO OUR MAN GERALDO RIVERA IN HIS KUWAIT CITY HOTEL ROOM...
GERALDO RECENTLY VOLUNTEERED TO LEAVE IRAQ BECAUSE THE MILITARY COULDN'T HANDLE THE TRUTH AS HE SAW IT!
BUT HE HASN'T STOPPED TELLING IT LIKE IT IS, ALBEIT FROM THE RELATIVE SAFETY OF KUWAIT, RIGHT, BUDDY?
THAT'S RIGHT, BRIT—EVEN HERE, THE WAR'S STILL ABOUT ME...
DAMN! LOOK AT THAT SUITE!
©B Trudeau

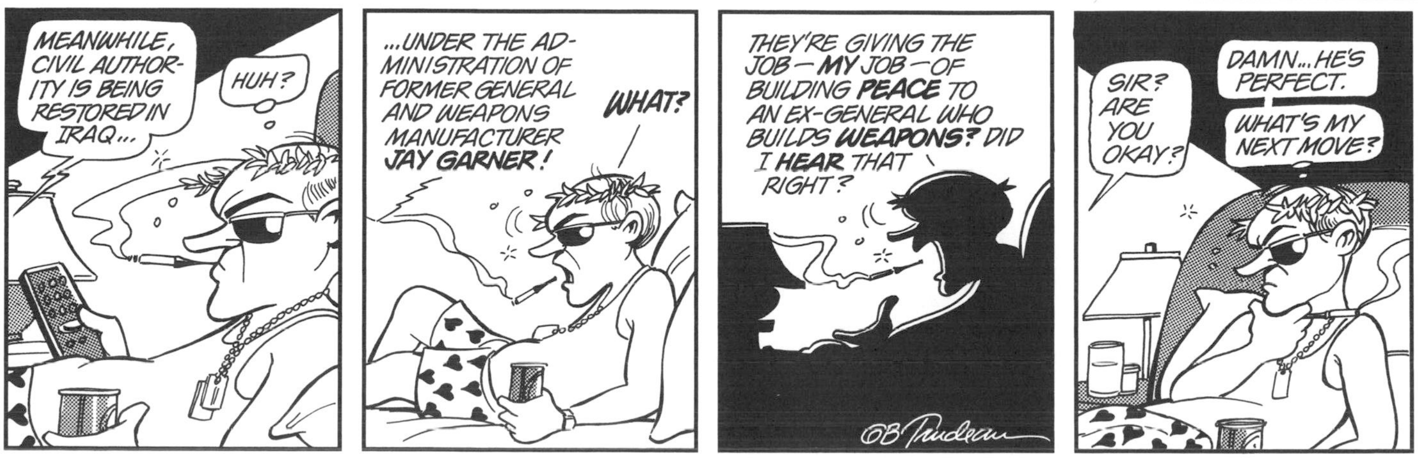
MEANWHILE, CIVIL AUTHORITY IS BEING RESTORED IN IRAQ...
HUH?
...UNDER THE ADMINISTRATION OF FORMER GENERAL AND WEAPONS MANUFACTURER JAY GARNER!
WHAT?
THEY'RE GIVING THE JOB—MY JOB—OF BUILDING PEACE TO AN EX-GENERAL WHO BUILDS WEAPONS? DID I HEAR THAT RIGHT?
SIR? ARE YOU OKAY?
DAMN... HE'S PERFECT.
WHAT'S MY NEXT MOVE?
©B Trudeau

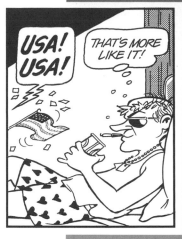

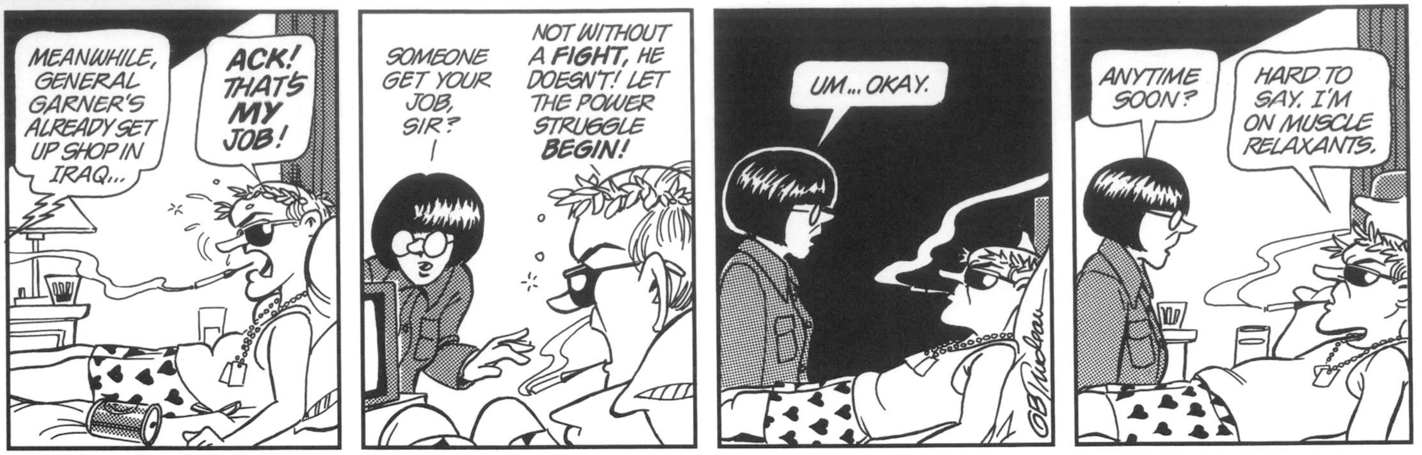

MEANWHILE, GENERAL GARNER'S ALREADY SET UP SHOP IN IRAQ...
ACK! THAT'S MY JOB!
SOMEONE GET YOUR JOB, SIR?
NOT WITHOUT A FIGHT, HE DOESN'T! LET THE POWER STRUGGLE BEGIN!
UM... OKAY.
ANYTIME SOON?
HARD TO SAY. I'M ON MUSCLE RELAXANTS.


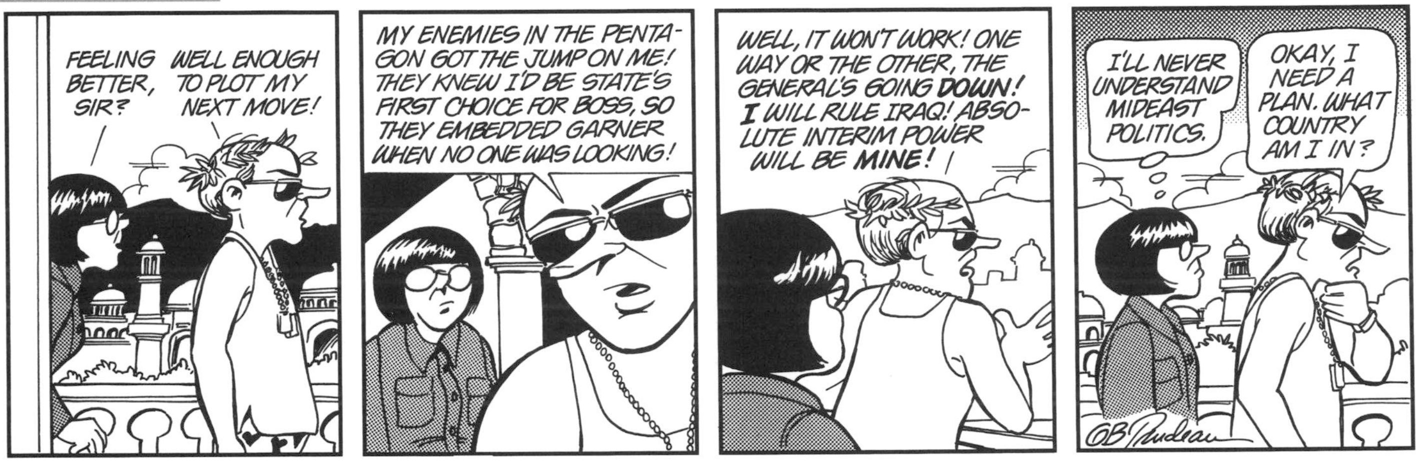

FEELING BETTER, SIR?
WELL ENOUGH TO PLOT MY NEXT MOVE!
MY ENEMIES IN THE PENTA-GON GOT THE JUMP ON ME! THEY KNEW I'D BE STATE'S FIRST CHOICE FOR BOSS, SO THEY EMBEDDED GARNER WHEN NO ONE WAS LOOKING!
WELL, IT WON'T WORK! ONE WAY OR THE OTHER, THE GENERAL'S GOING DOWN! I WILL RULE IRAQ! ABSO-LUTE INTERIM POWER WILL BE MINE!
I'LL NEVER UNDERSTAND MIDEAST POLITICS.
OKAY, I NEED A PLAN. WHAT COUNTRY AM I IN?


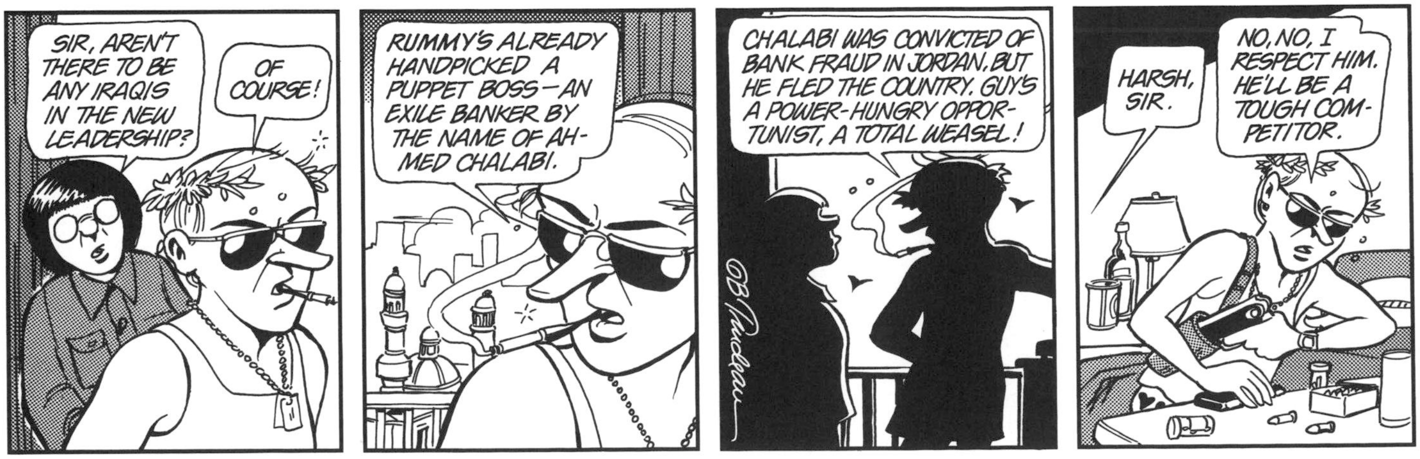

SIR, AREN'T THERE TO BE ANY IRAQIS IN THE NEW LEADERSHIP?
OF COURSE!
RUMMY'S ALREADY HANDPICKED A PUPPET BOSS—AN EXILE BANKER BY THE NAME OF AH-MED CHALABI.
CHALABI WAS CONVICTED OF BANK FRAUD IN JORDAN, BUT HE FLED THE COUNTRY. GUY'S A POWER-HUNGRY OPPOR-TUNIST, A TOTAL WEASEL!
HARSH, SIR.
NO, NO, I RESPECT HIM. HE'LL BE A TOUGH COM-PETITOR.

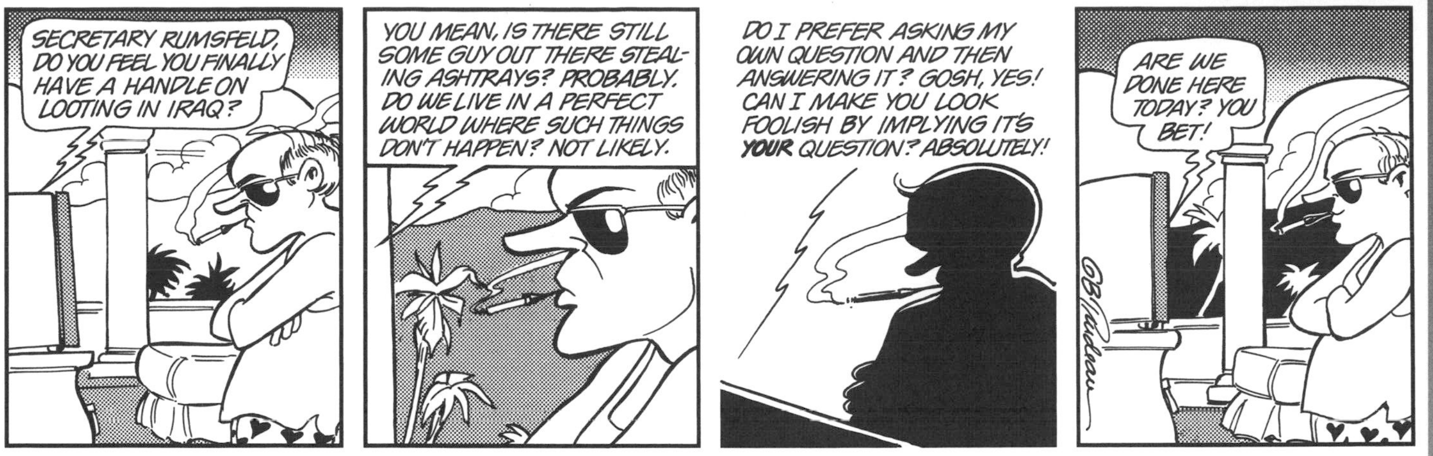
SECRETARY RUMSFELD, DO YOU FEEL YOU FINALLY HAVE A HANDLE ON LOOTING IN IRAQ?
YOU MEAN, IS THERE STILL SOME GUY OUT THERE STEALING ASHTRAYS? PROBABLY. DO WE LIVE IN A PERFECT WORLD WHERE SUCH THINGS DON'T HAPPEN? NOT LIKELY.
DO I PREFER ASKING MY OWN QUESTION AND THEN ANSWERING IT? GOSH, YES! CAN I MAKE YOU LOOK FOOLISH BY IMPLYING IT'S **YOUR** QUESTION? ABSOLUTELY!
ARE WE DONE HERE TODAY? YOU BET!

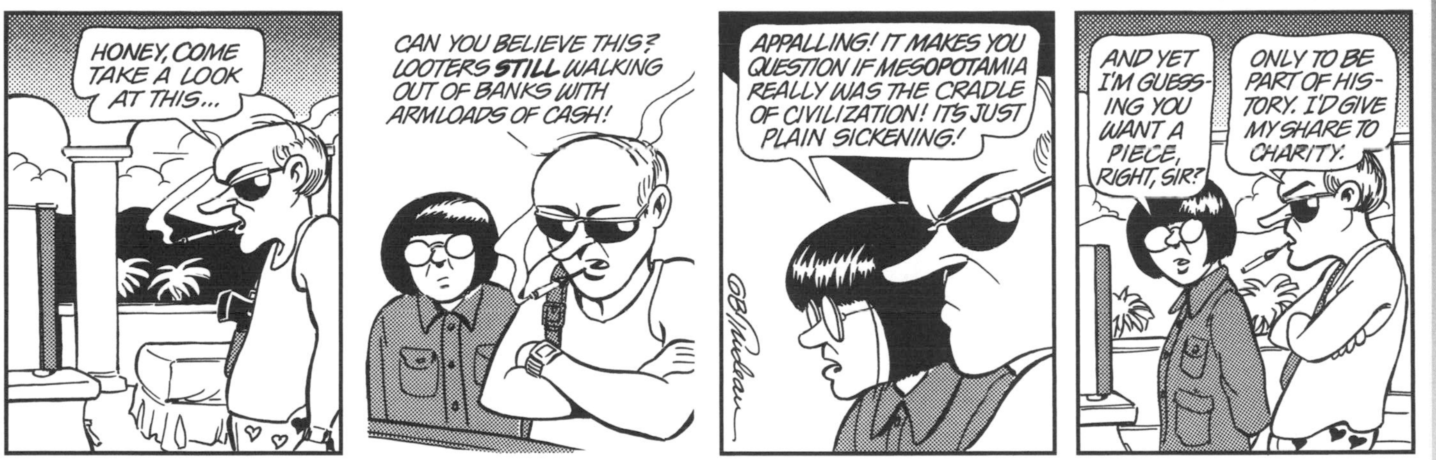
HONEY, COME TAKE A LOOK AT THIS...
CAN YOU BELIEVE THIS? LOOTERS **STILL** WALKING OUT OF BANKS WITH ARMLOADS OF CASH!
APPALLING! IT MAKES YOU QUESTION IF MESOPOTAMIA REALLY WAS THE CRADLE OF CIVILIZATION! IT'S JUST PLAIN SICKENING!
AND YET I'M GUESSING YOU WANT A PIECE, RIGHT, SIR?
ONLY TO BE PART OF HISTORY. I'D GIVE MY SHARE TO CHARITY.

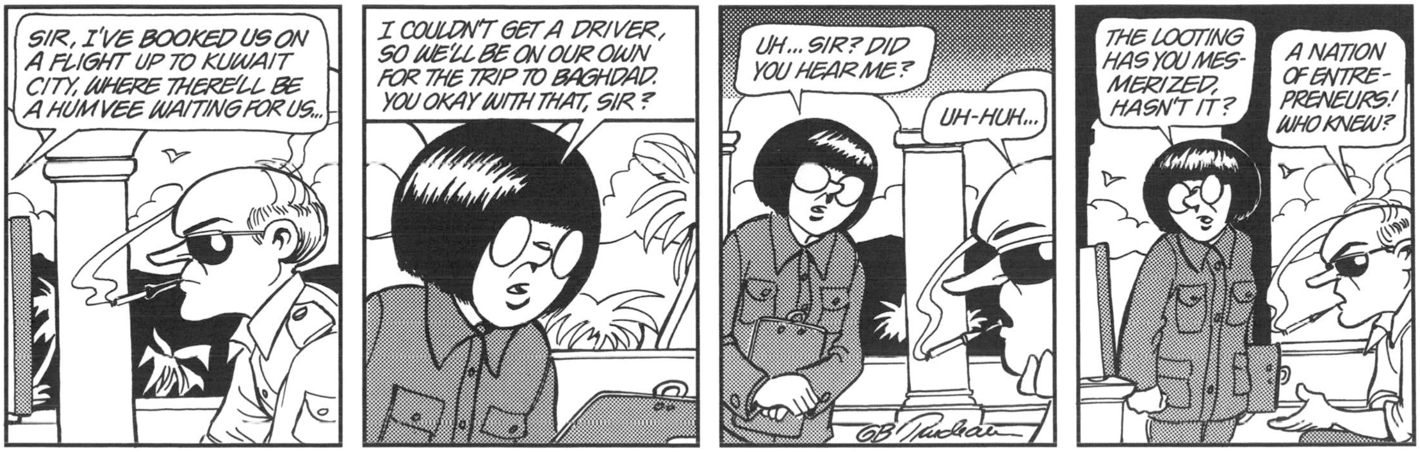
SIR, I'VE BOOKED US ON A FLIGHT UP TO KUWAIT CITY, WHERE THERE'LL BE A HUMVEE WAITING FOR US...
I COULDN'T GET A DRIVER, SO WE'LL BE ON OUR OWN FOR THE TRIP TO BAGHDAD. YOU OKAY WITH THAT, SIR?
UH... SIR? DID YOU HEAR ME?
UH-HUH...
THE LOOTING HAS YOU MESMERIZED, HASN'T IT?
A NATION OF ENTREPRENEURS! WHO KNEW?

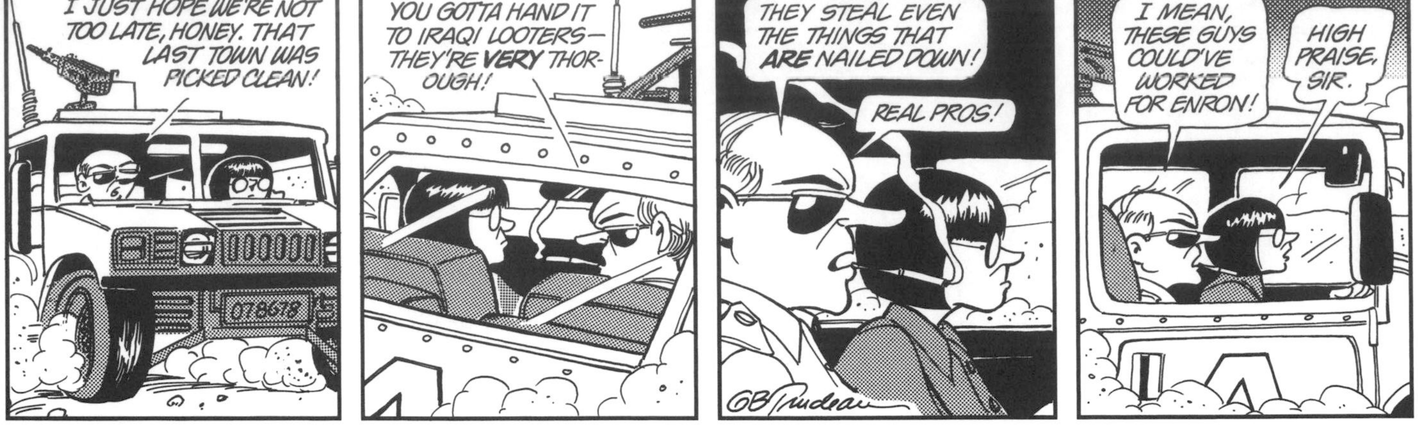
I JUST HOPE WE'RE NOT TOO LATE, HONEY. THAT LAST TOWN WAS PICKED CLEAN!
YOU GOTTA HAND IT TO IRAQI LOOTERS— THEY'RE **VERY** THOROUGH!
THEY STEAL EVEN THE THINGS THAT **ARE** NAILED DOWN!
REAL PROS!
I MEAN, THESE GUYS COULD'VE WORKED FOR ENRON!
HIGH PRAISE, SIR.

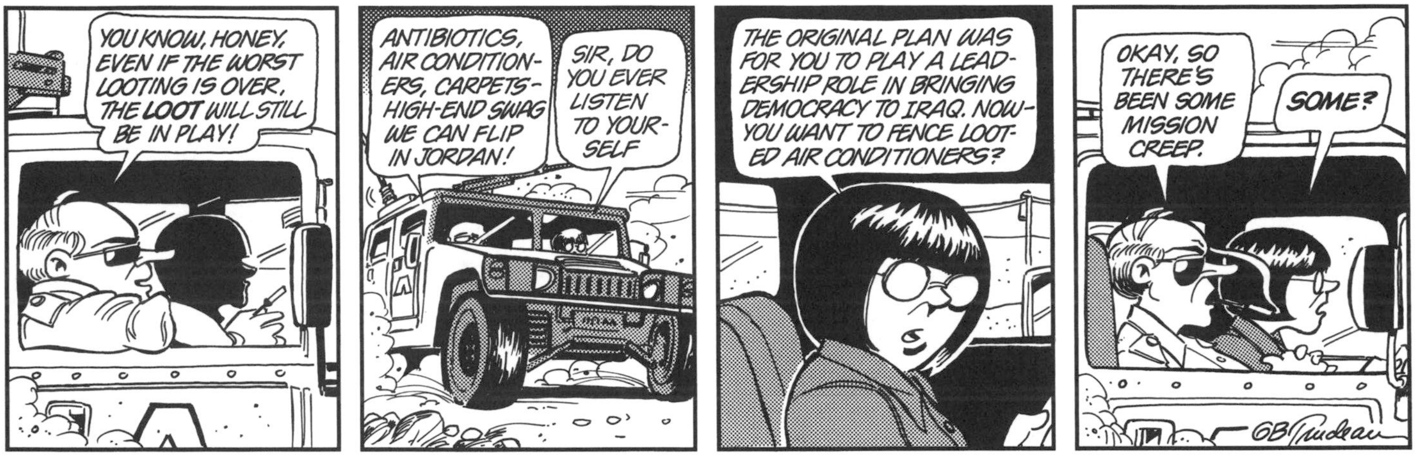
YOU KNOW, HONEY, EVEN IF THE WORST LOOTING IS OVER, THE **LOOT** WILL STILL BE IN PLAY!
ANTIBIOTICS, AIR CONDITIONERS, CARPETS-HIGH-END SWAG WE CAN FLIP IN JORDAN!
SIR, DO YOU EVER LISTEN TO YOURSELF
THE ORIGINAL PLAN WAS FOR YOU TO PLAY A LEADERSHIP ROLE IN BRINGING DEMOCRACY TO IRAQ. NOW-YOU WANT TO FENCE LOOTED AIR CONDITIONERS?
OKAY, SO THERE'S BEEN SOME MISSION CREEP.
**SOME?**

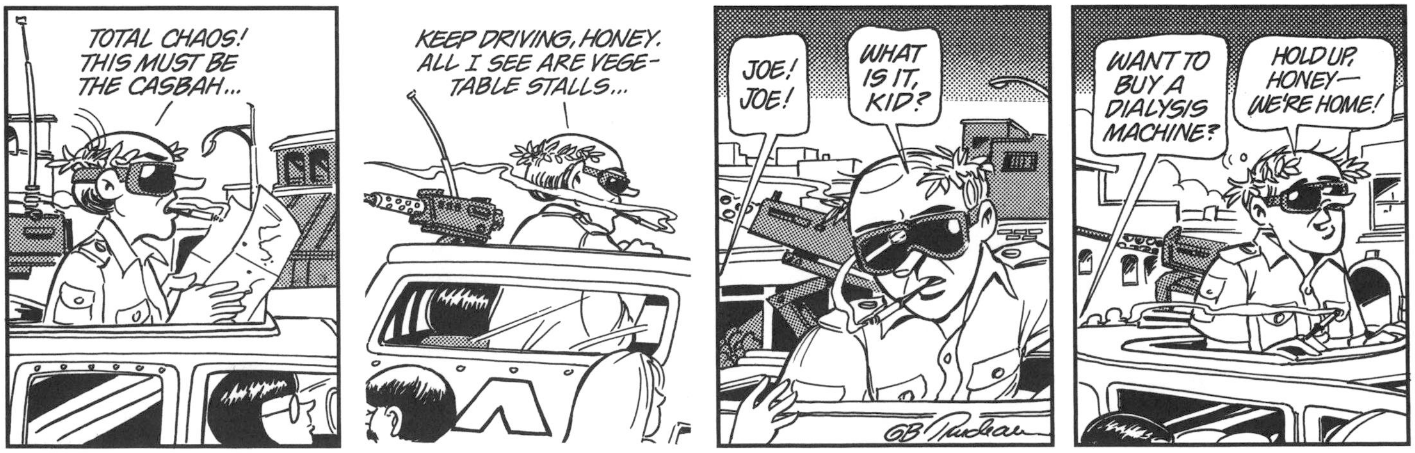
TOTAL CHAOS! THIS MUST BE THE CASBAH...
KEEP DRIVING, HONEY. ALL I SEE ARE VEGETABLE STALLS...
JOE! JOE!
WHAT IS IT, KID?
WANT TO BUY A DIALYSIS MACHINE?
HOLD UP, HONEY— WE'RE HOME!

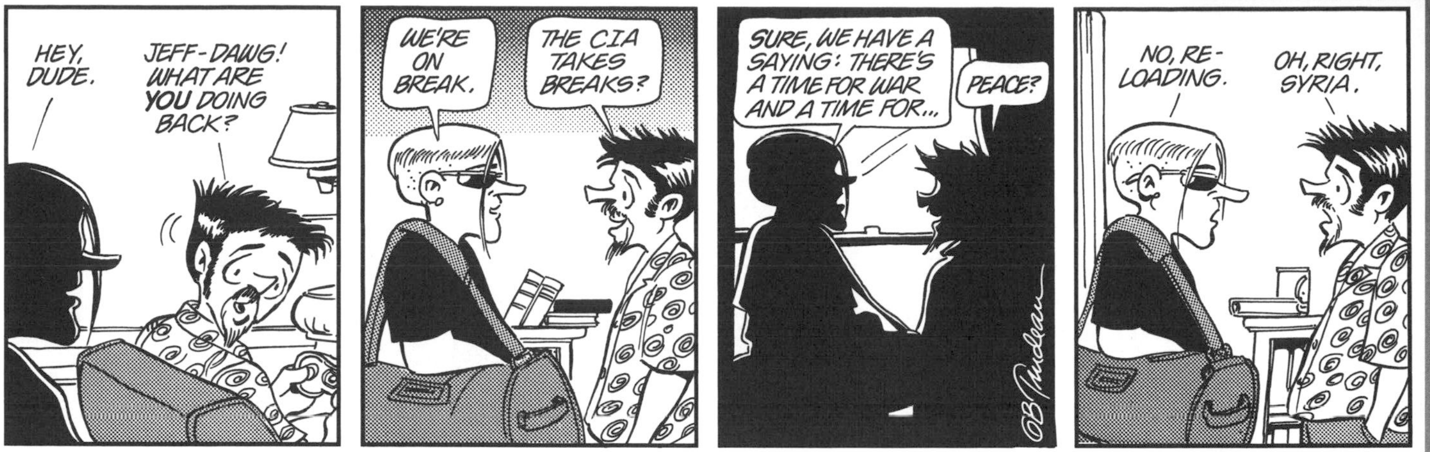
HEY, DUDE.
JEFF-DAWG! WHAT ARE YOU DOING BACK?
WE'RE ON BREAK.
THE CIA TAKES BREAKS?
SURE, WE HAVE A SAYING: THERE'S A TIME FOR WAR AND A TIME FOR...
PEACE?
NO, RE-LOADING.
OH, RIGHT, SYRIA.

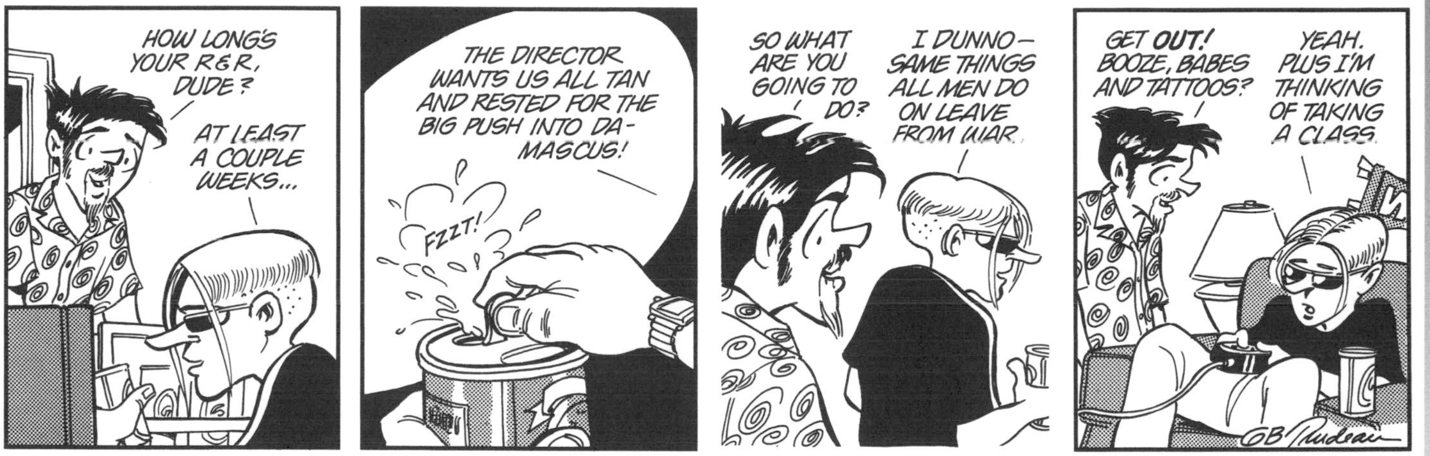
HOW LONG'S YOUR R&R, DUDE?
AT LEAST A COUPLE WEEKS...
THE DIRECTOR WANTS US ALL TAN AND RESTED FOR THE BIG PUSH INTO DAMASCUS!
FZZT!
SO WHAT ARE YOU GOING TO DO?
I DUNNO— SAME THINGS ALL MEN DO ON LEAVE FROM WAR.
GET OUT! BOOZE, BABES AND TATTOOS?
YEAH. PLUS I'M THINKING OF TAKING A CLASS.

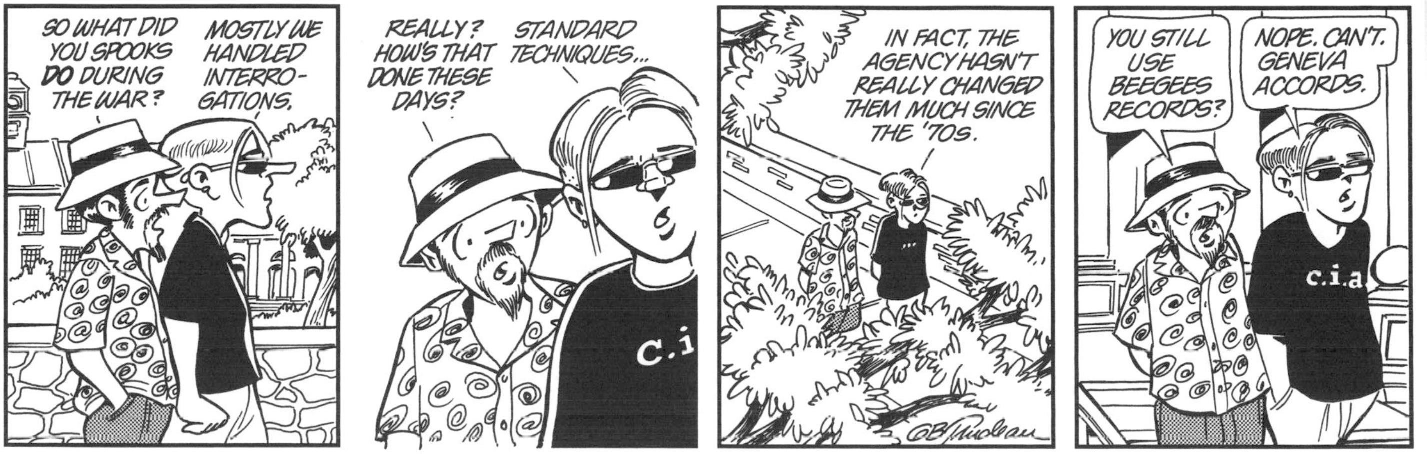
SO WHAT DID YOU SPOOKS DO DURING THE WAR?
MOSTLY WE HANDLED INTERRO-GATIONS.
REALLY? HOW'S THAT DONE THESE DAYS?
STANDARD TECHNIQUES...
C.I
IN FACT, THE AGENCY HASN'T REALLY CHANGED THEM MUCH SINCE THE '70S.
YOU STILL USE BEEGEES RECORDS?
NOPE. CAN'T. GENEVA ACCORDS.
c.i.a.

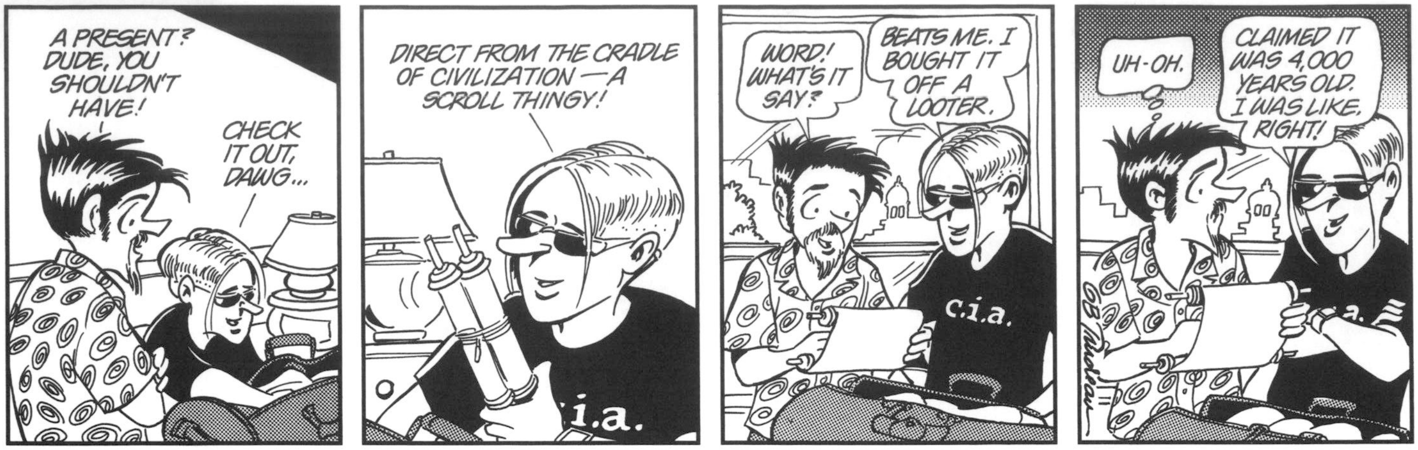
A PRESENT? DUDE, YOU SHOULDN'T HAVE!
CHECK IT OUT, DAWG...
DIRECT FROM THE CRADLE OF CIVILIZATION — A SCROLL THINGY!
WORD! WHAT'S IT SAY?
BEATS ME. I BOUGHT IT OFF A LOOTER.
UH-OH.
CLAIMED IT WAS 4,000 YEARS OLD. I WAS LIKE, RIGHT!
c.i.a.
GB Trudeau

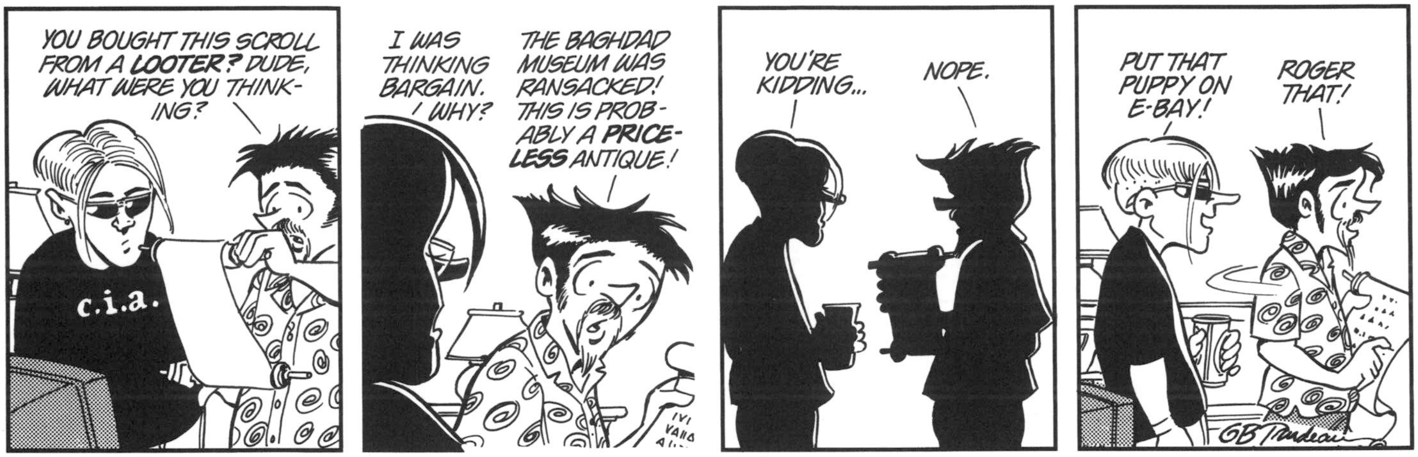
YOU BOUGHT THIS SCROLL FROM A **LOOTER?** DUDE, WHAT WERE YOU THINKING?
I WAS THINKING BARGAIN. WHY?
THE BAGHDAD MUSEUM WAS RANSACKED! THIS IS PROBABLY A **PRICELESS** ANTIQUE!
YOU'RE KIDDING...
NOPE.
PUT THAT PUPPY ON E-BAY!
ROGER THAT!
c.i.a.
GB Trudeau

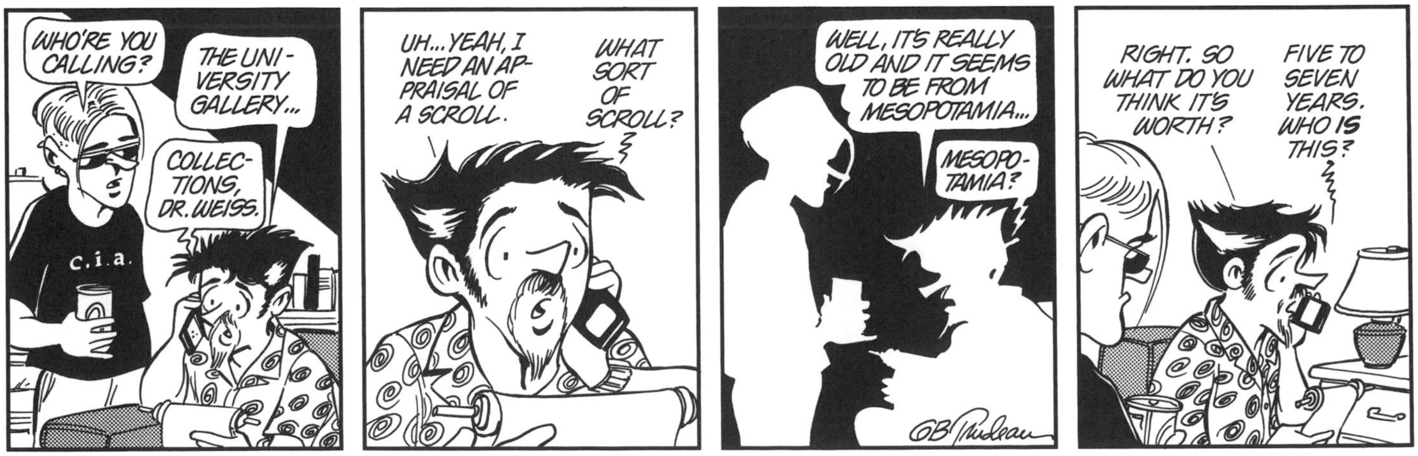
WHO'RE YOU CALLING?
THE UNIVERSITY GALLERY...
COLLECTIONS, DR. WEISS.
UH...YEAH, I NEED AN APPRAISAL OF A SCROLL.
WHAT SORT OF SCROLL?
WELL, IT'S REALLY OLD AND IT SEEMS TO BE FROM MESOPOTAMIA...
MESOPOTAMIA?
RIGHT. SO WHAT DO YOU THINK IT'S WORTH?
FIVE TO SEVEN YEARS. WHO **IS** THIS?
c.i.a.
GB Trudeau

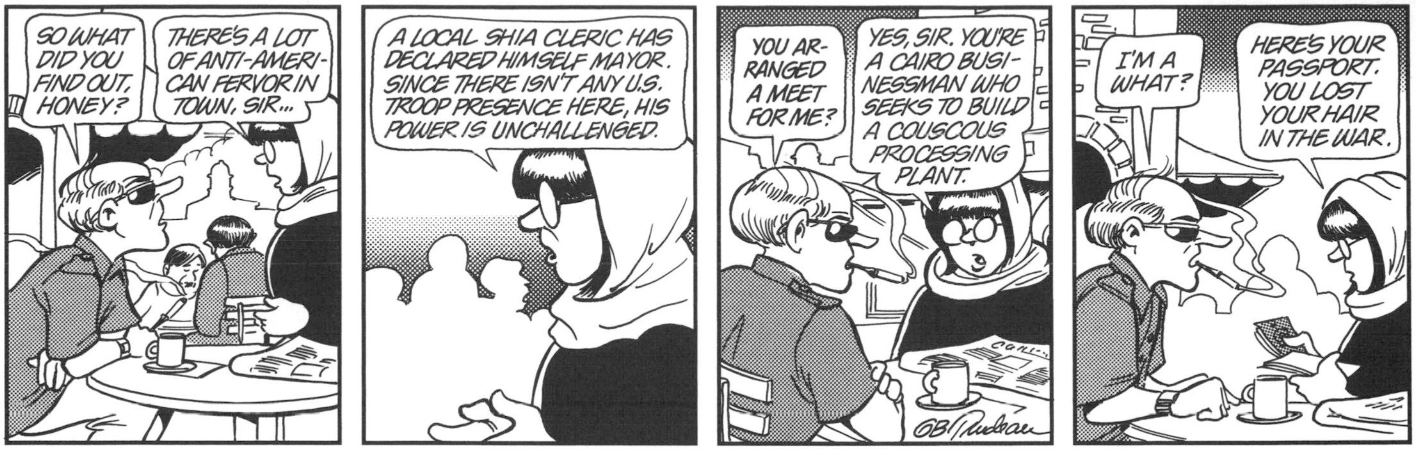
SO WHAT DID YOU FIND OUT, HONEY?
THERE'S A LOT OF ANTI-AMERICAN FERVOR IN TOWN, SIR...
A LOCAL SHIA CLERIC HAS DECLARED HIMSELF MAYOR. SINCE THERE ISN'T ANY U.S. TROOP PRESENCE HERE, HIS POWER IS UNCHALLENGED.
YOU ARRANGED A MEET FOR ME?
YES, SIR. YOU'RE A CAIRO BUSINESSMAN WHO SEEKS TO BUILD A COUSCOUS PROCESSING PLANT.
I'M A WHAT?
HERE'S YOUR PASSPORT. YOU LOST YOUR HAIR IN THE WAR.

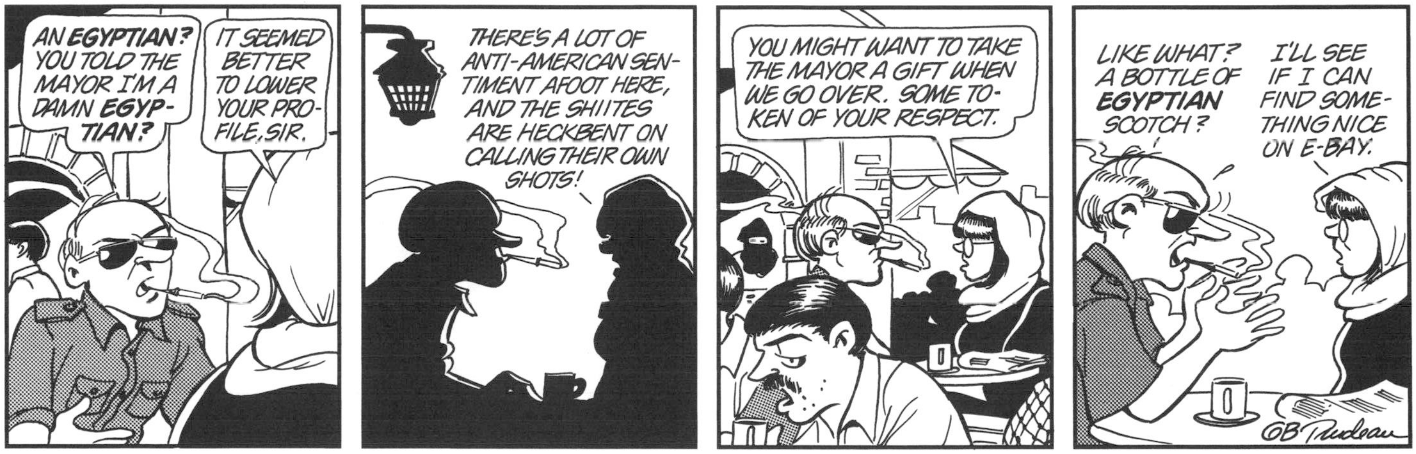
AN **EGYPTIAN**? YOU TOLD THE MAYOR I'M A DAMN **EGYPTIAN**?
IT SEEMED BETTER TO LOWER YOUR PROFILE, SIR.
THERE'S A LOT OF ANTI-AMERICAN SENTIMENT AFOOT HERE, AND THE SHIITES ARE HECKBENT ON CALLING THEIR OWN SHOTS!
YOU MIGHT WANT TO TAKE THE MAYOR A GIFT WHEN WE GO OVER. SOME TOKEN OF YOUR RESPECT.
LIKE WHAT? A BOTTLE OF **EGYPTIAN** SCOTCH?
I'LL SEE IF I CAN FIND SOMETHING NICE ON E-BAY.

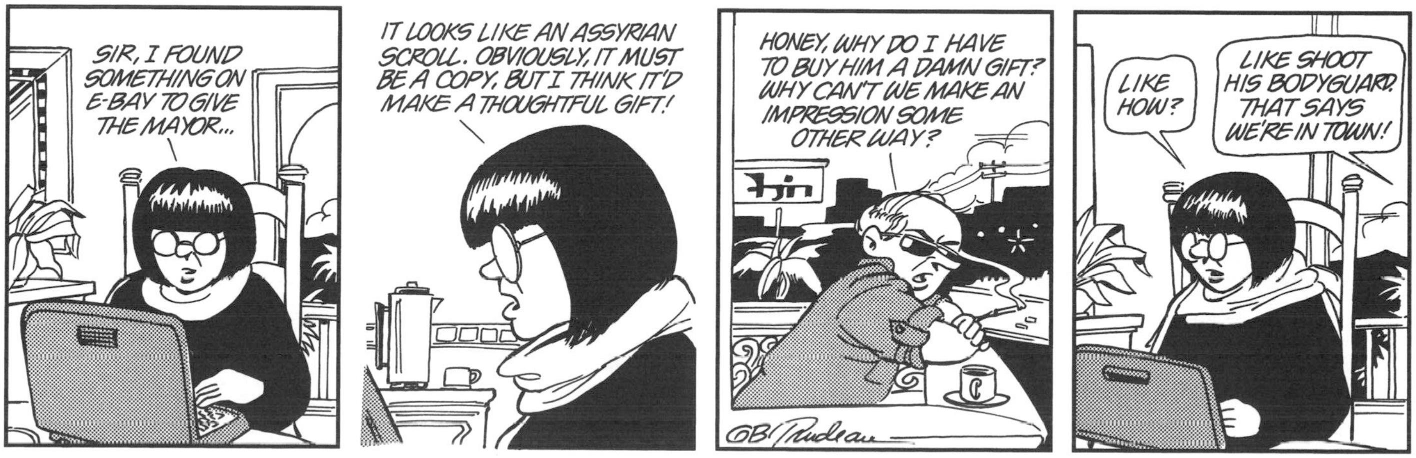
SIR, I FOUND SOMETHING ON E-BAY TO GIVE THE MAYOR...
IT LOOKS LIKE AN ASSYRIAN SCROLL.. OBVIOUSLY, IT MUST BE A COPY, BUT I THINK IT'D MAKE A THOUGHTFUL GIFT!
HONEY, WHY DO I HAVE TO BUY HIM A DAMN GIFT? WHY CAN'T WE MAKE AN IMPRESSION SOME OTHER WAY?
LIKE HOW?
LIKE SHOOT HIS BODYGUARD. THAT SAYS WE'RE IN TOWN!

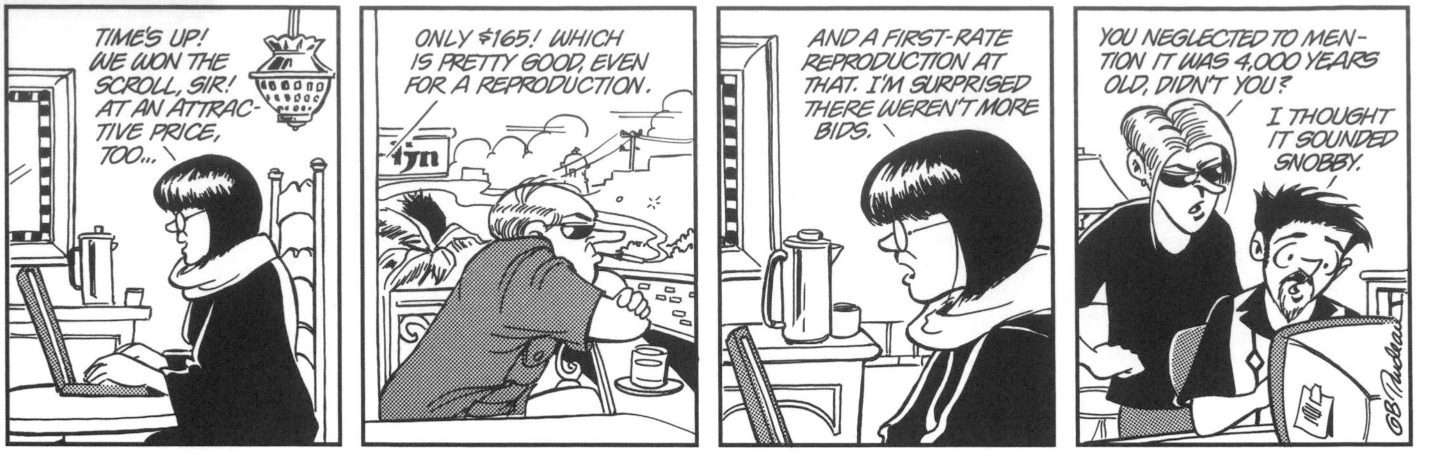
TIME'S UP! WE WON THE SCROLL, SIR! AT AN ATTRACTIVE PRICE, TOO...
ONLY $165! WHICH IS PRETTY GOOD, EVEN FOR A REPRODUCTION.
AND A FIRST-RATE REPRODUCTION AT THAT. I'M SURPRISED THERE WEREN'T MORE BIDS.
YOU NEGLECTED TO MENTION IT WAS 4,000 YEARS OLD, DIDN'T YOU?
I THOUGHT IT SOUNDED SNOBBY.

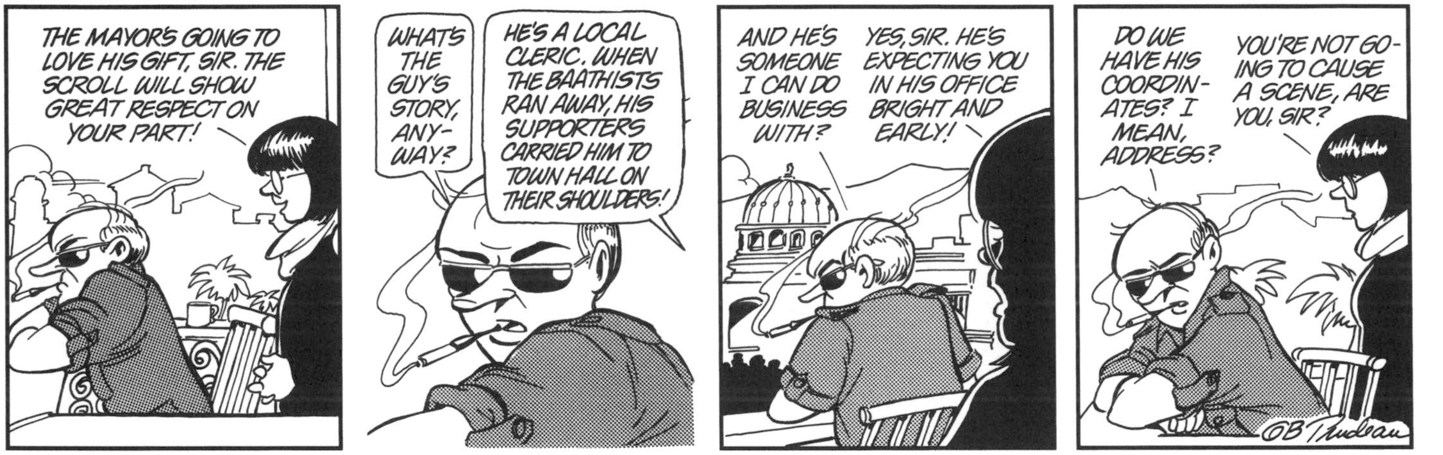
THE MAYOR'S GOING TO LOVE HIS GIFT, SIR. THE SCROLL WILL SHOW GREAT RESPECT ON YOUR PART!
WHAT'S THE GUY'S STORY, ANYWAY?
HE'S A LOCAL CLERIC. WHEN THE BAATHISTS RAN AWAY, HIS SUPPORTERS CARRIED HIM TO TOWN HALL ON THEIR SHOULDERS!
AND HE'S SOMEONE I CAN DO BUSINESS WITH?
YES, SIR. HE'S EXPECTING YOU IN HIS OFFICE BRIGHT AND EARLY!
DO WE HAVE HIS COORDINATES? I MEAN, ADDRESS?
YOU'RE NOT GOING TO CAUSE A SCENE, ARE YOU, SIR?

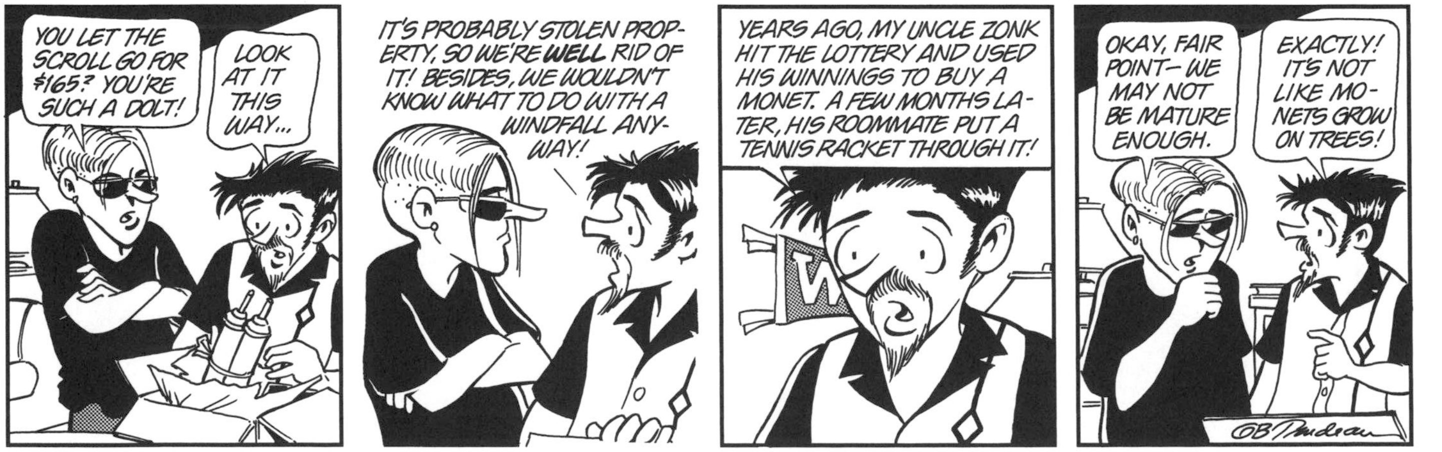
YOU LET THE SCROLL GO FOR $165? YOU'RE SUCH A DOLT!
LOOK AT IT THIS WAY...
IT'S PROBABLY STOLEN PROPERTY, SO WE'RE **WELL** RID OF IT! BESIDES, WE WOULDN'T KNOW WHAT TO DO WITH A WINDFALL ANYWAY!
YEARS AGO, MY UNCLE ZONK HIT THE LOTTERY AND USED HIS WINNINGS TO BUY A MONET. A FEW MONTHS LATER, HIS ROOMMATE PUT A TENNIS RACKET THROUGH IT!
OKAY, FAIR POINT– WE MAY NOT BE MATURE ENOUGH.
EXACTLY! IT'S NOT LIKE MONETS GROW ON TREES!

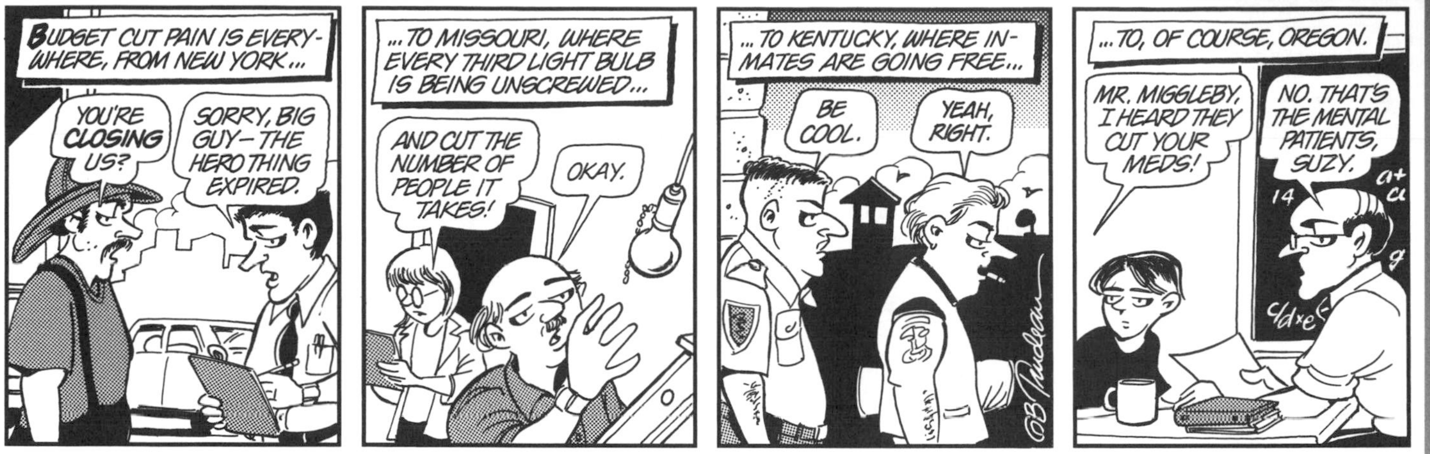
BUDGET CUT PAIN IS EVERYWHERE, FROM NEW YORK...
YOU'RE CLOSING US?
SORRY, BIG GUY—THE HERO THING EXPIRED.
...TO MISSOURI, WHERE EVERY THIRD LIGHT BULB IS BEING UNSCREWED...
AND CUT THE NUMBER OF PEOPLE IT TAKES!
OKAY.
...TO KENTUCKY, WHERE INMATES ARE GOING FREE...
BE COOL.
YEAH, RIGHT.
...TO, OF COURSE, OREGON.
MR. MIGGLEBY, I HEARD THEY CUT YOUR MEDS!
NO. THAT'S THE MENTAL PATIENTS, SUZY.

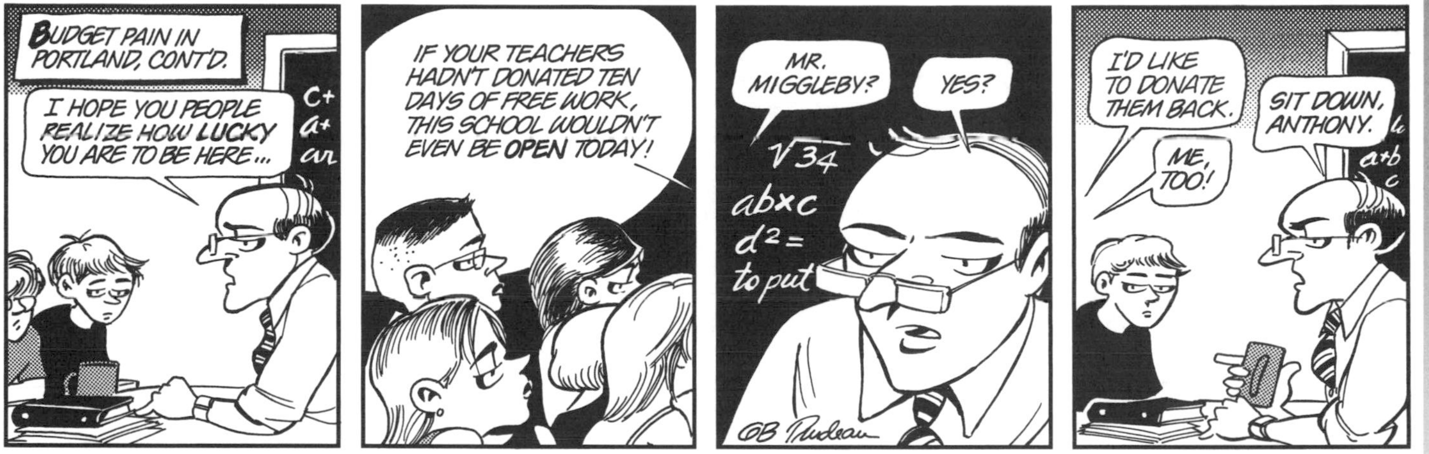
BUDGET PAIN IN PORTLAND, CONT'D.
I HOPE YOU PEOPLE REALIZE HOW LUCKY YOU ARE TO BE HERE...
IF YOUR TEACHERS HADN'T DONATED TEN DAYS OF FREE WORK, THIS SCHOOL WOULDN'T EVEN BE OPEN TODAY!
MR. MIGGLEBY?
YES?
I'D LIKE TO DONATE THEM BACK.
ME, TOO!
SIT DOWN, ANTHONY.

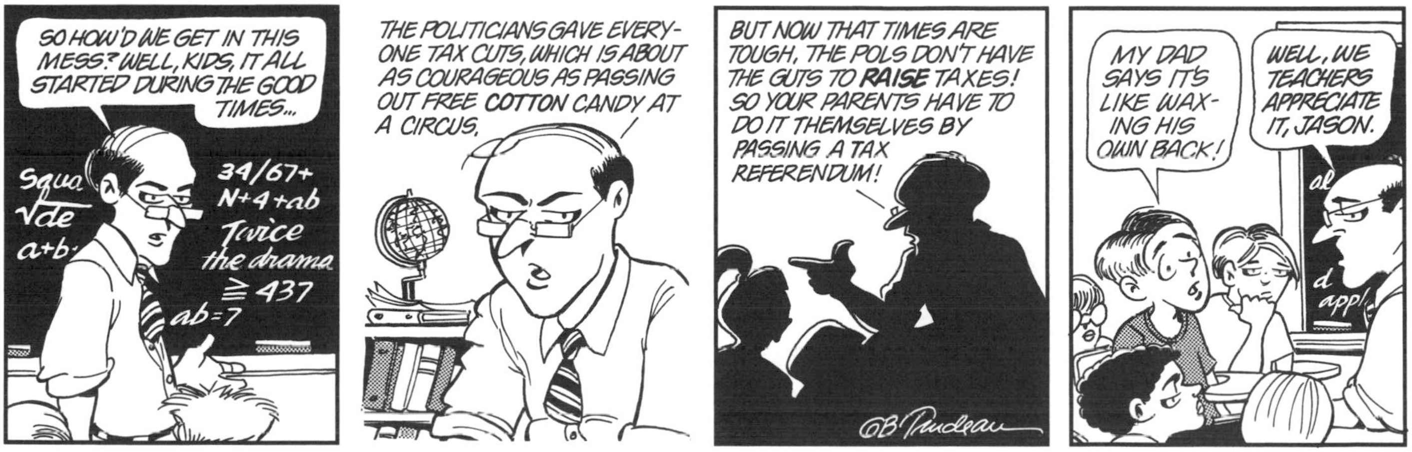
SO HOW'D WE GET IN THIS MESS? WELL, KIDS, IT ALL STARTED DURING THE GOOD TIMES...
THE POLITICIANS GAVE EVERYONE TAX CUTS, WHICH IS ABOUT AS COURAGEOUS AS PASSING OUT FREE COTTON CANDY AT A CIRCUS.
BUT NOW THAT TIMES ARE TOUGH, THE POLS DON'T HAVE THE GUTS TO RAISE TAXES! SO YOUR PARENTS HAVE TO DO IT THEMSELVES BY PASSING A TAX REFERENDUM!
MY DAD SAYS IT'S LIKE WAXING HIS OWN BACK!
WELL, WE TEACHERS APPRECIATE IT, JASON.

YOUR PARENTS FACE A STARK CHOICE, GUYS...

$14 + 7c$ $\geq 6$
$a^2 x$ $\sqrt{3}$
$c/d$ $14$

EITHER THEY VOTE TO INCREASE THEIR OWN TAXES, OR THE DISTRICT HAS TO START CUTTING...

$d\sqrt{z}$
$c^2$
$a+b$

...MEANING 600 FEWER TEACHERS, 30% BIGGER CLASSES AND NO ATHLETICS!

$\frac{a}{b} \times c$
$d^2$

COULDN'T WE JUST GET RID OF ALGEBRA? NO OFFENSE.

YEAH.

YEAH, WOULDN'T THAT SAVE A LOT?

SO I HOPE ALL YOU GUYS WILL TALK TO YOUR PARENTS ABOUT VOTING FOR THE FUNDING MEASURE!

IF THEY DON'T, THINGS **WILL** GET BAD! WE COULD END UP LOSING 17 DAYS OF SCHOOL, LIKE IN HILLSBORO!

$\frac{dee}{fed} \times \frac{7a}{5}$
$if\ the\ abst$
$for\ the$
$a+b = c-d$
$if\ d = 37$
$\sqrt{444}$

17 **FEWER** DAYS OF SCHOOL? REALLY?

IF YOUR PARENTS DON'T ACT, IT'S POSSIBLE!

UM...OKAY, I'LL MENTION IT.

I DON'T LIKE TO BOTHER MY PARENTS.

ME, NEITHER.

$a+b$
$\delta^2$
$\sqrt{d}$
$43$

PEOPLE, IT'S NOT JUST PORTLAND THAT'S IN TROUBLE. ALL ACROSS THE COUNTRY, STATES ARE MAKING DEEP CUTS!

$7$
$43$

THE SHORTFALL NATIONWIDE COULD BE $100 BILLION — JUST ABOUT WHAT WE'LL PAY THIS YEAR TO CRUSH AND REBUILD IRAQ!

$de + fg +$
$c^2 + 43$
$3b + 4k$
$if\ the$
$\frac{a}{b} = c$
$the$

WELL, MAYBE NOW THAT THE WAR'S OVER, THE PRESIDENT WILL TURN HIS ATTENTION TO US!

YEAH!

SIR? THE RICH ARE STILL HURTING.

I KNOW, I KNOW, I HEAR THEIR CRIES.

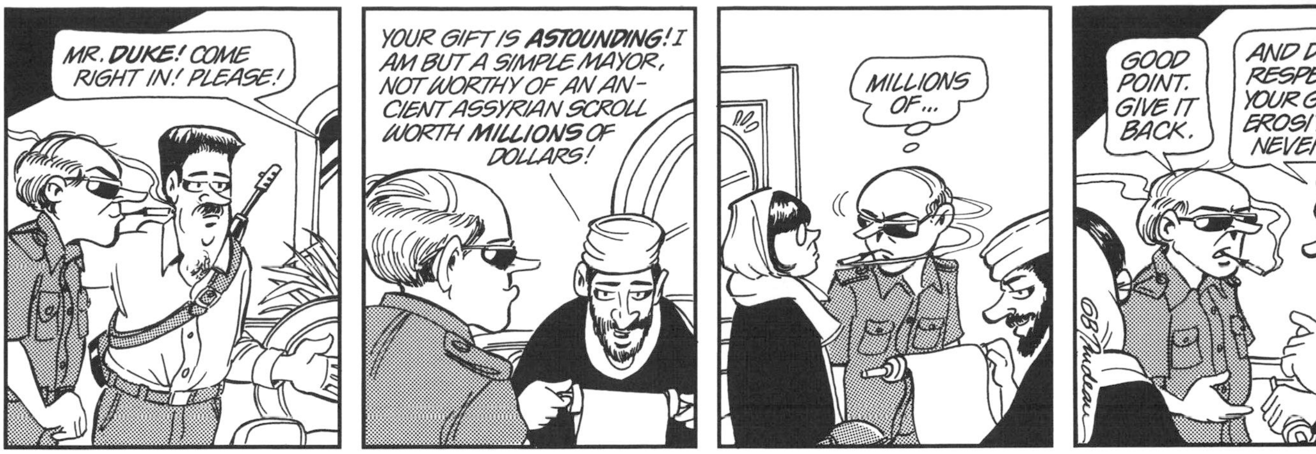
MR. DUKE! COME RIGHT IN! PLEASE!
YOUR GIFT IS ASTOUNDING! I AM BUT A SIMPLE MAYOR, NOT WORTHY OF AN ANCIENT ASSYRIAN SCROLL WORTH MILLIONS OF DOLLARS!
MILLIONS OF...
GOOD POINT. GIVE IT BACK.
AND DISRESPECT YOUR GENEROSITY? NEVER!

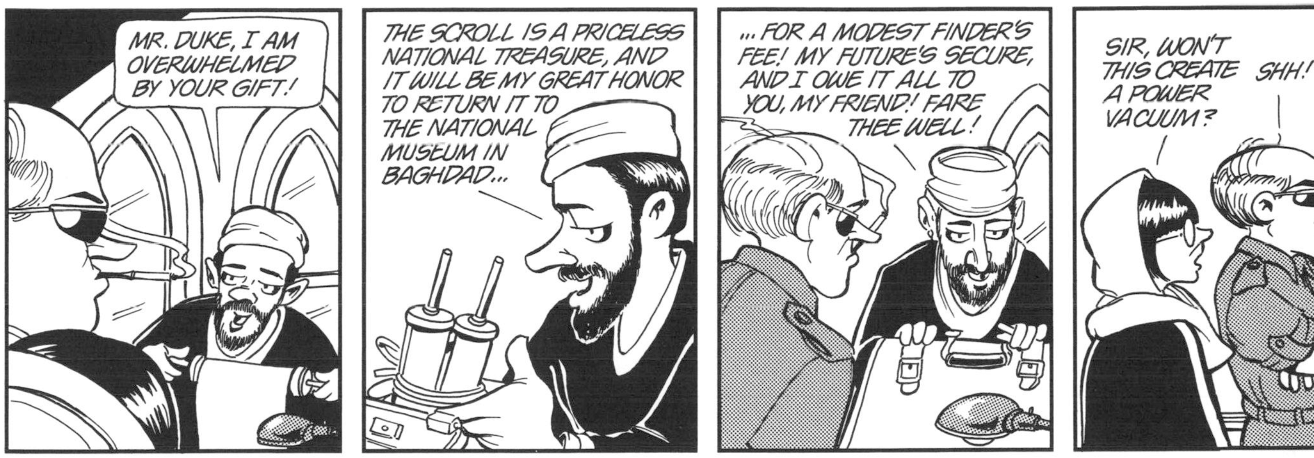
MR. DUKE, I AM OVERWHELMED BY YOUR GIFT!
THE SCROLL IS A PRICELESS NATIONAL TREASURE, AND IT WILL BE MY GREAT HONOR TO RETURN IT TO THE NATIONAL MUSEUM IN BAGHDAD...
...FOR A MODEST FINDER'S FEE! MY FUTURE'S SECURE, AND I OWE IT ALL TO YOU, MY FRIEND! FARE THEE WELL!
SIR, WON'T THIS CREATE A POWER VACUUM?
SHH!
TURN OUT THE LIGHTS, OKAY?

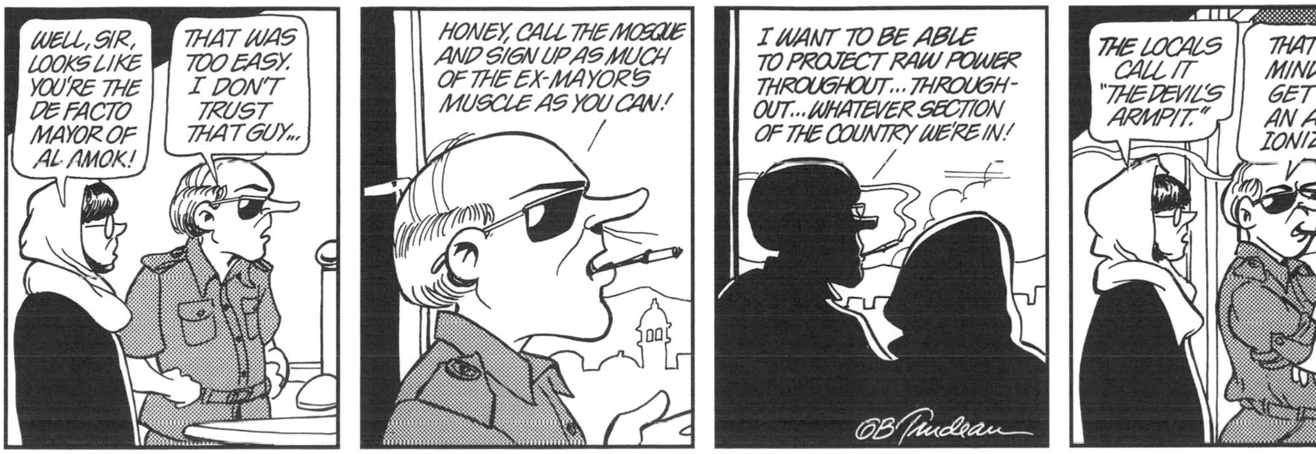
WELL, SIR, LOOKS LIKE YOU'RE THE DE FACTO MAYOR OF AL AMOK!
THAT WAS TOO EASY. I DON'T TRUST THAT GUY...
HONEY, CALL THE MOSQUE AND SIGN UP AS MUCH OF THE EX-MAYOR'S MUSCLE AS YOU CAN!
I WANT TO BE ABLE TO PROJECT RAW POWER THROUGHOUT... THROUGHOUT... WHATEVER SECTION OF THE COUNTRY WE'RE IN!
THE LOCALS CALL IT "THE DEVIL'S ARMPIT."
THAT REMINDS ME. GET ME AN AIR IONIZER.

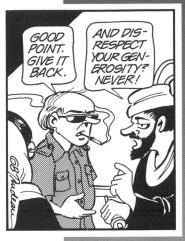

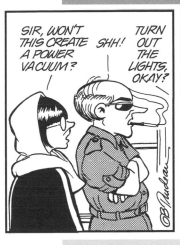

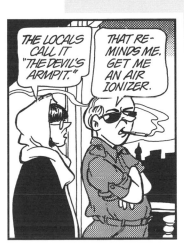

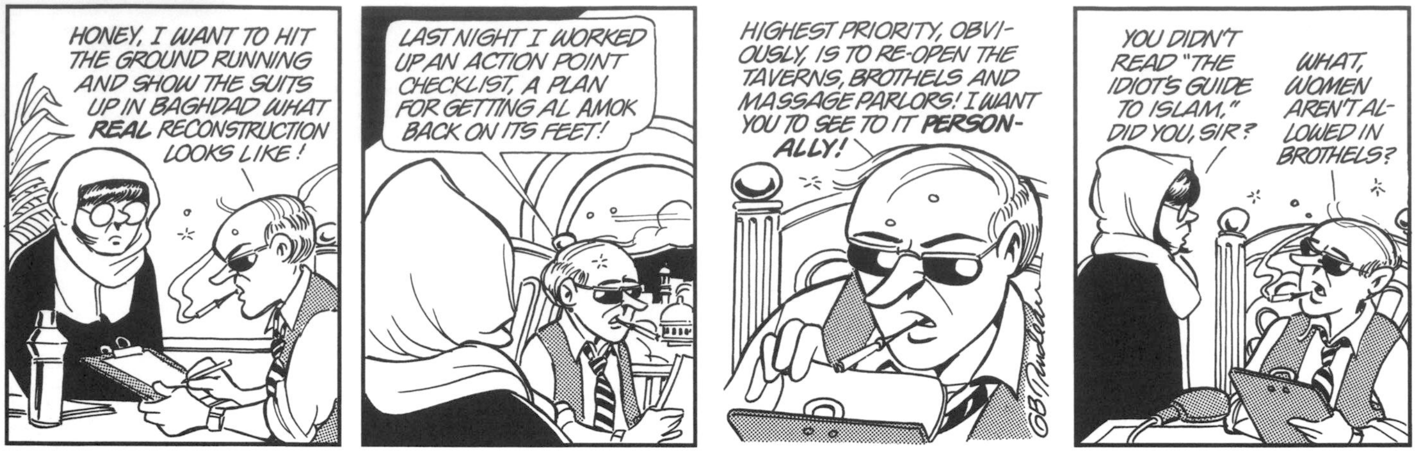
HONEY, I WANT TO HIT THE GROUND RUNNING AND SHOW THE SUITS UP IN BAGHDAD WHAT **REAL** RECONSTRUCTION LOOKS LIKE!
LAST NIGHT I WORKED UP AN ACTION POINT CHECKLIST, A PLAN FOR GETTING AL AMOK BACK ON ITS FEET!
HIGHEST PRIORITY, OBVIOUSLY, IS TO RE-OPEN THE TAVERNS, BROTHELS AND MASSAGE PARLORS! I WANT YOU TO SEE TO IT **PERSONALLY!**
YOU DIDN'T READ "THE IDIOT'S GUIDE TO ISLAM," DID YOU, SIR?
WHAT, WOMEN AREN'T ALLOWED IN BROTHELS?

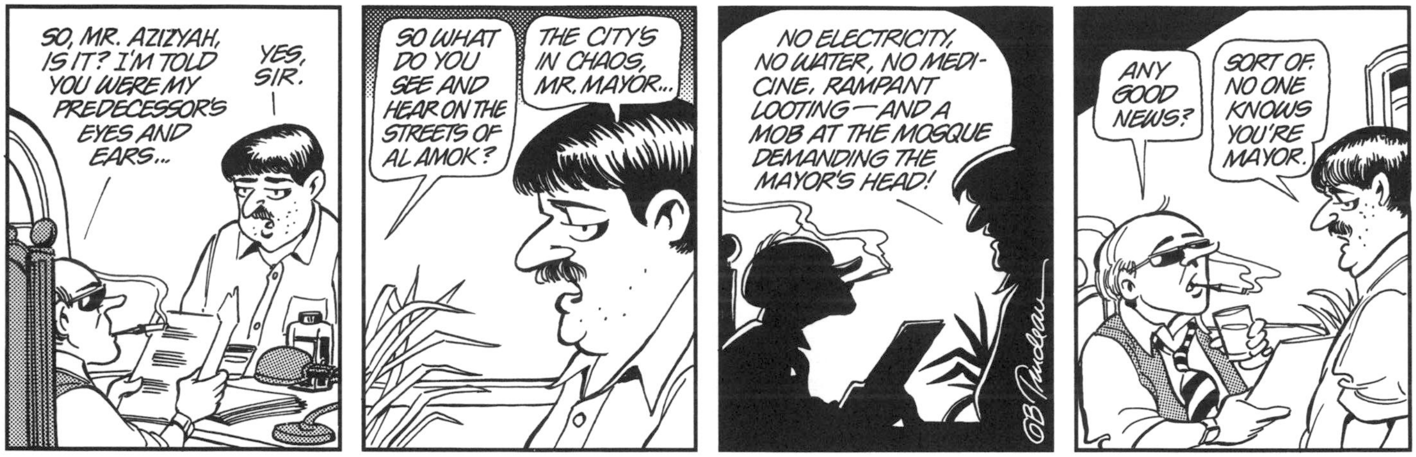
SO, MR. AZIZYAH, IS IT? I'M TOLD YOU WERE MY PREDECESSOR'S EYES AND EARS...
YES, SIR.
SO WHAT DO YOU SEE AND HEAR ON THE STREETS OF AL AMOK?
THE CITY'S IN CHAOS, MR. MAYOR...
NO ELECTRICITY, NO WATER, NO MEDICINE, RAMPANT LOOTING — AND A MOB AT THE MOSQUE DEMANDING THE MAYOR'S HEAD!
ANY GOOD NEWS?
SORT OF. NO ONE KNOWS YOU'RE MAYOR.

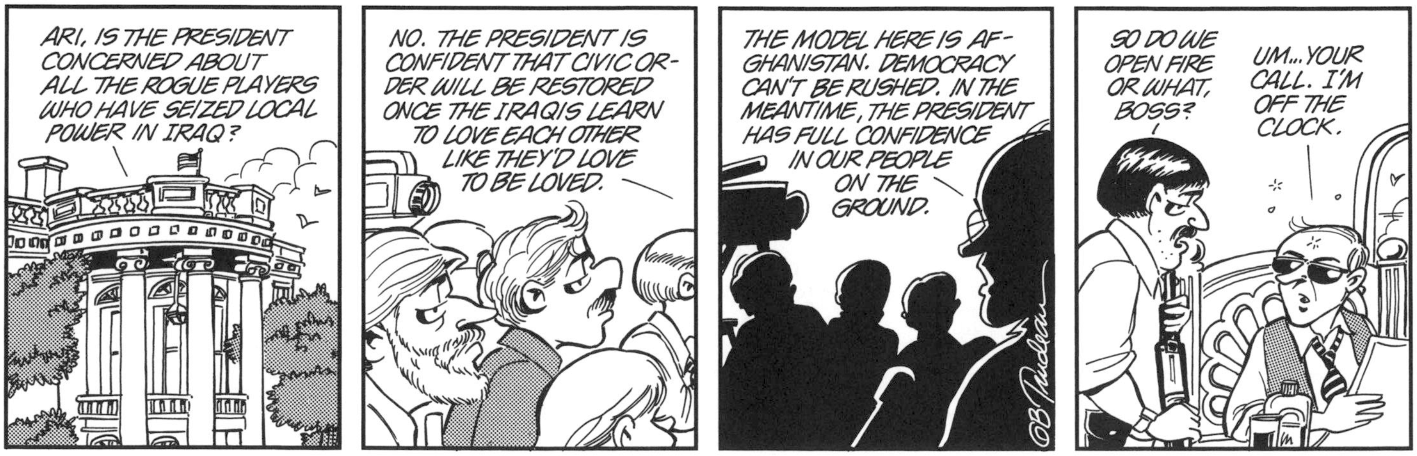
ARI, IS THE PRESIDENT CONCERNED ABOUT ALL THE ROGUE PLAYERS WHO HAVE SEIZED LOCAL POWER IN IRAQ?
NO. THE PRESIDENT IS CONFIDENT THAT CIVIC ORDER WILL BE RESTORED ONCE THE IRAQIS LEARN TO LOVE EACH OTHER LIKE THEY'D LOVE TO BE LOVED.
THE MODEL HERE IS AFGHANISTAN. DEMOCRACY CAN'T BE RUSHED. IN THE MEANTIME, THE PRESIDENT HAS FULL CONFIDENCE IN OUR PEOPLE ON THE GROUND.
SO DO WE OPEN FIRE OR WHAT, BOSS?
UM... YOUR CALL. I'M OFF THE CLOCK.

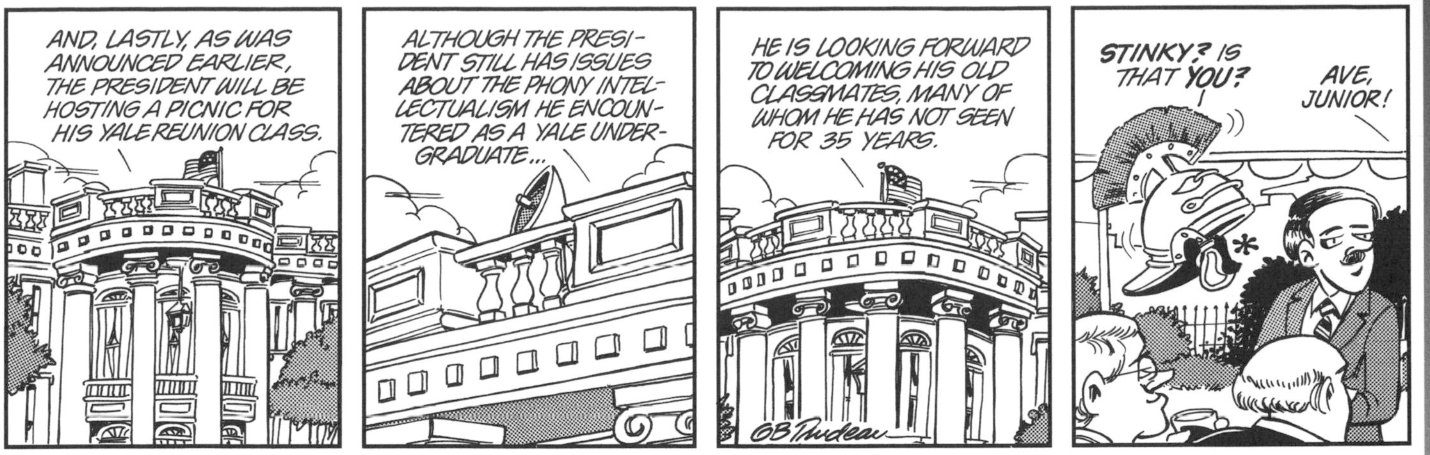
AND, LASTLY, AS WAS ANNOUNCED EARLIER, THE PRESIDENT WILL BE HOSTING A PICNIC FOR HIS YALE REUNION CLASS.
ALTHOUGH THE PRESIDENT STILL HAS ISSUES ABOUT THE PHONY INTELLECTUALISM HE ENCOUNTERED AS A YALE UNDERGRADUATE...
HE IS LOOKING FORWARD TO WELCOMING HIS OLD CLASSMATES, MANY OF WHOM HE HAS NOT SEEN FOR 35 YEARS.
STINKY? IS THAT YOU?
AVE, JUNIOR!

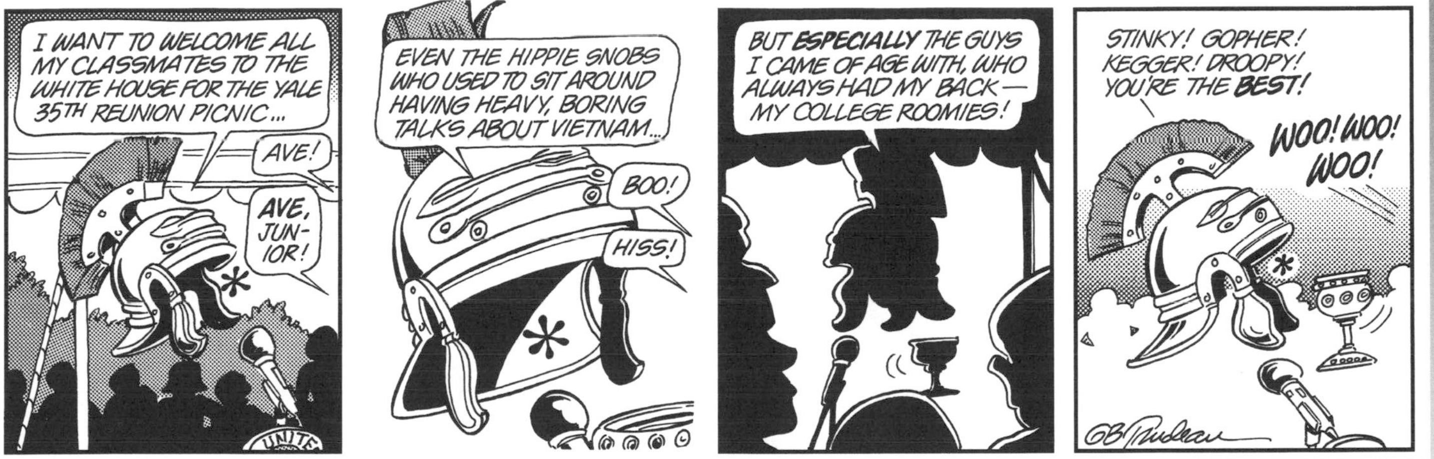
I WANT TO WELCOME ALL MY CLASSMATES TO THE WHITE HOUSE FOR THE YALE 35TH REUNION PICNIC...
AVE!
AVE, JUNIOR!
EVEN THE HIPPIE SNOBS WHO USED TO SIT AROUND HAVING HEAVY, BORING TALKS ABOUT VIETNAM...
BOO!
HISS!
BUT ESPECIALLY THE GUYS I CAME OF AGE WITH, WHO ALWAYS HAD MY BACK— MY COLLEGE ROOMIES!
STINKY! GOPHER! KEGGER! DROOPY! YOU'RE THE BEST!
WOO! WOO! WOO!

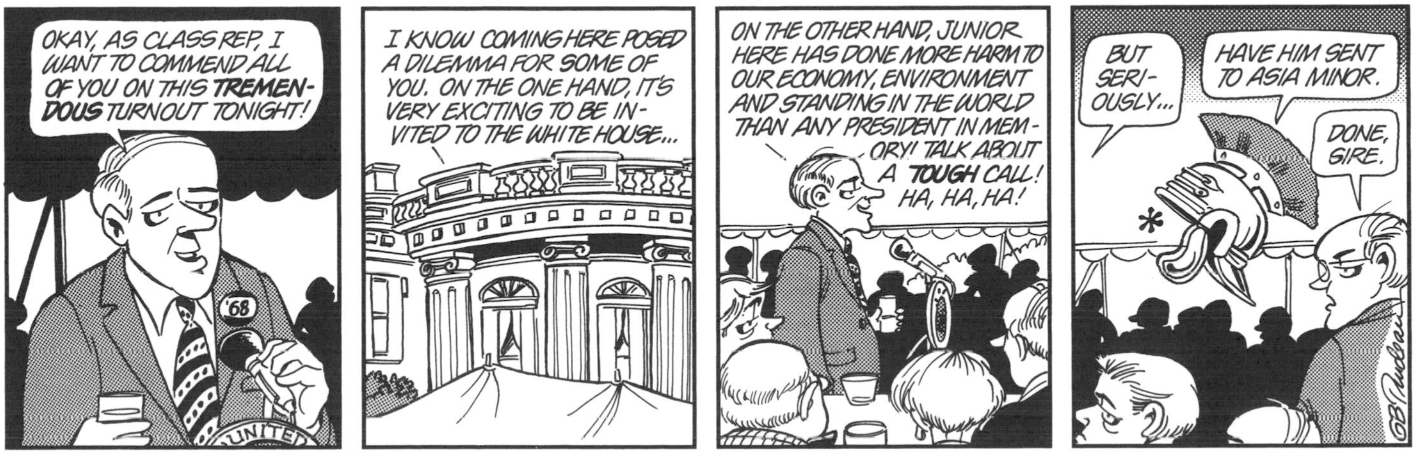
OKAY, AS CLASS REP, I WANT TO COMMEND ALL OF YOU ON THIS TREMENDOUS TURNOUT TONIGHT!
'68
I KNOW COMING HERE POSED A DILEMMA FOR SOME OF YOU. ON THE ONE HAND, IT'S VERY EXCITING TO BE INVITED TO THE WHITE HOUSE...
ON THE OTHER HAND, JUNIOR HERE HAS DONE MORE HARM TO OUR ECONOMY, ENVIRONMENT AND STANDING IN THE WORLD THAN ANY PRESIDENT IN MEMORY! TALK ABOUT A TOUGH CALL! HA, HA, HA!
BUT SERIOUSLY...
HAVE HIM SENT TO ASIA MINOR.
DONE, SIRE.

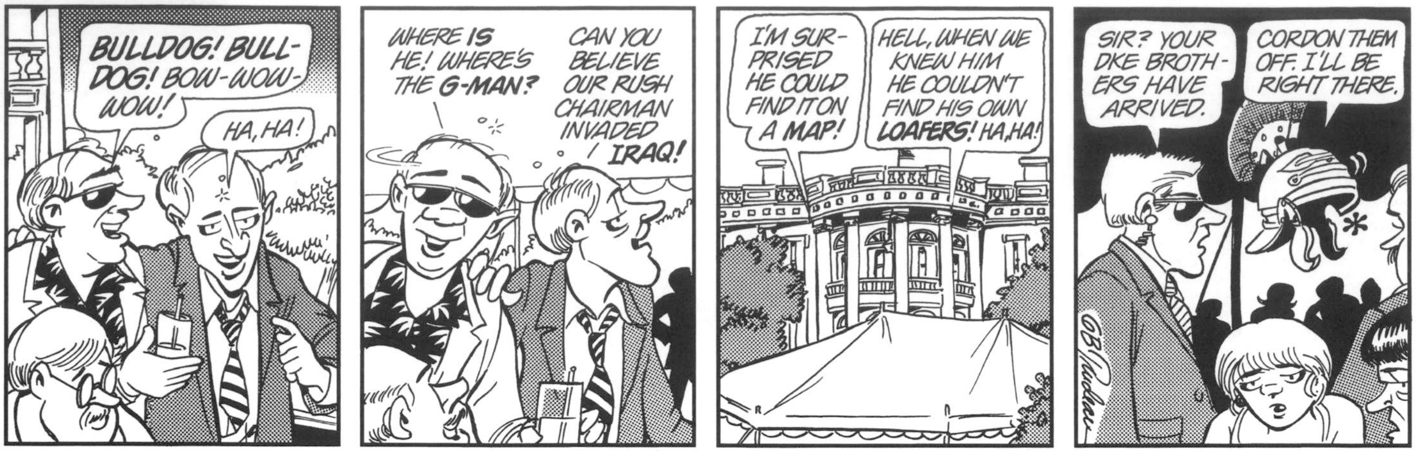
BULLDOG! BULL-DOG! BOW-WOW-WOW!
HA, HA!
WHERE IS HE! WHERE'S THE G-MAN?
CAN YOU BELIEVE OUR RUSH CHAIRMAN INVADED IRAQ!
I'M SUR-PRISED HE COULD FIND IT ON A MAP!
HELL, WHEN WE KNEW HIM HE COULDN'T FIND HIS OWN LOAFERS! HA, HA!
SIR? YOUR DKE BROTH-ERS HAVE ARRIVED.
CORDON THEM OFF. I'LL BE RIGHT THERE.

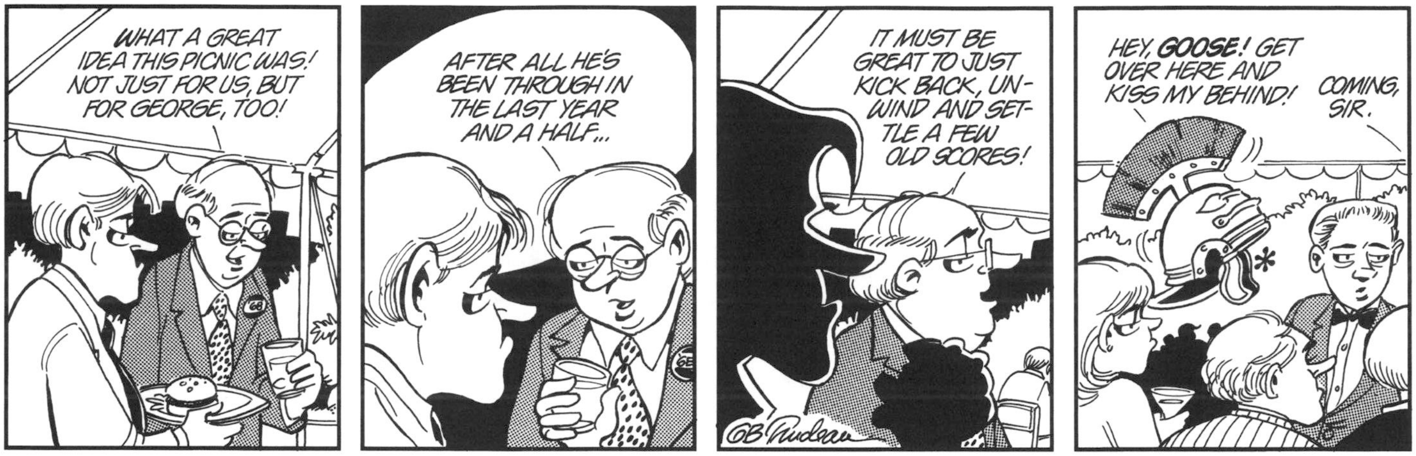
WHAT A GREAT IDEA THIS PICNIC WAS! NOT JUST FOR US, BUT FOR GEORGE, TOO!
AFTER ALL HE'S BEEN THROUGH IN THE LAST YEAR AND A HALF...
IT MUST BE GREAT TO JUST KICK BACK, UN-WIND AND SET-TLE A FEW OLD SCORES!
HEY, GOOSE! GET OVER HERE AND KISS MY BEHIND!
COMING, SIR.

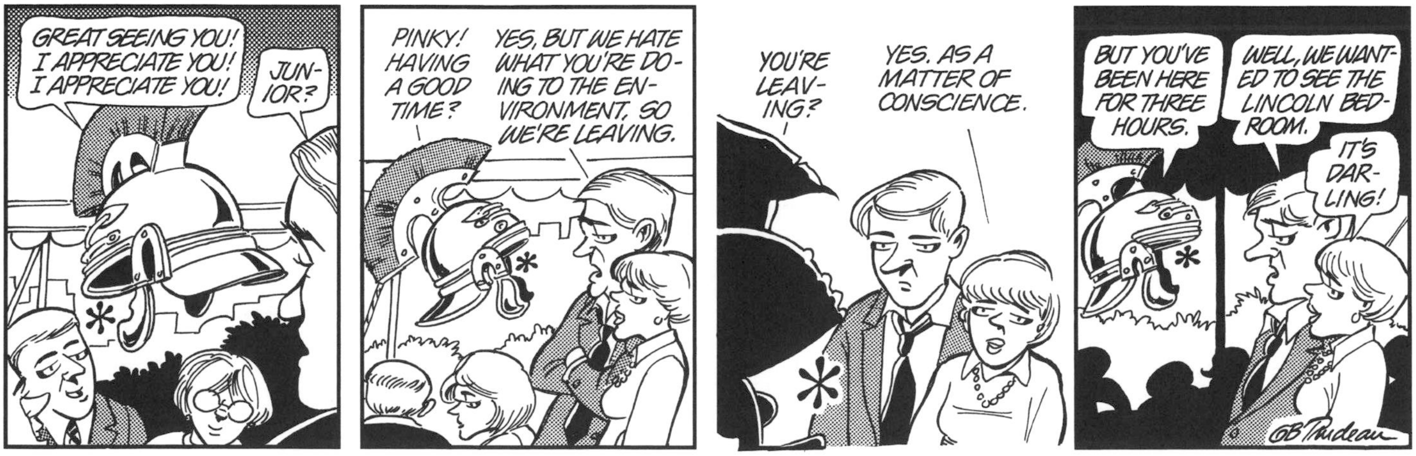
GREAT SEEING YOU! I APPRECIATE YOU! I APPRECIATE YOU!
JUN-IOR?
PINKY! HAVING A GOOD TIME?
YES, BUT WE HATE WHAT YOU'RE DO-ING TO THE EN-VIRONMENT, SO WE'RE LEAVING.
YOU'RE LEAV-ING?
YES. AS A MATTER OF CONSCIENCE.
BUT YOU'VE BEEN HERE FOR THREE HOURS.
WELL, WE WANT-ED TO SEE THE LINCOLN BED-ROOM.
IT'S DAR-LING!

THE ANGER'S STARTING TO BOIL OVER, BOSS! PEOPLE WANT **SERVICES**—WATER, ELECTRICITY, SECURITY, HOSPITALS...
OKAY, THIS CALLS FOR A LITTLE AMERICAN INGENUITY. HERE'S THE PLAN...
I WANT YOU TO IDENTIFY THE WEALTHIEST PEOPLE IN AL AMOK, TRACK 'EM DOWN, AND GIVE THEM ALL HUGE TAX CUTS!
THIS WORKS?
OF COURSE NOT. BUT THEN WE CAN'T AFFORD SERVICES.

YOU PEOPLE WANT TO BE LIKE US, RIGHT? WELL, IN AMERICA, THERE **IS** NO PROBLEM THAT CAN'T BE SOLVED BY TAX CUTS FOR THE RICH!
GOOD TIMES, BAD, SURPLUSES, DEFICITS—IT DOESN'T MATTER! TAX RELIEF IS THE ANSWER TO **EVERY** ECONOMIC QUESTION!
OH...
WHO GETS TO PAY FOR IT?
THAT'S THE BEAUTY PART— LAME-O GENERATION X!

BOSS, I DON'T MIND STICKING OUR KIDS WITH THE BILL FOR TAX RELIEF, BUT WHAT ARE WE GONNA DO FOR A CASH FLOW?
UH... BOSS?
GIVE HIM A MINUTE.
LOOTERS' FEES!
SEE? HE'S ALWAYS THINKING!

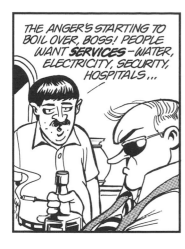

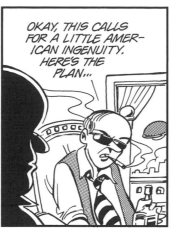

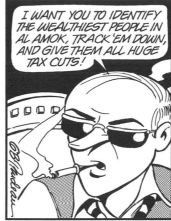

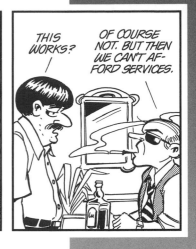

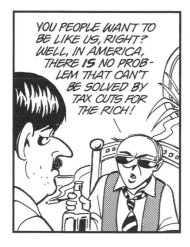

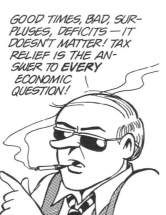

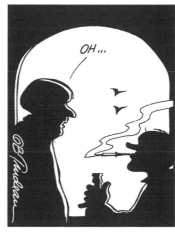

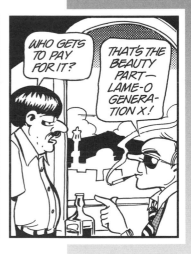

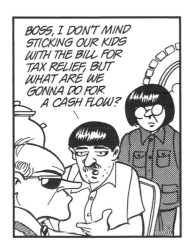

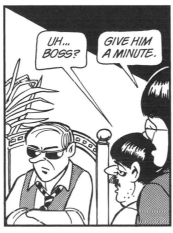

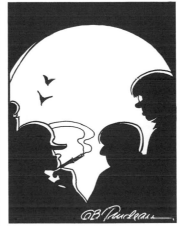

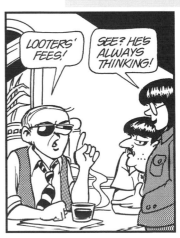

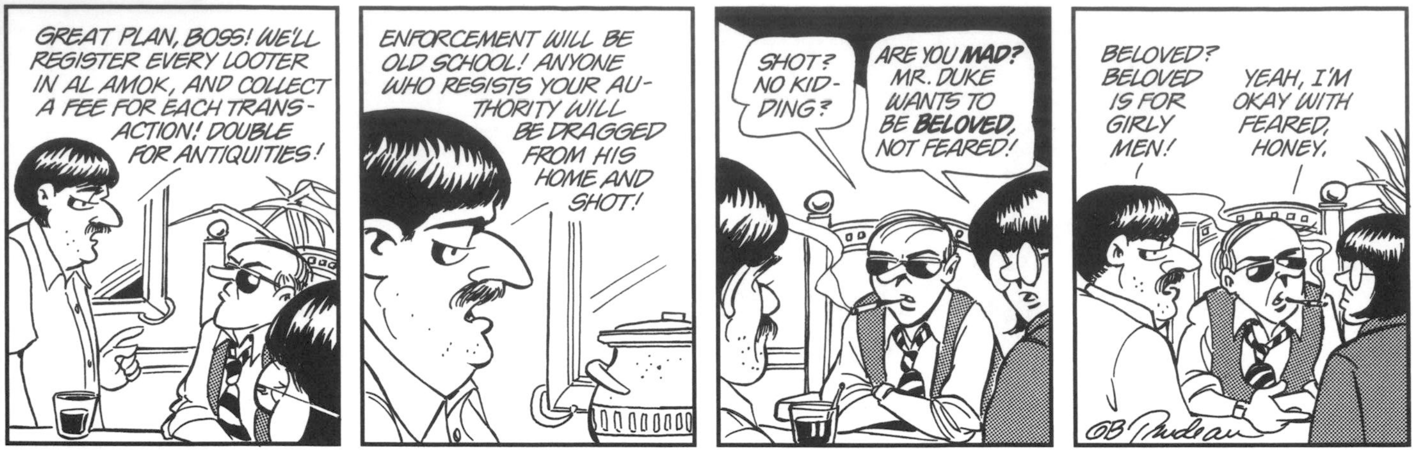
GREAT PLAN, BOSS! WE'LL REGISTER EVERY LOOTER IN AL AMOK, AND COLLECT A FEE FOR EACH TRANSACTION! DOUBLE FOR ANTIQUITIES!
ENFORCEMENT WILL BE OLD SCHOOL! ANYONE WHO RESISTS YOUR AUTHORITY WILL BE DRAGGED FROM HIS HOME AND SHOT!
SHOT? NO KIDDING?
ARE YOU MAD? MR. DUKE WANTS TO BE BELOVED, NOT FEARED!
BELOVED? BELOVED IS FOR GIRLY MEN!
YEAH, I'M OKAY WITH FEARED, HONEY.
©B Trudeau

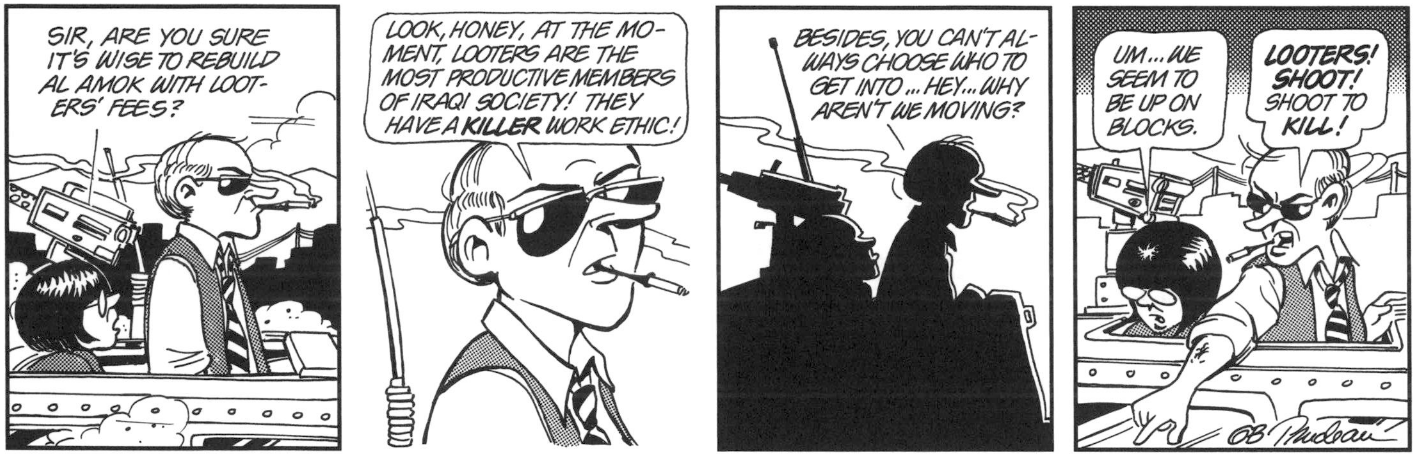
SIR, ARE YOU SURE IT'S WISE TO REBUILD AL AMOK WITH LOOTERS' FEES?
LOOK, HONEY, AT THE MOMENT, LOOTERS ARE THE MOST PRODUCTIVE MEMBERS OF IRAQI SOCIETY! THEY HAVE A KILLER WORK ETHIC!
BESIDES, YOU CAN'T ALWAYS CHOOSE WHO TO GET INTO... HEY... WHY AREN'T WE MOVING?
UM... WE SEEM TO BE UP ON BLOCKS.
LOOTERS! SHOOT! SHOOT TO KILL!
©B Trudeau

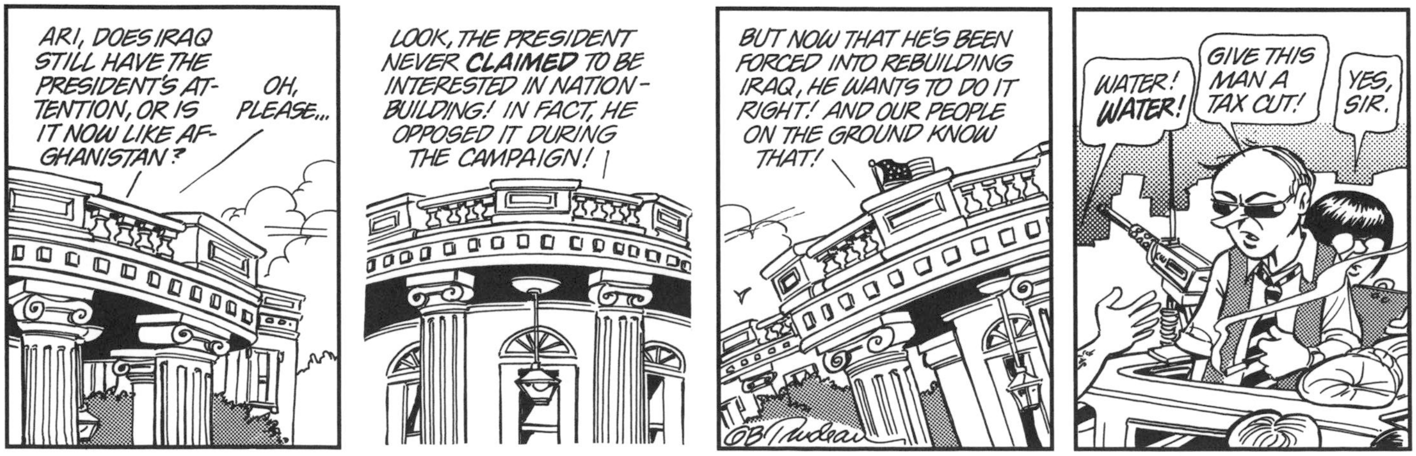
ARI, DOES IRAQ STILL HAVE THE PRESIDENT'S ATTENTION, OR IS IT NOW LIKE AFGHANISTAN?
OH, PLEASE...
LOOK, THE PRESIDENT NEVER CLAIMED TO BE INTERESTED IN NATION-BUILDING! IN FACT, HE OPPOSED IT DURING THE CAMPAIGN!
BUT NOW THAT HE'S BEEN FORCED INTO REBUILDING IRAQ, HE WANTS TO DO IT RIGHT! AND OUR PEOPLE ON THE GROUND KNOW THAT!
©B Trudeau
WATER! WATER!
GIVE THIS MAN A TAX CUT!
YES, SIR.

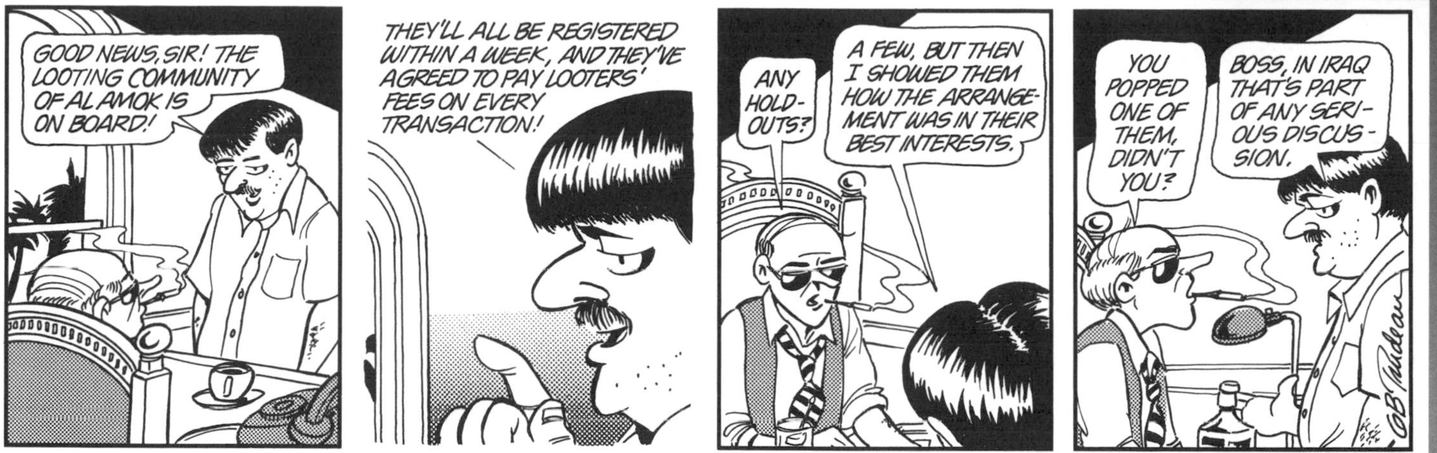
GOOD NEWS, SIR! THE LOOTING COMMUNITY OF AL AMOK IS ON BOARD!
THEY'LL ALL BE REGISTERED WITHIN A WEEK, AND THEY'VE AGREED TO PAY LOOTERS' FEES ON EVERY TRANSACTION!
ANY HOLD-OUTS?
A FEW, BUT THEN I SHOWED THEM HOW THE ARRANGEMENT WAS IN THEIR BEST INTERESTS.
YOU POPPED ONE OF THEM, DIDN'T YOU?
BOSS, IN IRAQ THAT'S PART OF ANY SERIOUS DISCUSSION.

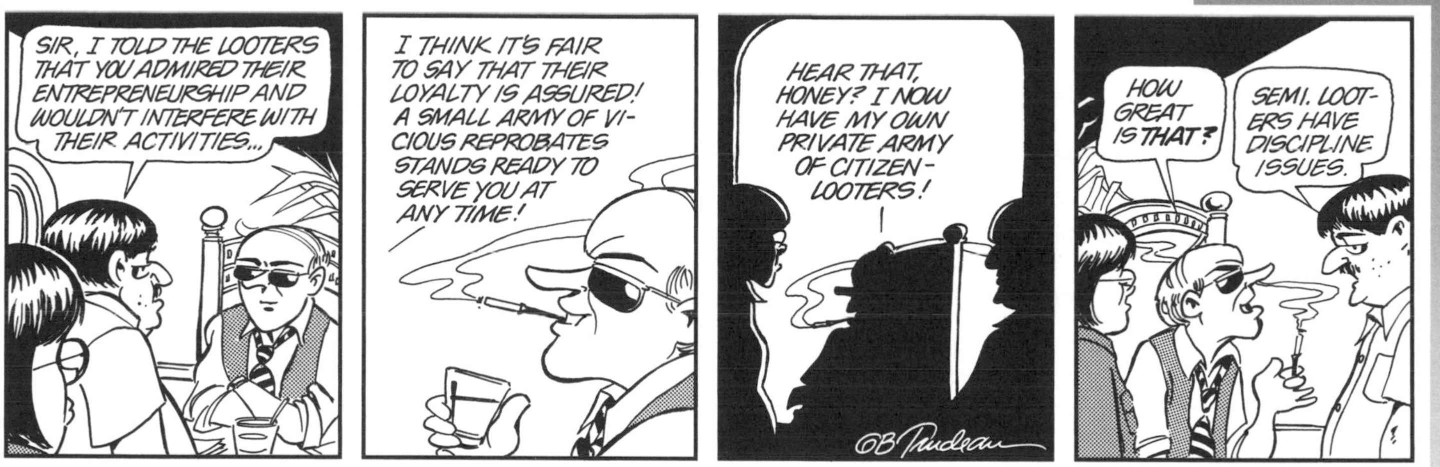
SIR, I TOLD THE LOOTERS THAT YOU ADMIRED THEIR ENTREPRENEURSHIP AND WOULDN'T INTERFERE WITH THEIR ACTIVITIES...
I THINK IT'S FAIR TO SAY THAT THEIR LOYALTY IS ASSURED! A SMALL ARMY OF VICIOUS REPROBATES STANDS READY TO SERVE YOU AT ANY TIME!
HEAR THAT, HONEY? I NOW HAVE MY OWN PRIVATE ARMY OF CITIZEN-LOOTERS!
HOW GREAT IS **THAT?**
SEMI. LOOTERS HAVE DISCIPLINE ISSUES.

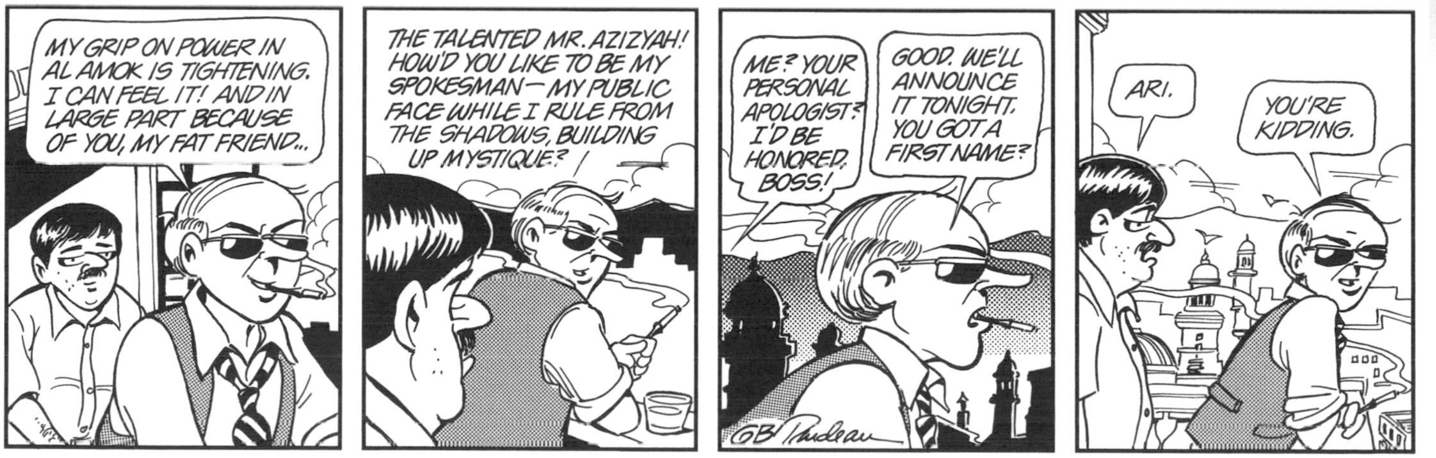
MY GRIP ON POWER IN AL AMOK IS TIGHTENING. I CAN FEEL IT! AND IN LARGE PART BECAUSE OF YOU, MY FAT FRIEND...
THE TALENTED MR. AZIZYAH! HOW'D YOU LIKE TO BE MY SPOKESMAN— MY PUBLIC FACE WHILE I RULE FROM THE SHADOWS, BUILDING UP MYSTIQUE?
ME? YOUR PERSONAL APOLOGIST? I'D BE HONORED, BOSS!
GOOD. WE'LL ANNOUNCE IT TONIGHT. YOU GOT A FIRST NAME?
ARI.
YOU'RE KIDDING.

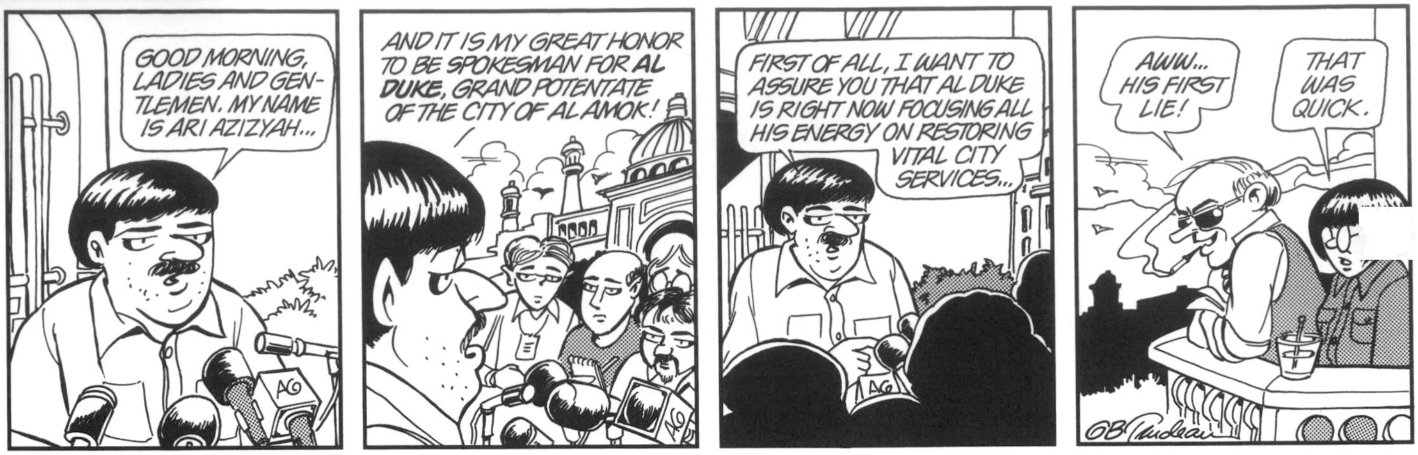
GOOD MORNING, LADIES AND GEN-TLEMEN. MY NAME IS ARI AZIZYAH...
AND IT IS MY GREAT HONOR TO BE SPOKESMAN FOR **AL DUKE**, GRAND POTENTATE OF THE CITY OF AL AMOK!
FIRST OF ALL, I WANT TO ASSURE YOU THAT AL DUKE IS RIGHT NOW FOCUSING ALL HIS ENERGY ON RESTORING VITAL CITY SERVICES...
AWW... HIS FIRST LIE!
THAT WAS QUICK.

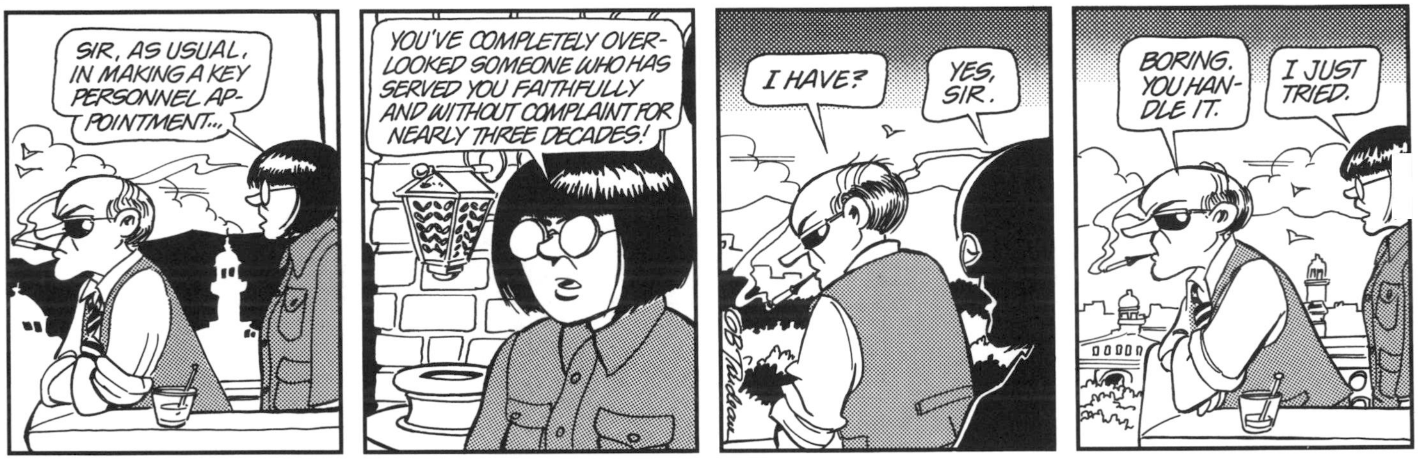
SIR, AS USUAL, IN MAKING A KEY PERSONNEL AP-POINTMENT...
YOU'VE COMPLETELY OVER-LOOKED SOMEONE WHO HAS SERVED YOU FAITHFULLY AND WITHOUT COMPLAINT FOR NEARLY THREE DECADES!
I HAVE?
YES, SIR.
BORING. YOU HAN-DLE IT.
I JUST TRIED.

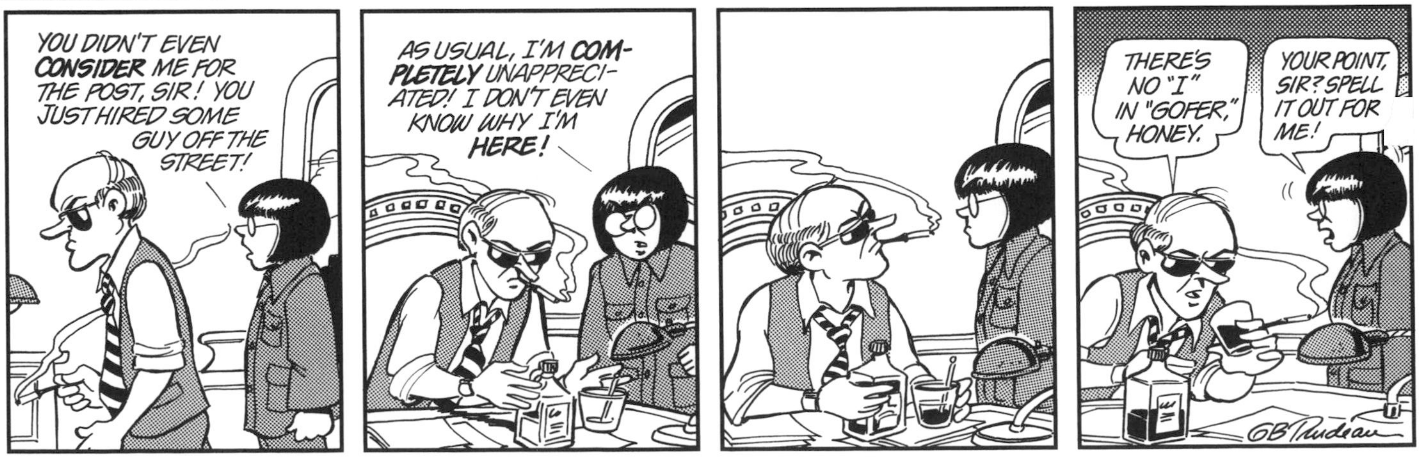
YOU DIDN'T EVEN **CONSIDER** ME FOR THE POST, SIR! YOU JUST HIRED SOME GUY OFF THE STREET!
AS USUAL, I'M **COM-PLETELY** UNAPPRECI-ATED! I DON'T EVEN KNOW WHY I'M **HERE**!
THERE'S NO "I" IN "GOFER," HONEY.
YOUR POINT, SIR? SPELL IT OUT FOR ME!

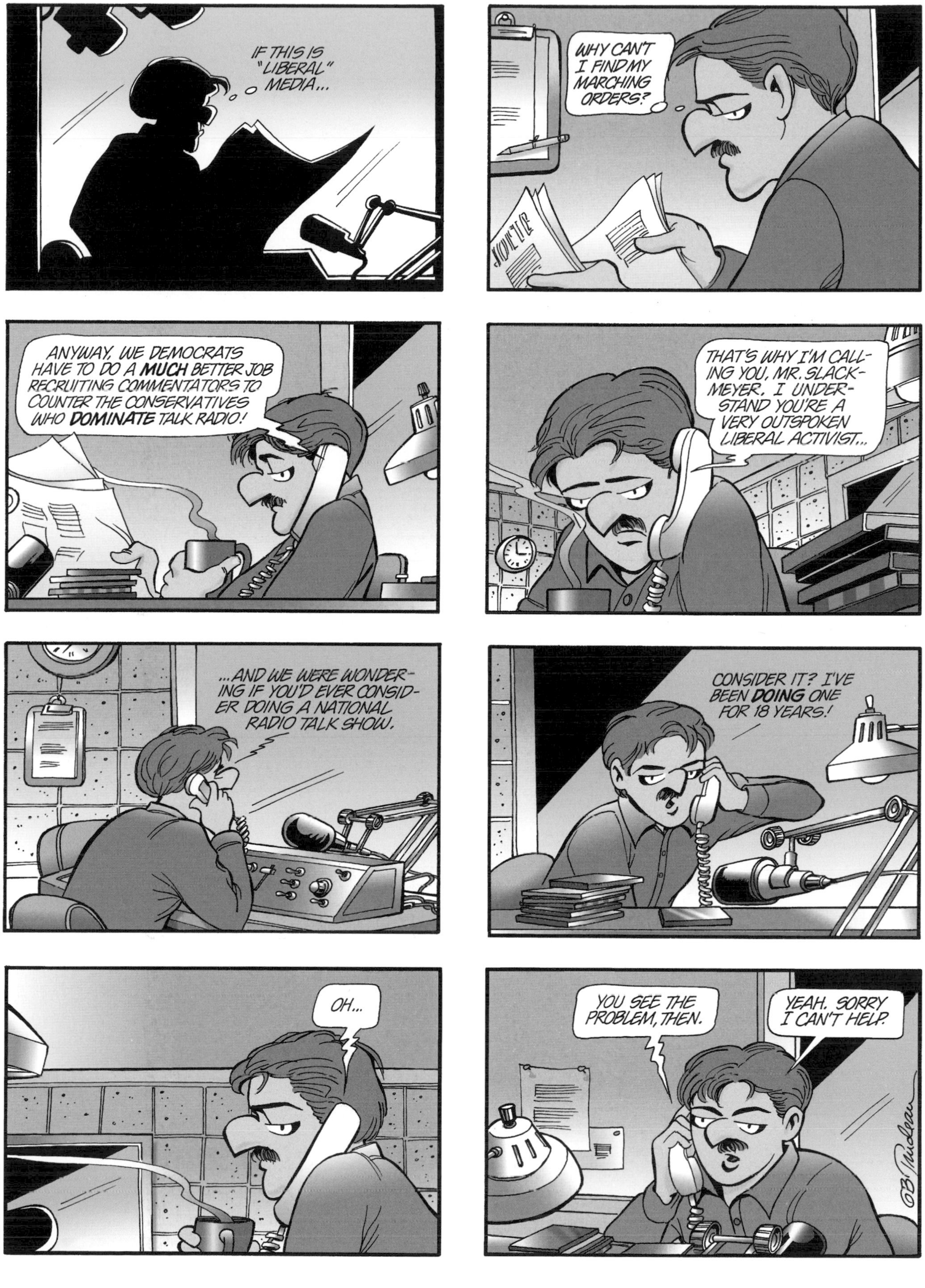
IF THIS IS "LIBERAL" MEDIA...
WHY CAN'T I FIND MY MARCHING ORDERS?
ANYWAY, WE DEMOCRATS HAVE TO DO A **MUCH** BETTER JOB RECRUITING COMMENTATORS TO COUNTER THE CONSERVATIVES WHO **DOMINATE** TALK RADIO!
THAT'S WHY I'M CALLING YOU, MR. SLACKMEYER. I UNDERSTAND YOU'RE A VERY OUTSPOKEN LIBERAL ACTIVIST...
...AND WE WERE WONDERING IF YOU'D EVER CONSIDER DOING A NATIONAL RADIO TALK SHOW.
CONSIDER IT? I'VE BEEN **DOING** ONE FOR 18 YEARS!
OH...
YOU SEE THE PROBLEM, THEN.
YEAH. SORRY I CAN'T HELP.

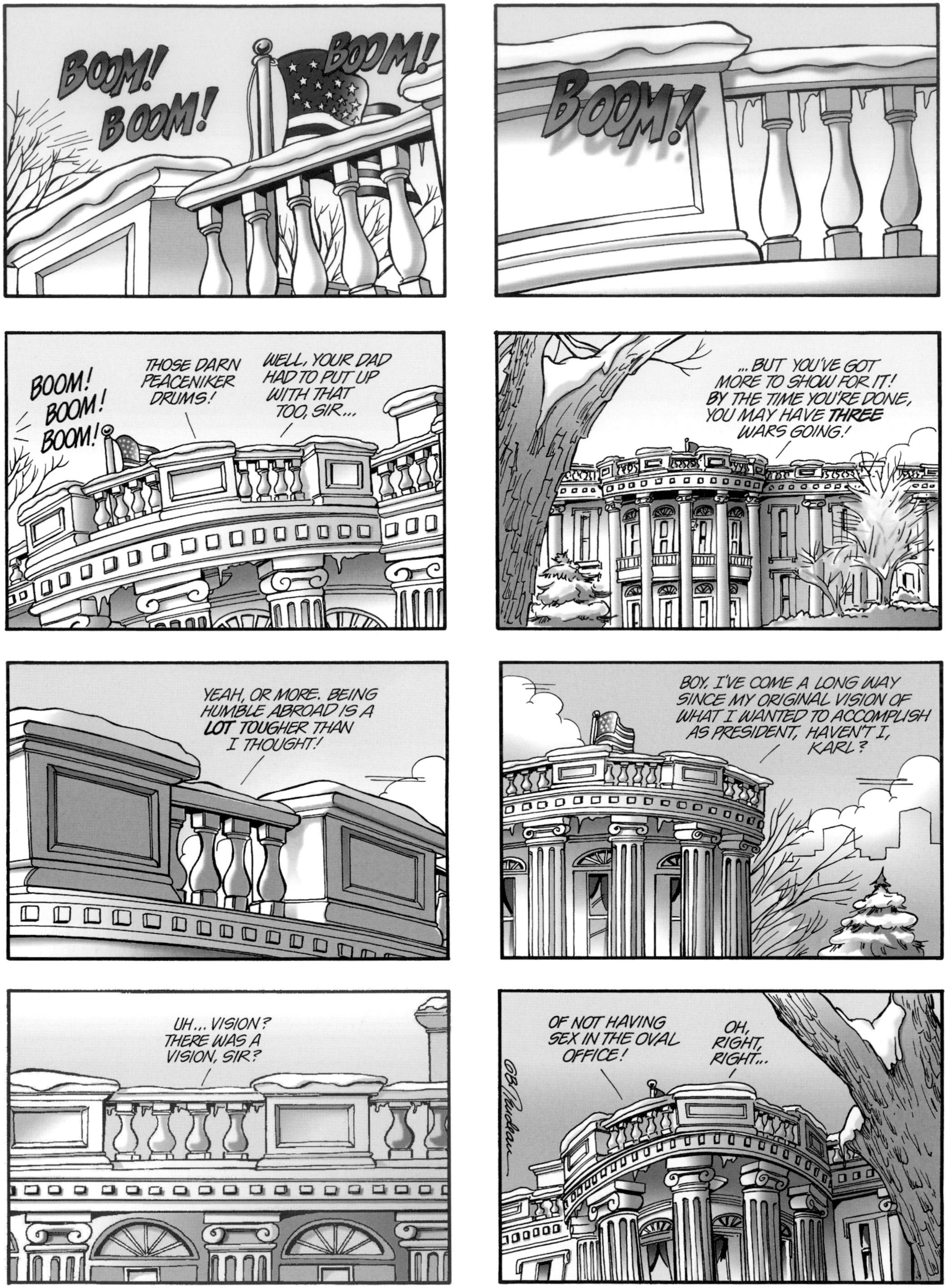
BOOM! BOOM!
BOOM!
BOOM!
BOOM! BOOM! BOOM!
THOSE DARN PEACENIKER DRUMS!
WELL, YOUR DAD HAD TO PUT UP WITH THAT TOO, SIR...
...BUT YOU'VE GOT MORE TO SHOW FOR IT! BY THE TIME YOU'RE DONE, YOU MAY HAVE THREE WARS GOING!
YEAH, OR MORE. BEING HUMBLE ABROAD IS A LOT TOUGHER THAN I THOUGHT!
BOY. I'VE COME A LONG WAY SINCE MY ORIGINAL VISION OF WHAT I WANTED TO ACCOMPLISH AS PRESIDENT, HAVEN'T I, KARL?
UH... VISION? THERE WAS A VISION, SIR?
OF NOT HAVING SEX IN THE OVAL OFFICE!
OH, RIGHT, RIGHT...

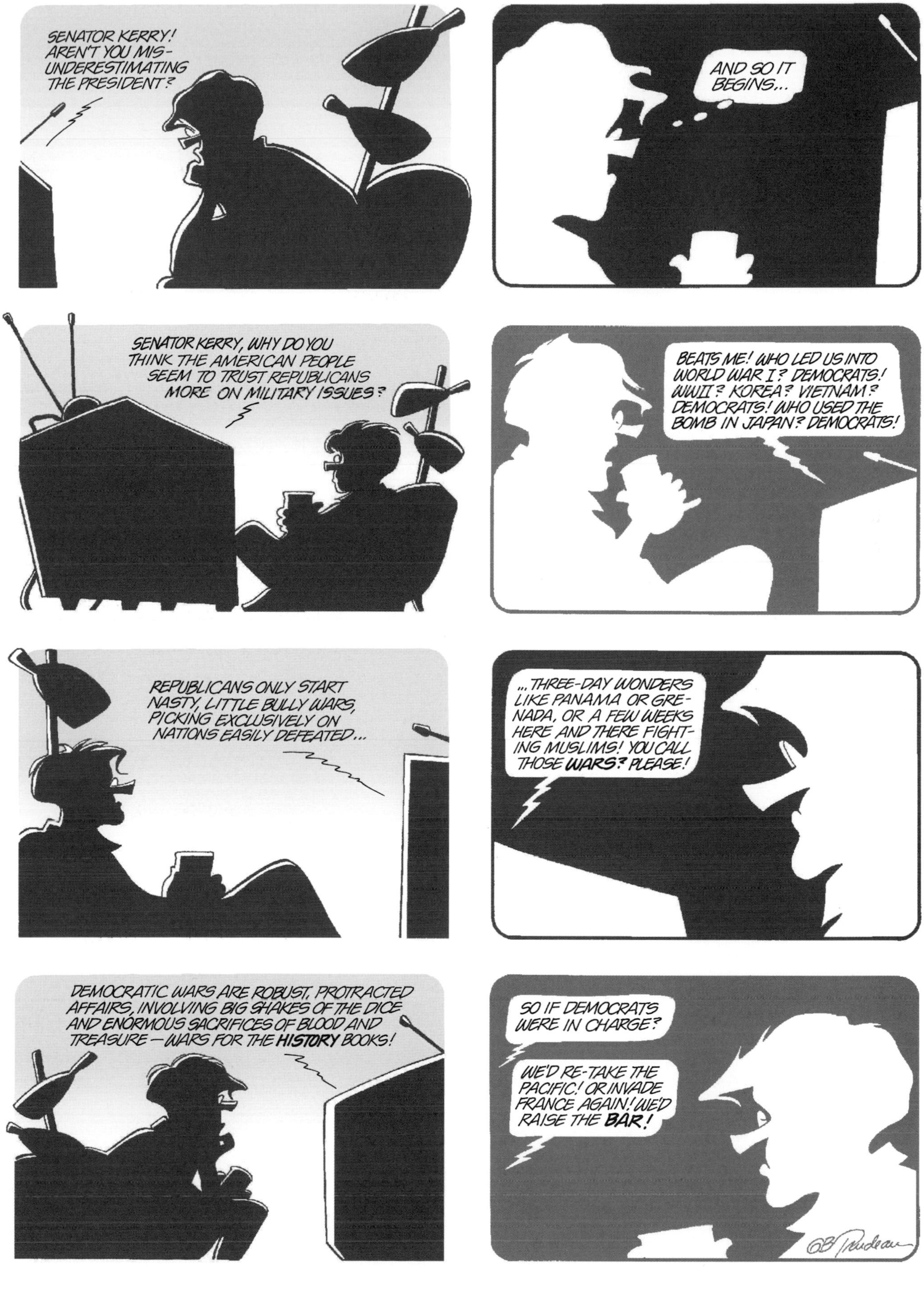
SENATOR KERRY! AREN'T YOU MIS-UNDERESTIMATING THE PRESIDENT?
AND SO IT BEGINS...
SENATOR KERRY, WHY DO YOU THINK THE AMERICAN PEOPLE SEEM TO TRUST REPUBLICANS MORE ON MILITARY ISSUES?
BEATS ME! WHO LED US INTO WORLD WAR I? DEMOCRATS! WWII? KOREA? VIETNAM? DEMOCRATS! WHO USED THE BOMB IN JAPAN? DEMOCRATS!
REPUBLICANS ONLY START NASTY, LITTLE BULLY WARS, PICKING EXCLUSIVELY ON NATIONS EASILY DEFEATED...
...THREE-DAY WONDERS LIKE PANAMA OR GRE-NADA, OR A FEW WEEKS HERE AND THERE FIGHT-ING MUSLIMS! YOU CALL THOSE WARS? PLEASE!
DEMOCRATIC WARS ARE ROBUST, PROTRACTED AFFAIRS, INVOLVING BIG SHAKES OF THE DICE AND ENORMOUS SACRIFICES OF BLOOD AND TREASURE—WARS FOR THE HISTORY BOOKS!
SO IF DEMOCRATS WERE IN CHARGE?
WE'D RE-TAKE THE PACIFIC! OR INVADE FRANCE AGAIN! WE'D RAISE THE BAR!

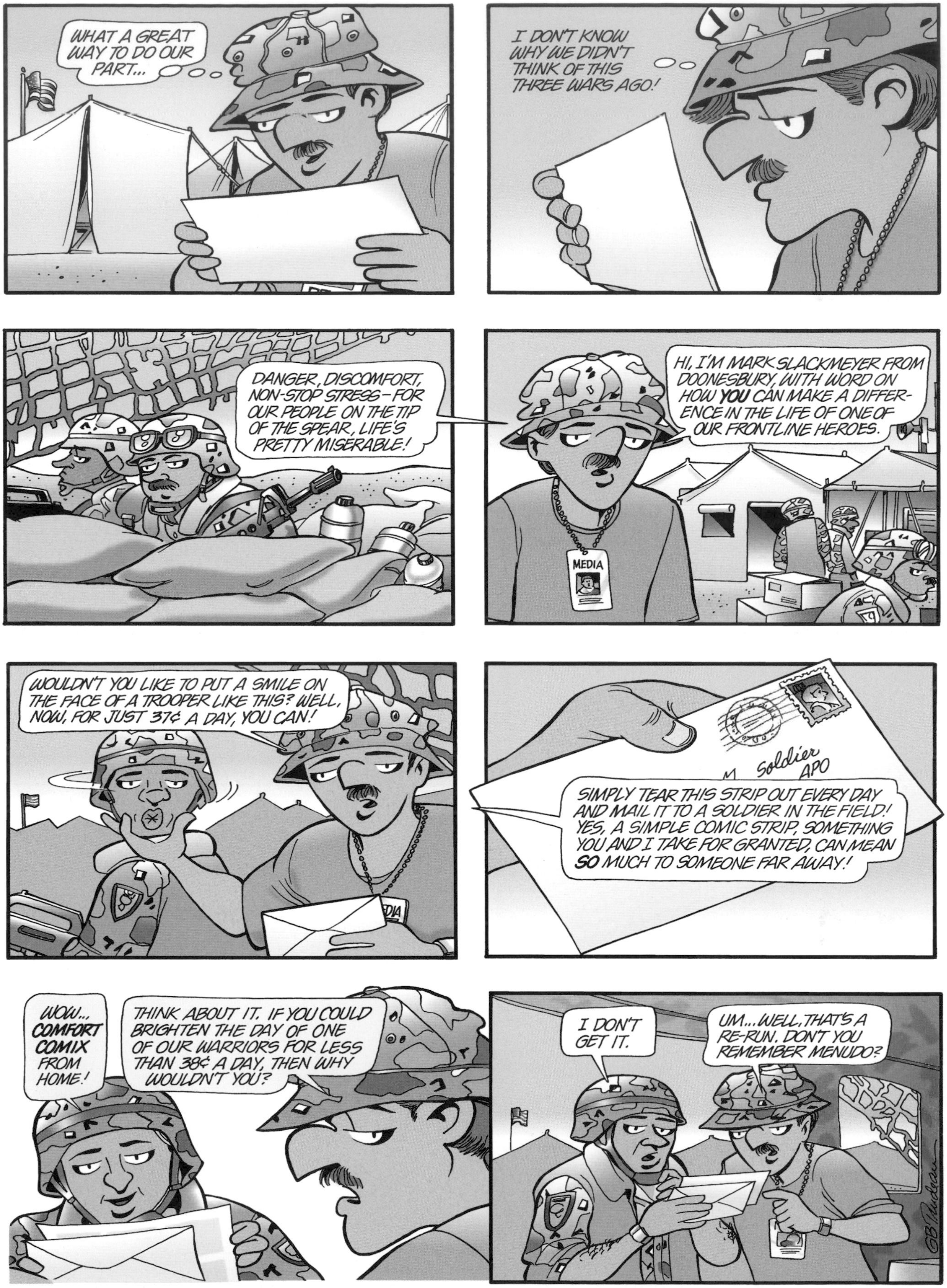
WHAT A GREAT WAY TO DO OUR PART...
I DON'T KNOW WHY WE DIDN'T THINK OF THIS THREE WARS AGO!
DANGER, DISCOMFORT, NON-STOP STRESS–FOR OUR PEOPLE ON THE TIP OF THE SPEAR, LIFE'S PRETTY MISERABLE!
HI, I'M MARK SLACKMEYER FROM DOONESBURY, WITH WORD ON HOW **YOU** CAN MAKE A DIFFERENCE IN THE LIFE OF ONE OF OUR FRONTLINE HEROES.
MEDIA
WOULDN'T YOU LIKE TO PUT A SMILE ON THE FACE OF A TROOPER LIKE THIS? WELL, NOW, FOR JUST 37¢ A DAY, YOU CAN!
Soldier APO
SIMPLY TEAR THIS STRIP OUT EVERY DAY AND MAIL IT TO A SOLDIER IN THE FIELD! YES, A SIMPLE COMIC STRIP, SOMETHING YOU AND I TAKE FOR GRANTED, CAN MEAN **SO** MUCH TO SOMEONE FAR AWAY!
WOW... **COMFORT COMIX** FROM HOME!
THINK ABOUT IT. IF YOU COULD BRIGHTEN THE DAY OF ONE OF OUR WARRIORS FOR LESS THAN 38¢ A DAY, THEN WHY WOULDN'T YOU?
I DON'T GET IT.
UM... WELL, THAT'S A RE-RUN. DON'T YOU REMEMBER MENUDO?

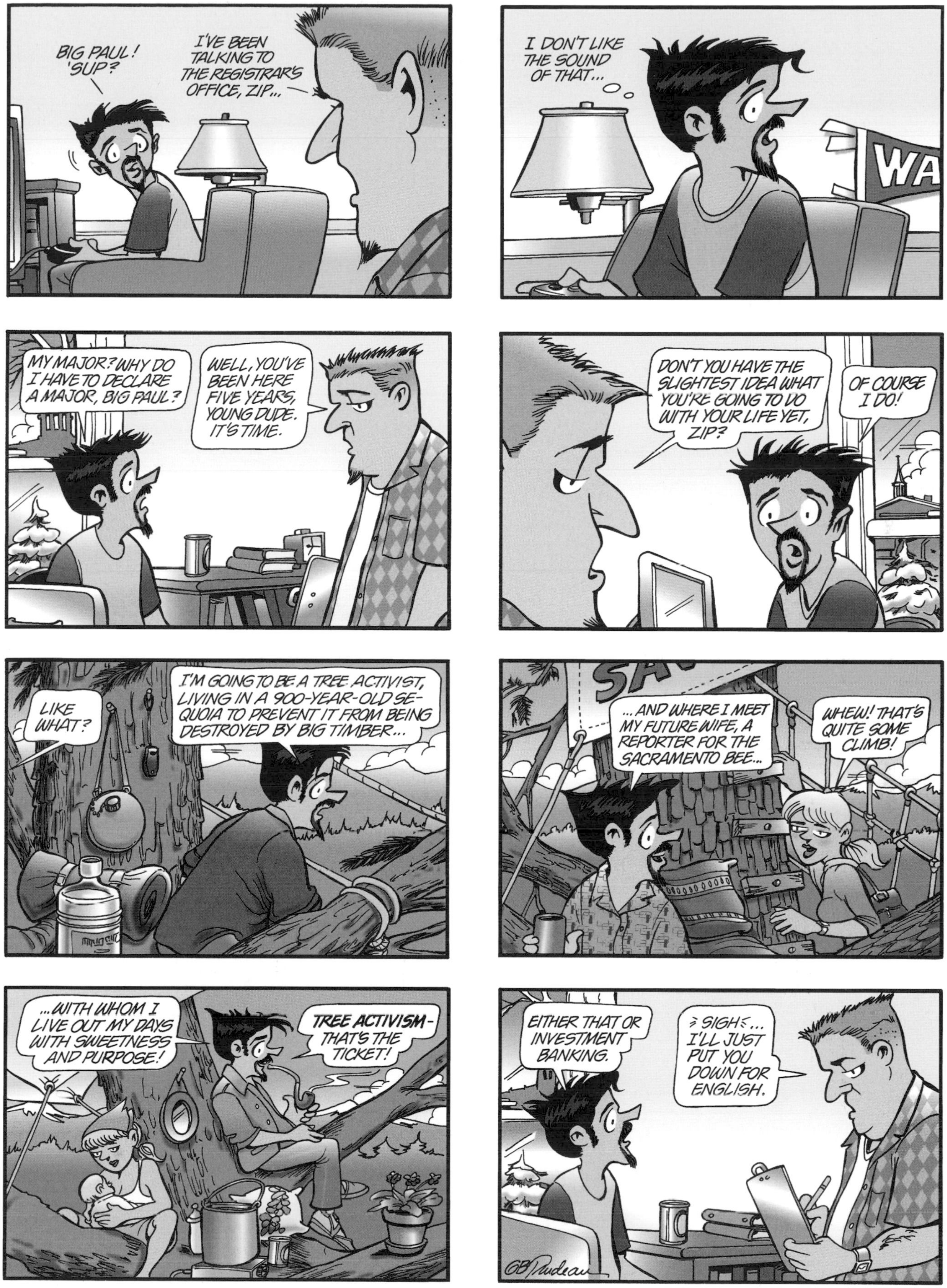

BIG PAUL! 'SUP?
I'VE BEEN TALKING TO THE REGISTRAR'S OFFICE, ZIP...
I DON'T LIKE THE SOUND OF THAT...
WA
MY MAJOR? WHY DO I HAVE TO DECLARE A MAJOR, BIG PAUL?
WELL, YOU'VE BEEN HERE FIVE YEARS, YOUNG DUDE. IT'S TIME.
DON'T YOU HAVE THE SLIGHTEST IDEA WHAT YOU'RE GOING TO DO WITH YOUR LIFE YET, ZIP?
OF COURSE I DO!
LIKE WHAT?
I'M GOING TO BE A TREE ACTIVIST, LIVING IN A 900-YEAR-OLD SEQUOIA TO PREVENT IT FROM BEING DESTROYED BY BIG TIMBER...
...AND WHERE I MEET MY FUTURE WIFE, A REPORTER FOR THE SACRAMENTO BEE...
WHEW! THAT'S QUITE SOME CLIMB!
...WITH WHOM I LIVE OUT MY DAYS WITH SWEETNESS AND PURPOSE!
TREE ACTIVISM - THAT'S THE TICKET!
EITHER THAT OR INVESTMENT BANKING.
SIGH... I'LL JUST PUT YOU DOWN FOR ENGLISH.
GBTrudeau

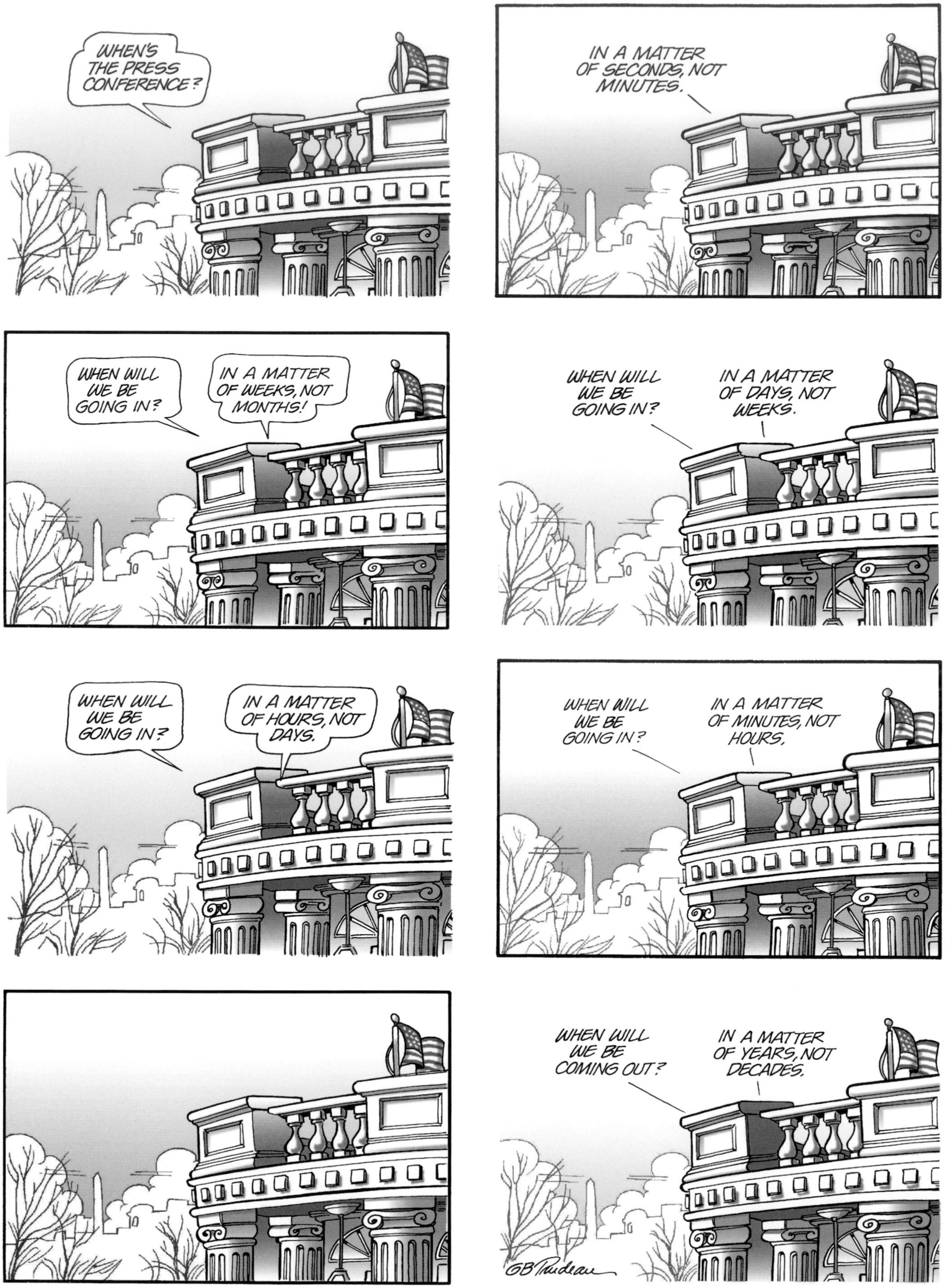

WHEN'S THE PRESS CONFERENCE?
IN A MATTER OF SECONDS, NOT MINUTES.
WHEN WILL WE BE GOING IN?
IN A MATTER OF WEEKS, NOT MONTHS!
WHEN WILL WE BE GOING IN?
IN A MATTER OF DAYS, NOT WEEKS.
WHEN WILL WE BE GOING IN?
IN A MATTER OF HOURS, NOT DAYS.
WHEN WILL WE BE GOING IN?
IN A MATTER OF MINUTES, NOT HOURS.
WHEN WILL WE BE COMING OUT?
IN A MATTER OF YEARS, NOT DECADES.
GB Trudeau

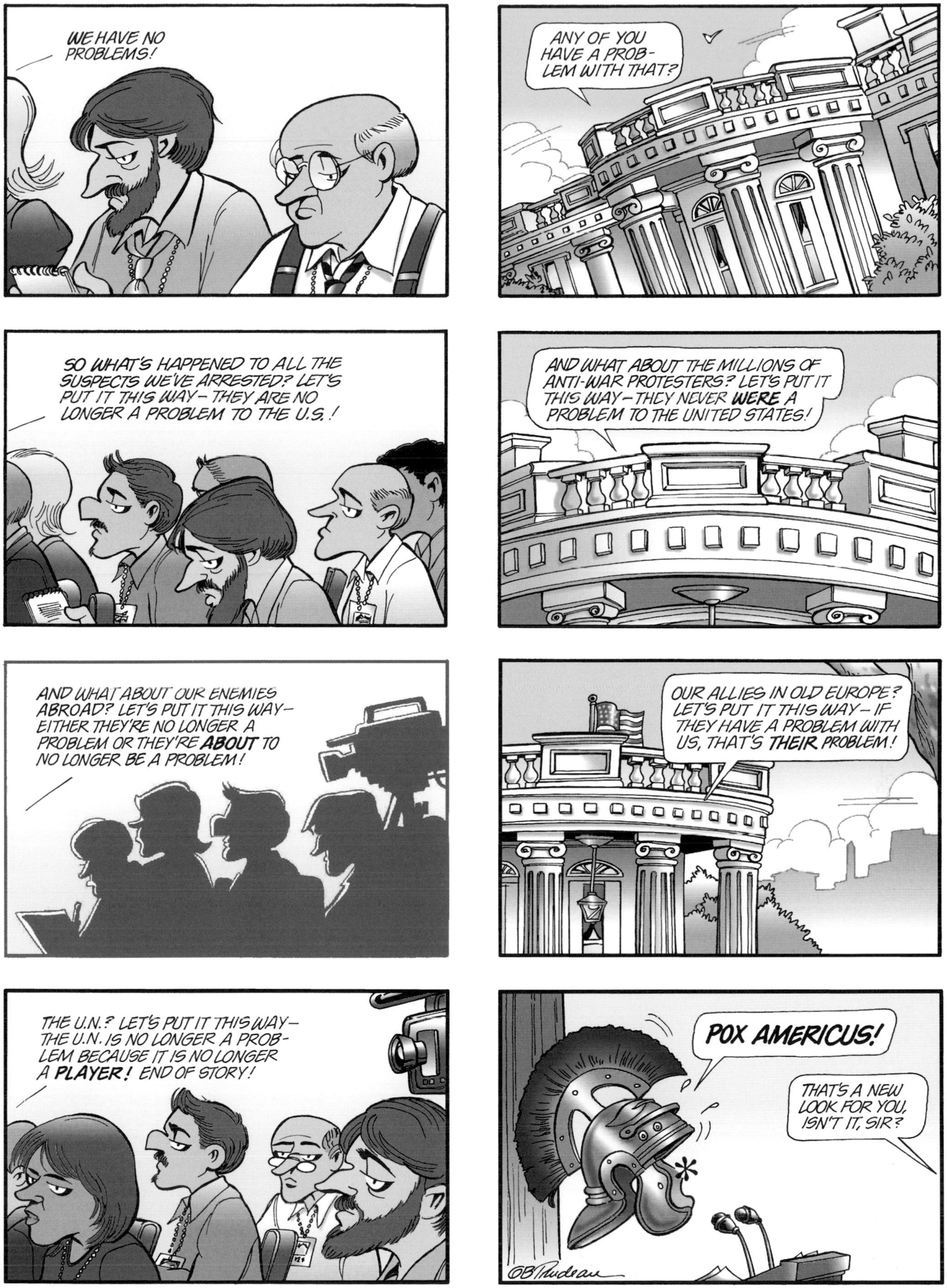
WE HAVE NO PROBLEMS!
ANY OF YOU HAVE A PROBLEM WITH THAT?
SO WHAT'S HAPPENED TO ALL THE SUSPECTS WE'VE ARRESTED? LET'S PUT IT THIS WAY – THEY ARE NO LONGER A PROBLEM TO THE U.S.!
AND WHAT ABOUT THE MILLIONS OF ANTI-WAR PROTESTERS? LET'S PUT IT THIS WAY – THEY NEVER WERE A PROBLEM TO THE UNITED STATES!
AND WHAT ABOUT OUR ENEMIES ABROAD? LET'S PUT IT THIS WAY – EITHER THEY'RE NO LONGER A PROBLEM OR THEY'RE ABOUT TO NO LONGER BE A PROBLEM!
OUR ALLIES IN OLD EUROPE? LET'S PUT IT THIS WAY – IF THEY HAVE A PROBLEM WITH US, THAT'S THEIR PROBLEM!
THE U.N.? LET'S PUT IT THIS WAY – THE U.N. IS NO LONGER A PROBLEM BECAUSE IT IS NO LONGER A PLAYER! END OF STORY!
POX AMERICUS!
THAT'S A NEW LOOK FOR YOU, ISN'T IT, SIR?
©B Trudeau

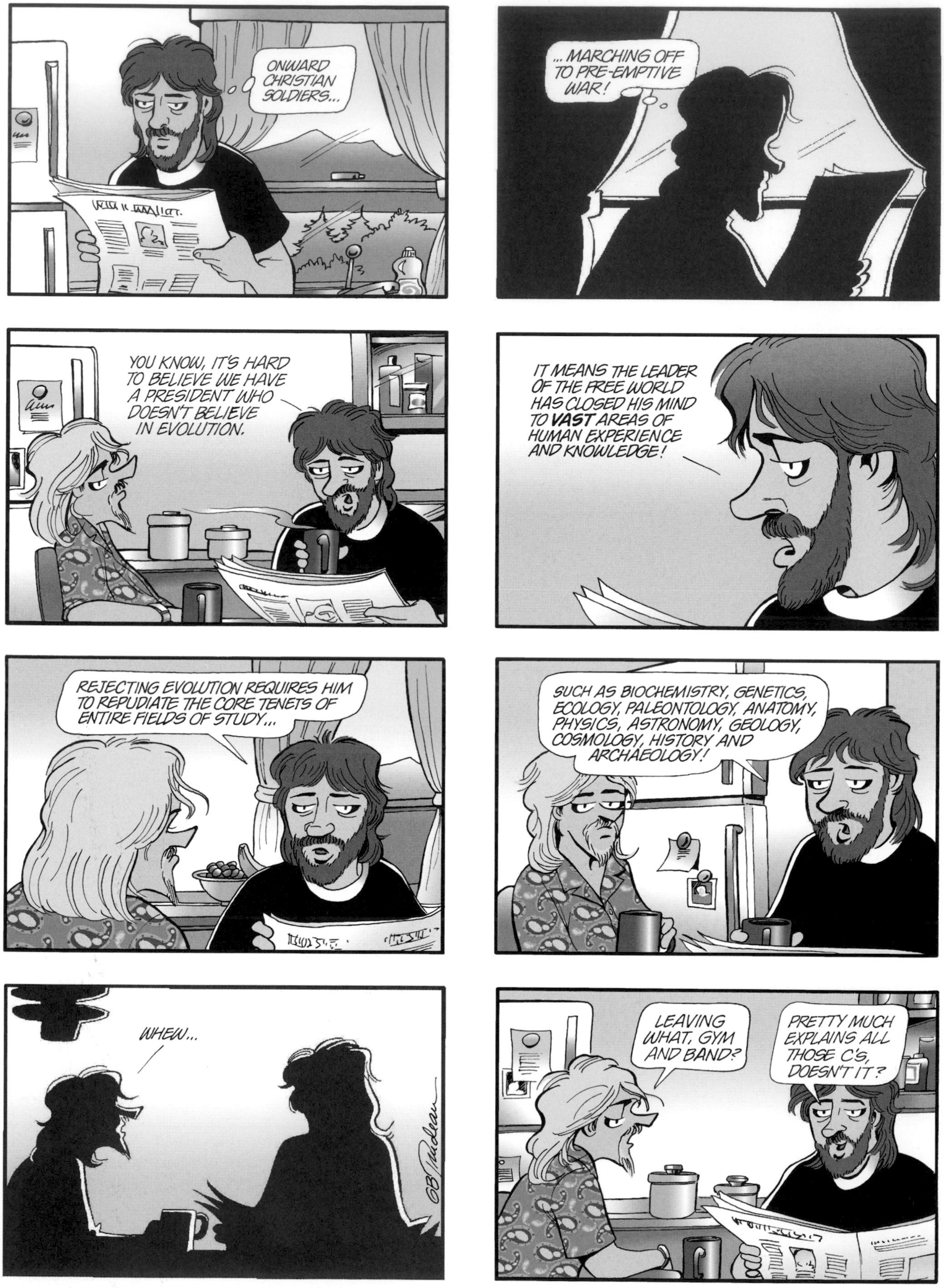
ONWARD CHRISTIAN SOLDIERS...
...MARCHING OFF TO PRE-EMPTIVE WAR!
YOU KNOW, IT'S HARD TO BELIEVE WE HAVE A PRESIDENT WHO DOESN'T BELIEVE IN EVOLUTION.
IT MEANS THE LEADER OF THE FREE WORLD HAS CLOSED HIS MIND TO VAST AREAS OF HUMAN EXPERIENCE AND KNOWLEDGE!
REJECTING EVOLUTION REQUIRES HIM TO REPUDIATE THE CORE TENETS OF ENTIRE FIELDS OF STUDY...
SUCH AS BIOCHEMISTRY, GENETICS, ECOLOGY, PALEONTOLOGY, ANATOMY, PHYSICS, ASTRONOMY, GEOLOGY, COSMOLOGY, HISTORY AND ARCHAEOLOGY!
WHEW...
GBTrudeau
LEAVING WHAT, GYM AND BAND?
PRETTY MUCH EXPLAINS ALL THOSE C'S, DOESN'T IT?

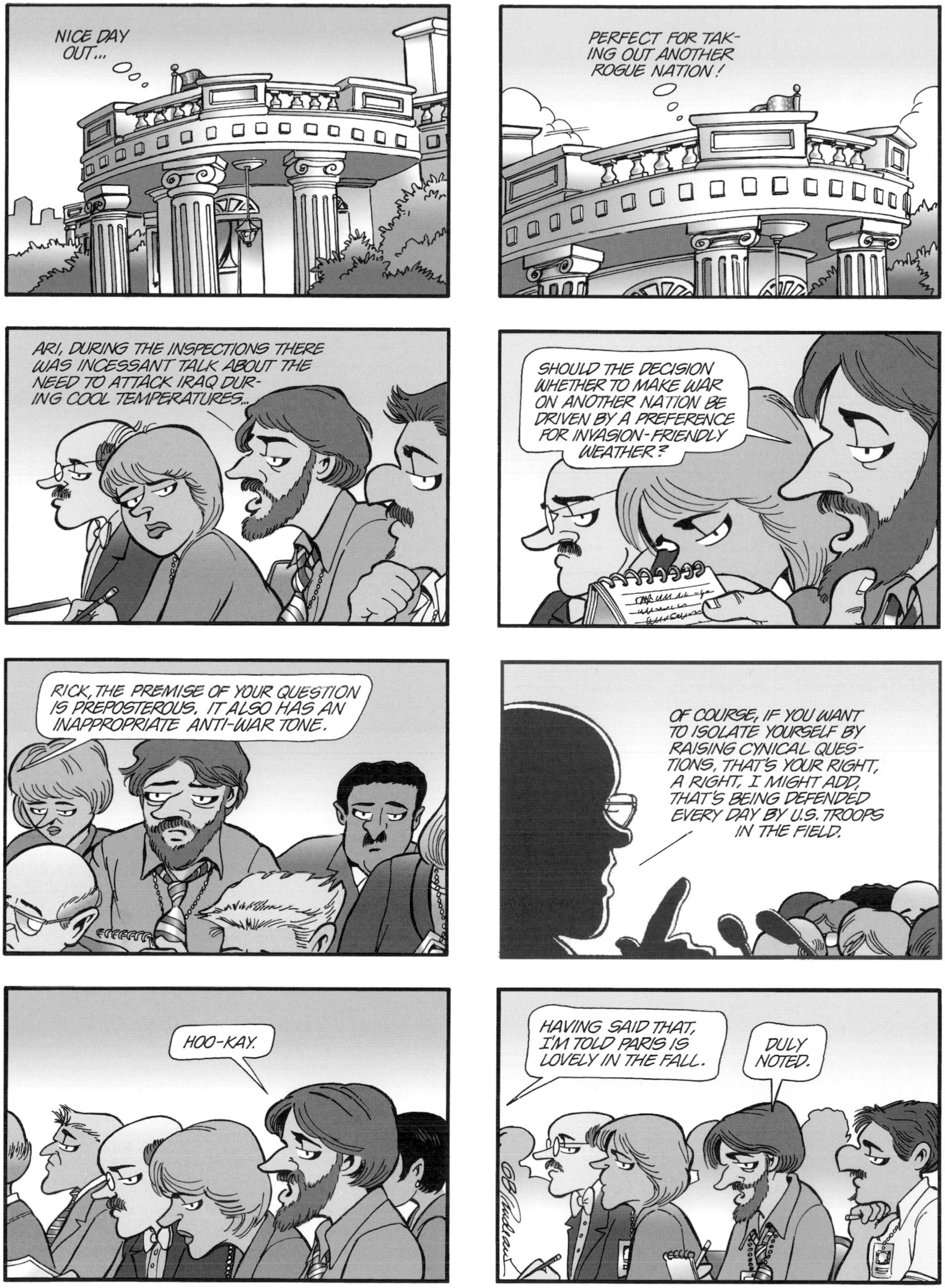
NICE DAY OUT...
PERFECT FOR TAKING OUT ANOTHER ROGUE NATION!
ARI, DURING THE INSPECTIONS THERE WAS INCESSANT TALK ABOUT THE NEED TO ATTACK IRAQ DURING COOL TEMPERATURES...
SHOULD THE DECISION WHETHER TO MAKE WAR ON ANOTHER NATION BE DRIVEN BY A PREFERENCE FOR INVASION-FRIENDLY WEATHER?
RICK, THE PREMISE OF YOUR QUESTION IS PREPOSTEROUS. IT ALSO HAS AN INAPPROPRIATE ANTI-WAR TONE.
OF COURSE, IF YOU WANT TO ISOLATE YOURSELF BY RAISING CYNICAL QUESTIONS, THAT'S YOUR RIGHT, A RIGHT, I MIGHT ADD, THAT'S BEING DEFENDED EVERY DAY BY U.S. TROOPS IN THE FIELD.
HOO-KAY.
HAVING SAID THAT, I'M TOLD PARIS IS LOVELY IN THE FALL.
DULY NOTED.

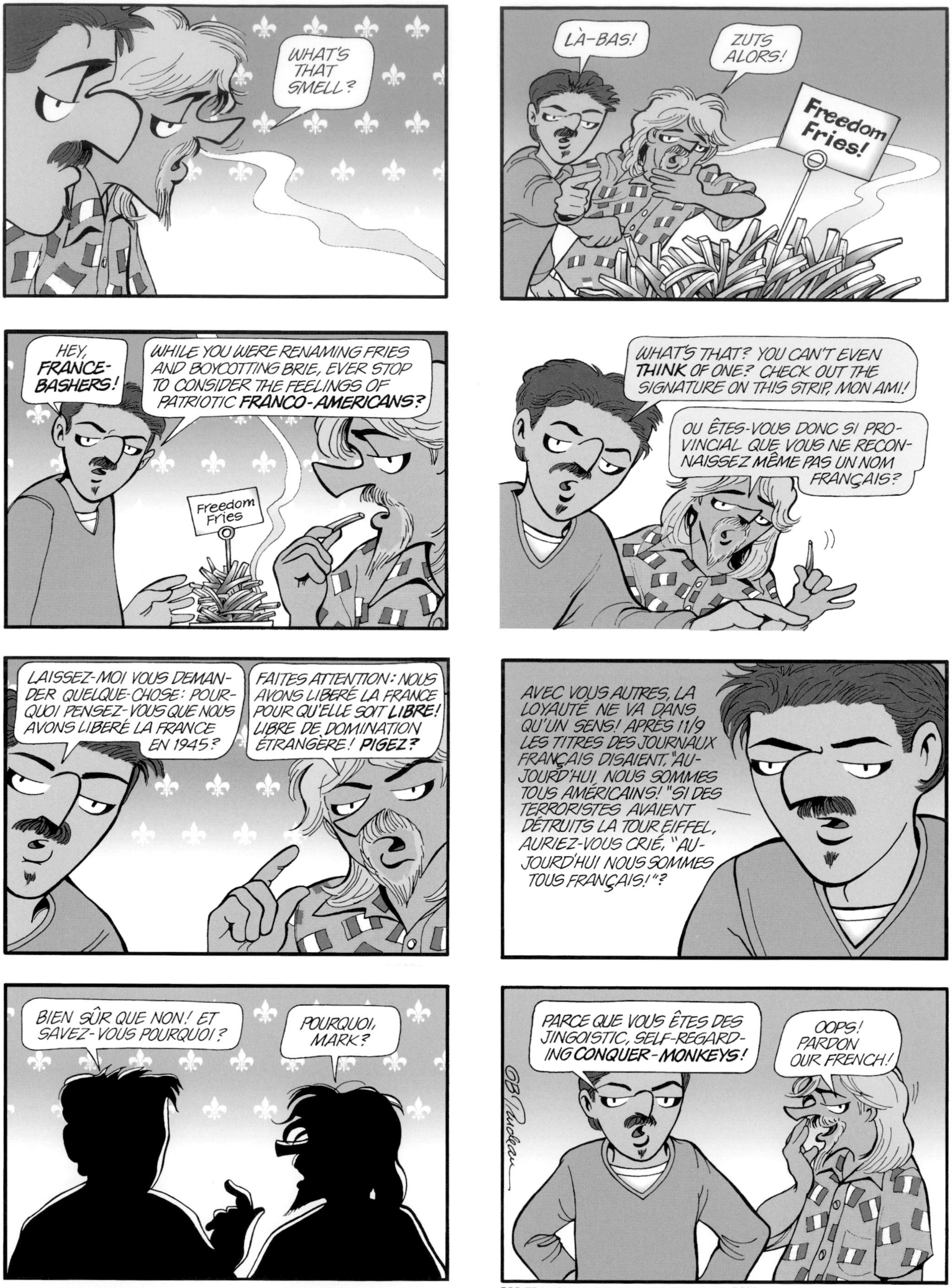
WHAT'S THAT SMELL?
LÀ-BAS!
ZUTS ALORS!
Freedom Fries!
HEY, FRANCE-BASHERS!
WHILE YOU WERE RENAMING FRIES AND BOYCOTTING BRIE, EVER STOP TO CONSIDER THE FEELINGS OF PATRIOTIC FRANCO-AMERICANS?
Freedom Fries
WHAT'S THAT? YOU CAN'T EVEN THINK OF ONE? CHECK OUT THE SIGNATURE ON THIS STRIP, MON AMI!
OU ÊTES-VOUS DONC SI PROVINCIAL QUE VOUS NE RECONNAISSEZ MÊME PAS UN NOM FRANÇAIS?
LAISSEZ-MOI VOUS DEMANDER QUELQUE-CHOSE: POURQUOI PENSEZ-VOUS QUE NOUS AVONS LIBERÉ LA FRANCE EN 1945?
FAITES ATTENTION: NOUS AVONS LIBERÉ LA FRANCE POUR QU'ELLE SOIT LIBRE! LIBRE DE DOMINATION ÉTRANGÈRE! PIGEZ?
AVEC VOUS AUTRES, LA LOYAUTÉ NE VA DANS QU'UN SENS! APRÈS 11/9 LES TITRES DES JOURNAUX FRANÇAIS DISAIENT, "AUJOURD'HUI, NOUS SOMMES TOUS AMÉRICAINS!" SI DES TERRORISTES AVAIENT DÉTRUITS LA TOUR EIFFEL, AURIEZ-VOUS CRIÉ, "AUJOURD'HUI NOUS SOMMES TOUS FRANÇAIS!"?
BIEN SÛR QUE NON! ET SAVEZ-VOUS POURQUOI?
POURQUOI, MARK?
PARCE QUE VOUS ÊTES DES JINGOISTIC, SELF-REGARDING CONQUER-MONKEYS!
OOPS! PARDON OUR FRENCH!

FOR TRANSLATION GO TO: DOONESBURY.COM

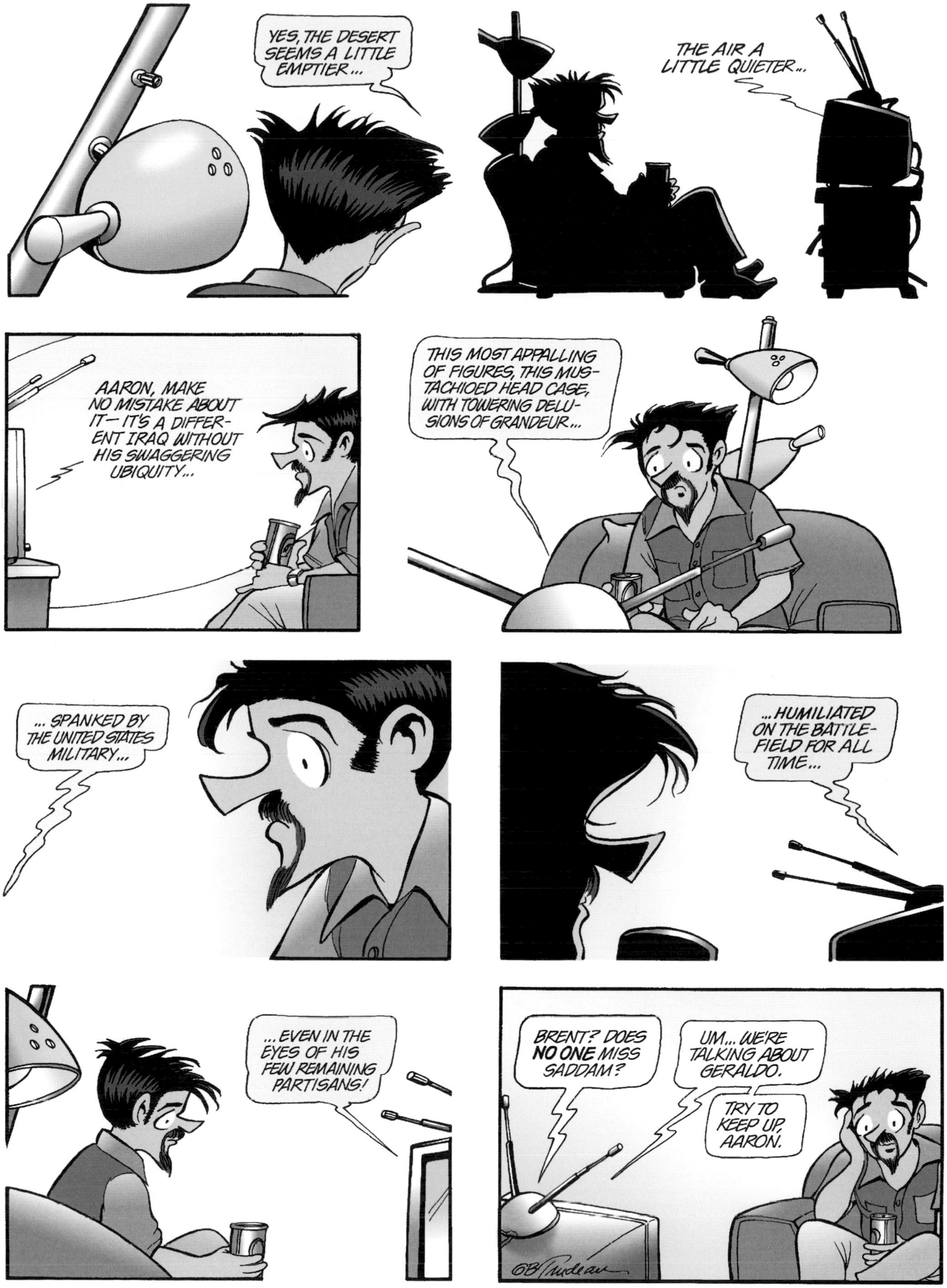
YES, THE DESERT SEEMS A LITTLE EMPTIER...
THE AIR A LITTLE QUIETER...
AARON, MAKE NO MISTAKE ABOUT IT— IT'S A DIFFERENT IRAQ WITHOUT HIS SWAGGERING UBIQUITY...
THIS MOST APPALLING OF FIGURES, THIS MUSTACHIOED HEAD CASE, WITH TOWERING DELUSIONS OF GRANDEUR...
... SPANKED BY THE UNITED STATES MILITARY...
... HUMILIATED ON THE BATTLEFIELD FOR ALL TIME...
... EVEN IN THE EYES OF HIS FEW REMAINING PARTISANS!
BRENT? DOES NO ONE MISS SADDAM?
UM... WE'RE TALKING ABOUT GERALDO.
TRY TO KEEP UP, AARON.
©B. Trudeau

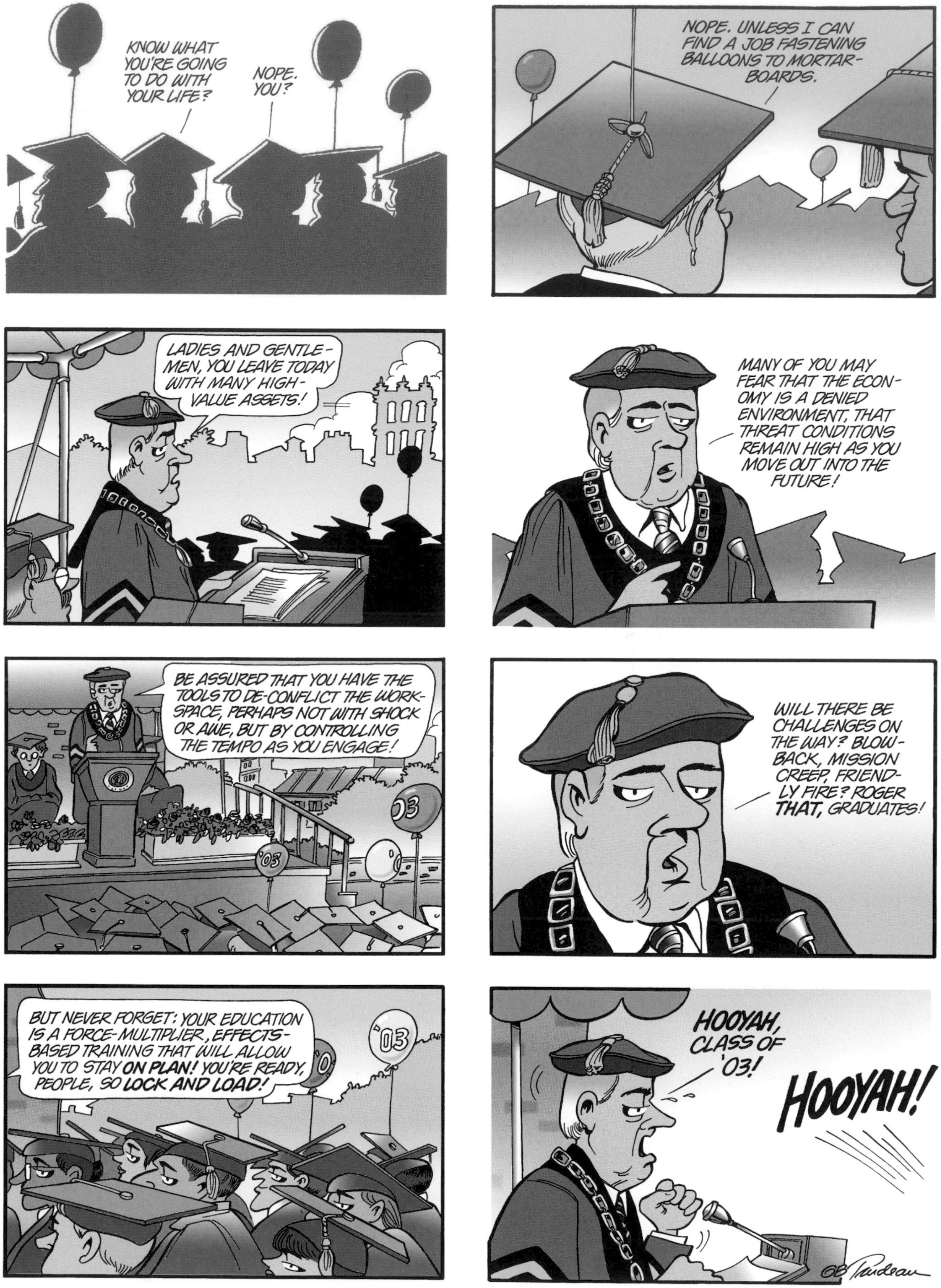
KNOW WHAT YOU'RE GOING TO DO WITH YOUR LIFE?
NOPE. YOU?
NOPE. UNLESS I CAN FIND A JOB FASTENING BALLOONS TO MORTAR-BOARDS.
LADIES AND GENTLE-MEN, YOU LEAVE TODAY WITH MANY HIGH-VALUE ASSETS!
MANY OF YOU MAY FEAR THAT THE ECON-OMY IS A DENIED ENVIRONMENT, THAT THREAT CONDITIONS REMAIN HIGH AS YOU MOVE OUT INTO THE FUTURE!
BE ASSURED THAT YOU HAVE THE TOOLS TO DE-CONFLICT THE WORK-SPACE, PERHAPS NOT WITH SHOCK OR AWE, BUT BY CONTROLLING THE TEMPO AS YOU ENGAGE!
'03
'03
WILL THERE BE CHALLENGES ON THE WAY? BLOW-BACK, MISSION CREEP, FRIEND-LY FIRE? ROGER **THAT,** GRADUATES!
BUT NEVER FORGET: YOUR EDUCATION IS A FORCE-MULTIPLIER, EFFECTS-BASED TRAINING THAT WILL ALLOW YOU TO STAY **ON PLAN!** YOU'RE READY, PEOPLE, SO **LOCK AND LOAD!**
'03
HOOYAH, CLASS OF '03!
HOOYAH!
©B Trudeau

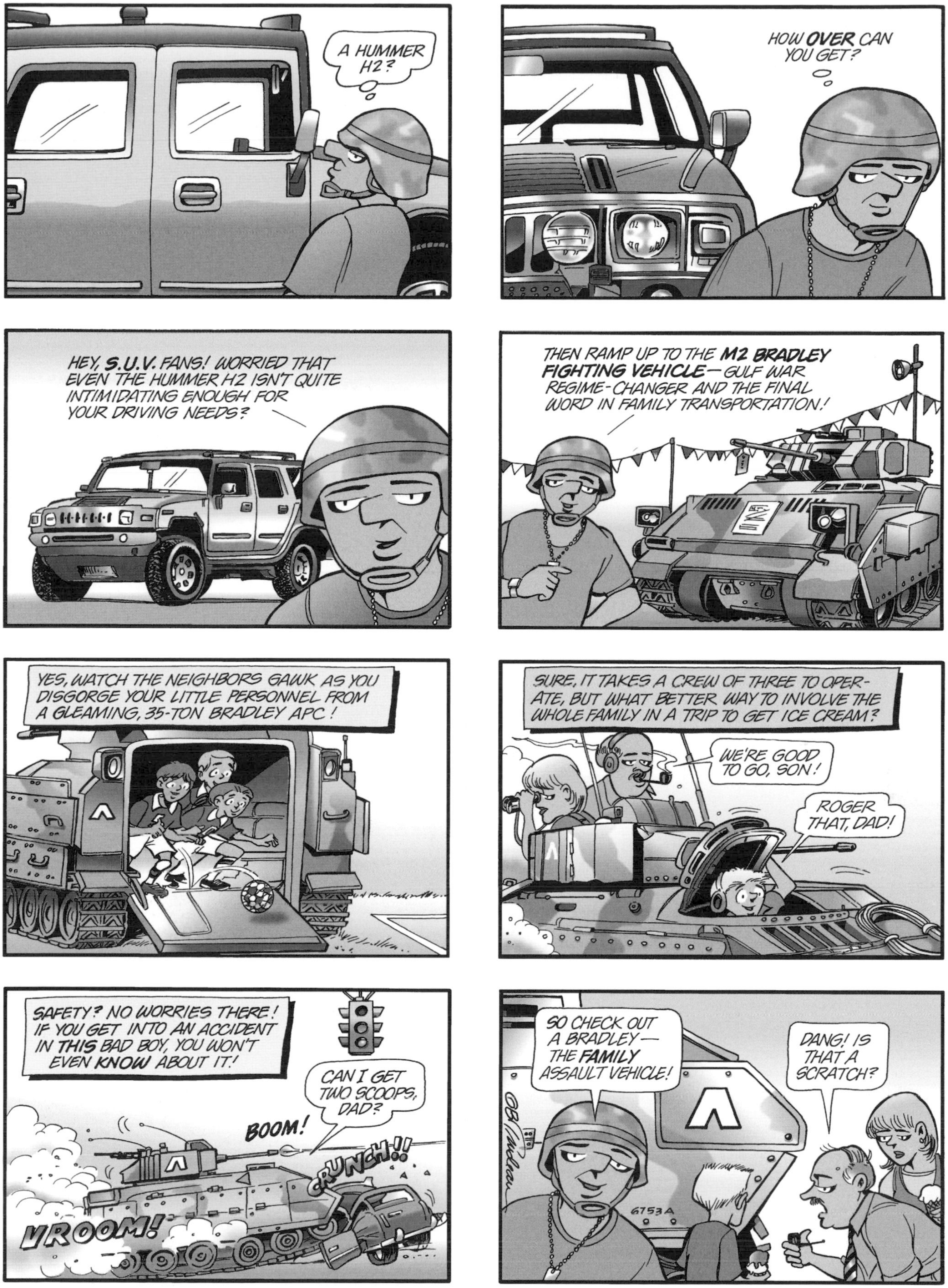

A HUMMER H2?
HOW OVER CAN YOU GET?
HEY, S.U.V. FANS! WORRIED THAT EVEN THE HUMMER H2 ISN'T QUITE INTIMIDATING ENOUGH FOR YOUR DRIVING NEEDS?
THEN RAMP UP TO THE M2 BRADLEY FIGHTING VEHICLE— GULF WAR REGIME-CHANGER AND THE FINAL WORD IN FAMILY TRANSPORTATION!
YES, WATCH THE NEIGHBORS GAWK AS YOU DISGORGE YOUR LITTLE PERSONNEL FROM A GLEAMING, 35-TON BRADLEY APC!
SURE, IT TAKES A CREW OF THREE TO OPERATE, BUT WHAT BETTER WAY TO INVOLVE THE WHOLE FAMILY IN A TRIP TO GET ICE CREAM?
WE'RE GOOD TO GO, SON!
ROGER THAT, DAD!
SAFETY? NO WORRIES THERE! IF YOU GET INTO AN ACCIDENT IN THIS BAD BOY, YOU WON'T EVEN KNOW ABOUT IT!
CAN I GET TWO SCOOPS, DAD?
BOOM!
CRUNCH!!
VROOM!
SO CHECK OUT A BRADLEY— THE FAMILY ASSAULT VEHICLE!
DANG! IS THAT A SCRATCH?
6753A

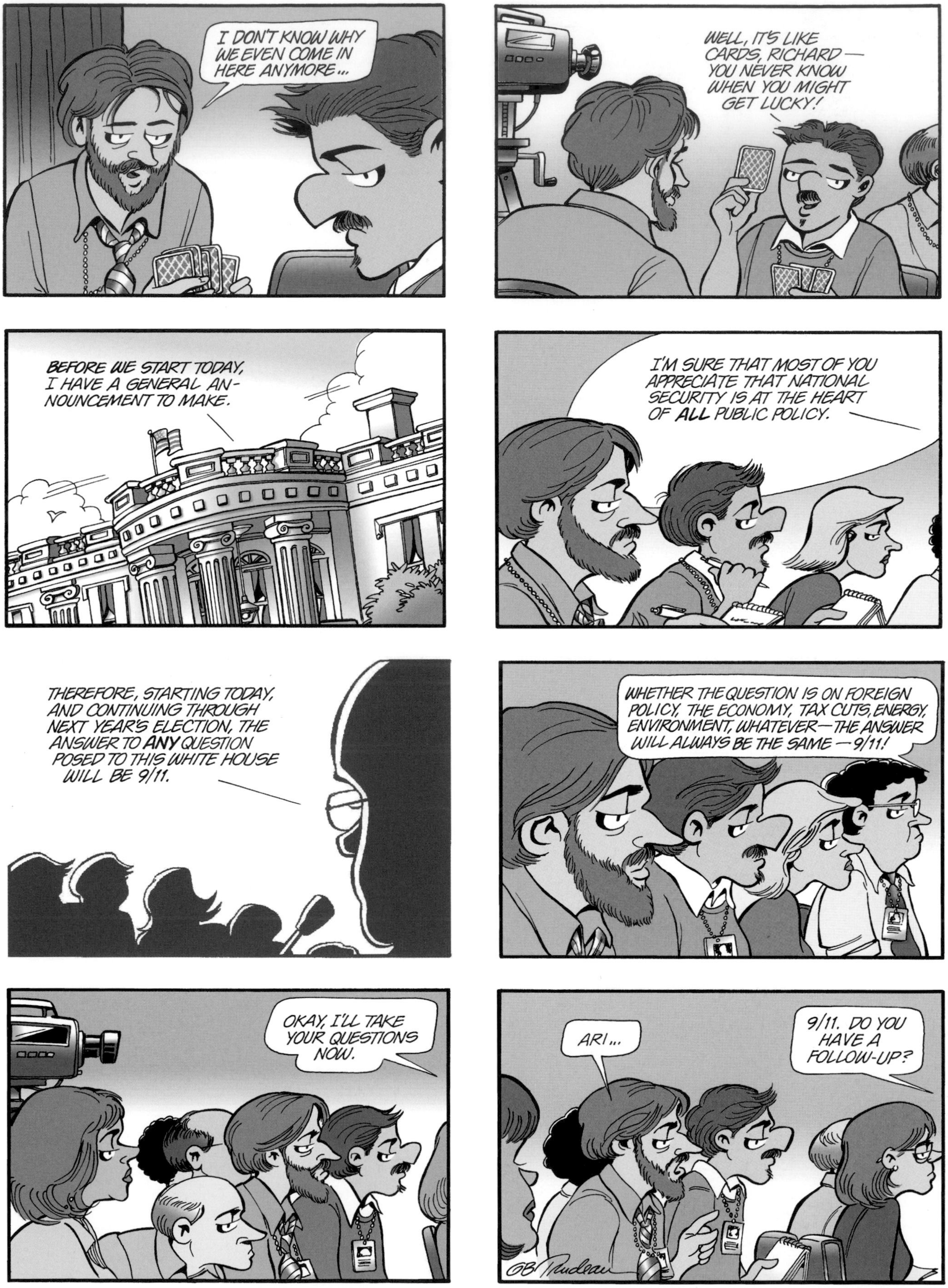

I DON'T KNOW WHY WE EVEN COME IN HERE ANYMORE...
WELL, IT'S LIKE CARDS, RICHARD— YOU NEVER KNOW WHEN YOU MIGHT GET LUCKY!
BEFORE WE START TODAY, I HAVE A GENERAL ANNOUNCEMENT TO MAKE.
I'M SURE THAT MOST OF YOU APPRECIATE THAT NATIONAL SECURITY IS AT THE HEART OF ALL PUBLIC POLICY.
THEREFORE, STARTING TODAY, AND CONTINUING THROUGH NEXT YEAR'S ELECTION, THE ANSWER TO ANY QUESTION POSED TO THIS WHITE HOUSE WILL BE 9/11.
WHETHER THE QUESTION IS ON FOREIGN POLICY, THE ECONOMY, TAX CUTS, ENERGY, ENVIRONMENT, WHATEVER—THE ANSWER WILL ALWAYS BE THE SAME—9/11!
OKAY, I'LL TAKE YOUR QUESTIONS NOW.
ARI...
9/11. DO YOU HAVE A FOLLOW-UP?

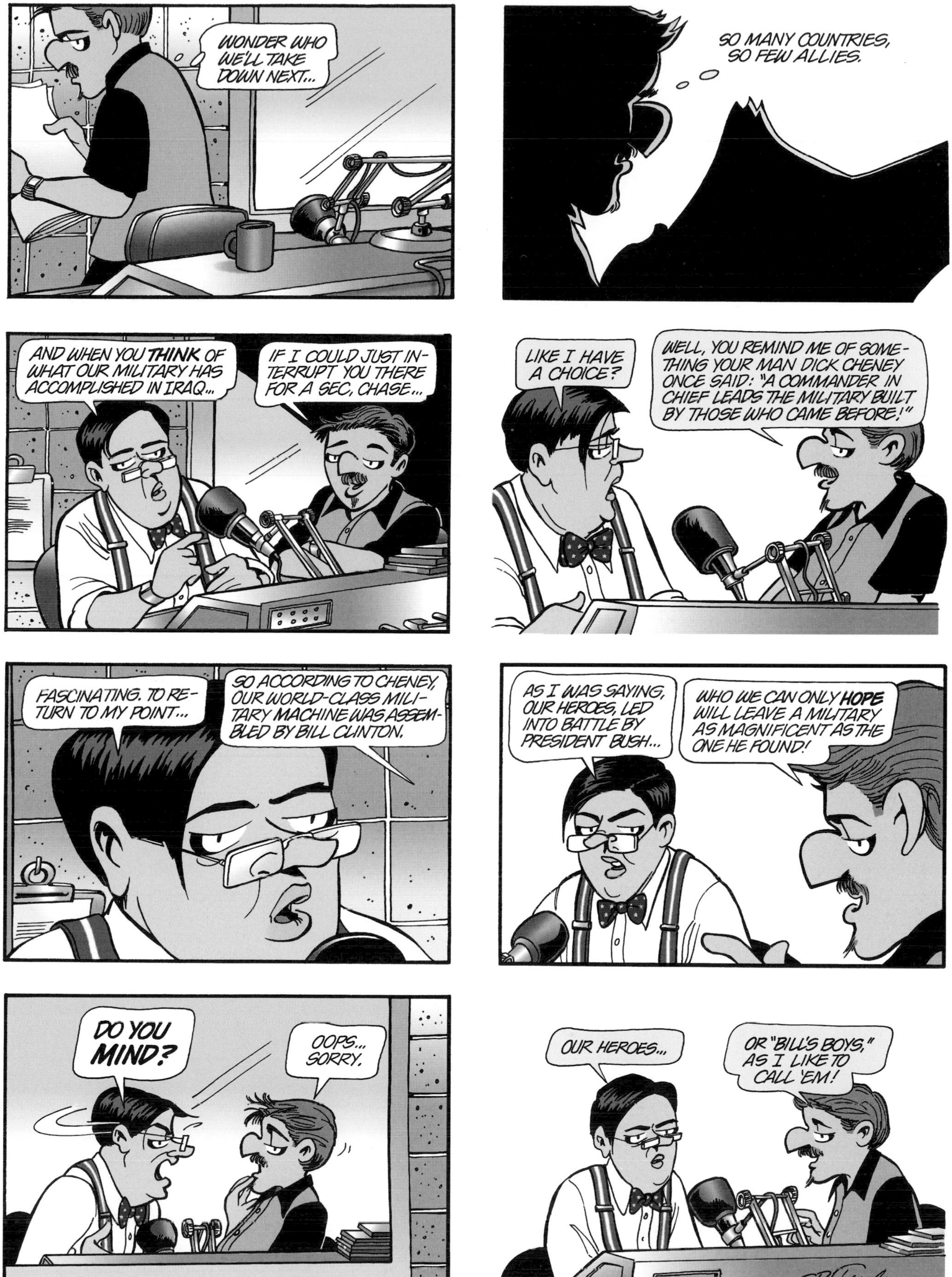
WONDER WHO WE'LL TAKE DOWN NEXT...
SO MANY COUNTRIES, SO FEW ALLIES.
AND WHEN YOU **THINK** OF WHAT OUR MILITARY HAS ACCOMPLISHED IN IRAQ...
IF I COULD JUST INTERRUPT YOU THERE FOR A SEC, CHASE...
LIKE I HAVE A CHOICE?
WELL, YOU REMIND ME OF SOMETHING YOUR MAN DICK CHENEY ONCE SAID: "A COMMANDER IN CHIEF LEADS THE MILITARY BUILT BY THOSE WHO CAME BEFORE!"
FASCINATING. TO RETURN TO MY POINT...
SO ACCORDING TO CHENEY, OUR WORLD-CLASS MILITARY MACHINE WAS ASSEMBLED BY BILL CLINTON.
AS I WAS SAYING, OUR HEROES, LED INTO BATTLE BY PRESIDENT BUSH...
WHO WE CAN ONLY **HOPE** WILL LEAVE A MILITARY AS MAGNIFICENT AS THE ONE HE FOUND!
**DO YOU MIND?**
OOPS... SORRY.
OUR HEROES...
OR "BILL'S BOYS," AS I LIKE TO CALL 'EM!
GB Trudeau

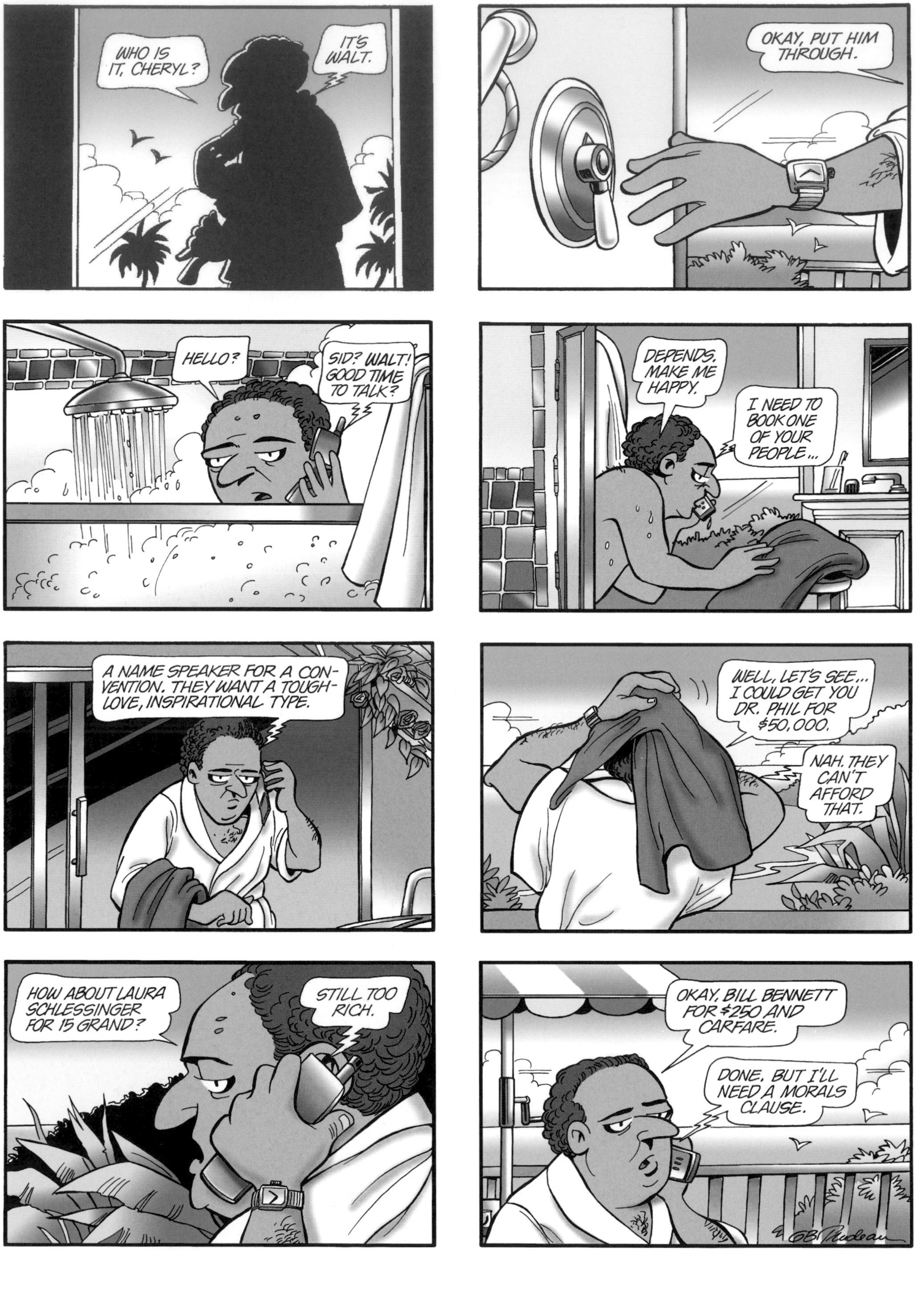
WHO IS IT, CHERYL?
IT'S WALT.
OKAY, PUT HIM THROUGH.
HELLO?
SID? WALT! GOOD TIME TO TALK?
DEPENDS. MAKE ME HAPPY.
I NEED TO BOOK ONE OF YOUR PEOPLE...
A NAME SPEAKER FOR A CONVENTION. THEY WANT A TOUGH-LOVE, INSPIRATIONAL TYPE.
WELL, LET'S SEE... I COULD GET YOU DR. PHIL FOR $50,000.
NAH. THEY CAN'T AFFORD THAT.
HOW ABOUT LAURA SCHLESSINGER FOR 15 GRAND?
STILL TOO RICH.
OKAY, BILL BENNETT FOR $250 AND CARFARE.
DONE, BUT I'LL NEED A MORALS CLAUSE.

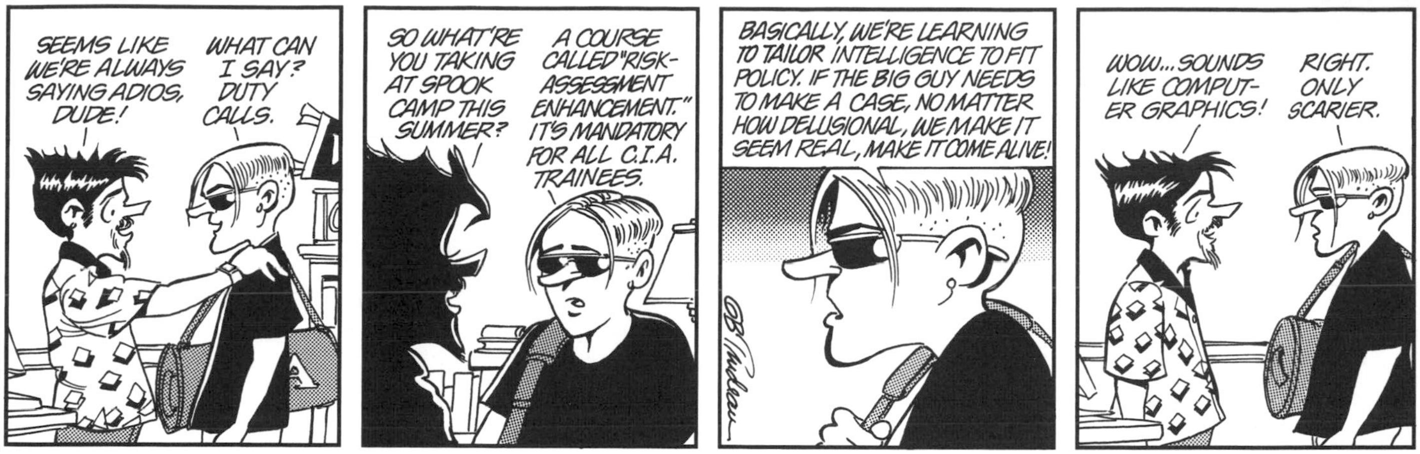
SEEMS LIKE WE'RE ALWAYS SAYING ADIOS, DUDE!
WHAT CAN I SAY? DUTY CALLS.
SO WHAT'RE YOU TAKING AT SPOOK CAMP THIS SUMMER?
A COURSE CALLED "RISK-ASSESSMENT ENHANCEMENT." IT'S MANDATORY FOR ALL C.I.A. TRAINEES.
BASICALLY, WE'RE LEARNING TO TAILOR INTELLIGENCE TO FIT POLICY. IF THE BIG GUY NEEDS TO MAKE A CASE, NO MATTER HOW DELUSIONAL, WE MAKE IT SEEM REAL, MAKE IT COME ALIVE!
WOW... SOUNDS LIKE COMPUTER GRAPHICS!
RIGHT. ONLY SCARIER.

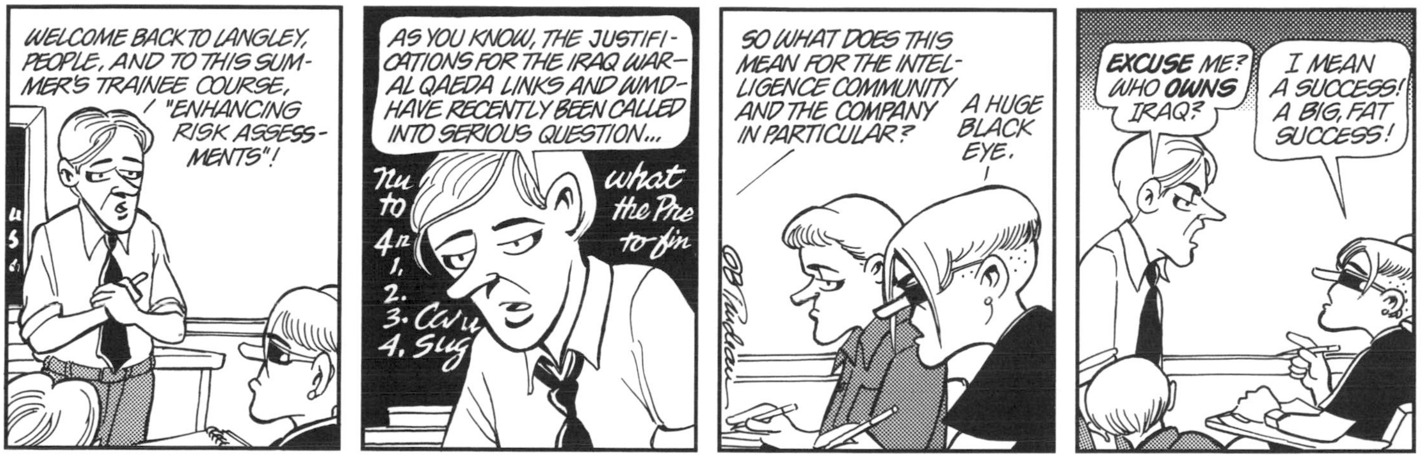
WELCOME BACK TO LANGLEY, PEOPLE, AND TO THIS SUMMER'S TRAINEE COURSE, "ENHANCING RISK ASSESSMENTS"!
AS YOU KNOW, THE JUSTIFICATIONS FOR THE IRAQ WAR—AL QAEDA LINKS AND WMD—HAVE RECENTLY BEEN CALLED INTO SERIOUS QUESTION...
SO WHAT DOES THIS MEAN FOR THE INTELLIGENCE COMMUNITY AND THE COMPANY IN PARTICULAR?
A HUGE BLACK EYE.
**EXCUSE** ME? WHO **OWNS** IRAQ?
I MEAN A SUCCESS! A BIG, FAT SUCCESS!

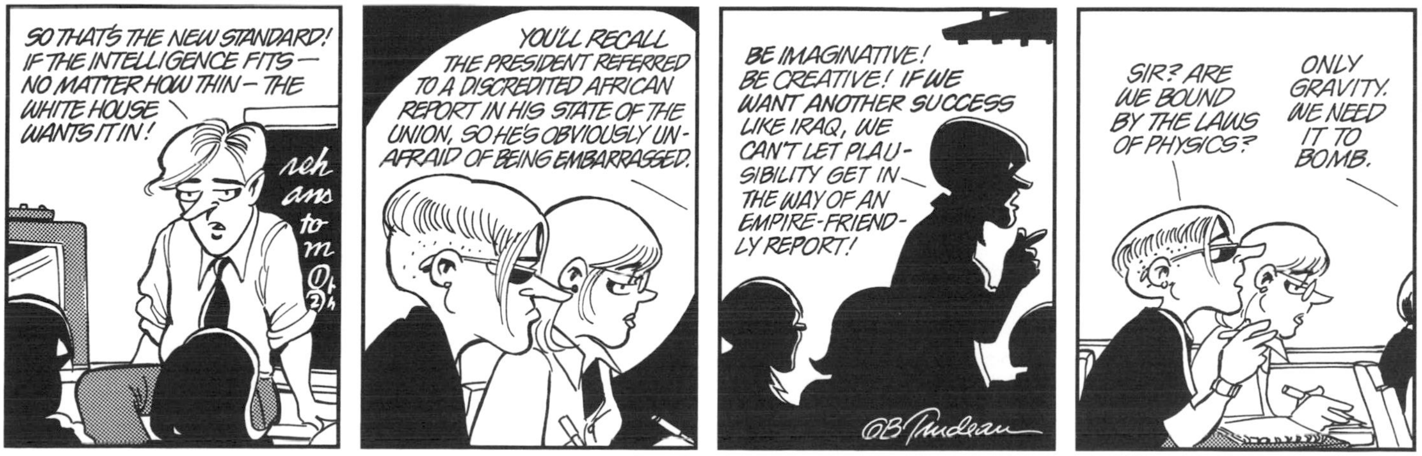
SO THAT'S THE NEW STANDARD! IF THE INTELLIGENCE FITS—NO MATTER HOW THIN—THE WHITE HOUSE WANTS IT IN!
YOU'LL RECALL THE PRESIDENT REFERRED TO A DISCREDITED AFRICAN REPORT IN HIS STATE OF THE UNION, SO HE'S OBVIOUSLY UNAFRAID OF BEING EMBARRASSED.
BE IMAGINATIVE! BE CREATIVE! IF WE WANT ANOTHER SUCCESS LIKE IRAQ, WE CAN'T LET PLAUSIBILITY GET IN THE WAY OF AN EMPIRE-FRIENDLY REPORT!
SIR? ARE WE BOUND BY THE LAWS OF PHYSICS?
ONLY GRAVITY. WE NEED IT TO BOMB.

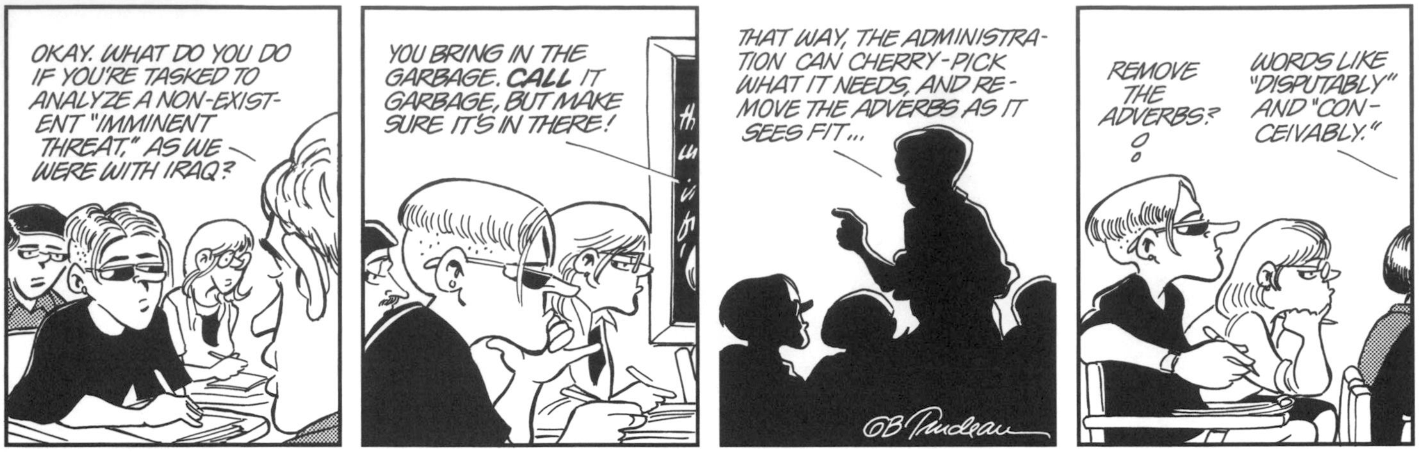
OKAY. WHAT DO YOU DO IF YOU'RE TASKED TO ANALYZE A NON-EXISTENT "IMMINENT THREAT," AS WE WERE WITH IRAQ?
YOU BRING IN THE GARBAGE. CALL IT GARBAGE, BUT MAKE SURE IT'S IN THERE!
THAT WAY, THE ADMINISTRATION CAN CHERRY-PICK WHAT IT NEEDS, AND REMOVE THE ADVERBS AS IT SEES FIT...
REMOVE THE ADVERBS?
WORDS LIKE "DISPUTABLY" AND "CONCEIVABLY."

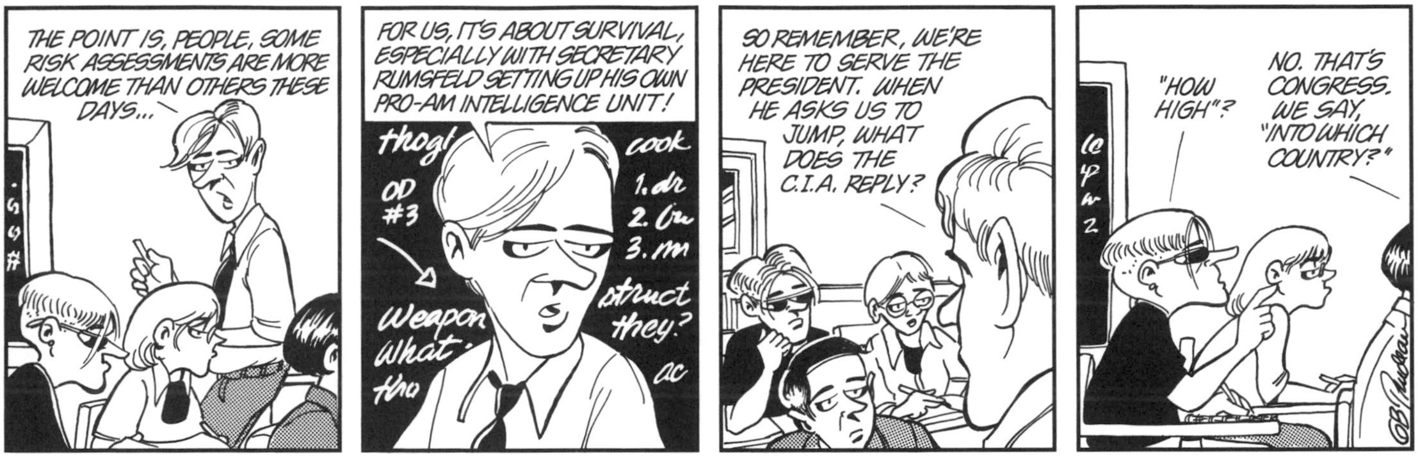
THE POINT IS, PEOPLE, SOME RISK ASSESSMENTS ARE MORE WELCOME THAN OTHERS THESE DAYS...
FOR US, IT'S ABOUT SURVIVAL, ESPECIALLY WITH SECRETARY RUMSFELD SETTING UP HIS OWN PRO-AM INTELLIGENCE UNIT!
thog! cook OD #3 1. dr 2. 3. m struct they? Weapon What tho ac
SO REMEMBER, WE'RE HERE TO SERVE THE PRESIDENT. WHEN HE ASKS US TO JUMP, WHAT DOES THE C.I.A. REPLY?
"HOW HIGH"?
NO. THAT'S CONGRESS. WE SAY, "INTO WHICH COUNTRY?"

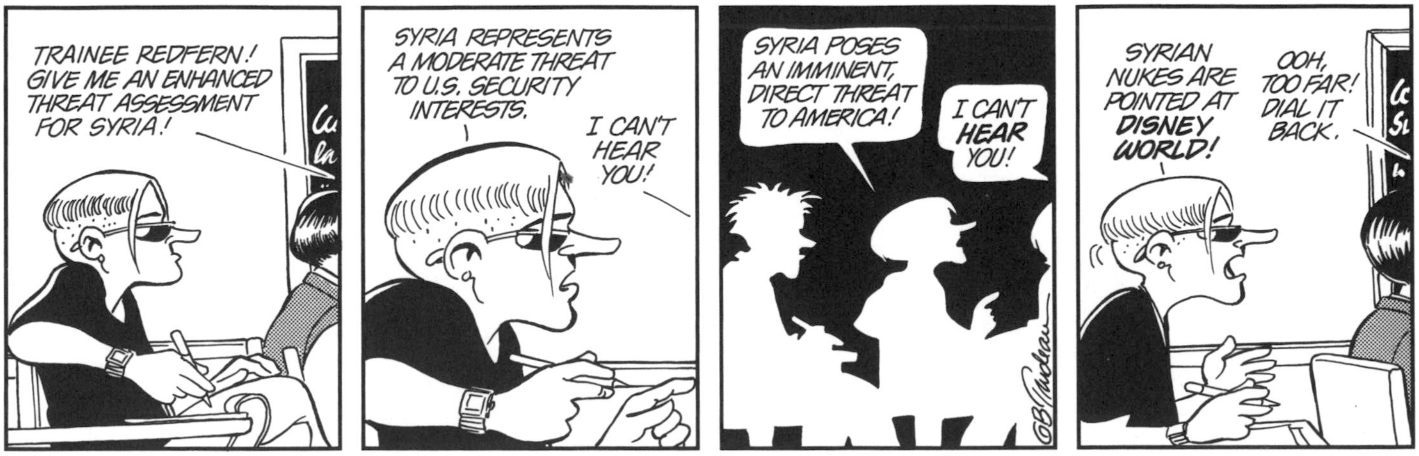
TRAINEE REDFERN! GIVE ME AN ENHANCED THREAT ASSESSMENT FOR SYRIA!
SYRIA REPRESENTS A MODERATE THREAT TO U.S. SECURITY INTERESTS.
I CAN'T HEAR YOU!
SYRIA POSES AN IMMINENT, DIRECT THREAT TO AMERICA!
I CAN'T HEAR YOU!
SYRIAN NUKES ARE POINTED AT DISNEY WORLD!
OOH, TOO FAR! DIAL IT BACK.

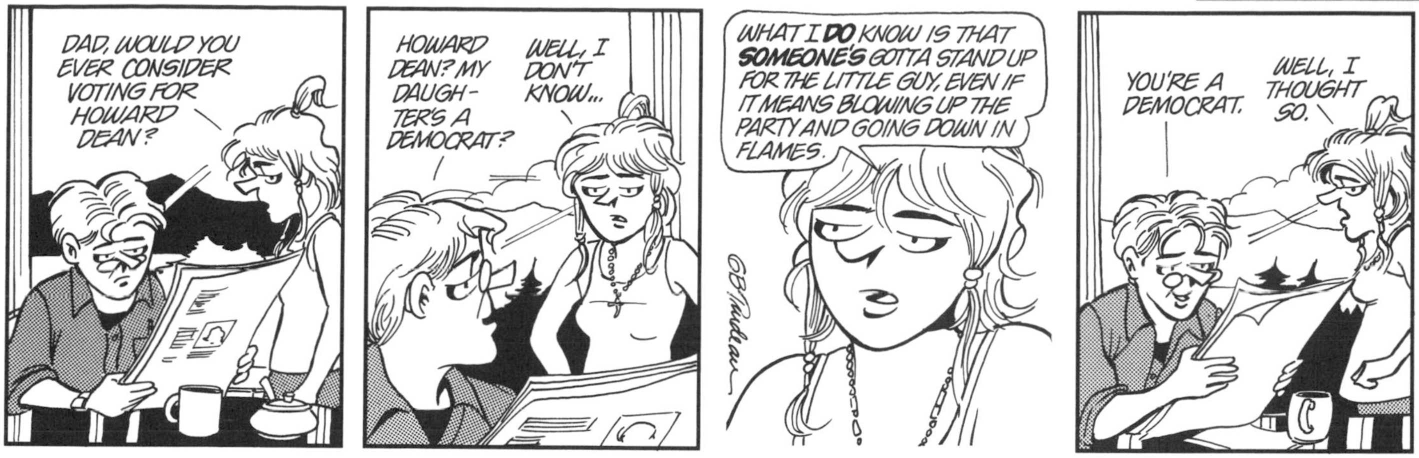
DAD, WOULD YOU EVER CONSIDER VOTING FOR HOWARD DEAN?
HOWARD DEAN? MY DAUGHTER'S A DEMOCRAT?
WELL, I DON'T KNOW...
WHAT I **DO** KNOW IS THAT **SOMEONE'S** GOTTA STAND UP FOR THE LITTLE GUY, EVEN IF IT MEANS BLOWING UP THE PARTY AND GOING DOWN IN FLAMES.
YOU'RE A DEMOCRAT.
WELL, I THOUGHT SO.

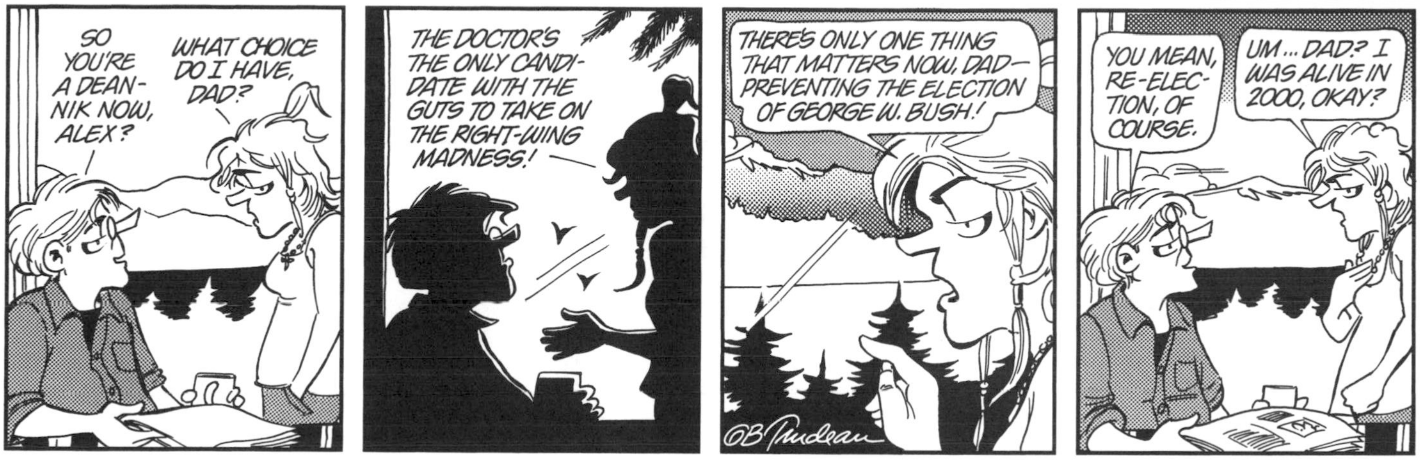
SO YOU'RE A DEANNIK NOW, ALEX?
WHAT CHOICE DO I HAVE, DAD?
THE DOCTOR'S THE ONLY CANDIDATE WITH THE GUTS TO TAKE ON THE RIGHT-WING MADNESS!
THERE'S ONLY ONE THING THAT MATTERS NOW, DAD— PREVENTING THE ELECTION OF GEORGE W. BUSH!
YOU MEAN, RE-ELECTION, OF COURSE.
UM ... DAD? I WAS ALIVE IN 2000, OKAY?

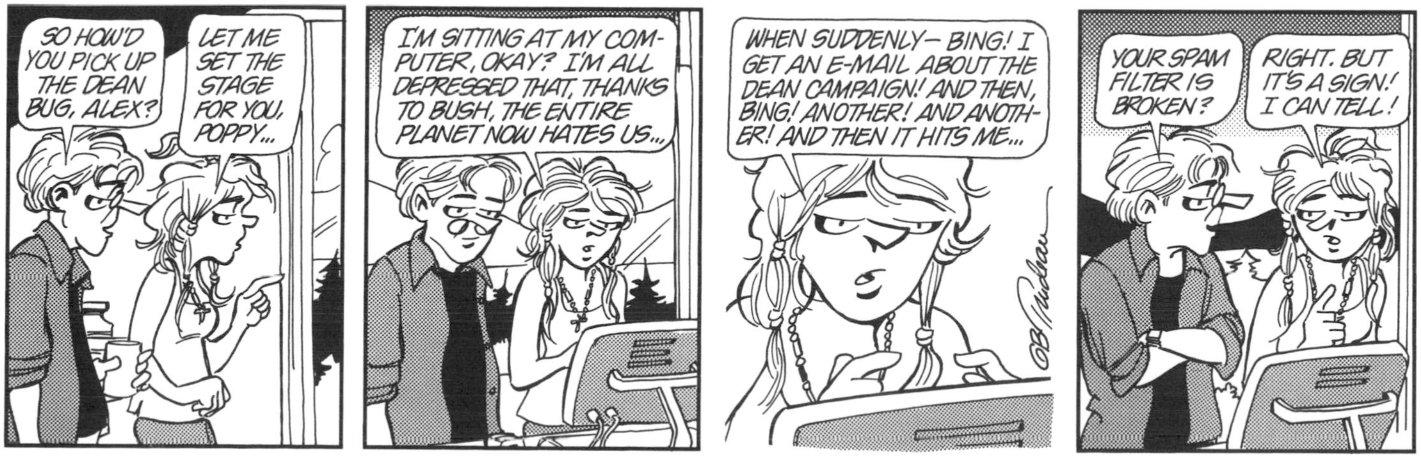
SO HOW'D YOU PICK UP THE DEAN BUG, ALEX?
LET ME SET THE STAGE FOR YOU, POPPY...
I'M SITTING AT MY COMPUTER, OKAY? I'M ALL DEPRESSED THAT, THANKS TO BUSH, THE ENTIRE PLANET NOW HATES US...
WHEN SUDDENLY— BING! I GET AN E-MAIL ABOUT THE DEAN CAMPAIGN! AND THEN, BING! ANOTHER! AND ANOTHER! AND THEN IT HITS ME...
YOUR SPAM FILTER IS BROKEN?
RIGHT. BUT IT'S A SIGN! I CAN TELL!

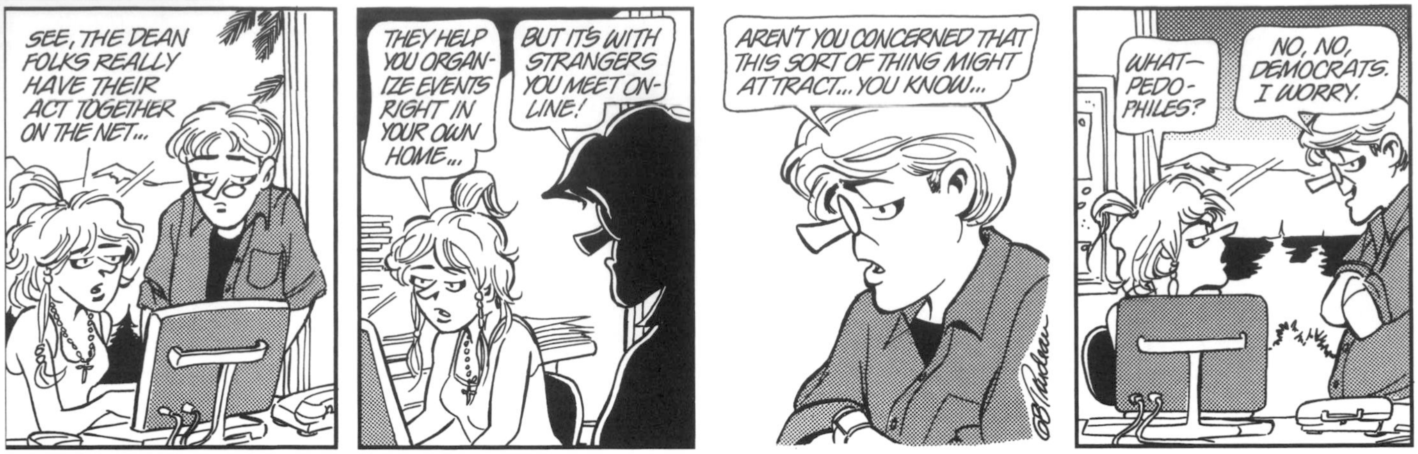
SEE, THE DEAN FOLKS REALLY HAVE THEIR ACT TOGETHER ON THE NET...
THEY HELP YOU ORGANIZE EVENTS RIGHT IN YOUR OWN HOME...
BUT IT'S WITH STRANGERS YOU MEET ON-LINE!
AREN'T YOU CONCERNED THAT THIS SORT OF THING MIGHT ATTRACT... YOU KNOW...
WHAT—PEDOPHILES?
NO, NO, DEMOCRATS. I WORRY.

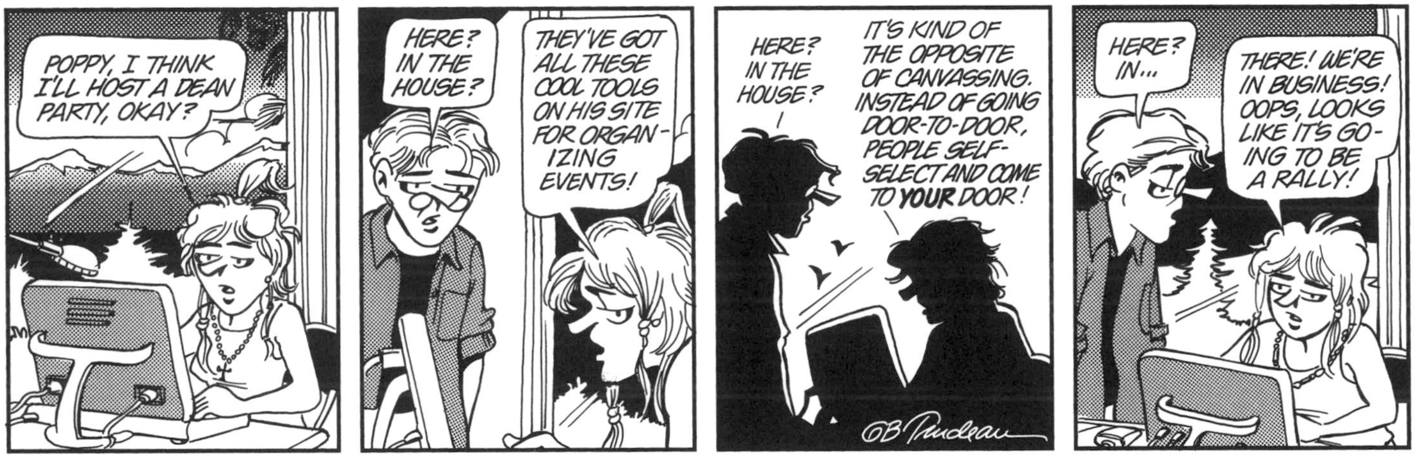
POPPY, I THINK I'LL HOST A DEAN PARTY, OKAY?
HERE? IN THE HOUSE?
THEY'VE GOT ALL THESE COOL TOOLS ON HIS SITE FOR ORGANIZING EVENTS!
HERE? IN THE HOUSE?
IT'S KIND OF THE OPPOSITE OF CANVASSING. INSTEAD OF GOING DOOR-TO-DOOR, PEOPLE SELF-SELECT AND COME TO YOUR DOOR!
HERE? IN...
THERE! WE'RE IN BUSINESS! OOPS, LOOKS LIKE IT'S GOING TO BE A RALLY!

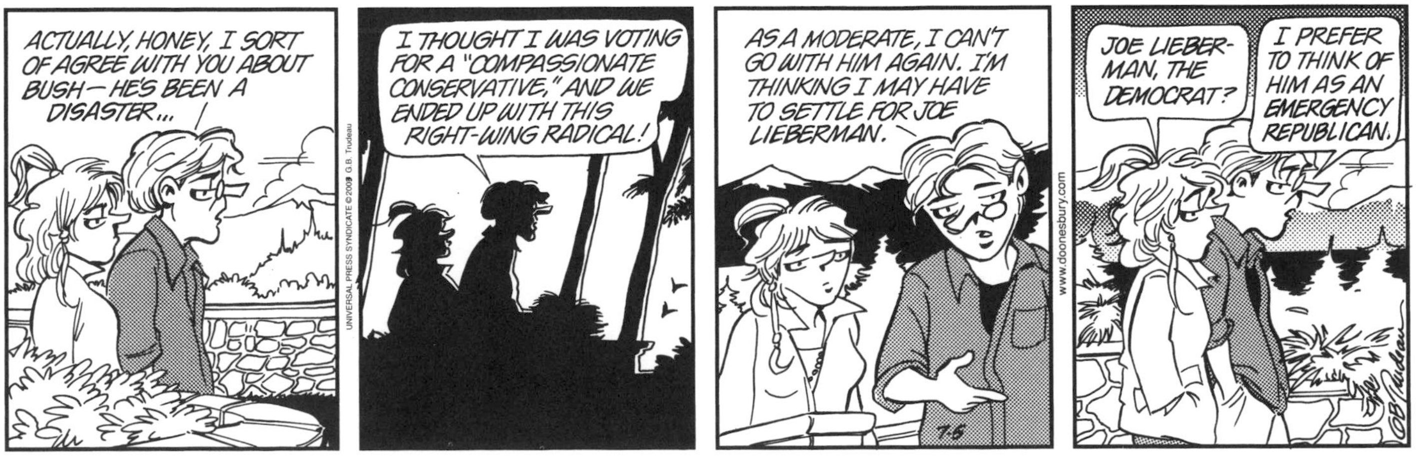
ACTUALLY, HONEY, I SORT OF AGREE WITH YOU ABOUT BUSH—HE'S BEEN A DISASTER...
I THOUGHT I WAS VOTING FOR A "COMPASSIONATE CONSERVATIVE," AND WE ENDED UP WITH THIS RIGHT-WING RADICAL!
AS A MODERATE, I CAN'T GO WITH HIM AGAIN. I'M THINKING I MAY HAVE TO SETTLE FOR JOE LIEBERMAN.
JOE LIEBERMAN, THE DEMOCRAT?
I PREFER TO THINK OF HIM AS AN EMERGENCY REPUBLICAN.
www.doonesbury.com

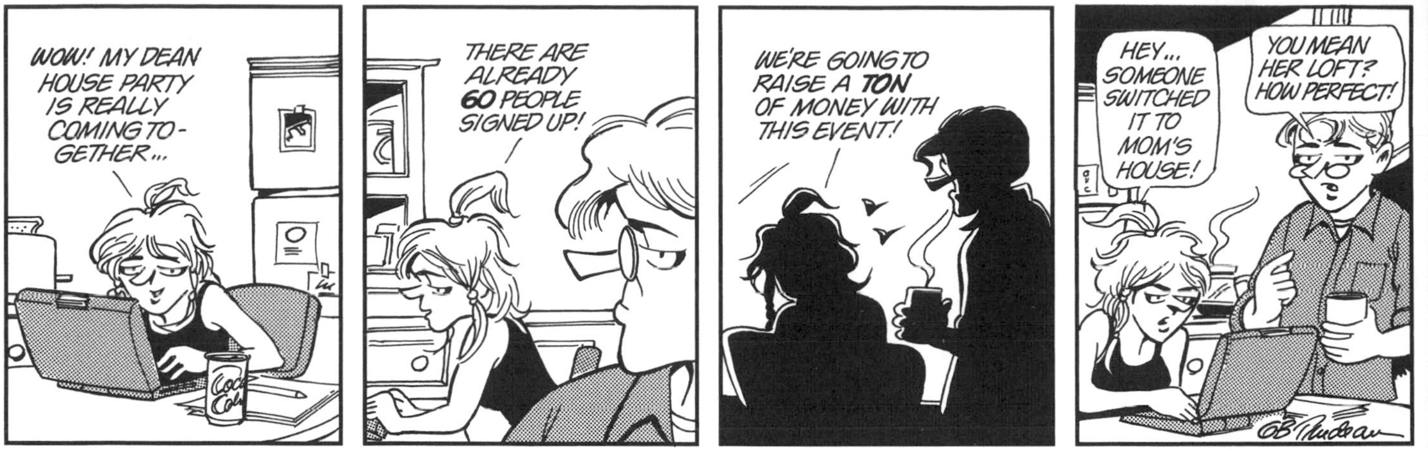
WOW! MY DEAN HOUSE PARTY IS REALLY COMING TOGETHER...
THERE ARE ALREADY 60 PEOPLE SIGNED UP!
WE'RE GOING TO RAISE A TON OF MONEY WITH THIS EVENT!
HEY... SOMEONE SWITCHED IT TO MOM'S HOUSE!
YOU MEAN HER LOFT? HOW PERFECT!

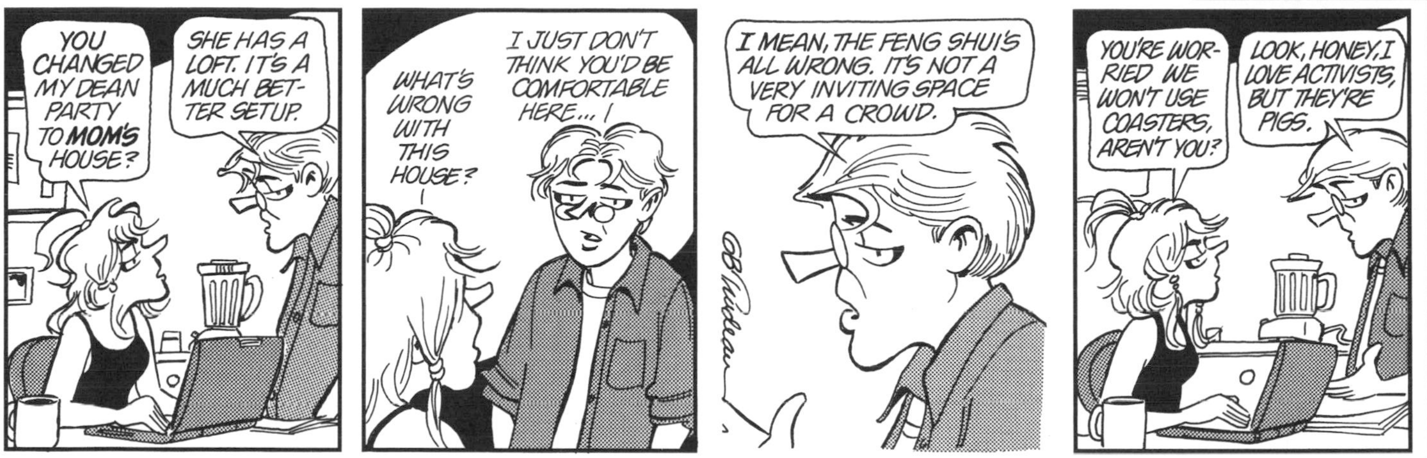
YOU CHANGED MY DEAN PARTY TO MOM'S HOUSE?
SHE HAS A LOFT. IT'S A MUCH BETTER SETUP.
WHAT'S WRONG WITH THIS HOUSE?
I JUST DON'T THINK YOU'D BE COMFORTABLE HERE...
I MEAN, THE FENG SHUI'S ALL WRONG. IT'S NOT A VERY INVITING SPACE FOR A CROWD.
YOU'RE WORRIED WE WON'T USE COASTERS, AREN'T YOU?
LOOK, HONEY, I LOVE ACTIVISTS, BUT THEY'RE PIGS.

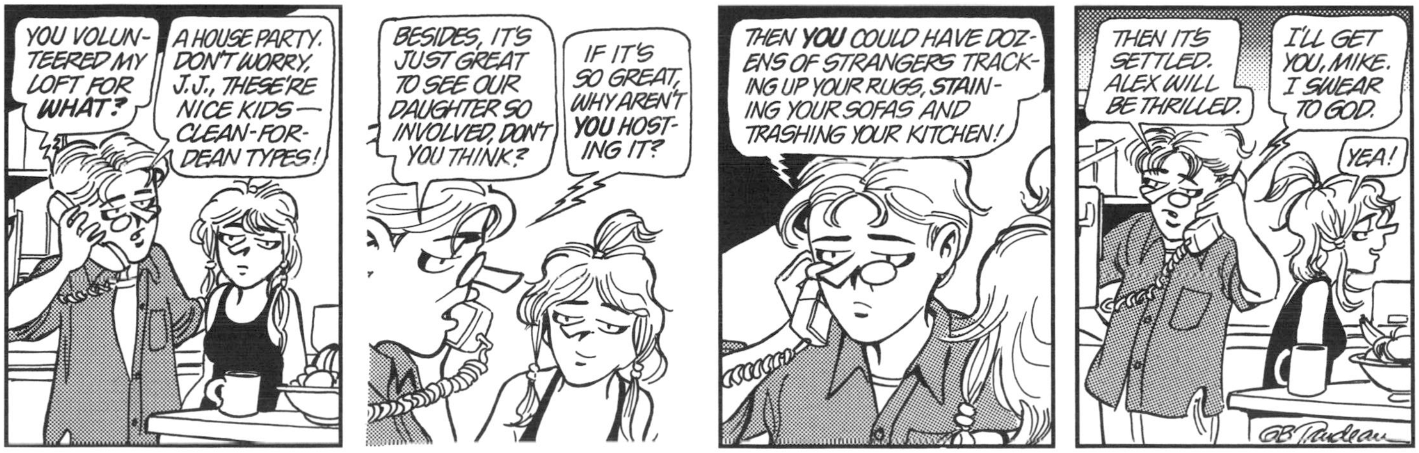
YOU VOLUNTEERED MY LOFT FOR WHAT?
A HOUSE PARTY. DON'T WORRY, J.J., THESE'RE NICE KIDS— CLEAN-FOR-DEAN TYPES!
BESIDES, IT'S JUST GREAT TO SEE OUR DAUGHTER SO INVOLVED, DON'T YOU THINK?
IF IT'S SO GREAT, WHY AREN'T YOU HOSTING IT?
THEN YOU COULD HAVE DOZENS OF STRANGERS TRACKING UP YOUR RUGS, STAINING YOUR SOFAS AND TRASHING YOUR KITCHEN!
THEN IT'S SETTLED. ALEX WILL BE THRILLED.
I'LL GET YOU, MIKE. I SWEAR TO GOD.
YEA!

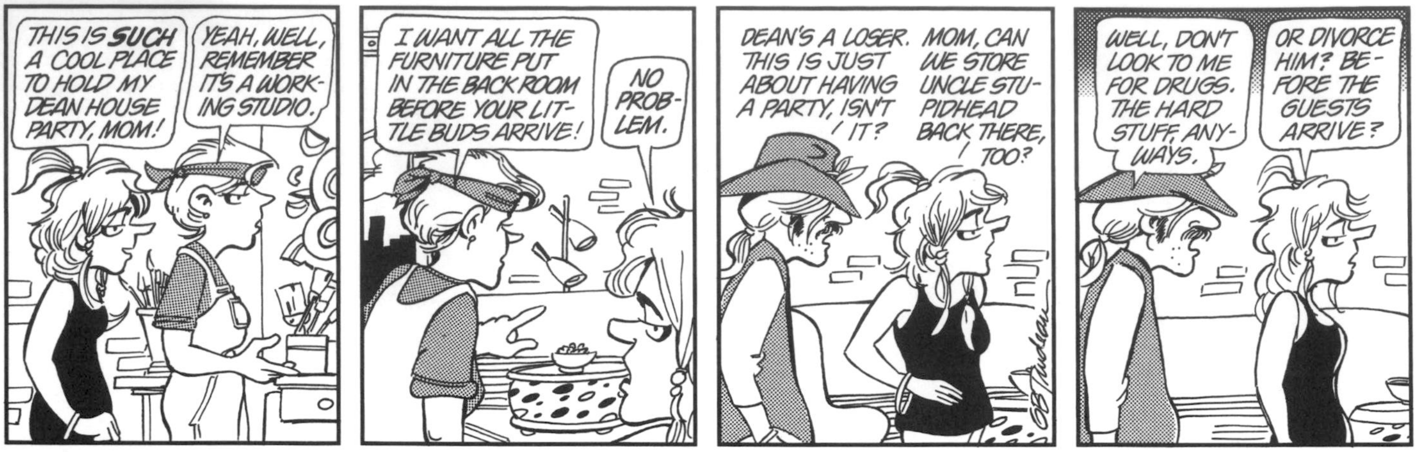
THIS IS **SUCH** A COOL PLACE TO HOLD MY DEAN HOUSE PARTY, MOM!
YEAH, WELL, REMEMBER IT'S A WORKING STUDIO.
I WANT ALL THE FURNITURE PUT IN THE BACK ROOM BEFORE YOUR LITTLE BUDS ARRIVE!
NO PROBLEM.
DEAN'S A LOSER. THIS IS JUST ABOUT HAVING A PARTY, ISN'T IT?
MOM, CAN WE STORE UNCLE STUPIDHEAD BACK THERE, TOO?
WELL, DON'T LOOK TO ME FOR DRUGS. THE HARD STUFF, ANYWAYS.
OR DIVORCE HIM? BEFORE THE GUESTS ARRIVE?

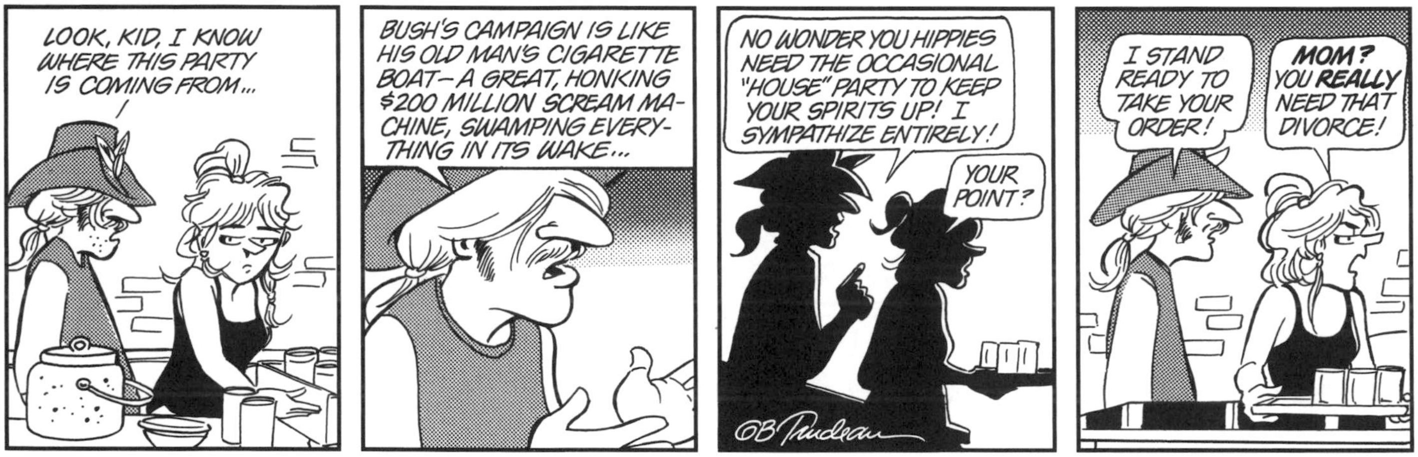
LOOK, KID, I KNOW WHERE THIS PARTY IS COMING FROM...
BUSH'S CAMPAIGN IS LIKE HIS OLD MAN'S CIGARETTE BOAT—A GREAT, HONKING $200 MILLION SCREAM MACHINE, SWAMPING EVERYTHING IN ITS WAKE...
NO WONDER YOU HIPPIES NEED THE OCCASIONAL "HOUSE" PARTY TO KEEP YOUR SPIRITS UP! I SYMPATHIZE ENTIRELY!
YOUR POINT?
I STAND READY TO TAKE YOUR ORDER!
**MOM?** YOU **REALLY** NEED THAT DIVORCE!

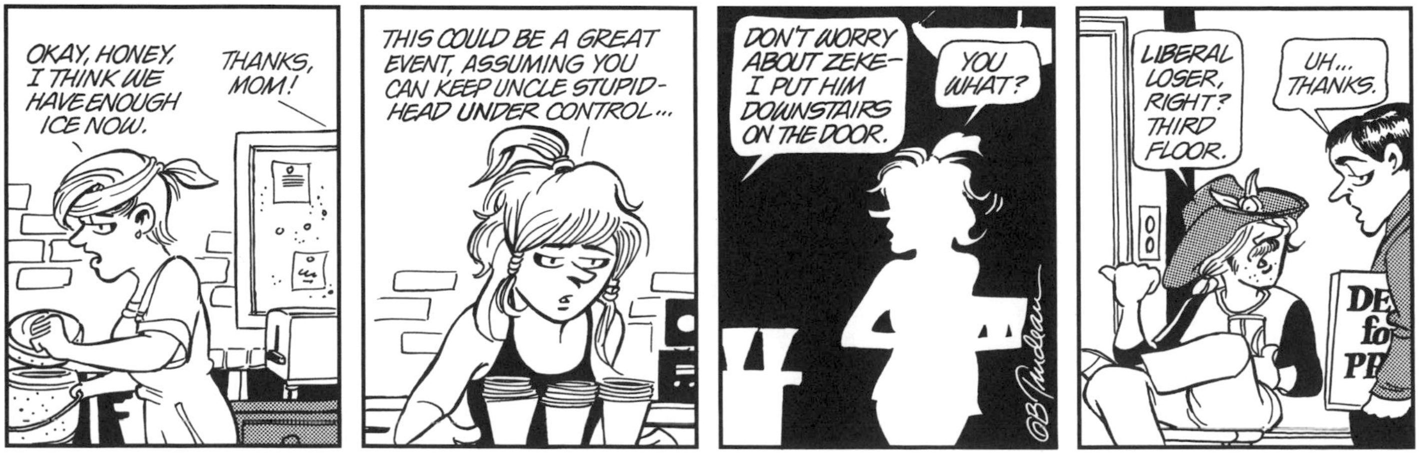
OKAY, HONEY. I THINK WE HAVE ENOUGH ICE NOW.
THANKS, MOM!
THIS COULD BE A GREAT EVENT, ASSUMING YOU CAN KEEP UNCLE STUPIDHEAD **UNDER** CONTROL...
DON'T WORRY ABOUT ZEKE—I PUT HIM DOWNSTAIRS ON THE DOOR.
YOU WHAT?
**LIBERAL** LOSER, RIGHT? THIRD FLOOR.
UH... THANKS.

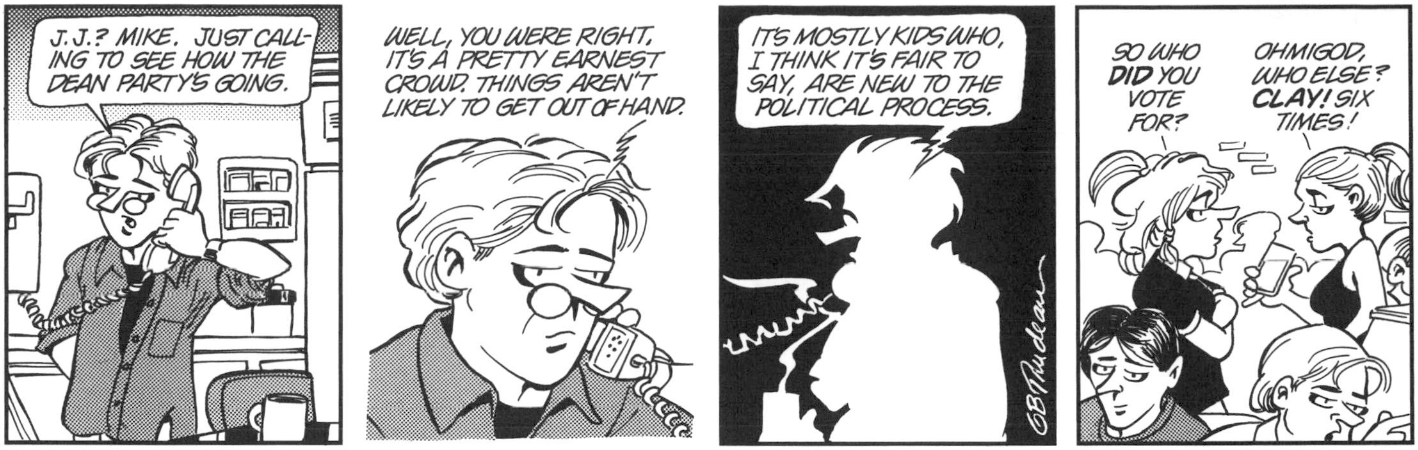
J.J.? MIKE. JUST CALLING TO SEE HOW THE DEAN PARTY'S GOING.
WELL, YOU WERE RIGHT. IT'S A PRETTY EARNEST CROWD. THINGS AREN'T LIKELY TO GET OUT OF HAND.
IT'S MOSTLY KIDS WHO, I THINK IT'S FAIR TO SAY, ARE NEW TO THE POLITICAL PROCESS.
SO WHO **DID** YOU VOTE FOR?
OHMIGOD, WHO ELSE? **CLAY!** SIX TIMES!

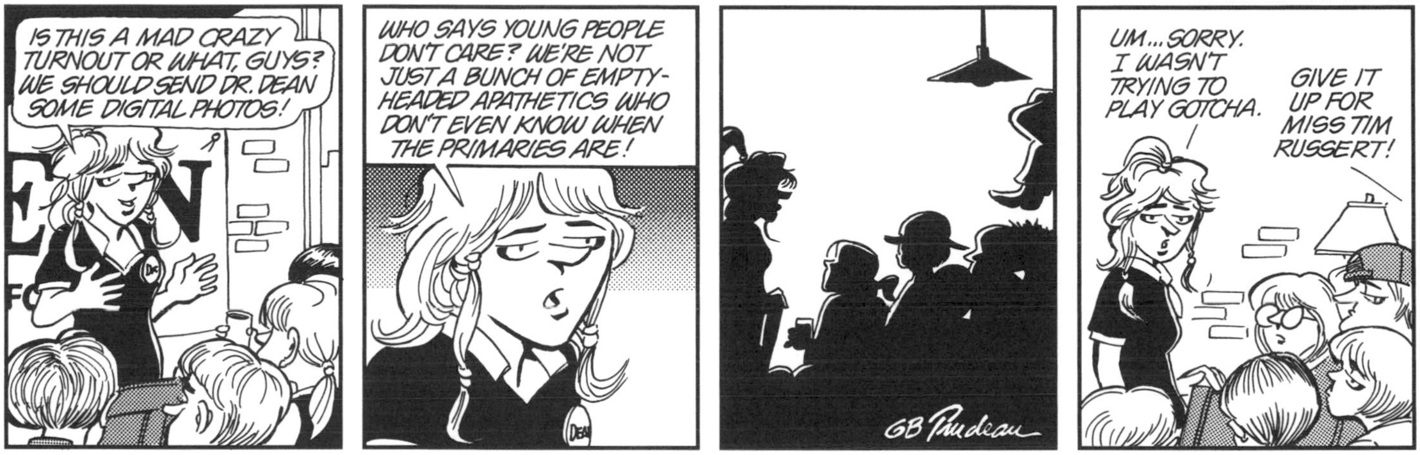
IS THIS A MAD CRAZY TURNOUT OR WHAT, GUYS? WE SHOULD SEND DR. DEAN SOME DIGITAL PHOTOS!
WHO SAYS YOUNG PEOPLE DON'T CARE? WE'RE NOT JUST A BUNCH OF EMPTY-HEADED APATHETICS WHO DON'T EVEN KNOW WHEN THE PRIMARIES ARE!
UM... SORRY. I WASN'T TRYING TO PLAY GOTCHA.
GIVE IT UP FOR MISS TIM RUSSERT!

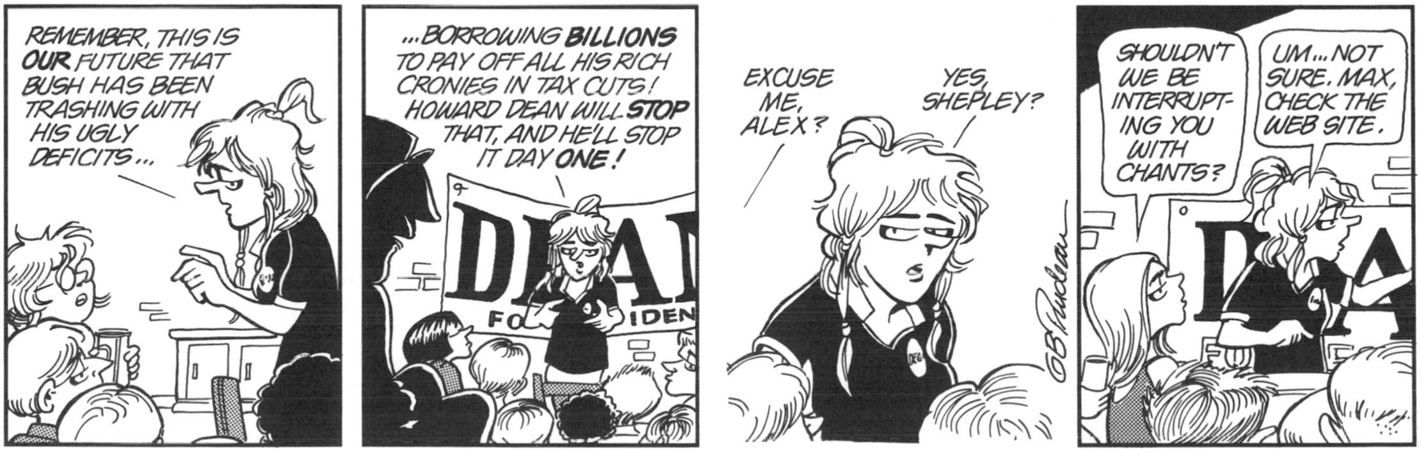
REMEMBER, THIS IS **OUR** FUTURE THAT BUSH HAS BEEN TRASHING WITH HIS UGLY DEFICITS...
...BORROWING **BILLIONS** TO PAY OFF ALL HIS RICH CRONIES IN TAX CUTS! HOWARD DEAN WILL **STOP** THAT, AND HE'LL STOP IT DAY **ONE**!
EXCUSE ME, ALEX?
YES, SHEPLEY?
SHOULDN'T WE BE INTERRUPTING YOU WITH CHANTS?
UM... NOT SURE. MAX, CHECK THE WEB SITE.

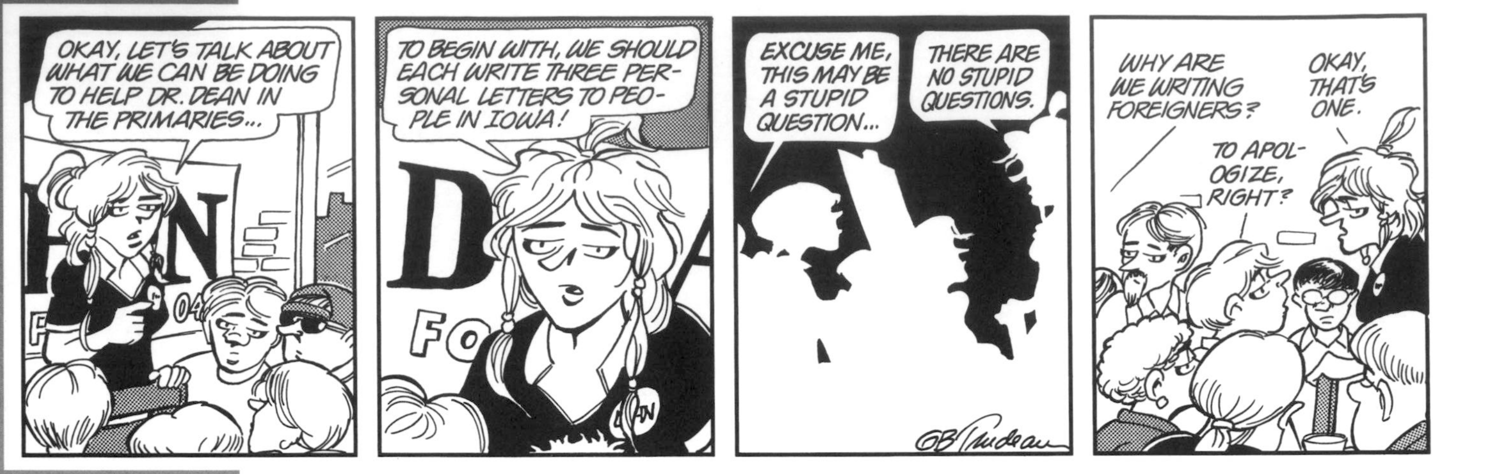
OKAY, LET'S TALK ABOUT WHAT WE CAN BE DOING TO HELP DR. DEAN IN THE PRIMARIES...
TO BEGIN WITH, WE SHOULD EACH WRITE THREE PERSONAL LETTERS TO PEOPLE IN IOWA!
EXCUSE ME, THIS MAY BE A STUPID QUESTION...
THERE ARE NO STUPID QUESTIONS.
WHY ARE WE WRITING FOREIGNERS?
TO APOLOGIZE, RIGHT?
OKAY, THAT'S ONE.

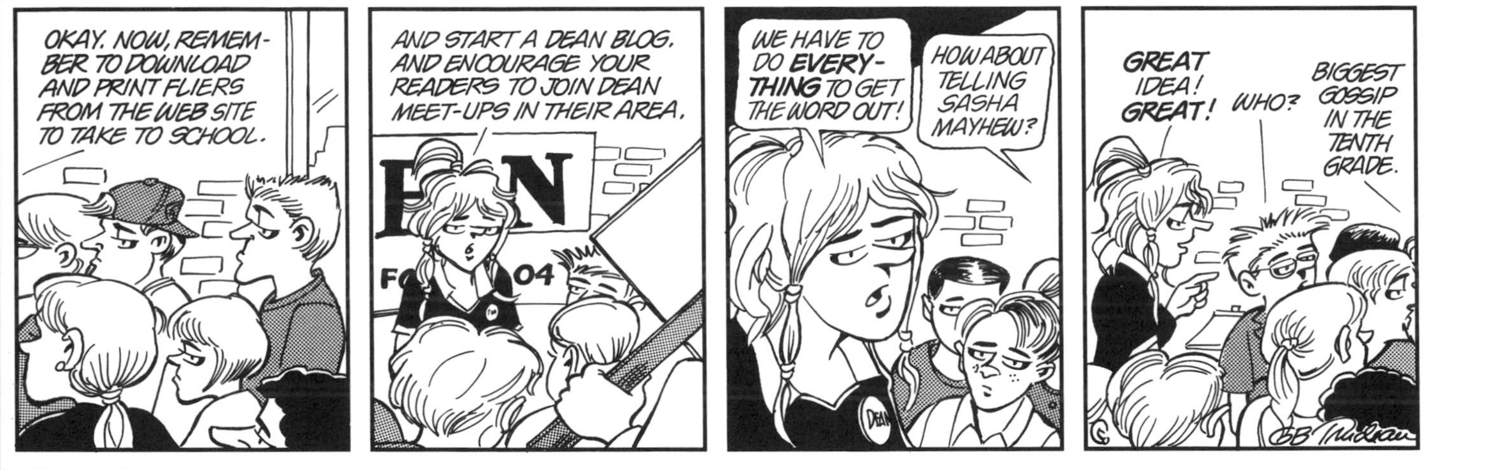
OKAY. NOW, REMEMBER TO DOWNLOAD AND PRINT FLIERS FROM THE WEB SITE TO TAKE TO SCHOOL.
AND START A DEAN BLOG. AND ENCOURAGE YOUR READERS TO JOIN DEAN MEET-UPS IN THEIR AREA.
WE HAVE TO DO EVERYTHING TO GET THE WORD OUT!
HOW ABOUT TELLING SASHA MAYHEW?
GREAT IDEA! GREAT!
WHO?
BIGGEST GOSSIP IN THE TENTH GRADE.

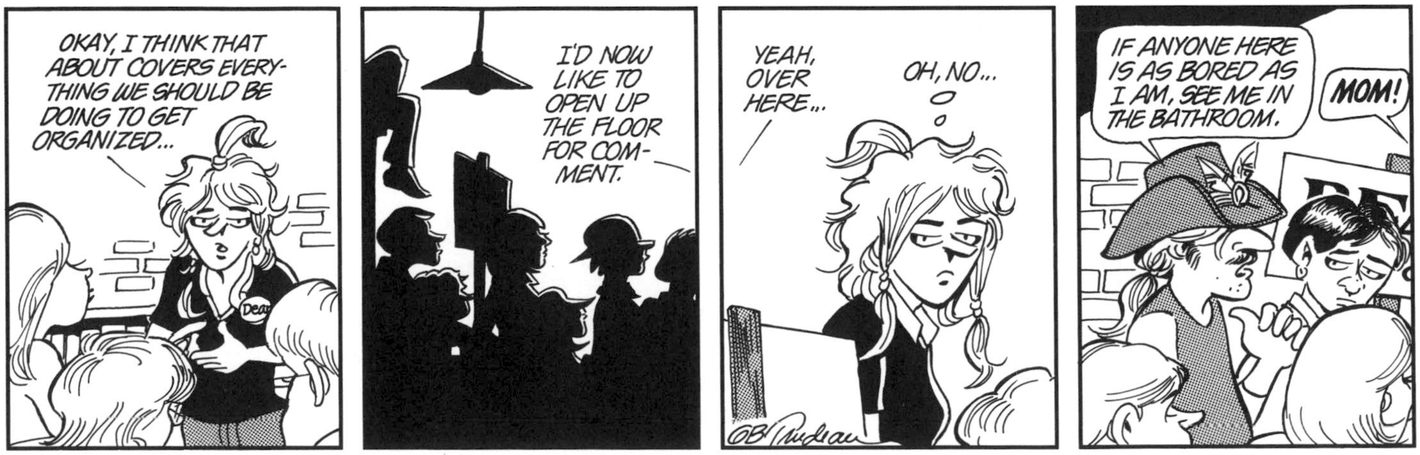
OKAY, I THINK THAT ABOUT COVERS EVERYTHING WE SHOULD BE DOING TO GET ORGANIZED...
I'D NOW LIKE TO OPEN UP THE FLOOR FOR COMMENT.
YEAH, OVER HERE...
OH, NO...
IF ANYONE HERE IS AS BORED AS I AM, SEE ME IN THE BATHROOM.
MOM!